T0140066

Lecture Notes in Artificial Intelligence 13069

Subseries of Lecture Notes in Computer Science

More information about this subseries at https://link.springer.com/bookseries/1244

Lu Fang · Yiran Chen · Guangtao Zhai ·
Jane Wang · Ruiping Wang ·
Weisheng Dong (Eds.)

Artificial Intelligence

First CAAI International Conference, CICAI 2021
Hangzhou, China, June 5–6, 2021
Proceedings, Part I

Springer

Editors
Lu Fang 🆔
Tsinghua University
Beijing, China

Yiran Chen 🆔
Duke University
Durham, NC, USA

Guangtao Zhai 🆔
Shanghai Jiao Tong University
Shanghai, China

Jane Wang 🆔
University of British Columbia
Vancouver, BC, Canada

Ruiping Wang 🆔
Institute of Computing Technology
Chinese Academy of Sciences
Beijing, China

Weisheng Dong 🆔
Xidian University
Xi'an, China

ISSN 0302-9743   ISSN 1611-3349 (electronic)
Lecture Notes in Artificial Intelligence
ISBN 978-3-030-93045-5   ISBN 978-3-030-93046-2 (eBook)
https://doi.org/10.1007/978-3-030-93046-2

LNCS Sublibrary: SL7 – Artificial Intelligence

This Springer imprint is published by the registered company Springer Nature Switzerland AG
The registered company address is: Gewerbestrasse 11, 6330 Cham, Switzerland

Preface

The present book includes extended and revised versions of papers selected from the 1st CAAI International Conference on Artificial Intelligence (CICAI 2021), held in Hangzhou, China, on June 6, 2021.

CICAI is a summit forum in the field of artificial intelligence and the 2021 forum was hosted by Chinese Association for Artificial Intelligence (CAAI). CICAI aims to establish a global platform for international academic exchange, promote advanced research in AI and its affiliated disciplines, and promote scientific exchanges among researchers, practitioners, scientists, students, and engineers in AI and its affiliated disciplines in order to provide interdisciplinary and regional opportunities for researchers around the world, enhance the depth and breadth of academic and industrial exchanges, inspire new ideas, cultivate new forces, implement new ideas, integrate into the new landscape, and join the new era.

The conference program included invited talks delivered by two distinguished speakers, Harry Shum and Song-Chun Zhu, as well as a panel discussion, followed by an oral session of 15 papers and a poster session of 90 papers. Those papers were selected from 307 submissions using a double-blind review process, and on average each submission received 3.2 reviews. The topics covered by these selected high-quality papers span the fields of machine learning, computer vision, natural language processing, and data mining, amongst others.

This book contains 101 papers selected and revised from the proceedings of CICAI 2021. We would like to thank the authors for contributing their novel ideas and visions that are recorded in this book.

June 2021

Lu Fang
Yiran Chen
Guangtao Zhai
Jane Wang
Ruiping Wang
Weisheng Dong

Organization

General Chairs

Lu Fang   Tsinghua University, China
Yiran Chen   Duke University, USA
Guangtao Zhai   Shanghai Jiao Tong University, China

Program Chairs

Jane Wang   University of British Columbia, Canada
Ruiping Wang   Chinese Academy of Sciences, China
Weisheng Dong   Xidian University, China

Publication Chairs

Yuchen Guo   Tsinghua University, China
Le Wu   Hefei University of Technology, China

Presentation Chairs

Xia Wu   Beijing Normal University, China
Jian Zhao   AMS, China

International Liaison Chair

Chunyan Miao   Nanyang Technological University, Singapore

Advisory Committee

C. L. Philip Chen   University of Macau, China
Xilin Chen   Institute of Computing Technology, Chinese Academy of Sciences, China
Yike Guo   Imperial College London, UK
Ping Ji   City University of New York, USA
Licheng Jiao   Xidian University, China
Ming Li   University of Waterloo, Canada
Chenglin Liu   Institute of Automation, Chinese Academy of Sciences, China
Derong Liu   University of Illinois at Chicago, USA

Hong Liu	Peking University, China
Hengtao Shen	University of Electronic Science and Technology of China
Yuanchun Shi	Tsinghua University, China
Yongduan Song	Chongqing University, China
Fuchun Sun	Tsinghua University, China
Jianhua Tao	Institute of Automation, Chinese Academy of Sciences, China
Guoyin Wang	Chongqing University of Posts and Telecommunications, China
Weining Wang	Beijing University of Posts and Telecommunications, China
Xiaokang Yang	Shanghai Jiao Tong University, China
Changshui Zhang	Tsinghua University, China
Lihua Zhang	Fudan University, China
Song-Chun Zhu	Peking University, China
Wenwu Zhu	Tsinghua University, China
Yueting Zhuang	Zhejiang University, China

Area Chairs

Badong Chen	Xi'an Jiaotong University, China
Peng Cui	Tsinghua University, China
Weihong Deng	Beijing University of Posts and Telecommunications, China
Yang Feng	Institute of Computing Technology, Chinese Academy of Sciences, China
Yulan Guo	National University of Defense Technology, China
Di Huang	Beihang University, China
Gao Huang	Tsinghua University, China
Qing Ling	Sun Yat-sen University, China
Qi Liu	University of Science and Technology of China, China
Risheng Liu	Dalian University of Technology, China
Deyu Meng	Xi'an Jiaotong University, China
Jinshan Pan	Nanjing University of Science and Technology, China
Xi Peng	Sichuan University, China
Chao Qian	Nanjing University, China
Boxin Shi	Peking University, China
Dong Wang	Dalian University of Technology, China
Jie Wang	University of Science and Technology of China, China

Contents – Part I

Computer Vision

Data Mining

Contents – Part II

Natural Language Processing

Robotics

Other AI Related Topics

Applications of AI

Comparative Sharpness Evaluation for Mobile Phone Photos

Qiang Lu[1], Guangtao Zhai[1(✉)], Yucheng Zhu[1], Xiongkuo Min[1], Tao Wang[1], and Xiao-Ping Zhang[2]

[1] Shanghai Jiao Tong University, Shanghai, China
{erislu,zhaiguangtao,zyc420,minxiongkuo,f1603011.wangtao}@sjtu.edu.cn
[2] Ryerson University, Toronto, Canada
xzhang@ee.ryerson.ca

Abstract. Mobile phones are the main source of a vast majority of digital photos nowadays. Photos taken by current mobile phones generally have fairly good visual quality without noticeable distortion. This progress benefits not only from the higher specification of camera sensor, but also the excellent imaging algorithm. Reliable and practical photo quality evaluation algorithm can guide the development of mobile phone photography to a higher level, which is also the key to this progress. Clearly, subjective photo quality assessment suffers from the drawbacks of productivity and reproducibility. Traditional objective image quality assessment algorithms can hardly discern the subtle quality difference between pictures photoed by different mobile phones. In this paper, we propose a comparative sharpness evaluation method based on an improved Siamese network with multilayer features for mobile phone photos. We employ Resnet-18 as the main feature extraction module. The features extracted from different layers of the two branches will be concatenated layer by layer and then passed to the final fully connected layer. The final output represents the sharpness comparison result of the two input pictures. Experimental results show that our sharpness evaluation algorithm achieves state-of-the-art performance on the SCPQD2020 database.

Keywords: Image sharpness · Comparative evaluation · Region selection · Image quality assessment

1 Introduction

With the advancement of mobile phone photography technology, mobile phone photo quality evaluation has gradually become a hot field. Among the attributes that affect image quality, sharpness is a critical one. A clearer picture can convey the information to the observer accurately. In the task of sharpness evaluation, traditional evaluation algorithms generally obtain a quantized value through measuring image gradient to represent the quality in terms of sharpness [23]. Some sharpness evaluation algorithms based on Deep Neural Network (DNN) like RankIQA [9] also tend to predict a specific value to represent image sharpness. However, such an evaluation idea is unreasonable in the sharpness assessment of mobile

© Springer Nature Switzerland AG 2021
L. Fang et al. (Eds.): CICAI 2021, LNAI 13069, pp. 3–14, 2021.
https://doi.org/10.1007/978-3-030-93046-2_1

(a) Photo A shot by device A   (b) Photo B shot by device B

(c) Local region of Photo A   (d) Local region of Photo B

Fig. 1. Comparison of global photos and local areas: (a) and (b) are photos of the same scene shot by two devices; (c) and (d) are the local areas selected. Compared to (a) and (b), it is easier to see the difference in sharpness between the two photos from (c) and (d).

phone photos. It is not appropriate to use a simple scalar to measure the sharpness, because the content of each photo is different [11]. The main purpose of mobile phone photo sharpness evaluation is to test the ability of the mobile phone camera system to capture details in different environments. Some mobile phone manufacturers often use their mobile phones and other phones to shoot the same scene and compare which photo is of better quality, and then optimize the camera algorithms of their mobile phones. There are some camera evaluation agencies like DxOMark [3] adopting the same approach. They shoot the same scene by using different mobile devices and compare which one has better sharpness subjectively. Therefore, comparative evaluation is a more appropriate and practical method for mobile photos sharpness assessment [22,24].

Traditional research of image quality mostly works with images with obvious distortion, and these methods are generally verified on some classic image quality evaluation databases, such as LIVE [16], TID2013 [15], CSIQ [7]. However, these databases cover only artificially and obviously distorted images but not natural ones. The distortion in mobile phone photos is not simple blur or Gaussian noise, but a combination of all possible distortion types in the mobile imaging system, and also includes the negative effects of some post-processing algorithms. All of these will have an impact on the photo sharpness [28]. W. Zhu et al. have established a brand new Smartphone Camera Photo Quality Database (SCPQD) including 1800 images of 120 scenes taken by 15 smartphones which is more close to the actual mobile phone photo quality evaluation [26]. Besides, the resolution of current mobile phone photos is quite high, usually tens of millions of pixels, which leads to a huge amount of computation on the traditional evaluation methods. Moreover, the imaging quality of some flagship mobile phones is relatively good, and the quality difference is so small that traditional sharpness evaluation algorithms can barely distinguish it.

In this paper, we propose a comparative evaluation algorithm for sharpness assessment of mobile phone photos. The main idea is to learn a function that maps input patterns into a target space such that the output in the target space approximates the sharpness relation in the input space. We first use an automatic area selection algorithm [10] to select a local area suitable for sharpness evaluation in two photos with the same scene, which is shown in Fig. 1, and then we input the two local regions into an improved Siamese network [1] to extract sharpness-related features. We employ the efficient Resnet-18 [6] as the backbone Convolutional Neural Network (CNN), and the weights of the network are shared in both branches. This model concatenates the outputs of each layer of Resnet-18 of both branches. Finally, the concatenated features of each layer are merged together and passed through a fully connected layer to get the sharpness comparison result. Experimental results show that our sharpness evaluation algorithm achieves state-of-the-art performance on the SCPQD2020 database [26].

2   The Comparative Evaluation Algorithm

In the evaluation of mobile phone photo quality, the absolute score of a photo is of little significance, but the relative order of the photo quality in the same scene is more useful. The purpose of comparative evaluation is to test the imaging quality of the mobile phone in a certain scene, and compare it with other mobile phones to distinguish the advantages and disadvantages. Therefore, we put forward a comparative evaluation algorithm in this paper. The inputs are two local patches with the same content selected from two pictures photoed by different phones. Resnet-18 is used as backbone to extract sharpness-related features. Considering that image sharpness is a relatively low-level image feature, not only deep layer features but also shallow layer features of Resnet have been fully utilized in our method. The final output represents the sharpness comparison result of the two photos. The overall framework of our model is shown in Fig. 2.

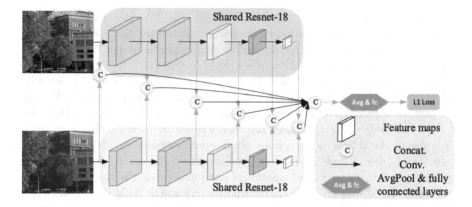

Fig. 2. The framework of our comparative sharpness evaluation model. Its backbone networks are two shared Resnets, followed by pooling layers and fully connected layers. The feature maps of each stage are concatenated for sharpness comparison.

2.1 Image Pre-processing

The resolution of current mobile phone photos is very high, generally with tens of millions of pixels. It is unrealistic to input such a large picture directly into CNN, because it requires too many computing resources. However, it is also inappropriate to directly resize the input picture as in the object detection task. This will have a great impact on sharpness, increasing the difficulty of evaluation to a certain extent. Due to the complexity of the shooting scene, not every area in the photo can reflect the quality in terms of sharpness [10]. Some relatively smooth areas in the actual scene, such as the sky, walls, etc. Cannot reflect the sharpness, but increase the amount of calculation. According to [10], we selected areas suitable for sharpness evaluation from the photos of each scene as input for the training and testing of subsequent comparative evaluation network. In each scene, the selected areas of each pair of photos are the same location to ensure that the main contents are the same. Images of each scene in the database are matched in pairs, with each pair labeled according to

$$Label(img_a, img_b) = \begin{cases} -1 & , if \quad q_a < q_b \\ 0 & , if \quad q_a = q_b \\ 1 & , if \quad q_a > q_b \end{cases} \quad (1)$$

where img_a, img_b are a pair of image patches, q_a, q_b are the sharpness qualities of two photos of this scene, which may be in the form of quality scores or rankings in different databases. The image patch pairs with labels are used as the training data of the comparative sharpness evaluation model.

2.2   The Comparative Sharpness Evaluation Model

The overall framework of our model is shown in Fig. 2. The main idea is to learn a function that maps input patterns into a target space such that the output in the target space approximates the sharpness relation in the input space. The first half of the network is somewhat similar to the Siamese network, containing two branches, and each branch extracts the features of every picture in the picture pair. Unlike the Siamese architecture, the latter part directly obtains the feature maps of all layers of the previous CNN, and then merges them together. The second half of the network is composed of the pooling layer and the fully connected layer, which map all the previous feature maps to a scalar output, and this output represents the sharpness comparison result of the photo pair. This model described above is defined as CompareNet.

As shown in Fig. 2, one pair of image patches are fed to two branches of the network separately. They are passed to the backbone CNN composed of Resnet-18, and the weights of the network are shared in both branches. Considering that sharpness belongs to the low-level feature of the picture after all, in this model we use the shallow layer feature maps in addition to the deep layer feature maps of Resnet. This network concatenates the intermediate feature maps of the two branches in each layer of Resnet to form a composite feature map. The composite feature maps of each layer are adjusted to the same size by custom convolutional layers, and then concatenated together to form a global feature map. After that, the global feature map outputs a feature scalar through the average pooling layer and the fully connected layer. The average pooling layer can not only quickly reduce the amount of parameters, but also ignore the influence of the input images that are not completely aligned. Finally this feature scalar is mapped to the interval from -1 to 1 through the tanh function. The model output and the dataset groudtruth are both scalars, so we choose smooth L1 loss as the model loss function, which is concise and efficient and can ensure the stability of gradient descent during the training process:

$$SmoothL1Loss = \begin{cases} 0.5x^2 & , \ if \ \ |x| < 1 \\ |x| - 0.5 & , \ otherwise \end{cases} \qquad (2)$$

In the model inference stage, we also input a pair of photos denoted by (img_a, img_b), assuming that the output of the model is denoted by y. If y is greater than 0, we think that the sharpness of picture img_a is worse than img_b; if y is less than 0, we think that picture img_a is clearer than img_b; if y is equal to 0, we think that the clarities of the two pictures are basically close, and it is difficult to distinguish the good from the bad. Of course, it is rare that y is equal to 0.

2.3   Ranking Method

As described above, our comparative sharpness evaluation model will only compare the sharpness of two photos once. In order to determine the order of the

---

Algorithm 1: The ranking method of photo sharpness for the same scene.

Data: All photos of the same scene; the number of photos is N.
Result: The order of sharpness qualities of all photos.

1 Use the automatic region selection algorithm [10] to obtain local areas suitable for sharpness assessment, denoted by img_i $(0 \leq i < N)$;
2 Use the $S[i]$ to store the number of comparative wins of each photo, $S[i] = 0$ $(0 \leq i < N)$;
3 $i = 0$;
4 **while** $i < N - 1$ **do**
5      $j = i + 1$;
6   **while** $j < N$ **do**
7          $y = model(img_i, img_j)$;
8   **if** $y < 0$ **then**
9              $S[i] = S[i] + 1$;
10   **end**
11   **else if** $y > 0$ **then**
12             $S[j] = S[j] + 1$;
13   **end**
14         $j = j + 1$;
15   **end**
16     $i = i + 1$;
17 **end**
18 Rank all pictures in this scenes according to the array S;

---

sharpness of all photos for a scene, we suppose that the number of photos is N, then maintain an array S whose length is equal to N and $S[i]$ stores the number of comparative wins of the ith photo $(0 \leq i < N)$. All elements of the array will be initialized to 0 at the beginning. Each picture is paired with all other pictures, and then the picture pairs are compared using the sharpness comparison evaluation model. Suppose the pair is denoted by (img_i, img_j) $(0 \leq i < N - 1, i + 1 \leq j < N)$, if the model output is less than 0, we add 1 to $S[i]$. If the output is bigger than 0, we add 1 to $S[j]$. The above calculation process can be summarized by

$$\begin{cases} 0 \leq i < N, i + 1 \leq j < N, \\ y = model(img_i, img_j), \\ if \quad y < 0, \ S[i] = S[i] + 1, \\ if \quad y > 0, \ S[j] = S[j] + 1. \end{cases} \quad (3)$$

After comparing all the picture pairs, all pictures in this scenes can be ranked according to the array S. The complete method for ranking the sharpness of mobile phone photos is summarized in the Algorithm 1.

Fig. 3. Some examples of selected regions by [10] in natural photos: the area within the green rectangle in the picture represents the area selected by the algorithm proposed in [10], which will replace the entire picture to participate in the sharpness evaluation.

3 Experimental Results

We have tested our sharpness evaluation algorithm on the SCPQD2020 database [26]. Exposure, color, noise and texture which are four dominant factors influencing the quality of mobile phone photos are evaluated in the subjective study of this database, respectively. In addition to photos, the quality rankings of photos of each evaluation attribute in each scene are also given. We select the texture sub-database as the basis for our sharpness comparison evaluation model. We compare the proposed method with some other sharpness evaluation algorithms and the naive Siamese networks for testing.

3.1 Implementation Details

The photos in SCPQD2020 are all common scenes in life. In order to select representative photo scenes for training, 120 scenes are marked as day and night, indoor and outdoor, bright and dark, etc. This process is summarized in Table 1. Then we select 100 scenes from this database as the training set according to the labels and the other 20 scenes remain as the test set. This can ensure that the scene types in the training set are sufficient, and the scene types in the test

Table 1. Some examples of scene labels: each scene will be labeled as day or night, indoor or outdoor, bright or dark, etc. According to the characteristics of the actual scene when shooting. The numbers in the last line represent the number of scenarios that belong to each attribute (Some scenes are not counted if it is difficult to distinguish which attribute belongs to according to the content).

Scene no.	Day/Night	Outdoor/Indoor	Bright/Dark
001	Day	Outdoor	Bright
002	Day	Outdoor	Bright
003	Day	Outdoor	Bright
...	...	...	...
119	Night	Outdoor	Dark
120	Night	Indoor	Bright
Numbers	75/21	81/38	98/21

set have all appeared in the training set [27]. Every two photos in each scene will be paired and each pair will be labeled according to their quality ranking like Eq. 1. Due to the excellent camera performance of current mobile phones, the sharpness of photos taken by some flagship mobile phones is very close, and it is sometimes difficult for photography experts to distinguish the difference. Such photos pairs will reduce the speed of convergence in the initial training, and are more suitable as a data source for fine-tuning in the future. So in order for the model to quickly learn the sharpness discrimination ability, some photo pairs with small sharpness differences and similar quality rankings in the training set are eliminated and do not participate in the training process. All picture pairs in the test set will be tested to verify the sharpness comparison accuracy of the model. The area selected by the automatic region selection algorithm from [10] will be used as input for training and testing, and Fig. 3 illustrates some examples of the selected regions.

Our CompareNet is implemented using the Pytorch framework [14]. In the training process, the initial learning rate is 1.5e-6, the selected optimizer is Adam optimizer, the weight delay is 1e-5, and the batch size is set to 64. The data enhancement methods include random flip, random rotation and random cropping with cropping patch size 224 × 224. The GPU used in the normal training process and the ablation experiment is an NVIDIA GTX 1080.

3.2   Performance Evaluation

We compare the proposed method with existing sharpness metrics including BRISQUE [12], CPBD [13], FISH [17], ARISM [5], JNB [4], S3 [2], BIBLE [8]. In order to reduce the computational complexity of these traditional algorithms, we also use the area selected by the automatic region selection algorithm [10] as the input for the evaluation of the traditional algorithms. Table 2 shows the performance comparison results which include average Spearman Rank Order

Table 2. Mobile phone photos sharpness evaluation performance of our algorithm and some traditional algorithms on SCPQD2020 with the selected region as input.

Algorithms	BRISQUE	CPBD	FISH	ARISM	JNB	S3	BIBLE	Our algorithm
Accuracy	0.6842	0.5419	0.6628	0.5628	0.6019	0.6219	0.6438	**0.7982**
SROCC	0.480	0.134	0.484	0.197	0.299	0.284	0.390	**0.766**

Table 3. Mobile phone photos sharpness evaluation performance of our algorithm and some other deep learning based algorithms on SCPQD2020.

Algorithms.	C. Yao et al.	Y. Zhou et al.	Z. Ying et al.	Z. Yuan et al.	S. Xu et al.	Ours
SROCC	0.4413	0.390	0.592	0.3738	0.3624	**0.766**

Correlation Coefficient (SROCC) and sharpness comparing accuracy of all scenes in test set. SROCC measures only the correlation of relative order between the predicted results and ground truth. The specific form of the comparison accuracy calculation is shown in Eq. 4, where Num_{all} is the number of all image pairs in test set and Num_{right} is the number of image pairs whose predictions given by the evaluation method are correct:

$$Accuracy = \frac{Num_{right}}{Num_{all}} \tag{4}$$

In addition to some traditional sharpness evaluation methods, our algorithm is also compared with some deep learning based sharpness evaluation methods. C. Yao et al. [19], Y. Zhou et al. [25], Z. Ying et al. [20], Z. Yuan et al. [21], S. Xu et al. [18] have all designed evaluation algorithms for the texture sub-database of SCPQD2020. Since some of these algorithms will not output the results of the sharpness comparison accuracy, Table 3 only shows the difference in SROCC between our algorithm and these algorithms.

The results in Table 2 show that our method has great superiority compared with traditional sharpness evaluation algorithms, whether it is in sharpness comparison accuracy or average SROCC. Table 3 demonstrates that our sharpness comparison evaluation model has achieved the best performance. Compared with the traditional algorithms with the selected area, the SROCC of the prediction result of our evaluation model has increased by more than 0.3 on average. Compared with other deep learning based evaluation algorithms, the evaluation performance of our model has improved by about 0.2 on average. Our sharpness comparison evaluation model combined with a suitable evaluation area can reach the highest sharpness comparison accuracy rate, and the most consistent evaluation result with subjective experiments. In the new field of mobile phone photo quality evaluation, our model can better distinguish the difference in sharpness of pictures.

Table 4. Sharpness comparing accuracy and average SROCC of our algorithm with different inputs and concatenated features on SCPQD2020, where 1 means that this method has concatenated middle layer features and 0 means that this method has not concatenated middle layer features.

Input	Middle layer features	Accuracy	SROCC
Global photo	0	0.5444	0.335
Selected region	0	0.7593	0.740
Global photo	1	0.6787	0.493
Selected region	1	**0.7982**	**0.766**

3.3 Ablation Study

In order to verify the effectiveness of the region selected by the automatic region selection algorithm, we also train and test our model on the global photo. Moreover, we also try to train and test the naive Siamese network on the same data to verify the role of Resnet's middle layer features in comparative sharpness evaluation of mobile photos.

Table 4 demonstrates that the area selected by the automatic area selection algorithm [10] can bring an average increase of 0.3 in SROCC, and bring an increase over 0.1 in comparing accuracy. It can be seen from Table 4 that our CompareNet brings much improvement in comparison accuracy and SROCC compared with the naive Siamese network, which proves that the middle layer feature maps of Resnet play a great role in sharpness evaluation. This also indicates that in the sharpness evaluation task, the deep network with too many layers does not necessarily bring great performance improvement.

4 Conclusion

In this paper, we propose a comparative sharpness evaluation model for mobile phone photos which maps input patterns into a target space such that the output in the target space approximates the sharpness relation in the input space. The regions selected by an automatic region selection algorithm are used as the inputs for training and testing. We employ Resnet-18 as the main feature extraction module. At the same time, the features of the middle layer extracted from the two branches of the network are merged and then passed to the final fully connected layer. The final output represents the sharpness comparison result of the two input pictures. By comparing the sharpness of all photos in a scene in pairs, the order of the sharpness quality of all photos in the scene can be calculated. Experimental results show that our sharpness evaluation algorithm achieves state-of-the-art performance on the SCPQD2020 database. Whether it is the traditional algorithm or the algorithm based on deep learning, the effect in the task of mobile phone photo sharpness evaluation is not ideal. In the future, the focus of our research work will be to further optimize the comparative evaluation algorithm and apply it to other fields, such as video quality evaluation.

References

1. Chopra, S., Hadsell, R., LeCun, Y.: Learning a similarity metric discriminatively, with application to face verification. In: 2005 IEEE Computer Society Conference on Computer Vision and Pattern Recognition (CVPR 2005), vol. 1, pp. 539–546. IEEE (2005)
2. Vu, C.T., T.D.P., Chandler, D.M.: S(3): A spectral and spatial measure of local perceived sharpness in natural images. IEEE Trans. Image Process. **21**(3), 934–945 (2011)
3. DxOMark: How DXOMARK scores smartphone rear cameras - explaining DXO-MARK Camera. https://www.dxomark.com/
4. Ferzli, R., Karam, L.J.: A no-reference objective image sharpness metric based on the notion of just noticeable blur (JNB). IEEE Trans. Image Process. Pub. IEEE Sig. Proces. Soc. **18**(4), 717–728 (2009)
5. Gu, K., Zhai, G., Lin, W., Yang, X., Zhang, W.: No-reference image sharpness assessment in autoregressive parameter space. IEEE Trans. Image Process. **24**(10), 3218–3231 (2015)
6. He, K., Zhang, X., Ren, S., Sun, J.: Deep residual learning for image recognition. In: Proceedings of the IEEE Conference on Computer Vision and Pattern Recognition, pp. 770–778 (2016)
7. Larson, E.C., Chandler, D.M.: Most apparent distortion: full-reference image quality assessment and the role of strategy. J. Electron. Imaging **19**(1), 011006 (2010)
8. Li, L., Lin, W., Wang, X., Yang, G., Bahrami, K., Kot, A.C.: No-reference image blur assessment based on discrete orthogonal moments. IEEE Trans. Cybern. **46**(1), 39–50 (2015)
9. Liu, X., van de Weijer, J., Bagdanov, A.D.: Rankiqa: Learning from rankings for no-reference image quality assessment. In: Proceedings of the IEEE International Conference on Computer Vision, pp. 1040–1049 (2017)
10. Lu, Q., et al.: Automatic region selection for objective sharpness assessment of mobile device photos. In: 2020 IEEE International Conference on Image Processing (ICIP), pp. 106–110. IEEE (2020)
11. Min, X., Zhai, G., Zhou, J., Farias, M.C., Bovik, A.C.: Study of subjective and objective quality assessment of audio-visual signals. IEEE Trans. Image Process. **29**, 6054-6068 (2020)
12. Mittal, A., Moorthy, A.K., Bovik, A.C.: No-reference image quality assessment in the spatial domain. IEEE Trans. Image Process. **21**(12), 4695–4708 (2012)
13. Narvekar, N.D., Karam, L.J.: A no-reference image blur metric based on the cumulative probability of blur detection (CPBD). IEEE Trans. Image Process. **20**(9), 2678–2683 (2011)
14. Paszke, A., et al.: Pytorch: an imperative style, high-performance deep learning library. In: Advances in Neural Information Processing Systems, pp. 8026–8037 (2019)
15. Ponomarenko, N., Ieremeiev, O., Lukin, V., Egiazarian, K., et al.: Color image database TID2013: peculiarities and preliminary results. In: European Workshop on Visual Information Processing (EUVIP), pp. 106–111. IEEE (2013)
16. Sheikh, H.R., Sabir, M.F., Bovik, A.C.: A statistical evaluation of recent full reference image quality assessment algorithms. IEEE Trans. Image Process. **15**(11), 3440–3451 (2006)
17. Vu, P.V., Chandler, D.M.: A fast wavelet-based algorithm for global and local image sharpness estimation. IEEE Sig. Process. Lett. **19**(7), 423–426 (2012)

18. Xu, S., Yan, J., Hu, M., Li, Q., Zhou, J.: Quality assessment model for smartphone camera photo based on inception network with residual module and batch normalization. In: 2020 IEEE International Conference on Multimedia & Expo Workshops (ICMEW), pp. 1–6. IEEE (2020)
19. Yao, C., Lu, Y., Liu, H., Hu, M., Li, Q.: Convolutional neural networks based on residual block for no-reference image quality assessment of smartphone camera images. In: 2020 IEEE International Conference on Multimedia & Expo Workshops (ICMEW), pp. 1–6. IEEE (2020)
20. Ying, Z., Pan, D., Shi, P.: Quality difference ranking model for smartphone camera photo quality assessment. In: 2020 IEEE International Conference on Multimedia & Expo Workshops (ICMEW), pp. 1–6. IEEE (2020)
21. Yuan, Z., Qi, Y., Hu, M., Li, Q.: Opinion-unaware no-reference image quality assessment of smartphone camera images based on aesthetics and human perception. In: 2020 IEEE International Conference on Multimedia & Expo Workshops (ICMEW), pp. 1–6. IEEE (2020)
22. Zhai, G., Kaup, A.: Comparative image quality assessment using free energy minimization. In: 2013 IEEE International Conference on Acoustics, Speech and Signal Processing, pp. 1884–1888. IEEE (2013)
23. Zhai, G., Min, X.: Perceptual image quality assessment: a survey. Sci. China Inf. Sci. **63**(11), 1–52 (2020). https://doi.org/10.1007/s11432-019-2757-1
24. Zhai, G., Zhu, Y., Min, X.: Comparative perceptual assessment of visual signals using free energy features. IEEE Trans. Multimedia **23**, 3700–3713 (2020)
25. Zhou, Y., Wang, Y., Kong, Y., Hu, M.: Multi-indicator image quality assessment of smartphone camera based on human subjective behavior and perception. In: 2020 IEEE International Conference on Multimedia & Expo Workshops (ICMEW), pp. 1–6. IEEE (2020)
26. Zhu, W., et al.: A multiple attributes image quality database for smartphone camera photo quality assessment. In: 2020 IEEE International Conference on Image Processing (ICIP), pp. 2990–2994 (2020). https://doi.org/10.1109/ICIP40778.2020.9191104
27. Zhu, W., Zhai, G., Hu, M., Liu, J., Yang, X.: Arrow's impossibility theorem inspired subjective image quality assessment approach. Sig. Process. **145**, 193–201 (2018)
28. Zhu, Y., Zhai, G., Ke, G., Che, Z.: No-reference image quality assessment for photographic images of consumer device. In: 2016 IEEE International Conference on Acoustics, Speech and Signal Processing (ICASSP) (2016)

DiffGNN: Capturing Different Behaviors in Multiplex Heterogeneous Networks for Recommendation

Tiankai Gu, Chaokun Wang$^{(\boxtimes)}$, and Cheng Wu

School of Software, Tsinghua University, Beijing 100084, China
{gtk18,c-wu19}@mails.tsinghua.edu.cn, chaokun@tsinghua.edu.cn

Abstract. Learning from multiplex heterogeneous networks is a crucial task in many real-world applications such as recommender systems. Usually, a multiplex heterogeneous network has multiple types of nodes and edges (or relations). Multiplex heterogeneous network embedding aims to learn from abundant structural and semantic information of a graph and embed nodes into low-dimensional representations. Existing works usually split the graph into several relation-specific subgraphs to distinguish different relations. However, these works either omit the important information of metapath in aggregation or fail to fully utilize the multiplex property in the network. To tackle the above challenges, we propose a novel model *DiffGNN*, which is designed to capture different behaviors in an elegant and efficient manner. *DiffGNN* adopts two powerful modules, i.e., the relation-specific attention (RsAtt) and metapath aware aggregation (MetAware), where MetAware aggregates information from different metapaths in each relation-specific subgraph and RsAtt combines and integrates the information with attentive weights. The experiments are conducted on three real-world datasets, and the experimental results show that our *DiffGNN* achieves significant improvement compared to the state-of-the-art models.

Keywords: Multiplex heterogeneous network · Graph neural network · Heterogeneous graph representation learning

1 Introduction

Recommender systems are designed to produce a list of personalized results that match user preferences with respect to their historical behaviors [3,4,28,29]. Learning the ability to accurately discover the potential interest of a user is a crucial task for the recommender systems, and the core task of improving the performance of models is to learn expressive representations of nodes. Therefore, recent works focus on deepening interactions with graph neural networks. Many works [12,27] introduce message aggregation through neighbors and stack these embeddings in multiple layers, aiming to capture high order relationships.

This work was supported by the National Natural Science Foundation of China (No. 61872207) and Kuaishou Inc.

L. Fang et al. (Eds.): CICAI 2021, LNAI 13069, pp. 15–26, 2021.
https://doi.org/10.1007/978-3-030-93046-2_2

Previous works such as [8,9,20,21] assume the graph to be homogeneous. The homogeneous assumption means that the network has only one node type and one edge type. In real-world applications, most of the networks consist of more than one node type and more than one edge type. For example, in a scientific collaboration network such as DBLP, we may have node types as *Author*, *Conference*. The relationship between two authors could be *co-author* and the relationship between an author and a conference could be *attend*. Moreover, in an online recommender system where users are recommended with several videos that they may be interested in, a graph could be constructed by the user, video interactions. Node types in such graph are naturally divided into *user* and *video*, and edge types could be defined as different user behaviors, such as a *view* behavior, a *comment* behavior and a *like* behavior. These networks are defined as heterogeneous information networks (HIN) in recent studies [7]. Intuitively, the heterogeneity in HINs is related to different types of relations. In order to capture the semantics in HINs, metapath2vec [6] is proposed to sample a series of metapaths, which are pre-defined paths with specified relations and node types $type_1 \xrightarrow{r_1} type_2 \xrightarrow{r_2} type_3 \cdots \xrightarrow{r_n} type_l$. The advanced sampling strategy helps to avoid meaningless paths.

However, although metapath based models show their better superiority in heterogeneous networks than the conventional graph neural networks, we notice that adopting metapath only in the sampling phase still fails to learn the heterogeneity completely. To fully utilize the information along the metapath and the graph structure, a better solution is to distinguish different metapaths in the aggregation stage, but most works simply learn the embedding of a node through the aggregation from its k-layer neighbors.

To address the above limitations, we propose a novel model *DiffGNN* for capturing and learning different behaviors in multiplex heterogeneous networks. *DiffGNN* learns the expressive representation of a node through relation-specific attention (RsAtt) and metapath aware aggregation (MetAware) (Fig. 1). Specifically, *DiffGNN* divided the multiplex heterogeneous network into several subgraphs according to the edge type in order to learn a unique representation of a node under each relation. In the aggregation stage, different from the previous works that aggregate k-layer neighbors in a uniform way, MetAware dynamically aggregates k-layer neighbors according to a specific meta scheme. This aggregation approach further learns a different metapath structure in each subgraph and performance aggregation according to the information along the metapath. We point out that *DiffGNN* is of high expressiveness and has a strong ability to learn the heterogeneity, especially when the graph is rich in node types and edge types. We also show that the degradation of *DiffGNN* still outperforms the state-of-the-art methods such as GATNE with ROC-AUC, FR-AUC and F1 scores to be $97.59, 97.35, 93.05$ in Amazon dataset respectively.

Overall, we summarize our contributions as follows.

(1) A novel model *DiffGNN* is proposed. *DiffGNN* is able to capture different user behaviors in multiplex heterogeneous networks and fully exploits the abundant semantics in both the sampling phase and the aggregation phase.

(2) Two powerful modules are proposed to efficiently utilize the heterogeneity of multiplex heterogeneous networks. The relation-specific attention (RsAtt) is to learn the importance of different subgraphs, and the metapath aware aggregation (MetAware) is to aggregate information from different metapaths.

(3) We conduct extensive experiments on three real-world datasets. The results in the benchmark datasets show the superiority of our *DiffGNN* model and illustrate a significant improvement compared to the state-of-the-art models.

2   Related Work

In this section, we discuss state-of-the-art models in network embedding, heterogeneous network embedding and models used in the recommender system.

2.1   Network Embedding

Several methods of network embedding have proven to be successful in recommender systems. These methods mainly consist of two categories. One of them is the graph embedding (GE) such as DeepWalk [20], LINE [21], Node2vec [8], Metapath2vec [6] and SDNE [24]. DeepWalk [20] is motivated by word2vec [19], which samples a series of paths by random walk on the graph and then trains the model using the skip-gram model. LINE [21] directly models the first-order and second-order proximity to learn the structural similarity for the node representations. Node2vec [8] designs an improved sampling strategy by considering both the BFS and the DFS search with flexible parameters for a diverse form of the node sequences. Another category used in recommender systems is the graph neural network. Representative models include GCN [15] and GraphSage [9]. In GCN [15], each node incorporates the node features from its neighbors and aggregates the information from these features and itself to learn the local structures in the network. While GraphSage [9] provides an inductive way. It also uses a mini-batch and the neighbor mapping function in the training procedure.

2.2   Heterogeneous Network Embedding

Heterogeneous network representation is one of the most challenging tasks in network embedding researches due to multiple types of nodes and links. There are several studies on heterogeneous network embedding such as Metagraph2vec [30], Change2vec [1], MV-URL [25], HeteSpaceyWalk [13] and RHINE [16]. Metapath2vec [6] formalizes the metapath based random walks and proposes a heterogeneous skip-gram model. Metagraph2vec [30] presents a new concept called metagraph to capture richer structural contexts and semantics at the same time, which may contain multiple paths. Change2vec [1] captures the dynamic heterogeneous networks, and timestamps are taken into consideration. In HeteSpacey-Walk [13], the metapath guided random walk is formalized as a higher-order

Markov chain process, and a new model called heterogeneous personalized spacy random walk is leveraged to learn the embeddings in heterogeneous networks. MNE [31] projects a node representation of different types into a unified embedding space and uses a common embedding with additional edge embedding to represent a node with different edge types.

2.3   GNN Models in Recommender Systems

The embeddings learned from graph neural networks are widely used in recommender systems with the thought of collaborative filtering such as [3,12,26,27]. CSE [3] is a unified framework for representation learning and recommendation. Two types of proximity relations are considered in its double proximity model, direct similarity and neighborhood similarity. The NGCF framework [26] is more expressive in modeling the high-order connectivity by propagating the embeddings on the user-item graph. DGCF [27] adopts intent-aware collaborative filtering, which pays special attention to user-item relationships and divides them into multiple possible latent intents. LightGCN [12] is a state-of-the-art model designed from the simplification of GCN and is more concise and appropriate for recommendation. GATNE [2] learns the heterogeneity through a multiplex network with a base embedding and an edge-specific embedding. MAGNN [7] also employs the metapath information to learn the abundant information in heterogeneous networks. However, as MAGNN aggregates a node embedding directly through multiple metapaths, it omits the importance of graph structure. Jin et al. [14] present an early summary issue in heterogeneous networks and propose NIRec to avoid explicit path reachability.

3   Methodology

In this section, we first give some useful preliminaries and notations used in this paper. Then, the metapath aware aggregation is introduced. Finally, we introduce the relation-specific attention.

A multiplex heterogeneous network is defined as a network $\mathcal{G} = (\mathcal{V}, \mathcal{E})$, where $\mathcal{V}$ is the node set and $\mathcal{E} = \bigcup_{r \in \mathcal{R}} \mathcal{E}_r$. $\mathcal{E}_r$ consists of all edges with edge type $r \in \mathcal{R}$, $|\mathcal{R}| > 1$ and $\mathcal{R}$ denotes the relation set in $\mathcal{G}$. Moreover, each node v in $\mathcal{G}$ is associated with a node type mapping function $\phi(v)$, $\phi \colon \mathcal{V} \to \mathcal{O}$, where $\mathcal{O}$ denotes all the node types in $\mathcal{G}$. We use $\kappa(v_i) = \{v_j | \forall v_j \in \mathcal{V}, \phi(v_j) = \phi(v_i)\}$ to denote the node set that contains the same node type $\phi(v_i)$ as v_i.

With the above definitions, the problem of multiplex heterogeneous network embedding is to generate a low-dimensional representation $m^*_{v_i,r}$ for each node $v_i \in \mathcal{V}$ under every relation $r \in \mathcal{R}$, $m^*_{v_i,r} \in \mathbb{R}^d$, where $d \ll |\mathcal{V}|$.

3.1   Metapath Aware Aggregation

Previous works [20, 21] use random walk to generate training sequences and learn the embedding for each node in a skip-gram paradigm. Metapath2vec [6] uses

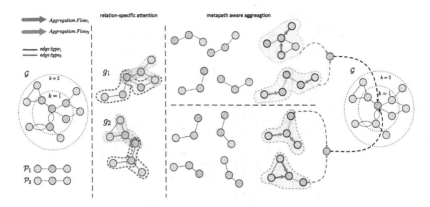

Fig. 1. The architecture of *DiffGNN*. We illustrate how RsAtt and MetAware modules work with 2-layer neighbors of a node. Note that different color of a node represents different node type and different color of an edge represents different edge type.

pre-defined metapaths $\mathcal{P}$ to guide the transition probability for generating the sequences for random walk. However, a metapath based random walk with such aggregation still fails to fully extract the heterogeneity in $\mathcal{G}$. As aggregators ignore the information of the metapaths, they simply treat the embedding from a node's k-layer neighbors in the same flow without distinction [2,9]. To tackle the problem of semantic-aware aggregation in multiplex heterogeneous network $\mathcal{G}$, we propose a metapath aware aggregation approach (MetAware) to effectively capture the semantics along the sampled paths.

As shown in Fig. 2, MetAware approach defines multiple aggregation flows for each node v_i in the k-layer aggregation phase. Specifically, the number of aggregation flows is equal to the number of metapaths defined with the same node type. Therefore, the aggregation layer is related to the length of the metapath. Such aggregations approach could be summarized as:

$$u_{v_i|\mathcal{P}_l}^{(k+1)} = Aggregation_{\mathcal{P}_i}(u_{v_i}^{(k)}, \{u_{v_j}^{(k)} : v_j \in \Gamma(\mathcal{N}_{v_i})\}), \qquad (1)$$

where $u_{v_i|\mathcal{P}_i}^{(k+1)}$ denotes the $(k+1)$-layer embedding vector of a node v_i under a specific scheme (i.e. metapath) $\mathcal{P}_l$, $\Gamma s(\cdot)$ is a node type matching function that picks the neighbors of v_i with the same node type in the scheme $\mathcal{P}_i$ at step k.

We concatenate the embedding of a node v_i conditioned on all the metapaths.

$$U_{v_i}^{(k+1)} = \left(u_{v_i|\mathcal{P}_1}^{(k+1)}, u_{v_i|\mathcal{P}_2}^{(k+1)}, \cdots, u_{v_i|\mathcal{P}_l}^{(k+1)} \right), \qquad (2)$$

where $U_{v_i}^{(k+1)}$ is an $l \times d_e$ dimensional embedding and d_e is the dimension of the edge embedding.

Self-attention mechanism [23] is adopted to learn the coefficients of different aggregation flows as:

$$\hat{U}_{v_i}^{(k+1)} = \mathcal{A}(Q, K, V) = softmax(\frac{QW^Q(KW^K)}{\sqrt{d_k}})VW^V, \qquad (3)$$

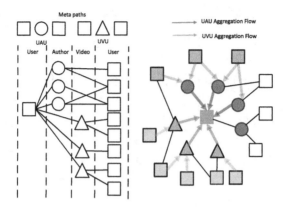

Fig. 2. Network schemes that illustrate the MetAware aggregations.

where $Q = U_{v_i}^{(k+1)} \in \mathbb{R}^{l \times d_e}$, $K = U_{v_i}^{(k+1)} \in \mathbb{R}^{l \times d_e}$, $V = U_{v_i}^{(k+1)} \in \mathbb{R}^{l \times d_e}$, $d_k = d_e/k$ is the embedding size of each head and k is the number of heads. W^Q, W^K, W^V are the parameters to be learned.

Thus we can employ a global aggregator to get the metapath aware aggregated embedding of a node v_i as:

$$\hat{u}_{v_i}^{(k+1)} = Aggregation_{Global}(\hat{U}_{v_i}^{(k+1)}). \tag{4}$$

Note that $Aggregation_{Global}(\hat{U}_{v_i}^{(k+1)})$ can be mean aggregator, sum aggregator or LSTM aggregator. In the rest of the paper, we focus on the mean aggregator as there are no significant differences in our experiments.

3.2 Relation-Specific Attention

In relation-specific attention, we split the original multiplex heterogeneous graph $\mathcal{G}$ according to its edge type, $g_r = (V_r, \mathcal{E}_r)$, where $V_r = V$ and $\mathcal{E}_r$ consists of all the edge that has the relation r. Each node has a corresponding embedding under each subgraph g_r. The attention mechanism is proposed to balance the attention weights.

To make the node embedding of a certain relationship able to capture the structure of both $\mathcal{G}$ and g_r. Following GATNE [2], we consider a node embedding of a certain relation as a global embedding and a local embedding via

$$m_{v_i, r_j} = \hat{u}_{v_i}^{(k+1)} \cdot W, \tag{5}$$

where W is the trainable parameters with dimensional $d_e \times d$ and m_{v_i, r_j} represents the embedding of node v_i w.r.t. relation r_j.

We then concatenate $m_{v_i, r}, r \in \mathcal{R}$ of all relations in $\mathcal{G}$ and also adopt self-attention to learn the coefficient along the relation dimension as:

$$\hat{M}_i = \mathcal{A}(Q, K, V) = softmax(\frac{QW^Q(KW^K)}{\sqrt{d_k}})VW^V, \tag{6}$$

Table 1. The statistics of datasets.

Datasets	$|\mathcal{V}|$	$|\mathcal{E}|$	$|\mathcal{O}|$	$|\mathcal{R}|$	$\mathcal{P}$
Amazon	10,099	148,659	1	2	I-I
Youtube	2,000	1,310,544	1	5	I-I
IMDb	11,616	34,212	3	1	M-D-M
					M-A-M
					D-M-D
					D-M-A-M-D
					A-M-A
					A-M-D-M-A

where $Q = K = V = [m_{v_i,r_1}; m_{v_i,r_2}; \cdots ; m_{v_i,r_n}]$, and W^Q, W^K, W^V are the parameters to be learned.

Then the node embedding $m^*_{v_i,r_j}$ under the relationship r_j is denoted as:

$$m^*_{v_i,r_j} = m^{global}_{v_i} + \hat{m}_{v_i,r_j}, \tag{7}$$

where $m^{global}_{v_i}$ is the global embedding under $\mathcal{G}$ with size d and $\hat{m}_{v_i,r_j}$ originates from $\hat{M}_i = [\hat{m}_{v_i,r_1}; \hat{m}_{v_i,r_2}; \cdots ; \hat{m}_{v_i,r_n}]$.

Our goal is to maximize the occurrence of a node v_i with its context. Following [6], we employ heterogeneous negative sampling, and the object function could be written as:

$$\mathcal{L} = -\log \sigma(c_h \cdot m^*_{v_i,r_j}) - \sum_{l=1}^{L} \mathbb{E}_{v_k \sim P_{Neg}} \left[\log \sigma(-c_k \cdot m^*_{v_i,r_j}) \right], \tag{8}$$

where c_h is the context embedding of node v_h and v_h is sampled from a window size of 5 in a path centered on v_i, $\sigma(\cdot)$ is the sigmoid function, represented as $\sigma(x) = \frac{1}{1+e^{-x}}$, P_{Neg} is the probability in negative sampling, c_k is the context embedding of v_k and v_k is the node sampled from P_{Neg}, and L is the number of negative sampling.

4   Experiments

In this section, we first introduce three real-world datasets and the state-of-the-art baselines. Then the performances of *DiffGNN* are illustrated. Finally, the parameter sensitivity and visualization of *DiffGNN* are also discussed.

4.1   Baselines and Experimental Settings

We discuss and analyze the performances of *DiffGNN* on three real-world datasets, which are Amazon [2,11,18], Youtube [22], and IMDB [7]. Amazon is an online shopping dataset that contains information about products. Youtube is the dataset that describes several types of interaction of users. IMDb is an online dataset of films, videos and television programs. The statistics are summarized in Table 1.

Table 2. The experimental results (%) on the Amazon and Youtube datasets ($|\mathcal{O}| = 1$ and $|\mathcal{R}| \geq 2$).

	Amazon			Youtube		
	ROC-AUC	PR-AUC	F1	ROC-AUC	PR-AUC	F1
DeepWalk	56.50	63.18	58.21	51.28	54.12	53.62
node2vec	95.16	94.13	89.34	77.14	72.13	70.75
LINE	68.59	69.32	63.90	61.95	59.06	59.40
MNE	90.28	91.74	83.25	82.30	82.18	75.03
GATNE	97.44	97.05	92.87	84.61	81.93	76.83
DiffGNN	**97.59**	**97.35**	**93.05**	**85.25**	**82.84**	**77.35**

- **Amazon.** Amazon dataset has $10,099$ nodes and $148,659$ edges. Note that $\mathcal{O} = \{product\}$ and $\mathcal{R} = \{also\ bought,\ also\ viewed\}$, which depicts the occurrence of two products. Amazon is the graph with $|\mathcal{O}| = 1$ and $|\mathcal{R}| \geq 2$.
- **Youtube.** Youtube dataset has $2,000$ nodes and $1,310,544$ edegs. Note that $\mathcal{O} = \{user\}$ and $\mathcal{R} = \{contact,\ shared\ friends,\ shared\ subscription,\ shared\ subscriber,\ shared\ videos\}$. Youtube is the graph with $|\mathcal{O}| = 1$ and $|\mathcal{R}| \geq 2$.
- **IMDb.** IMBb dataset has $11,616$ nodes and $34,212$ edges. Note that $\mathcal{O} = \{movie,\ director,\ actor\}$. IMDb is the graph with $|\mathcal{O}| \geq 2$ and $|\mathcal{R}| = 1$.

We compare our *DiffGNN* model with several graph embedding models. Specifically, the state-of-the-art models for the homogeneous network include DeepWalk [20], node2vec [8], and LINE [21]; the state-of-the-art models for the heterogenous network contain MNE [31] and GATNE [2].

Link prediction is one of the most important tasks in graphs as it helps to discover the latent relationship between two nodes that have not formed an edge yet. Furthermore, a recommender system usually incorporates a diversity of node types and edge types, which makes it easy to demonstrate our model outperforms other baselines in different types of heterogeneous networks. In Amazon and Youtube datasets, the train/validation/test ratio is $85\%/5\%/10\%$, while in IMDb, the ratio is set to $80\%/10\%/10\%$. All these nodes and corresponding edges are from the original processed graph. In validation and test set, we also randomly sample the same number of negative edge once a positive edge is generated. The parameter sensitivity is conducted under different hyper-parameter groups, and we adopt early stopping if the performance fails to improve in the lasting 5 epochs.

Following [2], we choose three criteria to evaluate the link prediction results. The evaluation metrics are ROC-AUC [10], PR-AUC [5] and F1 scores.

4.2 Experimental Results and Analysis

Link Prediction. *Results and analysis on the graph with $|\mathcal{O}| = 1$ and $|\mathcal{R}| \geq 2$.* Table 2 reports the performance of all models on the graph with a single node type and multiple edge types, namely the Amazon dataset and Youtube dataset.

Table 3. The experimental results (%) on the IMDb dataset ($|\mathcal{O}| \geq 2$ and $|\mathcal{R}| = 1$).

	ROC-AUC	PR-AUC	F1
DeepWalk	69.01	76.93	62.36
node2vec	90.43	94.86	86.75
LINE	50.38	49.97	50.01
GATNE-R	91.65	94.63	86.22
GATNE-M	90.67	94.05	85.32
DiffGNN-R	**92.33**	**95.04**	**86.78**
DiffGNN-M	91.91	94.84	86.43

For a fair comparison, we set the length of all the metapaths to be 2, which means all methods learn the information from the graph only depending on its first-order neighbors. The limitation on the length helps to exclude the improvement of the performance by the k-layer aggregations ($k > 2$). The results on Table 2 indicate that our *DiffGNN* model outperforms all the baselines. Compared to the models for homogeneous graph, *DiffGNN* achieves an uplift of $2.43 \sim 8.11\%$ in ROC-AUC, $3.22 \sim 10.71\%$ in PR-AUC and $3.71 \sim 6.60\%$ in F1 scores. Compared to the models for heterogeneous graph, *DiffGNN* achieves an uplift of around 0.15% in ROC-AUC, $0.30 \sim 0.91\%$ in PR-AUC and $0.18 \sim 0.52\%$ in F1 scores. The results indicate the importance of RsAtt, as MetaAware is degraded when $|\mathcal{O}| = 1$.

Results and analysis on the graph with $|\mathcal{O}| \geq 2$ and $|\mathcal{R}| = 1$. Table 3 reports the performance of all models on the graph with a single edge type and multiple node types. Both GATNE-R and *Diff*GNN-R represent we adopt random walk based sampling approach while GATNE-M and *DiffGNN*-M represent we adopt metapath based sampling approach. Compared with metapath based sampling approach, random walk based approach achieves better performance, with an uplift of 0.42% in ROC-AUC, 0.20% in PR-AUC and 0.35% in F1 score. This phenomenon illustrates the importance of learning local structures during the sampling stage. It also shows that *DiffGNN* achieves the best performance compared to previous state-of-the-art models, with a performance uplift of 1.24% in ROC-AUC, 0.79% in PR-AUC and 1.11% in F1 scores. It indicates that MetAware aggregation learns heterogeneity better as MetAware uses multi-flow to aggregate information from neighbors. In this experiment, the results indicates the importance of MetaAware ($|\mathcal{O}| \geq 2$), as RsAtt takes little effect when $|\mathcal{R}| = 1$.

Parameter Sensitivity. In *DiffGNN*, there are two hyper-parameters, namely the overall node embedding size d and the intermediate edge embedding size s. To illustrate the influence of these two hyper-parameters, we repeat the link prediction experiment on the amazon dataset with different values of d and s.

First, we fix d to 10 and vary s from 16 to 512. As shown in Fig. 3(a), the performance increases with the growth of s and reaches the top when s reaches 128. Then we fix s to 200 and change d from 2 to 64. We can see from Fig. 3(b)

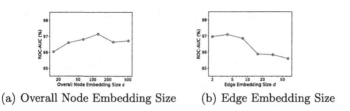

(a) Overall Node Embedding Size   (b) Edge Embedding Size

Fig. 3. The experimental results of parameter sensitivity.

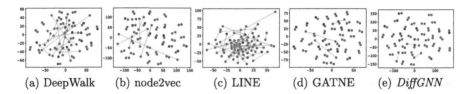

(a) DeepWalk   (b) node2vec   (c) LINE   (d) GATNE   (e) *DiffGNN*

Fig. 4. The Experimental results of visualization

that when $d = 10$, *DiffGNN* gains the best performance. Thus we conclude that neither too small nor too large node/edge embedding size could benefit *DiffGNN*.

Visualization on Node Embedding. We further conduct a visualization experiment to evaluate the similarity of two node embeddings on the IMDb dataset. We use t-SNE [17] to project the high dimensional node embedding to 2-dimensional embedding. Note that the color in Fig. 4 represents the node type, and the line represents two nodes that are connected in the test set. We point out that if a model achieves a good performance on the link prediction task, the distance between two connected nodes should be as closer as possible. Therefore, Fig. 4 also illustrates that *DiffGNN* outperforms all the other baselines. As shown in Fig. 4(e), the distance between two node embeddings connected in the test set is the closest among all the models, which indicates that *DiffGNN* captures the similarity of nodes in multiplex heterogeneous networks.

5   Conclusion

In this paper, we discussed the representation learning problem in multiplex heterogeneous networks in real-world applications. We proposed our *DiffGNN* model, with an aim to capture different behaviors elegantly and efficiently. We first adopted relation-specific attention to learn the attention weights among all split subgraphs, as different relations in the network represent different patterns. Then we proposed metapath aware aggregation to distinguish important patterns in the network. Finally, extensive results showed that *DiffGNN* achieved significantly better results compared to other state-of-the-art methods of both homogeneous network embedding and heterogeneous network embedding in the link prediction task.

References

1. Bian, R., Koh, Y.S., Dobbie, G., Divoli, A.: Network embedding and change modeling in dynamic heterogeneous networks. In: Proceedings of the 42nd SIGIR Conference on Research and Development in Information Retrieval, pp. 861–864 (2019)
2. Cen, Y., Zou, X., Zhang, J., Yang, H., Zhou, J., Tang, J.: Representation learning for attributed multiplex heterogeneous network. In: Proceedings of the 25th ACM SIGKDD International Conference on Knowledge Discovery & Data Mining, pp. 1358–1368 (2019)
3. Chen, C.M., Wang, C.J., Tsai, M.F., Yang, Y.H.: Collaborative similarity embedding for recommender systems. In: WWW Conference, pp. 2637–2643 (2019)
4. Chen, J., Zhang, H., He, X., Nie, L., Liu, W., Chua, T.S.: Attentive collaborative filtering: Multimedia recommendation with item-and component-level attention. In: Proceedings of the 40th SIGIR Conference on Research and Development in Information Retrieval, pp. 335–344 (2017)
5. Davis, J., Goadrich, M.: The relationship between precision-recall and roc curves. In: Proceedings of the 23rd International Conference on Machine Learning, pp. 233–240 (2006)
6. Dong, Y., Chawla, N.V., Swami, A.: metapath2vec: Scalable representation learning for heterogeneous networks. In: Proceedings of the 23rd ACM SIGKDD International Conference on Knowledge Discovery and Data Mining, pp. 135–144 (2017)
7. Fu, X., Zhang, J., Meng, Z., King, I.: Magnn: metapath aggregated graph neural network for heterogeneous graph embedding. In: Proceedings of The Web Conference 2020, pp. 2331–2341 (2020)
8. Grover, A., Leskovec, J.: node2vec: scalable feature learning for networks. In: Proceedings of the 22nd ACM SIGKDD International Conference on Knowledge Discovery and Data Mining, pp. 855–864 (2016)
9. Hamilton, W., Ying, Z., Leskovec, J.: Inductive representation learning on large graphs. In: Advances in Neural Information Processing Systems, pp. 1024–1034 (2017)
10. Hanley, J.A., McNeil, B.J.: The meaning and use of the area under a receiver operating characteristic (roc) curve. Radiology **143**(1), 29–36 (1982)
11. He, R., McAuley, J.: Ups and downs: modeling the visual evolution of fashion trends with one-class collaborative filtering. In: WWW Conference, pp. 507–517 (2016)
12. He, X., Deng, K., Wang, X., Li, Y., Zhang, Y., Wang, M.: Lightgcn: simplifying and powering graph convolution network for recommendation. arXiv preprint arXiv:2002.02126 (2020)
13. He, Y., Song, Y., Li, J., Ji, C., Peng, J., Peng, H.: Hetespaceywalk: a heterogeneous spacey random walk for heterogeneous information network embedding. In: Proceedings of the 28th ACM International Conference on Information and Knowledge Management, pp. 639–648 (2019)
14. Jin, J., et al.: An efficient neighborhood-based interaction model for recommendation on heterogeneous graph. In: Proceedings of the 26th ACM SIGKDD International Conference on Knowledge Discovery & Data Mining, pp. 75–84 (2020)
15. Kipf, T.N., Welling, M.: Semi-supervised classification with graph convolutional networks. arXiv preprint arXiv:1609.02907 (2016)
16. Lu, Y., Shi, C., Hu, L., Liu, Z.: Relation structure-aware heterogeneous information network embedding. In: Proceedings of the AAAI Conference on Artificial Intelligence, vol. 33, pp. 4456–4463 (2019)

17. Maaten, L.v.d., Hinton, G.: Visualizing data using t-SNE. J. Mach. Learn. Res. **9**(11), 2579–2605 (2008)
18. McAuley, J., Targett, C., Shi, Q., Van Den Hengel, A.: Image-based recommendations on styles and substitutes. In: Proceedings of the 38th SIGIR Conference on Research and Development in Information Retrieval, pp. 43–52 (2015)
19. Mikolov, T., Chen, K., Corrado, G., Dean, J.: Efficient estimation of word representations in vector space. arXiv preprint arXiv:1301.3781 (2013)
20. Perozzi, B., Al-Rfou, R., Skiena, S.: Deepwalk: Online learning of social representations. In: Proceedings of the 20th ACM SIGKDD International Conference on Knowledge Discovery and Data Mining, pp. 701–710 (2014)
21. Tang, J., Qu, M., Wang, M., Zhang, M., Yan, J., Mei, Q.: Line: Llarge-scale information network embedding. In: WWW Conference, pp. 1067–1077 (2015)
22. Tang, L., Liu, H.: Uncovering cross-dimension group structures in multidimensional networks. In: SDM Workshop on Analysis of Dynamic Networks, pp. 568–575 (2009)
23. Vaswani, A., et al.: Attention is all you need. In: Advances in Neural Information Processing Systems, pp. 5998–6008 (2017)
24. Wang, D., Cui, P., Zhu, W.: Structural deep network embedding. In: Proceedings of the 22nd ACM SIGKDD International Conference on Knowledge Discovery and Data Mining, pp. 1225–1234 (2016)
25. Wang, W., Yin, H., Du, X., Hua, W., Li, Y., Nguyen, Q.V.H.: Online user representation learning across heterogeneous social networks. In: Proceedings of the 42nd SIGIR Conference on Research and Development in Information Retrieval, pp. 545–554 (2019)
26. Wang, X., He, X., Wang, M., Feng, F., Chua, T.S.: Neural graph collaborative filtering. In: Proceedings of the 42nd SIGIR Conference on Research and Development in Information Retrieval, pp. 165–174 (2019)
27. Wang, X., Jin, H., Zhang, A., He, X., Xu, T., Chua, T.S.: Disentangled graph collaborative filtering. In: Proceedings of the 43rd SIGIR Conference on Research and Development in Information Retrieval, SIGIR 2020, pp. 1001–1010. Association for Computing Machinery, New York (2020)
28. Weston, J., Yee, H., Weiss, R.J.: Learning to rank recommendations with the k-order statistic loss. In: Proceedings of the 7th ACM Conference on Recommender Systems, pp. 245–248 (2013)
29. Ying, R., He, R., Chen, K., Eksombatchai, P., Hamilton, W.L., Leskovec, J.: Graph convolutional neural networks for web-scale recommender systems. In: Proceedings of the 24th ACM SIGKDD International Conference on Knowledge Discovery & Data Mining, pp. 974–983 (2018)
30. Zhang, D., Yin, J., Zhu, X., Zhang, C.: MetaGraph2Vec: complex semantic path augmented heterogeneous network embedding. In: Phung, D., Tseng, V.S., Webb, G.I., Ho, B., Ganji, M., Rashidi, L. (eds.) PAKDD 2018. LNCS (LNAI), vol. 10938, pp. 196–208. Springer, Cham (2018). https://doi.org/10.1007/978-3-319-93037-4_16
31. Zhang, H., Qiu, L., Yi, L., Song, Y.: Scalable multiplex network embedding. In: IJCAI, pp. 3082–3088 (2018)

Graph-Based Exercise- and Knowledge-Aware Learning Network for Student Performance Prediction

Mengfan Liu[1,2], Pengyang Shao[1,2], and Kun Zhang[1,2(✉)]

[1] Key Laboratory of Knowledge Engineering with Big Data,
Hefei University of Technology, Hefei, China
zhkun@hfut.edu.cn
[2] School of Computer Science and Information Engineering,
Hefei University of Technology, Hefei, China

Abstract. Predicting student performance is a fundamental task in Intelligent Tutoring Systems (ITSs), by which we can learn about students' knowledge level and provide personalized teaching strategies for them. Researchers have made plenty of efforts on this task. They either leverage educational psychology methods to predict students' scores according to the learned knowledge proficiency, or make full use of Collaborative Filtering (CF) models to represent latent factors of students and exercises. However, most of these methods either neglect the exercise-specific characteristics (e.g., exercise materials), or cannot fully explore the high-order interactions between students, exercises, as well as knowledge concepts. To this end, we propose a *Graph-based Exercise- and Knowledge-Aware Learning Network* for accurate student score prediction. Specifically, we learn students' mastery of exercises and knowledge concepts respectively to model the two-fold effects of exercises and knowledge concepts. Then, to model the high-order interactions, we apply graph convolution techniques in the prediction process. Extensive experiments on two real-world datasets prove the effectiveness of our proposed *Graph-EKLN*.

Keywords: Education data mining · Intelligent tutoring system · Collaborative filtering · Graph neural network

1 Introduction

Intelligent Tutoring Systems (ITSs) aim at providing personalized guidance for students [2,5], which can be treated as an important supplementary for traditional offline teaching mode. It has attracted enormous attention from both industry and academics [12,22].

Usually, researchers consider the issue from the educational psychology perspective and propose cognitive diagnosis models to discover students' knowledge proficiency [2]. Among them, the Deterministic Inputs, Noisy "And" Gate

© Springer Nature Switzerland AG 2021
L. Fang et al. (Eds.): CICAI 2021, LNAI 13069, pp. 27–38, 2021.
https://doi.org/10.1007/978-3-030-93046-2_3

(DINA) model is a representative method which uses multi-dimensional factors to represent students' knowledge states on specific knowledge concepts [10]. However, they ignore the influence of other exercise-specific characteristics. Knowledge proficiency is not the only factor that affects students' final scores. For example, exercise materials can also influence exercises' difficulty [17].

Moreover, motivated by the observation that students and exercises are collaboratively correlated, researchers borrow success of Matrix Factorization (MF) techniques in recommender systems to model the interactions between students and exercises [25,26]. For example, In [25], the authors applied MF to learn the latent embeddings of students and exercises and predicted the scores based on the inner products of them. Although MF based models achieve great success in ITSs, they still have some weaknesses. First of all, MF based methods are still inadequate in utilizing knowledge concept information, which is very important for student performance prediction. Second, MF based methods cannot deal with the high-order collaborative information between student and exercises.

Since students and exercises naturally form a bipartite graph structure, it is natural to apply Graph Convolutional Network (GCN) to model the high-order collaborative information in the student-exercise-knowledge graph. However, different from scale-free networks, distribution of exercise-knowledge data does not satisfy the power law distribution (i.e., shown in the middle part of Fig. 1). More specifically, the degree distribution of exercise is uniform, i.e., most exercises are related to around 1 to 2 knowledge concepts, as shown in the right part of Fig. 1. Furthermore, the number of knowledge concepts is relatively small. Therefore, knowledge concept nodes would link to many exercise nodes, leading to over smoothing when propagating information through dense links. To this end, in this paper, we propose a novel *Graph-based Exercise- and Knowledge-Aware Learning Network (Graph-EKLN)*, which takes the both influences of exercises and knowledge concepts into consideration for student performance prediction. For the effect of exercises, we apply GCN with link-specific aggregation functions [23] onto the student-exercise bipartite graph to explore the high-order collaborative information. For the effect of knowledge concepts, we replace exercises with their related knowledge concepts, and predict students' performance scores on knowledge concepts by MF. Along this line, the high-

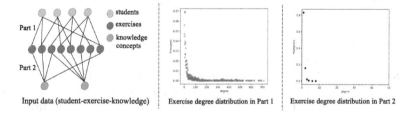

Fig. 1. Data structure of ITSs

order graph structure information and knowledge concept information can be fully explored for the final student performance prediction.

2   Related Work

2.1   Educational Psychology

Educational psychology models are mainly discussed from two sides: cognitive diagnosis models and knowledge tracing models [17,20]. Cognitive diagnosis models, assuming students' knowledge states are static throughout their practice, aim to discover students' proficiency to predict their future performance [5,8,10,18,28,36]. Item Response Theory (IRT) [5,11] was a typical and straightforward cognitive diagnosis model which used a one-dimensional continuous variable θ to indicate each student's knowledge state and used β to indicate each exercise's difficulty. In this way, $(\theta - \beta)$ was proportional to the predicted probability of the question being answered correctly. Another typical model was DINA [10]. DINA was a multi-dimensional discrete model to represent each student with a binary latent vector. We can know whether the student has mastered related knowledge concepts from students' knowledge states ('1' indicates the student has mastered the target knowledge concepts and vice versa). Recently, deep neural networks have been used for cognitive diagnosis. For example, Cheng et al. leveraged deep learning to enhance the process of diagnosing parameters [8]. Wang et al. proposed to incorporate neural networks to learn interaction functions between students and exercises [28]. Knowledge tracing models aims to track the changes of students' knowledge states during practice [9,14,17,24]. Researchers proposed a first-order Markov process model, in which knowledge states will change with transition probabilities after a learning opportunity [9]. Piech et al. introduced a recurrent neural network to describe the change of knowledge states [21]. Liu et al. explored the text content of exercises by integrating a bidirectional LSTM model [17].

2.2   Collaborative Filtering in Recommender Systems

Recommender systems have been widely utilized to help users find their potential interests in many areas [1,7,31]. Classical models utilize MF techniques to learn user and item embeddings [16]. Motivated by the observation that users and items naturally form a bipartite graph, researchers proposed to utilize Graph Convolution Networks (GCNs) to model high-order collaborative signals in user-item bipartite graph [6,23,29,34,35] and social networks [32,33] in recommender systems. E.g., Wang et al. used the graph convolution technique to encode collaborative signals in the propagation process [30]. Wu et al. modeled social diffusion process by propagating embeddings in the social network [33]. Chen et al. enhanced graph based recommendation by empirically removing non-linearities and proposed a residual network based structure [6].

2.3   Collaborative Filtering in ITS

Motivated by the observation that students and exercises are collaboratively correlated, researchers mapped educational data to user-item-rating triple data in recommender systems, then applied MF for predicting student performance [25]. To improve prediction results, Thai et al. proposed MRMF to explore the multiple relationships between students, exercises, and knowledge concepts by MF techniques [26]. Similarly, CRMF integrated the course relationships to update representations of exercises [15]. Moreover, researchers were inspired by social recommendation systems and used the SocialMF technique to improve the prediction accuracy [27]. Furthermore, Nakagawa et al. proposed GKT that viewed knowledge concepts and their dependencies as nodes and links in a graph, so that students' knowledge states on the answered concepts and their related concepts can be both updated over time [19]. Note that, students and exercises naturally form an interaction graph in ITSs. Considering that GCN can enhance recommendation performance in the user-item bipartite graph, we aim to propose a model that applies GCN onto the student-exercise bipartite graph in ITSs.

3   The Proposed Model

3.1   Problem Formulation

Suppose there are M students, N exercises, and O knowledge concepts. Interactions between students and exercises are represented with matrix $\mathbf{R} = \{r_{sp}\}_{M \times N}$, where r_{sp} represents the performance score that student s has on exercise p. In most cases, the observed part of $\mathbf{R}$ consists of 0 and 1, where $r_{sp} = 1$ if student s's answer to exercise p is correct and $r_{sp} = 0$ otherwise. As for relations between exercises and knowledge concepts, educational experts manually label each exercise with several knowledge concepts. We use matrix $\mathbf{Q} = \{q_{pk}\}_{N \times O}$ to denote the relations, where $q_{pk} = 1$ if exercise p is related to knowledge concept k and $q_{pk} = 0$ if there are no relations between them. Given observed interactions $\mathbf{R}$ and relations between exercises and knowledge concepts $\mathbf{Q}$, we aim to predict unobserved $\hat{r}_{sp}$, namely student s's score on non-interactive exercise p.

3.2   Overall Structure

The overall structure of *Graph-based Exercise- and Knowledge-Aware Learning Network* (*Graph-EKLN*) is shown in Fig. 2. In the left part of Fig. 2, links between students and exercises are established according to matrix R and links between exercises and knowledge concepts are established according to matrix Q. There two challenges in our task: how to handle with the different links (correct answer/wrong answer) between students and exercises and how to utilize knowledge concept information in MF based models.

To address these two challenges, we divide the task into two sub-tasks, as shown in the middle part of Fig. 2. The first sub-task is to predict student s's proficiency on exercise p itself $\hat{r}_{sp}^{\mathcal{P}}$. Note that, $\mathcal{P}$ denotes the predicted score $\hat{r}_{sp}^{\mathcal{P}}$ is in the exercise space. The second sub-task is to predict a student's proficiency on an exercise's related knowledge concepts $\hat{r}_{sp}^{\mathcal{K}}$. Note that, $\mathcal{K}$ denotes the predicted score $\hat{r}_{sp}^{\mathcal{K}}$ is in the knowledge space. The following two subsections describe the two sub-tasks respectively.

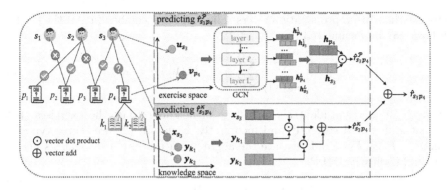

Fig. 2. The overall structure of our proposed *Graph-EKLN*.

3.3   Modeling High-Order Collaborative Information

Student embeddings and exercise embeddings in the exercise space are represented with $\mathbf{U} = [\mathbf{u}_1, ..., \mathbf{u}_s, ..., \mathbf{u}_M] \in \mathbb{R}^{M \times D}$, $\mathbf{V} = [\mathbf{v}_1, ..., \mathbf{v}_p, ..., \mathbf{v}_N] \in \mathbb{R}^{N \times D}$ respectively. D denotes the embedding size and $\mathbf{u}_s, \mathbf{v}_p$ represent the initial embeddings of student s and exercise p. To address the different-link problem mentioned in Subsect. 3.2, we follow R-GCN [23], which is proposed to learn representations of multi-relational graph.

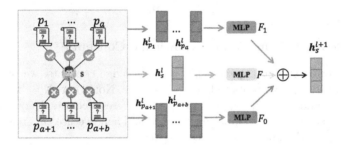

Fig. 3. The graph convolution layer in our model. Suppose student s has good performance scores on a exercises and bad performance scores on other b exercises. We show the information propagation process of the graph convolution layer on student s.

Figure 3 provides an overview of the one-layer GCN propagation process in our model. Specifically, we utilize link-specific aggregation functions based on multilayer perceptrons (MLPs) for two kinds of links, thus getting high-order students' and exercises' embeddings. Students' and exercises' initial embedding can be formulated as

$$\mathbf{h}_s^0 = \mathbf{u}_s, \mathbf{h}_p^0 = \mathbf{v}_p. \tag{1}$$

Suppose there are L propagation layers. The student s's embedding at the $(l+1)$-th layer can be formulated as:

$$\mathbf{h}_s^{(l+1)} = \sum_{n\in\{0,1\}} \sum_{p\in\mathcal{N}_s^n} \frac{1}{|\mathcal{N}_s^n|} F_n(\mathbf{h}_p^l) + F(\mathbf{h}_s^l), \tag{2}$$

where $\mathcal{N}_s^n$ denotes student s's n-th type of neighbors, i.e., the exercises that student s answered correctly and incorrectly. Equation (2) uses three types of functions F, F_0, F_1 to differentiate the aggregation process of student s's neighbors and itself with MLPs:

$$F_n(\mathbf{h}^l) = \sigma_2(\sigma_1(\mathbf{h}^l W_1))W_2, \tag{3}$$

where σ_1, σ_2 denote activation functions and W_1, W_2 denote the linear transformation. The exercise p's embedding can be obtained by aggregating embeddings of its neighbor nodes in the same way. After propagating information, we can obtain $[\mathbf{h}_s^0, ..., \mathbf{h}_s^l, .., \mathbf{h}_s^L]$ and $[\mathbf{h}_p^0, ..., \mathbf{h}_p^l, .., \mathbf{h}_p^L]$ as students' and exercises' embeddings of each layer. We concatenate embeddings of each layer as follows:

$$\mathbf{h}_s = \mathbf{h}_s^0||...||\mathbf{h}_s^l||...||\mathbf{h}_s^L, \quad \mathbf{h}_p = \mathbf{h}_p^0||...||\mathbf{h}_p^l||...||\mathbf{h}_p^L, \tag{4}$$

where $||$ is the concatenation operation. By calculating the inner dot of concatenated embeddings, we can get student s's proficiency on exercise p in the exercise space:

$$\hat{r}_{sp}^{\mathcal{P}} = \mathbf{h}_s^T \mathbf{h}_p. \tag{5}$$

3.4   Modeling Information of Knowledge Concepts

As for predicting students' proficiency on knowledge concepts, we project students and knowledge concepts to knowledge-space. Note that, $\mathbf{X} = [\mathbf{x}_1, ..., \mathbf{x}_s, ..., \mathbf{x}_M] \in \mathbb{R}^{M\times D}$ and $\mathbf{Y} = [\mathbf{y}_1, ..., \mathbf{y}_k, ..., \mathbf{y}_O] \in \mathbb{R}^{O\times D}$ respectively denote the representations of students and knowledge concepts. Then, we use the inner product to predict $\hat{r}_{sp}^{\mathcal{K}}$ in the knowledge concept space:

$$\hat{r}_{sp}^{\mathcal{K}} = \frac{1}{|\mathcal{K}_p|} \sum_{k\in\mathcal{K}_p} \mathbf{x}_s^{\mathrm{T}} \mathbf{y}_k, \tag{6}$$

where $|\mathcal{K}_p|$ denotes the set of knowledge concepts related to exercise p. It can be formulated as $\mathcal{K}_p = \{k|q_{pk} = 1\}$, while $q_{pk} \in \mathbf{Q}$. Please note that, we do not utilize GCN layer here. In fact, the number of knowledge concepts is much smaller than that of exercises. Thus, relations between students and knowledge concepts are not sparse enough. Therefore, we keep their original embeddings rather than utilizing GCN layers in Eq. (6) to avoid over smoothing.

3.5   Performance Prediction

In Subsect. 3.3, we model the effect of exercises by R-GCN technique. In Subsect. 3.4, we model the effect of knowledge concepts by inner product of student and knowledge concepts related to the target exercise. After obtaining $\hat{r}_{sp}^{\mathcal{P}}$ and $\hat{r}_{sp}^{\mathcal{K}}$, we can easily calculate student s's final predicted scores on exercise p. Thus the overall predicted function is defined as:

$$\hat{r}_{sp} = \hat{r}_{sp}^{\mathcal{P}} + \alpha \hat{r}_{sp}^{\mathcal{K}}, \tag{7}$$

where α is a hyper-parameter used to control the balance between the two subtasks. We use the point-wise based squared loss to optimize our model:

$$L = \frac{1}{T} \sum_{(s,p,r_{sp}) \in (S,P,\mathbf{R})} (r_{sp} - \hat{r}_{sp})^2, \tag{8}$$

where T denotes the number of (s, p, r_{sp}) triplets in training data.

4   Experiments

4.1   Dataset Description

Table 1. The statistics of the two datasets

Dataset	Students	Exercises	Concepts	Logs	Density
ASISST	4,163	17,746	123	278,868	0.37%
KDDcup	574	173,650	437	609,979	0.61%

We choose two widely-used datasets in our experiments. One dataset is ASSIST (ASSISTments 2009–2010 "skill builder")[1] provided by the online educational service ASSISTments. The other dataset is Algebra 2005–2006 from the Educational Data Mining Challenge of KDDCup[2]. The detailed statistics of two datasets are summarized in Table 1. Note that, we only consider exercises that are related to at least one knowledge concept. Specifically, we filter out exercises without related knowledge concepts for the two datasets. Because the number of concepts in KDDcup dataset is too small to make full use of concept information, we combine the knowledge concepts related to the same exercise as a new single concept. Please note that, these two datasets are extremely different. Specifically, in ASISST, each student has nearly 67 logs on average while in KDDcup, each student has nearly 1,063 logs.

---

[1] https://sites.google.com/site/assistmentsdata/home.
[2] http://pslcdatashop.web.cmu.edu/KDDCup/.

4.2   Experimental Settings

Evaluation Metrics. We adopt three widely used metrics (Accuracy, RMSE, and AUC) to measure the error between true ratings and predicted ratings [17,19,28]. Root mean square error (RMSE) is used to measure the absolute difference between predicted labels and real labels [3]. As students' performance scores are binary, we utilize the area under the curve (AUC) [4] as a metric.

Baselines. We compare our model with the following methods:

- **Student Average**: This method calculates students' average scores in training data and uses them as the predicted scores on exercises in testing data.
- **MF** [16]: It is a classical CF model in recommendations. This model utilizes MF techniques and learns latent representations of students and exercises. Note that knowledge concepts are not used in MF.
- **IRT** [11]: A classical cognitive diagnosis model that uses one-dimensional continuous variables to represent students' knowledge proficiency and exercises' difficulty, and uses the difference between them for score prediction.
- **NeuralCDM** [28]: This is an improved multi-dimensional cognitive diagnosis model that utilizes neural networks as the interaction function.
- **CRMF** [15]: This MF based model takes knowledge concepts into consideration by assuming that representations of exercises with the same knowledge concepts are more similar.
- **R-GCN** [23]: A substructure of our model that only uses R-GCN to predict scores but neglects students' proficiency on knowledge concepts.
- **R-GCN (hetero)**: In this method, We apply GCN in the whole student-exercise-knowledge heterogeneous graph in Fig. 1.

Parameter Settings. We implement our model in PyTorch-1.6.0. The embedding dimension is set to 128 for our model and other CF models. We initialize all parameters with Xavier initialization [13]. The learning rate is set to 0.001. We set the depth of GCN as two layers. We choose 2-layer MLPs to serve as F in Eq. (3) and LeakyReLU as the activation function. We also set the balancing parameter $\alpha = 1$.

4.3   Experimental Results

We list the results of our model and other baselines in Table 2. We have several observations from this table.

First, Student Average is the simplest baseline. It assumes that students have the same scores on different exercises, resulting in the worst performance. Second, classical MF based models (MF and CRMF) perform worse than our proposed *Graph-EKLN* on both two datasets. An obvious reason is that they ignore high-order collaborative information. Simultaneously, CRMF performs better than MF for considering course relations. Third, as for two cognitive diagnosis models (NeuralCDM and IRT), we observe that cognitive diagnosis models perform worse than all MF based model on the ASSIST dataset. MF based models explore similarity among students/exercises, and then provide suggested guidance for students based on the similarities. The reason is that lack of sufficient data brings trouble in cognitive diagnosis models while it has fewer effects on CF based models (MF, CRMF, R-GCN, and *Graph-EKLN*). Fourth, R-GCN (hetero) even performs worse than R-GCN on KDDcup. The reason is that data in the heterogeneous graph doesn't obey power law distribution, therefore, common graph based methods cannot be directly applied onto ITSs as mentioned in Sect. 1. Finally, our proposed *Graph-EKLN* has the best performance on both two datasets. The reason is that *Graph-EKLN* simultaneously utilizes information of high-order collaborative signals and related knowledge concepts.

Table 2. Overall performance. ↑ / ↓ denotes that the higher/lower, the better.

Model	ASSIST			KDDcup		
	Accuracy↑	RMSE↓	AUC↑	Accuracy↑	RMSE↓	AUC↑
Student average	0.6942	0.4483	0.6816	0.7679	0.4190	0.5891
MF	0.7399	0.4205	0.8105	0.7927	0.3841	0.8062
IRT	0.7181	0.4647	0.7394	0.7762	0.4835	0.7607
NeuralCDM	0.7249	0.4329	0.7561	0.8060	0.3713	0.8093
CRMF	0.7612	0.4134	0.8136	0.8014	0.3750	0.7968
R-GCN	0.7705	0.3982	0.8230	0.8205	0.3619	0.8239
R-GCN (hetero)	0.7748	0.3973	0.8232	0.8201	0.3642	0.8187
Graph-EKLN	**0.7782**	**0.3938**	**0.8298**	**0.8271**	**0.3591**	**0.8291**

4.4   Detailed Model Analyses

Ablation Study. We perform an ablation study to demonstrate the effectiveness of each component in our model. Specifically, we conduct four experiments to figure out whether graph based techniques (denoted as GCN) and utilizing knowledge concepts (KLG) are effective in ITSs. The basic model is MF, which only utilizes MF techniques. Besides MF techniques, MF-TEM follows Subsect. 3.4 to use knowledge concepts. MF and R-GCN are recorded in Subsect. 4.2. As shown in Table 3, MF-TEM performs better than MF. It proves that utilizing knowledge concepts is effective. Similarly, R-GCN also performs better than MF, which proves that capturing high-order collaborative signals is helpful for student score prediction. Finally, our proposed *Graph-EKLN* performs best to prove that simultaneously considering R-GCN and knowledge concepts has the most performance improvements.

Performance Under Different Balancing Parameter α. As mentioned in Eq. (7), α is a hyper-parameter that controls balance between two-fold effects. We try the parameter α in the range $\{0, 0.1, 1, 5, 10\}$. Note that, $\alpha = 0$ denotes only taking the exercise space into consideration, and *Graph-EKLN* degenerates

Table 3. The ablation study

Model	Components		ASSIST			KDDcup		
	KLG	GCN	Accuracy ↑	RMSE ↓	AUC ↑	Accuracy ↑	RMSE ↓	AUC ↑
MF	×	×	0.7399	0.4205	0.8105	0.7927	0.3841	0.8062
MF-TEM	✓	×	0.7664	0.3984	0.8288	0.8255	0.3626	0.8246
R-GCN	×	✓	0.7705	0.3982	0.8230	0.8205	0.3619	0.8239
Graph-EKLN	✓	✓	**0.7782**	**0.3938**	**0.8298**	**0.8271**	**0.3591**	**0.8291**

to R-GCN. As shown in Fig. 4, when $\alpha \to 0$, the results become worse; when α becomes higher (e.g., $\alpha = 5, 10$), the results also become worse. Finally, *Graph-EKLN* has the best performance on two datasets when $\alpha = 1$.

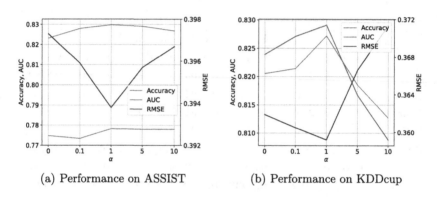

(a) Performance on ASSIST   (b) Performance on KDDcup

Fig. 4. Results of accuracy, AUC, and RMSE with different α

5   Conclusions

In this paper, we proposed a *Graph-based Exercise- and Knowledge-Aware Learning Network* to improve student performance prediction in ITSs. We borrowed the success of neural graph based models in recommender systems and successfully modeled two-fold effects of exercises and related knowledge concepts. Experimental results on two datasets showed the effectiveness of our model. Note that, we assumed that students' knowledge states are static in this paper. In the future, we are interested in extending our model to a dynamic model which can track the changes in knowledge states.

Acknowledgments. This work is supported in part by grants from iFLYTEK, P.R. China (Grant No. COGOS-20190002) and the Open Project Program of the National Laboratory of Pattern Recognition (NLPR).

References

1. An, M., Wu, F., Wu, C., Zhang, K., Liu, Z., Xie, X.: Neural news recommendation with long-and short-term user representations. In: Proceedings of the 57th Annual Meeting of the Association for Computational Linguistics, pp. 336–345 (2019)
2. Anderson, A., Huttenlocher, D., Kleinberg, J., Leskovec, J.: Engaging with massive online courses. In: Proceedings of WWW, pp. 687–698 (2014)
3. Barnston, A.G.: Correspondence among the correlation, RMSE, and Heidke forecast verification measures; refinement of the Heidke score. Weather Forecast. 7(4), 699–709 (1992)
4. Bradley, A.P.: The use of the area under the roc curve in the evaluation of machine learning algorithms. Pattern Recogn. 30(7), 1145–1159 (1997)
5. Burns, H., Luckhardt, C.A., Parlett, J.W., Redfield, C.L.: Intelligent Tutoring Systems: Evolutions in Design. Psychology Press, Hove (2014)
6. Chen, L., Wu, L., Hong, R., Zhang, K., Wang, M.: Revisiting graph based collaborative filtering: a linear residual graph convolutional network approach. In: Proceedings of AAAI, vol. 34, pp. 27–34 (2020)
7. Chen, L., Wu, L., Zhang, K., Hong, R., Wang, M.: Set2setrank: collaborative set to set ranking for implicit feedback based recommendation. arXiv preprint arXiv:2105.07377 (2021)
8. Cheng, S., et al..: Dirt: deep learning enhanced item response theory for cognitive diagnosis. In: Proceedings of CIKM, pp. 2397–2400 (2019)
9. Corbett, A.T., Anderson, J.R.: Knowledge tracing: modeling the acquisition of procedural knowledge. User Model. User-Adap. Inter. 4(4), 253–278 (1994)
10. De La Torre, J.: Dina model and parameter estimation: a didactic. J. Educ. Behav. Stat. 34(1), 115–130 (2009)
11. Embretson, S.E., Reise, S.P.: Item Response Theory. Psychology Press, Hove (2013)
12. Feng, M., Heffernan, N., Koedinger, K.: Addressing the assessment challenge with an online system that tutors as it assesses. User Model. User-Adap. Inter. 19(3), 243–266 (2009)
13. Glorot, X., Bengio, Y.: Understanding the difficulty of training deep feedforward neural networks. In: Proceedings of AISTATS, pp. 249–256 (2010)
14. Huang, Z., et al.: Learning or forgetting? A dynamic approach for tracking the knowledge proficiency of students. ACM Trans. Inf. Syst. (TOIS) 38(2), 1–33 (2020)
15. Huynh-Ly, T.N., Le, H.T., Nguyen, T.N.: Integrating courses' relationship into predicting student performance. Int. J. 9(4) (2020)
16. Koren, Y., Bell, R., Volinsky, C.: Matrix factorization techniques for recommender systems. Computer 42(8), 30–37 (2009)
17. Liu, Q., et al.: EKT: exercise-aware knowledge tracing for student performance prediction. IEEE Trans. Knowl. Data Eng. 33(1), 100–115 (2019)
18. Liu, Q., et al.: Fuzzy cognitive diagnosis for modelling examinee performance. ACM Trans. Intell. Syst. Technol. 9(4), 1–26 (2018)
19. Nakagawa, H., Iwasawa, Y., Matsuo, Y.: Graph-based knowledge tracing: modeling student proficiency using graph neural network. In: IEEE/WIC/ACM International Conference on Web Intelligence, pp. 156–163 (2019)
20. Pandey, S., Srivastava, J.: RKT: relation-aware self-attention for knowledge tracing. In: Proceedings of CIKM, pp. 1205–1214 (2020)
21. Piech, C., et al.: Deep knowledge tracing. arXiv preprint arXiv:1506.05908 (2015)

22. Romero, C., Ventura, S., Pechenizkiy, M., Baker, R.S.: Handbook of Educational Data Mining. CRC Press, Boca Raton (2010)
23. Schlichtkrull, M., Kipf, T.N., Bloem, P., Van Den Berg, R., Titov, I., Welling, M.: Modeling relational data with graph convolutional networks. In: ESWC, pp. 593–607 (2018)
24. Shen, S., et al.: Convolutional knowledge tracing: modeling individualization in student learning process. In: Proceedings of the 43rd International ACM SIGIR Conference on Research and Development in Information Retrieval, pp. 1857–1860 (2020)
25. Thai-Nghe, N., Drumond, L., Krohn-Grimberghe, A., Schmidt-Thieme, L.: Recommender system for predicting student performance. Procedia Comput. Sci. 1(2), 2811–2819 (2010)
26. Thai-Nghe, N., Schmidt-Thieme, L.: Multi-relational factorization models for student modeling in intelligent tutoring systems. In: IEEE KSE, pp. 61–66 (2015)
27. Thanh-Nhan, H.L., Huy-Thap, L., Thai-Nghe, N.: Toward integrating social networks into intelligent tutoring systems. In: IEEE KSE, pp. 112–117 (2017)
28. Wang, F., et al.: Neural cognitive diagnosis for intelligent education systems. In: Proceedings of AAAI, vol. 34, pp. 6153–6161 (2020)
29. Wang, S., Zhang, K., Wu, L., Ma, H., Hong, R., Wang, M.: Privileged graph distillation for cold start recommendation. arXiv preprint arXiv:2105.14975 (2021)
30. Wang, X., He, X., Wang, M., Feng, F., Chua, T.S.: Neural graph collaborative filtering. In: Proceedings of ACM SIGIR, pp. 165–174 (2019)
31. Wu, L., He, X., Wang, X., Zhang, K., Wang, M.: A survey on neural recommendation: From collaborative filtering to content and context enriched recommendation. arXiv preprint arXiv:2104.13030 (2021)
32. Wu, L., Li, J., Sun, P., Hong, R., Ge, Y., Wang, M.: Diffnet++: a neural influence and interest diffusion network for social recommendation. arXiv preprint arXiv:2002.00844 (2020)
33. Wu, L., Sun, P., Fu, Y., Hong, R., Wang, X., Wang, M.: A neural influence diffusion model for social recommendation. In: Proceedings of the 42nd International ACM SIGIR Conference on Research and Development in Information Retrieval, pp. 235–244 (2019)
34. Wu, L., Yang, Y., Chen, L., Lian, D., Hong, R., Wang, M.: Learning to transfer graph embeddings for inductive graph based recommendation. In: Proceedings of the 43rd International ACM SIGIR Conference on Research and Development in Information Retrieval, pp. 1211–1220 (2020)
35. Wu, L., Yang, Y., Zhang, K., Hong, R., Fu, Y., Wang, M.: Joint item recommendation and attribute inference: an adaptive graph convolutional network approach. In: Proceedings of the 43rd International ACM SIGIR Conference on Research and Development in Information Retrieval, pp. 679–688 (2020)
36. Zhu, T., et al.: MT-MCD: a multi-task cognitive diagnosis framework for student assessment. In: Pei, J., Manolopoulos, Y., Sadiq, S., Li, J. (eds.) DASFAA 2018. LNCS, vol. 10828, pp. 318–335. Springer, Cham (2018). https://doi.org/10.1007/978-3-319-91458-9_19

Increasing Oversampling Diversity
for Long-Tailed Visual Recognition

Liuyu Xiang[1,2], Guiguang Ding[1,2(✉)], and Jungong Han[3]

[1] School of Software, Tsinghua University, Beijing, China
xiangly17@mails.tsinghua.edu.cn
[2] Beijing National Research Center for Information Science
and Technology (BNRist), Beijing, China
dinggg@tsinghua.edu.cn
[3] Computer Science Department, Aberystwyth University,
Aberystwyth SY23 3FL, UK

Abstract. The long-tailed data distribution in real-world greatly increases the difficulty of training deep neural networks. Oversampling minority classes is one of the commonly used techniques to tackle this problem. In this paper, we first analyze that the commonly used oversampling technique tends to distort the representation learning and harm the network's generalizability. Then we propose two novel methods to increase the minority feature's diversity to alleviate such issue. Specifically, from the data perspective, we propose a mixup-based Synthetic Minority Over-sampling TEchnique called mixSMOTE, where tail class samples are synthesized from head classes so that a balanced training distribution can be obtained. Then from the model perspective, we propose Gradient Re-weighting Module (GRM) to re-distribute each instance's gradient contribution to the representation learning network. Extensive experiments on the long-tailed benchmark CIFAR10-LT, CIFAR100-LT and ImageNet-LT demonstrate the effectiveness of our proposed method.

Keywords: Long-tailed classification · Data imbalance · Oversampling

1 Introduction

In real-world scenarios, visual concepts usually tend to exhibit a long-tailed distribution, where instance-rich (or head) classes usually have abundant data while instance-scarce (or tail) classes only have few instances [1,4,9–11,16,20]. This long-tailed distribution usually brings profound negative impact for deep neural network training, as head classes tend to dominate the training process and lead to poor performance on tail classes.

In the literature, two widely used approaches for long-tailed classification are cost-sensitive learning and re-sampling. Cost-sensitive learning methods usually involve designing re-weighting loss functions [2,6,17,30] so that losses are re-weighted in a classwise manner. Re-sampling methods can either oversample

© Springer Nature Switzerland AG 2021
L. Fang et al. (Eds.): CICAI 2021, LNAI 13069, pp. 39–50, 2021.
https://doi.org/10.1007/978-3-030-93046-2_4

tail classes or undersample head classes. However, oversampling may lead to overfitting to the few samples in tail classes, while undersampling may cause information loss in head classes. Besides, recent methods also tackle this problem through head-to-tail knowledge transfer [15,18,25,26].

In this paper, we mainly focus on the commonly used oversampling technique where larger probabilities are assigned to sample tail class instances during training. While oversampling could alleviate head class dominance, it also distorts the underlying feature distribution and may hamper the representation learning.

To solve the dilemma between head class dominance and tail class overfitting in oversampling, we propose two techniques from both data and model level to enrich the oversampled tail feature diversity, so that a more generalizable representation can be obtained. Specifically, from the data perspective, we propose mixSMOTE to exploit the rich visual variations from the head classes and transfer them to the tail classes via mixup [29]. We demonstrate that mixSMOTE not only transfers the intra-class variations in a head-to-tail style, but also result in a less biased decision boundary which is beneficial for generalization.

Then from the perspective of network learning, we propose Gradient Re-weighting Module (GRM) to re-distribute each instance's contribution in the visual feature space. To be more specific, the GRM is plugged in between the feature learning network and the classifier and transforms the gradient distribution during the backward propagation via gradient re-weighting. In this way, the feature learning network will be less influenced by those oversampled tail class instances and the tail class overfitting is mitigated.

To verify the effectiveness of our proposed method, we conduct extensive experiments on the long-tailed benchmark CIFAR10-LT, CIFAR100-LT [2] and ImageNet-LT [18]. The results show that our method is able to achieve comparable or even superior results compared to the current state-of-the-art methods.

In summary, we make the following contributions: (1) We analyze that the commonly used oversampling will harm the feature learning network and lead to deteriorated generalizability. (2) We propose mixSMOTE to enrich the tail class diversity by exploiting the variation information from head classes. It is also beneficial for the deep network to have a more generalizable decision boundary. (3) We propose Gradient Re-weighting Module to re-distribute each instance's gradient contribution and down-weight those from oversampled instances, so that a more generalizable representation will be learned. (4) Extensive experiments demonstrate that our proposed method is able to achieve promising results on three long-tailed classification benchmarks. The effectiveness of each technique is also verified through ablation studies.

2   Related Work

The long-tailed classification problem has attracted increasing attention due to the prevalence of data imbalance. Current long-tailed classification methods mainly tackle this problem from the following three directions:

Re-sampling. These methods either oversample tail classes [3,5,28] or undersample head classes [7,11,22] to obtain a balanced training distribution. For undersampling methods, the most straightforward way is to randomly discard head class instances so that the training data is less imbalanced [11]. More recently, a trainable undersampling strategy is proposed in [22]. For oversampling methods, the most straightforward way is to sample duplicates of the tail class instances. Besides, Chawla et al. [3] propose the famous Synthetic Minority Oversampling TEchnique (SMOTE) to oversample minority samples by creating synthetic interpolated minority instances.

Cost-sensitive Re-weighting. Most re-weighting methods aim to design re-weighted loss functions such that head and tail classes are regularized at different levels [6,13,17,24,30]. Among these methods, Range Loss [30] minimizes the range of each category so that intra-class variations are reduced. Focal Loss [17] downweights the loss assigned to well-classified examples where LDAM (Label-Distribution-Aware Margin Loss) [2] encourages minority classes to have larger margins to achieve better generalization. Class-balanced Loss is proposed in [6] where the effective number of samples is calculated. Efforts have also been made to automatically learn a re-weighting function via meta learning [13,23,24,27].

Head-to-tail Knowledge Transfer. Another line of work tries to tackle the long-tailed problem from head-to-tail transfer [14,18,25,26]. Wang et al. [25] propose to progressively learn a transformation from head to tail classifiers. Liu et al. [18] propose to learn meta embedding equipped with a memory module for such knowledge transfer. Moreover, Kang et al. [14] propose to decouple the feature extractor and the classifier and train them sequentially in a two-stage manner.

3 Proposed Method

3.1 Problem Setup

Suppose we have a long-tailed distribution training set $\mathcal{D}_{train} = \{x_i, y_i\}$, $i \in \{1, ..., N\}$ where x_i is the i-th data point with label y_i, and N is the total number of training samples. We denote C as the total number of classes and N_c to be the number of samples for class c where $\sum_i N_i = N$. Without loss of generality, we assume that the classes are sorted by its cardinality in decreasing order, such that $N_1 \geq N_2 \geq ... \geq N_C$. Since the training set is long-tailed, we have $N_1 \gg N_C$. We also define tail classes $\{c | N_c \leq N_{th}\}$ with threshold N_{th}. For test-time evaluation, we have a balanced test set $\mathcal{D}_{test}$, such that $N_1^{test} \simeq N_C^{test}$.

For a deep neural network which learns a mapping function $y = F(x; \Theta)$, where Θ are model parameters. We denote its representation learning part as f_ϕ whose architecture is usually a deep CNN model. We denote its classifier as g_w where $g(f(x; \phi); w)$ outputs the model's prediction over classes $p(y|x)$.

Analysis of Oversampling Technique. While oversampling gives a more **class-wise** balanced training, we argue that, for feature learning network, it witnesses a distorted and highly-imbalanced **instance-wise** visual input distribution. Consider an extremely imbalanced case (which could be quite common in real-world) where only 5 samples are available for a certain tail class, and the head classes contain more than 1000 samples. If we adopt class-balanced oversampling, then for every epoch, the feature learning network will see 1000 variations of the head class, but only 5 variations of the tail class. In other words, the same visual inputs of this tail class will appear 200 times more than other head samples. This could lead to severe overfitting and harms the representation generalizability.

3.2   mixSMOTE

Method. The main idea of mixSMOTE is to interpolate between head and tail classes with different probabilities so that the diversity of the oversampled tail classes can be augmented. In order to do so, we first adopt a class-balanced oversampling strategy, where each class is sampled with equal probability within each mini-batch. While the class-balanced oversampling will result in a more balanced distribution for the classifier, it will cause representation overfitting to the tail instances. For an instance from class c, i.e. $(x_i, y_i), y_i = c$, the less class cardinality N_c is, the higher frequency x_i will be sampled, thus it will more likely to be overfitted. We then propose to select tail instances according to their class cardinalities to mixup with randomly selected head instances. Intuitively, a smaller class cardinality N_c will lead to severer overfitting, thus requires a higher probability to be selected for mixup.

Given the analysis above, for each tail instance in a class-balanced sampled mini-batch, the tail instances are selected for mixup according to Bernoulli(p_c) where p_c is the probability for class c that satisfies $\forall i, j \in$ tail class, if $N_i < N_j$, then $p_i > p_j$. In practice, we calculate p_c as follows:

$$p_c = \gamma \frac{\log(N_{min})}{\log(N_c)}$$

where γ is the hyperparameter and $N_{min} = N_C$ is the smallest class cardinality. Note that calculating p_c can have many choices and we choose the log() function to smooth the ratio between different N_c as N_{min} can be several magnitudes smaller than other N_c in the extremely imbalanced scenarios.

Once we acquire the selected tail instances $\{(x_i^t, y_i^t)\}$, we mix them up with randomly selected head instances $\{(x_j^h, y_j^h)\}$ within the same mini-batch:

$$\tilde{x}_i^t = \lambda x_i^t + (1 - \lambda)x_j^h \qquad \tilde{y}_i^t = \lambda y_i^t + (1 - \lambda)y_j^h$$

where $\lambda \sim$ uniform(a, b), $0 \leq a < b \leq 1$. Then we replace x_i^t with $\tilde{x}_i^t$ during the network training.

Toy Example. To see what mixSMOTE is actually doing, we illustrate two toy examples on the long-tailed *two moon* and *circle* datasets. We train a one hidden layer MLP with and without mixSMOTE, and plot $p(y|x)$ in Fig. 1. From the result of ordinary training without mixSMOTE (Fig. 1(a, c)), we find that the decision boundary is biased towards the head class (red points) because of the data imbalance, in which case the tail class instances may easily fall on the wrong side of the decision boundary (see the blue point on the top left in Fig. 1(a), the right side of the inner circle in Fig. 1(c)).

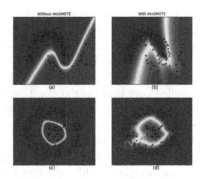

Fig. 1. Effect of mixSMOTE on two toy datasets.

Then by training with mixSMOTE (Fig. 1(b, d)) we find that the sharp decision boundary becomes smoother and less biased, and those misclassified blue points are able to fall on the right side of the decision boundary. The underlying reason is that **mixSMOTE smoothens and rectifies the decision boundary, so that the tail class acquires a larger margin away from the decision boundary**. This phenomenon is also in line with the spirit of LDAM [2], that encouraging a larger margin for tail classes will improve the generalization of the network.

3.3 Gradient Re-weighting Module

According to the previous analysis, while the feature space needs more diversity and the output space (classifier) needs to be more balanced, this is actually requiring **an instance-wise balanced representation learning and a class-wise balanced classifier**. Since oversampling already makes the distribution class-wise balanced, we wish to downweight those oversampled instances' contribution to the representation learning, so that the representation network will witness each visual instances as equally as possible.

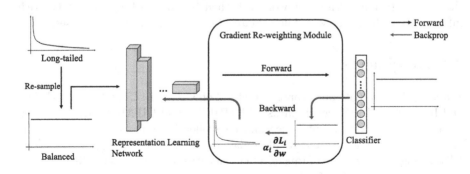

Fig. 2. Illustration of GRM.

To achieve the aforementioned goal, we propose to use gradient re-weighting for such distribution transformation, so that an instance-wise balanced representation distribution can be obtained.

Similar to previous analysis, a smaller class cardinality N_c indicates a higher frequency for x_i to be sampled. For those few samples from tail classes being sampled over and over again, they will not bring any new visual information to the representation network but will rather lead to overfitting. On the other hand, head classes contain more samples with more diversity thus should be emphasized during the representation learning. In other words, when backpropagating through the representation learning network, gradients from tail classes should be downweighted while gradients from head classes should be assigned with a larger weight.

Formally, the GRM layer can be formulated as a function $R(x; \alpha)$ whose forward and backward functions are:

$$\text{Forward} : R(x; \alpha) = x$$

$$\text{Backward} : \frac{dR(x; \alpha)}{dx} = \alpha_c I$$

where α is the gradient re-weighting factor, I is an identity matrix and c is the class x_i belongs to. The GRM is inserted between the feature extractor and the classifier for distribution transformation. While the forward pass of the network remains unchanged, the gradients are re-weighted according to class cardinality when backpropagated through GRM. Furthermore, from the previous analysis, α_c should be proportional to the class cardinality N_c. In practice, we define

$$\alpha_c = \beta \frac{\log(N_c)}{\log(N_{max})}$$

where β is the hyperparameter and N_{max} is the maximum class cardinality in the current mini-batch. A schematic illustration of the proposed GRM can be found in Fig. 2.

During the inference time, since GRM makes no changes during the forward pass, it will not bring any extra computational cost. By re-weighting the gradient, the representation learning network will then be able to fully exploit the rich information in head classes while also avoid overfitting to the tail classes.

4   Experiments

Datasets. We evaluate our proposed method on CIFAR10-LT, CIFAR100-LT [2] and ImageNet-LT [18] benchmarks. CIFAR10-LT and CIFAR100-LT is created with exponential decay imbalance and controllable imbalance ratio (i.e. the ratio between the largest and smallest class cardinality N_{max}/N_{min}). ImageNet-LT is a long-tailed version of ImageNet classification dataset by sampling a subset following the Pareto distribution with power value $\alpha = 6$. It is more challenging as the class cardinality ranges from 5 to 1280.

Baselines. For the experiments on CIFAR-LT, our baseline methods include (1) Standard Empirical Risk minimization (ERM) with Cross-Entropy Loss. (2) Focal Loss [17], a widely used re-weighting method. (3) Class-balanced (CB) re-weighting based on classwise effective number of samples [6]. (4) CB effective number based re-sampling. (5) CB effective number based Focal Loss. (6) Deferred re-sampling (DRS) [2] where ERM is first used and then switched to re-sampling. (7) LDAM [2] which is the current state-of-the-art method.

For the experiments on ImageNet-LT, our baseline methods include three re-weighting methods: Lifted Loss [19], Focal Loss [17] and Range Loss [30], three re-sampling methods: Class-balanced (CB) Re-sampling, mixup [29] and SMOTE [3], one state-of-the-art few-shot learning method FSLwF [8], as well as the recent state-of-the-art OLTR [18] and Decouple [14]. For the SMOTE baseline, we use the mini-batch neighborhood instead of global neighborhood.

Table 1. Results on CIFAR-LT. Baseline results are from [2].

Dataset	CIFAR10-LT		CIFAR100-LT	
Imbalance Ratio	100	10	100	10
ERM	70.36	86.39	38.32	55.70
Focal Loss [17]	70.38	86.67	38.41	55.78
CB RW	72.37	86.54	33.99	57.12
CB RS	70.55	86.79	33.44	55.06
CB Focal	74.57	87.10	36.02	57.99
DRS [2]	75.07	87.52	40.86	57.75
LDAM [2]	77.03	88.16	42.04	**58.71**
mixSMOTE	78.28	88.07	42.34	58.48
GRM	78.27	88.17	42.10	58.13
mixSMOTE + GRM	**78.81**	**88.67**	**42.50**	58.68

Implementation Details. We use PyTorch [21] framework for all experiments. The experiments are conducted on an NVIDIA GeForce 2080Ti GPU. In the experiments, we equally split all classes into head and tail classes, i.e. $N_{th} = N_{c/2}$. We choose the mixSMOTE hyperparameter $\gamma = 0.5$. The GRM hyperparameter β is set to 1.0 for CIFAR-LR and 0.1 for ImageNet-LT. The range of λ is set to $a = 0.4, b = 0.6$. For experiments on CIFAR-LT, we follow the same training rules in [2] for a fair comparison. Specifically, we choose the backbone network to be ResNet-32 [12], we train the network for 200 epochs with batch size 128, using SGD with momentum 0.9, weight decay of 2×10^{-4}.

For the experiments on ImageNet-LT, we choose the backbone network to be ResNet-10 [12]. We train the network for 90 epochs with batch size 512, using SGD with momentum 0.9. The initial learning rate is 0.2 with a cosine annealing learning rate schedule.

4.1   Results on Imbalanced CIFAR

The experimental results on CIFAR10-LT and CIFAR100-LT are shown in Table 1. Both mixSMOTE and GRM achieve comparable or superior results compared to the state-of-the-art methods such as LDAM [2]. Moreover, their combination will yield further improvements. We also observe that as the imbalance ratio gets larger, the proposed method demonstrates a better capability of addressing the long-tailed issue.

Table 2. Results on ImageNet-LT. *denotes reproduced results, other results are from [18]. We divide the baseline methods into two groups: one-stage and two-stage. Best results are formatted in bold where best one-stage results are underlined.

	Many $N_c > 100$	Medium $20 < N_C \leq 100$	Few $N_c < 20$	Overall
ERM	40.9	10.7	0.4	20.9
Lifted Loss [19]	35.8	30.4	17.9	30.8
Focal Loss [17]	36.4	29.9	16.0	30.5
Range Loss [30]	35.8	30.3	17.6	30.7
SMOTE * [3]	41.9	33.4	15.3	34.1
CB Re-sampling *	42.7	34.1	15.7	34.8
mixup * [29]	40.2	35.5	20.2	35.1
FSLwF [8]	40.9	22.1	15.0	28.4
OLTR [18]	43.2	35.1	18.5	35.6
Decouple [14]*	50.4	**37.9**	23.0	**40.6**
mixSMOTE	49.2	35.2	17.6	38.1
GRM	46.5	<u>37.2</u>	<u>**26.2**</u>	39.2
mixSMOTE + GRM	<u>**52.8**</u>	35.6	21.1	<u>40.2</u>

4.2   Results on ImageNet-LT

We evaluate the proposed method on ImageNet-LT which is more challenging as shown in Table 2, where many, medium, and few-shot are divided by class cardinality with thresholds 20 and 100. The first five methods are one-stage methods followed by three two-stage methods. The result shows that the proposed method outperforms all one-stage methods and achieves comparable accuracy with state-of-the-art two-stage methods. We also observe that in such extremely imbalanced scenarios, re-sampling is more effective than re-weighting methods, as tail class instances will hardly be sampled if ordinary random sampling is used. Moreover, both mixSMOTE and GRM bring large improvements compared to the class-balanced re-sampling baseline. Particularly, GRM achieves the best few-shot accuracy, demonstrating its effectiveness in reducing the overfitting in representation learning.

4.3   Ablation Study

Effectiveness of mixSMOTE. To analyze the effectiveness of mixSMOTE, we compare it with mixup, SMOTE and class-balanced re-sampling on ImageNet-LT shown in Table 2. Both mixup and SMOTE use class-balanced re-sampling for a fair comparison. The result shows that compared to the re-sampling baseline, mixup improves the few-shot accuracy but degrades the many-shot performance, while SMOTE on the other hand, slightly decreases the few-shot accuracy. Since ImageNet-LT is extremely long-tailed, this result indicates that mixup could help for few-shot generalization while SMOTE may lead to overfitting to the extremely scarce classes. Finally, our proposed mixSMOTE combines the advantages of them and improves both head and tail classes by a large margin.

t-SNE Visualization of GRM. We visualize the feature distribution on the CIFAR10-LT validation set as shown in Fig. 3. The class ids are sorted by its cardinality in decreasing order. Different colors denote different classes. From the results, we observe that tail class distribution (see the dark color

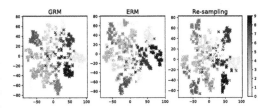

Fig. 3. t-SNE visualization.

points of class 7,8,9) in re-sampling and GRM become more clustered and centered compared to standard ERM. Meanwhile, re-sampling may lead to overfitting where tail classes are tangled with other classes (see the confusion between class 1 and 8 on the right). Finally, the feature distribution trained with GRM is more structured and discriminative.

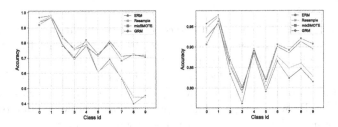

Fig. 4. Comparison of classwise accuracy on CIFAR10-LT with (a) imbalance ratio = 100 and (b) imbalance ratio = 10.

Classwise Accuracy. To further investigate how the proposed method improves the performance, we plot the per-class accuracy in Fig. 4. From the results, both mixSMOTE and GRM demonstrate great capability for tail class generalization, as most performance gains are from tail classes, indicating that our proposed mixSMOTE and GRM can effectively reduces tail class overfitting by increasing tail diversity.

Hyperparameter Sensitivity Analysis. Figure 5 shows the hyperparameter sensitivity analysis for γ in mixSMOTE and β in GRM. γ controls the maximum probability of a tail class instance to be selected for mixSMOTE and we observe the performance improves as γ increases. This result demonstrates the effectiveness of mixSMOTE as it improves the baseline by a large margin.

For the GRM gradient coefficient β, we show that the performance remains stable as β changes from 0.2 to 1.0. This result demonstrates the robustness of GRM as the performance is almost insensitive to the hyperparameter β.

For the range of mixSMOTE variable λ, we empirically observe that sampling from uniform$(0.4, 0.6)$ works slightly superior to uniform$(0, 1.0)$, which indicates that those *borderline* synthetic data points could be more important and informative in avoiding overfitting.

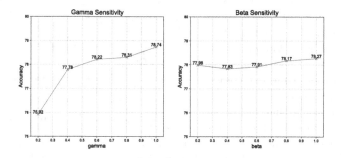

Fig. 5. Hyperparameter Sensitivity Analysis for γ in mixSMOTE and β in GRM.

5   Conclusion

In this paper, we first analyze that the core issue of overfitting in oversampling is the lack of tail class diversity. Then we propose two techniques from both data level and model level to introduce more tail class variations to alleviate tail class overfitting and promote generalizability. We first propose mixSMOTE to enrich the diversity of tail class samples by exploiting the rich head class variation. Then Gradient Re-weighting Module is proposed as a network component that serves to optimize the representation network with instance-wise balanced distribution, so that in the visual feature space, all training samples will contribute equally and diversely to the representation learning. Finally, we demonstrate the effectiveness of our proposed method both qualitatively and quantitatively by extensive experiments and visualization.

Acknowledgement. This work was supported by the National Natural Science Foundation of China (No. U1936202, 61925107).

References

1. Buda, M., Maki, A., Mazurowski, M.A.: A systematic study of the class imbalance problem in convolutional neural networks. Neural Netw. **106**, 249–259 (2018)
2. Cao, K., Wei, C., Gaidon, A., Arechiga, N., Ma, T.: Learning imbalanced datasets with label-distribution-aware margin loss. In: Advances in Neural Information Processing Systems, pp. 1565–1576 (2019)
3. Chawla, N.V., Bowyer, K.W., Hall, L.O., Kegelmeyer, W.P.: SMOTE: synthetic minority over-sampling technique. J. Artif. Intell. Res. **16**, 321–357 (2002)
4. Chawla, N.V., Japkowicz, N., Kotcz, A.: Special issue on learning from imbalanced data sets. ACM SIGKDD Explor. Newsl. **6**(1), 1–6 (2004)
5. Cohen, G., Hilario, M., Sax, H., Hugonnet, S., Geissbuhler, A.: Learning from imbalanced data in surveillance of nosocomial infection. Artif. Intell. Med. **37**(1), 7–18 (2006)
6. Cui, Y., Jia, M., Lin, T.Y., Song, Y., Belongie, S.: Class-balanced loss based on effective number of samples. In: Proceedings of the IEEE Conference on Computer Vision and Pattern Recognition, pp. 9268–9277 (2019)
7. Drummond, C., Holte, R.C., et al.: C4. 5, class imbalance, and cost sensitivity: why under-sampling beats over-sampling. In: Workshop on Learning from Imbalanced Datasets II, vol. 11, pp. 1–8. Citeseer (2003)
8. Gidaris, S., Komodakis, N.: Dynamic few-shot visual learning without forgetting. In: Proceedings of the IEEE Conference on Computer Vision and Pattern Recognition, pp. 4367–4375 (2018)
9. Gupta, A., Dollar, P., Girshick, R.: LVIS: a dataset for large vocabulary instance segmentation. In: Proceedings of the IEEE Conference on Computer Vision and Pattern Recognition, pp. 5356–5364 (2019)
10. Haixiang, G., Yijing, L., Jennifer Shang, G., Mingyun, H.Y., Bing, G.: Learning from class-imbalanced data: review of methods and applications. Expert Syst. Appl. **73**, 220–239 (2017)
11. He, H., Garcia, E.A.: Learning from imbalanced data. IEEE Trans. Knowl. Data Eng. **21**(9), 1263–1284 (2009)
12. He, K., Zhang, X., Ren, S., Sun, J.: Deep residual learning for image recognition. In: Proceedings of the IEEE Conference on Computer Vision and Pattern Recognition, pp. 770–778 (2016)
13. Jamal, M.A., Brown, M., Yang, M.H., Wang, L., Gong, B.: Rethinking class-balanced methods for long-tailed visual recognition from a domain adaptation perspective. In: Proceedings of the IEEE/CVF Conference on Computer Vision and Pattern Recognition, pp. 7610–7619 (2020)
14. Kang, B., et al.: Decoupling representation and classifier for long-tailed recognition. arXiv preprint arXiv:1910.09217 (2019)
15. Kim, J., Jeong, J., Shin, J.: M2m: imbalanced classification via major-to-minor translation. In: Proceedings of the IEEE/CVF Conference on Computer Vision and Pattern Recognition, pp. 13896–13905 (2020)
16. Krawczyk, B.: Learning from imbalanced data: open challenges and future directions. Prog. Artif. Intell. **5**(4), 221–232 (2016). https://doi.org/10.1007/s13748-016-0094-0
17. Lin, T.-Y., Goyal, P., Girshick, R., He, K., Dollár, P.: Focal loss for dense object detection. In: Proceedings of the IEEE International Conference on Computer Vision, pp. 2980–2988 (2017)

18. Liu, Z., Miao, Z., Zhan, X., Wang, J., Gong, B., Yu, S.X.: Large-scale long-tailed recognition in an open world. In: Proceedings of the IEEE Conference on Computer Vision and Pattern Recognition, pp. 2537–2546 (2019)
19. Oh Song, H., Xiang, Y., Jegelka, S., Savarese, S.: Deep metric learning via lifted structured feature embedding. In: Proceedings of the IEEE Conference on Computer Vision and Pattern Recognition, pp. 4004–4012 (2016)
20. Ouyang, W., Wang, X., Zhang, C., Yang, X.: Factors in finetuning deep model for object detection with long-tail distribution. In: Proceedings of the IEEE Conference on Computer Vision and Pattern Recognition, pp. 864–873 (2016)
21. Paszke, A., et al.: Automatic differentiation in pytorch (2017)
22. Peng, M., et al.: Trainable undersampling for class-imbalance learning. In: Proceedings of the AAAI Conference on Artificial Intelligence, vol. 33, pp. 4707–4714 (2019)
23. Ren, M., Zeng, W., Yang, B., Urtasun, R.: Learning to reweight examples for robust deep learning. arXiv preprint arXiv:1803.09050 (2018)
24. Shu, J., et al.: Meta-weight-net: learning an explicit mapping for sample weighting. In: Advances in Neural Information Processing Systems, pp. 1919–1930 (2019)
25. Wang, Y.-X., Ramanan, D., Hebert, M.: Learning to model the tail. In: Advances in Neural Information Processing Systems, pp. 7029–7039 (2017)
26. Xiang, L., Ding, G.: Learning from multiple experts: Self-paced knowledge distillation for long-tailed classification. arXiv preprint arXiv:2001.01536 (2020)
27. Xiang, L., Jin, X., Ding, G., Han, J., Li, L.: Incremental few-shot learning for pedestrian attribute recognition. In: IJCAI (2019)
28. Yan, Y., et al.: Oversampling for imbalanced data via optimal transport. In: Proceedings of the AAAI Conference on Artificial Intelligence, vol. 33, pp. 5605–5612 (2019)
29. Zhang, H., Cisse, M., Dauphin, Y.N., Lopez-Paz, D.: mixup: beyond empirical risk minimization. arXiv preprint arXiv:1710.09412 (2017)
30. Zhang, X., Fang, Z., Wen, Y., Li, Z., Qiao, Y.: Range loss for deep face recognition with long-tailed training data. In: Proceedings of the IEEE International Conference on Computer Vision, pp. 5409–5418 (2017)

Odds Estimating with Opponent Hand Belief for Texas Hold'em Poker Agents

Zhenzhen Hu, Jing Chen, Wanpeng Zhang[(✉)], Shaofei Chen, Weilin Yuan, Junren Luo, Jiahui Xu, and Xiang Ji

College of Intelligence Science and Technology, National University of Defense and Technology, Changsha 410073, China
`chenjing001@vip.sina.com`, {`wpzhang,yuanweilin12,`
`luojunren17,xjh,jixiang14`}`@nudt.edu.cn`

Abstract. Along with the great success of superhuman AI in succession, the development of Texas Hold'em poker agents is entering a new stage. The efforts to create indefectible AI transfers to develop new AIs which can exploit opponents and explain its own decisions better. Hand odds estimating used to state abstracting, situation evaluating, decision assisting is one of the key foundations for such new agents. But all the current methods implicitly assume a uniform distribution over the cards the opponent could be holding, which makes the win rate over-evaluated. In this paper three hand odds estimating methods considering the opponent hand belief are proposed to cope with this problem. We suggest the expected win rate algorithms with start hand range (EWR-SHR) and expected win rate algorithm with fold rate (EWR-FR) for preflop round and flop/turn/river round respectively. These two algorithms predict the opponent's hand range based on the opponent model and observed action not fold, their additional computation complexity is $O(1)$. The expected win rate algorithm with opponent hand distribution (EWR-HD) is the third method suitable for all rounds which uses the opponent model and observed action check/call/raise to infer the distribution of the opponent hand cards. Their features are compared, usages are summarized, and the experiment result indicates that all of them can evaluate the game situation more precisely than the current methods.

Keywords: Texas Hold'em · Poker agents · Hand odds estimating · Hand belief

1 Introduction

Strategic games are an interesting and challenging artificial intelligence domain, many theory, methods, techniques were created during the course of developing a program to play a strategic game, many areas of artificial intelligence have greatly benefited [2,3]. Games similar to chess is the best studied field including Chess, Checkers, Othello, Tic-tac-toe, and Go. The success of Alpha Go indicates this type of game with perfect information was solved [23].

© Springer Nature Switzerland AG 2021
L. Fang et al. (Eds.): CICAI 2021, LNAI 13069, pp. 51–64, 2021.
https://doi.org/10.1007/978-3-030-93046-2_5

Texas Hold'em poker is another class of game with imperfect information, which has characters such as hidden information, stochastic card dealing and potential deception [4,5]. Great achievements were obtained in recent years, the limited two-player Texas Hold'em was solved in 2015 [6], human professional player was defeated by Deepstack in no-limited two-player Texas Hold'em in 2017 [18], and Pluribus won the game with human in no-limited multi-player Texas Hold'em in 2019 [7]. These successes mean the algorithm based on CFR can find the approximate Nash equilibrium in a large state space, and a new stage for Texas Hold'em poker AI research is coming.

Although the approximate Nash equilibrium solving AIs can't be defeated by human, they are not guaranteed to win more chips than humans at same situation, and cannot exploit weakness of the opponents effectively and apply the deception strategy like humans [13,19], also there is no mechanism to explain their actions well for humans. Review the development of Texas Hold'em poker AI, it is necessary to rediscover the potential of approaches other than CFR based methods to cope with the opponent exploiting and decision explaining problem [1,11,16,17,21,28].

Hand odds estimating is one of the foundations of Texas Hold'em poker AI design. It is the base of state space abstraction and utility computation for leaf nodes of the game tree, it is also an important tool for feature detection in opponent modeling, and players usually use it to evaluate the situation and make decision. Based on the hand rank evaluating algorithms like Kev algorithm, TwoPlusTwo etc. [9,12,14,20,22,26,27,29], several methods were developed to estimating hand odds for different round in Texas Hold'em such as Chen algorithm [8], Expected win rate (EWR) algorithm [24], Effective hand strength (EHS) algorithm [21,24], Average rank strength (ARS) algorithm [25], Artificial neural network (ANN) approximate method [10]. But all these methods assume a uniform distribution over the cards the opponent could be holding, this is usually not correct as opponent will fold weak hands if his hand has little potential to be improved. Therefore, we must consider the hand belief if we want to make better odds estimating.

This paper describes three hand odds estimating methods considering hand belief based on start hand range, fold rate, hand distribution. These methods can improve the win rate evaluation and action risk management, allowing the agent to make better decisions. The rest of this paper is organized as follows: Sect. 2 describes the current common methods for hand odds estimating. Section 3 describes all the details of the proposed hand odds estimating methods considering hand holding belief. Section 4 assesses the proposed methods by win rate comparison with the current methods. Section 5 gives the paper's main conclusions and some suggestions for future work.

2   Related Work

People use hand odds estimating tools to solve the problems like situation judgement, decision assistant. Tools such as Pokerstove [20] can be used to calculate the win rate by inputting our own hand cards and the hand cards or range of opponents. Win rate is one of the indexes to describe the strength or potential of the card set consist of the cards in hand and on board. Because the cards on board is communal for all opponents, so we call the estimating work as hand odds estimating, and the next actions are heavily reliant upon it.

Hand odds estimating methods are constructed based on hand rank computation. According to the rule of Texas Hold'em poker, at the end round of a game, every player has 2 hand cards and 5 communal board cards, the player who has the best 5 cards in these 7 cards will win all the chips in the pot. Hand rank computation is used to calculate the rank of the best 5 cards and compare the ranks of the best 5 cards of opponents. The possible best 5 cards are classified to 9 categories such as Straight Flush, Four of a Kind and so on. A value or number assigned to all these 5 cards is called hand rank. Total ranks of 5 cards and 2 cards are 7462 and 169 respectively (See Table 1).

Table 1. Poker hand ranks with example

(a) 5-card rank		
Category	Example	sub-ranks
Straight Flush	As Ks Qs Js Ts	10
Four of a Kind	As Ah Ac Ad Ks	$\binom{13}{2}\binom{2}{1} = 156$
Full House	As Ah Kc Kd Ks	$\binom{13}{2}\binom{2}{1} = 156$
Flush	As Ks Qs Js 9s	$\binom{13}{5} - 10 = 1277$
Straight	As Kd Qs Jc Ts	10
Three of a Kind	As Ah Ac Kd Qs	$\binom{13}{3}\binom{3}{1} = 858$
Two pair	As Ah Kc Kd Qs	$\binom{13}{3}\binom{3}{2} = 858$
One pair	As Ah Kc Qd Js	$\binom{13}{4}\binom{4}{1} = 2860$
High Card	As Qh Jc Td 9s	$\binom{13}{5} - 10 = 1277$
	total:	7462

(b) 2-card rank		
Category	Example	sub-ranks
Pair	AsAh	$\binom{13}{1} = 13$
Non-pair	2d3c	$\binom{13}{1}\binom{12}{1} = 156$
	total:	169

A hand rank evaluator is used to compute the rank of a given hand, but a hand odds estimating tool is used to compute the probability of a certain hand being successful at the end of the game. Before computer was used to estimating the hand odds, human players concluded some empirical algorithms from their experience, like Chen algorithm [8]. Chen algorithm use a score of the two cards in hand to evaluate the hand strength for preflop round. In order to maintain consistency among odds evaluation methods, TEÓFILO et al. introduced a value normalization method [24]. Figure 1 (a) shows the normalized odds of Chen algorithm.

As the development of fast hand rank evaluator, the expected win rate algorithm (EWR) based on enumeration of opponents' hand cards and board cards was created naturally. At preflop round in a two-player game, by 2097572400 times of calculation and comparison of hand rank of both sides, we get the expected win rate by $P_w = n_{ahead}/n_{all}$. n_{ahead} is the number of cases in which our hand rank is greater than the opponent's hand rank, n_{all} is the number of

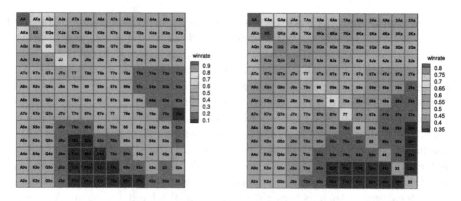

(a) Normalized odds of Chen algorithm   (b) Expected Win Rate algorithm

Fig. 1. Odds of hands at preflop round

all enumeration cases. Figure 1 (b) shows the expected win rate of preflop round for two-player game.

EHS algorithm is another enumeration-based method, which uses immediate hand strength and hand potential to compute effective hand strength. In the rounds after prefrop we can calculate the immediate hand strength with hand cards, board cards, and enumerated opponent hand cards: $IHS = \left(\frac{n_{ahead}+n_{tied}/2}{n_{all}}\right)^n$. n_{tied} is the number of tied cases. Because there are still one or two board cards in next rounds, the hand strength may change. So, the positive potential (all cases now is behind but finally ahead) and negative potential (all cases now is ahead but finally behind) are used to describe the hand potential: $P_P = \frac{n_{b-a}+n_{b-t}/2+n_{t-a}/2}{n_{behind}+n_{tied}/2}$. where, subscript a, b, t means ahead, behind, tied, $b-a$ means now is behind but ahead at end, and the others are similar. So, the effective hand strength (probability of the hand being the best or improving to become the best) is: $EHS = IHS + (1 - IHS)P_P$.

On account of the heavy computation expense of enumeration-based methods, several approximate methods were introduced to reduce the cost time. Monte Carlo method makes use of sampled cases to substitute the complete enumerated cases, experiments show that sampling 1000 board cards can produce a negligible error [24]. ARS is also an algorithm to avoid generating all combinations and computation [25], its key idea is storing pre-computed average future ranks in a table indexed by 169 kinds of 2-card combination ranks and 7462 kinds of 5-card combination ranks. So odds calculation transfers to a table look-up. Table 2 shows the look-up table's structure.

To make the space-time trade off, Silver uses deep learning to approximate the probabilities obtained from the Monte Carlo simulation with high accuracy [10]. The architecture of the network is p-24-12-k, where p = 29 is the dimensionality of the input vector, and k = 2 is the number of probabilities that we are predicting. The network only needs to store the weight matrices which take up

Table 2. Searching table structure of ARS algorithm

	5-card rank index	AKQJTs $\cdots$		234560
	2-card rank index		7462	
169 $\left\{\begin{array}{l}\\ \\ \\ \end{array}\right.$	AAs	.	.	.
	$\vdots$	.	.	.
	23o	.	.	.

8.4 KB of memory, while the ARS algorithm makes use of three pre-computed 10 MB lookup tables. Trained with a dataset of 250000 instances, the neural network model generalizes well and is able to approximate the majority of instances within 3% of the labels.

3   Methods Considering Hand Belief

All the above methods have an implicit assumption which assumes a uniform distribution over the cards the opponent could be holding. But it is not always correct because people usually fold the weak hand in no matter which round. So, if we estimate the odds based on uniform distribution assumption, the odds will be over-valued, which conduces to a higher risk to make aggressive decisions. Thus, we introduce three methods considering opponent's hand belief to make odds estimating more accurately. Opponent's hand belief can only be regarded after the opponent's action is observed, so it is highly depended on the opponent model. No matter start hand range, fold rate or opponent's action conditional probability for hand distribution, all of them have to be obtained through opponent modeling in the process of playing or from the off-line history data.

3.1   Expected Win Rate Algorithm with Start Hand Range (EWR-SHR)

In the real world, human player usually has a start hand range suitable for his own risk management in preflop round. If the rank or odds of the two cards in hand is in his start hand range, he will continue to play, otherwise he will give up. In the circumstances, if we have observed the opponent's action is not fold, we know the cards in opponent's hand is in his start range, thus we could use the start hand range to consider the opponent's hand belief.

The definition of start hand range may be different for humans. There are three common definitions. The first definition is a range defined in sort sequence of the 169 types of hand cards. If the lower bound of start hand range is r_L, the hand cards in the last r_L of the sequence will be folded. The second is sort the 169 types of hand cards by their expected win rate (see Fig. 1(b)), the hands with low win rate in the sequence will be folded. The third is using a sort sequence of all the 1326 combinations of 2-card hand by its expected win rate. Although the 1326 combinations can be mapped to 169 hand ranks, the number of hands related to each rank is not the same ("23o" include 12 types like "2s3d", "AA" include 6 types like "AsAd"), so using the third definition may be more exact but need more computation.

Take the third definition as an example. If we do not consider the start hand range, the set of all possible hands is $H_{all} = \{ho_1, \cdots, ho_n\}, n = 1225$ (size of the set is $\binom{50}{2}$ for 2-player game). ho is the opponent's hand. The range $r(ho)$ related to ho can be defined as the percent of the number of hands which has win rate lower than or equal to ho:

$$r(ho) = \frac{n_{\{Pw(h) \leq Pw(ho)\}}}{1326} \tag{1}$$

Where, $Pw(\cdot)$ is the win rate of the hand calculated by the common EWR algorithm. If considering the start hand range, the lower bound denoted as r_L, the opponent's hand set is determined by:

$$H_{rg} = \{ho|ho \in H_{all} \text{ and if } r(ho) \geq r_L\} \tag{2}$$

Based on this hand set, indexes like win rate can be calculated by enumeration or Monte Carlo method:

$$P_{win}(hs) = \sum_{i=1}^{m_{bc}} \sum_{ho \in H_{rg}} CpRk([hs, bc_i], [ho, bc_i]) \tag{3}$$

Where, P_{win} is the our win rate, hs is our hand, bc is board cards, m_{bc} is the number of combinations of board cards (for 2-player game preflop round is $\binom{48}{5}$), and the size of set H_{rg} is m_{ho}. Function $CpRk$ used to compare the rank of our hand and the opponent's hand to obtain the average win rate:

$$CpRk([hs, bc_i], [ho, bc_i]) = \begin{cases} \frac{1}{m_{bc}m_{ho}} & \text{if } Rank[hs, bc_i] > Rank[ho, bc_i] \\ 0 & \text{else} \end{cases} \tag{4}$$

The EWR-SHR described as Algorithm 1. Compared with the original EWR, the only added step for computing P_{win} is the judgement: $r(ho) \geq r_L$, if we use a hash table to story the $r(ho)$, the added computation complexity is $O(1)$.

3.2   Expected Win Rate Algorithm with Fold Rate (EWR-FR)

After entering the flop round, three board cards have been showed, players should do decision according to the 5-card rank. Sometimes if the player's 5-card is not strong enough and has little potential to improve for the next rounds, he may fold his hand. Actually, after the preflop round's decision, if the opponent's hand is weak enough, he might throw it early in preflop round. So, considering opponent hand belief after preflop is an additional processing on the foundation of the previous round.

Algorithm 1: Expected win rate with start hand range

Input   : hs: hand self, r_L: start hand range
Output: P_{win}: winrate

Function EWR-SHR(hs, r_L):
    $H_{all} \leftarrow 1225$ combinations of ho
    $H_{rg}, m_{ho} \leftarrow$ for ho in H_{all} if $r(ho) \geq r_L$, $Len(H_{rg})$
    $P_{win} \leftarrow 0$
    For ho in H_{rg} :
        $B_{all}, m_{bc} \leftarrow$ all or sampled combinations of cards not in $\{hs, ho\}$,
        $Len(B_{all})$
        For bc in B_{all} :
            If $rank[hs, bc] ¿ rank[ho, bc]$:
                $P_{win} + = 1/(m_{bc} m_{ho})$
    Return P_{win}

We introduce the opponent's fold rate as a criterion which can be modeled by doing statistics of the opponent's history data. Because the folded hand is usually a weak hand in the 7462 ranks of hand, we use the 7462 hands sort sequence and fold rate to obtain the remained hand set. A corresponding rate f of cards (ho, bc_s) defined as the percent of the number of hands which has rank lower than or equal to the rank of (ho, bc_s) is used to compare with fold rate f_r:

$$f(ho, bc_s) = \frac{n\{rank(h, bc_s) \leq rank(ho, bc_s)\}}{7462} \tag{5}$$

Where bc_s is the community cards have been showed on board. Thus, the opponent hand set for flop round is:

$$H_{fr} = \{ho | ho \in H_{rg} \text{ and if } f(ho, bc_s) \geq f_r\} \tag{6}$$

And for next rounds, the hand set is :

$$H_{fr} = \{ho | ho \in H_{fr,pre} \text{ and if } f(ho, bc_s) \geq f_r\} \tag{7}$$

Where $H_{fr,pre}$ means the hand range of the previous round. According to this hand set, the expected win rate can be computed by:

$$P_{win}(hs) = \sum_{i=1}^{m_{bc}} \sum_{ho \in H_{fr}} CpRk([hs, bc_s, bc_i], [ho, bc_s, bc_i]) \tag{8}$$

Where, bc_i is the community card need to be dealt, m_{bc} is the number of all combinations of the un-dealt board cards (for 2-player game in flop round $m_{bc} = \binom{45}{2}$). Function $CpRk$ has the same definition as preflop round (Eq. 4). The EWR-FR described as Algorithm 2.

Compared with the original EWR, the added step for computing P_{win} is $f[ho, bc_s] \geq f_r$, to calculate f need to compute the rank of card $[ho, bc_s]$, if we use two-plus-two algorithm, the added table searching complexity is $O(1)$. Then use a hash table to search the f value, the complexity is $O(1)$, so the total added computation complexity is $O(1)$.

Algorithm 2: Expected win rate with fold rate

Input : hs: hand self, r_f: fold rate, bc_s: board cards shown
Output: P_{win}: winrate

Function EWR-FR(hs,r_f,bc_s):
  $H_{fr}, m_{ho} \leftarrow$ for ho in H_{gr} or $H_{fr,pre}$ if $f(ho, bc_s) \geq f_r$, $Len(H_{fr})$
  $P_{win} \leftarrow 0$
  For ho in H_{fr} :
    $B_{all}, m_{bc} \leftarrow$ all or sampled combinations of cards not in $\{hs, ho, bc_s\}$,
    $Len(B_{all})$
    For bc in B_{all} :
      If $rank[hs, bc_s, bc] > rank[ho, bc_s, bc]$:
        $\mid$ $P_{win}+ = 1/(m_{bc}m_{ho})$
  Return P_{win}

3.3   Expected Win Rate Algorithm with Hand Distribution (EWR-HD)

The above two algorithms use the start hand range and fold rate to measure the opponent's hand belief, the key idea is that we can inference the hand range if the opponent has not given up. Actually, besides the action 'not fold' is an evidence, other actions like call, check, raise are also evidences can be used to inference. The difference of expected win rate algorithm with hand distribution from the above two algorithms is that the former make a hand distribution inference to calculate win rate but the latter makes a hand range inference.

Hand distribution inference using Bayes' principle sometimes called hand prediction is not a new idea, it has been used in poker AI [5,15] as a component of opponent modeling. Here we define it specially as a hand odds estimating technique and discuss it after formulating it.

By means of opponent modeling, we can obtain the probability of a specific action at a situation with specific hand cards, board cards, pot, action history: $P(a|ho, bc_s, pot, ha)$. a is an action may be check, call, raise x. The x after raise is the raise amount. The raise amount range is [100,20000], the pot is also a range [150,20000*number of players], and board cards has different number of states, for 2-player game preflop round has 1 state, flop round has $\binom{52}{3}$ states, turn round has $\binom{52}{4}$ states, river round has $\binom{52}{5}$ states. The action history ha also has a huge state space as each game may has different history.

Because of the huge state space, opponent modeling usually uses finite abstracted raise actions like raise 1 pot, 2 pots, 3 pots and all left chips, using the opponent win rate to substitute the opponent's hand cards and board cards, and take no account of pot and action history, so the opponent model can be simplified as: $P(a|Pw(ho, bc_s))$. If the opponent's action was observed, we can infer the opponent's hand distribution by Bayes formula:

$$P(ho|a) = \alpha P(ho)P(a|Pw(ho, bc_s)) \tag{9}$$

Where, $P(a|Pw(ho, bc_s))$ is the likelihood of the observed opponent's action come from opponent model, α is the normalization item. $P(ho)$ is the prior of opponent hand distribution can be initialized as uniform distribution for the first-time inference in a game:

$$P(ho) = \frac{1}{m_{ho}} \tag{10}$$

Where, $m_{ho} = \binom{50}{2}$ is number of all possible hand cards. If it's not the first time to reason, we use the previous inferred distribution as the prior. After the opponent's hand cards distribution has been obtained, the win rate can be calculated by enumerate all rest board cards combinations:

$$P_{win}(hs) = \sum_{i=1}^{m_{bc}} \sum_{j=1}^{m_{ho}} P(ho|a) CpRk([hs, bc_s, bc_i], [ho_j, bc_s, bc_i]) \tag{11}$$

Where, m_{bc} is the number of combinations of the rest board cards to be dealt, for 2-player game at perflop round the number of rest board cards is 5, thus $m_{bc} = \binom{48}{5}$. $m_{ho} = \binom{50}{2} = 1225$ is the number of all possible hand cards.

Algorithm 3: Expected win rate with hand distribution

Input : hs: hand self, $P(a|Pw(ho, bc_s))$: opponent model, a: opponent action
Output: P_{win}: winrate

Function EWR-HD($hs, P(a|Pw(ho, bc_s)), a$):
   | $H_{all}, m_{ho} \leftarrow$ 1225 combinations of ho, 1225
   | **For** ho in H_{all} :
   | | $P(ho) \leftarrow P_{init}(ho) = 1/1225$ or $P_{pre}(ho)$
   | | $P(ho|a) \leftarrow P(ho)P(a|Pw(ho, bc_s))$
   | $P(ho|a)$ normalization
   | $P_{win} \leftarrow 0$
   | **For** ho in H_{all} :
   | | $Pw_{ho} \leftarrow 0$
   | | $B_{all}, m_{bc} \leftarrow$ all or sampled combinations of cards not in $\{hs, ho, bc_s\}$,
   | | $Len(B_{all})$
   | | **For** bc in B_{all} :
   | | | **If** $rank[hs, bc_s, bc] > rank[ho, bc_s, bc]$:
   | | | | $Pw_{ho} += 1/(m_{bc}m_{ho})$
   | | $P_{win} = P_{win} + P(ho|a)Pw_{ho}$
   | Return P_{win}

The EWR-HD described as Algorithm 3. Compared with the original EWR, we need additional computation of $Pw(ho, bc_s)$, $P(a|Pw(ho, bc_s))$, $P(ho|a)$. Even for the computation of $Pw(ho, bc_s)$, m_{ho} times of computation of EWR is needed, so the complexity of EWR-HD is heavy.

4 Computation Experiments

Computation experiments for the above three algorithms were performed to evaluate the distinction from the original EWR method in this section.

Case I, assume we have obtained the opponent's start hand range is 15% from data statistics, so we can calculate our win rate for preflop round by Eq. (3). Figure 2(a) gives the heat map style range of the third definition for 1326 combinations of 2-card hand which shown in 169 ranks, Fig. 2(b) shows win rate of all the 169 ranks of hands we may hold. The red line is the expected win rate computed by original EWR, and the blue asterisk line is the result of EWR-SHR. It is obvious that the expected win rate of EWR-SHR is lower than the original one, and the lower the original win rate, the win rate value dropped-out is larger. It is consistent with the actual situation, because if the opponent does not fold, he may hold stronger hand, and our win probability will decrease.

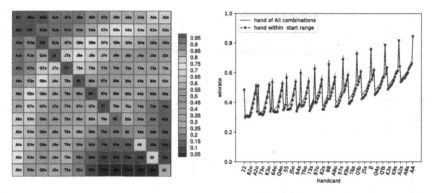

(a) Range of the third definition shown with 169 ranks

(b) Win rate compared with original EWR

Fig. 2. Result of EWR-SHR algorithm

Case II, at the flop round, a fold rate value 5% of the opponent has modeled from the previous games, expected win rate was computed by Eq. (8) and compared in Fig. 3 for 100 random sampled examples of our 2-card hand and 3-card board. In this case we did not consider the start hand range of the preflop round, so the opponent's hand set is only determined by the fold rate at flop round. The red line is computed by original EWR, while the blue asterisk line computed by EWR-FR. Result shows the similar changing after considering the opponent's hand belief, win rate with fold rate is lower than the original one, and the lower the original one, the win rate value dropped-out is larger (see the last sample with our hand "Kc7d" and board "Qc4d2d", win rate dropped from 0.41 to 0.28).

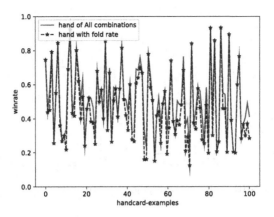

Fig. 3. Win rate of EWR-FR algorithm compared with original EWR

Case III, at the preflop round, we have obtained an opponent model with action raise 2 pots (see Fig. 4, the horizontal ordinate is expected win rate of the opponent, the vertical coordinate is PDF of action raise 2 pots). When an action of raise 2 pots was observed, we can predict the opponents hand distribution and compute the win rate by Eq. (11). The win rate with inferred hand distribution decreases obviously (See Fig. 5 (a)), the win rate decline percentage is commonly in range [30%, 50%], except several points which has very high original win rate (See Fig. 5 (b)).

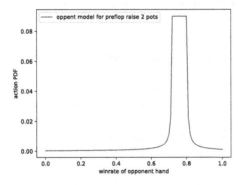

Fig. 4. Opponent model of action raise 2 pots at preflop round

These cases of experiment demonstrated that if the opponent's hand belief is considered, the evaluated expected win rate approaches to real value more closely. Hence it is clear that if we make decisions at the condition of not considering the information about the opponents, we will lose at higher probability, so we suffer higher failure risk naturally. Although these three algorithms all do

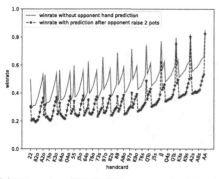 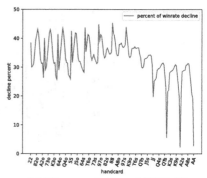

(a) Win rate of EWR-HD compared with original EWR

(b) Win rate decline of EWR-HD

Fig. 5. Result of EWR-HD algorithm

the prediction of the opponent's hand essentially, they use different things to consider the opponent's hand belief, and their features are compared in Table 3.

Opponent's hand belief can only be considered after the opponent's action is observed, because before the opponent's action we have none information to do an inference. Even we have constructed the opponent model through the previous games, if there is no opponent's action observed at the time when we are making decision, we cannot infer the opponent's hand belief. Therefore the above methods need to be used at a suitable time, Table 4 concludes the different occasions of applying, observation of opponent's action is the dividing point of applying these hand belief considered methods and the previous common methods.

Table 3. Comparison of three algorithms

Method	Action OB	Inference	Modeling	Computation complexity
EWR-SHR	not fold	hand range	easy	light
EWR-FR	not fold	hand range	easy	light
EWR-HD	check, call, raise	hand distribution	hard	heavy

All the three algorithms can be applied in multi-player games, because start hand range, fold rate and hand distribution can all be inferred for each opponent respectively, but for the sake of increased hidden hand cards, the immediate EWR computation accuracy will drop a little. Several types of AI can combine these algorithms, for rule-based AI they can be directly integrated to make a weighted decision for each round, for Integrated learning AI they can be used as a criterion to judge the situation or a input data for the neural network, for equilibrium solving AI the construction of the game tree will benefit from hand distribution, which makes utility evaluation of the tree more accurate.

Table 4. Usage of all hand estimating methods

Round		Without belief	With belief	Operation
Preflop	before OB	Chen algorithm		
		EWR algorithm		
	after OB		EWR-SHR	Init belief
			EWR-HD	Init belief
Flop Turn	before OB	EWR algorithm	EWR-FR/HD with saved belief	
		EHS algorithm		
		ARS algorithm		
	after OB		EWR-FR	Update belief
			EWR-HD	Update belief
River	before OB	EWR algorithm	EWR-FR/HD with saved belief	
	after OB		EWR-FR	Update belief
			EWR-HD	Update belief

5   Conclusion

Poker agents based on techniques other than approximate Nash equilibrium solving are still need to be studied oriented to the new trends of poker AI development. The common hand odds estimating methods as the foundation of poker AI were reviewed in this paper, and we proposed three expected win rate algorithms considering opponent's hand belief with start hand range, fold rate, and hand distribution to solve the win rate over-evaluation problem. By comparison with the common methods, we find that we will suffer greater failure risk if we do not take account of the opponent's hand belief. According to the premise of observing the opponent's action, we summarized the different usage and features of these algorithms. The work of this paper is a primary attempt to solve the hand odds over-evaluation problem, in the future these algorithms will be integrated into our poker AI and tested with different opponents, more results, comparison, and discussion will be done for opponent exploitation and decision explanation in Texas Hold'em and other fields.

References

1. Bard, N., Foerster, J.N., Chandar, S., Burch, N., Lanctot, M., et al.: The hanabi challenge: a new frontier for AI research. Artif. Intell. **1**, 1–35 (2019)
2. Billings, D.: Computer poker, pp. 1–46 (1995)
3. Billings, D.: Algorithms and assessment in computer poker, pp. 1–10 (2006)
4. Billings, D., Davidson, A., Schaeffer, J., Szafron, D.: The challenge of poker. Artif. Intell. **134**, 201–240 (2002)
5. Billings, D., Papp, D., Schaeffer, J., Szafron, D.: Opponent modeling in poker. In: AAAI 1998 Proceedings, pp. 1–7. American Association of Artificial Intelligence (1998)
6. Bowling, M., Burch, N., Johanson, M., Tammelin, O.: Heads-up limit Hold'em poker is solved. Science **347**(6218), 145–149 (2015)

7. Brown, N., Sandholm, T.: Superhuman AI for multiplayer poker. Science **365**(6456), 885–890 (2019)
8. Chen, W., Ankenman, J.: The mathematics of poker. Conjeleo (2006)
9. Coding the wheel: The great poker hand evaluator roundup (2008). https://www.codingthewheel.com/archives/poker-hand-evaluator-roundup/
10. Da Silva, B.: Approximating poker probabilities with deep learning. arXiv preprint arXiv:1808.07220 (2018)
11. Ganzfried, S., Sandholm, T.: Safe opponent exploitation. ACM Trans. Econ. Comput. **3**(2), 1–28 (2015)
12. Kev, C.: Cactus Kev's poker hand evaluator (2000). http://suffe.cool/poker/evaluator.html
13. Lake, B.M., Ullman, T.D., Tenenbaum, J.B., Gershman, S.J.: Building machines that learn and think like people, pp. 1–10. Two Plus Two Publishing (2016)
14. Lee, H.: Poker hand evaluator (2016). https://github.com/HenryRLee/PokerHandEvaluator
15. Li, X., Jiang, X.H., Chen, Y.Z., Bao, Y.J.: Game in multiplayer no-limit Texas Hold'em based on hands prediction. Chin. J. Comput. **41**(1), 1–18 (2018)
16. Li, X., Miikkulainen, R.: Opponent modeling and exploitation in poker using evolved recurrent neural networks. In: GECCO 2018, pp. 1–9. Association for Computing Machinery (2018)
17. Mealing, R., Shapiro, J.L.: Opponent modeling by expectation-maximization and sequence prediction in simplified poker. IEEE Trans. Comput. Intell. AI Games **9**(1), 11–25 (2017)
18. Moravík, M., Schmid, M., Burch, N., Lis, V., Bowling, M.: Deepstack: expert-level artificial intelligence in no-limit poker. Science **356**(6337), 508 (2017)
19. Newall, P.: Further limit Hold'em: exploring the model poker game, pp. 9–16. Two Plus Two Publishing (2013)
20. Prock, A.: Pokerstove (2002). https://github.com/andrewprock/pokerstove
21. Rubin, J., Watson, I.: Computer poker: a review. Artif. Intell. **175**(5–6), 958–987 (2011)
22. Senzee5: Paul senzee on software (2006). http://www.paulsenzee.com/2006/06/some-perfect-hash.html
23. Silver, D., Schrittwieser, J., Simonyan, K., Antonoglou, I., Hassabis, D.: Mastering the game of go without human knowledge. Nature **550**(7676), 354–359 (2017)
24. Teófilo, L.F., Reis, L.P., Cardoso, H.L.: Computing card probabilities in Texas Hold'em. In: 2013 8th Iberian Conference on Information Systems and Technologies (CISTI), pp. 1–6 (2013)
25. Teófilo, L.F., Reis, L.P., Cardoso, H.L.: Estimating the odds for Texas Hold'em poker agents. In: Proceedings of the 2013 IEEE/WIC/ACM International Joint Conferences on Web Intelligence (WI) and Intelligent Agent Technologies (IAT), vol. 2, pp. 369–374 (2013)
26. Timo, A.: Ompeval (2012). https://github.com/zekyll/OMPEval
27. Two Plus Two Newer Archives: Two plus two 7 card hand evaluators (2006). https://archives1.twoplustwo.com/showthread.php?t=288578
28. Wu, Z., Li, K., Zhao, E., et al.: L2e: learning to exploit your opponent, pp. 1–16 (2020)
29. XPokerEval: Xpokereval (2008). https://github.com/tangentforks/XPokerEval

Remote Sensing Image Recommendation Using Multi-attribute Embedding and Fusion Collaborative Filtering Network

Boce Chu[1,2], Jinyong Chen[2], Meirui Wang[2(✉)], Feng Gao[2], Qi Guo[2], and Feng Li[2]

[1] Beihang University, 37 Xueyuan Road, Beijing, China
[2] The 54th Research Institute of China Electronics Technology Group Corporation, 589 Zhongshanxi Road, Shijiazhuang, China

Abstract. With the popularization of remote sensing applications, the number of remote sensing users and their application requirements have increased explosively. Introducing recommendation systems into the distribution of remote sensing images can lower the threshold to obtain images for the public and subvert the traditional image service pattern. Different from other industries, users in the remote sensing field do not purchase data frequently in most cases, making it difficult to rely solely on order information to make recommendations. Therefore, how to use the semantic information of users and images as a foundation is an urgent problem. In this paper, we propose a feasible framework for personalized remote sensing image recommendation. We first describe remote sensing users and images through user duties, image semantics and order information; then, we complete the information modeling process via a knowledge graph. Next, we extract multidimensional features from the knowledge graphs of users and images with the help of knowledge representation learning and quantifiable features. Finally, using the high-dimensional spatial modeling capabilities of deep neural networks to perform a deep interaction exploration, we propose a Multi-attribute Fusion-based Collaborative Filtering Network, called MaF-CFNet. The model effectively fuses the multidimensional attribute features of users and images and obtains a recommendation score for each candidate image. The experimental results on our datasets demonstrate the effectiveness of MaF-CFNet compared to traditional methods.

Keywords: Remote sensing image recommendation · Multi-attribute fusion · Collaborative filtering

1 Introduction

In the past, users often obtained remote sensing images from data management systems primarily through manual queries and orders. However, a gradual

L. Fang et al. (Eds.): CICAI 2021, LNAI 13069, pp. 65–76, 2021.
https://doi.org/10.1007/978-3-030-93046-2_6

enrichment of application requirements and the rapid growth of remote sensing images make it inefficient to use artificial methods frequently to obtain interesting images from massive image databases. The development of personalized remote sensing image recommendation could simplify the process of obtaining images for users and improve the utilization rate of images, which would promote the corresponding business behavior. However, to date, no reasonable and feasible recommendation system exists in the field of remote sensing. The specific characteristics of remote sensing image recommendation are summarized below:

(1) Remote sensing users have multiple complex attributes. In contrast to typical existing recommendation tasks, which largely consider historical order operations, the interests of users in the remote sensing field is related more to their specific duties (for example: business, jurisdiction, etc.) and the corresponding businesses. To achieve accurate user modeling, it is necessary to conduct two-dimensional modeling based on semantic information regarding users' duties and businesses assisted by their historical ordering behaviors.

(2) Remote sensing images have multiple complex attributes. Conventional recommendation tasks usually consider only the meta-attributes of items. However, in the remote sensing field, the semantic information that users care about includes not only meta-attributes but also content attributes and quantifiable information. A remote sensing recommendation system should model the above three types of image attributes separately.

(3) The existing recommendation methods mainly address single-attribute matching problems, most of which are based on order information or simple semantic attributes. However, both users and images in the remote sensing field have multidimensional attributes, and these attributes do not exist in the same spatial dimension; thus, recommendation results cannot be obtained through direct matching methods. Therefore, our model must consider multidimensional spatial information fusion and perform high-precision matching.

To solve the above problems, using users' semantic information as the main basis and their order information as the auxiliary basis, this paper designs an effective framework for personalized remote sensing image recommendation. First, we design a semantic system that can obtain multidimensional semantic attributes for each image through semantic extraction methods. Then, we organize the semantic attributes and the order information of users and images into a knowledge graph, which can be quantified into multiple attribute feature vectors by representation learning methods. Finally, we propose a Multi-attribute Fusion-based Collaborative Filtering Network (MaF-CFNet), which embeds multiple vectors into the same spatial dimension for fusion by combining neural networks and collaborative filtering. The model computes a recommendation score for each candidate item based on the fused representation.

2   Related Works

The semantic relationships between attribute information can be used to effectively enhance the user interest and image features in the remote sensing field, which are difficult for traditional methods to mine. A knowledge graph can represent this multilayered semantic-related information reasonably, allow better modeling of the attribute information of users and images, and is more useful for deeper mining of the rich semantic information. Therefore, incorporating knowledge graphs into remote sensing image recommendations is a good idea.

In recent years, knowledge graphs have been applied to tasks such as information extraction [4], text classification [17], question answering [3,5], personalized recommendation [10,12,16] and many others with good results. Using a knowledge graph in recommendation systems has been effectively used to solve the sparsity problems. The existing knowledge-aware recommendation methods can be summarized into embedding-based methods [1,6,14,18,21] and path-based methods [15,20,22]. Path-based methods treat the knowledge graph as a heterogeneous information network and extract meta-path- or meta-graph-based latent features that represent the connectivity between users and items along various types of relation paths and graphs. Yu et al. [20] used matrix factorization to obtain the latent features of users and items based on different meta-paths to make recommendations. Zhao et al. [22] used a meta-graph to extract complex semantic relationships and then used matrix factorization to extract the latent features of users and items. The embedding-based methods use knowledge graph embedding (KGE) algorithms [13] to learn entity and relation embeddings and then integrate the learned embeddings into recommendation models. The KGE algorithm learns a low-dimensional vector for each entity and relationship in the knowledge graph while also maintaining the original structure and semantic information. In general, KGE algorithms can be divided into two categories: translational distance models [2,7,8,19] and semantic matching models [9,11]. Due to their excellent performances, KGE algorithms such as TransE [2], TransH [19], TransD [7], and TransR [8] have been widely used recently. Wang et al. [16] learned entity vectors and word vectors from a knowledge graph and then represents news by integrating these vectors in a CNN framework. Zhang et al. [21] combined items' structural embeddings, items' textual embeddings, and item's visual embeddings into a unified Bayesian network to jointly represent items.

Considering that users' and images' attributes and their relations are complicated, it is difficult to manually determine a comprehensive and clear meta-path or meta-graph using the path-based method. Moreover, this paper intends to model users and images from multiple perspectives and to characterize different attribute levels. Therefore, we prefer to use embedding-based representations to implement knowledge-aware remote sensing image recommendations.

3   Framework Overview

The remote sensing image recommendation task focuses on modeling the multi-attribute information for both users and images. Considering that knowledge graphs can model multidimensional semantic information effectively, we adopt the knowledge graph-based recommendation framework as a reference when designing our model. Because both remote sensing images and users have multiple complex attributes, when designing the recommendation framework, we conduct different semantic modeling and representation strategies for images and users. Figure 1 shows a schematic diagram of the proposed framework in this paper.

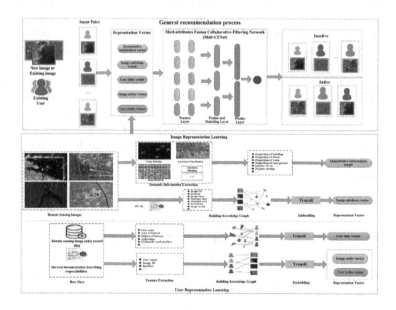

Fig. 1. The remote sensing image recommendation framework.

3.1   Image and User Semantic Information Extraction

This module mainly extracts semantic image information carried within the images themselves and their corresponding RPC configuration files; it obtains user-duty attributes through expert knowledge. For remote sensing images, we sort the semantic image information and design a semantic system for the recommendation task. We summarize all the information carried by remote sensing images into meta-attributes, content attributes, and quantifiable information. The meta attributes include time, resolution, satellite name, payload type and other information. The content attributes include culture, objects of interest, specific features, administrative areas, etc. The quantifiable information includes the proportion of land cover and the number of targets involved. First, we extract image content attributes and quantifiable information through object detection, land cover classification, location matching and so on. Simultaneously, we obtain useful meta-attributes from the RPC files that accompany the images.

3.2   Knowledge Graph Construction and Vector Representation

Through the preceding operations, we obtain user-duty attributes, image meta-attributes, image content attributes and quantifiable information. The quantifiable information is used to generate ground object proportion vectors that can be applied directly to the subsequent recommendation algorithm. Each bit of a ground object proportion vector represents a fixed culture or target class, and each digit represents its proportion or number in the image. This chapter organizes the image meta-attributes, content attributes, user-duty attributes and order information using three knowledge graphs: a user-duty graph, an order-information graph and an image-attribute graph. The image-attribute knowledge graph includes meta-attributes and content attributes such as the image name, image type, spatial resolution, administrative area, main culture, etc. The user-duty graph includes the user's name, main business, jurisdiction, objects of interest, etc. The entities in the order-information graph include username, image name, satellite, etc.

TransR maps relationship vectors to different spaces to ensure that the relationships that have different semantic angles, are represented in different planes. This approach better approximates the real situation. Therefore, this paper uses TransR to represent the user-duty knowledge graph, order-information knowledge graph and image-attribute knowledge graph. Finally, we obtain user-duty, user-order, image-order, and image-attribute embeddings.

3.3 Multi-attribute Fusion-Based Collaborative Filtering Network

To solve the problem of remote sensing image recommendation, we propose a Multi-attribute Fusion-based Collaborative Filtering Network (MaF-CFNet), as shown in Fig. 2. The model effectively fuses multidimensional input with the help of the high-dimensional spatial modeling ability of a neural network and embeds the feature vectors from different spaces into a unified vector space to achieve a better matching effect. Next, we introduce each part in detail.

Feature Representation Learning of Multi-attribute Information. For a user u and a remote sensing image i, we obtain the user-duty embedding u_{re}, user-order embedding u_{oe}, image-attribute embedding i_{ae} and image-order embedding i_{oe} (which contain graph semantic information) through knowledge graph representation learning, and we obtain the ground object proportion vector i_{ge} (which contains quantitative image information) through image interpretation. Note that the dimensions of the above vectors are not necessarily the same. To use this multi-attribute information in collaborative filtering methods, we must map the obtained vectors into a common space. To this end, MaF-CFNet adopts deep neural networks to learn richer latent features. Taking user-duty embedding u_{re} as an example, the representation learning part of its corresponding user-duty feature u_r can be defined as follows:

$$a_{ur0} = W_{ur0}^{\mathrm{T}} u_{re},$$
$$a_{ur1} = f(W_{ur1}^{\mathrm{T}} a_{ur0} + b_{ur1}),$$
$$\ldots \tag{1}$$
$$u_r = a_{urX} = f(W_{urX}^{\mathrm{T}} a_{urX-1} + b_{urX}),$$

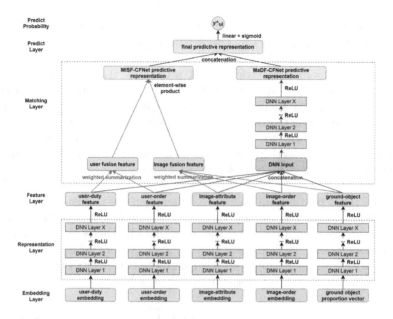

Fig. 2. The architecture of MaF-CFNet.

where W_{urX} and b_{urX} denote the weight matrix and bias vector for the x-th layer's neural network, respectively, $f()$ is the ReLU activation function. The user-order feature u_o, image-attribute feature i_a, image-order feature i_o and ground-object feature i_g are calculated in the same manner.

Multi-level Shallow Fusion. To acquire a comprehensive feature representation for both users and images, we fuse the multi-attribute information from these different objects separately. The obtained user fusion feature u_m and image fusion feature i_m can be regarded as latent vectors for user u and item i in the collaborative filtering process. Specifically, for user-duty feature u_r and user-order feature u_o, we construct the user fusion feature u_m and include a gate mechanism that can balance the relative importance of u_r and u_o:

$$u_m = \alpha_u u_r + \beta_u u_o, \tag{2}$$

where α_u and β_u are given by $[\alpha_u, \beta_u] = \mathrm{softmax}(W_r u_r + W_{uo} u_o)$, and $\alpha_u + \beta_u = 1$, respectively, and W_r and W_{uo} are weight matrices. Similarly, for the image-attribute feature i_a, the image-order feature i_o and the ground-object feature i_g, we construct an image fusion feature i_m and include a gate mechanism that can balance the relative importance of i_a, i_o and i_g:

$$i_m = \alpha_i i_a + \beta_i i_o + \lambda_i i_g, \tag{3}$$

where α_i, β_i and λ_i are given by $[\alpha_i, \beta_i, \lambda_i] = \mathrm{softmax}(W_a i_a + W_{io} i_o + W_g i_g)$, respectively, and $\alpha_i + \beta_i + \lambda_i = 1$. W_a, W_g and W_{io} are weight matrices. To mine the linear relations of user-image interaction, we can further integrate the user fusion feature u_m and the image fusion feature i_m. This fusion function is defined as follows:

$$p_{ui} = u_m \odot i_m, \tag{4}$$

where $\odot$ represents the elementwise product of vectors, and p_{ui} is a prediction vector based on multi-level shallow fusion. In summary, this subsection linearly fuses all the user and image features at the user and image levels and at the user-image level. We term this the Multi-level Shallow Fusion-based Collaborative Filtering Network (MlSF-CFNet).

Multi-attribute Deep Fusion. To further explore the deep relationships of multi-attribute fusion and model collaborative filtering using deep networks, we fuse all the user and image features into a unified vector and adopt this vector as the input to deep neural networks. The fusion strategy concatenates the user-duty feature u_r, user-order feature u_o, image-attribute feature i_a, image-order feature i_o and ground-object feature i_g into a joint representation:

$$q_0 = [u_r, u_o, i_a, i_o, i_g]. \tag{5}$$

Finally, we input this feature representation into a deep neural network, which expands the nonlinearity and flexibility of our model, with the goal of learning abstract user-image matching rules from the multi-attribute information. This deep learning portion of our multi-attribute fusion approach is defined as follows:

$$
\begin{aligned}
q_1 &= f(W_1^{\mathrm{T}} q_0 + b_1), \\
q_2 &= f(W_2^{\mathrm{T}} q_1 + b_2), \\
&\quad ... \\
q_{ui} = q_X &= f(W_X^{\mathrm{T}} q_{X-1} + b_X),
\end{aligned} \tag{6}
$$

where W_X and b_X denote the weight matrix and bias vector for the x-th layer's neural network, respectively, and $f()$ is the ReLU activation function. Finally, we obtain a prediction vector based on multi-attribute deep fusion q_{ui}. In this subsection, we conduct multilayer neural network training on the representation generated by fusing all the user and image features, allowing the network to more flexibly mine the complex associations among all the features. Therefore, this module is called the Multi-attribute Deep Fusion-based Collaborative Filtering Network, referred to as MaDF-CFNet.

Fusing MlSF-CFNet and MaDF-CFNet. Thus far, we have presented two types of multi-attribute fusion-based collaborative filtering algorithms (i.e., MlSF-CFNet and MaDF-CFNet). MlSF-CFNet achieves shallow fusion of the user and image levels and the user-image level; it can learn the low-rank relations between the user and the image but the elementwise product has limited expressiveness. MaDF-CFNet achieves deep fusion between all the user and image features; thus, it learns complex interactive relationships flexibly and nonlinearly but is weak at capturing the low-rank relations. We concatenate the prediction vectors of MlSF-CFNet and MaDF-CFNet to obtain a stronger and more expressive joint representation of the user-image matching rule. Then, the joint representation is passed into a fully connected layer, where each feature contained in the joint representation is assigned a different weight. Moreover, a subsequent sigmoid layer enables the model to calculate the probability that a given user will order a given image. Given the prediction vector based on multi-level shallow fusion p_{ui}, the prediction vector based on multi-attribute deep fusion q_{ui}, the output of MaF-CFNet is the probability that user u will order image i. This operation be defined as follows:

$$\widehat{y}_{ui} = \sigma(W_{out}^{\mathrm{T}}[p_{ui}, q_{ui}]), \tag{7}$$

where W_{out} is the weight matrix and $\sigma()$ is the activation function.

Objective Function. Given the training set $\mathbb{R} = <u_{re}, u_{oe}, i_{ae}, i_{oe}, i_{ge}, y_{ui}>$, our goal is to minimize the error between the actual category and the predicted probability; therefore, we use the cross-entropy loss function:

$$L = - \sum_{<u_{re}, u_{oe}, i_{ae}, i_{oe}, i_{ge}, y_{ui}>\in\mathbb{R}} (y_{ui} \log \widehat{y}_{ui} + (1 - y_{ui}) \log(1 - \widehat{y}_{ui})), \tag{8}$$

where u_{re}, u_{oe}, i_{ae}, i_{oe} and i_{ge} represent the user-duty embedding, user-order embedding, image-attribute embedding, image-order embedding, and the ground object proportion vector, respectively. $\widehat{y}_{ui}$ is the predicted probability value of user u ordering item i, while y_{ui} represents the ground truth. Thus, $y_{ui} = 1$ if user u actually ordered image i; otherwise, $y_{ui} = 0$.

4   Experiments and Evaluation

4.1   Data and Experimental Settings

Considering that no open source dataset exists for remote sensing image applications, we use 9,516 remote sensing image records and 2,578 user-order records acquired from June 2019 to May 2020 and stored in a business system as the dataset. By combining the detailed satellite parameters and relevant expert knowledge, we construct an image-attribute knowledge graph, a user-duty knowledge graph and an order-information knowledge graph. The hardware platform on which this experiment is executed is configured with a 64-bit Windows 7 operating system with 128 GB of RAM, a 1 TB hard-disk drive and an Nvidia P6000 GPU. The algorithm is written in Python and implemented on the TensorFlow framework. The following two parts describe the experiments to verify the proposed algorithm and framework.

4.2   Experimental Results and Discussion

In this paper, we use precision, recall, F1-score, and normalized discounted cumulative gain (NDCG) as metrics for top-K recommendation evaluation.

Table 1. Performance comparison of MaF-CFNet with baseline methods.

Methods	Precision@10	Recall@10	F1-score@10	NDCG@10
MaF-CFNet	0.7732	0.6356	0.6489	0.949089
Item-CF	0.4365	0.3484	0.3916	0.603189
User-CF	0.5862	0.4592	0.4953	0.719823

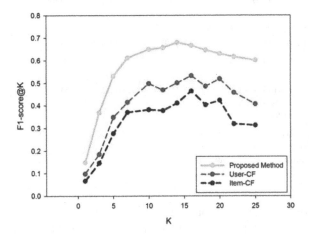

Fig. 3. F1-score comparison under different K values.

Performance Comparison of Recommendation Methods. To verify the superiority of our method, under the premise of a fixed top-10 selection, we compare our method with other methods according to the various metrics. Note that the application field of this paper resides at the intersection of remote sensing and recommendation; thus, it lacks baselines for comparison. Therefore, we use the most universal models (Item-CF and User-CF) as baselines for comparison purposes. From Table 1 and Fig. 3, it can be seen that our method outperforms Item-CF and User-CF on every metric, indicating that MaF-CFNet has better fusion and recommendation matching abilities.

Influence of Input Attributes. Our method takes multiple attributes as input and achieves remote sensing image recommendations through information fusion. Therefore, in our experiments, we compare methods with different inputs to determine the impacts of the various inputs on the recommendation task. By comparing the experimental results in Table 2, we reach the following conclusions. (1) As shown in ID (g), when taking all data as inputs, we obtain the best recommendation result, showing that all the inputs play a certain role in the recommendation task. (2) Comparing the recommendation results of (a), (b), and (c) with those of (d) (e) and (f) shows that the recommendation results when utilizing user-duty attributes as inputs are significantly better than the recommendation results when utilizing order information as inputs, which indicates

Table 2. Performance comparison under different inputs.

ID	Input	Precision@10	Recall@10	F1-score@10	NDCG@10
(a)	User-duty attributes + image quantifiable information	0.5431	0.5156	0.4828	0.80962
(b)	User-duty attributes + image attributes	0.7492	0.6074	0.6291	0.91472
(c)	User-duty attributes + image attributes + image quantifiable information	0.7522	0.6386	0.6431	0.92962
(d)	Order information	0.3497	0.2605	0.3254	0.60754
(e)	Order information + image attributes	0.4286	0.3004	0.3797	0.79213
(f)	Order information + image attributes + image quantifiable information	0.4425	0.3402	0.3995	0.80754
(g)	User-duty attributes + order information + image attributes +image quantifiable information	0.7732	0.6356	0.6489	0.949089

that the user-duty information plays a stronger role in the recommendation task than does the order information. (3) Comparing the recommendation results of (a) with (b) shows that the image attributes play a more important role in the recommendation task than do the image quantifiable information. (4) Comparing the recommendation results of (b) with (g) shows that when the inputs include only user-duty attributes and image attributes, the recommendation results are close to those when using all the inputs, indicating that the user-duty attributes and image attributes play important roles in user and image modeling.

5   Conclusion

To the best of our knowledge this is the first paper to propose a relatively complete and feasible recommendation framework for remote sensing image recommendation. Considering the essence of the remote sensing image recommendation task, this framework summarizes and models the relevant attributes of both users and images to make recommendations. We propose the MaF-CFNet model, which comprehensively considers the multidimensional attributes of users and images and identifies matching recommendations through both shallow and deep fusion. Extensive experiments on internal business datasets demonstrate the effectiveness of user modeling, image modeling and the MaF-CFNet model for the recommendation task. Compared with published recommendation methods, our method addresses the recommendation problem under multi-attribute input well. In the future, we plan to consider introducing a feature selection algorithm into the recommendation process and simplifying the multi-attribute inputs to improve the accuracy and speed of recommendation.

References

1. Ai, Q., Azizi, V., Chen, X., Zhang, Y.: Learning heterogeneous knowledge base embeddings for explainable recommendation. Algorithms **11**(9), 137 (2018)
2. Bordes, A., Usunier, N., Garcia-Duran, A., Weston, J., Yakhnenko, O.: Translating embeddings for modeling multi-relational data. In: Neural Information Processing Systems (NIPS), pp. 1–9 (2013)
3. Bordes, A., Weston, J., Usunier, N.: Open question answering with weakly supervised embedding models. In: Calders, T., Esposito, F., Hüllermeier, E., Meo, R. (eds.) ECML PKDD 2014, Part I. LNCS (LNAI), vol. 8724, pp. 165–180. Springer, Heidelberg (2014). https://doi.org/10.1007/978-3-662-44848-9_11
4. Daiber, J., Jakob, M., Hokamp, C., Mendes, P.N.: Improving efficiency and accuracy in multilingual entity extraction. In: Proceedings of the 9th International Conference on Semantic Systems, pp. 121–124 (2013)
5. Dong, L., Wei, F., Zhou, M., Xu, K.: Question answering over freebase with multi-column convolutional neural networks. In: Proceedings of the 53rd Annual Meeting of the Association for Computational Linguistics and the 7th International Joint Conference on Natural Language Processing, vol. 1: Long Papers, pp. 260–269 (2015)
6. Hongwei, W., et al.: Ripple network: propagating user preferences on the knowledge graph for recommender systems. In: Proceedings of 27th ACM International Conference on Information and Knowledge Management, CIKM 2018 (2018)
7. Ji, G., He, S., Xu, L., Liu, K., Zhao, J.: Knowledge graph embedding via dynamic mapping matrix. In: Proceedings of the 53rd Annual Meeting of the Association for Computational Linguistics and the 7th International Joint Conference on Natural Language Processing, vol. 1: Long papers, pp. 687–696 (2015)
8. Lin, Y., Liu, Z., Sun, M., Liu, Y., Zhu, X.: Learning entity and relation embeddings for knowledge graph completion. In: Proceedings of the AAAI Conference on Artificial Intelligence, vol. 29 (2015)
9. Liu, H., Wu, Y., Yang, Y.: Analogical inference for multi-relational embeddings. In: International Conference on Machine Learning, pp. 2168–2178. PMLR (2017)
10. Manrique, R., Marino, O.: Knowledge graph-based weighting strategies for a scholarly paper recommendation scenario. In: KaRS@ RecSys, pp. 5–8 (2018)
11. Nickel, M., Rosasco, L., Poggio, T.: Holographic embeddings of knowledge graphs. In: Proceedings of the AAAI Conference on Artificial Intelligence, vol. 30 (2016)
12. Oramas, S., Ostuni, V.C., Noia, T.D., Serra, X., Sciascio, E.D.: Sound and music recommendation with knowledge graphs. ACM Trans. Intell. Syst. Technol. (TIST) **8**(2), 1–21 (2016)
13. Wang, H., et al.: GraphGAN: graph representation learning with generative adversarial nets. In: Proceedings of the AAAI Conference on Artificial Intelligence, vol. 32 (2018)
14. Wang, H., Zhang, F., Hou, M., Xie, X., Guo, M., Liu, Q.: Shine: signed heterogeneous information network embedding for sentiment link prediction. In: Proceedings of the Eleventh ACM International Conference on Web Search and Data Mining, pp. 592–600 (2018)
15. Wang, H., et al.: RippleNet: propagating user preferences on the knowledge graph for recommender systems. In: Proceedings of the 27th ACM International Conference on Information and Knowledge Management, pp. 417–426 (2018)
16. Wang, H., Zhang, F., Xie, X., Guo, M.: DKN: deep knowledge-aware network for news recommendation. In: Proceedings of the 2018 World Wide Web Conference, pp. 1835–1844 (2018)

17. Wang, J., Wang, Z., Zhang, D., Yan, J.: Combining knowledge with deep convolutional neural networks for short text classification. In: IJCAI, vol. 350 (2017)
18. Wang, Q., Mao, Z., Wang, B., Guo, L.: Knowledge graph embedding: a survey of approaches and applications. IEEE Trans. Knowl. Data Eng. **29**(12), 2724–2743 (2017)
19. Wang, Z., Zhang, J., Feng, J., Chen, Z.: Knowledge graph embedding by translating on hyperplanes. In: Proceedings of the AAAI Conference on Artificial Intelligence, vol. 28 (2014)
20. Yu, X., et al.: Personalized entity recommendation: a heterogeneous information network approach. In: Proceedings of the 7th ACM International Conference on Web Search and Data Mining, pp. 283–292 (2014)
21. Zhang, F., Yuan, N.J., Lian, D., Xie, X., Ma, W.Y.: Collaborative knowledge base embedding for recommender systems. In: Proceedings of the 22nd ACM SIGKDD International Conference on Knowledge Discovery and Data Mining, pp. 353–362 (2016)
22. Zhao, H., Yao, Q., Li, J., Song, Y., Lee, D.L.: Meta-graph based recommendation fusion over heterogeneous information networks. In: Proceedings of the 23rd ACM SIGKDD International Conference on Knowledge Discovery and Data Mining, pp. 635–644 (2017)

Object Goal Visual Navigation Using Semantic Spatial Relationships

Jingwen Guo[1,2], Zhisheng Lu[1(✉)], Ti Wang[1,3], Weibo Huang[1], and Hong Liu[1]

[1] Peking University Shenzhen Graduate School, Shenzhen, China
`zhisheng_lu@pku.edu.cn`
[2] Soochow University, Suzhou, China
[3] Nanjing University of Science and Technology, Nanjing, China

Abstract. The target-driven visual navigation is a popular learning-based method and has been successfully applied to a wide range of applications. However, it has some disadvantages, including being ineffective at adapting to unseen environments. In this paper, a navigation method based on Semantic Spatial Relationships (SSR) is proposed and is shown to have more reliable performance when dealing with novel conditions. The construction of joint semantic hierarchical feature vector allows for learning implicit relationship between current observation and target objects, which benefits from construction of prior knowledge graph and semantic space. This differs from the traditional target driven methods, which integrate the visual input vector directly into the reinforcement learning path planning module. Moreover, the proposed method takes both local and global features of observed image into consideration and is thus less conservative and more robust in regards to random scenes. An additional analysis indicates that the proposed SSR performs well on classical metrics. The effectiveness of the proposed SSR model is demonstrated comparing with state-of-the-art methods in unknown scenes.

Keywords: Visual navigation · Semantic graph · Hierarchical relationship

1 Introduction

Vision-based mobile robot navigation has produced countless research contributions, both in the field of vision and in the field of control. However, it is difficult for mobile robots to run at high speeds due to the huge radar data and dimensionality disasters when processing real-time status information.

As a research hotspot in machine learning, deep reinforcement learning provides us with an important intelligent control method. It relies on the perception ability of deep learning without model information, and can collect sample data for learning during the navigation process of mobile robots. Interacting with the environment to obtain feedback for strategy is an effective method in field of

Supported by National Natural Science Foundation of China $No.62073004$, Science and Technology Plan of Shenzhen $No.JCYJ20190808182209321$.

mobile robot navigation. In recent years, many visual navigation methods based on reinforcement learning have emerged.

Traditional navigation algorithms firstly build the environment map, and then realize the path planning. Compared with these algorithms, using current environment observation and target information as prior conditional input of model, and planing the optimal path afterwords is a current research hotspot. These methods can be collectively referred to as end-to-end visual navigation. Zhu et al. [29] used a pre-trained residual network as feature extraction module and designed a twin network architecture to improve the goal and scenario generalization performance. Mirowski et al. [17] proposed a dual-path agent structure that uses end-to-end reinforcement learning for training and can handle real-world visual navigation tasks on city-level scale. Pathak et al. [20] exploited the collected samples to train general navigation strategies in a small range, and then used the expert teaching method to transfer the navigation target information to the agent, which can be summarized as an unsupervised learning mode.

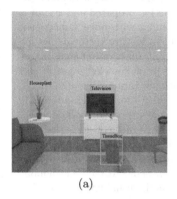
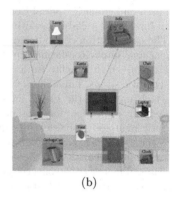

(a)   (b)

Fig. 1. Semantic Cues Based on Knowledge Graph. The navigation goal for agent is GarbageCan, which is invisible from observation (a). We use locational features as cues such as Television that can be easily detected. From prior semantic knowledge graph, we can learn that the connection between GarbageCan and TissueBox is strong as shown in (b). So their spatial locations should be very close. The agent can navigate to the target simply though it's invisible at the moment.

In above tasks, with target location and self-centered observations as input, the agent needs to persistently execute one possible action until it reaches the target. Target-driven visual semantic navigation is very challenging since the location and appearance of the target are unknown to the agent. The navigation system needs to estimate both the coordinates of the target and the path to it at the same time. Considering the disadvantages of current navigation methods, we propose an innovative visual navigation algorithm based on deep reinforcement learning and knowledge graph. The main idea is shown in Fig. 1. We capture the global semantic features and local location features of the current observation simultaneously. The prior knowledge graph can be used to perform semantic guidance and encode the spatial relationship of objects naturally, so that agent can infer the general direction of target even if the target is temporarily invisible.

We list the main contributions of this paper: (1) We propose an efficient end-to-end model Spatial Semantic Relationship (SSR) that takes visual images and target semantic labels as model inputs without map of the environment. (2) We use the deep graph neural network to introduce the external semantic prior information between objects, to encode the current visual observation of scene and the target information, learning the implicit relationships between these objects. (3) Our model improves the navigation performance and generalization ability to unknown environments and new target objects. (4) We construct the simulation environment as a robot navigation environment for algorithm comparison.

2   Related Work

Visual Navigation Without Map. Common navigation tasks are mainly divided into two categories. One task is actively exploring the environment, and the other is exploiting devices such as GPS sensors to send direction signals to the target. Visual navigation has powerful scene recognition capabilities because it can obtain massive amounts of environmental information through visual sensors. There have been some research recently in field of visual navigation. Lu et al. [14] proposed a novel abstract map Markov Network for deep reinforcement learning visual navigation method, and used graph neural network for probabilistic inference. It solved the problem that the agent is restricted in the new environment of acquiring the map and improved the success rate of navigation. Wu et al. [25] proposed a way to incorporate information theory regularization into deep reinforcement learning framework to improve the cross-target and cross-scene versatility of visual navigation. Gupta et al. [6] used visual information and self-motion to navigate in a vast indoor environment in the way of building potential map.

Deep Reinforcement Learning Methods for Navigation. Methods based on deep reinforcement learning have been combined with the traditional navigation algorithm [18] and achieved great process recently. Yu et al. [27] proposed a neural network and a hierarchical reinforcement learning mobile robot path planning model, which mapped the robot's actions and current state through hierarchical reinforcement learning. This method made robot perceive the environment and perform feature extraction to solve the problems of autonomous learning in path planning and slow path planning convergence speed. Mousavian et al. [19] proposed a deep reinforcement learning framework that used LSTM-based strategies for semantic target driven navigation, and learned navigation strategies based on capturing spatial layout and semantic contextual clues. Wen et al. [22] proposed an integrated navigation method Active SLAM which combined path planning with SLAM (simultaneous localization and mapping). They used fully convolutional residual network to identify obstacles to obtain depth images. They employed dual DQN algorithm to plan obstacle avoidance path and established 2D map of the environment based on FastSLAM at the same time during navigation process.

Object Goal Navigation. Object navigation is a valuable research problem, which refers to the robot autonomously navigating to a specific object. Different from point navigation related methods [23], the goal of object navigation is to navigate to the target category object, not global coordinates. Object navigation means that agent needs to make full use of the prior knowledge of the scene, which is very important for the efficiency of navigation. Chaplot et al. [2] proposed a modular system Goal-Oriented Semantic Exploration, which can effectively explore the environment by constructing episodic semantic maps and using it according to target object categories. Wortsman et al. [24] proposed Self-Adaptive Visual Navigation (SAVN) method, where the agent used meta-learning to adapt to the invisible environment. Martins et al. [15] solved the problem of enhanced metric representation by using semantic information from RGB-D images to construct scenes. They proposed a complete framework to use object-level information to create an enhanced map representation of the environment to assist robots in completing the object goal visual navigation. They exploited CNN-based object detector and 3D model-based segmentation technology to perform instance semantic segmentation, and used Kalman filter dictionaries to complete semantic class tracking and positioning.

Semantic Reasoning Using GNNs. Graph Neural Network (GNN) was first proposed by Gori et al. [5]. It is a deep learning method for processing graph data. GNNs have great effect on extracting features of data containing graph structures. Kawamoto et al. [9] proved that untrained GNN can perform well with a simple architecture. Deepmind [7] proved that the graph network supports relational reasoning and combinatorial generalization, which is of great significance for probabilistic reasoning. Guo et al. [28] pointed out that GNN is applied to tasks such as relation extraction and contextual reasoning, and the results are significantly better than other methods. Kim et al. [10] proposed a F-GCN module based on graph convolutional network, which used GNN to extract knowledge from multi-modal context and solve problem reasoning. In our proposed model, we adopt GCN to encode the prior knowledge graph and learn the spatial semantic relationship between agent and target object.

3   Proposed Approach

Our task is to introduce prior knowledge graph and spatial location information into the target-driven visual semantic navigation system. In order to achieve this goal, our method Spatial Semantic Relationship (SSR) contains three main components as shown in Fig. 2: (1) Spatial relationship between objects building module: we take local features observed by the agent and semantic label of the target object as input to explore the hidden internal spatial relationship and construct the context vector; (2) Semantic scene building module: we take the global visual features observed by agent and prior knowledge graph as input to form semantic scene representation; (3) Reinforcement learning navigation module: we combine the output of first two modules to obtain a joint visual semantic knowledge feature vector. We then input this vector into reinforcement learning navigation network, making the agent interact with environment and generate the next action strategy with judgement.

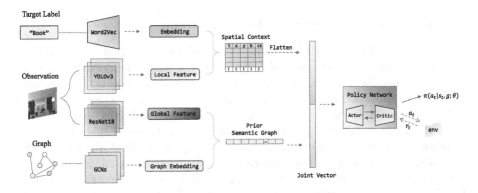

Fig. 2. Illustration of spatial semantic relationship model

3.1 Task Definition

We aim at training an agent, which receives RGB images as observation information, and semantic tags as target information. The agent is trained to look for an instance of the specificated target category object. During the navigation, agent perceives target location and environment through RGB images and finds the minimum length of action sequence to reach the target location while avoiding obstacles. Given the sequential decision characteristics of visual navigation, we can define this task as a Markov Decision Process (MDP) problem.

Considering $G = \{g_0, g_1, ..., g_n\}$ as the set of target objects, $S = \{s_0, s_1, ..., s_m\}$ as the set of states that agent may exist. s_t is defined by function $s_t = f(o_t; \alpha)$, where o_t is the current agent's observation of the environment from the first perspective, α is the network parameter. At each time step t, the agent needs to act according to the current state s_t and the target object g_i. Agent choose action a_t from set $A = \{MoveAhead, RotateRight, RotateLeft, LookUp, LookDown, DONE\}$ to achieve the maximum policy expectation π^* according to the strategy function $\pi(a_t|s_t, g; \theta)$, which is expressed as follows:

$$\pi^* = \arg\max_\pi E_\pi \left[\sum_k^N r_{k+t}|s_t = s, a_t = a \right], \forall s \in S, \forall a \in A, \forall t \geq 0 \quad (1)$$

The optimal strategy π^* represents the prediction of the maximum cumulative reward value that can be obtained in the future.

We add a special termination action $DONE$ to the agent's action set. If the agent executes $DONE$ and the target object is visible, then the navigation task is considered successful. If the agent executes $DONE$ while the target object is invisible, it is judged as failure. The target object is visible only when it is in the agent's view, and the geodestic distance between them is less than twice the width of the agent [1].

3.2 Construction of Semantic Relation Graph

Global Visual Feature Extraction. Visual feature extraction is divided into local visual representation and global feature extraction. The global features of image describe the spatial position relationship between objects. In contrast, the local features contain richer information of specific object. Therefore, we use different networks to extract the global and local features of objects at the same time, which are respectively used for the joint representation of spatial relationships and the construction of semantic relationship maps. He et al. [8] proposed a Residual Neural Network (ResNet) to learn features from visual images, which have shown excellent performance in a variety of computer vision tasks. We use ResNet18 [8] pre-trained in the ImageNet [4] to extract global feature vector of environment for each input observation to perceive surroundings. This vector will be input into the GCN later together with the knowledge graph embedding as a node feature to form the construction of prior semantic knowledge graph.

Prior Graph Embedding. We exploit the Visual Genome [13] to integrate semantic knowledge in the form of graph representation to construct a knowledge graph, and use GCNs [3] to calculate the relationship characteristics. GCN is an extension of the graph structure of CNN, and its goal is to learn the functional representation of a given graph $G = (V, E)$, where V is the set of nodes and E is the set of edges. The input of each node in V is a feature vector x_i. We summarize the input of all nodes into a matrix $X = [x_1, \ldots, x_{|V|}] \in \mathbb{R}^{|V| \times D}$, where D represents the dimension of the input feature. The graph structure is represented as a binary adjacency matrix $A \in \mathbb{R}^{|V| \times |V|}$. We normalize A to get $\bar{A}$. The structure of neural network can be expressed as follows:

$$H^{(l+1)} = f(\bar{A} \cdot H^{(l)} \cdot W^{(l)}) \tag{2}$$

where $f(\cdot)$ denotes the activation function, $W^{(l)}$ is the parameter of the lth layer, and l is the index of GCN layers. We construct a knowledge graph by including all object categories that appear in the simulation environment we use. Each object category is represented as a node in the graph. We input the global visual features extracted in the previous section into the GCNs together with the pre-built knowledge graph embedding. Consistent with [26], we use a three-layer GCN. The first two layers output the potential features of the joint input, and the last layer outputs a single value for each node. The final output is a $|V|$-dimensional feature vector. This feature vector basically encodes the global features of the current scene and the semantic priors in the environment.

3.3 Joint Representation of Spatial Context Information

We employ YOLOv3 [21] for local feature representation since it is a advanced real-time object detection system. The image of the current frame obtained by the agent is first input into YOLOv3 for target detection. We use the stacks of $[x, y, b, e]$ to represent the local features of the extracted image. For each detected object, x and y represent the center of the detected bounding box, and b represents the size of the bounding box; e represents the word vector corresponding to the category label of the object. Considering objects that are not in the current frame but may exist in the scene, we form the local feature representation of the current observation image $c_{embed} = [t, x, y, b, e]$, $t = 1$ if the object exists in the current frame. The target tag gets its word embedding through pretrained Word2Vec [16]. We then calculate the *Cosine Similarity* (CS) between each object and the target based on the embedding of their labels. The last column in c_{embed} is replaced with CS, so that we obtain the joint feature representation of the spatial relationship with five columns, which also called location-aware vector. After flattening the current local feature representation, we merge it with the global visual feature graph embedding of Sect. 3.2. The final vector is the visual representation of semantic knowledge of our environment. We introduce this vector into the policy network for decision making later.

3.4 Navigation Driven by Spatial Semantic Relationships of Objects

We use the Asynchronous Advantage Actor-Critic (A3C) [18] algorithm to predict the strategy and reward value of each time step. The input of our A3C module is the output feature of the joint representation, which consists of the current state, the prior relationship, and the semantic task goal. The A3C module produces two outputs, strategy and reward value. The hidden layer of the network consists of several fully connected layers and ReLU layers. The joint input is first mapped to the latent space, and then two branches of the network generate $|A|$ dimension of strategies and values, as shown in the Fig. 2. Different from previous researches using different strategy networks for different scenarios [29], we use a single strategy network for samples in different scenarios. This improves the navigation efficiency and generalization ability in unseen scenes.

4 Experiments

4.1 Datasets

The dataset used in this article is AI2-THOR (The House Of inteRactions) [12]. There are 120 scenes in the AI2-THOR environment, covering four different room categories: Kitchen, Living Room, Bedroom and Bathroom. Each category room has 30 different scenes. Each room has a set of objects that can be found. Certain object types can be found in all scenes of a given category, and certain object types can sometimes only be found in scenes of a specific category. Similar to [24], we use the first 20 scenes of each scene type as the training set, 5 scenes for verification, and the remaining 5 scenes for test. For each current state, the agent will take an action a_t from the set of actions A. For our experiment, we set the same target classes for different types of scenes. The initial position of the agent is randomly generated by the AI2-THOR framework, and then the navigation algorithm is trained and tested. We use 0.5 m to discretize the environment, meaning the distance between each location is 0.5 m.

4.2 Implementations and Evaluation Metircs

We use PyTorch to implement the framework partly based on the public implementation [29]. When learning navigation strategies, we use -0.01 to punish each action step. If an agent reaches a goal and sends a termination signal $DONE$, we will reward the agent with a reward value of 10. We use the Adam optimizer [11] to update the network parameters with a learning rate of $1e^{-4}$. In order to make meaningful comparison, we use the same hyperparameters in each experiment, such as episode number and reward function. We also use pretrained models like ResNet18 during the training process to speed up the process.

In this article, we refer to [1] and use two indicators to evaluate our method: *Success Rate (SR)* and *Success weighted by Path Length (SPL)*. *SR* is defined as the ratio of the number of times that the agent successfully navigates to the target to the total number of episodes:

$$SR = \frac{1}{N} \sum_{i=1}^{N} S_i \tag{3}$$

where N is the total number of episodes, S_i is the binary indicator of whether the ith episode is successful.

SPL is called normalized inverse path length weighted success, which considers both success rate and optimal path length:

$$SPL = \frac{1}{N} \sum_{i=1}^{N} S_i \frac{l_i}{p_i} \tag{4}$$

where N is the number of evaluations. $S_i = 1$ if the evaluation is successful, otherwise 0. l_i represents the length of the shortest path between the agent's starting position and one of its successful states, and p_i is the length of the current episode. The length used here is the number of operations, which means that performing an operation will increase the length by 1. This indicator can balance the length of the episode and the success rate.

4.3 Comparison Models

Here we describe models that are evaluated and compared in experiments. The following models are used: **Random Policy.** The agent randomly selects an action from the action set A at each time step, which is the simplest navigation method. **Pure DRL agent.** The classical deep reinforcement learning algorithm A3C is used to complete the navigation task. **Target-Driven.** This corresponds to the visual navigation model proposed by Zhu et al. [29]. They use the visual features from the last observation and the target image as input to predict the next action. **Scene Priors.** It uses prior knowledge in the form of a knowledge graph of object relationships to navigate. **SAVN.** The agent constantly understands its environment through the interactive loss function [24] in this model, even during inference time.

Table 1. Comparison with state-of-the-art models. We use the metrics of *Success Rate* (%) and *Success weight by Path Length* (%).

Methods	ALL		$L \geq 5$	
	SR	SPL	SR	SPL
Random policy	10.1	2.2	0.8	0.3
Pure DRL	21.8	6.9	12.1	6.5
Target-driven [29]	37.0	11.9	25.7	11.2
Scene priors [26]	35.6	10.7	22.9	10.4
SAVN [24]	37.2	11.2	26.7	10.3
Ours	**55.9**	**19.5**	**49.5**	**19.1**

4.4 Results

Quantitative Results. We show the evaluation results of five comparison models in Table 1, where $L \geq 5$ means that the length of the optimal navigation path is more than 5 steps. In order to make a fair comparison, when measuring the performance of this methods, we use the same episodes for training and test them on the same test set. The starting position of the agent is random. Table 1 shows the result on unseen tasks. We can see that the best results are obtained by using our SSR model, and its performance is better than Scene Priors and Target-Driven models. The SR of our model in unknown scene is 56%, SPL to 19%, which is better than other methods.

Table 2. The effect of action $DONE$ on navigation in different scenes.

Settings	Kitchen		Living room		Bedroom		Bathroom		Average	
	SR	SPL	SR	SPL	SR	SPL	SR	SPL	SR	SPL
With $DONE$	65.2	21.8	50.8	17.7	39.1	14.1	79.9	24.8	55.9	19.5
Without $DONE$	84.0	45.8	72.8	39.8	60.7	33.1	88.9	51.7	76.6	42.6

Since we use unseen scenes as test set, the experimental results in Table 1 also verify the generalization ability of our model for unknown situations. In fact, Target-Driven model's original extraction of visual features for positioning ability gradually lost because of multi-layer full connection layer. The generalization performance of the model for new targets is also reduced. Scene priors uses the knowledge graph of object relations to extract object relations, but fails to consider the hierarchical relationships between objects. However, we use different modules to learn local and global visual features, and combine them with target semantic information and prior knowledge graph respectively. By using the implicit spatial semantic relations, our model can overcome the shortcomings of previous methods and make the object search easier.

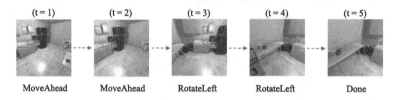

Fig. 3. Navigation example of SSR model.

We also evaluated our model with different stop criteria. In this case, the agent does not just rely on its $DONE$ actions to learn to terminate. On the contrary, it stops even when the environment signals that the target object has been found. Table 2 shows the evaluation results with and without $DONE$ signal respectively. If we don't use $DONE$ signal, the average SR of our model in four scenarios is about 76.6%. That's because in this simple environment, the agent will stop automatically when it reaches the goal.

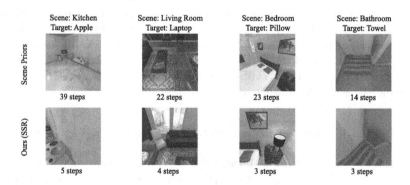

Fig. 4. Comparison between Ours (SSR) and Scene Priors

Case Study. Figure 3 is an example of the agent's view sequence when navigating to Bread in the Kinchen scene. The target object is displayed in red rectangle, and the objects detected in current observation are displayed in white box. If the target object exists in the object list of the current frame, the geometric distance between the agent and the target is less than the threshold, and the next decision of the agent is $DONE$, the navigation is considered successful and the episode is ended. Otherwise, the similarity between the object detected in the current frame and the target object will be calculated, and the spatial relation vector will be modified to make the next decision. Figure 4 shows the number of steps required for an agent to navigate to the same target object in four types of scenes. We compare our SSR model with Scene Priors model in unseen environment. Under the same setting, our model can achieve the target position with less operations.

5 Conclusion

We propose an effective target-driven visual navigation method. By learning the spatial visual semantic features and the prior relationship knowledge graph of the scene, our agent is capable of localizing target effectively. In our method, we extract the global and local visual features separately of the observation image through different network modules. Thus we get a joint representation of the spatial relationship to learn the potential connection between the target and the observation. Experiments demonstrate that our method provides obvious advantages for generalizing invisible scenes and targets in navigation.

References

1. Anderson, P., et al.: On evaluation of embodied navigation agents. arXiv preprint arXiv:1807.06757 (2018)
2. Chaplot, D.S., Gandhi, D.P., Gupta, A., Salakhutdinov, R.R.: Object goal navigation using goal-oriented semantic exploration. In: Advances in Neural Information Processing Systems, vol. 33 (2020)
3. Defferrard, M., Bresson, X., Vandergheynst, P.: Convolutional neural networks on graphs with fast localized spectral filtering. arXiv preprint arXiv:1606.09375 (2016)
4. Deng, J., Dong, W., Socher, R., Li, L.J., Li, K., Fei-Fei, L.: ImageNet: a large-scale hierarchical image database. In: 2009 IEEE Conference on Computer Vision and Pattern Recognition, pp. 248–255. IEEE (2009)
5. Gori, M., Monfardini, G., Scarselli, F.: A new model for learning in graph domains. In: Proceedings of 2005 IEEE International Joint Conference on Neural Networks, vol. 2, pp. 729–734. IEEE (2005)
6. Gupta, S., Davidson, J., Levine, S., Sukthankar, R., Malik, J.: Cognitive mapping and planning for visual navigation. In: Proceedings of the IEEE Conference on Computer Vision and Pattern Recognition, pp. 2616–2625 (2017)
7. Hamrick, J.B., et al.: Relational inductive bias for physical construction in humans and machines. arXiv preprint arXiv:1806.01203 (2018)
8. He, K., Zhang, X., Ren, S., Sun, J.: Deep residual learning for image recognition. In: Proceedings of the IEEE Conference on Computer Vision and Pattern Recognition, pp. 770–778 (2016)
9. Kawamoto, T., Tsubaki, M., Obuchi, T.: Mean-field theory of graph neural networks in graph partitioning. J. Stat. Mech: Theory Exp. **2019**(12), 124007 (2019)

10. Kim, D., Kim, S., Kwak, N.: Textbook question answering with multi-modal context graph understanding and self-supervised open-set comprehension. arXiv preprint arXiv:1811.00232 (2018)
11. Kingma, D.P., Ba, J.: Adam: a method for stochastic optimization. arXiv preprint arXiv:1412.6980 (2014)
12. Kolve, E., et al.: AI2-THOR: an interactive 3D environment for visual AI. arXiv preprint arXiv:1712.05474 (2017)
13. Krishna, R., et al.: Visual genome: connecting language and vision using crowd-sourced dense image annotations. Int. J. Comput. Vis. **123**(1), 32–73 (2017)
14. Lu, Y., Chen, Y., Zhao, D., Li, D.: MGRL: Graph neural network based inference in a Markov network with reinforcement learning for visual navigation. Neurocomputing **421**, 140–150 (2021)
15. Martins, R., Bersan, D., Campos, M.F., Nascimento, E.R.: Extending maps with semantic and contextual object information for robot navigation: a learning-based framework using visual and depth cues. J. Intell. Robot. Syst. **99**(3), 555–569 (2020)
16. Mikolov, T., Chen, K., Corrado, G., Dean, J.: Efficient estimation of word representations in vector space. arXiv preprint arXiv:1301.3781 (2013)
17. Mirowski, P., et al.: Learning to navigate in cities without a map. arXiv preprint arXiv:1804.00168 (2018)
18. Mnih, V., et al.: Asynchronous methods for deep reinforcement learning. In: International Conference on Machine Learning, pp. 1928–1937. PMLR (2016)
19. Mousavian, A., Toshev, A., Fišer, M., Košecká, J., Wahid, A., Davidson, J.: Visual representations for semantic target driven navigation. In: 2019 International Conference on Robotics and Automation (ICRA), pp. 8846–8852. IEEE (2019)
20. Pathak, D., et al.: Zero-shot visual imitation. In: Proceedings of the IEEE Conference on Computer Vision and Pattern Recognition Workshops, pp. 2050–2053 (2018)
21. Redmon, J., Farhadi, A.: Yolov3: an incremental improvement. arXiv preprint arXiv:1804.02767 (2018)
22. Wen, S., Zhao, Y., Yuan, X., Wang, Z., Zhang, D., Manfredi, L.: Path planning for active slam based on deep reinforcement learning under unknown environments. Intell. Serv. Robot. **13**, 263–272 (2020)
23. Wijmans, E., et al.: DD-PPO: learning near-perfect point goal navigators from 2.5 billion frames. arXiv preprint arXiv:1911.00357 (2019)
24. Wortsman, M., Ehsani, K., Rastegari, M., Farhadi, A., Mottaghi, R.: Learning to learn how to learn: Self-adaptive visual navigation using meta-learning. In: Proceedings of the IEEE/CVF Conference on Computer Vision and Pattern Recognition, pp. 6750–6759 (2019)
25. Wu, Q., Xu, K., Wang, J., Xu, M., Gong, X., Manocha, D.: Reinforcement learning-based visual navigation with information-theoretic regularization. IEEE Robot. Autom. Lett. **6**(2), 731–738 (2021)
26. Yang, W., Wang, X., Farhadi, A., Gupta, A., Mottaghi, R.: Visual semantic navigation using scene priors. arXiv preprint arXiv:1810.06543 (2018)
27. Yu, J., Su, Y., Liao, Y.: The path planning of mobile robot by neural networks and hierarchical reinforcement learning. Front. Neurorobotics **14**, 63 (2020)
28. Zhang, Y., Guo, Z., Lu, W.: Attention guided graph convolutional networks for relation extraction. arXiv preprint arXiv:1906.07510 (2019)
29. Zhu, Y., et al.: Target-driven visual navigation in indoor scenes using deep reinforcement learning. In: 2017 IEEE International Conference on Robotics and Automation (ICRA), pp. 3357–3364. IEEE (2017)

Classification of COVID-19 in CT Scans Using Image Smoothing and Improved Deep Residual Network

Changzu Chen[1], Zhongyi Hu[1(✉)], ShanJin[2], Lei Xiao[1], Mingzhe Hu[3], Qi Wu[1], Jingjing Shao[1], Zhenzhen Luo[1], and Mianlu Zou[1]

[1] Intelligent Information Systems Institute, Wenzhou University, Wenzhou 325035, China
[2] Zhejiang Topcheer Information Technology Co., Ltd, Hanzhou 310006, Zhejiang, China
[3] Department of Medical Imaging, Wenzhou People's Hospital, Wenzhou 325000, Zhejiang, China

Abstract. The global spread of coronavirus disease has become a major threat to global public health. There are more than 137 million confirmed cases worldwide at the time of writing. The spread of COVID-19 has resulted in a huge medical load due to the numerous suspected examinations and community screening. Deep learning methods to automatically classify COVID-19 have become an effective assistive technology. However, the current researches on data quality and the use of CT data to diagnose COVID-19 with convolutional neural networks are poor. This study is based on CT scan data of COVID-19 patients, patients with other lung diseases, and healthy people. In this work, we find that data smoothing can improve the quality of CT images of COVID-19 and improve the accuracy of the model. Specifically, an interpolation smoothing method is proposed using the bilinear interpolation algorithm. Besides, we propose an improved ResNet structure to improve the model feature extraction and fusion by optimizing the structure of the input stem and downsampling parts. Compared with the baseline ResNet, the model improves the accuracy of the three-class classification by 3.8% to 93.83%. Our research has particular significance for research on the automatic diagnosis of COVID-19 infectious diseases.

Keywords: COVID-19 · CT Scans · Classification · Deep learning

This work is supported in part by the Key Project of Zhejiang Provincial Natural Science Foundation under Grant LD21F020001, and the National Natural Science Foundation of China under Grant U1809209, and the Major Project of Wenzhou Natural Science Foundation under Grant ZY2019020, and the Key Project of Zhejiang Provincial Natural Science Foundation under Grant Z20F020022. We acknowledge the efforts and constructive comments of respected editors and anonymous reviewers.

© Springer Nature Switzerland AG 2021
L. Fang et al. (Eds.): CICAI 2021, LNAI 13069, pp. 89–100, 2021.
https://doi.org/10.1007/978-3-030-93046-2_8

1   Introduction and Related Work

Since December 2019, the outbreak of COVID-19 has posed a serious threat to global public health [7,10]. According to the World Health Organization data, as of mid-April 2021, there have been more than 137 million confirmed cases, and the global pandemic is still accelerating. [16]. It has spread inter-continentally in the first wave [15] and is suspected to be currently entering the second wave in various countries [1,5,15]. Some researches confirm that this problem may persist until 2024 [13]. Because of the strong infection rate of COVID-19, rapid and accurate diagnostic methods are urgently required to identify, isolate and treat the patients.

Real-time polymerase chain reaction(RT-PCR) test is considered a determinant for identifying COVID-19 infection [3], but the study has shown that the detection rate is low [6]. Computed tomography (CT) is a convenient diagnostic tool for pneumonia, which can effectively detect typical imaging features of COVID-19. Compared to RT-PCR test, it can produce faster results [12]. However, considering the large number of patients, the rate of spread of the disease, and the slow manual examination by professionals in hospitals [18], it is difficult for experts to respond to this number. For this reason, many researchers are focusing on artificial intelligence research that can accurately and quickly diagnose COVID-19.

Convolutional neural networks (CNNs) show good performance in many image classification tasks [14,21,22]. Therefore, the application of CNNs to the detection of COVID-19 has received extensive attention. Basic CNNs are used in some studies to provide a model for the computer-aided diagnosis of COVID-19. For example, Wang et al. [19] use the improved Inception neural network architecture for training to perform binary classification on healthy patients and patients with new crowns. Xu et al. use the classic ResNet architecture for feature extraction, and add a fully connected layer in the architecture to classify three categories (e.i. Health, COVID-19, and other types of pneumonia). Ozkaya et al. [17] perform a feature fusion using ResNet-50, GoogleNet, and VGG-16 deep architectures for effective COVID-19 detection using CT images. Jaiswal et al. [11] use a pre-trained DenseNet-201 architecture to get rid of the adverse effects of small datasets on CNN training. Automatic image analysis through the CNN model has great potential to optimize the role of CT images in the rapid diagnosis of COVID-19.

Note that the current model structures in the field of natural images have a perfect performance, including ResNeXt [20], attention mechanism [9], and dynamic convolution [4]. However, these models are not as effective as natural images on COVID-19 CT images. To this end, we design the Improved Deep Residual Network (I-ResNet) structure and combine it with our data pre-processing method to classify COVID-19 CT images. The contributions of this paper can be summarized as follows.

- From a pre-processing perspective, we find that smoothing image can improve the accuracy of the COVID-19 image classification model. And we propose a new method to eliminate irrelevant noise information.

- From a global perspective, we design a novel methodology based on Deep Residual Learning [8], named I-ResNet. This method has a strong generalization ability for COVID-19 classification based on CT images, and improves the results of the classification model.

2   Methods

In this section, we present a detailed description for the image smoothing pre-processing method of COVID-19 and I-ResNet in the classification of chest CT scan images. In the following, we first introduce the collection of chest CT data images, and then perform data preprocessing, which involves image smoothing. Finally, we propose I-ResNet for classification of chest CT scan images. An overview of our framework is illustrated in Fig. 1.

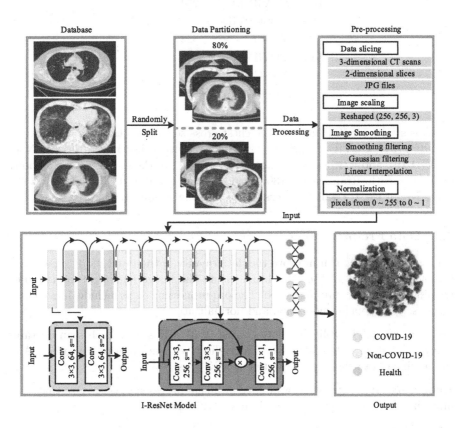

Fig. 1. An overview of the proposed method. The whole process consists of five main parts: database,data partitioning, pre-processing, training model, classification.

2.1 Dataset

In this study, a total of 1135 cross-sectional CT scans of the chest are collected. The data collection is divided into two parts. The data from COVID-19 diagnosed patient cases and other lung disease patient cases come from the relevant papers in medRxiv, bioRxiv, NEJM, JAMA, and The Lancet, etc. This part of the data is compiled and publicly provided by Yang et al. [22]. Sample data of healthy people are collected and provided by Wenzhou Kangning Hospital and Wenzhou People's Hospital. All data has been anonymized and meets the requirements of the Institutional Review Board of each participating institute.

Table 1. Statistics for the training and testing sets.

Split	Class	Num. Slices
Train	COVID-19	254
	Non-COVID-19	328
	Health	328
Test	COVID-19	63
	Non-COVID-19	69
	Health	93

This study uses CT slices of the chest cross-section for training and testing, including 317 COVID-19 images, 397 images with other lung diseases (Non-COVID-19), and 421 healthy images. The samples in the data set are randomly divided into the training set (80%) and testing set (20%). Table 1 shows the statistics for the CT sample slices in the training set and testing set.

2.2 Data Pre-processing

Data pre-processing can improve the data quality of the input model and maintain the uniformity of the model. To ensure the image quality of input model training, all data are pre-processed. The pre-processing steps include data slicing, image scaling, image smoothing, and normalization.

Data Slicing. The collected data consist of 3D CT scans. Each scan contains many axial slices. The dataset excludes slices with no information areas. And the retained data slices are exported as JPG files.

Image Scaling. To reduce variability in image processing, we ensure that each input image is reshaped to a standard size (256,256,3).

Image Smoothing. Data preprocessing uses image smoothing to reduce image noise. Image smoothing is usually achieved by an image convolution operation. It is also known as image filtering. The commonly used image smoothing methods are smoothing filtering and Gaussian filtering. In this work, we propose a new method of image smoothing - Linear Interpolation Filtering. In essence, it uses the bilinear difference to scale and recover the image to achieve the image smoothing effect. Bilinear interpolation is a linear interpolation extension of the bivariate interpolation function. The pixel values of the sampled points are calculated by the weights of the distances between the sampled points and the four surrounding neighboring points. The whole process consists of three steps: (i) Setting the fuzzy scale parameters W_1 and W_2 ; (ii) Using the bilinear interpolation algorithm to scale the original image (X, Y) to $(W_1 X, W_2 Y)$; (iii) Restoring to the original size to obtain an interpolated smoothed image.

Normalization. The original image is transformed into the corresponding unique standard form through a series of transformations. The normalization does not change the information storage of the image itself. However, the convergence of subsequent training networks can be accelerated by normalizing the range of pixel values from 0–255 to 0–1.

2.3 The Proposed Architecture

We adopt a highly modularized design following ResNet. Our network consists of a stack of residual blocks. These blocks have the same topology and are subject to two simple rules inspired by ResNet: (i) if producing spatial maps of the same size, the blocks share the same hyper-parameters (width and filter sizes), and (ii) each time when the spatial map is downsampled by a factor of 2, the width of the blocks is multiplied by a factor of 2.

As illustrated in Fig. 2, we design two modules to replace input stem and downsampling stage in ResNet. In this input stem, two 3×3 convolution modules replace the 7×7 convolution module. In downsampling, "Concat + 1×1 convolution" structure replaces "Add".

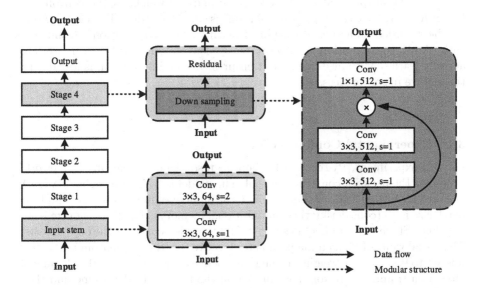

Fig. 2. The architecture of I-ResNet. The convolution kernel size, output channel size, and stride size (default is 1) are illustrated, similar for pooling layers.

Two 3×3 **replace** 7×7 : 7×7 convolution is expressed as

$$Z_{(7 \times 7)} = I * K_{(7 \times 7)}, \tag{1}$$

where $Z_{(7 \times 7)}$ and I are a matrix, $*$ means convolution operation, and $K_{(7 \times 7)}$ is 2D kernels. Two 3×3

$$Z_{2 \times (3 \times 3)} = F \left(I * K_{(3 \times 3)}^{(1)} \right) * K_{(3 \times 3)}^{(2)}, \tag{2}$$

where $Z_{2 \times (3 \times 3)}$ is a matrix, $K_{(3 \times 3)}^{(1)}$ and $K_{(3 \times 3)}^{(2)}$ are two 2D kernels, and F is the activation function. Stack the convolutional layer with two 3×3 size convolutional kernel instead of one with a 7×7 size. It has more nonlinearity (stacked convolutional layer contains an activation function), making the decision function more discriminative.

"Concat $+ 1 \times 1$ **convolution" replaces "Add"** : Suppose the two input channels are N and M. Then the single output channel of "Add" is

$$Z_{\text{add}} = \sum_{i=1}^{c} (N_i \oplus M_i), \tag{3}$$

where c is the number of input channels, Z_{add} is the output feature, and $\oplus$ is the element-wise addition of the kernel parameters on the corresponding positions.

The single output channel of "Concat $+ 1 \times 1$ convolution" is

$$Z_{\text{concat}} = \sum_{i=1}^{c} N_i * K_i' \oplus \sum_{j=1}^{d} M_j * K_{j+c}', \tag{4}$$

where d is the number of input channels, K_i' is the 1×1 convolution kernel, and Z_{concat} is the output feature. When $c = d$ and the weight of the convolution kernel K are 1, "Concat $+ 1 \times 1$ convolution" is equal to "Add". Therefore, "Add" can be regarded as a special case of "Concat$+ 1 \times 1$ convolution". Compared with "Add", the operation of "Concat $+ 1 \times 1$ convolution" allows the network to actively learn how to fuse features. It ensures that no information is lost during the feature fusion process.

3   Results

3.1   Experimental Configuration

For this experiment, PyTorch, a Python open-source deep learning framework, is used as the network construction tool. The model is trained using an NVIDIA GeForce RTX 2080 Ti GPU. For training, the number of iterations is 200, and the batch size is 16 (considering the computational memory). The learning rate is set to 0.0001. Stochastic gradient descent (SGD) is implemented for the experiments. The initial value of the gamma parameter is set to 0.1, the momentum parameter was set to 0.9, and the weight attenuation coefficient is set to 0.0001. The model after each training iteration is evaluated on the test set to determine and then store the best model.

3.2 Experimental Results and Analysis

To compare the advantages of our proposed model architecture and data pre-processing method, we selected four models, including ResNet [8], ResNext [20], SEResNet [9], DCResNet [4]. The results are shown in Table 2.

Table 2. Comparative results (ResNet, ResNext, SEResNet, DCResNet vs Ours).

Model	Test Acc. (%)
ResNet-18	90.75
ResNeXt-18	84.14
SEResNet-18	83.70
DCResNet-18	79.29
ResNet-18+ Image smoothing[a]	92.51
I-ResNet-18	93.39
I-ResNet-18+ Image smoothing[a]	93.83

[a] The image smooth method uses here is Gaussian smooth, and other smooth methods are discussed in Sect. 4.1

The accuracy is chosen as the main criterion for model performance comparison. Our experiments compare the effect of image smoothing on the accuracy of the classification model, and the superiority of I-ResNet network structure. Three points can be seen in Table 2.

- The model structures with good performance in the field of natural images, such as ResNeXt, SEResNet, and DCResNet, cannot be effectively applied in the classification of COVID-19 images.
- The preprocessing method of image smoothing can effectively improve the network model. Compared with the method without image smoothing, this method improves the accuracy by 1.76% on ResNet-18. And it improves the accuracy by 0.44% on I-ResNet.
- The I-ResNet model has the best accuracy. The accuracy is 2.64% higher than that of ResNet-18.

Table 3. Evaluation results of the best model (I-ResNet-18+ Image Smoothing) on the test set. ACC: accuracy, PRE: precision, SEN: sensitivity, F1-score is SEN and PRE harmonic averaging.

Classification	ACC	PRE	SEN	F1-score
COVID-19 vs Non-COVID-19	0.896	0.917	0.859	0.887
COVID-19 vs Health	1.000	1.000	1.000	1.000
Non-COVID-19 vs Health	1.000	1.000	1.000	1.000
3-way	0.938	–	–	–

The classification model trained by combining the image smoothing method and the I-ResNet network structure shows the detailed results of each evaluation index on the test set as shown in Table 3. The SEN of classification of COVID-19 and other diseases is 0.859, the SEN of classification of COVID-19 and health is 1.000. The results demonstrate that it has a high sensitivity to COVID-19, making the classification model more reliable for computer-aided diagnosis.

The confusion matrix of the proposed method on the classification task is shown in Fig. 3(a). It can be seen that our method distinguishes between these categories. In particular, it distinguishes all health categories. This provides a strong theoretical basis and tool for the community screening of COVID-19.

For this experiment, the area under the ROC curve (AUC) is calculated and is shown in Fig. 3(b). COVID-19 has an AUC of 0.913 relative to other data, 0.957 for Non-COVID-19, and 1.000 for health. It can be seen from this that the performance of the three-class model is excellent, and the overall performance of the model classification is good. The area under the micro-average ROC curve is 0.982 and the macro-average is 0.968, indicating that the overall performance of the model classification is good. This is of great help to the auxiliary diagnosis.

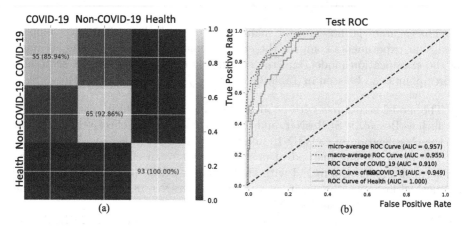

Fig. 3. The results of our proposed method. (a) Confusion matrix of the three classification results on the testing set. (b) ROC curve for the testing set.

4   Ablation Studies

The experiments validate the effectiveness of image smoothing and I-ResNet in improving the performance of classification on COVID-19 images. Concretely, we pick an off-the-shelf architecture as the baseline, build different counterparts, train it from scratch, and test it to collect the accuracy. For the comparability, all the models are trained until the complete convergence, and every pair of baseline and different counterparts use identical configurations, e.g., learning rate schedules and batch sizes.

4.1   Image Smoothing Contrast Results and Analysis

To preliminarily evaluate image smoothing on various architectures, we experiment with several representative benchmark models.

In Table 4, the performance of models is consistently lifted by a clear margin, suggesting that image smoothing can improve the accuracy of the new crown image classification model. Gaussian filtering has the best effect when the model has a higher accuracy rate. Linear interpolation filtering has universal effects.

Table 4. Comparison of validation accuracy (%) between different image smoothing methods and baseline models.

Image smoothing	Baseline	Linear interpolation filtering	Smoothing filtering	Gaussian filtering
ResNet-18	90.75	92.07	92.07	92.51
ResNext-18	84.14	85.02	83.70	83.70
SEResNet-18	83.70	86.78	85.90	86.34
DCResNet-18	79.29	80.62	80.62	79.74

In Fig. 4(a), the Gaussian filtering and the smoothing filtering have the best effect when the smooth radius is 3. In Fig. 4(b), the linear interpolation smooth has an improved effect in different models. In this ResNet-18, the model has the highest accuracy when the parameter is 0.6. In SEResNet-18, the model has the highest accuracy when the parameter is 0.2.

In sum, image smoothing has a great influence on the effect of models. Image smoothing can eliminate noise and affect the quality of data. It is a preprocessing method that can improve the value and accuracy of data.

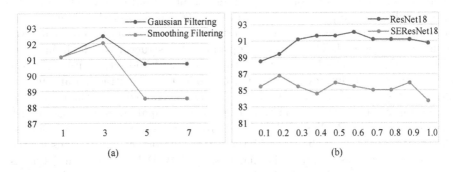

(a)   (b)

Fig. 4. Accuracy based on different image smooth parameters. (a) The effect of image smoothing methods with different smooth radii on ResNet-18. (b) The effect of linear interpolation smooth parameters ($W_1 = W_2$) on the model. A parameter of 1.0 means no operation on the image.

4.2   Improved Module Comparison Results and Analysis

To initially evaluate the effectiveness of I-ResNet, we try heuristic models on ResNet-18, including different structural parameters in the input stem, improved modules, and image smoothing.

The ablation study of all heuristics is shown in Table 5. The appropriate number of 3×3 convolutions to replace 7×7 convolutions has better results. In our classification task, two 3×3 convolutions with step 2 achieve the highest accuracy. Replacing "Add" with "Concat + 1×1 convolution" can increase by 0.88%, while stacking the three heuristics can increase to 93.83%.

Table 5. The breakdown effect for each effective training heuristic on ResNet-18.

Heuristic	Test Acc. (%)
7×7, s $= 2$ (baseline) + Add	90.75
7×7, s $= 2$ (baseline) + Concat+1×1	91.63
$2 \times (3 \times 3$, s $= 2) +$ Add	92.07
$(3 \times 3$, s $= 1$ 3×3, s $= 2) +$ Concat + 1×1	93.39
$(3 \times 3$, s $= 1$; 3×3, s $= 2) +$ Concat + 1×1 + Image smoothing	93.83

5   Conclusion

The outbreak has become a global concern due to the serious safety issues raised by the global spread of the COVID-19 outbreak. In the face of a possible second wave of the outbreak and the limitations of long nucleic acid testing time, low detection rate, and limited availability, there is an urgent need for alternative methods to help medical personnel perform rapid testing. Meanwhile, linear interpolation filtering is proposed to eliminate image noise. It is performed by using a bilinear interpolation algorithm to scale and recover the image. It can be well applied to different model structures. In addition, an improved ResNet structure is proposed. This structure optimizes the structure of the input stem and uses "Concat + 1×1 convolution" to replace the "Add" structure of the feature fusion part. It improves the ability of model feature extraction and fusion. These methods can be effectively fused. The model trained using these methods has better feature representation and classification capabilities. Compared with the baseline model ResNet, the model improves the accuracy of the three-class classification by 3.8% to 93.83%. The result has important implications for the development of tools to aid in the diagnosis of COVID-19. It helps in diagnosis and community screening for infectious diseases. Due to the limited data, computer vision has high accuracy in detecting COVID-19 in CT scans, and further research is needed given the limitations discussed.

References

1. Ali, I.: Covid-19: are we ready for the second wave? Disaster Med. Public Health Prep. **14**(5), e16–e18 (2020)
2. Butt, C., Gill, J., Chun, D., Babu, B.A.: Deep learning system to screen coronavirus disease 2019 Pneumonia. Appl. Intell. 1 (2020)
3. Chan, J.F.W., et al.: A familial cluster of pneumonia associated with the 2019 novel coronavirus indicating person-to-person transmission: a study of a family cluster. LANCET **395**(10223), 514–523 (2020)
4. Chen, Y., Dai, X., Liu, M., Chen, D., Yuan, L., Liu, Z.: Dynamic convolution: attention over convolution Kernels. In: Proceedings of the IEEE/CVF Conference on Computer Vision and Pattern Recognition, pp. 11030–11039 (2020)
5. Evenett, S.J., Winters, L.A.: Preparing for a second wave of COVID-19 a trade bargain to secure supplies of medical goods. Global Trade Alert (2020)
6. Fang, Y., et al.: Sensitivity of chest CT for Covid-19: comparison to RT-PCR. Radiology **296**(2), E115–E117 (2020)
7. Gorbalenya, A.E.: Severe acute respiratory syndrome-related coronavirus-the species and its viruses, a statement of the coronavirus study group. BioRxiv (2020)
8. He, K., Zhang, X., Ren, S., Sun, J.: Deep residual learning for image recognition. In: Proceedings of the IEEE Conference on Computer Vision and Pattern Recognition, pp. 770–778 (2016)
9. Hu, J., Shen, L., Sun, G.: Squeeze-and-excitation networks. In: Proceedings of the IEEE Conference on Computer Vision and Pattern Recognition, pp. 7132–7141 (2018)
10. Huang, C., et al.: Clinical features of patients infected with 2019 novel coronavirus in Wuhan, China. LANCET **395**(10223), 497–506 (2020)
11. Jaiswal, A., Gianchandani, N., Singh, D., Kumar, V., Kaur, M.: Classification of the COVID-19 infected patients using densenet201 based deep transfer learning. J. Biomol. Struct. Dyn. **39**(15), 5682–5689 (2020)
12. Khan, A.I., Shah, J.L., Bhat, M.M.: CoroNet: a deep neural network for detection and diagnosis of COVID-19 from chest X-ray images. Comput. Meth. Programs Biomed. **196**, 105581 (2020)
13. Kissler, S.M., Tedijanto, C., Goldstein, E., Grad, Y.H., Lipsitch, M.: Projecting the transmission dynamics of SARS-COV-2 through the post pandemic period. Science **368**(6493), 860–868 (2020)
14. LeCun, Y., Bengio, Y., Hinton, G.: Deep learning. Nature **521**(7553), 436–444 (2015)
15. Leung, K., Wu, J.T., Liu, D., Leung, G.M.: First-wave COVID-19 transmissibility and severity in China outside Hubei after control measures, and second-wave scenario planning: a modelling impact assessment. LANCET **395**(10233), 1382–1393 (2020)
16. World Health Organization: Coronavirus disease 2019 (COVID-19): situation report (2021)
17. Özkaya, U., Öztürk, Ş, Barstugan, M.: Coronavirus (COVID-19) classification using deep features fusion and ranking technique. In: Hassanien, A.-E., Dey, N., Elghamrawy, S. (eds.) Big Data Analytics and Artificial Intelligence Against COVID-19: Innovation Vision and Approach. SBD, vol. 78, pp. 281–295. Springer, Cham (2020). https://doi.org/10.1007/978-3-030-55258-9_17
18. Tanne, J.H., Hayasaki, E., Zastrow, M., Pulla, P., Smith, P., Rada, A.G.: COVID-19: how doctors and healthcare systems are tackling coronavirus worldwide. BMJ **368**, m1090 (2020)

19. Wang, S., et al.: A deep learning algorithm using CT images to screen for corona virus disease (COVID-19). MedRxiv (2020)
20. Xie, S., Girshick, R., Dollár, P., Tu, Z., He, K.: Aggregated residual transformations for deep neural networks. In: Proceedings of the IEEE Conference on Computer Vision and Pattern Recognition, pp. 1492–1500 (2017)
21. Zhang, X., Jiang, R., Wang, T., Huang, P., Zhao, L.: Attention-based interpolation network for video deblurring. Neurocomputing **453**, 865–875 (2020)
22. Zhao, J., Zhang, Y., He, X., Xie, P.: COVID-CT-dataset: a CT scan dataset about COVID-19. arXiv preprint arXiv:2003.13865 (2020)

Selected Sample Retraining Semi-supervised Learning Method for Aerial Scene Classification

Ye Tian[1], Jun Li[2], Liguo Zhang[1], Jianguo Sun[1(✉)], and Guisheng Yin[1]

[1] College of Computer Science and Technology, Harbin Engineering University,
Harbin 150001, China
sunjianguo@hrbeu.edu.cn
[2] China Industrial Control Systems Cyber Emergency Response Team,
Beijing 100040, China

Abstract. The performance of scene classification for remote sensing images based on deep neural networks is limited by the number of labeled data. To alleviate this problem, a variety of methods have been proposed to apply semi-supervised learning to exploit both labeled and unlabeled samples for training classifiers, but most of them still require a certain number of labeled samples considering the complex context relationship and huge spatial differences of remote sensing images. In this paper, we proposed a novel selected sample retraining semi-supervised learning method (S^2R) that is simple but works efficiently on scene classification remote sensing. First, we train several models independently, each model is trained for only a few epochs, and use them to label samples in the unlabeled data set. Then, the labeled unlabeled data set is divided into low-noise labeled data set and sub-unlabeled data set through the high probability sample selection method. Finally, the two segmented data sets are combined with the labeled data sets to train a scene classifier based on the semi-supervised learning method. To verify the effectiveness of the proposed method, it is further compared with several state-of-the-art semi-supervised classification approaches. The results demonstrate that our method consistently outperforms the previous methods on the condition of only a few labeled samples over the scene classification for remote sensing images.

Keywords: Remote sensing images · Scene classification · Semi-supervised classification

1 Introduction

With the improvement of unmanned aerial vehicle technologies and high-resolution visual sensors, a large amount of high-resolution remote sensing (HRRS) image data is available for analyzing the earth's surface [4]. In the field of HRRS, scene classification methods that can be used to solve practical

---

The original version of this chapter was revised: The author name has been corrected as "Jun Li". The correction to this chapter is available at
https://doi.org/10.1007/978-3-030-93046-2_67

problems, such as mapping and monitoring land types and city planning, have become an active research hotspot.

During the past few years, deep learning models, especially convolutional neural networks (CNNs), have received extensive attention in the field of scene classification [3,9]. However, CNNs usually require a large number of high-quality labeled samples in the training phase. Unfortunately, collecting the labeled data of training scene images is time and energy-consuming. In contrast, the acquisition of unlabeled images is much easier compared to acquire a manually-annotated dataset by experts and engineers.

In this case, the semi-supervised learning (SSL) methods have been introduced to jointly utilize labeled and unlabeled data in the context of HRRS images. For example, a semi-supervised generative framework is proposed in [5], it uses Residual network(Resnet) [6] and very deep CNNs (VGG) [11] as the feature extractors, uses the co-training-based self-labeled method to select and identical unlabeled data, and uses discriminatory evaluation to enhance the classification of the confusion classes with similar visualize features. In [2], it proposes an SSL method for HRRS classification based on CNNs and ensemble learning, the effective ResNet is adopted to extract preliminary HRRS image features, and the strategy of ensemble learning is utilized to establish discriminative image representations by exploring the intrinsic information of all labeled and unlabeled data, and finally supervised learning is performed for scene classification. Although the above methods have gained progress as well in semi-supervised scene classification, they need to use network ensembles to train multiple networks instead of one. And it cannot be ignored that these methods still require a certain number of labeled samples.

It is well known in the machine learning community that the consistency regularization [10,12] and mixing regularization [1,13] based SSL methods have proved to be simple while effective, achieving a number of state of the art results in the field of natural images over the last few years. Consistency regularization is driven by encouraging consistent predictions that two different augmentations of the same unsupervised image should lead to similar prediction probabilities. Mixing regularization is inspired by MixUp [16], it uses a blending factor from the Beta distribution to blend pairs of images and corresponding ground truth labels. Interpolation Consistency Training (ICT) [13] uses MixUp on a pair of pseudo-label unlabeled images which are predicted class probabilities by the exponential moving average (EMA) of the training model, and through consistent regularization to ensure that the prediction results of the training model on the mixed images are the same as the EMA model. MixMatch [1] works by guessing low-extropy labels for data-augmented unlabeled examples, mixing labeled and unlabeled data using MixUp, and then train an SSL classifier to output consistent predictions about linear interpolation of the data.

Contrary to natural images, however, HRRS images contain complex contextual relationships and large differences of object scale and are often affected by the camera angle, the direction of objects, illumination, and atmospheric conditions, which can result in high intra-class variations and in low inter-class variations. Therefore, SSL techniques based on consistent regularization methods are difficult to achieve good generalization performance in remote sensing images with few labeled samples (for example, only one or two samples per

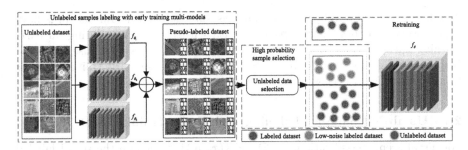

Fig. 1. Framework of the proposed semi-supervised selected samples retraining method, where the training procedure includes three phases: unlabeled samples labeling with early training multi-models, high probability sample selection, and retraining. Here, f_{θ_1}, f_{θ_2}, and f_{θ_3} are three pre-trained networks using labeled dataset and unlabeled dataset based on MixMatch method in a few epochs. f_θ is the final network retrained by using the labeled dataset, low-noise dataset, and sub-unlabeled dataset based on MixMatch method.

category). Moreover, as the training process deepens, the neural network will memorize the unlabeled data together with the false pseudo-labels, which will affect the recognition accuracy of the model [8].

To cope with this problem, in this paper, we propose a novel selected samples retraining semi-supervised learning method for aerial scene classification, namely S^2R. We use early-training multi-models to label partially unlabeled samples for HRRS images, inspired by the early-learning regularization [8]. First, initialize multiple independent ResNet networks with different parameters, and combine the MixMatch SSL method to independently train the model through only a few epochs, obtain multiple ResNet network models with different parameters after training, which are used to labeled unlabeled samples. Then, the pseudo-labeled unlabeled samples are divided into low-noise labeled datasets and unlabeled datasets through the high probability sample selection. To the best of our knowledge, it is the first time that the multiple Resnet models trained for only a few epochs have been used to label data in a semi-supervised scene classification task. Finally, SSL is carried out with the labeled data, pseudo-labeled data, and unlabeled data by combination with a pseudo-labeled loss function. The experiments on the AID dataset show that by adding the pseudo-labeled data filtered and labeled by multiple ResNet models trained in the early stage to SSL, the trained neural network can achieve higher classification accuracy.

The rest of this paper is organized as follows. The proposed method is described in Sect. 2. The experiments are described in Sect. 3, which is followed by our conclusions in Sect. 4

2   Methodology

SSL methods aim to improve the model's performance by leveraging unlabeled data. Current state-of-the-art SSL methods can be seen as noisy learning of pseudo-labeled data. When trained on noisy labels, deep neural networks have been observed to first fit the training data with clean labels during an early learning phase, before eventually memorizing the examples with false labels [8]. Inspired by this idea, we propose an SSL method that uses early training models to label data. An overview of the method is shown in Fig. 1

2.1   Unlabeled Samples Labeling with Early Training Multi-Models

For aerial scene classification, let $\mathcal{D}_L = \{(x_i, y_i)\}_{i=1}^{N_L}$ denote the set of labeled training data set, where x_i is the i-th sample, $y_i \in \{0, 1\}^C$ is the one-hot label over C classes, and N_L is the total number of labeled samples. Similarly, the set of unlabeled data can be represented as $\mathcal{D}_U = \{u_i\}_{i=1}^{N_U}$, where u_i is the i-th unlabeled sample, and N_U is the number of unlabeled samples. More formally, given a model with parameters θ, based on MixMatch [1] the combined loss $\mathcal{L}$ for SSL is computed as:

$$\mathcal{L} = \mathcal{L}_X + \lambda_U \mathcal{L}_U \tag{1}$$

$$\mathcal{L}_X = \frac{1}{|\mathcal{X}'|} \sum_{x,y \in \mathcal{X}'} \mathrm{H}\left(y, \mathrm{p}(x; \theta)\right) \tag{2}$$

$$\mathcal{L}_U = \frac{1}{C\,|\mathcal{U}'|} \sum_{u,q \in \mathcal{U}'} \|q - \mathrm{p}(u; \theta)\|_2^2 \tag{3}$$

where $\mathrm{H}(a, b)$ is the cross-entropy between distributions a and b, $\mathrm{p}(x; \theta)$ is the model's output softmax probability for class c, $\mathcal{X}'$ and $\mathcal{U}'$ are transformed from labeled data and unlabeled data through MixUp [16], and λ_U are hyperparameters.

Deep networks tend to learn clean samples faster than noisy samples [7], and we assume that this phenomenon also exists in SSL. Although SSL technology can improve the generalization performance of the model to a certain extent, when there is little labeled data, the model will be affected by the noise data in the unlabeled data. Our goal is to find a model or a combination of multiple models $P = \{\mathrm{p}(u; \theta_i)\}_{i=1}^M$ to label unlabeled samples. These models can not only learn clean data in SSL but also not overfit noisy data during the early training process of the model. Then select relatively clean labeled samples from pseudo-labeled samples, and convert them to one-hot labeled samples. Finally, the selected one-hot labeled samples are added to the SSL training process as low-noise labeled data, which is different from labeled data and unlabeled data to train a new model with better generalization performance.

In order to select low-noise labeled data with high labeled quality, according to the early-learning phenomenon [8], we adopt the MixMatch SSL method, using labeled data and unlabeled data to train the model for a few epochs. However, using an independent model to select low-noise samples, and then combining low-noise samples to train a new model may cause confirmation bias. Intuitively, two or multiple networks can filter different types of errors brought by noisy pseudo-labels since they have different learning abilities. Therefore, we use different initialization parameters and sample input order to independently and repeatedly train multiple models and use the predicted mean of these models for unlabeled samples as pseudo-labels for the samples. For a unlabeled sample u ($u \in \mathcal{D}_U$), we set

$$\hat{y} = \frac{1}{M} \sum_{i=1}^{M} \mathrm{p}(u; \theta_i) \tag{4}$$

where θ_i is the parameter of the early training model obtained by training only a few epochs using all data and different initialization parameters for the i-th time. Finally, we obtain the pseudo-labeled dataset $\mathcal{D}_{P_U} = \{(u_i, \hat{y}_i)\}_{i=1}^{N_U}$.

2.2 High Probability Sample Selection

In this section, We present a method to screen pseudo-labeled samples. In Sect. 2.1, through preliminary training, we obtained multiple scene classification models with different parameters and used these models to pseudo-label unlabeled samples. Intuitively, the pseudo-labeled dataset $\mathcal{D}_{P_U} = \{(u_i, \hat{y}_i)\}_{i=1}^{N_U}$ obtained in Sect. 2.1 contains a large amount of incorrectly labeled data and cannot be directly used to train the model. However, the performance of CNN will be better if the training data become less noisy. We aim to select some low-noise data in the pseudo-labeled data set $\mathcal{D}_{P_U}$ to optimize the classification model. From the view of [14], CNNs tend to learn simple patterns first, then gradually memorize all samples. And for unlabeled data, if the pseudo-labeling results of most models are the same, it should be correctly labeled Based on this observation, we select the low-noise pseudo-labels samples from $\mathcal{D}_{P_U}$ as follows:

$$\mathcal{D}_{P_s} = \arg\max_{\mathcal{D}_{P_U}:\{u_i, \hat{y}_i\}} \sum_{j=1}^{N_s} \sum_{i=1}^{C} \max(\hat{y}_i) \tag{5}$$

where N_s is the number of samples selected in each category. In other words, in the pseudo-labeled data set $\mathcal{D}_{P_U}$, we select the top N_s samples with the highest predicted probability of $\hat{y}$ in each category to form the low-noise pseudo-labeled dataset $\mathcal{D}_{P_s} = \{(u_i, \hat{y}_i)\}_{i=1}^{N_{P_s}}$ ($P_s = C \times N_s$). Particularly, we convert the pseudo-label into the low-noise pseudo-labeled dataset $\mathcal{D}_{P_s}$ into a one-hot label.

2.3 Retraining

After obtaining the low-noise pseudo-labeled dataset $\mathcal{D}_{P_s}$, we use labeled, low-noise pseudo-labeled and unlabeled datasets to train a new CNN model based on the MixMatch semi-supervised learning method. In order to make better use of the low-noise pseudo-labeled dataset, We rewrite the loss function as

$$\mathcal{L} = \mathcal{L}_{\mathcal{X}} + \lambda_{\mathcal{P}_s} \mathcal{L}_{\mathcal{P}_s} + \lambda_{\mathcal{U}} \mathcal{L}_{\mathcal{U}} \tag{6}$$

$$\mathcal{L}_{\mathcal{P}_s} = \frac{1}{|\mathcal{U}'_{\mathcal{P}_s}|} \sum_{u, \hat{y} \in \mathcal{U}'_{\mathcal{P}_s}} \mathrm{H}(\hat{y}, \mathrm{p}(u; \theta)) \tag{7}$$

where $\mathcal{U}'_{\mathcal{P}_s}$ is transformed from labeled data, low-noise pseudo-labeled data, and unlabeled data through MixUp [16], $\lambda_{\mathcal{P}_s}$ are hyperparameters. In order to ensure that the three data sets are mixed using mixup, in the actual training of the model, we use the same number of labeled data and low-noise pseudo labeled data in each mini-batch. And the number of unlabeled data is the sum of the number of labeled data and low-noise pseudo labeled data.

3 Experimental Results

In this section we first introduced the data set used for the experiment, then we compare S^{2}R with some state-of-the-art approaches. Finally, through sensitivity analysis, we analyzed the effects of the number of training epochs for early training of multiple models N_E, the number of early training models M, and the number of samples of each category N_s selected from the pseudo-label dataset on the performance of the final model.

3.1 Data Set Description

We evaluate the proposed model on both aerial image data set (AID) [15]. The AID has a number of 10,000 images and divided into 30 classes, which were collected from Google Earth imagery with the pixel-resolution changing from about half a meter to 8 m, the size was fixed as 600 × 600 pixels. The number of images in each category varies from 220 to 420. For these two data sets, we first randomly select 20% samples from each category as the test set. And then in order to verify the effectiveness of our semi-supervised learning method under different label sample numbers, we randomly select 1, 2, 3, and 5 samples in each category as the labeled dataset, and the remaining samples as the unlabeled dataset.

Table 1. Recognition accuracy (%) of Mean-teacher, ICT, MixMatch, and our proposed method with different Labeled data for each category. The best accuracies are indicated in bold in each column.

Method	AID			
	Num of labeled data for each category			
	1	2	3	5
Label propagation [2]	–	–	64.51	72.58
EL+LR [2]	–	–	72.18	78.87
Mean-Teacher [12]	19.38	31.31	40.02	51.66
ICT [13]	44.70	69.98	80.33	85.24
MixMatch [1]	48.66	74.72	87.37	91.63
S^{2}R(ours)	**53.87**	**79.14**	**88.31**	**92.34**

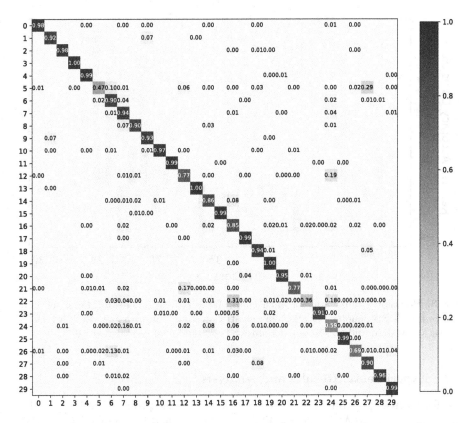

Fig. 2. Confusion matrix obtained by S^2R on AID testing set.

3.2   Implementation Details

Network Architecture. We use Resnet50 pre-trained on ImageNet as the backbone of our network architecture and we replace the last 1000 dimensional fully connected (FC) layer of Resnet50 by a C dimensional FC layer, while C is the number of classes for the training dataset.

Training Setup. For our experiments, we used a batch of 16 images and 200 batches as an epoch. The early training multiple models have only trained 10 epochs and the final model has trained 120 epochs by using the labeled dataset, low-noise pseudo-labeled dataset, and unlabeled dataset, where Adam optimizer is employed with a learning rate of 3×10^{-5} for all models. The selecting number of samples $N_s = 3$, and number of early training models $M = 3$. All the baseline SSL methods are trained by Adam optimizer with a 3×10^{-5} learning rate by 120 epochs, the learning rate remains constant during the training phase. Finally, we conduct 5 independent experiments on each dataset and record the average accuracy of each independent experiment as the final recognition accuracy of the SLL method.

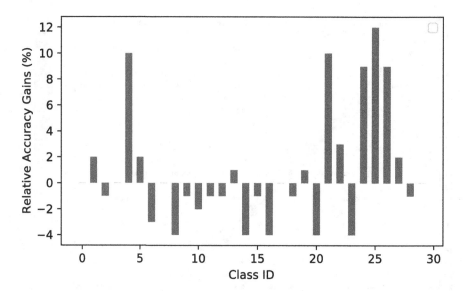

Fig. 3. Precision comparison for each class of the S^2R and the MixMatch method. Where the Y-axis denotes per class classification accuracy improvement of S^2R relative to the MixMatch, and the X-axis denotes the class index of each category.

3.3   Experimental Results and Analysis

Performance Comparison. The performance of the proposed SSL method is investigated on the AID dataset. The proposed method is compared with other state-of-the-art methods. The results are given in Table 1. As can be seen from Table 1, for the AID dataset, our method performs much better than its comparisons with 1, 2, and 3 labeled data per category. Also, it cannot be neglected that the results of the MixMatch method are close to our method when the number of labeled data goes up to 5 for each class, which indicates that when the labeled data are enough for SSL classification, the low-noise-pseudo-labeled data is not optimal any more considering the noise introduced by uncertainty. In general, when the number of tags for each category is 2, our method can best improve the model's aerial scene classification performance.

To further show the effectiveness of our proposed methods, Fig. 2 shows the confusion matrix obtained on AID by our method, with 3 labeled samples for each category. The recognition accuracy comparison of each category of our method and MixMatch when there are 3 labeled data for each category is shown in Fig. 3, which details the improvement of our method relative to the accuracy of MixMatch in each category. As shown in Fig. 2 and Fig. 3, our method has a certain improvement in the recognition accuracy of almost every category.

Table 2. Recognition accuracy (%) of the aerial scene classification using different number of training epochs N_E for early training of three models.

N_E	10	20	30	40
S²R	79.14	78.65	77.40	76.90

Influence of Parameters on Performance of S²R. In this section, The AID is used as an example to analyze the influences of three important parameters including N_E, M, and N_s on the performance of the final training model.

Table 3. Recognition accuracy (%) of the aerial scene classification using different selecting number of samples N_s for each category.

N_s	0	1	2	3	4	5	6
S²R	74.72	75.54	76.32	79.14	79.12	78.35	77.32

Table 4. Recognition accuracy (%) of the aerial scene classification using different number of early training models M.

M	1	2	3	4	5
S²R	77.86	78.38	79.14	78.92	78.75

Table 2 shows the changes of accuracy with the N_E changing over a wide range of values when the other two being fixed, $M = 3$ and $N_s = 4$. It can be seen from Table 2 that the performance of the model is best when $N_E = 10$. For N_S show in Table 3, the performance of the final model increases as N_S increases, and when $N_S = 4$, the accuracy reaches the maximum. For M show in Table 4, the 3 early training models have the best results, and the 4 models are the second. And it shows that it is not that the more models M, the better the training effect. In order to save computing resources and the performance of the three models is not much different from the four models, we used three models to label unlabeled data in the comparison experiment.

4   Conclusion

In this paper, we have presented a selected sample retraining semi-supervised learning method to reduce the demand for labeled samples in remote sensing image scene classification. A simple method is used to select unlabeled data labeled with multiple models that only train a few epochs, and the selected pseudo-labeled data is combined with labeled data and unlabeled data to train a new classification model. This model can greatly improve the classification performance of the model. The experimental results on the AID dataset show the superior performances of our method.

References

1. Berthelot, D., Carlini, N., Goodfellow, I., Papernot, N., Oliver, A., Raffel, C.A.: MixMatch: a holistic approach to semi-supervised learning. In: Proceedings Advances in Neural Information Processing Systems (NIPS), pp. 5049–5059 (2019)
2. Dai, X., Wu, X., Wang, B., Zhang, L.: Semisupervised scene classification for remote sensing images: a method based on convolutional neural networks and ensemble learning. IEEE Geosci. Remote Sens. Lett. **16**(6), 869–873 (2019). https://doi.org/10.1109/LGRS.2018.2886534
3. Dede, M.A., Aptoula, E., Genc, Y.: Deep network ensembles for aerial scene classification. IEEE Geosci. Remote Sens. Lett. **16**(5), 732–735 (2018). https://doi.org/10.1109/LGRS.2018.2880136
4. Dong, Y., Zhang, Q.: A combined deep learning model for the scene classification of high-resolution remote sensing image. IEEE Geosci. Remote Sens. Lett. **16**(10), 1540–1544 (2019). https://doi.org/10.1109/LGRS.2019.2902675
5. Han, W., Feng, R., Wang, L., Cheng, Y.: A semi-supervised generative framework with deep learning features for high-resolution remote sensing image scene classification. ISPRS-J. Photogramm. Remote Sens. **145**, 23–43 (2018). https://doi.org/10.1016/j.isprsjprs.2017.11.004
6. He, K., Zhang, X., Ren, S., Sun, J.: Deep residual learning for image recognition. In: Proceedings IEEE Conference (CVPR), pp. 770–778 (2016)
7. Li, J., Socher, R., Hoi, S.C.: DivideMix: learning with noisy labels as semi-supervised learning. In: Proceedings ICLR (2019)
8. Liu, S., Niles-Weed, J., Razavian, N., Fernandez-Granda, C.: Early-learning regularization prevents memorization of noisy labels. arXiv:2007.00151 (2020)
9. Liu, Y., Liu, Y., Ding, L.: Scene classification based on two-stage deep feature fusion. IEEE Geosci. Remote Sens. Lett. **15**(2), 183–186 (2017). https://doi.org/10.1109/LGRS.2017.2779469
10. Oliver, A., Odena, A., Raffel, C.A., Cubuk, E.D., Goodfellow, I.: Realistic evaluation of deep semi-supervised learning algorithms. In: Proceedings Advances in Neural Information Processing Systems (NIPS), pp. 3235–3246 (2018)
11. Simonyan, K., Zisserman, A.: Very deep convolutional networks for large-scale image recognition. In: Proceedings ICLR (2014)
12. Tarvainen, A., Valpola, H.: Mean teachers are better role models: weight-averaged consistency targets improve semi-supervised deep learning results. In: Proceedings Advances in Neural Information Processing Systems (NIPS), pp. 1195–1204 (2017)
13. Verma, V., Lamb, A., Kannala, J., Bengio, Y., Lopez-Paz, D.: Interpolation consistency training for semi-supervised learning. In: Proceedings Conference (AAAI), pp. 3635–3641 (2019)
14. Wei, H., Feng, L., Chen, X., An, B.: Combating noisy labels by agreement: a joint training method with co-regularization. In: Proceedings IEEE Conference (CVPR), pp. 13726–13735 (2020)
15. Xia, G.S., et al.: AID: a benchmark data set for performance evaluation of aerial scene classification. IEEE Trans. Geosci. Remote Sensing **55**(7), 3965–3981 (2017). https://doi.org/10.1109/TGRS.2017.2685945
16. Zhang, H., Cisse, M., Dauphin, Y.N., Lopez-Paz, D.: mixup: beyond empirical risk minimization. In: Proceedings ICLR (2018)

Knowledge Powered Cooperative Semantic Fusion for Patent Classification

Zhe Zhang[1], Tong Xu[1(✉)], Le Zhang[1], Yichao Du[1], Hui Xiong[2(✉)], and Enhong Chen[1]

[1] School of Computer Science and Technology, University of Science and Technology of China, Hefei, China
{tongxu,cheneh}@ustc.edu.cn, duyichao@mail.ustc.edu.cn
[2] The State University of New Jersey, New Brunswick, USA
hxiong@rutgers.edu

Abstract. Patent classification is beneficial for many patent applications, such as patent quality valuation, retrieval, and litigation analysis. Recently, many automatic patent classification methods have been proposed to save labor costs, which usually formulate this task as a multi-label text classification problem. In reality, patent language is highly terminological, full of scientific entities and domain knowledge. However, existing works seldom consider such unique property of patents, which reduces the classification performance. To this end, we propose a novel framework named Knowledge Powered Cooperative Semantic Fusion to capture deeper knowledge semantics for patent classification. Specifically, we first exploit knowledge graphs to enrich the patent with related entities. Then we design a mutual attention mechanism between entities and original texts to emphasize the crucial semantics of entities with the guide of texts, and vice versa. Finally, we introduce the graph convolutional network further to enhance the fusion representation of entities and texts. Extensive experiments on large-scale patent data demonstrate the superior performance of our model on the patent classification task.

Keywords: Patent classification · Knowledge graph · Attention mechanism · Graph convolutional network

1 Introduction

Patent classification is regarded as a basic task in the field of patent management, which can provide support for many downstream intelligent tasks, such as patent quality valuation [1], patent retrieval [2], and patent litigation analysis [3]. To avoid the ambiguity, patent classification schemes such as International Patent Classification (IPC[1]) and Cooperative Patent Classification (CPC[2]) are proposed to standardize patent categories. For instance, in CPC scheme, code

---

[1] https://www.wipo.int/classifications/ipc/en/.
[2] https://www.cooperativepatentclassification.org/index.

© Springer Nature Switzerland AG 2021
L. Fang et al. (Eds.): CICAI 2021, LNAI 13069, pp. 111–122, 2021.
https://doi.org/10.1007/978-3-030-93046-2_10

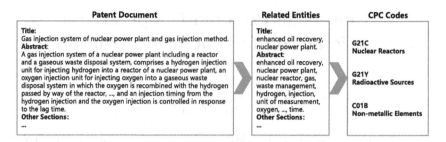

Fig. 1. A toy example of a patent document and its related entities.

"G06F 40/20" refers to category "Natural Language Analysis" and "G06F 40/56" refers to "Natural Language Generation". Traditionally, patent classification is completed by well-trained specialists, which is labor-intensive and sometimes error-prone because the code system is vast and growing.

Consequently, automatic patent classification has aroused widespread attention in the industry and academia [4,5]. Since the patent that contains title, abstract and other sections is usually long text and can be classified into multiple categories, most researchers have treated this task as a multi-label text classification problem. Concretely, shallow machine learning-based methods [6,7] usually focus on learning handcrafted feature combinations and deep learning-based methods [8,9] are dedicated to capturing the contextual semantics of patent texts. Although these methods have achieved great success by mining pure text semantics, they usually ignore the terminology of patents. Specifically, the patents are related to a large number of knowledge entities that can play an important role in patent classification. As shown in Fig. 1, it presents a patent, related entities discovered with entity linking technology [10,11], and CPC category codes of the patent. We can observe that the red entities are closely associated with code "G21C (Nuclear Reactors)" and "G21Y (Radioactive Sources)", while the blue ones are closely associated with "C01B (Non-metallic Elements)". In other words, these related entities can provide additional distinguishable semantics for patent classification besides original texts.

However, there are still many unique challenges in incorporating these entity semantics with pure text semantics into patent classification. First, it is difficult to mine such entity semantics with previous methods because the related entities may be very sparse in the patent corpus, which becomes the bottleneck of improving patent classification. Second, the importance of different entities to patent classification varies greatly, and domain-specific entities are usually more helpful. Take Fig. 1 as an example, "nuclear power plant" and "hydrogen" are strongly associated with target categories, while "gas" seems to be useless for classification. More seriously, due to the limitations of entity linking technology, some wrong entities may be introduced such as "enhanced oil recovery". Third, patent texts usually contain hundreds of words, but only a few key fragments can provide valuable information for classification. Extracting crucial fragments for target categories is as tricky as finding a needle in a haystack.

To address these challenges, we propose **K**nowledge Powered **C**ooperative **S**emantic **F**usion (KCSF) that jointly models the text semantics and entity semantics for more distinguishable representation of the patent. It achieves better performance on patent classification task by incorporating Knowledge Graphs (KG), mutual attention mechanism, and Graph Convolutional Network (GCN) [12]. The technical contributions of this paper are summarized as follows:

- We propose to employ entity linking and knowledge graph embedding techniques to introduce additional knowledge into semantic modeling so that the deeper entity semantics can be captured for patent classification.
- We design a novel mutual attention mechanism to extract the crucial semantics in texts with the help of entities and then reduce the bad influence of improper entities with the generated features of texts. Furthermore, we introduce the graph convolutional network to facilitate the fusion representation learning of texts and entities towards better classification performance.
- Extensive experiments on large-scale patent data clearly validate the effectiveness of our model, which also demonstrate the potentiality of knowledge-enhanced methods on patent classification task.

2 Related Work

2.1 Patent Classification

With the advances of natural language processing technology, many methods have been proposed to perform automatic multi-label patent classification such as KNN [13] and SVM [7]. These methods represent patent texts by contained words but ignore the contextual information and deep semantic information. To address this problem, deep learning techniques have been gradually applied on patent classification. For instance, based on TextCNN [14], DeepPatent [8] builds a deep convolutional neural network combined with the word embedding. BiGRU [15] is also used to encode patents based on domain-specific word embedding [4]. PatentBERT [9] utilizes pre-trained language model BERT [16] to represent the patent and then fine-tune it. In addition, A-GCN+A-NLSOA [5] attempts to study the patent classification with graph representation learning, which focuses on the links among patents and words. These methods usually take the original patent texts as input but ignore the scientific entities and common sense existing in patents, leading to limitations in their performance.

2.2 Knowledge-Enhanced Short Text Classification

Due to the lack of contextual semantics in short texts, researchers have gradually realized the importance of introducing knowledge as additional semantics [17,18]. Specifically, KPCNN [19] proposes to conceptualize the short texts as relevant concepts predefined in knowledge graphs and then stacks the words and concepts to obtain the embedding of the short texts. Based on that, STCKA [20] further introduces the attention mechanism to measure the importance of each

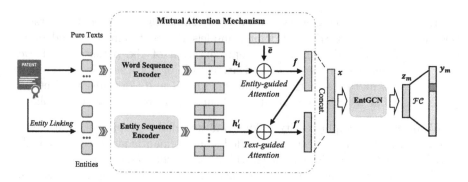

Fig. 2. The framework of KCSF for patent classification.

Fig. 3. Illustration of knowledge powered semantic augmentation process.

concept. Moreover, HGAT [21] attempts to model short texts, related entities, and contained topics simultaneously with heterogeneous information networks and adapts graph neural networks for semi-supervised classification. Inspired by these methods, we utilize knowledge graphs to enrich the semantic features of patents and design a dedicated cooperative semantic fusion framework.

3   The Proposed Model KCSF

Our model **KCSF** is a knowledge powered deep neural network as shown in Fig. 2. It consists of three key components: Knowledge Powered Semantic Augmentation, Mutual Attention Mechanism, and Entity-based Graph Convolutional Network (EntGCN).

3.1   Knowledge Powered Semantic Augmentation

The knowledge powered semantic augmentation aims at discovering and representing entities related to patent texts, which is shown in Fig. 3. First, entity linking tool TagMe[3] is used to recognize the entities in the patent texts. For example, in the patent title "Method for the contactless charging of the battery of an electric automobile", "charging" is linked with the entity "battery charger",

---
[3] https://sobigdata.d4science.org/web/tagme/.

while "electric" and "automobile" are linked with the entity "electric car". Second, based on all identified entities of all patents, we construct a sub-graph G by extracting all relations among them from KG DBpedia [22]. To enrich the relational information, we further expand G to all entities in the one-hop neighborhood of identified ones. Third, the KG embedding method TransE [23] is utilized to learn a low-dimensional embedding vector for each entity in G.

Specifically, the KG G consists of a large number of entity-relation-entity triples (h, r, t), where h, r, and t are the head entity, the relation, and the tail entity, respectively. TransE defines the score function as:

$$f_r(h, t) = \|\mathbf{h} + \mathbf{r} - \mathbf{t}\|_2^2, \tag{1}$$

where $\mathbf{h}$, $\mathbf{r}$, and $\mathbf{t}$ are the corresponding embedding vector of h, r, and t. The goal of TransE is to force $f_r(h, t)$ to be low if (h, r, t) is true, and high otherwise. In this manner, the embedding of each entity can be trained to preserve both relational information and structural information, which can provide additional distinguishable features for patent classification.

For a patent composed of a sequence of words, i.e., $s = [w_1, w_2, ..., w_n]$, each word may be associated with an entity in the KG. So the patent can be also processed as a sequence of entities, i.e., $s' = [e_1, e_2, ...e_{n'}]$ and each entity e_i can be represented as a vector via KG embedding.

3.2 Mutual Attention Mechanism

We design the mutual attention mechanism to model the original texts and related entities jointly. Specifically, we first employ two sequence encoders on word sequence and entity sequence respectively to get the corresponding hidden features. Then we employ two types of attention mechanisms consecutively to enhance the representation of entities with the guide of texts and vice versa.

Word/Entity Sequence Encoder. We construct the word sequence encoder based on word2vec [24] and Bidirectional Gated Recurrent Unit (BiGRU) [15]. First, given the word sequence $s = [w_1, w_2, ..., w_n]$, each word is mapped to an embedding vector $\mathbf{w}_i \in \mathbb{R}^{d_w}$ via word2vec, where d_w denotes the size of word embedding. Then we utilize BiGRU to encode patterns in word sequence to get the hidden features. Specifically, the input of BiGRU is a word embedding sequence $\mathbf{s} = [\mathbf{w}_1, \mathbf{w}_2, ..., \mathbf{w}_n]$, and the hidden feature $\mathbf{h}_i$ is calculated as follows:

$$\begin{aligned}
\overrightarrow{\mathbf{h}_i} &= \overrightarrow{\mathrm{GRU}}(\overrightarrow{\mathbf{h}_{i-1}}, \mathbf{w}_i) & \overrightarrow{\mathbf{h}_i} &\in \mathbb{R}^{d_h}, \\
\overleftarrow{\mathbf{h}_i} &= \overleftarrow{\mathrm{GRU}}(\overleftarrow{\mathbf{h}_{i+1}}, \mathbf{w}_i) & \overleftarrow{\mathbf{h}_i} &\in \mathbb{R}^{d_h}, \\
\mathbf{h}_i &= [\overrightarrow{\mathbf{h}_i}; \overleftarrow{\mathbf{h}_i}] & \mathbf{h}_i &\in \mathbb{R}^{2d_h},
\end{aligned} \tag{2}$$

where d_h is the hidden size of GRU and the semicolon refers to concatenation.

Next, we adopt a similar architecture to construct the entity sequence encoder. Given the entity sequence $s' = [e_1, e_2, ..., e_{n'}]$, each entity is mapped to an embedding vector $\mathbf{e}_i \in \mathbb{R}^{d_e}$ via TransE, where d_e is the size of entity embedding. Then we employ another BiGRU (i.e., $\overrightarrow{\mathrm{GRU'}}$ and $\overleftarrow{\mathrm{GRU'}}$) to get the hidden feature $\mathbf{h}'_i \in \mathbb{R}^{2d_h}$ for each entity. The detailed formula is similar to Eq. 2.

Entity-Guided Attention. Afterwards, we try to use the entities to enhance the representation of pure texts because the text semantics that are also reflected by entities are usually more crucial. To this end, we propose the entity-guided attention to evaluate the importance of different words with the help of entities. We first exploit the average pooling operation to merge n' entity embeddings into an average embedding $\bar{\mathbf{e}}$ and then feed it into vanilla attention [25] to calculate the attention weights α w.r.t each hidden feature $\mathbf{h}_i$ as follows:

$$\bar{\mathbf{e}} = \frac{1}{n'} \sum_{i=1}^{n'} \mathbf{e}_i,$$

$$\alpha_i = \mathrm{softmax}(\mathbf{v}^{(1)} \cdot \tanh(\mathbf{W}^{(1)}[\mathbf{h}_i; \bar{\mathbf{e}}] + \mathbf{b}^{(1)})), \tag{3}$$

where $\mathbf{W}^{(1)}$, $\mathbf{b}^{(1)}$, and $\mathbf{v}^{(1)}$ are trainable parameters. We combine all the hidden features of words to get the fusion feature $\mathbf{f}$ for word sequence as:

$$\mathbf{f} = \frac{1}{n} \sum_{i=1}^{n} \alpha_i \mathbf{h}_i. \tag{4}$$

Text-Guided Attention. To reduce the bad influence of improper entities introduced due to the complexity of patent language or the imprecision of entity linking, we further propose the text-guided attention as follows:

$$\alpha'_i = \mathrm{softmax}(\mathbf{v}^{(2)} \cdot \tanh(\mathbf{W}^{(2)}[\mathbf{h}'_i; \mathbf{f}] + \mathbf{b}^{(2)})), \tag{5}$$

$$\mathbf{f}' = \frac{1}{n'} \sum_{i=1}^{n'} \alpha_i \mathbf{h}'_i, \tag{6}$$

where $\mathbf{f}$ is the fusion feature of word sequence in Eq. 4 and $\mathbf{h}'_i(i \in \{1, ..., n'\})$ is the hidden feature for each entity obtained by BiGRU. The motivation is that the entities with semantics that are not similar to text semantics are usually insignificant or even noise, which is also observed in work [20]. Finally, we concatenate the two types of fusion features of patents to get the joint fusion feature $\mathbf{x} \in \mathbb{R}^{4d_h}$, i.e., $\mathbf{x} = [\mathbf{f}; \mathbf{f}']$.

3.3   Entity-Based Graph Convolutional Network

Intuitively, for patents with similar entities, their scientific fields are usually very similar, so they may have similar categories. Along this line, to further emphasize the crucial information in both the texts and entities, we consider the relations among different patents. Specifically, for the target patent p_m, we first compute the entity-based similarity between it and other patents, defined as the cosine similarity between their average entity embeddings, i.e., $\bar{\mathbf{e}}$ in Eq. 3. Next, we select the top K most similar patents of p_m and itself as the nodes and then compute the similarity scores between these $K+1$ patents as the weighted edges to constructed a neighborhood graph for p_m.

We use $\mathbf{A}$ to denote the adjacency matrix of the graph in which $\mathbf{A}(i,j)$ is the entity-based similarity between patent p_i and patent p_j. Let $\mathbf{D}$ denote the degree matrix. Moreover, we first obtain the joint fusion feature $\mathbf{x} \in \mathbb{R}^{4d_h}$ for each patent node and then stack them to get the feature matrix $\mathbf{X} \in \mathbb{R}^{(K+1) \times 4d_h}$. Because the graph only involves the one-hop neighbor nodes of p_m, we employ a single layer GCN [12] to enhance the presentation of p_m with its neighborhood:

$$\mathbf{Z} = \mathrm{ReLU}(\mathbf{D}^{-\frac{1}{2}} \mathbf{A} \mathbf{D}^{-\frac{1}{2}} \mathbf{X} \mathbf{W}^{(3)}). \tag{7}$$

Here, $\mathrm{ReLU}(\cdot)$ is rectified linear unit [26] and the m-th row of the output matrix $\mathbf{Z} \in \mathbb{R}^{(K+1) \times d_z}$ is the enhanced fusion feature of p_m. Let $\mathbf{z}_m \in \mathbb{R}^{d_z}$ denote the m-th row of $\mathbf{Z}$. We feed it into a fully connected layer for classification:

$$\hat{\mathbf{y}}_m = \mathrm{softmax}(\mathbf{W}^{(4)} \mathbf{z}_m + \mathbf{b}^{(3)}), \tag{8}$$

where $\hat{\mathbf{y}}_m$ is the predicted categories. Then we apply binary cross-entropy loss as the objective function, which is often used in multi-label text classification [27].

4   Experiments

4.1   Experimental Setup

Dataset and Evaluation Metrics. We built a dataset named USPTO-1M from the website of the United States Patent and Trademark Office (USPTO[4]), which has granted millions of USA patents since 1976. We first collected 1,441,172 patents from the USPTO website and only retained the patents containing both the title and abstract. Next, we adopted the exact same data cleaning process as DeepPatent [8], which included filtering low-frequency words, removing too short patents, etc. As a result, the USPTO-1M dataset contained 1,086,422 patents in 661 CPC subclass-level categories, and each patent had 1.88 categories averagely. We split the dataset into training and testing in an 80/20 ratio and further held 10% training data as the validation set to choose the optimal parameters.

We adopted the rank-based metrics including Precision@k, Recall@k, and NDCG@k (Normalized Discounted Cumulative Gain), which were widely used in multi-label text classification [5,28]. Particularly, we set k as 1, 3, and 5.

Implementation Details. For training KCSF, we used the Adam [29] optimizer and set the learning rate and weight decay to 1×10^{-3} and 5×10^{-5}, respectively. We set the dropout [30] probability to 0.4 and the batch size to 32. We also applied an early stop mechanism, in which the training would stop if

---

[4] www.uspto.gov.

the Precision@1 on the validation set did not improve in 10 continuous epochs. We trained word2vec [24] for word embeddings with $d_w = 100$ and trained TransE [23] for entity embeddings with $d_e = 100$. For the remaining parameters, we used the grid search for the optimal values. Specifically, we set $d_h = 256$ for the hidden states in BiGRU, $K = 8$ to construct the neighborhood graph, and $d_z = 384$ for the output of EntGCN.

Baselines. We compared our model KCSF with the following baselines, including general text classification models, patent classification models, knowledge-enhanced short text classification models and two variants of KCSF:

- FastText [31]: It is a widely used text classification model that makes full use of n-gram features for text representation.
- BiLSTM-SA [32]: It takes the benefit of BiLSTM and self-attention mechanism to mine deeper contextual semantics for classification.
- DeepPatent [8]: It is a deep learning-based patent classification model with core component based on the architecture of TextCNN [14].
- PatentBERT [9]: It applies BERT [16] to encode patent texts and classifies patents to multiple categories accurately by fine-tuning BERT.
- KPCNN [19]: It uses relevant concepts to enrich the semantics of short texts and adopts TextCNN to learn the coalesced embedding of concepts and texts.
- STCKA [20]: It is the state-of-the-art model for short texts classification, utilizing attention mechanism to evaluate the importance of each concept.
- KCSF-MAM: It is a variant of KCSF, without considering the mutual guidance between entities and texts. In other words, it uses the following formula to replace the mutual attention mechanism:

$$\mathbf{x} = [(\frac{1}{n}\sum_{i=1}^{n}\mathbf{h}_i); (\frac{1}{n'}\sum_{i=1}^{n'}\mathbf{h}_i')]. \tag{9}$$

- KCSF-GCN: It is a variant of KCSF, which discards the relations among different patents by removing the EntGCN module from our model.

4.2   Experimental Results and Ablation Studies

Comparison Between Different Models. We concatenated the title and abstract of the patent together as the original texts input into different models and focused on the subclass-level categories defined by the CPC schema. According to the results shown in Table 1, we have the following observations:

- Although both STCKA and BiLSTM-SA are BiLSTM-based models with attention mechanism, STCKA achieves an improvement of 3.6% on Precision@1 against BiLSTM-SA, which means that external knowledge can significantly improve the results of patent classification. The performance of KPCNN over DeepPatent, BiLSTM-SA, and FastText also proves this point.

Table 1. Results of multi-label patent classification on USPTO-1M.

Models	Precision@k (%)			Recall@k (%)			NDCG@k (%)		
	1	3	5	1	3	5	1	3	5
FastText	78.96	44.43	31.31	53.61	78.62	84.47	78.96	78.12	79.24
BiLSTM-SA	81.23	45.77	32.24	54.83	79.64	86.63	81.23	80.29	81.06
DeepPatent	81.38	45.93	32.48	54.80	79.86	86.53	81.38	80.66	81.41
PatentBERT	85.23	49.88	34.82	58.47	83.44	90.26	85.23	84.08	85.26
KPCNN	82.57	46.64	33.29	56.20	80.37	86.99	82.57	81.49	82.71
STCKA	84.78	49.21	34.73	57.49	83.22	89.16	84.78	83.66	85.29
KCSF	**87.82**	**51.27**	**36.76**	**59.91**	**84.23**	**91.74**	**87.82**	**86.04**	**87.73**

- The importance of different entities to patent classification varies greatly, and the attention mechanism can capture this difference well. Our model employs the mutual attention mechanism to evaluate the importance of different entities, and hence it performs much better than all baselines. On the contrary, KPCNN does not consider this issue, and thus it only performs a little bit better than another CNN-based model, i.e., DeepPatent.
- Our model obtains 3.0%, 2.1% and 2.0% improvements in precision and 3.0%, 2.4% and 2.4% in NDCG over STCKA. The reason is that our model is aware of the different roles of each fragment in patent texts and uses the entity-guided attention to emphasize the key fragments.
- PatentBERT outperforms all the other baselines because BERT can encode much more semantic information in word embeddings than common word2vec. KCSF still achieves better performance than PatentBERT, once again validating the effectiveness of cooperative semantic fusion.

Ablation Studies. We conducted ablation studies to evaluate the effectiveness of each module in our model KCSF, and the results are shown in Table 2. Particularly, KCSF-MAM ignores the harm of inappropriate entities and non-key words to the representation of patents, resulting in too much worthless semantic information being input into EntGCN. So its performance is much worse than KCSF. Moreover, KCSF-GCN discards the relations among patents, so that the fusion representation of texts and entities can not be further refined by aggregating additional semantic information from similar patents. That is the reason why KCSF-GCN performs worse than KCSF. In summary, the cooperation of our model is not only in the use of mutual attention mechanism to jointly model the entity semantics and text semantics, but also in the use of EntGCN to enhance each other between different patents.

4.3 Sensitivity Analysis on Neighborhood Graph Size

As mentioned in Sect. 3.3, the top K most similar patents of target patent p_m are selected to construct the neighborhood graph. In other words, K not only

Table 2. Ablation studies.

Models	Precision@k (%)			Recall@k (%)			NDCG@k (%)		
	1	3	5	1	3	5	1	3	5
KCSF-MAM	82.79	46.66	33.18	56.53	80.81	87.12	82.79	81.24	82.60
KCSF-GCN	85.49	49.76	34.95	58.50	83.69	90.14	85.49	84.55	85.54
KCSF	**87.82**	**51.27**	**36.76**	**59.91**	**84.23**	**91.74**	**87.82**	**86.04**	**87.73**

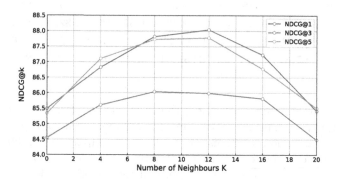

Fig. 4. Parameter sensitivity of KCSF.

determines the size of the graph but also reflects the quality of these neighbors. We tested all K in the set $\{0, 4, 8, 12, 16, 20\}$ by examining how they affect the performance of our model. According to Fig. 4, we realize that when $K < 12$, the performance keeps improving, but the improvement becomes more limited with larger K. Obviously, these similar patents can provide rich semantic information to enhance the representation of p_m. However, as more and more neighbors are considered, when a new neighbor is integrated, its contribution will be limited compared with the known information. More seriously, too large K may cause many patents that are not similar to p_m to be considered, resulting in a large amount of semantic noise being gathered by EntGCN into the representation of p_m. This is why the performance begins to deteriorate when $K > 12$.

5   Conclusion

In this paper, we proposed the KCSF framework to perform knowledge-enhanced patent classification. Specifically, we designed the mutual attention mechanism to capture the crucial semantics of entities with the guide of texts and vice versa. Moreover, we introduced the graph convolutional network to further enhance the fusion representation of entities and texts. Experimental results showed that our model had obtained substantial improvements on patent classification task.

Acknowledgement. This research was supported by the National Key Research and Development Program of China (Grant No. 2018YFB1402600), and the National Natural Science Foundation of China (Grant No. 91746301, 62072423).

References

1. Lin, H., Wang, H., Du, D., Wu, H., Chang, B., Chen, E.: Patent quality valuation with deep learning models. In: Pei, J., Manolopoulos, Y., Sadiq, S., Li, J. (eds.) DASFAA 2018. LNCS, vol. 10828, pp. 474–490. Springer, Cham (2018). https://doi.org/10.1007/978-3-319-91458-9_29

2. Fujii, A.: Enhancing patent retrieval by citation analysis. In: Proceedings of the 30th Annual International ACM SIGIR Conference on Research and Development in Information Retrieval, pp. 793–794 (2007)

3. Liu, Q., Wu, H., Ye, Y., Zhao, H., Liu, C., Du, D.: Patent litigation prediction: a convolutional tensor factorization approach. In: IJCAI, pp. 5052–5059 (2018)

4. Risch, J., Krestel, R.: Domain-specific word embeddings for patent classification. Data Technol. Appl. (2019)

5. Tang, P., Jiang, M., (Ning) Xia, B., Pitera, J.W., Welser, J., Chawla, N.V.: Multi-label patent categorization with non-local attention-based graph convolutional network. In: AAAI, pp. 9024–9031 (2020)

6. D'hondt, E., Verberne, S., Koster, C., Boves, L.: Text representations for patent classification. Comput. Linguist. **39**(3), 755–775 (2013)

7. Chih-Hung, W., Ken, Y., Huang, T.: Patent classification system using a new hybrid genetic algorithm support vector machine. Appl. Soft Comput. **10**(4), 1164–1177 (2010)

8. Li, S., Jie, H., Cui, Y., Jianjun, H.: DeepPatent: patent classification with convolutional neural networks and word embedding. Scientometrics **117**(2), 721–744 (2018)

9. Lee, J.-S., Hsiang, J.: Patent classification by fine-tuning BERT language model. World Patent Inf. **61**, 101965 (2020)

10. Milne, D., Witten, I.H.: Learning to link with Wikipedia. In: Proceedings of the 17th ACM Conference on Information and Knowledge Management, pp. 509–518 (2008)

11. Sil, A., Yates, A.: Re-ranking for joint named-entity recognition and linking. In: Proceedings of the 22nd ACM International Conference on Information & Knowledge Management, pp. 2369–2374 (2013)

12. Kipf, T.N., Welling, M.: Semi-supervised classification with graph convolutional networks. arXiv preprint arXiv:1609.02907 (2016)

13. Fall, C.J., Törcsvári, A., Benzineb, K., Karetka, G.: Automated categorization in the international patent classification. In: ACM SIGIR Forum, vol. 37, pp. 10–25. ACM, New York (2003)

14. Kim, Y.: Convolutional neural networks for sentence classification. arXiv preprint arXiv:1408.5882 (2014)

15. Cho, K., Van Merriënboer, B., Bahdanau, D., Bengio, Y.: On the properties of neural machine translation: encoder-decoder approaches. arXiv preprint arXiv:1409.1259 (2014)

16. Devlin, J., Chang, M.-W., Lee, K., Toutanova, K.: BERT: pre-training of deep bidirectional transformers for language understanding. arXiv preprint arXiv:1810.04805 (2018)

17. Jingyun, X., et al.: Incorporating context-relevant concepts into convolutional neural networks for short text classification. Neurocomputing **386**, 42–53 (2020)

18. Alam, M., Bie, Q., Türker, R., Sack, H.: Entity-based short text classification using convolutional neural networks. In: Keet, C.M., Dumontier, M. (eds.) EKAW 2020. LNCS (LNAI), vol. 12387, pp. 136–146. Springer, Cham (2020). https://doi.org/10.1007/978-3-030-61244-3_9

19. Wang, J., Wang, Z., Zhang, D., Yan, J.: Combining knowledge with deep convolutional neural networks for short text classification. In: IJCAI, vol. 350 (2017)
20. Chen, J., Yizhou, H., Liu, J., Xiao, Y., Jiang, H.: Deep short text classification with knowledge powered attention. In: Proceedings of the AAAI Conference on Artificial Intelligence vol. 33, pp. 6252–6259 (2019)
21. Linmei, H., Yang, T., Shi, C., Ji, H., Li, X.: Heterogeneous graph attention networks for semi-supervised short text classification. In: Proceedings of the 2019 Conference on Empirical Methods in Natural Language Processing and the 9th International Joint Conference on Natural Language Processing (EMNLP-IJCNLP), pp. 4823–4832 (2019)
22. Lehmann, J., et al.: DBpedia-a large-scale, multilingual knowledge base extracted from Wikipedia. Semantic Web **6**(2), 167–195 (2015)
23. Bordes, A., Usunier, N., Garcia-Duran, A., Weston, J., Yakhnenko, O.: Translating embeddings for modeling multi-relational data. In: Neural Information Processing Systems (NIPS), pp. 1–9 (2013)
24. Mikolov, T., Sutskever, I., Chen, K., Corrado, G.S., Dean, J.: Distributed representations of words and phrases and their compositionality. In: Advances in Neural Information Processing Systems, vol. 26, pp. 3111–3119 (2013)
25. Bahdanau, D., Cho, K., Bengio, Y.: Neural machine translation by jointly learning to align and translate. arXiv preprint arXiv:1409.0473 (2014)
26. Krizhevsky, A., Sutskever, I., Hinton, G.E.: ImageNet classification with deep convolutional neural networks. In: Advances in Neural Information Processing Systems, vol. 25, pp. 1097–1105 (2012)
27. Huang, W., et al.: Hierarchical multi-label text classification: an attention-based recurrent network approach. In: Proceedings of the 28th ACM International Conference on Information and Knowledge Management, pp. 1051–1060 (2019)
28. Prabhu, Y., Varma, M.: FastXML: a fast, accurate and stable tree-classifier for extreme multi-label learning. In: Proceedings of the 20th ACM SIGKDD International Conference on Knowledge Discovery and Data Mining, pp. 263–272 (2014)
29. Kingma, D.P., Adam, J.B.: A method for stochastic optimization. arXiv preprint arXiv:1412.6980 (2014)
30. Srivastava, N., Hinton, G., Krizhevsky, A., Sutskever, I., Salakhutdinov, R.: Dropout: a simple way to prevent neural networks from overfitting. J. Mach. Learn. Res. **15**(1), 1929–1958 (2014)
31. Joulin, A., Grave, E., Bojanowski, P., Mikolov, T.: Bag of tricks for efficient text classification. arXiv preprint arXiv:1607.01759 (2016)
32. Lin, Z., et al.: A structured self-attentive sentence embedding. arXiv preprint arXiv:1703.03130 (2017)

Diagnosis of Childhood Autism Using Multi-modal Functional Connectivity via Dynamic Hypergraph Learning

Zizhao Zhang[1], Jian Liu[2], Baojuan Li[2(✉)], and Yue Gao[1(✉)]

[1] BNRist, THUIBCS, KLISS, School of Software, Tsinghua University,
Beijing, China
zhangziz18@mails.tsinghua.edu.cn, gaoyue@tsinghua.edu.cn
[2] Fourth Military Medical University, Xi'an, China
liu-jian@fmmu.edu.cn

Abstract. Characterizations of atypical patterns of static functional connectivity (FC) have been widely observed in individuals with autism spectrum disorder (ASD). In recent years, some studies have hypothesized the stationary assumption and revealed the relevance of the time-varying anomaly in FC to the autistic traits. While most existing work focus on exploring properties of static FC (sFC) and dynamic FC (dFC) separately, little efforts have been made to investigate the correlation among these two modalities and combine their information to diagnose ASD. In this paper, we propose a multi-modal dynamic hypergraph learning framework for childhood autism diagnosis using both sFCs and dFCs. We collect a childhood ASD dataset including 91 ASD patients and 76 healthy controls (HC). After extracting features from the sFC and dFC for each subject, two hypergraphs are constructed to represent the complex correlation among different subjects under static and dynamic modalities, respectively. To further moderate inappropriate or even wrong connections, a multi-modal dynamic hypergraph learning process is conducted to jointly learn the data correlation and predict the subject labels, i.e., HC or ASD. Experimental results demonstrate that our method can achieve 75.6% accuracy with 5-fold cross validation and consistently outperform the conventional classifiers for autism diagnosis.

Keywords: Autism spectrum disorder · Multi-modal functional connectivity · Dynamic hypergraph learning

1 Introduction

Autism spectrum disorder (ASD) is a heterogeneous neurodevelopmental condition of increasing prevalence, with deficits in the social communication and restricted/repetitive/stereotyped patterns of behavior and interests [2]. Early diagnosis and treatment for ASD is essential to enable the patients to master new skills under the guidance of clinical. Currently, ASD diagnosis mainly relies

ⓒ Springer Nature Switzerland AG 2021
L. Fang et al. (Eds.): CICAI 2021, LNAI 13069, pp. 123–135, 2021.
https://doi.org/10.1007/978-3-030-93046-2_11

on general development screening and comprehensive evaluation by experienced doctors and health professionals. However, such experts is lacking in many areas. Increasing evidences suggest that ASD is related to the brain abnormalities in both anatomical and functional organization [1,3]. Towards this, functional magnetic resonance imaging (fMRI) has been widely used to investigate the atypical brain connectivity in ASD and has shown great promise for automated diagnosis of the brain developmental disease with less subjectivity and more availability. Such non-invasive imaging technique could be a candidate for defining reliable functional neurophenotypes for risk prognosis, prediction and monitoring of treatment response, and give insight into the pathophysiology of this disorder.

A body of studies have reported the static properties of the whole-brain functional network in ASD [5]. However, the static assumption ignores the dynamic nature of brain network, leading to highly inconsistently findings. For example, several previous studies have revealed exclusive sFC "under-connectivity" patterns in ASD [11,13,27], while some other studies have reported predominant over-connectivity or even mixed under-/over-connectivity in ASD [5,14,24]. Such inconsistencies maybe because the variability of functional connectivity across time affects the observed group difference. To tackle this issue, some recent works introduced to characterize the brain as a time-varying dynamic function network throughout the course of a resting state scan [25]. Wee et al. [26] first clustered R-fMRI time series into different groups to construct multiple FC networks. Then, the network matrices of each subject are concatenated together to learn a support vector machine (SVM) model. This SVM-based method achieves 71% accuracy under 10-fold cross validation on a dataset with 45 ASD and 47 socio-demographic-matched typically developing (TD) children. Price et al. [21] employed the sliding window connectivity into a multiple kernel SVM (MK-SVM) based multi-network multi-scale framework, which achieves an accuracy of 90% on a leave-one-out-cross-validation (LOOCV) setting on a dataset of 30 ASD and 30 TD children. dFC can offer unique temporal information that the traditional sFC cannot identify in ASD [9], and also has been applied in many other brain disorders, such as schizophrenia [28], epilepsy [17] and Alzheimer's disease [7].

A relatively recent trend is to apply graph-based models for ASD diagnosis at a subject level. In [16], each subject is modeled as a graph and all graphs have same structure but different signals at their nodes. A graph convolutional neural network is proposed to learn the similarity metric between pairs of graphs. The classification accuracy on ABIDE dataset is about 66% with 5-fold cross-validation. In [19,20], the population among subjects is represented by a sparse graph constructed according to the phenotypic information, such as age, sex and IQ. The graph structure and the features extracted from fMRI data are fed into the graph convolutional network [4] to infer the classes of unlabelled subjects, leading to 69.5% accuracy for ABIDE with 10-fold cross-validation. However, the graph-based models only consider pair-wise interaction between two subjects, losing sight of the high-order relationships among more than two subjects. What's more, these methods are mostly based on a static graph structure, which may not model the time-varying correlation accurately, giving rise to the poor diagnosis performance.

In this paper, we propose a multi-modal dynamic hypergraph learning framework for ASD diagnosis, which combines the information of both sFCs and dFCs to model the complex correlation among subjects. We have collected a childhood ASD dataset containing sFC and dFC data of 91 ASD patients and 76 healthy controls (HC). In our method, the complete time series of each subject are grouped into multiple sub-sequences and the dynamic properties are explored at the sub-sequence level. Two kinds of features are then extracted for each sub-sequence based on Lasso, which represent the static modality and dynamic modality, respectively. The complex correlation among sub-sequences under these two modalities are modeled by the hypergraph structure, and a multi-modal dynamic hypergraph learning model is proposed to accurately differentiate the children with ASD from HC. Experimental results show that our method can identify the ASD patients efficiently. We also report the selected brain regions that are potentially important for ASD diagnosis, which is consistent with the previous studies.

2   Methods

In principle, our method is composed of three stages, i.e., the data pre-processing stage to get the sFCs and dFCs of subjects, the feature selection stage to extract features and eliminate noisy ones, and the dynamic hypergraph learning stage to categorize the testing subjects for ASD diagnosis. Figure 1 shows the framework of our method. Given a population of N subjects with the imaging data, we first preprocess the raw fMRI time series and estimate the static FC and dynamic FC using sliding-window algorithm. Then, we select features from the FC matrices based on the Lasso regression model. An initial hypergraph $\mathcal{G} = (\mathcal{V}, \mathcal{E})$ is further constructed, in which each node represents a subject and each hyperedge can connect more than two subjects. We generate the hyperedges according to the similarity of imaging features to characterize the data correlation in different modalities. Finally, a multi-modal dynamic hypergrpah learning framework is proposed to simultaneously make diagnosis of ASD and update the hypergraph structure to model the dynamic population correlation.

2.1   Databases and Preprocessing

To validate the effectiveness of the model, we collect a private childhood autism database. In this part, we will first give the detailed description of the participants and preprocessing pipelines of the database, and then introduce the common approach to estimate the static functional connectivity and dynamic functional connectivity.

Participants. Two hundred and thirty-three children, aged 2–8 years, including 121 subjects with ASD and 112 HC participated in this study. Thirty ASD children and 36 healthy children were excluded due to left handedness, unsuccessful

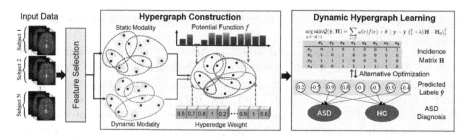

Fig. 1. The framework of our proposed ASD diagnosis method.

MRI scanning, excessive head motion, poor quality of spatial normalization, a family history of psychiatric disorders, current diagnosis of epilepsy, thalassemia, cyst or leukomalacia. Finally, the data from 91 ASD subjects and 76 matched HC were included in this work with sFCs and dFCs.

Data Acquisition. Data were collected in Shenzhen Children's Hospital. Both fMRI and T1 images were acquired on a Siemens Skyra 3.0T scanner during sleep. The high-resolution structural T1 images were collected with the following parameters: TR = 2300 ms, TE = 2.26 ms, FOV = 256 mm × 256 mm, matrix = 256 × 256, flip angle = 8°, number of slices = 176, slice thickness = 1 mm. The parameters for the fMRI session were as follows: TR = 2000 ms, TE = 30 ms, FOV = 230 mm × 230 mm, matrix = 64 × 64, flip angle = 90°, number of slices = 35, slice thickness = 3.6 mm, spacing = 0.72 mm.

Preprocessing. fMRI images were pre-processed using SPM12[1] and Gretna[2]. Slice timing were first performed to correct for the differences in the acquisition time of slices in a volume. Head motion was then corrected using rigid body transformation. This was followed by normalization of each subject's functional images to a standard MNI template. Next, fMRI images were spatially smoothed with a Gaussian kernel of 6 mm FWHM. Data were then temporally detrended and filtered with a band-pass filtering (0.01–0.1), while signals from the white matter and CSF with those caused by head motion were regressed out. Finally, data scrubbing was performed with a FD threshold of 0.5.

Static FC and Dynamic FC Estimation. Whole-brain sFC and dFC matrix for each subject were calculated using Gretna with a sliding-window algorithm. The brain was divided into 116 regions according to the AAL template. The window size for the sliding-window algorithm was set to 50 and the sliding window step was set to 2. Thus a 116 × 116 sFC matrix and a 116 × 116 × 96 dFC sequence were obtained for each subject.

---

[1] http://www.fil.ion.ucl.ac.uk/spm/software/spm12/.
[2] https://www.nitrc.org/projects/gretna/.

2.2 Feature Selection

Due to the functional connectivity matrix is symmetric, we only record its lower triangular part in a vector. For each subject, We first split the dFC sequence with τ time points into n sub-sequences in the following way: $\{1, n+1, 2n+1, \dots\}$ time points are divided into the first group, $\{2, n+2, 2n+2, \dots\}$ are divided into the second group, and so on. Then, we can obtain n sub-sequences of length $\tau' = \tau/n$. For each sub-sequence, the element-wise mean and variance of the functional connectivity matrix are extracted and concatenated together. The mean value over all time points indicates the average correlation among all ROIs, and the variance value shows the local stationary of the same scale's correlation.

Let $\bar{\mathbf{z}}_i^j$ denote the dFC feature vector of sub-sequence j from subject i. The label for the sub-sequences from the ASD group is set as 1, otherwise it is set as -1. The subjects in the ASD and HC groups are split into a training set and a testing set respectively. The least absolute shrinkage and selection operator (Lasso) is used here to conduct feature selection. Given the training set $\mathcal{P}$, the regression model can be written as

$$\min_{\beta_0, \beta} \left(\frac{1}{2\tau'|\mathcal{P}|} \sum_{i \in \mathcal{P}} \sum_{j=1}^{\tau'} \left(y_i - \beta_0 - \beta^T \bar{\mathbf{z}}_i^j \right)^2 + \mu |\beta|_1 \right), \tag{1}$$

where the hyperparameter μ is selected via 10-fold cross-validation on the training set. β is the fitted least-squares regression coefficients of the training data $\bar{\mathbf{z}}$ and the response y. We select the features with non-zero coefficients, referred to as $\mathbf{z}_i^j$.

For static modality, we extract the features of subject i from its sFC by Lasso as well. Specifically, the sFC feature vector of subject i is denoted as $\bar{\mathbf{x}}_i$. The Lasso model to select sFC features on the training set $\mathcal{P}$ can be written as

$$\min_{\gamma_0, \gamma} \left(\frac{1}{2|\mathcal{P}|} \sum_{i \in \mathcal{P}} \left(y_i - \gamma_0 - \gamma^T \bar{\mathbf{x}}_i \right)^2 + \eta |\gamma|_1 \right). \tag{2}$$

γ is the fitted least-squares regression coefficients of the training data $\bar{\mathbf{x}}$ and the response y and features corresponding to non-zero coefficients are selected, referred to as $\mathbf{x}_i$. We note that the hyperparameters μ in Eq. (1) and η in Eq. (2) are selected via 10-fold cross-validation on the training set.

2.3 Multi-modal Dynamic Hypergraph Learning for ASD Diagnosis

Hypergraph is an extension of simple graph, which is composed of a set of nodes and hyperedges. Different from the edge in simple graph which can only describe pair-wise relationship, the hyperedge can connect more than two vertices to represent the high-order correlation among subjects. Due to this advantage, hypergraph-based model has shown superior performance compared with graph-based model in many applications, such as classification [10], retrieval [31], detection [30] and segmentation [12]. In this part, the multi-modal dynamic hypergraph learning method is introduced for ASD diagnosis. First, an initial hypergraph structure is constructed to model the high-order correlation among sub-sequences, and each vertex (sub-sequence) for training data is given a label. As it is a challenging task to build high-order correlation accurately, we propose to jointly learn the hypergraph structure and the label projection matrix (the labels of all sub-sequences) under an alternative optimization framework. Finally, the labels of all sub-sequences are aggregated to get the labels of subjects for ASD diagnosis.

Hypergraph Construction. The hypergraph is constructed at a sub-sequence level, *i.e.*, each vertex represents a sub-sequence of some subject. Since the static modality feature vectors $\{\mathbf{x}_i\}$ is defined at the subject level, we let each sub-sequence inherit the static modality features from the subject to which it belongs. In other words, $\mathbf{x}_i^j$ represents the static modality of the j-th sub-sequence of object i, which equals to $\mathbf{x}_i$. In this way, each sub-sequence has two types of representations $\mathbf{x}_i^j$ and $\mathbf{z}_i^j$.

With the first representation $\{\mathbf{x}_i^j\}$, we first calculate the Euclidean distance between each pair of sub-sequences and construct a hypergraph $\mathcal{G}_1 = (\mathcal{V}, \mathcal{E}_1)$ accordingly. In this hypergraph, each vertex is connected to its k nearest neighbors ($k = 2n, 3n, \ldots, k_{max}n$) to generate $k_{max} - 1$ hyperedges. The second hypergraph $\mathcal{G}_2 = (\mathcal{V}, \mathcal{E}_2)$ is constructed based on the other representation $\{\mathbf{z}_i^j\}$ using the same k-nn scheme. Let $\mathcal{G}$ be the union of $\mathcal{G}_1$ and $\mathcal{G}_2$, *i.e.*, $\mathcal{G} = (\mathcal{V}, \mathcal{E}); \mathcal{E} = \mathcal{E}_1 \cup \mathcal{E}_2$. Once the hypergraph $\mathcal{G}$ is constructed, it can be represented by an incidence matrix $\mathbf{H}$, whose entries are defined as

$$\mathbf{H}(v, e) = \begin{cases} 1 \ if \ v \in e \\ 0 \ if \ v \notin e \end{cases}. \tag{3}$$

We denote the initial hypergraph structure as $\mathbf{H}_0$.

Multi-modal Dynamic Hypergraph Learning. Let y_v denote the true label of vertex v. For labeled data, $y_v = 1$ if the sub-sequence belongs to the ASD group, and it is -1 otherwise. For unlabeled data, y_v is set to zero. Let $\{\hat{y}_v\}$ denote the to-be-learned labels.

To predict these labels, a learning process is conducted on the hypergraph structure to optimize both label project matrix and hypergraph structure. We first define the potential function of a hyperedge e as

$$f(e) = \sum_{u,v \in \mathcal{V}} \frac{\mathbf{H}(u, e)\mathbf{H}(v, e)g(u, v)}{(1 + \alpha_1 + \alpha_2)\delta(e)}, \tag{4}$$

where

$$g(u, v) = \left\| \frac{\hat{y}_u}{\sqrt{d(u)}} - \frac{\hat{y}_v}{\sqrt{d(u)}} \right\|_2^2 + \alpha_1 \left\| \frac{\mathbf{x}_u}{\sqrt{d(u)}} - \frac{\mathbf{x}_v}{\sqrt{d(u)}} \right\|_2^2 + \alpha_2 \left\| \frac{\mathbf{z}_u}{\sqrt{d(u)}} - \frac{\mathbf{z}_v}{\sqrt{d(u)}} \right\|_2^2, \tag{5}$$

and $\delta(e)$ is the degree of hyperedge e. If the vertices in e share similar labels and features, its potential function will be lower than those with highly distincted labels/features. $f(e)$ estimates the data distribution on e from the sFC space, the dFC space and the label space, simultaneously.

Then, the objective function for learning on dynamic hypergraph can be written as the following dual optimization problem:

$$\underset{\hat{\mathbf{y}}, 0 \preceq \mathbf{H} \preceq 1}{\arg\min} \; \mathcal{Q}(\hat{\mathbf{y}}, \mathbf{H}) = \sum_{e \in \mathcal{E}} \omega(e) f(e) + \theta \|\mathbf{y} - \hat{\mathbf{y}}\|_2^2 + \lambda \|\mathbf{H} - \mathbf{H}_0\|_2^2, \qquad (6)$$

where $w(e)$ is the weight of hyperedge e. α_1, α_2, θ and λ are the trade-off hyperparameters selected via 10-fold cross-validation on the training set. The first term in Eq. 6 is the hypergraph-based loss function, which encourages hyperedges with lower potential have stronger connections, and the second and the third items are the empirical loss of $\hat{\mathbf{y}}$ and $\mathbf{H}$, respectively, under the assumption that the optimal $\hat{\mathbf{y}}$ and $\mathbf{H}$ don't change too much from the original one.

The optimization problem in Eq. 6 can be solved efficiently via alternative optimization. We first fix the hypergraph structure $\mathbf{H}$ and optimize $\hat{\mathbf{y}}$. This sub-problem has a closed-form solution

$$\hat{\mathbf{y}} = \left(\mathbf{I} + \frac{1}{\theta(1 + \alpha_1 + \alpha_2)} \mathbf{\Delta}\right)^{-1} \mathbf{y}, \qquad (7)$$

where $\mathbf{\Delta} = \mathbf{I} - \mathbf{D}_e^{-\frac{1}{2}} \mathbf{HWD}_e^{-1} \mathbf{H}^T \mathbf{D}_v^{-\frac{1}{2}}$. $\mathbf{D}_e$ and $\mathbf{D}_v$ is the diagonal matrices of the vertex degree and hyperedge degree, respectively. $\mathbf{D}_v = \text{diag}(\mathbf{HW1}); \mathbf{D}_e = \text{diag}(\mathbf{1}^T\mathbf{H})$. Then, $\hat{\mathbf{y}}$ is fixed and $\mathbf{H}$ is optimized, the sub-problem on optimizing $\mathbf{H}$ is bound constraint and can be addressed by the projected gradient method. The objective function is:

$$\arg \min_{0 \preceq \mathbf{H} \preceq 1} \mathcal{Q}(\mathbf{H}) = \text{tr}\left(\left(\mathbf{I} - \mathbf{D}_v^{-\frac{1}{2}} \mathbf{HWD}_e^{-1} \mathbf{H}^T \mathbf{D}_v^{-\frac{1}{2}}\right)\mathbf{K}\right) + \lambda \|\mathbf{H} - \mathbf{H}_0\|_2^2, \quad (8)$$

where $\mathbf{K} = \left(\hat{\mathbf{y}}\hat{\mathbf{y}}^T + \alpha_1 \mathbf{XX}^T + \alpha_2 \mathbf{ZZ}^T\right)/(1 + \alpha_1 + \alpha_2)$. Then, the iteration rule can be written as

$$\mathbf{H}_{k+1} = \mathbf{P}[\mathbf{H}_k - h_k \nabla \mathcal{Q}(\mathbf{H}_k)] \qquad (9)$$

$$\nabla \mathcal{Q}(\mathbf{H}) = 2\lambda(\mathbf{H} - \mathbf{H}_0) + \mathbf{J}\left(\mathbf{I} \otimes \mathbf{H}^T \mathbf{D}_v^{-\frac{1}{2}} \mathbf{KD}_v^{-\frac{1}{2}} \mathbf{H}\right) \mathbf{WD}_e^{-2}$$

$$+ \mathbf{D}_v^{-\frac{3}{2}} \mathbf{HWD}_e^{-1} \mathbf{H}^T \mathbf{D}_v^{-\frac{1}{2}} \mathbf{KJW} - 2\mathbf{D}_v^{-\frac{1}{2}} \mathbf{KD}_v^{-\frac{1}{2}} \mathbf{HWD}_e^{-1}, \tag{10}$$

where $\mathbf{J} = \mathbf{11}^T$ and h_k is the optimal step size at k-th iteration and $\mathbf{P}$ is the projection onto the feasible set $\{\mathbf{H}|0 \preceq \mathbf{H} \preceq 1\}$. The detailed derivation can refer to [29]. The procedure repeats until converges. Once the labels of all subsequences are learned, the class of one subject is finally decided by summarizing the label vectors of all its sub-sequences and getting the class with maximum score.

3   Experiments and Discussions

3.1   Experimental Settings

To evaluate the performance of the proposed multi-modal dynamic hypergraph learning method for ASD diagnosis, a 5-fold cross-validation scheme is used in our experiments. In experiments, we empirically set the parameter n for subsequence generation in the feature selection stage as 4. This procedure is repeated 10 times, and the average accuracy (ACC), sensitivity (SEN), specificity (SPEC), balance accuracy (BAC), positive predictive value (PPV), and negative predictive value (NPV) are reported for comparison.

We have compared our multi-modal based method (Multi+DHL) with those only using single modality (sFC/dFC+DHL). To show the superiority of DHL, we further compare with the following methods using single modal features extracted from sFC or dFC.

- Lasso. After training the Lasso models in Eq. 1 and Eq. 2 using the dFC and sFC information, respectively, we can directly obtain the classification results by calculating

$$\hat{y}_i^{dFC} = \text{Sgn}\left(\sum_j \beta \bar{\mathbf{z}}_i^j\right), \quad \hat{y}_i^{sFC} = \text{Sgn}\left(\gamma \bar{\mathbf{x}}_i\right). \tag{11}$$

- Random Forest (RF). We first select the sFC/dFC features using the Lasso model, and then employ the random forest model as the classifier. The hyperparameters in the Random Forest model are chosen by performing 10-fold cross-validation on the training set.
- Graph convolutional network (GCN) [15]. Following the feature selection stage using the Lasso model, we input the sFC/dFC features into a two-layer graph convolution network and output the classification results.

3.2   Experimental Results and Discussions

Table 1. Comparison of ASD diagnosis performance.

Method	ACC (%)	SEN (%)	SPEC (%)	BAC (%)	PPV (%)	NPV(%)
sFC+Lasso	68.26 ± 3.09	73.19 ± 3.44	62.37 ± 5.08	67.78 ± 3.18	70.02 ± 3.02	66.03 ± 3.52
dFC+Lasso	71.74 ± 2.41	75.16 ± 4.06	**67.63 ± 3.23**	71.4 ± 2.34	73.57 ± 2.04	69.62 ± 3.5
sFC+RF	72.87 ± 2.38	81.54 ± 3.94	62.5 ± 6.77	72.02 ± 2.61	72.42 ± 3.07	74.1 ± 3.46
dFC+RF	71.20 ± 4.07	81.43 ± 4.6	58.95 ± 6	70.19 ± 4.14	70.45 ± 3.6	72.77 ± 5.98
sFC+GCN	71.44 ± 3.7	77.47 ± 6.37	64.21 ± 5.36	70.84 ± 3.61	72.2 ± 2.98	70.86 ± 6.15
dFC+GCN	74.37 ± 3.11	83.63 ± 3.56	63.29 ± 4.94	73.46 ± 3.18	73.23 ± 2.86	76.46 ± 4.44
sFC+DHL	72.87 ± 2.38	79.89 ± 3.84	64.47 ± 3.67	72.18 ± 2.39	72.95 ± 2.02	72.95 ± 3.76
dFC+DHL	**74.67 ± 3.04**	80.88 ± 4.12	67.24 ± 4.27	**74.06 ± 3.04**	**74.76 ± 2.64**	74.74 ± 4.28
Multi+DHL	75.63 ± 2.2	**81.65 ± 2.38**	68.42 ± 4.98	75.03 ± 2.19	75.62 ± 2.17	**75.96 ± 2.23**

The best results are marked in red and the second best results are marked in blue.

On Comparison Between Single-Modality and Multi-modality. Experimental results are shown in Table 1. The proposed method (Multi+DHL) consistently achieves the highest or second highest performance for all the evaluation metrics, show that individuals with ASD can be reliably identified using multimodal FCs by dynamic hypergraph learning. We can observe that the method based on multi-modal FCs substantially outperform those only using sFC or dFC. For example, The improvement of multi+DHL on ACC is 3.79% and 1.29% compared with sFC+DHL and dFC+DHL, respectively. We note that the methods based on dynamic FC outperform those under assumptions of stationary FC under most circumstances. When only using Lasso, the improvement of dFC on ACC is 5.1% compared with sFC. For DHL, the classification accuracy of dFC is 2.47% higher than sFC. This conclusion is consistent with existing study [8].

On Comparison with State-of-the-Art Methods. As shown in these results, DHL can outperform the Lasso, RF and GCN in most cases, indicating the superiority of DHL over the state-of-the-art methods. Using the sFC features, the improvements of DHL on ACC, SEN, SPEC, BAC, PPV, NPV are 6.75%, 9.15%, 3.37%, 6.49%, 4.18% and 10.48% compared with Lasso, respectively. We note that the Random Forest method suffers from the class imbalance problem, although the data in our study are not strongly imbalanced. Compared with RF, DHL can achieve gains of 4.87% on ACC when dFC features are used. The error rate of DHL is 5.01% and 1.17% relatively lower than GCN using sFC and dFC modality, respectively, indicating the superiority of exploring high-order correlation over pair-wise correlation. The SPEC of dFC+GCN is 6.24% lower than dFC+DHL, while the SEN of dFC+GCN is 3.29% higher than dFC+DHL. It illustrates that GCN is more sensitive to the unbalance data than DHL. In general, our proposed method is more effective than GCN.

3.3 On Parameters

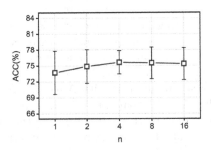

Fig. 2. The accuracy performance comparison with respect to different n selections.

To evaluate the influence of different parameter selections, we vary n from 1 to 16. Figure 2 provides the recognition accuracy performance curve with respect to the variation of parameter n. When n is 1, 2, 4, 8, 16, the classification accuracy of Multi+DHL is 73.7% ± 4.06%, 74.86% ± 3.17%, 75.63% ± 2.20%, 75.50% ± 2.99% and 75.33% ± 3.03%, respectively. When n is no less than 4, the performance becomes stable. When n is small, the performance is relatively poor. The grouping strategy can be considered as a way of data augmentation, based on the assumption that the sampled sub-sequences have the same distribution of dynamic properties (means and variables) as the original one. By this means, the extracted features are not sensitive to slight disturbances in the temporal signal, promoting robustness for ASD diagnosis.

3.4 Visualization

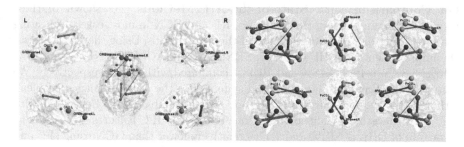

Fig. 3. Left: Connections whose time average is important for ASD diagnosis. Right: Connections whose time variance is important for ASD diagnosis.

Moreover, we visualize the important dynamic functional connections related to the mean values and the variance values in Fig. 3, respectively, by analyzing the learned β in Lasso. The results showed that the most discriminative connections included the connections between left and right caudate nucleus, between left and right superior frontal gyrus, between right posterior cingulate gyrus and middle temporal gyrus, etc., suggesting these brain connections may serve as potentially useful biomarkers for ASD. The findings are in line with the previous studies, that have observed similar abnormal functional connectivity patterns in patients with ASD [6,18]. Reduced functional connectivity between the forequarters and the caudate nucleus is observed in children with ASD [22]. In addition, one recent study has reported that in ASD patients, diminished functional connections among the frontal and forehead, the anterior gyrus, the superior parietal, the anterior and middle gyrus, and the forequarters and anterior/posterior cingulate gyrus [23]. In our study, classification using the crucial nodes is conducive to distinguish between HC and cohorts with ASD. Our results also reveal that aberrant functional connectivity within the crucial nodes could play a major role in diagnose for ASD.

4   Conclusion

The current study has developed a multi-modal FC based diagnosis system for children with ASD. In this study, the whole-brain sFC and dFC are calculated using a sliding-window algorithm, and two kinds of features are selected from the FC matrices using Lasso. A dynamic hypergraph learning algorithm is developed to explore subject correlation across different modalities and categorize the ASD subjects with HC. As shown in the results, we conclude that incorporating the high-order correlation among subjects into multi-modal FC analysis can provide a significantly improvement in the ASD diagnosis performance, and further may give a new perspective on understanding the mechanism of ASD.

Acknowledgments. This work was supported by National Natural Science Funds of China (U1701262).

References

1. Allen, G., Courchesne, E.: Differential effects of developmental cerebellar abnormality on cognitive and motor functions in the cerebellum: an fMRI study of autism. Am. J. Psychiatry **160**(2), 262–273 (2003)
2. Amaral, D.G., Schumann, C.M., Nordahl, C.W.: Neuroanatomy of autism. Trends Neurosci. **31**(3), 137–145 (2008)
3. Boddaert, N., Chabane, N., Gervais, H., Good, C., Bourgeois, M., Plumet, M., et al.: Superior temporal sulcus anatomical abnormalities in childhood autism: a voxel-based morphometry MRI study. Neuroimage **23**(1), 364–369 (2004)
4. Bruna, J., Zaremba, W., Szlam, A., LeCun, Y.: Spectral networks and locally connected networks on graphs. arXiv preprint arXiv:1312.6203 (2013)
5. Cerliani, L., Mennes, M., Thomas, R.M., Di Martino, A., Thioux, M., Keysers, C.: Increased functional connectivity between subcortical and cortical resting-state networks in autism spectrum disorder. JAMA Psychiat. **72**(8), 767–777 (2015)
6. Chen, H., Nomi, J.S., Uddin, L.Q., Duan, X., Chen, H.: Intrinsic functional connectivity variance and state-specific under-connectivity in autism. Hum. Brain Mapp. **38**(11), 5740–5755 (2017)
7. Chen, X., Zhang, H., Gao, Y., Wee, C.Y., Li, G., Shen, D.: High-order resting-state functional connectivity network for MCI classification. Hum. Brain Mapp. **37**(9), 3282–3296 (2016)
8. Demirtas, M., et al.: Dynamic functional connectivity reveals altered variability in functional connectivity among patients with major depressive disorder. Hum. Brain Mapp. **37**(8), 2918–2930 (2016)
9. Falahpour, M., Thompson, W.K., Abbott, A.E., Jahedi, A., Mulvey, M.E., et al.: Underconnected, but not broken? dynamic functional connectivity MRI shows underconnectivity in autism is linked to increased intra-individual variability across time. Brain Connectivity **6**(5), 403–414 (2016)
10. Gao, Y., Wang, M., Tao, D., Ji, R., Dai, Q.: 3-D object retrieval and recognition with hypergraph analysis. IEEE Trans. Image Process. **21**(9), 4290–4303 (2012)
11. von dem Hagen, E.A., Stoyanova, R.S., Baron-Cohen, S., Calder, A.J.: Reduced functional connectivity within and between 'social' resting state networks in autism spectrum conditions. Soc. Cogn. Affect. Neurosci. **8**(6), 694–701 (2012)

12. Huang, Y., Liu, Q., Zhang, S., Metaxas, D.N.: Image retrieval via probabilistic hypergraph ranking. In: Proceedings of IEEE Conference on Computer Vision and Pattern Recognition, pp. 3376–3383 (2010)

13. Jung, M., et al.: Default mode network in young male adults with autism spectrum disorder: relationship with autism spectrum traits. Molecular Autism **5**(1), 35 (2014)

14. Keown, C.L., Shih, P., Nair, A., Peterson, N., Mulvey, M.E., Müller, R.A.: Local functional overconnectivity in posterior brain regions is associated with symptom severity in autism spectrum disorders. Cell Rep. **5**(3), 567–572 (2013)

15. Kipf, T.N., Welling, M.: Semi-supervised classification with graph convolutional networks. arXiv preprint arXiv:1609.02907 (2016)

16. Ktena, S.I., et al.: Metric learning with spectral graph convolutions on brain connectivity networks. Neuroimage **169**, 431–442 (2018)

17. Laufs, H., Rodionov, R., Thornton, R., Duncan, J.S., Lemieux, L., Tagliazucchi, E.: Altered fMRI connectivity dynamics in temporal lobe epilepsy might explain seizure semiology. Front. Neurol. **5**, 175 (2014)

18. Monk, C.S., et al.: Abnormalities of intrinsic functional connectivity in autism spectrum disorders. Neuroimage **47**(2), 764–772 (2009)

19. Parisot, S., et al.: Spectral graph convolutions for population-based disease prediction. In: Descoteaux, M., Maier-Hein, L., Franz, A., Jannin, P., Collins, D.L., Duchesne, S. (eds.) MICCAI 2017. LNCS, vol. 10435, pp. 177–185. Springer, Cham (2017). https://doi.org/10.1007/978-3-319-66179-7_21

20. Parisot, S., et al.: Disease prediction using graph convolutional networks: application to autism spectrum disorder and Alzheimer's disease. Med. Image Anal. **48**, 117–130 (2018)

21. Price, T., Wee, C.-Y., Gao, W., Shen, D.: Multiple-network classification of childhood autism using functional connectivity dynamics. In: Golland, P., Hata, N., Barillot, C., Hornegger, J., Howe, R. (eds.) MICCAI 2014. LNCS, vol. 8675, pp. 177–184. Springer, Cham (2014). https://doi.org/10.1007/978-3-319-10443-0_23

22. Radulescu, E., et al.: Abnormalities in Fronto-striatal connectivity within language networks relate to differences in grey-matter heterogeneity in Asperger syndrome. NeuroImage Clin. **2**, 716–726 (2013)

23. Salmi, J., et al.: The brains of high functioning autistic individuals do not synchronize with those of others. NeuroImage Clin. **3**, 489–497 (2013)

24. Supekar, K., et al.: Brain hyperconnectivity in children with autism and its links to social deficits. Cell Rep. **5**(3), 738–747 (2013)

25. Watanabe, T., Rees, G.: Brain network dynamics in high-functioning individuals with autism. Nat. Commun. **8**, 16048 (2017)

26. Wee, C.Y., Yap, P.T., Shen, D.: Diagnosis of autism spectrum disorders using temporally distinct resting-state functional connectivity networks. CNS Neurosci. Therapeutics **22**(3), 212–9 (2016)

27. Yerys, B.E., et al.: Default mode network segregation and social deficits in autism spectrum disorder: evidence from non-medicated children. NeuroImage Clin. **9**, 223–232 (2015)

28. Yu, Q., et al.: Assessing dynamic brain graphs of time-varying connectivity in fMRI data: application to healthy controls and patients with schizophrenia. Neuroimage **107**, 345–355 (2015)

29. Zhang, Z., Lin, H., Gao, Y.: Dynamic hypergraph structure learning. In: Proceedings of International Joint Conference on Artificial Intelligence, pp. 3162–3169. International Joint Conferences on Artificial Intelligence Organization (2018)

30. Zhao, W., et al.: Learning to map social network users by unified manifold alignment on hypergraph. IEEE Trans. Neural Netw. Learn. Syst. **29**(12), 5834–5846 (2018)
31. Zhu, L., Shen, J., Jin, H., Zheng, R., Xie, L.: Content-based visual landmark search via multimodal hypergraph learning. IEEE Trans. Cybern. **45**(12), 2756–2769 (2015)

CARNet: Automatic Cerebral Aneurysm Classification in Time-of-Flight MR Angiography by Leveraging Recurrent Neural Networks

Yan Hu[1], Yuan Xu[2], Xiaosong Huang[2], Deqiao Gan[2], Haiyan Huang[2], Liyuan Shao[2], Qimin Cheng[2], and Deng Xianbo[3](✉)

[1] Wuhan University Press, Wuhan, China
[2] School of Electronic Information and Communications, Huazhong University of Science and Technology, Wuhan, China
[3] Wuhan Union Hospital, Wuhan, China

Abstract. Cerebral aneurysms (CAs) detection from unenhanced 3D time-of-flight magnetic resonance angiography (TOF MRA) images is time-consuming, laborious, and error-prone. In this paper we propose a novel architecture, Cerebral Aneurysm Recurrent Classification Network (CARNet), which integrates the spatial information over multi-view Maximum Intensity Projection (MIP) images by exploiting recurrent neural network (RNN). Specifically, CARNet first collects the region of interests (ROIs) around the aneurysms in 3D TOF MRA data via the conventional sliding window strategy. Then it detects CAs in MIP images from ROIs along 9 fixed planes via Maximum Intensity Projection which helps reduce computational cost. Afterwards CNN-GRU Aneurysm (CGA) Discrimination network recursively renews the high-level features of aneurysm extracted by CNN from all MIP images to make a decision by employing the RNN. Finally CARNet was evaluated on 213 patients of 480 samples with aneurysm acquired from the Radiology Department of Wuhan Union Hospital. Experimental results showed that CARNet outperforms the previous methods with a sensitivity of 85%–91%. In addition, the efficiency of CARNet is about twice that of 3D CNN.

Keywords: Cerebral aneurysm detection · Magnetic resonance angiography · Maximum intensity projection · Recurrent neural network

1 Introduction

Cerebral Aneurysm (CA) is one of the common diseases of cerebral vessels, which is a kind of tuberculous process caused by the abnormal enlargement of the arterial wall. The most dreaded complication of CA is a rupture and mortality. Moreover, the morbidity associated with aneurysm rupture remain high [1]. Therefore,

Supported by organization x.

it is of great significant task for radiologists to detect unruptured CAs. Three-dimensional time-of-flight magnetic resonance angiography (3D TOF MRA hereafter referred to as MRA) has been widely accepted as a non-invasive screening method for the detection of CAs [15]. For radiologists, a common method to detect the CA from MRA images is observing the blood vessels on the slices acquired by the maximum intensity projection (MIP) technology in MRA images along the axial plane. The radiologist can observe the slices from different angles (such as axial, coronal, and sagittal planes). However, it is difficult for radiologists to detect small (< 5 mm) unruptured CAs in typical MRA images since the adjacent intricate vessels may obscure the small CAs [3]. In addition, a physician may get fatigue when he faces lots of slices. It is reported that the sensitivities are about 64–70% for the radiologists to detect CAs in MRA images [6]. Therefore, to relieve the workload on radiologists as well as improve the efficiency and reliability, computer-aided detection (CAD) based methods have been devised.

Previous automatic CA detection methods mainly employed low-level hand-crafted features like vessel curvature, geodesic active regions, and shape difference through thresholding, morphological filter and region-growing algorithm. However, these hand-crafted features detection heavily depend on the domain knowledge of CAs. In addition, these low-level features are usually insufficient to capture the complicated characteristics of CAs. Recently, some investigations have been dedicated to learning features in a data-oriented way [7,14]. Among them, the convolutional neural network (CNN) is one of the most promising solutions due to its high capability in extracting powerful high-level features. Lately, CNNs have presented outstanding effectiveness on medical image such as Brain tumor segmentation [8], Thyroid nodules detection [5], Pulmonary nodule detection [12,19]. Ueda et al. [16] utilized the ResNet18 to detect CAs in MRA with the sensitivity of 91% and 93% for the internal and external test datasets, respectively. It shows that CNNs achieved great success in the detection of CA. However, this kind of method leverages feature information from serial slices and processes the slices independently, without considering the spatial information between neighboring slices.

As such, how to effectively employ CNNs to analyze 3D volumetric data still remains an open problem. A straightforward method is to employ a 3D conventional kernels CNN to represent the third dimension information from MRA images, such as Brain lesion segmentation [4] and Cerebral microbleed detection [2]. Alternatively, some researches adapt MIP images for processing 3D volumetric data [10]. The way is actually a 2.5D method [11] which uses MIP images to represent the 3D volumetric data. The approaches [9,17] aggregate orthogonal MIP images to reduce computer costs while preserving spatial information. In [9], the volumetric data are firstly decomposed into fixed triplane planes (axial, coronal, and sagittal planes) to obtain the MIP images. Arnaud et al. [12] further designed more comprehensive orthogonal planes to represent the volumetric data, which include 9 planes. Thereafter, each MIP images were processed using a multi-view architecture, and the output maps were combined through data fusion methods, such as late-fusion [9], committee-fusion [17] or the combination of both fusion methods [11]. Nakao et al. [7] directly concatenated the MIP images from 9 views vertically, and input it to CNN for aneurysm detection. It was effective for solving the computational complexity and the representation of 3D volumetric data. Nevertheless, the solution is still unable to make full use of the relationship between multi-view MIP images. Fortunately, a type of RNNs called Gated Recurrent Unit (GRU) is able to better exploit correlations in sequences. Information from multi-view MIP images can be integrated by the cyclic recursion. It is more reliable to make the most of the spatial information while enhancing complementary spatial correlation in multi-view MIP images.

Overall, in order to accurately and efficiently detect CAs in MRA images with low computational cost, we propose a novel architecture, CARNet, with the combination of the CNN to extract high-level hierarchical features and the RNN to integrate the spatial information on multi-view MIP images through cyclic recursion. The contributions of this paper are as follows: (1) We propose a novel architecture CARNet with the combination of CNN and RNN on multi-view MIP images for CA detection. To our knowledge, it is the first work to exploit RNN for the detection of aneurysms in MRA images, which recursively integrate the information of multi-view MIP images. (2) Our architecture tackles the underutilization of spatial information of 2D CNN and the huge computational cost of 3D CNN by leveraging MIP technology and cyclic recursion. (3) We demonstrated the superiority of our architecture through exhaustive comparative experiments with other state-of-the-art methods on dataset including 213 patients with CA acquired from radiology department of Wuhan Union Hospital.

2   Methods

To detect CAs from MRA images, we proposed a novel architecture CARNet based on the high-level features of CNN and the spatial information of RNN. An overview of the proposed architecture is shown in Fig. 1, composed of two stages: MIP Extracting and CGA Discrimination. The first stages, MIP Extracting aims to eliminate the background regions and rapidly locate ROIs of CA. Subsequently, CNN and RNN are integrated to make use of the spatial information between 9-view MIP images. The RNN features of MIP image from each view are fused and given to a softmax classifier to predict whether is an aneurysm or not.

2.1   MIP Extracting

The MIP extracting stage is for ROI screening, and the location of the ROI is obtained as follows. First, we employed the Otsu threshold segmentation and hessian matrix [18] to extract vessels in MRA images. Then, a sliding window with a size of $24 \times 24 \times 24$ around the vessel was used to generate a series of small cubes of $24 \times 24 \times 24$ (called ROI). Among the ROIs, the ROI centroids scattered around the CA were taken as positive samples and those without the CA were taken as negative samples under the guidance of the radiologist label information, leading to a total of 480 samples with 228 positive samples and

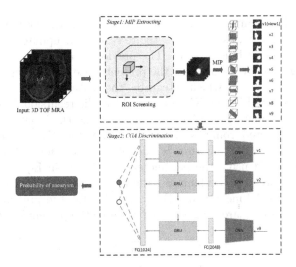

Fig. 1. An overview of the proposed CARNet architecture for CA Detection.

252 negative samples. For the samples with multiple aneurysms, the cropping process was executed for each aneurysm to acquire ROIs. After that, we extract the MIP images with the size of 24×24 of the VOI from 9 views by applying a MIP technology. Similar to [11], three planes of symmetry that are parallel to a pair of faces of the cube are used. These planes are commonly known as axial, sagittal, and coronal planes. The other six planes are the planes of symmetry that cut two opposite faces of cubes in diagonals. Such a plane contains two opposite edges of the cube and four vertices. Examples of extracted patches are shown at the top of Fig. 1.

2.2   CGA Discrimination

In the CGA discrimination stage, we propose a CNN-GRU Aneurysm(CGA) Discrimination network with the combination of CNN and RNN (as illustrated in Fig. 1), where the CNN network consists of the first 13 convolutional layers in the VGG16 network to extract features from each MIP image. The MIP images are resized to be 224×224 to fit the input of the VGG16. The CNN is formed by a sequence of five convolutional layers, followed by an average pool layer and fully connected (FC) layers. Rectified Linear Unit (ReLU) is taken as an activation function for all convolutional layers, because of its relative robustness to vanishing gradients and general applicability. The batch normalization (BN) is performed before each ReLU function. Feature maps from the 13 convolutional layers of VGG16 are extracted for each 9-view MIP image through a FC layer with a dropout of probability ($p = 0.5$).

Then, we combine 9-view feature maps into a batch as the input of RNN with a sequence layer to the process, and output the probability of CA. The applied RNN is addressed as a GRU layer, trained with a dropout of probability

$(p = 0.5)$. A GRU computes a present state h_v from the previous state h_{v-1} and the hidden state $\tilde{h}_v$, using the reset gate r_t and the update gate z_t to weigh the previous state and hidden state. The previous state $h_{(v-1)}$ is the previous view MIP image feature vector, and the present state h_v denotes the next view MIP image feature vector which integrates the feature vector of the previous view and the extracted from CNN through the cyclic recursion. Specifically, the reset gate r_t and update gate z_t are calculated using the input x_v (MIP image feature vector extracted from CNN) and the parameters $\{W_r, U_r, b_r, W_z, U_z, b_z\}$ in Eqs. 1, 2, 3, where the operator "$*$" denotes convolution. Then, the hidden state $\tilde{h}_v$ is calculated using the parameters W_h, U_h, b_h in Eqs. 4, 5, where the operator "$\circ$" denotes the Hadamard product and the activation function σ_h used Leaky Rectified Linear Units (LReLU). Finally, the previous state h_{v-1} and the hidden state $\tilde{h}_v$ are weighted to determine the present state h_v in Eq. 6.

$$r_t = \sigma_g(W_r * x_v + U_r * h_{v-1} + b_r) \tag{1}$$

$$z_t = \sigma_g(W_z * x_v + U_z * h_{v-1} + b_z) \tag{2}$$

$$\sigma_g(x) = \frac{e^x}{e^x + 1} \tag{3}$$

$$\tilde{h}_v = \sigma_h(W_h * x_v + U_h(r_t \circ h_{v-1}) + b_h) \tag{4}$$

$$\sigma_h(x) = LReLU(x) = \begin{cases} x & x > 0 \\ 0.2x & otherwise \end{cases} \tag{5}$$

$$h_v = z_t \circ h_{v-1} + (1 - z_t) \circ \tilde{h}_v \tag{6}$$

The composed RNN features of MIP image from each view are integrated and given to a softmax classifier. The last layer output is channeled through a softmax activation function to obtain the likelihood of 9-view MIP images. The application of BN layer and dropout layer can accelerate the learning rate, prevent overfitting and improve performance. In summary, our proposed network has the following architecture: input $(9 \times 224 \times 224 \times 3)$ – VGG – FC (2048) – dropout (0.5) – 9× GRU (1024) – dropout (0.5) – softmax (2).

During training and validation, the VGG16 parameters (initially configured to the pre-trained ImageNet weights) and all model parameters were fine-tuned on the MIP images. The model is trained on the basis of Adam algorithm, in which the parameters include learning rate = 0.01, $\beta_1 = 0.9$, $\beta_2 = 0.999$, epsilon $= 1 \times 10^{-8}$, schedule decay $= 1 \times 10^{-5}$ and a batch size of 16. 43 epochs can obtain a fine result with the loss function of cross-entropy.

3   Experiment and Setup

3.1   Dataset

In our paper, 3D TOF MRA source images were acquired from Wuhan Union Hospital during April 2018 through May 2019. Our CARNet was evaluated on

480 samples datasets obtained in 213 patients with CA that were verified with digital subtraction angiography (DSA). There are 228 positive samples and 252 negative samples. All original data were supplied in the DICOME format. In the selected 213 patients, 15 of them have two CAs, and the others only have one CA, bringing the total number of CAs to 228. The average, maximum and minimum size of the aneurysms are 7.7 mm, 2.4 mm and 23.0 mm.

The 3D TOF MRA data was collected by several magnetic resonance (MR) systems: (1) 1.5T MR scanners: MAGNETOM Aera, MAGNETOM Avanto, MAGNETOM SymphonyVision. (2) 3T MR scanners: Siemens Healthineers, MAGNETOM TrioTim, MAGNETOM Verio, Discovery MR750, Signa HDxt. The image parameter used in the MR system is presented in Table 1.

Table 1. The image parameters of the MR system

System	Magnetic intensity (T)	Matrix size (pixel)	Pixel spacing (mm)	Slice thickness (mm)
MAGNETOM Aera	1.5	512 × 480	0.39	0.50
MAGNETOM Avanto	1.5	512 × 512	0.35	0.50
MAGNETOM SymphonyVision	1.5	384 × 320	0.52	0.80
Siemens Healthineers	3.0	640 × 580	0.33	0.50
MAGNETOM TrioTim	3.0	768 × 672	0.26	0.60
MAGNETOM Verio	3.0	768 × 652	0.26	0.60
Discovery MR750	3.0	512 × 512	0.43	0.67
Signa HDxt	3.0	512 × 512	0.43	0.59

For each patient, a series of 2D slice images were sampled from DICOM MRA data on the axial plane. The average number of slice images for each patient is 123. The size of slice images ranges from 384 × 320 to 768 × 672, and the slice images were rescaled to a 512 × 512 matrix to facilitate the training. The slice images and empirically selected slice images of CA that were appropriate for diagnosis under the guidance of radiologists. For each image, the label is indicated by 1, 0, where "1" indicates with aneurysm and "0" with no aneurysm.

3.2 Evaluation Metrics

In this paper, we measured our CARNet testing performance for binary classification tasks using receiver-operating characteristic (ROC) curves with area under the curve (AUC) generated, and we calculated accuracy, sensitivity, and specificity of correctly classifying CA. The Kappa coefficient (k) was used to determine the reliability of the classification model. Cohen's kappa was calculated using the $k = (p_o - p_e)/(1 - p_e)$, where $p_o = $ *observed agreement among raters* and $p_e = $ *expected agreement* $= \frac{1}{N^2} \sum_k n_{k_1} n_{k_2}$ for categories k, number of items N, and n_{ki} the number of times rater i predicted category k. For the final evaluation we additionally computed recall and precision.

3.3   Data Augmentation

For the image augmentation, we made use of the extension packages skimage (https://scikit-image.org/) and transforms3d, which break the task down to matrix transformations. A total of 25 transformations per patient were performed on each image with the specified ranges. We keep the z-axis fixed and shifted around the $x - y$ plane within a range of $[-4, 4]$ degrees depending on the size of the aneurysm.

The detailed operation is as follows: (1) First, the MRA images are resampled to make the 3D TOF MRA image to an isotropic voxel size, while the slice images are rescaled to 512×512. (2) Then extracting the ROI with the size of $24 \times 24 \times 24$ around the blood vessels; For normal vessel patch without aneurysm, this cubic ROI is determined empirically, usually allowing vessels to be located in the middle of the ROI. For the patch of the vessel with the aneurysm attached, the aneurysm is placed in the middle of the ROI. (3) After determining the position of the ROI, it translates with 5-pixel sizes $(-4, -2, 0, 2, 4)$ which depends on the size of the aneurysm on the two planes. Then each ROI can be augmented to 25 (5×5). (4) After augmentation the images were normalized to [0,1] and guaranteed equal activation values for similar transitions in brain structures.

To validate the performance of the proposed CARNet, we create 4 datasets (called Original data, Augment data, MIP data, Augment MIP data) and split them into training, validation, and testing datasets, according to the ratio of 70%, 10%, and 20% respectively. The MIP data is the extraction of the original data from 9 views. The details of the datasets are shown in Table 2.

Table 2. Details of datasets and the split.

Datasets	Original data			Augment data (25 aug)			MIP data (9 views)			Augment MIP data (25 aug)		
	Aneurysm	Artery	Total	Aneurysm	Artery	Total	Aneurysm	Artery	Total	Aneurysm	Artery	Total
Training	160	175	335	4,000	4,375	8,375	1,440	1,575	3,015	36,000	39,375	75,375
Validation	22	26	48	550	650	1,200	198	234	432	4,950	5,850	10,800
Testing	46	51	97	1,150	1,275	2,425	414	459	873	10,350	11,475	21,825
Total	228	252	480	5,700	6,300	12,000	2,052	2,268	4,320	51,300	56,700	108,000

3.4   CARNet Training

The CARNet was trained on 335 training samples with different settings, summing up to a total training time of approximately 4 h. The number of epochs was chosen based on the results of the validation dataset. The validation dataset included 48 samples. The input consisted of the generated MIP images. We fixed the batch size at 16. The weights were adjusted after each epoch was processed.

The CARNET was trained using the propagation with stochastic gradient descent, which is an efficient training method to minimize the loss function between the true and predicted labels. Therefore, the improvement of the model depends to a large extent on the loss function as a representative of the predicted quality. We experimented with the two common loss functions as cross-entropy and dice coefficient in our tasks.

We took both objective functions into account and compared the results. The outcome were more successful for training with a cross-entropy loss function, as shown in Fig. 2. Therefore, the cross-entropy loss function was used in the training process.

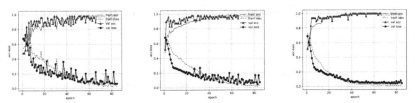

(a) weights initialized as zero and the loss function of cross-entropy

(b) weights randomly initialized and the loss function of dice coefficient

(c) weights randomly initialized and the loss function of cross-entropy

Fig. 2. Comparison of loss function for training initialized with zero and random weights. Accuracy of the training (red solid line) and validation (blue line with a triangle) and loss of the training (green dotted line) and validation (black line with a circle) sets show improvement with longer training (increasing epochs). (Color figure online)

4   Results

In this section, we first verified the benefit of RNN in CARNet by ablation experiments. For a fair comparison, our proposed CARNet on CA detection was compared with 2D CNN [16], 2.5D CNN [7], 3D CNN [13] using our dataset. Meanwhile, we revealed the scalability of CARNet and the superiority of data augmentation by conducting experiments on augmented data. In addition, we also validated the efficiency of our CARNet compared with 3D CNN [13].

1) The ablation experiments with CARNet: To validate the superiority of RNN in CARNet, we conducted ablation experiments for comparison. We tested the MIP images on VGG16 which is the CNN part of our CARNet for comparison. To facilitate the analysis, this method without RNN is named as CANet in Table 3. For the CANet network, a voting mechanism was used to get the final results on MIP images from 9 views of each sample. The threshold was set to 5, that is to say, a sample would be regarded as a positive sample when more than 5 of 9-view MIP images were detected to contain aneurysms.

The evaluation metrics including sensitivity (TPR), specificity (TNR), AUC, Kappa coefficient (Kp), accuracy (A), precision (P), recall (R), and F_1 score (F1) are summarized in Table 3. The accuracy of the CARNet reaches 93.8% and the sensitivity is 93.5%. The Receiver Operating Characteristic (ROC) curve is shown in Fig. 3(a). The corresponding area-under-the-curve (AUC) was calculated to be 0.938. After data augmentation, the sensitivity was improved to 94.2% and the ROC curves of AUC was 0.943, as shown in Fig. 3(b). The sensitivity was improved to 93.5% with false positive rate of 0.059 than 85.5% of CANet from Table 3. The results demonstrated that our architecture outperforms the single CNN in all metrics on the augmented datasets.

Table 3. The results of ablation experiments.

Model	Data	Shape	Train	Val	Test	Epoch	BS	TPR	FPR	AUC	Kp	A	P	R	F1
CANet	MIP	224 × 224 × 3	3015	432	97	54	128	85.5%	0.153	0.851	0.70	85.1%	85.1%	85.5%	85.1%
CANet	Aug_MIP	224 × 224 × 3	75375	10800	2425	85	256	87.3%	0.126	0.87	0.75	87.4%	87.4%	87.3%	87.4%
CARNet	MIP	9 × 224 × 224 × 3	335	48	97	43	16	93.5%	0.059	0.95	0.88	93.8%	93.5%	93.5%	93.8%
CARNet	Au_MIP	9 × 224 × 224 × 3	8375	1200	2425	48	32	**94.2%**	**0.056**	**0.94**	**0.89**	**94.3%**	**93.8%**	**94.2%**	**94.3%**

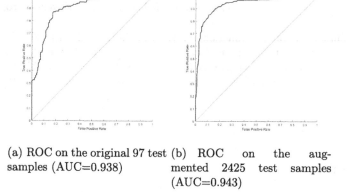

(a) ROC on the original 97 test samples (AUC=0.938)

(b) ROC on the augmented 2425 test samples (AUC=0.943)

Fig. 3. Receiver operating characteristic curve of CARNet.

2) Performance comparison with the previous methods: To validate the efficacy of CARNet, several experiments are conducted on the original and augmented datasets mentioned before (see Table 2 for details). Our CARNet were compared with the previous methods 2D CNN [16], 2.5D CNN [7], and 3D CNN [13]. The first one [16] employed Resnet18 on each MIP datasets. The second one [7] constructed a CNN on the MIP_con datasets. The third one [13] utilized a 3D CNN on the ROI datasets. Specifically, for the method of 2D CNN, we utilized the same network of ResNet18 as recommended in [16] and used the MIP images as input to the network. Similar to CANet before, the voting mechanism was adopted for the final results. For the 2.5D CNN, we referenced its volumes of interest (VOI) extraction and MIP image generation procedure on our dataset. The network adopted a similar network in [7], and the input images were generated by simply concatenating the MIP images of 9 views vertically (called MIP_con data). In case of 3D CNN, the network was extended from the VGG16 by replacing all 2D operations with the related 3D counterparts. Obviously, our CARNet was better than other methods including 2D CNN, 2.5D CNN, and 3D CNN from Table 4. The comparison results show that our CARNet benefits from the high-level representations which fuse richer spatial information between the MIP images by cyclic recursion resulting in higher CA detection performance.

In addition, we conducted experiments on the augmented dataset with 12,000 samples, as shown in Table 5. Our CARNet achieved the best performance on the augmented datasets in all evaluation metrics, which demonstrated the scalability of CARNet under the large datasets compared to the small datasets.

Table 4. Performance comparison with the different methods on the original dataset.

Model	Data	Shape	Train	Val	Test	Epoch	BS	TPR	FPR	AUC	Kp	A	P	R	F1
2D CNN [16]	MIP	224 × 224 × 3	3015	432	97	54	128	86.0%	0.135	0.862	0.72	86.3%	86.3%	86.0%	86.3%
2.5D CNN [7]	MIP_con	24 × 216 × 3	335	48	97	56	128	89.1%	0.098	0.90	0.79	89.7%	89.7%	89.1%	89.7%
3D CNN [13]	ROI	224 × 224 × 3	335	48	97	33	16	91.3%	0.078	0.92	0.83	91.8%	91.8%	91.3%	91.8%
Ours (CARNet)	MIP	9 × 224 × 224 × 3	335	48	97	43	16	**93.5%**	**0.059**	**0.94**	**0.88**	**93.8%**	**93.5%**	**93.5%**	**93.8%**

Table 5. Performance comparison with the different methods on the augmented dataset.

Model	Data	Shape	Train	Val	Test	Epoch	BS	TPR	FPR	AUC	Kp	A	P	R	F1
2D CNN [16]	Aug_MIP	224 × 224 × 3	75375	10800	2425	83	256	87.6%	0.112	0.88	0.76	88.3%	88.3%	87.6%	88.3%
2.5D CNN [7]	Aug_MIP_con	24 × 216 × 3	8375	1200	2425	88	256	90.1%	0.078	0.91	0.83	91.2%	91.2%	90.1%	91.2%
3D CNN [13]	Aug_ROI	224 × 224 × 3	8375	1200	2425	52	32	91.3%	0.059	0.93	0.86	92.8%	92.8%	91.3%	92.8%
Ours (CARNet)	Aug_MIP	9 × 224 × 224 × 3	8375	1200	2425	48	32	**94.2%**	**0.056**	**0.94**	**0.89**	**94.3%**	**93.8%**	**94.2%**	**94.3%**

3) Evaluation of the efficiency of CARNet: To validate the efficiency of CARNet, the experiments were conducted within NVIDIA TitanX environment compared with 3D CNN [13]. Table 6 illustrates the inference time for a single input sample and the computational complexity of the model. As evident from the numbers provided, CARNet can process the image at 31.1 fps on GPU with 27 ms. The efficiency of our CARNet is evident in the much lower number of operations per case and overall parameters. The CARNet is nearly 2× faster and 4× smaller than 3D CNN. However, although the results of efficiency reached a lower score for our CARNet than the VGG, the improvement in efficiency was remarkable from Table 3. The results indicate that the strategy of ROI screening of CARNet can remove massive computations and accelerate the detection process.

Table 6. Comparison with different model in term of implementation efficiency on the original dataset.

Model	Inference time (ms)	Speed (Fps)	FLOPs (G)	Para (M)
VGG	13	65.3	2.0	0.13
3D CNN [13]	53	18.7	15.4	1.61
Our CARNet	27	31.1	3.8	0.40

5   Conclusion

With the continuous accumulation of medical data, CNN provides a promising solution for many detections and segmentation tasks. However, the underutilization of three-dimensional spatial information by 2D CNN and the expensive computational cost of 3D CNN restrict their use in clinical practice. Therefore, we proposed a robust and efficient architecture CARNet with the combination of CNN and RNN for automatic detection CA on MIP images from 3D TOF MRA. The first stage MIP Extracting can remove massive redundant computations and reduce the computational cost. The CGA Discrimination makes the most of spatial information on multi-view MIP images to extract more representative high-level features for CAs by cyclic recursion, that dramatically improves the detection performance and speeds up the detection process compared with the previous methods that applied either 2D CNN or 3D CNN. The experiments conducted on the dataset with 480 samples collected from 213 patients, corroborated that our CARNet can significantly decrease false positive rate and accelerate the detection process with low computational cost while maintaining comparable or even superior sensitivity. Our CARNet, first proposed by exploiting the RNN to detect the CA based on multi-view MIP images is highly suitable for the detection of CAs on 3D TOF MRA images. The proposed architecture can be easily adapted to other detection tasks (such as cerebral microbleeds and pulmonary nodules) and boost the application of DCNNs on volumetric medical data. Future work will expand the approach to higher-dimensional datasets and include more training cases for better accuracy or segmentation of aneurysms for estimating the size.

Acknowledgment. The work of this paper was supported by National Key R&D Program of China (2018YFB0505401), and National Natural Science Foundation of China (No. 41771452).

References

1. Chalouhi, N., Hoh, B.L., Hasan, D.: Review of cerebral aneurysm formation, growth, and rupture. Stroke **44**(12), 3613–3622 (2013)
2. Dou, Q., et al.: Automatic detection of cerebral microbleeds from MR images via 3D convolutional neural networks. IEEE Trans. Med. Imaging **35**(5), 1182–1195 (2016)

3. Elmalem, V.I., Hudgins, P.A., Bruce, B.B., Newman, N.J., Biousse, V.: Underdiagnosis of posterior communicating artery aneurysm in non-invasive brain vascular studies. J. Neuroophthalmol. Official J. N. Am. Neuroophthalmol. Soc. **31**(2), 103 (2011)

4. Kamnitsas, K., Chen, L., Ledig, C., Rueckert, D., Glocker, B.: Multi-scale 3D convolutional neural networks for lesion segmentation in brain MRI. Ischemic Stroke Lesion Segment. **13**, 46 (2015)

5. Ma, J., Wu, F., Jiang, T., Zhu, J., Kong, D.: Cascade convolutional neural networks for automatic detection of thyroid nodules in ultrasound images. Med. Phys. **44**(5), 1678–1691 (2017)

6. Miki, S., et al.: Computer-assisted detection of cerebral aneurysms in MR angiography in a routine image-reading environment: effects on diagnosis by radiologists. Am. J. Neuroradiol. **37**(6), 1038–1043 (2016)

7. Nakao, T., et al.: Deep neural network-based computer-assisted detection of cerebral aneurysms in MR angiography. J. Magn. Reson. Imaging **47**(4), 948–953 (2018)

8. Pereira, S., Pinto, A., Alves, V., Silva, C.A.: Brain tumor segmentation using convolutional neural networks in MRI images. IEEE Trans. Med. Imaging **35**(5), 1240–1251 (2016)

9. Prasoon, A., Petersen, K., Igel, C., Lauze, F., Dam, E., Nielsen, M.: Deep feature learning for knee cartilage segmentation using a triplanar convolutional neural network. In: Mori, K., Sakuma, I., Sato, Y., Barillot, C., Navab, N. (eds.) MICCAI 2013. LNCS, vol. 8150, pp. 246–253. Springer, Heidelberg (2013). https://doi.org/10.1007/978-3-642-40763-5_31

10. Roth, H.R., et al.: Improving computer-aided detection using convolutional neural networks and random view aggregation. IEEE Trans. Med. Imaging **35**(5), 1170–1181 (2015)

11. Roth, H.R., et al.: A new 2.5D representation for lymph node detection using random sets of deep convolutional neural network observations. In: Golland, P., Hata, N., Barillot, C., Hornegger, J., Howe, R. (eds.) MICCAI 2014. LNCS, vol. 8673, pp. 520–527. Springer, Cham (2014). https://doi.org/10.1007/978-3-319-10404-1_65

12. Setio, A.A.A., et al.: Pulmonary nodule detection in CT images: false positive reduction using multi-view convolutional networks. IEEE Trans. Med. Imaging **35**(5), 1160–1169 (2016)

13. Standvoss, K., et al.: Cerebral microbleed detection in traumatic brain injury patients using 3d convolutional neural networks. In: Medical Imaging 2018: Computer-Aided Diagnosis, vol. 10575, p. 105751D. International Society for Optics and Photonics (2018)

14. Stember, J.N., et al.: Convolutional neural networks for the detection and measurement of cerebral aneurysms on magnetic resonance angiography. J. Digit. Imaging **32**(5), 808–815 (2019)

15. Štepán-Buksakowska, I., et al.: Computer-aided diagnosis improves detection of small intracranial aneurysms on MRA in a clinical setting. Am. J. Neuroradiol. **35**(10), 1897–1902 (2014)

16. Ueda, D., et al.: Deep learning for MR angiography: automated detection of cerebral aneurysms. Radiology **290**(1), 187–194 (2018)

17. Van Ginneken, B., Setio, A.A., Jacobs, C., Ciompi, F.: Off-the-shelf convolutional neural network features for pulmonary nodule detection in computed tomography scans. In: 2015 IEEE 12th International Symposium on Biomedical Imaging (ISBI), pp. 286–289. IEEE (2015)

18. Zeng, Y.Z., Zhao, Y.Q., Liao, M., Zou, B.J., Wang, X.F., Wang, W.: Liver vessel segmentation based on extreme learning machine. Physica Med. **32**(5), 709–716 (2016)
19. Zheng, S., Guo, J., Cui, X., Veldhuis, R.N.J., Oudkerk, M., van Ooijen, P.M.A.: Automatic pulmonary nodule detection in CT scans using convolutional neural networks based on maximum intensity projection. IEEE Trans. Med. Imaging **39**(3), 797–805 (2020). https://doi.org/10.1109/TMI.2019.2935553

White-Box Attacks on the CNN-Based Myoelectric Control System

Bo Xue, Le Wu, Aiping Liu, Xu Zhang, and Xun Chen[✉]

The School of Information Science and Technology, University of Science and Technology of China, Hefei 230027, China
xunchen@ustc.edu.cn

Abstract. Convolutional neural networks (CNN) have been widely used in myoelectric control field, such as prosthesis control, physical rehabilitation and human-computer interaction. Nevertheless, it was found that CNN models are very easily tricked by adversarial instances, which are normal instances with tiny intentional perturbations. In this study, an attack framework based on universal adversarial perturbations (UAP) was proposed to attack the CNN-based myoelectric control system. The performance of the proposed framework was evaluated with data recorded by a High-density surface EMG electrode array of 8 subjects during performing 6 finger and wrist extension movements. The experiment results demonstrated the effectiveness of two adversarial attack algorithms including DeepFool-based UAPs and Total Loss Minimization-based UAPs on the CNN-based EMG gesture recognition network for both target and non-target attacks. To our knowledge, this is the first work on the vulnerability of the CNN classifier in EMG-based gesture recognition system, which hopefully can draw more attention to the security of muscle-computer interface.

Keywords: Myoelectric pattern recognition · Surface electromyography · Gesture recognition · Universal adversarial perturbation · Convolutional neural network

1 Introduction

Surface electromyograpy (sEMG) is an electrical signal recorded by placing electrodes on the skin during muscle contraction. It contains rich motor control information that conveys the motion intentions of the user. It has been widely chosen as the control source of many human-machine interfaces such as powered prostheses, rehabilitation robots, and wearable devices since it is safe, non-invasive and easily implemented [1]. Myoelectric control is a technique which

Supported by the National Key Research and Development Program of China under Grant 2018YFB1005001, the National Natural Science Foundation of China under Grant 61922075 and the USTC Research Funds of the Double First-Class Initiative under Grant YD2100002004.

© Springer Nature Switzerland AG 2021
L. Fang et al. (Eds.): CICAI 2021, LNAI 13069, pp. 149–157, 2021.
https://doi.org/10.1007/978-3-030-93046-2_13

can translate the intensions and movements into commands to manipulate a prosthesis or other external robotic device. Myoelectric pattern recognition has long been known as a landmark technology which allows dexterous control of multiple degrees of freedom.

The myoelectric pattern recognition approaches can be catergorized into traditional approaches [2] and end-to-end deep learning approaches [3]. The traditional approaches usually include four stages: EMG signal acquisition, preprocessing and segmentation, feature extraction and gesture classification. However, some useful information may be dropped when the hand-crafted features are extracted. The end-to-end deep learning approaches typically take the original signal as input and utilize multi-layer nonlinear functions to represent the hidden relationships between the input and the output which address the shortcomings of the hand-crafted features based methods. Although promising performance can be achieved in well-controlled laboratory conditions, adversarial attacks may compromise the performance of the EMG control systems [4]. Specifically, the distribution of training and testing data is altered by the attack, resulting in malicious modification of the output instructions without any significant change in the signal and causing security problems.

In the field of myoelectric pattern recognition, the two-dimensional high density electrode arrays covering the entire muscle were ultilized to collect high-density sEMG (HD-sEMG) signals. Besides the conventional temporal and spectral information conveyed by sEMG signals, they can also provide valuable spatial information about muscle activity. The combination of convolutional neural networks (CNN) for EMG control can take full advantage of high-density electrode arrays and has received increasing attention from researchers. Park *et al.* were the first researchers to apply CNN to EMG pattern recognition [3]. Geng *et al.* used a deep CNN-based classification scheme to demonstrate that the patterns inside the instantaneous values of HD-sEMG enable gesture recognition [5]. In [6], Ding *et al.* proposed a parallel multiple-scale convolution architecture with larger sizes of kernel filters to achieve a recognition accuracy of 78.86% on the Ninapro DB2 dataset.

However, it has been found that deep learning models are susceptible to adversarial attacks [7]. In this attack, intentionally designed small perturbations, many of which are even imperceptible to humans, were added to the normal instances to trick the deep learning models, resulting in a dramatic performance degradation [8]. According to the purpose of the attacker, the attacks can be divided into two categories: target attacks and non-target attacks. For non-target attacks, it just forces the model to misclassify the adversary instances. Two typical non-target attack approaches are Fast Gradient Sign Method (FGSM) [7] and DeepFool [9]. And for target attacks, it forces the model to misclassify the adversary instances into a particular class. Some of typical target attack methods are the C&W's attack [10], adversarial transformation networks [11] and total loss minimization universal adversarial perturbation (TLM-based UAP) [12]. Many successful adversarial attacks have been reported in some areas, such as image classification and speech recognition [7]. As far as we know, the vulnerability of deep learning models in EMG control systems has not been investigated yet, but it is essential and imperative.

In this study, we propose an attack framework by injecting a jamming module between sEMG signal segmentation and CNN classifier for CNN-based myoelectric control system, as shown in Fig. 1. The jamming model can generate adversarial instances based on attack algorithms. And the DeepFool-based UAP and TLM-based UAP were ultilized to attack the CNN classifier with white-box attack under target and nontarget paradigms. We aim to explore the vulnerability of CNN classifier in EMG-based gesture recognition system and hopefully to design safer muscle-computer interface.

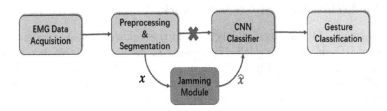

Fig. 1. Our proposed attack framework for CNN-based EMG gesture recognition system.

2   Methods

2.1   Date Collection

Eight subjects were recruited for data collection including five males and three females, with ages ranging from 24 to 35 years. And each of them signed an informed consent form which was approved by the Ethics Review Board of University of Science and Technology of China. As shown in Fig. 2, a flexible 10 × 10 electrode array placed on the surface of the extensor digitorum and extensor carpi ulnaris was used to record HD-sEMG in this study. Each electrode had a 3 mm diameter dry-contact probe with a 7 mm inter-electrode distance. Each channel was processed by a two-stage amplifier with a total gain of 60 dB, a built-in band-pass filter (20–500 Hz), and 16-bit digitalization at a sampling rate 1000 Hz [13].

A set of 6 classes of gestural movements including little finger extension, middle finger extension, index finger extension, extension of both index and middle fingers, extension of the last three fingers, and wrist extension was carried in the experiment. The subjects were instructed to do each gesture with 10 repetitions, and each repetition lasting approximately 5 s. For each repetition, the sEMG signal was segmented into about 40 frames using a sliding window of size 256 ms overlapping 128 ms. The subjects were allowed to rest for 5 min to avoid muscle fatigue between consecutive trials.

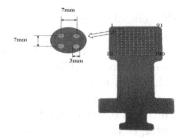

Fig. 2. The high-density electrode array we used for recording HD-sEMG data.

2.2   The Architecture of CNN Network

Lenet-5 network [14] has been widely used in the fields of gesture recognition on the basis of HD-sEMG image [15–17] because of its good performance in image classification. As shown in Fig. 3, the input to our network is sEMG image with the size of $N \times L_{row} \times L_{col}$. It contains two convolution blocks, and each block has a convolution layer, batch normalization layer, max pooling layer and dropout layer. The convolution layer is composed of several filters of 2×2 and a stride of 1 with no padding. The max pooling layer was designed with the filter of 2×2 and a stride of 1, also with no padding. To prevent the over-fitting problem, a dropout layer with a 0.2 rate was used after each max pooling layer. Then followed by the two convolution blocks were two fully-connected layers containing 128 units and 64 units separately. Two hidden layers were equipped with the Rectified Linear Unit(ReLU) activation function and the softmax activation was used in the last layer for prediction.

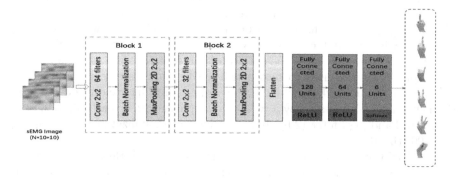

Fig. 3. The architecture of the CNN model.

2.3   Attack Algorithm

The universal adversarial perturbations (UAP) were chosen to attack the CNN-based EMG gesture recognition system because this attack approach is computed only once and be applicable to all EMG trials which is easy to use in practical applications. A successful UAP needs to satisfy two conditions:

$$\mathbb{P}_{x \sim \mu}\left(d\left(\mathbf{x}_i + \mathbf{v}\right) \neq d\left(\mathbf{x}_i\right)\right) \geq \delta \tag{1}$$

and

$$\|\mathbf{v}\|_p \leq \xi \tag{2}$$

where d $(\cdot)$ represents the classifier, $\mathbf{x}$ represents the signal, $\mathbf{v}$ represents the perturbation, δ represents the attack success rate (ASR) and ξ represents the maximum allowed strength of the UAP. In brief, (1) ensure that the UAP achieves a good attack performance and (2) ensure that perturbation is tiny [18].

DeepFool-Based UAP. DeepFool-based UAP is an attack algorithm based on decision hyperplane [18]. For a binary classification problem, suppose $\mathbf{x}$ is an input sample, and f is a classification function $f(x) = \mathbf{w}^T \mathbf{x} + \mathbf{b}$, the minimum perturbation can be given by

$$r^* = -\frac{f(x)}{\|\mathbf{w}\|_2^2} \mathbf{w} \tag{3}$$

For multi-class classification problem, the perturbation is the minimum distance of the sample to all decision hyperplanes. To ensure the constraint (2) is satisfied, the updated universal perturbation $\mathbf{v}$ is further projected onto the ℓ_p ball of radius ξ and centered at 0. The details of the DeepFool-based algorithm can be found in [18].

TLM-based UAP. TLM-based UAP directly optimize an objective function with respect to the UAP by batch gradient descent [12]. This algorithm can be summarized as solving the optimization problem below:

$$\min_{\mathbf{v}} \ E_{s \sim \mu} \ L(\mathbf{x} + \mathbf{v}, \mathbf{y}) + \beta \cdot R(\mathbf{x}, \mathbf{v}) \tag{4}$$

where $L(\mathbf{x}+\mathbf{v}, \mathbf{y})$ is the loss function, $\mathbf{y}$ is the label of the sample x, $R(\mathbf{x}, \mathbf{v})$ is the constraint on the perturbation $\mathbf{v}$, and β is the regularization coefficient. In our experiment, We set the $R(\mathbf{x}, \mathbf{v})$ as L2 regularization. For non-target attacks, L can be defined as $\log\left(p_y\left(x\right)\right)$ to minimize the predicted probability for the true class. And for target attacks, L can be defined as $-\log\left(p_y\left(x\right)\right)$ to maximum the predicted probability for the target class. The details of the TLM-based algorithm can be found in [12].

2.4 Performance Evaluation

Three metrics were employed to evaluate the test performance:

(1) Target Rate (TR), which is defined as the ratio of the number of the samples with target label to the overall number of the samples.

(2) Classification accuracy (CA), which is defined as the ratio of the overall number of properly classified samples to the overall number of samples.

(3) Signal-to-Perturbation Ratio (SPR), which can be defined as:

$$\text{SNR} = 10 \lg \left(\frac{\text{RMS}(\mathbf{X}_{EMG})}{\text{RMS}(\mathbf{X}_{The\ Adversarial\ Perturbation})} \right), \tag{5}$$

and where the root mean squared (RMS) value of $\mathbf{X}$ with the size of $P \times Q$ is defined as:

$$\text{RMS}(\mathbf{X}) = \sqrt{\frac{1}{P \cdot Q} \sum_{p=1}^{P} \sum_{q=1}^{Q} \mathbf{X}^2 (p, q)}. \tag{6}$$

3   Results and Discussions

We compare the UAP attack performance with two baselines. One is the performance of the CNN model on clean EMG signals, and the other is the performance of the CNN model on the EMG signals with Gaussian random noise $(-\xi, +\xi)$. If the classification performance can be significantly degraded by random noise under the same magnitude constraint, then there is no need to deliberately design the perturbation. Then we attack the CNN model in two ways, which are the target attack and non-target attack. We set $\xi = 0.05$ for the following experiments.

3.1   Non-target Attack on the CNN Network

Recall that the non-target attacks just force the model to misclassify the adversary instances into any class but a particular one. Figure 4 presents the classification accuracy of all subjects under two UAPs with non-target attack. The average classification rates of the CNN model on raw EMG signals, adding noise, adding DeepFool-based UAPs, adding TLM-UAPs are 93.91%, 93.80%, 34.98% and 18.32% respectively. It is obvious to see that the classification performance of the model for different gestures decreases substantially after adding UAPs, but adding the same magnitude of random noise has almost no impact on the classification ability of the CNN model. We also compute SPR of the perturbed EMG trials, which includes applying random noise, DeepFool-based UAP and TLM-based UAP with white-box attacks. The results are shown in Table 1. The perturbations generated by TLM-based UAP has the highest SPR compared to other perturbations. Figure 5 shows an example of the EMG signals for one sliding window of the diagonal channels of the electrode array before and after adversarial perturbation. The perturbation was tiny and hardly noticeable, making it difficult to detect.

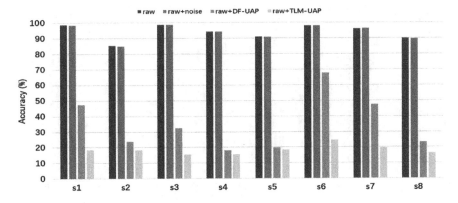

Fig. 4. The classification accuracy of all subjects with non-target attack.

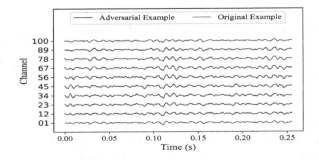

Fig. 5. An example of the EMG signals of one window before and after adversarial perturbation.

3.2 Target Attack on the CNN Network

The target attacks force the model to misclassify the adversary instances into a particular class. DF-based UAP can not perform target attack, so we only consider TLM-based UAP. In the experiment we totally have six gestures, so there are correspondingly six categories of targeted attacks. Figure 6 presents the TRs on different gestures of all subjects. The averaged TR is 86.85% of six gestures, and the TRs of the latter three categories of targeted attacks are close to 100%, which was very effective. The results indicate this method could manipulate the EMG-based control system to output any command the attacker wants, and it might be even more risky than non-target attacks.

Table 1. The SPR (dB) of EMG trials perturbed by DF-based UAP and TLM-based UAP in white-box attacks.

	Noise	DF-based UAP	TLM-based UAP
SPR	6.61	5.21	9.98

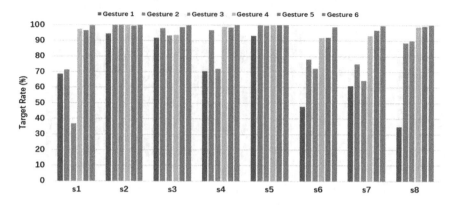

Fig. 6. The target rate of all subjects with target attack.

In this study, an attack framework based on two adversarial attack algorithms including DeepFool-based UAPs and TLM-based UAPs was proposed to attack the CNN-based EMG gesture recognition network with target and non-target paradigms. The experimental results demonstrated the vulnerability of CNN classifiers in EMG-based gesture recognition system, which exposes critical security concerns. Multiple approaches, such as gradients masking [19], auxiliary detection models [20], ensemble of classifiers [21] have been proposed to defend against adversarial instances in other fields. And what's more, the defense strategies based on adversarial training may be effective for universal adversarial perturbations, which is the direction of our future research.

References

1. Oskoei, M.A., Hu, H.: Myoelectric control systems-a survey. Biomed. Signal Process. Control **2**(4), 275–294 (2007)
2. Yang, X., Chen, X., Cao, X., Wei, S., Zhang, X.: Chinese sign language recognition based on an optimized tree-structure framework. IEEE J. Biomed. Health Inform. **21**(4), 994–1004 (2016)
3. Park, K.H., Lee, S.W.: Movement intention decoding based on deep learning for multiuser myoelectric interfaces. In: 2016 4th international winter conference on brain-computer Interface (BCI), pp. 1–2. IEEE (2016)
4. Zhang, X., Wu, D.: On the vulnerability of CNN classifiers in EEG-based BCIS. IEEE Trans. Neural Syst. Rehabil. Eng. **27**(5), 814–825 (2019)
5. Geng, W., Du, Y., Jin, W., Wei, W., Hu, Y., Li, J.: Gesture recognition by instantaneous surface EMG images. Sci. Rep. **6**(1), 1–8 (2016)
6. Ding, Z., Yang, C., Tian, Z., Yi, C., Fu, Y., Jiang, F.: SEMG-based gesture recognition with convolution neural networks. Sustainability **10**(6), 1865 (2018)
7. Goodfellow, I.J., Shlens, J., Szegedy, C.: Explaining and harnessing adversarial examples. arXiv preprint arXiv:1412.6572 (2014)
8. Kurakin, A., Goodfellow, I., Bengio, S., et al.: Adversarial examples in the physical world (2016)

9. Moosavi-Dezfooli, S.M., Fawzi, A., Frossard, P.: Deepfool: a simple and accurate method to fool deep neural networks. In: Proceedings of the IEEE Conference on Computer Vision and Pattern Recognition, pp. 2574–2582 (2016)
10. Carlini, N., Wagner, D.: Towards evaluating the robustness of neural networks. In: 2017 IEEE Symposium on Security and Privacy (SP), pp. 39–57. IEEE (2017)
11. Baluja, S., Fischer, I.: Adversarial transformation networks: learning to generate adversarial examples. arXiv preprint arXiv:1703.09387 (2017)
12. Liu, Z., Zhang, X., Meng, L., Wu, D.: Universal adversarial perturbations for CNN classifiers in EEG-based BCIS. arXiv preprint arXiv:1912.01171 (2019)
13. Zhang, X., Wu, L., Yu, B., Chen, X., Chen, X.: Adaptive calibration of electrode array shifts enables robust myoelectric control. IEEE Trans. Biomed. Eng. **67**(7), 1947–1957 (2019)
14. LeCun, Y., Bottou, L., Bengio, Y., Haffner, P.: Gradient-based learning applied to document recognition. Proc. IEEE **86**(11), 2278–2324 (1998)
15. Chen, X., Li, Y., Hu, R., Zhang, X., Chen, X.: Hand gesture recognition based on surface electromyography using convolutional neural network with transfer learning method. IEEE J. Biomed. Health Inform. **25**(4), 1292–1304 (2020)
16. Atzori, M., Cognolato, M., Müller, H.: Deep learning with convolutional neural networks applied to electromyography data: a resource for the classification of movements for prosthetic hands. Front. Neurorobot. **10**, 9 (2016)
17. Tam, S., Boukadoum, M., Campeau-Lecours, A., Gosselin, B.: A fully embedded adaptive real-time hand gesture classifier leveraging HD-SEMG and deep learning. IEEE Trans. Biomed. Circuits Syst. **14**(2), 232–243 (2019)
18. Moosavi-Dezfooli, S.M., Fawzi, A., Fawzi, O., Frossard, P.: Universal adversarial perturbations. In: Proceedings of the IEEE Conference on Computer Vision and Pattern Recognition, pp. 1765–1773 (2017)
19. Athalye, A., Carlini, N., Wagner, D.: Obfuscated gradients give a false sense of security: Circumventing defenses to adversarial examples. In: International Conference on Machine Learning, pp. 274–283. PMLR (2018)
20. Chen, J., Meng, Z., Sun, C., Tang, W., Zhu, Y.: ReabsNet: detecting and revising adversarial examples. arXiv preprint arXiv:1712.08250 (2017)
21. Abbasi, M., Gagné, C.: Robustness to adversarial examples through an ensemble of specialists. arXiv preprint arXiv:1702.06856 (2017)

MMG-HCI: A Non-contact Non-intrusive Real-Time Intelligent Human-Computer Interaction System

Peixian Gong[1,3], Chunyu Wang[1,4], and Lihua Zhang[1,2,5]([✉])

[1] Institute of AI and Robotics, Fudan University, Shanghai, China
{pxgong19,wangcy20,lihuazhang}@fudan.edu.cn
[2] Ji Hua Laboratory, Foshan, China
[3] Shanghai Engineering Research Center of AI and Robotics, Shanghai, China
[4] Engineering Research Center of AI and Robotics, Ministry of Education, Beijing, China
[5] Engineering Research Center of AI and Unmanned Vehicle Systems of Jilin Province, Changchun, China

Abstract. With the continuous development of science and technology, human-computer interaction (HCI) technology has been paid more and more attention by researchers. Traditional HCI methods, such as torch-screen, speech recognition and so on, have the problem of inconvenient application in some scenarios. The research of HCI technology based on millimeter-wave radar makes up for the deficiency of current HCI, and plays a very important role in its development. The main tasks of this paper are as follows: 1, Design of non-contact and non-invasive real-time human activity recognition system MMG-HCI. By analyzing the working features of millimeter-wave radar and combining them with the principle of computer multi-process synchronization, we designed a real-time system which integrates millimeter-wave radar data acquisition, point cloud data visualization, deep learning model inference and HCI. 2, Construction of millimeter-wave radar gesture dataset. Since there is no suitable open-source dataset at present, we collect and build our own dataset through the real-time system. 3, Training graph neural network (GNN) for HAR based on millimeter-wave radar. In order to classify the mmWave radar point cloud more accurately, we use the best performance MMPointGNN as the deep learning inference model of a real-time system. Experiments and demonstration show that we have designed an efficient, accurate, non-contact and non-invasive real-time HCI system.

Keywords: Human-computer interaction · Real-time system · Graph neural networks · Deep learning · mmWave radar

P. Gong and C. Wang—Contributed equally to this work.
This work is supported in part by the Shanghai Science and Technology Committee (STCSM) under Grant No. 19511132000 and Shanghai Municipal Science and Technology Major Project (2021SHZDZX0103).

L. Fang et al. (Eds.): CICAI 2021, LNAI 13069, pp. 158–167, 2021.
https://doi.org/10.1007/978-3-030-93046-2_14

1   Introduction

With the continuous development of science and technology, intelligent electronic devices have become an indispensable part of people's life. Improving the way of human-computer interaction (HCI) to make electronic devices more intelligent and widely used is on of the research hotspots in the field of HCI.

At present, the well-known traditional HCI methods mainly include torch screen and speech recognition. When people use smart phones, the vast majority of applications interact through the torch screen; and speech recognition technology, the most well-known is the "Siri" application developed by Apple, which can analyze people's voice through speech recognition and natural language processing (NLP) technology to achieve the specified functions. However, these HCI methods have some limitations. Touch screen technology is only used on the screen of the device, and it needs the contact and sliding between fingers and the screen; as for speech recognition technology, it collects people's voice print and other privacy information with identity recognition characteristics, which has strong invasion and privacy risk.

Radio frequency (RF) signal transceivers and environmental sensors can also be used for human activity recognition (HAR) and gesture recognition to a large extent, and they are non-contact and non-invasive. This makes up for the shortcomings of the traditional HCI methods. Researchers have proposed a WiFi-based gesture recognition system, which uses generative adversarial nets (GANs) to reduce time cost and increase sample diversity [8]. In several works [6,18,24], mmWave radar is also used for HAR and gesture recognition. Most of these technologies are designed for specific tasks and can only work in certain environments. Currently, there are only a few public datasets in the task of HAR or gesture recognition based on mmWave radar, such as MMActivity mentioned in [18]. But for HCI, ranges of motions in MMActivity are too large, and cannot bring users a good interactive experience. Therefore, we need to design our own interactive gestures and collect our own gesture recognition dataset based on mmWave radar. In our paper, mmWave radar is selected to explore its potential application in the field of HCI. We choose the mmWave radar IWR6843ISK produced by Texas Instruments (TI) to carry out the experiment.

There are many processing methods for point cloud, and the advanced deep learning methods can be divided into three categories: Convolution Neural Networks (CNNs) for voxeled point cloud, PointNet [12] and PointNet++ [13] for set representation of point cloud, Graph Neural Networks (GNNs) [6,17] for Graphical point cloud. The voxelized point cloud data contains a large number of empty voxels, and the computational cost of CNN will increase cubic with the increase of voxel resolution. The set representation of point cloud can be processed by PointNet/PointNet++. Although its computational cost is low, the accuracy of gesture recognition will also be reduced. In order to better classify the sparse point clouds generated by mmWave radar according to the time series, we use the MMPointGNN model proposed by [6] which has been proved to be highly efficient in point cloud feature extraction compared with other models.

MMPointGNN uses GNN to extract the spatial features of point clouds, and uses Bidirectional LSTM to extract the temporal features of point clouds.

In our work, we design a non-contact non-invasive real-time HCI system, which uses multiple sub processes to complete data collection, point cloud visualization and deep learning inference at the same time. The accuracy of the system if 87.27% on our own dataset. Our research shows that the final system has good stability and can be used in a variety of environments. The contributions of this paper can be summarized as follows:

1. We design an intelligent HCI system based on multi process, multi-stage pipeline and deep learning, which improves the user experience.
2. We use mmWave radar to build our own dataset as the training data of MMPointGNN, the core part of HCI system.
3. We use TI's IWR6843ISK radar to verify the performance of our system in the frequency range of 77-81 GHz. The classification accuracy of the proposed system is 87.27%, and the computing speed can reach 10 fps.

2   Related Works

2.1   Human Activity Recognition and Gesture Recognition

Human Activity Recognition (HAR) is a research hotspot in the field of computer vision in recent years, which is widely used in HCI [1–3], virtual reality [4,7,20] and video surveillance [14,15]. Although the research of HAR has made important progress in recent years, the high complexity and variability of human motion make the accuracy and efficiency of recognition not fully meet the practical requirements of related industries. Gesture is a special human activity, and it is also one of the ways to transfer information between people. The key to the success of any HCI lies in the degree of support for human intention. Compared with the traditional ways of interaction, gesture recognition [5,11,21] provides a more natural way for HCI interface.

2.2   Millimeter-Wave Radar

Gesture recognition based on mmWave radar is a method of automatic gesture recognition by using electromagnetic wave to obtain the motion features of human dynamic gesture. In recent years, it has been widely used as a simple and efficient way of information interaction. High accuracy recognition is the key of gesture recognition. Jih-Tsun [22] use mmWave radar based on range-angle image for gesture recognition. The proposed fusion model greatly improves the accuracy of mmWave radar gesture recognition. However, the dataset used in this method is a short distance dataset, which has high requirement for users. In addition, most works of gesture recognition using mmWave radar has not put forward practical workflow, but only optimizes the accuracy of classification model [9,10,16,19]. Our proposed workflow can make up for the shortcomings of previous works, and make them really available.

2.3   Graph Neural Networks

In the past few years, applications of neural network (NN) have promoted the research of pattern recognition and data mining. Many machine learning tasks that used to rely on manual feature extraction have been replaced by various deep learning models. Space based graph neural network (GNN) imitates the convolution operation of traditional convolution neural network (CNN) [23], and updates the vertex features according to the spatial relationship of vertices. MMPointGNN [6] is a network specially designed for gesture recognition based on mmWave radar. We choose it as the inference model of HCI system.

3   System Workflow

We implement a multi-process system to ensure the instantaneity of recognition. The workflow of the real-time human-computer interaction system MMG-HCI is shown in Fig. 1. It is written in Python with multiprocessing module and consists of following process instants.

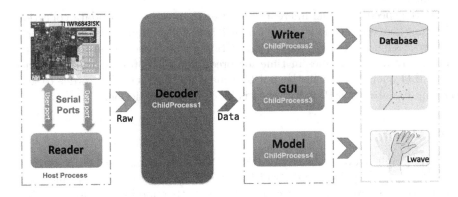

Fig. 1. Workflow of the real-time human-computer interaction system: MMG-HCI.

- **Reader:** This is the main(host) process of the system, which is mainly responsible for reading and writing millimeter-wave radar through the serial port, more specifically, loading configuration through user post and read data through data port. In addition, it will fork four child processes to handle further tasks.
- **Decoder:** This process receives bytes stream from *Reader* and decode them into structural data which contains several complete frames. Each of them consists of dozens of points described by coordinate information (x, y, z) and doppler information. These frames will be distributed to *Writer*, *GUI visualizer* and *Model predictor*.

- **Writer:** In the collection of the training data and test data, *Writer* process writes structural data into the database frame by frame. Moreover, we will also record and save video as memoisation using a RGB camera. Each entry in database contains the following fields:
  frameId,pointNum,posX,posY,posX,doppler,time.
- **GUI:** The GUI visualizer will display 3-D pointcloud frame by frame which is synchronized with radar. It provides a convenient approach for us to observe the data.
- **Model:** In the model inference part, we use a Graph Convolution Network MMPoint-GNN [6] to recognize a certain action. This model will be discussed in detail later.

3.1   Data Flow

Process safe message queues are used for interprocess communication. Process *Decoder* shares a message queue with Process *Reader* to get raw data from the radar. Process *Writer, GUI, Model* share three different message queues with Process *Decoder* but transmit the exact same data to avoid competition among consumers.

As the speed of model inference is slower than the speed of data collection, with time goes on, the model prediction will get a longer and longer delay without any processing. Therefor, a fixed length FIFO queue is used to ensure model get the exactly nearest frames in time for prediction. New frames will be pushed into FIFO queue and flush the tail to remain its fixed length in order to keep data up-to-date when Process *Model* is blocking for prediction.

3.2   Model

A novel graph neural network MMPointGNN with dynamic edges is used for processing sparse point clouds, which has been proved to be highly efficient in point cloud feature extraction compared with other models. It also combined with Bidirectional LSTM behind to build a whole recognition framework.

The MMPointGNN has improved on handling sparse point cloud data compared to primary PointGNN because of the dynamic edges selection which determines the connection of the edges among 3-D points. A Bi-LSTM is directly behind MMPointGNN, which has been proved to achieve a good performance in end-to-end learning of time sequence data.

Gesture recognition is a multi-classification problem, so we use the combination of softmax and cross entropy function as loss function.

$$loss(y, c) = -\log\left(\frac{\exp(y[c])}{\sum_{i=0}^{C-1}\exp(y[i])}\right)$$

where C is the number of classes, c is the ground truth, and $y = [y_0, ..., y_{C-1}]$ is the confidence vector predicted by the model.

4 Data Collection and Processing

4.1 Radar Configuration

We have used a TI's IWR6843ISK radar to collect our new gesture dataset which is called *mmlGesture* (millimeter-wave long-range Gesture) dataset. IWR6843ISK is an easy-to-use 60 GHz mmWave sensor which works in the 60-GHz to 64-GHz frequency range. It is a FMCW (Frequency Modulated Continuous Wave) radar which uses a chirp signal. And it includes 4 receive (RX) 3 transmit (TX) antenna with 120° azimuth field of view (FoV) and 30° elevation FoV. Also, it is able to work with or without a MMWAVEICBOOST board. So we connect the radar directly to the computer via a USB cable and communicate with it through serial ports.

4.2 Data Collection

In the part of data collection, the radar is mounted on a tripod stand at a height of 1.3 m, and the human body is about 1.3 m away from the radar, as shown in Fig. 2(a).

For better human-computer interaction experience, we designed a series of hands and arms movements corresponding to specific computer operations including *lwave, rwave, zoom in, zoom out,* as well as *click,* as shown in Fig. 2(b). All of these actions are mapped to specific computer operations respectively, such as *lwave* for hitting the left key of the keyboard while *rwave* for the right key. In addition, we collected a fair amount of *noise* data, which is under the environment of people's aimless movements. All the collected data is summarized in Table 1.

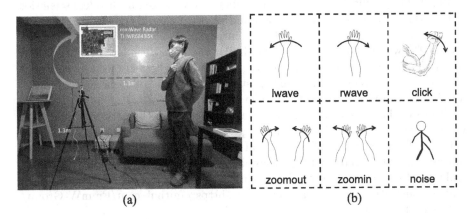

Fig. 2. Data collection. (a) devices setup and environment; (b) gestures and labels.

Table 1. Details of the mmGesture dataset.

Gesture	click	lwave	rwave	zoomin	zoomout	noise
Total frames	4196	2786	3507	4016	3882	4398
Duration (seconds)	419	279	351	401	389	440

4.3 Data Processing

The input to the model is a sequence of point cloud with the length of 20 frames which is consecutive and related to body movement. Since the data reading frequency 10 Hz, each action sequence takes approximately 2 s. For frames in an action sequence, the max-min normalization is made on x, y, z, and *doppler* axis. According to statistics, the maximum number of points (MP) in each frame of data is 105. Therefore, for frames in an action sequence whose number of points is less than MP, we will complete the frame with zero padding. While the number of points in a frame which is collected real-time may exceed MP, we will make a truncation for this frame. All actions in the training dataset were collected continuously in time, and a coherent movement may be repeated several times for minutes. To make the most of the data, we use a sliding window with a window length of 5 over the training dataset frames for a certain action when training.

5 Experiment and Demonstration

MMPointGNN algorithm achieves an accuracy of 87.27% on our own gesture dataset *mmlGesture*. The recognition accuracy of different gesture is indicated in Fig. 3. This result shows that the classifier can work well in the ideal scenarios (where the tester's location, direction and physical characteristics are the same as those of the training stage). The accuracy of *zoomin*, *click* and *noise* can reach 90%, while *lwave* and *rwave* are similar enough, which leads to insufficient discrimination between the two gestures. However, when the test environment changes, the accuracy of long-range gesture recognition will decline accordingly, and the test results will also have some fluctuations.

To solve this problem, we use a voting strategy from the latest 5 predictions. Once the voting result is identified as a gesture rather than noise, the system will enter a refractory period of 5 s to avoid reidentification. Although this measure makes the system have a little delay, it is very helpful for the accuracy and stability of the recognition results. For more information of open-source dataset and demonstration video, please access via: https://github.com/FmmW-Group/MMG-HCI.

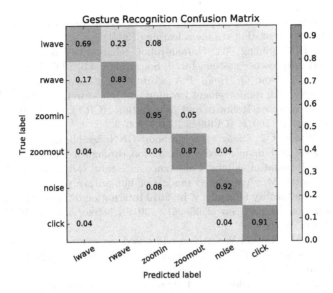

Fig. 3. The recognition accuracy of MMPointGNN for different gestures in the ideal dataset.

6 Conclusions

This paper starts with the field of HCI in the era of Internet of things, and analyzes the challenges in the field of HCI. Based on this background, our work focuses on the design of a novel non-contact, non-invasive real-time HCI system. The system adopts the method of multi-process and multi-stage pipeline architecture to realize the function integration of data collection, point cloud visualization and deep learning model inference. According to the features of sparse point cloud of mmWave radar, a new gesture dataset of mmWave radar is designed and collected. On this basis, MMPointGNN, which is more suitable for mmWave radar gesture recognition, is used as deep learning inference model. The intelligent HCI system proposed in this paper makes it possible for real-time gesture recognition based on mmWave radar to market, hoping to provide some reference for researchers in this field.

References

1. Zhdanova, M., Voronin, V., Semenishchev, E., Ilyukhin, Y., Zelensky, A.: Human activity recognition for efficient human-robot collaboration. In: Artificial Intelligence and Machine Learning in Defense Applications II (2020)
2. Anil, N., Sreeletha, S.H.: EMG based gesture recognition using machine learning. In: 2018 Second International Conference on Intelligent Computing and Control Systems (ICICCS), pp. 1560–1564 (2018). https://doi.org/10.1109/ICCONS.2018. 8662987

3. Ding, X., Jiang, T., Zhong, Y., Huang, Y., Li, Z.: Wi-fi-based location-independent human activity recognition via meta learning (2021)
4. Du, J., Do, H.M., Sheng, W.: Human-robot collaborative control in a virtual-reality-based telepresence system. Int. J. Soc. Robot. **13**, 1295–1306 (2020)
5. Gao, X., Jin, Y., Dou, Q., Heng, P.A.: Automatic gesture recognition in robot-assisted surgery with reinforcement learning and tree search. In: 2020 IEEE International Conference on Robotics and Automation (ICRA), pp. 8440–8446 (2020). https://doi.org/10.1109/ICRA40945.2020.9196674
6. Gong, P., Wang, C., Zhang, L.: Mmpoint-GNN: graph neural network with dynamic edges for human activity recognition through a millimeter-wave radar. In: 2021 The International Joint Conference on Neural Networks (IJCNN) (2021)
7. Haidu, A., Beetz, M.: Automated models of human everyday activity based on game and virtual reality technology. In: 2019 International Conference on Robotics and Automation (ICRA), pp. 2606–2612 (2019). https://doi.org/10.1109/ICRA.2019.8793859
8. Jiang, D., Li, M., Xu, C.: WiGAN: a wifi based gesture recognition system with GANs. Sensors **20**(17), 4757 (2020). https://doi.org/10.3390/s20174757, https://www.mdpi.com/1424-8220/20/17/4757
9. Li, Z., Lei, Z., Yan, A., Solovey, E., Pahlavan, K.: ThuMouse: a micro-gesture cursor input through mmWave radar-based interaction. In: 2020 IEEE International Conference on Consumer Electronics (ICCE), pp. 1–9 (2020). https://doi.org/10.1109/ICCE46568.2020.9043082
10. Liu, Y., Wang, Y., Liu, H., Zhou, A., Yang, N.: Long-Range Gesture Recognition Using Millimeter Wave Radar (2020)
11. Mahmoud, R., Belgacem, S., Omri, M.N.: Towards wide-scale continuous gesture recognition model for in-depth and grayscale input videos. Int. J. Mach. Learn. Cybern. **12**, 1–17 (2021)
12. Qi, C.R., Su, H., Mo, K., Guibas, L.J.: PointNet: deep learning on point sets for 3D classification and segmentation (2017)
13. Qi, C.R., Yi, L., Su, H., Guibas, L.J.: PointNet++: deep hierarchical feature learning on point sets in a metric space (2017)
14. Rashid, N., Demirel, B.U., Faruque, M.A.A.: AHAR: adaptive CNN for energy-efficient human activity recognition in low-power edge devices (2021)
15. Rodrigues, R., Bhargava, N., Velmurugan, R., Chaudhuri, S.: Multi-timescale trajectory prediction for abnormal human activity detection. In: 2020 IEEE Winter Conference on Applications of Computer Vision (WACV) (2020)
16. Senigagliesi, L., Ciattaglia, G., Gambi, E.: Contactless walking recognition based on MMwave radar. In: 2020 IEEE Symposium on Computers and Communications (ISCC), pp. 1–4 (2020). https://doi.org/10.1109/ISCC50000.2020.9219565
17. Shi, W., Ragunathan, R.: Point-GNN: graph neural network for 3D object detection in a point cloud. IEEE (2020)
18. Singh, A., Sandha, S., Garcia, L., Srivastava, M.: RadHAR: human activity recognition from point clouds generated through a millimeter-wave radar, pp. 51–56, October 2019. https://doi.org/10.1145/3349624.3356768
19. Smith, J.W., Thiagarajan, S., Willis, R., Makris, Y., Torlak, M.: Improved static hand gesture classification on deep convolutional neural networks using novel sterile training technique. IEEE Access **9**, 10893–10902 (2021)
20. Wang, Q., Jiao, W., Yu, R., Johnson, M.T., Zhang, Y.: Virtual reality robot-assisted welding based on human intention recognition. IEEE Trans. Autom. Sci. Eng. **17**(2), 799–808 (2020). https://doi.org/10.1109/TASE.2019.2945607

21. Xue, W.: Intelligent control system of picking robot based on visual gesture recognition. J. Agric. Mechanization Res. **42**, 249–253 (2020)
22. Yu, J., Yen, L., Tseng, P.: MMwave radar-based hand gesture recognition using range-angle image. In: 2020 IEEE 91st Vehicular Technology Conference (VTC2020-Spring), pp. 1–5 (2020). https://doi.org/10.1109/VTC2020-Spring48590.2020.9128573
23. Zhang, J.: Graph neural networks for small graph and giant network representation learning: an overview (2019)
24. Zhu, S., Xu, J., Guo, H., Liu, Q., Wu, S., Wang, H.: Indoor human activity recognition based on ambient radar with signal processing and machine learning. In: 2018 IEEE International Conference on Communications (ICC), pp. 1–6 (2018). https://doi.org/10.1109/ICC.2018.8422107

DSGSR: Dynamic Semantic Generation and Similarity Reasoning for Image-Text Matching

Xiaojing Li⬛, Bin Wang$^{(\boxtimes)}$⬛, Xiaohong Zhang⬛, and Xiaochun Yang⬛

Northeastern University, Shenyang 110819, China
{binwang,zhangxiaohong,yangxc}@mail.neu.edu.cn

Abstract. Cross-modal image-text matching is vital for building visual and language relationship. The biggest challenge is to eliminate the heterogeneity in image and text. Existing fine-grained image-text matching methods make great progress in exploring fine-grained correspondence. However, they only use the Cross-Attention method, which ignores the importance of image region semantics and dynamic image-text matching. In this paper, we propose a novel Dynamic Semantic Generation and Similarity Reasoning (DSGSR) network model for image-text matching. Specifically, we use intra-modal relations to enrich the regional features of the image. Then, in consideration of dynamic cross-modal matching, we dynamically generate the query text or image representation according to the retrieved image or text representation. We also introduce the Graph Convolutional Network (GCN) to deal with the effect of neighbor node information on matching accuracy when measuring the image-text similarity. A large number of experiments and analyses show that the DSGSR model surpass state-of-the-art methods on Flickr30K and MSCOCO datasets.

Keywords: Cross-modal · Regional semantics · Dynamic generation

1 Introduction

Due to the growth of social multimedia data, image-text matching is becoming more and more important. The task is to retrieve semantically similar text (image) for a given image (text). To a certain extent, it promotes the mutual understanding of language and vision. It can be applied to search engine platforms. The biggest challenge is how to measure the similarity of different modalities.

In order to solve the heterogeneity of different modalities, many methods are proposed. These methods can be roughly divided into coarse-grained matching

The work is partially supported by the National Natural Science Foundation of China (62072088), Ten Thousand Talent Program (ZX20200035), Liaoning Distinguished Professor (XLYC1902057), and CCF Huawei database innovation research program (No. CCF-HuaweiDBIR001A).

© Springer Nature Switzerland AG 2021
L. Fang et al. (Eds.): CICAI 2021, LNAI 13069, pp. 168–179, 2021.
https://doi.org/10.1007/978-3-030-93046-2_15

L$_1$: A younger man and an older man are shaking hands on a tennis court .

L$_2$: A man in a gray shirt and an older man are shaking hands.

L$_1$: A younger man and an older man are shaking hands on a tennis court .

L$_2$: A man in a gray shirt and an older man are shaking hands.

Fig. 1. L_1 and L_2 are texts about the image on the left. Salient regions of the image and important words of the sentence are selected on the right.

and fine-grained matching. For the coarse-grained method [8,15,17,19,20,24], the whole image and text are projected into a common embedding space respectively, and the similarity between image and text is measured by calculating vector distance. With the rapid development of deep learning, image and text features are extracted through deep neural network, and then the loss function is used to optimize the features [15,17]. That makes the distance between matching pairs smaller and smaller, and vice versa. In order to improve the accuracy, researchers introduce label information to supervise [24], and improve the loss function, such as triple loss [20], adversarial loss [19]. However, these methods hardly consider the influence of local correspondence, which may lead to sub-optimization of image-text matching. Subsequently, a large number of fine-grained research methods [5,6,9,10,12,13,22,23] are proposed and make great progress. The fine-grained approach is to divide the image into multiple regions and the text into words, aligned at the region and word levels. The similarity between image and text is measured by aggregating word-region similarity score. Karpathy et al. [9] propose that the maximum region-word similarity score correspond to each word. But it ignores the importance of different words in a sentence. Many methods [5,12] introduce attention mechanism, which explore fine-grained information better. Lee et al. [10] propose the SCAN model, introduce the attention mechanism to correspond one modal fragment to all fragments of another modality. It explores deeper fine-grained correspondence to achieve state-of-the-art performance over multiple benchmark datasets. In order to enhance the performance of the SCAN model, many methods [13,22,23] have improved the attention method.

However, the current approach has three shortcomings. Firstly, image region features are extracted through the convolution network and only the pixels of the region are analyzed. It hardly considers the relationships between regions of the image, unlike extracting word features which takes into account the relationship between words. In Fig. 1, for example, the image region *"pink"* has a certain relationship with *"old people"*, but there is no correlation between the feature representations of the two region. If the relationship between image regions can be considered, the representation of image region features will be semantic. In this way, we can better find the correlation between the image regions and the text words. Secondly, images and texts contain diversified semantics, which lack adaptability in retrieval. As shown in Fig. 1, an image corresponds to two sentences, where similar *"tennis court"* region is in L_1 but not in L_2. It may not be possible to retrieve L_2. Current methods cannot match positive samples with diverse semantics. Thirdly, they mostly rely on the similarity of significant matching fragments, without considering the influence of relevant neighbor information on the similarity score of image-text matching.

To solve these problems, this paper proposes a Dynamic Semantic Generation and Similarity Reasoning network model for image-text matching. Specifically, we first establish the intra-modality relationship for the region features of the image, and then capture the alignment between the regions and the words. Different from other methods, we use image modal relations to enrich the image representation. We also introduce the dynamic generation module to regenerate query representation, which fuses the matching information and reduces the interference of irrelevant information, so as to achieve the effect of adaptive matching. Gao et al. [4] use self-attention and cross-modal attention to realize dynamic information flow, which was different from our gating mechanism. Finally, we use vector instead of scalar when calculating similarity, because vector is conducive to further completing similarity reasoning. We introduce the GCN to further infer the image-text similarity by capturing the correlation between fragments. Our main contributions are summarized as follows:

- We propose attention mechanism for intra-modality relationship, which captures the contextual information of the image region to enrich the semantic feature representation of the image.
- We propose a dynamic generation module that generates feature representation with contextual semantic from another modal samples retrieved. It fuses with the query modal samples, selects the most semantically relevant matching information, and generates a new query representation, so as to achieve adaptive cross-modal image-text matching.
- In order to further improve the matching accuracy, we use the GCN to consider the influence of neighbor information.

2   Related Work

The essence of image-text matching is how to connect image and text and accurately measure their similarity. The existing research methods can be roughly divided into two categories: coarse-grained image-text matching and fine-grained image-text matching. Coarse-grained image-text matching is to learn the correspondence between the whole image and the text. Fine-grained image-text matching is to learn the correspondence between image regions and text words.

Coarse-Grained Image-Text Matching. Jiang et al. [8] use the methods of CNN and bag of words to extract the features of image and text, and then optimize the relationship between image and text matching pairs through the loss function. The similar pairs distance is minimized and the dissimilar pairs distance is maximized. Wang et al. [19] add adversarial network to achieve a common and effective subspace through the interaction between different modalities. Zhen et al. [24] add label constraints to optimize the network by minimizing the loss of label space and the loss between modalities. Faghri et al. [3] modify the triple ranking loss function and adopt hard negative pairs in the training process, which significantly improve the experimental performance.

Fine-Grained Image-Text Matching. Some research methods are devoted to learning the correspondence of salient objects. Karparthy et al. [9] used R-CNN for the first time to detect salient regions, and then aligned image regions with text words to optimize the most similar region-word pairs. Contextual Sentiment methods are applied in many task [7]. Anderson et al. [1] propose the application of bottom-up attention to image description and visual question-answering system. Many methods of image-text matching [2,10,18,21] are inspired by this method. Lee et al. [10] propose Stacked Cross Attention Network, which makes an image region correspond to multiple words and one word correspond to multiple regions by using the attention mechanism. It greatly improves the performance of image-text matching. In order to continue to find the image-text matching, the pre-training methods [11,14] are used to generate the representations of image and text, and good results are achieved. Nonetheless, these methods ignore image region relationship and dynamic matching of different modalities. And not considering relevant neighborhood information will affect the accuracy of image-text matching. By contrast, our method enrich regional semantic and dynamically regenerate query samples. Finally, the influence of neighbor information is also taken into account in measuring similarity.

3   Method

In this section, we describe the structural details of the DSGSR model for cross-modal image-text matching, as shown in Fig. 2.

3.1   Cross-Modal Feature Representation

Image Representation. Given an image, we extract image feature that consists of n region features f_i by bottom-up attentional pretrained on Visual Genome [1]. We further transform f_i into the feature v_i of d dimension by full connected layer. The image is represented as $V = \{v_i \mid i = 1, 2, \ldots, n, v_i \in R^d\}$, n is the number of regions in the image, $d = 1024$.

Text Representation. Given a text, the text consists of m words. A single-layer bidirectional GRU is used to extract d-dimensional word features. Each word feature t_j integrates the forward and backward context information in the text. The text is represented as $T = \{t_j \mid j = 1, 2, \ldots, m, t_j \in R^d\}$, $d = 1024$.

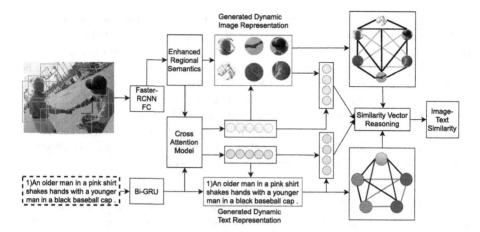

Fig. 2. Framework of the DSGSR model. A series of red circles represent word-based image features; A series of yellow circles represent region-based text features; A series of blue and purple circles represent the region-to-text similarity vector and word-to-image similarity vector respectively. (Color figure online)

3.2   Enriched Regional Semantics

Image region representation lack contextual semantics. We use the attention mechanism to aggregate the related messages between regions in the image modality, and achieve rich region feature representation. Specifically, the similarity between each region is calculated by cosine distance.

In order to make the generated region have contextual semantics, the similarity between regions is used as the weight of the corresponding region, and the new region feature representation is obtained by aggregation:

$$r_i = \sum_{j=0}^{n} \alpha_{ij} v_j, \tag{1}$$

where $\alpha_{ij} = \frac{\exp(\lambda s_{ij})}{\sum_{j=0}^{n} \exp(\lambda s_{ij})}$, s_{ij} is the similarity between i-th region and j-th region, and λ is a constant factor of the softmax function that facilitates the generation of regions with contextual semantics. The new image is represented as $R = \{r_i \mid i = 1, 2, \ldots, n, r_i \in R^d\}$.

3.3   Dynamic Generation Module

The dynamic generation module is used to generate new query representation to achieve the effect of flexible retrieval. Firstly, the attention retrieval sample representation is generated by the cross-modal attention mechanism [10]. Then it is fused with the query sample to generate a new query representation. For example, image-to-text matching, an image has five corresponding text. An image representation is updated once for a text, but the new image representation is only used to reason about the current text. The whole dynamic generation module includes dynamic image generation and dynamic text generation.

Dynamic Image Generation. In image-to-text matching, text representation focusing on each region of the image is generated by:

$$c_i^t = \sum_{j=0}^{m} \alpha_{ij}^v t_j, \tag{2}$$

where $\alpha_{ij}^v = \frac{\exp(\lambda s_{ij}^v)}{\sum_{j=0}^{m} \exp(\lambda s_{ij}^v)}$, s_{ij}^v is the similarity between i-th region and j-th word, and c_i^t is a textual representation of the i-th region by the cross-modal attention [10]. The text about all regions of the image is represented as $C^t = \{c_i^t \mid i = 1, 2, \ldots, n, c_i^t \in R^d\}$.

Region features are fused with similar textual features based the region, otherwise the region features are retained. Inspired by GRU, the gate mechanism is adopted to achieve. First calculate the update gate:

$$p_i^r = \sigma \left(w_{pr} \left[r_i, c_i^t \right] + b_{pr} \right), \tag{3}$$

where σ is the sigmoid activation function, and w_{pr}, b_{pr} are the learning parameters.

In order to enhance the similar information of region features and textual features about the region, the two are fused:

$$\begin{aligned} m_i &= r_i \oplus c_i^t \\ o_i^r &= \tanh \left(w_{or} m_i + b_{or} \right), \end{aligned} \tag{4}$$

where o_i^r is the fusion feature, w_{or} and b_{or} are learnable parameters, $\oplus$ denotes element-wise sum.

Finally, the Update Gate effectively integrates region features and fusion features to dynamically generate image region representations:

$$r_i^* = p_i^r * r_i + (1 - p_i^r) * o_i^r. \tag{5}$$

In the past, cosine similarity was used to get scalar to measure similarity, but it could not capture the finer grain correspondence of image-text. Therefore, we adopt the method of calculating the similarity vector between the new region r_i^* and the text representation c_i^t concerned with the image region:

$$\begin{aligned} \mathrm{srv}\left(r_i^*, c_i^t\right) &= \frac{W_{sr} \max\left(0, r_i^* * c_i^t\right)}{\left\| W_{sr} \max\left(0, r_i^* * c_i^t\right) \right\|_2}, \\ \mathrm{srv}_i &= \mathrm{srv}\left(r_i^*, c_i^t\right), \end{aligned} \tag{6}$$

where $w_{sr} \in R^{t \times d}$ is a learning parameter matrix, and $\| \cdot \|_2$ is l_2−norm. The image-to-text similar vector matrix denotes $S^r = \{srv_i^r \mid i = 1, \ldots, n, srv_i^r \in R^t\}$.

Dynamic Text Generation. In text-to-image matching, this process is completely symmetric with dynamic image generation. The word-image feature is c_j^v. Dynamic text representation is generated: $p_j^t = \sigma\left(w_{pt}\left[t_j, c_j^v\right] + b_{pt}\right)$; $m_j^* = t_j \oplus c_j^v$; $o_j^t = \tanh\left(w_{ot}m_j^* + b_{ot}\right)$; $t_j^* = p_j^t * t_j + \left(1 - p_j^t\right) * o_j^t$. Computing text similarity word and image region vector: $stv\left(t_j^*, c_j^v\right) = \dfrac{W_{st}\max\left(0, t_j^* * c_j^v\right)}{\left\|w_{st}\max\left(0, t_j^* * c_j^v\right)\right\|_2}$. The text-to-image similar vector matrix denotes that $S^t = \left\{stv_j^t \mid j = 1, 2, \dots, m, stv_j^t \in R^t\right\}$.

3.4 Similarity Reasoning Module

The word-region similarity is affected by the neighbor information, and the related neighbor relationship increases the similarity score of the matching pair. We construct a graph structure for regions (words), and then implement similarity reasoning using a layer of GCN on the graph structure.

Build a Graph. In a specified image, the region is regarded as a node to construct a full-connection graph, and the weight of edges $W_e^r \in R^{n \times n}$ is calculated by using cosine similarity. In a specified text, a word is regarded as a node, the graph is constructed with full connection, and the weight of edges $W_e^t \in R^{m \times m}$ is calculated by cosine similarity.

Graph Reasoning. In the image-to-text matching, we use adjacent information to find more similar matching on the visual graph. Specifically, the similarity vectors S^r is inferred by using the weight W_e^r. We use a layer of GCN to update similarity vectors S^r on the visual graph. Specific implementation is as follows:

$$S^{r*} = \tanh\left(W_e^r W_{gr} S^r\right), \tag{7}$$

where $W_{gr} \in R^{n \times n}$, $S^{r*} = \left\{s_j^{r*} \mid j = 1, 2, \dots, m, s_j^{r*} \in R^t\right\}$ is image-to-text similarity vector matrix.

In the text-to-image matching, GCN is used to make inference on the text graph to update similarity vector matrix $S^{t*} = \tanh\left(W_e^t W_{gt} S^t\right)$, where $W_{gt} \in R^{m \times m}$. Finally, in order to obtain the global similarity between the image and the text, we aggregate image-to-text global similarity and text-to-image global similarity scores. And we use the full connection layer to infer global similarity:

$$\begin{aligned} g_v &= \frac{1}{n}\sum_{i=1}^n \tanh\left(w_{hr}s_i^{r*} + b_{hr}\right) \\ g_t &= \frac{1}{m}\sum_{j=1}^m \tanh\left(w_{ht}s_j^{t*} + b_{ht}\right) \\ G(I, T) &= g_v + g_t, \end{aligned} \tag{8}$$

where $w_{hr} \in R^{1 \times t}$ and $w_{ht} \in R^{1 \times t}$, g_v is the global similarity of the image-to-text, g_t is the global similarity of the text-to-image, and $G(I, T)$ is the global similarity of the image and the text.

Objective Function. The hard triplet ranking loss function is very effective in the image-text matching task [3,23].

$$L = \sum_{i=0}^{B} [\beta - G\left(I_i, T_i\right) + G\left(I_i, T_{i*}\right)]_+ + \sum_{i=0}^{B} [\beta - G\left(I_i, T_i\right) + G\left(I_{i*}, T_i\right)]_+, \quad (9)$$

where T_{i*} and I_{i*} are the hard negatives, which are the highest score negatives. $[\cdot]_+$ represents max(), β is a margin value and B is the batch size.

4 Experiments

4.1 Datasets

We evaluate the model on two commonly used benchmark datasets, Flickr30k and MSCOCO. Each dataset is made up of an image corresponding to five pieces of text. Flickr30k collects $31,000$ images and $155,000$ texts from the Flickr website. According to the previous method [10], the dataset is divided into $29,000$ images for training, $1,000$ images for validation, and $1,000$ images for testing. The MSCOCO dataset consists of $123,287$ images and corresponding $616,435$ texts. We use $113,287$ images as the training set, $5,000$ images as the validation, and the remaining $5,000$ images as the training set. The test evaluation results of MSCOCO are averaged across 5 folders of $1,000$ image pairs.

4.2 Experimental Settings

The most commonly used evaluation criterion for image-text matching is Recall@K (R@K). In order to compare with the optimal model, we selected R@1, R@5, and R@10 to represent the percentage of real samples retrieved in the top 1, 5, and 10 to measure the performance of image-text bidirectional retrieval.

In this work, some of the parameters are set as follows. For the images, we used Fasters-RCNN [16] to detect and extract $n = 36$ salient regions with the feature of 2048 dimensions in each region by RESNET-101. For the text, the word vector size dimension is set to 300. The epoch for training is set to 30 and 20 respectively on Flickr30K and MSCOCO. The learning rate is set to 0.0002 and drops 10% for every 15 epochs on Flickr30K. The learning rate starts with a value of 0.0005 and decreases by 10% per 5 epochs in MSCOCO. Adam algorithm was used to optimize the training process, and the minimum batch was set to 64. Set the constant factor $\lambda = 9$ for softmax and $\beta = 0.2$ in the loss function. The dimension setting of the similarity vector is $t = 16$.

4.3 Experimental Results

Results in Flickr30K. Our method is compared with the experiment results of the previous method in Table 1. In contrast to SCAN, our model improves

Table 1. Comparisons of image-text matching results on Flickr30K and MSCOCO.

Methods	Flickr30K dataset						MSCOCO dataset					
	Sentence retrieval			Image retrieval			Sentence retrieval			Image retrieval		
	R@1	R@5	R@10	R@1	R@5	R@10	R@1	R@5	R@10	R@1	R@5	R@10
SCO [6]	55.5	82.0	89.3	41.1	70.5	80.1	69.9	92.9	97.5	56.7	87.5	94.8
SCAN [10]	67.4	90.3	95.8	48.6	77.7	85.2	72.7	94.8	98.4	58.8	88.4	94.8
BFAN [13]	68.1	91.4	–	50.8	78.4	–	74.9	95.2	–	59.4	88.4	–
PFAN [22]	70.0	91.8	95.0	50.4	78.7	86.1	76.5	**96.3**	**99.0**	61.6	89.6	95.2
CAAN [23]	70.1	91.6	97.2	52.8	79.0	**87.9**	75.5	95.4	98.5	61.3	89.7	95.2
DSGSR	**72.1**	**93.0**	**97.3**	**54.2**	**79.5**	87.0	**76.8**	95.7	98.5	**62.8**	**90.1**	**95.6**

Table 2. The effect of different network structres on Flickr30K and MSCOCO.

Methods	Flickr30K dataset						MSCOCO dataset					
	Sentence retrieval			Image retrieval			Sentence retrieval			Image retrieval		
	R@1	R@5	R@10	R@1	R@5	R@10	R@1	R@5	R@10	R@1	R@5	R@10
$w/o\ ER$	71.6	92.3	96.5	53.8	78.6	86.1	75.7	95.2	98.3	62.0	89.5	95.1
$w/o\ DG$	70.7	91.1	96.3	53.7	78.7	86.1	75.0	94.7	98.4	61.1	88.7	94.9
$w/o\ SR$	70.9	91.7	96.7	53.4	78.0	85.8	75.4	94.8	98.4	61.3	89.3	94.8
DSGSR	**72.1**	**93.0**	**97.3**	**54.2**	**79.5**	**87.0**	**76.8**	**95.7**	**98.5**	**62.8**	**90.1**	**95.6**

sentence retrieval by 4.7%(R@1) and image retrieval 5.6%(R@1). Compared with the BFAN and CAAN models that consider information intra-modality, and SCO models that consider semantics, the performance of our model is improved. Our method achieves 72.1%(R@1) and 93.0%(R@5) on text retrieval tasks, 54.2%(R@1) and 79.5%(R@5) on the image retrieval task.

Results in MSCOCO. Our model improved sentence retrieval by 4.1%(R@1) and image retrieval 4.0%(R@1) over the previous best model SCAN in Table 1. Compared with BFAN which takes into account intra-modal and inter-modal relationships, improved by 1.9%(R@1) and 1.7%(R@1) in both text retrieval and image retrieval respectively. Our method reached 76.8%(R@1) and 62.8%(R@1) in the text retrieval task and image retrieval task, respectively.

4.4 Ablation Studies

In this section, we conduct corresponding experiment analysis on the contribution of three modules, enriched regional semantics, dynamic generation module and similarity reasoning module. Firstly, replace the enriched region representation module with the region feature without context semantics, as "*w/o ER*" method. Secondly, the dynamic generated module is replaced by the stacked cross-attention in the SCAN model, as "*w/o DG*" method. Thirdly, the similarity vector reasoning module is removed, as "*w/o SR*" method.

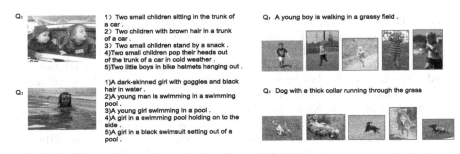

Fig. 3. Qualitative results of the image-to-text and text-to-image matching on Flickr30K. We show the ranking top-5 retrieval results, with green for positive and red for negative. (Color igure online)

From Table 2, we can see that "*w/o ER*", "*w/o DG*" and "*w/o SR*" reduce the overall model performance by 0.5%(R@1), 1.4%(R@1) and 1.2%(R@1) on Flickr30K, respectively. Meanwhile, "*w/o ER*", "*w/o DG*" and "*w/o SR*" reduced the overall performance of the model by 1.1%(R@1), 1.8%(R@1) and 1.4%(R@1) on MSCOCO, respectively. Therefore, each module plays a vital role in the overall model, and the lack of any module will reduce the model performance to a certain extent.

4.5   Qualitative Result

We present the qualitative results of image-text matching on Flickr30K in Fig. 3. Our model retrieves the best matching image in the text-to-image matching. Although there are four negative matches, they are similar to the query sentence. The text with the best match is also retrieved in the text-to-image. For example, it can find regions that include "*dog*", "*grass*", and "*run*" in the lower right corner of Fig. 3. It can be seen that our model can achieve the effect of dynamic matching and search for relevant semantic results to the greatest extent.

5   Conclusion

In this work, we propose Dynamic Semantic Generation and Similarity Reasoning (DSGSR) image-text matching to enrich image representation and address semantic diversity. We introduce a dynamic generation module to solve semantic diversity, enriched regional semantic representation and similarity vector reasoning to explore fine-grained correspondence. Therefore, the whole model considers the intra-modality and inter-modality relationship, and realizes dynamic matching. A large number of experiments on benchmark datasets demonstrate the effectiveness of our model.

References

1. Anderson, P., et al.: Bottom-up and top-down attention for image captioning and VQA. CoRR abs/1707.07998 (2017)

2. Chen, T., Luo, J.: Expressing objects just like words: recurrent visual embedding for image-text matching. In: The Thirty-Fourth AAAI Conference on Artificial Intelligence, AAAI 2020, The Thirty-Second Innovative Applications of Artificial Intelligence Conference, IAAI 2020, The Tenth AAAI Symposium on Educational Advances in Artificial Intelligence, EAAI 2020, New York, NY, USA, February 7–12, 2020, pp. 10583–10590. AAAI Press (2020)

3. Faghri, F., Fleet, D.J., Kiros, J.R., Fidler, S.: VSE++: improving visual-semantic embeddings with hard negatives. In: British Machine Vision Conference 2018, BMVC 2018, Newcastle, UK, September 3–6, 2018, p. 12. BMVA Press (2018)

4. Gao, P., et al.: Dynamic fusion with intra- and inter- modality attention flow for visual question answering. CoRR abs/1812.05252 (2018). http://arxiv.org/abs/1812.05252

5. Hu, Z., Luo, Y., Lin, J., Yan, Y., Chen, J.: Multi-level visual-semantic alignments with relation-wise dual attention network for image and text matching. In: Kraus, S. (ed.) Proceedings of the Twenty-Eighth International Joint Conference on Artificial Intelligence, IJCAI 2019, Macao, China, August 10–16, 2019, pp. 789–795. ijcai.org (2019)

6. Huang, Y., Wu, Q., Song, C., Wang, L.: Learning semantic concepts and order for image and sentence matching. In: 2018 IEEE Conference on Computer Vision and Pattern Recognition, CVPR 2018, Salt Lake City, UT, USA, June 18–22, 2018, pp. 6163–6171. IEEE Computer Society (2018)

7. Ito, T., Tsubouchi, K., Sakaji, H., Yamashita, T., Izumi, K.: Contextual sentiment neural network for document sentiment analysis. Data Sci. Eng. 5(2), 180–192 (2020). https://doi.org/10.1007/s41019-020-00122-4

8. Jiang, Q., Li, W.: Deep cross-modal hashing. CoRR abs/1602.02255 (2016)

9. Karpathy, A., Joulin, A., Li, F.: Deep fragment embeddings for bidirectional image sentence mapping. In: Ghahramani, Z., Welling, M., Cortes, C., Lawrence, N.D., Weinberger, K.Q. (eds.) Advances in Neural Information Processing Systems 27: Annual Conference on Neural Information Processing Systems 2014, December 8–13 2014, Montreal, Quebec, Canada, pp. 1889–1897 (2014)

10. Lee, K.-H., Chen, X., Hua, G., Hu, H., He, X.: Stacked cross attention for image-text matching. In: Ferrari, V., Hebert, M., Sminchisescu, C., Weiss, Y. (eds.) ECCV 2018. LNCS, vol. 11208, pp. 212–228. Springer, Cham (2018). https://doi.org/10.1007/978-3-030-01225-0_13

11. Li, G., Duan, N., Fang, Y., Gong, M., Jiang, D.: Unicoder-vl: a universal encoder for vision and language by cross-modal pre-training. In: The Thirty-Fourth AAAI Conference on Artificial Intelligence, AAAI 2020, The Thirty-Second Innovative Applications of Artificial Intelligence Conference, IAAI 2020, The Tenth AAAI Symposium on Educational Advances in Artificial Intelligence, EAAI 2020, New York, NY, USA, February 7–12, 2020, pp. 11336–11344. AAAI Press (2020)

12. Li, S., Xiao, T., Li, H., Yang, W., Wang, X.: Identity-aware textual-visual matching with latent co-attention. In: IEEE International Conference on Computer Vision, ICCV 2017, Venice, Italy, October 22–29, 2017, pp. 1908–1917. IEEE Computer Society (2017)

13. Liu, C., Mao, Z., Liu, A., Zhang, T., Wang, B., Zhang, Y.: Focus your attention: a bidirectional focal attention network for image-text matching. In: Amsaleg, L., et al. (eds.) Proceedings of the 27th ACM International Conference on Multimedia, MM 2019, Nice, France, October 21–25, 2019, pp. 3–11. ACM (2019)

14. Lu, J., Batra, D., Parikh, D., Lee, S.: Vilbert: pretraining task-agnostic visiolinguistic representations for vision-and-language tasks. In: Wallach, H.M., Larochelle, H., Beygelzimer, A., d'Alché-Buc, F., Fox, E.B., Garnett, R. (eds.) Advances in Neural Information Processing Systems 32: Annual Conference on Neural Information Processing Systems 2019, NeurIPS 2019, December 8–14, 2019, Vancouver, BC, Canada, pp. 13–23 (2019)

15. Mithun, N.C., Panda, R., Papalexakis, E.E., Roy-Chowdhury, A.K.: Webly supervised joint embedding for cross-modal image-text retrieval. In: Boll, S., et al. (eds.) 2018 ACM Multimedia Conference on Multimedia Conference, MM 2018, Seoul, Republic of Korea, October 22–26, 2018, pp. 1856–1864. ACM (2018)

16. Ren, S., He, K., Girshick, R.B., Sun, J.: Faster R-CNN: towards real-time object detection with region proposal networks. IEEE Trans. Pattern Anal. Mach. Intell. **39**(6), 1137–1149 (2017)

17. Sarafianos, N., Xu, X., Kakadiaris, I.A.: Adversarial representation learning for text-to-image matching. In: 2019 IEEE/CVF International Conference on Computer Vision, ICCV 2019, Seoul, Korea (South), October 27 - November 2, 2019, pp. 5813–5823. IEEE (2019)

18. Shi, B., Ji, L., Lu, P., Niu, Z., Duan, N.: Knowledge aware semantic concept expansion for image-text matching. In: Kraus, S. (ed.) Proceedings of the Twenty-Eighth International Joint Conference on Artificial Intelligence, IJCAI 2019, Macao, China, August 10–16, 2019, pp. 5182–5189. ijcai.org (2019)

19. Wang, B., Yang, Y., Xu, X., Hanjalic, A., Shen, H.T.: Adversarial cross-modal retrieval. In: Liu, Q., et al. (eds.) Proceedings of the 2017 ACM on Multimedia Conference, MM 2017, Mountain View, CA, USA, October 23–27, 2017, pp. 154–162. ACM (2017)

20. Wang, L., Li, Y., Huang, J., Lazebnik, S.: Learning two-branch neural networks for image-text matching tasks. IEEE Trans. Pattern Anal. Mach. Intell. **41**(2), 394–407 (2019)

21. Wang, S., Wang, R., Yao, Z., Shan, S., Chen, X.: Cross-modal scene graph matching for relationship-aware image-text retrieval. In: IEEE Winter Conference on Applications of Computer Vision, WACV 2020, Snowmass Village, CO, USA, March 1–5, 2020, pp. 1497–1506. IEEE (2020)

22. Wang, Y., et al.: Position focused attention network for image-text matching. In: Kraus, S. (ed.) Proceedings of the Twenty-Eighth International Joint Conference on Artificial Intelligence, IJCAI 2019, Macao, China, August 10–16, 2019, pp. 3792–3798. ijcai.org (2019)

23. Zhang, Q., Lei, Z., Zhang, Z., Li, S.Z.: Context-aware attention network for image-text retrieval. In: 2020 IEEE/CVF Conference on Computer Vision and Pattern Recognition, CVPR 2020, Seattle, WA, USA, June 13–19, 2020, pp. 3533–3542. IEEE (2020)

24. Zhen, L., Hu, P., Wang, X., Peng, D.: Deep supervised cross-modal retrieval. In: IEEE Conference on Computer Vision and Pattern Recognition, CVPR 2019, Long Beach, CA, USA, June 16–20, 2019, pp. 10394–10403. Computer Vision Foundation/IEEE (2019)

Phase Partition Based Virtual Metrology for Material Removal Rate Prediction in Chemical Mechanical Planarization Process

Wenlan Jiang, Chunpu Lv, Tao Zhang, and Huangang Wang[✉]

Department of Automation, Tsinghua University, Beijing, China
{jwl18,lvcp16}@mails.tsinghua.edu.cn, {taozhang,hgwang}@tsinghua.edu.cn

Abstract. In semiconductor manufacturing, the average Material Removal Rate (MRR) in Chemical Mechanical Planarization (CMP) process is important but difficult to measure. A useful method to predict MRR is to build a data-driven model for virtual metrology and a common step in virtual metrology is feature generation. However, few researches notice that the CMP process is a multi-phase batch process. Variable correlation varies with the phase variation. Thus, feature generation for the CMP process should consider the phase change to make the most of the process data. Inspired by this view, a phase partition-based virtual metrology method is proposed to predict MRR. In the proposed methodology, a novel phase partition and phase match method is first proposed to identify the stable phases in the batch process. And then statistical features are extracted from the time series of process variables and the filter-based feature selection method is designed to remove the irrelevant and redundant features. Based on the selected feature subset, a regression model is trained to predict the MRR. The effectiveness of the proposed method is evaluated on a challenge dataset.

Keywords: Chemical Mechanical Planarization · Material Removal Rate · Virtual metrology · Multi-phase character · Phase partition · Phase match

1 Introduction

In semiconductor manufacturing, Chemical Mechanical Planarization (CMP) process is one of the most important steps. The average Material Removal Rate (MRR) refers to the speed that the material is removed from the surface of the wafer in the CMP process and is recognized as a key indicator to assess the equipment status and polishing quality. However, the measurement of MRR will affect the production speed and extend the production cycle. Therefore, Virtual

Supported by National Science and Technology Innovation 2030 Major Project (2018AAA0101604) of the Ministry of Science and Technology of China.

L. Fang et al. (Eds.): CICAI 2021, LNAI 13069, pp. 180–190, 2021.
https://doi.org/10.1007/978-3-030-93046-2_16

Metrology (VM) has attracted the extensive attention of researchers. By virtual metrology, some hard-to-measure important quality indicators like MRR can be inferred through other variables easy to be obtained in the production process.

VM can be divided into physics-based methods and data-based methods. Taking the MRR prediction as an example, Preston Equation and Luo&Dornfeld Model are two typical physics-based VM models [7,15]. Compared to the physical models, data-driven models are much easier to constructed and widely applied in MRR prediction. Di et al. proposed an integrated model to predict MRR and reported improved prediction accuracy [3]. Jia et al. introduced the Group Method of Data Handling (GMDH) type polynomial Neural Network for adaptive feature selection and model selection for enhanced MRR prediction [6]. Deep Learning-based methods such as Deep Belief Network [16], and the Residual Convolutional Neural Network (ResCNN) [17] were applied, while ensemble-based approaches like random forest and stacking techniques were tried and acceptable prediction accuracy was given [11,12,19]. Some other researches focused on prediction uncertainty [1], just-in-time based VM [2], and automatic model updating for online prediction [4].

All the above-mentioned data-driven methods contain a common feature generation step but few consider the multi-phase character of the CMP process. As a typical batch process, the 3D data of the CMP process contains batch dimension, variable dimension, and time dimension. And with the multi-phase character, variable correlations vary with phase change. Extracting features for the whole time series of each process variable will lose much dynamic information and affect the prediction accuracy. Thus, feature extraction for each phase becomes significant. In this paper, a phase partition and phase match-based data-driven VM model is proposed for MRR prediction. Firstly, a Warped K-Means (WKM) algorithm combining with Phase Partition Combination Index (PPCI), called WKM-PPCI, is used for phase partition with uneven-length batch duration [9,13,14]. Then a four-step stable phase match algorithm is proposed since the phase partition results of WKM-PPCI are unequal. Given stable phase of the equal size, parallel feature extraction and parallel filter-based feature selection are conducted for each phase. Lastly, the remained feature sets are combined as the input to train the final regression model. The proposed method is evaluated on the PHM16 dataset and enhanced prediction performance is obtained with the phase partition and phase match.

The rest of this paper is organized as follows: Sect. 2 introduces the proposed method, including the detailed description for phase partition and phase match. Section 3 gives a case study and shows the effectiveness of the proposed method on the PHM16 dataset. Section 4 concludes.

2   Method

The flow of data processing and prediction is shown in Fig. 1. Data cleaning is the first step. When a batch process has MRR that deviates far from normal, or when the sampling length is too long or too short which means reworking or data missing, the corresponding batch process data needs to be removed.

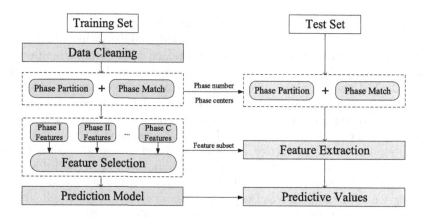

Fig. 1. The framework

The WKM algorithm incorporating the PPCI is used for phase partition and a novel phase match algorithm is adopted for consistent phase partition results, which are described in detail in Sect. 2.1 and 2.2.

Based on the consistent phase partition results, feature extraction and feature selection is used to generate feature vector with equal length and remove the irrelevant or redundant features, respectively. Finally, a regression model is used to fuse the multi-phase information and predict the final MRR.

2.1 Phase Partition Based on WKM and PPCI

Considering the more common scenarios, the phase partition methods for batch processes with uneven-length batch duration can be divided into PCA-based and clustering-based [10,13,14,18]. Compared to clustering-based phase partition methods, PCA-based phase partition methods for uneven batch duration are usually time-consuming and the minimum length requirements may not be met due to the rapid change of the transition phase [10,18]. So we apply the clustering-based phase partition method Warped K-means for uneven batch processes.

Considering a CMP batch process containing I normal batches, every batch has J variables and K_i timestamps, forming an irregular 3-dimensional matrix $\boldsymbol{X}$. The data of the i-th batch is $\boldsymbol{X}_i = [\boldsymbol{x}_1^i, \boldsymbol{x}_2^i, \dots, \boldsymbol{x}_{K_i}^i], \boldsymbol{x}_k^i \in \mathbb{R}^{J \times 1}$ is called a sampling point, $k = 1, 2, \dots, K_i$. Given the clustering number C, the optimization goal of WKM is to divide the process into time sequential clusters to minimize the Sum of Squared Error (SSE). The c-th cluster contains data of $\boldsymbol{X}_c = [\boldsymbol{x}_{b_c}, \boldsymbol{x}_{b_c+1}, \dots, \boldsymbol{x}_{b_c+n_c-1}]$, where b_c is the starting point, and n_c is the size of the c-the cluster. The objective function is shown as Eq. (1).

$$L = \sum_{c=1}^{C} L_c = \sum_{c=1}^{C} \sum_{k=b_c}^{b_c+n_c-1} (\boldsymbol{x}_k - \boldsymbol{\mu}_c)^{\mathrm{T}} (\boldsymbol{x}_k - \boldsymbol{\mu}_c) \tag{1}$$

where μ_c is the center of the c-th cluster, which is obtained by calculating the mean value of the sampling points belonging to the cluster.

In the WKM algorithm, the time sequence continuity is reflected by limiting the clusters that the sampling points attach to. For a specific cluster, sampling points in the first half can only be moved to the former cluster or remain unchanged. Sampling points in the second half can only be moved to the latter cluster or remain unchanged.

The WKM algorithm can only provide the clustering process of a single batch under the given clustering number C. But C needs to be determined by other methods. SSE decreases with the increase of C, but too large C will lead to scattered phases and the increase of computational complexity. Taking SSE and clustering number C into consideration, PPCI is presented to identify the turning point where SSE changes from rapid decline to weak decline or gradually remains stable. The calculation method of PPCI is shown in Eq. (2):

$$PPCI_C = \gamma \hat{L}_C + (1 - \gamma)\hat{C} \tag{2}$$

where $\hat{C}$ is the value of clustering number after normalization, and $\hat{L}_C$ is the normalized SSE after calculating the natural logarithm. The parameter $\gamma \in [0, 1]$ plays a key role in balancing SSE and the clustering number.

2.2   Phase Match

For batch data with dramatic changes in the transition phases, when C is very large, SSE will still significantly decrease. In this case, C corresponding to the minimum value of PPCI is the total number of stable phases and transition phases. Furthermore, as the transition phase partition is different, the clustering numbers are also different between batches. However, the characters of stable phases are usually continuous between batches and the number of stable phases is relatively constant. If the stable phases can be extracted, the phase partition can be unified accordingly and the process of stable phase extraction can be called phase match.

Given the WKM-based phase partition results of I batches, the left boundaries of i-th batch is denoted as $\{b_c^i | c = 1, 2, \ldots, C_i\}$, where C_i is the optimal number of phases selected by minimum PPCI, and the cluster centers are denoted as $\{\mu_c^i | c = 1, 2, \ldots, C_i\}$. The phase match algorithm is described as follows.

(1) **Determine the number of standard stable phases.** Setting the minimum sampling length L_S, and the number of phases with sampling length more than L_S of each batch is counted as $C_s = \{\tilde{n}_i | i = 1, 2, \ldots, I\}$. The mode of C_S, represented by C_s^* is selected as the number of standard stable phases.

(2) **Iterative adjustment of the RCSP.** RCSP is the abbreviation of representative centers of stable phases. The initial RCSP can be obtained by averaging the centers of the stable phases in batches that meets $C_i = C_S^*$, that is, $\mu_c^{initial} = mean(\{\mu_c^i | C_i = C_S^*, i = 1, 2, \ldots, I\})$. Then, RCSP is recalculated after excluding those batches with C_S^* stable phases but have large distances from RCSP, and the iteration is carried out until RCSP remains unchanged.

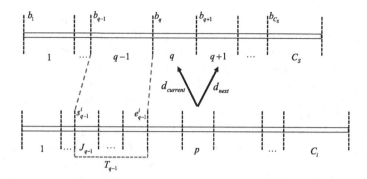

Fig. 2. The phase match algorithm

(3) **Match the phase partition of each batch with the RCSP.** This step is only for batches that do not participate in the final RCSP calculation in Step (2). Given the RCSP and the phase partition of each batch, the phase match of the i-th batch can be modeled as an optimization problem.

In the i-th batch, the c-th RCSP corresponds to continuous T_c phases from phase J_c, the distance from the centers of T_c phases to the c-th RCSP cannot be larger than the threshold θ. s_c^i and e_c^i are the start point and end point after match, $n_c^i = e_c^i - s_c^i$ represents the length, and $\tilde{\mu}_c^i$ is the updated phase center. The optimization problem can be solved by greedy algorithm.

As shown in Fig. 2, for the i-th batch, there are $q - 1$ stable phases and $p - 1$ phases have been matched. Along the direction of time dimension, the p-th phase and its phase center μ_p^i are first selected, and the distances between μ_p^i and two adjacent standard stable phase centers μ_q^s and μ_{q+1}^s, $d_{cur} = dist(\mu_p, \mu_q^s)$, $d_{next} = dist(\mu_p^i, \mu_{q+1}^s)$, are calculated successively. Comparing the relative sizes of these two distances to the threshold θ, and the suitable standard stable phase to match is determined. Only when $d_{next} < d_{cur}$ and $d_{next} < \theta$, $q = q + 1$. A balance parameter ρ is used to balance the match distance and the length of matched phase length. The match cost is defined as the match distance subtracts the match length times ρ. The continuous several phases with minimum match cost will be selected as the matched phase for the p-th stable phase.

(4) **Adjust the start and end points of the stable phases.** After the phase match in Step (3), some sampling points may fail to find a proper stable phase and can be mistakenly assigned to the transition phases. In the i-th batch, the range of the c-th stable phase is $[s_q^i, e_q^i]$, so the range of transition phases that need to be adjusted are (e_{q-1}^i, s_q^i) and (e_q^i, s_{q+1}^i).

2.3 Feature Extraction and Feature Selection

After phase partition and phase match, the statistics of each phase are calculated as the original feature set. Besides, the MRR of the time-nearest-neighbors and the usage-nearest-neighbors are extracted and added to the feature set. The usage-nearest-neighbors are emphasized for similar usages tend to generate similar MRRs. After the feature extraction, feature selection is also applied to remove irrelevant or redundant features. Here, a parallel feature selection for each phase is implemented. Considering the selection efficiency, the filter method is applied. Features with a single value, high multicollinearity, or low importance are removed.

2.4   Regression Model

The input of the final regression model is the concatenated feature vector of every single phase. Which kind of regression model to choose is decided by the cross-validation result on the train set or the validation result on the validation set. And the ensemble models tend to have better performance than the single regression model.

3   Case Study

3.1   Description of the Dataset

The PHM16 Dataset from the 2016 Prognostics and Health Management Data Challenge consisting of a training set, a validation set, and a test set. Wafers can be divided into three modes according to the chambers and the stages. The experiments are carried out on the mode with stage A and processed chambers [3–5]. Each wafer contains 25 variables, among which the pressure variables have the most abundant variation, as shown in Fig. 3. Therefore, the pressure variables are chosen to partition phases. In addition, the CMP process goes through three chambers, and the trajectories of variables in the first chamber and the next two chambers are similar. However, there are many gaps in the data of the latter two chambers, and the phase changes are not regular. Therefore, the phase partition is only conducted for the sampling points in the first chamber.

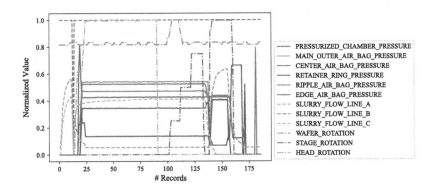

Fig. 3. The curves of different variables in a batch

3.2   Phase Partition and Phase Match

The phase partition result for a single batch obtained by WKM-PPCI are shown in Fig. 4 and the parameter γ for the PPCI calculation is empirically chosen to be 0.6. Figure 4(a) shows the variation curve of PPCI with the clustering number and the clustering number corresponding to the minimum PPCI is 15. As we can see in Fig. 4(b), the phase partition is too detailed with minimum PPCI.

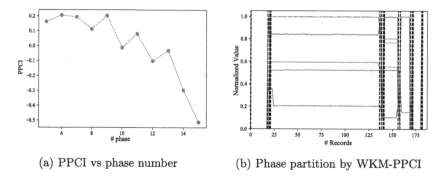

(a) PPCI vs phase number   (b) Phase partition by WKM-PPCI

Fig. 4. Phase partition results obtained by WKM-PPCI

In Fig. 5, the blue line shows the distribution of the number of whole phase while the red line shows the distribution of the number of stable phase with $L_S = 5$. It is obvious that the distribution of the number of stable phase is more concentrated than the number of whole phase, which explains why we could do phase match. Most of the batches have stable phases of 5 or 6. In this experiment, the standard number of stable phases is selected as $C_S^* = 5$. After C_S^* is determined, RCSP is calculated and the phase partition results of all batches are matched with RCSP using the algorithm in Sect. 2.2. Figure 6 shows the phase match results for three batches, and it can be seen that the results are consistent with the data variation trajectory and the stable phases are clearly distinguished from the short transient phases.

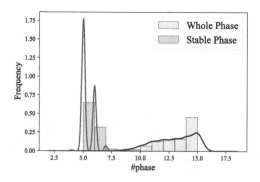

Fig. 5. Distribution of phase number with minimum PPCI (Color figure online)

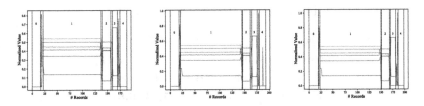

Fig. 6. Phase Match results of 3 batches

3.3 Feature Extraction and Feature Selection

On the basis of phase partition and phase match in Sect. 3.2, 70 features including statistics are extracted for each phase. We only use the filtered-based feature
selection here for fast feature selection. A parallel feature selection with single value identification, multicollinearity identification, and tree-based feature
importance identification is applied. Here, we apply the light gbm model with
cross-validation to calculate feature importance [8].

After the filter-based feature selection, 45, 26, 26, 31, and 49 features were
filtered out for the five phases, and the features remained were used to build
the regression model. As mentioned before, phase partition is only applied to
the first chamber of each batch. To use all information sufficiently, we extract
the same features for the first chamber and the last two chambers, respectively.
Based on the chamber extracted features and parallel feature selection, 23 features are filtered for the first chamber, and 35 features are filtered for the last
two chambers. Besides, the MRR of the usage-nearest-neighbors are extracted to
supply more precise predictions according to the previous researches. Here, we
extract 11 MRR of the usage-nearest-neighbors in the same mode and 3 neighbors from the other mode in PHM16 Dataset. Thus, there are 269 features are
used to build the final regression model.

3.4 Prediction Performance and Discussions

In our experiments, the performance metrics for regression prediction include
mean squared error $(MSE = \sum_{i=1}^{N}(y_i - \hat{y}_i)^2/N)$ and determination coefficient
$(r^2 = 1 - \sum_{i=1}^{N}(y_i - \hat{y}_i)^2/\sum_{i=1}^{N}(\bar{y} - \hat{y}_i)^2)$, where N is the number of batches, y_i
is the true value, $\hat{y}_i$ is the prediction value, and the $\bar{y}$ is the mean of y. Lower
MSE and higher r^2 indicate better prediction performance.

According to the 5-fold cross-validation results on the trainset, the Gradient
Boosting Deision Tree (GBDT) model offers the best prediction performance
and is selected as the final regression model [5].

Table 1. Phase GBDT vs Chamber GBDT.

Method	MSE	r^2
Non-phase GBDT	5.74	0.8599
Filter-based non-phase GBDT	5.44	0.8673
Phase GBDT	**5.33**	**0.8701**

To analyze the importance of phase partition and phase match, an ablation study is given. According to whether to use parallel feature selection, a GBDT model called *Non-phase GBDT* in Table 1 is trained without the phase extracted feature and *Filter-based non-phase GBDT* is trained based on the selected non-phase extracted features. Compared to the GBDT based on all extracted features, *Non-phase GBDT* without feature selection is much worse. Besides, with filter-based feature selection, the prediction performance is enhanced and the MSE of the filter chamber GBDT method could be 5.44. And the prediction performance of *Filter-based non-phase GBDT* is still worse than the proposed method called *Phase GBDT* in Table 1 with phase extracted features. It indicates that phase-based features can help to improve the prediction performance and feature selection is important even though the GBDT model contains adaptive feature selection.

Table 2. Comparisons of prediction performance with existing methods

Category	Methods	MSE
Deep learning	**CNN** [17]	**5.07**
	ResCNN [17]	**4.94**
	DBN [16]	6.76
Non deep learning	kNN-MTGP [1]	9.94
	Integrated Model [3]	5.89
	JIT-PF [2]	9.88
	GMDH [6]	5.90
	Phase GBDT	**5.33**

The final prediction performance of the proposed method on the test set is depicted in Fig. 7. Figure 7(a) shows that the predictions could fit the ground truths well and Fig. 7(b) draws the linear correlation between predictions and ground truths. Figure 7(c) depicts the distribution of the prediction error. As shown in Table 2, the phase GBDT method offers better prediction performance than most of the existing methods and is only worse than the CNN and ResCNN

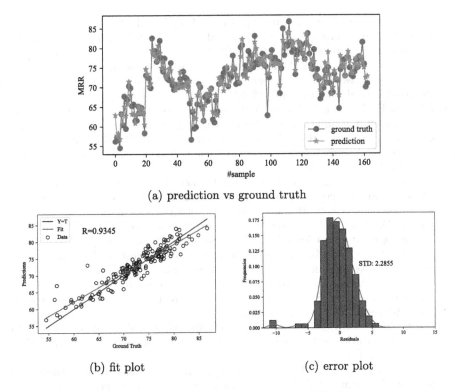

(a) prediction vs ground truth

(b) fit plot

(c) error plot

Fig. 7. The prediction performance of phase GBDT method.

based deep learning method but offers more interpretability. Although the proposed method doesn't give a better prediction performance than the deep learning method, it offers an insight that virtual metrology combining the multi-phase character of the batch process could offer better prediction performance.

4   Conclusion

Considering the multi-phase character of the CMP process, this paper proposes a phase partition and phase match-based VM method to predict MRR. After phase partition and phase match, parallel feature extraction and feature selection are conducted and the final regression model is trained to predict MRR. The proposed method gives improved prediction performance on the PHM16 Dataset with high prediction accuracy. Future work will focus on the effects of different phase importance and transition process on the prediction results.

References

1. Cai, H., Feng, J., Yang, Q., Li, W., Li, X., Lee, J.: A virtual metrology method with prediction uncertainty based on gaussian process for chemical mechanical planarization. Comput. Ind. **119**, 103228 (2020)

2. Cai, H., Feng, J., Zhu, F., Yang, Q., Li, X., Lee, J.: Adaptive virtual metrology method based on just-in-time reference and particle filter for semiconductor manufacturing. Measurement **168**, 108338 (2021)
3. Di, Y., Jia, X., Lee, J.: Enhanced virtual metrology on chemical mechanical planarization process using an integrated model and data-driven approach. Int. J. Prognostics Health Manag. **8**(2) (2017)
4. Feng, J., Jia, X., Zhu, F., Moyne, J., Iskandar, J., Lee, J.: An online virtual metrology model with sample selection for the tracking of dynamic manufacturing processes with slow drift. IEEE Trans. Semicond. Manuf. **32**(4), 574–582 (2019)
5. Friedman, J.: Greedy function approximation: a gradient boosting machine. Ann. Stat. **29**, 1189–1232 (2000)
6. Jia, X., Di, Y., Feng, J., Yang, Q., Dai, H., Lee, J.: Adaptive virtual metrology for semiconductor chemical mechanical planarization process using GMDH-type polynomial neural networks. J. Process Control **62**, 44–54 (2018)
7. Luo, J., Dornfeld, D.A.: Material removal mechanism in chemical mechanical polishing: theory and modeling. IEEE Trans. Semicond. Manuf. **14**(2), 112–133 (2001)
8. Ke, G., et al.: Lightgbm: a highly efficient gradient boosting decision tree. In: Advances in Neural Information Processing Systems, vol. 30 (2017)
9. Leiva, L.A., Vidal, E.: Warped k-means: an algorithm to cluster sequentially-distributed data. Inf. Sci. **237**, 196–210 (2013). Prediction, Control and Diagnosis using Advanced Neural Computations
10. Li, W., Zhao, C., Gao, F.: Sequential time slice alignment based unequal-length phase identification and modeling for fault detection of irregular batches. Ind. Eng. Chem. Res. **54**(41), 10020–10030 (2015)
11. Li, X., Wang, C., Zhang, L., Mo, X., Zhao, D., Li, C.: Assessment of physics-based and data-driven models for material removal rate prediction in chemical mechanical polishing. In: 2018 2nd International Conference on Electrical Engineering and Automation (ICEEA 2018). Atlantis Press (2018)
12. Li, Z., Wu, D., Yu, T.: Prediction of material removal rate for chemical mechanical planarization using decision tree-based ensemble learning. J. Manuf. Sci. Eng. Trans. Asme **141**(3) (2019). https://doi.org/10.1115/1.4042051
13. Luo, L.: Monitoring uneven multistage/multiphase batch processes using trajectory-based fuzzy phase partition and hybrid MPCA models. Can. J. Chem. Eng. **97**, 178–187 (2018)
14. Luo, L., Bao, S., Mao, J., Tang, D., Gao, Z.: Fuzzy phase partition and hybrid modeling based quality prediction and process monitoring methods for multiphase batch processes. Ind. Eng. Chem. Res. **55**(14), 4045–4058 (2016)
15. Preston, F.W.: The theory and design of plate glass polishing machines. J. Glass Technol. **11**(44), 214–256 (1927)
16. Wang, P., Gao, R.X., Yan, R.: A deep learning-based approach to material removal rate prediction in polishing. CIRP Ann. **66**(1), 429–432 (2017)
17. Zhang, J., Jiang, Y., Luo, H., Yin, S.: Prediction of material removal rate in chemical mechanical polishing via residual convolutional neural network. Control. Eng. Pract. **107**, 104673 (2021)
18. Zhang, S., Zhao, C., Wang, S., Wang, F.: Pseudo time-slice construction using a variable moving window k nearest neighbor rule for sequential uneven phase division and batch process monitoring. Ind. Eng. Chem. Res. **56**(3), 728–740 (2017)
19. Zhao, S., Huang, Y.: A stack fusion model for material removal rate prediction in chemical-mechanical planarization process. Int. J. Adv. Manuf. Technol. **99**(9–12), 2407–2416 (2018)

SAR Target Recognition Based on Model Transfer and Hinge Loss with Limited Data

Qishan He[1], Lingjun Zhao[1(✉)], Gangyao Kuang[1], and Li Liu[2,3]

[1] State Key Laboratory of Complex Electromagnetic Environment Effects on Electronics and Information System, College of Electronics Science and Technology, National University of Defense Technology, Changsha, China
[2] College of System Engineering, National University of Defense Technology, Changsha, China
[3] CMVS, Univeristy of Oulu, Oulu, Finland

Abstract. Convolutional neural networks have made great achievements in field of optical image classification during recent years. However, for Synthetic Aperture Radar automatic target recognition (SAR-ATR) tasks, the performance of deep learning networks is always degraded by the insufficient size of SAR images, which cause both severe over-fitting and low-capacity feature extraction model. On the other hand, models with high feature representation ability usually lose anti-overfitting capability to a certain extent, while enhancing the network's robustness leads to degradation in feature extraction capability. To balance above both problems, a network with model transfer using the GAN-WP and non-greedy loss is introduced in this paper. Firstly, inspired by the Support Vector Machine's mechanism, multi-hinge loss is used during training stage. Then, instead of directly training a deep neural network with the insufficient labeled SAR dataset, we pretrain the feature extraction network by an improved GAN, called Wasserstein GAN with gradient penalty and transfer the pre-trained layers to an all-convolutional network based on the fine-tune technique. Furthermore, experimental results on the MSTAR dataset illustrate the effectiveness of the proposed new method, which additional shows the classification accuracy can be improved more largely than other method in the case of sparse training dataset.

Keywords: SAR-ATR · Transfer learning · Generative adversial network

1 Introduction

Synthetic aperture radar (SAR) is an active imaging radar system, which has the characteristics of a variety of polarization modes and the imaging conditions are not affected by weather conditions. With the development of deep learning in thefield of optical image classification, a large number of classification networks have been applied to SAR image processing. Deep learning in Synthetic aperture

L. Fang et al. (Eds.): CICAI 2021, LNAI 13069, pp. 191–201, 2021.
https://doi.org/10.1007/978-3-030-93046-2_17

radar-Automatic Target Recognition (SAR-ATR) has made great achievements in SAR image preprocessing due to its automaticity and high accuracy from feature extraction. However, data-driven method is overly dependent on the scale of labeled data, and it will cause serious overfitting due to the scarce SAR dataset and the high cost and difficulty of manual annotation SAR data compared with the optical images.

The mainstream methods to improve the robustness of deep learning models in SAR-ATR can be mainly based on two ideas: 1) Strengthening the feature extraction ability of target network by augmenting dataset, 2) Reforming network structure to improve generalization ability. Chen proposed the all-convolutional networks [1] that substituted all full connection layers by convolutional layers, which greatly reduced the number of trainable parameters and increased the accuracy of MSTAR dataset under SOC conditions to 99% for the first time. Hai combined knowledge distillation with network quantization strategies. This method [2] greatly compressed the parameters of ResNet-18 to a three-layer network and outperformed other method's model with the same parameter's quantity. Zhong used the idea of filter based model pruning and transfer learning, which improved the generalization ability in small network and accelerated the forward propagation process [3]. Although the above methods reduce the model size to prevent from getting caught up in overfitting, training suchs model still demands a certain amount of training examples, moreover methods based on compressing model inevitably degrade network's representational capacity.

Huang [4] proposed a CNN using model transfer learning for the first time. By pretraining feature extraction model in unlabeled SAR scene images and then migrating to SAR target images, the accuracy of MSTAR under SOC and scarce training examples conditions reached to 97%. Zhang [5] showed that generative adversarial network could extract more universal features than autoencoder, by pre-training target network from unlabeled data through info-GAN. Liu [6] used electromagnetic simulation software and 3-D CAD models to generate a large number of SAR vehicle data. Although the above methods based on transfer learning improves the test accuracy using generated simulation data or unlabeled scene images, how to generate robust models relying on existing limited dataset is still a research difficulty. Qin [7] proposed the CAE-HL, which introduced the autoencoder to offset the feature extraction ability deficit with hinge loss. Wanger [8] combined SVM and CNN to obtain a network model with stronger robustness.

To improve both the anti-overfitting and feature extraction ability in the case of scarce training data, a network, called WGAN-HL-Convnet, consisting of an improved GAN, Wasserstein GAN with gradient penalty and multi-classification hinge loss, is proposed in this paper. Firstly, multi-classification hinge loss is introduced into the training stage of network model to adjust the decision of boundary determination. Whose optimization of the loss function is similar to the optimization problem under the constraint condition of SVM. When training samples are far away from the boundary margin, the network no longer pays attention to their contribution to the loss, which is the essential difference between the hinge loss and cross-entropy loss. Then, in order to make up for the degradation of feature extraction ability caused by the loss function, the pre-training model based on WGAN-GP is migrated, and the full connection layer in the discriminator of GAN is replaced with the convolution layer, which greatly reduces the number of model parameters and further improves the generalization ability of the network.

The remainder of this paper is organized as follows. Section 2 introduces the implementation of our method. Section 3 discusses the performance of the experimental results. Section 4 gives the conclusion.

2   Method

2.1   Multi-class Hinge Loss for SAR-ATR

In order to illustrate the applicability of hinge loss to the case of insufficient data, binary classification problem is discussed because of its convenience of feature visualization. Most loss function respond to all training data so as to extract information from existing data as much as possible and improve model's representational ability. While training sample reduces and the probability distribution of training samples and test samples has a certain deviation, as depicted in Fig. 1(a), however, such loss functions fail to obtain an appropriate judgement applicable to test sets, and the cause lies in that all of data characteristics generate a certain loss. In Fig. 1(b), it is showed not all data points are necessary to participate in the formation of decision line, and if only the feature points closed to the hyperplane are focused, the decision line obtained by limited training examples is more likely to be practical in the test samples.

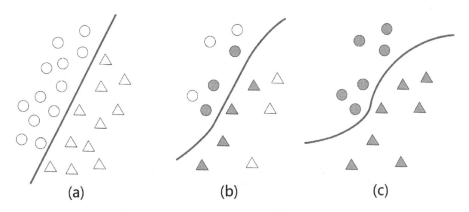

Fig. 1. Different decision lines under sufficient or unsufficient training examples with different loss functions. (a) under sufficient trainset; (b) under insufficient trainset with hinge loss; (c) under insufficient trainset with other loss

Given an input image x_i and its corresponding label $y_i \in \{+1, -1\}$ whose hinge loss can be expressed as $L(x_i, y_i) = \max(0, 1 - y_i f(x_i))$. When $y_i f(x_i) > 1$, the point is judged correctly and far from the judgement plane, so the loss is 0, that means it contributes nothing to the updating of model parameter. Other loss functions, such exponentially loss or cross-entropy loss, remain positive to all data points, as shown in Fig. 2, regardless of whether their predictions are right or wrong. This can lead the decision line in Fig. 1(c) to magnify its deviation degree after minimize the loss of all training data. Therefore, training network with Hinge loss rather than commonly used cross-entropy loss is more likely to improve the generalization ability and robustness in the case of insufficient SAR target images.

For multi-class classification problem, the multi-class hinge loss is used in this paper. Given an input image x_i, the corresponding loss function can be expressed as:

$$L(x_i, y_i) = \sum_{j \neq y_i} \max(0, f(x_i)_j - f(x_i)_{y_i} + \Delta) \tag{1}$$

where $f(x)$ is the output of network, $f(x)_j$ denotes each category score of the output, $j \in \{1, 2, ..., C\}$, and Δ denotes the threshold value.

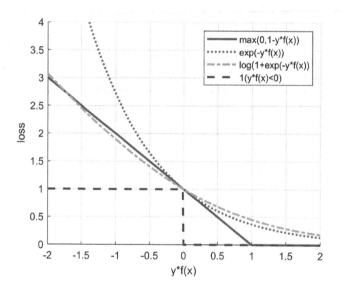

Fig. 2. Hinge loss and other loss functions

2.2 WGAN-HL-Convnet

Overflow of WGAN-HL-Convnet. Figure 3 demonstrates the overall architecture of the method. According to reference [9], although CNN based on hinge loss can avoid extracting redundant features under the condition of insufficient samples, the number of effective features extracted is much sparser than the

CNN based on ordinary cross-entropy loss. To enhance the representability of the target network, the unsupervised generative adversarial network and transfer learning technique are introduced to the proposed method. The classifier layers in the target classification are redesigned to make it capable of the SAR recognition tasks in the case of sparse training data.

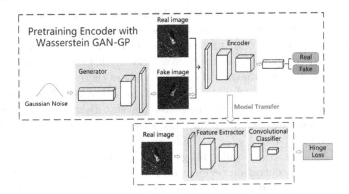

Fig. 3. Processing flow of the proposed method

According to the theory of transfer learning, the training stage can be divided into a pretraining phase and a fine-tuning phase. The typical GAN is known as an unsupervised learning framework to counterfeit images that visually looks like a real image. By means of adversarial training, the discriminator will have the representational ability to distinguish the authenticity of the input images. Meanwhile, the convolutional layers in the discriminator map the original input to the hidden feature space. Therefore, a GAN will be trained to learn universal features from the limited data as far as possible, and then based on the model transfer learning idea, a convolutional classifier will be added to create a SAR recognition model using the hinge loss. Lastly, the whole network will be finetuned to convergence. By combining pretraining technique using GAN and hinge loss, the model extracts a complete feature representation to compensate for the degradation in feature extraction ability, which reduces the over-fitting and owe-fitting risk.

Pretraining Encoder Using WGAN with Gradient Penalty. An unsupervised learning method based on Wasserstein GAN is adopted to improve feature extraction capability. Traditional GAN plays a 'minmax' game through alternately optimizing the following adversarial function:

$$\min_{G}\max_{D}\{V(D,G) = E_{x \sim p_{data}(x)}[\log D(x)] + E_{z \sim p_z(z)}[\log(1 - D(G(z)))]\} \quad (2)$$

where x denotes the sample from real probability distributionand $p_{data}(x)$ and z denotes the noise vector, of which the elements are produced randomly by a Gaussian distribution.

SAR target images have obvious background speckle noise and irregular scattering light spots, which make it hard for generator to generate visually similar SAR images. Since only a fraction of the background clutter and target contour images can be generated, it is difficult for discriminator to converge to ideal state. What's more, typical GAN usually uses Sigmod function, $f_{sig \bmod}(x) = \frac{1}{1+e^{-x}}$, as the activation function of the last layer, and the derivative $f'_{sig \bmod}(x) = f(x)(1 - f(x)) \le \frac{1}{4}$, which causes the gradient disappearing to zero due to the multiplicative effect of the gradient back propagation.

In order to train the discriminator fully, GAN based on Wasserstein distance with gradient penalty is used. Wasserstein distance, namely the bulldozer distance, can maintain smoothness even where there is no overlap between two distributions. To regression the Wasserstein distance in loss function, the sigmod activation function of the last layer in the discriminator is removed. Loss functions for the generator and the discriminator can be expressed as $-E_{z \sim P_z(z)}[D(G(z))]$ and $E_{z \sim p_z(z)}[D(G(z))] - E_{x \sim p_{data}(x)}[D(x)]$. In order to impose the Lipschitz constraint, the gradient penalty term focuses on generating the sample concentration region, and the real sample concentration region and the transition region between them are added to the discriminator's loss function, expressed as follows:

$$L(D) = E_{z \sim p_z(z)}[D(G(z))] - E_{x \sim p_{data}(x)}[D(x)] + \lambda E_{\widehat{x} \sim \widehat{X}}[\|\nabla_{\widehat{x}} D(\widehat{x})\|_p - 1]^2 \quad (3)$$

where $\widehat{x} = \varepsilon x + (1 - \varepsilon)G(z)$, ε is a random variable that obeys 0-1 uniform distribution, and λ is a proportion controlling hyperparameter.

All-Convolutional Network for Model Transfer. An all-convolutional network without fully connected layers is used in the proposed SAR target recognition model. The first five layers are transferred from the encoder of GAN, and the last two layers used to classify extracted features are initialized randomly. All connection layers adopt sparse connection instead of full connection, which effectively reduce the number of free parameters and avoid the severe overfitting due to limited training examples. The forward propagation of each convolutional kernel is express as:

$$O_j(w, h) = \sum_{i=1}^{N} \sum_{u,v=0}^{K-1} W_j^{(l)}(u, v) F_i^{(l)}(w - u, h - v) \quad (4)$$

where $O_j(w, h)$ denotes the output of the jth kernel, $F_i^{(l)}(w - u, h - v)$ refer to the pixel at the position $(w - u, h - v)$ of the ith feature map of the lth layer. And $W_j^{(l)}(u, v)$ is the trainable convolutional kernel with the size of K.

The overall flow architecture of the network is depicted in Fig. 4. For the feature extraction module, each convolutional block is followed by a leakRelu function to avoid the activation value falling in the interval where the gradient is zero, which is expressed as, $LeakyRELU(x) = \max(0.2x, x)$. The stride of each convolutional operation is set to 2 to compress the size of feature image.

The classification module is consist of two convolutional block. The size of the first convolutional block is 4, resulting in feature maps of size 1 × 1. The second one is a point-wise convolution block ensuring the final output size to be 1 × 1 × C, where C is the number of categories.

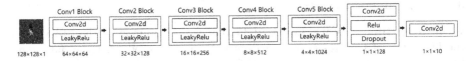

Fig. 4. The architecture of our model

3   Experiments and Results

3.1   Experimental Data Sets

The accuracy test is performed using the airborne Moving and Stationary Target Acquisition and Recognition (MSTAR) system. The dataset has released publicly 6 different categories of ground targets (armored personnel carrier, tank, rocket launcher, air defense unit, truck, bulldozer). To comprehensively assess the performance, the algorithm is tested both under standard operating conditions (SOC). SOC refers to that the serial numbers and target configurations in the test set are the same with those in the training set, but with different depression angles. The dataset under SOC consists of ten different of car targets, of which the optical and corresponding SAR images are shown in Fig. 5.

Fig. 5. SAR image examples and their corresponding optical images of ten types of targets in the MSTAR database

3.2   Training Details

The Adam optimizer is utilized for training GAN since it could adjust the learning rate dynamically. The batch size is 32, and initial learning rate of discriminator and generator is 0.003. The input noise of the generator is a 128-dimensional random vector of which the elements are produced by as Gaussian distribution. When training the classification, the initial learning rate is set to 0.001. Each

sample in the MSTAR dataset is resized to 128 × 128 and no image augmentation and preprocessing algorithm is applied to the SAR images. All experiments
are conducted on a Linux computer with a NVIDIA 3090 GPU card and 32 GB
of memory. The used neural network framework is Pytorch.

3.3   Experiment Results

Generated Images with Learned Features. A common method to verify
the feasibility of features extracted from GAN is to see whether the data can
be generated from the features derived from real images through discriminator.
We randomly enter some real images into encoder to get the feature vectors
and then feed the feature vectors into the generator to contrust the fake images
at different training stages of WGAN-gp. The generated images are given in
Fig. 6(b)–(c). It is suggested that the generated image turn to be identical to the
real image increasingly as the training epoches increases, which demonstrates
the effectiveness of the feature extraction through the discriminator.

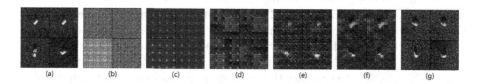

Fig. 6. Generated SAR images with WGAN-gp, where (a) is the real images. (b)–(g)
present the fake images at different training epoches

Testing Accuracy. This method mainly focuses in SAR target recognition
research on limited number of training samples. Therefore, based on the MSTAR
SOC dataset, training sets with smaller number of samples are constructed, we
contruct four subsets with 200, 500, 1000, 2000 samples have been established
by randomly extracted 20, 50, 100, 200 samples respectively from each class of
training dataset, and the testset is unchanged. We use subset-200, subset-500,
subset-1000, subset-2000 to denote the four training sets.

To illustrate the effectiveness of the proposed network under limited number
of training samples, three control trails, i.e. baseline-CNN, baseline-Convnet,
HL-Convnet, WGAN-HL-Convnet are set up. The specific implementation are
shown as follows: 1) baseline-CNN: directly training the random initialized target work of full connection layers in the classification modules with cross-entropy
loss function, 2) baseline-Convnet: directly training the random initialized target work of convolutonal layers in the classification modules with cross-entropy
function, 3) HL-Convnet: training the baseline-Convnet with hinge loss instead
of cross-entropy loss, 4) WGAN-HL-Convnet: training the HL-Convnet which is
initialized by the pretrained feature extraction module with WGAN-GP.

Table 1. Test accuracies of the trained models on SOC dataset.

Training set	baseline-CNN	baseline-Convnet	HL-Convnet	WGAN-HL-Convnet
subset-2000	95.63	96.86	96.37	**98.35**
subset-1000	91.22	93.73	94.15	**97.64**
subset-500	81.22	85.77	86.43	**93.64**
subset-200	64.55	65.07	72.20	**86.43**

Table 1 records the recognition accuracy of four networks trained on the four subsets. We repeat every experiment five times and choose the average value to mitigate the impact of fluctuation. The second row shows when the training data is abundant, the test accuracies of baseline-CNN, baseline-Convnet, HL-Convnet, WGAN-HL-Convnet are 95.63%, 95.75%, 94.06%, 97.19%. The performances of four methods are very close to each other, but our method still rank the first accuracy. The accuracy of baseline-Convnet surpasses that of HL-Convnet, which verifies cross-entropy loss accelerates in extracting useful features better than hinge loss under sufficient training data condition. As the number of training samples decreases, our method outperforms the other method significantly, exceeding the second highest accuracy over 5.49%, 7.21% and 14.23% under subset-1000, subset-500, subset-200 conditions respectively. Note that, in such three conditions the HL-Convnet behaves better than baseline-Convnet and our method behave better than HL-Convnet. The experiment demonstrates that in the case of scarce training samples, hinge loss is useful in improving the robustness of the classification network, and pretraining network through WGAN can further greatly improve the performance by enhancing the capability of feature extraction.

Table 2. Detailed accuracies of each categories on subset-2000.

Method	2S1	BMP2	BRDM2	BTR70	BTR60	D7	T62	T72	ZIL131	ZSU234
WGAN-HL-Convnet	98.54	100.00	**92.70**	99.48	98.46	99.27	98.16	98.97	99.27	99.27
HL-Convnet	94.89	**91.28**	95.62	94.89	97.43	98.54	94.87	97.95	97.81	98.90
baseline-Convnet	**93.79**	96.92	**93.06**	97.95	97.43	97.08	94.50	100.00	99.63	99.27

To analyse the classification accuracies in each categories, we enter all the test images into the model in batches by category and calculate the accuracy score on each type. The recall of each type is list in the Table 2 and 3. For WGAN-HL-Convnet, only the BRDM2 and BMP2 are relatively low, 92.7% and 92.82%, respectively in two tables. Other categories are all more than 95%. But for HL-Convnet, in Table 3, BRDM2, BTR60, T62 show lower scores than other types with accuracies of 84.30%, 84.61%. Similarly, baseline-Convnet has a poor

Table 3. Detailed accuracies of each categories on subset-1000.

Method	2S1	BMP2	BRDM2	BTR70	BTR60	D7	T62	T72	ZIL131	ZSU234
WGAN-HL-Convnet	95.25	**92.82**	97.44	97.44	95.89	98.9	98.9	98.46	99.63	99.63
HL-Convnet	98.9	93.33	**84.30**	94.89	92.82	97.44	**84.61**	100.00	97.44	98.90
baseline-Convnet	95.98	96.41	**80.29**	93.36	**90.25**	97.81	**90.84**	94.89	98.17	98.9

performance accuracies in BRDM2, BTR60, T62 in Table 3. The results shows that the GAN-HL-Convnet not only has higher recognition accuracies than the HL-Convnet and baseline-Convnet in the case of scarce training dataset, but alse performs more balanced in each categories.

4   Conclusion

In the present paper, a method based on the hinge loss and model transfer using Wasserstein GAN is proposed to address the limited label difficulty in SAR-ATR. We transfer the feature extraction module pre-trained from GAN and finetune the whole network with newly added convolutional classification module. The transfer method produces a higher performance on MSTAR dataset than other methods. This superiority becomes more apparent as the training set becomes sparser. Its reveals us that combining hinge loss functions and GAN's pretraining through model transfer is a good way to improve recognition in the case of scarce training samples.

References

1. Chen, S., Wang, H., Xu, F., et al.: Target classification using the deep convolutional networks for SAR images. IEEE Trans. Geosci. Remote Sens. **54**(8), 4806–4817 (2016)
2. Lan, H., Cui, Z., Cao, Z., et al.: SAR target recognition via micro convolutional neural network. In: IEEE International Geoscience and Remote Sensing Symposium (2019)
3. Zhong, C., Mu, X., He, X., et al.: SAR target image classification based on transfer learning and model compression. IEEE Trans. Geosci. Remote Sens. **16**(3), 412–416 (2019)
4. Huang, Z., Pan, Z., Lei, B.: Transfer learning with deep convolutional neural network for SAR target classification with limited labeled data. Remote Sens. **9**(9), 907 (2017)
5. Zhang, W., Zhu, Y., Fu, Q.: Deep transfer learning based on generative adversarial networks for SAR target recognition with label limitation. In: IEEE International Conference on Signal, Information and Data Processing (2019)
6. Liu, L., Pan, Z., Qiu, X., et al.: SAR target classification with CycleGAN transferred simulated samples. In: IEEE International Geoscience and Remote Sensing Symposium (2018)
7. Qin, R., Fu, X., Dong, J., et al.: A semi-greedy neural network CAE-HL-CNN for SAR target recognition with limited training data. Int. J. Remote Sens. **41**(20), 7889–7911 (2020)

8. Wagner, S.A.: SAR ATR by a combination of convolutional neural network and support vector machines. IEEE Trans. Aerosp. Electron. Syst. **52**(6), 2864–2872 (2016)

9. Zhang, W., Zhu, Y., Fu, Q.: Semi-supervised deep transfer learning-based on adversarial feature learning for label limited SAR target recognition. IEEE Access **7**, 152412–152420 (2019)

Neighborhood Search Acceleration Based on Deep Reinforcement Learning for SSCFLP

Zonghui Zhang, Zhangjin Huang[✉], and Lu Zou

University of Science and Technology of China, Hefei 230026, Anhui, China
zhuang@ustc.edu.cn

Abstract. This paper proposes a novel neighborhood search framework based on deep reinforcement learning to iteratively improve solutions to Single Source Capacitated Facility Location Problem (SSCFLP). Specifically, we construct a deep reinforcement learning model which learns a disturbing strategy to iteratively select the customers to be adjusted, and design a neighborhood operator to generate a new solution by reassigning the selected customers. The proposed model consists of an encoder and a decoder. The encoder is based on a bipartite graph attention network, which exchanges information between facilities and customers through a two-step information transfer mechanism, and extracts a feature vector as the state feature of the problem. The decoder is based on GRU, which takes the problem state feature as input and outputs a set of customers. After the customers being selected, the designed neighborhood operator reassigns these customers to form a new solution. Experiments on six generated datasets demonstrate that the proposed framework accelerates the process of neighborhood search, thereby finding better solutions in a shorter time. The results also show that the proposed framework outperforms the Simulated Annealing (SA) algorithm on all datasets and has achieved comparable performance with optimal solutions.

Keywords: Facility location · Graph attention network · Neighborhood search · Deep reinforcement learning

1 Introduction

The Single Source Capacitated Facility Location Problem (SSCFLP) is a classical combinatorial optimization problem, which can be applied to many domains, such as warehouse locating, city planning and so on. In recent years, there are many works be proposed to solve SSCFLP, such as exact methods, Lagrangian heuristics and meta heuristics. In [14], the author formulated the SSCFLP as a mixed integer linear programming model, and solved the problem exactly by the linear programming algorithms. However, the time consumption of exact algorithms makes it impossible to apply them on large-scale SSCFLP. In order to address the above problem, many works such as [2,7,10,12,13] presented heuristic methods based on the combination of Lagrangian relaxation and other algorithms to reduce the computation cost. In addition to Lagrangian relaxation, other heuristic based methods had been proposed, such as [1,6,11]. Compared with Lagrangian heuristics, these methods could find solutions efficiently, which is accompanied with the decline of quality.

L. Fang et al. (Eds.): CICAI 2021, LNAI 13069, pp. 202–212, 2021.
https://doi.org/10.1007/978-3-030-93046-2_18

With the rapid development of machine learning, some researchers proposed to utilize machine learning algorithms to solve combinatorial optimization problems, such as [3,4,8,9,17]. However, most of these works focus on Travelling Salesman Problem (TSP) and Vehicle Routing Problem (VRP), and they ignore the role of machine learning model in optimizing neighborhood search. In this paper, we present a deep reinforcement learning based heuristic neighborhood search approach to solve SSCFLP. The framework iteratively selects customers by a deep reinforcement learning model, and then adjusts these customers by a neighborhood operator. We evaluate our algorithm on six generated datasets, and the results show that the proposed method can accelerate the neighborhood search procedure and find high quality solutions in limited time.

2   Related Work

Existing works to solve SSCFLP can be divided into exact methods, approximation methods and heuristics. Due to the limited space, we only discuss neighborhood search related heuristics, which is most related to ours. There are three kinds of related methods: heuristics combined with Lagrangian relaxation, meta heuristics and machine learning based heuristics.

2.1   Lagrangian Relaxation Based Methods

The main idea of Lagrangian heuristic is to relax some particular constraints and constructs a new solution by solving the relaxed problem. Klincewicz and Luss [13] constructed uncapacitated facility location subproblem by relaxing the capacity constraints of SSCFLP, and applied dual ascent algorithm to solve the subproblem. Besides, the author applied an Add Heuristic to obtain an initial solution and an adjustment heuristic to improve the solution to the subproblem. Beasley and J.E. [2] relaxed both the capacity constraints and the assignment constraints, and presented a framework based on Lagrangian relaxation and subgradient optimisation. They applied their approach to four variants of FLP, and obtained good quality solutions to every variant. Despite achieving considerable performance, the core of these works is to solve linear programming models, which will consume a lot of time when the problem scale increases.

2.2   Meta Heuristics

Besides Lagrangian heuristic, many meta heuristics have been adopted to solve SSCFLP. Ahuja et al. [1] presented a large-scale neighborhood algorithm. In their work, the author utilized a greedy strategy which dynamically constructs a facility improvement graph and searches the graph to find negative subset-disjoint cycles. Contreras et al. [6] proposed a scatter search which is composed of four parts. Firstly, the Diversification Generation Method generates a set of trial solutions, and the Solution Combination Method combines these solutions. Then, the combined solution is improved iteratively during the improvement phase. Finally, a tabu search algorithm is applied to improve the best solution found. Ho and S.C. [11] proposed an iterated tabu search heuristic, which incorporated different perturbation operators into tabu search to explore more solution space. Meta heuristics greatly reduce the time of solving SSCFLP problems, nevertheless, the design of heuristics is a sophisticated work and needs plenty of expert knowledge. What's more, during the searching process, most searches are invalid since heuristics randomly selects actions, which results in a great time consumption.

2.3 Machine Learning Based Methods

The application of machine learning in combinatorial optimization is a promising area. Bello et al. [3] proposed a framework to solve TSP based on pointer network [17]. Results given by the framework are close to optimal results. Guo et al. [9] evaluated fitness function of evolutionary algorithm by extreme machine learning to solve two-stage capacitated facility location problems, and find optimal or near-optimal solutions in a reasonable computational time. Chen and Tian [4] combined Variable Large Neighborhood Search (VLNS) with reinforcement learning, and proposed a framework which iteratively performed removal and insertion operation to search better neighborhood solutions of the current solution. Gao et al. [8] solved Vehicle Routing Problem (VRP) by iteratively performing destroy-repair operation on the current solution, and their approach is able to tackle the large-scale dataset.

Being motivated by [8], in order to decrease invalid actions during neighborhood search of SSCFLP, we propose a deep reinforcement learning based neighborhood search framework, which iteratively chooses a set of customers and reassigns these customers to new facilities. Experimental results show that the proposed approach can obtain better solutions at lower searching cost, thus greatly improves the efficiency of neighborhood search.

3 Problem Definition

Let $F = \{1, \ldots, s_f\}$ denotes the indices set of facilities, and $C = \{1, \ldots, s_c\}$ denotes the indices set of customers, where s_f and s_c are sizes of facilities and customers, respectively. Each customer j has a demand d_j which should be satisfied by single facility, and each facility i has a capacity e_i, which denotes the maximum demand one can serve. Each facility i is associated with a fixed cost k_i which denotes the building cost of facility i. Moreover, if the demand of customer j is supplied by facility i, then there is a transportation cost t_{ij}. Therefore, the overall cost is composed of fixed costs for building facilities and transportation costs between open facilities and the customers these facilities supply for. The goal of SSCFLP is to minimize the overall cost by choosing appropriate potential facility locations and determining the allocation of customers, which can be modeled mathematically as:

$$COST = min \sum_{i \in F} \sum_{j \in C} t_{ij}x_{ij} + \sum_{i \in F} k_iy_i, \tag{1}$$

$$s.t. \quad \sum_{i \in F} x_{ij} = 1, \; for \; all \; j \in C, \tag{2}$$

$$\sum_{j \in C} d_jx_{ij} \leq e_iy_i, \; for \; all \; i \in F, \tag{3}$$

$$y_i \in \{0,1\}, \ \forall i \in F, \tag{4}$$

$$x_{ij} \in \{0,1\}, \ \forall i \in F, j \in C. \tag{5}$$

The decision variable y_i takes value 1 if facility i is open and 0 otherwise. Also, if customer j is supplied by facility i, then x_{ij} takes value 1 otherwise 0. Equation (2) ensures that the demand of each customer is only satisfied by single source. The meanings of Eq. (3) are embodied in two aspects. On the one hand, it ensures that the total customer demand served by a facility doesn't exceed the capacity. On the other hand, it guarantees that each customer can only be served by open facilities.

4 Proposed Approach

Given a single source capacitated facility location problem, firstly, we randomly generate an initial solution that satisfies the constraints mentioned in Sect. 3, and embed the current problem state into a deep reinforcement learning model. Then the model outputs a set of customers according to the current problem state. Finally, we utilize a neighborhood operator to generate a new solution based on the current solution, which will reassign customers choosen by the model. This process will be carried out iteratively until the predetermined exploration goal is reached. The whole procedure is depicted in Fig. 1.

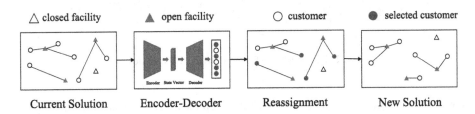

Fig. 1. The procedure of proposed algorithm in one iteration. The new solution will replace the current solution in the next iteration.

4.1 Graph Representation

There are two kinds of nodes in the graph which represent facilities and customers respectively. Let f_i denotes the node embedding of the i-th facility node. f_i is an 8-D vector with each element as: (1) e_i, which denotes the capacity of facility i; (2) k_i, which denotes the fixed cost of building facility i; (3) b_i, which denotes the total transportation cost between facility i and the customers it serves; (4) z_i, which denotes the number of customers served by facility i; (5) r_i, which denotes the remaining capacity of facility i; (6) y_i, which is a binary indicator about whether the facility is open or not; (7) m_i and n_i, which denote the x-axis and y-axis coordinates of facility i respectively. The node embedding of the j-th customer is represented as c_i, which is a 3-D vector including the demand and the coordinates of customer j. Beside facility nodes and customer nodes, the information of each edge is also taken into count. The embedding for the edge connecting facility i and customer j is denoted by a 2-D vector e_{ij}. e_{ij} consists of the transportation cost and a binary indicator x_{ij} about whether customer j is served by facility i.

4.2 Model

As illustrated in Fig. 1, the entire model is composed of a graph state encoder and a state vector decoder. The encoding part is constructed based on Graph Attention Network (GAT) [16] which takes original embeddings of the nodes (including facility nodes and customer nodes) and the edges of the graph as input, and outputs the encoded vector representation of the current graph state. Then, the Gated Recurrent Unit (GRU) [5] based decoder takes the state vector encoded by the encoder as input, and outputs a set of customers, which will be reassigned later by the neighborhood operator.

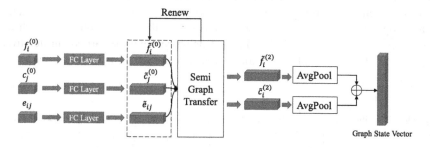

Fig. 2. The structure of the proposed state encoder.

Graph State Encoder. The structure of the graph state encoder is shown in Fig. 2. The original embeddings $(f_i^{(0)}, c_j^{(0)}, e_{ij})$ are firstly transformed by a fully connection layer to get the extended embeddings, then the extended embeddings $(\tilde{f}_i^{(0)}, \tilde{c}_j^{(0)}, \tilde{e}_{ij})$ are updated through a two-step information transfer mechanism, which is composed of two semi-graph information passing processes. The one passes information from facility nodes to customer nodes, and the other passes information in the opposite direction. The first semi-graph information passing process is calculated as:

$$\tilde{g}_{c,ij} = LeakyRelu(W_1[\tilde{c}_i^{(0)}||\tilde{f}_j^{(0)}||\tilde{e}_{ij}]), \tag{6}$$

$$p_{c,ij} = \frac{exp(\tilde{g}_{c,ij})}{\sum_j exp(\tilde{g}_{c,ij})}, \tag{7}$$

$$c_i^{(1)} = \tilde{c}_i^{(0)} + \sum_j p_{c,ij} \otimes \tilde{f}_j^{(0)}. \tag{8}$$

where $[\cdot||\cdot]$ represents a concat operation, $\otimes$ denotes element-wise multiplication between vectors and W_1 is a weight matrix. Since the second semi-graph information passing process transfers the integrated information from the customer nodes to the facility nodes, the formula is similar to the first process. Due to the limited space, we don't elaborate here.

The two information exchange phases mentioned above are carried out in the whole model to fully transfer information between facility nodes and customer nodes. After that, an average pooling layer is applied to both facility node embeddings and customer node embeddings, respectively. Finally, facility node embeddings and customer node embeddings are added together to generate the encoded graph state vector.

State Vector Decoder. We adopt a variant of the state vector decoder as explained in [17] to decode the graph state vector from the encoder and output the customer nodes to be adjusted. Specifically, we replace the Recurrent Neural Network (RNN) [18] in [17] with GRU, which is a variant of RNN with better performance. The structure of decoder is shown as Fig. 3. At step t, GRU takes the graph state vector and node embedding of the customer selected at step t-1 as input to update the graph state vector. Subsequently, the updated state vector together with all customer node embeddings are transformed into a solution state vector. Finally, the solution state is converted to a probability vector through a softmax layer to sample a new customer node.

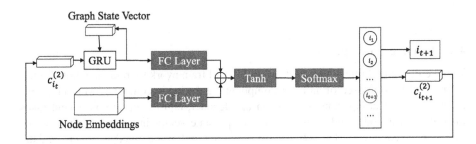

Fig. 3. The structure of the proposed state decoder.

4.3 Neighborhood Operator

After choosing customer nodes to be adjusted, the neighborhood operator reassigns these customers to construct a new solution based on the current solution. Firstly, the operator removes all customers in the candidate list and refreshes the state of facilities. Then a greedy strategy is applied to assign the removed customers to new facilities. We show the pseudocode of the whole procedure in Algorithm 1.

$Remove(c)$ is a function to remove customer c from its associated facility and refresh the state of the facility. If the remaining capacity of facility f is larger than the demand of customer c, $Satisfy(f,c)$ returns true and in other cases it returns false. $ComputeCost(f,c)$ computes the cost of assigning customer c to facility f. If the facility is open, the function returns the transportation cost between c and f, otherwise the total cost is the sum of k_f and t_{fc}. $GetMin(list)$ finds the facility with the least allocation cost. By iteratively selecting and reassigning customers, we will finally get a near-optimal solution to SSCFLP.

Algorithm 1. Algorithm of Neighborhood Operator

Input: Candidate customer list $L = \{c_{n_1}, \cdots, c_{n_k}\}, n_i \in \{1, \ldots, s_c\}$
Output: A new solution S_{new}
1: **for** $i \in \{1, \ldots, k\}$ **do**
2:     $Remove(c_{n_i})$
3: **end for**
4: **for** $i \in \{1, \ldots, k\}$ **do**
5:     $list = \{\}$
6:     **for** $f_j \in F$ **do**
7:         **if** $Satisfy(f_j, c_{n_i})$ **then**
8:             $ComputeCost(f_j, c_{n_i})$
9:             $Append(list, f_j)$
10:        **end if**
11:    **end for**
12:    $f_{new} = GetMin(list)$
13:    $S_{new} = Assign(c_{n_i}, f_{new})$
14: **end for**
15: **return** result

4.4 Training Procedure

We take Proximal Policy Optimization (PPO) [15] framework to train the whole framework. PPO is composed of an actor component and a critic component. In our experiment, the actor component is based on the decoder, and the critic component takes the output of encoder and transforms the graph state vector into a state value by two fully connected layers. At step t, the cost function $Cost^{(t)}$ is defined as Eq. (1), and the reward function $r(t)$ is defined as the reduction of cost, as shown below:

$$r^{(t)} = Cost^{(t)} - Cost^{(t-1)}. \tag{9}$$

The loss function of critic network L_c is calculated as:

$$L_c = [v_\phi(t) - v(t)]^2, v(t) = \sum_{i=t}^{t+k} \gamma^{i-t} r^i, \tag{10}$$

where $v(t)$ is the approximate state value, k is the length of sample sequence, γ is the discount factor, $v_\phi(t)$ is the state value at step t estimated by critic network. The actor network is trained by loss function proposed in [15]:

$$L_t^{CLIP} = \hat{\mathbf{E}}[min((r_t(\theta)v(t), clip(r_t(\theta), 1 - \epsilon, 1 + \epsilon)v(t))], \tag{11}$$

where L_t^{CLIP} is the loss function of the actor network, $r_t(\theta)$ is the ratio of new policy and old policy, and ϵ is a hyperparameter.

5 Experiments

5.1 Data Generation and Algorithm Settings

To evaluate the performance of our model, we set different data distributions to generate six datasets. The coordinates of all nodes are generated from $U(20, 200)$, where $U(a, b)$ is a uniform distribution in the interval $[a, b]$. The fixed costs are generated randomly from $U(300, 700)$. The transportation costs between facility i and customer j are determined as $c_{ij} = \rho h_{ij}$ where h_{ij} is the Euclidean distance between i and j, and ρ is a positive scalar. The customer demands and the facility capacities are generated from $U(10, 50)$ and $U(100, 500)$, respectively.

SSCFLP includes two levels of decision: deciding on the set of facilities to open and the allocation of customers. In order to increase the difficulty of the first level, we configure the settings to make the final solution open about half of the facilities. Besides, we configure the settings to balance the total fixed cost and the total transportation cost to increase the difficulty of the second level. Therefore, we generate different datasets with different ρ and different problem sizes. The statistical information about datasets is shown in Table 1. $\{S_f\}f\{S_c\}c$ means there are S_f facilities and S_c customers.

Table 1. Distribution of generated datasets. Number represents the number of instances in the dataset.

Dataset	Number	ρ	Capacity	Demand	Capacity/Demand	Transcost	Fixed cost
20f100c-1	128	0.04	299.79	29.53	2.05	3.75	499.43
20f100c-2	128	0.4	300.49	29.36	2.03	37.43	501.32
20f100c-3	64	4	301.00	29.53	2.04	376.71	497.87
30f150c	64	0.4	298.86	29.58	2.02	37.63	499.44
40f200c	64	0.4	299.50	29.52	2.03	37.65	504.30
100f100c	32	0.4	297.57	29.87	9.96	37.53	503.28

We compare our algorithm with SA on the datasets aforementioned (Sect. 5.1). Besides, we take the results obtained by Mixed Integer Linear Programming (MILP, mentioned in Sect. 3) as the lower bound of the solution. The time of computing solutions is limited to two hours. For SA, we set the decay coefficient $\lambda = 0.999$, the initial temperature $T_0 = 1000$ and the final temperature $T_1 = 0.1$. At every temperature, SA iterates 1500 times to find a good neighbor. Under these settings, the SA would search about 130 million times in the solution space. For the proposed framework, the primitive embeddings of both facility nodes and customer nodes are mapped to 32-D vectors, and the embeddings of edges are mapped to 16-D vectors.

During training data collection stage, 128 instances are created to interact with the reinforcement learning environment. In addition, we utilize a rollout strategy to generate training samples with respect to the instances. The rollout procedure repeats 20 times in total, and during one rollout, each instance generates 10 training samples. The batch size during the training period is set to 256, and the model is trained with Adam optimizer. The initial learning rate is 3e-4. Length of the candidate customer in Algorithm 1 is set to $k = 15$. A multiple restarting strategy is applied to our framework, which means that when the algorithm has reached the predetermined searching depth, it will randomly generate a new solution as the current solution.

5.2   Results and Analysis

Performance of Our Approach with Different Restarting Settings. We conduct three restarting settings for our algorithm on six datasets, which are named in form of model-{restarting times}*{searching depth}. Table 2 summarizes the results. We can infer from Tabel 2 that on the premise that all these three settings search about 10,000 solutions in the solution space, settings with more restarting times obtain better results. This is because that our approach quickly converges to the local optimal solution, hence under the same search times, settings with more restarting times make the algorithm jump out of the local optimal solution more easily, so as to explore wider solution space. In order to balance computation time and the quality of solutions, we choose model-100*100 to compare with other algorithms in the following experiments.

Table 2. Results of model on six generated datasets.

Dataset	Model-1*10,000	Model-10*1,000	Model-100*100
20f100c-1	3681.60	3627.23	3590.55
20f100c-2	5049.41	5003.71	4985.55
20f100c-3	15921.99	15911.88	15867.37
30f150c	7166.29	7110.26	7108.80
40f200c	9287.62	9207.18	9255.78
100f100c	4233.22	4050.87	4045.05

Comparison with SA on Datasets with Different Transportation Costs. In Table 3, we compare the performance of SA and our approach on datasets with different transportation distributions. Solutions obtained by MILP is taken as benchmark, and two different SA strategies are designed which are named as naive SA and greedy SA, separately. Both of the naive SA and the greedy SA select candidate customers to be adjusted randomly, but naive SA randomly reassigns customers to facilities while greedy SA follows Algorithm 1, which is the same as our approach.

Compared with naive SA, greedy SA obtains higher quality solutions, which indicates that Algorithm 1 can accelerate the convergence of neighborhood search. Additionally, solutions obtained by our approach is very close to the lower bound with a mean gap of only 1.3%, which is much less than 7.1% obtained by greedy SA.

Table 3. Results of SA and model on datasets with different transportation costs.

Dataset	MILP	Naive SA	Greedy SA	Model-100*100
20f100c-1	3547.28	5466.23	4009.14	3590.55
20f100c-2	4899.56	7820.56	5209.10	4985.55
20f100c-3	15703.61	24671.95	16036.24	15867.37

Results on Different Problem Scales. In order to test the generalization of our approach, Table 4 shows our results on different problem scales. As the results show, our approach outperforms greedy SA in all four problem scales. With the increase of customer scale, our approach becomes more and more advantageous. On 30f150c and 40f200c, our approach obtains better results than MILP, while on 100f100c, the performance of our model gets a little degradation. This is partly due to the fact that our neighborhood operator pays more attention to the assignment of customers. As a result, it is difficult to determine the facilities to open when the scale of facility is similar to that of customer.

Table 4. Results on datasets with different problem scales.

Dataset	MILP	Greedy SA	Model-100*100
20f100c-2	4899.56	5209.10	4985.55
30f150c	7143.94	7611.51	7108.80
40f200c	9711.56	10251.48	9255.78
100f100c	3787.45	4567.34	4045.05

6   Conclusion

In this paper, we combine graph attention network with deep reinforcement learning to construct an encoder-decoder based model. Based on the model, we present a neighborhood search framework to solve SSCFLP. The framework randomly generates an initial solution at first, and then, it iteratively utilizes the deep reinforcement model to select a candidate customer set. After that, a neighborhood operator reassigns these customers to construct a new solution based on the current solution. The results show that our approach can find better solutions while searches less solution space in comparison with classical simulated annealing algorithm. In further work, we will focus on exploring better neighborhood operators which could search in wider solution space, and apply our approach to more variants of facility location problem.

Acknowlegement. This work was supported in part by the National Natural Science Foundation of China (Nos. 71991464 / 71991460, and 61877056), and the Fundamental Research Funds for the Central Universities (Nos. WK6030000109 and WK5290000001).

References

1. Ahuja, R.K., Orlin, J.B., Pallottino, S., Scaparra, M.P., Scutellà, M.G.: A multi-exchange heuristic for the single-source capacitated facility location problem. Manage. Sci. **50**(6), 749–760 (2004)
2. Beasley, J.E.: Lagrangean heuristics for location problems. European J. Oper. Res. **65**(3), 383–399 (1993)
3. Bello, I., Pham, H., Le, Q.V., Norouzi, M., Bengio, S.: Neural combinatorial optimization with reinforcement learning. arXiv preprint arXiv:1611.09940 (2016)
4. Chen, X., Tian, Y.: Learning to perform local rewriting for combinatorial optimization. arXiv preprint arXiv:1810.00337 (2018)
5. Cho, K., et al.: Learning phrase representations using rnn encoder-decoder for statistical machine translation. arXiv preprint arXiv:1406.1078 (2014)
6. Contreras, I.A., Díaz, J.A.: Scatter search for the single source capacitated facility location problem. Ann. Oper. Res. **157**(1), 73–89 (2008)
7. Cortinhal, M.J., Captivo, M.E.: Upper and lower bounds for the single source capacitated location problem. European J. Oper. Res. **151**(2), 333–351 (2003)
8. Gao, L., Chen, M., Chen, Q., Luo, G., Zhu, N., Liu, Z.: Learn to design the heuristics for vehicle routing problem. arXiv preprint arXiv:2002.08539 (2020)
9. Guo, P., Cheng, W., Wang, Y.: Hybrid evolutionary algorithm with extreme machine learning fitness function evaluation for two-stage capacitated facility location problems. Expert Syst. Appl. **71**, 57–68 (2017)
10. Hindi, K., Pieńkosz, K.: Efficient solution of large scale, single-source, capacitated plant location problems. J. Oper. Res. Soc. **50**(3), 268–274 (1999)
11. Ho, S.C.: An iterated tabu search heuristic for the single source capacitated facility location problem. Appl. Soft Comput. **27**, 169–178 (2015)
12. Holmberg, K., Rönnqvist, M., Yuan, D.: An exact algorithm for the capacitated facility location problems with single sourcing. European J. Oper. Res. **113**(3), 544–559 (1999)
13. Klincewicz, J.G., Luss, H.: A lagrangian relaxation heuristic for capacitated facility location with single-source constraints. J. Oper. Res. Soc. **37**(5), 495–500 (1986)
14. Neebe, A., Rao, M.: An algorithm for the fixed-charge assigning users to sources problem. J. Oper. Res. Soc. **34**(11), 1107–1113 (1983)
15. Schulman, J., Wolski, F., Dhariwal, P., Radford, A., Klimov, O.: Proximal policy optimization algorithms. arXiv preprint arXiv:1707.06347 (2017)
16. Veličković, P., Cucurull, G., Casanova, A., Romero, A., Lio, P., Bengio, Y.: Graph attention networks. arXiv preprint arXiv:1710.10903 (2017)
17. Vinyals, O., Fortunato, M., Jaitly, N.: Pointer networks. arXiv preprint arXiv:1506.03134 (2015)
18. Zaremba, W., Sutskever, I., Vinyals, O.: Recurrent neural network regularization. arXiv preprint arXiv:1409.2329 (2014)

GBCI: Adaptive Frequency Band Learning for Gender Recognition in Brain-Computer Interfaces

Pengpai Wang, Yueying Zhou, Zhongnian Li, and Daoqiang Zhang$^{(\boxtimes)}$

College of Computer Science and Technology, MIIT Key Laboratory of Pattern Analysis and Machine Intelligence, Nanjing University of Aeronautics and Astronautics, Nanjing 211106, China
{pengpaiwang,dqzhang}@nuaa.edu.com

Abstract. In recent years, with the rapid development of brain-computer interface (BCI) technology, various applications based on BCI have generated significant interest. A motivating application of BCI is predicting human gender by electroencephalogram (EEG) analysis. However, most of the recent researches only identify the gender of EEG in the resting state. In real-life practice, it is difficult for the subjects to be at a full resting state when it mixes with motor imagery (MI). Therefore, we acquired two kinds of EEG activities data including 9 subjects (5 males and 4 females) with two state (i.e., resting state and MI) based on Chinese sign language. In this paper, to recognize gender form two state, an improved adaptive variational mode decomposition with long short term memory (AVMD-LSTM) network is developed to construct a hybrid state learning framework. Besides, the sample entropy (SE) is employed to select the channel of EEG data as the input of AVMD-LSTM. The recognition accuracy of gender classification was 89.21%. Comparing with the task of complete resting state, the model is validated with more robustness. Furthermore, the proposed algorithm has many applications, including biometrics, healthcare, and online entertainment advertising.

Keywords: Gender recognition · Brain-computer interface (BCI) · Electroencephalogram (EEG) · Sample entropy · Variational mode decomposition (VMD) · Shuffled frog leaping algorithm (SFLA)

1 Introduction

Brain-computer interface (BCI) is a communication method in which the brain can directly interact with the external environment or equipment [1]. The mature forms of brain signals for various applications include electroencephalogram (EEG) [2], magnetoencephalogram (MEG) [3], electrocorticogram

Supported by the National Natural Science Foundation of China under Grant 61876082, 61861130366, 61732006 and National Key R&D Program of China under Grant 2018YFC2001600, 2018YFC2001602. Thanks to Chinese sign language teacher Yinling Du for providing guidance.

L. Fang et al. (Eds.): CICAI 2021, LNAI 13069, pp. 213–224, 2021.
https://doi.org/10.1007/978-3-030-93046-2_19

(ECoG) [4], functional magnetic resonance imaging (fMRI) [5], near-infrared spectrum (NIRS) [6], etc. The major advantages of EEG signal are good real-time performance, easy access, and low cost which expand the scope of application. According to the response of brain nerves, the BCI system paradigm is divided into time-related potentials (ERP) [7], steady-state visual evoked potentials (SSVEP) [8], sensorimotor cortical potentials [9], etc. The sensorimotor cortex is a spontaneous neural response when doing tasks without external stimuli. In the BCI paradigm, body movement is an important field. Different limb movements of the human body will produce specific EEG signals, so they can be used as a transmission signal to control external devices.

The absolute difference between male and female genitalia has always been recognized. Recent studies [10,11] have shown that gender differences are attributed to distinctions in brain volume and density in total volume, total surface area, mean cortical thickness or height [12]. Furthermore, the structural connections of male and female brains are also different. The structure of male brain promotes the connection between perception and coordinated action, while the structure of female brain facilitates the communication between analytical and intuitive processing modes [13,14]. The prevalence and symptoms of many neuropsychiatric diseases are also different between men and women [15]. The study of brain differences may help to explain these gender divide.

Gender carries important information about male and female characteristics [16]. The research of gender identification has produced many potential applications, such as information security [17], human-computer interaction [18], disease diagnosis and treatment assistance [19], and demography [20]. However, for human beings, gender recognition can only rely on the characteristics of body parts and involves personal privacy, but for intelligent systems, there are no such problems. In addition to the discrepancy in physical characteristics between men and women, the differences in psychological and neural signals also provide new ideas for gender recognition.

In recent years, some researchers have used EEG signals to identify the gender characteristics of men and women. Hu et al. [21] achieved good classification results by using four entropy values to extract features from resting state EEG signals and then applying six traditional machine learning classifiers to classify them, and. Wang et al. [22] proposed a hybrid model of random forest and logistic regression to identify the gender of EEG signals in resting state. Kaushik et al. [23] proposed a deep BLSTM-LSTM hybrid learning framework to classify the gender-based EEG signals in the relaxation state which achieved a classification accuracy of 97.5%. Catrambone et al. [24] presented three different types of motion-related EEG signals to identify men and women where women had higher prediction accuracy for the prediction of intransitive, transitional and tool mediated actions. Kaur et al. [25] employed the resting EEG signals to identify gender, and obtain 96.66% classification accuracy.

However, in practice, when collecting and detecting EEG signals, it is difficult for the subjects to keep very calm, not thinking and even fixing their limbs. Therefore, we study gender recognition using the combined EEG signal of resting state and motor imagery, which make gender recognition of BCI conform to reality. The setting of motor imagination based on Chinese sign language is closer to real-word scene comparing with MI in general experiments. Due to the unlimited imagination activities and rich forms of expression, it is very suitable for gender recognition. Our contribution mainly includes the following three points: 1) It is more realistic and practical to apply motor imagery EEG signal for gender BCI recognition; 2) We use sample entropy (SE) to select effective channels as the input of proposed network; 3) Shuffled from the leading algorithm (SFLA) is used to improve the variational mode decomposition (VMD), optimize the number of band-limited intrinsic mode function (BIMF), and get the optimal EEG frequency band.

The structure of this paper is as follows. Section 2 describes the process of data acquisition and preprocessing in detail. Section 3 explains the methods we use for gender BCI recognition. Section 4 is the experimental results and discussion of this paper's character recognition of EEG signals. Finally, we make a conclusion and future directions in Section .

2 Materials

2.1 Participants and Equipment

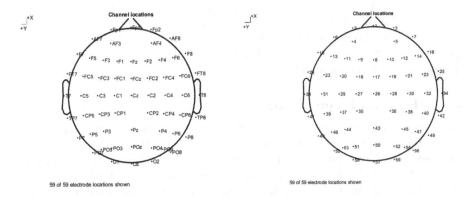

Fig. 1. Electrodes position based on the international 10–20 system standard.

A total of nine subjects (5 male, 4 female, 26±3 year old) participated in the gender BCI experiment. They are all students from our university. Participants signed the written informed consent before the day of the experiment. All subjects were healthy and had no related brain diseases. All protocols were approved by the Committee on Human Research at UCSF and experiments and data in this study complied with all relevant ethical regulations. After the completion of the sign language experiment, we give the participants a certain cash reward.

The experiment was carried out in the laboratory of our school in China. A portable wireless EEG amplifier (NeuSen.W64, Neuracle, China) with 64 electrodes was used to collect EEG signals. According to the international standard

10–20 system, the EEG data of 59 electrodes were recorded, shown as in Fig. 1. The sampling rate is set 1000 Hz. During the whole experiment, the impedance of all electrodes was kept below 5 KΩ.

2.2 Experimental Paradigm and Procedure

Each experimental phase consists of two runs with 15 min of rest. Each run includes 20 trials. There are 20 sign language sentences to execution 20 times in our experiment. One week before the experiment, the subjects were taught to complete Chinese sign language. To enable each subject to master sign language, and to carry out the corresponding execution smoothly in the sign language imagination experiment, the volunteers were required to imitate and complete the experimental personnel's sign language sentences again, before the beginning of each trial. These movements are practiced in a short window before the next resting phase begins. Each task consists of three sequences, as shown in Fig. 2. After the beginning of the sign language imagination experiment, the subjects kept their open for five minutes in the resting state and then after five minutes of rest, and then kept for five minutes in the resting state of closing their eyes. When an experiment starts, a Chinese prompt message of the sign language will appear in the center of the screen. Two seconds later, a cross prompt and a beep sound appeared on the screen. At this time, the subjects began to imagine sign language. After three seconds, the screen would stop and then enter a three second rest period. Before the experiment started, the subjects were asked to keep their eyes in the center of the screen to reduce the interference of eye movements. All subjects were told that they could not do any body movements unrelated to the experimental requirements.

2.3 EEG Data Preprocessing

To facilitate the subsequent processing and analysis of gender BCI, we preprocess it in advance, mainly including the following parts. Firstly, the EEG signal channels were selected, and 59 EEG channels were selected from 64 channels by removing 5 EOG channels. Then, the EEG signal is filtered from 0.1 Hz 100 Hz, and 50 Hz power frequency interference is removed. Next, the data is corrected by reference to the whole brain. The sign language imaginary sentences in the experiment have 3 s and are composed of three sign language words. To adapt to the training of gender BCI, we cut the imaginary sentences of sign language to 1 s or 2 s.

3   Methodology

In this section, we describe the architecture of channel selection and depth adaptive variational mode decomposition - long short term memory (AVMD-LSTM) model for gender recognition. The model is composed of an adaptive VMD algorithm and LSTM network to recognize the gender of individuals by analyzing EEG signals. Through the comparison of different frequency bands of adaptive VMD decomposition, the optimal frequency band of gender recognition is obtained. The experimental results have been compared with the original EEG data. The overall framework of our algorithm is shown in Fig. 3.

3.1   Channel Selection

To extract more information channels and speed up the calculation, we used SE to select channels, and extract 20 channels from 59 channels for gender analysis. The higher the value of SE, the richer the information contained in the signal. We selected the top 20 channels of EEG data containing males and females as materials.

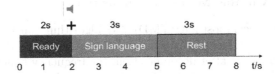

Fig. 2. Experimental paradigm.

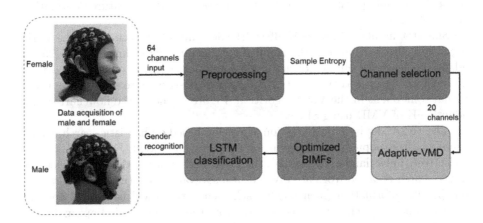

Fig. 3. The flowchart of model structure. Firstly, EEG data of males and females were collected by 64 channel neural, including resting state and sign language MI data. The data preprocessing includes filtering, re re-ference and segmentation. Then the SE is used to calculate the entropy value of each channel, and the top 20 with the largest entropy value are taken as the follow-up analysis data. The VMD optimized based on shuffled frog leading algorithm (SFLA) is used to decompose the data into five optimal frequency bands, which are input into LSTM for gender recognition.

SE method provides an evaluation of time series regularity. It allows comparison of measurements at different frequencies on datasets [26].

Suppose there is a primitive time series $\{u(j)\}$ consisting of N points, where N is length of time series, $1 \leq j \leq N$. The time series consists of $N - m + 1$ vector series $X_m(i)$, $\{i|1 \leq i \leq N - m + 1\}$, where m is the length of sequences.

$$X_m(i) = \{u(i+k), 0 \le k \le m-1\} \tag{1}$$

where $X_m(i)$ is the vector of the m-th data from $u(i)$ to $u(i+m-1)$.
SE can be estimated to be:

$$SampEn(m, r, N) = -\ln[\frac{A_m(r)}{B_m(r)}] \tag{2}$$

3.2   Adaptive Variable Mode Decomposition

Variational mode decomposition (VMD) [27] algorithm can decompose EEG signals into k uncertain band limited intrinsic mode functions. However, if there are too many sub modes after decomposition, the frequency bands overlap after signal decomposition, resulting in information redundancy in the results. On the contrary, too few sub mode decomposition will make it difficult to extract effective information from sub modes. Therefore, the key of VMD algorithm is to select the optimal parameters to eliminate noise and extract feature information effectively [28].

Since the number of modes K affects the decomposition accuracy of the VMD algorithm, this section uses the shuffled frog leaping algorithm (SFLA) [29] to adaptively learn the number of sub mode decomposition K to obtain the optimal parameters. An objective evaluation function is constructed to select the optimal modal component in the VMD algorithm. Figure 4 shown the flowchart of the adaptive K of VMD using SFLA.

The SFLA [30] is an optimization algorithm based on heuristic search, which simulates frog population iteration and searching for food. Frogs usually live collectively in wetland areas and get the most food by using the least movement in the search area. So frogs are divided into seveval groups (modules) and each one has its information (memes). In each meme, there will be a local optimal search strategy which is to forage by selecting the local or global optimal solutions for frogs to update the worst position to a better one. Local search can spread among local individuals, and hybrid strategy can exchange ideas among local individuals [31]. Using global information exchange and local depth exploration, the algorithm can jump out of the local extremum and move to the global optimal direction [32].

The SFLA algorithm first initializes the parameters and randomly generates the first frog population in the decision space. Then the fitness value of each frog can be calculated which is the basis to rank all populations.

$$Y_k = [(X_i)k|X_i = X(k + m * (i-1)), i = 1,..., n], k = 1,..., m \tag{3}$$

where m is the number of meme bundles and N is the number of members in each meme bundle. Equation 3 ensures that the members are evenly distributed in the memetic clusters. Let m = 3, then the first element becomes the first, the second element becomes the second, the third element becomes the third, the fourth element becomes the first, and so on.

The population is divided into meme bundles by the above formula, and the meme evolution process of each meme bundle is carried out. The new iteration will start from the reordering of the population until the termination condition is satisfied. The algorithm makes use of the characteristics of the meme distribution of wetland population to use a more effectively search in the solution space [33].

VMD is an adaptive and variational method, which can be used to decomposed signals to the mode by the minimization [34]. The models reproducing the input have specific sparsity properties [35]. Each mode is mostly compact around, a center pulsation, to access the bandwidth of a mode which can be determined by decomposition. Specifically, we first preset the order of modes. The original signal is decomposed into BIMF of preset order.

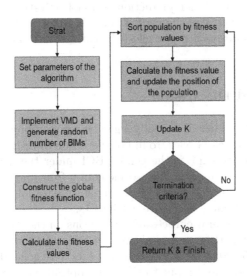

Fig. 4. The flowchart of the adaptive K in VMD using SFLA.

Introduce the quadratic penalty factor α and Lagrange multiplier. The constrained variational problem was transformed into a non-constrained variational problem.

The variational problem can be solved by alternate direction method of multipliers (ADMM). Seek out the saddle points for Lagrangian expressions by constantly updating the μ_k^{n+1}, ω_{kn+1} and λ_{n+1}. is converted to frequency domain by Parseval Fourier equidistance transform method obtained the frequency domain update of each mode. The decision expression is:

$$\sum_k \frac{\left\|\hat{\mu}_k^{n+1} - \hat{\mu}_k^n\right\|_2^2}{\left\|\hat{\mu}_k^n\right\|_2^2} < e \tag{4}$$

Finally, VMD will be analyzed signal f adaptive decomposition into K narrow band of the modal component $\mu_k(k = 1, 2, \cdots, K)$.

3.3   LSTM Network

In this paper, we adopt the open-source implementation of LSTM based on CUDA technology provided by NVIDIA. We used two hidden layers containing LSTM cells for the configuration. The LSTM architecture consists of three stacked LSTM layers with 512, 128 and 64 units, respectively. The learning rate is set to 0.001, decay is 1e-8 and the momentum is 0.7. In the first layer, the dropout is 0.2, and then batch normalization is performed, while the other two LSTM layers only perform batch normalization. Then there is a dense layer composed of 32 neurons, followed by another dense layer composed of one neuron. The last layer has only one neuron to classify the male and female gender. The model was trained by 500 epochs and cross-validated 10 times. The number of training parameters in gender prediction is 15300 (RestEEG: 4500, MI_EEG: 10800). If the performance of the verification set, which is the sum of squares of errors, does not improve after 50 cycles, the early stop strategy is used to stop the training.

4   Results and Discussion

The main idea of this article is to study a gender recognition method that can be more adaptable in the EEG background of the fusion of resting state and motor imagination, that is, to explore the gender BCI under the data fusion of EEG and EEG. The data set used in this article comes from the 64-channel EEG of 9 subjects. Each subject has 5 min of resting state data and 400 sign language sentence imagination data, which are cut into 1s.

We perform a series of preprocessing operations on the dataset, including filtering, re-referencing, artifact removal, segmentation and channel selection based on SE. A total of 15,300 male and female data sets were generated by 9 subjects. The data set is divided and input to the VMD optimized by SFLA for optimal frequency band decomposition, and finally the LSTM deep learning algorithm is used for gender recognition.

4.1   Results Using Our AVMD-LSTM Method Based on Different Data

To verify the effectiveness of the proposed model, we use the LSTM algorithm to classify and recognize the gender of the resting state and its mixed data with motor imagery. The classification accuracy of our proposed model reaches 89.12%, as shown in Fig. 5. Besides, we also conduct classification experiments on the five BIMFs decomposed by the improved VMD algorithm. Among them, the second sub mode is the highest. To verify the effectiveness of channel selection and frequency band decomposition, we use the original data without channel selection and frequency band selection in this experiment. As shown in Fig. 5, the classification accuracy is only 88.98% and 79.27%, which is lower than the classification accuracy of the proposed model. The experimental results show that the accuracy of gender recognition is the highest in a completely resting state. Although adding motor imagery EEG will reduce the accuracy, it will provide more practical significance for gender recognition because the brain of the subjects is activated in the awake state, and it is difficult to achieve the surprise state for a long time, the data added with motor imagery is more generalized.

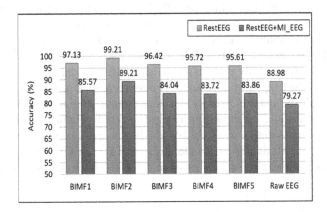

Fig. 5. Sample Entropy Results of 59 channels. The orange column indicates the top 20 channels with entropy higher than 40, and the blue column indicates the channels with entropy lower than 40. (Color figure online)

4.2 Channel Selection Based on Sample Entropy

To extract more useful channels with more information and speed up the calculation, we leverage the SE to calculate the entropy value of all samples' channels. The data obtained are shown in Fig. 6. We select the first 20 channels with an entropy value over 40, which are the 22nd, 23rd, 24th, 25th, 32nd, 33rd, 34th, 39th, 41nd, 42nd, 45th, 46th, 47th, 48th, 49th, 53rd, 54th, 55th, 56th and 59th channels. The corresponding electrode positions are shown in Fig. 1.

4.3 Efficacy of Our Model Structure

Table 1. six models gender recognition accuracy in two datasets.

EEG data	LSTM	SE-LSTM	Ours	CNN	SE-CNN	SE-AVMD-CNN
RestEEG (%)	94.72	97.08	99.21	92.44	96.51	97.62
RestEEG+MI_EEG (%)	75.27	82.57	89.21	73.48	77.66	85.59

In this section, the innovation of our model lines in the combination of the structural performance of SE, AVMD and LSTM algorithms. To verify the rationality of the AVMD-LSTM model structure, we reorganize these three parts. The first is to use only CNN algorithm for gender recognition. The second is to add the channel selection algorithm SE on top of the first one to validate the effectiveness of SE. The third is to add an adaptive VMD (AVMD) frequency band selection algorithm on the second basis to compare its performance. The next three methods are similar to LSTM, which are classified as CNN, SE-CNN, SE-AVMD-CNN, as shown in Table 1. The experimental results show that the two models based on the SE-AVMD module achieve the highest classification accuracy of the algorithms, which are 89.21% and 85.59% respectively.

The original signal is processed by the SE of the channel selection module to extract the useful channel, which not only increases the calculation time, but also eliminates the redundant information. The optimal frequency band selection of adaptive VMD can not only remove the noise in EEG but also select the best frequency band in the frequency domain for gender recognition. The addition of these two modules fully reflects that the model can extract rich hidden information from EEG and has outstanding signal representation ability, which makes the binary classification reach a higher level. Although the accuracy of gender recognition is reduced by adding MI data, it can make the model more adaptable and be applied to more scenarios under the condition of meeting the basic gender recognition.

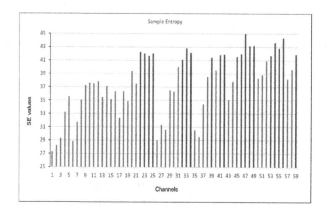

Fig. 6. Sample Entropy Results of 59 channels. The orange column indicates the top 20 channels with entropy higher than 40, and the blue column indicates the channels with entropy lower than 40. (Color figure online)

5   Conclusion

EEG signals of everyone are unique with a lot of meaningful information, including gender differences. The identification of human gender can be applied to many fields, such as online consumption, biometrics and health care. We try to establish a more generalized robust algorithm to predict individual gender by analyzing EEG signals that combine resting state and motor imagery. To make the gender recognition algorithm more generalized, the researchers recorded the EEG data of nine men and women sitting with their eyes open in a resting position and perform Chinese sign language motor imagery.

We developed a frequency band selection algorithm based on SFLA optimized VMD for gender recognition. To reduce computation time and extract more informative channels, we adopted SE to select 20 channels, and finally employed LSTM for gender classification. The accuracy of gender classification was 89.21%.

References

1. Gao, S.K., Wang, Y.J., Gao, X.R., et al.: Visual and auditory brain-computer interfaces. IEEE Trans. Biomed. Eng. **61**(5), 1436–1447 (2014)
2. Lu, N., Li, T., Ren, X., Miao, H.: A deep learning scheme for motor imagery classification based on restricted boltzmann machines. IEEE Trans. Neural Syst. Rehab. Eng .**25**(6), 566–576 (2017)
3. Kauhanen, L., Nykopp, T., Lehtonen, J., et al.: EEG and MEG brain-computer interface for tetraplegic patients. IEEE Trans. Neural Syst. Rehab. Eng. **14**(2), 190–193 (2006)
4. Mestais, C.S., Charvet, G., Sauter-Starace, F., Foerster, M., Ratel, D., Benabid, A.L.: WIMAGINE: wireless 64-Channel ECoG recording implant for long term clinical applications. IEEE Trans. Neural Syst. Rehab. Eng. **23**(1), 10–21 (2015)
5. Yuan, K., et al.: Interhemispheric functional reorganization and its structural base after BCI-Guided upper-limb training in chronic stroke. IEEE Trans. Neural Syst. Rehab. Eng. **28**(11), 2525–2536 (2020)
6. Han, C.-H., Müller, K.-R., Hwang, H.-J.: Enhanced performance of a brain switch by simultaneous use of EEG and NIRS Data for asynchronous brain-computer interface. IEEE Trans .Neural Syst. Rehab. Eng. **28**(10), 2102–2112 (2020)
7. Li, J., Yu, Z.L., Gu, Z., Wu, W., Li, Y., Jin, L.: A hybrid network for ERP detection and analysis based on restricted Boltzmann machine. IEEE Trans. Neural Syst. Rehab. Eng. **26**(3), 563–572 (2018)
8. Nakanishi, M., Wang, Y., Chen, X., et al.: Enhancing detection of SSVEPs for a high-speed brain speller using task-related component analysis. IEEE Trans. Biomed. Eng. **65**(1), 104–112 (2018)
9. He, B., Baxter, B., Edelman, B.J., Cline, C.C., Ye, W.W.: Noninvasive brain-computer interfaces based on sensorimotor rhythms. Proceed. IEEE **103**(6), 907–925 (2015)
10. Luders, E., et al.: Gender differences in cortical complexity. Nat. Neurosci. **7**(8), 799–800 (2004)
11. Chao, Z., et al.: Functional connectivity predicts gender: evidence for gender differences in resting brain connectivity. Human Brain Map. **39**(3), 1–11 (2018)
12. Ritchie, S.J., et al.: Sex differences in the adult human brain evidence from 5216 UK biobank participants. Cerebr. Cortex **28**(8), 2959–2975 (2018)
13. Ruigrok, A.N.V., et al.: A meta analysis of sex differences in human brain structure. Neurosci. Biobehav. Rev. **39**(1), 34–50 (2014)
14. Ingalhalikar, M., Smith, A., Parker, D., et al.: Sex differences in the structural connectome of the human brain. Proceed. National Acad. Sci. United States Am. **2**(111), 823–828 (2014
15. Jung, M., Choi, M., Lee, T.R.: Determinants of public phobia about infectious diseases in south korea effect of health communication and gender difference. Asia Pac. J. Public Health **27**(2), 1–12 (2015)
16. Kwon, N., Song, H.: Personality traits gender and information competency among college students. Malaysian J. Library Inf. Sci. **16**(1), 87–107 (2011)

17. Eidinger, E., et al.: Age and gender estimation of unfiltered faces. IEEE Trans. Inf. Forensics Secur. **9**(12), 2170–2179 (2014)

18. Volosyak, I., Valbuena, D., Luth, T., Malechka, T., Graser, A.: BCI demographics II how many (and What Kinds of) people can use a high-frequen cy SSVEP BCI. IEEE Trans. Neural Syst. Rehab. Eng. **19**(3), 232–239 (2011)

19. Raghavan, P., et al.: The role of robotic path assistance and weight support in facilitating 3D movements in individuals with oststroke Hemiparesis. Neurorehab. Neural Repair **34**(2), 1–12 (2020)

20. Sun, Y., Zhang, M., Sun, Z., et al.: Demographic analysis from biometric data: achievements, challenges, and new frontiers. IEEE Trans. Pattern Anal. Machine Intell. **40**(2), 332–351 (2018)

21. Hu, J.: An approach to EEG-based gender recognition using entropy measurement methods. Knowl. Based Syst. **140**(15), 134–141 (2018)

22. Wang, P., Hu, J.: A hybrid model for EEG-based gender recognition. Cognit. Neurodynam. **13**(6), 541–554 (2019). https://doi.org/10.1007/s11571-019-09543-y

23. Kaushik, P., et al.: EEG-Based age and gender prediction using deep BLSTM-LSTM network model. IEEE Sensors J. **19**(7), 2634–2641 (2019)

24. Catrambone, V., Greco, A., Averta, G., Bianchi, M., Valenza, G., Scilingo, E.P.: Predicting object-mediated gestures from brain activity: an EEG study on gender differences. IEEE Trans. Neural Syst. Rehab. Eng. **27**(3), 411–418 (2019)

25. Kaur, B., Singh, D., Roy, P.P.: Age and gender classification using brain-computer interface. Neural Comput. Appl. **31**, 5887–5900 (2019)

26. Cao, Z., Lin, C.-T.: Inherent fuzzy entropy for the improvement of EEG complexity evaluation. IEEE Trans. Fuzzy Syst. **26**, 1032–1035 (2018)

27. Subasi, A., Jukic, S., Kevric, J.: Comparison of EMD, DWT and WPD for the localization of Epileptogenic Foci using random forest classifier. Measurement **146**, 846–855 (2019)

28. Dora, C., Biswal, P.K.: An improved algorithm for efficient ocular artifact suppression from frontal EEG electrodes using VMD. Biocybern. Biomed. Eng. **40**(1), 148–161 (2019)

29. Xia, L., et al.: An improved shuffled frog-leaping algorithm with extremal optimisation for continuous optimisation. Inf. Sci. **192**, 143–151 (2012)

30. Hu, B., et al.: Feature selection for optimized high-dimensional biomedical data using an improved shuffled frog leaping algorithm. IEEE/ACM Trans. Comput. Biol. Bioinf. **15**(6), 1765–1773 (2018)

31. Fan, et al.: Self-adaptive kernel K-means algorithm based on the shuffled frog leaping algorithm. Soft Comput. Fusion Foundations Methodol. Appl. **22**(3), 861–872 (2018)

32. Rajamohana, S.P., Umamaheswari, K.: Hybrid approach of improved binary particle swarm optimization and shuffled frog leaping for feature selection. Comput. Electric. Eng. **67**, 497–508 (2018)

33. Huang, C., et al.: A new pulse coupled neural network (PCNN) for brain medical image fusion empowered by shuffled frog leaping algorithm. Front. Neurosci. **13**, 210 (2019)

34. Rehman, N.U., Aftab, H.: Multivariate variational mode decomposition. IEEE Trans. Signal Process. **67**(23), 6039–6052 (2019)

35. Taran, S., Bajaj, V.: Clustering variational mode decomposition for identification of focal EEG signals. IEEE Sensors Lett **2**(4), 1–4 (2018)

Computer Vision

Hybrid Domain Convolutional Neural Network for Memory Efficient Training

Bochen Guan[1(✉)], Yanli Liu[1], Jinnian Zhang[2], William A. Sethares[2],
Fang Liu[3], Qinwen Xu[1], Weiyi Li[1], and Shuxue Quan[1]

[1] OPPO US Research Center, InnoPeak Technology, Palo Alto, CA, USA
{bochen.guan,yanli.liu,qinwen.xu,weiyi.li,shuxue.quan}@oppo.com
[2] University of Wisconsin, Madison, WI, USA
{jinnian.zhang,sethares}@wisc.edu
[3] Harvard University, Cambridge, MA, USA
fliu12@mgh.harvard.edu

Abstract. For many popular Convolutional Neural Networks (CNNs), memory has become one of the major constraints for their efficient training and inference on edge devices. Recently, it is shown that the bottleneck lies in the feature maps generated by convolutional layers. In this work, we propose a hybrid domain Convolutional Neural Network (HyNet) to reduce the memory footprint. Specifically, HyNet prunes the filters in the spatial domain and sparsifies the feature maps in the frequency domain. HyNet also introduces a specifically designed activation function in the frequency domain to preserve the sparsity of the feature maps while effectively strengthening training convergence. We evaluate the performance of HyNet by testing on three state-of-the-art networks (VGG, DenseNet, and ResNet) on several competitive image classification benchmarks (CIFAR-10, and ImageNet). We also compare HyNet with several memory-efficient training approaches. Overall, HyNet can reduce memory consumption by about ∼50% without significant accuracy loss.

Keywords: Hybrid-domain · Memory-efficient training · CNN

1 Introduction

Deep Convolutional Neural Networks (CNNs) have made significant progress on various tasks such as image recognition [1,12,15,18], medical imaging [9] and object detection [10,33] in recent years. Current successful deep CNNs such as ResNet [12] and DenseNet [15] with a large number of parameters and typically involve over a great many layers. Therefore, their training process requires a lot of memory, which is a bottleneck when only limited resources are available

---

B. Guan, Y. Liu, J. Zhang—Equal contribution.
Jinnian Zhang was supported by the National Library of Medicine of the National Institutes of Health under award number R01LM013151.

© Springer Nature Switzerland AG 2021
L. Fang et al. (Eds.): CICAI 2021, LNAI 13069, pp. 227–239, 2021.
https://doi.org/10.1007/978-3-030-93046-2_20

[5]. On the other hand, network deployment and fine-tuning on edge devices become crucial due to privacy issues and under offline environments. Therefore, it is essential to develop an approach to reduce memory requirements to allow for training and deployment on embedded systems and cell phones.

It is demonstrated in [17,25] that the primary contributors to the memory bottleneck are the intermediate layer outputs (feature maps). In this work, we target reducing the memory cost of feature maps by resorting to the frequency domain, which is in contrast to the spatial domain approach proposed in [17]. Specifically, we exploit the fact that in the frequency domain, the energy of feature maps is often concentrated. We ask if it is possible to sparsely save the feature maps by enforcing entries less than a configurable threshold to zero. Thus, we propose a Hybrid domain Convolutional Neural Network (HyNet). We develop a memory-efficient convolutional block where the convolution and activation are implemented in hybrid (spatial and frequency) domains. The kernel is stored and pruned in the spatial domain, and feature maps are filtered and stored sparsely. The activation function is designed specially, such that it can preserve the sparsity and symmetry of the feature maps in the frequency domain. This also leads to an effective computation of the gradients during back propagation.

Overall, the key contributions of our work are summarized as follows:

1. We propose a new CNN (HyNet) for memory efficient training. The network performs convolution and activation in the frequency domain. Feature maps are compressed in hybrid (spatial and frequency) domains, and only non-zero entries are computed and saved.
2. We propose a frequency domain activation function, which is applied to both the real and imaginary parts of the input feature maps. It preserves the sparsity of feature maps and encourages convergence during training.
3. We conduct extensive experiments to show the effectiveness of HyNet with multiple computer vision tasks. For example, a HyNet implementation of the ResNet-18 network can achieve up to a 56.2% reduction in memory consumption on the ImageNet dataset without a significant loss of accuracy (68.48% top-1 accuracy compared with the baseline 69.57% top-1 accuracy).

2   Related Work

In the following section, we review several approaches to reduce memory cost during training, including memory scheduling, compact representation of feature maps, memory efficient CNN architectures, and model compression.

2.1   Memory Scheduling

To reduce the memory footprint of weights, [4] applies a simple hash function that groups connections into hash buckets and lets the connections in the same bucket share the same weight value. [28] dynamically allocates memory to convolutions and designs memory optimizations that reduce the peak memory usage.

Since the "life-time" of feature maps is different at each layer, several studies come up with approaches to reduce their memory consumption. In [21], feature maps are transferred between CPU and GPU, such that large-scale training with limited GPU memory is allowed, with a slightly slower training speed. In [23], the output of batch normalization, concatenation, and ReLU layers are stored in the shared memory, which leads to 75% memory reduction on DenseNet. [3] designs a more general memory sharing algorithm that is applicable to CNNs and RNNs, and a sublinear memory cost is achieved when compared with the original implementations. In [22], the authors identify the critical bottlenecks of the frequency convolutional layers and design a scheduling algorithm for FPGAs, which schedules on-chip memory access with minimum read conflicts.

Different from the above methods optimizing the memory footprint from hardware design, our proposed method focuses on compressing feature maps directly from the algorithmic design but still keeps the basic structure of the networks.

2.2 Compact Representation of Feature Maps

Another line of work focuses on constructing compact representations of feature maps. In [29], the authors propose a method to extract intrinsic representations of the feature maps, while preserving their discriminability. It achieves a high network compression ratio but requires additional modules to solve an optimization at each layer. On the other hand, [17] encodes and store the feature maps in the time domain by employing layer-specific encoding schemes, and performs decoding for back propagation. However, the additional encoding and decoding process increases computational complexity.

Compared with the above approaches, our HyNet does not require additional modules. Its architecture is designed for sparse storage of feature maps in the frequency domain, which is more computationally efficient.

2.3 Memory Efficient CNN Architectures

By modifying certain structures in popular CNN architectures, memory efficiency can be achieved. [26] combines the batch normalization and activation layers so that a single memory buffer can be used to store the feature maps. [31] proposes a novel CNN structural decoupling method. It decouples a CNN into sub-networks and eliminates the inter-layer data dependency, which reduces memory cost. In [19], several practical guidelines on network architecture design are provided for reducing memory access cost (MAC). Accordingly, ShuffleNet v2 is proposed, which is more efficient than ShuffleNet v1 and MobileNet v2. [2] introduces a limit on the number of input and output channels, resulting in both memory efficiency and low inference latency.

In comparison, HyNet involves a structural change in the convolutional block, where a sparse approximation and representation of the feature maps in the frequency domain is used, and a special activation function to preserve the symmetry property is incorporated.

2.4 CNN in the Frequency Domain

Several previous publications showed the feasibility of combining CNNs with Fast Fourier Transform (FFT) or Wavelet transforms [8, 11, 24]. These works are implemented by replacing the convolutional layer with the Fourier Transform and the dot product of the kernels and inputs in the frequency domain. Though some can accelerate the training process, it will take more memory in real implementation. Meanwhile, these works require inverse Fast Fourier Transform (iFFT) after convolutional layers, which will take additional computation.

In contrast, HyNet applies the FFT to reduce memory consumption. Different from the above-mentioned FFT-based CNNs, its computation complexity depends on certain input parameters.

2.5 Model Compression

Model compression can be achieved in several ways including quantization, pruning, and weight decomposition. Network quantization converts full-precision weights and the feature maps into a number of low-bit width integers. The key idea behind network pruning is to remove unimportant connections. Weight decomposition tries to find a low-rank decomposition of weights. Due to their different principles, we choose not to review their recent works here. We refer interested readers to a recent survey [7] for more details.

Overall, these methods compress weights to reduce the model size, and further reduce the size of feature maps. In comparison, HyNet directly reduces the memory consumption by sparsifying the feature maps and storing them efficiently. Model compression methods may be combined with our HyNet to save more memory.

3 The Proposed Method

HyNet is based on the observation that the feature maps for each CNN layer have compact energy in the frequency domain, just like natural images [30]. In Fig. 1, we compare feature maps after the first convolutional layer in DenseNet [15] with different inputs, and it is clear that the feature maps in the frequency domain are very compact. Inspired by this, we keep the non-trivial values while pruning small entries to zero and convert the maps back to the spatial domain. The compression of the feature maps in the frequency domain will not significantly impact the feature maps in the spatial domain. This idea gives rise to a new training framework, HyNet that works in the hybrid domain (spatial and frequency) to improve memory efficiency during training. It applies two thresholds β to feature maps and γ to filters, configuring the compression ratio where larger threshold values lead to more memory reduction. We demonstrate the core idea of HyNet in the bottom half of Fig. 2.

Notably, some previous works use the FFT to accelerate network training, but this requires additional memory [8, 20, 24]. In contrast, HyNet uses a different network architecture design for convolution, compression, activation, and

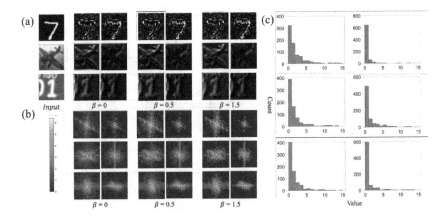

Fig. 1. Feature maps of HyNet after the first convolutional layer in DenseNet for different inputs. (a) Feature maps after two different filters in the frequency domain with three different thresholds β. (b) Feature maps, converted back to the spatial domain by the inverse Fourier transform with different thresholds β. Values of β have little effect on the visual appearance of the feature maps. (c) Distributions of absolute values in each feature map.

maxpooling in the frequency domain, which can be applied to both forward and backward propagation in network training and inference. HyNet is developed to reduce the memory consumption during training but not target on reducing the computational cost for inference.

In the following section, we present the convolution, activation, and maxpooling layers in HyNet.

3.1   Convolution

A standard 2D convolution with a stride of 1 is given by

$$y(i,j) = x * k = \sum_{m=0}^{M-1} \sum_{n=0}^{N-1} x(m,n)\, k(i - m, j - n), \tag{1}$$

where x is an input matrix with size (M, N); k is the kernel with size (N_k, N_k), and $*$ denotes the 2D convolution operator. y is the output with size (M', N'), where $M' = M + N_k - 1$ and $N' = N + N_k - 1$. This operation will cost $\mathcal{O}(M'N'N_k^2)$ multiplications. As described in [24], convolution can be implemented more efficiently in the frequency domain as

$$Y = X \odot K \tag{2}$$

where X and K are the 2D Fast-Fourier Transform (FFT) of x and k, respectively. For example, X is given by

$$X(p,q) = \mathcal{F}(x) = \sum_{m=0}^{M'-1} \sum_{n=0}^{N'-1} w_M^{pm} w_N^{qn} x(m,n) \tag{3}$$

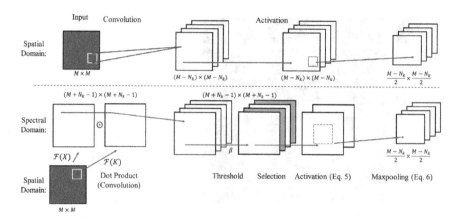

Fig. 2. The standard convolutional block in the spatial and frequency domain. The top figure shows the standard convolutional block with an input layer and a convolutional layer followed by an activation layer. The bottom figure shows the convolutional block in HyNet. To improve memory efficiency, the kernels are stored in the spatial domain while the feature maps are efficiently stored in the frequency domain.

where $w_M = e^{-2\pi i/(M+N_k-1)}$ and $w_N = e^{-2\pi i/(N+N_k-1)}$. Equation (2) requires that X and K share the same dimensions, so x and k should be zero padded to match their dimensions (M', N'). Equation (2) and (3) involve $\mathcal{O}(M'N' \log(M'N'))$ complex multiplications. In some cases, [24], frequency convolution has efficient computation over the spatial domain's reliance on the size of the kernels and inputs, but it also depends on the hardware implementation.

In HyNet, we define two thresholds $\gamma, \beta > 0$ to compress the network from both the spatial and frequency domains. Inspired by several pruning methods [6,16], we use l1-norm to select unimportant filter channels and physically prune them when the l1-norm is smaller than γ. The entries of the feature map Y with small absolute values smaller than β are pruned to zero.

The backward propagation of HyNet requires the calculation of the error δ_X for the previous layers, and the gradients Δ_K for k. Let δ_Y be the error from the next layer, and X_0, k_0 be the input and kernel of the convolutional layer stored in the forward propagation, respectively. Then,

$$\begin{aligned}
\delta_X &= \nabla_X L|_{X=X_0} = \delta_Y \odot K_0 \\
\Delta_K &= \nabla_K L|_{K=\mathcal{F}(k_0)} = \delta_Y \odot X_0,
\end{aligned} \quad (4)$$

where L is the loss function. After obtaining Δ_K, we apply IFFT and the $N_k \times N_k$ matrix for the update of k is given by

$$k_1 = k_0 + \lambda[\mathcal{F}^{-1}(\Delta_K)]_{N_k \times N_k}, \quad (5)$$

where λ is the learning rate. Since the kernel is not sparse in the frequency domain, we store it in the spatial domain to save memory.

3.2 Activation

Suppose the activation function A in the frequency domain can be written as

$$A(a + ib) = f(a) + ig(b) \qquad (6)$$

Each entry of a feature map in the frequency domain is a complex number. If a feature map X with a size of $(M + N_k - 1, N + N_k - 1)$ can be transformed back into a spatial domain without additional pseudo phases, it requires the following conjugate symmetry:

$$
\begin{aligned}
&X(M + N_k - 1 - p_0, N + N_k - 1 - q_0) \\
&= \sum_{m=0}^{M+N_k-2} \sum_{n=0}^{N+N_k-2} w_M^{(M+N_k-1-p_0)m} w_N^{(N+N_k-1-q_0)n} x(m,n) \\
&= \sum_{m=0}^{M+N_k-2} \sum_{n=0}^{N+N_k-2} w_M^{-p_0 m} w_N^{-q_0 n} x(m,n) \qquad (7) \\
&= \overline{X(p_0, q_0)}
\end{aligned}
$$

where $(p_0, q_0) \in X$.

To perform the activation function for a complex number, the activation should apply nonlinearity while maintaining the conjugate symmetry of the frequency feature maps, so that the maps after activation transformed into the spatial $(\mathcal{F}^{-1}(A(X)))$ can be real numbers. Therefore, we empirically conclude three requirements for the activation functions A:

1. f or g should be a non-linear function;
2. f and g should be monotonic non-decreasing;
3. g is an odd function.

In our study, we use $f(x) = x$ and $g(x) = \tanh(x)$ as a proof of concept for the activation function, and they might be replaced by any other activation functions that fulfill these two requirements. The error for the aforementioned activation in backward propagation is computed as

$$\delta_X = i(1 - (\tanh(\Im(X_0)))^2) \odot \Im(\delta_Y). \qquad (8)$$

3.3 Maxpooling

In the frequency domain, the high-frequency data is in the center and low frequencies are located towards the boundaries. In order to efficiently implement the network, HyNet does not transform the activated frequency feature maps back into the spatial domain using the IFFT. Instead, we introduce a Fourier maxpooling by truncating a small size of feature maps as shown in Fig. 2, which contains high-frequency data to retrain more spatial information [24]. If the pooling ratio in the spatial domain is κ, we set the truncating ratio s in the frequency domain as $s = \kappa \times \frac{M}{M+N_k-1}$, which leads to the same size after the pooling layer.

4 Experiments

Datasets and Baseline Model. To evaluate the memory efficiency of HyNet-during training, we conduct experiments on both small (CIFAR, SVHN) and large (ImageNet) datasets. We demonstrate that the effectiveness of HyNet on state-of-the-art architectures including VGG [18], DenseNet [15], and ResNet [12]. We also compare HyNet with several prior arts for memory efficient training.

Configurations. For all the networks, our settings are similar to those original implementations: we trained the network by stochastic gradient descent (SGD) with a momentum of 0.95, a weight decay of $5e-5$, and a batch size of 256 on CIFAR, SVHN, and ImageNet dataset. The network is trained by total of 120 epochs where the initial learning rate is set to 0.2 and is reduced by $1/10$ every 30 epochs. We use 4 NVIDIA Quadro P6000 cards for our experiment, and some customized operations of sparse tensors are developed on CUDA.

4.1 Results on CIFAR-10

Table 1. Comparison of memory consumption for different memory efficient implementations applied to VGG, DenseNet, and ResNet. All the methods are tested on CIFAR-10.

Network	Method	Memory (%) ↓	Acc. ↓
VGG-13	INPLACE-ABN [26]	47.9	1.66
	Chen Meng et al. [21]	34.4	0.96
	Nonuniform quantization [27]	20.0	1.36
	LQ-Net [32]	32.4	1.16
	HarDNet [2]	53.7	0.96
	vDNN [25]	45.9	0.96
	HyNet (ours)	61.0	0.97
DenseNet	INPLACE-ABN [26]	42.0	1.70
	Chen Meng et al. [21]	44.7	1.40
	Efficient-DenseNets [23]	55.7	1.30
	Nonuniform quantization [27]	22.9	2.40
	LQ-Net [32]	35.6	2.30
	HarDNet [2]	55.8	1.30
	vDNN [25]	40.8	1.30
	HyNet (ours)	63.0	1.33
ResNet-56	AMC [13]	50.0	0.91
	CP [14]	50.0	1.04
	HyNet (ours)	50.1	0.89

As shown in Table 1, we evaluate HyNet on VGG [18], ResNet [12], and DenseNet [15]. We also compare the average memory consumption and inference accuracy of HyNet with other related memory-efficient approaches. HyNet shows a low memory usage while maintaining a good performance. Some model pruning approaches such as AMC [13] and CP [14] show similar performance. However, these approaches either require pretrained models or reduce the memory progressively during training. Finally, the underlying idea of HyNet is different from those of the listed methods and it is able to combine HyNet with these methods.

4.2 Results on ImageNet

We evaluate HyNet for VGG [18], ResNet [12], and DenseNet [15] on the ImageNet dataset with the β value fixed to 0.8 and γ to 0.02 [16]. For a fair comparison, we keep the same image augmentation, hyper-parameter initialization, and optimization settings with the original network implementations [12,15,18].

Table 2 presents the comparison in memory usage and testing accuracy of HyNet on ImageNet dataset. The proposed method reports a slight top-1 accuracy drop and a negligible top-5 accuracy drop. It should be noted that HyNet can provide better performance or higher memory reduction by choosing different β and γ values (as demonstrated in Fig. 3).

Table 2 also shows the comparison between HyNet and other recently proposed memory-efficient algorithms on ImageNet. HyNet outperforms all the other algorithms and enjoys the largest memory reduction with acceptable accuracy loss. We would like to emphasize that HyNet can reduce the memory

Table 2. Comparison of memory consumption reduction for different memory efficient implementations applied to VGG, DenseNet, and ResNet. All of the methods are tested on ImageNet.

Network	Method	Memory (%) ↓	Top-1 Acc. ↓	Top-5 Acc. ↓
VGG-16	INPLACE-ABN	36.0	1.60	0.60
	Chen Meng et al.	40.6	1.00	0.00
	Nonuniform quantization	23.7	3.10	1.50
	LQ-Net	43.9	4.10	1.73
	HarDNet	49.9	1.30	0.10
	vDNN	42.3	1.40	0.23
	HyNet	52.1	0.90	0.10
DenseNet	INPLACE-ABN	43.0	1.50	0.03
	Chen Meng et al.	53.0	1.20	0.20
	Efficient-DenseNets	49.3	2.74	0.70
	Nonuniform quantization	24.1	3.70	1.50
	LQ-Net	48.7	6.60	3.70
	HarDNet	52.6	0.80	0.10
	vDNN	36.0	1.01	0.25
	HyNet	57.2	1.04	0.17
ResNet-18	SSS [16]	43.7	1.97	0.46
	LeGR [6]	53.0	1.17	0.40
	HyNet	56.5	1.09	0.31

requirements during the whole training process, which is different from other model compression approaches.

5   Ablation Study

We empirically investigate the relationship between memory compression and performance loss to the compression thresholds (β) in Fig. 3. Since there's almost no accuracy reduction for β less than 0.5, we set it from 0.5 to 1.5. We describe the memory consumption by using the memory of HyNet over the memory in the original implementations. HyNet is able to reduce training memory consumption by 50% with negligible performance loss. In addition, the memory consumption reduction rates are different among the different models, which is presumably due to the different feature representations of the various networks.

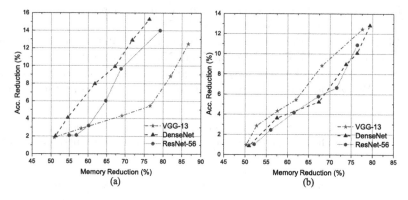

Fig. 3. Memory consumption and testing accuracy of HyNet on VGG-16 [18], DenseNet [15], and ResNet-56 [12] on (a) CIFAR-10 and (b) SVHN dataset.

6   Conclusion

In this work, we develop a new CNN architecture called HyNet, which saves memory by working in the hybrid domains. Especially, the filters are stored in the spatial domain and feature maps are stored sparsely in the frequency domain. By setting a configurable threshold to prune filter channels and another threshold to force small values in the feature maps in the frequency domain to zero, the feature maps of HyNet can be stored sparsely. HyNet also employs a designed activation function in the frequency domain to preserve the sparsity of the feature maps and help ensure training convergence. We evaluate HyNet on three competitive image classification benchmark datasets, and demonstrate its performance on three state-of-the-art networks. In some cases, HyNet can only use 50% memory without significant loss of performance. Notably, HyNet is focused on optimizing the memory of feature maps. It is worth trying to combine other methods, such as network scheduling, with HyNet to further improve memory efficiency during training and inference in the future.

References

1. Bao, F., Deng, Y., Kong, Y., Ren, Z., Suo, J., Dai, Q.: Learning deep landmarks for imbalanced classification. IEEE Trans. Neural Netw. Learn. Syst. **31**(8), 2691–2704 (2019)
2. Chao, P., Kao, C.Y., Ruan, Y.S., Huang, C.H., Lin, Y.L.: HarDNet: a low memory traffic network. In: The IEEE International Conference on Computer Vision (ICCV), October 2019
3. Chen, T., Xu, B., Zhang, C., Guestrin, C.: Training deep nets with sublinear memory cost. CoRR arXiv:1604.06174 (2016)
4. Chen, W., Wilson, J., Tyree, S., Weinberger, K., Chen, Y.: Compressing neural networks with the hashing trick. In: International Conference on Machine Learning, pp. 2285–2294. PMLR (2015)
5. Cheng, Y., Wang, D., Zhou, P., Zhang, T.: A survey of model compression and acceleration for deep neural networks. CoRR arXiv:1710.09282 (2017)
6. Chin, T.W., Ding, R., Zhang, C., Marculescu, D.: Towards efficient model compression via learned global ranking. In: Proceedings of the IEEE/CVF Conference on Computer Vision and Pattern Recognition, pp. 1518–1528 (2020)
7. Deng, L., Li, G., Han, S., Shi, L., Xie, Y.: Model compression and hardware acceleration for neural networks: a comprehensive survey. Proc. IEEE **108**(4), 485–532 (2020)
8. Fujieda, S., Takayama, K., Hachisuka, T.: Wavelet convolutional neural networks for texture classification. arXiv preprint arXiv:1707.07394 (2017)
9. Guan, B., et al.: Deep learning risk assessment models for predicting progression of radiographic medial joint space loss over a 48-month follow-up period. Osteoarthritis Cartilage **28**(4), 428–437 (2020)
10. Guan, B., Ye, H., Liu, H., Sethares, W.A.: Video logo retrieval based on local features. In: 2020 IEEE International Conference on Image Processing (ICIP), pp. 1396–1400. IEEE (2020)
11. Guan, B., Zhang, J., Sethares, W.A., Kijowski, R., Liu, F.: Spectral domain convolutional neural network. In: ICASSP 2021–2021 IEEE International Conference on Acoustics, Speech and Signal Processing (ICASSP), pp. 2795–2799. IEEE (2021)
12. He, K., Zhang, X., Ren, S., Sun, J.: Deep residual learning for image recognition. In: The IEEE Conference on Computer Vision and Pattern Recognition (CVPR), June 2016
13. He, Y., Lin, J., Liu, Z., Wang, H., Li, L.-J., Han, S.: AMC: AutoML for model compression and acceleration on mobile devices. In: Ferrari, V., Hebert, M., Sminchisescu, C., Weiss, Y. (eds.) ECCV 2018. LNCS, vol. 11211, pp. 815–832. Springer, Cham (2018). https://doi.org/10.1007/978-3-030-01234-2_48
14. He, Y., Zhang, X., Sun, J.: Channel pruning for accelerating very deep neural networks. In: Proceedings of the IEEE International Conference on Computer Vision, pp. 1389–1397 (2017)
15. Huang, G., Liu, Z., van der Maaten, L., Weinberger, K.Q.: Densely connected convolutional networks. In: The IEEE Conference on Computer Vision and Pattern Recognition (CVPR), July 2017

16. Huang, Z., Wang, N.: Data-driven sparse structure selection for deep neural networks. In: Ferrari, V., Hebert, M., Sminchisescu, C., Weiss, Y. (eds.) ECCV 2018. LNCS, vol. 11220, pp. 317–334. Springer, Cham (2018). https://doi.org/10.1007/978-3-030-01270-0_19

17. Jain, A., Phanishayee, A., Mars, J., Tang, L., Pekhimenko, G.: Gist: efficient data encoding for deep neural network training. In: 45th ACM/IEEE Annual International Symposium on Computer Architecture, ISCA 2018, Los Angeles, CA, USA, 1–6 June 2018, pp. 776–789 (2018). https://doi.org/10.1109/ISCA.2018.00070

18. Krizhevsky, A., Sutskever, I., Hinton, G.E.: ImageNet classification with deep convolutional neural networks. In: Pereira, F., Burges, C.J.C., Bottou, L., Weinberger, K.Q. (eds.) Advances in Neural Information Processing Systems, vol. 25, pp. 1097–1105. Curran Associates, Inc. (2012)

19. Ma, N., Zhang, X., Zheng, H.-T., Sun, J.: ShuffleNet V2: practical guidelines for efficient CNN architecture design. In: Ferrari, V., Hebert, M., Sminchisescu, C., Weiss, Y. (eds.) Computer Vision – ECCV 2018. LNCS, vol. 11218, pp. 122–138. Springer, Cham (2018). https://doi.org/10.1007/978-3-030-01264-9_8

20. Mathieu, M., Henaff, M., LeCun, Y.: Fast training of convolutional networks through FFTs. arXiv preprint arXiv:1312.5851 (2013)

21. Meng, C., Sun, M., Yang, J., Qiu, M., Gu, Y.: Training deeper models by GPU memory optimization on TensorFlow. In: Proceedings of ML Systems Workshop in NIPS (2017)

22. Niu, Y., Kannan, R., Srivastava, A., Prasanna, V.: Reuse kernels or activations? A flexible dataflow for low-latency spectral CNN acceleration. In: Proceedings of the 2020 ACM/SIGDA International Symposium on Field-Programmable Gate Arrays, pp. 266–276 (2020)

23. Pleiss, G., Chen, D., Huang, G., Li, T., van der Maaten, L., Weinberger, K.Q.: Memory-efficient implementation of DenseNets. arXiv preprint arXiv:1707.06990 (2017)

24. Pratt, H., Williams, B., Coenen, F., Zheng, Y.: FCNN: Fourier convolutional neural networks. In: Ceci, M., Hollmén, J., Todorovski, L., Vens, C., Džeroski, S. (eds.) ECML PKDD 2017. LNCS (LNAI), vol. 10534, pp. 786–798. Springer, Cham (2017). https://doi.org/10.1007/978-3-319-71249-9_47

25. Rhu, M., Gimelshein, N., Clemons, J., Zulfiqar, A., Keckler, S.W.: vDNN: virtualized deep neural networks for scalable, memory-efficient neural network design. In: The 49th Annual IEEE/ACM International Symposium on Microarchitecture, p. 18. IEEE Press (2016)

26. Rota Bulò, S., Porzi, L., Kontschieder, P.: In-place activated BatchNorm for memory-optimized training of DNNs. In: The IEEE Conference on Computer Vision and Pattern Recognition (CVPR), June 2018

27. Sun, F., Lin, J., Wang, Z.: Intra-layer nonuniform quantization for deep convolutional neural network (2016)

28. Wang, L., et al.: SuperNeurons: dynamic GPU memory management for training deep neural networks. In: ACM SIGPLAN Notices, vol. 53, pp. 41–53. ACM (2018)

29. Wang, Y., Xu, C., Xu, C., Tao, D.: Beyond filters: compact feature map for portable deep model. In: ICML. Proceedings of Machine Learning Research, vol. 70, pp. 3703–3711. PMLR (2017)

30. Weiss, Y., Freeman, W.T.: What makes a good model of natural images? In: 2007 IEEE Conference on Computer Vision and Pattern Recognition, pp. 1–8. IEEE (2007)

31. Yu, F., et al.: DC-CNN: computational flow redefinition for efficient CNN through structural decoupling. In: 2020 Design, Automation & Test in Europe Conference & Exhibition (DATE), pp. 1097–1102. IEEE (2020)

32. Zhang, D., Yang, J., Ye, D., Hua, G.: LQ-Nets: learned quantization for highly accurate and compact deep neural networks. In: Ferrari, V., Hebert, M., Sminchisescu, C., Weiss, Y. (eds.) ECCV 2018. LNCS, vol. 11212, pp. 373–390. Springer, Cham (2018). https://doi.org/10.1007/978-3-030-01237-3_23

33. Zhao, X., Ding, G.: Query expansion for object retrieval with active learning using bow and CNN feature. Multimedia Tools Appl. **76**(9), 12133–12147 (2017)

Brightening the Low-Light Images via a Dual Guided Network

Jianing Sun[2,3], Jiaao Zhang[2,3], Risheng Liu[1,2(✉)], and Fan Xin[1,2]

[1] DUT-RU International School of Information Science and Engineering,
Dalian University of Technology, Dalian, China
{rsliu,xin.fan}@dlut.edu.cn
[2] Key Laboratory for Ubiquitous Network and Service Software of Liaoning Province,
Dalian, China
[3] School of Software Technology, Dalian University of Technology, Dalian, China
{sunjn,jiaaozhang}@mail.dlut.edu.cn

Abstract. Illumination estimation based on the retinex theory is quite challenging in low-light image enhancement, and thus reflectance adjustment is necessary after illumination removal. In this paper, we propose a dual guided network to address low-light image enhancement. To be concrete, in the first stage of the method, a depth guide is introduced to constrain illumination. Based on their similarity of the smoothness, the accuracy of illumination estimation is improved. For the second stage, an attention guide is injected towards reflectance adjustment to obtain the final enhanced result. Through the guide of the attention module, details and color information lost when removing illumination can be well supplemented. Extensive ablation studies show the effectiveness and rationality of the proposed depth guide and attention guide. Qualitative and quantitative experiments demonstrate our superiority against existing state-of-the-art methods.

Keywords: Low-light image enhancement · Depth guide · Attention guide · Dual guide network · Deep learning

1 Introduction

Due to the large uncertainty in the brightness of the image shooting environment, images captured by ordinary shooting devices such as digital cameras or mobile devices may not achieve satisfactory visualization effects. Therefore, a low-light image enhancement algorithm with superior performance is of great significance to both industrial and academic research fields.

Conventional methods can be roughly divided into Histogram Equalization (HE) [5] based and Retinex based. HE methods [1,13,28,29] increase the dynamic range of pixel values through transforming the histogram of the original image into a uniform distribution. However, their contrast enhancement is often accompanied by increased noise, unnatural performance and overexposure problems. Retinex theory [6] assumes that an image can be represented by

© Springer Nature Switzerland AG 2021
L. Fang et al. (Eds.): CICAI 2021, LNAI 13069, pp. 240–251, 2021.
https://doi.org/10.1007/978-3-030-93046-2_21

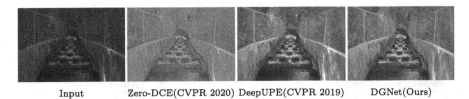

Input   Zero-DCE(CVPR 2020) DeepUPE(CVPR 2019)   DGNet(Ours)

Fig. 1. Visual comparison between the proposed method and two typical deep learning methods which estimate the illumination for enhancement (i.e., Zero-DCE, DeepUPE). For Zero-DCE, its illumination is actually a parameter of the curve. Obviously, the proposed method achieves the best visual performance with appropriate exposure.

element-wise multiplication of an illumination map (I) and a reflectance map (R). Based on this theory, many traditional methods enhance visual effects by estimating illumination and reflectance. The early works such as [15,16] directly used reflection as the final result and the enhanced images are often unnatural. Later methods [3,7,19,34] introduce priors as regularizations to ensure the required attributes of decomposing items. For example, LIME proposed in [11] refines illumination by a structure prior. Nevertheless, due to the lack of reflectance constraints, the results of these methods often have shortcomings such as under/over-exposure, color distortion and obvious artifacts (Fig. 1).

Methods based on deep learning [4,10,14,20–25,30,31,33,35] are also developed to address the low-light image enhancement task. Most of these methods are based on retinex theory and can be divided into two categories. One assumes that a pair of low/normal light images share consistent reflectance, such as RetinexNet [31], KinD [35], et al. The image is decomposed into illumination and reflectance through a decomposition-net, and two separate sub-networks are respectively constructed for optimize above two maps in parallel. Finally, the product of the two entries is taken as the result. However, the two parallel modules are not closely related, and the recombination operation implies that the obtained reflectance is overexposed. Another idea is to remove the well-learned illumination of the low-light images through element-wise division or inverse operation, which requires high capability of the designed network. The difficulty lies in how to accurately estimate the illumination. DeepUPE [30] directly uses the network to estimate the illumination and the only constraint on illumination is the smoothing constraint with low-light images. Actually, there are some drawbacks in using the low-light inputs for the smooth constraint. Since the structure of the input itself is not sharp, it is easy to cause the structure of the estimated illumination to be unclear. Thus in the work of Zero-DCE [10], TV loss is used for the loss function of illumination (it should be understood as a curve parameter in its method).

In this paper, we develop a dual guided network named DGNet to respectively inject depth guide [8,9] and attention guide [33] for illumination estimation and reflectance adjustment. The depth guide is obtained from the normal-light image through a depth estimation algorithm based on deep learning. We use it as a prior for smoothing constraints on illumination. In the first stage of the DGNet, the depth guide is used to assist the network to learn the illumination of the

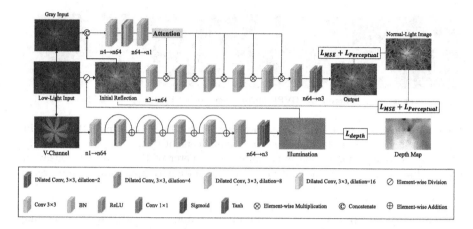

Fig. 2. The overall architecture of the DGNet. The lower part is the illumination estimation network of DGNet, where the input V-channel comes from the HSV color space. The upper part is the reflectance adjustment of DGNet. The "n3" denotes the channel of the feature is 3. And the red lines represent the loss items. (Color figure online)

low-light images. As mentioned above, the reflectance obtained after removing the illumination may have drawbacks like under/over-exposure, color distortion and obvious artifacts. Therefore, in the second stage of the DGNet, we design a reflectance adjustment network to restore the intrinsic property of objects and inject an attention module to guide the enhancement of reflectance. Under the guidance of attention, the reflection adjustment network realizes the accurate restoration of colors.

We summarize the main contributions of our work as follows:

- We propose a depth guided illumination estimation. Based on the similarity of global information, the depth map introduced in the training phase can effectively constrain the smoothness of the illumination as a prior.
- We propose an attention guided reflectance adjustment. The attention learned from the concatenation of the initial reflection and the grayscale of the low-light image can effectively supplement the details and color information lost caused by illumination removal, avoiding the unnatural restoration of colors.
- We conduct extensive ablation studies to prove the effectiveness and rationality of the proposed depth guide and attention guide. In addition, we also compare the proposed method with several state-of-the-art methods qualitatively and quantitatively to prove our superiority.

2   Methodology

In this section, the implementation details of the DGNet is introduced. We first present the specific network structure of illumination estimation and reflection adjustment and then introduce the loss function. The flowchart of the proposed method is detailed in Fig. 2. In the first stage, that is, the lower half of the network, we estimate illumination with a depth-guide. Then, we adjust reflection through an attention guide in the second stage, which is shown in the upper half.

2.1 Depth Guided Illumination Estimation

How to accurately estimate the illumination is a challenging problem and previous methods proposed some smooth constraints on illumination. In this paper, we propose a depth-guided illumination estimation. The depth map contains global semantic information. The illumination map depicts the global relationship of different brightness on the object. Since both of them contain global information and are smooth, we believe that the two maps have a certain similarity in smoothness. Thus, we use the depth map as a guide to solve the non-uniform illumination problem caused by incomplete low-light input information. In this paper, the monocular depth estimation method [9] is used to estimate the depth of normal-light images. What needs to be emphasized is that the illumination is constrained by depth guide through the loss function. Unlike other depth guided model [18], our depth guide is only introduced in the training phase, and does not need to be used in the testing phase. Therefore, we do not need to introduce additional computational costs, such as calculating the depth of images.

For the first stage of our DGNet, we first calculate the V channel in the HSV color space of the low-light input. The illumination estimation network first extracts features through a ConvBlock (Conv, Batch Normalization, Relu), and the number of feature channels of the output is 64. Then, an average pooling with a stride of 2 down-sample the extracted features. Then, four DilConvBlocks [32] (Dilated Conv, Batch Normalization, Relu) with dilations of 2, 4, 8, 16 and residual connection [12] are used where each DilConvBlocks is repeated four times. Next, upsampling is performed after a ConvBlock transition. For upsampling, we use linear interpolation to ensure feature continuity. Next, a ConvBlock with a kernel of 1×1 is used to transform the number of channels from 64 to 3. Finally, the sigmoid activation function is used to obtain the illumination.

2.2 Attention Guided Reflectance Enhancement

According to the retinex theory, by removing the illumination, we can get the reflectance of objects. However, due to the basis of the illumination estimation and the influence of element-wise division, the obtained reflections will expose some defects. Therefore, we call it the initial reflection and use the reflection adjustment network to optimize it. In order to restore the intrinsic property of the objects, we learn attention from the concatenation of the initial reflection and the grayscale of the low-light image, so as to make full use of the known information about the reflectance. It can be seen from Fig. 2 that in the adjustment network, the attention module is closely integrated to guide information supplementation and color correction. This can effectively improve the lack of detail and color distortion, so that the enhanced result has intrinsic property and more natural colors.

For the second stage of our DGNet, the initial reflection as input is obtained by dividing the low-light image by the illumination at the pixel level. We first concatenate the initial reflection and the grayscale of the low-light image into a 4-channel input for attention module. Then, a simple ConvBlock-DilConvBlock-ConvBlock structure is designed for attention learning, where the dilation is set as 2. For the adjustment network, a ConvBlock (Conv, Batch Normalization, Relu) is used to extract features from the initial reflection, and the number of feature channels is 64. Then, we multiply the attention on the feature. Next, similar to the illumination estimation network, four DilConvBlocks(Dilated Conv, Batch Normalization, Relu) with dilations of 2, 4, 8, 16 respectively, and residual connection (omitted in the flowchart for simplicity) are used. Each DilConvBlocks is repeated four times then multiply the attention. After a ConvBlock transition, a ConvBlock (Conv, Batch Normalization, Relu) with a kernel of 1×1 is used to transform the number of channels from 64 to 3. Finally, the tanh activation function is used to obtain the final enhancement result.

2.3 Loss Function

In the first stage of the network, illumination estimation is the main task. Considering the smooth similarity of illumination and depth, we use Depth-Guided Loss to constrain the illumination. In the second stage of the network, a rough reflectance and a final enhanced result will be produced. And we adopt the same constrained losses, including MSE Loss and Perceptual Loss to limit both.

Depth-Guided Loss. We believe that the depth map and illumination have similar glob information and smoothness. Thus, we uses a pre-trained VGG network [27] to measure feature distance between them. The depth-guided loss is defined as follows:

$$\mathcal{L}_{depth}(I, D) = \frac{1}{N_l} \|\mathcal{V}^l(I) - \mathcal{V}^l(D)\|^2, \tag{1}$$

where I denotes the illumination, D denotes the depth map, $\mathcal{V}^l$ represents the feature of the l-th layer output of VGG-16 network and N_l represents the number of features. Here, we use the features from the conv5_1 layer.

MSE Loss. We utilize the Mean Square Error (MSE) loss to constrain the initial reflectance and final enhanced output, described as

$$\mathcal{L}_{mse} = \|\hat{R} - G\|^2 + \|O - G\|^2, \tag{2}$$

where $\hat{R}$ represents the initial reflectance before adjustment network, O is the output enhanced image, and G presents the ground truth.

Perceptual Loss. We adopted the perceptual loss proposed in [17] for perceptual similarity guarantee. It also constrains both the initial reflectance and final enhanced output:

$$\mathcal{L}_{perce} = \mathcal{L}_{perceptual\_R} + \mathcal{L}_{perceptual\_O}, \tag{3}$$

| Input | w/o Depth Guide | w/ Depth Guide |

Fig. 3. Ablation study of the depth guide on LOL dataset [31]. The second column shows the visualized results of the method without the deep-guided loss. And the "w/Depth Guide" is the results enhanced by the proposed method.

Since it is difficult to learn a perfect illumination map in the first stage, we add mse loss and perceptual loss, which are commonly used in low-level image processing problems to the rough reflection obtained after element-wise division. Thus, in the process of backpropagation, the learning of illumination will also be promoted. Our entire loss function of can be formulated as:

$$\mathcal{L} = w_1\mathcal{L}_{depth} + w_2\mathcal{L}_{mse} + w_3\mathcal{L}_{perce}, \tag{4}$$

where w_1, w_2 and w_3 are the weights corresponding to the three loss functions mentioned above. In our training, we empirically set $w_1 = 1$, $w_2 = 1$ and $w_3 = 0.1$.

3   Experiment

In this section, we first introduced experimental details including benchmarks description and evaluated metrics. Then we conducted plenty of experiments to analyses about our method. Next, we executed extensive experiments to evaluate our proposed DGNet qualitatively and quantitatively.

3.1   Experimental Details

The proposed DGNet is implemented by PyTorch [26] and the entire network is conducted on a NVIDIA GeForce RTX 2060 SUPER GPU. We achieved the paired supervision training in LOL [31] and MIT 5K [2] datasets respectively. For the LOL dataset with 789 images, we randomly select 719 pairs for training and the remaining 70 images are used for evaluation. Considering that the LOL dataset generates normal light images by changing the exposure time, its

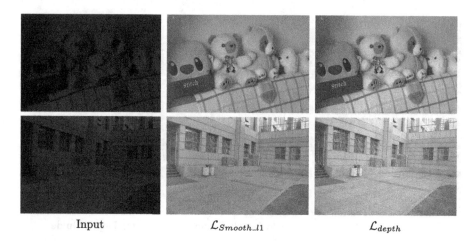

Input $\mathcal{L}_{Smooth\_l1}$ $\mathcal{L}_{depth}$

Fig. 4. Comparison results of $\mathcal{L}_{Smooth\_l1}$ and $\mathcal{L}_{depth}$ on LOL dataset [31].

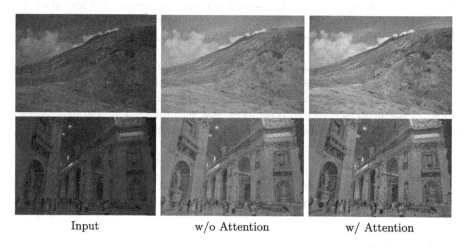

Input   w/o Attention   w/ Attention

Fig. 5. Ablation study of the attention guide on MIT 5k dataset [2]. The second column shows the visualized results of the method without the attention module. "w/attention" denotes that the reflectance adjustment network is guided by attention.

groundtruth is lack in professionalism, and thus we only compare the visual results on it. For the less challenging MIT 5K dataset, which includes 5000 raw images, we use the first 800 images to fine-tune the network with 50 epochs. And 500 images are randomly selected from the remaining 4,200 images as a test set. Noticing that the labels of MIT 5K are generated by expert-retouched, we not only tested the visual effects, but also evaluate numerical performance in terms of PSNR, SSIM and NIQE.

3.2 Ablation Study

In order to prove the effectiveness of our proposed methods for the low-light image enhancement problem, we conducted ablation experiments on both depth guide and attention guide strategies on two datasets. For the illumination estimation stage, we first remove $\mathcal{L}_{depth}$ as a control experiment to verify the effectiveness of the depth guide. The experimental results are shown in Fig. 3. We can find that the proposed method improves brightness, reduces shadows and restores richer details than the model without using the depth information. Besides, we also replace the $\mathcal{L}_{depth}$ with $\mathcal{L}_{Smooth\_l1}$ for comparison experiments. $\mathcal{L}_{Smooth\_l1}$ is also a commonly used loss function in low-level image processing problems, which can be expressed as $\mathcal{L}_{Smooth\_l1}(I,G) = \frac{1}{mn}\sum_{i=1}^{m}\sum_{j=1}^{n}\mathcal{S}\left(\mathbf{I}(i,j) - \mathbf{G}(i,j)\right)$. The definition of $\mathcal{S}(z)$ is described as, if $|z| \leq 1$, then $\mathcal{S}(z) = 0.5z^2$, otherwise $\mathcal{S}(z) = |z| - 0.5$. Visualization results in Fig. 4 prove that using the proposed depth guide strategy to estimation illumination is more effective than using $\mathcal{L}_{Smooth\_l1}$. For the reflectance adjustment stage, we remove the attention module for comparison. As shown in Fig. 5, compared with the proposed method, the result of the model without attention is prone to color distortion.

Fig. 6. Visual comparison on examples selected from MIT 5K dataset [2]. The image enhanced by our method can obtain the best visualization effect, compared with some state-of-the-art methods.

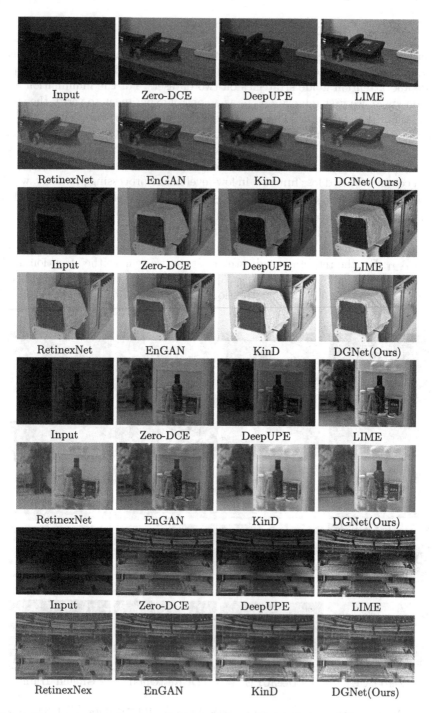

Fig. 7. Visual comparison on examples selected from LOL dataset [31]. The image enhanced by our method can obtain the best visualization effect, compared with state-of-the-art methods.

3.3   Performance Comparison

In order to prove the superiority of our DGNet, we compare it with 6 well-known low-light image enhancement methods quantitatively and qualitatively. They are LIME [11], RetinexNet [31], DeepUPE [30], KinD [35], Zero-DCE [10] and EnGAN [14]. For qualitative experiments, we analyze their performance through 500 test images from MIT 5K dataset and 70 test images from LOL dataset. Figure 6 and Fig. 7 demonstrate the visual comparison results respectively. As mentioned above, the labels of MIT 5K are retouched by expert, so we add the visual results of the ground truth. As shown in Fig. 6, the results of Zero-DCE and KinD has insufficient brightness, the results of EnGAN and DeepUPE have color distortion, and the results of LIME are overexposed. For the more challenging LOL database, the brightness of the restored results of Zero-ECE, DeepUPE, and LIME is insufficient. Results of RetinexNet and EnGAN has a lot of obvious noise, while the overexposure problem of KinD brings the unnatural color and blur of the image, resulting in the lack of details. On the contrast, our DGNet can better restore the color and details of the image while improving the brightness. Table 1 reports the numerical results on 500 MIT 5K testing images and the best result is in bold. Since the labels are not expert-generated, we omit the numerical results on LOL. The elaborated evaluations indicate that our DGNet is remarkably superior to the state-of-the-art deep networks in both visual quality and numerical performance.

Table 1. Quantitative performance on MIT 5K test dataset.

Method	SSIM ($\uparrow$)	PSNR ($\uparrow$)	NIQE ($\downarrow$)
LIME	0.8297	17.1818	5.9960
EnGAN	0.8279	17.9575	6.0242
DeepUPE	0.8220	19.8695	4.3794
Zero-DCE	0.7634	16.0706	5.6287
KinD	0.7629	15.3805	**4.3399**
DGNet (ours)	**0.8663**	**20.7338**	4.7517

4   Conclusion

In this paper, we proposed a dual guided network to tackle low-light image enhancement problem. In the illumination estimation stage, depth map is injected to well constrain the smoothness of illumination. Then, an attention module guides the reflectance adjustment to better learn the intrinsic properties and color information. Extensive evaluations and analysis show that our method could produce compelling results compared to the state-of-the-art methods. However, the current method does not consider the noise problem in the weak light environment, so we will focus on the denoising problem in the future work.

Acknowledgments. This work was partially supported by the National Natural Science Foundation of China (Nos. 61922019, 61733002 and 61672125), the LiaoNing Revitalization Talents Program (XLYC1807088) and the Fundamental Research Funds for the Central Universities.

References

1. Abdullah-Al-Wadud, M., Kabir, M.H., Dewan, M.A.A., Chae, O.: A dynamic histogram equalization for image contrast enhancement. IEEE Trans. Consum. Electron. **53**(2), 593–600 (2007)
2. Bychkovsky, V., Paris, S., Chan, E., Durand, F.: Learning photographic global tonal adjustment with a database of input/output image pairs. In: Proceedings of the IEEE Conference on Computer Vision and Pattern Recognition (2011)
3. Cai, B., Xu, X., Guo, K., Jia, K., et al.: A joint intrinsic-extrinsic prior model for retinex. In: Proceedings of the IEEE International Conference on Computer Vision, pp. 4020–4029 (2017)
4. Chen, C., Chen, Q., Xu, J., Koltun, V.: Learning to see in the dark. In: Proceedings of the IEEE Conference on Computer Vision and Pattern Recognition (2018)
5. Cheng, H., Shi, X.J.: A simple and effective histogram equalization approach to image enhancement. Digit. Signal Process. **14**(2), 158–170 (2004)
6. Land, E.H., McCann, J.J.: Lightness and retinex theory. J. Opt. Soc. Am. **61**, 1–11 (1971)
7. Fu, X., Zeng, D., Huang, Y., Zhang, X.P., Ding, X.: A weighted variational model for simultaneous reflectance and illumination estimation. In: Proceedings of the IEEE Conference on Computer Vision and Pattern Recognition (2016)
8. Godard, C., Mac Aodha, O., Brostow, G.J.: Unsupervised monocular depth estimation with left-right consistency. In: Proceedings of the IEEE Conference on Computer Vision and Pattern Recognition (2017)
9. Godard, C., Mac Aodha, O., Firman, M., Brostow, G.J.: Digging into self-supervised monocular depth prediction (2019)
10. Guo, C., Li, C., Guo, J., Loy, C.C., et al.: Zero-reference deep curve estimation for low-light image enhancement. In: Proceedings of the IEEE Conference on Computer Vision and Pattern Recognition, pp. 1780–1789 (2020)
11. Guo, X., Li, Y., Ling, H.: LIME: low-light image enhancement via illumination map estimation. IEEE Trans. Image Process. **26**(2), 982–993 (2017)
12. He, K., Zhang, X., Ren, S., Sun, J.: Deep residual learning for image recognition. arXiv preprint arXiv:1512.03385 (2015)
13. Ibrahim, H., Kong, N.S.P.: Brightness preserving dynamic histogram equalization for image contrast enhancement. IEEE Trans. Consum. Electron. **53**(4), 1752–1758 (2007)
14. Jiang, Y., Gong, X., Liu, D., Cheng, Y., et al.: EnlightenGAN: deep light enhancement without paired supervision. IEEE Trans. Image Process. **30**, 2340–2349 (2021)
15. Jobson, D.J., Rahman, Z., Woodell, G.A.: A multiscale retinex for bridging the gap between color images and the human observation of scenes. IEEE Trans. Image Process. **6**(7), 965–976 (1997)
16. Jobson, D.J., Rahman, Z., Woodell, G.A.: Properties and performance of a center/surround retinex. IEEE Trans. Image Process. **6**(3), 451–462 (1997)

17. Johnson, J., Alahi, A., Fei-Fei, L.: Perceptual losses for real-time style transfer and super-resolution. In: Leibe, B., Matas, J., Sebe, N., Welling, M. (eds.) ECCV 2016. LNCS, vol. 9906, pp. 694–711. Springer, Cham (2016). https://doi.org/10.1007/978-3-319-46475-6_43

18. Li, L., Pan, J., Lai, W., Gao, C., et al.: Dynamic scene deblurring by depth guided model. IEEE Trans. Image Process. **29**, 5273–5288 (2020)

19. Li, M., Liu, J., Yang, W., Sun, X., Guo, Z.: Structure-revealing low-light image enhancement via robust retinex model. IEEE Trans. Image Process. **27**(6), 2828–2841 (2018)

20. Liu, R., Cheng, S., He, Y., Fan, X., Lin, Z., Luo, Z.: On the convergence of learning-based iterative methods for nonconvex inverse problems. IEEE Trans. Pattern Anal. Mach. Intell. **42**(12), 3027–3039 (2019)

21. Liu, R., Fan, X., Hou, M., Jiang, Z., Luo, Z., Zhang, L.: Learning aggregated transmission propagation networks for haze removal and beyond. IEEE Trans. Neural Netw. Learn. Syst. **30**(10), 2973–2986 (2018)

22. Liu, R., Ma, L., Wang, Y., Zhang, L.: Learning converged propagations with deep prior ensemble for image enhancement. IEEE Trans. Image Process. **28**(3), 1528–1543 (2019)

23. Liu, R., Ma, L., Zhang, J., Fan, X., Luo, Z.: Retinex-inspired unrolling with cooperative prior architecture search for low-light image enhancement. In: Proceedings of the IEEE Conference on Computer Vision and Pattern Recognition (2021)

24. Liu, R., Ma, L., Zhang, Y., Fan, X., Luo, Z.: Underexposed image correction via hybrid priors navigated deep propagation. IEEE Trans. Neural Netw. Learn. Syst. (2021)

25. Ma, L., Liu, R., Zhang, J., Fan, X., Luo, Z.: Learning deep context-sensitive decomposition for low-light image enhancement. IEEE Trans. Neural Netw. Learn. Syst. (2021)

26. Paszke, A., Gross, S., Chintala, S., Chanan, G., et al.: Automatic differentiation in PyTorch (2017)

27. Simonyan, K., Zisserman, A.: Very deep convolutional networks for large-scale image recognition. In: International Conference on Learning Representations (2015)

28. Stark, J.A.: Adaptive image contrast enhancement using generalizations of histogram equalization. IEEE Trans. Image Process. **9**(5), 889–896 (2000)

29. Thomas, G., Flores-Tapia, D., Pistorius, S.: Histogram specification: a fast and flexible method to process digital images. IEEE Trans. Instrum. Meas. **60**(5), 1565–1578 (2011)

30. Wang, R., Zhang, Q., Fu, C., Shen, X., et al.: Underexposed photo enhancement using deep illumination estimation. In: Proceedings of the IEEE Conference on Computer Vision and Pattern Recognition, pp. 6849–6857 (2019)

31. Wei, C., Wang, W., Yang, W., Liu, J.: Deep retinex decomposition for low-light enhancement. In: British Machine Vision Conference, p. 155 (2018)

32. Yu, F., Koltun, V., Funkhouser, T.: Dilated residual networks. In: Proceedings of the IEEE Conference on Computer Vision and Pattern Recognition (2017)

33. Zhang, J., Liu, R., Ma, L., Zhong, W., et al.: Principle-inspired multi-scale aggregation network for extremely low-light image enhancement. In: IEEE International Conference on Acoustics, Speech and Signal Processing, pp. 2638–2642 (2020)

34. Zhang, Q., Yuan, G., Xiao, C., Zhu, L., Zheng, W.S.: High-quality exposure correction of underexposed photos. In: ACM Multimedia, pp. 582–590 (2018)

35. Zhang, Y., Zhang, J., Guo, X.: Kindling the darkness: a practical low-light image enhancer. In: ACM Multimedia, pp. 1632–1640

Learning Multi-scale Underexposure Image Correction

Wei Zhong[1,3]([✉]) [ID], Xiaodong Zhang[2,3] [ID], Long Ma[2,3] [ID], Risheng Liu[1,3] [ID], Xin Fan[1,3] [ID], and Zhongxuan Luo[1,3] [ID]

[1] International School of Information Science and Engineering,
Dalian University of Technology, Dalian, China
{zhongwei,rsliu,xin.fan,zxluo}@dlut.edu.cn
[2] School of Software Technology, Dalian University of Technology, Dalian, China
{ZXD123,longma}@mail.dlut.edu.cn
[3] Key Laboratory for Ubiquitous Network and Service Software of Liaoning Province,
Dalian, China

Abstract. Images captured in low light conditions usually suffer from color distortion and poor visibility. Although remarkable success has been made, existing methods are still unstable when applied to various scenes. Therefore, we propose a robust deep multi-scale network for underexposure image correction. We construct Gaussian pyramid to explore the complementary and redundant information in different scales, and further extract, fuse illuminations with progressive fusion strategy across scales. This process not only boosts the end-to-end training but also promotes the cooperative representation. Moreover, fine-fused illuminations in multi-scales bridge the gap between the restoration knowledge of underexposure images and the perceptual quality preference to normal light images. Extensive experiments with advanced methods and ablation studies demonstrate our method outperforms others under a variety of metrics in terms of qualitative and quantitative comparison.

Keywords: Underexposure image correction · Deep network · Illumination estimation

1 Introduction

Insufficient light in image capturing can degrade the visibility of images. These images not only cause unpleasant subjective feelings but also challenge computer vision tasks due to invisible details and low contrast of underexposed regions. To make hidden details visible and improve the usability for computer vision systems, underexposure image correction is necessary.

Many methods have been proposed to correct underexposure images. Conventional methods focus on brightness increase and contrast improvement to mitigate the degradation such as histogram equalization and Retinex-based methods.

This work was supported in part by National Natural Science Foundation of China (NSFC) under Grant 61906029, the Fundamental Research Funds for the Central Universities.

Input   ZeroDCE [2]

DeepUPE [3]   Ours

Fig. 1. An example underexposed image corrected by existing methods and ours.

Recently, learning-based approaches are proposed to adjust brightness, color, and contrast to produce more impressive results. However, these methods can't adapt to various scenes and have poor performance for severely underexposed regions.

Inspired by MSR-Net [1], we propose a novel method to correct underexposure images(see Fig. 1 for an example). Different from existing methods, we explore the multi-scale representation of image and design a deep underexposed image correction network that uncovers inherent features and fully exploits complementary details from multiple scales of image. As shown in Fig. 2, we first build Gaussian pyramid to downsample underexposure image in sequence and extract initial illuminations via extraction module. Secondly, we construct fusion module to fuse illuminations from multi-scales with progressive fusion strategy. Finally, restoration module aggregate illuminations to learn refined illumination map, which is the approximation of light distribution of image. The main contributions of this paper are summarized as follows:

- We propose a novel multi-scale underexposed image correction network. A simple but effective method which can uncover the inherent details and keep the perceptual consistency during images correction on multi-scales.
- The network is designed to extract, fuse, and estimate a series of illuminations from multi-scales. The estimation of these illuminations is mutually beneficial through the end-to-end training, capable of characterizing light distribution, denoising and correcting colors.
- We evaluate the performance of our method compared with various advanced methods on several datasets and perform adequate ablation studies. Results show that our method achieves state-of-the-art performance both on synthetic and real underexposure images.

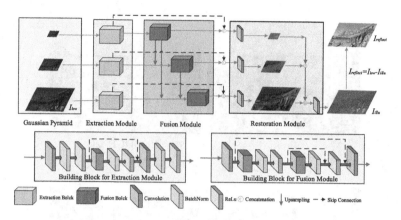

Fig. 2. The pipeline of multi-scale underexposed image correction network. Firstly, extraction module extracts initial illuminations from multi-scale representations of images generated by Gaussian pyramid. Then illuminations will be fused guided by progressive fusion strategy via fusion module. Finally, illuminations will be concatenated, adjusted by restoration module and get corrected images according to Retinex theory.

2   Related Work

2.1   Histogram-Based Methods

One of the most widely-used image correction methods is histogram equalization (HE) [4], which increases contrast of images by expanding the dynamic range of histograms. However, it tends to cause loss of contrast for regions with high frequencies in the entire image. To ameliorate the visual quality of results, Ibrahim *et al.* [5] and Coltuc *et al.* [6] adjusted histogram distribution of images in local regions while Pisano *et al.* [7] presented the contrast limited adaptive histogram equalization by setting a limit on the derivative of the slope of the transformation function. However, these methods are quite effective in contrast improvement and brightness increase while might induce ghosting artifacts. Although many HE-based variants have been proposed, they also might produce unsatisfying results for limited generalization ability.

2.2   Retinex-Based Methods

Retinex theory [8] regards an underexposure image as the pixel-wise product of reflectance and illumination. Retinex-based methods treat the reflectance as the corrected image approximately. Therefore, image correction can be considered as an illumination estimation to remove the influence of insufficient light on image. Jobson *et al.* [9] made an early attempt to this problem, but their results often look unnatural. Recently, Retinex-based methods [10,11] have been proposed to enhance the visibility of underexposure images. Although these methods solve the problem of dim brightness and color deviation, they ignore the suppression of noise, nonlinearity across color channels, and data complexity, resulting in halo phenomenon and color distortion. Our method also considers illumination estimation and yet it advances state-of-the-arts in two aspects. First, our network learns the illumination by exploiting complementary details from multi-scales and models a variety of illumination adjustments. Second, our method enables nonlinear color correction from multi-scale illuminations.

2.3 Learning-Based Methods

Learning-based methods have emerged for underexposure image correction and demonstrated impressive performance. For instance, Lore *et al.* [12] proposed LLNet to learn joint denoising for underexposure enhancement while Yan *et al.* [13] constructed a semantic map to enhance the image of semantic perception. Gharbi *et al.* [14] proposed HDR-Net, combining deep networks with local affine color transforms and bilateral grid processing with pairwise supervision. Cai *et al.* [15] learned a contrast enhancer from multi-exposure images. Recently, great effort on image correction is mostly focusing on unsupervised learning. Jiang *et al.* [16] introduced the EnlightenGAN for image enhancement, while Wang *et al.* [3] enhanced images by performing deep image decomposition. However, these methods may not work well on images that are significantly different from the training data.

3 Methodology

In Fig. 2, we show the outline of proposed method for underexposure image correction by excavating and exploiting the inherent correlations of illumination across different scales. The details of image correction and loss function are introduced as follows.

3.1 Underexposed Image Correction

Initial Illumination Extraction. For an underexposure image, our method first generates Gaussian pyramid to downsample it into different scales. Then extraction module takes each layer of pyramid as inputs to extract initial illuminations. As shown in Fig. 2, extraction module includes three building blocks, each block is composed of several Conv-BN-ReLu units with skip connection to help extract illumination. The reasons for designing extraction module are three folds: (a) To exploit the repetition of illumination in different scales, we apply residual learning to capture global texture information, making it possible to cooperatively represent target illumination. (b) The multi-scale structure provides an alternative solution to increase the receptive field to cover more features while maintaining a shallow depth. (c) The high resolution representations benefit from the outputs of previous stage as well as all low resolution pyramid layers by iterative sampling and fusion stage.

Progressive Illumination Fusion. The outputs of extraction module are fed to the fusion module for fusing the complementary information in different scales. Fusion module also takes multi-scale structure and includes several building blocks to improve the learning ability of network by focusing on the most informative scale-specific knowledge, making the cooperative representation more efficient. To alleviate the computation burden, we apply convolution to reduce the spatial dimension of features and utilize the deconvolution layer to increase the resolution to avoid losing resolution information, resulting in the U-shaped block. As shown in Fig. 2, the structure of building block helps the fine representation of multi-scale illumination. Moreover, long skip connections between cascaded blocks realize progressive fusion of multi-scale illuminations as well as to facilitate the effective backward propagation of gradient.

Refined Illumination Restoration. To estimate the final illumination map, we further integrate both low and high level multi-scale features from previous modules via restoration module. As shown in Fig. 2, the outputs of previous two modules are concatenated across scales and then a convolution layer is appended to rescale the illumination values from two modules and learns the channel interdependence. Finally, the iterative upsampling and concatenation of illuminations across different scales are implemented to estimate the refined illumination map and output corrected image according to Retinex theory.

3.2 Loss Function

Our proposed network learns the illumination map S from a set of underexposure images I. Then the corrected image $\tilde{I}$ can be obtained by $I = S * \tilde{I}$. We design a loss function $\mathcal{L}$ which includes three components and minimize it during the training state. It can be expressed as:

$$\mathcal{L} = \omega_{recon}\mathcal{L}_{recon} + \omega_{ss}\mathcal{L}_{ssim} + \omega_s\mathcal{L}_{smooth} \tag{1}$$

where $\mathcal{L}_{recon}$, $\mathcal{L}_{ssim}$, and $\mathcal{L}_{smooth}$ denote reconstruction loss, SSIM loss and smoothness loss, respectively. ω_{recon}, ω_{ss}, and ω_s are corresponding weights.

Mean squared error (MSE) is commonly used to train the network. However, MSE loss is not enough to express the visual perception and may produce a blurry and over-smoothed visual effect due to the squared penalty. Therefore, we replace MSE loss with SSIM [17] loss as a part of loss function. Moreover, we adopt reconstruction loss to metric the difference between enhanced image and ground truth. The reconstruction loss can be defined as:

$$\mathcal{L}_{recon} = \sum_{i=1}^{N} \left\| S_i * \tilde{I}_i - I_i \right\|_2 \tag{2}$$

where S_i, $\tilde{I}_i$ and I_i represent refined illumination map, ground truth, and underexposure image, respectively.

According to priors, illumination S in natural images should be locally smooth. Therefore, we take this prior into our method and it brings several benefits to corrected results. It not only enhances the contrast of images by preserving the monotonicity between neighboring pixels but also helps to reduce overfitting and improves the generalization ability of our network. The smoothness loss is defined as:

$$\mathcal{L}_{smooth} = \sum_{i=1}^{N} \sum_{p} \sum_{c} \omega_{x,c}^{p} \left(\nabla_x S_p\right)_c^2 + \omega_{y,c}^{p} \left(\nabla_y S_p\right)_c^2 \tag{3}$$

where p, c is the number of pixels and channels, $\nabla_x S$ and $\nabla_y S$ represent the horizontal and vertical gradient of illumination, ω_x and ω_y are gradient weight and empirically set to 1.0, respectively.

4   Experiments

In this section, we utilize MIT-Adobe FiveK dataset [18] as the training dataset with 5000 simulated low/label image pairs, and then randomly select 500 images pairs for testing, and train the network on the remaining 4500 image pairs. We evaluate the performance of it with other advanced methods including ZeroDCE [2], DeepUPE [3], EnlightenGAN [16], LightenNet [19] and KinD [20]. Moreover, we also make various ablation studies as well as explore additional applications.

4.1   Performance Evaluation

Firstly, we perform visual comparison with other methods and evaluate on MIT-Adobe FiveK [18], LIME [21], MEF [22], NPE [23], and VV[1] datasets. As shown in Fig. 3 and Fig. 4, our method recovers more clear details and better contrast in foreground and background without sacrificing the overexposed regions. Moreover, it displays vivid and natural colors to make results look more realistic.

Secondly, we perform quantitative comparison to evaluate the performance and generalization ability. We employ the Peak Signal-to-Noise Ratio (PSNR), Structural Similarity (SSIM) [17] and Natural Image Quality Evaluator (NIQE) [24] to metric advanced methods with ours on real underexposure datasets. Since MIT-Adobe FiveK dataset has label images, PSNR and SSIM are available, while other datasets only have low light images, only NIQE can be used. As shown in Table 1 and Table 2, our method achieves the highest PSNR/SSIM and lowest NIQE. For both comparisons, our method performs better, manifesting that it not only effectively learns the image adjustment for correcting underexposure images but also well generalizes to the unexposed images.

Finally, we show the colormaps of intermediate results from different scales and fine-fused illumination map. As shown in Fig. 5, our network generates illumination maps containing abundant information in multi-scales and can remove the redundant and exploit complementary texture details to make more impressive results.

---

[1] https://sites.google.com/site/vonikakis/datasets.

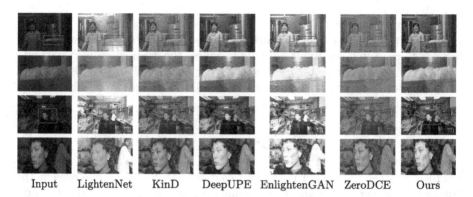

Input   LightenNet   KinD   DeepUPE   EnlightenGAN   ZeroDCE   Ours

Fig. 3. Visual comparison on MIT Adobe FiveK dataset. Red boxes indicate the obvious differences. (Color figure online)

Table 1. Quantitative comparison on MIT-Adobe FiveK dataset. The best result is in bold.

Method	PSNR	SSIM
LightenNet	20.086	0.728
DeepUPE	22.736	0.834
KinD	21.085	0.745
EnlightenGAN	21.685	0.789
ZeroDCE	19.036	0.704
Ours	**23.168**	**0.849**

4.2   Ablation Studies

Validation on Basic Modules. To verify the effectiveness of each module we design four networks and evaluate them on MIT-Adobe FiveK dataset. All cases include "EM", "EM+FM", "EM+RM", and "EM+FM+RM". As shown in Fig. 6, complete three modules achieve the best visual effect and the highest average PSNR/SSIM of testing dataset in upper right corner of figure. Our network progressively improves the correction performance by having more modules. These statistics convincingly demonstrate the effectiveness of each module in network.

Analysis on Different Loss Terms. Our loss function includes three main terms: reconstruction, SSIM, and smoothness losses, which are introduced to improve the perceptual quality of corrected images. To quantitatively evaluate the effect of different loss term on results, we retrain the network with and without each loss term. Table 3 shows that network with all terms achieves the highest average PSNR/SSIM than without them. The whole loss function not only helps provide a better interpretation of the task of each sub-module but also improves results.

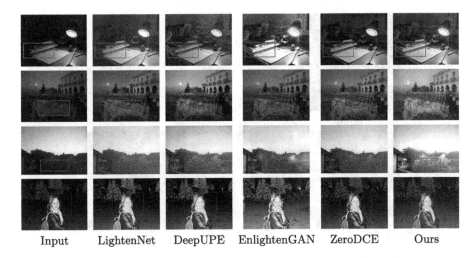

Input   LightenNet   DeepUPE   EnlightenGAN   ZeroDCE   Ours

Fig. 4. Visual comparison on real underexposure datasets. The images in first to fourth row come from MEF, LIME, NPE, VV datasets, respectively.

Table 2. Quantitative comparison on real underexposure datasets in terms of NIQE.

Method	LIME	MEF	NPE	VV	Avg
LightenNet	3.731	3.382	3.388	2.952	3.363
DeepUPE	3.928	3.532	3.797	3.008	3.566
KinD	3.387	3.375	3.346	3.556	3.416
EnlightenGAN	3.376	3.475	3.245	3.189	3.321
ZeroDCE	3.789	3.309	2.988	2.680	3.191
Ours	**3.246**	**3.186**	**2.920**	**2.484**	**2.959**

Table 3. Effects of all loss terms on corrected results. The best result is in bold.

Model	$\mathcal{L}_{recon}$	$\mathcal{L}_{SSIM}$	$\mathcal{L}_{smooth}$	PSNR	SSIM
A	✓	✗	✗	19.434	0.771
B	✗	✓	✗	18.546	0.768
C	✗	✗	✓	18.236	0.755
D	✓	✗	✓	21.892	0.827
E	✗	✓	✓	22.531	0.831
F	✓	✓	✗	22.445	0.833
G	✓	✓	✓	**23.168**	**0.849**

Effect of Number of Scales. Our network corrects images on multi-scales. To discuss the effect of different scales on results, we repeat the same experiment with a varying number of scales. Specifically, we set Gaussian pyramid level $n = 1$, the model is equivalent to a vanilla ResNet-like architecture at this time,

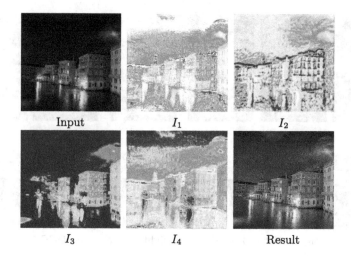

Fig. 5. Visualization of intermediate results. $I_1 - I_4$ are colormaps of multi-scale illuminations and refined illumination.

Fig. 6. Visual comparison of results with average PSNR and SSIM with different modules .

and also train another three models with scales $n = 2, 3$ and 4, respectively. As shown in Fig. 7, our method achieves the highest average PSNR/SSIM of testing dataset shown in the upper left corner and best perceptual quality of results when the network takes three scales.

4.3 Overexposed Image Correction

Our method is also applicable to overexposure correction. Underexposed image can be seen as the inverted version of an overexposed image which allows us to fix overexposed regions by enhancing the corresponding underexposed regions in the inverted image. For a given overexposed image I, we first compute its inverted image I' by $I' = 1 - I$. Then we perform illumination estimation on I' to obtain the illumination S', from which we recover the enhanced image R'. Finally, we get the corrected result R by performing inversion operation $R = 1 - R'$. Figure 8 shows two examples.

Fig. 7. Visual comparison of results with number of scales n.

Input   ZeroDCE   Ours

Fig. 8. Overexposed images corrected by ZeroDCE and ours.

5   Conclusion

In this paper, we propose and design a novel multi-scale deep neural network for underexposure image enhancement which fully leverages multi-scale feature information in images to learn the low-light image to illumination mapping. To accomplish our goal, we first design three basic modules with progressive fusion strategy to get refined illumination maps. Furthermore, we also design a novel loss function that takes various priors and constraints on fused illumination to make results have more clear details, vivid colors, and distinct contrast. Finally, we perform extensive experiments on benchmark datasets, showing that our method has great superiority in terms of quantitative and qualitative comparison over other advanced methods.

References

1. Shen, L., Yue, Z., Feng, F., et al.: MSR-net: low-light image enhancement using deep convolutional network. arXiv preprint arXiv:1711.02488 (2017)
2. Guo, C., Li, C., Guo, J., et al.: Zero-reference deep curve estimation for low-light image enhancement. In: Proceedings of the IEEE/CVF Conference on Computer Vision and Pattern Recognition, pp. 1780–1789 (2020)
3. Wang, R., Zhang, Q., Fu, C.W., et al.: Underexposed photo enhancement using deep illumination estimation. In: Proceedings of the IEEE/CVF Conference on Computer Vision and Pattern Recognition, pp. 6849–6857 (2019)
4. Pizer, S.M., Amburn, E.P., Austin, J.D., et al.: Adaptive histogram equalization and its variations. Comput. Vis. Graph. Image Process. **39**(3), 355–368 (1987)
5. Ibrahim, H., Kong, N.S.P.: Brightness preserving dynamic histogram equalization for image contrast enhancement. IEEE Trans. Consum. Electron. **53**(4), 1752–1758 (2007)
6. Coltuc, D., Bolon, P., Chassery, J.M.: Exact histogram specification. IEEE Trans. Image Process. **15**(5), 1143–1152 (2006)
7. Pisano, E.D., Zong, S., Hemminger, B.M., et al.: Contrast limited adaptive histogram equalization image processing to improve the detection of simulated spiculations in dense mammograms. J. Digit. Imaging **11**(4), 193 (1998). https://doi.org/10.1007/BF03178082
8. Land, E.H.: The retinex theory of color vision. Sci. Am. **237**(6), 108–129 (1977)
9. Jobson, D.J., Rahman, Z., Woodell, G.A.: Properties and performance of a center/surround retinex. IEEE Trans. Image Process. **6**(3), 451–462 (1997)
10. Fu, X., Zeng, D., Huang, Y., et al.: A weighted variational model for simultaneous reflectance and illumination estimation. In: Proceedings of the IEEE Conference on Computer Vision and Pattern Recognition, 2782–2790 (2016)
11. Cai, B., Xu, X., Guo, K., et al.: A joint intrinsic-extrinsic prior model for retinex. In: Proceedings of the IEEE International Conference on Computer Vision, pp. 4000–4009 (2017)
12. Lore, K.G., Akintayo, A., Sarkar, S.: LLNet: a deep autoencoder approach to natural low-light image enhancement. Pattern Recogn. **61**, 650–662 (2017)
13. Yan, Z., Zhang, H., Wang, B., et al.: Automatic photo adjustment using deep neural networks. ACM Trans. Graph. (TOG) **35**(2), 1–15 (2016)
14. Gharbi, M., Chen, J., Barron, J.T., et al.: Deep bilateral learning for real-time image enhancement. ACM Trans. Graph. (TOG) **36**(4), 1–12 (2017)
15. Cai, J., Gu, S., Zhang, L.: Learning a deep single image contrast enhancer from multi-exposure images. IEEE Trans. Image Process. **27**(4), 2049–2062 (2018)
16. Jiang, Y., Gong, X., Liu, D., et al.: EnlightenGAN: deep light enhancement without paired supervision. IEEE Trans. Image Process. **30**, 2340–2349 (2021)
17. Wang, Z., Bovik, A.C., Sheikh, H.R., et al.: Image quality assessment: from error visibility to structural similarity. IEEE Trans. Image Process. **13**(4), 600–612 (2004)
18. Bychkovsky, V., Paris, S., Chan, E., et al.: Learning photographic global tonal adjustment with a database of input/output image pairs. In: CVPR 2011, pp. 97–104. IEEE (2011)
19. Li, C., Guo, J., Porikli, F., et al.: LightenNet: a convolutional neural network for weakly illuminated image enhancement. Pattern Recogn. Lett. **104**, 15–22 (2018)
20. Zhang, Y., Zhang, J., Guo, X.: Kindling the darkness: a practical low-light image enhancer. In: Proceedings of the 27th ACM International Conference on Multimedia, pp. 1632–1640 (2019)

21. Guo, X., Li, Y., Ling, H.: LIME: low-light image enhancement via illumination map estimation. IEEE Trans. Image Process. **26**(2), 982–993 (2016)
22. Ma, K., Zeng, K., Wang, Z.: Perceptual quality assessment for multi-exposure image fusion. IEEE Trans. Image Process. **24**(11), 3345–3356 (2015)
23. Wang, S., Zheng, J., Hu, H.M., et al.: Naturalness preserved enhancement algorithm for non-uniform illumination images. IEEE Trans. Image Process. **22**(9), 3538–3548 (2013)
24. Mittal, A., Soundararajan, R., Bovik, A.C.: Making a "completely blind" image quality analyzer. IEEE Sig. Process. Lett. **20**(3), 209–212 (2012)

Optimizing Loss Function for Uni-modal and Multi-modal Medical Registration

Zi Li[2,3], Fan Xin[1,2(✉)], Risheng Liu[1,2], and Zhongxuan Luo[1,2,3]

[1] DUT-RU International School of Information Science and Engineering,
Dalian University of Technology, Dalian, China
`{xin.fan,rsliu,zxluo}@dlut.edu.cn`
[2] Key Laboratory for Ubiquitous Network and Service Software of Liaoning Province,
Dalian, China
[3] School of Software Technology, Dalian University of Technology, Dalian, China

Abstract. Recent learning-based methods render fast registration by leveraging deep networks to directly learn the spatial transformation fields between the source and target images. However, manually designing and tuning loss functions for multiple types of medical data need intensive labor and extensive experience, and automatic design of loss functions remains under-investigated. In this paper, we introduce a unified formulation of the loss function and raise automated techniques to search hyperparameters of losses to obtain the optimal loss function. Specifically, we take into consideration of the multifaceted properties of image pairs and propose a unified loss to constraint similarity from different aspects. Then, we propose a bilevel self-tuning training strategy, allowing the efficient search of hyperparameters of the loss function. Based on the adaptive degrees, the proposed unified loss would be applicable to the registration of arbitrary modalities and multiple tasks. Moreover, this training strategy also reduces computational and human burdens. We conduct uni-modal and multi-modal registration experiments on seven 3D MRI datasets, the networks trained with the searched loss functions deliver accuracy on par or even superior to those with the handcrafted losses. Extensive results demonstrate our advantages over state-of-the-art registration techniques in terms of accuracy with efficiency.

Keywords: Medical image analysis · Deformable image registration · Loss function optimizing · Computer vision · Deep learning

1 Introduction

Registration plays a critical role in medical image analysis and has been a topic of active research for decades. It transforms different images into one common coordinate system with matched contents by finding the spatial correspondence between images [24]. It is fundamental to many research and clinical tasks including anatomical change diagnosis [32], longitudinal studies [25] and statistical

L. Fang et al. (Eds.): CICAI 2021, LNAI 13069, pp. 264–275, 2021.
https://doi.org/10.1007/978-3-030-93046-2_23

atlas building [9]. Deformable registration methods compute a dense correspondence between image pairs [33]. Traditional image registration is formulated as an optimization problem to minimize image mismatching between a target image and a warped source image, subject to transformation constraints.

Conventional deformable registration techniques aim at solving the optimization problem. However, optimizing over high dimensional parameter space makes them computationally intensive and time-consuming [1–3,8]. Recent learning-based methods [7,10,23,36] replace the costly numerical optimization for image pairs with one step of prediction by learned deep networks so that they can provide fast deformation estimation. Hereafter, researchers combine the learning with diffeomorphic constraints in order to provide topology-preserving guarantee [10,23]. In different tasks, the deformation field varies largely as image pairs are of different types, thus limiting the effectiveness of most loss functions to specific tasks. Moreover, so far, tremendous progress has been made towards a more accurate method while the state-of-the-art deep models still rely on hand-crafted loss function designs. These approaches pose loss function tuning and choosing as a black-box problem and require considerable computational effort to perform many training runs. Nowadays, the strong ability of auto-machine learning techniques potentially helps to construct a self-tuning unified registration loss function, which will be explored in this study.

We propose a unified loss function to make use of both the structure and intensity distribution information to align image pairs. Then, to improve the efficiency of existing learning-based registration, this paper introduces a bilevel self-tuning training strategy. This bilevel training takes the loss function learning as the upper-level objective while formulates learning for model parameters as the lower-level objective. With the help of bilevel optimization, the varied information can be represented in our unified loss function with adaptive tuning. The characteristics and contributions of our work are summarized as follows:

- We propose a unified formulation of the loss function for various image registration tasks. More concretely, we take into consideration of the multi-faceted properties of image pairs and propose to constraint similarity from two aspects, i.e., the structure and intensity distribution.
- Rather than requiring substantial efforts to design loss functions, we introduce a bilevel training strategy to search loss function, leading to the increased model flexibility and reduced computational and human burdens.
- We test our method on seven datasets for uni-modal and multi-modal image registrations. Extensive evaluations on 3D brain MRI data demonstrate that our approach achieves state-of-the-art performance with extreme efficiency.

2   Related Work

2.1   Image Registration

Conventional registration methods [2,8,17,35] try to solve an optimization over the transformations. Common representations are displacement vector fields, such as the b-splines model with control points [31,34], elastic-type models [6].

Some algorithms perform TV-regularized image registration [17,35]. To capture large deformations and guarantee mathematical properties, such as topology-preserving, diffeomorphic registration [1–3,8] has been extensively developed. However, classical methods have very large numbers of parameters, too time-assuming and complicated to work with. Taking advantage of deep learning, deep registration methods have shown promising results [20–22,22]. Inspired by the spatial-transformer work [18], learning-based approaches [7,23] in recent have focused on replacing costly numerical optimization with unsupervised global function optimization. Some researches [10,23,36] further proposed to estimate the velocity fields or momentum fields to obtain diffeomorphic transformations. However, these approaches pose loss function designing as a black-box problem and require considerable computational effort to perform many training runs, especially when switching to other tasks and applications.

2.2   Loss Function Design

Loss function plays an important role in network learning of various computer vision tasks. When registering images of the same modality, standard similarity metrics include mean-squared error (MSE) and normalized cross-correlation (NCC) [28]. For cross-modality registration, because of the complex intensity relationship between different modalities, normalized mutual information (NMI) [30] are often used. However, as a global measure, it is difficult for local estimation, which may lead to many false local optima. To overcome the above issue, the modality independent neighborhood descriptor (MIND) [16] has been introduced. It allows the formulation of a descriptor, which is independent of the particular intensity distribution across two images and provides good representations of the local shape of an image feature. Although these artificially designed losses are successful under different scenarios, they heavily rely on careful design and expertise for analyzing the property of specific metrics. By contrast, we propose a unified formulation and introduce a bilevel training strategy for deriving loss functions for various registration.

3   The Proposed Method

In this section, we provide the background of image registration, design of unified loss functions, the technology of loss function searching, and network architecture.

Given a source image $\mathbf{s}$ and a target image $\mathbf{t}$ with a spatial domain $\Omega \in \mathbb{R}^d$, deformable image registration methods find a dense, non-linear correspondence feilds $\varphi : \Omega \times \mathbb{R} \to \Omega$. In this study, we follow current unsupervised learning-based registration methods and define a network with parameters that takes the image pair as input and outputs the deformation field.

3.1   Loss Function for Uni-modal and Multi-modal Data

Among existing methods, loss functions are mainly designed for training a single model, which is not applicable for multiple tasks. Our key idea is to propose a

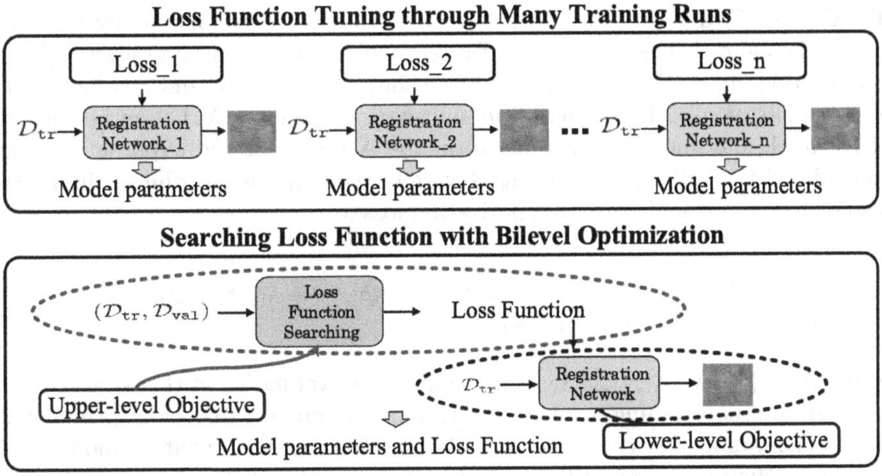

Loss Function Tuning through Many Training Runs

Searching Loss Function with Bilevel Optimization

Fig. 1. Illustration of our motivation and the proposed method. Top: to get the optimal losses, traditional approaches repeatedly train a registration model, each time with different loss combinations. Last: searching loss functions with bilevel optimization.

unified loss function for various registration tasks. To this end, we take into consideration of the multifaceted properties of image pairs and propose to constraint similarity from two aspects, i.e., the structure and intensity distribution.

Unified Similarity Loss. Given that the MSE is the most widely used metric that models the intensity relationship between the same modality, we use it to constrain the intensity distribution similarity between image pairs. While MSE focuses on the intensity distribution, it shows weaker constraints when meeting changes of contrast and structure, especially in different modalities. Therefore, we supplement the second item, which is defined by the MIND. Based on the similarity of small image patches within one image, it aims to extract the distinctive structure using the descriptor in a local neighborhood, which is preserved across modalities. Once the descriptors are extracted for both images, the similarity metric between the location in two images can be denoted as the sum of squared differences between their corresponding descriptors. MIND is able to distinguish between different types of structure such as corners, edges. It is also robust to the most considerable differences between modalities of nonfunctional intensity relations, making up for the issue of MSE loss. Hence, these two items compensate for each other. With the trade-off parameter, the proposed unified loss function consists of two parts is defined as follows:

$$\ell_{\mathtt{sim}}(.,.) = \ell_{\mathtt{MIND}}(.,.) + \lambda_{\mathtt{mse}}\ell_{\mathtt{MSE}(.,.)}, \tag{1}$$

where $\lambda_{\mathtt{mse}}$ is a hyperparameter to control the trade-off. In principle, this unified similarity loss would be applicable to the registration of arbitrary modalities.

Total Loss Function. In addition to similarity losses, we also apply regularization loss and defined it as the diffusion regularizer on spatial gradients [7] of deformation fields. The loss function regarding similarity loss and regularization loss consists of model parameters w and hyperparameters λ. Let w be the set of learnable parameters in the network, the λ represent the hyperparameters to trade off the different loss terms. Overall, we compute the sum of similarity losses at different scales and regularization loss as:

$$L_\lambda(w) = \sum_{(s,t)\in D_{tr}} \sum_{l=0}^{L} \lambda_l \ell_{\texttt{sim}}(s^l \circ \varphi^l, t^l) + \lambda_{\texttt{reg}} \ell_{\texttt{reg}}(\varphi), \qquad (2)$$

where $\lambda := \{\lambda_1, \lambda_2, \lambda_3, \lambda_{\texttt{reg}}, \lambda_{\texttt{mse}}\}$ (we apply a 3-level model in this study).

Conventional training involves tuning hyperparameters to decide optimal loss functions for multiple types of medical data, which significantly affect model performance. However, general training strategies mostly need many training runs with various loss function configurations, requiring considerably computational and human effort, as shown in the top part of Fig. 1. In the following, we introduce our self-tuning training strategy with bi-level optimization to tackle the inefficiency of loss function design and realize loss function automatic searching.

3.2   Self-tuning Training Strategy with Bi-level Optimization

To overcome the inefficiency of loss function choosing, we propose our bilevel self-tuning training, allowing the efficient search of the task-specific hyperparameters for loss functions, as shown in the bottom part of Fig. 1. We consider bilevel optimization problems [15] of the form to formulate the self-tuning learning, where we take optimization of task-specific hyperparameters λ as the upper-level subproblem, while lower-level subproblem denotes optimization of model parameters w. We start by denoting $\mathcal{D}_{tr}$ and $\mathcal{D}_{val}$ as the training and validation sets, respectively. In this setting, a prototypical choice for the lower-level objective is the regularized empirical error as:

$$L_\lambda(w) = \sum_{(s,t)\in\mathcal{D}_{tr}} \ell(w; s, t) + \ell_\lambda(w), \qquad (3)$$

where $\mathcal{D}_{\texttt{tr}} = \{(s_i, t_i)\}_{i=1}^n$ denotes source and target images in training data, ℓ denotes the prescribed loss function with respect to model parameter w, and ℓ_λ a regularizer parameterized by hyperparameters λ. The upper-level objective represents a proxy for the generalization error of w, and it may be given by the average loss on a validation set $\mathcal{D}_{\texttt{val}}$ as:

$$E(w, \lambda) = \sum_{(s,t)\in\mathcal{D}_{\texttt{val}}} \ell(w; s, t). \qquad (4)$$

Note that, although the upper-level objective does not depend explicitly on the hyperparameters λ, since λ is instrumental in finding a good model w which is our final goal. In this study, we use Eq. (2) as the specific example of Eq. (3), and define the upper-level objective as similarity loss without any hyperparameters.

Now, we try to solve the above bilevel problem. Due to its nested structure, evaluating exact gradients for the upper-level problem is difficult and computationally challenging. Finally, we follow [19] to apply approximation techniques to computation efficiently optimize the bilevel problem.

3.3   Network Architecture

The pipeline of network architecture is summarized in Fig. 2. We first use feature extractors to transform image pairs into the forms of two feature pyramids. Then, we use residual type estimators to generate deformation fields.

Feature Extractor. Given two input images, we generate L-level pyramids of feature representations. To generate feature representation at the lth layer, we use layers of convolutional filters to downsample the features at the $l - l$th pyramid level, by a factor of 2. Please refer to Table 1 for details.

Deformation Estimator. We consider a deep residual architecture, called the estimator, to generate deformation fields in a coarse-to-fine way. Its inputs are the features and upsampled deformation fields from the previous scale. This estimation process is repeated until the desired level. We parameterize the deformation field with a stationary velocity field and integrate it to obtain a diffeomorphism, which is invertible [1, 2]. The estimators at different levels share the same network structure but have their parameters. Table 2 shows details.

4   Experimental Results

4.1   Data Preparation and Evaluation Metric

For uni-modal registration, we used 528 T1 weighted brain MRI scans from five datasets: ABIDE [11], ADNI [27], HCP [13], OASIS [25], and PPMI [26]. We used the publicly available atlas from [7] as the target and aligned all the data to this common atlas. We divided our data into 377, 21 and 130 scans for training, validation and testing. Standard pre-processing operations were conducted including skull stripping with FreeSurfer [14] and affine normalization

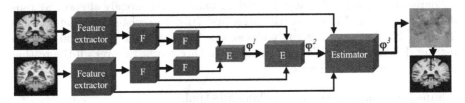

Fig. 2. Illustration of network architecture, which consists of series of feature extractors and estimators.

Table 1. The details of feature extractors architecture at level 1 and 2. Each convolution is followed by a LeakyReLU function.

Name	Stride	Ch I/O	In Res	Out Res	Input
conv0	2	1/16	$160 \times 192 \times 224$	$80 \times 96 \times 112$	Image
conv1	1	16/16	$80 \times 96 \times 112$	$80 \times 96 \times 112$	conv0
conv2	1	16/16	$80 \times 96 \times 112$	$80 \times 96 \times 112$	conv1
conv3	2	16/32	$80 \times 96 \times 112$	$40 \times 48 \times 56$	conv2
conv4	1	32/32	$40 \times 48 \times 56$	$40 \times 48 \times 56$	conv3
conv5	1	32/32	$40 \times 48 \times 56$	$40 \times 48 \times 56$	conv4

Table 2. The details of deformation estimator at level 1. Each convolution is followed by a LeakyReLU function except the one that outputs flows.

Name	Stride	Ch I/O	In Res	Out Res	Input
conv2_0	1	32/48	$80 \times 96 \times 112$	$80 \times 96 \times 112$	feature_s + feature_t
conv2_1	1	48/32	$80 \times 96 \times 112$	$80 \times 96 \times 112$	conv2_0
conv2_2	1	32/16	$80 \times 96 \times 112$	$80 \times 96 \times 112$	conv2_1
predict_flow	1	16/3	$80 \times 96 \times 112$	$80 \times 96 \times 112$	conv2_2
conv2_3	1	3/48	$80 \times 96 \times 112$	$80 \times 96 \times 112$	predict_flow
conv2_4	1	48/48	$80 \times 96 \times 112$	$80 \times 96 \times 112$	conv2_3
conv2_5	1	48/32	$80 \times 96 \times 112$	$80 \times 96 \times 112$	conv2_4
refine_flow	1	32/3	$80 \times 96 \times 112$	$80 \times 96 \times 112$	conv2_5
integrate	-	3/3	$80 \times 96 \times 112$	$80 \times 96 \times 112$	refine_flow
resize	-	3/3	$80 \times 96 \times 112$	$160 \times 192 \times 224$	integrate

with FSL [37]. We segmented the testing data with FreeSurfer, resulting in 29 anatomical structures in each volume. The images were cropped to $160 \times 192 \times 224$ with 1 mm isotropic resolution after cropping unnecessary areas. For multi-modal registration, we evaluate our method on datasets of brain scans acquired with T1 weighted and T2 weighted MRI, where T1 images do well to distinguish between different healthy tissues, whereas T2 images are best for highlighting abnormal structures in the brain such as tumors. We used 135 cases from BraTS18[1] and ISeg19[2] datasets, and each case includes two image modalities: T1 and T2 weighted brain images in size of $160 \times 160 \times 160$. Among them, 10 cases have segmentation ground truth. The set was split into 115, 10 and 10 for training, validation and testing. As most T1 and T2 images were already aligned, we randomly choose one T1 scan as the atlas and tried to register T2 scans to this T1 atlas. Similarly, we randomly choose one T2 scan as the atlas and tried to register T1 scans to it. We used the average Dice score [12] over all the testing pairs as the evaluation metric.

---

[1] https://www.med.upenn.edu/sbia/brats2018.html.
[2] https://iseg2019.web.unc.edu/.

Table 3. Quantitative comparisons in terms of Dice score.

Methods	SyN [4]	NiftyReg [34]	VM [7]	Ours
ABIDE	0.728 ± 0.029	0.747 ± 0.026	0.754 ± 0.016	**0.764 ± 0.011**
ADNI	0.761 ± 0.021	0.737 ± 0.035	0.761 ± 0.024	**0.772 ± 0.019**
HCP	0.767 ± 0.016	0.768 ± 0.013	0.761 ± 0.024	**0.772 ± 0.019**
OASIS	0.765 ± 0.010	0.748 ± 0.017	0.765 ± 0.010	**0.776 ± 0.006**
PPMI	0.778 ± 0.013	0.765 ± 0.015	0.775 ± 0.013	**0.784 ± 0.012**
T2-T1atlas	0.610 ± 0.010	0.619 ± 0.007	0.579 ± 0.013	**0.625 ± 0.009**
T1-T2atlas	0.610 ± 0.010	0.639 ± 0.011	0.579 ± 0.013	**0.644 ± 0.007**

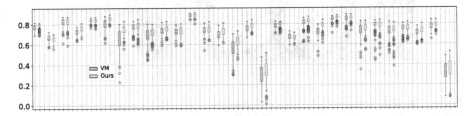

Fig. 3. Boxplots show the Dice scores for second-best VM and our method over sixteen anatomical structures including Cerebral White Matter (CblmWM), Cerebral Cortex (CblmC), Lateral Ventricle (LV), Inferior Lateral Ventricle (ILV), Cerebellum White Matter (CeblWM), Cerebellum Cortex (CereC), Thalamus (Tha), Caudate (Cau), Putamen (Pu), Pallidum (Pa), Hippocampus (Hi), Accumbens area (Am), Vessel, Third Ventricle (3V), Fourth Ventricle (4V), and Brain Stem (BS).

4.2 Top-performing Methods

We compared with top-performing Symmetric Normalization [4], NiftyReg [34], VoxelMorph [7], and refer them as SyN, NiftyReg and VM. For SyN, we used the version implemented in ANTs [5] and obtained hyperparameters from [7], which used a wide parameter sweep across datasets same to ours. We took cross correlation as the measure metric and used a step size of 0.25, Gaussian parameters (9, 0.2), at three scales with 201 iterations each. As for NiftyReg, we use the normalized mutual information cost function. We run it with 12 threads using 1500 iterations. We trained the VM model with recommended hyperparameters on the same datasets from scratch. Our experiments were performed using a 12 GB memory NVIDIA TITAN XP GPU with our implementation in PyTorch [29].

4.3 Comparisons Results

Table 3 depicts the accuracy and stability in terms of Dice score. As for unimodal data, our method gives an obvious higher mean and lower variance of Dice score on most datasets, indicating a more accurate and stable registration. As for multi-modal data, our algorithm may successfully auto-adapt to this new

Table 4. Quantitative comparisons in terms of running time in second.

Methods	SyN [4]	NiftyReg [34]	VM [7]	Ours
Uni-modal	4529 ± 1010	486 ± 40	0.615 ± 0.010	**0.170 ± 0.006**
Multi-modal	542 ± 170	195 ± 22	0.403 ± 0.007	**0.134 ± 0.003**

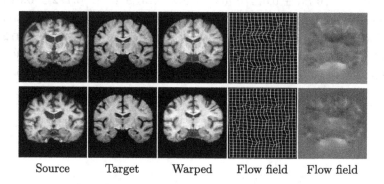

Source   Target   Warped   Flow field   Flow field

Fig. 4. Example slices extracted from uni-modal data. The five columns refer to the source, target, registered images and deformation fields.

scene without manual burdens, thanks to our automatic search that may perform the task-specific adjustment. As for uni-modal data, to take a deeper perspective of the alignment of anatomical segmentation. We illustrate the Dice score of several anatomical structures in Fig. 3. Limited by space, we take the second-best VM method as the representatives. We can see that VM gives evenly accuracy but performs much less stable among different anatomical segmentations. By contrast, our method achieves a good balance between accuracy and stability. Table 4 compares the running time under uni-modal and multi-modal registration tasks whereas our method needs the least inference time, even faster much than deep methods. Figure 4 and Fig. 5 illustrate our representative registration results from uni-modal and multi-modal data. As shown, although large deformation exists between image pairs, the source images and labels are well aligned to the targets, demonstrating our excellent performance. Overall, not only does our algorithm achieve state-of-the-art accuracy, but also the fastest runtimes.

4.4   Ablation Analysis

we conducted a series of ablation experiments in Table 5 to explore self-tuning training strategy. In the ablation experiment of uni-modal data, we set all the image size to (160, 160, 160) and select a 120-images small-scale dataset for training. We compared the results of experiments using MSE loss, MIND loss, the unified loss with manually selected hyperparameters, the unified loss using hyperparameters obtained by self-tuning training strategy. Results indicate that the networks trained with the searched loss functions deliver accuracy on par

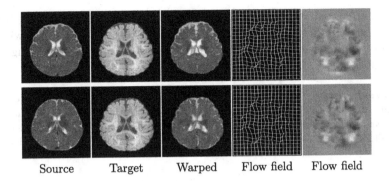

Source   Target   Warped   Flow field   Flow field

Fig. 5. Example slices extracted from multi-modal data. The five columns refer to the source, target, registered images and deformation fields.

Table 5. Ablation experiments on self-tuning training strategy.

Methods	W/MSE	W/MIND	W/UNIFIED	W/UNIFIED*
ABIDE	0.757 ± 0.014	0.737 ± 0.019	0.758 ±0.012	**0.764 ± 0.011**
ADNI	0.738 ± 0.028	0.702 ± 0.038	0.725 ± 0.030	**0.755 ± 0.019**
HCP	0.619 ± 0.091	0.655 ± 0.047	**0.684 ± 0.035**	0.681 ± 0.041
OASIS	0.755 ± 0.014	0.722 ± 0.019	0.743 ± 0.012	**0.768 ± 0.007**
PPMI	0.765 ± 0.016	0.739 ± 0.022	0.754 ± 0.017	**0.772 ± 0.012**
T2-T1atlas	0.495 ± 0.006	0.607 ± 0.007	0.500 ± 0.006	**0.625 ± 0.009**
T1-T2atlas	0.391 ± 0.045	0.600 ± 0.006	0.392 ± 0.049	**0.644 ± 0.007**

or even superior to those with the handcrafted losses. When switching to multi-modal data, generally, manually loss function tuning will be executed, which requires many training runs. Due to the joint learning of the task-specific hyper-parameters of losses and model parameters, the proposed self-tuned training could auto-adapt to this new scene and achieve satisfying performance.

5   Conclusion

In this work, we propose a unified loss function and self-tuning training strategy for the registration network to solve multiple registration problems. First, the diverse properties of image pairs within our unified loss function are utilized to constraint similarity between image pairs. Then, we propose a self-tuning bilevel training strategy, allowing the efficient search of hyperparameters of losses. In particular, the adaptive degrees allow the network to be trained to adaptively adjust loss function with respect to image pairs. This training strategy also reduces computational and human burdens. Extensive uni-modal and multi-modal experiments have shown that our method achieves state-of-the-art performance with extreme efficiency. Moreover, we offer a compelling path towards automated loss function designing for registration networks. We believe our method will drastically alleviate the burden of retraining networks with different loss combinations and thereby enable the development of learning-based registration.

Acknowledgments. This work was partially supported by the National Key R&D Program of China (2020YFB1313503), the National Natural Science Foundation of China (Nos. 61922019, 61733002, and 61672125), LiaoNing Revitalization Talents Program (XLYC1807088) and the Fundamental Research Funds for the Central Universities.

References

1. Arsigny, V., et al.: A log-euclidean framework for statistics on diffeomorphisms. In: MICCAI, pp. 924–931 (2006)
2. Ashburner, J.: A fast diffeomorphic image registration algorithm. Neuroimage **38**(1), 95–113 (2007)
3. Avants, B.B., Epstein, C.L., Grossman, M., Gee, J.C.: Symmetric diffeomorphic image registration with cross-correlation: evaluating automated labeling of elderly and neurodegenerative brain. Med. Image Anal. **12**(1), 26–41 (2008)
4. Avants, B.B., et al.: Symmetric diffeomorphic image registration with cross-correlation: evaluating automated eling of elderly and neurodegenerative brain. Med. Image Anal. **12**(1), 26–41 (2008)
5. Avants, B.B., et al.: A reproducible evaluation of ants similarity metric performance in brain image registration. Neuroimage **54**(3), 2033–2044 (2011)
6. Bajcsy, R., Kovacic, S.: Multiresolution elastic matching. Comput. Vis. Graph. Image Process. **46**(1), 1–21 (1989)
7. Balakrishnan, G., et al.: Voxelmorph: a learning framework for deformable medical image registration. IEEE Trans. Med. Imaging **38**(8), 1788–1800 (2019)
8. Beg, M.F., Miller, M.I., Trouvé, A., Younes, L.: Computing large deformation metric mappings via geodesic flows of diffeomorphisms. Int. J. Comput. Vision **61**(2), 139–157 (2005)
9. Dalca, A., et al.: Learning conditional deformable templates with convolutional networks. In: NeurIPS, pp. 806–818 (2019)
10. Dalca, A., et al.: Unsupervised learning of probabilistic diffeomorphic registration for images and surfaces. Med. Image Anal. **57**, 226–236 (2019)
11. Di Martino, A., et al.: The Autism brain imaging data exchange: towards a large-scale evaluation of the intrinsic brain architecture in Autism. Mol. Psychiatry **19**(6), 659–667 (2014)
12. Dice, L.: Measures of the amount of ecologic association between species. Ecology **26**(3), 297–302 (1945)
13. Essen, D.C.V., et al.: The WU-Minn human connectome project: an overview. Neuroimage **80**, 62–79 (2013)
14. Fischl, B.: Freesurfer. Neuroimage **62**(2), 774–781 (2012)
15. Franceschi, L., Donini, M., Frasconi, P., Pontil, M.: Forward and reverse gradient-based hyperparameter optimization. In: International Conference on Machine Learning, vol. 70, pp. 1165–1173 (2017)
16. Heinrich, M.P., et al.: MIND: modality independent neighbourhood descriptor for multi-modal deformable registration. Med. Image Anal. **16**(7), 1423–1435 (2012)

17. Hermann, S., Werner, R.: Tv-l1-based 3D medical image registration with the census cost function. In: Pacific-Rim Symposium on Image and Video Technology, pp. 149–161 (2013)
18. Jaderberg, M., et al.: Spatial transformer networks. In: NeurIPS, pp. 2017–2025 (2015)
19. Liu, H., et al.: DARTS: differentiable architecture search. In: ICLR (2019)
20. Liu, R., Cheng, S., He, Y., Fan, X., Lin, Z., Luo, Z.: On the convergence of learning-based iterative methods for nonconvex inverse problems. IEEE Trans. Pattern Anal. Mach. Intell. **42**(12), 3027–3039 (2020)
21. Liu, R., Li, Z., Fan, X., Zhao, C., Huang, H., Luo, Z.: Learning deformable image registration from optimization: perspective, modules, bilevel training and beyond. CoRR abs/2004.14557 (2020)
22. Liu, R., Liu, J., Jiang, Z., Fan, X., Luo, Z.: A bilevel integrated model with data-driven layer ensemble for multi-modality image fusion. IEEE Trans. Image Process. **30**, 1261–1274 (2021)
23. Liu, R., et al.: Bi-level probabilistic feature learning for deformable image registration. In: IJCAI, pp. 723–730 (2020)
24. Maintz, J.B.A., Viergever, M.A.: A survey of medical image registration. Med. Image Anal. **2**(1), 1–36 (1998)
25. Marcus, D.S., et al.: Open access series of imaging studies: longitudinal MRI data in nondemented and demented older adults. J. Cogn. Neurosci. **22**(12), 2677–2684 (2010)
26. Marek, K., et al.: The Parkinson progression marker initiative (PPMI). Prog. Neurobiol. **95**(4), 629–635 (2011)
27. Mueller, S.G., et al.: Ways toward an early diagnosis in Alzheimer's disease: The Alzheimer's disease neuroimaging initiative (ADNI). Alzheimer's Dementia **1**(1), 55–66 (2005)
28. Murphy, K., et al.: Evaluation of registration methods on thoracic CT: the EMPIRE10 challenge. IEEE Trans. Med. Imaging **30**(11), 1901–1920 (2011)
29. Paszke, A., et al.: Pytorch: an imperative style, high-performance deep learning library. In: NeurIPS, pp. 8024–8035 (2019)
30. Pluim, J.P.W., et al.: Mutual information based registration of medical images: a survey. IEEE Trans. Med. Imaging **22**(8), 986–1004 (2003)
31. Rueckert, D., et al.: Nonrigid registration using free-form deformation: application to breast MR images. IEEE Trans. Med. Imaging **18**(8), 712–721 (1999)
32. Sermesant, M., Forest, C., Pennec, X., Delingette, H., Ayache, N.: Deformable biomechanical models: application to 4D cardiac image analysis. Med. Image Anal. **7**(4), 475–488 (2003)
33. Sotiras, A., et al.: Deformable medical image registration: a survey. IEEE Trans. Med. Imaging **32**(7), 1153–1190 (2013)
34. Sun, W., et al.: Free-form deformation using lower-order b-spline for nonrigid image registration. In: MICCAI, pp. 194–201 (2014)
35. Vishnevskiy, V., Gass, T., Szekely, G., Tanner, C., Goksel, O.: Isotropic total variation regularization of displacements in parametric image registration. IEEE Trans. Med. Imaging **36**(2), 385–395 (2017)
36. Wang, J., Zhang, M.: Deepflash: an efficient network for learning-based medical image registration. In: CVPR, pp. 4443–4451 (2020)
37. Woolrich, M.W., et al.: Bayesian analysis of neuroimaging data in FSL. Neuroimage **45**(1), S173–S186 (2009)

Registration of 3D Point Clouds Based on Voxelization Simplify and Accelerated Iterative Closest Point Algorithm

Jiayu Wang and Hongjun Li[(✉)]

College of Science, Beijing Forestry University, Beijing 100083, China
lihongjun69@bjfu.edu.cn

Abstract. 3D point clouds have lots of applications in the fields of reverse engineering, laser remote sensing and automatic driving. The registration of point clouds scanned form different positions or different angles is the basis for shape understanding and analysis. However, due to the complex environment and the large amount of data, the automatic registration of different scans is still a challenging problem. In this work, we propose a fast registration algorithm using the prior information under a voxel structure. In this algorithm, the point cloud is firstly voxelized and organized with a 3D voxel structure. Then, we take an initial alignment based on reliable parts according to prior information. Finally we refine registration using kd-tree to accelerate Iterative Closest Point algorithm. To evaluate our algorithm, we take both synthetic data and real data experiments. The results show that our algorithm is higher efficiency and robustness.

Keywords: Point cloud registration · ICP · Structural features · Voxelization

1 Introduction

In the past decades, 3D scanning technology has been applied in digital city, autonomous vehicles, intelligent monitoring, non-contact measurement and 3D modeling due to its high precision 3D information and fast data acquisition. Generally, the collected data consist of a large number of points and each point is represented by 3D coordinates $P(x,y,z)$, so the data are often referred to as point clouds. In the view of the scanning way, there are three common ways of laser scanning: hand held laser scanning, fixed-position laser scanning and moving scanning. Moving scanning includes vehicle laser scanning and airborne laser scanning.

Different point clouds belong to different coordinate system due to the change of scanner position, which results in the demand of point cloud registration. This is a basic step before 3D modeling, 3D reconstruction, shape analysis, scene understanding, and so on. The goal of point cloud registration is to find the accurate coordinate transformation formula between those two different coordinate systems. The challenge of this task comes from the lack of accurate corresponding points because of self-occlusion or occlusions of the object been scanned, and the density inconsistency since the scanners are not the same one [5,28].

© Springer Nature Switzerland AG 2021
L. Fang et al. (Eds.): CICAI 2021, LNAI 13069, pp. 276–288, 2021.
https://doi.org/10.1007/978-3-030-93046-2_24

For overcoming this challenge, some literatures used point to point registering method, for example, the Iterative Closest Point algorithm (ICP) [5]. Others used preprocessing as coarse registration before point to point registering, which results in a multi-steps methods. However, most existing methods of point cloud registration were time consuming and even had large error, which are illustrated in our experimental section.

In fact, in practical engineering application, both fixed-position laser scanner and moving scanner are horizontally placed in general. So the z-axis in the collected point cloud is roughly upwards. Based on the priori information, we propose a fast automatic registration algorithm. Its highlights are:

(1) This algorithm based on voxelization simplify and accelerated ICP is a multi-steps method. Both time efficiency and accuracy are improved comparing to several existing methods.
(2) A rule of calculating the length of voxel edge is proposed. By this way, voxels are the same size for both two point clouds that need to be registered. This method has two advantages: firstly, the influence of non-uniform density is decreased; secondly, the number of points used to register is reduced, which accelerates the subsequent register processing.
(3) An approach for coarse registration is proposed. This method uses prior reliable region to roughly align the two point clouds, which can void the reflection transformation, an error that occurs in some global optimal orthogonal transformation methods.

In addition, we use the kd-tree structure to improve the efficiency of registration.

2 Related Work

Early 3D registration algorithms were reviewed in some survey papers [22]. We here only explore some closed to us, which can be roughly classified into three categories: geometric descriptors-based, ICP related, and hybrid methods. In addition, we briefly explore the evaluation index of the registration effect.

2.1 Geometric Descriptors-Based

A lot of registration methods are based on the geometric information of point cloud. The reconstructed polygon surface can be used as coordinate transformation invariant feature descriptors [16]. The angle between the normal vector and its neighbor is an invariant to scale and rotation transformation, which is used to construct the angular-based registration algorithm [12]. Given the use of projective transform allows to handle perspective effects, a contour-based algorithm is proposed [2]. A 3D shape descriptor, Regional Curvature Map that is discriminative and robust against normal errors and varying point cloud density, is proposed [26] for automatic 3D point cloud registration.

In addition, some registration methods are proposed by defining maximally stable shape index regions [17], combining local shape geometries with statistical properties

[34], integrating geometric structure into a deep neural network [5], using normals of points [24], etc.

Although these methods have made full use of the geometrical information, the results of registration are a little coarse alignment and often used as pre-registering in some algorithms.

2.2 ICP Related

Iterative Closest Point (ICP) algorithm performs a fine registration of two overlapping point clouds by iteratively estimating the transformation parameters, assuming good a priori alignment is provided. Many progresses were made to improve each step of the process, including selecting, matching, rejecting, weighting, minimizing, using the knowledge of the shape [9]. By considering the normal and curvature features, the Normal ICP method was presented [25]. By introducing the deletion mask, the classical ICP algorithm is modified [19]. By transforming a point cloud into image using spherical polar coordinates, Levenberg-Marquardt-ICP algorithm was proposed [29]. In addition, geometric metric, transformation compatibility measure were also employed [27].

A priori alignment is helpful for the convergence of ICP algorithm, so a process of registration can be roughly classified into two steps: coarse registration and fine registration with ICP [6]. In the step of coarse registration, there were some novel approaches, for example, feature similarity [7], key points and zero-mean normalized cross-correlation coefficient registration criterion [36].

2.3 Hybrid Methods

Hybrid methods include geometrical, statistical, optimal methods and deep learning technology. Registration can be formulated as a branch-and-bound problem with mixed-integer linear programming [35], treated as a rigid transformation [1], performed using Gaussian mixtures [31], or achieved by combining Newton iteration with the improved 3D normal distribution transformation [11]. In recent years, Simultaneous Localization and Mapping (SLAM) technique [13], bidirectional Maximum Correntropy Criterion [37], learning-based methods including deep neural network [4,5,10], general graph-theoretic framework [33], were employed for point cloud registration.

Multi-stage registering methods include two-stage pipeline, i.e. the initial pairwise alignment and the globally consistent refinement [8]; three steps that consist of extract the planar surfaces, the registration by combining heuristic search, and the transformation is refined using weighted least squares [30]; and four major steps that are the voxelization of the point cloud, the approximation of planar patches, the matching of corresponding patches, and the estimation of transformation parameters [32].

Different form the above literatures which focused on algorithm accuracy, some papers emphasised on the speed of registration. A simple way is to reduce the number of points, for instance, using guaranteed outlier removal [21] as a preprocessing step. Inspired by those methods, our method dramatically reduces the number of points by voxelization, and uses the center points of voxels to get the rigid transformation which works for original point clouds.

2.4   Evaluation

The registration performance can be evaluated by accuracy, robustness and speed. Among the indexes, accuracy is not easy to define. The representative approaches include using the consistent point clouds [14], or the compare software [23], or the deviation of registered planar surfaces, or the mean square point-to-point distance [15].

In this paper, we evaluate the accuracy by comparing the estimated transform formula to the ground truth one which is obtained using virtual point cloud.

3   Method

Let input point clouds consist of the target point cloud (Ω_t) and the source point cloud (Ω_s). The main steps of our registration algorithm are as follow. Firstly, both Ω_t and Ω_s are voxelized by an adaptive 3D grids to reduce massive data. Secondly, the voxel point cloud V_t and V_s, generated from Ω_t and Ω_s, are initially aligned by the optimal horizontal rotation angle, which is determined by prior reliable region. The relative rigid body transformation parameters are obtained. Then, we use kd-tree-accelerated ICP to register the pre-aligned voxel point cloud. The transformation formula for the registration of Ω_t and Ω_s is derived. Lastly, a simplified point model is obtained by re-sampling from the registered point clouds.

3.1   Voxelization

First, we calculate the axis-aligned bounding box (AABB-box) of Ω_t as

$$[x_{min}, x_{max}] \times [y_{min}, y_{max}] \times [z_{min}, z_{max}] \tag{1}$$

The number of voxel along each axis direction is a key factor for balancing the sampling resolution and the algorithm efficiency. Let N_{fav} and N_{min} be the favorite voxel number along the longest edge B_{long} and the minimum number along the shortest edge B_{short} of the AABB-box.

$$B_{long} = max\{x_{max} - x_{min}, y_{max} - y_{min}, z_{max} - z_{min}\} \tag{2}$$

$$B_{short} = min\{x_{max} - x_{min}, y_{max} - y_{min}, z_{max} - z_{min}\} \tag{3}$$

Each voxel has the same size and its length V_L is calculated as

$$V_L = min\{\frac{B_{long}}{N_{fav}}, \frac{B_{short}}{N_{min}}\} \tag{4}$$

According to the voxel length V_L, the target point cloud Ω_t can be voxelized. Then, we take the centual point from each voxel and make them form a new point cloud V_t. Using the same voxel length V_L, the source point cloud Ω_s can be voxelized and its voxel point cloud V_s can be obtained using the same method as V_t. In practice, parameters N_{fav} and N_{min} are specified by user according to his algorithm requirements on speed and accuracy. Voxels are the same size for both V_t and V_s, which decreases the influence of non-uniform density of Ω_t and Ω_s due to occlusion in scanning procession.

3.2   Initial Alignment

The initial registration is to roughly align the two voxel point clouds V_t and V_s using a method, named APRR (Alignment guided by Prior Reliable Region).

In scanning practice, some regions are more reliable than other regions because the position of the scanner and scanning direction, as well as the occlusion. For instance, when an object needs to be scanned, the lower region of the object is more reliable if the scanner is placed at a low position, as shown in Fig. 1(a). On the contrary, if the scanner is placed at a top position (Fig. 1(b)), the upper region of the object is more reliable.

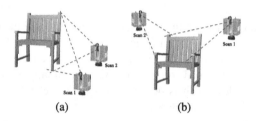

(a)   (b)

Fig. 1. Reliable region is related to the position of scanner.

Guided by this kind of prior information, both V_t and V_s are translated to their base centers, C_t and C_s. Then, we define the reliable region in both voxel point clouds V_t and V_s, which are similar to the scanning point clouds Ω_t and Ω_s. In our experiments, we assume that the upper region is reliable and the average position vector $\overrightarrow{v_t}$ is consistent to the average position vector $\overrightarrow{v_s}$ of points in the upper region of V_t and V_s respectively. Using $\overrightarrow{v_t}$ and $\overrightarrow{v_s}$, a rotation transform T_r is obtained. Then, we get

$$V_t' = T_r \cdot (V_t - C_t), \quad V_s' = I_s \cdot (V_s - C_s), \tag{5}$$

where I_s is the unit transform; V_t' and V_s' are the initial aligned point clouds. Note that formula (5) derived from APRR is a rigid body transformation, avoiding reflection error which occurs in an optimal question without reflection constraint [18].

3.3   Refine with ICP

In order to improve the registration efficiency of ICP algorithm, we establish kd-tree structure to search the nearest point pairs. Based on literature [5], the ICP algorithm combining with kd-tree is as follows:

S1: the initial nearest neighbor point is set as the node stored at the top of the stack, and the nearest distance is calculated;

S2: calculate the distance between the current node and the target point, and compare it with the nearest distance to judge whether it is updated as the nearest neighbor;

S3: in the index space, a spherical bounding box is formed with the target point as the center of the ball and the nearest distance as the radius, and the space ball is judged to intersect with the segmentation plane of the top node of the stack.

S4: repeat steps (S1) and (S2) until the stack is empty and the solution is finished and the transform formula is obtained as

$$V_t' = T_{Ricp} \cdot V_s' + T_{Ticp}, \tag{6}$$

where T_{Ricp} is the rotation and T_{Ticp} is the translational item.

3.4   The Transformation Formula

In our algorithm, there are two steps that generate transform formulae (5) and (6). For convenient to use, a full transform function can be calculated by the composition of formulae (5) and (6) as

$$V_t = R_{full} \cdot V_s + T_{full}, \tag{7}$$

where,

$$R_{full} = T_r^{-1} \cdot T_{Ricp}, \tag{8}$$

and

$$T_{full} = T_r^{-1} \cdot (T_{Ticp} - T_{Ricp} \cdot C_s) + C_t. \tag{9}$$

Note that formula (7) works not only for the registration of V_t and V_s, but also for the registration of input point cloud Ω_t and Ω_s, i.e.

$$\Omega_t = R_{full} \Omega_s + T_{full}, \tag{10}$$

3.5   Accuracy Indexes

The registration of point clouds is evaluated by rotation error ε_A and the translational transform error ε_D. ε_A is the maixmum deviation angle. By comparing the estimated transform formula to the ground truth one from virtual point cloud data or actual scanning data. Referring formula (10), let the ground truth transform function be

$$\Gamma_g : \ \Omega_t = [\alpha_1, \alpha_2, \alpha_3]\Omega_s + \alpha_0. \tag{11}$$

and an estimated transform function

$$\Gamma_e : \ \Omega_t = [\beta_1, \beta_2, \beta_3]\Omega_s + \beta_0. \tag{12}$$

where α_i and β_i, $i = 1, 2, 3$, are unit vectors.

Then the rotation error ε_A of the estimated transform function Γ_e is defined as

$$\varepsilon_A = \max\{\arccos(\alpha_i \cdot \beta_i), i = 1, 2, 3\}. \tag{13}$$

where $(\alpha_i \cdot \beta_i)$ represents the inner product of two vectors.

The translational transform error ε_D of the estimated transform function Γ_e is defined as

$$\varepsilon_D = \sqrt{(\alpha_0 - \beta_0)^T (\alpha_0 - \beta_0)}. \tag{14}$$

3.6 Simplification

After the registration of input point cloud Ω_t and Ω_s, there are many redundancy points, especially in the overlap regions. For removing those redundancy points and simplifying point cloud, one of the fast methods is to voxelize the registered point cloud. The size of each voxel can be calculated using formula (4) and the parameter N_{fav} should be bigger. For example, in Fig. 2(a), the number of points in Ω_t and Ω_s are 239,808 and 190,468 respectively. So there are 430,276 points in the registered point cloud as show in Fig. 2(b). After removing those redundancy points, there are only 55,386 points in simplified point cloud (Fig. 2(c)) which is enough to represent the 3D chair model.

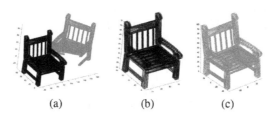

(a)   (b)   (c)

Fig. 2. Model simplification after registered. The simplified model (c) has point number only 12.87% of that in registered model (b).

4 Experiment

In order to verify the validity of our algorithm, we carry out experiments on both simulated data and actual scanning data. The algorithm is implemented using MATLAB R2016b programming, and the experiments are carried out in a laptop.

4.1 Parameter Analysis

In our algorithm, parameters N_{fav} and N_{min} are the favorite voxel number along the longest edge and the minimum number along the shortest edge of the AABB-box. They are specified by users. N_{min} works only for very thin point cloud and in our experiments, it is set as a constant number ($N_{min} = 13$) for avoiding trivial case.

Here we use a chair data (Chair1a, in Fig. 4) to illustrate the relation between the favorite voxel number N_{fav} and the time efficiency in our algorithm. Figure 3 shows four types of running time (voxelization, rough pre-alignment, registration and total time) when N_{fav} increases from 16 to 256 exponentially. We can find that the rough pre-alignment time is quite stable at different values of N_{fav}, which is shorter than one second. Specifically, the rough pre-alignment time is positively correlated with the voxelization time. When $N_{fav} > 32$, the total time and the registration time increase significantly. Therefore, we let $N_{fav} = 32$ as the default value in our algorithm. Apparently, the registration time takes most part of the total time and when $N_{fav} = 128$, it reaches the highest percent 94.51%. That means we can take more researches on registration part to improve the efficiency.

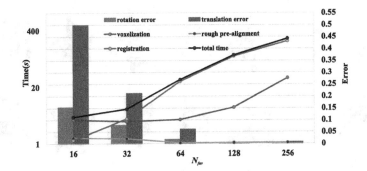

Fig. 3. The time efficiency and the error of our algorithm corresponding to different voxel number. The rotation error ε_A is shown as $(180\varepsilon_A/\pi)°$.

The histogram in Fig. 3 shows the rotation error ε_A and the translational transform error ε_D of our method with different N_{fav}. For visual effect, ε_A is represented by degree, i.e. $(180\varepsilon_A/\pi)°$ in Fig. 3. It can be found that both the rotation error and the translational transform error decrease as N_{fav} increases.

4.2 Comparison

We compare our method to 5 representative algorithms: CPD2010 [20], SurR2010 [14], FRS2014 [3], RICP2015 [18], SDRSAC2019 [38]. Experiment data consist of 6 pair point clouds, as shown in the most left column of Fig. 4. The first 3 pair point clouds (From the 1st row through the 3rd row in the figure) randomly generated from a mesh chair by rotating, translating and cutting. Point clouds from the 4th row to the 5th row are randomly generated from another mesh chair by rotating, translating and cutting. The last row is a tree which were scanned by a laser scanner from different directions.

Experiment results are shown in Fig. 4. Parameter $N_{fav} = 32$ and other parameters in other algorithms are default values they proposed. From Fig. 4, we can find that in the view of visual effect, our algorithm works well for all point cloud data. FRS2014 and RICP2015 algorithm are ranked second, which register 4 point cloud data correctly. CPD2010, SurR2010 and SDRSAC2019 each registers one point cloud data correctly.

As for the evaluation of efficiency, we list the run time (unit: s) in Table 1. In the table, *Tar.Pts* and *Sou.Pts* mean the number of points in target point cloud and source point cloud respectively. As can be seen, the run time of Ours is very close to CPD2010, though Ours consistently attains higher solution quality. Their average time is 3.7539s and Ours spends 2.3410s. The average time of SurR2010 is 41.1058s and RICP2015 spends about half as much time as SurR2010. Moreover, SDRSAC2019 is very time consuming, which spend more than 4000 s. Both Ours and FRS2014 obtain higher matches compared to other competitors, but Ours takes 99.47 % less time than FRS2014 on average. This clearly shows the efficiency of our method. We calculate standard deviation δ of the time of these algorithms and find that Ours is the most stable method ($\delta_{Ours} = 0.77$), and CPD2010 performs good with $\delta_{CPD} = 2.10$. Running time of FRS2014 and SDRSAC2019 are extremely unstable, whose δ are larger than 400.

Input   CPD2010 [20]   SurR2010 [14]   FRS2014 [3]   RICP2015 [18]   SDRSAC2019 [?]   Ours

Fig. 4. Comparing our method with 5 representative algorithms. From top to down, the point clouds are Chair1a, Chair1b, Chair1c, Chair2a, Chair2b, and Tree, corresponding to Table 1.

For evaluating accuracy, the rotation error ε_A (Formula (13)) and the translational transform error ε_D (Formula (14)) of those 6 algorithms are listed in Table 2 and Table 3. As shown in Table 2, ε_A of our approach can achieve a large improvement compared to other methods. In all chair registration tasks, ε_A of Ours are the minimum, whose magnitude is 10^{-3}. ε_A of Ours in Tree task is 0.054, little larger than RICP's rotation error, 0.0538. The average of Ours rotation error is 0.01 and the best among 6 algorithms.

Table 1. Comparing the running time (unit: s) of our method with 5 representative algorithms.

Data	Tar.Pts	Sou.Pts	CPD2010	SurR2010	FRS2014	RICP2015	SDRSAC2019	Ours
Chair1a	239,808	190,468	3.0975	61.1964	652.4600	148.3290	4909.6000	3.5015
Chair1b	224,530	192,318	2.4898	57.0994	94.9460	108.7808	4021.1000	2.5756
Chair1c	224,530	190,468	2.3117	61.6668	1055.0728	100.4179	4351.1000	2.8589
Chair2a	135,751	120,492	3.2219	38.0111	71.5560	61.3787	3759.5000	1.8480
Chair2b	120,492	102,151	3.4558	22.5115	414.0710	50.6407	4936.9000	1.5029
Tree	93,696	113,887	7.9467	6.1494	0.0243	12.1838	4554.0000	1.7591

Table 2. Comparison of the rotation error ε_A of 6 algorithms.

Data	CPD	SurR	FRS	RICP	SDRSAC	Ours
Chair1a	0.6080	1.4585	0.0539	2.4806	2.2069	**0.0014**
Chair1b	2.9842	3.0708	3.1329	0.0972	1.7148	**0.0027**
Chair1c	1.4955	1.3949	0.0559	2.1682	0.0093	**0.0027**
Chair2a	1.8197	1.8159	0.0201	0.0028	2.5294	**0.0019**
Chair2b	0.9237	0.6518	0.0611	0.0475	2.4854	**0.0056**
Tree	0.0649	0.0639	0.1160	**0.0538**	2.1666	0.0540

As for the translational transform error, Table 3 shows that ε_D of Ours are the minimum in all registration tasks and the average error of Ours is 0.36. ε_D of Ours are 97.45%, 89.78%, 87.79%, 56.66%, 80.46% and 2.5% less than the second smallest translation error in each row of the table.

Table 3. Comparison of the translational transform error ε_D of 6 algorithms.

Data	CPD	SurR	FRS	RICP	SDRSAC	Ours
Chair1a	101.85	178.415	8.30	313.04	236.92	**0.212**
Chair1b	71.577	72.601	74.97	6.047	90.30	**0.618**
Chair1c	188.63	169.143	7.36	59.78	4.177	**0.51**
Chair2a	165.46	164.34	2.585	0.293	255.5	**0.127**
Chair2b	60.508	48.63	3.24	4.75	79.37	**0.633**
Tree	0.102	0.086	0.79	0.079	4.692	**0.077**

5 Conclusion

An algorithm for the registration of point clouds which are from roughly upright scanner(s) is proposed in this paper. The algorithm accelerates the registering process by voxelizing the point clouds and reduces the influence of nonuniform density using the same size of voxel. An initial align guided by prior reliable region is helpful for avoiding reflection transform error. Experiments show that our method greatly speeds up the registration and has the smallest deviation of the rotation and the translational errors.

Our method has its limitations which are future works. The first is the assumption that the upwards direction of the target and source point clouds should be approximately consistent. Although the assumption is true for most cases, including the airborne laser scanning and the terrestrial laser scanning, it does not work when the angle between the z-axis of target and source point cloud is too large. Another limitation is that there is at least one prior reliable region in input point clouds.

Acknowledgments. The work was supported by the National College Students innovation and entrepreneurship training program No. G201910022067.

References

1. Torre-Ferrero, C., Llata, J.R., Alonso, L., Robla, S., Sarabia, E.G.: 3D point cloud registration based on a purpose-designed similarity measure. Eurasip J. Adv. Signal Process. **2012**(1), 1–15 (2012)
2. Bennis, A., Bombardier, V., Thiriet, P., Brie, D.: Contours based approach for thermal image and terrestrial point cloud registration. ISPRS Int. Arch. Photogramm. Remote Sens. Spatial Inf. Sci. **40**(5), 97–101 (2013)
3. Bustos, A.J.P., Chin, T.J., Suter, D.: Fast rotation search with stereographic projections for 3D registration. In: Proceedings of the 2014 IEEE Conference on Computer Vision and Pattern Recognition, CVPR 2014, pp. 3930–3937. IEEE Computer Society, USA (2014)
4. Chang, W.C., Pham, V.T.: 3-D point cloud registration using convolutional neural networks. Appl. Sci. **9**(16), 3273.1–20 (2019)
5. Elbaz, G., Avraham, T., Fischer, A.: 3D point cloud registration for localization using a deep neural network auto-encoder. In: 2017 IEEE Conference on Computer Vision and Pattern Recognition (CVPR), pp. 2472–2481 (2017)
6. Fukai, H., Xu, G.: Fast and robust registration of multiple 3D point clouds. In: 2011 RO-MAN, pp. 331–336 (2011)
7. Geng, N., Ma, F., Yang, H., Li, B., Zhang, Z.: Neighboring constraint-based pairwise point cloud registration algorithm. Multimedia Tools Appl. **75**(24), 16763–16780 (2015). https://doi.org/10.1007/s11042-015-2941-6
8. Gojcic, Z., Zhou, C., Wegner, J.D., Guibas, L.J., Birdal, T.: Learning multiview 3D point cloud registration. In: 2020 IEEE Conference on CVPR (2020)
9. Gressin, A., Mallet, C., Demantke, J., David, N.: Towards 3D lidar point cloud registration improvement using optimal neighborhood knowledge. ISPRS J. Photogramm. Remote. Sens. **79**(May), 240–251 (2013)
10. Groß, J., Ošep, A., Leibe, B.: Alignnet-3D: fast point cloud registration of partially observed objects. In: International Conference on 3D Vision (3DV) (2019)
11. Hu, F., Ren, T., Shi, S.: Discrete point cloud registration using the 3D normal distribution transformation based newton iteration. J. Multimed. **9**(7), 934–940 (2014)
12. Jiang, J., Cheng, J., Chen, X.: Registration for 3-D point cloud using angular-invariant feature. Neurocomputing **72**(16–18), 3839–3844 (2009)

13. Kim, P., Chen, J., Cho, Y.K.: Slam-driven robotic mapping and registration of 3D point clouds. Autom. Constr. **89**(May), 38–48 (2018)

14. Kjer, H.M., Wilm, J.: Evaluation of surface registration algorithms for PET motion correction. Ph.D. thesis, Technical University of Denmark Kgs Lyngby Denmark (2010)

15. Lachhani, K., Duan, J., Baghsiahi, H., Willman, E., Selviah, D.: Error metric for indoor 3D point cloud registration. In: Irish Machine Vision and Image Processing Conference (2014)

16. Li, N., Cheng, P., Sutton, M.A., Mcneill, S.R.: Three-dimensional point cloud registration by matching surface features with relaxation labeling method. Exp. Mech. **45**, 71–82 (2005)

17. Manafzade, M.M., Harati, A.: Point cloud registration using MSSIR: maximally stable shape index regions. In: 2013 21st Iranian Conference on Electrical Engineering (ICEE), pp. 1–6 (2013)

18. Manu: Rigid ICP registration. https://www.mathworks.com/matlabcentral/fileexchange/40888-rigid-icp-registration. Accessed 18 Aug 2020

19. Marina, R., Reno, V., Nitti, M., DÓrazio, T., Stella, E.: A modified iterative closest point algorithm for 3D point cloud registration. Comput. Aided Civil Infrastruct. Eng. **31**(7), 515–534 (2016)

20. Myronenko, A., Song, X.: Point set registration: coherent point drift. IEEE Trans. Pattern Anal. Mach. Intell. **32**(12), 2262–2275 (2010)

21. Parra Bustos, A., Chin, T.: Guaranteed outlier removal for point cloud registration with correspondences. IEEE Trans. Pattern Anal. Mach. Intell. **40**(12), 2868–2882 (2018)

22. Pomerleau, F., Colas, F., Siegwart, R.: A review of point cloud registration algorithms for mobile robotics. Found. Trends Robot **4**(1), 1–104 (2015)

23. Rajendra, Y.D., et al.: Evaluation of partially overlapping 3D point cloud's registration by using ICP variant and cloudcompare. In: ISPRS-International Archives of the Photogrammetry, Remote Sensing and Spatial Information Sciences, pp. 891–897 (2014)

24. Raposo, C., Barreto, J.P.: Using 2 point+normal sets for fast registration of point clouds with small overlap. In: 2017 IEEE International Conference on Robotics and Automation (ICRA), pp. 5652–5658 (2017)

25. Serafin, J., Grisetti, G.: NICP: dense normal based point cloud registration. In: IEEE/RSJ International Conference on Intelligent Robots and Systems, pp. 742–749 (2015)

26. Sun, J., Zhang, J., Zhang, G.: An automatic 3D point cloud registration method based on regional curvature maps. Image Vision Comput. **56**, 49–58 (2016)

27. Thomas, A., Sunilkumar, A., Shylesh, S., Methirumangalath, S., Chen, D., Peethambaran, J.: TCM-ICP: transformation compatibility measure for registering multiple LIDAR scans. CoRR abs/2001.01129 (2020)

28. Watanabe, T., Niwa, T., Masuda, H.: Registration of point-clouds from terrestrial and portable laser scanners. Int. J. Autom. Technol. **10**(2), 163–171 (2016)

29. Xian, Y., Xiao, J., Wang, Y.: A fast registration algorithm of rock point cloud based on spherical projection and feature extraction. Front. Comput. Sci. **13**(1), 170–182 (2019). https://doi.org/10.1007/s11704-016-6191-1

30. Xiao, J., Adler, B., Zhang, H.: 3D point cloud registration based on planar surfaces. In: 2012 IEEE International Conference on Multisensor Fusion and Integration for Intelligent Systems (MFI), pp. 40–45 (2012)

31. Xiong, H., Szedmak, S., Piater, J.: A study of point cloud registration with probability product kernel functions. In: Proceedings of the 2013 International Conference on 3D Vision, 3DV 2013, pp. 207–214. IEEE Computer Society, USA (2013)

32. Xu, Y., Boerner, R., Yao, W., Hoegner, L., Stilla, U.: Automated coarse registration of point clouds in 3D urban scenes using voxel based plane constraint. ISPRS Ann. Photogramm. Remote Sens. Spatial Inf. Sci. **IV-2/W4**, 185–191 (2017)

33. Yang, H., Shi, J., Carlone, L.: Teaser: fast and certifiable point cloud registration (2020)

34. Yang, J., Cao, Z., Zhang, Q.: A fast and robust local descriptor for 3D point cloud registration. Inf. Sci. **346**, 163–179 (2016)
35. Yu, C., Da, J.: A maximum feasible subsystem for globally optimal 3D point cloud registration. Sensors **18**(2), 544.1–19 (2018)
36. Huang, Y., Da, F.P., Tang, L.: Research on algorithm of point cloud coarse registration. In: 2016 2nd IEEE International Conference on Computer and Communications (ICCC), pp. 1335–1339 (2016)
37. Zhang, X., Jian, L., Xu, M.: Robust 3D point cloud registration based on bidirectional maximum correntropy criterion. PLoS ONE **13**(5), 1–15 (2018)
38. Le, H.M., Do, T.-T., Hoang, T., Cheung, N.-M.: SDRSAC: semidefinite-based randomized approach for robust point cloud registration without correspondences. In: IEEE Conference on CVPR, pp. 124–133 (2019)

Few-shot Weighted Style Matching for Glaucoma Detection

Jinhui Liu[1]([✉]) and Xin Yu[2]

[1] BNRist and School of Software, Tsinghua University, Beijing, China
[2] University of Technology Sydney, Ultimo, Australia

Abstract. Glaucoma is a harmful eye disease that can lead to irreversible blindness. Color fundus photography (CFP) is the most popular non-invasive and low-cost imaging modality to detect glaucoma. However, diagnosing glaucoma from fundus images is not an easy task and only clinicians with years of experience can do it. Deep neural network (DNN), especially convolutional neural network (CNN), has shown great power in medical image processing and has great potential for efficient glaucoma diagnosis. Nevertheless, fundus images captured by different cameras and devices may have different characteristics, which causes domain shift problem and severely affects CNN generalizing across different datasets. In this paper, we exploit unsupervised domain adaptation to address domain shift. Here, we assume only few target unlabeled samples are available, which is a more realistic and challenging problem. We present a novel few-shot weighted style matching framework (few-shot WSM) to robustly detect glaucoma from different fundus image datasets. The few-short WSM module reduces domain shift by matching the style of the source domain images and the target domain images. Experiment results show our framework effectively reduces the domain shift problem and significantly improves the glaucoma classification performance.

Keywords: Glaucoma classification · Few-shot domain adaptation · Style transfer

1 Introduction

Glaucoma is a leading cause of irreversible blindness and is predicted to affect 112 million people by 2040 [22]. Since glaucoma does not always have physical symptoms in the early stage, having a regular test for glaucoma is an important way to detect it as soon as possible. Among all the techniques to detect glaucoma, Color fundus photography (CFP) is the most popular non-invasive low-cost imaging modality to detect glaucoma and is widely performed by clinicians. However, diagnosing glaucoma from fundus images is a professional task and only clinicians with years of experience can do it. Recently, deep neural networks (DNNs), especially Convolutional Neural Networks (CNNs), have shown

© Springer Nature Switzerland AG 2021
L. Fang et al. (Eds.): CICAI 2021, LNAI 13069, pp. 289–300, 2021.
https://doi.org/10.1007/978-3-030-93046-2_25

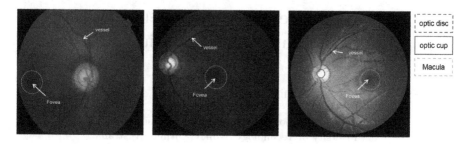

Fig. 1. Appearance of fundus image from Drishti (left), REFUGE Train (middle) and REFUGE Val/Test (right) dataset. They all contain the same structure whereas different style.

great power in glaucoma classification using fundus images, and previous works have shown that DNNs can diagnose glaucoma with high accuracy competing to human clinicians [5,9].

However, fundus images captured by different cameras and institutions have obvious appearance discrepancy due to different parameter settings, which causes the domain shift problem. Domain shift is the main cause for the poor generalization capability of DNNs across different datasets.

To reduce the effect of domain shift, domain adaptation (DA) methods are developed to improve the cross-domain performance of DNNs. Among all the proposed methods, unsupervised domain adaptation (UDA) is the most common method because it is free of annotations on the target domain, which is especially valuable in the medical image processing area due to the lack of labeled data. However, we are focusing on a more challenging and realistic problem that only few unlabeled samples of the target domain are available. Under this circumstance, most UDA methods are prone to failure because of the scarce of target domain data.

We propose a novel framework to handle the problem. First, we notice that fundus images captured by different cameras all have the same content information, the fundus structure such as optic disc and cup, vessel and macula, but different styles with different colors and textures, etc., as shown in Fig. 1. We assume the domain shift is mainly on style differences. Based on this assumption, we decide to adopt style transfer technique to match the styles of fundus images from different datasets. The goal of style transfer is to change visual style information of an image while preserving its semantic content. [6] proposed the seminal idea of combining content loss and style loss to realize style transfer. [7] found that the mean and variance statistics of the latent embedding represent the style of images, and designed AdaIN module to achieve arbitrary style transfer. [13] focused on one-shot style transfer and proposed the Adversarial Style Mining (ASM) architecture utilizing only one image on the target domain.

In this work, We follow [7] and [13,25] and bring up a few-shot weighted style matching framework to narrow down the domain shift of the source domain and the target domain of the fundus image datasets. We believe each fundus image has its own distance to the center of its dataset, so we utilize the MeanShift [3] algorithm to calculate the distance of each target training sample and use the distance to guide the style transfer procedure. Afterward, style-matched source domain images are utilized to train a CNN classification model. The main contributions of this paper are:

(1) To the best of our knowledge, we are the first to handle domain shift problem of different fundus image datasets under the few-shot setting for the purpose of glaucoma detection;
(2) We observe style discrepancy of different fundus images and design a novel few-shot weighted style matching framework to effectively reduce the domain shift of different fundus image datasets;
(3) We take sample-to-dataset distance into consideration and adopt MeanShift algorithm to measure the distance of each target training sample to the target domain dataset.

2   Related Work

2.1   Glaucoma Detection in Deep Learning

Deep learning plays an increasingly important role in medical imaging analysis, especially fundus image diagnosis. Glaucoma as a disease endangering human health needs to be detected and treated as early as possible. Plenty of works are exploring using deep learning to help detect glaucoma [1,2,5,9,11,26].

[2] trained a CNN model in an end-to-end manner for glaucoma detection. [11] used a deep CNN architecture and approximately 40 thousand annotated fundus images proving the effectiveness of deep learning on glaucoma diagnosis. [9] adopted evidence map to help the network focus on pathological area to detect glaucoma. [5] and [1] considered using a multi-branch network that combines results from different branches to achieve high accuracy. [26] chose to directly estimate the vertical cup-to-disc ratio (CDR) from optic disc and optic cup to detect glaucoma. A larger CDR leads to more suspicion of glaucoma. However, these works do not consider domain shift problem and assume training and test images have the same distribution, which is hardly satisfied in clinical practice. [23] first explored domain adaptation for glaucoma detection, they proposed a pOSAL framework to jointly segment optic disc and cup and utilize the vertical CDR as an indicator to classify glaucoma, but their method need a large amount of target domain samples for training.

2.2   Few-shot Domain Adaptation

few-shot domain adaptation manages to handle domain shift problem with only few samples on target domain [4,10,13–15,20,24]. [15] brought up a classification and contrastive semantic alignment (CCSA) loss to learn an embedding subspace that semantically aligns different domains while maintaining discriminative. [14] exploited adversarial learning to maximize the confusion between two domains

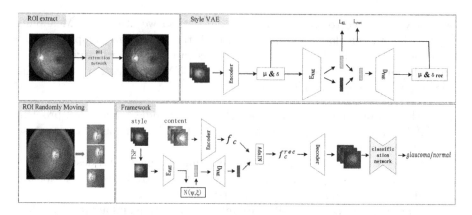

Fig. 2. Overview of the few-shot WSM framework (see Right Bottom). We extract optic disc area from original fundus image (see Left Top) as Region-of-Interest (ROI). Based on ROI, we employ an VAE to learn the "style" distribution where each style is regarded as mean μ and variance σ of encoded features (see Right Top).

to learn a domain invariant embedding subspace. Both [15] and [14] need annotations of target samples. Recently, [13] and [24] proposed to leverage only one shot unlabeled target sample to bridge the gap between source and target domain. They designed a RAIN module to explore the target domain style distribution with the one target sample and transferred the style of source domain images to the explored target domain. However, they only use one sample for domain adaptation and if more target samples are acquired, they regard these samples equally important. We argue that each target sample should have a different priority according to its distance to the center of target dataset.

3   Methodology

3.1   Framework

In this section, we discuss our proposed few-shot WSM framework. Our framework contains three modules: a Region-of-Interest (ROI) extraction module, a few-shot weighted style transfer module and a CNN-based classification module.

3.2   ROI Extraction Module

To perform accurate classification, we first locate and extract the optic disc region, see in Fig. 2 (Left Top). Previous works and clinical experience have shown that optic disc is the most discriminative region for glaucoma diagnosis. Meanwhile, since fundus images normally have very large resolution, it is low-efficient to directly utilize the whole image. Furthermore, due to memory limitation, images need downsampling which will lose valuable information and lower classification accuracy.

To achieve precise detection, We adopt Faster-RCNN [18] as ROI extraction network with ground-truth bounding box annotations. We only use source domain images to train the network. Excitingly, we find the module generalizes well on target domain images since optic disc shows clear structure characteristics in both source and target domain.

3.3   Target Sample Prioritization

We believe that each target sample has a different distance to the center of the target dataset. The sample closer to the target dataset should be assigned with higher weight and priority when used for adapting to the target dataset.

Accordingly, we deploy MeanShift algorithm to measure the distance. Mean-Shift is a non-parametric clustering technique that can locate the center of the densest region of data. Specifically, we first adopt an ImageNet pre-trained VGG [12] to encode target samples into latent features. We utilize MeanShift algorithm to locate the cluster center of the features and measure the distance from each feature to the center. We normalize the distances as weights to represent the priority of target samples for being selected in the few-shot weighted style transfer module. Note that since the few-shot target samples are uniformly selected from the target dataset in our work, the center of these samples can be regarded as the center of the whole target dataset with confidence.

3.4   Few-shot Weighted Style Transfer

Based on our assumption that the domain shift in fundus images is mainly due to style discrepancy, we propose a few-shot weighted style transfer module to minimize the style difference of source and target fundus datasets. Our module consists of two parts: style-VAE network and AdaIN network.

Firstly, we enlarge and randomly move the bounding box detected by the ROI extraction network without losing the optic disc region to increase the diversity of samples, as shown in Fig. 2 (Left Bottom).

We use the enlarged ROIs of few target domain samples to train the style-VAE network to learn the style distribution of target domain. The style-VAE is composed of an encoder E_{VAE} and a decoder D_{VAE}, both are fully-connected networks. ROIs are first put through an ImageNet pre-trained VGG to extract features f_s. Following [7], we calculate the mean and variance statistics of f_s and concatenate them as style. The E_{VAE} encodes style to Gaussian distribution $N(\psi, \xi)$ and D_{VAE} aims at decoding samples from such distribution to reconstruct the original style. KL divergence $\mathcal{L}_{KL}$ and reconstruction loss $\mathcal{L}_{rec}$ are utilized to train the style VAE:

$$\mathcal{L}_{style-VAE} = \lambda_k \mathcal{L}_{KL} + \lambda_r \mathcal{L}_{rec} \tag{1}$$

$$\mathcal{L}_{KL} = KL[N(\psi, \xi) || N(0, I)] \tag{2}$$

$$\mathcal{L}_{rec} = ||\mu(f_s) \oplus \sigma(f_s), \hat{\mu}(f_s) \oplus \hat{\sigma}(f_s)||_2 \tag{3}$$

where $\hat{\mu}(f_s)$ and $\hat{\sigma}(f_s)$ denotes mean and variance of the reconstructed style and $\oplus$ denotes concatenate operation.

After style-VAE is trained, We sample content images from source domain images and style images from few-shot target domain images to train AdaIN network. We sample style image I_s with our target sample prioritization strategy and obtain its style distribution $N(\psi, \xi)$ through E_{VAE}. Then we sample ε from $N(\psi, \xi)$ and decode it with D_{VAE} to acquire more diverse styles. Similar to [7], We train AdaIN network with content loss $\mathcal{L}_c$ and style loss $\mathcal{L}_s$:

$$\mathcal{L}_{AdaIN} = \mathcal{L}_c + \lambda_s \mathcal{L}_s \tag{4}$$

4   Experiment

4.1   Dataset and Evaluation Metrics

Dataset. We conduct experiments on two public glaucoma classification datasets, Drishti-GS dataset [21] and the REFUGE challenge dataset [16]. The statistics of these two datasets are listed in Table 1. Since we believe that the domain shift in fundus image dataset is mainly due to different camera parameters, we split REFUGE dataset into two parts, REFUGE Train dataset and REFUGE Val/test dataset, because they are captured by two different cameras. We extensively evaluate our method on two adaptation tasks: REFUGE Val/test → Drishti-GS, REFUGE Train → Drishti-GS.

Table 1. The statistics of datasets to evaluate our proposed method.

Dataset	Size	Image resolution	Cameras
Drishti-GS	101	2047×1760	Fundus camera with FOV 30°
REFUGE Train	400	2124×2056	Zeiss Visucam 500
REFUGE Val/Test	800	1634×1634	Canon CR-2

Evaluation Metrics. We adopt REFUGE challenge evaluation metrics for glaucoma classification to evaluate our proposed method. Specifically, the receiver operating characteristic curve (ROC) and the area under the curve (AUC) are used as the main criteria for evaluation. Additionally, a reference sensitivity value at a specificity of 0.85 is also reported to assess the overall performance of our method. The sensitivity and specificity are defined as:

$$Sensitivity = \frac{TP}{TP + FN}, \tag{5}$$

$$Specificity = \frac{TN}{TN + FP} \tag{6}$$

where TP, FP, TN and FN represent true/false positives and true/false negatives, respectively.

4.2   Implementation Details

We use Pytorch [17] Framework to implement our method. Our training process is composed of three stages. In the first stage, we use source domain images to train the ROI extraction network. We use SGD [19] optimizer with a momentum of 0.9 and set the learning rate as $1e - 4$ with a batch size of 2. We train the network for 40k iterations with the first 4k as warm-up stage. In the second stage, we use source images and few target samples to train the few-shot weighted style transfer module. We split the training procedure into two steps. We first use the few shot target samples to train the style-VAE network then fix the style-VAE and train AdaIN network of our module. We use Adam [8] optimizer and set the learning rate as $1e - 4$ with a batch size of 4. In the third stage, we fix the whole few-shot weighted style transfer module to train the classification network. We employ Resnet-50 as backbone and also SGD as an optimizer. We set learning rate as $2.5e - 4$ with a batch size of 2. We train the network for a total of 100 epochs, with the first 20 as warm-up stage. All experiments are conducted on a computer with an Intel(R) Core(TM) i7-7820X CPU @3.60GHz and a single GeForce RTX 2080 Ti GPU.

4.3   Experiment Results on Glaucoma Detection

In this section, we evaluate the effectiveness of our few-shot WSM framework on task REFUGE Val/test $\rightarrow$ Drishti-GS and REFUGE Train $\rightarrow$ Drishti-GS. We compare with [23] which also evaluate their framework on the Drishti-GS dataset. We randomly select 5 shot, 10 shot and 20 shot samples from training split of Drishti-GS dataset as target domain training samples. We use REFUGE Train or REFUGE Val/Test dataset as source domain and few target samples as target domain to train our framework. We present the classification performance of our method on the testing split of Drishti-GS in Table 2.

It is observed that the few-shot WSM can significantly improve classification performance and achieve consistent improvement with more target samples. Our method easily outperforms pOSAL with fewer target samples which indicates that our few-shot WSM method achieves better adaptation performance. In addition, Fig. 3 plots the ROC curves of our method, for visualizing the trade-off between sensitivity and specificity.

Table 2. AUC performance on Drishti Dataset. TS denotes the number of target samples. R_T denotes REFUGE Train dataset. R_VT denotes REFUGE Val/Test dataset. D denotes Drishti-GS dataset.

Method	TS	R_T $\rightarrow$ D	R_VT $\rightarrow$ D
Source Only	–	0.8071	0.8524
pOSAL [23]	50	0.8583	–
few-shot WSM (ours)	5	0.8706	0.9178
few-shot WSM (ours)	10	0.8929	0.9213
few-shot WSM (ours)	20	0.9008	0.9379

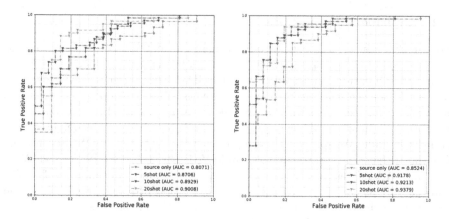

Fig. 3. The ROC curve of our method. Left: REFUGE Train → Drishti-GS. Right: REFUGE Val/test → Drishti-GS

4.4 Effectiveness of Target Sample Prioritization Strategy

In this section, we mainly illustrate the impact of our target sample prioritization (TSP) strategy. We conduct experiments on both REFUGE Train → Drishti-GS and REFUGE Val/test → Drishti-GS tasks with 5 shot, 10 shot and 20 shot target domain samples to extensively verify the effectiveness of the TSP strategy. We assign the same weight to each target sample for comparison. The results of are given in Table 3 and Fig. 4. As we can see, the TSP strategy can boost classification performance in both tasks under every scenario which proves the effectiveness and necessity of the TSP strategy in our few-shot WSM approach.

Table 3. Effectiveness of target sample prioritization strategy. Ref Sen denotes reference sensitivity.

Task	Method	5 shot		10 shot		20 shot	
		AUC	Ref Sen	AUC	Ref Sen	AUC	Ref Sen
R_T → D	w/o TSP	0.8341	0.5833	0.8562	0.7385	0.8643	0.7667
	w/ TSP	0.8706	0.7000	0.8929	0.8154	0.9008	0.8833
R_VT → D	w/o TSP	0.8905	0.7833	0.9071	0.7846	0.9071	0.8000
	w/ TSP	0.9178	0.8501	0.9213	0.8769	0.9379	0.8615

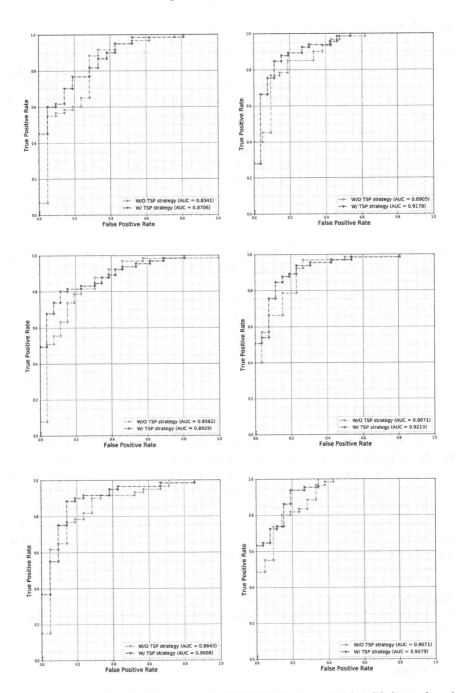

Fig. 4. Effectiveness of TSP strategy in REFUGE Train → Drishti-GS (1*st* column) and REFUGE Val/test → Drishti-GS (2*nd* column) under 5 shot (top), 10 shot (middle) and 20 shot (bottom) scenarios.

4.5 Ablation Study

In the ablation experiments, we illustrate the impact of ROI extraction module E and few-shot weighted style transfer module S. We first remove module E and directly use the whole fundus image for style transfer and glaucoma classification, then remove module S and use ROI of fundus images only to train classification network. We conduct experiments in REFUGE Val/test → Drishti-GS task and utilize 10 target samples for training. The results are shown in Table 4.

As seen in the table, the performance heavily decreases once module S is removed (AUC −5.78%; reference sensitivity −21.02%), which proves the necessity of our module S. The performance also drops after removing module E. It verifies that focusing on optic disc area can reduce the domain shift between different fundus images.

Table 4. Ablation results over the test set of Drishti-GS dataset. E denotes ROI Extraction module. S denotes few-shot weighted Style Transfer module

Method	TS	AUC	Reference sensitivity
full	10	0.9213	0.8769
w/o E w/ S	10	0.8889	0.8167
w/ E w/o S	10	0.8635	0.6667

5 Conclusion

In this paper, we propose a novel few-shot weighted style matching (few-shot WSM) approach to handle the domain shift problem of different fundus image datasets in the case of the target-data-scarce scenario. To reduce the domain shift between source and target domain, we employ a few-shot weighted style transfer module to narrow down the style discrepancy. We argue that each target sample has a different distance to the center of the target dataset. So we propose a target sample prioritization strategy for better domain adaptation performance. We conduct extensive experiments on two public fundus image datasets to demonstrate the effectiveness of our few-shot WSM framework.

Acknowledgement. This work was supported by the National Key R&D Program of China 2018YFA0704000, the NSFC (No. 61822111, 61727808) and Beijing Natural Science Foundation (JQ19015).

References

1. Chai, Y., Liu, H., Xu, J.: Glaucoma diagnosis based on both hidden features and domain knowledge through deep learning models. Knowl.-Based Syst. **161**, 147–156 (2018). https://doi.org/10.1016/j.knosys.2018.07.043

2. Chen, X., Xu, Y., Kee Wong, D.W., Wong, T.Y., Liu, J.: Glaucoma detection based on deep convolutional neural network. In: 2015 37th Annual International Conference of the IEEE Engineering in Medicine and Biology Society (EMBC), pp. 715–718 (2015). https://doi.org/10.1109/EMBC.2015.7318462

3. Comaniciu, D., Meer, P.: Mean shift: a robust approach toward feature space analysis. IEEE Trans. Pattern Anal. Mach. Intell. **24**(5), 603–619 (2002). https://doi.org/10.1109/34.1000236

4. Ding, Y., Yu, X., Yang, Y.: Modeling the probabilistic distribution of unlabeled data for one-shot medical image segmentation (2021)

5. Fu, H., et al.: Disc-aware ensemble network for glaucoma screening from fundus image. IEEE Trans. Med. Imaging (2018). https://doi.org/10.1109/TMI.2018.2837012

6. Gatys, L.A., Ecker, A.S., Bethge, M.: A neural algorithm of artistic style. CoRR abs/1508.06576 (2015). http://arxiv.org/abs/1508.06576

7. Huang, X., Belongie, S.: Arbitrary style transfer in real-time with adaptive instance normalization. In: 2017 IEEE International Conference on Computer Vision (ICCV), pp. 1510–1519 (2017). https://doi.org/10.1109/ICCV.2017.167

8. Kingma, D.P., Ba, J.: Adam: a method for stochastic optimization (2014). http://arxiv.org/abs/1412.6980, cite arxiv 1412.6980Comment: Published as a conference paper at the 3rd International Conference for Learning Representations, San Diego (2015)

9. Li, L., Xu, M., Wang, X., Jiang, L., Liu, H.: Attention based glaucoma detection: a large-scale database and CNN model (2019)

10. Li, P., Yu, X., Yang, Y.: Super-resolving cross-domain face miniatures by peeking at one-shot exemplar. arXiv preprint arXiv:2103.08863 (2021)

11. Li, Z., He, Y., Keel, S., Meng, W., Chang, R.T., He, M.: Efficacy of a deep learning system for detecting glaucomatous optic neuropathy based on color fundus photographs. Ophthalmology **125**(8), 1199–1206 (2018). https://doi.org/10.1016/j.ophtha.2018.01.023. https://www.sciencedirect.com/science/article/pii/S0161642017335650

12. Liu, S., Deng, W.: Very deep convolutional neural network based image classification using small training sample size. In: 2015 3rd IAPR Asian Conference on Pattern Recognition (ACPR), pp. 730–734 (2015). https://doi.org/10.1109/ACPR.2015.7486599

13. Luo, Y., Liu, P., Guan, T., Yu, J., Yang, Y.: Adversarial style mining for one-shot unsupervised domain adaptation. In: Advances in Neural Information Processing Systems (2020)

14. Motiian, S., Jones, Q., Iranmanesh, S.M., Doretto, G.: Few-shot adversarial domain adaptation (2017)

15. Motiian, S., Piccirilli, M., Adjeroh, D.A., Doretto, G.: Unified deep supervised domain adaptation and generalization. In: Proceedings of the IEEE International Conference on Computer Vision (ICCV), October 2017

16. Orlando, J.I., et al.: Refuge challenge: a unified framework for evaluating automated methods for glaucoma assessment from fundus photographs. Med. Image Anal. **59**, 101570 (2020). https://doi.org/10.1016/j.media.2019.101570. https://www.sciencedirect.com/science/article/pii/S1361841519301100

17. Paszke, A., et al.: Automatic differentiation in pytorch (2017)

18. Ren, S., He, K., Girshick, R., Sun, J.: Faster R-CNN: towards real-time object detection with region proposal networks. IEEE Trans. Pattern Anal. Mach. Intell. **39**, 1137–1149 (2015). https://doi.org/10.1109/TPAMI.2016.2577031

19. Ruder, S.: An overview of gradient descent optimization algorithms. arXiv preprint arXiv:1609.04747 (2016)

20. Shiri, F., Yu, X., Porikli, F., Hartley, R., Koniusz, P.: Identity-preserving face recovery from stylized portraits. Int. J. Comput. Vision **127**(6), 863–883 (2019)

21. Sivaswamy, J., Krishnadas, S., Chakravarty, A., Joshi, G., Tabish, A.S.: A comprehensive retinal image dataset for the assessment of glaucoma from the optic nerve head analysis. JSM Biomed. Imaging Data Papers **2**(1), 1004 (2015)

22. Tham, Y.C., Li, X., Wong, T.Y., Quigley, H., Aung, T., Cheng, C.Y.: Global prevalence of glaucoma and projections of glaucoma burden through 2040 a systematic review and meta-analysis. Ophthalmology **121**, 2081–2090 (2014). https://doi.org/10.1016/j.ophtha.2014.05.013

23. Wang, S., Yu, L., Yang, X., Fu, C.W., Heng, P.A.: Patch-based output space adversarial learning for joint optic disc and cup segmentation. IEEE Trans. Med. Imaging **38**(11), 2485–2495 (2019). https://doi.org/10.1109/TMI.2019.2899910

24. Zhang, Y., Tsang, I., Luo, Y., Hu, C., Lu, X., Yu, X.: Recursive copy and paste GAN: face hallucination from shaded thumbnails. IEEE Trans. Pattern Anal. Mach. Intell. (2021)

25. Zhang, Y., Tsang, I.W., Luo, Y., Hu, C.H., Lu, X., Yu, X.: Copy and paste GAN: face hallucination from shaded thumbnails. In: Proceedings of the IEEE/CVF Conference on Computer Vision and Pattern Recognition, pp. 7355–7364 (2020)

26. Zhao, R., Chen, X., Liu, X., Chen, Z., Guo, F., Li, S.: Direct cup-to-disc ratio estimation for glaucoma screening via semi-supervised learning. IEEE J. Biomed. Health Inform. **24**, 1104–1113 (2020)

Lightweight Convolutional SNN for Address Event Representation Signal Recognition

Zhaoxin Liu[1], Bangbo Huang[2], Jinjian Wu[1(✉)], and Guangming Shi[1]

[1] School of Artificial Intelligence, Xidian University, Shanxi, China
`zxliu9931@stu.xidian.edu.cn, jinjian.wu@mail.xidian.edu.cn,`
`gmshi@xidian.edu.cn`
[2] X Lab, The Second Academy of CASIC, Beijing, China

Abstract. SNN (Spiking Neural Network) is well suited for DVS (Dynamic Vision Sensor) object recognition because the output of the DVS sensor is the spike. The existing SNNs usually build networks by fully connection with a large number of parameters. However, the deep network is unable to train with this connection and large parameter networks cannot be deployed where storage is limited. To overcome these shortcomings, we introduce a new model called Fire module. There are two structures in Fire module. One is a combination of weight sharing layers and the other is a skip connection, which reduces the number of parameters and makes deep network trainable respectively. We compare our method with existing SNNs and show that our method achieves competitive performance with 1800x fewer parameters against fully connection on TMV3-DVS and N-CARS datasets. Moreover, we combine the DVS sensor and our lightweight SNN object recognition network to produce an object recognition hardware system.

Keywords: Spiking neural network · Lightweight network · Object recognition · Hardware system

1 Introduction

DVS is an event-based Sensor, which has the characteristics of high frame rate, small storage space required, low delay, large dynamic range, and low power consumption [3,13]. The outputs from such sensor are spikes with high temporal resolution. However, current algorithms for processing such signals cannot balance performance and computational speed. As a mainstream image processing method, CNN has achieved remarkable results in processing traditional images, but it cannot handle spikes directly. If spikes are converted into images, the high frame rate and low delay characteristics of the DVS sensor will be lost. In addition, CNNs require high-powered computers to compute, which limits the

This work was partially supported by the NSF of China (No. 62022063, No. 61772388 and No. 61632019).

L. Fang et al. (Eds.): CICAI 2021, LNAI 13069, pp. 301–310, 2021.
https://doi.org/10.1007/978-3-030-93046-2_26

use of DVS in low-power scenarios. Spiking neural network is a kind of neuromorphic network that processes signals in the format of spikes. In recent years, there has been great progress in neuromorphic processors [1,11], which enables networks to have the characteristics such as fast processing speed and low power consumption. Therefore, SNN is very suitable for processing spike signals output by DVS. However, there are two other problems with SNN. The first one, most of the existing SNNs are not able to train deep network structures, as using fully connection. The second, computing spiking neurons under the von Neumann architecture is very complex, too many parameters are unacceptable. Directly reducing the network size leads to performance degradation, and the large-scale network cannot be used in MEC (Mobile Edge Computing).

To solve the existing problems of SNN, this paper proposes a lightweight spiking neural network based on Fire module. Fire module consists of multiple spiking convolutions with skip connection. Skip connection makes multiscale information fusion and prevents the vanishing gradient which makes deep networks training possible. The two parts of spiking convolution connected by skip connection reduce and increase the number of channels respectively. So that the number of network parameters is effectively reduced, and a lightweight DVS object recognition network is achieved. We evaluate the performance of our framework on N-CARS [16]. We build a traffic vehicle recognition database to verify the effectiveness of our method. We deploy our framework in a hardware system to implement a set of object recognition system. The system can acquire DVS event data and realize object recognition through the lightweight recognition network. We summarize our contributions as follows:

1. We propose a Fire module structure with a skip connection to prevent the vanishing gradient during the training process, solving the problem that full connection cannot train deep network.
2. We reduce the number of parameters by combining weight-sharing layers without affecting the performance.
3. We deploy our framework in a hardware system that consists of a DVS sensor and lightweight SNN. We captured data of traffic vehicles in real scenes to evaluate the performance of the algorithm for real scenes.

The rest of the paper is organized as follows. In Sect. 2 we review related work. Section 3 introduces a general Spike neuron model and Spiking convolution. Section 4 details our Fire module. In Sect. 5, we demonstrate the effectiveness of our framework and introduces the object recognition hardware system before concluding in Sect. 6.

2   Related Work

SNN, as the third-generation artificial neural network, has the characteristics of fast response, low power consumption, and strong ability to process temporal signals. It can take full advantage of DVS cameras, and it is an important development trend to use SNN to process DVS signals. There are two main ideas to solve the SNN training problem: conversion-based approaches and spike-based approaches.

The idea of the conversion-based approaches method is to design CNN networks with the same input-output mapping as SNNs. Essentially, the trained CNN networks can be converted to SNN by matching the feature parameters of CNN neurons with features of SNN neurons such as the leak time constants, refractory period, membrane threshold [2,4,14]. This approach achieves a relatively good performance in the initial stage, but there are no biologically interpretive rules. The parameter matching is not very simple to do, for the complex network adaptability is relatively poor.

There are two kinds of spike-based methods: supervised learning and unsupervised learning. The unsupervised learning method is based on the STDP rule and simulates the variation of brain neurons. However, this training approach is difficult to form a large-scale network structure and the performance is generally poor. Some scholars proposed multi-layer unsupervised learning networks [17,18], which effectively improved the performance on MNIST data sets, but could not achieve good results for larger data. The supervised learning approach for SNN is very difficult due to the discontinuous signal of spike. The idea of the first supervised methods was to imitate STDP for training [6,12], and these methods could only do single-layer networks due to their own limitations, and the performance was not satisfactory. However, they provided inspiration for later supervised training methods. Since then, research on supervised learning has turned to simulate spike-based gradient to enable supervised learning in multi-layer SNNs by spike-based gradient descent [7–10]. SLAYER is a more representative approach [15], which uses the stochastic spiking neuron approximation for backpropagating errors. This approach is highly adaptable and has achieved good results on multiple datasets. However, it consumes large resources and cannot achieve real-time data processing. The SNN lightweight network structure introduced in this paper is a solution to this problem.

3   Spiking Neuron Connection

SNNs are more bionic than CNNs, and the biggest difference is the neuron. In this section, we introduce a model for a spiking neuron and the structure of convolutional layer of spiking neurons.

3.1   Spike Response Model

Spiking neurons communicate with each other by voltage spikes. The input and output formats of a neuron are all spikes. Spikes affect the neuronal membrane voltage and thus output new spikes. In this paper, we use a simple yet versatile spiking neuron model named Spike Response Model (SRM) [5], Details are as follows.

The neuron's state is membrane potential $u(t)$, which is obtained by scaled input spike by synaptic weight w_i. Defining a spike train, $s_i(t) = \sum_f \delta(t - t_i^{(f)})$. Where t is the time of the fth spike of the ith input. Before entering the neuron, the spike is converted by a spike response kernel $\varepsilon(\cdot)$. The refractory response can be represented as $(\nu * s)(t)$ by refractory kernel $\nu(\cdot)$ and output spike train $s(t)$. So, we can get membrane potential $u(t)$

$$u(t) = \sum_i w_i(\varepsilon * s_i)(t) + (\nu * s)(t) \tag{1}$$

The neuron outputs a spike when membrane potential $u(t)$ reaches threshold ϑ

$$f_s(u) : u \rightarrow s, s(t) := s(t) + \delta(t - t^{f+1})$$
$$where \; t^{f+1} = min\left\{t : u(t) = \vartheta, \; t > t^{(f)}\right\} \tag{2}$$

3.2 Spiking Convolution Layer

The difference between SNNs and CNNs is the neuron. However, neurons do not affect the network topology. Existing SNN usually connects two layers of neurons with full connection. However, this type of connection has a very large number of parameters and the network structure is related to the input data. Consider that the input feature size is $x * y$ and the number of channels is equal to m. The output size is the same as the input and the number of channels is equal to n. The number of parameters for this connection N_f is $x * y * m * n$

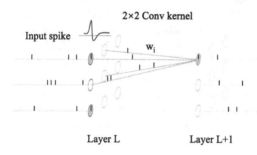

Layer L   Layer L+1

Fig. 1. The figure shows the spiking convolution with the number of channels in the input and output layers as 1. The size of the convolution kernel is $2^2 * 1 * 1$. Input spike raises the membrane voltage of neurons in Layer L. When the membrane voltage reaches a threshold, the neuron is activated and output a spike. Output spikes of Layer L are scaled by convolution kernel and transmitted to Layer L+1 as input spike.

Inspired by CNNs, SNN convolutional structure is proposed. This structure makes sparse connections between neurons in the form of weight sharing. Each neuron is connected only to neurons at adjacent locations and shares a set of parameters called the convolutional kernel W. As shown in Fig. 1, spiking convolution can effectively reduce the number of parameters. The number of convolutional layers is related to the number of channels in the input and output layers. Consider that the number of input channels is m and the number of output layers is n, convolution kernel W size is $k * k$. The number of parameters in the convolution layer N_c is $k^2 \times m \times n$.

4   Lightweight SNN Object Recognition Network

Although spiking convolution can reduce the number of parameters in the network, there are still too many parameters for large-scale networks and deep networks cannot be trained. We propose a Fire module structure to prevent the vanishing gradient and reduce the number of parameters in the convolutional layer.

4.1   Fire Module

In Sect. 3.2, we discussed the number of parameters in the spike convolution layer, which is $k^2 * m * n$. The number of parameters of the convolution kernel will be very large when the number of input and output layer Channels is large. In order to reduce the parameters without changing the receptive field of neurons, three convolution structures are used instead of the original convolution.

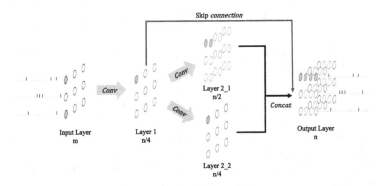

Fig. 2. This is a Fire module structure with the same input and output dimensions as the normal convolution.

The Fire module is divided into two parts shown in Fig. 2. The first part serves to reduce the input layer channel with $1 * 1$ convolution. This is reasonable because $1 * 1$ convolution can integrate the information of each channel in the input layer while reducing the number of channels. This convolution kernel has $n/4$ channels so the number of channels in the output layer is $n/4$ which is denoted as layer 1.

The second part consists of two convolutions in parallel, and their input is the output of the first part. The size of the first convolution of this part is $k * k$ (k is usually taken as 3). This convolution ensures that Fire module has the same receptive field as the original convolution. The number of channels is $n/2$ and the output layer is denoted layer 2_1. The second is $1 * 1$ convolution with $n/4$ channels whose output is labeled as layer 2_2. The purpose of this part is to get the required number of channels without adding too many parameters.

The output of the entire Fire module consists of three convolutional outputs in two parts. Skip-connection structure is added inside the structure to prevent the vanishing gradient and to facilitate multi-scale feature information fusion. Therefore, the number of parameters of Fire module N_{cc} is

$$
\begin{aligned}
N_{cc} &= 1^2 \times m \times \frac{n}{4} + k^2 \times \frac{n}{4} \times \frac{n}{2} + 1^2 \times \frac{n}{4} \times \frac{n}{4} \\
&= m \times n/4 + (\frac{k^2}{8} + \frac{1}{16}) \times n^2
\end{aligned}
\tag{3}
$$

When k is equal to 3, Ncc becomes

$$
N_{cc} = m \times n/4 + \frac{19}{16} \times n^2
\tag{4}
$$

Next, we analyze the parameter number of ordinary convolution and Fire module. The ratio of the number of Fire module parameters N_{cc} to the number of ordinary convolution parameters N_c is

$$
R_1 = \frac{N_{cc}}{N_c} = \frac{\frac{mn}{4} + \frac{19}{16}n^2}{9mn} = \frac{1}{36}(1 + \frac{19n}{4m})
\tag{5}
$$

The ratio of the number of Fire module parameters N_{cc} to the number of fully connection parameters N_f is

$$
R_2 = \frac{N_{cc}}{N_f} = \frac{\frac{mn}{4} + \frac{19}{16}n^2}{xymn} = \frac{1}{4xy}(1 + \frac{19n}{4m})
\tag{6}
$$

Generally speaking, the channels of adjacent convolutions are the same, and the ratio $R1$ is equal to **0.159** when $m = n$. In the case of N-CARS, the average size of the feature map is $56 * 48$. The ratio $R2$ is **0.00053** (1800x smaller than fully connection). This compression rate is very competitive.

4.2   Lightweight Object Recognition

SNNs do not require an activation layer because Spike neurons are highly nonlinear. So, the SNN structure only needs three structures: convolutional, sampling, and fully connected to complete the function. In this paper, Fire module replaces the normal convolution in the network.

Like the structure of a normal classification network, this paper uses a network consisting of two parts: feature extraction and classifier. The feature extraction part consists of a combination of convolution and sampling. The classification section consists of multiple fully connected layers.

5   Experiments and Results

In this section, we evaluate the performance of our framework. In Sect. 5.1, we introduce the traffic dataset TMV3-DVS. In Sects. 5.2 and 5.3, we present results for object recognition and hardware system of our framework.

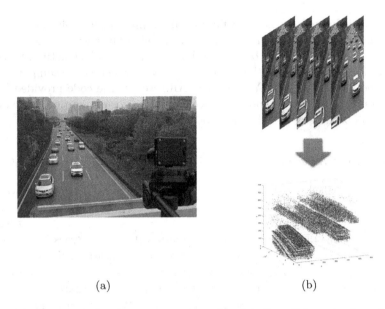

(a)   (b)

Fig. 3. (a) We use the hardware system introduced in Sect. 5.3 to simulate the traffic monitoring scene at the flyover. (b) The DVS sensor captures vehicle signals and outputs event streams.

5.1 Traffic Monitoring Vehicle 3

Vehicle recognition in traffic monitoring scenarios is very useful. However, conventional cameras store a large amount of data and have difficulty in capturing fast-moving objects. DVS sensor only captures moving objects, requiring little storage space with high temporal resolution. So, the DVS sensor is suitable for traffic monitoring. We captured vehicle data from a traffic monitoring perspective named Traffic Monitoring Vehicle 3 (TMV3-DVS), shown in Fig. 3. We divide vehicles into three classes: large cars like buses, small cars, and motorcycles. Vehicles do not move in a relatively short time, so the crop of vehicles is taken out for recognition. For each class, we collected 50 samples (total of 150 samples) and each sample lasts for approximately 20 milliseconds. The sample size is 225 * 205 and the maximum timestamp is 324593.

5.2 Object Recognition Performance

We compared the accuracy and backbone parameter number of the fully connected SNN method, normal convolution SNN method, and Fire module. There are very few DVS datasets taken in real-life scenarios so we not only tested our method on N-CARS but also evaluated our performance on the traffic dataset TMV3-DVS that we built. The result is shown in Table 1. In the backbone layer normal convolution layer is represented by C, the Fire module is represented by F, and P stands for pooling layer. For example, 32C3 represents convolution layer with 32 channels of the 3×3 filters. 16F3 represents convolution layer with 16 channels of the 3×3 filters. 2P indicates pooling layer with 2×2 filters. FC is a fully connected network built according to our network structure. Since the number of parameters is too large to train, only parameters are compared here. For the performance of SLAYER on N-CARS we use the code provided by the authors online. H-First is hand-coded spiking model for recognition so we do not compare its parametric number with other methods.

Table 1. Top-1 Accuracy and number of parameters on TMV3-DVS and N-CARs.

Dataset	Method	Backbone layers	Parameter	Accuracy
N-CARs	H-First [9]	–	–	56.10%
	Gabor-SNN [16]	–	–	78.90%
	SLAYER [15]	16C3-2P-32C3-2P-64C3-2P	23328	84.00%
	FC	60*50*16-2P-30*25*32-2P-15*13*64	1.03E+10	-
	Ours	16F3-p2-32F3-p2-64F3-p2	7032	**84.10%**
TMV3- DVS	SLAYER [15]	16C3-2P-32C3-2P-64C3-2P	23328	97.50%
	FC	60*50*16-2P-30*25*32-2P-15*13*64	1.03E+10	-
	Ours	16F3-p2-32F3-p2-64F3-p2	7032	**97.50%**

In order to visualize the comparison between the performance and the parameters of each method, we plot the number of parameters as the x-axis and the accuracy as the y-axis in Fig. 4. Since the parameters of H-First and Gabor-SNN cannot be directly compared with each other, these two methods only care about the comparison of accuracy. From the experimental results, we can see that our method can reduce the number of parameters without reducing the accuracy.

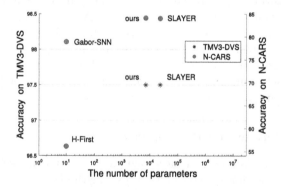

Fig. 4. Performance and parameters of each method.

5.3   Recognition Hardware System

The hardware system captures DVS data of the object and identifies the object with Lightweight SNN. The system consists of DVS sensor, denoising algorithm, SNN recognition network and display module, the specific structure is shown in Fig. 5. The advantages of the system include:

- Fast imaging speed, it can identify high-speed moving objects.
- Low power consumption, more flexible use scenarios.
- Small space requirement for storage.

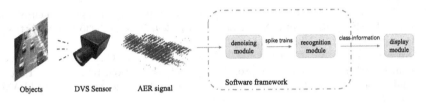

Fig. 5. System flow diagram of the recognition system consisting of the DVS sensor.

6   Conclusion

In this paper, we propose a Fire module structure to reduce parameters. Compared with normal spike convolution, this structure has a compression rate of 0.159 when the input and output channels are the same. The network structure with low number of parameters solves the problem that SNN cannot be applied in MEC. To evaluate our approach, we built a traffic vehicle dataset and implemented an object recognition hardware system. We compared the accuracy and parameters of our method with recent SNN methods on the N-CARs and TMV3-DVS datasets. Our method significantly reduces the parameters without a significant reduction in accuracy.

References

1. Bauer, F.C., Muir, D.R., Indiveri, G.: Real-time ultra-low power ECG anomaly detection using an event-driven neuromorphic processor. IEEE Trans. Biomed. Circuits Syst. **13**(6), 1575–1582 (2019). https://doi.org/10.1109/TBCAS.2019.2953001
2. Cao, Y., Chen, Y., Khosla, D.: Spiking deep convolutional neural networks for energy-efficient object recognition. Int. J. Comput. Vision **113**(1), 54–66 (2014). https://doi.org/10.1007/s11263-014-0788-3
3. Delbrück, T., Linares-Barranco, B., Culurciello, E., Posch, C.: Activity-driven, event-based vision sensors. In: Proceedings of 2010 IEEE International Symposium on Circuits and Systems, pp. 2426–2429 (2010). https://doi.org/10.1109/ISCAS.2010.5537149

4. Diehl, P.U., Neil, D., Binas, J., Cook, M., Liu, S., Pfeiffer, M.: Fast-classifying, high-accuracy spiking deep networks through weight and threshold balancing. In: 2015 International Joint Conference on Neural Networks (IJCNN), pp. 1–8 (2015). https://doi.org/10.1109/IJCNN.2015.7280696

5. Gerstner, W.: Time structure of the activity in neural network models. Phys. Rev. E **51**(1), 738–758 (1995). https://doi.org/10.1103/PhysRevE.51.738

6. Gütig, R., Sompolinsky, H.: The tempotron: a neuron that learns spike timing–based decisions. Nat. Neurosci. **9**(3), 420–428 (2006). https://doi.org/10.1038/nn1643

7. Lee, J.H., Delbruck, T., Pfeiffer, M.: Training deep spiking neural networks using backpropagation. Front. Neurosci. **10**, 508 (2016). https://doi.org/10.3389/fnins.2016.00508

8. Mostafa, H.: Supervised learning based on temporal coding in spiking neural networks. IEEE Trans. Neural Netw. Learn. Syst. **29**(7), 3227–3235 (2018). https://doi.org/10.1109/TNNLS.2017.2726060

9. Orchard, G., Meyer, C., Etienne-Cummings, R., Posch, C., Thakor, N., Benosman, R.: HFirst: a temporal approach to object recognition. IEEE Trans. Pattern Anal. Mach. Intell. **37**(10), 2028–2040 (2015). https://doi.org/10.1109/TPAMI.2015.2392947

10. Panda, P., Roy, K.: Unsupervised regenerative learning of hierarchical features in Spiking Deep Networks for object recognition. In: 2016 International Joint Conference on Neural Networks (IJCNN), pp. 299–306 (2016). https://doi.org/10.1109/IJCNN.2016.7727212

11. Pei, J., et al.: Towards artificial general intelligence with hybrid Tianjic chip architecture. Nature **572**(7767), 106–111 (2019). https://doi.org/10.1038/s41586-019-1424-8

12. Ponulak, F., Kasiński, A.: Supervised learning in spiking neural networks with ReSuMe: sequence learning, classification, and spike shifting. Neural Comput. **22**(2), 467–510 (2010). https://doi.org/10.1162/neco.2009.11-08-901

13. Posch, C., Matolin, D., Wohlgenannt, R.: A QVGA 143 dB dynamic range frame-free PWM image sensor with lossless pixel-level video compression and time-domain CDS. IEEE J. Solid-State Circuits **46**(1), 259–275 (2011). https://doi.org/10.1109/JSSC.2010.2085952

14. Rueckauer, B., Lungu, I.A., Hu, Y., Pfeiffer, M., Liu, S.C.: Conversion of continuous-valued deep networks to efficient event-driven networks for image classification. Front. Neurosci. **11**, 682 (2017). https://doi.org/10.3389/fnins.2017.00682

15. Shrestha, S.B., Orchard, G.: SLAYER: spike layer error reassignment in time. arXiv:1810.08646 [cs, stat] (2018)

16. Sironi, A., Brambilla, M., Bourdis, N., Lagorce, X., Benosman, R.: HATS: histograms of averaged time surfaces for robust event-based object classification. In: Proceedings of the IEEE Conference on Computer Vision and Pattern Recognition, pp. 1731–1740 (2018)

17. Zeng, Y., Zhang, T., Xu, B.: Improving multi-layer spiking neural networks by incorporating brain-inspired rules. Sci. China Inf. Sci. **60**(5), 1–11 (2017). https://doi.org/10.1007/s11432-016-0439-4

18. Zhang, T., Zeng, Y., Zhao, D., Shi, M.: A plasticity-centric approach to train the non-differential spiking neural networks. In: Proceedings of the AAAI Conference on Artificial Intelligence, vol. 32(1) (2018)

In-the-Wild Facial Highlight Removal via Generative Adversarial Networks

Zhibo Wang[1,2], Ming Lu[3], Feng Xu[1,4], and Xun Cao[2(✉)]

[1] BNRist and School of Software, Tsinghua University, Beijing, China
[2] School of Electronic Science and Engineering, Nanjing University, Nanjing, China
caoxun@nju.edu.cn
[3] Intel Labs, Beijing, China
[4] Beijing Laboratory of Brain and Cognitive Intelligence, Beijing Municipal
Education Commission, Beijing, China

Abstract. Facial highlight removal techniques aim to remove the specular highlight from facial images, which could improve image quality and facilitate tasks, *e.g.*, face recognition and reconstruction. However, previous learning-based techniques often fail on the in-the-wild images, as their models are often trained on paired synthetic or laboratory images due to the requirement on paired training data (images with and without highlight). In contrast to these methods, we propose a highlight removal network, which is pre-trained on a synthetic dataset but finetuned on the unpaired in-the-wild images. To achieve this, we propose a highlight mask guidance training technique, which enables Generative Adversarial Networks (GANs) to utilize in-the-wild images in training a highlight removal network. We have an observation that although almost all in-the-wild images contain some highlights on some regions, small patches without highlight can still provide useful information to guide the highlight removal procedure. This motivates us to train a region-based discriminator to distinguish highlight and non-highlight for a facial image and use it to finetune the generator. From the experiments, our technique achieves high-quality results compared with the state-of-the-art highlight removal techniques, especially on the in-the-wild images.

Keywords: Generative Adversarial Networks · Highlight removal

1 Introduction

Highlights always lead to deviations from skin colors in facial images, which causes problems in many tasks including face recognition and reconstruction. However, capturing specular-free images in the wild is almost impossible, as these images require special equipments such as polarizing filters or *Light Stage* [3], which can only be acquired in a laboratory environment. Hence, portrait

Supplementary Information The online version contains supplementary material available at https://doi.org/10.1007/978-3-030-93046-2_27.

L. Fang et al. (Eds.): CICAI 2021, LNAI 13069, pp. 311–322, 2021.
https://doi.org/10.1007/978-3-030-93046-2_27

highlight removal techniques are necessary to facilitate consumer-level access to specular-free in-the-wild facial images. Traditional methods on highlight removal [30,31] usually require strict assumptions on lighting conditions. However, facial images are normally captured in natural environments and thus the violations of the assumptions lead to obvious artifacts in the results. [17] develops a portrait highlight removal method by using some weak lighting assumptions and achieves state-of-the-art results by a complicated model of facial skins. However, it is time-consuming to solve the non-linear optimization of their facial skin model.

Recently, more efficient methods based on deep neural networks [32,34] have been proposed to remove highlight from facial images. As they require paired images (images with and without highlight) for training, they both construct a synthetic dataset to pre-train their network in a supervised manner. To make the models more applicable to real images, [32] finetunes their network on real images, constrained by the low-rank property of diffuse components. However, this property does not hold for facial images due to the complexity of facial reflectance, which limits the diversity of their output diffuse colors. [34] further captures 150 paired real images under laboratory environment for network fine-tuning and achieves good performance on their laboratory testing images. Due to the limitations of their real training samples, their methods do not work well on the in-the-wild images.

In this paper, we propose a facial highlight removal method based on the Generative Adversarial Network (GAN) [6]. We first pre-train the generator using a high-quality synthetic dataset from [29]. Then, we develop a highlight mask guidance training technique to utilize in-the-wild facial images in the GAN training. As trained with real in-the-wild facial images, our method can generate convincing results on these inputs. However, adopting traditional GAN in the highlight removal cannot directly utilize in-the-wild images, as it requires real and fake image samples: one with highlight and one without highlight. Therefore, directly introducing GAN is hindered by the difficulty in capturing highlight-free in-the-wild images. In this paper, we have an observation that for a daily-recorded facial image, there are always some local regions without highlight. These regions can be indicated by a highlight mask and used for training a discriminator. When the discriminator learns the prior knowledge from the non-highlight facial regions, it lets the generator generate photo-realistic non-highlight facial regions. To extract these highlight masks, we use a traditional highlight extraction method [31]. We observe that although [31] may generate artifacts for facial highlight removal, its extracted highlight shares a strong correlation with the real highlight distribution as shown in Fig. 2. We use a tactful strategy to convert the extracted highlight to highlight mask.

Our method is evaluated through extensive experiments. We evaluate the highlight mask guidance training technique with comprehensive ablation studies. We compare our methods with state-of-the-art techniques both qualitatively and quantitatively. To validate the effectiveness of our method, we present a large amount of highlight removal results on the in-the-wild images.

2   Related Work

2.1   Highlight Removal

There are many previous works about separating highlights from the input image. Early methods [1,13] rely on color segmentation. However, algorithms based on color segmentation cannot handle complicate textured images. Based on the observation that highlight pixels contain useful information, [20] proposes to combine illumination-based constraints and image inpainting to remove highlights. [11] uses the dark channel prior to generate a specular-free image. [31] proposes a real-time highlight removal method based on bilateral filtering.

When the above methods are applied to face images, they usually generate obvious artifacts or lose the photo-realism. The reason is that they are not designed for face images and utilize some assumptions which do not work on highlights on faces. [17] proposes a method based on a skin model of human faces, which achieves the state-of-the-art highlight removal effect for facial images. However, it is time-consuming to solve the optimization. [32,34] speed up facial highlight removal techniques based on deep neural networks. They both use synthetic images to pre-train their networks. [32] uses a low-rank assumption [7] when finetuning their network on real images but this assumption does not hold well on facial images. [34] introduces GAN into highlight removal methods. However, as they require paired training data, the real images used in their training are captured in a laboratory environment with limited numbers and lighting conditions.

Our method takes one step further. With a highlight mask guidance, our method facilitates the usage of in-the-wild images in the GAN training. Thus, our network can be trained with images captured under much more varieties of environments and lightings.

2.2   Generative Adversarial Networks

Generative models have always been an important topic in the field of computer vision. In recent years, more and more studies on deep neural networks show their potential in image generation [5,12]. Generative adversarial networks [6] is an important method to train a certain generative model. The adversarial training between the generator and the discriminator enables the generator to output photo-realistic images [4,22]. An important application of GANs is image-to-image translation [8,27]. It can be applied to a variety of tasks such as super-resolution [15] and style transfer [9]. Instead of directly generating images, [14,25] generate the corresponding residual image between the input and output. Residual learning helps to stabilize the training process. We also adopt the residual learning inspired by these pioneering works.

Specialized in face image processing, [19] uses conditional GAN [18] to control the attributes of the faces in output images. MaskGAN [16] provides more freedom in facial image manipulation. StyleGAN [10] can synthesize high resolution photorealistic facial images. [34] also uses GAN in the task of highlight removal. Indicated by CycleGAN like methods [8,33], GANs have the potential to be trained using unpaired images. To the best of our knowledge, training GAN using unpaired

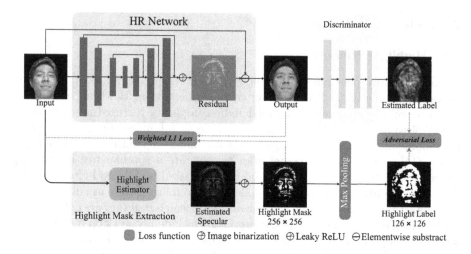

Fig. 1. The overall architecture of our method. Our network has a generator $\mathcal{G}$ and a discriminator $\mathcal{D}$. The generator is first pre-trained on a synthetic dataset and finetuned on the in-the-wild images using our highlight mask guided training technique. We use the highlight mask extraction module to generate binary highlight masks. A Leaky ReLU layer is added at the end of the generator to encourage positive outputs.

images has never been explored in the field of highlight removal. The proposed method fills the gap in this field and achieves visually pleasing results.

2.3 Face Color Transfer

Highlights have always been a limitation in the field of face color transfer. In [23], quotient image technique is proposed to change the lightings in facial images. Using this technique, the lightings of the input images can be changed by multiplying the ratio of two reference images captured under the target lighting and the source lighting. 3D reconstruction can also be used to edit the lighting in the facial images. This method uses a three-dimensional face morphable model [2] to fit the face geometry in the input image and estimate the albedo of faces and environment lighting and output a relighted facial image by re-rendering the facial image under the target lighting. However, the spherical harmonic light model [21] and the Lambertian surface assumption make it impossible to recover albedo under extreme lighting such as highlights. To further handle this problem, [28] unless a Markov random field to model face texture. Mass transport approaches are also used to transfer color from a reference facial image to the target one. Using mass transport, [26] remaps the color of the input image according to the facial geometry. By constructing a synthetic face dataset with multiple reflectance channels, [29] generates convincing specular and shadow of target lightings.

3   Our Method

In this section, we will present the details of our technique. The pipeline of our method is illustrated in Fig. 1, we use a Highlight Mask Extraction module to extract the highlight masks as guidance for GAN training. We first assume the highlight masks as existing values and introduce the highlight mask guided GAN in Sect. 3.1. Then, we introduce Highlight Mask Extraction module in Sect. 3.2. Our implementation details are given in Sect. 3.3.

3.1   Highlight Mask Guided GAN

Given an input facial image I, facial highlight removal aims to change the pixel values of the facial highlight regions to show the original skin colors while preserving the values of other pixels. As shown in Fig. 1, we propose a highlight removal architecture using generative adversarial networks. The generator $\mathcal{G}$ outputs the residual between the input image I and the estimated highlight removal result $\hat{I}_d$:

$$\hat{I}_d = I - \mathcal{G}(I). \tag{1}$$

The generator $\mathcal{G}$ is composed of an encoder-decoder architecture. Considering that highlight components in an image will always have positive values, we add a leaky rectified linear unit (Leaky ReLU) activation function in the last layer of $\mathcal{G}$.

For the discriminator, directly using traditional GAN methods in highlight removal requires the discriminator to tell whether the input image contains or does not contain highlights. However, we observe that a whole face region without any highlights is difficult to capture in a non-laboratory environment, so it is difficult to collect enough positive samples to train a discriminator that can determine whether an input facial image contains highlights or not. To empower the GAN training in highlight removal with in-the-wild images, we design our network architecture based on the following consideration. As most natural facial images contain both highlight and highlight-free regions, we can train a region-based discriminator $\mathcal{D}$ which outputs a low-resolution highlight mask M_L to indicate highlight and highlight-free regions. To be noted, we call the low-resolution highlight mask "highlight label map" to distinguish it from the original highlight mask M_H. By minimizing the size of the highlight regions obtained by the discriminator, the generator could be trained to perform the highlight removal task.

We also adopt the two-stage training strategy from [3,7]. Before trained on real images with highlight mask guidance, the network is pre-trained in a supervised manner on a synthetic dataset [29], which contains about 270,000 paired images with and without highlight.

Supervised Loss. Given a synthetic image I^s and its corresponding image without highlight I_d^s, the estimated $\hat{I}_d^s$ should be similar to I_d^s. We directly employ L_1 loss as follows,

$$\mathcal{L}_{sup} = \|\hat{I}_d^s - I_d^s\|_1. \tag{2}$$

Weighted-L1 Loss. When trained on real images I^r, we use a weighted-L_1 loss to constrain the highlight removal results $\hat{I}^r_d$ should have the same content as I^r. As highlights have different intensities in I^r, the intensity of each pixel in the residual $\mathcal{G}(I^r)$ should varies with facial regions. Therefore, for non-highlight regions, large weights are applied. For highlight regions, we use small weights for highlight regions. With the highlight mask indicating highlight regions, the weighted-L_1 loss are defined as follows,

$$\mathcal{L}_{wL_1} = \lambda_H \|M_H \odot (\hat{I}^r_d - I^r)\| + \lambda_{NH} \|(1 - M_H) \odot (\hat{I}^r_d - I^r)\|, \qquad (3)$$

where $\odot$ represent the element-wise multiplication operator.

Adversarial Loss. We apply the different adversarial loss in training $\mathcal{G}$ and $\mathcal{D}$,

$$\mathcal{L}_{adv} = \mathcal{L}_{\mathcal{G}} + \mathcal{L}_{\mathcal{D}}, \qquad (4)$$

where $\mathcal{L}_{\mathcal{G}}$ is for training the generator $\mathcal{G}$ and $\mathcal{L}_{\mathcal{D}}$ is for training the discriminator $\mathcal{D}$. As the non-highlight regions change little after the highlight removal, the discriminator should recognize these regions as real samples before and after the highlight removal. For highlight regions, the discriminator should not only distinguish them in the input image but also recognize the fake non-highlight regions generated by the generator. Therefore, the highlight regions should always be treated as fake samples. When training the generator, we require that the highlight removal result $\hat{I}^r_d$ can fake the discriminator over all facial regions. We define the adversarial loss functions as follows,

$$\mathcal{L}_{\mathcal{D}} = \mathrm{BCE}(\mathcal{D}(I^r), M_L) + \mathrm{BCE}(\mathcal{D}(\hat{I}^r_d), M_L), \qquad (5)$$

$$\mathcal{L}_{\mathcal{G}} = \mathrm{BCE}(\mathcal{D}(\hat{I}^r), \mathbf{0}), \qquad (6)$$

where BCE represent the Binary Cross Entropy loss and $\mathbf{0}$ represent a map filled with 0 with the same size as the highlight label map M_L. Here, 0 represent real while 1 represents fake.

Overall, our total loss function is expressed as,

$$\mathcal{L} = \lambda_{sup}\mathcal{L}_{sup} + \mathcal{L}_{wL_1} + \mathcal{L}_{adv}. \qquad (7)$$

3.2   Highlight Mask Extraction

In this subsection, we detail how we extract the highlight mask of a given input image. Although previous methods [31] fail to remove highlight from facial images, their extracted highlights can still represent an approximate distribution of highlights. As shown in Figs. 1 and 2, we first estimate the specular component from the input facial using [31]. Then, we use a threshold t to convert the estimated specular into a binary highlight mask M_H. As for the low-resolution highlight label map M_L, it is converted from the highlight mask M_H using a max pooling layer $\mathcal{M}$. To be noticed, although the reception field of the max pooling layer $\mathcal{M}$ is smaller than that of the discriminator D, the center points of both $\mathcal{M}$ and $\mathcal{D}$ are set to be the same. This can make the highlight label map has the same size as the output of $\mathcal{D}$. We apply the highlight mask extraction on real images from the FFHQ dataset [10] and use them in the finetuning stage.

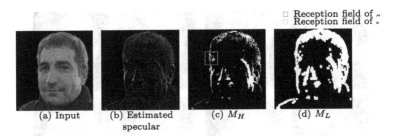

Reception field of $\mathcal{M}$
Reception field of $\mathcal{D}$

(a) Input   (b) Estimated   (c) M_H (d) M_L
                  specular

Fig. 2. The intermediate results and the final output of the highlight mask extraction module. The center point (indicated by the red points) of the reception field of the max pooling layer $\mathcal{M}$ is set to be the same as that of the discriminator $\mathcal{D}$. Besides, M_L and $\mathcal{D}$ have the same size. (Color figure online)

3.3 Implementation Details

To train our highlight removal network, we use a two-stage training strategy. In the pre-training stage, we set the learning rate to 0.002 only with the supervised loss on the synthetic dataset. Then, in the finetuning stage, the learning rate is decreased to 0.0002 with our total loss function $\mathcal{L}$. Our model is implemented in Pytorch and trained using one NVIDIA GTX 1080Ti GPU for 20 h. We set the threshold t in the highlight mask extraction module to 0.02, λ_{sup} to 10, λ_H to 10 and λ_L to 0.1. In the max pooling layer $\mathcal{L}$, we set its kernel size to 6, stride to 2 and padding size to 0. The average running time is about 8ms during testing with a 512×512 input image.

4 Experiments

In this section, we will first evaluate the key contributions of our proposed method. Then, we compare our method with the state-of-the-art highlight removal methods qualitatively and quantitatively. Especially, we present the comparisons on the photorealistic in-the-wild images generated by StyleGAN [10] to show that our method can improve the performance on the in-the-wild images. For quantitative experiments, as most previous methods do not release their codes or models and highlight-free images are difficult to capture, we perform the experiments based on the results reported in their paper.

4.1 Ablation Study

To illustrate the effectiveness of our highlight mask guided training strategy, we present the results of different setups. The baseline method is trained only with the supervised loss $\mathcal{L}_{sup}$. Then, we add a traditional adversarial loss, in which the discriminator distinguishes whether its input image is in the real image distribution or generated by the generator. We compare these two methods with our final method.

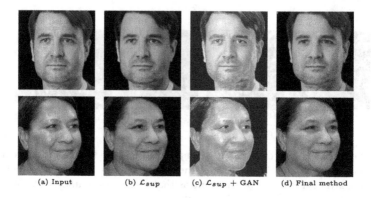

(a) Input   (b) $\mathcal{L}_{sup}$ (c) $\mathcal{L}_{sup}$ + GAN   (d) Final method

Fig. 3. Qualitative evaluation of the proposed highlight masked guided GAN training on in-the-wild images. (b) shows the results of a highlight removal network only trained with supervised loss $\mathcal{L}_{sup}$. (c) represents the incorporation of traditional GAN training. (d) indicates our final method.

We present some qualitative comparisons in Fig. 3. The results in Fig. 3(c) demonstrate that directly implementing traditional GAN training in the highlight removal task will lead to meaningless results. Since the synthetic dataset [29] cannot explicitly model the eyes in their data synthesis, the network trained only with the supervised synthetic data fail to handle the highlights in the eyes as shown in the first row in Fig. 3(b). Besides, when highlight leads to information loss in the input, the highlight masked guided GAN training enables the network to recover the missing content and generating visually pleasing results. However, only using the supervised loss $\mathcal{L}_{sup}$ itself will lead to color deviation or unresolved highlight as shown in Fig. 3(b). These comparisons manifest that with the help of the highlight masked guided GAN training, we improve the highlight removal effect of our method.

4.2   Comparisons with Previous Techniques

To demonstrate the effect of the proposed method, we present both quantitative and qualitative comparisons with previous highlight removal techniques. The compared methods include some traditional general highlight removal methods [24,31] and highlight removal methods designed for facial highlight removal [17,32].

For quantitative experiments, since [17,32] do not release their codes, we directly compare our methods with previous techniques based on laboratory images presented in [32]. To be noted, the RMSE and SSIM metrics differ from those reported in [32] as we crop the image for better visualization and recompute these metrics between all the results and the ground truth for a fair comparison. The results are shown in Fig. 4. As we can see, our method achieves better performance compared to [17,24,31]. When compared to [32], our method generates comparable result in the first row of Fig. 4. Although the metrics in the second row are not as good as [32], our method still generates visually pleasing results.

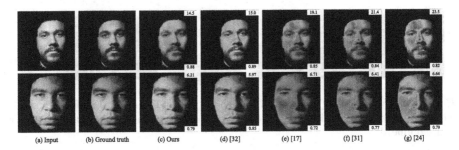

Fig. 4. Quantitative evaluation comparisons with the state-of-the-art on laboratory images. We compare our methods (c) with general highlight removal methods (f) [31] and (g) [24], and facial highlight removal techniques (d) [32] and (e) [17]. The performance is measured by RMSE (upper right) and SSIM (lower right). As the codes of [17,32] are not released, the input, ground truth and the results of these methods are from the paper of [32] for comparison convenience.

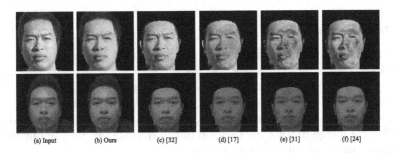

Fig. 5. Qualitative evaluation comparisons with the state-of-the-art on in-the-wild images. As our network is trained with highlight mask guided GAN on the in-the-wild images, our results outperforms all the state-of-the-art methods on the in-the-wild images.

The above quantitative experiments are performed on laboratory images while our method mainly focuses on the in-the-wild images. Therefore, we further make comparisons based on the in-the-wild images from [32] to demonstrate the advantages of our methods. As shown in Fig. 5, our method generates more visually pleasing results compared to all the state-of-the-art methods. Although [32] works well on the laboratory images, it fails to handle the highlight around the nose and the mouth region in these in-the-wild images. Benefitting from our proposed highlight mask guided training technique, our method is still robust on these inputs and generates convincing results.

Fig. 6. Limitations of our methods. Although our method works well on facial regions, white hair and white clothes might be recognized as highlight by our network. (Color figure online)

4.3 More Results

We also provide more highlight removal results in our supplemental material to demonstrate the robustness of our method. In these results, we can see that our method can handle in-the-wild images with different races, genders, ages, and input lightings.

4.4 Limitations

Our method improves the highlight removal effect on the facial regions, especially on the in-the-wild images. However, as the highlight mask extraction module is designed for facial regions, other white objects in an image might be recognized as highlight. This will lead to color deviation in these regions. As shown in Fig. 6, white hair and the white collar turn yellow after the highlight removal. If we add extra image parsing information in the training, we believe our method can achieve more visually pleasing results.

5   Conclusions

In this paper, we proposed a highlight removal method based on generative adversarial networks. Our method achieves high-quality results in facial highlight removal compared with the state-of-the-art, especially on the in-the-wild images. To avoid the lack of images that have no highlights, with the proposed highlight mask guided GAN training technique, our network is finetuned on the unpaired in-the-wild images. Experiments on laboratory images and in-the-wild images validate the effectiveness of our method. We hope the proposed approach can inspire future works on related problems.

Acknowledgements. This work was supported by the National Key R&D Program of China 2018YFA0704000, the NSFC (No. 61822111, 61727808, 61671268, 62025108) and Beijing Natural Science Foundation (JQ19015, L182052).

References

1. Bajcsy, R., Lee, S.W., Leonardis, A.: Detection of diffuse and specular interface reflections and inter-reflections by color image segmentation. Int. J. Comput. Vis. **17**(3), 241–272 (1996)

2. Blanz, V., Vetter, T.: A morphable model for the synthesis of 3D faces. In: Proceedings of the 26th Annual Conference on Computer Graphics and Interactive Techniques, pp. 187–194 (1999)
3. Debevec, P., Hawkins, T., Tchou, C., Duiker, H.P., Sarokin, W., Sagar, M.: Acquiring the reflectance field of a human face. In: Proceedings of the 27th Annual Conference on Computer Graphics and Interactive Techniques, pp. 145–156 (2000)
4. Denton, E.L., Chintala, S., Fergus, R., et al.: Deep generative image models using a Laplacian pyramid of adversarial networks. In: Advances in Neural Information Processing Systems, pp. 1486–1494 (2015)
5. Dosovitskiy, A., Springenberg, J.T., Brox, T.: Learning to generate chairs with convolutional neural networks. In: 2015 IEEE Conference on Computer Vision and Pattern Recognition (CVPR), pp. 1538–1546. IEEE (2015)
6. Goodfellow, I., et al.: Generative adversarial nets. In: Advances in Neural Information Processing Systems, pp. 2672–2680 (2014)
7. Guo, J., Zhou, Z., Wang, L.: Single image highlight removal with a sparse and low-rank reflection model. In: Ferrari, V., Hebert, M., Sminchisescu, C., Weiss, Y. (eds.) ECCV 2018. LNCS, vol. 11208, pp. 282–298. Springer, Cham (2018). https://doi.org/10.1007/978-3-030-01225-0_17
8. Isola, P., Zhu, J.Y., Zhou, T., Efros, A.A.: Image-to-image translation with conditional adversarial networks. In: Proceedings of the IEEE Conference on Computer Vision and Pattern Recognition, pp. 1125–1134 (2017)
9. Johnson, J., Alahi, A., Fei-Fei, L.: Perceptual losses for real-time style transfer and super-resolution. In: Leibe, B., Matas, J., Sebe, N., Welling, M. (eds.) ECCV 2016. LNCS, vol. 9906, pp. 694–711. Springer, Cham (2016). https://doi.org/10.1007/978-3-319-46475-6_43
10. Karras, T., Laine, S., Aila, T.: A style-based generator architecture for generative adversarial networks. In: Proceedings of the IEEE/CVF Conference on Computer Vision and Pattern Recognition, pp. 4401–4410 (2019)
11. Kim, H., Jin, H., Hadap, S., Kweon, I.: Specular reflection separation using dark channel prior. In: 2013 IEEE Conference on Computer Vision and Pattern Recognition (CVPR), pp. 1460–1467. IEEE (2013)
12. Kingma, D.P., Welling, M.: Auto-encoding variational bayes. arXiv preprint arXiv:1312.6114 (2013)
13. Klinker, G.J., Shafer, S.A., Kanade, T.: The measurement of highlights in color images. Int. J. Comput. Vis. **2**(1), 7–32 (1988)
14. Kupyn, O., Budzan, V., Mykhailych, M., Mishkin, D., Matas, J.: Deblurgan: blind motion deblurring using conditional adversarial networks. In: Proceedings of the IEEE Conference on Computer Vision and Pattern Recognition, pp. 8183–8192 (2018)
15. Ledig, C., et al.: Photo-realistic single image super-resolution using a generative adversarial network. In: Proceedings of the IEEE Conference on Computer Vision and Pattern Recognition, pp. 4681–4690 (2017)
16. Lee, C.H., Liu, Z., Wu, L., Luo, P.: MaskGAN: towards diverse and interactive facial image manipulation. In: Proceedings of the IEEE/CVF Conference on Computer Vision and Pattern Recognition (CVPR), June 2020
17. Li, C., Lin, S., Zhou, K., Ikeuchi, K.: Specular highlight removal in facial images. In: Proceedings of the IEEE Conference on Computer Vision and Pattern Recognition, pp. 3107–3116 (2017)
18. Mirza, M., Osindero, S.: Conditional generative adversarial nets. arXiv preprint arXiv:1411.1784 (2014)

19. Perarnau, G., van de Weijer, J., Raducanu, B., Álvarez, J.M.: Invertible conditional gans for image editing. arXiv preprint arXiv:1611.06355 (2016)
20. Quan, L., Shum, H.Y., et al.: Highlight removal by illumination-constrained inpainting. In: Ninth IEEE International Conference on Computer Vision, Proceedings, pp. 164–169. IEEE (2003)
21. Ramamoorthi, R., Hanrahan, P.: A signal-processing framework for inverse rendering. In: Computer Graphics Proceedings, SIGGRAPH 2001 pp. 117–128 (2001)
22. Salimans, T., Goodfellow, I., Zaremba, W., Cheung, V., Radford, A., Chen, X.: Improved techniques for training GANs. In: Advances in Neural Information Processing Systems, pp. 2234–2242 (2016)
23. Shashua, A., Riklin-Raviv, T.: The quotient image: class-based re-rendering and recognition with varying illuminations. IEEE Trans. Pattern Anal. Mach. Intell. **23**(2), 129–139 (2001)
24. Shen, H.L., Zheng, Z.H.: Real-time highlight removal using intensity ratio. Appl. Opt. **52**(19), 4483–4493 (2013)
25. Shen, W., Liu, R.: Learning residual images for face attribute manipulation. In: 2017 IEEE Conference on Computer Vision and Pattern Recognition (CVPR), pp. 1225–1233. IEEE (2017)
26. Shu, Z., Hadap, S., Shechtman, E., Sunkavalli, K., Paris, S., Samaras, D.: Portrait lighting transfer using a mass transport approach. ACM Trans. Graph. (TOG) **37**(1), 2 (2018)
27. Taigman, Y., Polyak, A., Wolf, L.: Unsupervised cross-domain image generation. arXiv preprint arXiv:1611.02200 (2016)
28. Wang, Y., et al.: Face relighting from a single image under arbitrary unknown lighting conditions. IEEE Trans. Pattern Anal. Mach. Intell. **31**(11), 1968–1984 (2008)
29. Wang, Z., Yu, X., Lu, M., Wang, Q., Qian, C., Xu, F.: Single image portrait relighting via explicit multiple reflectance channel modeling. ACM Trans. Graph. (TOG) **39**(6), 1–13 (2020)
30. Yang, Q., Tang, J., Ahuja, N.: Efficient and robust specular highlight removal. IEEE Trans. Pattern Anal. Mach. Intell. **37**(6), 1304–1311 (2015)
31. Yang, Q., Wang, S., Ahuja, N.: Real-time specular highlight removal using bilateral filtering. In: Daniilidis, K., Maragos, P., Paragios, N. (eds.) ECCV 2010. LNCS, vol. 6314, pp. 87–100. Springer, Heidelberg (2010). https://doi.org/10.1007/978-3-642-15561-1_7
32. Yi, R., Zhu, C., Tan, P., Lin, S.: Faces as lighting probes via unsupervised deep highlight extraction. In: Proceedings of the European Conference on Computer Vision (ECCV), pp. 317–333 (2018)
33. Zhu, J.Y., Park, T., Isola, P., Efros, A.A.: Unpaired image-to-image translation using cycle-consistent adversarial networks. In: Proceedings of the IEEE International Conference on Computer Vision, pp. 2223–2232 (2017)
34. Zhu, T., Xia, S., Bian, Z., Lu, C.: Highlight removal in facial images. In: Peng, Y. (ed.) PRCV 2020. LNCS, vol. 12305, pp. 422–433. Springer, Cham (2020). https://doi.org/10.1007/978-3-030-60633-6_35

A Cross-Layer Fusion Multi-target Detection and Recognition Method Based on Improved FPN Model in Complex Traffic Environment

Cuijin Li$^{(\boxtimes)}$, Dewei Chen, Junji Chen, and Hongying Dai

Chongqing Institute of Engineering, Chongqing 400056, China
http://www.cqie.edu.cn/

Abstract. According to the low accuracy and speed of multi-target detection in complex traffic environment, this paper proposes a multeature Pyramid Networks) to improve the target detection accuracy and network generalization ability. Firstly, the five-layer architecture of ResNet101 is adopted to construct a top-down feature map by 2×-sampling the spatial resolution, and the up-sampling map and the bottom-up feature map are combined by mixing of their elements to construct a feature layer, which has both integrating high-level semantic information and low-level geometric information. Secondly according to the imbalance of training samples in BBox regression, an improved Focal EIOU Loss function is proposed by using Efficient IOU Loss function and Focal Loss function. Finally, manual annotation of mixed data set is used for training by considering the actual situation of complex traffic environment. The experimental results show that this model has better detection effect than the other current models in complex traffic environment. The average detection accuracy and speed of the model are 2.5% and 2 FPS higher than FPN on KITTI test set, respectively. And the average detection accuracy and speed are 1.4% and 4 FPS higher than FPN on Cityscale test set.

Keywords: Multi target detection · Multi target recognition · Weighted balanced samples · Feature Pyramid Networks

1 Introduction

Target detection is the key technique of vehicle in dealing with complex scenes reasonably and safely [1], and is also one of the hot spots of computer vision research [2,3]. Lots of research on target detection methods has been studied by

Supported by the Scientific and Technological Research Program of Chongqing Municipal Education Commission (KJQN202101907), the Chongqing Institute of technology high tech Talents Program (2019gckv04) and the research projects of Chongqing Institute of Technology (2020xzky04).

L. Fang et al. (Eds.): CICAI 2021, LNAI 13069, pp. 323–334, 2021.
https://doi.org/10.1007/978-3-030-93046-2_28

researchers [4,5]. Traditional detectors usually approach sparse regions recommend box from the clustering of sliding windows, as the preferred object detection [6,7]. For example, the classic Harr [8] features and Adaboosting [9] classifiers are selected, and the sliding window [10,11] search strategy is used for face detection. The features extracted from the Histogram of Gradients (HOG) [12] and processed by Support Vector Machine (SVM) [13,14] are used in pedestrian detection. For general object detection, HOG feature plus multi-scale Deformable Part Model (DPM) [15,16] algorithm is used. Although these methods use fewer features to improve time efficiency, but they have obvious limitations and inaccuracies [17]. In recent years, with the development of deep learning technology, Convolutional Neural Network(CNN) has become the latest research hotspot, due to its superior to traditional methods in accuracy [18,19]. Kong et al. [20] proposed HyperNet, which combines the Hyper Features of the bottom layer, middle layer and high layer, achieve better results in the processing of small objects. Zhao et al. [21] proposed Cascaded R-CNN by analyzing the relationship between the two IOU of input proposal ground truth and of the detection model to define the positive and negative samples. Hou et al. [22] proposed a method of short link salient target detection based on depth monitoring. Jin et al. [23] proposed a deep multi model rail inspection system DM-RIS by using the improved Fast R-CNN.

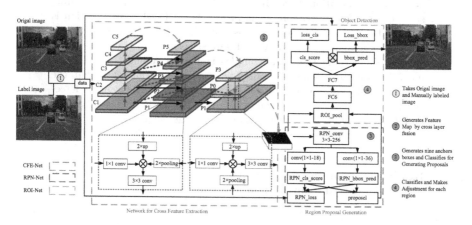

Fig. 1. The improvement architecture of the Faster R-CNN network.

Faster R-CNN algorithm has high precision and strong expansibility. In recent years, many papers have also been improved based on Faster R-CNN algorithm. In this paper, aiming at the problems of low accuracy and speed of multi-objective detection in the complex traffic environment, a multi-layer fusion multi-objective detection and recognition algorithm based on Faster R-CNN is proposed to improve the accuracy of target detection and network generalization. The whole structure of the model proposed in this paper is shown in Fig. 1. The main contributions of this paper are as follows.

(1) The Five-Layer basic architecture of ResNet101 is adopted to construct the top-down feature map by 2×-sampling the spatial resolution. The upper sampling map and the bottom-up feature map are combined by mixing of their elements. And a feature layer integrating high-level semantic information and low-level geometric information is constructed. In order to reduce the overlapping effect of the upper sampling, each combined feature map is followed by a 3 × 3 convolution. Finally, the P1 feature layer, which is rich in geometric information, is sampled by up-sampling, and the P3 feature layer, which is rich in semantic information, is sampled by down-sampling, and their sampling results are used to fuse with P2 feature layer by mixing of their pixel, and the final feature layer P0 is obtained by a 3 × 3 convolution.

(2) According to the imbalance of training samples in BBox regression, the Efficient IOU Loss function is selected. The penalty term splits the influence factors of aspect ratio to calculate the length and width of the target frame and anchor frame respectively, including overlap loss, center distance loss and width height loss. And an improved Focal EIOU Loss is proposed by combined with Focal Loss.

(3) Considering the actual situation of complex traffic environment, training and a large number of tests are carried out by manually labeling mixed data sets. Experimental results show that the average detection accuracy and speed of the model on KITTI test set are 2.4% and 5 FPS higher than FPN, respectively. On Cityscale test set, the average detection accuracy and speed are 1.9% and 4 FPS higher than FPN.

The rest of this paper is arranged as follows. In the second section, FPN and Resnet101 are introduced. The third section introduces the improved FPN model network structure and the improved Focal EIOU Loss. The fourth section gives the training process and experimental results, and evaluates the proposed method. Finally, the discussion and conclusion are given in the fifth section.

2   Related Works

2.1   Feature Pyramid Networks

As a common scheme, in order to solve the problem of multi-scale target detection, different size feature maps is generated and image pyramid is constructed according to the original image. And detect different size targets on the corresponding feature maps. It is widely used in target detection and recognition, but the detection accuracy of small targets and occluded targets needs to be improved. As shown in Fig. 2, occluded cars and distant cars are not recognized.

2.2   ResNet101

ResNet101 network mainly uses the basic ResNet structure and the bottleneck structure. The basic structure is generally used for less than 30 layers, and the bottleneck structure is generally used for more than 30 layers, which can reduce the network parameters. The dimensions of the addition part of the infrastructure are the same, where expansion is 1; while the dimensions of the bottleneck structure are different, so they cannot be added directly. They can only be added directly after down-sampling, where expansion is 4.

3   Improved FPN

The five-layer architecture of ResNet101 is adopted based on Feature Pyramid Networks to construct a top-down feature map by 2×-sampling the spatial resolution and the up-sampling map and the bottom-up feature map are combined by mixing of their elements to construct a feature layer in this paper. The algorithm is divided into four parts. The first one is the input of any size and any angle image, including the original image and manual calibration image. The second one is the cross layer fusion convolution neural network based on ResNet101. The third one is the RPN network for extracting candidate frames. The fourth one is the ROI network for classification and regression, in which the improved Focal EIOU Loss is set in order to improve the detection accuracy.

3.1   Cross Layer Fusion CNN

ResNet101 is used to build the Bottom-Up network in this paper, as shown in Fig. 3. C5 generates the feature map with the lowest resolution through a 1×1 convolution layer. And then merge the up-sampling feature map with the top-down path shallow feature map by 2× sampling. Finally, in order to reduce the aliasing effect caused by up sampling, each merged feature graph generates the final feature graph P5, P4, P3, P2, P1 through a 3×3 convolution, corresponding to C5, C4, C3, C2, C1 has the same space size. By sampling P3 feature layer rich in semantic information (2× up-simpling) and P1 feature layer rich in geometric information (2× pooling), it is fused with P2 feature layer by pixel addition. Finally, the final feature layer P0 is obtained by a 3×3 convolution of the fused features. The pixel values of each layer of the network are shown in Fig. 2.

3.2   Improved Focal EIOU Loss

Considering the imbalance of training samples in BBox regression, that is, the number of high-quality anchor frames with small regression error is far less than that of low-quality samples with large regression error in an image, and the poor quality sampling will produce too large gradient to affect the training process, EIOU loss function is selected. The penalty term of this function splits the influence factor of aspect ratio and calculates the length and width of the target box and the anchor box respectively, which includes three parts: overlap loss, center distance loss and width height loss. The first two parts continue the method in CIOU, but the width height loss directly minimizes the difference between the width and height of the target box and the anchor box, which makes the convergence speed faster. Based on EIOU and focal loss, an improved

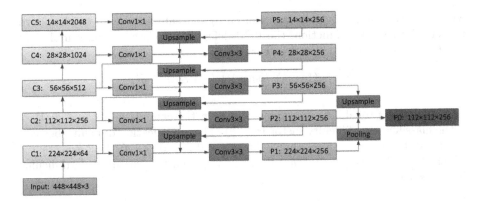

Fig. 2. Cross layer convergence CNN architecture diagram.

focal EIOU loss is proposed. From the angle of gradient, the high-quality anchor frame is separated from the low-quality anchor frame. The penalty term is shown in Formula (1),

$$L_{Focal-EIOU} = IOU^{\gamma} L_{EIOU} \tag{1}$$

$$L_{EIOU} = L_{CIOU} + L_{dis} + L_{asp} \tag{2}$$

$$L_{CIOU} = 1 - IOU + R_{CIOU} \tag{3}$$

$$R_{CIOU} = \frac{P^2(b, b^{gt})}{c^2} + \alpha v \tag{4}$$

where α is the parameter used to do trade-off, $v = \frac{4}{\pi}(arctan\frac{w^{gt}}{h^{gt}} - arctan\frac{w}{h})^2$ is a parameter used to measure the consistency of aspect ratio, distance loss $L_{dis} = \frac{p^2(w,w^{gt})}{c_w^2}$ and aspect loss $L_{asp} = \frac{p^2(h,h^{gt})}{c_h^2}$.

Classification loss comes with to the error of candidate box classification (target or background). In order to solve the problem of class imbalance between positive and negative samples, a weighting factor α is introduced, as shown in Formula (5). The positive and negative samples are balanced through α, but it does not differentiate between easy sample and hard sample. Therefore, this paper uses the Focal-loss function to reduce the loss of easy samples and increase the weight of hard samples in the loss function. The Focal-loss function is shown in Formula (6),

$$CE = \begin{cases} -\alpha log(p), & if \quad y = 1 \\ -(1-\alpha)log(1-p), & otherwise \end{cases} \tag{5}$$

where α is the positive/negative sample balance factor, p is the probability of $y = 1$.

$$FL = \begin{cases} -\alpha(1-P)^{\gamma} log(p), & if \quad y = 1 \\ -(1-\alpha)P^{\gamma} log(1-p), & otherwise \end{cases} \tag{6}$$

where γ is the sample balance factor of hard/easy samples. Based on the above two classification loss function, the PCB defect multi classification sample loss function is obtained and shown in Formula (7),

$$L_{cls} = \sum_i (\alpha_i(1 - p_i)^\gamma log(p_i) + (1 - \alpha_i)p_i^\gamma log(1 - p_i)), \tag{7}$$

where p is the probability that the target is in the candidate box, $p \in [0,1]$, γ is the classification difficulty factor ($\gamma > 0$). The classification difficulty become greater if the positive sample threshold is close 0.7, and $(1-p)^\gamma$ becomes greater which lead p is closer 1. $(1 - p)^\gamma$ is close to 0 when the classification difficulty becomes small.

3.3   Data Set

Aiming at the above problems, the performance of the improved Faster R-CNN model is fully verified. Cityscapes data set and KITTI data set are used to train and test. Considering the actual situation, this paper divides the data set into five categories: person, car, bus, bicycle and motorcycle. The number of training samples manually labeled in Cityscapes and KITTI data sets is shown in Table 1.

Table 1. The manually label sampling number of data set

Dataset	Car	Bus	Person	Bicycle	Motorcycle
Cityscapes	5670	1107	6765	4740	4131
KITTI	8217	1146	6153	4675	1077

In deep learning, the quality of data set directly affects the final detection effect. At the same time, because the network wants to fully learn the characteristics of the target to be detected, it needs a large number of samples. In this paper, the data sets used in the experiment, such as bicycles, motorcycles and buses, are less than those of motor vehicles, which will lead to over fitting problems, and the generalization ability of the final trained detection model is poor. To solve this problem, this paper uses the mixed data set training method in the experiment. In Cityscapes data set and KITTI data set, VOC07 data set is added respectively, and 1000 images including bicycle, motorcycle and bus sample training set are manually labeled. Finally, 4000 images of Cityscapes + VOC2007 data set and 5000 images of KITTI + VOC2007 data set are selected as the training data set, and 2000 images are selected as the test set.

4   Experimental Result

4.1   Experimental Environment

The experiments in this paper are carried out in the fast feature embedded cafe software environment under the condition of Ubuntu 18.04 and convolutional architecture. The hardware environment is i7 8700k, and the GPU is GTX 1070TI 8G memory.

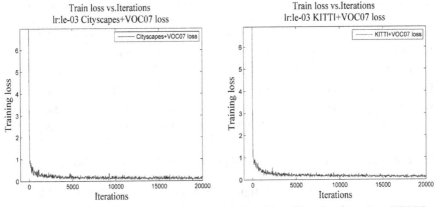

(a) Total loss function based on Cityscapes + VOC07 data set

(b) Total loss function based on KITTI + VOC07 data set

Fig. 3. Total loss function in training process.

4.2 Training Process

In order to verify the influence of multi-scale fusion, weighted balance multi class cross entropy loss function and soft-NMS on the model detection performance, the training process is divided into the following five steps.

1. Prepare manually labeled training data sets Cityscapes, KITTI and VOC07.
2. Use Caffe framework to define training and testing model, and modify loss function, soft NMS function and feature extraction network related code.
3. When the loss reaches the maximum number of iterations or the loss value is less than the threshold, the training is stopped and the script file of Caffe model is obtained.
4. The Caffe-model is used to initialize the parameters of the test model, and the labeled test data set is used to obtain the final effect output.
5. The evaluation model obtains the output image from the corresponding data set, and obtains some mapping tables, average accuracy indexes of various categories, and the evaluation result chart of IOU confidence score covering the object positioning frame, etc.

4.3 Loss Function

As shown in Fig. 3, the initial value of the total loss in the training process of the improved FPN algorithm is 6.8. With the increase of the number of iterations, the loss value drops sharply to about 1.1. When the loss cost slowly approaches 0.3, the whole gradient tends to be smooth. Therefore, the loss value of the whole training process is decreasing, and there is no adverse trend of up and down vibration in the whole process, so the network parameters of the whole model training are the most suitable parameters in the improved FPN network structure.

Table 2. Detection accuracy of each category under the different backbone network

Backbone	Input size	Car	Person	Bus	Bicycle	Motorcycle	mAP	Rate
VGG16	448×448	88.5	83.9	89.9	73.3	83.8	83.8	1
Resnet50	448×448	99.1	90.2	99.5	84.8	86.1	91.9	10
Resnet50+FPN	448×448	99.5	90.7	99.9	88.6	90.2	93.8	15
Resnet101	448×448	99.6	91.6	99.9	89.2	91.5	94.3	20
Resnet101+FPN	448×448	99.7	92.8	99.9	90.4	93.8	96.8	22+

Table 3. Detection results mAP(%) and Recall(%) on Cityscapes dataset

Method	Backbone	Input size	Model size	$mAP(\%)$	Recall(%)
Faster R-CNN	X-101	448×448	130M	81.2	72.6
Libra R-CNN	R-101	448×448	135M	86.4	73.8
Mask R-CNN	X-101	448×448	205M	87.1	78.5
R-FCN	R-101	448×448	235M	90.8	79.2
TridentNet	R-101	448×448	117M	91.5	79.3
Cascade R-CNN	R-101	448×448	189M	92.7	80.8
FPN	R-101	448×448	289M	95.4	83.6
Our method	R-101	448×448	198M	96.8	85.6

4.4   Test Results of Cityscapes Dataset

Figure 4 shows the target detection and classification output of Cityscapes data set based on the improved Faster R-CNN network. As shown in Fig. 6, when multiple objects are located in the same scene image, the network can still capture the characteristics and location of objects, the confidence of IOU can reach more than 0.9, and the objects can be accurately classified.

Compared with the original Faster R-CNN network structure, Small target acquisition and long-range target location can also get better scores through their own classification function. The output results in RPN network make full use of the feature information between 0.5 and 0.7. The output contains rich positive sample information and eliminates a lot of non object information, so the image target classification is more clear and accurate. Compared with the output object of the original Faster R-CNN, the network effect based on the improved FPN is closer to the real tag value of ground truth.

Table 2 shows the detection accuracy of each category under the different backbone network, because the bus category are relatively large and easy to detect, the accuracy of the bus category is up to 99.9%, while the bicycle category features are not easy to capture. When facing the shooting point, there are fewer features, so the accuracy of the bicycle category is at least 90.4%.

Fig. 4. The output images with the improved network in the Cityscapes.

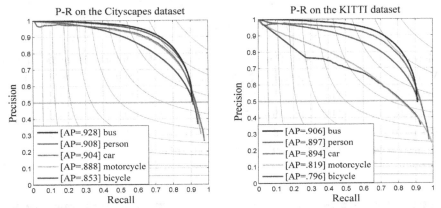

(a) Five types of target P-R curves based on Cityscapes data set

(b) Five types of target P-R curves based on KITTI data set

Fig. 5. Each type of target P-R curves.

As shown in Table 3, compared with the Fast R-CNN network, the improved network structure uses five types of targets on Cityscapes + VOC07 data set for training. The data set covers a variety of scenarios in the field of transportation, and the performance is measured by the class average accuracy and speed on the test set. The improved FPN map achieves a maximum of 96.8%, which is 2.5 points higher than the original ResNet101. Through Cityscapes dataset training, the map of the improved FPN network is 87.7%, which is also higher than that of the original Faster R-CNN. This is because the improved Fast R-CNN combines multi-layer feature map, which can make the model obtain more low-level and high-level image feature information, and improve the detection accuracy of small targets.

As shown in Fig. 5, the P-R curve of all kinds of targets in the improved FPN algorithm is relatively large and easy to detect. Therefore, the highest accuracy of bus category is 99.9%, while the feature of bicycle category is not easy to capture. When it is facing the shooting point, the feature is less. Therefore, the lowest accuracy of bicycle category is 90.4%.

4.5   Test Results of KITTI Dataset

Figure 6 shows the detection results on KITTI dataset using the improved FPN model. The convolution feature extraction network is ResNet101, and the training data set is VOC07 + KITTI. Each output box is related to a category label and softmax score [0,1], and the score threshold of these images is set to 0.6. As shown in Table 4, compared with Fast R-CNN in KITTI data set, the speed of the improved FPN is improved (rate = 21 fps), and mAP is 10.9% higher than VGG16.

Table 4. Detection results $mAP(\%)$ and Rate(fps) on KITTI test

Method	Input size	Car	Person	Bus	Bicycle	Motorcycle	mAP	Rate
VGG16	448×448	72.7	71.7	81.2	76.6	79.6	78.7	1
Resnet50	448×448	87.3	84.2	88.3	77.2	78.5	83.8	10
Resnet50+FPN	448×448	89.1	85.7	89.6	78.2	80.9	86.2	14
Resnet101	448×448	89.3	87.8	90.3	79.1	81.4	88.2	17
Resnet101+FPN	448×448	89.4	89.7	90.9	79.6	81.9	89.6	21

Fig. 6. The output images with the improved network on the KITTI.

5   Conclusion

An improved FPN multi-target detection and recognition scheme based on ResNet101 in this paper. Experimental results and data show that the improved FPN neural network has better performance R-CNN model combines low-level and high-level image semantic features, so that the model can obtain more information, thus improving the positioning accuracy of target pixel features. In addition, the weighted multi classification cross entropy loss function is improved when the samples are divided into categories, and the soft NMS algorithm is used when the anchor frame is selected, which improves the detection results of small targets and occluded targets The mixed data sets were labeled manually. (Experimental data mapping in cityscapes test shows that VGG16: 0.838, OUR-Cross: 0.968, OUR-Cross-FPS: 22 +).

Improved FPN image target classification and recognition model in manually annotated Cityscapes and KITTI datasets has been improved, but it is not the best network model for more complex scenes (moving targets, weather, lighting and human factors change). In the future, we will deeply study the generation of confrontation network (GAN) [24] to solve the problem of target detection and recognition in more complex traffic scenes distinguish.

References

1. Liqiang, L., Jianzhong, C.: End-to-end learning interpolation for object tracking in low frame-rate video. IET Image Process. **14**(6), 1066–1072 (2020)
2. Gaurang, B., Vinay, C., Pratik, N., Subham, K., Sundaresan, R.: Deep3DSCan: deep residual network and morphological descriptor based framework for lung cancer classification and 3D segmentation. IET Image Process. **14**(7), 1240–1247 (2020)
3. Yang, F., Zhang, L., Yu, S., Prokhorov, D., Mei, X., Ling, H.: Feature pyramid and hierarchical boosting network for pavement crack detection. IEEE Trans. Pattern Anal. Mach. Intell. **21**(4), 1525–1535 (2020)
4. Liu, S., Huang, D., Wang, Y.: Pay attention to them: deep reinforcement learning-based cascade object detection. IEEE Trans. Neural. Netw. Learn. Syst. **21**(7), 2544–2556 (2020)
5. Xun, H., Hong, L., Xinrong, L., Wang, C.: MobileNet-SSD microscope using adaptive error correction algorithm: real-time detection of license plates on mobile devices. IET Intell. Transp. Syst. **14**(2), 110–118 (2020)
6. Lienhart, R., Maydt, J.: An extended set of Harr-like features for rapid object detection. In: International Conference on Image Processing, pp. 900–903. IEEE (2002)
7. Viola, P., Jones, M.: Rapid object detection using a boosted cascade of simple features. In: Proceedings of the 2001 IEEE Computer Society Conference on Computer Vision and Pattern Recognition (CVPR 2001), pp. 511–518. IEEE (2003)
8. Shan, J., Zhang, H., Liu, W., Liu, Q.: Online active learning ensemble framework for drifted data streams. IEEE Trans. Neural Network. Learn **30**(2), 486–498 (2019)
9. Sestito, G.S., Turcato, A.C., Dias, A.L., Rocha, M.S.: A method for anomalies detection in real-time ethernet data traffic applied to profinet. IEEE Trans. Ind. Inform. **14**(5), 2171–2180 (2018)
10. Dalal, N., Triggs, B.: Histograms of oriented gradients for human detection. In: IEEE Computer Society Conference on Computer Vision and Pattern Recognition (CVPR 2005), pp. 886–893. IEEE (2005)
11. Cortes, C., Vapnik, V.: Support-vector networks. Mach. Learn. **20**(3), 273–297 (1995)
12. Lin, C.F., Wang, S.D.: Fuzzy support vector machines. IEEE Trans. Neural Netw. **13**(2), 464 (2002)
13. Felzenszwalb, P.F., Girshick, R.B., Mcallester, D., et al.: Object detection with discriminatively trained part-based models. Computer **47**(2), 6–7 (2014)
14. Girshick, R., Donahue, J., Darrell, T., Malik, J.: Rich feature hierarchies for accurate object detection and semantic segmentation. In: 2014 IEEE Conference on Computer Vision and Pattern Recognition, Columbus, OH, pp. 580–587 (2014)
15. He, K., Zhang, X., Ren, S., Sun, J.: Spatial pyramid pooling in deep convolutional networks for visual recognition. IEEE Trans. Pattern Anal. Mach. Intell. **37**(9), 1904–1916 (2015)

16. Lin, T., Goyal, P., Girshick, R., He, K., Dollar, P.: Focal loss for dense object detection. IEEE Trans. Pattern Anal. Mach. Intell. **42**(2), 318–327 (2020)

17. Yu, B., Tao, D.: Anchor cascade for efficient face detection. IEEE Trans. Trans. Image. Process. **28**(5), 2490–2501 (2018)

18. Kong, T., Sun, F., Liu, H., Jiang, Y., Li, L., Shi, J.: Foveabox: beyound anchor-based object detection. IEEE Trans. Image. Process. **29**(2), 7389–7398 (2020)

19. Li, Y., Wang, X., Liu, W., Feng, B.: Pose anchor: a single-stage hand keypoint detection network. IEEE Trans. Circ. Syst. Video Technol. **20**(7), 2104–2113 (2020)

20. Kong, T., Yao, A., Chen, Y., Sun, F.: Hypernet: towards accurate region proposal generation and joint object detection. In: Proceedings of IEEE Conference on Computer Vision and Pattern Recognition, pp. 1063–6919, Las Vegas, NV (2018)

21. Cai, Z., Vasconcelos, N.: Cascade R-CNN: delving into high quality object detection. In: 2018 IEEE/CVF Conference on Computer Vision and Pattern Recognition, Salt Lake City, UT, pp. 6154–6162 (2018)

22. Hou, Q., Cheng, M.-M., Hu, X., Borji, A., Tu, Z., Torr, P.H.S.: Deeply supervised salient object detection with short connections. IEEE Trans. Pattern Anal. Mach. **41**(4), 815–828 (2019)

23. Jin, X.T., Wang, Y.N., Zhang, H., et al.: DM-RIS: deep multimodel rail inspection system with improved MRF-GMM and CNN. IEEE Trans. Instrum. Measure. **69**(4), 1051–1064 (2020)

24. Li, X., et al.: Multi-task structure-aware context modeling for robust keypoint-based object tracking. IEEE Trans. Pattern Anal. Mach. Intell. **41**(4), 915–927 (2020)

Various Plug-and-Play Algorithms with Diverse Total Variation Methods for Video Snapshot Compressive Imaging

Xin Yuan$^{(\boxtimes)}$ (iD)

Westlake University, Hangzhou 310024, Zhejiang, China
xyuan@westlake.edu.cn
https://xyvirtualgroup.github.io/

Abstract. Sampling high-dimensional images is challenging due to limited availability of sensors; scanning is usually necessary in these cases. To mitigate this challenge, snapshot compressive imaging (SCI) was proposed to capture the high-dimensional (usually 3D) images using a 2D sensor (detector). Via novel optical design, the *measurement* captured by the sensor is an encoded image of multiple frames of the 3D desired signal. Following this, reconstruction algorithms are employed to retrieve the high-dimensional data. In this paper, we consider different plug-and-play (PnP) algorithms for SCI reconstruction, where various denoisers can be used into diverse solvers, such as ISTA, FISTA, TwIST, ADMM and GAP. Regarding the denoisers, though various algorithms have been proposed, the total variation (TV) based method is still the most efficient one due to a good trade-off between computational time and performance. This paper aims to answer the question of which TV penalty (anisotropic TV, isotropic TV and vectorized TV) works best for video SCI reconstruction? Various TV denoising and solvers are developed and tested for video SCI reconstruction on both simulation and real datasets.

Keywords: Computational imaging · Snapshot compressive imaging (SCI) · Coded aperture compressive temporal imaging (CACTI) · Compressive sensing · Total variation · Plug-and-Play (PnP)

1 Introduction

Snapshot compressive imaging (SCI) [33] refers to compressive imaging systems where multiple frames are mapped into a single measurement, with video SCI [15, 22–24, 26, 27, 34] and spectral SCI [17, 19, 20, 28, 35] as two representative applications. In video SCI shown in Fig. 1, high-speed frames are modulated at a higher frequency than the capture rate of the camera; in this manner, each captured measurement frame can recover a number of high-speed frames, which is dependent on the coding strategy, *e.g.*, 148 frames reconstructed from a snapshot in [15]. In spectral SCI, the wavelength dependent coding is implemented by

© Springer Nature Switzerland AG 2021
L. Fang et al. (Eds.): CICAI 2021, LNAI 13069, pp. 335–346, 2021.
https://doi.org/10.1007/978-3-030-93046-2_29

a coded aperture (physical mask) and a disperser [28]; more than 30 hyperspectral images have been reconstructed from a snapshot measurement. Though it is fair to say that SCI was inspired by compressive sensing (CS) [11], the theory of SCI has just been developed in [12] due to the special structure of the sensing matrix. In this paper, we focus on the practically applicable (e.g., easy to use, flexible and robust) algorithms rather than state-of-the-art results, which have been achieved by deep learning based methods with massive training data.

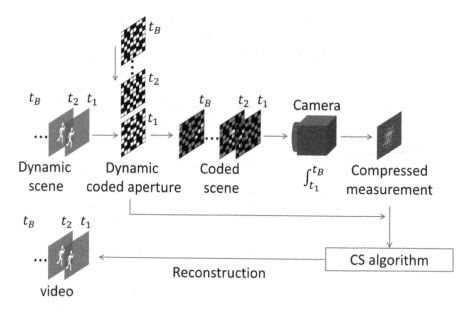

Fig. 1. Principle of snapshot video compressive sensing

Mathematically, the measurement in the SCI systems can be modeled by

$$y = \Phi x + g, \tag{1}$$

where $\Phi \in \mathbb{R}^{n \times nB}$ is the sensing matrix, $x \in \mathbb{R}^{nB}$ is the desired signal, and $g \in \mathbb{R}^n$ denotes the noise. Unlike traditional CS, the sensing matrix considered here is not a dense matrix. In SCI, e.g., video CS as in CACTI [15,34], the matrix Φ has a very specific structure and can be written as

$$\Phi = [\mathbf{D}_1, \ldots, \mathbf{D}_B], \tag{2}$$

where $\{\mathbf{D}_k\}_{k=1}^B$ are diagonal matrices.

As in Fig. 1, consider that B high-speed frames $\{\mathbf{X}_k\}_{k=1}^B \in \mathbb{R}^{n_x \times n_y}$ (at timestamp $t_1, \ldots, t_B$) are modulated by the masks $\{\mathbf{C}_k\}_{k=1}^B \in \mathbb{R}^{n_x \times n_y}$, correspondingly. The 2D measurement $\mathbf{Y} \in \mathbb{R}^{n_x \times n_y}$ captured by the camera is given by

$$\mathbf{Y} = \sum_{k=1}^B \mathbf{X}_k \odot \mathbf{C}_k + \mathbf{G}, \tag{3}$$

where $\odot$ denotes the Hadamard (element-wise) product. For all B pixels (in the B frames) at position (i,j), $i = 1,\dots,n_x$; $j = 1,\dots,n_y$, they are collapsed to form one pixel in the measurement (in one shot) as

$$y_{i,j} = \sum_{k=1}^{B} c_{i,j,k} x_{i,j,k} + g_{i,j} \,. \tag{4}$$

By defining

$$x = [x_1,\dots,x_B]\,, \tag{5}$$

where $x_k = \mathrm{vec}(\mathbf{X}_k)$, and $\mathbf{D}_k = \mathrm{diag}(\mathrm{vec}(\mathbf{C}_k))$, for $k = 1,\dots,B$, we have the vector formulation of Eq. (1), where $n = n_x n_y$. Therefore, $x \in \mathbb{R}^{n_x n_y B}$, $\boldsymbol{\Phi} \in \mathbb{R}^{n_x n_y \times (n_x n_y B)}$, and the compressive sampling rate in SCI is equal to $1/B$, which is defined by the hardware design. It has recently been proved that even when $B > 1$, reconstruction can be achieved with overwhelming probability [12].

The following task for the algorithm is to reconstruct the desired signal x given the measurement y and the special sensing matrix $\boldsymbol{\Phi}$ determined by the physical masks $\{\mathbf{C}_k\}_{k=1}^{B}$.

2   Solve SCI by Total Variation Regularization

Obviously, Eq. (1) is an ill-posed problem and a regularizer is usually utilized to confine the solution. Though recently, various algorithms including GMM [30, 31], DeSCI [14] and deep learning algorithms [9,10,16,18,21,21,24,29] have been proposed, they either need to run a long time or a large amount of training data. It has been noticed that for real data, the flexible and efficient algorithms are still based on the total variation (TV) regularization.

Therefore, in this paper, we focus on the TV regularization and solve the following problem,

$$\hat{x} = \arg\min_{x} \frac{1}{2}\|y - \boldsymbol{\Phi}x\|_2^2 + \mathrm{TV}(x), \tag{6}$$

where TV( ) denotes the TV regularizer. Since x inherently is a 3D data-cube in SCI, various TV can be used. For example, the *Anisotropic TV* (ATV) and the *Isotropic TV* (ITV) and moreover the TV can be imposed on each 2D frame of the video or on the entire 3D cube.

For the ease of notation, in the following, we first define the operators:

$$\mathcal{D}_h x_k = \mathbf{X}_k \mathbf{D}_h\,, \quad \mathcal{D}_v x_k = \mathbf{D}_v \mathbf{X}_k, \tag{7}$$

where $\{\mathbf{D}_h \in \mathbb{R}^{(n_y-1)\times n_y}, \mathbf{D}_v \in \mathbb{R}^{(n_x-1)\times n_x}\}$ as the gradient operator to perform differentiation on the desired frame horizontally and vertically, respectively.

2.1   Different TV Formulations

In the literature, different TVs can thus be summarized as follows:

– ATV:

$$\text{ATV}(\boldsymbol{x}) = \sum_{k=1}^{B} \left(\|\mathcal{D}_h \boldsymbol{x}_k\|_1 + \|\mathcal{D}_v \boldsymbol{x}_k\|_1 \right). \tag{8}$$

Note that the formulation of ATV2D is the same as ATV3D.

– ITV2D:

$$\text{ITV2D}(\boldsymbol{x}) = \sum_{k=1}^{B} \sqrt{\|\mathcal{D}_h \boldsymbol{x}_k\|_2^2 + \|\mathcal{D}_v \boldsymbol{x}_k\|_2^2}. \tag{9}$$

– ITV3D:

$$\text{ITV3D}(\boldsymbol{x}) = \sqrt{\sum_{k=1}^{B} \left(\|\mathcal{D}_h \boldsymbol{x}_k\|_2^2 + \|\mathcal{D}_v \boldsymbol{x}_k\|_2^2 \right)}. \tag{10}$$

We thus have the following problems to solve the SCI reconstruction using various TVs:

1) ATV:

$$\hat{\boldsymbol{x}} = \arg\min_{\boldsymbol{x}} \frac{1}{2} \|\boldsymbol{y} - \boldsymbol{\Phi}\boldsymbol{x}\|_2^2 + \lambda \sum_{k=1}^{B} \text{ATV2D}(\boldsymbol{x}_k). \tag{11}$$

2) ITV2D:

$$\hat{\boldsymbol{x}} = \arg\min_{\boldsymbol{x}} \frac{1}{2} \|\boldsymbol{y} - \boldsymbol{\Phi}\boldsymbol{x}\|_2^2 + \lambda \sum_{k=1}^{B} \text{ITV2D}(\boldsymbol{x}_k). \tag{12}$$

3) ITV3D:

$$\hat{\boldsymbol{x}} = \arg\min_{\boldsymbol{x}} \frac{1}{2} \|\boldsymbol{y} - \boldsymbol{\Phi}\boldsymbol{x}\|_2^2 + \lambda \text{ITV3D}(\boldsymbol{x}). \tag{13}$$

2.2   Different Plug-and-Play Solvers

It has been demonstrated that Plug-and-Play [8] (PnP) algorithms can provide a flexible solution for SCI problems [36]. The previous section have presented different TV norms and here we present different popular solvers (we are not seeking for a thorough survey here) in the literature. The SCI reconstruction problem in Eq. (11)–Eq. (13) can be solved using different frameworks.

– FISTA [2]: It consists the following steps

$$\boldsymbol{z}^{(t)} = \boldsymbol{\theta}^{(t)} + \frac{1}{L(f)} \boldsymbol{\Phi} \left(\boldsymbol{y} - \boldsymbol{\Phi}\boldsymbol{\theta}^{(t)} \right), \tag{14}$$

$$\boldsymbol{x}^{(t)} = \text{TVdenoise}(\boldsymbol{z}^{(t)}), \tag{15}$$

$$\tau^{(t+1)} = \frac{1 + \sqrt{1 + 4(\tau^{(t)})^2}}{2}, \tag{16}$$

$$\boldsymbol{\theta}^{(t+1)} = \boldsymbol{x}^{(t)} + \frac{\tau^{(t)} - 1}{\tau^{(t+1)}} \left(\boldsymbol{x}^{(t+1)} - \boldsymbol{x}^{(t)} \right), \tag{17}$$

where $\tau^{(1)} = 1$ is introduced in FISTA and various TV norms in Sect. 2.1 (with solutions in Sect. 2.3) can be used. $f(\boldsymbol{x}) = \frac{1}{2}\|\boldsymbol{y} - \boldsymbol{\Phi}\boldsymbol{x}\|_2^2$ is continuously differentiable with Lipschitz continuous gradient $L(f)$ (derived elsewhere).

- TwIST [3]: It consists the following steps

$$z^{(t)} = x^{(t)} + \boldsymbol{\Phi}(y - \boldsymbol{\Phi}x^{(t)}), \tag{18}$$

$$\boldsymbol{\theta}^{(t)} = \text{TVdenoise}(z^{(t)}), \tag{19}$$

$$x^{(t+1)} = (1 - \alpha)x^{(t-1)} + (\alpha - \beta)x^{(t)} + \beta\boldsymbol{\theta}^{(t)}, \tag{20}$$

where $\{\alpha, \beta\}$ are TwIST parameters and can be determined by the eigenvalues of $\boldsymbol{\Phi}\boldsymbol{\Phi}$.

- GAP [13]: It consists the following steps:

$$x^{(t+1)} = \boldsymbol{\theta}^{(t)} + \boldsymbol{\Phi}(\boldsymbol{\Phi}\boldsymbol{\Phi})^{-1}(y - \boldsymbol{\Phi}\boldsymbol{\theta}^{(t)}) \tag{21}$$

$$\boldsymbol{\theta}^{(t+1)} = \text{TVdenoise}(x^{(t+1)}). \tag{22}$$

- ADMM [4]: We derive the ADMM framework by formulating the problem as

$$\hat{x} = \underset{x}{\operatorname{argmin}} \frac{1}{2}\|y - \boldsymbol{\Phi}x\|_2^2 + \lambda\text{TV}(\boldsymbol{\theta}), \quad \text{s.t. } \boldsymbol{\theta} = x. \tag{23}$$

This can be solved by the following sub-problems:

$$x^{(t+1)} = \underset{x}{\operatorname{argmin}} \frac{1}{2}\|y - \boldsymbol{\Phi}x\|_2^2 + \frac{\rho}{2}\|x - \boldsymbol{\theta}^{(t)} + u^{(t)}\|_2^2, \tag{24}$$

$$\boldsymbol{\theta}^{(t+1)} = \text{TVdenoise}(u^{(t)} + x^{(t+1)}), \tag{25}$$

$$u^{(t+1)} = u^{(t)} + x^{(t+1)} - \boldsymbol{\theta}^{(t+1)}. \tag{26}$$

As derived in [32], since in SCI, $\boldsymbol{\Phi}\boldsymbol{\Phi}$ is a diagonal matrix, Eq. (24) can be solved element-wise and thus very efficiently and when $\rho = 0$, it will degrade to GAP.

Note that in each framework, there is a "TVdenoise" step and various TV priors in previous subsection can be used, thus leading to the Plug-and-Play framework. In the following, we present various solutions of different "TVdenoise".

2.3 Solutions of TV Denoising

We now present different solvers for various TV denoising.

- ATV:
    - Clip: The iterative clipping algorithm [25] was employed in GAP-TV [32]. It was derived by the min-max property and the majorization-minimization procedure and inspired by [1,7,38]. The full algorithm is listed in Algorithm 1. One key step is to introduce variables $\{w_h, w_v\}$, with $\{|w_h| \leq 1, |w_v| \leq 1\}$.
    - Chambolle: in [6,7] (denoted as **ATV-Cham**).

Algorithm 1. GAP-ATV-Clip/Cham/FGP for SCI

Require: Input measurements $\boldsymbol{y}$, sensing matrix $\boldsymbol{\Phi}$.
  Initialize $\boldsymbol{\theta}^{(0)} = \boldsymbol{\Phi}\boldsymbol{y} = \boldsymbol{v}^{(0)}, \boldsymbol{u}^{(0)} = \boldsymbol{0}, \boldsymbol{w}_h^{(0)} = \boldsymbol{w}_v^{(0)} = \boldsymbol{0}, \rho, \lambda$, MaxIter and In-Iter (for TV denoising).
  for $t = 0$ **to** MaxIter **do**
    $\boldsymbol{x}^{(t+1)} = \boldsymbol{\theta}^{(t)} + \boldsymbol{\Phi}(\boldsymbol{\Phi}\boldsymbol{\Phi})^{-1}(\boldsymbol{y} - \boldsymbol{\Phi}\boldsymbol{\theta}^{(t)})$.
    Select one algorithm from the following boxes.

% ATV-Clip
for $s = 0$ **to** In-Iter **do**
  $\boldsymbol{\theta}_h^{(s+1)} = \boldsymbol{x}^{(t+1)} - \mathcal{D}_h \boldsymbol{w}_h^{(s)}, \quad \boldsymbol{\theta}_v^{(s+1)} = \boldsymbol{x}^{(t+1)} - \mathcal{D}_v \boldsymbol{w}_v^{(s)},$
  $\boldsymbol{w}_h^{(s+1)} = \text{clip}\left(\boldsymbol{w}_h^{(s)} + \frac{1}{\alpha}\mathcal{D}_h \boldsymbol{\theta}_h^{(s+1)}, 2\lambda\right),$
  $\boldsymbol{w}_v^{(s+1)} = \text{clip}\left(\boldsymbol{w}_v^{(s)} + \frac{1}{\alpha}\mathcal{D}_v \boldsymbol{\theta}_v^{(s+1)}, 2\lambda\right).$
end for
$\boldsymbol{\theta}^{(t+1)} = \boldsymbol{\theta}_h + \boldsymbol{\theta}_v - \boldsymbol{x}^{(t+1)}.$

% ATV-Cham
Initialize $\delta t = 1/8, \boldsymbol{p}_d = 0$.
for $s = 0$ **to** In-Iter **do**
  $\boldsymbol{z}^{(s+1)} = \boldsymbol{p}_d^{(s)} - \frac{\boldsymbol{x}^{(t+1)}}{\lambda},$
  $\boldsymbol{z}_h^{(s+1)} = \mathcal{D}_h \boldsymbol{z}^{(s+1)},$
  $\boldsymbol{z}_v^{(s+1)} = \mathcal{D}_v \boldsymbol{z}^{(s+1)},$
  $\boldsymbol{w}_h^{(s+1)} = \frac{\boldsymbol{w}_h^{(s)} + \delta t \boldsymbol{z}_h^{(s+1)}}{\max(1, |\boldsymbol{w}_h^{(s)} + \delta t \boldsymbol{z}_h^{(s+1)}|)},$
  $\boldsymbol{w}_v^{(s+1)} = \frac{\boldsymbol{w}_v^{(s)} + \delta t \boldsymbol{z}_v^{(s+1)}}{\max(1, |\boldsymbol{w}_v^{(s)} + \delta t \boldsymbol{z}_v^{(s+1)}|)},$
  $\boldsymbol{p}_d^{(s+1)} = \mathcal{D}_h \boldsymbol{w}_h^{(s+1)} + \mathcal{D}_v \boldsymbol{w}_v^{(s+1)}.$
end for
$\boldsymbol{\theta}^{(t+1)} = \boldsymbol{x}^{(t+1)} - \lambda \boldsymbol{p}_d^{(s+1)}.$

% ATV-FGP
Initialize $\nu^{(0)}$.
for $s = 0$ **to** In-Iter **do**
  $\boldsymbol{\theta}^{(s+1)} = \boldsymbol{x}^{(t+1)} - \lambda(\mathcal{D}_h \boldsymbol{w}_h^{(s)} + \mathcal{D}_v \boldsymbol{w}_v^{(s)}),$
  $\boldsymbol{z}_h^{(s+1)} = \mathcal{D}_h \boldsymbol{\theta}^{(s+1)}, \quad \boldsymbol{z}_v^{(s+1)} = \mathcal{D}_v \boldsymbol{\theta}^{(s+1)},$
  $\boldsymbol{p}_h^{(s+1)} = \frac{\boldsymbol{w}_h^{(s)} + \frac{1}{8\lambda}\boldsymbol{z}_h^{(s+1)}}{\max(1, |\boldsymbol{w}_h^{(s)} + \frac{1}{8\lambda}\boldsymbol{z}_h^{(s+1)}|)},$
  $\boldsymbol{p}_v^{(s+1)} = \frac{\boldsymbol{w}_v^{(s)} + \frac{1}{8\lambda}\boldsymbol{z}_v^{(s+1)}}{\max(1, |\boldsymbol{w}_v^{(s)} + \frac{1}{8\lambda}\boldsymbol{z}_v^{(s+1)}|)},$
  $\nu^{(s+1)} = \frac{1 + \sqrt{1 + 4(\nu^{(s)})^2}}{2},$
  $\boldsymbol{w}_h^{(s+1)} = \boldsymbol{p}_h^{(s+1)} + \frac{\nu^{(s)} - 1}{\nu^{(s+1)}}(\boldsymbol{p}_h^{(s+1)} - \boldsymbol{p}_h^{(s)}),$
  $\boldsymbol{w}_v^{(s+1)} = \boldsymbol{p}_v^{(s+1)} + \frac{\nu^{(s)} - 1}{\nu^{(s+1)}}(\boldsymbol{p}_v^{(s+1)} - \boldsymbol{p}_v^{(s)}).$
end for
$\boldsymbol{\theta}^{(t+1)} = \boldsymbol{\theta}^{(s+1)}.$

---

end for
Output $\boldsymbol{x}$.

- FGP: (fast gradient projection) proposed in [1] (denoted as **ATV-FGP**) with solutions summarized in Algorithm 1. Note we have used $\max(1, |\boldsymbol{w}_h^{(s)} + \delta t \boldsymbol{z}_h^{(s+1)}|)$ in the denominator of the update pf $\boldsymbol{w}_h$ and similar for $\boldsymbol{w}$, which is recommended in [7]. This can also be changed to $1 + \delta t |\boldsymbol{z}_h^{(s+1)}|$ as originally derived in [6]. This also holds true for the following derivations on ITV2D and ITV3D.
- ITV2D:
  - ITV2D-Cham: Following ATV-Cham, Let

$$\tilde{\boldsymbol{w}}_h^{(s+1)} = \boldsymbol{w}_h^{(s)} + \delta t \boldsymbol{z}_h^{(s+1)}, \tag{27}$$

$$\tilde{\boldsymbol{w}}_v^{(s+1)} = \boldsymbol{w}_v^{(s)} + \delta t \boldsymbol{z}_v^{(s+1)}. \tag{28}$$

Recall that $\tilde{\boldsymbol{w}}_h^{(s+1)}$ can be a 3D video and we reshape it to $\tilde{\mathbf{W}}_h \in \mathbb{R}^{n_x \times n_y \times B}$ by ignoring the boundary effects (and also dropping the index $(s+1)$), and similar to $\tilde{\mathbf{W}}_v$. We further let $[\tilde{\mathbf{W}}_h]_{i,j,k}$ denote the (i,j)-th pixel or voxel in k-th frame and similar for $[\tilde{\mathbf{W}}_v]_{i,j,k}$. We now have the update equations for $[\mathbf{W}_h]_{i,j,k}$ and $[\mathbf{W}_v]_{i,j,k}$, which correspond to $\boldsymbol{w}_h$ and $\boldsymbol{w}_v$, respectively.

$$[\mathbf{W}_h]_{i,j,k} = \frac{[\tilde{\mathbf{W}}_h]_{i,j,k}}{\max\left(1, \sqrt{[\tilde{\mathbf{W}}_h]_{i,j,k}^2 + [\tilde{\mathbf{W}}_v]_{i,j,k}^2}\right)}, \tag{29}$$

$$[\mathbf{W}_v]_{i,j,k} = \frac{[\tilde{\mathbf{W}}_v]_{i,j,k}}{\max\left(1, \sqrt{[\tilde{\mathbf{W}}_h]_{i,j,k}^2 + [\tilde{\mathbf{W}}_v]_{i,j,k}^2}\right)}. \tag{30}$$

- ITV2D-FGP: Similar to ITV2D-Cham, we only need to change the update equations of $\boldsymbol{p}_h$ and $\boldsymbol{p}_v$ in ATV-FGP.

3) ITV3D: The ITV3D denosing step can be solved by the algorithm proposed in [5] (denoted as **ITV3D-VTV**), or the FGP (fast gradient projection) proposed in [1] (denoted as **ITV3D-FGP**). Regarding the solution, the difference lies in Eqs. (29) and (30) and we now have

$$[\mathbf{W}_h]_{i,j,k} = \frac{[\tilde{\mathbf{W}}_h]_{i,j,k}}{\max\left(1, \sqrt{\sum_{k=1}^B \left([\tilde{\mathbf{W}}_h]_{i,j,k}^2 + [\tilde{\mathbf{W}}_v]_{i,j,k}^2\right)}\right)}, \tag{31}$$

$$[\mathbf{W}_v]_{i,j,k} = \frac{[\tilde{\mathbf{W}}_v]_{i,j,k}}{\max\left(1, \sqrt{\sum_{k=1}^B \left([\tilde{\mathbf{W}}_h]_{i,j,k}^2 + [\tilde{\mathbf{W}}_v]_{i,j,k}^2\right)}\right)}. \tag{32}$$

Similar changes will happen for $\boldsymbol{p}_h$ and $\boldsymbol{p}_v$ for ITV3D-FGP.

Algorithm 1 gives the full algorithm of GAP with ATV using different denoising algorithms. It is easy to replace GAP with ADMM/TwIST/FISTA and replace ATV with ITV. We thus achieve the various compositions of frameworks for SCI reconstruction with different TV denoising algorithms summarized in Table 1.

3   Experimental Results

Now, we apply various TV algorithms and projection frameworks to video SCI on both simulation and real data.

Table 1. Different frameworks and various TV denoising algorithms to solve SCI. PSNR results of 4 datasets used in [14], in each cell, top-left: `Kobe`, top-right: `Traffic`, middle-left: `Runner`, middle-right: `Drop`, bottom: average. The bold number denotes the highest PSNR (based on the 0.001 precision) for each projection algorithm per video dataset. The red number denotes the highest PSNR for each dataset across all the algorithms. *Italian* denotes the highest average PSNR for each row and the *blue Italian* one is the highest average PSNR across all algorithms.

	ATV			ITV2D		ITV3D	
	Clip	Cham	FGP	Cham	FGP	Cham	FGP
FISTA	22.49, 18.80 25.61, 29.40 24.07	22.75, 18.80 25.85, 29.62 24.25	24.50, 19.97 27.82, 32.13 26.11	23.11, 19.14 26.50, 30.33 24.77	**24.50**, 19.97 27.82, 32.13 26.11	23.29, 19.29 26.47, 30.85 24.97	24.50, 20.06 **27.84, 32.14** *26.13*
TwIST	25.38, 20.44 28.12, 32.79 26.68	25.47, 20.34 28.24, 32.72 26.69	25.83, 20.57 **28.89, 33.56** 27.21	25.50, 20.37 28.62, 32.97 26.86	25.83, 20.56 28.89, 33.56 27.21	24.98, 20.39 28.02, 31.65 26.26	25.78, 20.75 28.86, 33.53 *27.23*
GAP	26.71, 20.75 28.81, 33.97 *27.56*	26.72, 20.64 28.91, 33.83 27.53	26.17, 20.67 29.13, 33.91 27.47	26.28, 20.53 29.13, 33.74 27.42	26.17, 20.65 29.12, 33.91 27.46	25.38, 20.55 28.33, 32.07 26.58	26.10, 20.85 29.08, 33.87 27.48
ADMM	25.88, 20.42 28.61, 33.39 27.08	26.05, 20.52 28.58, 33.27 27.10	26.00, 20.62 **29.01, 33.74** 27.34	25.87, 20.44 28.87, 33.36 27.14	25.99, 20.61 29.01, 33.74 27.34	25.18, 20.47 28.18, 31.94 26.44	25.94, **20.80** 28.98, 33.71 *27.36*

3.1 Simulation

We used four datasets, *i.e.*, `Kobe, Traffic, Runner, Drop` in [14], where $B = 8$ video frames are compressed into a single measurement and the same sensing matrix is used. The results are summarized in Table 1. It can be observed that, in general, the ITV3D algorithm works well in all scenarios. On average, the best result is obtained by GAP-ATV-Clip, though the gains over other approaches are very limited. For each dataset, GAP provides the best result. Due to space limit, we did not show the reconstructed video frames here. We also notice that only (In-Iter) 2 iterations can give good results of FPG while other TV solvers need 5 iterations.

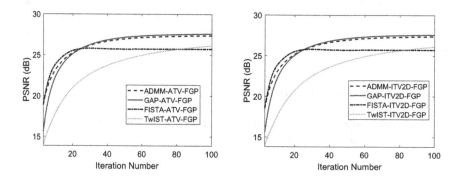

Fig. 2. PSNR vs. Iteration Number for different algorithms.

Another metric to compare different algorithms is the speed. As a good candidate for each row, we select ATV-FGP and ITV2D-FGP as the TV denoising algorithm and the first measurement in Drop is employed to show the reconstruction PSNR vs. iteration number in Fig. 2. It can be observed that TwIST always converges slowest and it usually needs 500 iterations to get a good result. FISTA converges fastest but cannot lead to good results while GAP and ADMM converge similarly to FISTA and GAP leads to the best results in about 60 iterations.

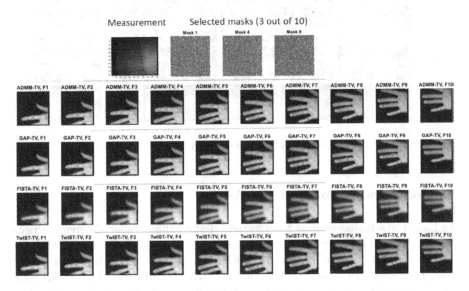

Fig. 3. Real data results. A hand is moving in front of a SCI camera and 10 frames are reconstructed from a snapshot measurement (top-left). 3 masks out of 10 are shown in the first row.

3.2 Real Data

We now test different methods on the real data captured by our video SCI camera at https://github.com/mq0829/DL-CACTI. In total, $B = 10$ frames are modulated and compressed to a snapshot measurement (Fig. 3 top-left) with a spatial resolution of 512×512. A hand is moving fast in front of the camera being a high-speed scene.

ITV3D-FGP is used for the TV denoising and we run the algorithms for 150 iterations, which takes about 3 min on an Intel i7 CPU laptop with 32G memory. It can be seen that the all algorithms can reconstruction the motion clearly from the smashed (blurry) single measurement. FISTA results suffer from blurry and the other 3 results look similar while GAP seems providing the best one.

We again test the speed of different algorithms but this time by visualizing the results for every 10 iterations in Fig. 4. It can be seen that FISTA can provide decent results in 40 iterations. However, it does not get improved with more iterations. This is similar to the simulation results. ADMM is the second efficient one to give good results in 50 iterations and they are getting better with more iterations. TwIST is slowest and it needs over 100 iterations to get good results.

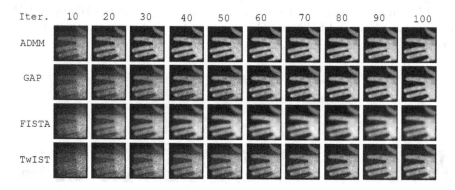

Fig. 4. Results by plotting Frame 6 every 10 iterations.

4   Conclusions and Future Work

We have investigated diverse total variation algorithms under different projection frameworks for video snapshot compressive imaging. GAP and ADMM are recommended for decent results while FISTA is a choice with limited running time. Regrading the total variation solver, FGP is recommended for different cases because it is faster. We notice that using these algorithms to initialize complicated algorithms like DeSCI can achieve better results as shown in [36].

Another interesting direction is to use this TV based algorithm to initialize the untrained neural network to improve the results but without any training data [23]. This is an elegant way to combine optimization based methods with deep learning based algorithms.

Regarding the future work, we will derive the convergence results of these algorithms and develop integration frameworks of TV and deep learning [37].

References

1. Beck, A., Teboulle, M.: Fast gradient-based algorithms for constrained total variation image denoising and deblurring problems. IEEE Trans. Image Process. **18**(11), 2419–2434 (2009)
2. Beck, A., Teboulle, M.: A fast iterative shrinkage-thresholding algorithm for linear inverse problems. SIAM J. Imaging Sci. **2**(1), 183–202 (2009)
3. Bioucas-Dias, J., Figueiredo, M.: A new TwIST: two-step iterative shrinkage/thresholding algorithms for image restoration. IEEE Trans. Image Process. **16**(12), 2992–3004 (2007)

4. Boyd, S., Parikh, N., Chu, E., Peleato, B., Eckstein, J.: Distributed optimization and statistical learning via the alternating direction method of multipliers. Found. Trends Mach. Learn. **3**(1), 1–122 (2011)

5. Bresson, X., Chan, T.F.: Fast dual minimization of the vectorial total variation norm and applications to color image processing. Inverse Probl. Imaging **2**, 455 (2008)

6. Chambolle, A.: An algorithm for total variation minimization and applications. J. Math. Imaging Vis. **20**(1–2), 89–97 (2004)

7. Chambolle, A.: Total variation minimization and a class of binary MRF models. In: Rangarajan, A., Vemuri, B., Yuille, A.L. (eds.) EMMCVPR 2005. LNCS, vol. 3757, pp. 136–152. Springer, Heidelberg (2005). https://doi.org/10.1007/11585978_10

8. Chan, S.H., Wang, X., Elgendy, O.A.: Plug-and-play ADMM for image restoration: fixed-point convergence and applications. IEEE Trans. Comput. Imaging **3**, 84–98 (2017)

9. Cheng, Z., et al.: Memory-efficient network for large-scale video compressive sensing. In: IEEE/CVF Conference on Computer Vision and Pattern Recognition (CVPR), June 2021

10. Cheng, Z., et al.: BIRNAT: bidirectional recurrent neural networks with adversarial training for video snapshot compressive imaging. In: Vedaldi, A., Bischof, H., Brox, T., Frahm, J.-M. (eds.) ECCV 2020. LNCS, vol. 12369, pp. 258–275. Springer, Cham (2020). https://doi.org/10.1007/978-3-030-58586-0_16

11. Donoho, D.L.: Compressed sensing. IEEE Trans. Inf. Theory **52**(4), 1289–1306 (2006)

12. Jalali, S., Yuan, X.: Snapshot compressed sensing: performance bounds and algorithms. IEEE Trans. Inf. Theory **65**(12), 8005–8024 (2019)

13. Liao, X., Li, H., Carin, L.: Generalized alternating projection for weighted-$\ell_{2,1}$ minimization with applications to model-based compressive sensing. SIAM J. Imaging Sci. **7**(2), 797–823 (2014)

14. Liu, Y., Yuan, X., Suo, J., Brady, D., Dai, Q.: Rank minimization for snapshot compressive imaging. IEEE Trans. Pattern Anal. Mach. Intell. **41**(12), 2990–3006 (2019)

15. Llull, P., et al.: Coded aperture compressive temporal imaging. Opt. Express **21**(9), 10526–10545 (2013)

16. Ma, J., Liu, X., Shou, Z., Yuan, X.: Deep tensor ADMM-Net for snapshot compressive imaging. In: IEEE/CVF Conference on Computer Vision (ICCV) (2019)

17. Ma, X., Yuan, X., Fu, C., Arce, G.R.: Led-based compressive spectral-temporal imaging. Opt. Express **29**(7), 10698–10715 (2021)

18. Meng, Z., Jalali, S., Yuan, X.: Gap-net for snapshot compressive imaging. arXiv:2012:08364 (2020)

19. Meng, Z., Ma, J., Yuan, X.: End-to-end low cost compressive spectral imaging with spatial-spectral self-attention. In: Vedaldi, A., Bischof, H., Brox, T., Frahm, J.-M. (eds.) ECCV 2020. LNCS, vol. 12368, pp. 187–204. Springer, Cham (2020). https://doi.org/10.1007/978-3-030-58592-1_12

20. Meng, Z., Qiao, M., Ma, J., Yu, Z., Xu, K., Yuan, X.: Snapshot multispectral endomicroscopy. Opt. Lett. **45**(14), 3897–3900 (2020)

21. Miao, X., Yuan, X., Pu, Y., Athitsos, V.: λ-Net: reconstruct hyperspectral images from a snapshot measurement. In: IEEE/CVF Conference on Computer Vision (ICCV) (2019)

22. Qiao, M., Liu, X., Yuan, X.: Snapshot spatial-temporal compressive imaging. Opt. Lett. **45**(7), 1659–1662 (2020)

23. Qiao, M., Liu, X., Yuan, X.: Snapshot temporal compressive microscopy using an iterative algorithm with untrained neural networks. Opt. Lett. **46**(8), 1888–1891 (2021)
24. Qiao, M., Meng, Z., Ma, J., Yuan, X.: Deep learning for video compressive sensing. APL Photonics **5**(3), 030801 (2020)
25. Selesnick, I., Bayram, I.: Total variation filtering. Connexions (2009)
26. Sun, Y., Yuan, X., Pang, S.: Compressive high-speed stereo imaging. Opt. Express **25**(15), 18182–18190 (2017)
27. Sun, Y., Yuan, X., Pang, S.: High-speed compressive range imaging based on active illumination. Opt. Express **24**(20), 22836–22846 (2016)
28. Wagadarikar, A., Pitsianis, N., Sun, X., Brady, D.: Video rate spectral imaging using a coded aperture snapshot spectral imager. Opt. Express **17**(8), 6368–6388 (2009)
29. Wang, Z., Zhang, H., Cheng, Z., Chen, B., Yuan, X.: MetaSCI: scalable and adaptive reconstruction for video compressive sensing. In: IEEE/CVF Conference on Computer Vision and Pattern Recognition (CVPR), June 2021
30. Yang, J., et al.: Compressive sensing by learning a Gaussian mixture model from measurements. IEEE Trans. Image Process. **24**(1), 106–119 (2015)
31. Yang, J., et al.: Video compressive sensing using Gaussian mixture models. IEEE Trans. Image Process. **23**(11), 4863–4878 (2014)
32. Yuan, X.: Generalized alternating projection based total variation minimization for compressive sensing. In: 2016 IEEE International Conference on Image Processing (ICIP), pp. 2539–2543, September 2016
33. Yuan, X., Brady, D.J., Katsaggelos, A.K.: Snapshot compressive imaging: theory, algorithms, and applications. IEEE Sig. Process. Mag. **38**(2), 65–88 (2021)
34. Yuan, X., et al.: Low-cost compressive sensing for color video and depth. In: IEEE Conference on Computer Vision and Pattern Recognition (CVPR) (2014)
35. Yuan, X., Tsai, T.H., Zhu, R., Llull, P., Brady, D.J., Carin, L.: Compressive hyperspectral imaging with side information. IEEE J. Sel. Top. Sig. Process. **9**(6), 964–976 (2015)
36. Yuan, X., Liu, Y., Suo, J., Dai, Q.: Plug-and-Play algorithms for large-scale snapshot compressive imaging. In: The IEEE/CVF Conference on Computer Vision and Pattern Recognition (CVPR), June 2020
37. Yuan, X., Yang Liu, J.S., Durand, F., Dai, Q.: Plug-and-Play algorithms for video snapshot compressive imaging. arXiv: 2101.04822, January 2021
38. Zhu, M., Wright, S.J., Chan, T.F.: Duality-based algorithms for total-variation-regularized image restoration. Comput. Optim. Appl. **47**(3), 377–400 (2010). https://doi.org/10.1007/s10589-008-9225-2

EEG Signals Classification in Time-Frequency Images by Fusing Rotation-Invariant Local Binary Pattern and Gray Level Co-occurrence Matrix Features

Zhongyi Hu[1]($\boxtimes$), Zhenzhen Luo[1], Shan Jin[2], and Zuoyong Li[3]

[1] College of Computer and Artificial Intelligence, Intelligent Information Systems Institute, Wenzhou University, Wenzhou, China
[2] Zhejiang Topcheer Information Technology Co., Ltd, Zhejiang, China
[3] Fujian Provincial Key Laboratory of Information Processing and Intelligent Control, College of Computer and Control Engineering, Minjiang University, Fuzhou, China

Abstract. Automatic epilepsy diagnosis system based on EEG signals is critical in the classification of epilepsy. This disease classification through doctors' visual observation of transient EEG signals is more art than science. This paper proposes a novel EEG signals classification method based on time-frequency images by fusing rotation-invariant local binary pattern and gray level co-occurrence matrix features. Specifically , a continuous wavelet transform is applied to perform wavelet decomposition of mutated EEG signals and obtain their time-frequency images. Then, the binary particle swarm optimization algorithm is used to eliminate redundant features in feature selection and optimize the hyperparameters of SVM. The proposed method was verified by its comparison with other available cutting-edge classification methods. The proposed EEG signals classification framework achieved a better classification effect, which will help expert clinicians and neuroscientists to make more accurate and rapid epilepsy diagnosis.

Keywords: EEG signals · Epilepsy classification · Local binary pattern (LBP) · Gray level co-occurrence matrix (GLCM) · Binary particle swarm optimization algorithm (BPSO)

This work was supported by the Key Project of Zhejiang Provincial Natural Science Foundation under Grant LD21F020001, Grant LSZ19F020001, and the National Natural Science Foundation of China under Grant U1809209, Grant 61702376, Grant 61972187, Grant 61772254, and the Major Project of Wenzhou Natural Science Foundation under Grant ZY2019020, and Natural Science Foundation of Fujian Province under Grant 2020J02024, Grant 2019J01756, and Fuzhou Science and Technology Project under Grant 2020-RC-186. We acknowledge the efforts and constructive comments of respected editors and anonymous reviewers.

L. Fang et al. (Eds.): CICAI 2021, LNAI 13069, pp. 347–358, 2021.
https://doi.org/10.1007/978-3-030-93046-2_30

1   Introduction

Epilepsy is a neurological disorder with impaired brain function caused by abnormal discharge of brain neurons [1]. It is suffered by over 50 million people all over the world, which makes is the second-largest neurological disorder after cerebrovascular disease. Due to the repetitive and non-stationary nature of epilepsy during the disease onset, an accurate diagnosis of the epilepsy area by visual observation, labeling, and analyzing of electroencephalographic (EEG) signals is quite problematic and time-consuming [2]. This makes topical the elaboration and large-scale implementation of an artificial intelligence technology to solve the epilepsy EEG classification problem and develop an automatic epilepsy diagnosis system [3, 4].

An electroencephalography is an important tool for the diagnosis of epilepsy. Since EEG signals of patients with epilepsy have such specific features as sharp waves, spikes, and spike-and-wave complexes, one can identify epilepsy by analyzing amplitude and frequency. There are several common signal processing methods, including Fourier Transform (FT), Short-time Fourier Transform (STFT), and Wavelet Transform (WT). Among them, STFT is more suitable than TF for processing non-stationary EEG signals. However, the fixed window size of STFT fails to simultaneously provide high time resolution and high frequency resolution. In view of the above reasons, WT method is used to obtain high resolution in time domain and frequency domain [5]. Time-frequency images (TFs) have rich spatial information, and it is very important to extract and select discriminant features effectively. For example, Li et al. [6] proposed a gray level co-occurrence matrix (GLCM) descriptor for extracting time-frequency features. Furthermore, several authors extracted time-frequency features based on weighted permutation entropy, fuzzy approximate entropy, and energy spectrum entropy [7–11]. The feature selection methods can be classified into the following three types (Filter, Wrapper, and Embedded ones), including the binary particle swarm optimization (BPSO), recursive feature elimination (RFE), principal component analysis (PCA), and ReliefF [6, 12–15].

In this paper, the CWT method is firstly used to get five frequency parts and corresponding time-frequency image from the mutated signals. Then, LBP and GLCM descriptors are applied to extract texture features from the local and global perspectives, respectively. Considering that too high dimensions are not conducive to epilepsy classification, BPSO and RFE feature selection algorithms are combined to find the effective subset. BPSO can search for a local optimal solution in a certain range, and then find the optimal global solution after multiple iterations. By this method, the optimal parameters of the SVM are found. Finally, the optimal feature set is incorporated into a support vector machine based on radial basis functions (SVM-RBF) for classification. In this paper, four classification performance evaluation indexes of accuracy (ACC), sensitivity (SEN), specificity (SPE), and the area under the curve (AUC) are used to compare and analyze the six epilepsy classification problems. The acceptable accuracy of all six classification problems are achieved: 100% for four cases and 99.44% and 99.59% for the remaining two cases. This shows that the proposed method has certain advantages in the epilepsy classification over other available methods and provides promising classification results.

The rest of this paper is organized as follows. Section 2 describes the dataset used in the experiment. In Sect. 3, the proposed method is introduced, including CWT, the feature fusion of LBP and GLCM descriptor, feature selection and SVM parameters optimization via BPSO-RFE-SVM. Sections 4 and 5 present experiment results and discussion, respectively. Finally, the findings of this paper are summarized in Sect. 6.

2   Database Description

The epilepsy dataset used in the experiment was acquired from the EEG database of the Department of Epileptology of the University of Bonn, Germany, which is described in [16] and is available online publicly. The EEG dataset is composed of five subsets, which are Z, O, N, F, and S, respectively. Subsets Z and O were collected from five healthy people when their eyes were open and closed, respectively. Subsets N, F, and S were collected from five epilepsy patients with no other disease history. Among them, Subsets N and F were recorded during the seizure-free interval period from epilepsy patients. Subset S comprised the cerebral EEG dataset of the epilepsy area from five epilepsy patients during seizures. According to the international standard electrode placement of the 10–20 system, each subset contains 100 single-channel data with sampling time of 23.6s, and sampling frequency of 173.61 Hz.

3   Methodology

The aim of this study is to achieve high-precision epilepsy classification of EEG signals through time-frequency images obtained by CWT. In order to accomplish the classification task, firstly, feature extraction is performed on TFs by fusing LBP and GLCM descriptors. Then, the effective feature subset is first extracted using the RFE algorithm to reduce the computational complexity, and then the BPSO-SVM-RBF algorithm is applied to provide a simultaneous feature subset optimization and optimization of SVM parameters. Finally, the optimized SVM classifier is used to achieve the EEG classification in healthy people and patients with epilepsy. The framework of the proposed method is depicted in Fig. 1.

3.1   Time-Frequency Analysis Using the CWT Method

The continuous wavelet transform (CWT) is applicable for the non-stationary and non-periodic transformation of mutant signals, therefore, it is widely applied to EEG signals classification.

The mathematical definition of CWT for EEG signal $f(t)$ is as follows:

$$CWT(s, \tau) = < f(t), \psi_{s,\tau}(t) > = \frac{1}{\sqrt{s}} \int_{-\infty}^{+\infty} f(t)\psi^*(\frac{t - \tau}{s})dt \qquad (1)$$

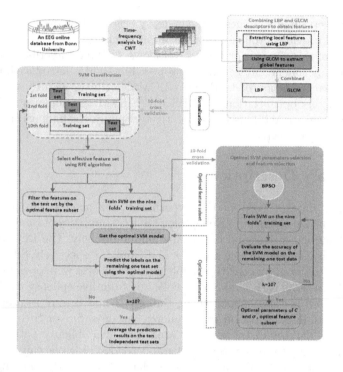

Fig. 1. The entire framework of the proposed approach required for the experiment

where $\psi_{s,\tau}(t)$ is mother wave; s is scale, which can change the scaling transformation of the wavelet function; τ is as a translation variable, which corresponds to the time variable t and controls the wavelet function translation transformation.

In the time-frequency analysis using CWT, the complex Morlet wavelet basis is the most commonly used as wavelet basis function. It not only has a symmetry but also achieves a good resolution in the time and frequency domains [17]. Given this, a complex Morlet wavelet basis is used to conduct a time-frequency analysis of EEG signals. Its expression is as follows:

$$\psi_{s,\tau}(t) = \frac{1}{\sqrt{\pi f_b}} exp(2\pi i f_c t - t^2/f_b) \qquad (2)$$

Here, settings $f_b = 25$ and $f_c = 1$ are applied.

3.2 Feature Extraction Based on LBP and GLCM Descriptors

Local Binary Pattern Descriptor. The local binary pattern (LBP) is an algorithm proposed by Ojala et al. to describe image texture features [18,19]. The application range of image texture extraction based on the LBP algorithm includes natural, medical, and time-frequency images of EEG signals.

Set the center pixel of the image as the threshold and compare it with the value of its neighborhood. According to formula (2), calculate and adopt the obtained value as feature value of the image. The calculation formula is:

$$LBP_{r,p} = \sum_{i=0}^{P-1} s(g_i - g_c)2^i, \; s(x) = \begin{cases} 1, & x \geqslant 0 \\ 0, & x < 0 \end{cases} \tag{3}$$

where r is the neighborhood radius, P is the total number of neighborhood points on a circle of radius r, g_i and g_c represent gray values of the image neighborhood and center pixel, respectively.

However, the basic LBP algorithm has the following drawback: the center pixel of an image changes with its rotation, so the calculated texture feature values are different. Furthermore, considering that the LBP algorithm obtains high-dimensional feature vectors. In order to reduce the feature dimension, Ojala et al. proposed uniform and non-uniform mode based on the rotation-invariant mode. The formula is defined as follows:

$$LBP_{r,p}^{riu2} = \begin{cases} \sum_{i=0}^{P-1} s(g_i - g_c), & U(LBP_{r,p}) \leqslant 2 \\ p+1, & otherwise \end{cases} \tag{4}$$

$$U(LBP_{r,p}) = |s(g_{p-1} - g_c) - s(g_0 - g_c)| + \sum_{i=0}^{P-1} |s(g_i - g_c) - s(g_{i-1} - g_c)| \tag{5}$$

where $U(LBP_{r,p})$ represents the number of conversions of two neighboring values 1 to 0 (or 0 to 1) on a circle of radius r. If $U(LBP_{r,p}) \leqslant 2$, the uniform pattern belongs to the $p+1$ class, otherwise, all non-uniform patterns belong to the one class. The feature vector dimension of the texture histogram is $p+2$.

Fusing LBP and GLCM Descriptors to Extract Features. The application of efficient and comprehensive EEG feature extraction method has a decisive effect on subsequent feature selection and classification. Because LBP can only extract local texture features, this causes the overall time-frequency texture features to be ignored, resulting in lower classification performance. Therefore, GLCM descriptors were introduced to extract global features.

The GLCM obtains the digital feature matrix of the texture by setting two variables, namely direction θ and distance d, and uses the joint probability density function between two position pixels to define GLCM. A pair of image gray values that meet the direction θ and distance d corresponds to the probability value of the sum, which is defined as:

$$P(i, j; d, \theta) = \{(x, y), (x + d_x, y + d_y)|f(x, y) = i, \\ f(x + d_x, y + d_y) = j\} \tag{6}$$

where $f(x, y) = i$ is the gray value of the pixel at the position (x, y), and $f(x + d_x, y + d_y) = j$ is the gray value of the pixel at the adjacent position $(x + d_x, y + d_y)$ when (x, y) satisfies the fixed values θ and d.

The feature vectors jointly obtained by the two methods are subjected to one-dimensional vector merging, which is defined as follows:

$$\begin{cases} X_i = (L_i, G_i) \\ L_i = (l_{i,1}, l_{i,2}, \cdots, l_{i,j}), & 1 \leqslant j \leqslant 50 \\ G_i = (g_{i,1}, g_{i,2}, \cdots, g_{i,k}), & 1 \leqslant k \leqslant 80 \end{cases} \tag{7}$$

Here j and k are dimensional subscripts of the LBP and GLCM feature parameter vectors, respectively; L_i and G_i are time-frequency feature vectors obtained via the LBP and GLCM methods, respectively, and X_i is a feature vector combining LBP and GLCM, whose dimension is 130.

3.3   Optimization of Feature Subset and SVM Parameters Based on the BPSO-RFE-SVM Algorithm

Considering the time complexity of most classification algorithms and high dimensionality of data, this section proposes the BPSO-RFE method for feature selection, which can effectively decrease the computational complexity and feature dimensionality, and has a good model generalization. BPSO-RFE is a hybrid feature selection algorithm, i.e., a comprehensive combination of BPSO and RFE algorithms. RFE takes less time in the process of feature selection, but the obtained classification accuracy is low. On the contrary, BPSO can achieve a high classification effect but requires multiple iterations to find the global optimal solution (or approximate optimal solution), which makes its time complexity much higher than that of the RFE algorithm. If these two algorithms are combined, the effect of complementary advantages can be achieved. Firstly, the RFE algorithm preliminarily select features extracted by the LBP and GLCM descriptors. Finally, for the purpose of eliminating redundant features, the BPSO algorithm is applied to further optimize the obtained effective features.

The support vector machine (SVM) is one of the most utilized classifiers to solve classification problems. It is interchangeable for both supervised machine learning and unsupervised model training. In contrast to traditional neural network algorithms, the SVM classifier can achieve the high-precision classification of small-scale sample data in a short time. In order to improve the classification accuracy, it is essential to choose the appropriate SVM parameters (C, σ). The first parameter C is the penalty factor of SVM objective function. Its role is to adjust the error and convert the original problem into an unrestricted optimization problem. Another parameter σ is the radius of RBF.

4   Experimental Results

The entire experimental study was conducted using the international standard epilepsy EEG database. Based on the prior knowledge of signal preprocessing, the wavelet threshold method was used to denoise EEG signals. Then, the CWT method was introduced to subdivide the entire frequency band into five parts

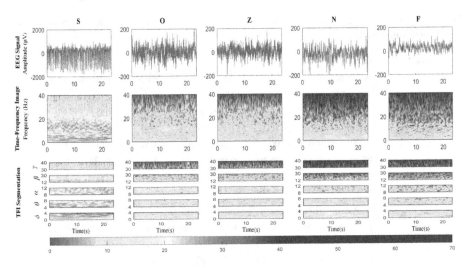

Fig. 2. The overall time-frequency images of EEG signals and their segmentations

(δ, θ, α, β, and γ) and generate TFI of the corresponding frequency band. EEG signal images of five datasets (S, O, Z, N, F) and their corresponding TFI are given in Fig. 2.

When LBP and GLCM descriptors are combined to extract texture features, each EEG segment can furnish (4*4+10)*5=130 feature parameters. The feature sets of frequency sub-bands (δ, θ, α, β, and γ) and the overall feature sets of TFI (combined with all sub-band feature sets) are obtained by this method. Table 1 shows the performance index values received from six sub-problems in different feature sets, including binary classification problems (O-S, Z-S, and OZ-S) among healthy people and epilepsy patients in the seizure period, as well as binary classification problems (N-S, F-S, and NF-S) among epileptic patients with seizure-free interval and epileptic seizure. A single sub-band feature set is far less accurate than the classification accuracy obtained by all sub-band feature sets. Therefore, the entire study uses features from all sub-bands to classify epilepsy.

Given the fact that feature extraction may have redundant features and classifier performance, the experiment based on the BPSO-RFE-SVM algorithm for feature selection and parameter optimization can enhance the accuracy of SVM classification and reduce time loss. The classification result of ACC (%) based on different feature extraction methods and parameters optimization using the BPSO algorithm in Table 2. The action can achieve a better classification effect, which proves that LBP and GLCM algorithms have a complementary result. The fourth row of Table 2 utilizes the grid search to optimize SVM parameters, and the remaining methods exploit the heuristic optimization algorithm BPSO. In this work, the classification result obtained upon the training of SVM's optimal parameters (C, σ) is the best.

Table 1. The comparison of classification performance for different sub-bands and combined sub-bands

Feature set	O-S				Z-S			
	ACC(%)	SEN(%)	SPE(%)	AUC	ACC(%)	SEN(%)	SPE(%)	AUC
δ	100	100	100	1	99.37	100	95.23	0.993
θ	97.77	100	95.24	0.999	100	100	100	1
α	100	100	100	1	100	100	100	1
β	96.12	100	90.91	0.994	100	100	100	1
γ	95.50	98.90	90.91	0.992	99.31	100	95.38	0.998
Combined	100	100	100	1	100	100	100	1
	N-S				F-S			
	ACC(%)	SEN(%)	SPE(%)	AUC	ACC(%)	SEN(%)	SPE(%)	AUC
δ	97.77	98.86	96.73	0.994	97.50	100	95.23	0.999
θ	98.33	98.88	97.80	0.997	96.11	95.60	96.63	0.988
α	97.50	98.75	98.75	0.999	97.78	97.70	97.79	0.995
β	98.88	98.87	97.80	0.996	98.33	97.80	98.88	0.999
γ	98.89	100	97.83	0.999	97.22	98.85	95.69	0.997
Combined	100	100	100	1	99.44	99.33	99.23	0.998
	OZ-S				NF-S			
	ACC(%)	SEN(%)	SPE(%)	AUC	ACC(%)	SEN(%)	SPE(%)	AUC
δ	100	100	100	1	96.25	98.34	96.04	0.985
θ	100	100	100	1	95.00	90.47	97.43	0.991
α	98.51	100	96.80	0.995	96.66	95.00	97.50	0.993
β	97.04	99.86	96.67	0.993	97.50	90.91	100	0.996
γ	98.89	99.90	100	0.996	98.30	100	97.56	0.998
Combined	100	100	100	1	99.59	99.96	99.62	0.998

Table 2. The classification result of ACC (%) based on different feature extraction methods and parameters optimization using the BPSO algorithm

Methods	Dataset					
	O-S	Z-S	N-S	F-S	OZ-S	NF-S
GLCM, BPSO-REF-SVM	100	100	100	97.50	100	98.50
LBP, BPSO-REF-SVM	100	100	99.38	99.33	100	99.25
LBP+GLCM, RFE-SVM	100	100	99.50	99.35	100	99.07
LBP+GLCM, BPSO-RFE-SVM	**100**	**100**	**100**	**99.44**	**100**	**99.59**

Note: bold values indicate the best results.

5   Discussion

This study is carried out using the epileptic EEG dataset of the Department of Epileptology, University of Bonn, Germany. In order to verify feasibility of the proposed method feasibility, we select some cutting-edge epileptic classification

Table 3. Implementation of six classification problems and performance comparison based on Epilepsy EEG dataset from the Department of Epileptology, University of Bonn, Germany

Dataset	Authors	Methods	ACC (%)
O-S	Zhu et al. [20]	FWHVA	97.00
	Swami et al. [21]	DTCWT and GRNN	99.00
	Kumar et al. [5]	DWT, fApEn and SVM	99.65
	This work	**CWT, LBP+GLCM, BPSO-RFE-SVM**	**100**
Z-S	Fu et al. [22]	HHT based on TFIs and SVM-RFE	99.13
	Kaya et al. [23]	Uniform and non-uniform 1D-LBP	99.50
	Li et al. [6]	CWT, GMM, GLCM, ReliefF and RFE-SVM	100
	This work	**CWT, LBP+GLCM, BPSO-RFE-SVM**	**100**
OZ-S	Chen [24]	DTCWT and FT	100
	Tiwari et al. [18]	LBP and SVM	100
	This work	**CWT, LBP+GLCM, BPSO-RFE-SVM**	**100**
N-S	Sharma et al. [25]	ATFFWT and FD	99.00
	Kumar et al. [5]	DWT, fApEn and SVM	99.60
	Zhu et al. [20]	FWHVA	99.60
	This work	**CWT, LBP+GLCM, BPSO-RFE-SVM**	**100**
F-S	Hassan et al. [26]	CEEMDAN and LPBoost	97.00
	Jia et al. [27]	CEEMDAN and random forest classifier	98.00
	Li et al. [12]	MRBF-MPSO-OLS, GLCM+FV, and SVM	99.30
	This work	**CWT, LBP+GLCM, BPSO-RFE-SVM**	**99.44**
NF-S	Kaya et al. [23]	Uniform and non-uniform 1D-LBP	97.00
	Kumar et al. [5]	DWT, fApEn and SVM	98.33
	Tiwari et al. [18]	LBP and SVM	99.45
	This work	**CWT, LBP+GLCM, BPSO-RFE-SVM**	**99.59**

Note: bold values correspond to results obtained via the proposed method.

methods and results for performance comparison using the same dataset, as shown in Table 3.

In view of the differences in EEG signals obtained from healthy people and epileptic patients, and the diversity of epileptic patients between seizure-free interval and epileptic seizure period, the whole experiment is split into two subtasks: (i) healthy people and epileptic patients in the seizure period, (ii) epileptic patients in the seizure-free interval and seizure periods. The first subtask includes three categories to consider. For solving the first binary classification problem of datasets O and S, several researchers proposed particular approaches, which could achieve good classification accuracy but failed to reach 100%. For example, Kumar et al. [5] proposed the fuzzy approximate entropy-based wavelet to realize the classification of epileptic EEG signals. Signal was decomposed into five frequency sub-bands by discrete wavelet transform (DWT) and adopted fuzzy approximate entropy for five parts to get feature set, and the radial basis function as the kernel function of support vector machine (SVM) to achieve the best accuracy of 99.65%. For the two classification problems of datasets Z-S and OZ-S, Kaya et al. [23] proposed the local binary pattern for feature extraction, while the classifier selected by Fu et al. [22] and Li et al. [6] was the SVM-RBF. Feature extraction can also be achieved by using the double-tree complex wavelet transform. As can be seen in Table 3, this proposed method achieves a classification accuracy of 100% for three problems.

The second subtask can also be reduced to the following three classification problems. The first problem is the classification of datasets N and S. In the study, authors [25] put forward a flexible analysis of WT for time-frequency decomposition of mutated signals and calculated the fractal dimension of each sub-band, while the least-squares support vector machine used as a classifier yielded only a 99% accuracy of classification. Kumar et al. [5] and Zhu et al. [20] also made some progress in the classification effect improvement. For the classification of datasets F and S, the method adopted by Li et al. [12] outperformed those proposed by other researchers [26,27]. Authors [5,18,23] proposed various methods to solve the classification problem of NF-S, but their accuracy was below 100%. However, Tiwari et al. [18] adopted LBP and SVM methods, with the classification accuracy of 99.45%, which proved that LBP descriptors could effectively extract EEG features. In this study, not only LBP was used to extract the local texture features of image, but GLCM was also introduced to gain global features. By fusing two feature sets, the classification problem of NF-S yielded the accuracy of 99.59%, i.e., higher by 0.14% than that of [18]. Experimental results confirm that the proposed method has a higher accuracy.

6   Conclusion

The aim of this study is to fuse local and global texture features. The classification of EEG signals that can be applied in an automatic epilepsy diagnosis system by using a popular EEG database: Bonn. Furthermore, the EEG database was used to prove efficiency of our proposed classification framework. A novel study was conducted by fusing features, and using BPSO-RFE-SVM to select discriminative features and optimize SVM' parameters. As a feature extractor, we propose the combination of LBP and GLCM since it outperformed a single descriptor in six classification problems. As a feature selection, we propose RFE-SVM and BPSO to select discriminative features. In terms of the classifier, we propose BPSO to optimize parameters of SVM-RBF since the optimal classifier result in good classification accuracy. For above six classification problems of EEG signals, experimental results demonstrate that our proposed method has a better classification effect with comparing other researchers' classification methods. In addition, we also expect that the proposed framework can be effectively applied to other neurological disease classification problems.

References

1. Iasemidis, L.D., et al.: Adaptive epileptic seizure prediction system. IEEE Trans. Biomed. Eng. **50**(5), 616–627 (2003)

2. Martis, R.J., et al.: Computer aided diagnosis of atrial arrhythmia using dimensionality reduction methods on transform domain representation. Biomed. Sign. Process. Control **13**(9), 295–305 (2014)
3. Li, Y., Liu, Y., Cui, W.G., Guo, Y.Z., Huang, H., Hu, Z.Y.: Epileptic seizure detection in eeg signals using a unified temporal-spectral squeeze-and-excitation network. IEEE Transactions on Neural Systems & Rehabilitation Engineering (2020)
4. Schuyler, R., White, A., Staley, K., Cios, K.J.: Epileptic seizure detection. IEEE Eng. Med. Biol. Mag. **26**(2), 74–81 (2007)
5. Kumar, Y., Dewal, M.L., Anand, R.S.: Epileptic seizure detection using dwt based fuzzy approximate entropy and support vector machine. Neurocomputing **133**(8), 271–279 (2014)
6. Li, Y., Cui, W.G., Luo, M.L., Li, K., Wang, L.: Epileptic seizure detection based on time-frequency images of eeg signals using gaussian mixture model and gray level co-occurrence matrix features. International Journal of Neural Systems, p. 1850003 (2018)
7. Guo, L., Rivero, D., Pazos, A.: Epileptic seizure detection using multiwavelet transform based approximate entropy and artificial neural networks. J. Neurosci. Methods **193**(1), 156–163 (2010)
8. Mohammadpoory, Z., Haddadnia, J., Nasrolahzadeh, M.: Epileptic seizure detection in eegs signals based on the weighted visibility graph entropy. Seizure **50**, 202–208 (2017)
9. Li, Y., Lei, M.Y., Cui, W.G., Guo, Y.Z., Wei, H.L.: A parametric time frequency-conditional granger causality method using ultra-regularized orthogonal least squares and multiwavelets for dynamic connectivity analysis in eegs. IEEE Trans. Biomed. Eng. **66**(12), 3509–3525 (2019)
10. Singh, G., Kaur, M., Singh, B.: Detection of epileptic seizure eeg signal using multiscale entropies and complete ensemble empirical mode decomposition. Wireless Personal Commun. **116**(1), 845–864 (2021)
11. Chen, S., Zhang, X., Chen, L., Yang, Z.: Automatic diagnosis of epileptic seizure in electroencephalography signals using nonlinear dynamics features. IEEE Access **7**, 61046–61056 (2019)
12. Li, Y., Cui, W.G., Huang, H., Guo, Y.Z., Li, K., Tan, T.: Epileptic seizure detection in eeg signals using sparse multiscale radial basis function networks and the fisher vector approach. Knowl.-Based Syst. **164**, 96–106 (2019)
13. Wang, L., et al.: Automatic epileptic seizure detection in eeg signals using multi-domain feature extraction and nonlinear analysis. Entropy **19**(6), 222 (2017)
14. Huang, H., et al.: A new fruit fly optimization algorithm enhanced support vector machine for diagnosis of breast cancer based on high-level features. BMC Bioinform. **20**(8), 290 (2019)
15. Omidvar, M., Zahedi, A., Bakhshi, H.: Eeg signal processing for epilepsy seizure detection using 5-level db4 discrete wavelet transform, ga-based feature selection and ann/svm classifiers. Journal of Ambient Intelligence and Humanized Computing, pp. 1–9 (2021)
16. Andrzejak, R.G., Lehnertz, K., Mormann, F., Rieke, C., David, P., Elger, C.E.: Indications of nonlinear deterministic and finite-dimensional structures in time series of brain electrical activity: Dependence on recording region and brain state. Phys. Rev. E Stat. Nonlin. Soft. Matter Phys. **64**(6), 061907 (2001)
17. Zhang, Z.G., Hung, Y.S., Chan, S.C.: Local polynomial modeling of time-varying autoregressive models with application to time-frequency analysis of event-related eeg. IEEE Trans. Biomed. Eng. **58**(3), 557–566 (2011)

18. Tiwari, A., Pachori, R.B., Kanhangad, V., Panigrahi, B.: Automated diagnosis of epilepsy using key-point based local binary pattern of eeg signals. IEEE Journal of Biomedical and Health Informatics, pp. 1–1 (2016)
19. Boubchir, L., Al-Maadeed, S., Bouridane, A., Cherif, A.A.: Classification of eeg signals for detection of epileptic seizure activities based on lbp descriptor of time-frequency images. In: 2015 IEEE International Conference on Image Processing (ICIP) (2015)
20. Zhu, G., Li, Y., Wen, P.P.: Epileptic seizure detection in eegs signals using a fast weighted horizontal visibility algorithm. Comput. Methods Programs Biomed. **115**(2), 64–75 (2014)
21. Swami, P., Gandhi, T.K., Panigrahi, B.K., Tripathi, M., Anand, S.: A novel robust diagnostic model to detect seizures in electroencephalography. Expert Syst. Appl. **56**, 116–130 (2016)
22. Fu, K., Qu, J.F., Chai, Y., Dong, Y.: Classification of seizure based on the time-frequency image of eeg signals using hht and svm. Biomed. Sign. Process. Control **13**, 15–22 (2014)
23. Kaya, Y., Uyar, M., Tekin, R., Yildirim, S.: 1d-local binary pattern based feature extraction for classification of epileptic eeg signals. Appl. Math. Comput. **243**, 209–219 (2014)
24. Chen, G.Y.: Automatic eeg seizure detection using dual-tree complex wavelet-fourier features. Expert Syst. Appl. **41**(5), 2391–2394 (2014)
25. Sharma, M., Pachori, R.B., Acharya, U.R.: A new approach to characterize epileptic seizures using analytic time-frequency flexible wavelet transform and fractal dimension. Pattern Recogn. Lett. **94**, 172–179 (2017)
26. Hassan, A.R., Subasi, A.: Automatic identification of epileptic seizures from eeg signals using linear programming boosting. Comput. Methods Programs Biomed. **136**, 65–77 (2016)
27. Jia, J., Goparaju, B., Song, J.L., Zhang, R., Brandon, M.: Automated identification of epileptic seizures in eeg signals based on phase space representation and statistical features in the ceemd domain. Biomed. Sign. Process. Control **38**, 148–157 (2017)

Reduced-reference Perceptual Discrepancy Learning for Image Restoration Quality Assessment

Leida Li[1(✉)], Bo Hu[2], Yipo Huang[1], and Hancheng Zhu[3]

[1] Xidian University, Xi'an 710071, China
ldli@xidian.edu.cn
[2] Chongqing University of Posts and Telecommunications, Chongqing 400065, China
hubo90@cqupt.edu.cn
[3] China University of Mining and Technology, Xuzhou 221116, China
zhuhancheng@cumt.edu.cn

Abstract. Image restoration has been receiving extensive attention owing to its widespread applications, and numerous restoration algorithms have been proposed. However, how to accurately evaluate the performances of image restoration algorithms remains largely unexplored. Current image restoration quality metrics make predictions solely based on the restored images without making full use of the original degraded image, which we believe also provides valuable information. For image restoration quality assessment, accurate measurement of the perceptual discrepancy between the degraded image and the restored images is crucial. Motivated by this, this paper presents a perceptual discrepancy learning (PDL) framework for image restoration quality assessment, where the original degraded image is utilized as reduced-reference to achieve reliable predictions. First, a large-scale paired image quality database with weakly annotated labels is built, based on which a prior quality model is trained using Siamese network. Then, based on the prior model, the degraded-restored image pairs (DRIPs) are further used to train the perceptual discrepancy prediction model in an end-to-end manner. Finally, the performances of image restoration algorithms can be obtained based on the predicted relative perceptual discrepancy (RPD) values directly. Experimental results on four image restoration quality databases demonstrate the advantage of the proposed metric over the state-of-the-arts.

Keywords: Image restoration · Quality assessment · Perceptual discrepancy · Convolutional neural network

1 Introduction

Image restoration, aiming at recovering a latent clear image from one or several degraded images, has been receiving extensive attention owing to its widespread applications, e.g., autonomous driving, remote sensing and medical imaging. In the past few years, a large number of image restoration algorithms have been developed for various applications, including denoising [1], deblurring [2], super resolution [3] and dehazing [4], etc.

© Springer Nature Switzerland AG 2021
L. Fang et al. (Eds.): CICAI 2021, LNAI 13069, pp. 359–370, 2021.
https://doi.org/10.1007/978-3-030-93046-2_31

(a) B-T score = -1.678   (b) B-T score = -2.638

(c) B-T score = 0.157   (d) B-T score = 2.555

Fig. 1. An example of image deblurring in the MURID database [5]. (a) is the original blurred image, (b) to (d) are deblurred images with different deblurring approaches. Deblurred image (b) has worse quality of the original image, which is indicated by the Bradley-Terry (B-T) scores. Higher B-T score indicates better quality.

Although significant progress has been achieved, there is not a single image restoration algorithm that can perform consistently well on diversified visual contents. With so many image restoration algorithms at hand, how to *fairly* evaluate their performances, or just to pick out the best-performing one, becomes challenging. To this end, an accurate image quality assessment (IQA) model is highly desired, which can perform comprehensive evaluations on a large number of images with diversified contents and distortions.

While the current IQA models have achieved superior performance on legacy image quality databases, e.g. LIVE [6], CSIQ [7] and TID2013 [8], they are still quite limited in evaluating the quality of image restoration [9]. This is mainly because that restored images are characterized by multiple distortions. Specifically, although the distortion in the original image will be weakened after restoration, the restoration process often introduces new distortions, such as blurring, ringing effect, etc. This makes the quality evaluation of image restoration more complicated, so the current IQA models do not work well, which will be shown in the experiment section.

In the image restoration community, the related work on the quality evaluation can be categorized into four popular restoration tasks, including image denoising, image deblurring, image super-resolution reconstruction and image dehazing. Typically, [10] proposed a NR image content metric Q for the parameter selection of image denoising algorithms, which is based on the singular value decomposition of local image gradients. In [11], a NR-IQA metric was proposed for motion deblurring by measuring image naturalness and sharpness. Hu *et al.* [12] proposed a new NR quality metric for motion deblurring by measuring noise, ringing and residual blur. In [13], Hautiere *et al.*. proposed three popular quality indices for image dehazing by measuring the change of visible edges between the restored image and the original image, including the percentage of pixels that become pure black or white, the rate of appearance of new edges and the mean ratio of the gradients at the visible edges. [14] proposed a FR image dehazing quality metric by measuring the structure recovering, color rendition, and over-enhancement of low-contrast areas.

The quality assessment of image restoration is slightly different from the conventional IQA. In image restoration, it is very likely that an algorithm may not necessarily achieve satisfactory restoration result, some even produce restored images with worse quality than the original degraded image. Figure 1 shows such an example, where the quality of restored image (b) gets worse than the original image. Therefore, compared to generating an absolute quality score for a restored image, it is more desirable to measure the relative perceptual discrepancy (RPD) between the degraded image and the corresponding restored image, which we call degraded-restored image pair (DRIP). By this means, we can easily know: (1) whether the quality of a restored image is better or worse than that of the original degraded image; (2) the extent to which the quality of a restored image is better or worse than that of the original degraded image. Motivated by this, this paper presents a reduced-reference Perceptual Discrepancy Learning (PDL) framework for image restoration quality assessment, with emphasize on benchmarking the performances of image restoration algorithms. A large-scale paired image quality database with weakly annotated labels is first built to train a prior quality model with high discriminative ability between distorted images from the same visual content. Based on the prior quality model, degraded-restored image pairs and the associated ground-truth relative perceptual discrepancy values are further used to train the PDL model in an end-to-end manner. Finally, the quality of restored images, and accordingly the performances of image restoration algorithms, can be easily determined based on the predicted RPD values. Extensive experimental results on four public image restoration quality databases demonstrate the superiority of the proposed PDL model over the state-of-the-arts.

2 Proposed Method

In this section, we introduce the proposed reduced-reference perceptual discrepancy learning approach in detail. The diagram of the proposed model is illustrated in Fig. 2. We use the term "reduced-reference" because the reference used here is the original degraded image, which is intrinsically different from the perfect-quality image used in conventional FR-IQA.

2.1 Paired Image Quality Database and Prior Model

To train a reliable deep learning-based relative perceptual discrepancy prediction model, a large number of discriminative image pairs are needed. However, the number of images in the current image restoration quality databases is typically limited. To address the problem, we first build a large-scale paired image quality database, based on which an effective prior quality model for perceptual discrepancy learning can be established. The paired image quality database contains 630,000 image pairs from 36,000 distorted images, which are generated based on 1,000 high quality reference images.

Data Preparation. We first choose 1,000 high quality images from a legacy image quality database CSIQ [7] and the Internet, which cover diversified contents, including people, animal, vehicle, building and natural scenery, etc. Then, three types of

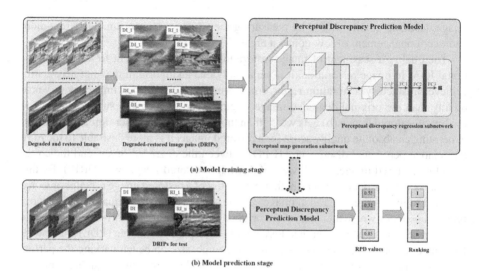

Fig. 2. Framework of the proposed perceptual discrepancy learning (PDL) approach.

representative distortions are added to the 1,000 reference images to generate the distorted images, including blur (Gaussian blur, motion blur), noise (white Gaussian noise, salt and pepper noise) and compression distortion (JPEG, JPEG2K). Considering the distortion diversity in real applications, we further set six different levels for each distortion type. In this way, 36,000 distorted images are obtained with diversified contents, distortion types and distortion levels. Figure 3 shows two sets of distorted images with Gaussian blur and JPEG compression in the database.

Data Annotation. After obtaining the distorted images, a FR-IQA metric is employed to generate the quality labels. The reasons are two-fold. First, with so many images, it is extremely laborious to annotate them by subjective experiment. Second, it has been demonstrated that current FR-IQA metrics have been able to predict quality scores highly consistent with human perception on synthetic distortions [15]. In this paper, we employ the well-known SSIM metric [16] to generate the labels for the distorted images. In Fig. 3, we also list the SSIM scores between the distorted images and the corresponding reference images. It is observed that the SSIM scores are highly consistent with the distortion levels.

Prior Quality Model. After annotation, we construct image pairs for training the prior quality model. Since we mainly care about the quality of restored images from the same original image, we also construct image pairs using distorted images with the same visual content. For a specific reference image, all the 36 distorted versions are referred to as an image group. For each image group, we can construct C_{36}^2 image pairs, which constitutes a paired image set:

$$\mathbf{A} = \{(I_i, I_j), i = 1, 2, ..., 35, i < j \le 36\}, \tag{1}$$

where $C_a^b = \frac{a!}{b!(a-b)!}$, $(a \ge b)$ is the combinatorial number function. For image pair set $\mathbf{A}$, the corresponding quality label (relative perceptual discrepancy) set is calculated as:

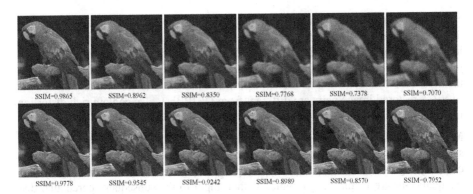

Fig. 3. Example images with Gaussian blur (upper row) and JPEG (bottom row) in the paired image quality database. From left to right, distortions in the images are increasing.

$$\mathbf{D} = \{D_{i,j} = Q_i - Q_j, i = 1, 2, ..., 35, i < j \leq 36\}, \tag{2}$$

where Q_i and Q_j are the SSIM scores of image pair (I_i, I_j). In this way, we can obtain the distorted image pairs and the corresponding quality labels for all image groups. Finally, $C_{36}^2 \times 1000 = 630000$ image pairs can be produced.

With the distorted image pairs and associated annotations, we first train a prior quality model based on the Siamese network. The prior model functions as a pre-trained model, which will be further used to train the relative perceptual discrepancy prediction model. Since the prior model is trained using paired images with the same contents, it is expected to have good discrimination ability of distortion intensity, which is important for image restoration quality assessment.

2.2 PDL Model Training

With the above prior quality model, the PDL model can be further obtained by performing a fine-tuning using degraded-restored image pairs.

DRIP Preparation. Assume we have $m \times n$ restored images from m degraded images by n restoration algorithms, each degraded image and its restored versions are called an image group. For each image group, the degraded image is paired with the corresponding n restored images. So n DRIPs can be obtained:

$$\mathbf{A}_{\mathrm{DRIP}} = \{(I_d, I_r^i), i = 1, 2, ..., n\}, \tag{3}$$

where I_d and I_r^i denote the degraded image and the restored image generated by the ith restoration algorithm, respectively. The corresponding quality label set of $\mathbf{A}_{\mathrm{DRIP}}$ is denoted by:

$$\mathbf{D}_{\mathrm{DRIP}} = \{D_p^i = Q_r^i - Q_d, i = 1, 2, ..., n\}, \tag{4}$$

where Q_d and Q_r^i denote the quality scores of the degraded image and its ith restored image, respectively. In this way, we can construct $m \times n$ DRIPs for all image groups.

In implementation, to obtain more training samples, the n restored images from each degraded image are also paired with each other. For each image group, C_n^2 restored image pairs can be further obtained from the n restored images. Therefore, $m \times C_n^2$ restored image pairs can be further generated in this way. Finally, in combination with the $m \times n$ DRIPs, we obtain $m \times (n + C_n^2)$ image pairs in total. Note that although the $m \times C_n^2$ restored image pairs are different from DRIP, they also contain rich distortion information, which are beneficial for training the PDL model.

Model Training. As illustrated in Fig. 2, the proposed PDL framework consists of two subnetworks, including a perceptual map generation subnetwork and a perceptual discrepancy regression subnetwork. The perceptual map generation subnetwork generates the quality-aware feature maps, which is then input to the subsequent perceptual discrepancy regression subnetwork to predict the relative perceptual discrepancy value between the input image pair. The perceptual map generation subnetwork consists of two identical branches with shared weights. In implementation, we use the VGG19 network [17] as the backbone. Specifically, we remove all the fully-connected layers and the last four convolutional layers. Then, we use the remaining layers to build the perceptual map generation subnetwork. For each branch, the network generates a set of feature maps, denoting by $\mathbf{M} \in \mathbb{R}^{w \times h \times c}$, where w, h and c are the width, height and channel of the feature maps. Here, w and h are determined by the size of the input image, and c is determined by the backbone network.

The perceptual discrepancy regression subnetwork consists of one fusion layer and three fully-connected layers. The fusion layer calculates the spatial discrepancy between the two branches, which is defined by:

$$\mathbf{M}_f^i = \mathbf{M}_u^i - \mathbf{M}_d^i, \tag{5}$$

where $\mathbf{M}_u^i$ and $\mathbf{M}_d^i$ denote the ith ($i = 1, 2, ..., c$) feature map of the two (up and down) branches. After the fusion layer, the Global Average Pooling (GAP) operation is employed to extract features from the fused feature maps, and the GAP is defined as:

$$x = \frac{1}{w \times h} \sum_{i=1}^{w} \sum_{j=1}^{h} \mathbf{M}_f(i, j). \tag{6}$$

In this way, c features can be generated from the fused feature maps, which are denoted by $\mathbf{X} = \{x_i, i = 1, 2, ..., c\}$. Then, the feature vector $\mathbf{X}$ is fed to the subsequent fully-connected (FC) layer. After each FC layer, the Rectified Linear Unit (ReLU) is used as the activation function, and the dropout ratio is set to be 0.5 to alleviate overfitting. The last FC layer with a linear operator produces the predicted discrepancy value of an input image pair. In implementation, the first two FC layers contain 512 nodes each, and the output of the last FC layer is the final prediction result.

The objective of model training is to find a function F that can predict the RPD value of an input image pair (I_r, I_d) as close as to the ground truth, i.e. D_p. This is a regression task, so we adopt the mean squared error (MSE) loss to train the model:

$$L = \frac{1}{N} \sum_{i=1}^{N} (F(\mathbf{I}_r, \mathbf{I}_d)^i - D_p^i)^2, \tag{7}$$

where N is the number of training image pairs.

2.3   Model Prediction

In the model prediction stage, we first prepare a set of DRIP pairs. Then, the RPD values are predicted using the proposed PDL model. Based on the RPD values, the quality of restored images, and accordingly the performance of restoration algorithms, can be obtained. Specifically, given $k \times n$ restored images generated by n image restoration algorithms from k degraded images, we can construct $k \times n$ DRIP pairs. Then, the PDL model is used to generate the predicted RPD results. For better understanding, we define a prediction matrix as follows

$$
\mathbf{P} = \begin{pmatrix} p_{11} & p_{12} & \cdots & p_{1n} \\ p_{21} & p_{22} & \cdots & p_{2n} \\ \vdots & \vdots & \ddots & \vdots \\ p_{k1} & p_{k2} & \cdots & p_{kn} \end{pmatrix}, \tag{8}
$$

where $\mathbf{P}(i,j) = p_{ij}$, $i = 1, 2, ..., k$ $j = 1, 2, ..., n$, denotes the predicted RPD value of the DRIP pair comprised of the ith degraded image and its jth restored image.

The performance ranking of image restoration algorithms can be easily determined based on the prediction matrix, either in image level or database level. For image level evaluation, the performance ranking of restoration algorithms on the ith image can be obtained from the RPD values in the ith row of the prediction matrix, and higher value indicates better performance. For database level evaluation, a simple statistical analysis is sufficient. Specifically, to evaluate the overall performance of the jth restoration algorithm, we first calculate the average of the predicted RPD values for all images restored by the algorithm:

$$
R_j = \frac{1}{k} \sum_{i=1}^{k} \mathbf{P}(i,j). \tag{9}
$$

For each of the n restoration algorithms, an average RPD value can be calculated and denoted by $(R_1, R_2, \cdots, R_n)$. Then, the overall performance ranking of the n algorithms can be obtained after performing a sorting.

3   Experimental Results

3.1   Experimental Settings

We evaluate the performance of the proposed PDL metric on four public image restoration quality databases, including three image motion deblurring databases and one image dehazing database. In these databases, both the original degraded image and the restored images are annotated, so the ground truth perceptual discrepancy values can be easily calculated, which are needed in model training.

Image Deblurring Databases. In [5], Lai *et al.* built three motion deblurring databases, including Motion Deblurring for Real Image Database (MDRID), Motion Deblurring for Non-uniform blurred Image Database (MDNID) and Motion Deblurring for Uniform blurred Image Database (MDUID). In MDRID, 100 real blurred images were

Table 1. Performance comparison of the proposed metric and four types of image quality metrics on four image restoration quality databases. The best results are marked in boldface.

Metric	Type	Motion deblurring						Image dehazing	
		MDRID		MDNID		MDUID		DHID	
		SRCC	KRCC	SRCC	KRCC	SRCC	KRCC	SRCC	KRCC
BIQI [20]	GNR	0.284	0.218	0.379	0.301	0.479	0.364	0.038	0.046
DESIQUE [21]	GNR	0.249	0.189	0.200	0.149	0.553	0.438	0.012	0.010
DIIVINE [22]	GNR	0.234	0.176	0.208	0.157	0.417	0.309	0.070	0.059
BLIIND2 [23]	GNR	0.318	0.245	0.253	0.197	0.486	0.368	0.068	0.049
BRISQUE [24]	GNR	0.251	0.192	0.359	0.268	0.447	0.346	0.092	0.076
NFERM [25]	GNR	0.366	0.281	0.411	0.316	0.585	0.459	0.182	0.160
CORNIA [26]	GNR	0.159	0.116	0.119	0.086	0.479	0.352	0.239	0.182
GMLOG [27]	GNR	0.293	0.219	0.198	0.145	0.541	0.423	0.046	0.041
FISBLIM [28]	MLD	−0.132	−0.101	−0.086	−0.067	−0.164	−0.118	0.142	0.123
SISBLIM [29]	MLD	−0.072	−0.060	−0.166	−0.130	−0.227	−0.172	−0.065	−0.032
GWH-GLBP [30]	MLD	0.262	0.197	0.325	0.253	0.450	0.344	0.057	0.047
MMD [11]	MD	0.212	0.156	0.439	0.332	0.599	0.479	-	-
NRRB [12]	MD	0.083	0.096	0.194	0.167	0.274	0.223	-	-
e [13]	ID	-	-	-	-	-	-	-0.209	-0.176
Σ [13]	ID	-	-	-	-	-	-	0.334	0.267
γ [13]	ID	-	-	-	-	-	-	0.039	0.025
Ref. [14]	ID	-	-	-	-	-	-	0.252	0.207
MetricQ [10]	GIR	0.148	0.124	0.333	0.270	0.284	0.219	0.129	0.103
Ref. [31]	GIR	0.522	0.416	0.579	0.467	0.759	0.614	0.411	0.335
Proposed PDL	GIR	**0.538**	**0.425**	**0.591**	**0.471**	**0.762**	**0.622**	**0.412**	**0.341**

collected from diversified scenes. In MDNID and MDUID, 25 sharp images from the Internet were selected to synthesize blurred images, respectively. Moreover, the Bradley-Terry [18] scores were calculated as the ground truth.

Image Dehazing Database. In [19], a dehazed image quality database (DHID) was built. First, 25 hazy images covering diverse outdoor scenes and distortion degrees were processed by 8 image dehazing algorithms, producing 200 dehazed images. Then, subjective study was conducted using the multi-stimulus method by showing each group of 9 images simultaneously, including 1 original hazy image and 8 dehazed versions. Finally, the mean opinion score (MOS) was calculated as the ground truth.

Two popular monotonicity criteria are employed in the experiment, including the Spearman rank order correlation coefficient (SRCC) and the Kendalls rank order correlation coefficient (KRCC). A better quality metric is expected to produce higher SRCC and KRCC values.

3.2 Performance Evaluation

The performance of the proposed model is compared with four types of state-of-the-art quality metrics. First, eight representative general-purpose NR-IQA metrics are compared, including BIQI [20], DESIQUE [21], DIIVINE [22], BLIIND-II [23], BRISQUE [24], NFERM [25], CORNIA [26] and GM-LOG [27]. Then, since restored images

Table 2. Cross-database validation results of the proposed PDL model and three popular image quality metrics based on three motion deblurring databases.

Training database	Test database	Metric	SRCC	KRCC
MDRID	MDNID	BRISQUE [24]	−0.063	−0.045
		NFERM [25]	0.247	0.186
		Ref. [31]	0.465	0.369
		PDL	**0.571**	**0.452**
	MDUID	BRISQUE [24]	0.107	0.091
		NFERM [25]	0.416	0.318
		Ref. [31]	0.613	0.491
		PDL	**0.762**	**0.624**
MDNID	MDRID	BRISQUE [24]	0.054	0.040
		NFERM [25]	0.203	0.155
		Ref. [31]	**0.418**	**0.326**
		PDL	0.335	0.252
	MDUID	BRISQUE [24]	0.386	0.294
		NFERM [25]	0.402	0.315
		Ref. [31]	0.645	0.506
		PDL	**0.646**	**0.522**
MDUID	MDRID	BRISQUE [24]	0.081	0.062
		NFERM [25]	0.267	0.198
		Ref. [31]	0.243	0.189
		PDL	**0.366**	**0.288**
	MDNID	BRISQUE [24]	0.147	0.109
		NFERM [25]	0.414	0.319
		Ref. [31]	0.314	0.235
		PDL	**0.532**	**0.417**

typically contain multiple distortions, three top-performing multiple distortion quality metrics are compared, including FISBLIM [28], SISBLIM [29] and GWH-GLBP [30]. Furthermore, two metrics for motion deblurring are compared, including MMD [11] and NRRB [12]. Four metrics for image dehazing are compared, icluding the three metrics (e, Σ, γ) in [13] and one metric in Ref. [14]. Finally, two metrics of this type are compared, including MetricQ [10] and Ref. [31]. In implementation, all restored images are divided into two non-overlapping groups according to the original degraded images used, i.e., 80% images are used for model training and the remaining 20% images are used for testing. This avoids content bias because the images used for model training are not used for model test. Following the setting in [15,32], we repeat the training-testing process by 20 times and the mean values are reported in this paper. The experimental results are summarized in Table 1, where the best performances are marked in boldface. In the table, "GNR" represents the general-purpose NR quality metric, "MLD" represents the metric for multiply distorted images, "MD" represents the metric for motion deblurring, "ID" represents the metric for image dehazing, and "GIR" represents the general-purpose image restoration quality metric.

From Table 1, we know that the proposed PDL metric outperforms the existing quality metrics on all the four databases. For motion deblurring, Ref. [31] also delivers very encouraging results. The other metrics do not perform very well on motion deblurring. Moreover, it can be observed that the MDRID and MDNID databases are more challenging than MDUID. This is easy to understand in that realistic blurring and non-uniform blurring are more difficult than uniform blurring for image deblurring models. On the image dehazing database, the proposed metric outperforms Ref. [31] slightly. Other quality metrics are very limited in evaluating the quality of image dehazing.

3.3 Generalization Ability

For a learning-based quality metric, generalization ability is an important performance criterion and is alo highly desired in practical applications. To this end, we further test the generalization ability of the proposed model using cross-database validation for motion deblurring. Specifically, we train the PDL model using one database and test its performance on the other two databases. We repeat this experiment three times to ensure that all three databases are used for model training. Meantime, we also test three of the existing metrics under the same setting for comparison, including two popular general-purpose NR-IQA metrics BRISQUE [24], NFERM [25], and one general-purpose image restoration quality metric, i.e. Ref. [31]. Table 2 summarizes the experimental results, where the best results are marked in boldface.

From Table 2, we know that the proposed PDL model achieves the best generalization ability among the compared quality metrics in 5 of the 6 cross-validation test. When the model is trained on MDNID database and tested on the MDRID database, Ref. [31] achieves better performance than the proposed model. From these results, it can be concluded that the proposed PDL model has the best generalization ability.

4   Conclusion

In this paper, we have proposed a reduced-reference perceptual discrepancy learning model for the quality assessment of image restoration. The proposed metric has been inspired by the fact that quantifying the relative perceptual discrepancy between the degraded image and the corresponding restored image is highly needed in this task. Instead of predicting an absolute quality score for a restored image, the relative perceptual discrepancy between the degraded-restored image pair is measured to investigate the extent to which the quality of a restored image is better or worse than the original degraded image. In addition, a large-scale paired image quality database with weakly annotated labels has been built to address the problem of insufficient training data, which is used to train a prior quality model. The experiments conducted on four public image restoration databases have demonstrated the advantage of the proposed model over the state-of-the-art metrics.

Acknowledgment. This work was supported by the National Natural Science Foundation of China under Grants 61771473, 61991451 and 61379143, Natural Science Foundation of

Jiangsu Province under Grant BK20181354, the Fundamental Research Funds for the Central Universities under Grant JBF211902, the Key Project of Shaanxi Provincial Department of Education under Grant 20JY024, the Science and Technology Plan of Xian under Grant 20191122015KYPT011JC013, and the Six Talent Peaks High- level Talents in Jiangsu Province under Grant XYDXX-063.

References

1. Zhang, K., Zuo, W.M., Chen, Y.J., Meng, D.Y., Zhang, L.: Beyond a Gaussian denoiser: Residual learning of deep CNN for image denoising. IEEE Trans. Image Process. **26**(7), 3142–3155 (2017)
2. Pan, J.S., Sun, D.Q., Pfister, H., Yang, M.-H.: Deblurring images via dark channel prior. IEEE Trans. Pattern Anal. Mach. Intell. **40**(10), 2315–2328 (2018)
3. Dong, C., Loy, C.C., He, K.M., Tang, X.O.: Image super-resolution using deep convolutional networks. IEEE Trans. Pattern Anal. Mach. Intell. **38**(2), 295–307 (2016)
4. He, K.M., Sun, J., Tang, X.O.: Single image haze removal using dark channel prior. Int. Conf. Comput. Vis. Pattern Recognit. **33**(12), 1956–1963 (2009)
5. Lai, W.S., Huang, J.B., Hu, Z., Ahuja, N., Yang, M.-H.: A comparative study for single image blind deblurring. In: International Conference on Computer Vision and Pattern Recognition, pp. 1701–1709. Las Vegas, USA (2016)
6. Sheikh, H.R., Sabir, M.F., Bovik, A.C.: A statistical evaluation of recent full reference image quality assessment algorithms. IEEE Trans. Image Process. **15**(11), 3440–3451 (2006)
7. Larson, E.C., Chandler, D.M.: Most apparent distortion: full reference image quality assessment and the role of strategy. J. Electron. Imaging **19**(1), 1–21 (2010)
8. Ponomarenko, N., et al.: Color image database TID2013: peculiarities and preliminary results. In: 4th European Workshop Visual Information Processing (EUVIP), pp. 106–111. IEEE, Paris, France (2013)
9. Hu, B., Li, L.D., Wu, J.J., Qian, J.S.: Subjective and objective quality assessment for image restoration: a critical survey. Signal Process. Image Commun. **85**, 1–19 (2020)
10. Zhu, X., Milanfar, P.: Automatic parameter selection for denoising algorithms using a no-reference measure of image content. IEEE Trans. Image Process. **19**(12), 3116–3132 (2010)
11. Liu, Y.M., Wang, J., Cho, S., Finkelstein, A., Rusinkiewicz, S.: A no-reference metric for evaluating the quality of motion deblurring. ACM Trans. Graph. **32**(6), 1–12 (2013)
12. Hu, B., Li, L.D., Qian, J.S.: Perceptual quality evaluation for motion deblurring. IET Comput. Vis. **12**(6), 796–805 (2018)
13. Hautiere, N., Tarel, J.-P., Aubert, D., Dumont, E.: Blind contrast enhancement assessment by gradient ratioing at visible edges. J. Image Anal. Stereol. **27**(2), 87–95 (2008)
14. Min, X.K., Zhai, G.T., Gu, K., et al.: Quality evaluation of image dehazing methods using synthetic hazy images. IEEE Trans. Multimedia **21**(9), 2319–2333 (2019)
15. Kim, J., Lee, S.: Fully deep blind image quality predictor. IEEE J. Sel. Top. Sign. Process. **11**(1), 206–220 (2017)
16. Wang, Z., Bovik, A.C., Sheikh, H.R., Simoncelli, E.P.: Image quality assessment: from error visibility to structural similarity. IEEE Trans. Image Process. **13**(4), 600–612 (2004)
17. Simonyan, K., Zisserman, A.: Very deep convolutional networks for largescale image recognition. In: International Conference on Learning Representations. San Diego, CA (2015)
18. Bradley, R.A., Terry, M.E.: Rank analysis of incomplete block designs the method of paired comparisons. Biometrika **39**(3–4), 324–345 (1952)
19. Ma, K.D., Liu, W.T., Wang, Z.: Perceptual evaluation of single image dehazing algorithms. In: IEEE International Conference on Image Processing, pp. 3600–3604. IEEE, Quebec City, Canada (2015)

20. Moorthy, A.K., Bovik, A.C.: A two-step framework for constructing blind image quality indices. IEEE Signal Process. Lett. **17**(5), 513–516 (2010)
21. Zhang, Y., Chandler, D.M.: "No-reference image quality assessment based on log derivative statistics of natural scenes. J. Electr. Imag. **22**(4), 1–11 (2013)
22. Moorthy, A.K., Bovik, A.C.: Blind image quality assessment: from natural scene statistics to perceptual quality. IEEE Trans. Image Process. **20**(12), 3350–3364 (2011)
23. Saad, M.A., Bovik, A.C.: Blind image quality assessment: a natural scene statistics approach in the DCT domain. IEEE Trans. Image Process. **21**(8), 3339–3352 (2012)
24. Mittal, A., Moorthy, A.K., Bovik, A.C.: No-reference image quality assessment in the spatial domain. IEEE Trans. Image Process. **21**(12), 4695–4708 (2012)
25. Gu, K., Zhai, G.T., Yang, X.K., Zhang, W.J.: Using free energy principle for blind image quality assessment. IEEE Trans. Multimedia **17**(1), 50–63 (2015)
26. Ye, P., Kumar, J., Kang, L., Doermann, D.: Unsupervised feature learning framework for no-reference image quality assessment. In: Int. Conf. Comput. Vis. Pattern Recognit. (CVPR), pp. 1098–1105. IEEE, Providence, USA (2012)
27. Xue, W.F., Mou, X.Q., Zhang, L., Bovik, A.C., Feng, X.C.: Blind image quality assessment using joint statistics of gradient magnitude and laplacian features. IEEE Trans. Image Process. **23**(11), 4850–4862 (2014)
28. Gu, K., et al.: FISBLIM: a five-step blind metric for quality assessment of multiply distorted images. In: IEEE Workshop on Signal Processing Systems (SiPS 2013), pp. 241–246. IEEE, Taipei City, Taiwan, China (2013)
29. Gu, K., Zhai, G.T., Yang, X.K., Zhang, W.J.: Hybrid no-reference quality metric for singly and multiply distorted images. IEEE Trans. Broadcast. **60**(3), 555–567 (2014)
30. Li, Q.H., Lin, W.S., Fang, Y.M.: No-reference quality assessment for multiply-distorted images in gradient domain. IEEE Signal Process. Lett. **23**(4), 541–545 (2016)
31. Hu, B., Li, L.D., Liu, H.T., Lin, W.S., Qian, J.S.: Pairwise-comparison-based rank learning for benchmarking image restoration algorithms. IEEE Trans. Multimedia **21**(8), 2042–2056 (2019)
32. Kim, J., Lee, S.: Deep learning of human visual sensitivity in image quality assessment framework. In: International Conference on Computer Vision and Pattern Recognition (CVPR), pp. 1969–1977. IEEE, Honolulu, USA (2017)

EFENet: Reference-Based Video Super-Resolution with Enhanced Flow Estimation

Yaping Zhao[1], Mengqi Ji[1], Ruqi Huang[1(✉)], Bin Wang[2], and Shengjin Wang[1]

[1] Tsinghua University, Beijing, China
ruqihuang@sz.tsinghua.edu.cn
[2] Hikvision, Hangzhou, China

Abstract. In this paper, we consider the problem of reference-based video super-resolution(RefVSR), i.e., how to utilize a high-resolution (HR) reference frame to super-resolve a low-resolution (LR) video sequence. The existing approaches to RefVSR essentially attempt to align the reference and the input sequence, in the presence of resolution gap and long temporal range. However, they either ignore temporal structure within the input sequence, or suffer accumulative alignment errors. To address these issues, we propose EFENet to exploit simultaneously the visual cues contained in the HR reference and the temporal information contained in the LR sequence. EFENet first globally estimates cross-scale flow between the reference and each LR frame. Then our novel flow refinement module of EFENet refines the flow regarding the furthest frame using all the estimated flows, which leverages the global temporal information within the sequence and therefore effectively reduces the alignment errors. We provide comprehensive evaluations to validate the strengths of our approach, and to demonstrate that the proposed framework outperforms the state-of-the-art methods.

Keywords: Super-resolution · Reference-based video synthesis · Video enhancement · Image fusion

1 Introduction

In this paper, we consider the problem of reference-based video super-resolution (RefVSR), which is strongly motivated by the recent advances of hybrid camera systems. In general, our goal is to utilize a high-resolution (HR) reference frame to super-resolve a low-resolution (LR) video sequence captured by cameras at similar viewpoints (see, e.g., Fig. 1). While numerous methods [3,15,29,30] have been proposed for reference-based super-resolution (RefSR), some of them even have been applied in practice such as giga-pixel imaging [4,25,26] and light-field reconstruction [3,20]. The RefSR task for *videos* remains challenging, due to the following two factors: 1) the large parallax and resolution gap (e.g., 4×) makes it difficult to transfer details from HR frame to LR ones; 2) the potential large temporal

© Springer Nature Switzerland AG 2021
L. Fang et al. (Eds.): CICAI 2021, LNAI 13069, pp. 371–383, 2021.
https://doi.org/10.1007/978-3-030-93046-2_32

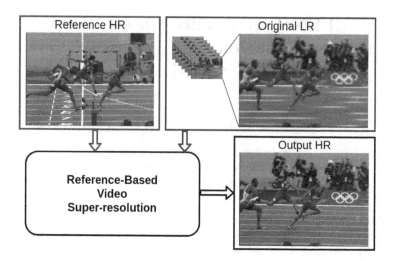

Fig. 1. Given a high-resolution (HR) and multiple low-resolution (LR) frames as input, we propose a reference-based video super-resolution algorithm to output the HR frame.

gap between the HR and LR frames can lead to significant viewpoint drift among frames, therefore makes the regarding correspondence estimation error-prone.

To better align frames across different resolutions, recent works [15,30] for RefSR apply a flow estimator from [7] to estimate the correspondence. Though such methods can be used in RefVSR by dividing the RefVSR task into multiple separated RefSR tasks, they discard the important temporal information contained in video sequence. Therefore, they have trouble handling long input sequence, as it is increasingly difficult to estimate correspondence between the reference and the LR frames as the temporal gap increases. On the other hand, to exploit the temporal information from the input sequence, several works [12,16,17] are proposed to leverage the temporal information between LR frames by flow estimation and motion compensation. However, they suffer the resolution discrepancy between the HR reference and the LR frames, hindering the usage of the rich visual cues from the reference.

To overcome the aforementioned difficulties, we propose an end-to-end neural network, EFENet[1], for RefVSR. EFENet takes advantage of the state-of-the-art RefSR method *CrossNet++* [15], but, more crucially, introduces a novel flow refinement module to improve the furthest frame alignment with *all* the prior ones, allowing the usage of temporal information for long range video synthesis on top of the powerful correspondence estimation module. In the end, EFENet decodes the refined flow to output super-resolved video sequences. Note that, the existing video super-resolution methods [12,16,17] locally estimate the correspondence between adjacent frames and propagate the information to the furthest frame accumulatively. In contrast to them, EFENet leverages the temporal

---

[1] Code is available at https://github.com/IndigoPurple/EFENet.

information in a global manner, effectively reducing the accumulative alignment errors. We test our pipeline and several strong baselines on Vimeo90K and MPII datasets. Extensive experimental results show the substantial improvements of our method over the state-of-the-art methods.

Our contributions are listed as follows:

- We propose an end-to-end network, EFENet, for RefVSR. By combining *CrossNet++* with a novel flow refinement module, EFENet effectively improves long sequence video synthesis quality for cross-scale camera systems.
- The flow refinement module of EFENet exploits globally the temporal information for flow enhancement, and therefore reduces alignment errors.
- Extensive experiments demonstrate the superior performance of our method in comparison to the state-of-the-art methods.

2   Related Work

2.1   Single-Image Super-Resolution

Since recovering the HR content from a single image is ill-posed, a large amount of image priors are proposed for single image super-resolution (SISR). Image priors proposed for the SR task include: gradient prior [14], sparsity prior [24], patch dictionary prior [18], etc. With the development of deep learning, Dong *et al.* adapt a three-layers convolutional network [6] for SISR. Later, more advanced network structures are proposed to improve SISR results. To further improve realism of SR outputs, Ledig *et al.* [10] use a generative adversarial network to generate photo realistic SR result. Later, Sajjadi *et al.* propose EnhanceNet [13] to leverage adversarial loss and perceptual loss to generate realistic textures. However, SISR is limited to generate sharp image, especially for large scale factors, as it is essentially highly ill-posed.

2.2   Reference-Based Super-Resolution

From the other perspective, the performance of SISR can be improved if an additional HR reference image similar to the LR image is given as input. Boominathan *et al.* [3] adopt high-resolution images captured by cameras from similar viewpoints as the reference, and propose a patch-based synthesis algorithm via non-local mean [5] for super-resolving the low-resolution light-field images. Wu *et al.* [22] further improve it by employing patch registration before the nearest neighbor searching, then apply dictionary learning for reconstruction. Wang *et al.* [20] iterate the patch synthesizing step of [3] for enriching the reference patch database. Zheng *et al.* [28] decompose images into sub-bands by frequencies and apply patch matching for high-frequency sub-band reconstruction. In addition, Zheng *et al.* [28] propose a cross-resolution patch matching and synthesis scheme for RefSR. To improve RefSR, more recent works [15,30] utilize cross-scale optical flow networks and a warping-synthesis framework to perform RefSR prediction. Aslo there is work [27] leveraging patch-based correlation to perform non-rigid feature swapping for reference-based SR.

2.3   Video Super-Resolution

Compared to the image SR task, video SR enjoys extra cues given by the correlation between temporally adjacent frames. Essentially, video SR can be regarded as yet another temporal variant of reference-based SR task. Recent methods [9,12,16,17] leverage the temporal consistency between LR frames for video SR. Those works typically combine flow estimation and motion compensation to propagate the correspondence from previous time step to the current time step. However, the existing works have difficulty leveraging the high-resolution visual information of additional reference frames. Moreover, the optical flow are estimated between low-resolution frames, resulting in degenerated correspondence.

3   Method

In this section, we start by giving a conceptual comparison among different RefVSR strategies (Sect. 3.1). And then we provide details of our pipeline, including the network structure (Sect. 3.2) and the optimization objective (Sect. 3.3).

3.1   RefVSR Strategies Analysis

Given an HR reference I_t^H at time step t and an LR video sequence $\{I_{t+1}^L, \cdots, I_{t+n}^L\}$, our goal is to generate an HR frame $\widehat{I}_{t+n}^H$ corresponding to the LR frame I_{t+n}^L at time step $t+n$.

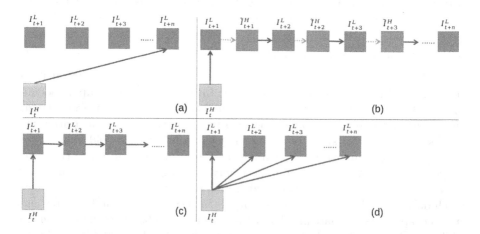

Fig. 2. Different strategies for cross-scale correspondence estimation: (a) direct estimation [15,30]; (b) recursive warping following local correspondence estimation [12,16]; (c) sequential local correspondence composition [8]; (d) refinement based on all global correspondence.

A central issue of the RefVSR task is how to accurately estimate correspondence among frames that both across different resolutions and undergoing significant temporal (and thus viewpoint) drifts. To see this, we first analyze different
strategies taken in the prior arts, as shown in Fig. 2: (a) each correspondence of
the input frame pairs is estimated independently, limiting the ability to utilize
temporal consistency [15,30];(b) the reference is processed and warped multiple
times, resulting in increasing alignment errors [12,16], and (c) correspondence is
estimated on the adjacent LR frames [8], hindering the usage of the rich visual
cues from the reference and resulting in degenerated correspondence.

To overcome the limitations of above methods, we propose a new one shown
in Fig. 2 (d). On one hand, different from (a), our method leverages temporal
information to facilitate long range video synthesis. On the other hand, different
from (b) and (c), our method estimates cross-scale flow between the reference
frame and *each* of the LR frames, achieving full exploitation of visual cues from
the reference. And then, we propose a flow refinement module that takes all
the estimated flows as input and globally leverage the temporal information to
reduce the alignment error.

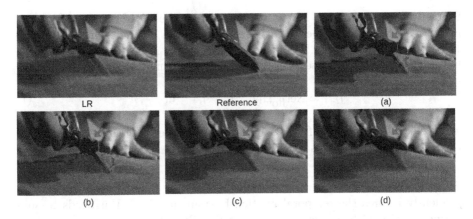

Fig. 3. Given the LR frame and the reference, the image alignment results using different strategies: (a) direct estimation; (b) recursive warping; (c) sequential composition;
(d) ours. Obviously, our strategy performs the best, see the discrepancies pointed out
by the red arrows for comparison. (Color figure online)

To illustrate the effectiveness of our method, we re-implement the competing methods with the state-of-the-art flow estimator [7]. As shown in Fig. 3,
our method (e) significantly improves the flow estimations method (a) of *Cross-
Net++* [15] by taking temporal information into consideration. Moreover, the
way we leverage such information is superior to the naive combination of *Cross-
Net++* [15] and the existing VSR methods [8,12,16] (b, c).

3.2   Network Structure

Figure 4 illustrates the architecture of EFENet, which contains a flow estimator, a flow refinement module, and a synthesis network.

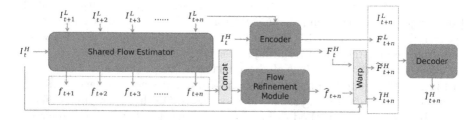

Fig. 4. Our deep neural network for RefVSR. It contains a shared flow estimator (left), a flow refinement module (middle), and an encoder-decoder synthesis network (right).

Shared Flow Estimator Module. As shown on the left of Fig. 4, we first estimate the correspondence between the reference frame I_t^H and each of LR frames $\{I_{t+1}^L, \cdots, I_{t+n}^L\}$, resulting n flow maps $\{f_{t+1}, \cdots, f_{t+n}\}$. Our flow estimator is based on a recently proposed the cross-scale flow estimator [15]. Formally,

$$f_{t+i} = \mathrm{Net}_{\mathrm{flow}}(I_t^H, {I_{t+i}^L}^{\uparrow}), i = 0, \cdots, n \tag{1}$$

where $\mathrm{Net}_{\mathrm{flow}}$ denotes the flow estimator, ${I_{t+i}^L}^{\uparrow}$ denotes the bicubicly upsampled LR frame and f_{t+i} denotes the output flow.

Flow Refinement Module. Obviously, estimating flow for each frame independently ignores the temporal relationships among them, thus leads to suboptimal results in the presence of large motion. To address this issue, we propose a flow refinement module which takes the concatenation of the generated flow maps at multiple time steps as input and output the refined flow at time step $t + n$.

In order to globally leverage prior flows to refine the temporally furthest flow, we adopt a U-Net [11] like structure with 4 strided convolution and deconvolution layers as an encoder-decoder. In fact, using such an encoder-decoder have two advantages: on one hand, the encoder can capture high-level information, including semantic and temporal information, in the hierarchical convolution process; on the other hand, the decoder, which uses skip-connections in the de-convolution process, integrates features at different scales to ensure the enhancement of the reconstructed flow.

Specifically, we let

$$\hat{f}_{t+n} = \text{Net}_{\text{refine}}([f_{t+1}, \cdots, f_{t+n}]), \tag{2}$$

where $[\cdot, \cdot]$ represents concatenation operation, $\text{Net}_{\text{refine}}$ represents the refinement module and $\hat{f}_{t+n}$ is the refined optical flow.

Encoder-Decoder Synthesis Network. After the flow refinement, we use another U-Net like encoder-decoder with 4 strided convolution and deconvolution layers to synthesize the SR result. Specifically, we first apply an encoder Net_E to extract the feature map at scale 1 from $I_{t+n}^{L}{}^{\uparrow}$ and I_t^H, and repeatedly convolve the feature map at the scale $i-1$ (for $1 < i \leq 4$) to extract the feature map at scale i:

$$\begin{aligned} \{F_{t+n,s}^{L}\} &= \text{Net}_E(I_{t+n}^{L}{}^{\uparrow}), \\ \{F_{t,s}^{H}\} &= \text{Net}_E(I_t^H), s = 1, 2, 3, 4, \end{aligned} \tag{3}$$

where $F_{t+n,s}^{L}$ is the feature map of up-sampled LR frame $I_{t+n,s}^{L}{}^{\uparrow}$ at scale s, and $F_{t,s}^{H}$ is the feature map of reference image I_t^H at scale s.

After the feature encoding, we leverage the refined flow $\hat{f}_{t+n}$ from the previous step to warp the reference image I_t^H and reference feature maps $\{F_{t,s}^{H}\}$:

$$\begin{aligned} \widetilde{I}_{t+n}^{H} &= \mathcal{W}(I_t^H, \hat{f}_{t+n}), \\ \{\widetilde{F}_{t+n,s}^{H}\} &= \mathcal{W}(\{F_{t,s}^{H}\}, \hat{f}_{t+n}), s = 1, 2, 3, 4, \end{aligned} \tag{4}$$

where $\mathcal{W}(\cdot, f)$ denotes backward warping operation that warps an image or feature maps according to the flow f.

Finally, we design a decoder Net_D to generate the final output. Specifically, the feature maps $\{F_{t+n,s}^{L}\}$, upsampled LR frame $I_{t+n}^{L}{}^{\uparrow}$, warped reference features $\{\widetilde{F}_{t+n,s}^{H}\}$ and warped reference $\widetilde{I}_{t+n}^{H}$ are concatenated to generate $\hat{I}_{t+n}^{H}$:

$$\hat{I}_{t+n}^{H} = \text{Net}_D([I_{t+n}^{L}{}^{\uparrow}, \widetilde{I}_{t+n}^{H}, \{F_{t+n,s}^{L}\}, \{\widetilde{F}_{t+n,s}^{H}\}]), s = 1, 2, 3, 4. \tag{5}$$

3.3 Loss Function

To train the network, we employ a combination of reconstruction loss and a set of warping loss. Specifically, let $\{I_{t+1}^{H}, \cdots, I_{t+n}^{H}\}$ denote the HR ground-truth (GT) of LR frames $\{I_{t+1}^{L}, \cdots, I_{t+n}^{L}\}$, we first formulate a reconstruction loss:

$$\mathcal{L}_{SR} = \frac{1}{N} \sum_{j=1}^{N} \sum_{k} \rho(\hat{I}_{t+n}^{H} - I_{t+n}^{H}), \tag{6}$$

where $\rho(x) = \sqrt{x^2 + 0.001^2}$ is the Charbonnier penalty function, N is the number of samples, j and k iterate over samples and spatial locations respectively.

In addition, to regularize the estimated flow at each time step, we impose constraint on the estimated optical flows $f_{t+1}, \cdots, f_{t+n}$. Specifically,

$$\mathcal{L}_{\text{flow1}} = \frac{1}{2N} \sum_{i=1}^{n} \sum_{j=1}^{N} \sum_{k} ||\mathcal{W}(I_t^H, f_{t+i}) - I_{t+i}^H)||_2^2, \tag{7}$$

where $\mathcal{W}(I_{t+i}^H, f_{t+i})$ denotes backward version of I_{t+i}^H using flow f_{t+i}; n is the number of time steps, N is the number of samples, i, j and k iterate over time steps, training samples and spatial locations respectively.

Similarly, we impose constraint on the enhanced flow $\hat{f}_{t+n}$:

$$\mathcal{L}_{\text{flow2}} = ||\mathcal{W}(I_t^H, \hat{f}_{t+n}) - I_{t+n}^H||_2^2. \tag{8}$$

4   Experiment

4.1   Evaluation

We evaluate our approach on the large-scale and representative datasets including Vimeo90K [23] and MPII [1]. Vimeo90K contains 89,800 video clips with 7 frames, while most sequences of MPII have about 40 frames. We take the initial frame from each video clip as the reference, and down-sample the remaining frames as the LR inputs. Following [15,30], we set the resolution gap as 4×. Finally, to quantitatively evaluate the results, we use image quality metrics PSNR and SSIM [21].

We train our network for 150,000 iterations on Vimeo90K, and apply the Adam [9] with $\beta_1 = 0.9, \beta_2 = 0.999$ as the optimizer. For comparison, we test RefSR methods including *CrossNet* [30], *CrossNet++* [15], *SRNTT* [27] and VSR methods including *ToFlow* [23], *MEMC-Net* [2], *RBPN* [9], and *EDVR* [19]. In addition, we train a variant of RBPN [8] such that its input contains the HR reference, resulting a method called *RBPN w/ ref*.

From Table 1, it is evident that our method outperforms all the baselines. Moreover, we observe that: i) our method outperforms the existing reference-based method as we leverage the temporal information across frames to estimate better correspondence; ii) our method outperforms the RefVSR approach *RBPN w/ ref* which leverages sequential local correspondence composition, showing the advantage of our proposed flow estimation module.

We also provide qualitative comparisons in Fig. 5, 6. From the figures, we observe that: i) among the reference-based approaches including *CrossNet*, *CrossNet++*, *SRNTT* and *RBPN w/ ref*, our method generates the most sharp and visually plausible images; ii) while *CrossNet++* achieves good performance on super-resolving static objects (e.g., text, buildings), it fails in non-rigid deformation cases (e.g., human body, face).

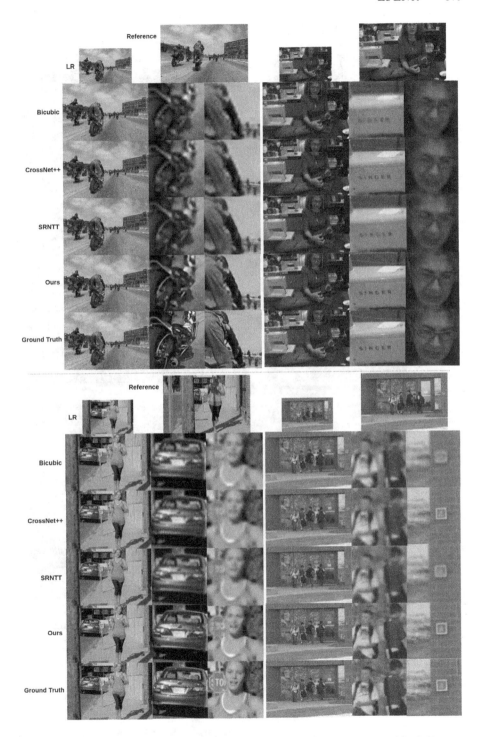

Fig. 5. Comparisons on MPII dataset under the cross-scale 4× settings.

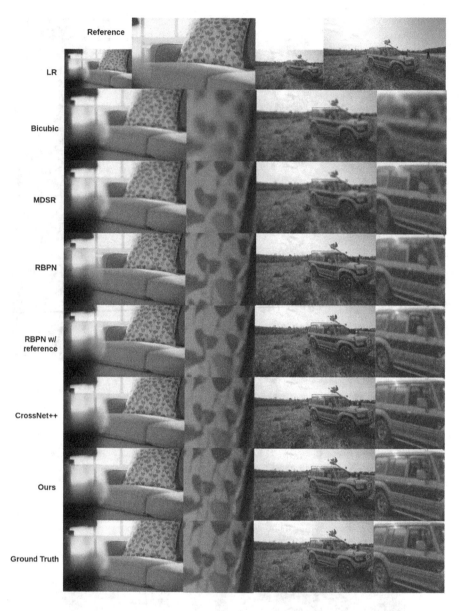

Fig. 6. Comparisons on Vimeo90K dataset under the cross-scale 4× settings.

Table 1. Left: quantitative evaluations of existing SR methods on Vimeo90K dataset. Right: quantitative evaluations of ablation methods on Vimeo90K and MPII datasets.

Inputs	Methods	PSNR	SSIM
1 LR	Bicubic	29.79	0.90
7 LR	TOFlow [23]	33.08	0.94
	MEMC-Net [2]	33.47	0.95
	RBPN [8]	35.32	0.95
	EDVR [19]	35.79	0.94
1 LR+1 HR	CrossNet [30]	36.71	0.95
	CrossNet++ [15]	38.95	**0.97**
7 LR+1 HR	RBPN w/ ref	36.60	0.95
	ours	**39.25**	**0.97**

Dataset	Methods	PSNR	SSIM
Vimeo	CrossNet++ [15]	38.95	0.97
	Setup1	38.85	0.97
	Setup2	39.14	0.97
	ours	**39.25**	**0.97**
MPII	CrossNet++ [15]	30.19	0.87
	Setup1	30.11	0.87
	Setup2	30.60	0.88
	ours	**30.76**	**0.89**

4.2 Ablation Study

To compare different correspondence estimation designs, we propose a set of ablation experiments. Specifically, similar to Fig. 2 (a), we use the original network of *CrossNet++* for synthesis. We also implemented alignment modules based on the diagram of (b) and (c) in Fig. 2, resulting two variants of *CrossNet++* called *Setup 1* and *Setup 2*. From Table 1, we observe that: i) when facing long temporal ranges on MPII dataset, the performance of *CrossNet++* decayed more than ours; ii) naively combining *CrossNet++* with existing VSR strategies performs worse than our method, and even causes degeneration to original *CrossNet++*.

5 Conclusion

We present an end-to-end network EFENet for RefVSR, which globally estimates cross-scale flow between the reference frame and each LR frame, and then improves the flow estimation with a novel flow refinement module. The core of EFENet is a novel flow refinement module, which exploit simultaneously the visual cues contained in the HR reference and the temporal information contained in the LR sequence to boost the super-resolution performance. Finally, we provide comprehensive evaluations and comparisons with previous methods to validate the strengths of our approach and demonstrate that the proposed network is able to outperform the state-of-the-art methods.

References

1. Andriluka, M., Pishchulin, L., Gehler, P., Schiele, B.: 2D human pose estimation: new benchmark and state of the art analysis. In: IEEE Conference on Computer Vision and Pattern Recognition (CVPR), June 2014
2. Bao, W., Lai, W.S., Zhang, X., Gao, Z., Yang, M.H.: MEMC-Net: motion estimation and motion compensation driven neural network for video interpolation and enhancement. IEEE Trans. Pattern Anal. Mach. Intell. (2018). https://doi.org/10.1109/TPAMI.2019.2941941

3. Boominathan, V., Mitra, K., Veeraraghavan, A.: Improving resolution and depth-of-field of light field cameras using a hybrid imaging system. In: 2014 IEEE International Conference on Computational Photography (ICCP), pp. 1–10. IEEE (2014)

4. Brady, D.J., et al.: Multiscale gigapixel photography. Nature **486**(7403), 386–389 (2012)

5. Buades, A., Coll, B., Morel, J.M.: Non-local means denoising. Image Process. Line **1**, 208–212 (2011)

6. Dong, C., Loy, C.C., He, K., Tang, X.: Learning a deep convolutional network for image super-resolution. In: Fleet, D., Pajdla, T., Schiele, B., Tuytelaars, T. (eds.) ECCV 2014. LNCS, vol. 8692, pp. 184–199. Springer, Cham (2014). https://doi.org/10.1007/978-3-319-10593-2_13

7. Dosovitskiy, A., et al.: FlowNet: learning optical flow with convolutional networks. In: IEEE International Conference on Computer Vision, pp. 2758–2766 (2015)

8. Haris, M., Shakhnarovich, G., Ukita, N.: Recurrent back-projection network for video super-resolution. In: IEEE Conference on Computer Vision and Pattern Recognition (CVPR) (2019)

9. Haris, M., Shakhnarovich, G., Ukita, N.: Recurrent back-projection network for video super-resolution. In: Proceedings of the IEEE/CVF Conference on Computer Vision and Pattern Recognition (CVPR), June 2019

10. Ledig, C., et al.: Photo-realistic single image super-resolution using a generative adversarial network. In: Proceedings of the IEEE Conference on Computer Vision and Pattern Recognition, pp. 4681–4690 (2017)

11. Ronneberger, O., Fischer, P., Brox, T.: U-Net: convolutional networks for biomedical image segmentation. In: International Conference on Medical Image Computing and Computer-Assisted Intervention, pp. 234–241 (2015)

12. Sajjadi, M.S.M., Vemulapalli, R., Brown, M.: Frame-recurrent video super-resolution. In: IEEE Conference on Computer Vision and Pattern Recognition, pp. 6626–6634 (2018)

13. Sajjadi, M.S., Scholkopf, B., Hirsch, M.: EnhanceNet: single image super-resolution through automated texture synthesis. In: Proceedings of the IEEE International Conference on Computer Vision, pp. 4491–4500 (2017)

14. Sun, J., Xu, Z., Shum, H.Y.: Image super-resolution using gradient profile prior. In: 2008 IEEE Conference on Computer Vision and Pattern Recognition, pp. 1–8. IEEE (2008)

15. Tan, Y., et al.: CrossNet++: cross-scale large-parallax warping for reference-based super-resolution. IEEE Comput. Archit. Lett. **01**, 1–1 (2020)

16. Tao, X., Gao, H., Liao, R., Wang, J., Jia, J.: Detail-revealing deep video super-resolution. In: IEEE International Conference on Computer Vision, pp. 4482–4490 (2017)

17. Tao, X., Gao, H., Liao, R., Wang, J., Jia, J.: Detail-revealing deep video super-resolution. In: Proceedings of the IEEE International Conference on Computer Vision, pp. 4472–4480 (2017)

18. Timofte, R., De Smet, V., Van Gool, L.: Anchored neighborhood regression for fast example-based super-resolution. In: Proceedings of the IEEE International Conference on Computer Vision, pp. 1920–1927 (2013)

19. Wang, X., Chan, K.C., Yu, K., Dong, C., Loy, C.C.: EDVR: video restoration with enhanced deformable convolutional networks. In: The IEEE Conference on Computer Vision and Pattern Recognition Workshops (CVPRW), June 2019

20. Wang, Y., Liu, Y., Heidrich, W., Dai, Q.: The light field attachment: turning a DSLR into a light field camera using a low budget camera ring. IEEE Trans. Visual Comput. Graphics **23**(10), 2357–2364 (2016)

21. Wang, Z., Bovik, A.C., Sheikh, H.R., Simoncelli, E.P.: Image quality assessment: from error visibility to structural similarity. IEEE Trans. Image Process. **13**(4), 600–612 (2004)

22. Wu, J., Wang, H., Wang, X., Zhang, Y.: A novel light field super-resolution framework based on hybrid imaging system. In: 2015 Visual Communications and Image Processing (VCIP), pp. 1–4. IEEE (2015)

23. Xue, T., Chen, B., Wu, J., Wei, D., Freeman, W.T.: Video enhancement with task-oriented flow. Int. J. Comput. Vis. **127**, 1–20 (2019)

24. Yang, J., Wright, J., Huang, T., Ma, Y.: Image super-resolution as sparse representation of raw image patches. In: 2008 IEEE Conference on Computer Vision and Pattern Recognition, pp. 1–8. Citeseer (2008)

25. Yuan, X., Fang, L., Dai, Q., Brady, D.J., Liu, Y.: Multiscale gigapixel video: a cross resolution image matching and warping approach. In: 2017 IEEE International Conference on Computational Photography (ICCP), pp. 1–9. IEEE (2017)

26. Zhang, J., et al.: Multiscale-VR: multiscale gigapixel 3D panoramic videography for virtual reality. In: IEEE International Conference on Computational Photography (2020)

27. Zhang, Z., Wang, Z., Lin, Z., Qi, H.: Image super-resolution by neural texture transfer. arXiv:1903.00834v1 (2019)

28. Zheng, H., Guo, M., Wang, H., Liu, Y., Fang, L.: Combining exemplar-based approach and learning-based approach for light field super-resolution using a hybrid imaging system. In: Proceedings of the IEEE International Conference on Computer Vision Workshops, pp. 2481–2486 (2017)

29. Zheng, H., Ji, M., Wang, H., Liu, Y., Fang, L.: Learning cross-scale correspondence and patch-based synthesis for reference-based super-resolution. In: BMVC (2017)

30. Zheng, H., Ji, M., Wang, H., Liu, Y., Fang, L.: CrossNet: an end-to-end reference-based super resolution network using cross-scale warping. In: Ferrari, V., Hebert, M., Sminchisescu, C., Weiss, Y. (eds.) ECCV 2018. LNCS, vol. 11210, pp. 87–104. Springer, Cham (2018). https://doi.org/10.1007/978-3-030-01231-1_6

Multi-label Aerial Image Classification via Adjacency-Based Label and Feature Co-embedding

Xiangrong Zhang$^{(\boxtimes)}$, Shouping Shan, Jing Gu, Xu Tang, and Licheng Jiao

School of Artificial Intelligence, Xidian University, Xi'an, China
{xrzhang,lchjiao}@mail.xidian.edu.cn, jgu@xidian.edu.cn

Abstract. Multi-label image classification is a fundamental task in aerial image processing, which automatically generates image annotations for better image content interpretation. Many existing methods realize multi-label classification through an image level, while they ignore the dependencies among labels and the cross-modal relations between labels and image features. In this paper, we propose a simple and intuitive multi-label classification method via adjacency-based label and feature co-embedding for aerial images. To be specific, we introduce an adjacency-based label embedding module to maintain the original label relationships in the semantic space. A label and feature co-embedding module is designed to enhance the text-image cross-modal interactions and to obtain the attention-based label-specific vectors, which effectively excavate the response relations between labels and images. Experiments on two benchmark aerial image multi-label datasets show that our approach achieves considerable performance compared with seven previous approaches. Besides, visualization analyses indicate the label embeddings learned by our model maintain a meaningful semantic topology, which explicitly exploit label-feature dependencies.

Keywords: Aerial images · Multi-label classification · Adjacency-based label embedding · Label and feature co-embedding

1 Introduction

Multi-label aerial image classification (MLAIC) tries to assign labels on multiple objects in an image, which is a fundamental task in computer vision. Recently, MLAIC boosted massive applications such as image retrieval and urban cartography [11,15,16,18,24]. One way to tackle the MLAIC problem is to separate the multi-label task into several isolated single-label classification tasks [6,10].

Supported by the National Natural Science Foundation of China under Grant 61772400, Grant 61802295, Grant 61772399, Grant 61801351, and Grant 61871306; and in part by the Key Research and Development Program in Shaanxi Province of China under Grant 2019ZDLGY03-08.

© Springer Nature Switzerland AG 2021
L. Fang et al. (Eds.): CICAI 2021, LNAI 13069, pp. 384–395, 2021.
https://doi.org/10.1007/978-3-030-93046-2_33

However, these methods cannot make full use of the label dependencies, which are significant for modeling multiple label relationships.

To solve these problems, Recurrent Neural Networks (RNNs) [8,21,22] are proposed to capture the label relations by considering the label co-occurrence as long-term sequential dependence. While these approaches neglect to fully exploit the visual-spatial image information. To learn the label-specific semantic characterizations, several works like Relation Network [9] and SRN [32] try to learn the local correlations between labels and images, but ignore the prior global correlations among labels.

In this paper, we propose a multi-label classification method via the adjacency-based label and feature co-embedding. Specifically, to excavate the multiple label relations, we introduce a label embedding module (LEM) based on the statistical label co-occurrence matrix to utilize the global relationships between labels. In the LEM, we study a label distance measurement mechanism to improve the interpretability of label embedding by considering the local mini-batch label relations. Besides, to facilitate modeling the relations between labels and features, a label and feature co-embedding module is also designed. Finally, the verified experiments show that the adjacency-based label and feature co-embedding algorithm obtains competitive performance on MLAIC task.

The major contributions of this paper can be briefly summarized as follows:

- An adjacency-based label embedding module is proposed to maintain the global correlations among labels during the label embedding process. Moreover, to better utilize the local label relations, a label distance measurement mechanism is studied to constrain label embedding module, which can shorten the distance between interdependent labels and separate unrelated labels farther.
- A label and feature co-embedding module is designed to model the label-specific relationships with image features, through which the cross-modal response relations between labels and features can be effectively excavated.
- We evaluate our method on two benchmark aerial image multi-label datasets, the experiments indicate that our proposed method achieves competitive performance compared with previous approaches.

2   Related Work

The MLAIC task has attracted increasing interest recently. Boutell [1] and Read [20] considered to handle multi-label classification by transforming the problem into multiple single-label classification tasks [30]. Benefited from the great success of deep Conventional Neural Network (CNNs) in the single-label image classification task, this strategy largely improves the performance of multi-label image classification [6,10]. However, these methods ignore the topological structure between labels, which is an important rule to reflect the relationship between labels.

To explore the dependencies between labels, RNNs-based approaches are proposed [8,21,22,31] to embed label vectors by exploiting the correlations between labels, while those methods need to pre-define or learn the label orders [3]. Recently, Graph Convolutional Networks (GCNs) [5,12,14,28] are also proposed for multi-label image classification. Chen et al. [5] used multi-layer GCNs to mine the dependencies between label vectors. However, the proposed ML-GCN only considers the global features of the image, and the different labels relative to the image features are ignored.

In addition, several approaches [4,7,9,23,29] are proposed to capture the spatial dependence between labels, and to locate the positions of the distinguishing features of each label. Hua et al. [7,9] applied relation network to the MLAIC task, in which a label relational inference module is proposed. It has the ability to locate the specific regions of labels and model the semantic label dependence. However, the matching process between the image feature parcels and labels requires a amount of calculations. Besides, image features and labels co-projection [23,29] methods are also popular. You et al. [29] proposed a cross-modal attention and semantic graph embedding method for multi-label classification, which utilizes the global label relationships for label embedding process, while neglect to consider the local label dependencies among mini-batch samples. Chen et al. [4] proposed a specific semantic graph representation learning method to deeply explore the label-image relationships, while such approach ignores the prior information of the global label dependencies.

3   Approach

The overall structure of the proposed method is shown in Fig. 1, which includes several stages. Firstly, the LEM with label distance measurement mechanism takes the GloVe vectors [19] as input to generate label embeddings, which maintains the original label relationships. The feature embeddings are obtained by two 1×1 convolution layers. Then the learned label and feature embeddings are fed into the co-embedding module to obtain the attention-based label-specific vectors which can be used for final prediction. We will describe our LEM and the label and feature co-embedding module in detail.

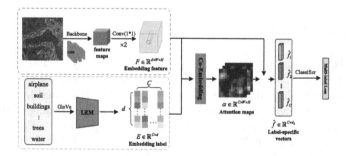

Fig. 1. Pipeline of adjacency-based label and feature co-embedding model.

3.1 Adjacency-Based Label Embedding

The statistic label co-occurrence matrix contains global dependencies between labels, which is instructive for the label embedding process to maintain the original prior global label relations.

The relationships among labels can be built in a data-driven way [5]. To model the co-occurrence patterns between labels, we build the label adjacency matrix $A \in \mathbb{R}^{C \times C}$ from the training set which equals the conditional probability matrix by setting $A_{ij} = P(L_i|L_j)$, where C is the number of the labels and $P(L_i|L_j)$ denotes the probability of label L_j when label L_i appears.

In the following discussion, Let X be the input aerial images, let Y be the corresponding ground-truth labelings, and let L be the original text labels.

Given labels L we adopt GloVe [19] to obtain the original label representations $G \in \mathbb{R}^{C \times N}$, where N is the dimension of GloVe vectors. This label representation preserves more information than one-hot embeddings. To get the label embeddings $E = \{e_i\}_{i=1}^{C}$, where $e_i \in \mathbb{R}^d$ and d is the dimension of label embeddings, the obtained G are then fed into a mapping layer $\Phi(\cdot)$ which contains two fully-connected layers and a batch normalization layer followed by ReLU activations.

$$G = GloVe(L) \in \mathbb{R}^{C \times N} \tag{1}$$

$$E = \Phi(G) \in \mathbb{R}^{C \times d} \tag{2}$$

We define the relationships among labels upon the embeddings E, so that the relations between e_i and e_j is defined as $cos(e_i, e_j)$ and we consider that $cos(e_i, e_j)$ is close to the adjacency A_{ij} in A to utilize the global label relations as shown in Fig. 2. The label embedding loss $\mathcal{L}_{lem}$ formulates as:

$$\mathcal{L}_{lem} = \sum_{i=1}^{C} \sum_{j=1}^{C} \sigma_{ij} \left(\frac{e_i^\top e_j}{\|e_i\| \|e_j\|} - A_{ij} \right)^2 \tag{3}$$

where σ_{ij} donates an indicator function to relax the constraint by

$$\sigma_{ij} = \begin{cases} 0, A_{ij} < \tau \quad and \quad \frac{e_i^\top e_j}{\|e_i\|\|e_j\|} < \tau \\ 1, \quad otherwise \end{cases} \tag{4}$$

where τ is a small hyperparameter to ignore the noisy co-occurrence label pairs, which makes the module focus more on the strong relationships.

Label Distance Measurement Mechanism. The label embedding module ensures that the generated label embedding vectors maintain the original label dependencies. While these dependencies only reflect the global statistical information of samples which ignore the local label co-occurrence. Thereby, we propose a label distance measurement mechanism to enhance the related label embeddings to be more compact in a mini-batch.

The distance between higher relevant embedding labels should be closer than lower relevant embedding labels. For examples, if label L_i and label L_j are in

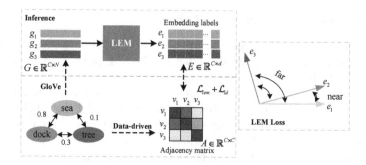

Fig. 2. Illustration of the adjacency-based label embedding module. The LEM loss means that $cos(\mathbf{e}_i, \mathbf{e}_j)$ among label embeddings should be close to A_{ij}.

the same image rather than label L_k, we consider that the distance between L_i and L_j in the semantic space should be shortened, whereas the distance between L_i and L_k should be widened [23]. It can be formulated as:

$$p\left(\mathbf{e}_i^+, \mathbf{e}_j^+\right) + \delta \leq p\left(\mathbf{e}_i^+, \mathbf{e}_k^-\right), \quad \forall \mathbf{e}_i^+, \mathbf{e}_j^+ \in L^+ \quad \forall \mathbf{e}_k^- \in L^- \qquad (5)$$

where $\mathbf{e}_i^+$ and $\mathbf{e}_j^+$ indicates label L_i and L_j are co-appearing labels, while $\mathbf{e}_k^-$ is the absent label. $p(\mathbf{e}_i^+, \mathbf{e}_j^+)$ denotes the Euclidean distance of all pairs of appearing labels, and $p(\mathbf{e}_i^+, \mathbf{e}_k^-)$ indicates the distance of the cartesian product combinations between the co-appearing labels and absent labels. Finally, the label distance measurement loss $\mathcal{L}_{ld}$ is defined as follows:

$$\mathcal{L}_{ld} = \frac{\sum p(\mathbf{e}_i^+, \mathbf{e}_j^+) - \sum p(\mathbf{e}_i^+, \mathbf{e}_k^-) + \delta}{n} \qquad (6)$$

where δ is a hyperparameter and n indicates the size of mini-batch.

3.2   Label and Feature Co-embedding

Previous LEM obtains the label embeddings $E \in \mathbb{R}^{C \times d}$, while images X and E are still belong to different modalities. Thereby, a label and feature co-embedding module is studied to fully excavate the response relationships between labels and image features.

Given input images X we obtain features $F_{cnn} \in \mathbb{R}^{D \times W \times H}$ by CNN (e.g., ResNet 50), where W, H and D denote the width, height, and channel of features. We then apply the map $\Psi(\cdot)$ which contains two 1×1 convolution layers to project the image features to the same dimension as semantic labels embedding space by

$$F = \Psi(F_{cnn}) \in \mathbb{R}^{d \times W \times H} \qquad (7)$$

The corresponding image feature embeddings $F = \{\mathbf{f}_{wh}\}_{w=1,h=1}^{W,H}$ and label embeddings $E = \{\mathbf{e}_i\}_{i=1}^{C}$ are fused by using a low-rank bilinear pooling method

[13] to guide the embedding label $\mathbf{e}_i$ focusing on the semantic-aware feature region $\mathbf{f}_{wh}$ by

$$\mathbf{f}_{i,wh} = \mathbf{U}^T \left(\tanh\left(\mathbf{f}_{wh} \odot \mathbf{e}_i \right) \right) + \mathbf{b} \tag{8}$$

where $\odot$ is the element-wise multiplication operation and $tanh(\cdot)$ is the hyperbolic tangent function, (w, h) is the location of image feature projection. $\mathbf{U} \in \mathbb{R}^{d \times d_2}$ and $\mathbf{b} \in \mathbb{R}^{d_2}$ are learnable parameters in a fully connected layer, and d_2 is the dimension of output features. Thereby, we can obtain the feature's response coefficient with each label $\mathbf{e}_i$ by a fully connected network as follows:

$$\alpha_{i,wh} = f_{fc}(\mathbf{f}_{i,wh}) \tag{9}$$

where the coefficient $\alpha_{i,wh}$ indicates the i_{th} label embedding's response of location (w, h) in feature embedding, and larger value of $\alpha_{i,wh}$ means that feature embedding $\mathbf{f}_{wh}$ has greater relevance with label embedding $\mathbf{e}_i$. We normalize the coefficients over all positions using a softmax function [4] by

$$\hat{\alpha}_{i,wh} = \frac{exp(\alpha_{i,wh})}{\sum\limits_{w,h} exp(\alpha_{i,wh})} \tag{10}$$

The final attention-based label-specific vector can be formulated as:

$$\hat{\mathbf{f}}_i = \sum_{w,h} \hat{\alpha}_{i,wh} \mathbf{f}_{i,wh} \tag{11}$$

where $\hat{\mathbf{f}}_i$ indicates the response vector between feature embedding $\mathbf{f}_{w,h}$ and label embedding $\mathbf{e}_i$, which is fed into a linear classifier for final multi-label classification.

Training Loss. Finally, the whole object function in our model for MLAIC is defined as follows:

$$\mathcal{L} = \mathcal{L}_{CE} + \mathcal{L}_{lem} + \lambda \mathcal{L}_{ld} \tag{12}$$

where $\mathcal{L}_{CE}$ is the multi-label cross-entropy loss function. and λ is the hyperparameter to balance losses.

4   Experiments

To assess the performance of our method, experiments on the two benchmark aerial image multi-label datasets are conducted. Specifically, we compare the proposed approach with seven state-of-the-art methods, including ResNet-50 [6], ResNet-RBFNN [30], CA-ResNet-BiLSTM [8], AL-RN-ResNet [9], ML-GCN [5], SSGRL [4], ADD-GCN [28], in which ResNet50 is chosen as the backbone network.

Datasets. The datasets in our experiments are UCM and AID multi-label datasets. Specifically, UCM multi-label dataset [2] is reproduced by assigning all aerial images collected in the UCM dataset [27] with newly defined object labels. AID multi-label dataset [9] is reproduced by AID scene classification dataset [26]. The number of categories in both datasets is 17: soil, airplane, building, car, chaparral, court, dock, field, grass, limousine, pavement, sand, sea, ship, tank, tree, and water.

Experimental Setup. In our experiments, the input and output dimensions of the two fully connected layers of the label embedding module are 300 to 150 and 150 to 300, respectively. 80% of the images are used as the training set and 20% are used as the test set. The input images are scaled, cropped, and rotated randomly during the training process, and the image resolution is expanded to 448×448 during the test uniformly. The initial learning rate during training is 0.01, among which the learning rate of the backbone network is set to 0.001. After 20th iteration of total 80 epochs, the learning rate drops to 10% of the origin. The batch size is 8, and the SGD optimizer with momentum is chosen for optimization, in which the momentum is 0.9. The parameters d, d_2, δ and τ are set as 300, 300, 0.1, 0.01 respectively. λ in UCM and AID multi-label datasets are 1 and 10 respectively.

Evaluation Metrics. In the experiment, we apply example-based mF_1 [25], example-based mP_e, and example-based mR_e scores to quantitatively assess the performance of different models. Furthermore, the category-based precision mP_l and category-based recall mR_l are also considered.

4.1 Experimental Results

UCM Classification Results. The comparisons of classification performance on UCM multi-label dataset are shown in Table 1. We can observe that our model surpasses all competitors in mF_1 and mPe scores. Specifically, our method increases mF_1 score by 0.28% compared to AL-RN-ResNet, which is the state-of-the-art method in MLAIC, but ignores the global dependencies between labels.

Compared with the graph-based ML-GCN approach, which only considers the global label relations, Our model outperforms ML-GCN by 0.43% in mF_1 score. Similarly, the proposed approach improves SSGRL and ADD-GCN, which are state-of-art methods in natural scene images by 0.30%, and 0.93% in mF_1 score respectively. This indicates that our method is more suitable for MLAIC task.

The predictions of several samples in UCM multi-label dataset are presented in Table 2, where blue color represents the missing labels in the prediction results, and red color represents the incorrectly predicted labels in the prediction results.

AID Classification Results. In the AID multi-label dataset, our model obtains an improvement of 0.79% in the mF_1 score compared to AL-RN-ResNet (see Table 3). Although our approach performs superiorly to most of the competitors,

Table 1. Comparisons of the classification performance on UCM multi-label dataset.

Method	mF_1	mP_e	mR_e	mP_l	mR_l
ResNet-50 [6]	79.68	80.86	81.95	88.78	78.98
ResNet-RBFNN [30]	80.58	79.92	84.59	86.21	83.72
CA-ResNet-BiLSTM [8]	81.47	77.94	89.02	86.12	84.26
AL-RN-ResNet [9]	86.76	88.81	87.07	**92.33**	85.26
ML-GCN [5]	86.61	86.51	**89.04**	89.88	86.12
SSGRL [4]	86.74	88.89	86.93	92.27	82.44
ADD-GCN [28]	86.12	88.05	86.72	90.18	**86.43**
Ours	**87.04**	**89.49**	87.75	90.63	84.72

Table 2. Example images and predicted labels on the UCM multi-label data set.

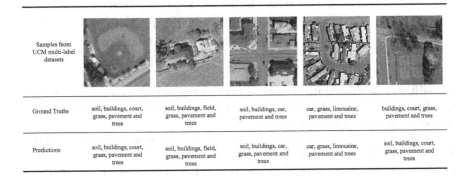

Samples feom UCM multi-label datasets					
Ground Truths	soil, buildings, court, grass, pavement and trees	soil, buildings, field, grass, pavement and trees	soil, buildings, car, pavement and trees	car, grass, limousine, pavement and trees	buildings, court, grass, pavement and trees
Predictions	soil, buildings, court, grass, pavement and trees	soil, buildings, field, grass, pavement and trees	soil, buildings, car, grass, pavement and trees	car, grass, limousine, pavement and trees	soil, buildings, court, grass, pavement and trees

Table 3. Comparisons of the classification performance on AID multi-label dataset.

Method	mF_1	mP_e	mR_e	mP_l	mR_l
ResNet-50 [6]	86.23	89.31	85.65	72.39	52.82
ResNet-RBFNN [30]	83.77	82.84	88.32	60.85	70.45
CA-ResNet-BiLSTM [8]	87.63	89.03	88.99	79.5	65.6
AL-RN-ResNet [9]	88.72	91	88.95	80.81	71.12
ML-GCN [5]	**89.6**	91.39	**90.31**	82.1	70.72
SSGRL [4]	89.14	91.23	89.69	78.41	70.89
ADD-GCN [28]	88.71	89.93	90.23	**84.69**	**73.68**
Ours	89.51	**91.8**	89.76	82.3	71.46

ML-GCN obtains the best mF_1 performance in which GCN is applied to model the label relationships. Compared to the graph-based methods, our algorithm is more intuitive and easy-understanding. Besides, our label and feature co-embedding method effectively considers the response between each label and each feature pixel rather than global image contents.

4.2   Ablation Study

We perform an ablation study on UCM multi-label dataset where LD is the label distance measurement loss. As observed in Table 4, the label embeddings learned by LEM obtain an improvement by 0.45% in mF_1 score compared with the original GloVe vectors, which means the label embeddings are more discriminative. Besides, the LEM with label distance measurement mechanism achieves the best performance compared with single LEM and original GloVe vectors, which indicates the proposed label distance measurement mechanism is helpful for guiding LEM as expected.

Table 4. Effects of different chosen modules in UCM multi-label dataset.

LEM	LD	mF_1	mP_e	mR_e	mP_l	mR_l
×	×	86.38	89.16	86.73	90.13	85.06
√	×	86.83	89.07	87.65	**91.32**	**86.88**
√	√	**87.04**	**89.49**	**87.75**	90.63	84.72

Classifier Visualization. To dive deep into the model, we visualize the label-specific attention maps learned from our label and feature co-embedding module on the UCM multi-label dataset.

As shown in Fig. 3, the regions with label-specific semantics are highlighted. For instance, the regions of the tennis court are considered as discriminative regions for label 'court' even if the court's region in the first image is obscured. Meanwhile, the residential and industrial areas are strongly activated in feature maps for recognizing label 'building'. We can observe that the relevant semantic area about 'car' can still be found although the car is small, which indicates our approach can not only obtain competitive performance but also build a bridge to align information between different modalities.

In Fig. 4, we adopt the Principal Component Analysis (PCA) [17] to visualize the label embeddings learned by adjacency-based label embedding module with label distance measurement mechanism based on the UCM multi-label dataset. It is clear to see that the learned embedding vectors (see Fig. 4(b)) in semantic space contain much more meaningful correlations compared to GloVe vectors in Fig. 4(a). For instance, labels 'water', 'ship', and 'dock' gather closer than original GloVe vectors in projection space, which is consistent with common sense, and indicates that the module successfully embeds the vectors as expected.

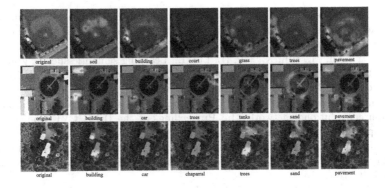

Fig. 3. Label-specific attention maps from UCM multi-label dataset visualization.

(a) GloVe label vectors visualization   (b) Learned label embedding vectors visualization

Fig. 4. Visualization of the label vectors PCA projection.

5   Conclusion

In this paper, we propose a simple and intuitive multi-label aerial image classification method based on the adjacency-based label and feature co-embedding.
This work comprises two components: an adjacency-based label embedding module with label distance measurement mechanism to guide label embedding, and
a label and feature co-embedding module to model the cross-modality interaction between labels and images. In order to assess the performance of our
method, experiments on the UCM and AID multi-label datasets are conducted.
In comparison with previous works, our method obtains competitive classification results. In addition, the visualization of the label-specific attention maps
learned by co-embedding module indicates that our approach can align cross-
modality information.

References

1. Boutell, M.R., Luo, J., Shen, X., Brown, C.M.: Learning multi-label scene classification. Pattern Recogn. **37**(9), 1757–1771 (2004)
2. Chaudhuri, B., Demir, B., Chaudhuri, S., Bruzzone, L.: Multilabel remote sensing image retrieval using a semisupervised graph-theoretic method. IEEE Trans.
Geosci. Remote Sens. **56**(2), 1144–1158 (2017)

3. Chen, S.F., Chen, Y.C., Yeh, C.K., Wang, Y.C.: Order-free rnn with visual attention for multi-label classification. In: Proceedings of the AAAI Conference on Artificial Intelligence. vol. 32 (2018)
4. Chen, T., Xu, M., Hui, X., Wu, H., Lin, L.: Learning semantic-specific graph representation for multi-label image recognition. In: Proceedings of the IEEE/CVF International Conference on Computer Vision. pp. 522–531 (2019)
5. Chen, Z.M., Wei, X.S., Wang, P., Guo, Y.: Multi-label image recognition with graph convolutional networks. In: Proceedings of the IEEE/CVF Conference on Computer Vision and Pattern Recognition. pp. 5177–5186 (2019)
6. He, K., Zhang, X., Ren, S., Sun, J.: Deep residual learning for image recognition. In: Proceedings of the IEEE conference on computer vision and pattern recognition. pp. 770–778 (2016)
7. Hua, Y., Mou, L., Zhu, X.X.: Label relation inference for multi-label aerial image classification. In: IGARSS 2019–2019 IEEE International Geoscience and Remote Sensing Symposium. pp. 5244–5247. IEEE (2019)
8. Hua, Y., Mou, L., Zhu, X.X.: Recurrently exploring class-wise attention in a hybrid convolutional and bidirectional lstm network for multi-label aerial image classification. ISPRS J. Photogramm. Remote. Sens. **149**, 188–199 (2019)
9. Hua, Y., Mou, L., Zhu, X.X.: Relation network for multilabel aerial image classification. IEEE Trans. Geosci. Remote Sens. **58**(7), 4558–4572 (2020)
10. Huang, G., Liu, Z., Van Der Maaten, L., Weinberger, K.Q.: Densely connected convolutional networks. In: Proceedings of the IEEE conference on computer vision and pattern recognition. pp. 4700–4708 (2017)
11. Kang, J., Fernandez-Beltran, R., Hong, D., Chanussot, J., Plaza, A.: Graph relation network: Modeling relations between scenes for multilabel remote-sensing image classification and retrieval. IEEE Transactions on Geoscience and Remote Sensing (2020)
12. Khan, N., Chaudhuri, U., Banerjee, B., Chaudhuri, S.: Graph convolutional network for multi-label vhr remote sensing scene recognition. Neurocomputing **357**, 36–46 (2019)
13. Kim, J.H., On, K.W., Lim, W., Kim, J., Ha, J.W., Zhang, B.T.: Hadamard product for low-rank bilinear pooling. arXiv preprint arXiv:1610.04325 (2016)
14. Li, Q., Peng, X., Qiao, Y., Peng, Q.: Learning category correlations for multi-label image recognition with graph networks. arXiv preprint arXiv:1909.13005 (2019)
15. Li, X., Zhao, F., Guo, Y.: Multi-label image classification with a probabilistic label enhancement model. In: UAI, vol. 1, pp. 1–10 (2014)
16. Ma, J., Wu, L., Tang, X., Liu, F., Zhang, X., Jiao, L.: Building extraction of aerial images by a global and multi-scale encoder-decoder network. Remote Sens. **12**(15), 2350 (2020)
17. Maćkiewicz, A., Ratajczak, W.: Principal components analysis (PCA). Comput. Geosci. **19**(3), 303–342 (1993)
18. Marcos, D., Volpi, M., Kellenberger, B., Tuia, D.: Land cover mapping at very high resolution with rotation equivariant CNNs: towards small yet accurate models. ISPRS J. Photogramm. Remote. Sens. **145**, 96–107 (2018)
19. Pennington, J., Socher, R., Manning, C.D.: Glove: global vectors for word representation. In: Proceedings of the 2014 Conference on Empirical Methods in Natural Language Processing (EMNLP), pp. 1532–1543 (2014)
20. Read, J., Pfahringer, B., Holmes, G., Frank, E.: Classifier chains for multi-label classification. Mach. Learn. **85**(3), 333 (2011)

21. Sumbul, G., Demir, B.: A CNN-RNN framework with a novel patch-based multi-attention mechanism for multi-label image classification in remote sensing. arXiv preprint arXiv:1902.11274 (2019)

22. Wang, J., Yang, Y., Mao, J., Huang, Z., Huang, C., Xu, W.: CNN-RNN: a unified framework for multi-label image classification. In: Proceedings of the IEEE Conference on Computer Vision and Pattern Recognition, pp. 2285–2294 (2016)

23. Wen, S., et al.: Multilabel image classification via feature/label co-projection. IEEE Trans. Syst. Man Cybern. Syst. **51**, 7250–7259 (2020)

24. Wu, J., et al.: Multi-label active learning algorithms for image classification: overview and future promise. ACM Comput. Surv. (CSUR) **53**(2), 1–35 (2020)

25. Wu, X.Z., Zhou, Z.H.: A unified view of multi-label performance measures. In: International Conference on Machine Learning, pp. 3780–3788. PMLR (2017)

26. Xia, G.S., et al.: AID: a benchmark data set for performance evaluation of aerial scene classification. IEEE Trans. Geosci. Remote Sens. **55**(7), 3965–3981 (2017)

27. Yang, Y., Newsam, S.: Bag-of-visual-words and spatial extensions for land-use classification. In: Proceedings of the 18th SIGSPATIAL International Conference on Advances in Geographic Information Systems, pp. 270–279 (2010)

28. Ye, J., He, J., Peng, X., Wu, W., Qiao, Yu.: Attention-driven dynamic graph convolutional network for multi-label image recognition. In: Vedaldi, A., Bischof, H., Brox, T., Frahm, J.-M. (eds.) ECCV 2020. LNCS, vol. 12366, pp. 649–665. Springer, Cham (2020). https://doi.org/10.1007/978-3-030-58589-1_39

29. You, R., Guo, Z., Cui, L., Long, X., Bao, Y., Wen, S.: Cross-modality attention with semantic graph embedding for multi-label classification. In: Proceedings of the AAAI Conference on Artificial Intelligence, vol. 34, pp. 12709–12716 (2020)

30. Zeggada, A., Melgani, F., Bazi, Y.: A deep learning approach to UAV image multilabeling. IEEE Geosci. Remote Sens. Lett. **14**(5), 694–698 (2017)

31. Zhang, X., Sun, Y., Kai, J., Chen, L., Jiao, L., Zhou, H.: Spatial sequential recurrent neural network for hyperspectral image classification. IEEE J. Sel. Top. Appl. Earth Obs. Remote Sens. **11**, 1–15 (2018)

32. Zhu, F., Li, H., Ouyang, W., Yu, N., Wang, X.: Learning spatial regularization with image-level supervisions for multi-label image classification. In: Proceedings of the IEEE Conference on Computer Vision and Pattern Recognition, pp. 5513–5522 (2017)

Coarse-to-Fine Attribute Editing
for Fashion Images

Qinghu Wang[1], Jianjun Qian[1]([✉]), Xingxing Zou[2,3], Jian Yang[1],
and Waikeung Wong[2,3]

[1] PCA Lab, Key Lab of Intelligent Perception and Systems for High-Dimensional
Information of Ministry of Education, Nanjing University of Science and Technology,
Nanjing, China
{wangqinghu,csjqian,csjyang}@njust.edu.cn

[2] Institute of Textiles and Clothing, The Hong Kong Polytechnic University,
Hung Hom, Hong Kong, Special Administrative Region of China
calvin.wong@polyu.edu.hk

[3] Laboratory for Artificial Intelligence in Design, Hung Hom,
Hong Kong, Special Administrative Region of China
xingxingzou@aidlab.hk

Abstract. With the development of Generative Adversarial Networks,
attribute editing has been more and more popular in computer vision.
The previous works employed the multi-domain image-to-image translation framework to solve attribute editing. However, it is difficult to generate consistent texture with the original images. Meanwhile, the un-target
attribute regions are changed by using these methods. To address these
problems, this paper presents a coarse-to-fine attribute editing scheme
(CFAE) for fashion images. CFAE is composed of coarse stage and refine
stage. In the coarse stage, we design a landmark-based attention scheme
in conjunction with StarGAN [5] to locate and edit the target attribute
regions. Subsequently, DeepFillv2 [16] is employed in the refine stage to
make the target attribute regions consistent with the original image. In
experiment section, we compare our method with several state-of-the-art
methods on OUTFIT Dataset and the results demonstrate the effectiveness of CFAE.

Keywords: Deep learning · GAN · Fashion · Attribute editing

1 Introduction

Attribute editing aims to make translations to images according to the target
attributes. In this paper, we focus on the attribute editing for fashion images
which have several attributes such as neckline, sleeve length and their corresponding values: V-neckline, long-sleeve. It has important potential values to
edit attributes of the fashion images. For one thing, consumers can change some

This research is funded by the Laboratory for Artificial Intelligence in Design (Project
Code: RP3-1), Hong Kong Special Administrative Region.

L. Fang et al. (Eds.): CICAI 2021, LNAI 13069, pp. 396–407, 2021.
https://doi.org/10.1007/978-3-030-93046-2_34

Fig. 1. Attributes editing examples of our method on OUTFIT Dataset. The edited images are realistic and corresponding with the target attributes.

attributes of current clothes to retrieve new clothes online. For another thing, designers can design new garments by using different attributes. In [18], the authors study the attribute editing task in the perspective of image retrieval. Based on this, Kenan E et al. propose a weakly supervised localization method to handle region-specific attribute editing [1]. However, with the increasing number of attributes, these image retrieval methods have to collect more fashion images to enlarge the dataset. As Generative Adversarial Networks (GANs) [8] becoming more prevalent, the image-to-image translation frameworks are used to solve the attribute editing task. Pix2pix [11] and CycleGAN [20] can only translate images between two domains and they have limited scalability when handling image translation across multiple domains. The StarGAN [5] is able to perform multi-domain image-to-image translations with a single generative network by introducing an auxiliary classifier in the discriminator. Ganimation [14] and SaGAN [17] incorporate an attention mechanism in the generative network to focus on the target attribute regions. The difference between these two methods is SaGAN [17] uses an additional branch to generate the attention map. The goal of above mentioned methods is editing facial attributes rather than fashion attributes. AMGAN [2] proposes the CAM-based attention mechanism to improve the translation performance for fashion images. It uses the pre-trained classification network to obtain the class activation maps (CAMs) [19] and uses them to locate the target attribute regions during training the generator. However, the CAMs [19] can not locate the attributes accurately just using the convolutional neural network, leading to unnecessary translations in un-target attribute regions. Although AMGAN [2] achieves better results in attribute editing, it generates blurry textures inconsistent with surrounding areas in the target attribute regions.

Motivated by the above works, this paper presents a coarse-to-fine attribute editing scheme (CFAE) for fashion images. Different from AMGAN [2], CFAE utilizes landmarks to locate the target attribute regions. It is more accurate to locate the target attribute regions with landmarks. We first use an pre-trained landmark predictor to predict the key points of a cloth. Then some specific points are connected according to the target attribute to obtain the target attribute regions mask. Additionally, CFAE adopts DeepFillv2 [16] to solve the texture inconsistent problems by borrowing the idea of image inpainting.

We evaluate our method on the fashion dataset: OUTFIT. Some available fashion datasets such as DeepFashion [12] often consists of complex scenes including variations of the scale, illumination, and occlusion. These complex scenes will affect the performance of fashion images synthesize or attribute editing. In OUTFIT dataset, the fashion images only consist of the clothes and clean background. Figure 1 illustrates some examples of attribute editing results of our method on the OUTFIT dataset. From Fig. 1, CFAE can translate the input images into new ones based on the target attributes and the new generated regions are consistent with the surrounding areas.

Our contributions are summarized as follows:

- We propose a coarse-to-fine attribute editing scheme (CFAE) for fashion images. CFAE can generate photorealistic images based on the target attributes.
- The landmark-based attention scheme is introduced to locate the attribute regions accurately.
- We conduct experiments on the fashion dataset: OUTFIT. Experimental results on the OUTFIT demonstrate the advantages of the proposed CFAE over state-of-the-art methods.

2   Method

In this section, we describe the details of CFAE. The framework of CFAE is shown in Fig. 2. CFAE is composed of coarse stage and refine stage. For coarse stage, we incorporate landmark-based attention scheme in StarGAN [5] to translate the image based on the target attribute. For refine stage, the inpainting model DeepFillv2 [16] is used to refine the generated results.

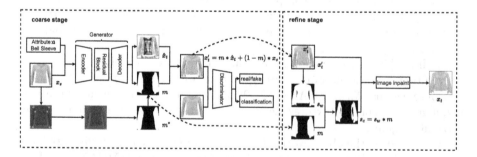

Fig. 2. The framework of CFAE. The coarse stage incorporates encoder-decoder and generative adversarial networks to edit the input images based on the target attribute. In the refine stage, we employ the inpainting model to refine the edited regions for preserving the texture consistency of the fashion image.

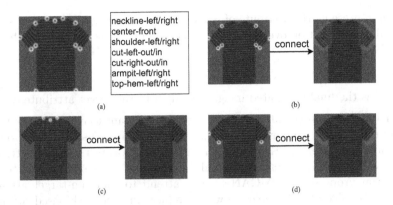

neckline-left/right
center-front
shoulder-left/right
cut-left-out/in
cut-right-out/in
armpit-left/right
top-hem-left/right

(a)

connect

(b)

connect

(c)

connect

(d)

Fig. 3. All estimated thirteen landmarks are listed in (a), (b), (c), (d) respectively show the specific landmarks of attributes: sleeve, neckline, sleeve cuff and their corresponding masks.

2.1   Coarse Stage

Overview. In the coarse stage, we combine landmark-based attention scheme with StarGAN [5] to edit attribute of fashion image. From Fig. 2, we can see that the generator G is an encoder-decoder structure. Based on G, the $\hat{x}_t$ and attention map m are achieved according to the image x_s and target attribute a(one-hot vector). Then we obtain the final result by combining the generated target attribute regions and the original image as follows

$$x'_t = m * \hat{x}_t + (1 - m) * x_s \tag{1}$$

The discriminator is used to compute adversarial loss and attribute classification loss.

Adversarial Loss. Inspired by WGAN-GP [9], the adversarial loss is defined as
$$\mathcal{L}_{adv} = \mathbb{E}_x \left[D_{src}(x) \right] - \mathbb{E}_{x'_t} \left[D_{src}(x'_t) \right]$$
$$- \lambda_{gp} \mathbb{E}_{\tilde{x}} \left[\left(\| \nabla_{\tilde{x}} D_{src}(\tilde{x}) \|_2 - 1 \right)^2 \right] \tag{2}$$

where x represents the source images, x'_t represents the final results of generator and $\tilde{x}$ is sampled uniformly along a straight line between real and generated images. The generator G is trained to minimize the adversarial objective while the discriminator D is trained to maximize it.

Classification Loss. Here, we use the same classification loss as StarGAN [5], which is decomposed into two terms: one term calculated from real images for optimizing D, another is calculated from fake images for optimizing G. The former is defined as
$$\mathcal{L}_{cls}^D = \mathbb{E}_{x,a'} \left[-\log D_{cls} \left(a' | x \right) \right] \tag{3}$$

where a' represents the attribute of source images x and $D_{cls}(a'|x)$ represents a probability distribution over attribute labels computed by D. The classification loss of G is defined as

$$\mathcal{L}_{cls}^G = \mathbb{E}_{x_t',a}\left[-\log D_{cls}(a|x_t')\right] \tag{4}$$

where x_t' is the final translated image according to the target attribute a.

Attention Loss. In the attribute editing task, we want to edit only the target attribute regions. Therefore, the attention mechanism is used to focus on the target attribute regions. However, it is difficult to locate the target attribute regions without extra supervision signal. In addition, The CAM-based attention mechanism proposed in AMGAN [2] will attend to some un-target attribute regions. To solve these problems, we introduce an landmark-based attention scheme. We use a pre-trained model to predict the landmarks of garments. Then some specific landmarks are connected with certain width line to generate the target attribute regions mask. We combine the target attribute regions mask with attention loss to guide the generation of the attention map. The attention loss is defined as

$$L_{attn}^G = \|m - m^*\|_1 \tag{5}$$

where m^* represents the target attribute regions mask and m represents the attention map.

Landmark-Based Attention Scheme. Here, we can locate the different parts of the clothes based on landmarks. As illustrated in Fig. 3(a) we first estimate thirteen landmarks of a cloth and connect the relative landmarks according to the target attribute. Specifically, for sleeve length or sleeve shape attribute, we connect the four landmarks in sequence: shoulder-left/right, cuff-left/right-out, cuff-left/right-in, armpit-left/right as shown in Fig. 3(b). For neckline attribute, the three landmarks are connected in sequence: neckline-left, neckline-right, center-front as shown in Fig. 3(c). The two landmarks: cut-left/right-out, cut-left/right-in are used to locate the sleeve cuff regions as illustrated in Fig. 3(d). We thus employ the target attribute regions masks to locate the different attributes. Then these masks are used to supervise the generation of attention maps, keeping the attribute-irrelevant regions unchanged.

Reconstruction Loss. In addition, we use the cycle consistency loss to help generator to preserve the un-target attribute regions. The reconstruction loss is defined as

$$\mathcal{L}_{rec}^G = \mathbb{E}_{x,a,a'}\left[\|x - G(G(x,a),a')\|_1\right] \tag{6}$$

where G transform the source image x according to the target attribute a and then reconstruct x based on the original attribute a'.

Overall, the loss functions of D and G can be written respectively as

$$\mathcal{L}_D = -\mathcal{L}_{adv} + \lambda_{cls}\mathcal{L}_{cls}^D \tag{7}$$

$$\mathcal{L}_G = \mathcal{L}_{adv} + \lambda_{cls}\mathcal{L}_{cls}^G + \lambda_{attn}\mathcal{L}_{attn}^G + \lambda_{rec}\mathcal{L}_{rec}^G \tag{8}$$

where λ_{cls}, λ_{attn}, λ_{rec} are used to control the importance of their corresponding loss.

2.2 Refine Stage

Although the shape of translated image is consistent with the target attribute, the texture of generated part is often different with the surrounding area. To overcome this problem, we propose a refine module. Our key insight is to transform this problem to an image inpainting problem. Intuitively, a cloth image can be decomposed into the shape and texture. We can first obtain the shape mask and then fill the shape mask with consistent texture. As shown in Fig. 2, We first segment the whole cloth from the background to obtain the segmentation map s_w, then we multiply the segmentation map and the attention map generated from coarse stage to get the inpainting mask s_c, which is defined as

$$s_c = s_w * m \tag{9}$$

The translated image x_t' from coarse stage is fed together with the inpainting mask s_c into the image inpainting model. The image inpainting model will fill the inpainting mask with consistent texture and output the final result x_t.

Image Inpainting model. Image inpainting is mainly studied in two perspective: non-learning-based methods and learning-based methods. Traditional non-learning-based methods such as [3,4,6,7], they typically fill the holes by propagating neighboring information or pasting the similar patches of the background. Learning-based approaches mainly use deep convolutional neural network and generative adversarial networks to solve the inpainting problem. In [13], the authors firstly introduce the deep learning into image inpainting task. Due to the success of the attention mechanism in vision tasks, Jiahui Yu et al. propose Deepfillv1 to solve the image inpainting task [15]. The contextual attention module in Deepfillv1 can borrow the distant patches to make better predictions. Additionally, they propose the gated convolution in DeepFillv2 to improve the performance for solving the free form image painting problem [16]. Based on this, we employ DeepFillv2 [16] as the inpainting model in our refine stage. In the train step, as illustrated in Fig. 4, we use the target attribute regions mask m^* to replace the attention map to obtain the inpainting mask. Which is defined as

$$s_c = s_w * m^* \tag{10}$$

The inpainting model includes a generator to complete the mask and a discriminator to distinguish between the completed image and the original image. We train the inpainting model by jointly optimizing the adversarial loss and the L1 loss.

3 Experiments

In this section, we compare our proposed method with some baseline models including StarGAN [5], Ganimation [14] and AMGAN [2].

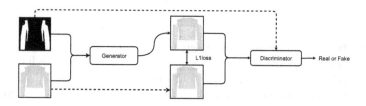

Fig. 4. In the training step, we use the target attribute regions masks connected by landmarks to substitute the attention maps generated in coarse stage. The inpainting model is trained by jointly optimize the L1 loss and the adversarial loss.

3.1 OUTFIT Dataset

Compared with the available fashion dataset DeepFashion [12], the fashion images in OUTFIT are only composed with clothes and clean background. Some samples are shown in Fig. 5(a). These clean fashion images will be helpful for the attribute editing task. Additionally, most fashion dataset are labeled in the perspective of consumers. The labels of OUTFIT is more professional and more fine-grained, which will be helpful for the fashion designers.

The OUTFIT includes 68,958 images and 15 attributes. In our experiments, we conduct the editing of three different attributes: Sleeve length, Sleeve shape and Neckline. These attributes and their corresponding values and number of samples are listed in the Fig. 5(b). We randomly select 2000 images for test and 32479 images for training.

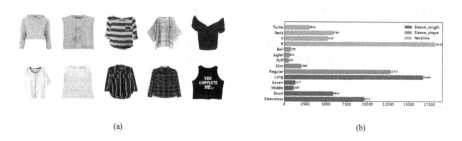

(a)   (b)

Fig. 5. (a) Some samples of the OUTFIT dataset. All images are composed of clothes and clean background. (b) Sample number of different attributes

3.2 Baseline Models

StarGAN. [5] introduces an auxiliary classifier in the discriminator to recognize the attributes of the input image, which extends the CycleGAN [20] to solve multi-domain image-to-image translation.

Ganimation. [14] modifies the generator of StarGAN, outputting an additional attention map. Through the attention map, the Ganimation can focus on the target attribute regions.

AMGAN. [2] uses CAMs from the pre-trained classifier as the supervisor of the attention map, making the generated attention map locate the specific attribute more accurately.

Fig. 6. Qualitative results of sleeve length and sleeve shape. The first row is the target attribute. Comparing with other methods, our method can translate the attributes accurately and can generate the consistent texture with the original image.

3.3   Qualitative Evaluation

Figure 6 shows the editing results of sleeve related attributes respectively: Sleeve length, Sleeve shape. Because of lacking attention mechanism, StarGAN [5] always changes un-target attribute regions and the overall color. For Ganimation [14], the authors introduce an attention mechanism without additional supervisory signal. Although Ganimation can preserve the un-target attribute regions unchanged, it can not generate good results in the target attribute regions. When using the CAMs as the supervisor of the attention map, the results become much better. However, in some cases, the CAMs [19] will attend to some unrelated regions, such as the seventh and eighth column of the Fig. 6. Meanwhile, it is difficult to generate consistent texture with the original cloth for CAMs. Our method introduces the landmark-based attention scheme to locate the target attribute region. For example, for sleeve shape attribute, the AMGAN [2] often attend the chest regions while our method only focus on the sleeve regions. All methods mentioned above can not generate the textures consistent with the original image. We use the image inpainting method to refine the generated results in coarse stage and obtain the best results which keep the shape of coarse stage and have the consistent texture.

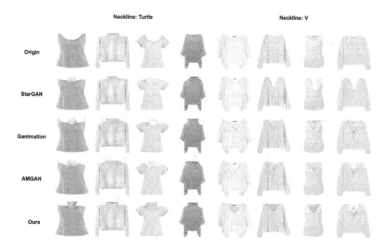

Fig. 7. Qualitative results of neckline. The first four columns translate the neckline to Turtle and the others translate the neckline to V. The results generated of our method are much better than these baseline models.

In Fig. 7, we demonstrate the editing results of neckline. The results are consistent with results of Fig. 6. The baseline methods can hardly generate the right neckline shape according to the target neckline values. The changes they conduct in the neckline area are both blurry and unrealistic. Our method not only translate the neckline to right shape, but also generate the coherent texture.

3.4   Quantitative Evaluation

In this section, we use the FID [10] as the evaluation metrics. In [10], FID has been shown more consistent with human evaluation than Inception Score(IS). FID measures the quality of generated images by comparing the distribution with the real images. The low FID represents the high quality of the generated images. In our experiments, we calculate the FID between the translated image sets and the training data set. The results are listed in Table 1. For the lack of attention mechanism, StarGAN [5] gets the worst performance because it change a lot in the unrelated regions while can not translate these regions to be realistic. Ganimation [14] obtain the lowest FID in all methods. However, from the attention map generated by Ganimation [14], we observe that it only change a little in the original image, resulting poor performance in the attribute translation as shown in Fig. 8. AMGAN performs better than StarGAN through the introduction of the CAMs. But it can not generate the consistent texture in the target attribute regions. Our approach handles this problem and gets the lowest FID except for Ganimation [14] which is consistent with the quantitative results.

Table 1. The FID of all methods. The low FID represents the high quality of the generated images. Our method get the lowest FID except for Ganimation [14]. The low FID obtained by Ganimation attributes to the little changes in the original images.

Method	Sleeve length	Sleeve shape	Neckline
StarGAN	23.5880	34.8146	18.9614
Ganimation	**10.8010**	**26.6254**	**9.7987**
AMGAN	15.2416	29.5742	11.8355
Ours	**11.9848**	**27.5830**	**10.3818**

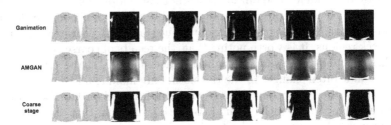

Fig. 8. Sleeve length editing results and attention map of three methods. The Ganimation [14] only do little changes on the original image and can not edit the attribute correctly.

3.5 Ablation Study

In this section, we analyze the individual effect of each proposed components of our method: landmark-based attention scheme and refine module. Figure 9(a) shows the results of our method without attention, and without refine stage of sleeve. Firstly, the proposed method degenerates into StarGAN [5] without landmark-based attention scheme. As mentioned above, StarGAN [5] changes the unrelated regions and the overall color of the cloth. Secondly, it is difficult to generate consistent texture with the whole cloth for our model without refine stage.

Fig. 9. (a) Qualitative ablation results of sleeve length and sleeve shape. (b) Qualitative ablation results of neckline.

Table 2. The FID of our full model and full model without attention and refine stage.

Method	Sleeve length	Sleeve shape	Neckline
w/o attention	23.5880	34.8146	18.9614
w/o refine	14.7653	28.4033	11.4456
Full model	**11.9848**	**27.5830**	**10.3818**

In Fig. 9(b), we compare the results of our model without attention and without refine stage of neckline. The full model without attention can not generate good results according to the target attribute because they can not locate the target attribute regions. And the model without refine stage will generate some artifacts in the neck regions. It is worth noting that, the results of coarse stage and refine stage has little difference when changing the neckline to V shape. This is because the V neckline often changes inside the cloth, only making a little area to refine. Table 2 shows the FID of our full model and full model without attention and refine stage. Our full model get the lowest FID, meaning that the effectiveness of our proposed landmark-based attention scheme and coarse-to-fine framework.

4   Conclusion

In this paper, we propose a coarse-to-fine model to edit the attributes of fashion images. The landmark-based attention scheme and the coarse-to-fine framework are introduced to improve the performance of attribute editing. The experimental results on OUTFIT dataset evaluate the advantages of CFAE over other competed methods. The landmark-based attention scheme can help to locate the target attribute regions and the coarse-to-fine framework can generate consistent texture with the original images. So the proposed CFAE can generate realistic fashion images according to the user-specific attributes. This will help the consumers to retrieve their target clothes and assist the fashion designers to design different attributes clothes.

References

1. Ak, K.E., Kassim, A.A., Hwee Lim, J., Yew Tham, J.: Learning attribute representations with localization for flexible fashion search. In: Proceedings of the IEEE Conference on Computer Vision and Pattern Recognition, pp. 7708–7717 (2018)
2. Ak, K.E., Lim, J.H., Tham, J.Y., Kassim, A.A.: Attribute manipulation generative adversarial networks for fashion images. In: Proceedings of the IEEE International Conference on Computer Vision, pp. 10541–10550 (2019)
3. Ballester, C., Bertalmio, M., Caselles, V., Sapiro, G., Verdera, J.: Filling-in by joint interpolation of vector fields and gray levels. IEEE Trans. Image Process. **10**(8), 1200–1211 (2001)
4. Bertalmio, M., Sapiro, G., Caselles, V., Ballester, C.: Image inpainting. In: Proceedings of the 27th Annual Conference on Computer Graphics and Interactive Techniques, pp. 417–424 (2000)

5. Choi, Y., Choi, M., Kim, M., Ha, J.W., Kim, S., Choo, J.: StarGAN: unified generative adversarial networks for multi-domain image-to-image translation. In: Proceedings of the IEEE Conference on Computer Vision and Pattern Recognition, pp. 8789–8797 (2018)
6. Efros, A.A., Freeman, W.T.: Image quilting for texture synthesis and transfer. In: Proceedings of the 28th Annual Conference on Computer Graphics and Interactive Techniques, pp. 341–346 (2001)
7. Efros, A.A., Leung, T.K.: Texture synthesis by non-parametric sampling. In: Proceedings of the seventh IEEE International Conference on Computer Vision, vol. 2, pp. 1033–1038. IEEE (1999)
8. Goodfellow, I., et al.: Generative adversarial nets. In: Advances in Neural Information Processing Systems, pp. 2672–2680 (2014)
9. Gulrajani, I., Ahmed, F., Arjovsky, M., Dumoulin, V., Courville, A.C.: Improved training of Wasserstein GANs. In: Advances in Neural Information Processing Systems, pp. 5767–5777 (2017)
10. Heusel, M., Ramsauer, H., Unterthiner, T., Nessler, B., Hochreiter, S.: GANs trained by a two time-scale update rule converge to a local Nash equilibrium. In: Advances in Neural Information Processing Systems, pp. 6626–6637 (2017)
11. Isola, P., Zhu, J.Y., Zhou, T., Efros, A.A.: Image-to-image translation with conditional adversarial networks. In: Proceedings of the IEEE Conference on Computer Vision and Pattern Recognition, pp. 1125–1134 (2017)
12. Liu, Z., Luo, P., Qiu, S., Wang, X., Tang, X.: DeepFashion: powering robust clothes recognition and retrieval with rich annotations. In: Proceedings of the IEEE Conference on Computer Vision and Pattern Recognition, pp. 1096–1104 (2016)
13. Pathak, D., Krahenbuhl, P., Donahue, J., Darrell, T., Efros, A.A.: Context encoders: feature learning by inpainting. In: Proceedings of the IEEE Conference on Computer Vision and Pattern Recognition, pp. 2536–2544 (2016)
14. Pumarola, A., Agudo, A., Martinez, A.M., Sanfeliu, A., Moreno-Noguer, F.: GANimation: anatomically-aware facial animation from a single image. In: Ferrari, V., Hebert, M., Sminchisescu, C., Weiss, Y. (eds.) ECCV 2018. LNCS, vol. 11214, pp. 835–851. Springer, Cham (2018). https://doi.org/10.1007/978-3-030-01249-6_50
15. Yu, J., Lin, Z., Yang, J., Shen, X., Lu, X., Huang, T.S.: Generative image inpainting with contextual attention. In: Proceedings of the IEEE Conference on Computer Vision and Pattern Recognition, pp. 5505–5514 (2018)
16. Yu, J., Lin, Z., Yang, J., Shen, X., Lu, X., Huang, T.S.: Free-form image inpainting with gated convolution. In: Proceedings of the IEEE International Conference on Computer Vision, pp. 4471–4480 (2019)
17. Zhang, G., Kan, M., Shan, S., Chen, X.: Generative adversarial network with spatial attention for face attribute editing. In: Ferrari, V., Hebert, M., Sminchisescu, C., Weiss, Y. (eds.) ECCV 2018. LNCS, vol. 11210, pp. 422–437. Springer, Cham (2018). https://doi.org/10.1007/978-3-030-01231-1_26
18. Zhao, B., Feng, J., Wu, X., Yan, S.: Memory-augmented attribute manipulation networks for interactive fashion search. In: Proceedings of the IEEE Conference on Computer Vision and Pattern Recognition, pp. 1520–1528 (2017)
19. Zhou, B., Khosla, A., Lapedriza, A., Oliva, A., Torralba, A.: Learning deep features for discriminative localization. In: Proceedings of the IEEE Conference on Computer Vision and Pattern Recognition, pp. 2921–2929 (2016)
20. Zhu, J.Y., Park, T., Isola, P., Efros, A.A.: Unpaired image-to-image translation using cycle-consistent adversarial networks. In: Proceedings of the IEEE International Conference on Computer Vision, pp. 2223–2232 (2017)

PSS: Point Semantic Saliency for 3D Object Detection

Jiajing Cen, Pei An, Gaojie Chen, Junxiong Liang, and Jie Ma[✉]

National Key Laboratory of Science and Technology on Multi-spectral Information
Processing, School of Artificial Intelligence and Automation, Huazhong University
of Science and Technology, Wuhan, China
majie@hust.edu.cn

Abstract. Efficient fusion on LiDAR-camera data for 3D object detection is a challenging task. Although RGB image provides sufficient texture and semantic features, some of them are unrelated to the targeted objects, which are useless and even misleading for detection task. In this paper, point semantic saliency (PSS) is proposed for precise fusion. In this scheme, physical receptive field (PRF) constraint is built to establish the relation of 2D and 3D receptive fields from camera projection model. To increase the saliency of the pixel from targeted object, we propose PSS to extract salient point feature with the guidance of RGB and semantic segmentation images, which provides 2D supplementary information for 3D detection. Comparison results and ablation studies demonstrate that PSS improves the detection performance in both localization and classification. Among the current single stage detectors, our method improves APs by 0.62% for *hard* level and mAP by 0.31%.

Keywords: 3D object detection · Multiple sensors · Autonomous driving

1 Introduction

3D object detection has wide applications in the fields of autonomous driving and industrial robotics. Its task is to determine the 3D bounding box of target object from the different type of sensors, such as monocular camera, stereo, Radar, and LiDAR. Among the sensors, LiDAR is widely used, for it is convenient to generate 3D structure information of the surroundings.

In terms of LiDAR data representation, LiDAR based 3D detectors can be classified into three categories. (i) Point based methods exploit point-aware backbone networks, such as PointNet [15] or PointNet++ [16], to generate deep point features from point cloud. (ii) For high computation efficiency, view based method represents point cloud as a series of 2D maps in Front View (FV) or Bird's Eye View (BEV), and then uses 2D convolution layers for feature extraction. PIXOR [22] is an anchor-free detection method with using height-encode

This work is supported by the National Natural Science Foundation of China (61991412).

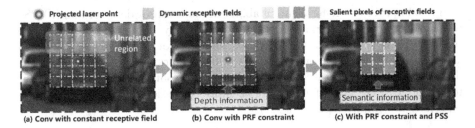

Fig. 1. Comparison with existing multi-sensor method. Instead of using a RGB backbone for the whole image or extracting feature from a constant field, our method uses PSS to extract image feature of a laser point in the dynamic receptive field, which generates accurate RGB feature of only significant objects.

BEV map. However, due to the rounding error in 2D map generation, some structure information of point cloud is missing. (iii) Therefore, voxel based method converts point cloud into voxel representation to preserve spatial information. VoxelNet [26] extracts local voxel-wise features for non-empty voxels by several voxel feature encoding layers. Sparse convolution [4] has been proposed to compute voxel feature with considering the sparse structure of point cloud. Recently, voxel based methods exploiting sparse convolution layers as their backbone networks are high ranking on KITTI, such as SA-SSD [5] and PV-RCNN [17].

Although LiDAR based methods have made great progress, there exist some challenges for consumer grade inexpensive LiDAR sensor which generates low-resolution point cloud. And RGB image provides sufficient and discriminative texture features for this object that benefit for object detection. Based on this fact, multi-sensor based detector has been proposed to improve the object detection performance with fusing sparse point cloud and dense RGB image [7]. How to design an efficient module to utilize LiDAR and camera data is the key problem for multi-sensor based detectors. The main difficulty is the inconsistent data form of point cloud and RGB image. Alternatively, some parts of image are not belong to target objects, as presented in Fig. 1 (a), introducing unrelated 2D texture features. For adjacent fields, semantic parts of cars are more notable for target objects.

Motivated by this, we propose an efficient multi-sensor fusion framework to select the optimal 2D supplementary information of 3D target object and fuse them under the same representation in the early stage. The main challenge of LiDAR-based 3D detection comes from far and small objects. On the one hand, small objects have few points in LiDAR representation. On the other hand, we have more close range samples in training dataset. Based on the physical projection model of LiDAR-camera system, we establish physical receptive field (PRF) constraint between 2D and 3D receptive fields building dynamic receptive fields to filter out RGB information of background in Fig. 1 (b). To restrain irrelevant information, we propose PSS module to guide 3D detector learning salient area of targets in Fig. 1 (c). Our contributions can be summarized into two-fold: (i) PRF constraint based dynamic receptive field selection strategy in RGB image to improve the generalization ability of multi-sensor detector and (ii) PSS to guide contextual information learning attentively via generating high-level semantic prior knowledge. The proposed multi-sensor fusion strategy is evaluated on KITTI 3D/BEV object detection benchmarks. Extensive experiments demonstrate that our strategy outperforms current single stage methods on the metric of 3D mAP and achieve more accurate regression and higher confidence especially in complex scenes.

2   Related Works

According to the type of fusion approach, LiDAR-camera 3D object detection methods can be divided into three categories.

2.1   Multi-view Fusion

LiDAR has different 2D representations according to the direction of projection, such as FV and BEV. MV3D [2] is the pioneering work of multi-view based fusion which leverages BEV to obtain 3D proposal, then the region-wise features of FV and image are combined via ROI pooling. Inspired by MV3D, AVOD [6] does some improvement by only fusing BEV and image anchors' features. ContFuse [8] exploits continuous convolutions to add RGB features into BEV feature map at different resolutions. Differ from above methods declaring BEV is an effective representation of 3D objects, LaserNet [12] considers the sparsity of BEV selecting compact range view data as the detector's input. Aiming at the occlusion and scale variation of range view, they also provide contextual information and predict a probability distribution over 3D bounding box. Most multi-view based methods are two stage architecture (proposals generation and refinement stage) that tend to be time-consuming and cumbersome.

2.2   Bounding Box Fusion

These methods first generate 2D detection regions and then fuse point clouds region information for further 3D box estimation. Frustum pointNets [14] generates a series of frustums from 2D image and extracts each frustum's features for 3D segmentation and box bounding output. AM3D [11], unlike image-based methods extracting 2D image features, reconstructs 3D space with 2D boxes and depth map to exploit 3D attention contexts. PI-RCNN [20] puts a strategy based on image semantic results. Instead of concatenating original points, they act on 3D proposals for calibration. CLOCs [13] first obtains 2D and 3D proposals through pre-training 2D and 3D detectors and then is trained to leverage their geometric and semantic consistencies producing final detection results more accurately. Although they could focus on the potential area fast, 2D detectors affect their performances seriously.

2.3   Point Feature Fusion

Point feature fusion methods directly mix the RGB features into raw point clouds before the 3D detector framework with 3D structure immovable. IPOD [23] applies existing 2D semantic segmentation results to predict foreground pixels, thus removing background point clouds. MVX-Net [18] proposes multimodal VoxelNet pipeline [26] fusing sensors at different stages. PointFusion [21] crops RGB image box regression and related raw 3D points extracting their features separately, then regards the fusion features as spatial anchors for dense and 3D bounding box prediction. PointPainting [19] projected point clouds into the output of image semantic segmentation and appended the pixels class score to points directly. In comparison, our method enhances the quality of points' feature from camera for more discriminative detector.

3   Method

In this section, we propose a multi-sensor fusion method with PRF constraint and PSS to exploit the effective supplementary information. Compared with state-of-the-art 3D detection methods, our proposed framework makes up for the above LiDAR missing information and has good generalization to full distance detection especially in outdoor scene.

3.1   Physical Receptive Fields Constraint

As objects have different depths in a scene, feature extraction with constant receptive field invariant of depth does not benefit for objects far from LiDAR-camera system. By projecting point clouds onto image in Fig. 2 (a), the feature extraction area contains unrelated surrounding if given inappropriate receptive fields. In view of this phenomenon, we propose PRF constraint and establish a dynamic receptive field for structure-aware feature extraction. Let $\mathbb{P} = \{p_i\}_{i=1}^{N}$ be the i-th point of LiDAR point clouds. N is the number of point clouds. $p_i = (x_i, y_i, z_i)^T$ represent the p_i position. Camera intrinsic matrix $\mathbf{K}$ has been calibrated, presented as:

$$\mathbf{K} = \begin{pmatrix} f_u & 0 & u_0 \\ 0 & f_v & v_0 \\ 0 & 0 & 1 \end{pmatrix}, \tag{1}$$

where f_u and f_v are focal lengths. $(u_0, v_0, 1)^T$ is the pixel coordinates of the principle point. It is assumed that the extrinsic parameters of LiDAR-camera system, such as the rotation matrix $\mathbf{R}$ and the translation vector T, have been calibrated. Let $I_i = (u_i, v_i, 1)^T$ be the pixel coordinates of the i-th projected point. From pinhole projection model, I_i is computed as [25]:

$$d_i I_i = \mathbf{K} \cdot (\mathbf{R} p_i + T), \tag{2}$$

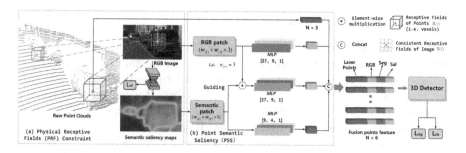

Fig. 2. PSS 3D object detection network: The network takes original LiDAR point clouds and images as input. Mining the scale correspondence to generate consistent receptive fields between point clouds and image. Semantic saliency patches are used to guide RGB feature extraction through tuning layers.

where d_i is the depth of p_i. As 3D sparse convolution plays an important role in 3D object detection [4], we take it for illustration. Receptive field $\mathbb{R}(i)$ of sparse convolution is a cubic space of p_i. Supposed point $p' = (x_i + \delta x, y_i + \delta y, z_i + \delta z)$ is in $\mathbb{R}(i)$, p' satisfies such constraints:

$$\delta x \in [-\frac{v_x}{2}, \frac{v_x}{2}], \delta y \in [-\frac{v_y}{2}, \frac{v_y}{2}], \delta z \in [-\frac{v_z}{2}, \frac{v_z}{2}], \tag{3}$$

where v_x, v_y, and v_z are the width, length, and height of the cubic space $\mathbb{R}(i)$, respectively. Pixel coordinate I' of p' is marked as $I + \delta I$. Using Eq.(2), $\delta I = (\delta u, \delta v, 0)^T$ is approximately computed as Eq. (4). For all points in $\mathbb{R}(i)$, their projected pixels form an area $\mathbb{R}_p(i)$ in image plane. It is the projection of $\mathbb{R}(i)$. From $\mathbb{R}_p(i)$, we establish the PRF constraint:

$$|\delta u| \le f_u \frac{\delta x}{d_i - \delta z}, |\delta v| \le f_v \frac{\delta y}{d_i - \delta z}, \tag{4}$$

However, $\mathbb{R}_p(i)$ has complex contour, thus making PRF constraint high complexity. For the practical applications, a tight $w(i) \times w(i)$ square $\mathbb{S}(i) \supset \mathbb{R}_p(i)$ is exploited for convolution instead of $\mathbb{R}_p(i)$ whose center point is I_i. $\mathbb{S}(i)$ is the dynamic receptive field derived from PRF constraint. From Eq. (4), size $w(i)$ is computed as:

$$w(i) = \max(f_u \frac{v_x}{d_i}, f_v \frac{v_y}{d_i}), \tag{5}$$

where v_x, v_y, and v_z are set as 0.05 m, 0.05 m, and 0.1 m for 3D sparse convolution [4]. Using the focal lengths of the camera in KITTI dataset [3], from Eq. (5), $w(i) = 7, 5, 3$ while $d(i) = 5$ m, 7 m, 12 m. With PRF constraint, image features extracted from $\mathbb{S}(i)$ contain least scene features as well.

3.2 Point Semantic Saliency

As discussed in Sect. 3.1, we establish the image receptive fields consistent with each laser points depth to construct dynamic receptive fields. In this section, we develop PSS to make up for the deficiency of LiDAR data for further detection network. Generally, point clouds contain abundant spatial information but lack dense semantic information. One common practice is introducing semantic segmentation for pixels classification, and [19, 20] apply image segmentation as calibrated points features for 3D detection. However, the accuracy of 2D semantic segmentation network has great influence on the detection results while most reliable segmentation networks are time consuming. Therefore, our PSS module utilizes lightly semantic salient maps as the guiding layer for feature guidance learning automatically.

Given original point clouds $\mathbb{P}$, dynamic image receptive fields $\mathbb{S}_{rgb}$ and semantic receptive fields $\mathbb{S}_{sal}$ which is obtained by DeepLabv3+ segmentation network [1] as inputs, we adopt multi-Layer perceptron (MLP) to extract image points features and then aggregate them into structure features f_i. f_i is the input of 3D detectors that contains both LiDAR and image points features. For neural networks, low-level RGB image contains rich spatial information and good perception of detailed objects while feature maps tend to semantic information [24]. To retain the original image and dig for more specific semantic information, our PSS module encodes local feature from the tail of each stage and concentrates multidimensional information to laser points, which improves the ability of generalization (shown in Fig. 2 (b)). The aggregated point features f_i can be expressed as *PSS algorithm* where $f_i^{(rgb)}$ and $f_i^{(seg)}$ are multidimensional RGB and segmentation features. p_i is original laser point information.

Algorithm 1. PSS

Input:
LiDAR point clouds $\mathbb{P} \in \mathbb{R}^{N,D}$ with N points and $D = 3$, RGB fields $\mathbb{S}_{rgb} \in \mathbb{R}^{N,w,w,3}$, Semantic fields $\mathbb{S}_{sal} \in \mathbb{R}^{N,w,w,1}$.
Output:
$F \in \mathbb{R}^{N,6}$

1: **for** i in range N **do**
2:   $p_i = P[i,:]$, $\mathbb{S}_{rgb}(i) = \mathbb{S}_{rgb}[i]$, $\mathbb{S}_{sal}(i) = \mathbb{S}_{sal}[i]$
3:   $f_i^{(rgb)} = \sigma(\mathbf{MLP}(\mathbb{S}_{rgb}(i)))$
4:   $f_i^{(seg)} = \sigma(\mathbf{MLP}(\mathbb{S}_{sal}(i)))$
5:   $f_i^{(sal)} = \sigma(\mathbf{MLP}(\mathbb{S}_{rgb}(i) \odot \mathbb{S}_{sal}(i)))$
6:   $f_i = \mathbf{Concat}(p_i, f_i^{(rgb)}, f_i^{(seg)}, f_i^{(sal)})$
7: **end for**

Besides encoding separately, we come up with salient feature $f_i^{(sal)}$ to discriminate if the grid belong to corresponding object regions while the training process, which has different scale according to point range. We regard segmentation results as a salient guiding patch imposed at RGB patch to tune MLP for contextual information significantly. The whole fusion feature is generated through *PSS algorithm* where σ refers to the sigmoid function and $\odot$ denotes the element-wise multiplication. f_i is the a fusion point feature for further 3D detection network which provides more contextual information to suppress false region as well as enhance saliency of targets.

3.3   Loss Function

The loss function applies the common anchor-based setting [26] to optimize our proposed network: the regression loss $\mathcal{L}_{\text{reg}}$ and classification loss $\mathcal{L}_{\text{cls}}$ to supervise the regression and classification tasks. $\mathcal{L}_{\text{reg}}$ is a Smooth-$l1$ loss [10] and $\mathcal{L}_{\text{cls}}$ is a focal loss [9]. The loss of 3D object detection is defined as:

$$\mathcal{L}_{\text{obj}} = \mathcal{L}_{\text{reg}} + \mathcal{L}_{\text{cls}}. \tag{6}$$

For PSS training, we regard it as segmentation network using image semantic segmentation label for supervision to tune the parameter. In the point clouds scene, points segmentation are labeled by 3D object label, then we can obtain a sparse segmentation mask through the projection relation. To address the imbalance number between foreground and background label, we employ focal loss as:

$$\mathcal{L}_{\text{sal}} = -\alpha_t \left(1 - p_t\right)^\gamma \log\left(p_t\right), \tag{7}$$

where

$$p_t = \begin{cases} p & \text{if } p_t \text{ is foreground point} \\ 1 - p & \text{otherwise} \end{cases}. \tag{8}$$

Therefore, the total loss is:

$$\mathcal{L} = \mathcal{L}_{\text{obj}} + \lambda \mathcal{L}_{\text{sal}}, \tag{9}$$

where λ is the weight of salient network loss.

4   Experiments

In this section, we evaluate our proposed PSS on the KITTI 3D/BEV object detection benchmark [3]. KITTI dataset contains 7,481 training samples and 7,518 test samples and provides an outdoor benchmark for 3D object detection. Further, we divide the training samples into a training set with 3,712 samples and a validation set with 3,769 samples following the common protocol. We conduct experiments on **car** category and compare PSS with state-of-the-art 3D detectors on use average precision (AP) with IoU threshold 0.7 as evaluation metric. According to objects size, occlusion level and truncation level, the benchmark is split into three levels of difficulties: *easy, moderate* and *hard*. For the official test benchmark, the mAP with 40 recall positions is reported. And on the validation set, the mAP with 11 recall positions is used to compare with previous methods.

4.1   Implementation Details

PSS network takes LiDAR points as well as the corresponding images as inputs. Following the common setting in previous detection network [5], we select the LiDAR points between the range $(0.0\,\text{m}, 70.4\,\text{m})$, $(-40.0\,\text{m}, 40.0\,\text{m})$, $(-3.0\,\text{m}, 1.0\,\text{m})$ along the X_l, Y_l and Z_l axes respectively, which are visible in the

Table 1. Performance comparison of 3D/BEV AP and mAP with previous methods on KITTI test server (cars).

Method	Modality	Single stage	3D mAP	Cars-3D			Cars-BEV		
				Easy	Moderate	Hard	Easy	Moderate	Hard
PointRCNN	LiDAR		77.76	86.96	75.64	70.70	92.13	87.39	82.72
STD	LiDAR		80.92	87.95	79.71	75.09	94.74	89.19	86.42
PV-RCNN	LiDAR		82.83	90.25	81.43	76.82	94.98	90.65	86.14
MV3D	LiDAR+Image		64.20	74.97	63.63	54.00	86.62	78.93	69.80
AVOD	LiDAR+Image		67.70	76.39	66.47	60.23	90.99	84.82	79.62
MMF	LiDAR+Image		78.68	88.40	77.43	70.22	93.67	88.21	81.99
EPNet	LiDAR+Image		81.23	89.81	79.28	74.59	94.22	88.47	83.69
PointPainting	LiDAR+Image		71.38	82.11	73.63	67.08	92.45	88.11	83.36
SECOND	LiDAR	✓	73.90	83.34	72.55	65.82	89.39	83.77	78.59
PointPillars	LiDAR	✓	75.29	82.58	74.31	68.99	90.07	86.56	82.81
VoxelNet	LiDAR	✓	66.77	77.47	65.11	57.73	89.35	79.26	77.39
SA-SSD	LiDAR	✓	80.90	88.75	**79.79**	74.16	95.03	91.03	85.96
3DSSD	LiDAR	✓	80.82	88.36	79.57	74.55	92.66	89.02	85.86
ContFuse	LiDAR+Image	✓	71.38	83.68	68.78	61.67	94.07	85.35	75.88
PSS (ours)	LiDAR+Image	✓	**81.21**	**89.13**	79.71	**74.78**	93.17	89.28	84.38

RGB image views. And the resolution of input RGB images is 1280×384. The overall 3D detector framework follows the voxel based method [5] where voxel size is set as $v_w = 0.05$ m, $v_l = 0.05$ m and $v_h = 0.10$ m. The matching thresholds for the positive and negative anchors are 0.6 and 0.45, respectively. The anchor length, width and height of car are set as 1.6 m, 3.9 m and 1.56 m. Anchors that contain no point are filtered out. For semantic segmentation sub-network, we pretrain the DeepLabv3+ segmentation network on the KITTI semantic segmentation benchmark, then fine-tuned it during the 3D detection network training. We select the weight $\lambda = 0.5$ in Eq. (9).

We implement the proposed PSS with Pytorch. The network is trained end-to-end with ADAM optimizer. We train the entire network with the batch size 1, learning rate 0.008, and weight decay 0.001 for 75 epoch on 1 GTX 2080 Ti GPU, which takes about 22 h. The learning rate is decayed with a one-cycle strategy. Bounding boxes with low-confidence are filtered out by threshold of 0.3 at inference stage. The non-maximum suppression (NMS) with IoU threshold of 0.1 is applied for final detection results. Data augmentation is used to avoid model over-fitting including rotation, flipping and scale transformation. Specifically, the point cloud is randomly rotated within the range of $[-\pi/15, \pi/15]$ and flipped. Each ground truth box is randomly scaled following the uniform distribution of $[0.95, 1.05]$.

4.2 Experiments on KITTI Dataset

All detection results are measured using the official KITTI test server evaluation for 3D and BEV detection tasks. As shown in Table 1, we compare our PSS with other state-of-the-art methods. Generally, two stage detectors have lower

Fig. 3. 3D detection and confidence score visualization of our method (left) and the top single stage method SA-SSD (right) prediction. Red rectangle means true-negatives and red ellipse is false-positives. (Color figure online)

Fig. 4. Precision-recall curve of the proposed method, current multi-sensor or single stage methods for hard-level car category on KITTI test dataset (left). The distribution of target confidence score compared with SA-SSD (right).

computation efficiency for more precise classification and localization. As a single stage and multi-sensor detector, our PSS ranks 1*st* on the easy-level and hard-level object detection, *i.e.* 89.13% and 74.78%, and achieves the best performance (81.21%) in 3D mAP among current single stage methods, which is the most important index of 3D detection. We present 3D prediction results by projecting 3D bounding boxes to the RGB images for visualization in Fig. 3. Compared with the top method SA-SSD, the columns on the left show our method has outstanding performance in recall rates at long distance. The two columns on the right demonstrate the effectiveness of false objects removing. Besides, our method produces higher confidence localization and classification scores in test dataset in Fig. 4. With RGB information fused, PSS has a stable performance in the detection of far objects that filter based on bounding box height in the image plane. Owing to the PRF constraint of scale, irrelevant information are suppressed at early stage leading the whole training process based on corresponding scope. The guiding of PSS also optimizes the false alarm results in some degree.

4.3   Ablation Study

In this section, we conduct extensive ablation studies on the validation set of KITTI dataset to study the contribution of PRF constraint and the PSS module separately. The 3D detector is based on SA-SSD, which is the same for all the variants.

Table 2. Ablation experiments of PRF constraint and PSS in KITTI validation dataset.

	Easy	Moderate	Hard	3D mAP	Gain
LiDAR only	95.38	86.59	83.93	88.63	–
RGB points	94.97	86.22	84.02	88.40	−0.23
5 × 5	95.16	87.29	84.17	88.88	+0.25
PRF	95.87	88.16	85.98	90.00	+1.37
PRF+PSS (label)	95.63	87.92	85.27	89.61	+0.98
PRF+PSS	97.54	88.92	88.31	91.59	+2.96

Effects of PRF Constraint. In Sect. 3.1, we define the length of dynamic square $\mathbb{S}(i)$. Here, we compare a set of receptive fields size in $\{1 \times 1, 5 \times 5, \text{PRF}\}$ to validate the necessity of selecting appropriate receptive fields. Table 2 presents the results. The $1st$ row shows the performance of LiDAR-only method SA-SSD which uses voxelized sparse convolution as its backbone. The $2nd$ row appends image pixels information yielding decrease of 3D mAP 0.24% over the baseline, since single corresponding pixels are independent and meaningless as well as point clouds. The $3rd$ and $4th$ row show performances of fixed fields. Our PRF significantly outperforms above experiments and achieves 1.56% improvement in 3D mAP.

Effects of PSS. In PSS module, we utilize the segmentation results as supervision of image features. We investigate the effects of segmentation prediction format of PSS. Semantic segmentation network provides class score of cars, and one hot encoding convert it into class label. In Table 2, the label-driving PSS leads to worse detection while score-driving PSS makes a robust improvement of $(2.16\%, 2.33\%, 4.38\%)$ on *Easy*, *Moderate* and *Hard* level.

5   Conclusion

We have proposed a multi-sensor fusion model with point semantic saliency for 3D object detection in the outdoor scene. Considering the challenge of extracting effective features from multiple sensors, our method analyzes the physical relationship and integrates semantic saliency map for attentively learning. Experimental results on the KITTI dataset demonstrate that our fusion framework improves the 3D detection performance compared with previous fusion method.

References

1. Chen, L., Zhu, Y., Papandreou, G., et al.: Encoder-decoder with atrous separable convolution for semantic image segmentation. In: Proceedings of ECCV, pp. 833–851 (2018)
2. Chen, X., Ma, H., Wan, J., et al.: Multi-view 3D object detection network for autonomous driving. In: Proceedings of CVPR, pp. 1–10 (2017)
3. Geiger, A., Lenz, P., Urtasun, R.: Are we ready for autonomous driving? The KITTI vision benchmark suite. In: Proceedings of CVPR, pp. 3354–3361 (2012)
4. Graham, B., Engelcke, M., van der Maaten, L.: 3D semantic segmentation with submanifold sparse convolutional networks. In: Proceedings of CVPR, pp. 9224–9232 (2018)
5. He, C., Zeng, H., Huang, J., et al.: Structure aware single-stage 3D object detection from point cloud. In: Proceedings of CVPR, pp. 11870–11879 (2020)
6. Ku, J., Mozifian, M., Lee, J., et al.: Joint 3D proposal generation and object detection from view aggregation. In: Proceedings of IROS, pp. 1–8 (2018)
7. Liang, M., Yang, B., Chen, Y., et al.: Multi-task multi-sensor fusion for 3D object detection. In: Proceedings of CVPR, pp. 7345–7353 (2019)
8. Liang, M., Yang, B., Wang, S., Urtasun, R.: Deep continuous fusion for multi-sensor 3D object detection. In: Proceedings of ECCV, pp. 663–678 (2018)
9. Lin, T., Goyal, P., Girshick, R.B., et al.: Focal loss for dense object detection. In: Proceedings of CVPR, pp. 2999–3007 (2017)
10. Liu, W., et al.: SSD: single shot MultiBox detector. In: Leibe, B., Matas, J., Sebe, N., Welling, M. (eds.) ECCV 2016. LNCS, vol. 9905, pp. 21–37. Springer, Cham (2016). https://doi.org/10.1007/978-3-319-46448-0_2
11. Ma, X., Wang, Z., Li, H., et al.: Accurate monocular 3D object detection via color-embedded 3D reconstruction for autonomous driving. In: Proceedings of ICCV, pp. 6850–6859 (2019)
12. Meyer, G.P., Laddha, A., Kee, E., et al.: LaserNet: an efficient probabilistic 3D object detector for autonomous driving. In: Proceedings of CVPR, pp. 12677–12686 (2019)
13. Pang, S., Morris, D., Radha, H.: CLOCs: camera-LiDAR object candidates fusion for 3D object detection. In: Proceedings of IROS, pp. 1–8 (2020)
14. Qi, C.R., Liu, W., Wu, C., et al.: Frustum PointNets for 3D object detection from RGB-D data. In: Proceedings of CVPR, pp. 918–927 (2018)
15. Qi, C.R., Su, H., Mo, K., Guibas, L.J.: PointNet: deep learning on point sets for 3D classification and segmentation. In: Proceedings of CVPR, pp. 77–85 (2017)
16. Qi, C.R., Yi, L., Su, H., Guibas, L.J.: PointNet++: deep hierarchical feature learning on point sets in a metric space. In: Proceedings of NIPS, pp. 5099–5108 (2017)
17. Shi, S., Guo, C., Jiang, L., et al.: PV-RCNN: point-voxel feature set abstraction for 3D object detection. In: Proceedings of CVPR, pp. 10526–10535 (2020)
18. Sindagi, V.A., Zhou, Y., Tuzel, O.: MVX-Net: multimodal VoxelNet for 3D object detection. In: Proceedings of ICRA, pp. 7276–7282 (2019)
19. Vora, S., Lang, A.H., Helou, B., Beijbom, O.: PointPainting: sequential fusion for 3D object detection. In: Proceedings of CVPR, pp. 4603–4611 (2020)
20. Xie, L., Xiang, C., Yu, Z., et al.: PI-RCNN: an efficient multi-sensor 3D object detector with point-based attentive Cont-conv fusion module. In: Proceedings of AAAI, pp. 12460–12467 (2020)
21. Xu, D., Anguelov, D., Jain, A.: PointFusion: deep sensor fusion for 3D bounding box estimation. In: Proceedings of CVPR, pp. 244–253 (2018)

22. Yang, B., Luo, W., Urtasun, R.: PIXOR: real-time 3D object detection from point clouds. In: Proceedings of CVPR, pp. 7652–7660 (2018)
23. Yang, Z., Sun, Y., Liu, S., et al.: IPOD: intensive point-based object detector for point cloud. CoRR arXiv:1812.05276 (2018)
24. Zeiler, M.D., Fergus, R.: Visualizing and understanding convolutional networks. In: Fleet, D., Pajdla, T., Schiele, B., Tuytelaars, T. (eds.) ECCV 2014. LNCS, vol. 8689, pp. 818–833. Springer, Cham (2014). https://doi.org/10.1007/978-3-319-10590-1_53
25. Zhang, Z.: A flexible new technique for camera calibration. IEEE Trans. Pattern Anal. Mach. Intell. **22**(11), 1330–1334 (2000)
26. Zhou, Y., Tuzel, O.: VoxelNet: end-to-end learning for point cloud based 3D object detection. In: Proceedings of CVPR, pp. 4490–4499 (2018)

Image Segmentation Based on Non-convex Low Rank Multiple Kernel Clustering

Xuqian Xue[1], Xiao Wang[2], Xiaoqian Zhang[2,3], Jing Wang[2], and Zhigui Liu[2(✉)]

[1] School of Computer Science and Technology, Southwest University of Science and Technology, Mianyang 621010, People's Republic of China
[2] School of Information Engineering, Southwest University of Science and Technology, Mianyang 621010, People's Republic of China
liuzhigui@swust.edu.cn
[3] School of Computer Science and Engineering, Nanjing University of Science and Technology, Nanjing 210094, People's Republic of China

Abstract. Subspace clustering has been widely used in image segmentation. These methods usually use superpixel segmentation to pre-segment image, while the superpixel segmentation method always divides image into superpixel blocks of similar shape and size, which results in poor segmentation and is time-consuming. In addition, the existing image segmentation methods based on subspace clustering don't consider processing nonlinear structure data and complex noise. In order to solve the above problems, this paper proposes an image segmentation method (AMR_WT_NLMSC) based on non-convex low-rank multi-kernel clustering, which uses the adaptive morphological reconstruction seed segmentation (AMR_WT) for pre-segmentation, and designs non-convex low-rank multi-kernel subspace clustering (NLMSC) achieves the final segmentation. Experiments on real image datasets show that AMR_WT _NLMSC method has the more accurate segmentation effect.

Keywords: Subspace clustering · Low rank · Multi-kernel · Image segmentation

1 Introduction

Image segmentation based on subspace clustering is a region segmentation method, and its process consists of three parts: pre-segmentation, feature extraction and subspace clustering. (I) Superpixel segmentation is a general pre-segmentation method, which groups pixels into superpixel blocks. Its representative algorithms include normalized cuts(N-Cuts) [1] and simple linear iterative

This work has been supported in part by the National Natural Science Foundation of China under Grant 62102331, the National Natural Science Foundation of China under Grant 61772272, the Sichuan Province Science and Technology Support Program under Grant Nos. 2020YJ0432, 2020YFS0360, 18YYJC1688 and 18ZB0611, and the Postgraduate Innovation Fund Project by Southwest University of Science and Technology under Grant 20ycx0032.

L. Fang et al. (Eds.): CICAI 2021, LNAI 13069, pp. 420–431, 2021.
https://doi.org/10.1007/978-3-030-93046-2_36

clustering(SLIC) [2]. Among them, N-Cuts is a typical superpixel segmentation method based on graph theory, and SLIC is widely used due to its simplicity and efficiency. (II) In order to facilitate subsequent processing of superpixel images, it is usually necessary to extract the image feature of each superpixel to form a feature matrix. (III) Image segmentation based on subspace clustering is clustering the feature data of the image essentially. Input the feature matrix into the subspace clustering model to get the affinity matrix of the data, and then use spectral clustering to complete the final segmentation. In summary, the process of image segmentation based on subspace clustering is shown in Fig. 1. In recent years, Cheng et al. [3] proposed a multi-task low-rank similarity image segmentation method, which extracts multiple features from the image and derives a unified affinity matrix from the multi-feature space. Tao et al. [4] proposed an image segmentation method based on weighted sparse subspace clustering. Li et al. [5] proposed an image segmentation method based on improved sparse subspace clustering. However, the pre-segmentation methods of these image segmentation methods need to be optimized, and the subspace clustering methods cannot handle noise and nonlinear structure data.

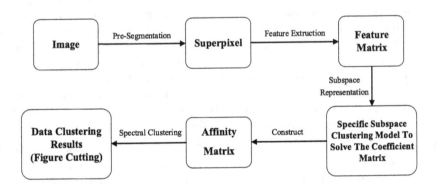

Fig. 1. Image segmentation process based on subspace clustering.

For the pre-segmentation, the superpixel segmentation method [6] divides the superpixel blocks into regular regions with similar shapes and sizes, which destroys the real local spatial structure of image. To overcome this problem, we use AMR_WT [7] for the pre-segmentation, which has better pre-segmentation effect. For the existing subspace clustering methods, they ignore complex noise, the nonlinear structure data. This paper proposes a robust subspace clustering method (NLMSC) based on non-convex low-rank multi-kernel, which uses "kernel trick" to achieve nonlinear subspace clustering, and uses mixture correntropy induced metric (MCIM) to deal with complex noise. In addition, block diagonal constraint is imposed on the coefficient matrix to determine the block diagonal structure of the affinity matrix. In the process of nonlinear data mapping, Schatten-p norm is applied to the kernel matrix to ensure that the data in the feature space has multiple low-dimensional subspaces.

The rest of this paper is organized as follows. In Sect. 2, the related content of AMR_WT and self-representation low-rank kernel subspace clustering are introduced. In Sect. 3, the NLMSC method and AMR_WT_NLMSC image segmentation method are introduced in detail. The experiment is given in Sect. 4 and then summarized in Sect. 5.

2   Related Work

2.1   Adaptive Morphological Reconstruction for Seed Segmentation

Seed segmentation algorithms, such as graph cuts (GC) [8], random walker (RW) [9], and watershed transformation (WT) [10], are widely used in image segmentation. WT is an image region segmentation method based on topological theory and mathematical morphology. Its basic idea is to take the similarity between neighboring pixels as an important reference in the segmentation process, so as to make the spatial position similar and pixels with similar gray values (seeking gradient) are connected to each other to form a closed contour. The common operation steps of the WT are grayscale the color image, then find the gradient map, and finally perform the WT algorithm on the basis of the gradient map to find the edge line of the segmented image. The useless seeds of gradient images in WT leads to over-segmentation. Lei et al. [7] proposed an adaptive morphological reconstruction of seed image segmentation algorithm (AMR_WT) to solve over-segmentation. AMR uses multi-scale structural elements to reconstruct the gradient images, and then performs a pointwise maximum operation on these reconstruction gradient images to obtain the final adaptive reconstruction results. The specific definition is as follows:

Definition 1. *Let $b_s \subseteq \cdots b_i \subseteq b_{i+1} \subseteq \cdots \subseteq b_m$ be a series of nested structuring elements, where i is the scale parameter of a structuring element, $1 \leq s \leq i \leq m$, $s, i, m \in N^+$. For a gradient image g such that $f = \varepsilon_{b_i}(g)$ and $f \leq g$, the adaptive morphological reconstruction denoted by ψ of g from f is defined as:*

$$\psi(g, s, m) = \vee_{s \leq i \leq m} \left\{ R_g^\phi(f)_{b_i} \right\} \tag{1}$$

2.2   Self-representing Low-rank Kernel Subspace Clustering

The SSC [11] algorithm takes advantage of the "self-expression" of data, i.e., data points in the same subspace can be expressed linearly with each other. Unfortunately, its model is only applicable to linear (or affine) subspaces. Therefore, using the kernel trick [12], nonlinear structural data can be mapped to linear feature space (as shown in Fig. 2). The nonlinear extension of SSC is given by:

$$\min_{H, Z} \|\phi(X)\|_* + \lambda \|Z\|_1 \quad \text{s.t.} \ \phi(X) = \phi(X)Z, Z_{ii} = 0 \tag{2}$$

where $H = \phi(X)^T \phi(X)$ is the Gram matrix, Z is the self-expressive coefficient matrix, X is the data matrix, $\phi(X) = [\phi(x_1), \phi(x_2), \cdots, \phi(x_N)]$ represents the mapped feature space, and $\boldsymbol{\lambda}$ is the trade-off parameter. $\|\phi(\boldsymbol{X})\|_*$ is the convex approximation of rank $(\phi(\boldsymbol{X}))$, which ensures that the mapped data is contained in multiple linear subspaces.

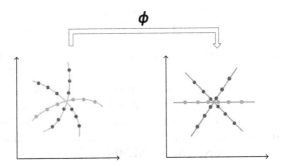

Fig. 2. The subspace structure retains the feature map: the nonlinear subspace maps to the linear subspace in the high dimensional Hilbert space.

3   Proposed Method

3.1   Robust Subspace Clustering Based on Non-convex Low-rank Multi-kernel (NLMSC)

Mapping non-linear structure data to Reproducing Kernel Hilbert Space (RKHS) can perform linear analysis. Through the graph learning framework based on self-expression, we can learn affinity matrices for spectral clustering. Considering the self-expression and kernel mapping, the kernel self-expression optimization problem is formulated as:

$$\min_{\boldsymbol{Z}} \frac{1}{2}\|\phi(\boldsymbol{X}) - \phi(\boldsymbol{X})\boldsymbol{Z}\|_F^2 + \alpha R(\boldsymbol{Z}), \text{ s.t. } \boldsymbol{Z} \geq 0, \text{diag}(\boldsymbol{Z}) = 0 \qquad (3)$$

where α is the regularization parameter and $R(\boldsymbol{Z})$ is the regularization term on self-expression coefficient $\boldsymbol{Z}$.

Based on kernel trick, in kernel space, we mainly rely on the kernel matrix $\boldsymbol{H} = \phi(\boldsymbol{X})^T\phi(\boldsymbol{X})$, the $(i,j)-th$ element of $\boldsymbol{H}$ is $\boldsymbol{H}_{ij} = \langle \phi(\boldsymbol{x}_i), \phi(\boldsymbol{x}_j)\rangle$. Therefore, problem (3) can be expressed as:

$$\|\phi(\boldsymbol{X}) - \phi(\boldsymbol{X})\boldsymbol{Z}\|_F^2 = Trace\left(\phi(\boldsymbol{X})^T\phi(\boldsymbol{X}) - 2\phi(\boldsymbol{X})^T\phi(\boldsymbol{X})\boldsymbol{Z} + \boldsymbol{Z}^T\phi(\boldsymbol{X})^T\phi(\boldsymbol{X})\boldsymbol{Z}\right)$$

$$= Trace\left(\boldsymbol{H} - 2\boldsymbol{H}\boldsymbol{Z} + \boldsymbol{Z}^T\boldsymbol{H}\boldsymbol{Z}\right)$$

$$(4)$$

Inspired by [13], we introduce BDR to make Z maintain block diagonal property when the underlying subspace is independent. BDR is defined as the sum of the k smallest eigenvalues of L, i.e.,

$$\|Z\|_{\boxed{k}} = \sum_{i=N-k-1}^{N} \alpha_i(L) \tag{5}$$

In the multi-kernel learning model, it is assumed that each basic kernel H^i is a small perturbation of the desired consensus kernel H, expressed as $\min\|H^i - H\|_F^2$, and the weight of each kernel should be robust to noise. Hence, we use the mixture correntropy induced metric(MCIM) to solve the weight vector to learn the purer optimal consensus kernel. In addition, the Schatten-p constraint is imposed on the optimal consensus kernel to maintain the low-rank structure of the feature space. Finally, NLMSC model can be formulated as:

$$\min_{Z,H,w} \frac{1}{2}Trace\left(H - 2HZ + Z^T HZ\right) + \alpha\|Z\|_{\boxed{k}} + \beta\sum_{h=1}^{r} w_i \left\|H^i - H\right\|_F^2 \tag{6}$$
$$+ \lambda\|H\|_{Sp}^p \quad s.t. Z \geq 0, \mathrm{diag}(Z) = 0, Z = Z^T$$

where α and β are the non-negative trade-off parameters, w_i is the weight of the $i - th$ predefined basic kernel H^i, and $\lambda > 0$.

In (6), in order to satisfy the necessary property of BDR, the constraint of the kernel self-expression coefficient matrix Z is symmetric and non-negative, which may affect its expression ability. In addition, we notice that Z and H both involve two items, which makes the solution difficult. Therefore, we introduce two auxiliary matrices A and B to separate variables and to solve subproblems independently, let $Z = A$ and $H = B$, then the optimization problem of formula (6) is transformed into:

$$\min_{Z,H,w,A,B} \frac{1}{2}Trace\left(H - 2HZ + Z^T HZ\right) + \alpha\|A\|_{\boxed{k}} + \lambda\|B\|_{Sp}^p$$
$$+ \beta\sum_{h=1}^{r} w_i \left\|H^i - H\right\|_F^2 \quad s.t. \ A \geq 0, \mathrm{diag}(A) = 0, A = A^T, Z = A, H = B \tag{7}$$

Next, the corresponding augmented Lagrangian function of (7) is expressed as:

$$L(Z, H, w, A, B) = \frac{1}{2}Trace\left(H - 2HZ + Z^T HZ\right) + \alpha\|A\|_{\boxed{k}} + \lambda\|B\|_{Sp}^p$$
$$+ \beta\sum_{h=1}^{r} w_i \left\|H^i - H\right\|_F^2 + \frac{\mu}{2}\left(\|A - Z + Y_1/\mu\|_F^2 + \|B - H + Y_2/\mu\|_F^2\right),$$
$$s.t. \ Z \geq 0, \mathrm{diag}(Z) = 0, Z = Z^T \tag{8}$$

where $\mu > 0$ is the penalty parameter, Y_1 and Y_2 are Lagrange multipliers.

We use the Alternating Direction Method of Multipliers (ADMM) [14] to solve the optimization problem, then need to update $\boldsymbol{Z}, \boldsymbol{H}, \boldsymbol{w}, \boldsymbol{A}, \boldsymbol{B}$ in sequence, while fixing other variables and finally get:

$$\boldsymbol{Z}^{t+1} = (\mu\boldsymbol{I} + \boldsymbol{H})\backslash(\boldsymbol{H} + \mu\boldsymbol{A} + \boldsymbol{Y}_1)$$
$$\boldsymbol{A}^{t+1} = \max\left(0, \frac{\tilde{\boldsymbol{M}} + \tilde{\boldsymbol{M}}^T}{2}\right)$$
$$\boldsymbol{H}^{t+1} = \frac{2\beta\sum_{i=1}^{r} \boldsymbol{w}_i \boldsymbol{H}^i + \mu\boldsymbol{B} + \boldsymbol{Y}_2 - \frac{\boldsymbol{I}}{2} + \boldsymbol{Z}^T - \frac{\boldsymbol{Z}\boldsymbol{Z}^T}{2}}{\mu + 2\beta\sum_{i=1}^{r} \boldsymbol{w}_i} \qquad (9)$$
$$\boldsymbol{w}_i^{t+1} = 1 - \mathrm{MCIM}\left(\boldsymbol{H}^i, \boldsymbol{H}\right)$$
$$\boldsymbol{B}^{t+1} = \boldsymbol{\Gamma}^* \boldsymbol{V}^T$$

In view of the length of the paper, the solution process of each variable is not uniformly given here. The closed-form solution of $\boldsymbol{A}$ can be referred to [15], and the closed-form solution of $\boldsymbol{B}$ can be referred to [16]. Equation (9) gives the closed-form solutions of the update variables to solve the problem (8), they will cyclically calculate the corresponding values of algorithm, value until the convergence condition is reached or the maximum number of iterations is exceeded. In each iteration, the convergence criterion for stopping is:

$$\mathrm{diff}_Z = \left\|\boldsymbol{Z}^{t+1} - \boldsymbol{Z}^t\right\|_F, \mathrm{diff}_A = \left\|\boldsymbol{A}^{t+1} - \boldsymbol{A}^t\right\|_F, \mathrm{diff}_B = \left\|\boldsymbol{B}^{t+1} - \boldsymbol{B}^t\right\|_F,$$
$$\mathrm{diff}_H = \left\|\boldsymbol{H}^{t+1} - \boldsymbol{H}^t\right\|_F, \max(\mathrm{diff}_Z, \mathrm{diff}_A, \mathrm{diff}_B, \mathrm{diff}_H) \le \varepsilon \qquad (10)$$

where ε is the threshold.

3.2 AMR_WT_NLMSC Method

In this section, by combining the pre-segmentation method AMR_WT and the NLMSC method, we propose a new image segmentation method AMR_WT_NLMSC based on subspace clustering. First, for the input original image, AMR uses multi-scale structural elements to reconstruct the gradient image. Secondly, the pointwise maximum operation is performed on these reconstructed gradient images to obtain the final adaptive reconstruction result. The WT algorithm uses the adaptive reconstruction results provided by AMR to obtain super-pixel images with precise contours. Suppose that AMR_WT divides the image into N super-pixels, and extracts the color features of each super-pixel to form a feature matrix $\boldsymbol{X} = [\boldsymbol{x}_1, \boldsymbol{x}_2, \ldots, \boldsymbol{x}_N]$. Input $\boldsymbol{X}$ into the NLMSC model to obtain the coefficient matrix $\boldsymbol{A} = [\boldsymbol{A}_1, \boldsymbol{A}_2, \ldots, \boldsymbol{A}_N]$, by $\boldsymbol{W} = |\boldsymbol{A}| + \left|\boldsymbol{A}^T\right|$ constructing the similarity matrix, finally inputting into spectral clustering for graph segmentation to obtain the segmentation result of the original image. Figure 3 clearly shows the AMR_WT_NLMSC image segmentation process.

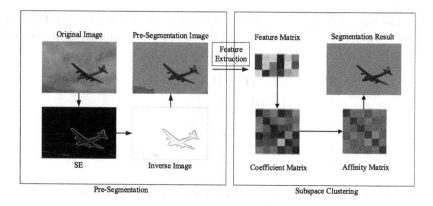

Fig. 3. AMR_WT_NLMSC image segmentation process.

4 Experiments

In this section, we have verified the good clustering performance of the NLMSC model and the effective segmentation effect of AMR_WT_NLMSC.

4.1 NLMSC Clustering Experiment Analysis

We use Yale[1] and ORL[2] datasets to test the effectiveness of NLMSC. The Yale dataset contains 38 faces, and each face contains 64 facial images taken under different light. The ORL dataset contains 400 facial images from 40 different subjects. Some sample images of the Yale, ORL datasets are shown in Fig. 4. Due to specular reflection, most of the images in the two datasets are damaged by shadows and noise. In addition, when images are taken for the same face, facial poses and expressions are not exactly the same, resulting in non-linear structure data. Therefore, these two datasets can be used to verify the clustering performance of NLMSC in processing large-scale damage and nonlinear structure data. Compare the NLMSC method with the following methods: MKKM [17], RMKKM [18], SCMK [19], LKGr [20], SMKL [21], LRKSC [22], and JMKSC [15]. The metrics include clustering accuracy (ACC), normalized mutual information(NMI) and purity. Among these three indicators, the higher the value, the better the algorithm performance. For the above comparison methods, we either use the parameters suggested in the respective original papers (if parameters are provided), or manually adjust them to retain the best performing parameters and adjust the algorithm to the best level.

For all comparative clustering methods, we set the number of clusters to the true number of clusters k, independently repeat the experiment 20 times with random initializations, and report the final result. Table 1 shows the clustering results in terms of ACC, NMI, and Purity for all datasets. The best results of the

---

[1] http://vision.ucsd.edu/datasetsAll.

[2] https://git-disl.github.io/GTDLBench/datasets.

a.Yale dataset   b.ORL dataset

Fig. 4. Example images of the corresponding dataset.

experiment are highlighted in bold. SCMK, LKGr, SMKL, LRKSC obtain better clustering results than MKKM and RMKKM, which shows that methods based on spectral clustering usually have better performance than methods based on k-means. The clustering performance of JMKSC is better than SCMK, LKGr, SMKL, LRKSC, which shows that multi-kernel learning is better than single-kernel learning when processing nonlinear structure data to a certain extent. Among all the methods, NLMSC obtains the best clustering performance. This is because NLMSC not only uses multi-kernel learning to process nonlinear structure data, but also uses MCIM to solve the weight vector to suppress noise. In addition, the Schatten-p low-rank constraint is imposed on the optimal consensus kernel to ensure that the feature space has multiple low-dimensional subspaces.

Table 1. Clustering results on benchmark datasets.

	Metrics	MKKM	RMKKM	SCMK	LKGr	SMKL	LRKSC	JMKSC	NLMSC
Yale	ACC	0.457	0.521	0.582	0.540	0.582	0.623	0.630	**0.661**
	NMI	0.501	0.556	0.576	0.566	0.614	0.628	0.631	**0.669**
	Purity	0.475	0.536	0.610	0.554	0.667	0.669	0.673	**0.721**
ORL	ACC	0.475	0.556	0.656	0.616	0.573	0.718	**0.725**	0.720
	NMI	0.689	0.748	0.808	0.794	0.733	0.849	0.852	**0.861**
	Purity	0.514	0.602	0.699	0.658	0.648	0.749	0.753	**0.810**

4.2   AMR_WT_NLMSC Segmentation Experiment Analysis

In order to verify the segmentation performance of AMR_WT_NLMSC method, we conducted experiments on some color images of the BSDS500 dataset. The classic superpixel segmentation method SLIC is used as the comparison algorithm for the pre-segmentation part, and LRKSC is used as the comparison

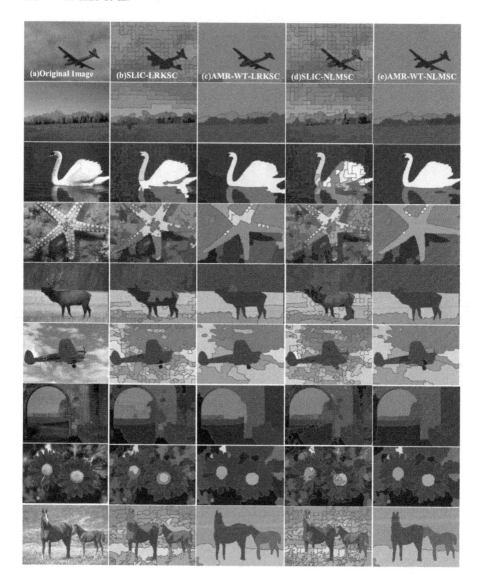

Fig. 5. Image segmentation results.

algorithm for the subspace clustering part. The following comparison experiments are designed respectively, SLIC_LRKSC, AMR_WT_LRKSC, SLIC_NLMSC, AMR_WT_NLMSC. The segmentation result is shown in Fig. 5. Take the aircraft image in the first column as an example to analyze:

(1) Comparing SLIC_NLMSC and AMR_WT_NLMSC, the subspace clustering models of these two methods are the same, and the pre-segmentation are SLIC and AMR_WT respectively. Through observation, it is found that although SLIC_LRKSC outlines the outline of the aircraft, the background area is messy, which is affected by the SLIC segmentation result. AMR_WT_LRKSC distinguished the aircraft from the background and segmented the aircraft outline, which proved that AMR removed some meaningless seeds. Compared with SLIC, AMR_WT is a more effective pre-segmentation. This is because SLIC divides the image into regular regions of similar shape and size, destroying the local spatial structure of the real image, while AMR_WT adaptively divides the image into areas of different sizes.

(2) Comparing AMR_WT_LRKSC and AMR_WT_NLMSC, the pre-segmentation method of these two methods is AMR_WT, and the subspace clustering model are LRKSC and NLMSC respectively. AMR_WT_LRKSC segmented the contour of the aircraft, but did not completely separate the aircraft from the background area, while AMR_WT_NLMSC completely distinguished the aircraft from the background, which shows that NLMSC has a better segmentation effect than LRKSC.

In order to quantitatively measure the performance of AMR_WT_NLMSC, we use two evaluation indicators of probability Rand index (PRI) and variability of information (VOI) to report the experimental results, as shown in Table 2. The higher the PRI, the better the segmentation effect, and the lower the VOI, the better the segmentation effect. By comparing SLIC_NLMSC and AMR_WT_NLMSC, it is found that the PRI value of AMR_WT_NLMSC is larger than that of SLIC_NLMSC, and the VOI value is smaller than that of SLIC_NLMSC, which fully proves the effectiveness of the pre-segmentation method AMR_WT. In addition, comparing AMR_WT_LRKSC and AMR_WT _NLMSC, it is found that the PRI value of AMR_WT_NLMSC is larger than that of AMR_WT_LRKSC, and the VOI value is smaller than that of AMR_WT_LRKSC, which proves the good clustering performance of NLMSC. Therefore, among all methods, AMR_WT_NLMSC obtains the best segmentation results.

Table 2. Evaluation index of image segmentation results of each algorithm.

Metrics	SLIC_LRKSC	AMR_WT_LRKSC	SLIC_NLMSC	AMR_WT_NLMSC
PRI	0.51123	0.5405	0.5623	**0.8542**
VOI	3.39865	2.6729	3.5465	**1.0123**

4.3 Run Time Experiment

We have verified the operating efficiency of NLMSC and AMR_WT_NLMSC respectively. Figure 6a shows that the operating efficiency of NLMSC is lower than that of MKKM. This is because MKKM is a simple subspace clustering model, and the clustering performance of NLMSC is much higher than that of MKKM. Compared with JMKSC, NLMSC imposes a non-convex low-rank constraint on the kernel matrix, which takes some time. Except for MKKM and JMKSC, NLMSC not only has better clustering performance, but also runs more efficiently. Figure 6b shows that the operating efficiency of SLIC is much lower than that of AMR_WT, and AMR_WT_NLMSC obtains the highest operating efficiency.

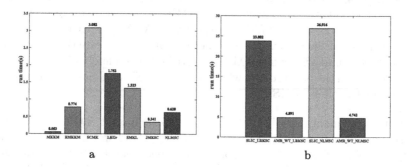

Fig. 6. A refers running time of subspace clustering method, b refers the running time of the image segmentation method.

5 Conclusion

In this work, we propose an image segmentation method based on non-convex low-rank multi-kernel clustering. This paper firstly combines the adaptive morphological reconstruction seed segmentation algorithm with the subspace clustering method to achieve efficient image segmentation. In particular, we design a subspace clustering method based on non-convex low-rank multi-kernel to better deal with nonlinear structure data and complex noise. The experimental results show that the proposed method NLMSC has the good clustering performance, and AMR_WT_NLMSC has the good image segmentation effect.

References

1. Ren, X., Malik, J.: Learning a classification model for segmentation. In: IEEE International Conference on Computer Vision, vol. 2, pp. 10–17. IEEE Computer Society (2003)
2. Achanta, R., Shaji, A., Smith, K., Lucchi, A., Fua, P., Süsstrunk, S.: SLIC superpixels. Technical report (2010)

3. Cheng, B., Liu, G., Wang, J., Huang, Z.Y., Yan, S.: Multi-task low-rank affinity pursuit for image segmentation. In: IEEE International Conference on Computer Vision (2011)

4. Li, T., Wang, W.W., Zhai, D., Jia, X.X., et al.: Weighted-sparse subspace clustering method for image segmentation. Syst. Eng. Electron. **36**(3), 580–585 (2014)

5. Li, X.P., Wang, W.W., Luo, L., Wang, S.Q., et al.: Improved sparse subspace clustering method for image segmentation. Syst. Eng. Electron. **37**(10), 2418–2424 (2010)

6. Al-Azawi, R.J., Al-Jubouri, Q.S., Mohammed, Y.A.: Enhanced algorithm of super-pixel segmentation using simple linear iterative clustering. In: 2019 12th International Conference on Developments in eSystems Engineering (DeSE) (2020)

7. Lei, T., Jia, X., Liu, T., Liu, S., Meng, H., Nandi, A.K.: Adaptive morphological reconstruction for seeded image segmentation. IEEE Trans. Image Process. **28**(11), 5510–5523 (2019)

8. Boykov, Y., Funka-Lea, G.: Graph cuts and efficient ND image segmentation. Int. J. Comput. Vis. **70**(2), 109–131 (2006)

9. Grady, L.: Random walks for image segmentation. IEEE Trans. Pattern Anal. Mach. Intell. **28**(11), 1768–1783 (2006)

10. Vincent, L., Soille, P.: Watersheds in digital spaces: an efficient algorithm based on immersion simulations. IEEE Comput. Archit. Lett. **13**(06), 583–598 (1991)

11. Elhamifar, E., Vidal, R.: Sparse subspace clustering: algorithm, theory, and applications. IEEE Trans. Pattern Anal. Mach. Intell. **35**(11), 2765–2781 (2013)

12. Patel, V.M., Vidal, R.: Kernel sparse subspace clustering, pp. 2849–2853. IEEE (2014)

13. Lu, C., Feng, J., Lin, Z., Mei, T., Yan, S.: Subspace clustering by block diagonal representation. IEEE Trans. Pattern Anal. Mach. Intell. **41**(2), 487–501 (2018)

14. Boyd, S., Parikh, N., Chu, E.: Distributed Optimization and Statistical Learning via the Alternating Direction Method of Multipliers. Now Publishers Inc., Norwell (2011)

15. Yang, C., Ren, Z., Sun, Q., Wu, M., Yin, M., Sun, Y.: Joint correntropy metric weighting and block diagonal regularizer for robust multiple kernel subspace clustering. Inf. Sci. **500**, 48–66 (2019)

16. Xue, X., Zhang, X., Feng, X., Sun, H., Chen, W., Liu, Z.: Robust subspace clustering based on non-convex low-rank approximation and adaptive kernel. Inf. Sci. **513**, 190–205 (2020)

17. Huang, H., Chuang, Y., Chen, C.: Multiple kernel fuzzy clustering. IEEE Trans. Fuzzy Syst. **20**(1), 120–134 (2012)

18. Du, L., et al.: Robust multiple kernel k-means using l21-norm (2015)

19. Kang, Z., Peng, C., Cheng, Q., Xu, Z.: Unified spectral clustering with optimal graph. Learning. arXiv:1711.04258 (2017)

20. Kang, Z., Wen, L., Chen, W., Xu, Z.: Low-rank kernel learning for graph-based clustering. Knowl. Based Syst. **163**, 510–517 (2019)

21. Kang, Z., Lu, X., Yi, J., Xu, Z.: Self-weighted multiple kernel learning for graph-based clustering and semi-supervised classification. Machine Learning arXiv:1806.07697 (2018)

22. Ji, P., Reid, I., Garg, R., Li, H., Salzmann, M.: Low-rank kernel subspace clustering. CoRR (2017)

Novel View Synthesis of Dynamic Human with Sparse Cameras

Xun Lv[1], Yuan Wang[1], Feiyi Xu[1], Jianhui Nie[1], Feng Xu[2,3], and Hao Gao[1,3(✉)]

[1] Nanjing University of Posts and Telecommunications, Nanjing, China
[2] Tsinghua University, Beijing, China
[3] Hangzhou Zhouxi Institute of Brain and Intelligence, Hangzhou, China

Abstract. This paper proposes a new method to synthesize a novel view of a human in motion. For image-based rendering, the challenging problem is to synthesize an image of a novel view with sparse images. As the number of cameras decreases, there will exist missing regions in the synthetic image. To address this challenge, we use a skinned multi-person linear model (SMPL) model to represent the surface and posture of the human body in motion and correlate the images of the human in different poses. If the missing pixel at the novel view is visible at other times, we can use spatio-temporal sequence information to complete it. Therefore, we choose images from different frames to synthesize images of the novel view. Then, we use deformable convolutional network to align these images and take advantage of ConvLSTM to perform temporal aggregation. Finally, we can obtain a more realistic free-view image of the human. This method allows us to freely move the camera view in time and space to synthesize free-view video.

Keywords: Novel view synthesis · Image-based rendering

1 Introduction

In the fields of film and television production, sports competitions, etc., the demand for interactive free-view video is constantly increasing. When watching the video, we hope to freely shuttle in the dynamic scene and change the camera view. Most free-view video systems require high-quality 3D reconstruction. However, due to expensive equipments and constrained environments, it is difficult to reconstruct a high-precision geometric model in the real world. If the resolution of the geometric model is relatively low, it is not enough to render an ideal image.

Image-based rendering (IBR) can synthesize such realistic interactive images. At present, the application areas of the most existing view synthesis methods are largely limited to static scenes. However, there are few methods related to free-view video of changing contents (such as human). In this paper, we focus on the novel view synthesis of human in dynamic scenes. Due to the occlusion between the body parts of human, there are invisible areas in an image of novel

© Springer Nature Switzerland AG 2021
L. Fang et al. (Eds.): CICAI 2021, LNAI 13069, pp. 432–443, 2021.
https://doi.org/10.1007/978-3-030-93046-2_37

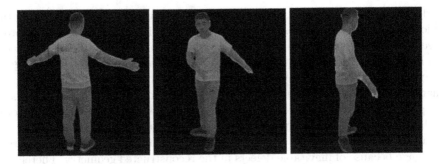

Fig. 1. The experimental results on our own data. Our method can achieve good performance given sparse views.

view, especially when the camera perspective is sparse. To overcome the issue, we make full use of the complementarity of temporal and spatial information in human movement.

We propose a free-view synthesis method for human in a dynamic scene to synthesize images of any time and view. An acquisition system containing 20 cameras is used to capture multi-view images, and we use the SMPL [16] model to represent the shape and posture of humans. After mapping the information from the source images to the target view through the SMPL model, we use a deep-blending network to synthesize novel view of the static scene. However, the synthesized new perspective images are often missing or blurred due to mutual occlusion of humans, especially when the number of cameras is sparse. In order to solve this problem, we use the temporal and spatial consistency of people in dynamic scenes to enhance the quality of image on condition that the missing part is visible in time sequence. We use the SMPL model to map the collected images of the person in other frames to the target view. Then, the deformation network can align layers from different frames. Finally, ConvLSTM [22] is used to synthesize the ideal novel view. This method enables our perspective to move freely in time and space in a dynamic scene. As is shown in Fig. 1, the experimental results indicate that our method performs well in challenging real datasets.

2   Related Work

Human Capture. At present, most of the traditional 3D modeling methods [5,11] are based on images of a scene, which use structure-from-motion [1,21] to register images and adopt multi-view stereo technique [7,9] to reconstruct geometry. However, the reconstructed geometry may not represent the underlying scene perfectly. Therefore, they must rely on depth sensors [19,29,30] or dense camera arrays [5,11] to reconstruct high-precision models. In recent years, deep-learning based methods have been successfully applied to monocular depth estimation [8] or binocular stereo depth estimation [25]. At the same time, some works [12,28] combines the advantages of the both types of methods for depth fusion or geometry refinement. In addition, the statistical model SMPL is proposed to reconstruct the human model, which can provide a prior model of the human. In order to capture the human model in sparse multi-view images, template-based methods [13] deforms the shape of the template to fit the input image to reconstruct a dynamic human. However, in most cases, the deformed template can only describe the basic geometry of the human and cannot restore its high-precision model. Then, texture mapping [15,24] is essential for creating realistic models without increasing geometric complexity. But this is a large challenge because of inevitable defects in the reconstructed geometry. Therefore, image-based rendering methods are utilized to synthesize novel view.

Image-Based Rendering. Recently, convolutional neural networks (CNN) and deep learning have been applied to solve problems of novel view synthesis. Image-based rendering methods aim to synthesize novel views without detailed 3D geometry. With rough scene geometry, they generally warp the source images into the target view according to the depth. Therefore, deep-blending [12] proposes a deep blending network to learn blending weights to generate realistic images. Then, FVS [20] shows the improvements on this basis and achieves good results. Given densely sampled images, some works [17,18] apply light field functions to obtain novel views without geometric models. Although their rendering results are impressive, they require intensive sampling, which limits the application scenarios of this method. At the same time, the range of viewpoints that can be rendered is limited.

4D Human. Nowadays, a lot of works are devoted to the synthesis of novel view in static scenes. However, in reality, dynamic scenes commonly exist in our life. The method [28] proposes a deep blender rendering network for fusion of foreground and background to generate novel view of dynamic scenes. 4D Visualization [2] can visualize dynamic events in 4D time and space, which is interactive. And it performs well on challenging in-the-wild scenes.

3   Method

To begin with, we perform a preprocessing step that calculates the geometry and mesh from the set of input images. Next, we select source images which are close to the novel view, namely target view. Then, we map them into the target view and a blending network is applied to synthesis an image of target view. However, there are some blurry and missing areas in the image of target view due to the lack of sufficient views. Therefore, we capture temporal information to improve the quality of image. The source images in other frames are selected and mapped into the target view, and we synthesize images of the target view from these frames separately. After that, we use the deformable convolution network [6,31] to align these images and take advantage of ConvLSTM to blend their aligned feature maps. Finally, these modules will output the corresponding refined an image of novel view. The overall pipeline of the proposed method is shown in Fig. 2.

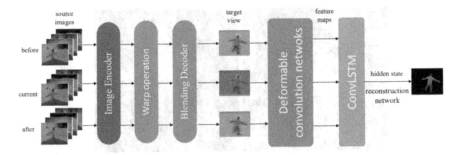

Fig. 2. Overview of our method. The input is three sets of source images from different times. The network can finally generate a single image of novel view.

3.1 Preprocessing

We firstly adopt a set of multi-view images from different frames. Then, SFM is utilized to register the images and obtain the intrinsic parameters K and extrinsic parameters $T(R \mid t)$.

In this paper, we focus on the human in dynamic scenes. Therefore, we adopt foreground segmentation technology [3,10] to obtain the silhouettes of human in the images that we are interested in, as shown in Fig. 3a. Given the geometry, we can generate the depth map of the corresponding known view and perform interpolation to supplement the depth based on the contour.

Given sparse views, we can estimate the 3D human pose, and reconstruct the rough geometry through multi-view stereo or the silhouettes, as shown in Fig. 3b. Based on this, SMPL [16] is applied to describe the pose and shape of the human. The SMPL is a statistical model with 10 shape parameters and 24 pose parameters, which is driven by the rotation of the joints. It is widely used in various fields related to the human motion capture. Therefore, we only need reconstruct a human geometry in the first frame. In other frames, we can estimate the pose and shape parameters and use the parameters to obtain the human geometry.

3.2 Selection

In actual situations, not all images are overlapped with the target view. Therefore, we have to choose the source images which are close to the target view. Based on extrinsic parameters, we sort the sources images according to the difference of position and direction with the target view. In every frame, we select several source images that have more overlap with the target view.

With the aid of [20], we can synthesize a detailed novel view from dense views. However, as the number of known views decreases, the synthesized images will become worse. Therefore, we select source images before and after the current frame. Based on the geometry, we derive the depth map for each target view. The depth of each pixel at target view is projected into the source images. Then

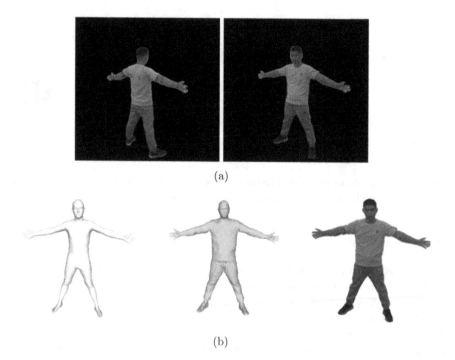

Fig. 3. (a) Silhouettes of human; (b) Human geometry for novel view synthesis. Given multi-view images, we first obtain a SMPL model (left) with multi-view images and then reconstruct a deformable model (middle). In order to present the effect of the model, we put a real image (right).

we count the number of visible pixels in each of the source images and sort them. The top ones are used to synthesize images of the target view.

3.3 Mapping and Blending Images of Novel View

As mentioned above, we have selected the source images. In the first part of the network, we encode these images with feature extraction network which is composed of VGG network. Then, they are be mapped into the target view. For a pixel (u_t, v_t) in the target view, we can find the pixel (u, v) in source images by the formula:

$$s_c^k \begin{bmatrix} u_c^k \\ v_c^k \\ 1 \end{bmatrix} = K_c T_c T_{\text{SMPL}} T_t^{-1} K_t^{-1} s_t \begin{bmatrix} u_t \\ v_t \\ 1 \end{bmatrix} \tag{1}$$

where t represents the target view, c is the camera index, k is the frame in sequence, s is the value of depth, K and T denotes the intrinsic and extrinsic parameters of the camera separately. T_{SMPL} is the transformation matrix is derived by SMPL joints. Now, we have the feature maps of source images warped into target view. We utilize a U-Net based convolutional architecture with gated recurrent units (GRU) to blend them in each frame to synthesis novel views I_t^k, $k = \{$before, current, after$\}$.

3.4 Alignment and Aggregation

At this point, we have 3 synthetic images of novel view at the current frame. Our goal is to generate a qualified novel view with the 3 images. We adopt the deformable convolution network to align these images and make use of ConvLSTM to blend their feature maps. Finally, these modules will output the corresponding refined image of novel view.

Alignment Module. Given 3 images of a novel view, we need to aggregate them to obtain a single blended novel view. However, these synthetic images are not aligned due to the errors or differences in the warping operation and the process of blending. Inspired by [27], we adopt the deformable convolutional networks to align the images of a novel view. Comparing 3 images of novel view, we find that the human pose of I_t^{current} is closely to that of the ground truth. Therefore, we align I_t^{before} and I_t^{after} with I_t^{current}. In the first part of the network, we respectively encode these images with one convolutional layer and 5 residual blocks followed by LeakyRelus. The features F_t^{before}, F_t^{current} and F_t^{after} are obtained. Then, the deformable align modules can use these features to dynamically predict offsets of sampling convolution kernels. To accurately align features of different scales, we adopt a Pyramid, Cascading and Deformable (PCD) structure [26]. For simplicity, we use F_t^{before} and F_t^{current} as an example. The module takes the F_t^{before} and F_t^{current} as inputs to predict the offsets for sampling F_t^{after}:

$$\Delta p = g\left(\left[F_t^{\text{before}}, F_t^{\text{current}}\right]\right) \tag{2}$$

$$F_t^{\text{align}} = D\,Conv\left(F_t^{\text{before}}, \Delta p\right) \tag{3}$$

where g denotes the function of convolutional layers, [,] denotes the channel-wise concatenation and Δp is the offset of convolutional kernels. After applying to the deformable function, the F_t^{before} can be aligned. In the same way, we can obtain the aligned F_t^{after}.

Aggregation Module. At the moment, we have the 2 aligned feature maps and the feature map at the current frame. Therefore, we can generate an image of novel view with feature maps in other frames instead of individual feature maps. ConvLSTM is a popular sequence data model which can efficiently process temper information. Therefore, we choose it to blend the 2 aligned feature maps and F_t^{current}. According to the time index, the 2 aligned features and F_t^{current} are successively fed into the networks. Then we can obtain the hidden state of current frame. Finally, we use a reconstruct module which consists of 10 stacked residual blocks. The module takes the individual hidden state h_t as input and outputs the deep features. The final estimated novel view I_t will be obtained by a convolutional layer from deep features.

3.5   Training

Loss Function. To train the network, we use the perceptual loss functions [4]. Since our novel view only focus on the human motion, we compare our estimated image with the ground truth by utilizing the mask of ground truth. Before computing the loss, we firstly set the background of the estimated images and ground truth to zero according to the mask. Then the loss function is described as the following formula:

$$L = \left\| I_t^{GT} - I_t \right\|_1 + \sum_l \lambda_l \left\| \varphi_l \left(I_t^{GT} \right) - \varphi_l \left(I_t \right) \right\|_1 \tag{4}$$

where ϕ_l are the outputs of the layers 'conv1-2', 'conv2-2', 'conv3-2', 'conv4-2', and 'conv5-2' of a pre-trained VGG-19 network [23]. We set the weighting coefficients $\{\lambda_l\}_{l=1}^5$ as in [4].

4   Experiments

4.1   Experimental Settings

Dataset. To evaluate our method, we create a multi-view dataset which include two scenes. The dataset is captured by a multi-view camera system which is composed of 20 cameras. The sequence in each scene has a length of 300 frames. To generate an image of the novel view at different times, the dataset includes source images, depth maps, human masks and ground truth. We select 5 of 20 cameras which are uniformly distributed as source images for training and use the remaining cameras as target views for testing. Limited by the GPU memory, we train the network with the part of the images of dataset. We crop patches of size 480 × 300 according to the location of the mask. This can help us capture the most part of the human.

Evaluation Metrics. In our evaluations, we use two standard metrics, including peak signal-to noise ratio (PSNR) and structural similarity index (SSIM). Since our method mainly focus on the dynamic human, we only care about the part of human. To validate the effectiveness of our network, we evaluate synthetic view and ground truth in mask. According to the mask of human, we obtain the bounding box and the pixels of background are set to zero. Then we evaluate the quality of novel view in the bounding box by computing the two metrics.

Implementation Details. We use Adam [14] optimizer with $b_1 = 0.9$, $b_2 = 0.999$ and $\epsilon = 10^{-8}$. The learning rate is set to 10^{-4}. We train the model with a batch size of 1. All networks converge after about 50 epochs of our training set. For 5 source images in current frame, we select 4 of them to be projected into the target view according to the ranking. The experiments are all conducted on a server with Python3.6, Pytorch1.3 and Nvidia Tesla M40.

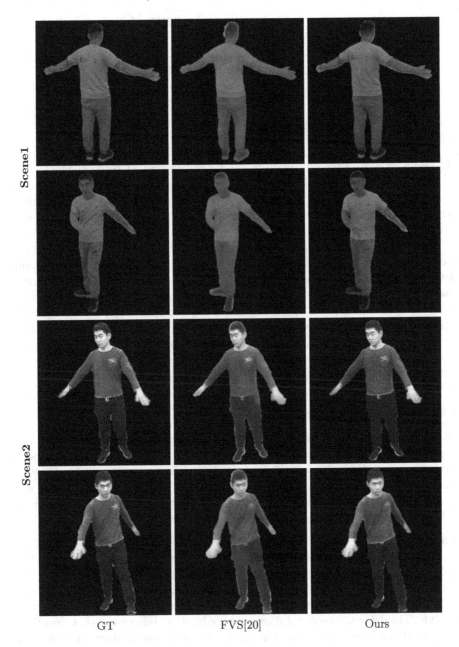

Scene1

Scene2

GT   FVS[20]   Ours

Fig. 4. Qualitative results on different methods. We select one novel view for qualitative results comparison. Our method significantly outperforms [20].

Table 1. Quantitative results (PSNR (dB) and SSIM) of different methods.

	Scene1	Scene2
FVS [20]	24.79/0.9254	21.57/0.8854
Ours	30.02/0.9574	25.06/0.9286

4.2   Comparisons

We compare with FVS [20] in terms of PSNR and SSIM respectively on two scenes. There are obvious differences in the characteristics of the human in each scene. For each scene, we train a separate model. Table 1 shows that our method achieves remarkable improvements on both metrics, about 4.36 in PSNR and 0.0376 in SSIM on average.

The visual results are presented in Fig. 4. The results indicate that our method achieves noticeably visual improvements and restore structures and details of a human. FVS uses a static 3D geometry which can only integrate spatial information at the current frame. Given sparse views, the results of FVS are blurred or lack of parts of human body because source images have less overlap with target view. However, we reconstruct a dynamic human model which can correlate information between different frames. Therefore, after combining temporal and spatial information, there exists less blurry or artifacts in the images our method generated.

4.3   Ablation Study

To further demonstrate the effectiveness of different modules in alignment and aggregation, we perform an ablation study on Scene1. We train three models to demonstrate the effect of different modules. Ours w/o alignment does not use deformable convolutional networks to align other feature maps. Ours w/o ConvLSTM uses no ConvLSTM to aggregate information. Ours full uses both deformable convolutional networks and ConvLSTM.

Effective of Alignment Module. To evaluate the effect of alignment, we use Ours w/o alignment to aggregate these synthetic images of the novel view. Table 2 shows that adding an alignment module achieves better performance, about 0.08 in PSNR and 0.013 in SSIM on average. By comparing, we find that there will be missing or blurred areas in the final results without an alignment module. The deformable convolution network has the ability to predict the offsets between different feature maps. Therefore, the alignment module can utilize the predicted offsets to more accurately extract the features from other feature maps in other frames. This can contribute to effectively exploiting information from other frames.

Effective of ConvLSTM. To investigate the effect of ConvLSTM, we adopt another method, namely Ours w/o ConvLSTM. After aligning the feature maps of these images of novel view, we concatenate all the feature maps and feed

Table 2. Ablation study on different modules.

Methods	Ours w/o alignment	Ours w/o ConvLSTM	Ours full
PSNR	29.90	29.22	**30.02**
SSIM	0.9558	0.9535	**0.9574**

them into a 3 × 3 convolutional layer to obtain the fused feature map. Then, the reconstruction network will finally output a single blended image. Table 2 shows that adding ConvLSTM module can gain boost in performance about 27.79/0.8474 in PSNR/SSIM. Experiments show that directly concatenating all feature maps may produce ghosting and other artifacts. However, ConvLSTM can select useful information from previous frames to improve the novel view quality.

4.4 Limitations

In our experiment, the number of samples in training set is too small. Although our method can refine the novel view quality, the trained model is not strong enough to match all scenes. Because the characteristics of humans in each scene are different, we train a model separately for different dynamic scenes. Besides, we only focus on the human in scenes and do not consider the changes in background information, which will limit the application of our method.

5 Conclusion

In this paper, we propose a new method to obtain a novel view of human motion. To achieve this, we reconstruct a dynamic human geometry to estimate the depth map of different views and the human pose at other times. Utilizing novel synthesis in static scenes, we can obtain several images of a novel view with different sets of source images. Furthermore, a deformable sampling module can align these images. To better leverage information in these images, we use ConvLSTM to aggregate them. Experiments show that our method can refine the novel view synthesis quality by integrating temporal and spatial information and outperform the state-of-the-art method.

Acknowlegements. The authors acknowledge much support by the National Nature Science Foundation of China (No. 61931012), Open Program of National Key Laboratory of Science and Technology on Space Intelligent Control (KGJZDSYS-2018-02), and Postgraduate Research and Practice Innovation Program of Jiangsu Province (KYCX20-0822, SJCX20-0255).

References

1. Agarwal, S., et al.: Building Rome in a day. Commun. ACM **54**(10), 105–112 (2011)
2. Bansal, A., Vo, M., Sheikh, Y., Ramanan, D., Narasimhan, S.: 4D visualization of dynamic events from unconstrained multi-view videos. In: Proceedings of the IEEE/CVF Conference on Computer Vision and Pattern Recognition, pp. 5366–5375 (2020)
3. Chen, L.C., Papandreou, G., Kokkinos, I., Murphy, K., Yuille, A.L.: DeepLab: semantic image segmentation with deep convolutional nets, atrous convolution, and fully connected CRFs. IEEE Trans. Pattern Anal. Mach. Intell. **40**(4), 834–848 (2017)
4. Chen, Q., Koltun, V.: Photographic image synthesis with cascaded refinement networks. In: Proceedings of the IEEE International Conference on Computer Vision, pp. 1511–1520 (2017)
5. Collet, A., et al.: High-quality streamable free-viewpoint video. ACM Trans. Graph. (ToG) **34**(4), 1–13 (2015)
6. Dai, J., et al.: Deformable convolutional networks. In: Proceedings of the IEEE International Conference on Computer Vision, pp. 764–773 (2017)
7. Frahm, J., et al.: Building Rome on a cloudless day. In: Daniilidis, K., Maragos, P., Paragios, N. (eds.) ECCV 2010. LNCS, vol. 6314, pp. 368–381. Springer, Heidelberg (2010). https://doi.org/10.1007/978-3-642-15561-1_27
8. Fu, H., Gong, M., Wang, C., Batmanghelich, K., Tao, D.: Deep ordinal regression network for monocular depth estimation. In: Proceedings of the IEEE Conference on Computer Vision and Pattern Recognition, pp. 2002–2011 (2018)
9. Furukawa, Y., Curless, B., Seitz, S.M., Szeliski, R.: Towards internet-scale multi-view stereo. In: 2010 IEEE Computer Society Conference on Computer Vision and Pattern Recognition, pp. 1434–1441. IEEE (2010)
10. Gong, K., Liang, X., Li, Y., Chen, Y., Yang, M., Lin, L.: Instance-level human parsing via part grouping network. In: Proceedings of the European Conference on Computer Vision (ECCV), pp. 770–785 (2018)
11. Guo, K., et al.: The relightables: volumetric performance capture of humans with realistic relighting. ACM Trans. Graph. (TOG) **38**(6), 1–19 (2019)
12. Hedman, P., Philip, J., Price, T., Frahm, J.M., Drettakis, G., Brostow, G.: Deep blending for free-viewpoint image-based rendering. ACM Trans. Graph. (TOG) **37**(6), 1–15 (2018)
13. Joo, H., Simon, T., Sheikh, Y.: Total capture: a 3D deformation model for tracking faces, hands, and bodies. In: Proceedings of the IEEE Conference on Computer Vision and Pattern Recognition, pp. 8320–8329 (2018)
14. Kingma, D.P., Ba, J.: Adam: a method for stochastic optimization. arXiv preprint arXiv:1412.6980 (2014)
15. Lempitsky, V., Ivanov, D.: Seamless mosaicing of image-based texture maps. In: 2007 IEEE Conference on Computer Vision and Pattern Recognition, pp. 1–6. IEEE (2007)
16. Loper, M., Mahmood, N., Romero, J., Pons-Moll, G., Black, M.J.: SMPL: a skinned multi-person linear model. ACM Trans. Graph. (TOG) **34**(6), 1–16 (2015)
17. Mildenhall, B., et al.: Local light field fusion: practical view synthesis with prescriptive sampling guidelines. ACM Trans. Graph. (TOG) **38**(4), 1–14 (2019)

18. Mildenhall, B., Srinivasan, P.P., Tancik, M., Barron, J.T., Ramamoorthi, R., Ng, R.: NeRF: representing scenes as neural radiance fields for view synthesis. In: Vedaldi, A., Bischof, H., Brox, T., Frahm, J.-M. (eds.) ECCV 2020. LNCS, vol. 12346, pp. 405–421. Springer, Cham (2020). https://doi.org/10.1007/978-3-030-58452-8_24

19. Newcombe, R.A., Fox, D., Seitz, S.M.: DynamicFusion: reconstruction and tracking of non-rigid scenes in real-time. In: Proceedings of the IEEE Conference on Computer Vision and Pattern Recognition, pp. 343–352 (2015)

20. Riegler, G., Koltun, V.: Free view synthesis. In: Vedaldi, A., Bischof, H., Brox, T., Frahm, J.-M. (eds.) ECCV 2020. LNCS, vol. 12364, pp. 623–640. Springer, Cham (2020). https://doi.org/10.1007/978-3-030-58529-7_37

21. Schonberger, J.L., Frahm, J.M.: Structure-from-motion revisited. In: Proceedings of the IEEE Conference on Computer Vision and Pattern Recognition, pp. 4104–4113 (2016)

22. Shi, X., Chen, Z., Wang, H., Yeung, D.Y., Wong, W.K., Woo, W.C.: Convolutional LSTM network: a machine learning approach for precipitation nowcasting. In: Advances in Neural Information Processing Systems, vol. 2015, pp. 802–810 (2015)

23. Simonyan, K., Zisserman, A.: Very deep convolutional networks for large-scale image recognition. arXiv preprint arXiv:1409.1556 (2014)

24. Waechter, M., Moehrle, N., Goesele, M.: Let there be color! Large-scale texturing of 3D reconstructions. In: Fleet, D., Pajdla, T., Schiele, B., Tuytelaars, T. (eds.) ECCV 2014. LNCS, vol. 8693, pp. 836–850. Springer, Cham (2014). https://doi.org/10.1007/978-3-319-10602-1_54

25. Wang, K., Shen, S.: MVDepthNet: real-time multiview depth estimation neural network. In: 2018 International conference on 3D vision (3DV), pp. 248–257. IEEE (2018)

26. Wang, X., Chan, K.C., Yu, K., Dong, C., Change Loy, C.: EDVR: video restoration with enhanced deformable convolutional networks. In: Proceedings of the IEEE/CVF Conference on Computer Vision and Pattern Recognition Workshops, pp. 1954–1963 (2019)

27. Xiang, X., Tian, Y., Zhang, Y., Fu, Y., Allebach, J.P., Xu, C.: Zooming Slow-Mo: fast and accurate one-stage space-time video super-resolution. In: Proceedings of the IEEE/CVF Conference on Computer Vision and Pattern Recognition, pp. 3370–3379 (2020)

28. Yoon, J.S., Kim, K., Gallo, O., Park, H.S., Kautz, J.: Novel view synthesis of dynamic scenes with globally coherent depths from a monocular camera. In: Proceedings of the IEEE/CVF Conference on Computer Vision and Pattern Recognition, pp. 5336–5345 (2020)

29. Yu, T., et al.: BodyFusion: real-time capture of human motion and surface geometry using a single depth camera. In: Proceedings of the IEEE International Conference on Computer Vision, pp. 910–919 (2017)

30. Yu, T., et al.: DoubleFusion: real-time capture of human performances with inner body shapes from a single depth sensor. In: Proceedings of the IEEE Conference on Computer Vision and Pattern Recognition, pp. 7287–7296 (2018)

31. Zhu, X., Hu, H., Lin, S., Dai, J.: Deformable ConvNets v2: more deformable, better results. In: Proceedings of the IEEE/CVF Conference on Computer Vision and Pattern Recognition, pp. 9308–9316 (2019)

Attention Guided Retinex Architecture Search for Robust Low-light Image Enhancement

Xiaoke Shang[1,2(✉)], Jingjie Shang[2], Long Ma[2], Shaomin Zhang[1], and Nai Ding[1,3]

[1] Zhejiang University, Zhejiang 310058, China
sxk-1212@zju.edu.cn
[2] Dalian University of Technology, Dalian 116024, China
[3] Zhejiang Lab, Zhejiang 311121, China

Abstract. In recent years, learning-based low-light image enhancement approaches have shown superior performance, but they mostly heavily depend on proficient engineering skills and need expensive testing costs to acquire a satisfying architecture. To settle these issues, we aim at automatically discovering an efficient architecture towards robust low-light image enhancement. Specifically, by integrating the domain knowledge to depict the task requirements, we establish an attention guided Retinex supernet that contains the Retinex-inspired architecture and attention architecture. Then we construct a distillation-based search space as the basic composition for these three modules. Subsequently, we develop a bilevel optimization-based hierarchical differentiable architecture search scheme to progressively optimize the architecture of each module by explicitly expressing the inherent relationship between these modules. Extensive quantitative and qualitative experiments fully reveal our superiority against other state-of-the-art methods. A series of analytical evaluations are further conducted to indicate the effectiveness of our proposed algorithm.

Keywords: Low-light image enhancement · Attention architecture search · Bilevel optimization · Information distillation

1 Introduction

The demand for high-quality images have became increasingly urgent in many real-world applications, e.g., visual tracking [4], object segmentation [21], and recognition [8]. Unfortunately, there exist many diverse conditions to degrade the image quality. One of the most common degraded scenarios is the low-light, which causes the captured images to suffer from low visibility, low contrast and intensive noise. Therefore, enhancing low-light images has drawn much attention in academia and industry communities. There emerge many algorithms by developing different mechanisms, to satisfy the goal. In the following, we will briefly introduce existing works related to low-light image enhancement. Our main contributions are described in the end.

Supported by the Major Scientific Research Project of Zhejiang Lab 2019KB0AC02.

L. Fang et al. (Eds.): CICAI 2021, LNAI 13069, pp. 444–455, 2021.
https://doi.org/10.1007/978-3-030-93046-2_38

Input   EnGAN (TIP '21)   ZeroDCE (TPAMI '21)   Ours

Fig. 1. Visual results of state-of-the-art methods (including EnGAN [10] and ZeroDCE [14]) and our proposed method on a challenging low-light image from the LOL dataset [3].

1.1   Related Works

According to the algorithmic principle, existing low-light image enhancement can be roughly divided into two categories, model-based [2,5,16] and learning-based methods [20,22,25].

Retinex theory is the core modeling rule in model-based approaches. In the early stage, researchers tend to adopt the simple filter to generate the key component (i.e., illumination) by the domain conversion. By performing the Gaussian filter on the low-light inputs in the log-domain, Jobson *et al.* developed Single-Scale Retinex (SSR) [12] to generate the illumination, then obtained the enhanced results by subtraction operation. Further, Rahman *et al.* constructed Multi-scale Retinex (MSR) [24] by multiply executing the Gaussian filtering to generate multiple illuminations in the log-domain, then derived the final outputs by presenting the weighted sum on the enhanced results based on SSR. Considering the color distortion, Jobson *et al.* designed Multi-scale Retinex with Color Restoration (MSRCR) [11] by introducing an effective weighting function to correct the color.

Designing the model with fidelity and regularization is the mainstream measure in model-based methods. This type of method focus on defining the prior regularizations for different components. In the past few decades, researchers have developed a variety of regularization forms for this task. A simple convex form ℓ_2-norm was early built to constrain the illumination in some works [5,6]. Unfortunately, because of the weak characterization for the edge-preserving property, causing the estimated illumination cannot satisfy the actual demand. Benefiting from the stronger edge-aware ability, ℓ_1-norm and its variants [2,9,16] were further developed to constrain the illumination. Indeed, the performance realized the significant promotion. However, these model-based methods always needed to manually adjust plenty of parameters towards different scenarios. Additionally, their computational procedures were also complex and time-consuming.

On the basis of massive training data, learning-based methods treat architecture design and loss definition as the main goal. In the low-light image enhancement field, there exist less training data for pushing forward the development of learning-based methods. Until recent few years, Wang *et al.* [25] established the DeepUPE by designing an illumination estimation network. This work utilized the MIT-Adobe 5K dataset [1] (a well-known image enhancement dataset) to train DeepUPE, and it also provided a new dataset by using the same generation way with MIT-Adobe 5K dataset. Chen *et al.* created the LOL dataset [3] (a widely-used low-light image enhancement dataset) that was acquired by adjusting the exposure time. They also designed the RetinexNet by performing the Retinex theory in the architecture design. Considering the unnatural performance, Zhang *et al.* designed some training loss functions and tuned up the architecture of RetinexNet to receive the better performance. LightenNet [15] acquired the training pairs by performing the uniform illuminations based on the Retinex theory, then designed a lightweight network architecture to solve low-light image enhancement. But its enhanced effects were limited because of the unreal synthetic data. By used the global-local discriminator [23], EnlightenGAN [10] built a U-Net type generator with the attention mechanism to obtain enhanced results under the unpaired supervision. Similarly, DRBN [26] constructed a semi-supervised learning framework for low-light image enhancement. The work in [28] proposed a decomposition-based network that was able to restore image objects in the low-frequency layer, and enhanced high-frequency details on the restored image.

Undoubtedly, learning-based methods are superior to model-based methods. But actually, learning-based works were mostly heuristically designed, which heavily relies on proficient engineering skills and it needs to throw into a great number of energies to excavate a satisfying architecture.

1.2 Our Contributions

To avoid the expensive testing cost brought by the heuristic design, we aim at automatically discovering a attention guided Retinex architecture for robust low-light image enhancement. As shown in Fig. 1, our discovered architecture can significantly improve the visual quality than other newest heuristically-designed methods. More concretely, we construct an attention guided Retinex supernet that contains the illumination optimization, attention generation, and reflectance optimization modules. Different from existing heuristically-designed works, we further design a distillation-based search space and a bilevel optimization-based hierarchical differentiable architecture search scheme for automatically discovering these three modules. Evaluations on the well-known and challenging LOL dataset and comprehensive analysis are conducted to verify our superiority and effectiveness, respectively. Briefly, our contributions can be summarized as follows:

- We construct an attention guided robust low-light image enhancement framework towards the challenging low-light scenarios with noises/artifacts.
- We establish a joint network architecture with Retinex-inspired architecture and attention architecture and a distillation-based search space towards low-light image enhancement.
- We design a bilevel optimization-based hierarchical differentiable architecture search paradigm to handle the challenges on joint searching of Retinex-inspired and attention architectures.

2 The Proposed Algorithm

We first establish an attention guided Retinex supernet to handle low-light image enhancement proceeding from the task requirements. Then we introduce a

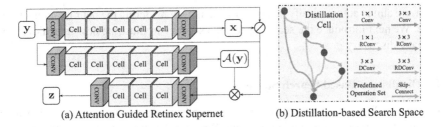

(a) Attention Guided Retinex Supernet   (b) Distillation-based Search Space

Fig. 2. Illustration of the proposed attention guided Retinex supernet and distillation-based search space. Note that our cell acts on the feature with 64 channels. The CONV in the first and last layers of the subfigure (a) represent the feature extraction (from 3 channels to 64 channels) and reconstruction (from 64 channels to 3 channels), respectively. We also define a new distillation-based search space.

distillation-based search space. Finally, we design a hierarchical bilevel optimization scheme for automatically discovering the architecture of our built supernet.

2.1 Attention Guided Retinex Supernet

Retinex theory is the commonly adopted low-light image enhancement model, it describes the inherent relationship between low-light and normal-light images. This model can be formulated as $y = x \otimes z$, where y, x, and z represent the low-light observation, the illumination image, and reflectance image (i.e., normal light image). $\otimes$ is the element-wise multiplication. Generally, the illumination is the research emphasis, and then the reflectance can be directly derived from the estimated illumination according to the Retinex theory. But in some real-world scenarios, the reflectance may be polluted by some unknown noises/artifacts. To this end, we construct the following model

$$\begin{cases} x = \mathcal{M}_x(y), \\ z = \mathcal{M}_z(y \oslash x), \end{cases} \tag{1}$$

where $\mathcal{M}_x$ and $\mathcal{M}_z$ are the optimization module for the illumination and reflectance, respectively. The goal of this model is to optimize these two components separately to ensure accurate estimation. But unfortunately, this intuitive model cannot obtain the ideal performance because the process $y \oslash x$ may bring about some inappropriate exposure. To suppress it, we propose an attention-aware reflectance optimization module by introducing the attention mechanism. The formulation can be written as

$$z = \mathcal{M}_z\big((y \oslash x) \otimes v\big), v = \mathcal{G}(y \oslash x), \tag{2}$$

where $\mathcal{G}$ represents the attention generation module. v is the generated attention map.

Up to now, we have clearly described all details of our proposed attention guided Retinex supernet, the next is to explore how to define these three mappings (i.e., $\mathcal{M}_x$, $\mathcal{M}_z$, and $\mathcal{A}$). The commonly adopted strategy is to heuristically design them based on engineering experiences. To avoid the expensive testing cost by using the heuristic design, we aim at automatically discovering them by considering the neural architecture search. We next introduce the search space and strategy to illustrate how to achieve the automatic discovery process.

2.2 Distillation-Based Search Space

As shown in Fig. 2, these three modules all need to perform feature extraction and reconstruction in the beginning and ending. We consider the same cell for three modules, but the number of cells is different. Inspired by the feature distillation techniques [19], we define a distillation-based search space by introducing a distillation cell (the specific form can be seen in Fig. 2 (b)). It can be observed that each node are related to the final node, this way realizes the information distillation, to further improve utilization.

The candidate operations contain 1×1 and 3×3 Convolution (Conv), 1×1 and 3×3 Residual Convolution (RConv), 3×3 Dilation Convolution with dilation rate of 2 (DConv), 3×3 Residual Dilation Convolution with dilation rate of 2 (RDConv), and Skip Connection. By adopting the continuous relaxation technique used in differentiable NAS literature [17,18,27], we introduce the vectorized form $\alpha = \{\alpha_x, \alpha_z, \alpha_v\}$ to encode architectures in our search space (denoted as $\mathcal{A}$) for these modules. We also present the network parameters for these modules as $\omega = \{\omega_x, \omega_z, \omega_v\}$ which is associated with α. Next, we detail the search strategy under the search space.

Table 1. PSNR and SSIM results among recently-proposed methods and ours on the LOL dataset.

Metrics	DeepUPE	DRBN	FIDE	EnGAN	KinD	ZeroDCE	Ours
	(CVPR '19)	(CVPR '20)	(CVPR '20)	(TIP '21)	(IJCV '21)	(TPAMI '21)	
PSNR	14.7466	18.0319	18.3129	17.3119	14.3810	16.2824	**19.4953**
SSIM	0.4821	**0.7887**	0.6596	0.5649	0.6159	0.5009	0.7541

2.3 Hierarchical Differentiable Architecture Search Strategy

Indeed, we can directly search the built attention guided Retinex supernet under the defined distillation-based search space. Unfortunately, because of the complex coupling effects between different modules, these architectures are actually hard to optimize by a naive search scheme[1]. Here we establish a newly-designed hierarchical bilevel optimization search strategy toward the inherent connection between each module. The optimized model can be described by the following bilevel optimization

$$\min_{\alpha \in \mathcal{A}} \mathcal{L}_{\text{val}}(\alpha; \omega^*),$$
$$\text{s.t. } \omega^* = \arg\min_{\omega} \mathcal{L}_{\text{tr}}(\omega; \alpha), \tag{3}$$

---

[1] In the experimental section, we have presented the results of this naive search scheme.

Fig. 3. Visual comparison on the low-light image from the LOL dataset.

Table 2. Quantitative comparison of ablation study.

Metric	w/o α_v	w/o α_z	Ours
PSNR	11.3199	16.5226	**19.4953**
SSIM	0.3673	0.4635	**0.7541**

where $\alpha = \{\alpha_x, \alpha_z, \alpha_v\}$, $\omega = \{\omega_x, \omega_z, \omega_v\}$, $\mathcal{L}_{val}$ and $\mathcal{L}_{tr}$ are the loss function on the validation and training dataset, respectively. As for the loss definition, we just use the MSE loss for the illumination optimization and attention generation module. For the reflectance optimization module, we also consider the VGG-based perceptual loss [13].

Actually, as for Eq. 3, it is absolutely different from the existing neural architecture search techniques [7,29]. This model contains multiple architectures that need to be optimized, rather than the single one architecture [7,29]. More importantly, for $\alpha = \{\alpha_x, \alpha_z, \alpha_v\}$, these sub-architectures exist the interactive together to bring about the challenging. To settle it, we propose a hierarchical mechanism to gradually optimize these architectures. Specifically, we first present the inherent relationship between these modules, that is, the illumination optimization as the basic composition that decides to the form of other two modules. The attention generation influences the input of the reflectance optimization module. Based on these inherent relationship, we first optimize the architecture of α_x, and train this obtained architecture to generate ω_x. Then we fix this module, to optimize the architecture of α_v, and train this obtained architecture to generate ω_v. Next, we fix these two modules, to optimize the architecture of α_z, and train this obtained architecture to generate ω_z. In this hierarchical bilevel optimization mechanism, we can realize a accurate optimization for these modules.

3   Experimental Results

In this section, we first introduce the implementation details. Then we conduct a series of experiments to verify our actual performance by compared it with many recently-proposed state-of-the-art methods. Finally, we conduct a sequence of algorithmic

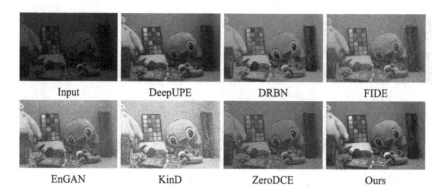

| Input | DeepUPE | DRBN | FIDE |
| EnGAN | KinD | ZeroDCE | Ours |

Fig. 4. Visual comparison on the noisy low-light image from the LOL dataset.

analysis to verify our effectiveness from different perspectives, including ablation study for different modules, the analysis of search strategy and intermediate results.

3.1 Implementation Details

As for training process, we randomly sampled 689 image pairs from LOL dataset for searching and training, and the remaining 100 image pairs were used for testing. SGD optimizer was carried out in the searching phase and Adam optimizer was carried out in the training phase. The maximum number of epoch was set as 200. The learning rate was set to 1e-5 at the beginning, and decreased by a factor of 10 until to 0 after 100 epoch. All experiments were conducted on a single GPU of NVIDIA Tesla V100.

3.2 Comparison with State-of-the-Arts

In this part, we conducted the quantitative performance on the 100 low-light images that were randomly sampled from the LOL dataset [3], by comparing our proposed method with latest state-of-the-art network-based methods including DeepUPE [25], DRBN [28], FIDE [26], EnGAN [10], KinD [30], ZeroDCE [14]. Following the setting in existing works [26,28], the well-known and commonly-used PSNR and SSIM were adopted as evaluated metrics. As illustrated in Table 1, our proposed method obtained a competitive performance against other state-of-the-art methods. This experiment fully indicates that our superiority from the perspective of statistics.

To fully evaluate the qualitative performance, we first performed the visual results on the low-light image (without noises) sampled from the LOL dataset [3]. As demonstrated in Fig. 3, the results of DeepUPE and ZeroDCE cannot come to a satisfying lightness, the results of DRBN and FIDE appeared some unknown artifacts, the results of EnGAN and KinD occurred color distortion with different levels. In contrast, our proposed method performed the best visual quality with the appropriate exposure, clear structures, and vivid colors. Further, we considered a challenging example (with the visible noises) that was sampled from the LOL dataset. As shown in Fig. 4, we can easily observe that the compared methods cannot remove noises well, except DRBN.

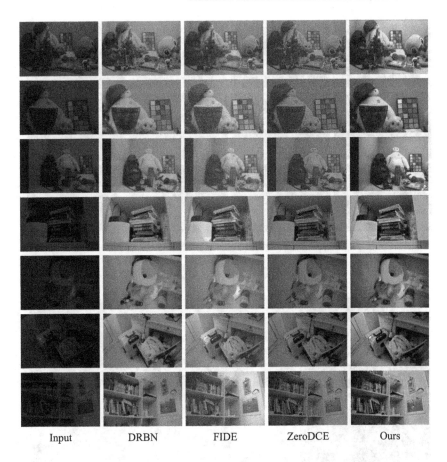

Input   DRBN   FIDE   ZeroDCE   Ours

Fig. 5. Visual results of state-of-the-art methods and ours on the LOL dataset.

But DRBN appeared the blur and artifacts, especially in the rectangular color plate. Compared with them, our proposed algorithm can significantly remove the undesired noises, and retain the important textures and details. More visual results on the LOL dataset were demonstrated in Fig. 5.

3.3 Ablation Study and Analysis

In our designed attention guided Retinex supernet, which contains three main components, i.e., illumination optimization, attention generation and reflectance optimization modules. In which, the illumination optimization is the essential component which cannot be removed. Here we explored the effects of the attention generation and reflectance optimization modules. As shown in Table 2, the attention generation module heavily influenced the performance, which illustrated that the attention generation was indeed important for addressing low-light image enhancement. Further, the reflectance optimization actually removed noises to better improve the visual quality. We also presented

Input   w/o α_v w/o α_z Ours

Fig. 6. Qualitative comparison of ablation study.

Input   Naive Search   Hierarchical Search

Fig. 7. Analyzing the search strategy.

the visual comparison for these cases. As shown in Fig. 6, it can be easily seen that w/o α_v cannot perform an appropriate exposure, w/o α_z appeared some non-ignorable visible noises. In a word, these two modules are essential in our designed framework.

In our designed method, the newly-defined bilevel optimization search strategy is one of the important contribution. Here we analyzed the effects and effectiveness of this strategy by compared it with a simple naive search strategy, i.e., viewing the attention guided Retinex supernet as a whole network, and just searching once. As shown in Fig. 7, we can easily see that the naive search strategy cannot well describe the structural information, causing some unknown artifacts to degrade the visual quality. Our hierarchical bilevel optimization search strategy successfully overcame this issues by fully exploiting the inherent relationship between different modules.

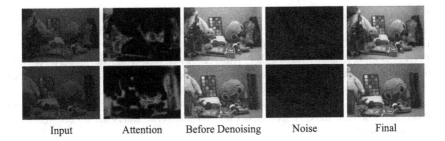

| Input | Attention | Before Denoising | Noise | Final |

Fig. 8. Visual results of the intermediate outputs.

Figure 8 demonstrated the visual results of the intermediate results. We can easily see that the attention map indeed characterized the structural information to strengthen the structural expression. The noise map presented most of the undesired components with less background information to ensure the improvement in visual quality.

4   Conclusion and Future Works

In this work, we first constructed an attention guided Retinex supernet that contains the illumination optimization, attention generation, and reflectance optimization modules to accurately characterize the task demand for robust low-light image enhancement. We then designed a distillation-based search space to improve the information utilization on spatial scales. We also established a hierarchical bilevel optimization search strategy to automatically discover the desired architecture by exploiting the inherent relationship between different modules. Extensive evaluated experiments were conducted to verify our superiority against other state-of-the-art methods. A series of analytical verification were also conducted to illustrate our effectiveness.

In the future, we will apply the attention architecture search mechanism which is newly designed in this work to settle other low-level vision applications, e.g., image deraining, dehazing, and so on. Additionally, we also will introduce the hardware constraints (e.g., latency) in the architecture search procedure, to establish a more practical low-light image enhancement algorithm.

References

1. Bychkovsky, V., Paris, S., Chan, E., Durand, F.: Learning photographic global tonal adjustment with a database of input/output image pairs. In: Proceedings of the IEEE/CVF Conference on Computer Vision and Pattern Recognition, pp. 97–104 (2011)
2. Cai, B., Xu, X., Guo, K., Jia, K., Hu, B., Tao, D.: A joint intrinsic-extrinsic prior model for retinex. In: International Conference on Computer Vision, pp. 4000–4009 (2017)
3. Chen, W., Wang, W., Yang, W., Liu, J.: Deep retinex decomposition for low-light enhancement. In: British Machine Vision Conference, pp. 1–12 (2018)
4. Danelljan, M., Gool, L.V., Timofte, R.: Probabilistic regression for visual tracking. In: Proceedings of the IEEE/CVF Conference on Computer Vision and Pattern Recognition, pp. 7183–7192 (2020)

5. Fu, X., Liao, Y., Zeng, D., Huang, Y., Zhang, X.P., Ding, X.: A probabilistic method for image enhancement with simultaneous illumination and reflectance estimation. IEEE Trans. Image Process. **24**(12), 4965–4977 (2015)
6. Fu, X., Zeng, D., Huang, Y., Zhang, X.P., Ding, X.: A weighted variational model for simultaneous reflectance and illumination estimation. In: Proceedings of the IEEE/CVF Conference on Computer Vision and Pattern Recognition, pp. 2782–2790 (2016)
7. Guo, J., et al.: Hit-detector: Hierarchical trinity architecture search for object detection. In: Proceedings of the IEEE/CVF Conference on Computer Vision and Pattern Recognition, pp. 11405–11414 (2020)
8. Guo, J., Zhu, X., Zhao, C., Cao, D., Lei, Z., Li, S.Z.: Learning meta face recognition in unseen domains. In: Proceedings of the IEEE/CVF Conference on Computer Vision and Pattern Recognition, pp. 6163–6172 (2020)
9. Guo, X., Li, Y., Ling, H.: Lime: low-light image enhancement via illumination map estimation. IEEE Trans. Image Process. **26**(2), 982–993 (2017)
10. Jiang, Y., Gong, X., Liu, D., et al.: EnlightenGAN: deep light enhancement without paired supervision. arXiv preprint arXiv:1906.06972 (2019)
11. Jobson, D.J., Rahman, Z.U., Woodell, G.A.: A multiscale retinex for bridging the gap between color images and the human observation of scenes. IEEE Trans. Image Process. **6**(7), 965–976 (1997)
12. Jobson, D.J., Rahman, Z.U., Woodell, G.A.: Properties and performance of a center/surround retinex. IEEE Trans. Image Process. **6**(3), 451–462 (1997)
13. Johnson, J., Alahi, A., Fei-Fei, L.: Perceptual losses for real-time style transfer and super-resolution. In: ECCV, pp. 694–711 (2016)
14. Li, C., Guo, C., Chen, C.L.: Learning to enhance low-light image via zero-reference deep curve estimation. IEEE Trans. Pattern Anal. Mach. Intell. **01**, 1–1 (2021)
15. Li, C., Guo, J., Porikli, F., Pang, Y.: Lightennet: a convolutional neural network for weakly illuminated image enhancement. Pattern Recogn. Lett. **104**, 15–22 (2018)
16. Li, M., Liu, J., Yang, W., Sun, X., Guo, Z.: Structure-revealing low-light image enhancement via robust retinex model. IEEE Trans. Image Process. **27**(6), 2828–2841 (2018)
17. Liang, H., et al.: Darts+: improved differentiable architecture search with early stopping. arXiv preprint arXiv:1909.06035 (2019)
18. Liu, H., Simonyan, K., Yang, Y.: Darts: Differentiable architecture search. In: International Conference on Learning Representations (2018)
19. Liu, J., Tang, J., Wu, G.: Residual feature distillation network for lightweight image super-resolution. arXiv preprint arXiv:2009.11551 (2020)
20. Liu, R., Ma, L., Zhang, Y., Fan, X., Luo, Z.: Underexposed image correction via hybrid priors navigated deep propagation. IEEE Trans. Neural Netw. Learn. Syst. (2021)
21. Lu, X., Wang, W., Shen, J., Tai, Y.W., Crandall, D.J., Hoi, S.C.: Learning video object segmentation from unlabeled videos. In: Proceedings of the IEEE/CVF Conference on Computer Vision and Pattern Recognition, pp. 8960–8970 (2020)
22. Ma, L., Liu, R., Zhang, J., Fan, X., Luo, Z.: Learning deep context-sensitive decomposition for low-light image enhancement. IEEE Trans. Neural Netw. Learn. Syst. (2021)
23. Mao, X., Li, Q., Xie, H., et al.: Least squares generative adversarial networks. In: International Conference on Computer Vision, pp. 2794–2802 (2017)
24. Rahman, Z.U., Jobson, D.J., Woodell, G.A.: Multi-scale retinex for color image enhancement. In: International Conference on Image Processing, pp. 1003–1006 (1996)
25. Wang, R., Zhang, Q., Fu, C.W., Shen, X., Zheng, W.S., Jia, J.: Underexposed photo enhancement using deep illumination estimation. In: Proceedings of the IEEE/CVF Conference on Computer Vision and Pattern Recognition, pp. 6849–6857 (2019)

26. Xu, K., Yang, X., Yin, B., Lau, R.W.: Learning to restore low-light images via decomposition-and-enhancement. In: Proceedings of the IEEE/CVF Conference on Computer Vision and Pattern Recognition, pp. 2281–2290 (2020)
27. Xu, Y., Xie, L., Zhang, X., Chen, X., Qi, G.J., Tian, Q., Xiong, H.: PC-darts: partial channel connections for memory-efficient differentiable architecture search. In: International Conference on Learning Representations (2020)
28. Yang, W., Wang, S., Fang, Y., Wang, Y., Liu, J.: From fidelity to perceptual quality: a semi-supervised approach for low-light image enhancement. In: Proceedings of the IEEE/CVF Conference on Computer Vision and Pattern Recognition, pp. 3063–3072 (2020)
29. Zhang, H., Li, Y., Chen, H., Shen, C.: Memory-efficient hierarchical neural architecture search for image denoising. In: Proceedings of the IEEE/CVF Conference on Computer Vision and Pattern Recognition, pp. 3657–3666 (2020)
30. Zhang, Y., Zhang, J., Guo, X.: Kindling the darkness: a practical low-light image enhancer. In: ACM MM, pp. 1632–1640 (2019)

Dual Attention Feature Fusion Network for Monocular Depth Estimation

Yifang Xu[1,2], Ming Li[1,2], Chenglei Peng[1,2(✉)], Yang Li[1,2], and Sidan Du[1,2(✉)]

[1] Nanjing University, Nanjing, China
{pcl,coff128}@nju.edu.cn
[2] Nanjing Institute of Advanced Artificial Intelligence, Nanjing, China

Abstract. Monocular depth estimation is a traditional computer vision task, which plays a crucial role in 3D reconstruction and scene understanding. Recent works based on deep convolutional neural networks (DCNNs) have achieved great success. However, these works did not make full use of structural information, resulting in discontinuity of depth and ambiguity of boundaries. This paper proposes Dual Attention Feature Fusion Network (DAFFNet), which utilizes the structural relationship between the RGB image and the predicted depth to solve the above problems. It contains two critical modules, Dual Attention Fusion Module (DAFM) and Iterative Dual Attention Fusion Module (IDAFM). Specifically, DAFM includes two blocks (spatial attention block and channel attention block), which fuse global context and local information respectively. To aggregate information of different encoder and decoder levels, we design IDAFM, an iterative version of DAFM. Extensive experimental results on the KITTI dataset show that our model achieves the competitive performance with recent state-of-the-art models.

Keywords: Depth estimation · Attention mechanism · Feature fusion · Deep learning

1 Introduction

Estimating depth from 2D images is one of the most basic computer vision task, and has many applications such as 3D reconstruction, scene understanding, autonomous driving and intelligent robots [1]. For better depth estimation, those applications usually use stereo images pairs [2], multiple frames from video sequences [3] or multi-view images [4]. Although the above methods have achieved impressive progress, these methods require additional cost (e.g. camera motion and depth sensor technologies), so it is natural to develop monocular depth estimation (MDE) which demands less cost and constraint [5]. However, MDE is a challenging task, because it is a technically ill-posed problem as a single image can be projected from an infinite number of different 3D scenes [6]. To solve this inherent ambiguity, people considered using prior auxiliary information such as texture information, occlusion, object sizes, object locations, perspective, and defocus [1, 7].

© Springer Nature Switzerland AG 2021
L. Fang et al. (Eds.): CICAI 2021, LNAI 13069, pp. 456–468, 2021.
https://doi.org/10.1007/978-3-030-93046-2_39

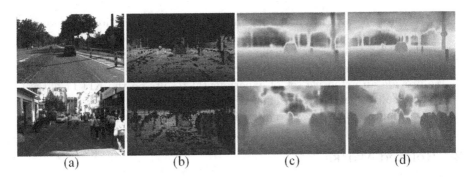

Fig. 1. Example of monocular depth estimation on KITTI dataset [8]. (a) Input RGB image; (b) Ground truth depth; (c) Fu et al. [7]; (d) Ours.

More recently, some works on MDE have shown significant improvements in performance by using deep convolutional neural networks (DCNNs) based on encoder-decoder architecture [9–11]. To increase the receptive field and generate high-dimension global information, DCNNs in encoder phase contains multiple convolutional layers and downsampling layers. However, the downsampling layers reduce the size of feature maps, which lead to ambiguous object edges, discontinuous depth in predicted depth map. To address the above problems, state-of-the-art (SOTA) MDE models use pre-trained convolutional backbones such as ResNet [12], DenseNet [13] and ResNext [14] with upsampling, skip-connection [15], depth-to-space [16], attention module [17], ordinal regression [7] and local planar assumption for upsampling operation [5]. Besides the improvements on models, some works introduce multiple loss functions leading models to better structural information [18].

Compared to exiting MDE models, in this paper, we propose a novel attention network, named Dual Attention Feature Fusion Network (DAFFNet, see Fig. 2). It is based on encoder-decoder architecture and contains multiple attention module, which exploits structural information in RGB images. Inspired by the attention mechanism [17,19], we propose a new attention module, named Dual Attention Feature Module (DAFM, see Fig. 3), which improves the structural information of high dimension. To generate dual attention feature, we sequentially utilize this module at different levels in the encoding stage. We also design an iterative version of DAFM (IDAFM, see Fig. 4) to exploit the mixed cross-channel information in the decoding phase. While existing research has been improved consistency between RGB image input and predicted depth, they usually work poorly on the boundaries of different objects, which leads to lots of quantitative details error. We demonstrate that using loss function to optimize depth gradient can effectively address this issue [15,18].

In conclusion, our contributions are as follows:

- We design a novel encoder-decoder network (DAFFNet) that applies the concept of attention feature fusion mechanism.

- We propose a new attention module (DAFM) and its iterative version (IDAFM) which effectively integrates local information and global context. Besides, we combine scale-invariant gradient loss in loss function, which lead to model to capture structural information in object boundaries.
- We provide an extensive set of experimental results on the KITTI dataset. These results show the high efficiency and performance of our model. Our model achieves competitive results with recent SOTA models.

2   Related Works

2.1   Supervised Monocular Depth Estimations

In MDE, supervised learning uses a single RGB as input, and utilizes depth data measured by depth sensing technologies (such as ToF, LiDAR, RADAR) as ground truth for supervision. Early MDE works mainly leverage hand-crafted features. Saxena et al. [1] design a supervised model to learn depth from visual cues. This model is based on discriminatively-trained Markov Random Field (MRF) that fuses multiscale local and global information. Saxena et al. [20] also develop the model based on MRF to plane parameter algorithm that captures 3D location and 3D orientation at homogeneous patch in a single image. Eigen et al. [6] propose a deep learning network that cascade coarse global prediction module and refined local prediction module. Unlike previous works, their work use scale-invariant error as loss function to help measure depth relations rather than scale. Since then, given the success of deep convolutional neural networks (DCNNs) in MDE, increasingly depth estimation networks have been proposed [15,21–23]. Laina et al. [21] introduce a fully convolutional architecture with residual up-convolutional layers to reduce number of parameters for training samples required. Some works [24,25] are based on Conditional Random Fields (CRFs) and use multi-scale feature fusion to improve the reconstruction accuracy and positioning of occlusion boundaries. To address the increasing error in depth magnitude, Fu et al. [7] propose spacing-increasing discretization (SID) strategy to model MDE as an ordinal regression problem. The latest SOTA model is designed by Lee et al. [5] based on local planar guidance assumption to replace upsampling layers, which use 4D plane coefficients to define explicit relations internal features and the final output.

2.2   Unsupervised/Self-supervised Monocular Depth Estimation

In addition to supervised learning, some methods try to utilize unsupervised learning for MDE, since unsupervised learning does not require additional supervised signals (such as depth, self-motion, optical flow ground truth), it needs more geometric constraints derived from 3D scene and 2D image. Garg et al. [26] proposed to learn the right view generated from the given left view by supervision of stereo image pairs, and apply Taylor expansion to approximate the gradient of depth. Mahjourian et al. [27] introduce 3D point cloud method to infer depth and ego-motion from monocular videos, and this method is suitable

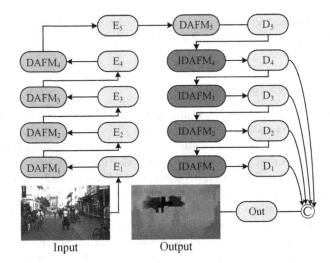

Input   Output

Fig. 2. Overview of our network architecture. The network consists of E_i/D_i (the i-th encoder/decoder), DAFM$_i$ (the i-level dual attention feature module), IDAFM$_i$ (the i-level iterative dual attention feature module). IDAFM is iterative version of DAFM, which couples the high-level feature from D_i with the low-level feature from E_i. ⓒ is the concatenate operation for upsampling feature from decoder.

for low-quality uncalibrated video datasets. Yang et al. [28] builds the inherent relationship between depth and normal based on the 3D as-smooth-as-possible prior. By jointly learning depth, normal, and edge, their network can effectively reduce the discontinuity of depth value and the deterioration of the normal vector. Zheng et al. [29] use synthetic image depth pairs and unpaired real images as input, and concatenate Generative Adversarial Network (GAN) and depth prediction network to enhance the realism of the input images.

2.3 Attention Mechanism

Attention mechanism is derived from human visual perception, since the human visual system cannot process the entire scene simultaneously, but it can selectively focus on the prominent parts to capture useful information. Similarly, attention mechanism is also suitable for various computer vision tasks with different scale features, such as image classification, saliency detection, face recognition and monocular depth estimation [30]. Hu et al. [31] propose to extract local information by fusing channel-wise feature of different levels together in local receptive fields. Woo et al. [19] introduce spatial attention module based on channel attention module, and concatenates two modules for adaptive feature refinement.

3   Our Method

In this section, we describe the proposed monocular estimation network with a novel dual attention feature module and iterative dual attention feature module located on multiple stages in the decoding phase. And finally we detail how the network output can be improved by the scale-invariant loss and the scale-invariant gradient loss.

3.1 Network Architecture

We illustrate our network architecture in Fig. 2. The network is based on an encoder-decoder architecture. And we utilize different models pre-trained on ImageNet [32] as backbone, such as ResNet [12], DenseNet [13] and ResNext [14], and add skip connection from encoder to decoder for multi-level attention feature fusion. A light-weight attention- based DAFM sequentially follows encoder in every encoding stage to combine spatial attention with channel attention features. Then, at each stage in decoding phase, high-level features from decoder and low-level features from encoder are fused in IDAFM to make the network focus on both global information and the detailed spatial cues. From a structural point of view, channel attention pays more attention to global semantic information, while spatial attention more emphasizes local texture details. Decoders are stack of upsampling layer and multiple convolutional layers. The output features of the four-stage of decoder are upsampled by a factor of 2, 4, 8, 16 times respectively by the pixel-shuffling operation [33], and then concatenate to feed into the final convolutional layer to get the depth estimation.

3.2 Dual Attention Feature Module

One key idea in this work is to lead the network to focus on global context without losing local information, which to exploit structural information (i.e., depth cues and semantic information) from different levels. Unlike the previous attention mechanism model, we propose DAFM (see Fig. 3), which contains two attention mechanisms, used to capture the semantic features of space and channel respectively. To reduce computational cost, we choose point-wise convolution as convolutional layer, which only utilizes point-wise channel interactions for each spatial position. Suppose input $x \in \mathbb{R}^{C \times W \times H}$, where C, W, H is the channel, width, height of input feature map respectively.

In spatial attention block, input feature reduced to $C/r \times H \times W$ by 1×1 convolution layer, and finally output spatial attention map $S_A(x) \in \mathbb{R}^{1 \times W \times H}$ via another 1×1 convolution layer. This way can effectively compress spatial information.

$$S_A(x) = c_2(\delta[c_1(x)]) \tag{1}$$

where δ denotes ReLU function. c_1 and c_2 refers to convolution layer.

In channel attention block, local information leads to poor global semantic understanding. Thus, channel attention block is proposed to model depth cues between channels and get global context. And this is based on global average pooling (GAP), which aggregates structural information into an attentive vector. Input feature via GAP and two 1×1 convolution layers to output $C_A(x) \in \mathbb{R}^{C \times 1 \times 1}$.

$$C_A(x) = c_2(\delta[c_1(g(x))]) \tag{2}$$

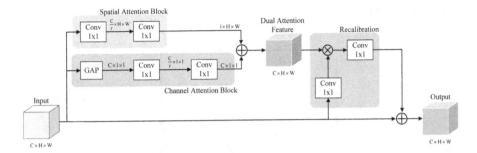

Fig. 3. The architecture of Dual Attention Feature Module (DAFM). The shape of the feature maps are shown in their tensors, e.g., $C \times W \times H$. GAP is abbreviation of global average pooling. $\oplus$ denotes element-wise addition and $\otimes$ denotes element-wise product.

where g denotes global average pooling.

Spatial attention map and channel attention vector are merged into a dual attention feature $D_A(x) \in \mathbb{R}^{C \times W \times H}$ in the following way:

$$D_A(k, w, h) = S_A(1, w, h) \times C_A(k, 1, 1) \tag{3}$$

where $k \in 1, 2...C, w \in 1, 2...W, h \in 1, 2...H$.

To further extract structural information from high-dimensional feature, we recalibrate dual attention feature, which is shown in (4) And final output of DAFM is shown in (5).

$$\widetilde{D_A} = D_A \otimes c(\delta[x]) \tag{4}$$

$$O_A = c(\delta[\widetilde{D_A}]) \oplus x \tag{5}$$

where $\otimes$ denotes element-wise product and $\oplus$ denotes element-wise sum. c refers to convolution layer.

3.3 Iterative Dual Attention Feature Module

Given two feature maps $x, y \in \mathbb{R}^{C \times W \times H}$, we assume x is feature map from decoder with a larger receptive field, y is feature map from encoder with low-level semantic information.

Based on dual attention feature module D, output of iterative dual attention feature module can be expressed as:

$$z = D(x + y) \otimes x + (1 - D(x + y)) \otimes y \tag{6}$$

where $z \in \mathbb{R}^{C \times W \times H}$ is output of IDAFM. Output z can also be regarded as addition of the adaptive weights of x and y after via DAFM. As can be seen from Fig. 4, the architecture of IDAFM adaptive balance between high-level features and low-level features, which aggregate global context and local information.

High-level feature

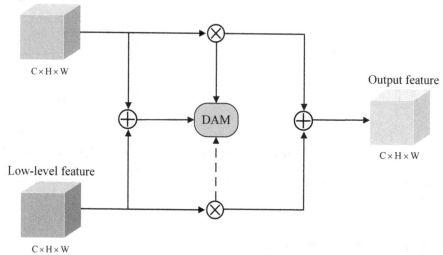

Fig. 4. The architecture of Iterative Dual Attention Feature Module (IDAFM). The shape of the feature maps are shown in their tensors such as $C \times W \times H$. $\oplus$ denotes element-wise addition and $\otimes$ denotes element-wise product.

3.4   Training Loss

The loss function to constraint our network includes two terms, i.e., scale-invariant loss L_d (in log space) and scale-invariant gradient loss L_g. We describe in detail each loss item as follows.

Scale-Invariant Loss. Eigen et al. propose scale invariant loss in [6], as shown in (7).

$$L_d(e) = \frac{1}{T} \sum_i e_i^2 - \frac{\lambda}{T^2} (\sum_i e_i)^2 \tag{7}$$

where $e_i = log(\tilde{d}_i) - log(d_i)$. d_i and $\tilde{d}_i$ denote the ground truth depth and output depth in a pixel. $\lambda = 0.5$, and T refers to the number of pixels having valid ground truth depth value. Inspired by [5], we rewrite (7),

$$L_d(e) = \frac{1}{T} \sum_i e_i^2 - \frac{1}{T^2} (\sum_i e_i)^2 + \frac{(1 - \lambda)}{T^2} (\sum_i e_i)^2 \tag{8}$$

and we can think of (8) as the sum of the variance and weighted mean square error. Setting $\lambda = 0$, equation (8) is L2-norm, and setting $\lambda = 1$ is scale invariant error. Thus, to focus on minimizing the variance of error and keep nonlinear in error, we set $\lambda = 0.8$ in this work.

Fig. 5. Visualization of the different methods and our proposed method on KITTI dataset. (a) Input RGB image; (b) Fu et al. [7]; (c) Lee et al. [5]; (d) Ours. The results of our method show clearer object boundaries and more continuous depth values in homogenous fields.

Scale-Invariant Gradient Loss. Ummenhofer et al. [18] define scale-invariant gradient loss L_g based on gradient loss, as shown in (9). The loss function enhance sharpness at inhomogeneous object boundaries and emphasizes smoothness in homogeneous fields. In this loss function, we utilize 4 different spacings $s \in \{1, 2, 4, 8\}$ to cover all gradients at different scales.

$$L_g(g) = \frac{1}{T} \sum_{s \in \{1,2,4,8\}} \sum_{i,j} \|\tilde{g}_s(i,j) - g_s(i,j)\|_2 \tag{9}$$

$$g_s(i,j) = \left(\frac{d_{i+s,j} - d_{i,j}}{|d_{i+s,j} + d_{i,j}|}, \frac{d_{i,j+s} - d_{i,j}}{|d_{i,j+s} + d_{i,j}|}\right)^T \tag{10}$$

where g_s is gradient of pixel (i, j) in ground truth and $\widetilde{g_s}$ is gradient in predicted depth map at different spacings.

Total Loss. Our total loss function L_t is defined as follows:

$$L_t = \alpha L_d + \beta L_g \tag{11}$$

where α and β are both constants, and we set to 5 and 2 in this work.

4   Experiments

4.1   KITTI Dataset

The KITTI [8] dataset is an outdoor dataset, which contains 61 scenes images with 375×1241 resolution captured by depth cameras. All scenes are composed of 6 categories (city, residential, road, campus, person, and calibration). Since previous models mostly are based on the training and testing set split by Eigen et al. [6], we also use the same split dataset in this work. The training set includes 23488 images from 36 different scenes, and testing set contains 697 images from 25 different scenes. For some other details, we set the maximum depth of images to 80 and 50 in the KITTI dataset. We randomly crop image size to 352×704 to feed into our network. To avoid over-fitting, before input image to the network, we augment images with 50 probability using random horizontal flip, random contrast and random brightness adjustment.

Table 1. Quantitative results on KITTI using Eigen split.

Method	Depth	Accuracy metric (higher is better)			Error metric (lower is better)			
		$\delta < 1.25^1$	$\delta < 1.25^2$	$\delta < 1.25^3$	Abs Rel	Sq Rel	RMSE	RMSE(log)
Saxena et al. [20]	0–80 m	0.601	0.820	0.926	0.280	3.012	8.734	0.361
Eigen et al. [6]	0–80 m	0.702	0.898	0.967	0.203	1.548	6.307	0.282
Godard et al. [2]	0–80 m	0.879	0.961	0.982	0.115	0.882	4.701	0.190
Alhashim et al. [15]	0–80 m	0.886	0.965	0.986	0.093	0.589	4.170	0.171
Fu et al. [7]	0–80 m	0.936	0.985	0.995	0.071	0.268	2.271	0.116
Lee et al. [5]	0–80 m	**0.956**	0.993	0.998	**0.059**	**0.245**	2.756	**0.096**
Ours-ResNext	0–80 m	**0.956**	**0.994**	**0.999**	0.062	0.249	**2.735**	0.098
Godard et al. [2]	0–50 m	0.873	0.954	0.979	0.108	0.657	3.729	0.194
Fu et al. [7]	0–50 m	0.936	0.985	0.995	0.071	0.268	2.271	0.116
Lee et al. [5]	0–50 m	**0.964**	**0.994**	**0.999**	0.056	0.169	**1.925**	**0.087**
Ours-ResNext	0–50 m	0.963	**0.994**	**0.999**	**0.054**	**0.154**	1.962	0.089

4.2 Implementation Details

Specifically, we implement our network in the open source deep learning framework PyTorch. In training phase, we use Adam optimizer [34] with $\beta_1 = 0.9$, $\beta_2 = 0.99$ and $\epsilon = 10^{-6}$. The training strategy uses polynomial decay with initial learning rate and power. We train the proposed network on two NVIDIA 2080Ti GPU with 24 GB memory. Epoch is set to 50 with batch size 16, which apply to all experiments in this work. In encoding phase, we utilize ResNet [12], ResNext [14] and DenseNet [13] pretrained in the ILSVRC dataset as backbone. Upconvolutional layers in decoder use the bilinear neighbor upsampling operation followed by convolutional layers.

4.3 Evaluation Result

The quantitative results of our method with other previous related methods are shown in Table 1. In some evaluation metrics, Our Resnext-based model already outperforms the SOTA model proposed in [5] which use ResNext101 as their backbone network. Since the proposed method achieves improvements in accuracy metrics (i.e., $\delta < t$), which means more correct pixels appear in the depth map. As it can be seen from Fig. 5, the results of our method show clearer object boundaries and more continuous depth values in homogenous fields. However,

Table 2. Experimental results using KITTI's Eigen split with various backbone networks. The best results are bold. In this experiment, we set the depth range to 0–80 m.

Method	#Params	Accuracy metric (higher is better)			Error metric (lower is better)			
		$\delta < 1.25$	$\delta < 1.25^2$	$\delta < 1.25^3$	Abs Rel	Sq Rel	RMSE	RMSE(log)
DenseNet-121 [13]	13.3M	0.948	0.992	0.998	0.067	0.272	2.854	0.103
DenseNet-161 [13]	39.5M	0.954	**0.994**	**0.999**	**0.061**	0.258	2.807	0.099
ResNet-50 [12]	39.8M	0.947	0.992	0.998	0.066	0.268	2.868	0.104
ResNet-101 [12]	58.8M	0.951	0.992	0.998	0.065	0.261	2.783	0.100
ResNext-50 [14]	39.3M	0.953	0.993	**0.999**	0.065	0.260	2.818	0.102
ResNext-101 [14]	103.0M	**0.956**	**0.994**	**0.999**	0.062	**0.249**	**2.735**	**0.098**

Table 3. Result from the ablation study using KITTI dataset. Baseline: a network composed of only encoder and decoder; D: using dual attention feature module after every encoder at different levels; I: using iterative dual attention feature module in every decoder at different levels; L: the network introduce scale-invariant gradient loss. The loss function of all methods without scale-invariant gradient loss apply to scale-invariant loss. All methods use ResNext-101 as encoder. In this experiment, we set the depth range to 0–80 m.

Method	#Params	Accuracy metric (higher is better)			Error metric (lower is better)			
		$\delta < 1.25$	$\delta < 1.25^2$	$\delta < 1.25^3$	Abs Rel	Sq Rel	RMSE	RMSE(log)
Baseline	62.8M	0.928	0.981	0.992	0.086	0.338	3.437	0.158
Baseline+D	78.5M	0.942	0.989	0.996	0.070	0.298	3.015	0.112
Baseline+I	87.3M	0.946	0.990	0.997	0.068	0.253	2.841	0.106
Baseline+D+I	103.0M	0.952	0.992	0.998	0.065	0.252	2.753	**0.097**
Baseline+D+I+L	103.0M	**0.956**	**0.994**	**0.999**	**0.062**	**0.249**	**2.735**	0.098

in experimental results from Fig. 5, we can see the artifacts in the upper part of the images. We consider this is due to the ground truth of the KITTI dataset is sparse depth data. Our model does not train well on the pixels missing the ground truth. Since DAFFNet adopts existing network (i.e., ResNext [14]) as an encoder, it is wondered to see the performance of DAFFNet using different backbones. So we change encoder and save all the settings, the results are shown in Table 2. Various experimental results show that our model can be widely applied to different backbone networks. And our Resnext-based model achieves the best result.

4.4   Ablation Study

To demonstrate the importance of different modules in our model, we perform ablation experiments. From the baseline network, which only consists of backbone network (i.e., ResNext-101) and decoder (i.e., upconvolutional layers and convolutional layers), we increase the network with the core modules to see how the added factor improves the evaluation metrics. It can be seen from Table 3 the proposed models contains all modules (i.e., DAFM, IDAFM, scale-invariant gradient loss) to achieve the best performance. It proves that our model makes full use of structural information. All modules are necessary to get the best monocular depth estimation result.

5 Conclusion

In this paper, we propose a novel monocular depth estimation network named Dual Attention Feature Fusion Network to address ambiguous object boundaries and discontinuous depth value issues. It contains two critical modules, the Dual Attention Feature module and the Iterative Attention Feature module. Ablation study shows that the modules exploit structural information from different levels and improve evaluation metrics. Extensive experimental results on the KITTI dataset show that our model achieves the competitive performance with recent state-of-the-art models.

References

1. Saxena, A., Chung, S.H., Ng, A.: Learning depth from single monocular images. In: NIPS (2005)
2. Godard, C., Aodha, O.M., Brostow, G.J.: Unsupervised monocular depth estimation with left-right consistency. In: CVPR, pp. 6602–6611. IEEE Computer Society (2017)
3. Ranftl, R., Vineet, V., Chen, Q., Koltun, V.: Dense monocular depth estimation in complex dynamic scenes. In: CVPR, pp. 4058–4066. IEEE Computer Society (2016). https://doi.org/10.1109/CVPR.2016.440
4. Yang, J., Mao, W., Alvarez, J.M., Liu, M.: Cost volume pyramid based depth inference for multi-view stereo. In: CVPR, pp. 4876–4885. IEEE (2020). https://doi.org/10.1109/CVPR42600.2020.00493
5. Lee, J.H., Han, M., Ko, D.W., Suh, I.H.: From big to small: multi-scale local planar guidance for monocular depth estimation. CoRR abs/1907.10326 (2019)
6. Eigen, D., Puhrsch, C., Fergus, R.: Depth map prediction from a single image using a multi-scale deep network. In: NIPS, pp. 2366–2374 (2014)
7. Fu, H., Gong, M., Wang, C., Batmanghelich, K., Tao, D.: Deep ordinal regression network for monocular depth estimation. In: CVPR, pp. 2002–2011. IEEE Computer Society (2018)
8. Geiger, A., Lenz, P., Stiller, C., Urtasun, R.: Vision meets robotics: the Kitti dataset. Int. J. Robot. Res. **32**, 1231–1237 (2013)
9. Fácil, J.M., Ummenhofer, B., Zhou, H., Montesano, L., Brox, T., Civera, J.: CAM-Convs: camera-aware multi-scale convolutions for single-view depth. In: CVPR, pp. 11826–11835. Computer Vision Foundation. IEEE (2019)
10. Lee, J., Kim, C.: Monocular depth estimation using relative depth maps. In: CVPR, pp. 9729–9738. Computer Vision Foundation/IEEE (2019)
11. Zhou, T., Brown, M., Snavely, N., Lowe, D.: Unsupervised learning of depth and ego-motion from video. In: CVPR, pp. 6612–6619 (2017)
12. He, K., Zhang, X., Ren, S., Sun, J.: Deep residual learning for image recognition. In: CVPR, pp. 770–778. IEEE Computer Society (2016)
13. Huang, G., Liu, Z., Weinberger, K.Q.: Densely connected convolutional networks. In: CVPR, pp. 2261–2269 (2017)

14. Xie, S., Girshick, R.B., Dollár, P., Tu, Z., He, K.: Aggregated residual transformations for deep neural networks. In: CVPR, pp. 5987–5995. IEEE Computer Society (2017)
15. Alhashim, I., Wonka, P.: High quality monocular depth estimation via transfer learning. CoRR abs/1812.11941 (2018)
16. Aich, S., Vianney, J.M.U., Islam, M.A., Kaur, M., Liu, B.: Bidirectional attention network for monocular depth estimation. CoRR abs/2009.00743 (2020)
17. Chen, T., et al.: Improving monocular depth estimation by leveraging structural awareness and complementary datasets (2020)
18. Ummenhofer, B., et al.: Demon: depth and motion network for learning monocular stereo. In: CVPR, pp. 5622–5631. IEEE Computer Society (2017)
19. Woo, S., Park, J., Lee, J.-Y., Kweon, I.S.: CBAM: convolutional block attention module. In: Ferrari, V., Hebert, M., Sminchisescu, C., Weiss, Y. (eds.) ECCV 2018. LNCS, vol. 11211, pp. 3–19. Springer, Cham (2018). https://doi.org/10.1007/978-3-030-01234-2_1
20. Saxena, A., Sun, M., Ng, A.Y.: Make3D: learning 3D scene structure from a single still image. IEEE Trans. Pattern Anal. Mach. Intell. **31**(5), 824–840 (2009). https://doi.org/10.1109/TPAMI.2008.132
21. Laina, I., Rupprecht, C., Belagiannis, V., Tombari, F., Navab, N.: Deeper depth prediction with fully convolutional residual networks. In: 3DV, pp. 239–248. IEEE Computer Society (2016)
22. Li, R., Xian, K., Shen, C., Cao, Z., Lu, H., Hang, L.: Deep attention-based classification network for robust depth prediction. In: Jawahar, C.V., Li, H., Mori, G., Schindler, K. (eds.) ACCV 2018. LNCS, vol. 11364, pp. 663–678. Springer, Cham (2019). https://doi.org/10.1007/978-3-030-20870-7_41
23. Eigen, D., Fergus, R.: Predicting depth, surface normals and semantic labels with a common multi-scale convolutional architecture. In: ICCV, pp. 2650–2658. IEEE Computer Society (2015)
24. Ramamonjisoa, M., Du, Y., Lepetit, V.: Predicting sharp and accurate occlusion boundaries in monocular depth estimation using displacement fields. In: CVPR, pp. 14636–14645. IEEE (2020)
25. Xu, D., Ricci, E., Ouyang, W., Wang, X., Sebe, N.: Multi-scale continuous CRFS as sequential deep networks for monocular depth estimation. In: CVPR, pp. 161–169. IEEE Computer Society (2017)
26. Garg, R., B.G., V.K., Carneiro, G., Reid, I.: Unsupervised CNN for single view depth estimation: geometry to the rescue. In: Leibe, B., Matas, J., Sebe, N., Welling, M. (eds.) ECCV 2016. LNCS, vol. 9912, pp. 740–756. Springer, Cham (2016). https://doi.org/10.1007/978-3-319-46484-8_45
27. Mahjourian, R., Wicke, M., Angelova, A.: Unsupervised learning of depth and ego-motion from monocular video using 3D geometric constraints. In: CVPR, pp. 5667–5675. IEEE Computer Society (2018)
28. Yang, Z., Wang, P., Wang, Y., Xu, W., Nevatia, R.: LEGO: learning edge with geometry all at once by watching videos. In: CVPR, pp. 225–234. IEEE Computer Society (2018)
29. Zheng, C., Cham, T., Cai, J.: T2Net: synthetic-to-realistic translation for solving single-image depth estimation tasks. In: ECCV (2018)
30. Wang, Q., Guo, G.: LS-CNN: characterizing local patches at multiple scales for face recognition. IEEE Trans. Inf. Forensics Secur. **15**, 1640–1653 (2020)
31. Hu, J., Shen, L., Sun, G.: Squeeze-and-excitation networks. In: CVPR, pp. 7132–7141. IEEE Computer Society (2018). https://doi.org/10.1109/CVPR.2018.00745

32. Russakovsky, O., et al.: ImageNet large scale visual recognition challenge. IJCV **115**(3), 211–252 (2015). https://doi.org/10.1007/s11263-015-0816-y
33. Kong, S., Fowlkes, C.C.: Pixel-wise attentional gating for parsimonious pixel labeling. CoRR abs/1805.01556 (2018)
34. Kingma, D.P., Ba, J.: Adam: a method for stochastic optimization. In: Bengio, Y., LeCun, Y. (eds.) ICLR (2015)

A Strong Baseline Based on Adaptive Mining Sample Loss for Person Re-identification

Yongchang Gong, Liejun Wang[✉], Shuli Cheng, and Yongming Li

College of Information Science and Engineering, Xinjiang University, Ürümqi, China
{gyc,slcaydxju}@stu.xju.edu.cn, wljxju@xju.edu.cn

Abstract. At present, deep learning has made great progress in Person re-identification task. Many advanced models can achieve high performance. However, only a few scholars pay attention to studying the baseline. We find that embedding the same module into different baselines can lead to huge performance gaps between models. Therefore, the baseline is an extremely important component of the model. By studying the existing methods, we designed a powerful baseline with a simple structure. The proposed baseline uses resnet-50 as the backbone to extract the global features of people. To mine the information of the samples and make the model converge quickly, we designed an Adaptive Mining Sample Loss (AMSL), which allocates weights adaptively based on the Euclidean distance between samples. Compared with the triple loss, AMSL can not only push the positive point pairs closer, concentrate the samples of each class into the hypersphere to prevent the structural information from being destroyed. Experimental results indicate that the mAP and Rank-1 of the proposed baseline are 19.0% and 19.6% higher than the most powerful baseline BagTricks on CUHK-03, respectively.

Keywords: Deep learning · Person re-identification · Loss function · Baseline

1 Introduction

Person re-identification (Re-ID) has been widely used in large-scale people search, criminal investigation, and other fields. In recent years, Re-ID models [1,2] based on deep learning have made great progress,and many novel and effective modules have been proposed. However, we find that only a small number of researchers [3–6] focus on studies with a valid baseline. The functions of these baselines are no longer sufficient to support the development of pedestrian re-identification. As we all know, BagTricks [6] is the baseline with the best performance. As shown in Fig. 1, we visualize the retrieval results and heat map of BagTricks [6]. We see that in Fig. 1(a), the target is obscured by a tree, which leads to the performance degradation of BagTricks [6]. In Fig. 1(b) and (c), the query images are very similar to the pedestrians in the gallery, which

© Springer Nature Switzerland AG 2021
L. Fang et al. (Eds.): CICAI 2021, LNAI 13069, pp. 469–480, 2021.
https://doi.org/10.1007/978-3-030-93046-2_40

makes BagTricks [6] retrieve some disturbing images. In the current study, we analyze the performance of existing baselines and design a powerful and effective baseline for Re-ID.

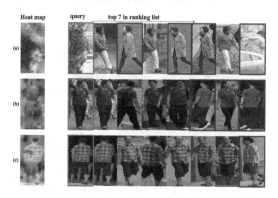

Fig. 1. Heat maps and search results of BagTricks on Market-1501 and DukeMTMC-ReID.

There are three intentions for this study. First, in order to extract rich discriminative features (which can effectively distinguish human features), most scholars' research mainly focuses on the construction of deep convolutional neural networks [7–9]. Especially, Zheng et al. [8] proposed a coarse-to-fine pyramid network, which can effectively extract local and global information. Alemu et al. [9] proposed a constrained clustering scheme to alleviate the Re-ID problem. Zhang et al. [10] designed a densely semantically aligned framework (DSA), which can solve the problem of body dislocation. In order to extract semantic context information, Zhang et al. [11] proposed the Relation-Aware Global Attention (RAG). These authors embed the novel methods into their baselines and achieve high performance. Through experiments, we find that when the same module is embedded with different baselines, their performance is very different. Therefore, a simple and powerful baseline is extremely important for the development of Re-ID.

Second, we investigate articles about designing effective baselines [3–6]. Especially, Sun et al. [5] designed a strong Partial Convolutional Baseline (PCB), which adopts the partition strategy to extract part features through multiple classifiers. BagTricks [6] is a powerful baseline, which uses some effective training skills to learn rich global features. Ye et al. [12] designed a strong AGW baseline, which consists of non-local attention [13] and resnet-50 [14]. We find that these baselines are trained by different loss functions, and perform poorly on datasets with few samples. In Re-ID, classification loss (ID loss) and triple loss [15] are often used. The effect of the triple loss is to bring the positive samples as close as possible to the input image and push away the negative samples. Wu et al. [16] believed that triple loss destroyed the structural information of samples, hard negative samples are likely to cause the model to collapse. Therefore, they proposed a pairwise margin loss. In order to mine the positive and negative sample information, we propose an Adaptive Mining Sample Loss (AMSL) on the top of the pairwise margin loss. AMSL can dynamically allocate weights according to the distance between samples to optimize the model, so as to avoid misjudging negative samples as positive ones. In order to protect the structural information of samples, AMSL can learn a hypersphere for each class and keep a certain interval between different classes. In the baseline, we replace the triple loss with AMSL, which greatly improves the performance of the baseline.

Third, in industry, simple and efficient models are preferred. However, in the academic community, in order to pursue high precision, researchers continue to add some modules to extract multiple local features and semantic information. Such models bring additional consumption. In Tricks [17], Luo et al. summarized some effective training techniques, which did not change the structure of the model but improved the performance of the model. Therefore, we used these training techniques and designed a strong baseline.

In summary, the main contributions of this paper are as follows:

(1) Compared with the triple loss, the designed AMSL can greatly improve the performance of the model, and has better practicability and accuracy.
(2) We propose a simple and powerful baseline, which reaches 75.6% mAP and 78.4% Rank-1 on CUHK-03. This result is 19.0% and 19.6% higher than the current strongest baseline BagTricks [6] on mAP and Rank-1, respectively.
(3) We designed some extended experiments, such as replacing the backbone and embedding some novel methods, to prove that our baseline is an effective baseline for Re-ID tasks.

2   The Proposed Baseline

In this section, we focus on the pipeline of our baseline and discuss the proposed adaptive mining sample loss in detail.

2.1   The Pipeline of Baseline

The proposed baseline is a simple and powerful model. The existing advanced models take resnet-50 [14] as their backbone, because the residual module of resnet-50 can prevent the network gradient explosion and improve the model performance. In order to compare with existing advanced models, we also take resnet-50 as our backbone. Figure 2 shows the pipline of the proposed baseline, which has five key parts: ResNet-50, GAP, adaptive mining sample loss, BN layers, and ID loss+label smooth. The adaptive mining sample loss is added after the generalized average pooling layer.

During the training process, we adopt some training strategies, which do not change the structure of the baseline and can effectively improve the performance of the baseline. Training strategies include: random erasing data augmentation [18], label smoothing [19], warmup Learning Rate [20], and last Stride [5]. In

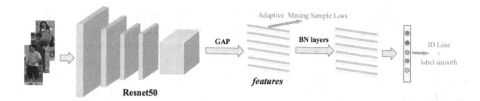

Fig. 2. The pipeline of the proposed baseline.

warmup Learning Rate, when the epoch is in the interval 0 to 10, the learning rate increases linearly. When the epoch is in the interval 10 to 40, the learning rate is 3.0×10^{-4}. After that, the learning rate will gradually decrease as the epoch increases. The changes in the learning rate lr(t) are as follows:

$$lr(t) = \begin{cases} 3.0 \times 10^{-4} \times \frac{t}{10}, & t \leq 10 \\ 3.0 \times 10^{-4}, & 10 < t \leq 40 \\ 6.0 \times 10^{-5}, & 40 < t \leq 70 \\ 1.2 \times 10^{-5}, & 70 < t \end{cases} \tag{1}$$

2.2 Adaptive Mining Sample Loss

In this section, we focus on discussing the designed adaptive mining sample loss. It concentrates positive and negative samples in the hypersphere, which can effectively protect the structure of the sample set. In order to mine hard positive and negative samples, the loss function of positive and negative samples is weighted adaptively by measuring the distance between samples, which effectively prevents the model from misjudging samples. Specifically, when the input image is very similar to the hard negative sample, AMSL will assign a large weight to the negative sample loss. When the input image is very different from the hard positive sample, AMSL will allocate a large weight to the positive sample loss, so that the model can focus on extracting the hard positive and negative sample features.

Before introducing the AMSL, we first explain some formula symbols. f represents a discriminant function, which brings the input image closer to the positive sample and pushes the negative sample away. $D_{ij} = |f(x_i) - f(x_j)|$ is the Euclidean distance between sample x_i and sample x_j. y_i is the label of sample x_i. x_i^c represents the ith sample in category C. $P_{c,i}^*$ and $N_{c,i}^*$ represent positive and negative sample sets respectively.

The contrastive loss [27] directly optimizes the distance between the input image and the positive sample by the following formula to make it equal to 0, while keeping the distance from the negative sample above α:

$$L_{\text{contrast}}(x_i, x_j, f) = y_{ij} D_{ij}^2 + (1 - y_{ij}) [\alpha - D_{ij}]_+^2 \tag{2}$$

One disadvantage of this formula is that in order to make the distance between the input image and the positive sample as zero as possible, the contrast loss destroys the spatial structure of the dataset.

Given an image x_i, the main idea of designing the AMSL is to make the input image close to its positive samples, and take the input image as the center of the sphere to gather all the positive samples into a hypersphere with α radius of $\alpha - m$. To keep the input image away from the negative sample, the radius of the input image to the negative sample is at least α. Therefore, the minimum distance between positive and negative sample sets is m. The formula is as follows:

$$L_{amsl}\left(x_i, x_j, f\right) = \left(\alpha + y_{ij}\left(D_{ij} - m\right) + \left(y_{ij} - 1\right)D_{ij}\right)_+ \tag{3}$$

Where $y_{ij} \in \{0, 1\}$. When $y_i = y_j$, $y_{ij} = 1$, otherwise, $y_{ij} = 0$.

Our basic equation is L_{amsl}. Based on L_{amsl}, we design a positive sample loss, which can make the query image x_i^c close to its positive sample set, far away from the negative sample set, and force the boundary distance between the positive sample set and the negative sample set to be m. By the positive sample loss, all the positive samples of x_i^c are concentrated in a hypersphere with $\alpha - m$ radius. In order to mine the hard positive sample information, we first calculate the Euclidean distance D_{ij}^n between the positive sample and x_i^c, and then allocate the weight for the positive sample loss by softmax. The formula is as follows:

$$L_P\left(x_i^c, f\right) = \sum_{x_j^c \in P_{c,i}^*} \frac{\exp\left(D_{ij}^n\right)}{\sum_{x_j^c \in P_{c,i}^*} \exp\left(D_{ij}^n\right)} L_{amsl}\left(x_i^c; x_j^c; f\right) \tag{4}$$

In order to keep x_i^c away from the negative sample set and make the distance between them at least α, we design a negative sample loss. There are a large number of negative hard samples in the dataset. If the hard negative sample information can not be effectively mined, the performance of the model will be degraded. Therefore, we use the softmin function to assign weights adaptively. The formula is as follows:

$$L_N\left(x_i^c, f\right) = \sum_{x_j \in N_{c,i}^*} \frac{\exp\left(-D_{ij}^n\right)}{\sum_{x_j^c \in N_{c,i}^*} \exp\left(-D_{ij}^n\right)} L_{amsl}\left(x_i^c; x_j^c; f\right) \tag{5}$$

It is worth noting that the partial derivative of L_{amsl} is always one. Therefore, in training, the model is influenced by our weighting strategy. The calculation is as follows:

$$\left|\frac{\partial L_{amsl}\left(x_i, x_j, f\right)}{\partial f\left(x_i\right)}\right| = \left|\frac{\alpha + D_{ij} - y_{ij}\beta}{\partial f\left(x_i\right)}\right| = \left|\frac{2\left(f\left(x_i\right) - f\left(x_j\right)\right)}{2\left|f\left(x_i\right) - f\left(x_j\right)\right|}\right| = 1 \tag{6}$$

In AMSL, we treat these positive and negative sample losses equally and optimize them.

$$L_{AMSL}\left(x_i^c, f\right) = L_P\left(x_i^c, f\right) + L_N\left(x_i^c, f\right) \tag{7}$$

In the proposed baseline, we adopt ID loss and AMSL joint learning strategy, as shown below:

$$L_{\text{Total}} = L_{ID} + w * L_{\text{AMSL}} \tag{8}$$

Where w controls the degree of contribution between ID loss and AMSL. We set w to 0.5, which performs well in our experiments.

3   Experimental Results and Analysis

We conduct many experiments on a teslav 100 GPU with 16 GB RAM and compare with the existing advanced Re-ID methods. Our baseline is implemented in Pytorch 0.4.1. Specially, the methods of AWTL [3], GP [4], PCB [5], BagTricks [6], SONA [7], DSA-reID [10], AGW [12], RAG-SC [11], Pyramid [8], DCDS [9], AANet [1], Tricks [17] and OSNet [21] are selected for comparison.

3.1   Datasets and Evaluation Metrics

We conduct experiments on three authoritative datasets. Among them, Market-1501 [22] and DukeMTMC-ReID [23] are two large-scale person re-identification datasets, and CUHK-03 (Detected) [24] is a re-identification dataset with a relatively small number of samples.In order to measure whether the proposed baseline performs well in re-identification tasks, we use the Cumulative Match Characteristic curve (CMC) [25] and mean Average Precision (mAP) [22] to evaluate the performance of the baseline.

3.2   Network Settings and Hyper-parameter Optimization

The input picture size is 256×128, the initial learning rate is 0.0003, and the epoch is 180. When training the model, the Adam optimizer is used, the training batch is set to $B = P \times K$. P and K represent the number of people with different identities and the number of different images for each person, respectively. In Market-1501 [22], P $= 16$ and K$= 4$.

In Eq. 3, hyper-parameters α and m control the spatial distribution of positive and negative sample sets. In order to evaluate the impact of these two parameters on the proposed baseline performance, we have done a large number of ablation experiments on three datasets. Figure 3(a) and (d) show the optimization results of hyper-parameters α and m on Market-1501. We observe that hyper-parameters α and m have a great impact on baseline performance. When hyper-parameters α and m are set to 2.2 and 1.4 respectively, the baseline performance is the best, that is, mAP reaches 88.1% and Rank-1 reaches 95.1%. Figure 3(b) and (e) show the optimization results of hyper-parameters α and m on DukeMTMC-ReID. We observe that if the distance between hyper-parameters α and m is too small or too large, the baseline performance will be degraded. When hyper-parameters α and m are set to 1.8 and 1.0 respectively, the baseline performance is the best, that is, mAP reaches 78.2% and Rank-1 reaches

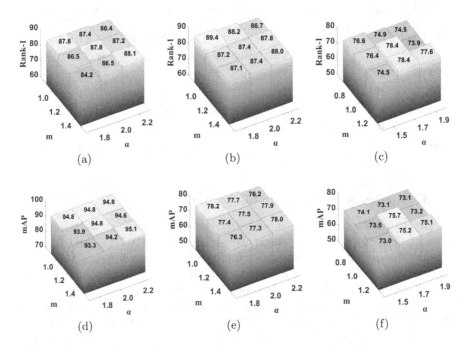

Fig. 3. Optimize hyper-parameters α and m on three datasets.

89.4%. Figure 3(c) and (f) show the optimization results of hyper-parameters α and m on CUHK-03. When hyper-parameters α and m are set to 1.7 and 1.0 respectively, the baseline performance is the best, that is, mAP reaches 75.7% and Rank-1 reaches 78.4%.

3.3 Compared with Advanced Baselines

In order to verify that the proposed baseline is the most powerful, we have selected advanced baselines in recent years for comparison. AWTL [3] uses triple loss to guide model training. GP [4] and PCB [5] all use ID loss to guide model training. BagTricks [6] uses ID loss, triple loss, and center loss [26] to guide model training. Table 1 shows the comparison results of our baseline with other baselines on the three datasets. On CUHK-03, our baseline reaches 75.6% mAP and 78.4% Rank-1. Our baseline improves mAP and Rank-1 by 19.0% and 19.6%, respectively, over BagTricks. Experiments show that AMSL is effective, and our baseline performs better than the best available baseline.

Table 1. Compare with different advanced baselines on three experimental datasets

Baseline	Loss	Market-1501		DukeMTMC-ReID		CUHK-03	
		mAP	Rank-1	mAP	Rank-1	mAP	Rank-1
AWTL	Trip	75.7	89.5	63.4	79.8	–	–
GP	ID	78.8	91.7	68.8	83.4	–	–
PCB	ID	81.6	93.8	69.2	83.3	57.5	63.7
BagTricks	ID+Trip+Center	86.0	94.8	74.8	86.6	56.6	58.8
Our	ID+AMSL	**88.1**	**95.1**	**78.2**	**89.4**	**75.6**	**78.4**

3.4   Compared with the State-of-the-Art

In order to assess the effectiveness of the proposed baseline, we select some advanced algorithms for comparison. DSA-reID [10], AGW [12], and RAG-SC [11] embed their proposed modules into their baseline to improve the performance of the model. We embed the Relation-Aware Global Attention (RAG) in the RAG-SC [11] algorithm into the proposed baseline.Table 2 shows the comparison results of our baseline+RAG with other methods on the three datasets.On DukeMTMC-ReID, our baseline+RAG reaches 81.0% mAP and 90.8% Rank-1. Compared with AGW [12], our baseline+RAG improves mAP and Rank-1 by 1.4% and 1.8%, respectively. On CUHK-03, our baseline+RAG reaches 78.6% mAP and 81.9% Rank-1. Compared with RAG-SC [11], our baseline+RAG improves mAP and Rank-1 by 4.1% and 2.3%, respectively. Experiments show that our baseline can further improve the performance of other methods.During the model training process, RAG-SC [11] needs to train 600 epochs, while our baseline+RAG only needs 180 epochs, which indicates that our baseline can make the model converge quickly.

Table 2. Compare with different advanced methods on three experimental datasets.

Methods	Publication	Market-1501		DukeMTMC-ReID		CUHK-03	
		mAP	Rank-1	mAP	Rank-1	mAP	Rank-1
SONA	ICCV 2019	88.8	95.6	78.3	89.5	77.3	79.9
DSA	CVPR 2019	87.6	95.7	74.3	86.2	73.1	78.2
AGW	PAMI 2021	87.8	95.1	79.6	89.0	62.0	63.6
RAG-SC	CVPR 2020	88.4	**96.1**	–	–	74.5	79.6
Ours+RAG [11]	–	**89.7**	95.6	**81.0**	**90.8**	**78.6**	**81.9**

3.5   Compared with Different Backbone Methods

For experimental fairness, the backbone network of all the above ablation experiments and comparison algorithms is ResNet-50 [11]. However, some methods use ResNet101, ResNet152 or IBN-Net50-a as their backbone network. Based on different backbones, the performance of the model will be different, mainly because

Table 3. Compare with different advanced methods on three experimental datasets.

Methods	Backbone	Market-1501		DukeMTMC-ReID		CUHK-03	
		mAP	Rank-1	mAP	Rank-1	mAP	Rank-1
Pyramid	ResNet101	88.2	**95.7**	79.0	89.0	74.8	78.9
DCDS	ResNet101	85.8	94.8	75.5	87.5	–	–
AANet	ResNet152	83.4	93.9	74.3	87.7	–	–
Tricks	SEResNet101	87.3	94.6	78.0	87.5	68.0	69.6
OSNet	OSNet	84.9	94.8	73.5	88.6	67.8	72.3
BagTricks	IBN-Net50-a	88.2	95.0	79.1	90.1	62.8	64.5
Ours	IBN-Net50-a	**89.5**	95.6	**81.5**	**91.3**	**80.6**	**83.4**

different backbones will have a great impact on the model. In order to evaluate the performance of our baseline on different backbones, we selected some advanced methods for comparison, which have different backbone networks. In particular, OSNet [21] is the backbone built by the authors themselves (Table 3).

3.6 Influences of Adaptive Mining Sample Loss

In order to evaluate intuitively the effectiveness of adaptive mining sample loss (AMSL), we constructed a model, which consists of a convolution layer, a ReLU, a maximum pooling layer, a BN layer and a fully connected layer. It is respectively guided by ID loss, ID loss+triple loss, and ID loss+AMSL to train on MNIST dataset, and visualize the sample distribution. Figure 4 shows the distribution of samples. We observe that the model is only guided by ID loss, which leads to a loose sample distribution. The model is guided by ID loss+triple loss. The intra class structure of samples is very compact, but the distance between classes is very small. To some extent, triple loss destroys the structural information of samples. However, the model is guided by ID loss + AMSL, the internal structure of each sample is more compact, and the distance between classes is larger, which intuitively reflects that our AMSL is effective, and fully protects structural information of samples.

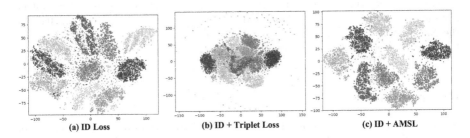

(a) ID Loss   (b) ID + Triplet Loss   (c) ID + AMSL

Fig. 4. Under the supervision of different losses, visualize the distribution of samples on MNIST dataset.

To show the effectiveness of our proposed baseline visually, we visualize the ranking results of the baseline. As shown in Fig. 5, we observe that compared to BagTricks [6], our baseline has no matching errors, which shows that our method is feasible.

Fig. 5. Visualization of ranking results: BagTricks vs. Ours.

4   Conclusions

In this paper, we design a simple and powerful baseline for person Re-ID tasks. Our baseline reaches 75.6% mAP and 78.4% Rank-1 on CUHK-03. This result is much higher than the best existing baseline performance. In addition, our baseline training time only takes 3.5 h, and some advanced modules embedded in the proposed baseline perform better than the original model. Most of the existing models are supervised by ID+triplet losses. Through experiments, we find that ID+triplet losses destroy the spatial structure of the sample. To solve this problem, we design an adaptive sample mining loss, which can make the model converge quickly. It enables the model to fully mine sample information and protect the spatial structure of samples, which makes it perform well on the dataset with few samples. We hope that our baseline can promote development of Re-ID in the community of scholars and industry.

Aconwledgment. This research was funded by the Natural Science Foundation of Xinjiang Uygur Autonomous Region grant number 2020D01C034, Tianshan Innovation Team of Xinjiang Uygur Autonomous Region grant number 2020D14044, National Science Foundation of China under Grant U1903213, 61771416 and 62041110, the National Key R&D Program of China under Grant 2018YFB1403202, Creative Research Groups of Higher Education of Xinjiang Uygur Autonomous Region under Grant XJEDU2017T002.

References

1. Tay, C.-P., Roy, S., Yap, K.-H.: AANET: Attribute attention network for person re-identifications. In: Proceedings of the Computer Vision and Pattern Recognition (CVPR), pp. 7134–7143. IEEE, Long Beach, (2019)

2. Gong, Y., Wang, L., Li, Y., Du, A.F.: A discriminative person re-identification model with global-local attention and adaptive weighted rank list loss. IEEE Access **8**, 203700–203711 (2020)
3. Ristani, E., Tomasi, C.: Features for multi-target multi-camera tracking and re-identification. In: Proceedings of the IEEE Conference on Computer Vision and Pattern Recognition, pp. 6036–6046. IEEE, Salt Lake City (2018)
4. Xiong, F., Xiao, Y., Cao, Z., Gong, K., Fang, Z., Zhou, J.T.: Good practices on building effective CNN baseline model for person re-identification. In: International Society for Optics and Photonics, ICGIP 2018, pp. 1–2 (2019)
5. Sun, Y., Zheng, L., Yang, Y., Tian, Q., Wang, S.: Beyond part models: person retrieval with refined part pooling (and a strong convolutional baseline). In: Proceedings of the European Conference on Computer Vision (ECCV), pp. 480–496. IEEE, Munich (2018)
6. Luo, H., et al.: A strong baseline and batch normalization neck for deep person re-identification. IEEE Trans. Multimedia **10**(22), 2597–2609 (2019)
7. Xia, B.N., Gong, Y., Zhang, Y., Poellabauer, C.: Second-order non-local attention networks for person re-identification. In: CVPR, pp. 3760–3769. IEEE, Long Beach (2019)
8. Zheng, F., et al.: Pyramidal person re-identification via multi-loss dynamic training. In: CVPR, pp. 8514–8522. IEEE, Long Beach (2019)
9. Alemu, L.T., Pelillo, M., Shah, M.: Deep constrained dominant sets for person re-identification. In: Proceedings of the Conference on Computer Vision, pp. 9855–9864. IEEE, Long Beach (2019)
10. Zhang, Z., Lan, C., Zeng, W., Chen, Z.: Densely semantically aligned person re-identification. In: CVPR, pp. 667–676. IEEE, Long Beach (2019)
11. Zhang, Z., Lan, C., Zeng, W., Chen, Z.: Relation-aware global attention for person re-identification. In: CVPR, pp. 3186–3195. IEEE, Washington (2020)
12. Ye, M., Shen, J., Lin, G., Xiang, T., Shao, L., Hoi, S.C.: Deep learning for person re-identification: a survey and outlook. IEEE Trans. Pattern Anal. Mach. Intell. (2021)
13. Wang, X., Girshick, R., Gupta, A., He, K.: Non-local neural networks. In: CVPR, pp. 7794–7803. IEEE, Salt Lake City (2018)
14. He, K., Zhang, X., Ren, S., Sun, J.: Deep residual learning for image recognition. In: Proceedings of on Computer Vision and Pattern Recognition, pp. 770–778. IEEE, Las Vegas (2016)
15. Liu, H., Feng, J., Qi, M., Jiang, J., Yan, S.: End-to-end comparative attention networks for person re-identification. IEEE Trans. Image Process. **7**(26), 3492–3506 (2017)
16. Wu, C.Y., Manmatha, R., Smola, A.J., Krahenbuhl, P.: Sampling matters in deep embedding learning. In: CVPR, pp. 2840–2848. IEEE, Venice (2017)
17. Luo, H., Gu, Y., Liao, X., Lai, S., Jiang, W.: Bag of tricks and a strong baseline for deep person re-identification. In: CVPR. IEEE, Long Beach (2019)
18. Zhong, Z., Zheng, L., Kang, G., Li, S., Yang, Y.: Random erasing data augmentation. In: Proceedings of the AAAI Conference on Artificial Intelligence, pp. 13001–13008. IEEE, New York (2020)
19. Zheng, Z., Zheng, L., Yang, Y.: A discriminatively learned CNN embedding for person reidentification. ACM Trans. Multimedia Comput. Commun. Appl. (TOMM) **1**(14), 1–20 (2017)
20. Fan, X., Jiang, W., Luo, H., Fei, M.: Spherereid: deep hypersphere manifold embedding for person re-identification. J. Vis. Commun. Image Represent. **20**, 51–58 (2019)

21. Zhou, K., Yang, Y., Cavallaro, A., Xiang, T.: Omni-scale feature learning for person re-identification. In: CVPR, pp. 3702–3712. IEEE, Seoul, Korea (2019)

22. Zheng, L., Shen, L., Tian, L., Wang, S., Wang, J., Tian, Q.: Scalable person re-identification: a benchmark. In: Proceedings of the IEEE International Conference on Computer Vision, pp. 1116–1124. IEEE, Santiago (2015)

23. Ristani, E., Solera, F., Zou, R., Cucchiara, R., Tomasi, C.: Performance measures and a data set for multi-target, multi-camera tracking. In: Hua, G., Jégou, H. (eds.) ECCV 2016, Part II. LNCS, vol. 9914, pp. 17–35. Springer, Cham (2016). https://doi.org/10.1007/978-3-319-48881-3_2

24. Li, W., Zhao, R., Xiao, T., Wang, X.: Deepreid: deep filter pairing neural network for person re-identification. In: The Computer Vision and Pattern Recognition, pp. 152–159. IEEE, Columbus (2014)

25. Bolle, R.M., Connell, J.H., Pankanti, S., Ratha, N.K., Senior, A.W.: The relation between the ROC curve and the CMC. In: Fourth IEEE Workshop on Automatic Identification Advanced Technologies (AutoID 2005), vol. 2, issue 5 (2005)

26. Wen, Y., Zhang, K., Li, Z., Qiao, Y.: A discriminative feature learning approach for deep face recognition. In: Leibe, B., Matas, J., Sebe, N., Welling, M. (eds.) ECCV 2016, Part VII. LNCS, vol. 9911, pp. 499–515. Springer, Cham (2016). https://doi.org/10.1007/978-3-319-46478-7_31

27. Hadsell, R., Chopra, S., LeCun, Y.: Dimensionality reduction by learning an invariant mapping. In: CVPR 2006, pp. 1735–1742. IEEE, New York (2006)

Unsupervised Domain Adaptation via Attention Augmented Mutual Networks for Person Re-identification

Hui Tian[1] and Junlin Hu[2(✉)]

[1] College of Information Science and Technology, Beijing University of Chemical Technology, Beijing, China
[2] School of Software, Beihang University, Beijing, China
`hujunlin@buaa.edu.cn`

Abstract. Supervised learning has limited generalization ability across scenes due to its high cost of data annotation, and unsupervised learning and unsupervised domain adaptation have become the hot topics in recent years. With the applications of deep learning in the field of unsupervised domain adaptation (UDA) for person re-identification, pseudo label methods via clustering techniques have become the mainstream route. However, the clustering procedure inevitably leads to noisy pseudo-labels. To reduce the interference of clustering noise, mutual mean-teaching (MMT) is introduced to generate reliable soft pseudo labels, however, this method is easy to fall into the local optimum. In this paper, we propose a novel Attention Random Variation (ARV) module that can be integrated into the MMT framework to develop Attention Augmented Mutual Networks (AAMN). Our ARV module generates random differences between two collaborative networks under the MMT framework to avoid the networks converging to the same kind of noise. Specifically, we propose a parameter-free Random Variation module to produce differences by randomly enhancing units of feature maps, and then combine it with an attention mechanism to enlarge networks differences and complementarity. Experimental results show that our AAMN method improves mAP of baseline method by 1.9% and 6.3% on Market-to-Duke and Duke-to-Market UDA tasks respectively.

Keywords: Person re-identification · Unsupervised domain adaptation · Domain adaptation · Attention mechanism

1 Introduction

Person re-identification (Re-ID) aims to match person images of the same identity across different cameras. It plays an important role in public security and intelligent surveillance. In the past decade, most Re-ID research work focuses on supervised learning, which is trained on the labeled datasets. Although supervised learning-based methods, such as [21,22], have achieved

© Springer Nature Switzerland AG 2021
L. Fang et al. (Eds.): CICAI 2021, LNAI 13069, pp. 481–491, 2021.
https://doi.org/10.1007/978-3-030-93046-2_41

breakthrough progress, there are still several unsolved problems. First, supervised methods require large-scale labeled data where data annotation is an expensive and time-consuming task. Second, these methods cannot be well generalized to other scenarios and have significant performance drop because of the domain gaps of different datasets. Therefore, unsupervised domain adaptation (UDA) [1,12,13,16,31] methods are proposed to eliminate or reduce the domain gaps, which utilize the labeled source domain data to learn model parameters in training step and apply the learned models to the unlabeled target domain.

With the development of deep learning, different kinds of UDA methods based on deep neural network techniques are proposed, such as image-level adaptation [3,24,32] and feature-level methods [2,15,17]. The image-level based methods solve domain adaptation from the perspective of style transfer between different datasets or cameras. Feature-level based methods transfer discriminative feature information from the source domain to the target domain to reduce the domain gaps. However, the improvement of these methods is not significant in UDA task. At present, the mainstream UDA methods [6,14,25] for person re-identification aim to generate pseudo labels by clustering algorithms. Although clustering-based methods show the promising performance, these methods inevitably lead to noisy pseudo-labels, which greatly affects the subsequent network training and recognition accuracy.

To generate high-quality pseudo labels and reduce label noise, mutual mean-teaching (MMT) framework [7] is proposed, which generates reliable soft pseudo labels by collaboratively training two networks. In addition, to avoid two networks converging to the same kind of noise and increase the independence of output, this method adopts the temporally average model and different initializations to train the coupled networks. Although these schemes reduce two networks' bias to the same training noise to some degree, the independence and complementarity of their output feature maps are still weak, which may affect further performance improvement.

To effectively address the above problem, we propose a novel attention random variation (ARV) module integrated into the MMT framework. The key idea behind ARV is to create random differences between the output feature maps of two neural networks to enhance the complementary characteristics of the same identity pedestrians. First, we design a random variation (RV) module, which is inspired by the Random Erasing approaches [30] to generate differences by randomly enhancing a block of feature maps. The design of this module is different from that of hard-attention [4,19] (image-level data augmentation), but they have similar functions, which have strong prediction randomness and dynamic variability. As a result, augmented features with various can be generated to well make differences between the two networks. Then, we further lead the soft-attention mechanism [10,23], which are widely used in the deep learning model, into the dual networks to emphasize important information and suppress noise ones. Finally, the RV and the non-local attention [23] are incorporated to form the attention random variation (ARV) module, and we present an attention augmented mutual networks (AAMN) by integrating ARV module into the MMT framework. Our contributions can be summarized as follows:

- A random variation (RV) scheme is designed to randomly enhance units in feature maps, which well makes differences between the two networks.
- A non-local attention is utilized to learn discriminate information, combined with the RV to form the ARV module to enlarge the feature differences.
- Our proposed ARV module significantly improves performances on different challenging UDA tasks for person Re-ID, which achieves improvements of 1.9% and 6.3% in terms of mAP on Market-to-Duke and Duke-to-Market UDA tasks, respectively.

2   Related Works

In this section, we briefly review the methods related unsupervised domain adaptation for person Re-ID, data augmentation, and attention mechanism.

2.1   Unsupervised Domain Adaptation for Person Re-ID

Due to the difference in data distribution between the source domain and target domain and the weak generalization ability of the supervised learning models. In recent years, UDA methods have attracted much attention. UDA methods can be roughly divided into three categories. The first is image-level methods, which learns invariant features by transferring styles from different databases or cameras. For example, PTGAN [24] transfers knowledge, while SPGAN [3] considers maintaining the original person IDs by self-similarity and domain-dissimilarity. Unlike domain-invariant style transfer, CamStyle [32] learns a camera-invariant subspace aided by labeled training images. These methods largely depend on the quality of the generated images, so the improvement of performance is limited in the unsupervised setting. The second is feature-level methods, which learn the feature information from the source domain and perform domain adaptation to the target dataset. For instance, Lin et al. [15] propose a multi-task mid-level feature alignment network (MMFA) to dig a deeper representation of mid-level features of each domain. Delorme et al. [2] and Qi et al. [17] propose conditional adversarial network and camera-aware domain adaptation framework respectively to match distributions from different domains. Compared with image-level methods, this kind of method has better performance. The last category is clustering-based methods. Fu et al. [6] propose the SSG method by iteratively alternating clustering and network training process. Ding et al. [5] propose dispersion-based automatically generated clusters considering both intra-cluster and inter-cluster dispersion. This kind of method inevitably generates noisy pseudo-labels. To overcome this problem, Yang et al. [27] design an asymmetric co-teaching framework with a sample filtering procedure after the clustering and Ge et al. [7] introduce an MMT framework, which generates reliable soft pseudo labels by collaboratively training two networks. However, co-training networks tend to bias the same training noise. It is necessary to enhance the independence and complementarity of feature maps of two networks. We propose a novel attention random variation (ARV) module to deal with this issue.

2.2 Data Augmentation

In image pre-processing, data augmentation produces various kinds of image samples, which can make the model learning feature invariant to a certain extent, so this technology has been widely used to improve the generalization ability of deep networks. One common data augmentation method includes cropping the image or flipping the image horizontally [11], which enhances data by creating a variety of image samples. Another method randomly erases or mask a block of the image regions to make models robust to occlusions, such as Random Erasing [30] that randomly selects a rectangle region in an image and erases its units with random values, Cutout [4] and Hide-and-Seek [19] that randomly hide square regions of an input image and set these pixels with fixed values. Different from these methods which aim at solving a specific variation problem (e.g., the pose or occlusion variations), our random variation module creates differences by randomly enhancing a continuous region in feature maps, learning discriminative features from two same networks.

2.3 Attention Mechanism

In the field of image recognition, attention mechanism is a critical technology, which makes deep learning model extract more discriminant information, and has been widely used. There are three main categories of attention methods: temporal attention, channel attention and spatial attention mechanism. The latter two attention mechanisms [10,23] are more suitable for image-based person Re-ID. For instance, classic non-local operations [23] computes responsive weights based on relationships between different locations. Hu et al. [10] propose a squeeze-and-excitation network to learn the correlation between channels and adjust the channel weights of the feature maps. Further, some supervised learning methods for person Re-ID such as SONA [26] adopt an attention scheme. As mentioned above, attention mechanism has been proved to be effective in many models. In this paper, we adopt non-local scheme combined with a random variation module to encourage the dual networks to create differences.

3 Our Approach

In this section, we introduce our attention augmented mutual networks (AAMN) that mainly consists of three parts: mutual mean-teaching (MMT) framework [7], random variation module and attention mechanism.

3.1 MMT Framework

MMT framework can alleviate noisy pseudo-labels problems to some degree, which is briefly reviewed as follows. Stage 1: given the source domain data and person identity labels, the network is trained to learn the knowledge of the source domain in a supervised way. Stage 2: the MMT framework alternately conducts hard pseudo label generation and soft pseudo label generation. Specifically, clustering technique is used to obtain hard pseudo-labels as the supervised class signals, then the MMT framework collaboratively trains two same networks with different initializations to generate soft pseudo labels. Stage 3: both hard pseudo labels and soft pseudo labels are generated by one network to conduct the other network training. Stage 4: the past average model is used to estimate performance for UDA person Re-ID.

The core technology of this framework is to use the past temporally average model of each network instead of the current model to avoid two networks quickly converge to each other. The past average model updates the weights by accumulating the values of iteration, so it is insensitive to the change of the current-iteration prediction values. The parameters can be updated by:

$$E^{(T)}[\boldsymbol{\theta}_1] = \alpha E^{(T-1)}[\boldsymbol{\theta}_1] + (1-\alpha)\boldsymbol{\theta}_1, \tag{1}$$

$$E^{(T)}[\boldsymbol{\theta}_2] = \alpha E^{(T-1)}[\boldsymbol{\theta}_2] + (1-\alpha)\boldsymbol{\theta}_2, \tag{2}$$

where T denotes current iterations, $\boldsymbol{\theta}_1$ and $\boldsymbol{\theta}_2$ indicate the current parameters generated by the two networks, $E^{(T)}[\boldsymbol{\theta}_1]$ and $E^{(T)}[\boldsymbol{\theta}_2]$ indicate the weight parameters of the average models of the two networks in the iteration T, and α is the momentum super-parameter.

3.2 Random Variation

To create random differences between the output feature maps of two neural networks, we introduce the random variation (RV) module. Different from random erasing [30] that randomly erases image-level pixels with random values and DropBlock [8] which drops contiguous regions from a feature map, RV randomly selects a contiguous region of a feature map, and then modulates this feature map by different multiples. The RV is modulated on a feature map by the following steps.

Step 1: randomly select the modulation region. Given a feature map $\mathbf{F} \in \mathbb{R}^{c \times h \times w}$, where c is the number of channels, h and w are height and width of the feature map respectively, we randomly select a region with the area of s_e and the aspect ratio r, then we set height $h_e = \sqrt{s_e \times r}$ and weight $w_e = \sqrt{\frac{s_e}{r}}$, and initialize a point (x_e, y_e) in $\mathbf{F}$. If $x_e + w_e \leq w$ and $y_e + h_e \leq h$, the region $(x_e, y_e, x_e + w_e, y_e + h_e)$ is selected as $\mathbf{F}_e$. Otherwise, the above procedure is repeated execution until an appropriate region is selected.

Step 2: The feature map $\mathbf{F}$ is modulated as $\mathbf{F}^*$ by the following formula:

$$F_{chw}^* = \begin{cases} F_{chw}, & F_{chw} \in \mathbf{F}_e, \\ bF_{chw}, & \text{otherwise,} \end{cases} \tag{3}$$

where b is a hyper-parameter controlling the degree of modulation. The RV module not only creates differences between the features of two neural networks, but also retains the original feature information.

For a feature map $\mathbf{F}$, let P be the probability of its undergoing RV. In this process, differences between the features of two networks are generated. We analyze the differences when this module is applied to two networks in the following three different cases: 1) the RV module does not modulate the difference between two networks with probability P^2; 2) the module makes a difference in one of the two feature maps of two networks with probability P; and 3) the RV module modulates two feature maps of two networks respectively with probability P^2. In summary, the two randomly selected regions $\mathbf{F}_e$ are not the same.

3.3 Attention Random Variation

Our proposed random variation module can be combined with attention mechanisms. In this paper, we adopt the Non-local block [23] attention to increase the difference between two networks. Here we employ its dot-product version. The response signal $\mathbf{y}_i$ of $\mathbf{x}_i$ at the position i is defined as:

$$\mathbf{y}_i = \frac{1}{N} \sum_{\forall j} f\left(\mathbf{x}_i, \mathbf{x}_j\right) g\left(\mathbf{x}_j\right), \tag{4}$$

where $\mathbf{x}$ denotes the input signal, g is 1×1 convolution operation, N is the number of positions in $\mathbf{x}$, and f is a dot-product operation that is calculated as:

$$f\left(\mathbf{x}_i, \mathbf{x}_j\right) = \theta\left(\mathbf{x}_i\right)^T \phi\left(\mathbf{x}_j\right), \tag{5}$$

in which θ and ϕ denote two different 1×1 convolutions. Then a Non-local block is defined as:

$$\mathbf{z}_i = \mathbf{W}_z \mathbf{y}_i + \mathbf{x}_i, \tag{6}$$

where $\mathbf{W}_z$ is a weight matrix to be learned, and $\mathbf{z}_i$ is the final output of the Non-local block corresponding to $\mathbf{x}_i$.

The RV module creates different features of two networks. The Non-local block selectively emphasizes discriminative features and suppresses less useful ones. We arrange the Non-local block after the random variation to form our attention random variation (ARV) module. Specifically, given a feature map $\mathbf{F}$, we first pass it through the RV module obtaining $\mathbf{F}^* = \mathrm{RV}(\mathbf{F})$ and then through the Non-local block reaching $\mathbf{F}' = \mathrm{Attention}(\mathbf{F}^*)$. The whole procedure of our ARV module is denoted by $\mathbf{F}' = \mathrm{Attention}(\mathrm{RV}(\mathbf{F}))$.

We further integrate our ARV module into the MMT framework and propose an attention augmented mutual networks (AAMN) for person Re-ID.

4 Experiments

In this section, we evaluate our ARV and AAMN methods on the platform of Ubuntu 16.04 system and two NVIDIA GeForce RTX2080Ti GPUs.

4.1 Datasets and Protocols

Market1501 [29]: This dataset is collected by six cameras, consisting of 32,668 images of 1,501 person identities. Among them, Training set contains of 12936 pictures of 751 pedestrian identities and the rest is test data.

DukeMTMC-reID [18]: It collects 36,411 person images from eight cameras, for which contains 1402 persons. There are 16,522 images of 702 pedestrian for training and remaining images out of another 702 pedestrian for testing.

To evaluate our method, we implement domain adaptation tasks on the two settings, i.e., Duke-to-Market and Market-to-Duke. We adopt Rank-k and mean average precision (mAP) to assess the performances of our method.

4.2 Experimental Settings

We choose Resnet50 [9] as the backbone of our method. To make a fair comparison, we follow the same initial experimental settings as literature [7]. By default, we set the probability of RV module to 0.5 and hyper-parameter b to 1.5.

The detailed training process is summarized as follows: First, we train two Resnet50 backbone networks separately in the labeled source domain by supervised way to obtain the pre-trained weights of MMT, where the neural networks are trained with 80 epochs. Then, we plug the non-local block into Layer 2 and Layer 3 of the Resnet50 backbone. We use 8 epochs to train the non-local block with other parameters frozen. Finally, the RV module is added into Layer 3 before the non-local block of the Resnet50 to train AAMN on the unlabeled target domain with 30 epochs, and we adopt 500 pseudo-classes generated by the k-means clustering algorithm. It is noted that randomly erasing method is employed in the training process, which does not conflict with our proposed RV method.

4.3 Comparison with State-of-the-Art Methods

We compare our proposed method with state-of-the-art methods on the two domain adaptation tasks. Table 1 reports the performances of different approaches. Experimental results of this table verify the effectiveness of our method. Specifically, by adopting the attention random variation (ARV) module, our proposed AAMN performs better than MMT method. For mAP, we obtain the improvements by 6.3% and 1.9% on Duke-to-Market and Market-to-Duke, respectively. These results further demonstrate the importance of our proposed ARV module for creating a difference between two neural networks.

4.4 Analysis of Probability P in the RV Module

Our AAMN method with different probability values P (i.e., 0.3, 0.5, 0.7 and 1) of the RV operation are evaluated in Table 2. When P is increased from 0.3 to 0.5, the performance improve slightly from 77.0% to 77.5% (mAP) on the Duke-to-Market task. However, if P is increased to 0.7 and 1, the mAP of AAMN is evidently decreased from 75.1% to 72.6% on the Duke-to-Market task.

Table 1. Comparison (%) of mAP with the state-of-the-art methods on Market1501 and DukeMTMC-reID datasets

Methods	Duke-to-Market				Market-to-Duke			
	mAP	rank-1	rank-5	rank-10	mAP	rank-1	rank-5	rank-10
SPGAN [3]	22.8	51.5	70.1	76.8	22.3	41.1	56.6	63.0
CFSM [1]	28.3	26.2	–	–	27.3	49.8	–	–
HHL [31]	31.4	62.2	78.8	84.0	27.2	46.9	61.0	66.7
BUC [16]	38.3	66.2	79.6	84.5	27.5	47.4	62.6	68.4
CDS [25]	39.9	71.6	81.2	84.7	42.7	67.2	75.9	79.4
TAUDL [12]	41.2	63.7	–	–	43.5	61.7	–	–
UTAL [13]	46.2	69.2	–	–	44.6	62.3	–	–
PDA-Net [14]	47.6	75.2	86.3	90.2	45.1	63.2	77.0	82.5
UDAP [20]	53.7	75.8	89.5	93.2	49.0	68.4	80.1	83.5
PCB-PAST [28]	54.6	78.4	–	–	54.3	72.4	–	–
SSG [6]	58.3	80.0	90.0	92.4	53.4	73.0	80.6	83.2
MMT [7]	71.2	87.7	94.9	96.9	65.1	78.0	88.8	92.5
AAMN	77.5	89.6	96.2	97.4	67.0	79.7	89.1	92.9

Table 2. Different probability P

P	Duke-to-Market	
	mAP	Rank-1
0.3	77.0	88.9
0.5	77.5	89.6
0.7	75.1	88.0
1	72.6	87.7

Table 3. Different components

Models	Market-to-Duke	
	mAP	Rank-1
MMT	65.1	78.0
Only Att	66.2	78.6
ARV	67.0	79.7

4.5   Analysis of Different Components of AAMN

Our proposed ARV module mainly consists of two components: the RV module and the attention (i.e., non-local block). We conduct comparative experiments to verify the effectiveness of each component. Table 3 reports the mAP and Rank-1 of different components. We can see that 1) when the attention (i.e., Only Att.) is added, the performance increases slightly on the Market-to-Duke task; and 2) the performance of AAMN is further improved when the ARV module is utilized.

5 Conclusion

This paper presents a parameter-free module, called random variation (RV), and then combines it with an attention mechanism to form ARV module. The proposed ARV can control the feature maps to bias the same noise effectively by enhancing the differences of feature maps of the dual networks. We further propose an Attention Augmented Mutual Networks (AAMN) by applying the ARV to the MMT framework. Experimental results on various UDA tasks have demonstrated the effectiveness of the proposed method.

Acknowledgments. This work was supported by the National Natural Science Foundation of China under Grant 62006013.

References

1. Chang, X., Yang, Y., Xiang, T., Hospedales, T.M.: Disjoint label space transfer learning with common factorised space. In: AAAI Conference on Artificial Intelligence, pp. 3288–3295 (2019)
2. Delorme, G., Xu, Y., Lathuilière, S., Horaud, R., Alameda-Pineda, X.: CANU-ReID: a conditional adversarial network for unsupervised person re-identification. In: International Conference on Pattern Recognition (2021)
3. Deng, W., Zheng, L., Ye, Q., Kang, G., Yang, Y., Jiao, J.: Image-image domain adaptation with preserved self-similarity and domain-dissimilarity for person re-identification. In: IEEE Conference on Computer Vision and Pattern Recognition, pp. 994–1003 (2018)
4. DeVries, T., Taylor, G.W.: Improved regularization of convolutional neural networks with cutout. arXiv preprint arXiv: 1708.04552 (2017)
5. Ding, G., Khan, S., Tang, Z., Zhang, J., Porikli, F.: Towards better validity: Dispersion based clustering for unsupervised person re-identification. arXiv preprint arXiv: 1906.01308 (2019)
6. Fu, Y., Wei, Y., Wang, G., Zhou, Y., Shi, H., Huang, T.S.: Self-similarity grouping: a simple unsupervised cross domain adaptation approach for person re-identification. In: IEEE/CVF International Conference on Computer Vision, pp. 6112–6121 (2019)
7. Ge, Y., Chen, D., Li, H.: Mutual mean-teaching: Pseudo label refinery for unsupervised domain adaptation on person re-identification. arXiv preprint arXiv: 2001.01526 (2020)
8. Ghiasi, G., Lin, T.Y., Le, Q.V.: Dropblock: A regularization method for convolutional networks. arXiv preprint arXiv: 1810.12890 (2018)
9. He, K., Zhang, X., Ren, S., Sun, J.: Deep residual learning for image recognition. In: IEEE Conference on Computer Vision and Pattern Recognition, pp. 770–778 (2016)
10. Hu, J., Shen, L., Sun, G.: Squeeze-and-excitation networks. In: IEEE Conference on Computer Vision and Pattern Recognition, pp. 7132–7141 (2018)
11. Krizhevsky, A., Hinton, G., et al.: Learning multiple layers of features from tiny images. University of Toronto (2009)
12. Li, M., Zhu, X., Gong, S.: Unsupervised person re-identification by deep learning tracklet association. In: Ferrari, V., Hebert, M., Sminchisescu, C., Weiss, Y. (eds.) ECCV 2018, Part IV. LNCS, vol. 11208, pp. 772–788. Springer, Cham (2018). https://doi.org/10.1007/978-3-030-01225-0_45

13. Li, M., Zhu, X., Gong, S.: Unsupervised tracklet person re-identification. IEEE Trans. Pattern Anal. Mach. Intell. **42**(7), 1770–1782 (2019)
14. Li, Y.J., Lin, C.S., Lin, Y.B., Wang, Y.C.F.: Cross-dataset person re-identification via unsupervised pose disentanglement and adaptation. In: IEEE/CVF International Conference on Computer Vision, pp. 7919–7929 (2019)
15. Lin, S., Li, H., Li, C.T., Kot, A.C.: Multi-task mid-level feature alignment network for unsupervised cross-dataset person re-identification. arXiv preprint arXiv: 1807.01440 (2018)
16. Lin, Y., Dong, X., Zheng, L., Yan, Y., Yang, Y.: A bottom-up clustering approach to unsupervised person re-identification. In: AAAI Conference on Artificial Intelligence, pp. 8738–8745 (2019)
17. Qi, L., Wang, L., Huo, J., Zhou, L., Shi, Y., Gao, Y.: A novel unsupervised camera-aware domain adaptation framework for person re-identification. In: IEEE/CVF International Conference on Computer Vision, pp. 8080–8089 (2019)
18. Ristani, E., Solera, F., Zou, R., Cucchiara, R., Tomasi, C.: Performance measures and a data set for multi-target, multi-camera tracking. In: Hua, G., Jégou, H. (eds.) ECCV 2016, Part II. LNCS, vol. 9914, pp. 17–35. Springer, Cham (2016). https://doi.org/10.1007/978-3-319-48881-3_2
19. Singh, K.K., Lee, Y.J.: Hide-and-seek: forcing a network to be meticulous for weakly-supervised object and action localization. In: IEEE International Conference on Computer Vision, pp. 3544–3553 (2017)
20. Song, L., et al.: Unsupervised domain adaptive re-identification: theory and practice. Pattern Recognit. **102**, 107173 (2020)
21. Sun, Y., Zheng, L., Yang, Y., Tian, Q., Wang, S.: Beyond part models: person retrieval with refined part pooling (and a strong convolutional baseline). In: European Conference on Computer Vision, pp. 480–496 (2018)
22. Wang, G., Yuan, Y., Chen, X., Li, J., Zhou, X.: Learning discriminative features with multiple granularities for person re-identification. In: ACM International Conference on Multimedia, pp. 274–282 (2018)
23. Wang, X., Girshick, R., Gupta, A., He, K.: Non-local neural networks. In: IEEE Conference on Computer Vision and Pattern Recognition, pp. 7794–7803 (2018)
24. Wei, L., Zhang, S., Gao, W., Tian, Q.: Person transfer GAN to bridge domain gap for person re-identification. In: IEEE Conference on Computer Vision and Pattern Recognition, pp. 79–88 (2018)
25. Wu, J., Liao, S., Wang, X., Yang, Y., Li, S.Z.: Clustering and dynamic sampling based unsupervised domain adaptation for person re-identification. In: IEEE International Conference on Multimedia and Expo, pp. 886–891 (2019)
26. Xia, B.N., Gong, Y., Zhang, Y., Poellabauer, C.: Second-order non-local attention networks for person re-identification. In: IEEE/CVF International Conference on Computer Vision, pp. 3760–3769 (2019)
27. Yang, F., et al.: Asymmetric co-teaching for unsupervised cross-domain person re-identification. In: AAAI Conference on Artificial Intelligence, pp. 12597–12604 (2020)
28. Zhang, X., Cao, J., Shen, C., You, M.: Self-training with progressive augmentation for unsupervised cross-domain person re-identification. In: IEEE/CVF International Conference on Computer Vision, pp. 8222–8231 (2019)
29. Zheng, L., Shen, L., Tian, L., Wang, S., Wang, J., Tian, Q.: Scalable person re-identification: a benchmark. In: IEEE international Conference on Computer Vision, pp. 1116–1124 (2015)
30. Zhong, Z., Zheng, L., Kang, G., Li, S., Yang, Y.: Random erasing data augmentation. In: AAAI Conference on Artificial Intelligence, pp. 13001–13008 (2020)

31. Zhong, Z., Zheng, L., Li, S., Yang, Y.: Generalizing a person retrieval model hetero- and homogeneously. In: Ferrari, V., Hebert, M., Sminchisescu, C., Weiss, Y. (eds.) ECCV 2018, Part XIII. LNCS, vol. 11217, pp. 176–192. Springer, Cham (2018). https://doi.org/10.1007/978-3-030-01261-8_11

32. Zhong, Z., Zheng, L., Zheng, Z., Li, S., Yang, Y.: Camera style adaptation for person re-identification. In: IEEE Conference on Computer Vision and Pattern Recognition, pp. 5157–5166 (2018)

MPNet: Multi-scale Parallel Codec Net for Medical Image Segmentation

Bin Huang[1], Jian Xue[1], Ke Lu[1,2(✉)], Yanhao Tan[1], and Yang Zhao[1]

[1] University of Chinese Academy of Sciences, Beijing, China
{huangbin181,tanyanhao15,zhaoyang196}@mails.ucas.ac.cn,
{xuejian,luk}@ucas.ac.cn
[2] Peng Cheng Laboratory, Vanke Cloud City Phase I Building 8, Xili Street, Nanshan District, Shenzhen, China

Abstract. Medical image segmentation based on the deep learning codec network achieves highly accurate segmentation. However, the structure of the tandem decoder at different scales makes it difficult for the model to segment detailed regions well. Although such detailed areas are small, they are very important in clinical medicine, and therefore one current challenge is to improve detail segmentation. In this paper, we propose a method called the MPNet (Multi-scale Parallel Codec Net), which contains a structure with parallel encoder-decoder routes that respectively comprise a scale transformer and convolution. They extract characteristics at various scales, and the feature maps of each scale are fused through an intersection module to predict the output. The parallel multi-scale routes increase the width of the model, and thus a deep architecture is not needed to obtain precise segmentation. These shallow paths independently learn semantic features at different scales and make the gradient back-propagation faster and more stable. Moreover, a new time-varying loss function is also proposed to speed up network convergence further. Experimental results on four public datasets show that the proposed method performs better than some state-of-the-art methods.

Keywords: Deep learning · Semantic segmentation · Medical image · Multi-scale Parallel Codec Net

1 Introduction

At present, deep learning models have been widely used in medical image segmentation, and the development of the codec network has promoted the development of deep learning image segmentation [5,16]. The encoding path and decoding path structure combined with a skip link structure proposed by UNet [15] has achieved great success in many medical segmentation tasks. V-Net [14] and

This research was supported by the National Natural Science Foundation of China (62027827, 62032022, 61929104, 61972375, 61671426), the Beijing Natural Science Foundation (4182071) and Scientific Research Program of Beijing Municipal Education Commission (KZ201911417048).

L. Fang et al. (Eds.): CICAI 2021, LNAI 13069, pp. 492–503, 2021.
https://doi.org/10.1007/978-3-030-93046-2_42

UNet++ [23] improves the structure based on UNet to achieve better image segmentation accuracy. All of the improved networks are based on improvements in the serial codec combined with a skip link structure and have been very successful. However, it has been found in many studies that deep codec-based CNN networks are smooth, blurry, and fuzzy [2,10,20]. That is, some information is lost on the encoding and decoding paths. To improve the network's ability to segment details, some studies on multi-scale methods have been proposed. In DeepLab [1], a space pyramid pooling module is used to further extract multi-scale information, which is achieved using hollow convolution at different rates. PSPnet [22] also uses a multi-scale method: a pyramid parsing module is applied to harvest different sub-region representations. MS-Dual-Guided [18] uses guided self-attention mechanisms to capture richer multi-scale contextual dependencies, and overcome the limitations of deep encoder-decoder architectures. SegAN [21] is based on GAN and proposes a multi-scale loss function for both segmentor and critic. The min-max adversarial learning mode is adopted to train the segment and loss networks to overcome the problems with category imbalance in medical images. However, these models are too complex for learning 3D images, and there is still room for improvement in the segmentation performance.

In this paper, an end-to-end image segmentation network named MPNet (Multi-scale Parallel Codec Net) is proposed to improve the segmentation results in the important but small detailed regions of medical images. In the proposed network, feature extraction and scale transformations are completely performed in the parallel shallow codec routes instead of a deep network codec path, which improves the ability of MPNet to learn scale. Moreover, the parallel scale learning routes can extract the semantic information at different scales. In summary, the main contributions of this paper are as follows:

- An innovative universal codec network called MPNet is proposed that can be applied to medical images to achieve end-to-end segmentation. The number of paths, scales, and internal feature extractor depths in the model are all variable and can be changed to handle different modalities of medical images.
- MPNet uses a multi-scale parallel structure instead of the classical tandem coding method. This network learns the features of each scale more independently and segments details better. In addition, the shallow parallel scale routes can avoid disappearing and exploding gradients so that the network converges to the optimal solution very quickly.
- A new time-varying loss function is proposed to help the parallel routes quickly focus on the main target regions of the image in the training process, and speed up the process of convergence further.

2   The Proposed Method

In order to improve the accuracy of image segmentation, especially the small detailed regions of the segmentation results, many adjustments have been made to the codec architecture in the proposed MPNet model.

Basically, the prediction process of image segmentation by a N-layer "codec path + skip pathways" network structure (such as UNet [15]) can be simply described as:

$$\begin{aligned}
\mathbf{m}_i &= E_i(\mathbf{m}_{i-1}) \\
\mathbf{m}'_{i-1} &= D_i(\mathbf{m}'_i \oplus \mathbf{m}_i) \\
\mathbf{m}_0 &= E_0(I) \\
O &= D_0(\mathbf{m}'_0)
\end{aligned} \tag{1}$$

where $\mathbf{m}_i$ and $\mathbf{m}'_i$ denote the feature maps of the i-th layer on the encoding path and decoding path respectively, E_i and D_i are the convolution operation of the encoder and decoder of the i-th layer, $\oplus$ denotes the concatenation layer, I and O are the input and output images. These equations reveal that the feature maps in the codec framework are computed synchronously, that is, in the process of gradient back-propagation, the derivative of D_i contains the derivative of D_{i-1}, and the derivative of E_i contains the derivatives of E_{i+1} and D_i. This synchronous computing makes information unavoidably lost in the gradient back-propagation process, because $\mathbf{m}_i$ and $\mathbf{m}'_i$ themselves represent semantic features at different scales.

The proposed MPNet is constructed by multi-scale parallel codec routes, for which the feature maps $\mathbf{m}_s$ are taken out corresponding to the scale space $\mathbf{S}$, instead of $\mathbf{m}_i$ for the i-th layer in the traditional network structure. By this way, $\mathbf{m}_s$ are learned by MPNet in parallel to avoid losing semantic information at different scales. Moreover, scale transformation is performed on the input to obtain feature maps of n scales independently, and feature extraction is performed on each scale separately. Finally, the results of extraction are concatenated together and the output is predicted. The overall prediction process can be described as:

$$O = \mathcal{F}[H_{s_0}(\mathbf{m}_{s_0}), ..., H_{s_i}(\mathbf{m}_{s_i}), ..., H_{s_n}(\mathbf{m}_{s_n})] \tag{2}$$

where H_{s_i} represents the feature extraction procedure on each scale $s_i \in \mathbf{S}$ and $\mathcal{F}$ represents the multi-scale intersection convolution. By this formula, MPNet independently processes the semantic information at different scales, which can improve the accuracy of the segmentation, especially the details of the segmented regions, compared with conventional codec networks.

2.1   The Overall Network Structure

Figure 1 provides a schematic representation of the proposed MPNet applied to 3D segmentation. The MPNet consists of two main parts.

The first part contains multi-scale parallel codec routes. Input images are respectively fed into the convolutional layers at the beginning of the parallel routes. These layers are responsible for converting the input image into a multi-channel feature map and preparing for the training of the multi-scale parallel routes. The input image and output feature maps of the routes have a consistent shape. The feature learning of the determined scale is completed within each route, which contains an encoder, a decoder, and a feature learner.

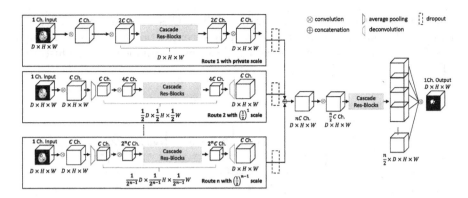

Fig. 1. Network structure of the MPNet for 3D medical image segmentation.

These independent structures can extract features at different scales within parallel routes, and such structures also provide good dynamic adjustment, that is, the model can improve segmentation performance by adjusting the parameters of a route individually or by adding/deleting a route.

The second part is an intersection convolution and output part: it concatenates the output of the routes and performs a convolution to fuse the semantics at different scales. The final prediction is output by intersection convolution module.

2.2 Multi-scale Parallel Codec Routes

The network model contains multi-scale parallel codec routes. Their encoders, decoders, and feature learners are independent of each other, and the scale is determined by the convolution kernel of the respective encoders and decoders per the actual situation.

The encoder consists of a pooling layer and a convolutional layer. In addition to dealing with the role of scale, the convolutional layer needs to transform channels to extend the ability to learn the features of the routes. The decoder is composed of a transposed convolutional layer which also needs to transform channels to ensure that the output channels of routes are the same.

The feature learner is composed of cascading residual blocks proposed by He et al. in [4]. The number of cascades can be adjusted according to the actual situation, although cascading many more modules will increase the computational complexity and the convergence difficulty of the network while hardly improving network performance. This structure can learn residual information and has good gradient conduction while maintaining a relatively shallow structure, which is conducive to gradient conduction in parallel structures and makes it easier for training at all scales to converge.

The number of cascades of the feature learner determines the depth of the route. In MPNet, each route should maintain a shallow depth so that the scale learner can cover all receptive fields from small to large. In addition, the shallow structure will not have a strong learning ability. This can cause a scale learner in a parallel structure pay more attention to the extraction for self-scale feature. Therefore, in most cases, two cascading blocks are recommended, as illustrated in Fig. 2.

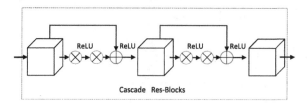

Fig. 2. The recommend feature learners involve two cascading residual blocks.

This structure is used as a feature extractor to accelerate convergence. In particular, this part has one original scale learning route using special "encoder and decoder", which are convolutional layers with kernel size of 1 to carry out convolution learning at the original scale. The independent learning at the original scale improves the segmentation of the details. We prove in the experimental results that learning using a small receptive field substantially improves the details in the results, and learning using a large receptive field substantially improves global consistency.

In these multi-scale parallel codec routes, a wider channel should be used at a smaller scale to maintain similar parameter counting and learning capabilities. The up-sampler of each path will convolve the semantic learning results into a feature map of the same size to ensure that the semantic information at each scale is equal. This important feature enables MPNet to have a strong learning ability for semantics at various scales. It also substantially improves the segmentation of detailed regions.

2.3   Intersection Convolution

The processing results of the multi-scale parallel codec routes are feature maps with the same shape and number of channels. Therefore, when fusing feature maps, they have the same number of parameters, and thus the network has consistent feature learning capabilities for the semantics at different scales.

To improve computational efficiency, the feature maps are concatenated together and one layer of convolution is applied to distill a feature map with fewer channels. Further convolution is performed using the cascading ResNet blocks to extract the fused features. The ResNet blocks are also cascaded here to reduce the depth of the network and the difficulty of training.

The final predicted image is then output using fully connected layers based on convolution with a kernel size of 1. A fully connected layer is used to reduce the number of dimensions and map the learned "distributed feature representation" to the label space. Similar applications have been used in the method described in [9,11,19].

2.4   Time-Varying Loss Function

The loss function used for this model is a mixed loss function combining time-varying Dice loss and cross entropy loss [3], which can be written as: $L_{\text{total}} = \alpha L_{\text{Dice}}(t) + \beta L_{\text{bce}}$, where α and β are hyper-parameters. α and β are recommended to take empirical values of 0.8 and 0.4 respectively, and can be fine-tuned for particular scenarios. Dice loss was proposed in [14], which focuses well on true positives, but lacks the ability to correct false negatives. The utilization of Binary Cross-Entropy (BCE) loss L_{bce} addresses this problem. The optimal selection of the hyper-parameters is related to the level of balance in the data categories. When categories are balanced, such as in larger organ segmentation tasks, the BCE loss function will play a greater role, whereas in tasks with a small target area such as lesion segmentation, the Dice loss performs better.

In this paper, the Dice loss function is further improved by adding a time-varying factor $s(t)$, and the new Dice loss is written as:

$$L_{\text{Dice}}(t) = 1 - \frac{2 \sum_{i=1}^{P} (p_i q_i + s(t))}{\sum_{i=1}^{P} p_i^2 + \sum_{i=1}^{P} q_i^2 + s(t)} \tag{3}$$

where p_i and q_i are the voxels in the predicted image and annotated image respectively, and P is the total number of the voxels. The time-varying factor $s(t)$ is defined as:

$$s(t) = \begin{cases} \dfrac{s_0}{10^{\lambda t}} & \text{if } a(t-1) > a' \\[2ex] s(t-1) & \text{otherwise} \end{cases} \tag{4}$$

where s_0 is the initial value for the iterative computation of $s(t)$ which can be chosen in $[10^{-2}, 10^{-5}]$ according to the significance of the target region. λ is a hyper-parameter to adjust the value of t which is usually set to 10^{-1} empirically. $a(t)$ is the accuracy at time t on validation set with size N, which is defined as:

$$a(t) = \frac{\sum_{i=1}^{N} (1 - L_{\text{Dice}}^i(t))}{N} \tag{5}$$

At the end of some training epoch when a exceeds the threshold a', $s(t)$ will be updated to a smaller value defined in (4). The factor $s(t)$ has two main effects: 1) In the early stage of training, $s(t)$ plays a dominant role in the calculation for smoothing the gradients around the points of extreme cases (for example, the voxels p and q which are both very close to 0). Moreover, $s(t)$ can help MPNet automatically ignore some target regions in the image that are difficult to be optimized; 2) In the later stage of training, the value of $s(t)$ is almost 0 which does not affect the results anymore, and the training process is also close to convergence. Therefore, the target areas with "prominent features" are computed prior to other areas of the image, and the process of convergence is faster and more stable.

3   Experiments

The proposed method of this paper was implemented based on PyTorch, and two Titan V GPUs were used to train the network and carry out the experiments.

MPNet performs better on several open datasets than some state-of-the-art methods. The experiments were based on four public datasets: CHAOS [8], Brain Tumor (Phase 1) [17], Prostate (Phase 1) [17], and Fluo-C3DH-A549-SIM [13]. These datasets include computed tomography, nuclear magnetic resonance imaging, and electron microscope imaging, and include the tasks of lesion segmentation and organ segmentation. These labeled data sets were divided into training and test sets at a ratio of 8:2. The networks for comparison were trained on the training set and their performance was tested on the test set.

Table 1. Comparison on the segmentation performance of the methods.

Datasets	Methods	Average dice	mAP
Brain tumor	nnU-Net [6]	0.6771	–
	MS-Dual-Guided (2D) [18]	0.8037	–
	V-Net [14]	0.8495	0.8510
	SegAN (2D) [21]	0.85	–
	UNet++ [23]	**0.8944**	0.8918
	Ours	0.8902	**0.8989**
Prostate	nnU-Net [6]	0.7581	–
	V-Net [14]	0.7976	0.7433
	UNet++ [23]	0.8220	0.7838
	Ours	**0.8263**	**0.7906**
CHAOS	V-Net [14]	0.8639	0.8075
	MS-Dual-Guided (2D) [18]	0.8675	–
	UNet++ [23]	0.9074	0.8646
	Ours	**0.9112**	**0.8783**
Cells	V-Net [14]	0.9689	0.9224
	UNet++ [23]	0.9684	0.9546
	Ours	**0.9710**	**0.9554**

Some experimental results are shown in Table 1. We reproduced the V-Net and UNet++ methods as comparison methods in our experiments. In addition, all factors not related to the models such as preprocessing (e.g., resizing and normalization) and training, (e.g., experimental installations and the optimizer setting) were the same. The partial results of some methods (e.g. nnU-Net, MS-Dual-Guided and SegAN) are directly taken from [6,18,21] (results of some methods for some of the datasets have not been reported in these papers). With respect to the Dice coefficient and mAP, MPNet obtains much better results than most state-of-the-art methods. Moreover, the main improvement is in the segmentation of small detailed regions, as can be seen in Fig. 3.

At the same time, MPNet is easier to train than V-Net and UNet++. Figure 4 shows the curves of the Dice coefficient with respect to the test set and epochs.

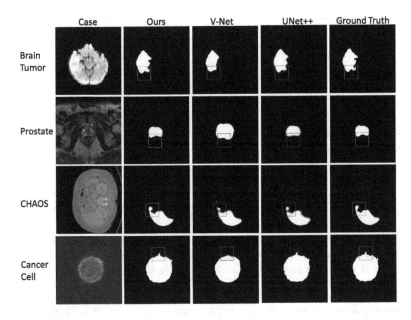

Fig. 3. The comparison of some segmentation results on small and detailed areas performed by the proposed MPNet and other conventional methods on four public datasets. The colored rectangles illustrate the segmentation results of the small detailed regions by different methods, which indicate the superiority of the proposed method (red rectangles indicate the examples of other methods with less precision). (Color figure online)

In most tasks, MPNet needs fewer epochs to converge to the optimal point. This proves that multi-scale routes with shallow learners can effectively and quickly learn the features at each scale of the image.

The route dealing with small-scale feature maps has big receptive fields and pays more attention to the overall information, whereas the modules dealing with large-scale feature maps have small receptive fields and pay more attention to local details, as pointed out by [7,12]. In the experimental models based on U-Net, a $\frac{1}{2}$ scale feature map was obtained using sampling or pooling with a convolution kernel size of 2 in the encoding path. Moreover, on the i-th layer of the network, the corresponding scale is $\frac{1}{2^i}$. Therefore, to implement a training process with the same scale, five routes were used in MPNet and 2^{n-1} was used as the codec kernel size in the n-th route. This obtains a $\frac{1}{2^{n-1}}$ scale feature map after the encoder, which is then output to the original scale by the corresponding decoder after passing through the cascading residual blocks learner. The receptive field size of the feature learner ranges from 9 to 176 before passing through the decoders, as shown in Table 2.

Though the encoders of the improved models based on U-Net have a wider range of receptive fields, for example, the receptive field of the "L-Stages" of V-Net ranges from 5 to 372 as reported in [14], these tandem structures cannot learn

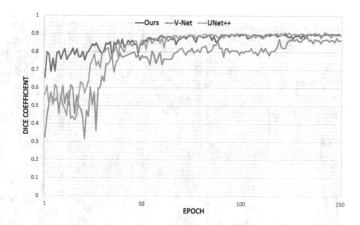

Fig. 4. Curves showing the change of Dice coefficient on the test set as the epochs increasing (in the first 150 epochs). Obviously, MPNet benefits from the parallel shallow structure, which is easier to converge and thus easier to be trained.

Table 2. Theoretical receptive fields of the parallel routes using two cascaded Res-Block feature learners. The column "**RF1**" shows the receptive field of the feature map after passing through the encoder and the column "**RF2**" shows the receptive field after passing through the feature learners (before decoder). In this way, MPNet realizes a feature learner covering a range of receptive fields from small to large.

Route	RF1	Channels	RF2
1	$1 \times 1 \times 1$	16	$9 \times 9 \times 9$
2	$2 \times 2 \times 2$	32	$22 \times 22 \times 22$
3	$4 \times 4 \times 4$	64	$44 \times 44 \times 44$
4	$8 \times 8 \times 8$	128	$88 \times 88 \times 88$
5	$16 \times 16 \times 16$	256	$176 \times 176 \times 176$

the information separately, and the biggest receptive field is much larger than the input image itself. Moreover, larger receptive field means that a lot of edge features and complement zeros are incorporated in the convolution process, and these almost useless values are disadvantageous to feature extraction. However, a more compact receptive field makes MPNet to learn semantic features better at various scales. Experience shows that parallel structures combined with compact receptive fields retain more detailed semantic features while training and perform better than other kinds of structures.

Experiments were carried out to reveal the contribution of each route to the segmentation results, as shown in Fig. 5. In the task of brain tumor segmentation, where the location of the target area is random and the details of the target area are rich, we removed the 1st original scale route and the 5th large-receptive-field route, and obtained average Dice coefficients of 0.8861 and 0.8750 on the test set, respectively, whereas the Dice coefficient of the complete five-way model is

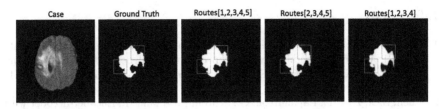

Fig. 5. Some experimental results for the case of Brain Tumor segmentation. The 4th and 5th sub-figures (labeled with "Routes [2, 3, 4, 5]" and "Routes [1, 2, 3, 4]" on the top) illustrate the segmentation results by removing the 1st route and the 5th route respectively. The colored rectangles show the difference on the detailed areas of the segmentation result. (Color figure online)

0.8902. It can be inferred that the original scale improves the detail segmentation, whereas the 5th largest scale has a substantial improvement on overall segmentation. In the absence of a large-receptive-field route, the convolution of a smaller receptive field will be distracted from processing the overall information, and therefore the loss of the 5th route will lead to a large performance loss. In contrast, in the absence of the 1st route, the mere loss of detailed information will not lead to much difference in the metrics. As can also be seen from the segmentation results, the segmentation loss of the model without the 1st route is reflected in the detail areas. This proves that the parallel routes of MPNet have a more independent ability to learn semantic information at various scales.

4 Conclusion

The MPNet model proposed in this paper adopts a multi-scale parallel structure in which each scale-learning route independently completes the encoding and decoding and learns the image features of the corresponding scale. The aim is to improve the overall image segmentation and detail segmentation effects simultaneously. The routes use a shallow cascade ResNet block as the feature learner, which maintains good gradient conductivity, and with the help of the time-varying loss function, the network can quickly converge to a local optimal point. In an actual scenario, the number of routes of the network and the depth of the learning module can be dynamically adjusted depending on the available computing resources. Compared with the baseline method, the proposed method performs better on public datasets and can be applied to a variety of segmentation tasks in practical scenarios. In the experiments, we proved that the parallel structure and small receptive field route strongly contribute to the segmentation of small detailed regions, which will be of great significance to future research in medical image segmentation models.

However, there are still points that can be studied in MPNet. In general, choosing more routes at different scales will improve segmentation. However, considering that computing resources are limited, how to choose the appropriate width and depth of the routes in various tasks of the model remains to be explored.

References

1. Chen, L.C., Papandreou, G., Kokkinos, I., Murphy, K., Yuille, A.L.: DeepLab: semantic image segmentation with deep convolutional nets, atrous convolution, and fully connected CRFs. IEEE Trans. Pattern Anal. Mach. Intell. **40**(4), 834–848 (2017)
2. Chen, L.C., Zhu, Y., Papandreou, G., Schroff, F., Adam, H.: Encoder-decoder with atrous separable convolution for semantic image segmentation. In: Proceedings of the European Conference on Computer Vision (ECCV), pp. 801–818 (2018)
3. Drozdzal, M., Vorontsov, E., Chartrand, G., Kadoury, S., Pal, C.: The importance of skip connections in biomedical image segmentation. In: Carneiro, G., et al. (eds.) LABELS/DLMIA -2016. LNCS, vol. 10008, pp. 179–187. Springer, Cham (2016). https://doi.org/10.1007/978-3-319-46976-8_19
4. He, K., Zhang, X., Ren, S., Sun, J.: Deep residual learning for image recognition. In: 2016 IEEE Conference on Computer Vision and Pattern Recognition (CVPR), pp. 770–778 (2016). https://doi.org/10.1109/CVPR.2016.90
5. Hesamian, M.H., Jia, W., He, X., Kennedy, P.: Deep learning techniques for medical image segmentation: achievements and challenges. J. Digit. Imaging **32**(4), 582–596 (2019)
6. Isensee, F., et al.: nnU-Net: self-adapting framework for U-Net-based medical image segmentation. arXiv preprint arXiv:1809.10486 (2018)
7. Jia, Y., Huang, C., Darrell, T.: Beyond spatial pyramids: receptive field learning for pooled image features. In: 2012 IEEE Conference on Computer Vision and Pattern Recognition, pp. 3370–3377. IEEE (2012)
8. Kavur, A.E., Selver, M.A., Dicle, O., Barış, M., Gezer, N.S.: CHAOS - combined (CT-MR) healthy abdominal organ segmentation challenge data, April 2019. https://doi.org/10.5281/zenodo.3362844
9. Krizhevsky, A., Sutskever, I., Hinton, G.E.: ImageNet classification with deep convolutional neural networks. Commun. ACM **60**(6), 84–90 (2017)
10. Lin, G., Milan, A., Shen, C., Reid, I.: RefineNet: multi-path refinement networks for high-resolution semantic segmentation. In: Proceedings of the IEEE Conference on Computer Vision and Pattern Recognition, pp. 1925–1934 (2017)
11. Long, J., Shelhamer, E., Darrell, T.: Fully convolutional networks for semantic segmentation. In: Proceedings of the IEEE Conference on Computer Vision and Pattern Recognition, pp. 3431–3440 (2015)
12. Luo, W., Li, Y., Urtasun, R., Zemel, R.: Understanding the effective receptive field in deep convolutional neural networks. Adv. Neural. Inf. Process. Syst. **29**, 4898–4906 (2016)
13. Maška, M., et al.: A benchmark for comparison of cell tracking algorithms. Bioinformatics **30**(11), 1609–1617 (2014)
14. Milletari, F., Navab, N., Ahmadi, S.A.: V-net: fully convolutional neural networks for volumetric medical image segmentation. In: 2016 Fourth International Conference on 3D Vision (3DV), pp. 565–571. IEEE (2016)
15. Ronneberger, O., Fischer, P., Brox, T.: U-net: convolutional networks for biomedical image segmentation. In: Navab, N., Hornegger, J., Wells, W.M., Frangi, A.F. (eds.) MICCAI 2015. LNCS, vol. 9351, pp. 234–241. Springer, Cham (2015). https://doi.org/10.1007/978-3-319-24574-4_28
16. Shvets, A.A., Rakhlin, A., Kalinin, A.A., Iglovikov, V.I.: Automatic instrument segmentation in robot-assisted surgery using deep learning. In: 2018 17th IEEE International Conference on Machine Learning and Applications (ICMLA), pp. 624–628. IEEE (2018)

17. Simpson, A.L., et al.: A large annotated medical image dataset for the development and evaluation of segmentation algorithms. arXiv preprint arXiv:1902.09063 (2019)
18. Sinha, A., Dolz, J.: Multi-scale self-guided attention for medical image segmentation. IEEE J. Biomed. Health Inform. **25**, 121–130 (2020)
19. Szegedy, C., et al.: Going deeper with convolutions. In: 2015 IEEE Conference on Computer Vision and Pattern Recognition (CVPR), pp. 1–9 (2015). https://doi. org/10.1109/CVPR.2015.7298594
20. Wang, G., Sun, C., Sowmya, A.: ERL-net: entangled representation learning for single image de-raining. In: 2019 IEEE/CVF International Conference on Computer Vision (ICCV), pp. 5643–5651 (2019). https://doi.org/10.1109/ICCV.2019. 00574
21. Xue, Y., Xu, T., Zhang, H., Long, L.R., Huang, X.: SegAN: adversarial network with multi-scale l 1 loss for medical image segmentation. Neuroinformatics **16**(3), 383–392 (2018)
22. Zhao, H., Shi, J., Qi, X., Wang, X., Jia, J.: Pyramid scene parsing network. In: Proceedings of the IEEE Conference on Computer Vision and Pattern Recognition, pp. 2881–2890 (2017)
23. Zhou, Z., Rahman Siddiquee, M.M., Tajbakhsh, N., Liang, J.: UNet++: a nested U-net architecture for medical image segmentation. In: Stoyanov, D., et al. (eds.) DLMIA/ML-CDS -2018. LNCS, vol. 11045, pp. 3–11. Springer, Cham (2018). https://doi.org/10.1007/978-3-030-00889-5_1

Part-Aware Spatial-Temporal Graph Convolutional Network for Group Activity Recognition

Qi Wang, Xianglong Lang, Ye Xiang, and Lifang Wu[✉]

Faculty of Information Technology, Beijing University of Technology, Beijing, China
lfwu@bjut.edu.cn

Abstract. Group activity recognition, a challenging task that requires not only recognizing the individual actions of each person but also inferring relationships among persons, has received considerable attention. Previous methods infer coarse-level relations based on holistic features of individuals. This paper goes one step further beyond existing methods by learning part-aware spatial-temporal graph convolutional network (PSTGCN) to model fine-grained relations using part-level features. The PSTGCN includes two core graphs, the locally-connected graph, and the fully-connected graph. The locally-connected graph in which all parts of the same person are connected mines structural information of individuals. The fully-connected graph in which all parts of persons are connected extracts the latent relationships among individuals in part-level. Extensive experiments on two widely-used datasets: the Volleyball dataset and the Collective Activity dataset, are conducted to evaluate our PSTGCN, and the improved performance demonstrates the effectiveness of our approach. Visualizations of the part-based relation graph and the group-level features indicate our method can capture the discriminative information for group activity recognition.

Keywords: Group activity recognition · Part-aware · Graph convolutional network

1 Introduction

Group activity recognition aims to understand what activity a group of people performs, which has drawn increasing attention from both industry and academia as it has many practical applications such as sports video analysis, video surveillance and video retrieval [7, 12, 24, 29].

The earlier approaches tackle down this task mostly based on hand-crafted features of persons, which are then processed by graphical probability models to capture interaction relationships among persons [16, 17]. With the recent impressive success of CNN/RNN in the field of computer vision [4, 10, 18, 19],

---

Q. Wang and X. Lang—Indicates equal contribution.

© Springer Nature Switzerland AG 2021
L. Fang et al. (Eds.): CICAI 2021, LNAI 13069, pp. 504–515, 2021.
https://doi.org/10.1007/978-3-030-93046-2_43

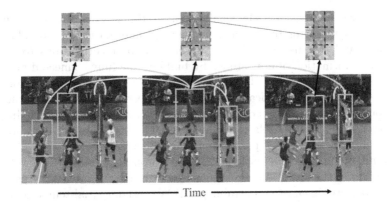

Fig. 1. Left spike in the volleyball game. For the spiking player in the orange bounding box, we can see his dynamic changes across frames. The dotted cells denote the body parts. The spatial and temporal dependencies (red lines) among body parts provide discriminative information for individual representation. Meanwhile, context information among persons (green lines) is also a critical cue. (Color figure online)

several deep learning based methods are proposed and made significant progress on group activity recognition [13,14,30]. Typically, these methods follow a two-stage pipeline, which extracts individual-level features by a convolutional neural network (CNN) firstly and then aggregates these individual-level features into the group-level features using a basic pooling strategy. To model the temporal dynamics, the recurrent neural network (RNN) is exploited to capture temporal evolution of individual-level features and group-level features [6,30], without considering the relations among individuals.

Recently, some works [8,28] adopt advanced relation modeling technique, such as graph convolutional network (GCN) [15] and Transformer [25], to model the interaction relations among individuals and achieve promising performance. Despite the progress of the existing methods, they utilize holistic appearance features to construct relation representations and neglect the spatiotemporal part-level dependencies. As shown in Fig. 1, the person who is spiking the ball must swing up the arm over time to spike the ball. The part-level features of an individual determine action. Meanwhile, a group of people cooperates to complete the activity. The interactions among persons bring context information in the scene. Recent approaches often construct relations based on coarse-level features which cannot effectively represent the local details information of individuals to some extent, leading to the limited performance of individual action and group activity recognition.

To this end, we propose a part-aware spatial-temporal graph convolutional network (PSTGCN) for group activity recognition, which can take advantage of two fine-grained part-level relationships, including intra- and inter-actor part interactions. Specifically, we decompose the feature maps of each actor extract by RoIAlign into a set of part features, which can preserve the spatial pattern of appearance. We construct the locally-connected part graph by connecting all parts of the same actor to model the structural information of individual. On the other hand, we also consider the inter-actor part correlations to provide contextual information of appearance by building the fully-connected graph for each part of different actors. To capture temporal context information of video frames, we further extend locally- and fully-connected part graphs to the temporal domain by connecting nodes in the graph across different frames. Inspired by the excellent ability of relation modeling of GCN [15], we use it to infer the spatial-temporal relations of part-level features automatically.

Overall, the major contributions are: (i) we propose a unified framework that jointly captures the fine-grained relationships for intra- and inter-actor parts and is able to perform in end-to-end training. (ii) We design spatial-temporal locally- and fully-connected part graphs to model the potential relations of different part features across frames, providing more discriminative individual representations and context information for group activity recognition. (iii) We conduct experiments on two widely-used datasets [5,14], on which our proposed method outperforms state-of-the-art approaches and demonstrates the effectiveness.

2   Related Work

Initially, the traditional methods for group activity recognition relied on hand-crafted features and utilized probability graph models to capture the structures of group activity. Choi et al. [5] introduced a spatiotemporal local (STL) descriptor to capture the posture and spatial-temporal distribution of individuals in the video. Amer et al. [1] proposed a AND-OR graph to model objects occurring in the scene, individual action and group activity simultaneously. However, these methods require strong prior knowledge and have limited representation ability.

Later, the deep learning based methods [3,6,14,22,23] have demonstrated impressive results on group activity recognition. Ibrahim et al. [14] proposed a two-stage hierarchical deep temporal model where the first stage LSTM capture individual-level dynamics, and the group-level dynamics are modeled in the second stage. Tang et al. [23] exploited LSTM to model individual action and suppressed irrelevant motions in videos. However, the methods mentioned above ignore the relations among individuals.

Recently, several works attempt to model relationships in the group activity. Qi et al. [21] proposed an attentive semantic recurrent neural network to build the temporal and spatial relationships. Hu et al. [11] applied deep reinforcement learning for relation learning and proposed two agents to refine the relation graph. Wu et al. [28] proposed to build relation graphs by the visual similarity and location of actors in the scene and refine features of actors by GCN. [20] proposed a graph attention interaction model with graph attention blocks to explore potential interaction relationships between individuals and subgroups. Gavrilyuk et al. [8] utilized the transformer to learn interactions between the actors and adaptively extract the critical information for group activity recognition.

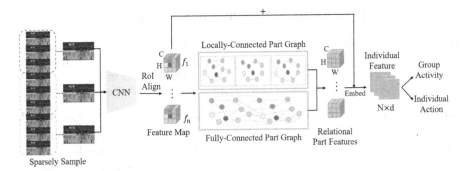

Fig. 2. The proposed part-aware spatial-temporal graph convolutional network

3 Method

3.1 Overall Framework

The existing methods construct relationships based on coarse-level features and are limited to represent the detailed information of persons. In this paper, we aim at modeling fine-grained relationships based on part-level features to explore intra- and inter-actor correlations. The framework is shown in Fig. 2. Our method takes three steps: (i) the actors are decomposed into a set of parts; (ii) we design two kinds of graphs, namely locally-connected graph and fully-connected graph. The locally-connected graph models the structural information of different parts for each individual. The fully-connected graph explores the interactions among parts of different individuals, providing part-level interaction context information. (iii) we perform relational reasoning and inference for individual action and group activity recognition.

3.2 Part-Level Feature Extraction

Given a video sequence with bounding boxes indicating the locations of actors, we first divide the video sequence into K segments and then sample K frames uniformly from K segments. Then we adopt Inception-v3 to extract feature map for each frame and utilize RoIAlign to slice out individual feature maps $F = \{f^{(n)}\}_{n=1}^{N}$, where N is the number of actors in the scene and the size of feature map is $H \times W$. Previous methods process the feature maps by fully-connected layer to extract holistic feature vector and consider the actor as a whole. Unlike these methods, we decompose the feature map and take each grid in the $H \times W$ feature maps as a part-level features, which preserves the local appearance information. We denote the part features of n-th actor by $f^{(n)} = \{f_p^{(n)}\}_{p=1}^{P}$, where $P = H \times W$ is the number of parts of an actor; $f_p^{(n)} \in \mathcal{R}^D$ is the p-th part of the n-th actor; D is the dimension of part features.

3.3   Building Part-Aware Spatial-Temporal Graphs

Graph neural network has been successfully applied to relational reasoning and previous work has proved it effective. Inspired by these works, we use graph structure to establish the relationships among part-level features.

Graph Definition. In our graph, the nodes are the set of actors' part features $V = \{f_p^{(n)} | n = 1, \ldots, N; p = 1, \ldots, P\}$, where $f_p^{(n)}$ is the p-th part feature of the n-th actor, N is the number of actors, P is the number of parts for an actor. $G \in \mathcal{R}^{(N \times P) \times (N \times P)}$ is the adjacency matrix where each element represents the pairwise relationship between part features. We represent the pairwise relations between every two part features in the graph as follows:

$$G_{ij} = g\left(f_i, f_j\right) \tag{1}$$

where $g()$ denotes the relation function, G_{ij} represents the importance of the j-th part feature f_j to the i-th part feature f_i. In the experiment, We attempt the dot-product and embedded dot-product as [15] introduced to compute relation values.

Locally-Connected Part Graph (LCPG). In the existing methods, the inferior performance of individual action recognition prevents further improvement of group activity recognition. However, these methods failed to consider the structural information of actors which can bring discriminative information for individual representation. In order to explore the interactions between different parts of the same individual, we propose a locally-connected part graph in which part features within the same actor are connected while the part features between different actors are disconnected. Firstly, we construct an original graph G_{ori} following the method introduced above. Then we impose constraints M_{self} to the original graph and use the softmax function to normalize the relation values so that the sum of all relation values for each part features is 1. It can be written as:

$$G_{self} = softmax\left(G_{ori} \odot M_{self}\right) \tag{2}$$

where $\odot$ stands for Hadamard product, M_{self} is a binary mask with the same size of G_{ori}. If part region i and part region j belong to the same actor, $M_{self}^{ij} = 1$, and vice versa.

Fully-Connected Part Graph (FCPG). Previous approaches model relations among actors using the holistic appearance features which lose the local detailed information to some extent and will bring redundancy in the message passing. Motivated by the Non-Local network [27] in which the feature at a target position is refined by a weighted sum of features from all positions, we propose a fully-connected part graph. The objective of the fully-connected part graph is to explore the interaction relationships among individuals in a fine-grained way.

The original graph G_{ori} is constructed following the method introduced in graph definition. Then we apply softmax function to normalize the relation values. The fully-connected part graph can be computed as $G_{fully} = softmax\,(G_{ori})$.

Temporal Modeling. Temporal information is important for activity recognition. We now extend our model to the temporal domain. We follow the sparse sampling strategy in [26]. We divide the video sequence into $K = 3$ segments and then sample 3 frames uniformly. Then we build spatial-temporal graphs upon part features of actors in the scene across frames. In the spatial-temporal graphs, we take totally $N \times K \times P$ part features of all actors as nodes, where N is the number of actors in the scene and P denotes the number of parts for each actor. Following the way of building the graph we previously mentioned, the spatial-temporal LCPG and FCPG can be created.

3.4   Inference on Graphs

After the construction of LCPG and FCPG, we perform relational inferring on graphs. Inspired by [15], we employ GCN, a feature refining structure, to pass message across part-level features and output the high-level relational features. The formulation of conventional GCN can be written as:

$$X^{(l)} = \sigma\left(GX^{(l-1)}W^{(l)}\right) \tag{3}$$

where G is the adjacent matrix of graph, $X^{(l)}$ and $W^{(l)}$ is the features of nodes and the learnable weight matrix in the l-th layer. σ denotes the ReLU activation function.

Our PSTGCN includes two kinds of graph structures: locally- and fully connected graphs. According to our experiment, we use late fusion and adopt max pooling as a fusion function:

$$F^{(l)} = maxpool\left(\sigma\left(G_{locally}F^{(l-1)}W^{(l)}_{locally}\right), \sigma\left(G_{fully}F^{(l-1)}W^{(l)}_{fully}\right)\right) \tag{4}$$

where $F^{(l)} \in \mathcal{R}^{(N \times K \times P) \times D}$ is the part features of individuals in the l-th layer, N is the number of actors, K denotes the number of frames, P denotes the number of parts, D is the dimension of features, $G_{locally}$, $G_{fully} \in \mathcal{R}^{(N \times K \times P) \times (N \times K \times P)}$ are the matrix representation of locally- and fully-connected graph, $W^{(l)}_{locally}$, $W^{(l)}_{fully} \in \mathcal{R}^{D \times D}$ are the layer-specific learnable weight matrix of locally- and fully-connected part graph, respectively. In the experiment, we also explore other fusion functions.

Inspired by residual network [9], the relational part features are fused with original part features by summation to form the final actor part representation. We then embed the part representations into individual representations with d dimensions for each actor. The activity representation is obtained by max pooling among individuals. Two classifiers are used for individual action and group activity recognition. The whole framework can be trained in an end-to-end way with backpropagation and standard cross entropy loss.

4   Experiment

4.1   Datasets and Settings

Datasets. The Volleyball dataset (VD) [14] contains 55 videos and 4830 clips, with 3493 for training and 1337 for testing. The middle frame of each clip is annotated with bounding box of players, individual actions from 9 action labels and one of 8 group activity labels. For the unannotated frames, we use the tracklets provided by [3]. Following previous methods, we use a temporal window of 10 frames to train the network, which corresponds to 5 frames before the middle frame and 4 frames after.

The Collective Activity dataset (CAD) [5] is composed of 44 videos sequences from 5 group activity labels (crossing, waiting, queueing, walking and talking). The training set and testing set split follows [21]. The middle frame of every ten frames is annotated with group activity label, bounding box of individuals and their action labels (N.A., crossing, waiting, queueing, walking and talking).

4.2   Implement Details

We employ inception-v3 network as backbone. Besides, we also experimented with VGG networks to compare with other works fairly. The number of sampled frames $K = 3$. RoIAlign is used to extract feature map of individuals with size of $H = W = 3$. The dimension d of feature which is used for classification is set to 1024. We adopt the stochastic gradient descent with ADAM optimizer with fixed hyperparameters to $\beta_1 = 0.9$, $\beta_2 = 0.999$, $\epsilon = 10^{-8}$. For the Volleyball dataset, we train the network in 200 epochs using minibatch size of 4 and the learning rate ranging from 0.0003 to 0.00005. For the Collective Activity dataset, we use batch size of 12 with a learning rate of 0.00001 and train the network in 50 epochs.

4.3   Ablation Studies

In this section, we will introduce the ablation study of the proposed method on the Volleyball dataset to understand the contributions of each component. We use group activity recognition accuracy as the evaluation metric.

Part-Level Relation. Firstly, we explore the effect of two kinds of part graphs and different relations functions to calculate relation values. As shown in Table 1, based on the single frame, the Non-Part-Aware model performs group activity and individual actions on original appearance features without part-aware graph reasoning. We can find that group activity recognition accuracy can be improved by adding the LCPG and FCPG in the Non-part Aware model. The Non-Part-Aware model ignores the rich part-level interactions and results in a performance drop. Compared with dot-product, embedding dot-product can get better results on two types of graphs.

Table 1. Comparison of two types of graphs using different relation functions

Method	Accuracy
Non-part-aware	90.3
LCPG-dot-product	91.2
LCPG-embedded dot-product	**91.3**
FCPG-dot-product	91.3
FCPG-embedded dot-product	**91.5**

Fusion of Graphs. We further study the strategy of fusing two kinds of graphs. The results are presented in Table 2. Our model reaches the best performance when using the late fusion by max pooling which can preserve significant values of the two types of relational part features. It also indicated that the two types of graphs, LCPG and FCPG, can complement each other.

Table 2. Performance comparison of different fusion strategies

Method	Accuracy
Early fusion	91.5
Late fusion-sum	92.0
Late fusion-concat	91.7
Late fusion-max pooling	**92.3**

Temporal Modeling. Previous experiments are based on a single frame without considering temporal information. Now, we investigate the temporal modeling of our part-aware graph model. The results are list in Table 3. We have the similar observation as [28], the sparsely sampling frames is better than using densely frames because of the limited size and diversity of existing datasets. We build spatial-temporal graphs which further improve the performance to 92.7%.

Table 3. Comparison of different temporal modeling strategies

Method	Accuracy
Single frame	92.3
Densely frames (10 frames)	92.5
Sparsely sample frames (3 frames)	92.6
Spatial-temporal graphs (3 frames)	**92.7**

4.4   Comparison with the State of the Art

Results on the Volleyball Dataset. Table 4 shows the comparison of our model with other state-of-the-art methods on the volleyball datasets. For a fair comparison, we only report results of some methods [2,8] with the input of RGB frames. We provide the results using three different backbones, Inception-v3, VGG16, and VGG19. Our method surpasses other existing methods and improves group activity recognition performance to 93.2%. ARG [28] and GAIM [20] are both GCN based methods to capture the interaction information between individuals. However, they only use coarse-level features and are limited to represent the detailed information of persons while our model is able to capture fine-grained relationships, which improves the performance. Meanwhile, we also achieve the best performance in individual action recognition since our LCPG can explore structured information for individuals which improves the discrimination of individual representation.

Table 4. Comparison with state-of-the-arts on Volleyball dataset (VD) and Collective Activity dataset (CAD). The G-MCA and I-MCA denote the accuracy of group activity and individual action recognition respectively

Method	Backbone	G-MCA(VD)	I-MCA(VD)	G-MCA(CAD)
stagNet [21]	VGG16	89.3	–	89.1
PRL [11]	VGG16	91.4	–	–
GAIM [20]	Inveption-v3	92.1	82.6	90.6
ARG [28]	Inception-v3	92.5	83.0	91.0
ARG [28]	VGG19	92.6	82.6	–
HRN [13]	VGG19	89.5	–	–
CRM [2]	I3D	92.1	–	83.4
Actor-Transformer [8]	I3D	91.4	–	90.8
Ours	Inception-v3	92.7	83.1	**91.4**
Ours	VGG16	92.5	82.8	90.6
Ours	VGG19	**93.2**	**83.6**	–

Results on the Collective Activity Dataset. We further compare our method with the state-of-the-art methods on the Collective Activity dataset. Our approach again reaches 91.4 % for group activity recognition and achieves state-of-the-art results. When using the same backbone, our method outperforms the ARG [28]. Besides, our method is better than CRM [2] and Actor-Transformer [8] which use a more powerful backbone. The results show the effectiveness and generality of our proposed method.

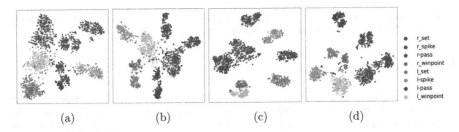

(a)   (b)   (c)   (d)

Fig. 3. t-SNE visualization of embedding of video representation on the Volleyball dataset learned by different model variants: (a) Non-Part-Aware (b) FCPG (single frame) (c) LCPG+FCPG (single frame) (d) Our final PSTGCN model.

4.5 Visualization

To better understand the performance of our method, we demonstrate the t-SNE visualization of group-level features learned by the variants of our model on the validation set of Volleyball dataset in Fig. 3. We can discover that the group-level representation learned by our part-aware graph model can be better separated and the LCPG and FCPG can help to improve the classification performance.

We also visualize some examples of the fully-connected part graph in Fig. 4. To better visualize, we sum the relation values of different parts of the same individual and describe the relationships among individuals as a $N \times N$ matrix. We can see that our model can focus on the key actor in the scene.

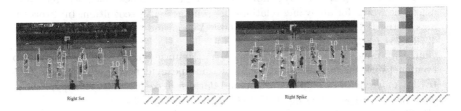

Fig. 4. Visualization of the learned fully-connected graph. We present two examples. For each example, the left is a frame with bounding boxes and group activity label and the key actor is denoted by the red star. The right is an adjacent matrix to represent the learned relation among pairwise individuals. The values change from large to small along with the colors changing from blue to white. (Color figure online)

5 Conclusion

This work demonstrates the effectiveness of leveraging the spatial-temporal relations of parts of persons for individual action and group activity recognition. Specifically, we propose a part-aware spatial-temporal graph convolutional network (PSTGCN) to model the fine-grained relationships composed of two core graphs. The locally-connected part graph learns the structural information of parts of an individual. The fully-connected part graph explores the interaction relationships among individuals using part-level features. We evaluate the proposed model on two datasets, and the results demonstrate the effectiveness and generalization ability of our model.

Acknowledgement. This paper is partially supported by Natural Science Foundation of China (NSFC) under Grant No.61976010, 62106011 and 61802011.

References

1. Amer, M.R., Xie, D., Zhao, M., Todorovic, S., Zhu, S.-C.: Cost-sensitive top-down/bottom-up inference for multiscale activity recognition. In: Fitzgibbon, A., Lazebnik, S., Perona, P., Sato, Y., Schmid, C. (eds.) ECCV 2012. LNCS, vol. 7575, pp. 187–200. Springer, Heidelberg (2012). https://doi.org/10.1007/978-3-642-33765-9_14
2. Azar, S.M., Atigh, M.G., Nickabadi, A., Alahi, A.: Convolutional relational machine for group activity recognition. In: Proceedings of the IEEE/CVF Conference on Computer Vision and Pattern Recognition, pp. 7892–7901 (2019)
3. Bagautdinov, T., Alahi, A., Fleuret, F., Fua, P., Savarese, S.: Social scene understanding: end-to-end multi-person action localization and collective activity recognition. In: Proceedings of the IEEE Conference on Computer Vision and Pattern Recognition, pp. 4315–4324 (2017)
4. Cao, Z., Hidalgo, G., Simon, T., Wei, S.E., Sheikh, Y.: OpenPose: realtime multi-person 2D pose estimation using part affinity fields. IEEE Trans. Pattern Anal. Mach. Intell. **43**(1), 172–186 (2019)
5. Choi, W., Shahid, K., Savarese, S.: What are they doing?: collective activity classification using spatio-temporal relationship among people. In: 2009 IEEE 12th International Conference on Computer Vision Workshops, ICCV Workshops, pp. 1282–1289. IEEE (2009)
6. Deng, Z., Vahdat, A., Hu, H., Mori, G.: Structure inference machines: recurrent neural networks for analyzing relations in group activity recognition. In: Proceedings of the IEEE Conference on Computer Vision and Pattern Recognition, pp. 4772–4781 (2016)
7. Gan, C., Wang, N., Yang, Y., Yeung, D.-Y., Hauptmann, A.G.: DevNet: a deep event network for multimedia event detection and evidence recounting. In: 2015 IEEE Conference on Computer Vision and Pattern Recognition (CVPR), pp. 2568–2577 (2015). https://doi.org/10.1109/CVPR.2015.7298872
8. Gavrilyuk, K., Sanford, R., Javan, M., Snoek, C.G.: Actor-transformers for group activity recognition. In: Proceedings of the IEEE/CVF Conference on Computer Vision and Pattern Recognition, pp. 839–848 (2020)
9. He, K., Zhang, X., Ren, S., Sun, J.: Deep residual learning for image recognition. In: 2016 IEEE Conference on Computer Vision and Pattern Recognition (CVPR), pp. 770–778 (2016). https://doi.org/10.1109/CVPR.2016.90
10. He, K., Gkioxari, G., Dollár, P., Girshick, R.: Mask R-CNN. In: Proceedings of the IEEE International Conference on Computer Vision, pp. 2961–2969 (2017)
11. Hu, G., Cui, B., He, Y., Yu, S.: Progressive relation learning for group activity recognition. In: Proceedings of the IEEE/CVF Conference on Computer Vision and Pattern Recognition, pp. 980–989 (2020)
12. Liu, H.-Y., Zhang, H.: A sports video browsing and retrieval system based on multi-modal analysis: SportsBR. In: 2005 International Conference on Machine Learning and Cybernetics, vol. 8, pp. 5077–5081 (2005). https://doi.org/10.1109/ICMLC.2005.1527838
13. Ibrahim, M.S., Mori, G.: Hierarchical relational networks for group activity recognition and retrieval. In: Proceedings of the European Conference on Computer Vision (ECCV), pp. 721–736 (2018)

14. Ibrahim, M.S., Muralidharan, S., Deng, Z., Vahdat, A., Mori, G.: A hierarchical deep temporal model for group activity recognition. In: Proceedings of the IEEE Conference on Computer Vision and Pattern Recognition, pp. 1971–1980 (2016)

15. Kipf, T.N., Welling, M.: Semi-supervised classification with graph convolutional networks. arXiv preprint arXiv:1609.02907 (2016)

16. Lan, T., Sigal, L., Mori, G.: Social roles in hierarchical models for human activity recognition. In: 2012 IEEE Conference on Computer Vision and Pattern Recognition, pp. 1354–1361. IEEE (2012)

17. Lan, T., Wang, Y., Yang, W., Robinovitch, S.N., Mori, G.: Discriminative latent models for recognizing contextual group activities. IEEE Trans. Pattern Anal. Mach. Intell. **34**(8), 1549–1562 (2011)

18. Liu, W., et al.: SSD: single shot multibox detector. In: Leibe, B., Matas, J., Sebe, N., Welling, M. (eds.) ECCV 2016. LNCS, vol. 9905, pp. 21–37. Springer, Cham (2016). https://doi.org/10.1007/978-3-319-46448-0_2

19. Lou, G., Shi, H.: Face image recognition based on convolutional neural network. China Commun. **17**(2), 117–124 (2020). https://doi.org/10.23919/JCC.2020.02.010

20. Lu, L., Lu, Y., Yu, R., Di, H., Zhang, L., Wang, S.: GAIM: graph attention interaction model for collective activity recognition. IEEE Trans. Multimed. **22**(2), 524–539 (2019)

21. Qi, M., Qin, J., Li, A., Wang, Y., Luo, J., Van Gool, L.: stagNet: an attentive semantic RNN for group activity recognition. In: Proceedings of the European Conference on Computer Vision (ECCV), pp. 101–117 (2018)

22. Shu, X., Zhang, L., Sun, Y., Tang, J.: Host-parasite: graph LSTM-in-LSTM for group activity recognition. IEEE Trans. Neural Netw. Learn. Syst. **32**, 663–674 (2020)

23. Tang, Y., Wang, Z., Li, P., Lu, J., Yang, M., Zhou, J.: Mining semantics-preserving attention for group activity recognition. In: Proceedings of the 26th ACM International Conference on Multimedia, pp. 1283–1291 (2018)

24. Tran, D., Bourdev, L., Fergus, R., Torresani, L., Paluri, M.: Learning spatiotemporal features with 3D convolutional networks. In: Proceedings of the IEEE International Conference on Computer Vision, pp. 4489–4497 (2015)

25. Vaswani, A., et al.: Attention is all you need. arXiv preprint arXiv:1706.03762 (2017)

26. Wang, L., et al.: Temporal segment networks: towards good practices for deep action recognition. In: Leibe, B., Matas, J., Sebe, N., Welling, M. (eds.) ECCV 2016. LNCS, vol. 9912, pp. 20–36. Springer, Cham (2016). https://doi.org/10.1007/978-3-319-46484-8_2

27. Wang, X., Girshick, R., Gupta, A., He, K.: Non-local neural networks. In: Proceedings of the IEEE Conference on Computer Vision and Pattern Recognition, pp. 7794–7803 (2018)

28. Wu, J., Wang, L., Wang, L., Guo, J., Wu, G.: Learning actor relation graphs for group activity recognition. In: Proceedings of the IEEE/CVF Conference on Computer Vision and Pattern Recognition, pp. 9964–9974 (2019)

29. Wu, L.F., Wang, Q., Jian, M., Qiao, Y., Zhao, B.X.: A comprehensive review of group activity recognition in videos. Int. J. Autom. Comput. **18**(3), 334–350 (2021)

30. Yan, R., et al.: Participation-Contributed Temporal Dynamic Model for Group Activity Recognition. In: 2018 ACM Multimedia Conference, pp. 1292–1300 (2018)

A Loop Closure Detection Algorithm Based on Geometric Constraint in Dynamic Scenes

Cheng Hang$^{(\boxtimes)}$, Bo Zhao, and Baoyun Wang

College of Automation and College of Artificial Intelligence, Nanjing University
of Posts and Telecommunications, Nanjing 210046, China
tracymayday15@163.com, bywang@njupt.edu.cn

Abstract. In visual SLAM (Simultaneous Localization and Mapping),
the loop closure detection module is mainly applied for eliminating the
pose drift and obtaining globally consistent maps. In dynamic environments, conventional loop closure detection algorithms may be unstable. In this paper, an algorithm for accurately detecting closed loops in
dynamic scenes is proposed. Firstly, the classification scheme of dynamic
and static feature points based on geometric constraints is improved to
obtain the precise division of dynamic and static points. Secondly, the
clustering of images is performed after excluding all the dynamic points.
Thirdly, for each node in the visual dictionary tree, an improved pyramid term frequency-inverse document frequency (TF-IDF) is employed
to represent the score weight of the images. Then the vector description
of the images can be obtained after the above procedure. Finally, the similarity calculation function between images is modified to obtain images
with higher similarity scores. The experimental results illustrate that this
algorithm can effectively reduce the influence of perceptual aliasing and
greatly increase the recall rate of the loop closure detection.

Keywords: Loop closure detection · Geometric constraint · TF-IDF
entropy · Similarity score

1 Introduction

In the visual SLAM system, which has attracted much attention in autonomous
driving, UAV (Unmanned Aerial Vehicle) navigation and 3D reconstruction [1–
3], errors of pose estimation will accumulate as the tracking time grows. The loop
closure detection algorithm, a key aspect and fundamental problem in SLAM
system [4], is very effective in eliminating the accumulated errors in robot pose
estimation and maintaining the accuracy of the map over a long period of time
by the judgement of whether the robot has returned to the revisited environment
area [5].

Supported by National Natural Science Foundation of China under the Grant number
61803210.

L. Fang et al. (Eds.): CICAI 2021, LNAI 13069, pp. 516–527, 2021.
https://doi.org/10.1007/978-3-030-93046-2_44

Loop closure detection using the bag-of-visual words (BOVW) model is one of the most typical approaches for mainstream SLAM systems [6]. The methodology extracts image features and clusters them to obtain a visual dictionary tree. When a new image arrives, it is projected into the visual dictionary tree and represented by a vector composed of the words represented by the nodes in the tree and the weights of words. Then, the similarity between images is calculated by computing the distance between these vectors. The smaller the distance, the higher the similarity and the more likely to generate closed loops [7].

A lot of research has been undertaken to tackle the loop closure detection problem on the basic of BOVW schemes. The most pioneering work falling into this direction was proposed by Cummins et al. [8]. They integrated the Chou-Liu tree probabilistic model with the BOVW scheme to improve the accuracy of the algorithm by comparing the current frame with the historical frames individually and detected the closed loop accurately from an image library of 10,000 frames; The solution presented by Milford et al. [9]. Adopted image sequences instead of single frames for matching. Labbe et al. [10] used a memory partitioning scheme to perform the loop closure process, with only part of the historical frame information stored in the Working-Memory being used to effectively improve the real-time performance of the algorithm; Lin et al. [11] improved the efficiency of the loop closure detection using spatial information to select the candidate matches, avoiding the global search range. Li et al. [12] made improvements to the TF-IDF score calculation scheme for visual dictionary trees to effectively reduce the perceptual aliasing problems in the BOVW model; Research [13] based on the spatial distribution information among visual words was also effectively introduced into the BOVW model to increase the distinction between visual word scores, which was useful for accuracy improvement; Zhang et al. [14] used a swarm intelligence optimization algorithm to build a mathematical model to transform the problem of calculating similarity into a maximum optimization problem, which improved the efficiency and accuracy of loop closure detection.

In order to reduce the difficulty of data association as well as to improve the efficiency of the system, the SLAM system is mostly performed in a small range of static scene. However, when there are moving objects constantly existing in the scene, the environment information will be veiled or appear suddenly, which will lead to a decrease in the accuracy of loop closure detection and even cause the failure [15]. Tan et al. [16] determine the dynamic static points by the judgment of the distance through the scheme of reprojection error, which projects the features in the image to the current frame and measures their distance from the tracked features. Alcantarilla et al. [17] introduced the scheme of scene flow to compare the changes of scene flow of feature points by performing additional scene flow calculation on the image so as to detect dynamic feature points; Zhang et al. [18] used the combination of scene flow and geometric relationship to effectively distinguish dynamic feature points in the scene, which is good for improving the localization accuracy; Gao et al. [19] used the double single Gaussian model to distinguish the foreground and background in the image so as to complete the differentiation of dynamic feature points; Yang et al. [20] used the triangular principle method to have a good filtering effect on the dynamic points in the image and improve the performance of the whole system.

Based on the above analysis, in order to increase the accuracy of loop closure detection in dynamic scenes, this paper proposes a loop closure detection algorithm combining geometric constraint and BOVW method based on the literature [20]. Firstly, the dynamic and static features in the scene are divided with an improved geometric constraint scheme. Secondly, the presentations of score weights of different words are improved to obtain the description vector of the current image which only contains static feature points, and then the similarity calculation function of the two images is improved to get images with higher similarity scores. In the loop closure detection experiments, this algorithm reduces the influence of perceptual aliasing between images and effectively increases the recall rate of the loop closure detection.

The overall structure of the rest of this paper takes the form of four sections. Section 2 uses the improved geometric constraint method to divide the dynamic and static points in the image. The improved loop closure detection algorithm is described in detail in Sect. 3. And the experimental results on two open datasets are shown in Sect. 4. Section 5 gives a brief summary of our work and the future work.

2 Improved Geometric Constraint-Based Dynamic and Static Feature Points Segmentation

When the feature points matching is accomplished, Not only the feature points are matched accurately, but also the dynamic points in the environments are retained. Since these dynamic points can lead to a great impact on the subsequence loop closure detection algorithm. In this paper, an improved geometric constraint model of feature points is applied for extracting them from the image. As presented in Fig. 1, image I_{k-1} and image I_k are two adjoining frames that have been matched. The three vertices forming the triangle $\triangle p_1 p_2 p_3$ and $\triangle q_1 q_2 q_3$ in the two images represent the ORB feature points extracted from the images. The vertices p_1, p_2, p_3 in image I_{k-1} are matched with q_1, q_2, q_3 in image I_k respectively. Each side of the triangle represents the Euclidean distance between the feature points and is denoted by the letter d.

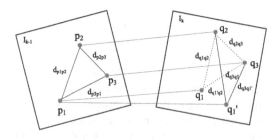

Fig. 1. Bi-directional geometric voting model.

When there are no dynamic objects in the environment, the difference between the corresponding sides of the two triangles should belong to a small interval, which can be expressed by the following equation

$$|d_{p_m p_n} - d_{q_m q_n}| \in (d_{min}, d_{max}),\tag{1}$$

for $m, n \in \{1, 2, 3, \cdots\}$ representing the feature points' number. In order to present the change of the corresponding edge more clearly in the presence of dynamic points, the geometrically constrained score function of an edge is further defined in an exponential form as follows

$$s_{mn} = e^{\left|\frac{d_{p_m p_n} - d_{q_m q_n}}{A_{mn}}\right|},\tag{2}$$

where $d_{p_m p_n}$ denotes the Euclidean distance between feature points p_m, p_n, and A_{mn} can be expressed as

$$A_{mn} = \frac{d_{p_m p_n} + d_{q_m q_n}}{2}.\tag{3}$$

As depicted in Fig. 1, when the dynamic feature point q_1 in the scene moves to q_1', its Euclidean distance from the other two feature points q_2, q_3 will change. Because of the movement of q_1, the value of geometrically constrained score function (2) will inevitably become larger. By observing the change of the value, the changed edges can be obtained, and then the dynamic feature points are determined. However, since each edge involves two feature points, it is difficult to determine which point is the real dynamic point. Based on this problem, a bi-directional geometric voting model of feature points is proposed to determine the real dynamic feature points in the scene. The main idea of this method is described as follows: a score value $q_u(m)$ is defined for the feature point m, and when the geometrically constrained score function of an edge changes, the score values of vertices are each added with an abnormal score value increment $q_a(mn)$. As the judgments continue, there is a large gap between the scores of truly dynamic points with those of static points. The expression of the score value of a feature point can be expressed as follows

$$q_u(m) = \sum_{n=0}^{z} q_a(mn),\tag{4}$$

where $q_u(m)$ represents the score value of the feature point m, z represents the number of feature points connected to the feature point m, and $q_a(mn)$ represents the increment of abnormal score value expressed by

$$q_a(mn) = \begin{cases} 1, & s_{mn} > \gamma \cdot A_s \\ 0, & otherwise. \end{cases}\tag{5}$$

And γ represents the ratio factor of the geometric constraint average score, A_s represents the average geometric constraint score between points on the image expressed as

$$A_s = \frac{\sum_{m=1, n=1}^{N} \omega_{mn} s_{mn}}{N},\tag{6}$$

where N denotes the number of the matched feature points in the image, ω_{mn} denotes the geometric error weighting factor, which is used to reduce the effect of larger geometric constraint scores on the calculation of the average score

$$\omega_{mn} = \begin{cases} 0, & s_{mn} > \theta, \\ 1, & otherwise, \end{cases} \tag{7}$$

where θ is the set threshold of the geometric score, when the geometric constraint score is larger than this set threshold, this score will not participate in the calculation of the average geometric constraint score.

In order to increase the accuracy of the score value $q_u(m)$ of the feature point m in the current frame, considering the time factor, the score of this feature point in the historical frames are weighted with the current score to obtain an improved score $q_u^t(m)$, which is represented as follows

$$q_u^t(m) = (1 - \alpha_t)\, q_u^{k-1}(m) + \alpha_t q_u^k(m), \tag{8}$$

where α_t represents the temporal learning rate, $q_u^{k-1}(m)$ represents the score value of the feature point m at the moment $k - 1$, and $q_u^k(m)$ represents the score value of the feature point m at the moment k.

Considering the spatial factor, the score of the feature point in the current frame is weighted with the score of others around it to obtain the score $q_u^s(m)$, namely

$$q_u^s(m) = (1 - \beta_s)\, q_u(m) + \beta_s \frac{1}{r^2} \sum_{i \in \mathcal{N}_{(m)}} q_u(i), \tag{9}$$

where β_s represents the spatial learning rate, $q_u(m)$ represents the score value of the feature point m, $N_{(m)}$ represents a spatial region adjacent to the feature point m, r^2 represents the area of this spatial region, and $q_u(i)$ represents the score value of the feature point i belonging to this region.

The score value of the feature point m is then finally defined as $q_u^f(m)$. This paper uses Algorithm 1 to get the final score value.

$$q_u^f(m) = \sqrt{q_u^t(m) \cdot q_u^s(m)}. \tag{10}$$

3   Improved Bag-of-Visual-Words Based Loop Closure Detection Algorithm

Loop closure detection algorithm can add constraints between the current pose and previous poses to reduce the cumulative error caused by the system. In order to increase the adaptability of the traditional loop closure detection algorithm in dynamic scenes, this paper proposes an improved BOVW detection scheme that contains two main aspects: (1) scene modeling after eliminating dynamic points (2) an improved method for calculating the similarity between images.

Algorithm 1. Score values of the feature points

Input: Matched feature points
Output: Score values of the feature points
    for all matched feature points **do**
        Calculate the distance s_{mn} between the feature points p_m, p_n;
        if $s_{mn} >$ threshold **then**
            add abnormal score value increment $q_a(mn)$ to the score value $q_u(m)$ and
$q_u(n)$;
        end if
    end for
    for each feature point p_m **do**
        Calculate the score value $q_u^t(m)$ considering the time factor;
        Calculate the score value $q_u^s(m)$ considering the spatial factor;
        Calculate the score value $q_u^f(m)$ considering the time and spatial factor;
    end for

3.1 Scene Modeling After Eliminating Dynamic Points

In a static environment, the classical BOVW algorithm uses a large number of features from images for training to obtain a visual dictionary tree with k branches and l layers. Then it extracts the image features from the acquired image and projects the features to the visual dictionary to obtain the visual word description vector for that image. According to the literature [12], the score weights of images in different tree nodes can be represented by the TF-IDF entropy of each tree node. TF represents the frequency of a word in an image. The higher the frequency, the higher the word is distinguished; IDF represents the frequency of a word in the dictionary. The lower the frequency, the more differentiated the classification of the image. Define TF-IDF entropy as

$$w_i^l(P) = \frac{n_i}{n} \log \frac{N}{N_i}. \tag{11}$$

In the above equation, for $l \in \{1, 2, 3, \cdots, L\}$ represents the number of layers of the visual dictionary tree, for $i \in \{1, 2, 3, \cdots, k^l\}$ represents the number of nodes in the l layer, $w_i^l(P)$ represents the score weight of the ith node of image P on the lth layer of the tree, n_i and n respectively represent the number of feature points projected to node i and the total number of feature points. N and N_i represent the total number of images that require to be processed and the number of images that appear to have features projected to the node i respectively.

    Although the TF-IDF entropy defined in the above equation works in most cases, there is still a problem as shown in Table 1. The three words w_1, w_2, and w_3 have the same IDF value according to the above equation. From the perspective of TF value, w_1 appears the most and its score has the highest weight, w_2 owns the second and w_3 has the smallest. However, in terms of word differentiation, w_3 should get the highest weight because of its larger span of appearances in each image compared to w_1 and w_2. Obviously these two situations are contradictory.

Table 1. Number of each word in the database image.

Word	Image1	Image2	Image3	$\cdots$	ImageX
w_1	20	20	20	$\cdots$	20
w_2	18	16	17	$\cdots$	19
w_3	11	15	16	$\cdots$	18

Based on this problem, a propelled coefficient of variation is introduced to get a precise score weighting for each word. The coefficient of variation is defined as

$$CV = \frac{\sigma}{\mu}, \tag{12}$$

where, σ means the standard deviation of the number of times the word appears. μ represents the average number of the occurrences of the word. For the case of w_1 whose standard deviation is 0 in Table 1, the coefficient of variation is improved and redefined as λ_i.

$$\lambda_i = \begin{cases} 1 & CV_i = 0, \\ 1 + \alpha \frac{CV_i}{\sum_{i=1}^{K^l} CV_i} & CV_i \neq 0, \end{cases} \tag{13}$$

where CV_i represents the coefficient of variation of the word represented by the ith node. α is the average scale factor of the coefficient of variation, and K^l represents the total number of visual words.

The improved TF-IDF entropy is expressed as

$$w_i^l(P) = \lambda_i \frac{n_i}{n} \log \frac{N}{N_i}. \tag{14}$$

The score vector of image P in the whole visual dictionary tree is represented as

$$w(P) = \left(w^1(P), w^2(P), \ldots, w^L(P) \right), \tag{15}$$

where $w^l(P)$ represents the score vector of the image on the lth layer, denoted as

$$w^l(P) = \left(w_1^l(P), w_2^l(P), \ldots, w_{k^l}^l(P) \right). \tag{16}$$

3.2   Improved Similarity Score Algorithm

In [12], the similarity score function for image P and Q at the ith node is defined as

$$S_i^l(P, Q) = \min \left\{ w_i^l(P), w_i^l(Q) \right\}. \tag{17}$$

Although the equation representing the similarity score can be a good way to determine the similarity of individual nodes, there still exists a little problem. According to (17), if there are three images satisfying $w_i^l(M) > w_i^l(P) > w_i^l(Q)$, the similarity score between image M and image Q will be the same as that between image P and image Q, which causes perceptual aliasing. In order to avoid the above problem, the expression of the above similarity score function is redefined. At the same time, because the number of words present in each image is much smaller than the number of all words in the visual dictionary tree, the score of many words present in the image is 0. In order to improve the computational efficiency of the whole algorithm, the above expression of the similarity score function is improved as

$$S_i^l(P,Q) = \begin{cases} 0, & w_i^l(P) = 0 \ or \ w_i^l(Q) = 0, \\ e^{-|w_i^l(P)-w_i^l(Q)|}, & otherwise. \end{cases} \qquad (18)$$

4   Experiments and Analysis

4.1   Dynamic and Static Feature Points Differentiation Experiments

In order to verify the effectiveness of the proposed algorithm in dynamic scenes, this paper selects the fr3 highly dynamic scene sequence dataset walking-xyz from the TUM RGB-D public dataset [21] as the experimental data. 450 ORB feature points are extracted from one of the frames and the score of each feature point is calculated using the method proposed in Sect. 2. The score threshold is 300, which means that when the score of a feature point exceeds this score threshold, it will be judged as a dynamic feature point. The dynamic feature points are represented by red points, and the green points represent static points. Comparing the feature extraction result of the proposed method with that of ORB-SLAM, it can be seen that the method in this paper can effectively detect the feature points on dynamic objects. Figure 2 shows the feature extraction results. Figure 2(a) is the image obtained after feature extraction by ORB-SLAM, and Fig. 2(b) represents the feature extraction image obtained by the algorithm of this paper. Figure 2(c) shows the calculation result of the score distribution of feature points. All the experiments are performed on a laptop CPU(Intel Core i5-8265U, 8 GB RAM), and the system is Ubuntu 16.04.

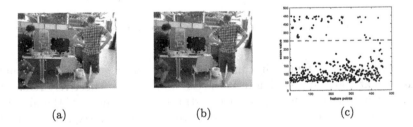

(a)	(b)	(c)

Fig. 2. Feature extraction results. (a) ORB-SLAM, (b) Ours, (c) Score distribution of feature points.

4.2 Experiments of Loop Closure Detection

An important criterion to evaluate the performance of loop closure detection is the precision-recall curve. Precision rate refers to the percentage of true closed-loops among all closed-loops detected by the algorithm. Recall rate indicates the percentage of closed-loops correctly detected by the algorithm among all actual closed-loops. The formulas for precision and recall are respectively shown in the following equations:

$$precision = \frac{TP}{TP + FP},$$ (19)

$$recall = \frac{TP}{TP + FN}.$$ (20)

To demonstrate the usefulness of the improved TF-IDF entropy as well as the similarity function proposed in this paper, two datasets from TUM RGB-D were selected for experimental validation. The first one is a sequence named fr3_long_office_household collected in a complex indoor environment, and the other one is called fr2_pioneer_slam2 collected in an extremely similar environment, which is prone to perceptual aliasing. The loop closure detection algorithm in this paper is compared with classical algorithms like IAB-MAP, FAB-MAP and RTAB-MAP. Figure 3 shows the results of the precision- recall curve.

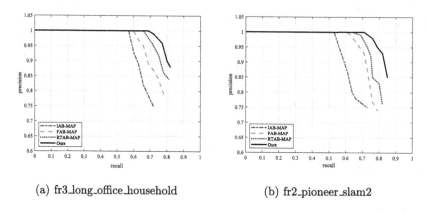

(a) fr3_long_office_household   (b) fr2_pioneer_slam2

Fig. 3. Comparison of precision-recall curves in two sequences of TUM dataest.

From the above figure, it can be seen that the algorithm has a higher recall rate at 100% of precision in both scenes, which can effectively reduce the impact of perceptual aliasing. To demonstrate the usefulness of the algorithm in dynamic scenes, experiments are conducted by selecting sequences from the KITTI dataset [22], an open source odometry dataset collected by GPS and laser. These sequences contain dynamic objects like pedestrians and cars. Sequences 00, 02, 05, 06, and 07 all contain closed-loop paths. In this paper, two sequences 00 and 05 are selected for the experiment. Figure 4 presents the precision-recall curves of the three algorithms in KITTI 00 and KITTI 05.

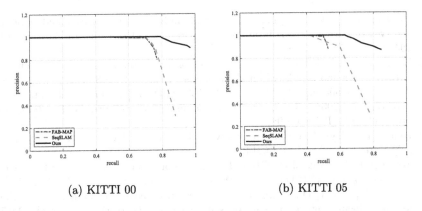

(a) KITTI 00   (b) KITTI 05

Fig. 4. Comparison of precision-recall curves in two sequences of KITTI dataest.

As depicted in Fig. 4, when the proposed algorithm is accurate to 100% of precision, the recall rate is still 79% compared with others in the KITTI 00 dataset. Therefore, the proposed algorithm has better recall performance in dynamic scenes than the other two algorithms, which verifies the effectiveness of the algorithm in dynamic environments.

5   Conclusion

This paper proposes an improved loop closure detection algorithm for the problem of moving objects and perceptual aliasing. For the sake of avoiding the unstability in dynamic scenes, the improved geometric constraint scheme is adopted to clearly delineate the dynamic and static feature points. Then the improved TF-IDF entropy is used to clearly describe the scene with the dynamic feature points removed, followed by calculating the similarity score between two frames with the improved similarity calculation function. Experiments on the datasets verify the effectiveness of the algorithm.

In the future, we are going to fuse the inertial measurement data to propel the robustness of this algorithm in dynamic scenes. Besides, in order to get the complete image, the image inpainting algorithm can be considered to repair the part of dynamic feature points removed from the scene. In addition, the greedy algorithm can be taken into consideration for the loop closure detection to improve the real-time performance of this algorithm. Finally, the closed-loop results can be applied to further optimize the camera poses and the generated map information.

References

1. Yang, X., Zhou, L., Jiang, H., Tang, Z., Zhang, G.: Mobile3DRecon: real-time monocular 3D reconstruction on a mobile phone. IEEE Trans. Vis. Comput. Graph. **26**(12), 3446–3456 (2020)

2. Bresson, G., Alsayed, Z., Yu, L., Glaser, S.: Simultaneous localization and mapping: a survey of current trends in autonomous driving. IEEE Trans. Intell. Veh. **2**(3), 194–220 (2017)
3. Kanellakis, C., Nikolakopoulos, G.: Survey on computer vision for UAVs: current developments and trends. J. Intell. Rob. Syst. **87**(1), 141–168 (2017)
4. Angeli, A., Doncieux, S., Meyer, J. A., Filliat, D.: Real-time visual loop-closure detection. In: 2008 IEEE International Conference on Robotics and Automation, pp. 1842–1847. IEEE (2008)
5. Huang, B., Zhao, J., Liu, J.: A survey of simultaneous localization and mapping. arXiv preprint arXiv:1909.05214 (2019)
6. Mur-Artal, R., Tards, J.D.: ORB-SLAM2: an open-source slam system for monocular, stereo, and RGB-D cameras. IEEE Trans. Rob. **33**(5), 1255–1262 (2017)
7. Angeli, A., Filliat, D., Doncieux, S., Meyer, J.A.: Fast and incremental method for loop-closure detection using bags of visual words. IEEE Trans. Rob. **24**(5), 1027–1037 (2008)
8. Cummins, M., Newman, P.: Appearance-only SLAM at large scale with FAB-MAP 2.0. Int. J. Rob. Res. **30**(9), 1100–1123 (2011)
9. Milford, M. J., Wyeth, G. F.: SeqSLAM: visual route-based navigation for sunny summer days and stormy winter nights. In: 2012 IEEE International Conference on Robotics and Automation, pp. 1643–1649. IEEE (2012)
10. Labbe, M., Michaud, F.: Appearance-based loop closure detection for online large-scale and long-term operation. IEEE Trans. Rob. **29**(3), 734–745 (2013)
11. Lin, J., Han, B., Luo, Q.: SLAM research based on NDT matching and improved loop closure detection. Opt. Tech. **44**(2), 152–157 (2018)
12. Li, B., Yang, D., Deng, L.: Visual vocabulary tree with pyramid TF-IDF scoring match scheme for loop closure detection. Acta Autom. Sinica **37**(6), 665–673 (2011)
13. Li, W., Zhang, G., Xu, J., Yao, E.: Improved loop closure detection algorithm for VSLAM with spatial coordinate index. DEStech Trans. Mater. Sci. Eng. (2016)
14. Zhang, C., Zhang, Y.: Research on SLAM loop closure detection Based on HHO algorithm. Laser Optoelectron. Progr. **58**(12), 452–460 (2021)
15. Saputra, M.R.U., Markham, A., Trigoni, N.: Visual SLAM and structure from motion in dynamic environments: a survey. ACM Comput. Surv. (CSUR) **51**(2), 1–36 (2018)
16. Tan, W., Liu, H., Dong, Z., Zhang, G., Bao, H.: Robust monocular SLAM in dynamic environments. In: 2013 IEEE International Symposium on Mixed and Augmented Reality (ISMAR), pp. 209–218. IEEE (2013)
17. Alcantarilla, P. F., Yebes, J. J., Almazn, J., Bergasa, L. M.: On combining visual SLAM and dense scene flow to increase the robustness of localization and mapping in dynamic environments. In: 2012 IEEE International Conference on Robotics and Automation, pp. 1290–1297. IEEE (2012)
18. Zhang, H., Xu, H., Yao, E., Song, H., Zhao, X.: Robust stereo visual odometry algorithm in dynamic scenes. Chin. J. Sci. Instr. **39**(9), 246–254 (2018)
19. Gao, C., Zhang, Y., Wang, X., Deng, Y., Jiang, H.: Semi-direct RGB-D SLAM algorithm for dynamic indoor environments. Robot **41**(3), 372–383 (2019)
20. Yang, S., Fan, G., Bai, L., Li, R., Li, D.: MGC-VSLAM: a meshing-based and geometric constraint VSLAM for dynamic indoor environments. IEEE Access **8**(8), 1007–1021 (2020)

21. Sturm, J., Engelhard, N., Endres, F., Burgard, W., Cremers, D.: A benchmark for the evaluation of RGB-D SLAM systems. In: 2012 IEEE/RSJ International Conference on Intelligent Robots and Systems, pp. 573–580. IEEE (2012)
22. Geiger, A., Lenz, P., Stiller, C., Urtasun, R.: MGC-VSLAM: vision meets robotics: the KITTI dataset. Int. J. Rob. Res. **32**(11), 1231–1237 (2013)

Unsupervised Deep Plane-Aware Multi-homography Learning for Image Alignment

Tao Cai, Yunde Jia, Huijun Di$^{(\boxtimes)}$, and Yuwei Wu

School of Computer Science, Beijing Institute of Technology, Beijing, China
{caitaoo,jiayunde,ajon,wuyuwei}@bit.edu.cn

Abstract. Due to its feature representation capabilities, deep learning has been applied to homography estimation in the field of image alignment. Most deep homography learning methods focus on estimating a single global homography, and cannot deal with the problem of parallax when the scene contains multiple different planes, and the translation of the camera's optical center is not negligible. In this paper, we propose an unsupervised multi-homography learning method with a plane-perception trait to mitigate this parallax problem. In our model, the problem of multi-homography learning and plane perception are jointly considered, which can benefit from each other. To make the learning process stable under unsupervised setting, we design a special attention mechanism to bootstrap the collaboration between multi-homography learning and plane perception. We construct a new dataset that is captured in real scenes, having many challenges such as multiple planes, large parallax, etc. Quantitative and qualitative results show that our proposed method can better align images with large parallax and multiple planes.

Keywords: Multi-homography · Plane aware · Image alignment · Unsupervised learning

1 Introduction

Image alignment is a fundamental task in computer vision, with various applications such as image stitching [4,33], high dynamic range imaging [7,23], multi-frame super-resolution [1,30], medical image analysis [25], virtual reality [3,5], etc. The goal of image alignment is to find 2D warps to align the content of images. Homography is a popular warp wildly used in image alignment [27]. It maps the pixels in one image to the corresponding pixels in another image, through projective transformation. The estimation of homography usually depends on the matched feature points. Traditional features cannot cope with various scenarios. For scenes with few textures or with repetitive textures, traditional features will be insufficient or unstable for homography estimation. In contrast, deep learning has excellent feature representation capabilities and

© Springer Nature Switzerland AG 2021
L. Fang et al. (Eds.): CICAI 2021, LNAI 13069, pp. 528–539, 2021.
https://doi.org/10.1007/978-3-030-93046-2_45

has been successful in many computer vision tasks. Therefore, homography estimation based on deep learning is an inevitable trend and brings new vitality to image alignment.

Existing works have designed various deep models to estimate homography. However, most models [6,10,11,15,16,19–22,28,31,34,35] focus on estimating a single global homography, and the image can be aligned only when the camera is rotated around its optical center or the scene is planar. When the scene contains multiple different planes, and the translation of the camera's optical center is not negligible, it will cause the problem of parallax, that is, no single transformation can bring images into alignment. Although some promising methods have been proposed to estimate multiple homographies, such as DeepMeshFlow [32], they can only compensate for the misalignment problem caused by small parallax.

In this paper, we propose a plane-aware unsupervised deep multi-homography learning method to mitigate the large parallax problem. Without loss of generality, we assume that the whole scene is composed of several plane regions. We can estimate a local homography for each plane region, then fuse the estimated homographies to align the entire scene. However, if we do not have any other information, such as the depth information of the scene, it is difficult to stably segment all planar regions in the scene. We tackle this problem from another viewpoint. It is not our purpose to find plane regions, but to facilitate the learning of homographies that fits plane regions. Inspired by the idea of the classic EM algorithm [9], we jointly consider the problem of multi-homography learning and plane perception in our model. On the one hand, the learned multiple homographies can help to infer different planes through the alignment effect of different homography. On the other hand, the results of plane inference can guide the fusion of the learned multiple homographies to align the entire scene. In other words, plane perception can drive the multi-homography learning to reduce the overall alignment error. Nevertheless, under unsupervised setting, it is difficult to stably learn such a deep model. The key to make the learning process stable is that we design a special attention mechanism to drive the learned multiple homographies to adapt to different local regions. Such an attention mechanism can ensure that all the learned homographies have a plane bias, thus bootstrapping the collaboration between multi-homography learning and plane perception.

Besides, the dataset used in existing works is usually generated through the MS-COCO dataset [17], which lacks some challenging problems in the real scene, especially the large parallax. In this paper, we also construct a real scene dataset with various challenges, such as large parallax, multiple planes, large viewpoint change, and so on, to facilitate the development of image alignment community. Comprehensive experiments show that our proposed method can better align images with large parallax and multiple planes.

In summary, the contributions of this paper mainly include two:

- We propose a plane-aware unsupervised deep multi-homography learning method for image alignment, which can better align images with large parallax and multiple planes.

- We construct a real scene dataset with various challenges, such as large parallax, multiple planes, large viewpoint change, and so on, to facilitate image alignment community.

2 Related Work

DeTone et al. [10] applied deep learning to estimate homography at first. With the help of deep features, they obtained more accurate and robust results. Chang et al. [6] combined the differentiable Lucas-Kanade algorithm [18] with CNN, and utilized a coarse-to-fine strategy on the feature level. Nowruzi et al. [11] believed that there is no need to use a complex model to estimate homography. They proposed to cascade multiple simple models through a hierarchical structure, and achieved good estimation accuracy. Nie et al. [22] proposed a deep image stitching method, where its alignment can solve the challenges of large baseline and arbitrary image size. In [19,21], they believed that noises in real scenes would affect the robustness of homography estimation. Therefore, they proposed to introduce various noises into the training of network to mitigate this weakness. Zeng et al. [34] thought that the 4-point parameterization [2] representing homography ignores the spatial structure among pixel correspondences. So they proposed the perspective field to improve the homography representation. Ye et al. [31] also attempted to find a more efficient homography representation. They proposed to use a weighted sum of predefined bases in view of that the freedom of homography is largely less than deep features. In [16,24], they argued that there is a gap between image appearance features and homography (geometric information). They explicitly utilized feature correlation to find correspondences, and then estimated the homography to fill the gap. [15,35] considered that moving objects, low illumination, large foreground, and so on will result in homography estimation failure or with low accuracy. They proposed to simultaneously identify those ill-posed regions and estimate robust homography.

Nguyen et al. [20] proposed the first unsupervised deep homography estimation model, which leverages the STN [14] to calculate a photometric loss. Based on this work, Wang et al. [28] argued that the homography invertibility should also be used in deep model training. In [32,35], the proposed deep feature loss substituted the above photometric loss to handle low-light and texture-less scenes. Moreover, Ye et al. [32] used mesh flow to describe the image transformation and can handle the small parallax. Shen et al. [26] proposed an alignment method which combines the homography and the flow to deal with large motions and local transformation deviations.

In contrast, our method focuses on solving the problem of large parallax in real scenes. By utilizing the characteristic that homography can only align a single plane, our model can perceive planes in scenes. Then, the model learns accurate multi-homography for all planes and thus can align images with large parallax.

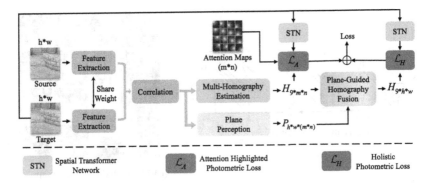

Fig. 1. The overview of our proposed model. In a multi-task way, we can achieve plane-aware multi-homography estimation. At first, predefined attention maps facilitate the estimation of multiple location-aware homographies. Those homographies can then help the plane prediction module to find planes. In return, the plane module assists the estimation module in refocusing locations.

3   Plane-Aware Multi-homography Learning

We will introduce our two main modules (Fig. 1), the plane prediction module, and the multi-homography estimation module. The two modules work together in a manner similar to multi-task. Differently, we need predefined attention maps to obtain a coarse initialization of multi-homography, without which the plane prediction probably fails. In return, the predicted planes will gradually make those homographies focusing on planes rather than predefined regions. Finally, gained from each other, the two modules can estimate plane-aware multi-homography and predict planes.

3.1   Attention-Driven Multi-homography Estimation

Feature Extraction. Deep features perform better in many tasks than traditional hand-designed ones. We use the image features output by the layer3 of ResNet-34 [12] in consideration of that too deep features lose too much spatial information and can damage the accuracy of estimation. The final feature map size is one-sixteenth of the input image size.

Feature Correlation. There is a gap between image appearance features and the geometry information (homography) [16]. Therefore, it may be difficult for a model to learn accurate and robust estimation of homography, especially in a real scene dataset with large parallax, multiple planes, and other challenges. To fill the gap, we explicitly compute correspondences in our model, named feature correlation [24], as shown in Fig. 2a. Feature correlation denotes by

$$C_{ij}^{kl} = \left\langle \frac{F_s^{ij}}{||F_s^{ij}||_2}, \frac{F_t^{kl}}{||F_t^{kl}||_2} \right\rangle, \tag{1}$$

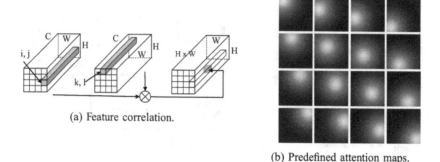

(a) Feature correlation.

(b) Predefined attention maps.

Fig. 2. The feature correlation and all predefined attention maps for an image pair to be aligned. The attention belongs to the Gaussian distribution with $\sigma = 64$ for an image size of 256×256.

where F_s and F_t represent the reference image features and the target ones respectively, and the C_{ij}^{kl} is one element in the final correlation results. We search possible correspondences in the whole feature map for each pixel. This improves the capability of our model to meet the large motion challenge.

Homography Regression. Our homography estimation module mainly consists of four BasicBlock [12] to smooth the correlation map and eliminate outliers since neighbors usually have similar correspondences. Then this module uses a 2D convolution layer and an adaptive average pooling to obtain an output with the size $4 \times 4 \times 8$. This output is the motions of four corners, which can then utilize the Tensor DLT [20] to calculate the corresponding multiple homographies. More detailed configurations of this module are shown in Table 1a.

Inspired by HVS [8,13], we design various attention maps for all estimated homographies based on the Gaussian distribution. In Fig. 2b, we give examples of attention maps. For one input image pair, we can use 4×4 or other numbers of attention maps to guide those homographies. On the one hand, we need to guide those multiple homographies to align different local regions. On the other hand, only focusing on local regions maybe confuse those homographies because texture-less, low-light, large motion, large parallax, and others in real scenes are very hard to align, which means that the global information is non-trivial. The final loss function of this estimation module is an attention highlighted photometric loss, denoted as

$$\mathcal{L}_A = \sum_{k=1}^{m*n} \frac{M_k \cdot |I_{ref} - F(H_k, I_{tgt})|}{\sum M_k}, \tag{2}$$

in which M_k is the k-th attention map, F is the STN [14], H_k is the k-th homography, I_{ref} is the reference image, and I_{tgt} is the target image.

Table 1. The network architecture of multi-homography estimator, plane perception.

(a) Multi-homography estimator

No.	Type	Kernel	Channel
1	BasicBlock	3	128
2	BasicBlock	3	64
3	BasicBlock	3	32
4	BasicBlock	3	16
5	Conv2D	1	8
6	AdaptAvgpool	–	–

(b) Plane perception module

No.	Type	Kernel	Channel
1	Bilinear x2	–	–
2	BasicBlock, Bilinear x2	3	128
3	BasicBlock, Bilinear x2	3	64
4	BasicBlock, Bilinear x2	3	32
5	BasicBlock	3	16
6	Softmax	–	–

3.2   Plane Perception and Homography Fusion

Although the predefined attention maps can urge multiple homographies to focus on different regions, those maps are coarse and can not be aware of planes in scenes. The plane perception module can obtain its initial coarse predictions with the help of those location-aware homographies. And then give feedback to the homography estimation module to further fit planes. In such a positive way, the two modules rely on each other and finally achieve the ultimate goal of plane-aware multi-homography estimation.

Based on the correlation map, this module performs the plane classification for each pixel. In Table 1b, we give its architecture which mainly consists of the bilinear interpolation to scale up and the BasicBlock [12] to obtain smooth planes. The final homography for the pixel in (i, j) can be denoted as

$$H_{ij} = \sum_{k=1}^{m*n} P_{ij}^k \cdot H_k, \tag{3}$$

where P_{ij} is a vector which represents the probability on all planes. This final homography field is the output of our model to align the whole input image pair. Also, we calculate the holistic photometric loss utilizing the STN [14], given by

$$\mathcal{L}_H = \frac{1}{N} \sum |I_{ref} - F(H, I_{tgt})|, \tag{4}$$

in which F is the STN [14], H is the final homography field, and N is for computing the average error spatially. The final loss function is given by

$$\mathcal{L} = \mathcal{L}_A + \mathcal{L}_H. \tag{5}$$

Implementation Details. We implement our model using PyTorch. We use the Adam optimizer to train our model with an initial learning rate of 1e−3. Training after 30 epochs and 80 epochs, we reduce the learning rate to half. In the first 50 epochs, we train only the multi-homography estimation module, the feature extraction module, the feature correlation layer. After this, we start to train the plane perception module. The batch size we use is 4 and the total epoch of training is 285.

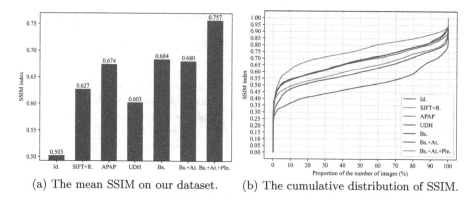

(a) The mean SSIM on our dataset.   (b) The cumulative distribution of SSIM.

Fig. 3. Quantitative comparisons among methods on the SSIM index testing on our built large parallax dataset. Methods include the identity matrix, SIFT+RANSAC, APAP [33], UDH [20], the baseline, the baseline with our attention maps, and our method (having attentions and the plane-perception).

Ref   Tgt   SIFT+RANSAC   APAP   UDH   Baseline   Ours

Fig. 4. A case with almost one single plane. For each method, we overlay the reference image (in green) with the aligned image (in magenta) to highlight misalignment. Normal color similar to input images represents small differences. The SITF+RANSAC, APAP [33], UDH [20] are almost failed. (Color figure online)

4   Experiments

In this section, we will compare different methods for image alignment quantitatively and qualitatively, including the identity matrix, SIFT+RANSAC, APAP [33], UDH [20], the baseline (Fig. 5), our model without plane-perception and our model.

Dataset. The existing dataset generated using MS-COCO [17] only contains a single plane and no parallax. So we built a new dataset with large parallax and multiple planes in real scenes, named PLMP. The PLMP dataset contains 20 outdoor scenes, with about 11k training image pairs and about 2k testing image pairs. The original resolution of images is 1920×1080. In experiments, we reduce it to a quarter, i.e., 480×270. To reveal possible structural misalignment, we use the SSIM [29] to quantitatively evaluate methods. In our experiments, given two images, we calculate the SSIM map using a window size of 3 for each pixel and then compute the average as the final SSIM result.

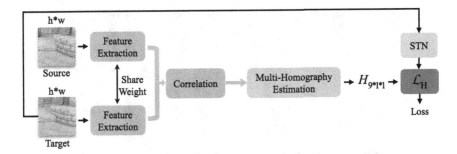

Fig. 5. Our baseline deep single-homography model.

4.1 Comparisons on PLMP Dataset

Quantitative Evaluation. In Fig. 3, we give both the mean SSIM results and the cumulative distribution of SSIM on the dataset. The mean SSIM results in Fig. 3a show that our method outperforms others. In Fig. 3b, we give the cumulative distribution of SSIM on the test dataset. According to the results of the identity matrix, about 70% of image pairs have the mean SSIM less than 0.55, revealing that the dataset has a large misalignment. We deeply compare methods by analyzing the proportion of results under two SSIM thresholds. With the SSIM below 0.60, SIFT+RANSAC has about 40% of results and UDH [20] has about 50%. APAP [33] has more than 20%. In contrast, our method only has less than 10%. With the SSIM above 0.80, our method has about 40%. And APAP [33] has only about 10%. For SIFT+RANSAC and UDH [20], they have less than 5%. So without plane perception, we cannot mostly mitigate large parallax and obtain further improvement. This is what our model does and it outperforms others.

Qualitative Evaluation. In Fig. 6, we give alignment results in parallax scenes. We overlay the input reference image with the warped target image by each method to reveal misalignment. The green channel shows the reference image and the magenta channel shows the warped target image. Normal intensities represent that difference is small. We found that using a global homography like SIFT+RANSAC, the baseline, and UDH [20] can coarsely align images. Using local adaptations based on local feature matches, such as APAP, still cannot solve the parallax problem in real scenes. In contrast, our method almost aligns those samples. Sometimes, traditional features may fail and further challenge methods based on them, like what we show in Fig. 4.

In Fig. 7, we show our predicted plane masks in one testing case. The 16 homographies have their plane masks, representing regions they can align. Those predicted plane masks generally agree with planes in the scene. They are learned by the plane-perception module, utilizing a trait of the homography, that is, one homography can only align a planar region. With multi-homography estimation and plane perception, our proposed method can handle large parallax scenes with multiple planes.

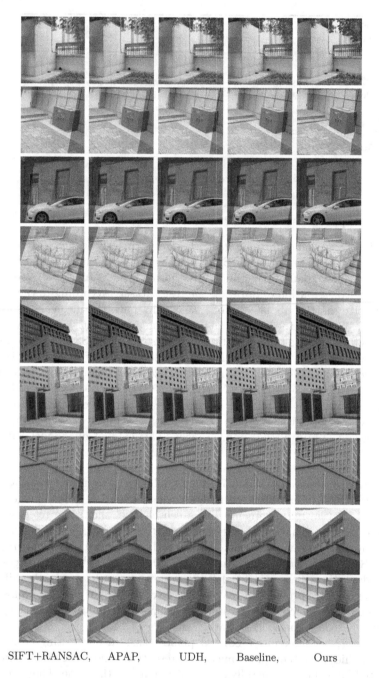

SIFT+RANSAC,   APAP,   UDH,   Baseline,   Ours

Fig. 6. Qualitative comparisons among SIFT+RANSAC, APAP [33], UDH [20], the baseline model, and our proposed plane-aware multi-homography model. Green and magenta color show differences. Normal intensities represent small differences, which means that there is almost no misalignment.

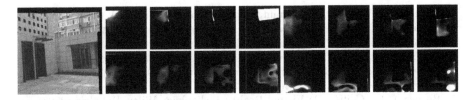

Fig. 7. Plane masks predicted in one case. The 4-th mask shows a pleasing plane. And those masks generally agree with planes in the scene.

4.2 Ablation Studies

Here we will analyze the function of the plane-perception module. The model training will not converge without predefined attention maps. So we do comparisons among the baseline model, the baseline model with only attention maps, and the full model (with the plane-perception) in Fig. 3. We found that the baseline model can estimate a good global homography. If the model only uses predefined attention maps without plane-perception, the performance becomes slightly lower due to a limited global fitting capability. With the plane perception, the full model achieves a better performance than the baseline. It means the plane-perception module can truly help the multi-homography estimation and fusion.

5 Conclusion

We have proposed a plane-aware multi-homography estimation model for image alignment in large parallax scenes. We urged a multi-homography estimation module to find planes in images through attention maps. Then we utilized the trait that a homography can only align a single plane to tell another plane-perception module all the plane locations. Finally, this perception module can refine plane locations, and give feedback to the estimation module for refocusing planar regions. In such a positive way, our method can simultaneously perceive planes and estimate accurate multiple homographies to handle large parallax. Quantitative and qualitative experiments on our new real scene dataset show that our method can handle large parallax.

Acknowledgment. This work was supported in part by the Natural Science Foundation of China (NSFC) under Grants No. 61773062.

References

1. Arefin, M.R., et al.: Multi-image super-resolution for remote sensing using deep recurrent networks. In: Proceedings of the IEEE/CVF Conference on Computer Vision and Pattern Recognition Workshops, pp. 206–207 (2020)
2. Baker, S., Datta, A., Kanade, T.: Parameterizing homographies. In: Technical Report CMU-RI-TR-06-11 (2006)

3. Bonetti, F., Warnaby, G., Quinn, L.: Augmented reality and virtual reality in physical and online retailing: a review, synthesis and research agenda. In: Jung, T., tom Dieck, M.C. (eds.) Augmented Reality and Virtual Reality. PI, pp. 119–132. Springer, Cham (2018). https://doi.org/10.1007/978-3-319-64027-3_9

4. Brown, M., Lowe, D.G.: Automatic panoramic image stitching using invariant features. Int. J. Comput. Vis. **74**(1), 59–73 (2007)

5. Burdea, G.C., Coiffet, P.: Virtual Reality Technology. Wiley, Hoboken (2003)

6. Chang, C.H., Chou, C.N., Chang, E.Y.: CLKN: cascaded Lucas-Kanade networks for image alignment. In: Proceedings of the IEEE Conference on Computer Vision and Pattern Recognition, pp. 2213–2221 (2017)

7. Chen, S.Y., Chuang, Y.Y.: Deep exposure fusion with deghosting via homography estimation and attention learning. In: ICASSP 2020–2020 IEEE International Conference on Acoustics, Speech and Signal Processing (ICASSP), pp. 1464–1468. IEEE (2020)

8. Corbetta, M., Shulman, G.L.: Control of goal-directed and stimulus-driven attention in the brain. Nat. Rev. Neurosci. **3**(3), 201–215 (2002)

9. Dempster, A.P., Laird, N.M., Rubin, D.B.: Maximum likelihood from incomplete data via the EM algorithm. J. Roy. Stat. Soc.: Ser. B (Methodol.) **39**(1), 1–22 (1977)

10. DeTone, D., Malisiewicz, T., Rabinovich, A.: Deep image homography estimation. arXiv preprint arXiv:1606.03798 (2016)

11. Erlik Nowruzi, F., Laganiere, R., Japkowicz, N.: Homography estimation from image pairs with hierarchical convolutional networks. In: Proceedings of the IEEE International Conference on Computer Vision Workshops, pp. 913–920 (2017)

12. He, K., Zhang, X., Ren, S., Sun, J.: Deep residual learning for image recognition. In: Proceedings of the IEEE Conference on Computer Vision and Pattern Recognition, pp. 770–778 (2016)

13. Itti, L., Koch, C., Niebur, E.: A model of saliency-based visual attention for rapid scene analysis. IEEE Trans. Pattern Anal. Mach. Intell. **20**(11), 1254–1259 (1998)

14. Jaderberg, M., Simonyan, K., Zisserman, A., Kavukcuoglu, K.: Spatial transformer networks. In: Proceedings of the 28th International Conference on Neural Information Processing Systems, vol. 2, pp. 2017–2025 (2015)

15. Le, H., Liu, F., Zhang, S., Agarwala, A.: Deep homography estimation for dynamic scenes. In: Proceedings of the IEEE/CVF Conference on Computer Vision and Pattern Recognition, pp. 7652–7661 (2020)

16. Li, Y., Pei, W., He, Z.: SRHEN: stepwise-refining homography estimation network via parsing geometric correspondences in deep latent space. In: Proceedings of the 28th ACM International Conference on Multimedia, pp. 3063–3071 (2020)

17. Lin, T.-Y., et al.: Microsoft COCO: common objects in context. In: Fleet, D., Pajdla, T., Schiele, B., Tuytelaars, T. (eds.) ECCV 2014. LNCS, vol. 8693, pp. 740–755. Springer, Cham (2014). https://doi.org/10.1007/978-3-319-10602-1_48

18. Lucas, B.D., Kanade, T.: An iterative image registration technique with an application to stereo vision. In: Proceedings of the 7th International Joint Conference on Artificial Intelligence, IJCAI 1981, vol. 2, pp. 674–679. Morgan Kaufmann Publishers Inc., San Francisco (1981)

19. Molina-Cabello, M.A., Elizondo, D.A., Luque Baena, R.M., López-Rubio, E., et al.: Homography estimation with deep convolutional neural networks by random color transformations. In: British Machine Vision Conference, pp. 1–11 (2019)

20. Nguyen, T., Chen, S.W., Shivakumar, S.S., Taylor, C.J., Kumar, V.: Unsupervised deep homography: a fast and robust homography estimation model. IEEE Robot. Autom. Lett. **3**(3), 2346–2353 (2018)

21. Niblick, D., Kak, A.: Homography estimation with convolutional neural networks under conditions of variance. arXiv preprint arXiv:2010.01041 (2020)

22. Nie, L., Lin, C., Liao, K., Zhao, Y.: Learning edge-preserved image stitching from large-baseline deep homography. arXiv preprint arXiv:2012.06194 (2020)

23. Reinhard, E., Heidrich, W., Debevec, P., Pattanaik, S., Ward, G., Myszkowski, K.: High Dynamic Range Imaging: Acquisition, Display, and Image-based Lighting. Morgan Kaufmann, Burlington (2010)

24. Rocco, I., Arandjelovic, R., Sivic, J.: Convolutional neural network architecture for geometric matching. In: Proceedings of the IEEE Conference on Computer Vision and Pattern Recognition, pp. 6148–6157 (2017)

25. Shen, D., Wu, G., Suk, H.I.: Deep learning in medical image analysis. Ann. Rev. Biomed. Eng. **19**, 221–248 (2017)

26. Shen, X., Darmon, F., Efros, A.A., Aubry, M.: RANSAC-flow: generic two-stage image alignment. In: Vedaldi, A., Bischof, H., Brox, T., Frahm, J.-M. (eds.) ECCV 2020. LNCS, vol. 12349, pp. 618–637. Springer, Cham (2020). https://doi.org/10.1007/978-3-030-58548-8_36

27. Szeliski, R.: Image alignment and stitching: a tutorial. Found. Trends® Comput. Graph. Vis. **2**(1), 1–104 (2006)

28. Wang, C., Wang, X., Bai, X., Liu, Y., Zhou, J.: Self-supervised deep homography estimation with invertibility constraints. Pattern Recogn. Lett. **128**, 355–360 (2019)

29. Wang, Z., Bovik, A.C., Sheikh, H.R., Simoncelli, E.P.: Image quality assessment: from error visibility to structural similarity. IEEE Trans. Image Process. **13**(4), 600–612 (2004)

30. Wronski, B., et al.: Handheld multi-frame super-resolution. ACM Trans. Graph. (TOG) **38**(4), 1–18 (2019)

31. Ye, N., Wang, C., Fan, H., Liu, S.: Motion basis learning for unsupervised deep homography estimation with subspace projection. arXiv preprint arXiv:2103.15346 (2021)

32. Ye, N., Wang, C., Liu, S., Jia, L., Wang, J., Cui, Y.: DeepMeshFlow: content adaptive mesh deformation for robust image registration. arXiv preprint arXiv:1912.05131 (2019)

33. Zaragoza, J., Chin, T.J., Brown, M.S., Suter, D.: As-projective-as-possible image stitching with moving DLT. In: Proceedings of the IEEE Conference on Computer Vision and Pattern Recognition, pp. 2339–2346 (2013)

34. Zeng, R., Denman, S., Sridharan, S., Fookes, C.: Rethinking planar homography estimation using perspective fields. In: Jawahar, C.V., Li, H., Mori, G., Schindler, K. (eds.) ACCV 2018. LNCS, vol. 11366, pp. 571–586. Springer, Cham (2019). https://doi.org/10.1007/978-3-030-20876-9_36

35. Zhang, J., et al.: Content-aware unsupervised deep homography estimation. In: Vedaldi, A., Bischof, H., Brox, T., Frahm, J.-M. (eds.) ECCV 2020. LNCS, vol. 12346, pp. 653–669. Springer, Cham (2020). https://doi.org/10.1007/978-3-030-58452-8_38

3D Hand Pose Estimation via Regularized Graph Representation Learning

Yiming He and Wei Hu$^{(\boxtimes)}$

Wangxuan Institute of Computer Technology, Peking University, Beijing, China
forhuwei@pku.edu.cn

Abstract. This paper addresses the problem of 3D hand pose estimation from a monocular RGB image. While previous methods have shown great success, the structure of hands has not been fully exploited, which is critical in pose estimation. To this end, we propose a regularized graph representation learning under a conditional adversarial learning framework for 3D hand pose estimation, aiming to capture structural interdependencies of hand joints. In particular, we estimate an initial hand pose from a parametric hand model as a prior of hand structure, which regularizes the inference of the structural deformation in the prior pose for accurate graph representation learning via residual graph convolution. To optimize the hand structure further, we propose two bone-constrained loss functions, which characterize the morphable structure of hand poses explicitly. Also, we introduce an adversarial learning framework conditioned on the input image with a multi-source discriminator, which imposes the structural constraints onto the distribution of generated 3D hand poses for anthropomorphically valid hand poses. Extensive experiments demonstrate that our model sets the new state-of-the-art in 3D hand pose estimation from a monocular image on five standard benchmarks.

Keywords: 3D hand pose estimation · Graph refinement · Prior pose · Adversarial learning · Bone-constrained loss

1 Introduction

3D human hand pose estimation is a long-standing problem in computer vision, which is critical for various applications such as virtual reality and augmented reality [15, 25]. Previous works attempt to estimate hand pose from depth images

This work was supported by National Natural Science Foundation of China under contract No. 61972009.

Supplementary Information The online version contains supplementary material available at https://doi.org/10.1007/978-3-030-93046-2_46.

© Springer Nature Switzerland AG 2021
L. Fang et al. (Eds.): CICAI 2021, LNAI 13069, pp. 540–552, 2021.
https://doi.org/10.1007/978-3-030-93046-2_46

Input   Prior Pose   Output Pose

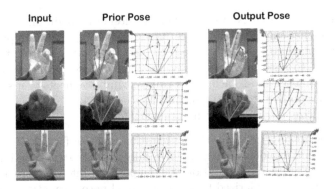

Fig. 1. The proposed method estimates 3D hand pose from a monocular image based on regularized graph representation learning. A parametric hand model generates a *prior pose*, which regularizes the learning of deformations in graph topology under a conditional adversarial learning framework.

[10,11] or in multi-view setups [24,33]. However, due to the diversity and complexity of hand shape, gesture, occlusion, *etc.*, it still remains a challenging problem despite years of studies [14].

As RGB cameras are more widely accessible than depth sensors, recent works focus mostly on 3D hand pose estimation from a monocular RGB image and have shown their efficiency [3–5,8,12]. While some early works [4,5] did not explicitly exploit the structure of hands, some recent methods [8,12] have shown the crucial role of hand structure in pose estimation, but may resort to an additional synthetic dataset. Also, unlike bodies and faces that have obvious local characteristics (*e.g.*, eyes on a face), hands exhibit almost uniform appearance. Consequently, estimated hand poses from existing methods are sometimes distorted and unnatural.

To fully exploit the structure of hands, we propose to represent the irregular topology of 3D hand poses naturally on graphs, and learn the graph representation regularized by a prior pose from the monocular image input under a conditional generative adversarial learning framework, aiming to capture the structural dependencies among hand joints. Moreover, while most existing works [4,5,12] deploy 3D Euclidean distance between joints as the loss function for 3D annotation, we propose two *bone loss functions* that constrain the length and orientation of each bone connected by adjacent joints so as to preserve hand structure explicitly. Besides, unlike some recent works [5,12,18], we estimate 3D hand poses *without* resorting to ground truth meshes or depth maps, which is more suitable for datasets in the wild.

Specifically, given an input monocular image, our framework consists of a hand pose generator and a conditional discriminator. The generator is composed of a MANO hand model module [26] that provides an initial pose estimation as prior pose and a deformation learning module regularized by the prior pose. In particular, taking the prior pose and image features as input, the deformation learning module learns the deformation in the prior pose to further refine the hand structure, by our designed residual graph convolution that leverages on the recently proposed ResGCN [19]. Further, we design a conditional multi-source discriminator that employs hand poses, hand bones computed from poses as well as the input image to distinguish the predicted 3D hand pose from the ground-truth, leading to anthropomorphically valid hand pose. Experimental results demonstrate that our model achieves significant improvements over state-of-the-art approaches on five standard benchmarks.

To summarize, our main contributions include

- We propose regularized graph representation learning for 3D hand pose estimation from a monocular image, which fully exploits structural information.
- We learn the graph representation of hand poses by inferring structural deformation, which is regularized by an initial hand pose estimation from a parametric hand model.
- We introduce two bone-constrained loss functions, which optimize the estimation of hand structures by explicitly enforcing constrains on the topology of bones.
- We present a conditional adversarial learning framework to impose structural constraints onto the distribution of generated 3D hand poses, which is able to address the challenge of uniform appearance in hands.

2   Related Work

According to the input modalities, previous works on 3D hand pose estimation can be classified into two categories: 1) 3D hand pose estimation from depth images; 2) 3D hand pose estimation from a monocular RGB image.

2.1   Estimation from Depth Images

Depth images contain rich 3D information for hand pose estimation [28], which has shown promising accuracy [32]. There is a rich literature on 3D hand pose estimation with depth images as input [6,7,9–11,16,21]. Among them, some earlier works such as [7,16] are based on a deformable hand model with an iterative optimization training approach. Due to the effectiveness of deep learning, some recent works like [21] leverage CNN to learn the shape and pose parameters for a proposed model (LBS hand model).

2.2   Estimation from a Monocular Image

Compared with the aforementioned two categories, a monocular RGB image is more accessible. Early works [2] propose complex model-fitting approaches, which are based on dynamics and multiple hypotheses and depend on restricted requirements. These model-fitting approaches have proposed many hand models, based on assembled geometric primitives [23] or sphere meshes [29], *etc.* Our work deploys the MANO hand model [26] as our prior, which models both hand shape and pose as well as generates meshes. Nevertheless, these sophisticated approaches suffer from low estimation accuracy.

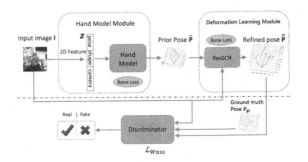

Fig. 2. Architecture of the proposed regularized graph representation learning under a conditional adversarial learning framework for 3D hand pose estimation.

With the advance of deep learning, many recent works estimate 3D hand pose from a monocular RGB image using neural networks [3–5,12,18]. Among them, some recent works [12,18] directly reconstruct the 3D hand mesh and then generate the 3D hand pose through a pose regressor. Kulon *et al.* [18] reconstruct the hand pose based on an auto-encoder, which employs an encoder to extract the latent code and feeds the latent code into the decoder to reconstruct hand mesh. Ge *et al.* [12] propose to estimate vertices of 3D meshes from GCNs [17] in order to learn nonlinear variations in hand shape. The latent feature of the input RGB image is extracted via several networks and then fed into a GCN to directly infer the 3D coordinates of mesh vertices. However, since the accuracy of the output hand mesh is critical for both methods, they need an extra dataset which provides ground truth hand meshes as supervision. Also, the upsampling layer used in [12] to reconstruct the hand mesh will cause a non-uniform distribution of vertices in mesh, which influences the accuracy of hand pose.

In contrast, we take a prior pose estimated from a parametric hand model as regularization for graph representation learning over hand poses rather than directly reconstructing hand poses from latent features. Besides, our method does not require any additional supervision such as mesh supervision [12,18] or depth image supervision [5,12]. Hence, our method is more suitable for datasets in the wild. Further, we introduce conditional adversarial training for 3D hand pose estimation, which enables learning a real distribution of 3D hand poses.

3 Methodology

3.1 Overview of the Proposed Approach

We aim to infer 3D hand pose via regularized graph representation learning under an adversarial learning framework. The entire framework consists of a hand pose generator $\mathbb{G}$ and a conditional discriminator $\mathbb{D}$, as illustrated in Fig. 2.

The multi-source discriminator $\mathbb{D}$ imposes structural constraints onto the distribution of generated 3D hand poses conditioned on the input image, which distinguishes the ground-truth 3D poses from the predicted ones.

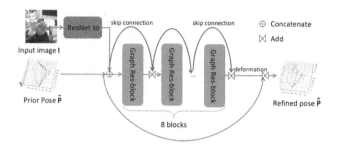

Fig. 3. Architecture of the deformation learning module in our generator.

3.2 The Proposed Hand Pose Generator $\mathbb{G}$

Given the observed input image $\mathbf{I}$ and ground truth hand pose $\mathbf{P}_{\mathrm{gt}}$, we formulate the training of hand pose estimation from a monocular image as a Maximum a Posteriori (MAP) estimation problem:

$$\hat{\mathbf{P}}_{\mathrm{MAP}}(\mathbf{I}, \mathbf{P}_{\mathrm{gt}}) = \underset{\mathbf{P}}{\mathrm{argmax}}\, f(\mathbf{I}, \mathbf{P}_{\mathrm{gt}}|\mathbf{P})g(\mathbf{P}), \tag{1}$$

where $\mathbf{P}$ denotes the hand pose to estimate. In (1), $g(\mathbf{P})$ represents the prior probability distribution of the hand pose, which provides the prior knowledge of $\mathbf{P}$. $f(\mathbf{I}, \mathbf{P}_{\mathrm{gt}}|\mathbf{P})$ denotes the likelihood function, which is the probability of obtaining the observed image $\mathbf{I}$ and ground truth hand pose $\mathbf{P}_{\mathrm{gt}}$ given the estimated hand pose $\mathbf{P}$.

We define the likelihood function as an exponential function of the distance between the estimated pose and the ground truth pose/input image:

$$f(\mathbf{I}, \mathbf{P}_{\mathrm{gt}}|\mathbf{P}) = \exp\{-d_1(\mathbf{P}_{\mathrm{gt}}, \mathbf{P}) - d_2(\mathbf{I}, \mathbf{P})\}, \tag{2}$$

where $d_1(\cdot)$ is the distance metric between the estimated hand pose and the ground truth, and $d_2(\cdot)$ is the distance metric between the estimated hand pose and the input image. Regarding $g(\mathbf{P})$, it is a constant C after we acquire a prior pose from a parametric hand model. Hence, when we substitute (2) and $g(\mathbf{P}) = C$ into (1), take the logarithm and multiply by -1, we have

$$\min_{\mathbf{P}} d_1(\mathbf{P}_{\mathrm{gt}}, \mathbf{P}) + d_2(\mathbf{I}, \mathbf{P}). \tag{3}$$

$d_1(\cdot)$ and $d_2(\cdot)$ will be discussed in Sect. 3.4 in detail.

Specifically, we employ a parametric hand model to provide the prior of $\mathbf{P}$, and designate a Deformation Learning Module to learn the pose under the supervision of the ground-truth pose and input image. We discuss the two modules of the generator in detail as follows.

The Hand Model Module. Given an input monocular image, this module aims to generate an initial estimation of 3D hand pose $\tilde{\mathbf{P}}$ as a prior. A hand

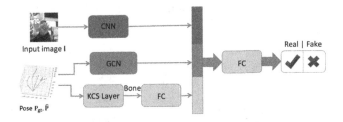

Fig. 4. Architecture of the conditional discriminator.

model is able to represent both hand shape and pose with a few parameters, which is thus a suitable prior for hand pose estimation.

We first predict parameters of the hand model. Specifically, we crop and resize the input image to a salient region of the hand, which is fed into the ResNet-50 network [13] to extract features for the construction of the latent code $\mathbf{z}$, $i.e.$, parameters of the hand model. Then, we employ a modified MANO hand model [26], which is based on the SMPL model [20] for human bodies.

The Deformation Learning Module. This module aims at accurate graph representation learning for hand pose estimation, which is conditional on the prior and under the supervision of the input image and ground truth pose as in (1). In particular, conditioned on the prior $\tilde{\mathbf{P}}$, we learn the structural *deformation* in $\tilde{\mathbf{P}}$ instead of the holistic hand pose.

We first construct an unweighted graph over $\tilde{\mathbf{P}}$, where the irregularly sampled key points ($i.e.$, joints) on the hand are projected onto nodes. The graph signal on each node is the concatenation of the global feature vector of the input image and the 3-dimensional coordinate vector of each joint in the input prior pose. Nodes are connected if they represent adjacent key points of the hand, where the adjacency relations follow the human hand structure as presented in Fig. 5, leading to an adjacency matrix $\mathbf{A} \in \mathbb{R}^{N \times N}$.

Based on the graph representation $\mathbf{A}$, the finally refined pose is

$$\hat{\mathbf{P}} = \tilde{\mathbf{P}} + \mathrm{GCN}(\tilde{\mathbf{P}} \oplus \mathbf{F}, \mathbf{A}), \tag{4}$$

where $\mathbf{F} \in \mathbb{R}^{N \times F}$ denotes the F-dimensional global feature vector of the image repeated N times, and $\oplus$ denotes the feature-wise concatenation operation. $\mathrm{GCN}(\tilde{\mathbf{P}} \oplus \mathbf{F}, \mathbf{A})$ represents the learned deformation between the prior $\tilde{\mathbf{P}}$ and the ground truth. The sum of the prior pose $\tilde{\mathbf{P}}$ and its deformation thus leads to the refined hand pose.

Let $\mathbf{X}^l$ denote the input of the l-th Graph Res-block, then the output of the l-th Graph Res-block takes the form

$$\mathbf{X}^{l+1} = N\left(g(N(g(\mathbf{X}^l, \mathbf{A})), \mathbf{A})\right) + \mathrm{skip}(\mathbf{X}^l), \tag{5}$$

where $g(\cdot)$ represents a single GCN layer as in [17], $N(\cdot)$ represents a single normalization layer, and $\mathrm{skip}(\cdot)$ denotes the skip connection which is a GCN

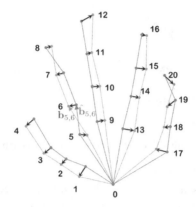

Fig. 5. Illustration of the residual between the ground truth hand pose (marked in green) and the predicted one (marked in red). Each hand pose has 21 key joints. We denote a bone vector connecting two key joints i and j by $\mathbf{b}_{i,j}$, such as $\mathbf{b}_{5,6}$ in the figure. (Color figure online)

layer to match the dimension of the two terms in (5). We then stack several layers of Graph Res-blocks to learn the deformation of the prior pose, as demonstrated in Fig. 3.

3.3 The Proposed Conditional Discriminator $\mathbb{D}$

A simple architecture of a discriminator is a fully-connected (FC) network with the hand pose as input, which however has two shortcomings: 1) the relation between the RGB image and inferred hand pose is neglected; 2) structural properties of the hand pose are not taken into account explicitly. Instead, inspired by the multi-source architecture in [31], we design a conditional multi-source discriminator with three inputs to address the aforementioned issues. As illustrated in Fig. 4, the inputs include: 1) features of the input monocular image; 2) features of the refined hand pose $\hat{\mathbf{P}}$ or the ground truth pose $\mathbf{P}_{\mathrm{gt}}$; 3) features of bones via the KCS layer as in [30], which computes the bone matrix from $\hat{\mathbf{P}}$ or $\mathbf{P}_{\mathrm{gt}}$ via a simple matrix multiplication. The bone features contain prominent structural information such as the length and direction of bones, thus characterizing the hand structure accurately.

The loss function of the conditional discriminator follows the definition of the Wasserstein loss [1] conditioned on the input image $\mathbf{I}$:

$$\mathcal{L}_{\mathrm{Wass}} = -\mathbb{E}_{\mathbf{P}_{\mathrm{gt}} \sim p_{data}(\mathbf{P}_{\mathrm{gt}})} \mathbb{D}(\mathbf{P}_{\mathrm{gt}}|\mathbf{I}) + \mathbb{E}_{\hat{\mathbf{P}} \sim p(\hat{\mathbf{P}})} \mathbb{D}(\hat{\mathbf{P}}|\mathbf{I}), \qquad (6)$$

where $\mathbb{D}$ takes the generated (fake) pose $\hat{\mathbf{P}}$ and ground-truth pose $\mathbf{P}_{\mathrm{gt}}$ as input, $\mathbf{P}_{\mathrm{gt}}$ is a sample following the ground-truth pose distribution $p_{data}(\mathbf{P}_{\mathrm{gt}})$ and $\hat{\mathbf{P}}$ is a sample from the refined pose distribution $p(\hat{\mathbf{P}})$.

3.4   The Proposed Bone-Constrained Loss Functions

As presented in (3), we have two types of loss functions for the MAP estimation of hand pose. We employ the commonly adopted Euclidean distance in the coordinates of joints of 3D hand pose $\mathcal{L}_{\text{pose}}$ [12] as well as two proposed bone-constrained metrics as $d_1(\cdot)$ to measure the distortion of the estimated 3D hand pose compared to the ground truth, and apply the commonly used Euclidean distance in the coordinates of joints of projected 2D hand pose $\mathcal{L}_{\text{proj}}$ [12] as $d_2(\cdot)$ to measure the distance between the estimation and the 2D image,

$$\mathcal{L}_{\text{pose}} = \sum_i ||\mathbf{j}_i - \hat{\mathbf{j}}_i||_2, \mathcal{L}_{\text{proj}} = \sum_i ||\mathbf{j}'_i - \hat{\mathbf{j}}'_i||_2, \tag{7}$$

where $\mathbf{j}_i \in \mathbb{R}^{3\times1}, \mathbf{j}'_i \in \mathbb{R}^{2\times1}$ are 3D and 2D coordinates of joint i respectively.

Since $\mathcal{L}_{\text{pose}}$ and $\mathcal{L}_{\text{proj}}$ cannot capture the structural properties of hand pose explicitly, we propose two novel bone-constrained loss functions to characterize the length and direction of each bone.

As illustrated in Fig. 5, we first define a bone vector $\mathbf{b}_{i,j} \in \mathbb{R}^{3\times1}$ between hand joint i and j as

$$\mathbf{b}_{i,j} = \mathbf{j}_i - \mathbf{j}_j, \tag{8}$$

The first bone-constrained loss $\mathcal{L}_{\text{len}}$ quantifies the distance in *bone length* between the ground truth hand and its estimate, which we define as

$$\mathcal{L}_{\text{len}} = \sum_{i,j} \left| ||\mathbf{b}_{i,j}||_2 - ||\hat{\mathbf{b}}_{i,j}||_2 \right|, \tag{9}$$

where $\mathbf{b}_{i,j}$ and $\hat{\mathbf{b}}_{i,j}$ are the bone vectors of the ground truth and the predicted bone respectively.

The second bone-constrained loss $\mathcal{L}_{\text{dir}}$ measures the deviation in the *direction of bones*:

$$\mathcal{L}_{\text{dir}} = \sum_{i,j} \left| \left| \mathbf{b}_{i,j}/||\mathbf{b}_{i,j}||_2 - \hat{\mathbf{b}}_{i,j}/||\hat{\mathbf{b}}_{i,j}||_2 \right| \right|_2. \tag{10}$$

Besides, as we adopt the framework of adversarial learning, we also introduce the Wasserstein loss $\mathcal{L}_{\text{Wass}}$ in (6) into the loss function for adversarial training. Hence, the overall loss function $\mathcal{L}$ is

$$\mathcal{L} = \mathcal{L}_{\text{pose}} + \lambda_{\text{proj}}\mathcal{L}_{\text{proj}} + \lambda_{\text{len}}\mathcal{L}_{\text{len}} + \lambda_{\text{dir}}\mathcal{L}_{\text{dir}} + \lambda_{\text{Wass}}\mathcal{L}_{\text{Wass}}, \tag{11}$$

where λ_{proj}, λ_{len}, λ_{dir} and λ_{Wass} are hyperparameters for the trade-off among these losses. In accordance with (3), $d_1 = \mathcal{L}_{\text{pose}} + \lambda_{\text{len}}\mathcal{L}_{\text{len}} + \lambda_{\text{dir}}\mathcal{L}_{\text{dir}}$, and $d_2 = \lambda_{\text{proj}}\mathcal{L}_{\text{proj}}$.

4 Experimental Results

4.1 Implementation Details

In our experiments, we first pretrain the hand model module and then train the entire network end-to-end. In particular, the training process can be divided into three stages.

Stage I. We pretrain the hand model module, which is randomly initialized and trained for 100 epochs using the Adam optimizer with learning rate 0.001. Then, we freeze the parameters of this stage to evaluate the effectiveness of the deformation learning module.

Stage II. We train the generator $\mathbb{G}$ end-to-end without the discriminator $\mathbb{D}$. In $\mathbb{G}$, the hand model module is initialized with the trained model in the first stage and the deformation learning module is randomly initialized. $\mathbb{G}$ is then trained with 100 epochs using the Adam optimizer with learning rate 0.0001.

Stage III. We adopt the framework of SNGAN [22] for the conditional adversarial training, and train our model end-to-end. $\mathbb{G}$ and $\mathbb{D}$ are trained with 100 epochs using the Adam optimizer with learning rate 0.0001.

Regarding the hyper-parameters in (11), we set $\lambda_{\mathrm{len}} = 0.01, \lambda_{\mathrm{dir}} = 0.1, \lambda_{\mathrm{proj}} = 0.1, \lambda_{\mathrm{Wass}} = 0.01$.

4.2 Experimental Results

We compare our method with competitive 3D hand pose estimation approaches on the five datasets. We list the results in 3D Euclidean distance for comparison with the state-of-the-arts in Table 1. Compared to these works which directly reconstruct the 3D hand pose [4,5,12], our method performs much better mainly due to the proposed regularized graph representation learning and conditional adversarial learning. We show the qualitative results and PCK results in the supplementary material.

Table 1. Comparison with state-of-the-art methods on the five datasets. Note that MPII+ZNSL only provides 2D annotation, thus we employ the 2D distance (px) metric on this dataset.

	STB	RHD	MPII+ZNSL(px)	Dexter+Object	EgoDexter
[12]	6.37	15.33	–	–	–
[4]	9.76	–	18.95	25.53	45.33
[27]	8.56	19.73	–	40.20	56.92
[34]	–	–	59.40	34.75	52.77
Ours	**3.97**	**12.40**	**9.87**	**16.12**	**34.98**

Table 2. The performance of different stages in our model on three datasets (measured in 3D Euclidean distance (mm)).

Stage	Hand model	Deformation	Discriminator	STB	RHD	EGODEXTER
I	✓			24.15	83.37	52.32
II	✓	✓		5.12	15.84	43.26
III	✓	✓	✓	**3.97**	**12.40**	**34.98**

Table 3. Ablation studies on the Deformation Learning Module, with comparison between the Deformation Learning Module and the simple FC Refinement Module in 3D Euclidean distance (mm).

Model	GCN Deformation	FC Deformation	Discriminator	STB	RHD	EGODEXTER
1		✓		15.11	37.59	52.34
2	✓			5.12	15.84	40.12
3		✓	✓	10.23	25.15	44.23
4	✓		✓	**3.97**	**12.40**	**34.98**

4.3 Ablation Studies

We perform ablation studies on the performance of different stages, the deformation learning module, the discriminator and loss functions. Due to the page limit, we present all the results in 3D Euclidean distance (mm). Please refer to the supplementary material for the results measured in 3D PCK.

On Different Stages. We present the results of three training stages in average 3D Euclidean distance, as listed in Table 2. The performance of **Stage II** significantly outperforms **Stage I**, which demonstrates that the proposed deformation learning module plays the most critical role in our model. The adversarial training scheme (**Stage III**) further improves the result, by learning a real distribution of the 3D hand pose.

On the Deformation Learning Module. We compare the deformation learning module with a simple fully-connected deformation learning module (FC Deformation Module) to refine the prior pose. We train the deformation learning modules in different experimental settings: 1) without our discriminator, *i.e.*, without adversarial learning; and 2) with our discriminator. As presented in Table 3, the GCN deformation learning module leads to significant gain over the simple FC deformation module on both datasets in different settings, thus validating the superiority of the proposed deformation learning module.

On the Conditional Discriminator. We compare with a single-source discriminator which only takes the 3D hand pose as the input. As presented in Table 4, the multi-source discriminator outperforms the single-source one on both datasets, which gives credits to exploring the structure of hand bones and the relation between the image and pose.

Table 4. Ablation studies on the discriminator (3D Euclidean distance (mm)).

Model	Deformation Learning	Multi-source	Single-source	STB	RHD	EGODEXTER
1	✓	✓		**3.97**	**12.40**	**34.98**
2	✓		✓	4.54	15.10	37.46

Table 5. Ablation studies on the proposed bone-constrained loss functions at three stages.

Model	$\mathcal{L}_{pose} + \mathcal{L}_{proj}$	$\mathcal{L}_{len}$	$\mathcal{L}_{dir}$	STB			RHD		
				Stage I	Stage II	Stage III	Stage I	Stage II	Stage III
1	✓			32.75	9.11	5.35	99.24	25.96	15.07
2	✓	✓		30.32	8.00	5.02	95.19	22.96	14.76
3	✓		✓	27.65	6.91	5.00	89.76	21.63	14.01
4	✓	✓	✓	24.15	5.12	**3.97**	83.37	15.84	**12.40**

On Loss Functions. We also evaluate the proposed bone-constrained loss functions $\mathcal{L}_{len}$ and $\mathcal{L}_{dir}$ separately. We train the network with different combinations of loss functions on the STB and RHD datasets in three stages respectively. As reported in Table 5, the network trained with our proposed bone-constrained loss functions performs better in all the three stages on both datasets. We also notice that $\mathcal{L}_{dir}$ plays a more significant role compared to $\mathcal{L}_{len}$. This gives credits to the constraint on the orientation of bones that explicitly takes structural properties of hands into consideration.

5   Conclusion

In this paper, we propose regularized graph representation learning under a conditional adversarial learning framework for 3D hand pose estimation from a monocular image. Based on the MAP estimation formulation, we take an initial estimation of hand pose as prior pose, and further learn the structural deformation in the prior pose via residual graph convolution. Also, we propose two bone-constrained loss functions to enforce constraints on the bone structures explicitly. Extensive experiments demonstrate the superiority of the proposed method.

References

1. Arjovsky, M., Chintala, S., Bottou, L.: Wasserstein generative adversarial networks. In: Precup, D., Teh, Y.W. (eds.) Proceedings of the 34th International Conference on Machine Learning. Proceedings of Machine Learning Research, vol. 70, pp. 214–223. PMLR, International Convention Centre, Sydney, Australia, 06–11 August 2017

2. Athitsos, V., Sclaroff, S.: Estimating 3d hand pose from a cluttered image. In: IEEE Computer Society Conference on Computer Vision & Pattern Recognition (2003)

3. Baek, S., Kim, K.I., Kim, T.K.: Pushing the envelope for rgb-based dense 3d hand pose estimation via neural rendering. In: The IEEE Conference on Computer Vision and Pattern Recognition (CVPR) (June 2019)

4. Boukhayma, A., Bem, R.D., Torr, P.H.: 3D hand shape and pose from images in the wild. In: The IEEE Conference on Computer Vision and Pattern Recognition (CVPR) (June 2019)

5. Cai, Y., Ge, L., Cai, J., Yuan, J.: Weakly-supervised 3d hand pose estimation from monocular rgb images. In: The European Conference on Computer Vision (ECCV) (September 2018)

6. Choi, C.: Deephand: robust hand pose estimation by completing a matrix imputed with deep features. In: Computer Vision & Pattern Recognition (2016)

7. De, L.G.M., Fleet, D.J., Paragios, N.: Model-based 3d hand pose estimation from monocular video. IEEE Trans. Pattern Anal. Mach. Intell. **33**(9), 1793–1805 (2011)

8. Doosti, B., Naha, S., Mirbagheri, M., Crandall, D.J.: Hope-net: a graph-based model for hand-object pose estimation. In: IEEE/CVF Conference on Computer Vision and Pattern Recognition (CVPR) (June 2020)

9. Fitzgibbon, A.: Accurate, robust, and flexible real-time hand tracking. In: Proceedings, pp. 3633–3642 (2015)

10. Ge, L., Cai, Y., Weng, J., Yuan, J.: Hand pointnet: 3d hand pose estimation using point sets, pp. 8417–8426 (June 2018). https://doi.org/10.1109/CVPR.2018.00878

11. Ge, L., Liang, H., Yuan, J., Thalmann, D.: Robust 3d hand pose estimation in single depth images: from single-view cnn to multi-view cnns. In: The IEEE Conference on Computer Vision and Pattern Recognition (CVPR) (June 2016)

12. Ge, L., et al.: 3D hand shape and pose estimation from a single rgb image. In: The IEEE Conference on Computer Vision and Pattern Recognition (CVPR) (June 2019)

13. He, K., Zhang, X., Ren, S., Sun, J.: Deep residual learning for image recognition. In: The IEEE Conference on Computer Vision and Pattern Recognition (CVPR) (June 2016)

14. Hui, L., Yuan, J., Lee, J., Ge, L., Thalmann, D.: Hough forest with optimized leaves for global hand pose estimation with arbitrary postures. IEEE Trans. Cybern. **PP**(99), 1–15 (2017)

15. Hürst, W., van Wezel, C.: Gesture-based interaction via finger tracking for mobile augmented reality. Multimed. Tools Appl. **62**, 233–258 (2011)

16. Khamis, S., Taylor, J., Shotton, J., Keskin, C., Izadi, S., Fitzgibbon, A.: Learning an efficient model of hand shape variation from depth images. In: IEEE Conference on Computer Vision & Pattern Recognition (2015)

17. Kipf, T.N., Welling, M.: Semi-supervised classification with graph convolutional networks. In: International Conference on Learning Representations (ICLR) (2017)

18. Kulon, D., Wang, H., Güler, R.A., Bronstein, M.M., Zafeiriou, S.: Single image 3d hand reconstruction with mesh convolutions. In: BMVC (September 2019)

19. Li, G., Muller, M., Thabet, A., Ghanem, B.: Deepgcns: can gcns go as deep as cnns? In: The IEEE International Conference on Computer Vision (ICCV) (October 2019)

20. Loper, M., Mahmood, N., Romero, J., Pons-Moll, G., Black, M.J.: Smpl: a skinned multi-person linear model. ACM Trans. Graph. **34**(6), 248:1–248:16 (2015). https://doi.org/10.1145/2816795.2818013, http://doi.acm.org/10.1145/2816795.2818013

21. Malik, J., Elhayek, A., Nunnari, F., Varanasi, K., Stricker, D.: Deephps: end-to-end estimation of 3d hand pose and shape by learning from synthetic depth. In: 2018 International Conference on 3D Vision (3DV) (2018)
22. Miyato, T., Kataoka, T., Koyama, M., Yoshida, Y.: Spectral normalization for generative adversarial networks. In: International Conference on Learning Representations (2018). https://openreview.net/forum?id=B1QRgziT-
23. Oikonomidis, I., Kyriazis, N., Argyros, A.: Efficient model-based 3d tracking of hand articulations using kinect, vol. 1 (January 2011). https://doi.org/10.5244/C.25.101
24. Panteleris, P., Argyros, A.A.: Back to RGB: 3d tracking of hands and hand-object interactions based on short-baseline stereo. CoRR abs/1705.05301 (2017). http://arxiv.org/abs/1705.05301
25. Piumsomboon, T., Clark, A., Billinghurst, M., Cockburn, A.: User-defined gestures for augmented reality. In: Kotzé, P., Marsden, G., Lindgaard, G., Wesson, J., Winckler, M. (eds.) INTERACT 2013. LNCS, vol. 8118, pp. 282–299. Springer, Heidelberg (2013). https://doi.org/10.1007/978-3-642-40480-1_18
26. Romero, J., Tzionas, D., Black, M.J.: Embodied hands: modeling and capturing hands and bodies together. ACM Trans. Graph. **36**(6), 245:1–245:17 (2017). https://doi.org/10.1145/3130800.3130883, http://doi.acm.org/10.1145/3130800.3130883
27. Spurr, A., Song, J., Park, S., Hilliges, O.: Cross-modal deep variational hand pose estimation. CoRR abs/1803.11404 (2018). http://arxiv.org/abs/1803.11404
28. Tang, D., Yu, T.H., Kim, T.K.: Real-time articulated hand pose estimation using semi-supervised transductive regression forests. In: IEEE International Conference on Computer Vision (2013)
29. Tkach, A., Pauly, M., Tagliasacchi, A.: Sphere-meshes for real-time hand modeling and tracking. ACM Trans. Graph. **35**(6), 222:1–222:11 (2016). https://doi.org/10.1145/2980179.2980226, http://doi.acm.org/10.1145/2980179.2980226
30. Wandt, B., Ackermann, H., Rosenhahn, B.: A kinematic chain space for monocular motion capture (February 2017)
31. Yang, W., Ouyang, W., Wang, X., Ren, J., Li, H., Wang, X.: 3D human pose estimation in the wild by adversarial learning. In: The IEEE Conference on Computer Vision and Pattern Recognition (CVPR) (June 2018)
32. Yuan, S., et al.: Depth-based 3d hand pose estimation: from current achievements to future goals, pp. 2636–2645 (June 2018). https://doi.org/10.1109/CVPR.2018.00279
33. Zhang, J., Jiao, J., Chen, M., Qu, L., Xu, X., Yang, Q.: 3d hand pose tracking and estimation using stereo matching (October 2016)
34. Zimmermann, C., Brox, T.: Learning to estimate 3d hand pose from single rgb images. In: The IEEE International Conference on Computer Vision (ICCV) (October 2017)

Emotion Class-Wise Aware Loss for Image Emotion Classification

Sinuo Deng[1], Lifang Wu[1], Ge Shi[1(✉)], Heng Zhang[1], Wenjin Hu[1], and Ruihai Dong[2]

[1] Faculty of Information Technology, Beijing University of Technology, Beijing, China
[2] Insight Centre for Data Analytics, University College Dublin, Dublin, Ireland

Abstract. With the increasing number of images containing rich emotional information in social media and the urgent demand for faster and more accurate image emotional information mining, some researchers have begun to pay attention to image emotion classification research. However, most of the work focuses on the complex model design, neglecting the proper consideration of the loss function, which is common in the research of image emotion classification task. Simultaneously, the widely used loss function, such as the Softmax Loss, ignores the difference in the concentration of the inner-class features in image emotion and object classification, which causes the problem of lacking inner-class feature distance converging data imbalance leading to more misclassifications of affective images. We explored the problem of inner-class feature constraints in the loss function design for image classification tasks. Based on the existing loss improvement, we propose a method with the Emotion Class-wise Aware (ECWA) loss to get better accuracy and robustness on more occasions. Results show that the method we proposed is more effective in the image emotion classification task, especially in the emotion category with few samples.

Keywords: Image emotion classification · Convolutional neural network · Deep metric learning · Loss function

1 Introduction

With social media development and the increasing amount of data with affective information, more accurate algorithms are needed to replace manual methods to retrieve and analyze this information [4,18]. Earlier studies have analyzed the emotional trend characteristics of images from basic characteristics or traditional aesthetic evaluation and used traditional machine learning methods to form a classifier to determine the emotional category of images. With the introduction of deep models and deep frameworks such as AlexNet [14], GoogleNet [24], and ResNet [10], deep learning models as the basic feature extractor for image feature analysis have been widely used. In recent years, various model applications and framework adjustments have been continuously proposed [1].

© Springer Nature Switzerland AG 2021
L. Fang et al. (Eds.): CICAI 2021, LNAI 13069, pp. 553–564, 2021.
https://doi.org/10.1007/978-3-030-93046-2_47

CAT   BYCYCLE   CONTENTMENT   SADNESS

Fig. 1. Example images of the two different object categories in the ILSVRC dataset [8] (left) and two different emotion categories Flickr & Instagram dataset [28] (right).

Although it can play a certain role, the main backbone mentioned above mainly sources from image object classification, which is essentially different from emotion classification. There should be a more targeted loss function corresponding to it. However, these deep neural network models have a relatively concise way of judging the loss in classification problems, and most of them use the softmax loss as the loss function, which refers to the cross-entropy loss function with softmax as the activation function [7,14].

We find that the loss function used in the emotional image classification task needs to be analyzed for its own purpose that constraints on the extracted features. Traditional image object classification has relatively clearer distinctions at the pixel contour level, such as shape, and its own characteristics have certain constraints, just like Fig. 1. The problem can be solved only by considering the distance between classes, such as the commonly used cross-entropy loss. However, for multi-category emotional images, the features such as the contours of the same category are relatively inconspicuous, and certain constraints need to be placed to make the distinction between different categories more obvious. Therefore, it is necessary to improve the method of narrowing the distance within the class. Moreover, emotional images are currently more of a carrier that expresses human emotions on the Internet, and their appearance is more random and uneven. Taking category imbalance into consideration in the loss function design will make the resulting model more robust.

Therefore, this paper designs the loss function in the deep learning framework from the perspective of the affective image category imbalance and lacking inner-class constraint. ECWA Loss, a modified loss function of inner-class constraint with emotion class-wise awareness. Experiments on four differnet type but widely used image emotion classification datasets show that our proposed method exhibits a promising performance.

The main contributions of this work can be summarized as follow: 1) different from designing a complex framework, we propose a loss function to constraint the inner-class feature discriminatively from a more practical perspective on image emotion classification task; 2) unlike the existing work that only design for special dataset or occasion, we employ a general method in image emotion classification, which performs better on four widely used data sets compared with SOTA methods under the same conditions. The remainder of the paper is organized as follows. First, we summarize the related work of image emotion classification. Second, we present the framework of our proposed method and its principle in detail. Finally, the experiment results are reported, followed by the conclusion.

2   Related Work

2.1   Image Emotion Classification

With the popularity of social media platforms, such as Twitter and Flickr, Image emotion recognition has attracted increasing research interest. As an important research area of artificial intelligence, image emotion recognition aims to predict the aroused emotion of people after they view images [11,12]. While visual emotion recognition has been studied for many years, the research lags on cognitive content analysis [29].

Existing image emotion analysis research can be grouped into two emotional expression models of psychology, the Dimensional Emotion Space (DES) and the Categorical Emotion States (CES) [30]. CES approaches classify emotions into representative categories, such as Mikel's wheel [17] or Ekman's model [9], which is the theoretical basis for the classification of most emotion data sets.

Compared with traditional hand-crafted features [20], features learned by deep neural networks are highly discriminative. Last few years, several works exploit deep features and achieve significant progress due to the better ability of feature extraction of CNN architectures. Campos et al. [5,6] proposed fine-tune state-of-the-art CNNs pretrained on the large-scale general dataset [8] for visual emotion prediction.

Recently, there are more researches on complex framework design. She et al. [23] developed a weakly supervised framework for sentiment detection and classification and gained the SOTA results on several datasets. Considering the additional region and vote information of the image emotion dataset, Rao et al. [21] proposed an image emotion classification model with better results.

2.2   Metric Learning

Metric learning has been extensively studied in pattern analysis and image recognition during past decades [2]. Recently, deep metric learning methods that capturing semantic similarity have been successfully applied to a variety of domains, e.g., face verification [25], image retrieval [13], and classification tasks [26].

In image emotion anasysis, few researchers have explored the combination of metric learning and image emotion classification. More recently, Yao et al. developed a unified multi-task framework which is jointly optimized by softmax and designed multi-constraint sentiment similarity losses [26]. They showed that it took better results on image emotion classification task by InceptionV3 CNN backbone. However, this method has certain limitations. It relied on the slide of data and selection of anchor points picture like the triplet loss method [22].

As the work of loss function design, both center loss [25] and focal loss [15] have similar research goals as ours. Considering the unobvious difference between any two different person faces and any two face images from the same person. Center loss is proposed to minimize the intra-class distances of the deep features. The research combined center loss and softmax loss to enhance the discriminative power of features for face recognition. Although center loss function achieve better performance on constraint deep feature distances of inner-intra class, it lacks consideration on data imbalance, which often appears in the field of image emotion analysis as illustrated in introduction. On the contrary, the focal loss performs the opposite of center loss. Although it is designed to deal with the data imbalance problem in the object detection tasks, it is not special strength on the feature distance problem, including the image emotion classification task.

Inspired by [15,25], we design the Emotion Class-wise Aware (ECWA) method, which integrates a class-wise aware module based on center loss to solve data imbalance caused by different emotion classes, to improve the classification accuracy by constraining the inner-class feature distance according to different classes and expand the intra-class ones between different emotion classes.

3   Method

To solve the above problems, we designed an emotion image classification framework that is simultaneously optimized by the emotion class-wise aware loss and softmax loss for image emotion classification. Figure 2 show the architecture of our proposed method.

3.1   Framework

In this work, our goal is to get a more accurate model of affective image classification task through a loss-designed-based framework with a concise backbone architecture. The model is trained with the joint supervision of the inner- and intra-class constraint loss. Given N training images $\{(x_i, y^{x_i})\}_{i=1}^{N}$ of K categories, x_i denotes the ith training image, and $y^{x_i} \in \{0, 1, \cdots, K-1\}$ represents the corresponding emotion labels. And the category distribution $l_i \in \{1, 2, \cdots, K\}$ of these K categories training images can get from the training dataset directly. Then, for image x_i, we maximize the confidence score p_{x_i} of the ground-truth y^{x_i} by optimizing the joint loss, which enforces that a distance is maintained between the deep features of different classes. By leveraging the advantages of the intra- and inner- class loss (i.e., L_{ECWA} and $L_{softmax}$), we can obtain more discriminative features for classification tasks in the end-to-end framework.

The architecture in Fig. 2 is comprised of five key steps: a. The data collected from the dataset preprocess into the convolutional network in the correct form; b. The feature extracted before the last fully connected layer is sent to the ECWA module to calculate the loss value and the weight value; c. The category distribution of the training set is used to calculate the weight value in Class-wise

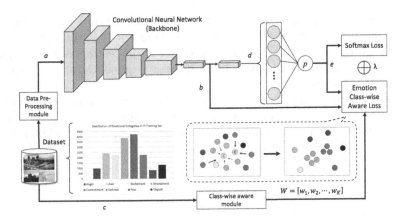

Fig. 2. The architecture of our proposed method.

aware module; d. Get the category of the maximum value in the last FC layer; e. The original softmax loss and the designed ECWA loss are used to calculate the total loss, and the backbone network in step b and the subsequent fully connected layer are updated by feedback until the model converges to complete the model training.

3.2 Emotion Class-Wise Aware Module

As a key part of the inner-class constraints loss, the Emotion Class-wise Aware module is used to calculate weight value w_i of each category according to the distribution l_i which includes the amount of each category in the training dataset. After then, join the weight coefficients of each category together to obtain the emotion category weight vector W:

$$W = [w_1, w_2, \cdots, w_K], \quad w_i = \frac{\sum_{i=1}^{K} l_i}{l_i K}, \forall i = 1, 2, \cdots, K. \tag{1}$$

3.3 Emotion Class-Wise Aware Loss

Spired by [25], we constraint the feature by calculate the distance between the emotion feature of the input image with the initialized center feature of the class which the image belongs of. However, apart from of this, the Emotion Class-wise Aware weight are incorporated into this basic inner-class constraints loss. It is aware of the loss to condense the deep features within the different categories discriminately, which may reduces the impact caused by the unbalanced sample categories. The specific loss function is as follows:

$$L_{ECWA} = \frac{1}{2N} \sum_{i=1}^{N} \left(w_i \| f_i - C_{y_i} \|_2 \right)^2, \tag{2}$$

where w_i is get from Eq. 1, f_i is the feature of the image before the classification layer through the basic backbone network in step b, C_{y_i} is the feature center when the category is y_i, and the feature center is the feature vector composed of the mean values of the features obtained from images of the same category in the current batch in each dimension.

As the common classification loss function to provide the intra-class classification constraint, the softmax loss is optimized to maximize the probability of the correct class in the training process. The fine-tuning of the backbone model is done by minimizing the softmax loss:

$$L_{\text{softmax}} = -\frac{1}{N} \sum_{i=1}^{N} \log \frac{e^{f_{y_i}}}{\sum_{j=1}^{K} e^{f_j}}, \tag{3}$$

where f_y is the output of y category by the softmax layer.

The softmax loss can be seen as the sum of the negative log-likelihood over all training images, which penalizes the classification error for each class equally and thus ignore the intra-class variance, while ECWA loss can provide enough corresponding constraint. Thus, these two loss can supplement each other to optimizing the classification framework in both inner- and intra-class ways. The total loss function is integrated with two losses the Eq. 2 and Eq. 3 via a weighted combination:

$$Loss = \lambda * L_{softmax} + (1 - \lambda) * L_{ECWA}, \tag{4}$$

where λ is the weight to control the tradeoff between the two losses.

4   Experiment

4.1   Dataset and Implementation Details

We evaluate the proposed ECWA method on four different widely used public affective datasets: FI, EmotionROI, Twitter I, Twitter II datasets.

FI [28] is consists of 23,308 pictures by 8 imbalance scale emotion categories from Flickr and Instagram, the situation in the actual situation of social media.

EmotionROI [20] has balanced number of images, a total of 1980 images of 6 emotion categories, as a multi-category and Flickr-sourced data set.

Twitter I [27] is a two-category data set which has 1,269 pictures selected from the Twitter platform.

Twitter II [3] is a 603-images Small-scale data sets which is also always used for testing the model performance of image emotion classification task.

It is worth mentioning that the names of Twitter I and Twitter II are not proposed by this article or the original author but are given by other researchers in the experiment for the convenience of distinction. This article uses the same name for the convenience of explanation and comparison experiments.

We implement ECWA based on the PyTorch framework [19] and adopt the AlexNet, InceptionV3 and ResNet101 architectures as the backbone for comparison methods on an NVIDIA GTX 1080Ti GPU with 32 GB on-board memory.

Table 1. Different setting of training parameters on different backbone.

Backbone	Croped Size	Batchsize	Initial Learning Rate
AlexNet [14]	227 × 227	32	0.01
InceptionV3 [24]	299 × 299	16	0.001
ResNet101 [10]	448 × 448	16	0.0001

To deal with the limited training data, we apply random horizontal flips and crop a random patch with fixed size as a form of data augmentation to reduce overfitting, which is based on the same preprocessing of WSCNet. The setting details of different backbone as show in Table 1.

To compare performance more fairly, the all datasets are split same with the best performance work, WSCNet. The FI datasets are split by randomly into 80% training, 5% validation and 15% testing sets. The other datasets are split into 80% training and 20% testing sets respectively. For the classification performance of models got by each method fairly, we use accuracy for the universally-agreed metric when testing. To ensure stability, the results of the whole experiment are obtained by averaging repeated experiments with 3–5 random seeds.

4.2 Compared Methods and Analysis

We compare the proposed ECWA by accuracy with two state-of-the-art method of image emotion classification, WSCNet [23] and Yang et al. [26], and compare with more details on focal loss [15] which is designed from similar target. The comparisons are performed with codes uploaded by the authors or results provided by the corresponding paper.

Classification Performance. As can be seen from the Table 2, original ImageNet pretrained model and fine-tuned model don't have good enough performance, while the fine-tuned one has obviously better result. It shows that the image emotion classification task is much more different from the original object classification task. Even after fine-tuned training, the accuracy rate has been improved, but it is not enough to make up for the gap caused by the different of the task. From another point of view, the CNN backbone is a simple feature extraction module that can be significantly improved after proper training in some degree. Compare with the WSCNet, the ECWA method has better performance on all four datasets, which means the ECWA method is effective and robust for image emotion classification task.

Comparison with Other Loss Function. In the Table 3, focal loss and center loss have higher accuracy than softmax loss on all three backbone, but compared to ECWA loss these three loss are significantly lower. Even if Yang [26]. only has public results on the InceptionV3 backbone, it is still not as good as our results.

Table 2. Results of different methods tested on different datasets by same ResNet101 backbone architecture. The number of categories is annotated behind the dataset name.

Method	FI (8)	Twitter I (2)	Twitter II (2)	EmotionROI (6)
ImageNet pretrained backbone [10]	0.5001	0.7255	0.7042	0.4079
Fine-tuned backbone	0.6616	0.7813	0.7823	0.5160
WSCNet [23]	0.7007	0.8425	0.8135	0.5825
Center loss [25]	0.6994	0.8440	0.8151	0.5808
ECWA based	**0.7087**	**0.8479**	**0.8167**	**0.5909**

Table 3. Results of different loss on FI dataset by different backbone.

Method	AlexNet [14]	InceptionV3 [24]	ResNet101 [10]
Softmax loss	0.5813	0.6525	0.6616
Focal loss [15]	0.5994	0.6841	0.6984
Center loss [25]	0.6069	0.6823	0.6994
Yang et al. [26]	–	0.6837	–
ECWA	**0.6101**	**0.6938**	**0.7087**

Influence of Hyper-parameters. We systematically analyze the influence of hyper-parameter λ in Eq. 4, where λ controls the relative importance between the inner-class constraint loss and inter-class distance constraint loss. In the optimization function, the lower the value λ is, the more important the inner-class constraint term is. We illustrate how λ influences the performance of the total loss using Accuracy on the FI dataset. Since the two losses are mutually related, we consider the results for λ ranging from 0.1 to 0.9. This ensures that the two constraints simultaneously exist in our framework. As shown in Fig. 3, we present the accuracy on the FI dataset when λ is set to different values and compare with the SOTA method performance by line chart. We can make the following observations from the results: (1) ResNet101 based models have best average performance in this task. (2) Our model takes higher Accuracy than the normal Center Loss, which does not have the emotion classes aware module based on the same backbone. (3) The best results are obtained when $\lambda = 0.6$.

In general, the proposed method is robust for different backbones. There are no large fluctuations in the experimental results with changes in the hyper-parameter λ, especially from 0.4 to 0.8, and get the best result of 0.6. The overall trends of different models are basically the same.

Results Analysis of Classification Details. In addition to comparing the overall accuracy rate, since we have taken measures with different categories

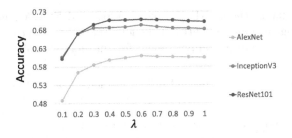

Fig. 3. Accuracy of different Hyper-parameters with different backbones on FI dataset.

and different constraint methods, we hope to see the changes brought to the accuracy performance of each category by applying our loss. For this reason, in the unbalanced multi-category FI dataset, we used ResNet101 with the best performance among these comparison methods as the backbone to compare the classification accuracy of the original method and the focal loss method that solves the problem of sample imbalance in each sentiment category.

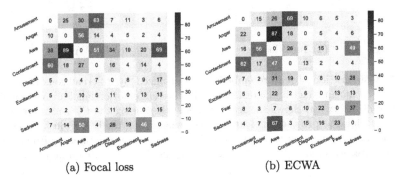

Fig. 4. Visualization confusion metric of misclassified by different method on the test set of FI. The different colors distinguish different misclassified degree as each color bar. (a) shows the results of focal loss, while (b) presents the our work.

The Fig. 4 above is the confusion matrix of the misclassified results, and the results for different classification situations can be seen intuitively. We found that compared with the focal loss method, which is also used to solve the problem of sample imbalance, for the ECWA method, in addition to slight performance degradation in individual categories, there is a more significant improvement in the small sample category, which increases in the anger and fear categories respectively. Just like the quantitative results in Table 4, the classification accuracy rate of the two categories anger and fear has been improved as high as 26.88% and 30%. It is not difficult to see that in the processing of emotional images by this method, especially for categories with a small number of samples, better classification accuracy can be obtained through more distance constraints.

We also visualize the t-SNE [16] of focal loss and ECWA method on FI in Fig. 5. From Fig. 5(a) and Fig. 5(b), it demonstrates that this quite obvious that the ECWA has a significant improvement for the small sample category.

Table 4. Comparison of focal loss and ECWA method on each category of FI dataset.

Method	Amusement	Awe	Contentment	Excitement	Anger	Disgust	Fear	Sadness
Focal loss	0.8244	0.6710	0.7730	0.6557	0.4140	0.6777	0.2867	0.6974
ECWA	0.8299	0.7800	0.6381	0.6580	0.6828	0.6942	0.5867	0.6690
Difference	0.0055	0.1090	−0.1349	0.0023	**0.2688**	0.0165	**0.3000**	−0.0284

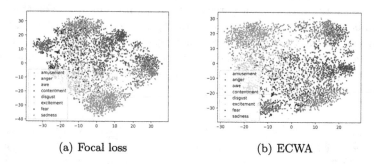

(a) Focal loss   (b) ECWA

Fig. 5. Visualization of feature embeddings optimized by different constraints. Each point represents an image in the test set of FI. Different emotion labels are distinguished by different colors. (a) shows the feature space when using the FC feature learned by focal loss, while (b) presents the feature space when using the ECWA loss learned from our framework. It is observed that the ECWA can separate the images from different emotion categories more effectively than Focal loss. (Color figure online)

5   Conclusion

In this paper, to solve the problem of lacking inner-class feature distance converging and data imbalance caused by using traditional loss functions, we propose an ECWA method, which expands the feature distance of intra-classes and constraints the inner-classes ones differently. The results show that against the comparison method under the same conditions, the ECWA method has achieved better results in four data sets of different backbones, data imbalance levels, and data sources. This work effectively explores the loss function of the image emotion classification task. It provides a choice of the loss function and related discussion issues for future research of image emotion classification and other directions, such as image emotion retrieval and social media analysis.

Acknowledgement. This work was supported in part by the National Natural Science Foundation of China (61976010, 61802011, 61702022), Beijing Municipal Education Committee Science Foundation (KM201910005024).

References

1. Ain, Q.T., et al.: Sentiment analysis using deep learning techniques: a review. Int. J. Adv. Comput. Sci. Appl. **8**(6), 424 (2017)
2. Bellet, A., Habrard, A., Sebban, M.: A survey on metric learning for feature vectors and structured data. arXiv preprint arXiv:1306.6709 (2013)
3. Borth, D., Ji, R., Chen, T., Breuel, T., Chang, S.F.: Large-scale visual sentiment ontology and detectors using adjective noun pairs. In: Proceedings of the 21st ACM International Conference on Multimedia, pp. 223–232 (2013)
4. Cambria, E., Das, D., Bandyopadhyay, S., Feraco, A.: Affective computing and sentiment analysis. In: Cambria, E., Das, D., Bandyopadhyay, S., Feraco, A. (eds.) A Practical Guide to Sentiment Analysis. Socio-Affective Computing, vol. 5, pp. 1–10. Springer, Cham (2017). https://doi.org/10.1007/978-3-319-55394-8_1
5. Campos, V., Jou, B., Giro-i Nieto, X.: From pixels to sentiment: fine-tuning cnns for visual sentiment prediction. Image Vis. Comput. **65**, 15–22 (2017)
6. Campos, V., Salvador, A., Giró-i Nieto, X., Jou, B.: Diving deep into sentiment: understanding fine-tuned cnns for visual sentiment prediction. In: Proceedings of the 1st International Workshop on Affect & Sentiment in Multimedia, pp. 57–62 (2015)
7. De Boer, P.T., Kroese, D.P., Mannor, S., Rubinstein, R.Y.: A tutorial on the cross-entropy method. Ann. Oper. Res. **134**(1), 19–67 (2005)
8. Deng, J., Dong, W., Socher, R., Li, L.J., Li, K., Fei-Fei, L.: Imagenet: a large-scale hierarchical image database. In: 2009 IEEE Conference on Computer Vision and Pattern Recognition, pp. 248–255. IEEE (2009)
9. Ekman, P.: An argument for basic emotions. Cogn. Emot. **6**(3–4), 169–200 (1992)
10. He, K., Zhang, X., Ren, S., Sun, J.: Deep residual learning for image recognition. In: Proceedings of the IEEE Conference on Computer Vision and Pattern Recognition, pp. 770–778 (2016)
11. Jia, J., Wu, S., Wang, X., Hu, P., Cai, L., Tang, J.: Can we understand van gogh's mood? Learning to infer affects from images in social networks. In: Proceedings of the 20th ACM International Conference on Multimedia, pp. 857–860 (2012)
12. Joshi, D., et al.: Aesthetics and emotions in images. IEEE Signal Process. Mag. **28**(5), 94–115 (2011)
13. Kaya, M., Bilge, H.Ş: Deep metric learning: a survey. Symmetry **11**(9), 1066 (2019)
14. Krizhevsky, A., Sutskever, I., Hinton, G.E.: Imagenet classification with deep convolutional neural networks. Adv. Neural Inf. Process. Syst. **25**, 1097–1105 (2012)
15. Lin, T.Y., Goyal, P., Girshick, R., He, K., Dollár, P.: Focal loss for dense object detection. In: Proceedings of the IEEE International Conference on Computer Vision, pp. 2980–2988 (2017)
16. Van der Maaten, L., Hinton, G.: Visualizing data using t-sne. J. Mach. Learn. Res. **9**(11) (2008)
17. Mikels, J.A., Fredrickson, B.L., Larkin, G.R., Lindberg, C.M., Maglio, S.J., Reuter-Lorenz, P.A.: Emotional category data on images from the international affective picture system. Behav. Res. Methods **37**(4), 626–630 (2005)
18. Ortis, A., Farinella, G.M., Battiato, S.: Survey on visual sentiment analysis. IET Image Process. **14**(8), 1440–1456 (2020)
19. Paszke, A., et al.: Pytorch: An imperative style, high-performance deep learning library. arXiv preprint arXiv:1912.01703 (2019)
20. Peng, K.C., Sadovnik, A., Gallagher, A., Chen, T.: Where do emotions come from? Predicting the emotion stimuli map. In: 2016 IEEE International Conference on Image Processing (ICIP), pp. 614–618. IEEE (2016)

21. Rao, T., Li, X., Zhang, H., Xu, M.: Multi-level region-based convolutional neural network for image emotion classification. Neurocomputing **333**, 429–439 (2019)
22. Schroff, F., Kalenichenko, D., Philbin, J.: Facenet: a unified embedding for face recognition and clustering. In: Proceedings of the IEEE Conference on Computer Vision and Pattern Recognition, pp. 815–823 (2015)
23. She, D., Yang, J., Cheng, M.M., Lai, Y.K., Rosin, P.L., Wang, L.: Wscnet: weakly supervised coupled networks for visual sentiment classification and detection. IEEE Trans. Multimed. **22**(5), 1358–1371 (2019)
24. Szegedy, C., Vanhoucke, V., Ioffe, S., Shlens, J., Wojna, Z.: Rethinking the inception architecture for computer vision. In: Proceedings of the IEEE Conference on Computer Vision and Pattern Recognition, pp. 2818–2826 (2016)
25. Wen, Y., Zhang, K., Li, Z., Qiao, Yu.: A discriminative feature learning approach for deep face recognition. In: Leibe, B., Matas, J., Sebe, N., Welling, M. (eds.) ECCV 2016. LNCS, vol. 9911, pp. 499–515. Springer, Cham (2016). https://doi.org/10.1007/978-3-319-46478-7_31
26. Yao, X., She, D., Zhang, H., Yang, J., Cheng, M.M., Wang, L.: Adaptive deep metric learning for affective image retrieval and classification. IEEE Trans. Multimed. (2020)
27. You, Q., Luo, J., Jin, H., Yang, J.: Robust image sentiment analysis using progressively trained and domain transferred deep networks. In: Proceedings of the AAAI Conference on Artificial Intelligence, vol. 29 (2015)
28. You, Q., Luo, J., Jin, H., Yang, J.: Building a large scale dataset for image emotion recognition: the fine print and the benchmark. In: Proceedings of the AAAI Conference on Artificial Intelligence, vol. 30 (2016)
29. Zhao, S., Ding, G., Huang, Q., Chua, T.S., Schuller, B.W., Keutzer, K.: Affective image content analysis: a comprehensive survey. In: IJCAI, pp. 5534–5541 (2018)
30. Zhao, S., Gao, Y., Jiang, X., Yao, H., Chua, T.S., Sun, X.: Exploring principles-of-art features for image emotion recognition. In: Proceedings of the 22nd ACM International Conference on Multimedia, pp. 47–56 (2014)

Image Style Recognition Using Graph Network and Perception Layer

Quan Wang and Guorui Feng[✉]

School of Communication and Information Engineering, Shanghai University,
Shanghai 200444, China
fgr2082@aliyun.com

Abstract. Art images can usually convey the background of the times, culture and the personal emotions of the painter. Appreciating visual art can not only close the distance with the artist, but also enrich our life. It becomes very meaningful to recognition the visual style through computer-aided means. However, the existing methods have not fully explored the correlation between regional styles, and it is difficult to fully describe the style information of artistic images. In this paper, we propose a two-branch network structure, which can aggregate graph style features and global style features. Specially, a graph network is introduced to construct the correlation between the styles of artistic image regions to capture graph style. In addition, we design a perceptual layer to learn cross-layer correlation features to capture global style. The experimental results demonstrate the superiority of the proposed method in three style datasets.

Keywords: Style representation · Graph network · Style recognition

1 Introduction

Image art creation often conveys more meaning than semantic content, and the visual style of image occupies an important role [6]. Generally, the visual style reflects the history, culture and personality of the creator. Accurate recognition of style allows more non-artists to understand art and participate in creation [20]. However, modeling the visual style is still a challenge at this stage. In this work, we have two classification tasks, one is to identify the pictorial styles (e.g. expressionism, cubism, etc.), and the other is to identify the author of oil painting (e.g. Amedeo Modigliani, Monet, etc.) [1]. Figure 1 shows different styles of paintings by different painters.

Existing style recognition methods can be divided into two categories, they are handcrafted feature-based [7,11,15,18] and deep learning-based [1–3,14,17,20]. Handcrafted feature-based still use traditional feature description operators, such as local binary patterns (LBP), Generalized Search Trees

This work was supported by the National Natural Science Foundation of China under Grants 62072295 and Natural Science Foundation of Shanghai under Grant 19ZR1419000.

L. Fang et al. (Eds.): CICAI 2021, LNAI 13069, pp. 565–574, 2021.
https://doi.org/10.1007/978-3-030-93046-2_48

Fig. 1. Sample oil paintings of different styles. (a) shows the categories divided by artistic style, from top to bottom: Impressionism, Naive Art, Cubism. (b) shows the categories divided by artist, from top to bottom: van Gogh, Titian, Pablo Picasso.

(GIST), histogram of oriented gradient (HOG), etc. Since there is no unique representation algorithm designed for visual style, handcrafted feature-based can not handle this problem. Recently, by introducing deep convolutional neural networks (CNN) [9], more and more methods adopt deep features to describe style. For example, Wei et al. [2] use VGG [16] to extract the depth features of the style image, and employ the Gram matrix to calculate the correlation between each feature channel to express the style. After that, Wei et al. [3] design a learning framework to automatically learn correlations between feature maps. Yang et al. [20] propose a method of visual style recognition via label distribution learning. Additional style information can be learned using the label distribution of the historical context. Bianco et al. [1] construct a two-branch style classification network, which realize the combination of deep features and traditional handcrafted features. While these methods have improved the accuracy of style recognition to a certain extent, they have not fully explored the correlation between regional styles. Therefore, the existing methods of expressing styles with more complex semantic targets are still limited.

In order to take advantage of the global style consistency of artistic images, it is necessary to explore the correlation between regional styles. We further found that the styles of different regions are more like web structures in the feature space, where the style information of an image consists of multiple style nodes. Hence, we introduce graph convolutional network (GCN) [8] to model the relations of different regions. This is mainly inspired by the powerful neighborhood correlation modeling capabilities of GCN. Specifically, we use a pretrained network to extract the depth features of the input image and perform block operations on the depth features. Furthermore, we construct graph by the Gram matrix of different blocks to build the correlation between regional styles. In addition to using the graph network to capture graph style feature, we also design a perceptual layer to learn to cross-layer correlation feature weights, which can improve the ability of cross-layer related features to represent style. In summary, the contributions of proposed method are the following.

- We introduce GCN to model the potential relationship between the local style of paintings, so as to capture more discriminative and robust style information.
- We design a perceptual layer to learn cross-layer correlation features to achieve a stronger global style representation.

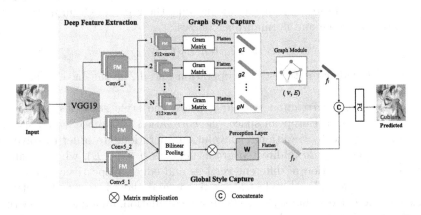

Fig. 2. Overview of proposed method, The framework consists of three modules, including deep feature extraction module, graph style capture module, global style module and fully connected module.

2 Our Method

In this section, we discuss the details of the proposed method. An illustration of the framework is depicted in Fig. 2. We first introduce the deep feature extraction module and the selection of feature layers. Then, we describe the process of graph style feature capture, including regional style representation and regional style correlation modeling. Finally, we elaborate on the design of the perception layer and its effectiveness for global style feature capture.

2.1 Preliminary

In our work, the pre-trained VGG19 is used in our method to extract deep feature map. We choose the feature map of conv5_1 and conv5_2 as the subsequent input, which proved to be very effective in the next experiments. These two feature maps are denoted as F_1 and F_2, where $F_1, F_2 \in \mathbb{R}^{C \times H \times W}$ in which C, H, W denote the channel number, height and width of feature map, respectively. F_1 is evenly cut into N patches, the i-th feature map block of F_1 can be defined as F_1^i.

2.2   Graph Style Capture

Regional style representation: Inspired by [4], we utilize Gram matrix to represent style characteristics. Gram-based statistical features of style are obtained by calculating the correlation of different feature channels of each layer of VGG19. In this paper, we define the regional Gram matrix G^i as follows:

$$G^i_{ab} = \sum_P F^i_{ap} F^i_{bp}, \qquad (1)$$

where F^i_{ap} and F^i_{bp} represent feature map a and b in the patch i, respectively. p represents the location of the feature map. P is the total number of channels per layer. To facilitate subsequent calculations, the regional Gram matrix G^i is performed to stretch and normalize as follows:

$$\bar{G}^i = Flatten(L_2(G^i)), \qquad (2)$$

where $Flatten$ denotes the stretch operation and $L2$ is the L2 normalization operation.

Regional style correlation modeling: Since the style statistics of different regions are not in a European space, the correlation between regional styles is often not captured by traditional convolution operations. In order to solve this problem, we employ an undirected graph network $g = (V, E)$, where V and E represent the collection of different vertices and edges, respectively. Here, each vertex denotes a regional style feature vector and the edges are the relations between different regional style. To facilitate calculation, an adjacency matrix A is defined in a graph model, where each element corresponds to a pair of edge relations.

Refer to the design experience of adjacency matrix in [5], we adopt a nonlinearity module to establish the relationship between the vertices $V = [\bar{G}^1, \bar{G}^2, ..., \bar{G}^N]$. The module contains three operations. First, learn the distance between different nodes by using the learnable weight w, then adopt the $ReLU$ activation function to ensure the nonlinearity of the whole process, and finally use the $Softmax$ operation to normalize and generate $A \in \mathbb{R}^{N \times N}$. The adjacency matrix A can be defined as follows:

$$A_{i,j} = Softmax(ReLU(w(\bar{G}^i - \bar{G}^j)^2)), \qquad (3)$$

where $A_{i,j}$ is the element at position (i, j) in A. Following yang et al. [19], let $\bar{A} = A + I_n$ denote the self-loop adjacency matrix, where I_n represent the identity matrix. The graph laplacian L can be described as follows:

$$L = D^{-1/2} \bar{A} D^{-1/2}, \qquad (4)$$

where $D = \sum_j \bar{A}_{i,j}$. In our study, the l-th layer graph style matrix can be realized by

$$X^l = ReLU(LX^{l-1} * \Phi), \qquad (5)$$

where Φ is the graph convolution kernel, $*$ denotes the standard convolution operation. For classification, the graph style feature matrix X will finally be stretched into a style vector g_l.

2.3 Global Style Capture

The previous methods with better performance are to express the style by calculating the correlation of channels from cross-layer. Motivated by this, we also adopt cross-layer correlation in the following branch to capture the global style of the image. The difference is that we designed a perceptual layer W to learn the weights of the correlation matrix instead of the previous Euclidean distance. The global style feature f_g is defined as follows:

$$f_g = Flatten(BP(F_1, F_2) \otimes W), \tag{6}$$

where the BP operator means bilinear pooling [10]. BP is used to calculate the correlation between different feature layers, similar to the Gram matrix. $W \in \mathbb{R}^{M \times N}$, M and N represents the number channel of F_1 and F_2, respectively. The $\otimes$ operator denotes matrix multiplication. $Flatten$ executes to stretch the matrix into a vector.

2.4 Fully Connected Module

The fully connected module is used as a classifier to predict the style vector. The fully connected module also affects the classification accuracy of the network. If the module is not designed properly, it will cause the network to overfit. The final style vector $f_s = \phi(f_l, f_g)$ will be input to the fully connected module for classification, where ϕ represents *concatenate* operation. Refer to the design experience of other classification networks [3], our fully connected module is depicted in Fig. 2 (Fig. 3).

3 Experiments

3.1 Datasets and Implementation Details

For the performance evaluation, we use three style datasets, including Painting_Styles [7], Painting_Artists [7] and OilPainting [2]. These datasets are collected by different authors on WikiArt.org. The dataset includes two forms, one is classified by style and the other is classified by artist. The specific information is shown in Table 1. To train our model, we adopt the cross entropy loss function and Adam optimizer, respectively. Compared with other optimizers, Adam can control the learning speed, which makes the parameters relatively stable. The batch size will be set from 8 to 64 for different datasets. To be fair, our strategy for selecting the training and testing sets is the same as the comparison method. For Painting_Artists, the training and test images are 2275 and 1991, respectively. In Painting_Styles, 1250 is used for training and the rest for testing. Experiments performed in OilPainting with five-fold cross-validation.

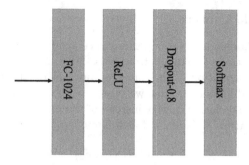

Fig. 3. Structure of fully connected modules.

Table 1. Details of the three datasets.

Dataset	Style	Artists	Images
Painting_Styles	13	–	2338
Painting_Artists	–	91	4266
OilPainting	–	104	15357

3.2   Style Classification Based on Different Layers

Before verifying the proposed network model, we first discuss the classification performance of style vectors from different layers. The Gram matrix and the direct convolution layer are used to generate the style vectors, which are denote by VGG_FC and Gram, respectively. We choose one convolutional layer from each of the four convolutional modules, which are conv1_1, conv2_1, conv3_1 and conv4_1. Furthermore, in order to prove the pros and cons of different convolutions of the same convolution module, covn5_1, conv5_2, conv5_3 and conv5_4 are also selected.

The experimental results in Painting91_Styles dataset and OilPainting_ Artists dataset are shown in Table 2. It can be clearly seen that the style classification accuracy is higher with the increase of the network depth in different convolution modules. The reason is mainly that the image information becomes refined during the continuous convolution process. Therefore, many classification methods directly use higher-level features as the representation vector. In addition, the classification performance of conv5_1, conv5_2, conv5_3 and conv5_4 is relatively close. This also shows that the expression ability of a certain deep network will be suppressed. We choose conv5_1 and conv5_2 as the input to our model.

Table 2. Performance of VGG_FC and Gram on Painting_Styles dataset and Painting_Artists dataset.

Layer	Painting91_Styles(%)		OilPainting_Artists(%)	
	VGG_FC	Gram	VGG_FC	Gram
conv1_1	29.91	40.07	18.18	30.49
conv2_1	32.75	44.43	24.35	36.69
conv3_1	48.23	61.66	39.80	53.09
conv4_1	52.21	66.18	44.84	58.15
conv5_1	63.43	75.23	55.68	68.48
conv5_2	62.51	74.12	55.57	67.54
conv5_3	62.86	74.53	55.32	68.28
conv5_4	62.72	74.32	54.09	67.33

3.3 Comparison to Previous Work

We compare our proposed method with eight style recognition methods, including Khan et al. [7] and SCMFA [15] two conventional algorithms and six deep learning based algorithms: MSCNN [13], CNNF [12], Peng et al. [14], Gram [2], Gram_learn [3], Yang et al. [20]. Furthermore, in order to examine the effectiveness of the proposed module, we adopt the cross-layer correlation representation without the perception layer as a baseline. We add the perceptual layer to the baseline as Ours-1. Ours-2 is to increase the graph branch on the basis of Ours-1. As shown in Tables 3 and 4, compared with other methods, our method obtains the highest recognition accuracy in all three datasets. Moreover, in the experiment of the influence of different modules on our method, ours-1 and ours-2 are improved compared to baseline. It shows that the ability to express style can be effectively enhanced by establishing the correlation between local styles and learning cross-layer style representation.

In order to further prove the effectiveness of the proposed method, we analyze the classification results of individual categories. The confusion matrix in Fig. 4 shows the classification results of each style, in which (a) and (b) represent the confusion matrix baseline and Ours-2, respectively. It can be seen that our method is very effective on Abstract, Cubbism, Impressionism, Popart and Post Impressionismits, and its recognition accuracy exceeds 80%. Furthermore, compared with baseline, our method achieves improvements in Abstract, Cubbism, Impressionism, etc. Figure 4 shows the sample of Abstract, Cubbism and Impressionism.

Table 3. Comparison of the proposed method with prior work on Painting_Styles dataset and Painting_Artists dataset.

Method	Painting_Styles(%)	Painting_Artists(%)
Khan et al. [7]	62.02	53.10
MSCNN [13]	70.96	57.91
CNNF [12]	69.21	56.35
Peng et al. [14]	71.05	57.51
SCMFA [15]	73.16	65.78
Yang et al. [20]	77.76	–
Baseline	74.05	63.46
Ours-1	76.68	67.32
Ours-2	**77.86**	**68.19**

Table 4. Comparison of the proposed method with prior work on OilPainting dataset.

Method	OilPainting_Artists(%)
CNNF [12]	57.00
Gram [2]	63.17
Gram_leran [3]	69.74
Baseline	68.91
Ours-1	71.58
Ours-2	**72.32**

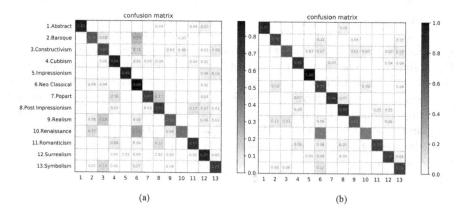

(a)   (b)

Fig. 4. The confusion matrix for Painting_Styles. (a) and (b) represent the confusion matrix baseline and Ours-2, respectively.

4   Conclusion

With the rapid development of deep learning, more and more visual tasks have received widespread attention. In this paper, we propose a new two-branch network to recognition the visual style. The proposed network has made two improvements on the basis of existing methods. On the one hand, it introduces a graph network to construct correlations between different regional styles to obtain graph style features. On the other hand, it designs a perceptual layer to learn cross-layer correlation features to capture global style features. Our method makes full use of the global consistency of the visual style, and combines the graphic style features with the global style features to achieve a better style expression. The experimental results prove the superiority of this method on three style datasets.

References

1. Bianco, S., Mazzini, D., Napoletano, P., Schettini, R.: Multitask painting categorization by deep multibranch neural network. Expert Syst. Appl. **135**, 90–101 (2019)
2. Chu, W., Wu, Y.: Deep correlation features for image style classification. In: ACMMM, pp. 402–406 (2016)
3. Chu, W., Wu, Y.: Image style classification based on learnt deep correlation features. IEEE Trans. Multimed. **20**(9), 2491–2502 (2018)
4. Gatys, L.A., Ecker, A.S., Bethge, M.: Image style transfer using convolutional neural networks. In: CVPR, pp. 2414–2423 (2016)
5. Jia, Z., et al.: Graphsleepnet: adaptive spatial-temporal graph convolutional networks for sleep stage classification. In: IJCAI, pp. 1324–1330 (2020)
6. Karayev, S., et al.: Recognizing image style. In: BMVC, pp. 1–11 (2014)
7. Khan, F.S., Beigpour, S., van de Weijer, J., Felsberg, M.: Painting-91: a large scale database for computational painting categorization. Mach. Vis. Appl. **25**(6), 1385–1397 (2014). https://doi.org/10.1007/s00138-014-0621-6
8. Kipf, T.N., Welling, M.: Semi-supervised classification with graph convolutional networks. In: ICLR (2017)
9. Krizhevsky, A., Sutskever, I., Hinton, G.E.: Imagenet classification with deep convolutional neural networks. In: NIPS, pp. 1106–1114 (2012)
10. Lin, T., RoyChowdhury, A., Maji, S.: Bilinear CNN models for fine-grained visual recognition. In: ICCV, pp. 1449–1457 (2015)
11. Ojala, T., Pietikäinen, M., Mäenpää, T.: Multiresolution gray-scale and rotation invariant texture classification with local binary patterns. IEEE Trans. PAMI **24**(7), 971–987 (2002)
12. Peng, K., Chen, T.: Cross-layer features in convolutional neural networks for generic classification tasks. In: ICIP, pp. 3057–3061 (2015)
13. Peng, K., Chen, T.: A framework of extracting multi-scale features using multiple convolutional neural networks. In: ICME, pp. 1–6 (2015)
14. Peng, K., Chen, T.: Toward correlating and solving abstract tasks using convolutional neural networks. In: WACV, pp. 1–9 (2016)
15. Puthenputhussery, A., Liu, Q., Liu, C.: Sparse representation based complete kernel marginal fisher analysis framework for computational art painting categorization. In: ECCV, vol. 9912, pp. 612–627 (2016)

16. Simonyan, K., Zisserman, A.: Very deep convolutional networks for large-scale image recognition. In: Bengio, Y., LeCun, Y. (eds.) ICLR (2015)
17. Tan, W.R., Chan, C.S., Aguirre, H.E., Tanaka, K.: A deep convolutional network for fine-art paintings classification. In: ICIP, pp. 3703–3707 (2016)
18. Tseng, T., Chang, W., Chen, C., Wang, Y.F.: Style retrieval from natural images. In: ICASSP, pp. 1561–1565 (2016)
19. Yang, J., Zheng, W., Yang, Q., Chen, Y., Tian, Q.: Spatial-temporal graph convolutional network for video-based person re-identification. In: CVPR, pp. 3286–3296 (2020)
20. Yang, J., et al.: Historical context-based style classification of painting images via label distribution learning. In: 2018 ACM Multimedia Conference on Multimedia Conference, MM 2018, Seoul, Republic of Korea, 22–26 October 2018, pp. 1154–1162. ACM (2018)

Arable Land Change Detection Using Landsat Data and Deep Learning

Mei Huang and Wenzhong Yang[✉]

School of Information Science and Engineering, Xinjiang University,
Urumqi 830046, China

Abstract. Arable land is closely related to people's livelihood. Protecting arable land is very urgent. Thus, rapid and accurate detection of arable land changes is especially important for arable land protection. However, most existing deep learning-based methods can easily lead to the accumulation of errors, low accuracy, and have poor anti-noise ability. In this study, we proposed an improved U-Net model for arable land change detection. This is an end-to-end network that is briefer and more intuitive. The model was trained and tested on three arable land areas in Xinjiang. We trained Landsat 8 images of exuberant arable land areas with RGB and 15 m spatial resolution. The improved U-Net model has some advantages compared to other methods: the deeper U-Net has a larger field of perception, with greater noise immunity, and deep convolution can capture more complex spectral features, thus improving feature differentiation. Considering that the deeper the network, the easier the gradient disappears, we use residual units to prevent gradients from disappearing. Moreover, the model parameters were adjusted to reduce the complexity of the model. The experimental results show superior performance on change detection tasks compared to other traditional models with 96.00% accuracy, precision, recall, and FI score, 93.54%, 85.07%, 88.29%. Through experiments, we found that the network can detect the change of cultivated land well. Thus, the proposed model can effectively implement arable land change detection.

Keywords: Change detection · Arable land · U-Net · VGGNet · ResNet

1 Introduction

Arable land is always been human existence's basic dependency. With the increase of population and social development, arable land is continuously

This research was funded by [the National Natural Science Foundation of China] grant number [No. U1603115], [the National Key Research and Development Program of China] grant number [No. 2017YFBO504203], [the Science and Technology Planning Project of Sichuan Province] grant number [No. 18SXHZ0054] and [National Engineering Laboratory for Public Safety Risk Perception and Control by Big Data] grant number [PSRPC: No. XJ201810101].

L. Fang et al. (Eds.): CICAI 2021, LNAI 13069, pp. 575–588, 2021.
https://doi.org/10.1007/978-3-030-93046-2_49

decreasing [1]. As a country with a large population, if China cannot ensure enough arable lands, malnutrition will become a serious problem [2]. Today, the per capita area of China is comparatively small, and the tension between people and land is becoming ever more acute. The quality of arable land has deteriorated, and the resources that can be reclaimed from arable land are very limited [3]. To achieve sustainable development, arable land protection is imminent [4]. Quickly and accurately detect changes of arable land is well situated to efficiently evaluate the specific status of arable land. Remote sensing is a suitable methods for the detection of arable land changes. It can estimate arable land use without actual ground measurement [5–7].

There are various researches on the identification of remote sensing image changes at home and abroad, mainly including object-based methods and pixel-based methods [8]. The former methods use a cluster of pixels as a processing unit. Several scholars have performed work on object-level methods for change detection [9–12]. Object-based methods can use spatial information well so that it is not easily affected by noise. But those algorithms that can be used are relatively limited. What's more, image segmentation is very important for object-level change detection. But current segmentation methods rely on a single scale parameter, which can easily lead to "over-segmentation" or "under segmentation". The generalization ability is weak and cannot perform well within single category segmentation. The latter methods use pixel as a processing unit. The pixel-based methods include the traditional pixel-based methods and deep learning-based methods [8]. The traditional pixel-based methods are widely used for its simplicity, but it sensitives to noise. The ratio methods and differential methods are commonly used methods. It uses those methods to get the different images and then uses the threshold segmentation methods to extract the change information. Those ways demand high-precision thresholds selection and characteristic indicators criteria and are easily influenced by noise (such as brightness or atmospheric conditions) [13]. The accuracy is often poor.

In recent years, deep learning has gradually become popular in computer areas. Many scholars have applied deep learning to solve practical problems and have achieved good results [14–16]. But traditional convolution networks also have the problems of high storage overhead, low efficiency, and limited sensing area size. In 2015, Olaf Ronneberger et al. [17] proposed a U-Net based on FCN [18] architecture, which combines deep and shallow features with impressive achievements in the field of medical image segmentation.

U-Net uses multi-channel convolution and adds a skip connection between the encoder layer and its corresponding decoder layer, which makes it possible to fuse shallow features obtained by down-sampling and deep features obtained by up-sampling features. That is why U-Net can better learn the details of the image features, making the output prediction outcomes boundary clearer. U-Net model has some advantages compared to other methods: Firstly, it only requires a set of 30 images (512×512) samples to train the network, which makes it have absolute advantages over other networks that require a large number of samples. Secondly, it is an end-to-end network framework that can completely maintain context information, so it can provide accurate segment outcomes. Thirdly, its encoder-decoder structure can compress images, remove noise, and make detection edges clearer. U-Net was originally used for segmentation of medical images [19–21], then, widely used in remote sensing image segmentation and remote sensing image change detection. Based on their work material, many scholars [22–25] have realized that a model with a good segmentation performance for medical images is not the best structure for remote sensing images with complex data features. Zayd Mahmoud Hamdi et al. [26] find the most suitable U-Net architecture for evaluating forest damage after continuously adjusted network parameters. Raveerat Jaturapitpornchai et al. [27] transformed U-Net construction and weighed the loss function according to positive class percentage and negative class percentage to detect newly built construction; Daifeng Peng et al. [28] combined maps from different semantic levels for change detection; To our knowledge, there exist a few publications on the arable land change detection based on U-Net. For this task, common U-Net is impossible to extract the complex features of the remote sensing image, resulting in the inability to accurately detect the change of cultivated land. Recently, Xu Yue et al. [29] combined VGGNet [30] and U-Net to propose a new network model (D-Unet) for segmenting remote sensing images, which is very effective. The detection results are also good, so that this architecture may provide better performance in change detection.

2   Data Pre-processing

2.1   Image Registration

Before change detection, the images need to be accurately registered. If the registration isn't accurate, it will cause some false changes in the detection results. To reduce the error, images were firstly corrected on ENVI through radiometric correction and FLAASH atmospheric correction to make the color of the remote sensing images more in line with the actual situation. What's more, the spatial resolution of RGB images that we can acquire on United States Geological Survey was 30 m. We use image sharpening to make the picture clearer. The GS fusion approach renders the image's spatial resolution 15 m.

2.2   Visual Interpretation

ROI tool was used to manually label the research area. The generated labels are RGB images. Both the training data and test data images are divided into a patch size of 128 × 128, and training data are flipped upside down, left and right to increase the robustness of the model and boost the generalization ability of the model. The test data is not enhanced. In the new model training, it merely reads the pixel value of one channel (R channel) in the label images. We divided each pixel value by 255 to get a binary image, so the pixel value is 0 and 1. Then we connected two images before passing them through the network, treating them as different color channels. When the image is read, the shape of the training data and the test data is (128, 128, 6), and the shape of the label is (128, 128, 1). The overall workflow of preprocessing, model training, and model testing are shown in Fig. 1.

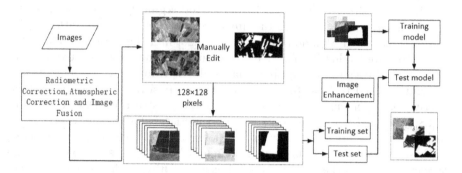

Fig. 1. Flowchart showing the analytical workflow of the study.

3   Network Structure

For arable land change detection, we proposed an improved U-Net architecture. Firstly, considering U-Net is unable to extract the complex features of the remote sensing image, we use a deep U-Net to capture more efficient features, What's more, this way can also enlarge the receptive field and enhance anti-noise ability. Secondly, as the number of network layers deepens, problems such as Gradient Vanish, network degradation, and over-fitting problems will appear. In order to prevent these phenomena from happening and make the network converge quickly, we did not use the original conv, but use a residual network as the convolution unit. Due to the number of each neural network layer is different, this paper uses different layers of the residual network. Finally, the number of convolution cores in the last convolution layer of each module in the decoding part is halved to reduce the number of parameters and the complexity of the model.

This structure has been used to change detection and achieved good perfor-mance. The new improved U-Net consists of two parts, the encoding path and the decoding path (Fig. 2).

The coding path consists of two residual units with a step size of two (1, 2 layers) and four residual units with a step size of three (3, 4, 5 layers). The residual network structure is shown in Fig. 2, with the exception of the fifth layer. (The fifth layer consists of two three-layer residual networks). The center of the encoding path contains 5 sets of convolution, of which 1, 2 groups perform 2 times 3×3 convolutions, and 64, 128 are the corresponding number of convolution kernels. 3, 4, groups perform 3 times 3×3 conv. The number of convolution kernels used in the convolution operation is 256, 512. The 5 layer perform 6 times 3×3 conv with 512 kernels. It should be noted that it contains two three-level residual units. The activation functions are Relu functions. In order to

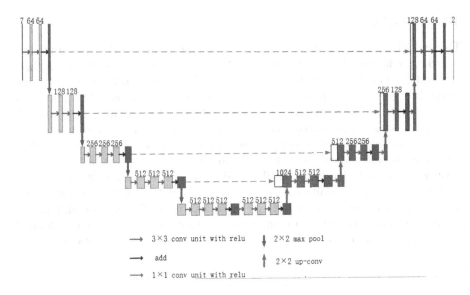

Fig. 2. Detail of network architecture.

improve the model's robustness and reduce the dimension of the feature map, convolutions are accompanied by 2 × 2 pooling. After each layer of convolution operation, a BN layer is added to prevent overfitting, while at the same time improving the convergence speed of the network and making the model training more stable.

The decoding path input of each layer conv includes not only the deep feature map obtained by up-sampling but also the shallow feature map created by the corresponding encoding component. The features that are obtained with the network's deeper layers will be more effective, more abstract, and more original image information is lost. This methods of fusing two feature maps through the methods of channel connection can combine high-resolution rate images with low-resolution images to obtain richer information. The convolution methods used in the decoding path is consists of two residual units with a step size of three (6, 7 layer) and two residual units with a step size of two (8, 9 layer). The center of the decoding path includes 4 sets of up-convolutions, of which 6, 7 groups perform 3 times 3 × 3 convolutions, and the corresponding number of convolution kernels used is 512, 512, 256, and 256, 256, 128. 8, 9 groups perform 2 times 3 × 3 convolutions. The number of convolution kernels used during convolution is 256, 256, 128, and 64, 64, 2. The network's last layer uses 1 × 1 convolution to get the result of binary classification.

3.1 VGGNet

This model incorporates VGGNet [30] to increase the network depth and thus improve the feature discrimination. VGGNet model uses 3×3 convolutional kernels and 2×2 pool-ing kernels, which does not degrade network performance due to the increased depth, nor does it cause parameter explosion. This small convolutional kernel series method (Fig. 3) can convert the parameters of a small area into a single value for comparison, which can well address the registration problems caused by the different perspectives of the reason sensor and other factors. The size of the perceptual field of three tandem 3×3 convolutional layers is the same as that of a 7×7 convolutional layer, but the sum of the parameters of the three 3×3 convolutional layers is only about half of the one 7×7. And the use of three non-linear operations will make the ability of network learning features stronger. This structure increases the receptive field without increasing the complexity of the network so that more information can be obtained.

Fig. 3. The receptive field of three convolutional in series.

3.2 ResNet

ResNet was proposed by Kaiming He et al. [31] in 2015. It made a reference between the input and output of each layer to form a residual function. This residual function can be optimized more easily and is suitable for deep network structures. To get a good segmentation effect, many scholars combined the residual network with U-Net. Kaili Cao et al. [32] proposed an improved Res-UNet for tree species classification by change of convolutional method and copy and crop way. Jiachen Yang et al. [33] using a deep residual network and Super-Vector coding detect aircraft. In view of the fact that deepening the U-Net model would cause the network to produce more errors during training, the speed of the model training may slow, and is likely to cause the gradient to vanish. We are trying to combine residual network with U-Net in this paper. The residual network extracts features by adding the input and output of different convolutional layers. It may reduce model parameters to some extent, thereby reducing model training time, and may better prevent the gradient from disappearing. The residual network structure used in this paper is as follows (Fig. 4):

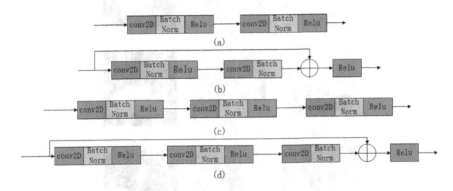

Fig. 4. (a) Two-level common convolution unit, (b) Three-level common convolution unit, (c) Two-level residual unit, (d) Three-level residual unit.

4   Measurement

To evaluate the model's performance, we use a confusion matrix to analyze the results of each pixel classification. There are four types of results of pixel classification: TP, FP, TN, and FN represent the number of true positives, the number of false positives, the number of true negatives, and the number of false negatives. Calculate on the basis of these four indicators: accuracy (A) and Precision (P), Recall (R), F1 score (F1), as follows:

$$A = \frac{TP + TN}{TP + TN + FP + FN} \tag{1}$$

$$P = \frac{TP}{TP + FP} \tag{2}$$

$$R = \frac{TP}{TP + FN} \tag{3}$$

$$F1 = \frac{2PR}{P + R} \tag{4}$$

5   Ground Truth Data

The Landsat-8 data are from United States Geological Survey and Geospatial Data Cloud, which time span is 16 days. It contains 11 bands, of which band 8 has a spatial resolution of 15 m, and the remaining bands have a resolution of 30

Fig. 5. Figure Examples of landsat-8 dataset :(a) time1 image from Bayingol Mongolian; (b) time2 image from Bayingol Mongolian; (c) label image of a and b; (d) time1 image from Changji Hui Autonomous Prefecture; (e) time2 image from Changji Hui Autonomous Prefecture; (f) label image of d and e; (g) time1 image from Wusu; (h) time2 image from Wusu; (i) label image of g and h.

m spatially. Images were acquired with three spectral bands (red, green, blue) and 15 m spatial resolution. The process of creating the ground truth was entirely manual and done by authors. All of the ground truths were created by comparing images of the same location from different times and directly drawing polygons onto the images. White represents the changed area, representing the unchanged area (Fig. 5c, Fig. 5f, Fig. 5i). The study area is three places in Xinjiang: Bayingol Mongolian Autonomous Prefecture (25 June 2013, 10 June 2019), Changji Hui Autonomous Prefecture (28 August 2013, 7 August 2017), and Wusu (21 July 2013, 7 July 2017). Orthophoto and corresponding labels were divided into a total of 500 tiles of 128 × 128 pixels (Fig. 5a Fig. 5f). 2/3 of the samples from each region as the training set, and do data enhancement, the remaining as the test set. This process generated a total of 1152 training samples and 200 test samples. The number of patches for each study area is shown in Table 1.

Table 1. Aquisition information of dataset.

Location	Acquisition Date of Landsat 8 Images (Time1-Time2)	Number of Patches
Bayingol Mongolian Autonomous Prefecture	25 June2013–10 June 2019	138
Changji Hui Autonomous Prefecture	28 August 2013–7 August 2017	168
Wusu	21 July 2013–7 July 2017	194

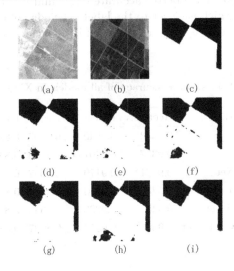

Fig. 6. Change detection results using different methods for Karamay area: (a) time 1 Landsat images; (b) time 2 Landsat images; (c) ground truth; (d) the result of FCN; (e) the result of UNet; (f) the result of Res-UNet; (g) the result of D-Unet; (h) the result of Res-D-Unet; (i) the result of improved U-Net.

6   Result and Discussion

The hardware environment for this experiment is Intel(R) Core(TM) i9-9900K CPU (3.6 GHz, 8 cores, and 32 GB RAM) and a single NVIDIA-SMI GeForce GTX 2080 Ti GPU, memory 64 GB, and Ubuntu 18.04.3, Python3.6, tensorflow1.14.0 software system. First of all, data enhancement is performed on the cut training data, including up and down swapping, left and right swapping, random cutting, rotation, and other operations. This will generate 1152 128×128 size image blocks. The test data consists of 200 image blocks of 128×128 size. We merge the channels of the two time-phase images and put this merged 6-channel image and the single channel of labels (pixel values were converted into 0 and 1) into the model training. The model is processed in batches images, the batch size is 16. We use the Adam optimizer with a learning rate of 0.001 to update the weights continuously until it finds the best global. The model training stops when the loss function decreases and is likely to be flat. The loss function used in this paper is the cross-entropy of the network model's prediction outcome pixel value and the true pixel value of the label. This loss function is often used in classification problems, in conjunction with the softmax function.

We select 1/3 datasets as test data and use the visual interpretation results as the reference. Within the same training data, visual comparisons are made with the other traditional approaches in order to check the efficacy and superiority of the proposed approach, as illustrated in Fig. 6, 7 and 8. It is obvious that the proposed method achieves the best change detection performance. The results of the improved U-Net have better accurate edges and fewer missed detections than other models, which is closer to the label. The edge of the results detected by those existing models is very irregular, and the occurrence of holes is more serious.

Table 2. Four species accuracy of all models in Xinjiang area.

Network	Accuracy	Precision	Recall	F1 score
FCN	0.9333	0.9340	0.7397	0.8256
U-Net	0.9357	0.9307	0.7553	0.8339
Res-UNet	0.9431	0.9179	0.8057	0.8581
D-Unet	0.9337	0.9373	0.7389	0.8264
Res-D-Unet	0.9452	0.9200	0.8348	0.8753
Improved U-Net	0.9600	0.9354	0.8507	0.8829

Four quantitative evaluation metrics (A, P, R, and F1) were calculated and summarized in Table 2 for quantitative comparisons. We conclude that the FCN model has the lowest A, P, R, and F1 value among those network models (Fig. 6d, Fig. 7d, and Fig. 8d), and then U-Net (Fig. 6e, Fig. 7e, and Fig. 8e). Other models get better change detection results than U-Net, Res-UNet model (Fig. 6f, Fig. 7f, and Fig. 8f) does not use traditional convolutional blocks, but uses the residual connection, which greatly promotes the training of deep networks and improves the spatial accuracy; D-Unet model (Fig. 6g, Fig. 7g, and Fig. 8g) add some layers to U-Net, which ability to get richer features. Res-D-Unet model (Fig. 6h, Fig. 7h, and Fig. 8h) is the model that we combined ResNet and D-Unet, which can reduce the complexity of the model as well as prevent the disappearance of the gradient in the deep network. Obviously, the accuracy is better than ResNet and D-Unet. The improved U-Net (Fig. 6i, Fig. 7i, and Fig. 8i) model not only deepen the U-Net but also use the residual unit and reduced the parameters of the model, which greatly promoted the training of deep networks and improved the spatial accuracy, with the highest A, P, R and F1 values. It's evident that the improved U-Net achieved the best performance among all methods, with A, P, R, and F1 values reaching 96.00%, 93.54%, 85.07%, and 88.29%. It proved that the improved U-Net in this paper is better for the detection of arable land changes.

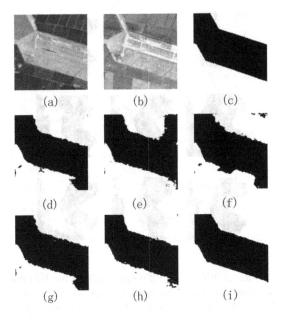

Fig. 7. Change detection results using different methods for Bazhou area: (a) time 1 Landsat images; (b) time 2 Landsat images; (c) ground truth; (d) the result of FCN; (e) the result of UNet; (f) the result of Res-UNet; (g) the result of D-Unet; (h) the result of Res-D-Unet; (i) the result of improved U-net.

Table 3 shows the number of parameters that need to be trained during each model training, as well as training time and prediction time. With the deepening of the network, the parameters of the model will become more and the training speed will slow down. The residual structure will also increase the network parameters and the training time. but the prediction time seems equal. In this model, after increasing the depth of the model and adding the residual module, the parameters in the decoding part are reduced. It can be seen that the reduction of parameters can improve the training time of the model to some extent.

Table 3. Parameters, training, and prediction time of the different models.

Model	Number of parameters	Prediction time(s)	Training time(min)
FCN	141,915,411	10	175
U-Net	31,045,314	7	78
Res-UNet	31,809,876	6	79
D-Unet	35,902,658	6	86
Res-D-Unet	36,762,818	7	82
Improved U-Net	34,008,962	6	80

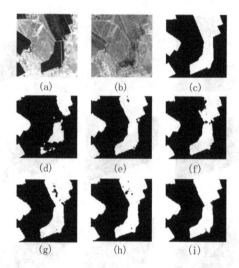

Fig. 8. Change detection results using different methods for Urumuqi area: (a) time 1 Landsat images; (b) time 2 Landsat images; (c) ground truth; (d) the result of FCN; (e) the result of UNet; (f) the result of Res-UNet; (g) the result of D-Unet; (h) the result of Res-D-Unet; (i) the result of improved U-Net.

7   Conclusion

Given the enormous workload of changes in regional arable land through human-made detection, which takes plenty of time and consumes manpower and material resources, this paper proposed an improved convolutional neural network based on U-Net, which can detect arable land changes on remote sensing images. The network performs remote sensing image classification at pixel-level. At first, image registration is performed on the Landsat 8 images to avoid false change detection. Then, the image will be pre-processed by cropping and data enhancement, and the processed image will be put into an improved U-Net model for training. The high-resolution features and semantic features are fused together. Compared to the manually labeled test set labels, it is found that the result detected by our method is more consistent with the label compared to other methods. Our model can accurately detect the changing area of arable land between two images as well as manually unmarked area, which is effective and feasible. However, due to the limited requirements of hardware equipment, the training period of the model is a bit long, and the edge fineness of the segmentation results needs to be improved. The main content of the following research work is to reduce the training time and prediction time of the model while improving edge accuracy.

References

1. Zhang, L., Cheng, J.: Arable land protection based on the change of Chinese culti-vated land in 2015. The Great Western Development (Land Development Project Research) (2018)
2. Wang, J., Li, P., Zhan, Y.Q., Tian, S.Y.: Study on the protection and improvement of cultivated land quality in China. China Popul. Resour. Environ. **29**, 87–93 (2019)
3. Ge, Y., Hu, S., Ren, Z., Jia, Y., Chen, Y.: Mapping annual land use changes in china's poverty-stricken areas from 2013 to 2018. Remote Sens. Environ. **232**, 111285 (2019)
4. Liu, D., Gong, Q., Yang, W.: The evolution of farmland protection policy and optimization path from 1978 to 2018. Chinese Rural Economy (2018)
5. Mou, L., Bruzzone, L., Zhu, X.X.: Learning spectral-spatial-temporal features via a recurrent convolutional neural network for change detection in multispectral imagery. IEEE Trans. Geosci. Remote Sens. (2019)
6. Lv, P., Zhong, Y., Zhao, J., Zhang, L.: Unsupervised change detection based on hybrid conditional random field model for high spatial resolution remote sensing imagery. IEEE Trans. Geosci. Remote Sens. 1–14 (2018)
7. Anniballe, R., et al.: Earthquake damage mapping: an overall assessment of ground surveys and VHR image change detection after L'Aquila 2009 earthquake. Remote Sens. Environ. Interdiscip. J. **210**, 166–178 (2018)
8. Tong, G.F., Li, Y., Ding, W.L., Yue, X.Y.: Review of remote sensing image change detection. J. Image Graph. (2015)
9. Cai and Liu: A comparison of object-based and contextual pixel-based classifica-tions using high and medium spatial resolution images. Remote Sens. Lett. **4**(10), 998–1007 (2013)
10. Zhang, P., Lv, Z., Shi, W.: Object-based spatial feature for classification of very high resolution remote sensing images. IEEE Geosci. Remote Sens. Lett. **10**(6), 1572–1576 (2013)
11. Mahmoudi, F.T., Samadzadegan, F., Reinartz, P.: Context aware modification on the object based image analysis. J. Indian Soc. Remote Sens. **43**(4), 709–717 (2015)
12. Gong, J.Y., Sui, H.G., Sun, K.M., Ma, G.R., Liu, J.Y.: Object-level change detec-tion based on full-scale image segmentation and its application to wenchuan earth-quake. Sci. China **51**(2 Supplement), 110–122 (2008)
13. Sui, H., Feng, W., Wenzhuo, L.I., Sun, K., Chuan, X.U.: Review of change detection methods for multi-temporal remote sensing imagery. Wuhan Daxue Xuebao (Xinxi Kexue Ban)/Geomatics Inf. Sci. Wuhan Univ. **43**(12), 1885–1898 (2018)
14. Haobo, L., Lu, H., Mou, L.: Learning a transferable change rule from a recurrent neural network for land cover change detection. Remote Sens. **8**(6), 506 (2016)
15. Sublime, J., Kalinicheva, E.: Automatic post-disaster damage mapping using deep-learning techniques for change detection: case study of the tohoku tsunami. Remote Sens. **11**(9), 1123 (2019)
16. De Bem, P.P., De Carvalho Junior, O.A., Fontes Guimarães, R., Trancoso Gomes, R.A.: Change detection of deforestation in the Brazilian Amazon using landsat data and convolutional neural networks. Remote Sens. **12**(6), 901 (2020)
17. Ronneberger, O., Fischer, P., Brox, T.: U-Net: convolutional networks for biomed-ical image segmentation. In: Navab, N., Hornegger, J., Wells, W.M., Frangi, A.F. (eds.) MICCAI 2015. LNCS, vol. 9351, pp. 234–241. Springer, Cham (2015). https://doi.org/10.1007/978-3-319-24574-4_28

18. Long, J., Shelhamer, E., Darrell, T.: Fully convolutional networks for semantic segmentation. IEEE Trans. Pattern Anal. Mach. Intell. **39**(4), 640–651 (2015)
19. Alom, M.Z., Yakopcic, C., Taha, T.M., Asari, V.K.: Recurrent residual convolutional neural network based on u-net (r2u-net) for medical image segmentation (2018)
20. Li, H., Chen, D., Nailon, W.H., Davies, M.E., Laurenson, D.: Improved breast mass segmentation in mammograms with conditional residual U-Net. In: Stoyanov, D., et al. (eds.) RAMBO/BIA/TIA -2018. LNCS, vol. 11040, pp. 81–89. Springer, Cham (2018). https://doi.org/10.1007/978-3-030-00946-5_9
21. Kolařík, M., Burget, R., Uher, V., Říha, K., Dutta, M.: Optimized high resolution 3d dense-u-net network for brain and spine segmentation. Appl. Sci. **9**(3) (2019)
22. Daudt, R.C., Le Saux, B., Boulch, A.: Fully convolutional siamese networks for change detection. IEEE (2018)
23. Xu, Y., Feng, M., Pi, J., Chen, Y.: Remote sensing image segmentation method based on deep learning model (2019)
24. Gu, L., Xu, S.Q., Zhu, L.Q.: Detection of building changes in remote sensing images via flows-unet. Acta Autom. Sin. **46**(6), 1291–1300
25. Flood, N., Watson, F., Collett, L.: Using a u-net convolutional neural network to map woody vegetation extent from high resolution satellite imagery across Queensland, Australia. Int. J. Appl. Earth Obs. Geoinf. **82**, 101897 (2019)
26. Hamdi, Z.M., Brandmeier, M., Straub, C.: Forest damage assessment using deep learning on high resolution remote sensing data. Remote Sens. **11**(17), 1976 (2019)
27. Jaturapitpornchai, R., Matsuoka, M., Kanemoto, N., Kuzuoka, S., Ito, R., Nakamura, R.: Newly built construction detection in SAR images using deep learning. Remote Sens. **11**(12), 1444 (2019)
28. Peng, D., Zhang, Y., Guan, H.: End-to-end change detection for high resolution satellite images using improved UNet++. Remote Sens. **11**(11), 1382 (2019)
29. Pan, Z., Xu, J., Guo, Y., Hu, Y., Wang, G.: Deep learning segmentation and classification for urban village using a worldview satellite image based on u-net. Remote Sens. **12**(1574) (2020)
30. Simonyan, K., Zisserman, A.: Very deep convolutional networks for large-scale image recognition. arXiv preprint arXiv:1409.1556 (2014)
31. He, K., Zhang, X., Ren, S., Sun, J.: Deep residual learning for image recognition. In: Proceedings of the IEEE Conference on Computer Vision and Pattern Recognition, pp. 770–778 (2016)
32. Cao, K., Zhang, X.: An improved res-unet model for tree species classification using airborne high-resolution images. Remote Sens. **12**(7), 1128 (2020)
33. Yang, J., Zhu, Y., Jiang, B., Gao, L., Xiao, L., Zheng, Z.: Aircraft detection in remote sensing images based on a deep residual network and super-vector coding. Remote Sens. Lett. **9**(3), 228–236 (2018)

Attention Scale-Aware Deformable Network for Inshore Ship Detection in Surveillance Videos

Di Liu[1], Yan Zhang[1(✉)], Yan Zhao[2], and Yu Zhang[1]

[1] National Key Laboratory of Science and Technology on Automatic Target Recognition, College of Electronic Science and Technology, National University of Defense Technology, Changsha 410073, China
atrthreefire@sina.com

[2] State Key Laboratory of Complex Electromagnetic Environment Effects on Electronics and Information System, College of Electronic Science and Technology, National University of Defense Technology, Changsha 410073, China

Abstract. Aiming at detecting multi-scale inshore ships in surveillance videos, a one-stage detector namely Attention Scale-aware Deformable Network (ASDN) is proposed in this paper by employing two primary components including Attention Scale-aware Module (ASM) and Deformable Convolutional Network (DCN). Moreover, ASM composed of several branches of convolutions with specially designed kernels and a Convolutional Block Attention Modules (CBAM), is designed for extracting and refining non-local features of multi-scale inshore ships with large aspect ratios at the topmost feature layer. DCN is adopted to capture irregular significant features of ships by modulating input features using parameterized offsets and amplitudes at lateral connections of fine-grained feature pyramid. Experiments conducted on public Seaships7000 dataset demonstrate the contributions of ASM and DCN, and the effectiveness of our method for multi-scale inshore ship detection in surveillance videos in comparison with other Convolutional Neural Network (CNN) based methods, e.g., FPN, Libra R-CNN, SSD, YOLOv3, RefineDet.

Keywords: Attention scale-aware deformable network (ASDN) · Attention scale-aware module (ASM) · Deformable convolutional network (DCN) · Multi-scale inshore ship detection · Surveillance videos

1 Introduction

Video surveillance system has been widely used in modern societies [5,6] benefiting from its advantages of stability, high-resolution and real-time imaging capabilities. Identifying multi-scale inshore ships from surveillance videos could acquire much detailed information than that of from remote sensing images and is crucial for effective channel utilization and port managements.

L. Fang et al. (Eds.): CICAI 2021, LNAI 13069, pp. 589–600, 2021.
https://doi.org/10.1007/978-3-030-93046-2_50

Currently, methods for inshore ship detection in surveillance videos could be divided into traditional methods and Convolutional Neural Network (CNN) based methods. In traditional methods, background [1,22] and foreground [2,20] modeling by handcrafted features are two mainstream ways. Although these methods could figure out inshore ships to some extend, their performance degenerated sharply due to diversified structures of ship, complex surroundings and various weather conditions. Besides, the generalization ability of these methods are restricted by their inflexible parameters. Recently, CNN-based methods have achieved expressive performance in many computer vision tasks [7,16] because of their powerful feature representation and discrimination abilities. As for inshore ship detection, Shao et al. [17] proposed a Saliency-Aware Convolutional Neural Network (SACNN), in which a coarse-to-fine inshore ship detection pipeline was designed based on YOLOv2 [14], as well as a public domain-specific dataset called Seaships7000 [18]. Besides, a variant of YOLOv3 [12] is proposed by designing a prediction box uncertain regression and a redesigned a binary cross entropy losses. Besides, a data augmentation strategy for synthesizing inshore ships at low illumination weather environments is proposed for inshore ship detection at various weather conditions [11]. As shown in Fig. 1, the extremely large aspect ratios of inshore ships, complex background and diversified couple relationships between ships and surroundings or themselves cause serious difficulties for ship detection undoubtedly. Although the above tricks and networks improve detection performance of CNN-based methods, the influence of special geometric shapes of inshore ships has not been further considered.

Fig. 1. Multi-scale inshore ships under various background conditions.

In this paper, an algorithm called Attention Scale-aware Deformable Network (ASDN) is proposed to alleviate these problems. Most specifically, an Attention Scale-aware Module (ASM) is carefully designed for extracting and refining non-local representative features of inshore ships with various scales and aspect ratios by designing several branches of convolutional operations with specific kernels followed by a Convolutional Block Attention Module (CBAM) [23]. Considering that traditional convolutional kernels may be hard to capture rich and transformable characteristics of inshore ships due to their restricted respective fields, a Deformable Convolutional Network (DCN) [25] is adopted to grab deformable information of ships. By utilizing ASM and DCN reasonably at the topmost feature map and the lateral connections of feature pyramid network separately, our method is obtained. Experiments conducted on public Seaships7000 dataset demonstrate the contributions of ASM and DCN and the effectiveness of our method for multi-scale inshore ship detection in surveillance videos in comparison with other CNN-based methods such as FPN [8], Libra R-CNN [13], YOLOv3 [15], SSD [10], RefineDet [24].

2   Attention Scale-Aware Deformable Network

2.1   Network Architecture

Our method belongs to a one-stage detector, of which the overall architecture is shown in Fig. 2.

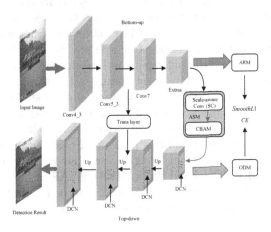

Fig. 2. Structure of Attention Scale-aware Deformable Network (ASDN).

In the bottom-up pathway, a VGG-16 [19] network is acted as a backbone to extract basic features from input images. And three intermediate layers of VGG-16, i.e., $Conv4\_3$, $Conv5\_3$, $Conv7$, and a newly added extra layer are selected to acquire hierarchical information of ships. The sizes of these four feature maps are 80×80, 40×40, 20×20 and 10×10 in sequence. To further represent multi-scale inshore ships, an Attention Scale-aware Module (ASM) consisting of a Scale-aware Convolution (SC) and a Convolutional Block Attention Module (CBAM) is attached behind the extra layer. In the top-down pathway, a feature pyramid network is established by constructing four levels of fine-grained feature layers by combining corresponding basic features from transformation layers with up-sampled features from former fine-grained feature layers. To capture irregular informative features of inshore ships and alleviate misalignment problem between anchors and features, four layers of Deformable Convolutional Networks (DCN) are employed in lateral connections of fine-grained feature maps instead of vanilla convolutional layers. Similar to RefineDet, a cascade anchor refinement mechanism, which consists of Anchor Refinement Module (ARM) and Object Detection Module (ODM), is adopted in our method to detect inshore ships in surveillance videos progressively. In the inference phase, final detection results are obtained after several post-processing operations, e.g., confidence threshold and Non-Maximum Suppression (NMS) [4].

2.2   Inner Module Description

Attention Scale-Aware Module. An Attention Scale-aware Module (ASM) is carefully designed to fully exploit representative features of multi-scale inshore ships at the topmost feature map. As shown in Fig. 3, ASM is consists of four branches of convolutional operations with various kernel sizes and dilated rates followed by a Convolutional Block Attention Module (CBAM). Specifically, the first convolutional branch with a kernel size of 3 is use for grabbing local semantic features. In the second branch, three stacked convolutional layers with dilated rates of 1, 2 and 4 are adopted to enlarge respective fields for extracting non-local features of ships as well as and reduce parameter capacities. The last two convolutional branches, which consists of asymmetric convolutional kernels of 1×3 and 3×1 with large dilated rates, are introduced to handle inshore ships with extreme aspect ratios. After concatenating features from the four branches, different areas of semantic information is fused and boosted deeply. Besides, a CBAM is attached on the concatenated features to further highlight prominent features of inshore ships and weaken interference introduced by background. After smoothing confusion of features by a plain convolutional layer, the final refined features are obtained. Comparing some current multi-scale feature extraction modules, i.e., Receptive Field Block (RFB) [9], ASPP [3] and Stem [21], the asymmetric convolutional kernels of ASM are properly designed for inshore ships and features could be propagated effectively after processed by CBAM.

Deformable Convolutional Network. Due to the inflexible and axis-aligned kernels of traditional convolutions, representing inshore ships with extremely large aspect ratios accurately is exhausted. To tackle the problem, several Deformable Convolutional Networks (DCN) are adopted in lateral connections when building the fine-grained feature pyramid instead of plain convolution. As depicted in Fig. 4, to represent irregular significant information of objects on a feature map X, a traditional convolution layer is utilized to predict two-dimensional offsets and a mask of for deformable modeling. Then, sampling points of DCN's kernels at input feature map X are adjusted by this deviation. Finally, the output feature O is produced by a regular convolutional layer modulated by the learned mask. The processing steps of DCN could be summarized as Eq. 1, where X and Y are input and output features separately. Δp_k and Δm_k are learned offsets and mask. In a regular convolutional operation with a regular kernel 3×3, K is 9 and p_k refers to locations of convolutional operation where $k = (i, j)$ $i, j \in -1, 0, 1$.

$$Y(p_n) = \sum_{k=1}^{K} W_k \cdot X(p_n + p_k + \Delta p_k) \cdot \Delta m_k \tag{1}$$

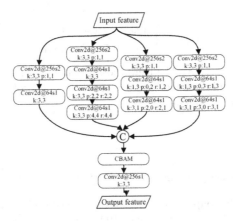

Fig. 3. Structure of Attention Scale-aware Module (ASM).

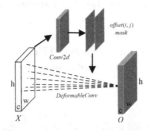

Fig. 4. Structure of Deformable Convolutional Network (DCN).

2.3 Loss Functions

Similar to [24], the overall loss function defined as Eq. 2, contains the losses of ARM and ODM. The detailed definition of each item is similar to that in [10] and is formulated as Eq. 3.

$$L_{total} = L_{ARM} + L_{ODM} \tag{2}$$

$$L(x, c, l, g) = \frac{1}{N} \left(L_{conf}(x, c) + \alpha L_{loc}(x, l, g) \right) \tag{3}$$

N refers to the number of positive anchors matched to the ground truth objects. L_{conf} is the cross entropy loss between predicted class c and label c, which is given by Eq. 4. Here $x_{i,j}^p$ is 1 if i_{th} anchor is matched to j_{th} the ground truth object. $\hat{c}_i^p$ refers to the Softmax loss defined as Eq. 5. The L_{loc} refers to $SmoothL1$ loss defined in Eq. 6.

$$L_{conf}(x, c) = -\sum_{i \in Pos}^{N} x_{ij}^p \log\left(\hat{c}_i^p\right) - \sum_{i \in Ne.g.} \log\left(\hat{c}_i^0\right) \tag{4}$$

$$\hat{c}_i^p = \frac{\exp\left(c_i^p\right)}{\sum_p \exp\left(c_i^p\right)} \tag{5}$$

$$L_{loc} = \begin{cases} 0.5x^2, if \ |x| < 1 \\ |x| - 0.5, otherwise \end{cases} \tag{6}$$

In the training phase, ARM filters redundant initial anchors according to a preset threshold θ. Only refined anchors of which the probabilities higher than θ will make contributes to loss of ODM.

3   Experiment

3.1   Dataset and Hyperparameter Settings

All experiments in this paper are conducted on Seaships7000 dataset. It contains 7000 high-resolution images with size of 1920×1080 captured by a real-deployed video surveillance system around Zhuhai Hengqin New Area. The annotated inshore ships in the dataset could be divided into six classes, i.e., ore carrier, bulk cargo carrier, general cargo carrier, container ship, fishing ship and passenger ship. Figure 5 shows different types of inshore ships captured under various weather conditions. We randomly selected 1750, 1750 and 3500 no-overlapped images as training, valid and testing sets separately.

Fig. 5. Different types of inshore ships in Seaships7000 dataset.

In training stage, all input images are resized to 640×640 pixels. Data augmentation strategies like mirroring, random cropping, contrast and illumination distorting and random expanding are adopted to enrich diversity of training set. Scales and aspect ratios of default anchors are $32, 64, 128, 256$ and $1, 1.414, 0.707$ separately. All the models are trained by 200 epochs through a Stochastic Gradient Descent (SGD) optimizer and the batch-size is 6. The initial learning rate is 0.001 and multiplied by 0.1 at steps of 75 and 150 respectively. In inference stage, the threshold of confidence and Intersection of Union between predictions and ground truths are set to 0.05 and 0.5, respectively and only the top 100 detection results sorted by the confidence scores are collected for evaluation.

3.2 Evaluation Metrics

In all experiments, Precision (P), Recall (R) and F score (F_1) are adopted to evaluate the detection performance of different methods and could be defined as Eq. 7, 8 and 9 separately. TP and FN refer to how many real ships are detected or missed. FP is number of false alarms. Besides, frame-per-second (FPS) and parameter capacity (Params) are recorded to judge the running speed and model complexity of compared methods, which are formulated as Eq. 10 and 11, respectively.

$$P = TP/(TP + FP) \tag{7}$$

$$R = TP/(TP + FN) \tag{8}$$

$$Fscore(F_1) = \frac{2PR}{P + R} \tag{9}$$

$$FPS = 1/t_{img} \tag{10}$$

$$Params = C_{out} \cdot (k_w k_h \cdot C_{in} + 1) \tag{11}$$

4 Result and Analysis

4.1 Effects of Inner Modules

Table 1 shows the detection performance of variants of ASDN equipped with different inner modules. For a fair and clear comparison, RefineDet is chosen as a baseline considering the similar network structures and data processing schemes between ASDN and RefineDet. It's obvious that the detection accuracy of our method increases gradually by combining ASM and DCN together. Furthermore, scores of precision and F_1 of ASDN are 0.838 and 0.900, which are 2.5%, 1.4% higher than those of the baseline separately. However, after removing ASM from ASDN, scores of precision, recall rates and F_1 all decrease by 0.7%, 0.3% and 0.6%, respectively. After removing DCN from ASDN, the detection performance of ASDN(w/o DCN) comes to a distinct decrease especially for the precision rate, which is 1.8% lower than that of ASDN. Based on these comparisons, it could be concluded that the multi-scale feature extraction and refinement abilities introduced by the ASM and deformable modeling ability in DCN are effective for improving the detection accuracy of our method. Furthermore, we replaced ASM with other multi-scale feature extraction strategies, e.g., RFB, ASPP and Stem. It could be seen that the detection performance of these variants of ASDN are still unsatisfied. Additionally, the recall rate of ASDN(w/o CBAM) decreases to 0.958, which is 1.3% lower than that of ASDN. It may be because that CBAM, in which channel and spatial attentions involved, highlights significant features of inshore ships and helps our method figure out more ground truth ships. Additionally, according to the last two columns of Table 1, a large number of parameters is introduced by ASM, which slow the detection speed of our method are due to its complex structures our method achieves 56 FPS and is slower than that of RefineDet due to much more parameters involved, i.e., 37.05M.

Table 1. Effects of inner modules in ASDN.

Models	P	R	F_1	Params(G)	FPS
ASDN	0.838	0.971	0.900	37.05	56
ASDN(w/o ASM)	0.831	0.968	0.894	34.30	62
ASDN(w/o DCN)	0.820	0.974	0.890	36.75	59
ASDN(w/o CBAM)	0.836	0.958	0.893	37.00	59
ASDN(w/ RFB)	0.835	0.964	0.895	36.89	53
ASDN(w/ ASPP)	0.821	0.947	0.880	36.21	58
ASDN(w/ Stem)	0.827	0.965	0.891	36.70	60
RefineDet	0.813	0.975	0.886	34.05	65

4.2 Compared with Other CNN-Based Methods

Table 2 illustrates the detection results of our method and compared CNN-based methods. In terms of detection accuracy, all the one-stage and two-stage methods obtain considerable recall rates because of the low threshold of confidence. In all experiments, precision rates acquired by the compared methods are notably different due to different levels of feature discrimination abilities owned by these algorithms. Most specifically, in comparison with one-stage object detectors, i.e., SSD, YOLOv3 and RefineDet, due to the lack of feature fusion strategies in SSD and inadequate feature representation ability for inshore ships with extreme aspect ratios in YOLOv3, scores of precision rate and F_1 are only 0.728 and 0.780, respectively. In comparison with two-stage object detectors, i.e., FPN, Libra R-CNN, even though multi-level of backbone features are combined together and an iterative top-down feature fusion operation is adopted in Libra R-CNN and FPN respectively, however, redundant information may also be introduced further. As for the detection speed, our method could detect inshore ships faster than the two stage detectors,e.g., Libra R-CNN and FPN, by a large margin and performs moderately among SSD, YOLOv3 and RefineDet resulting from limited capacities of parameters.

Furthermore, Table 3 illustrates scores of F_1 achieved by different algorithms for detecting each classes of inshore ships. It could be seen that certain differences exist for detecting different classes of inshore ships by the same algorithm due to diversified structures of ships and complex coupled relationships between surroundings and objects. Among these methods, our method achieves the topmost scores of F_1 at most types of inshore ships, which further demonstrate its effectiveness for detecting inshore ships in surveillance videos.

Table 2. Evaluation results of CNN-based methods on various metrics.

Models	P	R	F_1	Params(M)	FPS
FPN	0.739	0.966	0.837	60.04	16
Libra R-CNN	0.834	0.967	0.896	60.41	15
YOLOv3	0.780	0.944	0.854	61.55	34
SSD	0.728	0.973	0.833	25.22	200
RefineDet	0.813	0.975	0.886	34.05	65
Ours	0.838	0.971	0.900	37.05	56

Table 3. Scores F_1 achieved by different CNN-based methods on each class of inshore ships.

Models	PS	GCC	FB	BCC	OC	CS
FPN	0.792	0.826	0.865	0.796	0.854	0.883
Libra R-CNN	0.875	0.893	**0.880**	0.836	**0.918**	0.965
YOLOv3	0.780	0.867	0.863	0.834	0.874	0.906
SSD	0.825	0.839	0.800	0.809	0.796	0.922
RefineDet	0.869	0.919	0.856	0.845	0.870	0.958
Ours	**0.879**	**0.921**	0.879	**0.862**	0.887	**0.974**

Figure 6 shows the detection results of different inshore ships at three conditions by CNN-based methods. Firstly, our method could extract representative features from partial targets. In Fig. 6 (a), ships are with large aspect ratios and truncated. RefineDet, YOLOv3, SSD and Libra R-CNN all fail to detect the ship A out and ship B is missed by YOLOv3. However, our method could detect ships A and B accurately. Secondly, our method could represent small inshore ships well. In Fig. 6 (b), characteristics of ships are fuzzy due to far distances between sensors and ships. Ships A and B are all missed by YOLOv3 and SSD. However, all these small fishing boats are detected because of the fine-grained feature pyramid in FPN, Libra R-CNN and our method. Thirdly, our method could distinguish the confusing characteristics of overlapping ships. In Fig. 6 (c), there exist several occlusions between the three ships. Due to the serious interference among them, false alarms exist in the detection results of RefineDet and FPN. Besides, YOLOv3 fails to detect ship A out. SSD and Libra R-CNN locate ship A inaccurately. However, our method could detect the three ships accurately.

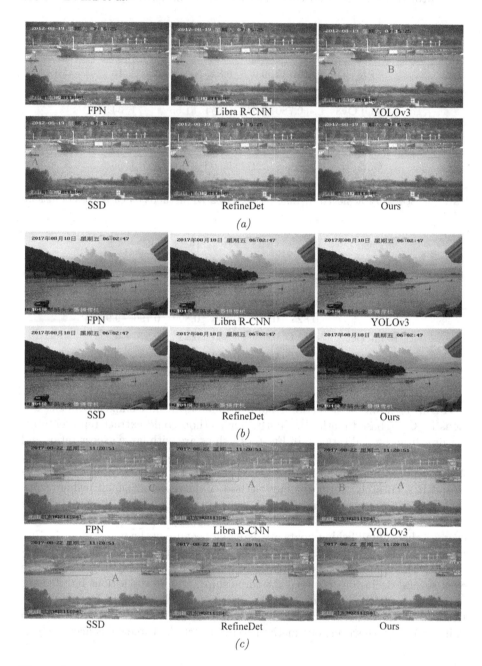

Fig. 6. Detection results of multi-scale inshore ships at three conditions by different CNN-based methods. Blue and red rectangles refer to ground truths and detection results, separately. (Color figure online)

5   Conclusion

In this paper, a one-stage detector, Attention Scale-aware Deformable Network (ASDN), is proposed for multi-scale inshore ship detection in surveillance videos by carefully combining two primary components including Attention Scale-aware Module (ASM) and Deformable Convolutional Network (DCN). ASM combining multi-branch convolutional layers with various kernel sizes and CBAM together, is designed for grabbing and refining informative features of multi-scale inshore ships with large aspect ratios. DCN is adopted for alleviating feature misalignment problems between refined anchors and features as well as extracting irregular characteristics of inshore ships. Experimental results on Seaships7000 dataset illustrate the effectiveness of our method for inshore ship detection in surveillance videos compared with other CNN-based methods, e.g., FPN, Libra R-CNN, YOLOv3, SSD and RefineDet. In the future, we will combine the imaging properties of inshore ships with network design tightly to improve the detection performance for inshore ships in surveillance videos further.

References

1. Arshad, N., Moon, K.S., Kim, J.N.: An adaptive moving ship detection and tracking based on edge information and morphological operations. In: International Conference on Graphic and Image Processing (ICGIP 2011), vol. 8285, p. 82851X. International Society for Optics and Photonics (2011)
2. Bao, X., Zinger, S., Wijnhoven, R., et al.: Ship detection in port surveillance based on context and motion saliency analysis. In: Video Surveillance and Transportation Imaging Applications, vol. 8663, p. 86630D. International Society for Optics and Photonics (2013)
3. Chen, L.C., Papandreou, G., Schroff, F., Adam, H.: Rethinking atrous convolution for semantic image segmentation. arXiv preprint arXiv:1706.05587 (2017)
4. Hosang, J., Benenson, R., Schiele, B.: Learning non-maximum suppression. In: Proceedings of the IEEE Conference on Computer Vision and Pattern Recognition, pp. 4507–4515 (2017)
5. Hyla, T., Wawrzyniak, N.: Ships detection on inland waters using video surveillance system. In: Saeed, K., Chaki, R., Janev, V. (eds.) CISIM 2019. LNCS, vol. 11703, pp. 39–49. Springer, Cham (2019). https://doi.org/10.1007/978-3-030-28957-7_4
6. Hyla, T., Wawrzyniak, N.: Identification of vessels on inland waters using low-quality video streams. In: International Conference on System Sciences, p. 7269 (2021)
7. Krizhevsky, A., Sutskever, I., Hinton, G.E.: Imagenet classification with deep convolutional neural networks. Adv. Neural Inf. Process. Syst. **25**, 1097–1105 (2012)
8. Lin, T.Y., Dollár, P., Girshick, R., He, K., Hariharan, B., Belongie, S.: Feature pyramid networks for object detection. In: Proceedings of the IEEE Conference on Computer Vision and Pattern Recognition, pp. 2117–2125 (2017)
9. Liu, S., Huang, D., Wang, Y.: Receptive field block net for accurate and fast object detection. In: Ferrari, V., Hebert, M., Sminchisescu, C., Weiss, Y. (eds.) ECCV 2018. LNCS, vol. 11215, pp. 404–419. Springer, Cham (2018). https://doi.org/10.1007/978-3-030-01252-6_24

10. Liu, W., et al.: SSD: single shot multibox detector. In: Leibe, B., Matas, J., Sebe, N., Welling, M. (eds.) ECCV 2016. LNCS, vol. 9905, pp. 21–37. Springer, Cham (2016). https://doi.org/10.1007/978-3-319-46448-0_2

11. Nie, X., Yang, M., Liu, R.W.: Deep neural network-based robust ship detection under different weather conditions. In: 2019 IEEE Intelligent Transportation Systems Conference (ITSC), pp. 47–52. IEEE (2019)

12. Nie, X., Liu, W., Wu, W.: Ship detection based on enhanced YOLOv3 under complex environments. JOCA **40**, 2561–2570 (2020)

13. Pang, J., Chen, K., Shi, J., Feng, H., Ouyang, W., Lin, D.: Libra R-CNN: towards balanced learning for object detection. In: Proceedings of the IEEE/CVF Conference on Computer Vision and Pattern Recognition, pp. 821–830 (2019)

14. Redmon, J., Farhadi, A.: YOLO9000: better, faster, stronger. In: Proceedings of the IEEE Conference on Computer Vision and Pattern Recognition, pp. 7263–7271 (2017)

15. Redmon, J., Farhadi, A.: YOLOv3: an incremental improvement. arXiv preprint arXiv:1804.02767 (2018)

16. Ren, S., He, K., Girshick, R., Sun, J.: Faster R-CNN: towards real-time object detection with region proposal networks. arXiv preprint arXiv:1506.01497 (2015)

17. Shao, Z., Wang, L., Wang, Z., Du, W., Wu, W.: Saliency-aware convolution neural network for ship detection in surveillance video. IEEE Trans. Circuits Syst. Video Technol. **30**(3), 781–794 (2019)

18. Shao, Z., Wu, W., Wang, Z., Du, W., Li, C.: Seaships: a large-scale precisely annotated dataset for ship detection. IEEE Trans. Multimedia **20**(10), 2593–2604 (2018)

19. Simonyan, K., Zisserman, A.: Very deep convolutional networks for large-scale image recognition. arXiv preprint arXiv:1409.1556 (2014)

20. Sullivan, M.D.R., Shah, M.: Visual surveillance in maritime port facilities. In: Visual Information Processing XVII, vol. 6978, p. 697811. International Society for Optics and Photonics (2008)

21. Szegedy, C., et al.: Going deeper with convolutions. In: Proceedings of the IEEE Conference on Computer Vision and Pattern Recognition, pp. 1–9 (2015)

22. Wei, H., Nguyen, H., Ramu, P., Raju, C., Liu, X., Yadegar, J.: Automated intelligent video surveillance system for ships. In: Optics and Photonics in Global Homeland Security V and Biometric Technology for Human Identification VI, vol. 7306, p. 73061N. International Society for Optics and Photonics (2009)

23. Woo, S., Park, J., Lee, J.-Y., Kweon, I.S.: CBAM: convolutional block attention module. In: Ferrari, V., Hebert, M., Sminchisescu, C., Weiss, Y. (eds.) ECCV 2018. LNCS, vol. 11211, pp. 3–19. Springer, Cham (2018). https://doi.org/10.1007/978-3-030-01234-2_1

24. Zhang, S., Wen, L., Bian, X., Lei, Z., Li, S.Z.: Single-shot refinement neural network for object detection. In: Proceedings of the IEEE Conference on Computer Vision and Pattern Recognition, pp. 4203–4212 (2018)

25. Zhu, X., Hu, H., Lin, S., Dai, J.: Deformable convnets v2: More deformable, better results. In: Proceedings of the IEEE/CVF Conference on Computer Vision and Pattern Recognition, pp. 9308–9316 (2019)

Context-BMN for Temporal Action Proposal Generation

Baoqing Tang[1,2], Shengye Yan[1,2(✉)] (iD), Yihua Ni[1,2], Yongjia Yang[1,2], and Kang Pan[1,2]

[1] Jiangsu Collaborative Innovation Center of Atmospheric Environment and Equipment Technology (CICAEET), Nanjing University of Information Science and Technology, Nanjing 210044, China
[2] Jiangsu Key Laboratory of Big Data Analysis Technology, Nanjing 210044, China

Abstract. Temporal Action Proposal Generation (TAPG) is a challenging task which locates the pair of starting and ending point of each action in an untrimmed video. In this article, a novel network named Context-BMN is proposed to better take advantage of the contextual semantic information in action features. To explicitly encode the starting/ending point of an action, context-BMN introduces extra proposal-level action features in addition to local-level action features for action feature extraction. To balance the positive/negative training samples, a novel loss function called Free-Focal Loss is proposed for the training of Context-BMN which utilizes different IOU interval of the sample to judge its contribution in the loss function. To address the problem that large gradients of difficult samples are detrimental to co-training of classification and regression, a "Balanced L1 Loss" is proposed to improve the regression gradients of specific samples. Comprehensive experiments are conducted on the well-known ActivityNet-1.3 dataset. The experimental results demonstrate the effectiveness of Context-BMN. Specifically, Context-BMN promotes the AR@100 from 75.01% to 76.56%, which is comparable to the state-of-the-art performance [21] on this dataset (76.75%).

Keywords: Temporal action proposal generation · Context-BMN · Deep learning

1 Introduction

Temporal Action Proposal Generation (TAPG) is an important task of computer vision. It has received a lot of attention and excellent results have been achieved [3–6,8]. TPAG takes untrimmed videos as input, and output the action segments in the videos. On one hand, TPAG itself can be used for action clip extraction. On the other hand, it can be followed with other modules such as action classification to fulfil more specific jobs. The solo or combo of TPAG have various real-world applications such as video recommendation, video highlight detection and smart surveillance. Several TAPG-related competitions are organized including the famous ActivityNet challenge and PaddlePaddle AI competition.

© Springer Nature Switzerland AG 2021
L. Fang et al. (Eds.): CICAI 2021, LNAI 13069, pp. 601–612, 2021.
https://doi.org/10.1007/978-3-030-93046-2_51

Current methods to deal with TAPG can be divided into two categories: anchor-based [1,2,7] and boundary-based [13,18,20] methods. In anchor-based methods, a set of anchors of different scales are designed in advance to generate candidate segments by regularly assigning candidate segments in the video sequence. In Boundary-based methods, temporal probability sequences containing rich local semantic information are usually generated by evaluating each temporal location in the video sequence, which helps to generate accurate boundaries and duration. For example, Boundary-Matching Network (BMN) [20] proposes a boundary matching mechanism to generate features and confidence scores of candidate proposals efficiently and achieves very good results. However, BMN abandons the actionness probability sequences that contain rich contextual semantic information, which is not conducive to handling complex activities and chaotic contexts. Besides, BMN ignores the rich contextual semantic information contained in the proposal-level features. Whats more, BMN suffers from severe sample imbalance during training, which makes the model pay too much attention to the background and not enough to grasp the contextual semantic information of the whole video.

To deal with the upper-mentioned problems, we propose Context-BMN. The overall framework is illustrated in Fig. 1. Context-BMN can capture the proposal-level features with rich contextual semantic information to predict boundary sequences. Besides, a novel Focal Loss [11] called Free-Focal loss is proposed to solve the sample imbalance problem in the training process. Finally, we use Balanced L1 Loss [12] as the regression loss function when evaluating the confidence scores of candidate proposals, which helps to rebalance the tasks and samples involved to achieve better convergence.

2   Our Approach

2.1   Pipeline of Our Framework

Figure 1 illustrates the detailed pipeline of the proposed method. For feature extraction, we use a two-stream network to encode video visual contents as shown on the top-right in the figure. The outputs of the two-stream network are then fed into the Context-BMN network as RGB and optical flow characteristics respectively. Context-BMN consists of three modules: Context Feature Generator (CFG), Boundary Prediction (BP) and Proposal Evaluation (PE), which are shown in the bottom-right in the figure. CFG is the backbone of the entire network to explore the rich local semantic information in video sequences. CFG outputs two types of features: shallow-level boundary feature and deep-level actionness feature. Boundary Matching (BM) layer is used to extract global proposal-level features from two kinds of local-level features, which is shown under the CFG module in the figure. BP takes boundary features as input to generate starting and ending probability of each location in the sequence. PE generates proposal confidence scores for densely distributed proposals based on actionness feature. In the last, a post-processing step is used to fuse the scores by

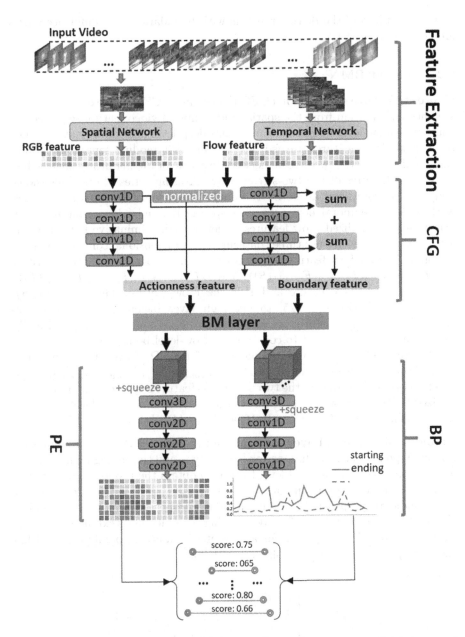

Fig. 1. The pipeline of our method. (a) Feature Extraction: we use spatial & temporal network to encode video visual feature. (b) Context-BMN network: It contains Context Feature Generator (CFG), Boundary Prediction (BP) and Proposal Evaluation (PE).

Soft-NMS [15], and the dense proposals with boundaries and confidence scores are generated.

2.2 Context-BMN

Context Feature Generator (CFG). The aim of CFG is to extract rich local semantic information from the spatial and temporal video feature sequences. It outputs shallow-level boundary feature and deep-level actionness feature. Then the two kinds of features are fed into BP and PE module separately. Unlike BMN which splits the two-stream network features for further utilization, we fuse the output features of the two-stream network using series of one-dimensional temporal convolutional layers on the output features of the spatial flow network and the temporal flow network respectively. And add normalized RGB feature and normalized Flow features to generate discriminative boundary and actionness features. We use three consecutive one-dimensional convolutional layers on RGB and flow feature sequences to explore local information, written as $Sf = F_{conv13}(F_{conv12}(F_{conv11}(S)))$ and $Df = F_{conv23}(F_{conv22}(F_{conv21}(T)))$, where S is the RGB feature and T is the Flow feature. Then, we fuse Sf, Df by element-wise sum [25] to get high layer fusion feature denoted as $Hf = F_{sum(Sf,Df)}$, Similarly, we can get $Lf = F_{conv11(S)} + F_{conv21(T)}$. Finally, we concatenate Hf and Lf to construct shallow-level boundary feature.

We use two following convolutional layers for Sf,Df to generate two actionness feature sequences, denoted as $P^a = (F_{conv14}(Sf), F_{conv24}(Df))$. In inference, we take the average of the two actionness feature sequences along with normalized RGB feature and Flow feature to generate the final deep-level actionness feature, denoted as $Af = (F_{conv14}(Sf) + F_{conv24}(Df))/2 + nor_{RGB} + nor_{Flow}$.

Boundary-Matching Layer. As shown in Fig. 2, we use BM layer to uniformly sample N points between the starting boundary t_s and the ending boundary t_e of each proposal $\phi_{i,j}$ in the local level feature to obtain the proposal-level feature.

In BM mechanism, a sampling mask weight $w_{i,j} \in R^{N \times T}$ is predefined for each candidate proposal. For each candidate proposal sampling mask weight $w_{i,j} \in R^{N \times T}$, we get it by uniformly sampling N points on its extended temporal region $[t_s - 0.25d, t_e = 0.25d]$. For a non-integer sampling points t_n, we define the corresponding sampling mask $w_{i,j,n} \in R^T$ as:

$$w_{i,j,n}[t] = \begin{cases} 1 - dec(t_n) & \text{if t} = \text{floor}(t_n) \\ dec(t_n) & \text{if t} = \text{floor}(t_n) + 1 \\ 0 & \text{otherwise} \end{cases}$$

Boundary Prediction (BP). The goal of BP is to take the proposal-level boundary feature as input, and then evaluate the starting and ending probabilities of each location in temporal sequence. The BM layer transforms the shallow-level boundary feature into four-dimensional proposal-level feature tensor. Then we pass it into several stacked convolutional layers to generate an $L \times 2$

boundary probability sequences. For each location of the sequence, we supervise the training with Free-Focal loss to predict precise temporal boundaries.

Proposal Evaluation (PE). The goal of PE module is to take the proposal-level actionness feature as input and outputs the proposal confidence map, where the confidence scores represent the overlap between candidate proposals and ground truth action instances. We use a series of 3d and 2d convolutional layers to explore semantic information in proposal-level feature. The BM layer converts deep-level actionness feature into an four-dimensional proposal-level feature tensor. Multi-convolutional layers are stacked to generate two types of proposal confidence maps m_{CC} and m_{CR} with shape $L \times L \times 2$. For each proposal in confidence map m_{CC} and m_{CR}, we use binary classification loss and regression loss to supervise training separately to generate reliable proposal confidence score.

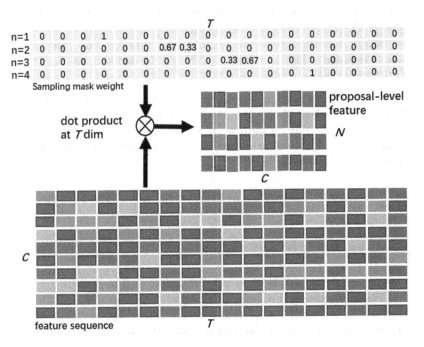

Fig. 2. Illustration of BM layer. For each proposal, we conduct dot product at T dimension between sampling weight and temporal feature sequence, to generate proposal-level feature of shape $C \times N$.

2.3 Training of Context-BMN

In order to jointly learn CFG, BP and PE, a unified multi-task learning scheme is proposed for optimization.

Label Assignment. With respect to CFG, in order to generate accurate P^a, we compose actionness label g^a for training actionness classification loss. With respect to BP, following BMN [20], we need to generate boundary label sequence g^s, g^e for boundary classification loss. With respect to PE, we need to generate action confidence label map g^c for classification loss and regression loss. For a ground-truth action instance $\varphi_g = (t_s, t_e)$ with duration $d_g = t_e - t_s$ in annotation set ψ_w, we define its action region as $r_A = (t_s, t_e)$, starting and ending region as $r_S = [t_s - d_g/10, t_s + d_g/10]$ and $r_e = [t_e - d_g/10, t_e + d_g/10]$ separately.

Loss of CFG. For each temporal location i of actionness score feature sequence P^a, we denote its local region as $r_i = [i - d_f/2, i + d_f/2]$, where d_f is the two temporal locations intervals. Then we calculate maximum overlap ration IoR between r_i and r_A, where IoR is defined as the overlap ratio with ground-truth proportional to the duration of this region. If the value of this ratio is bigger than the overlap threshold, we set the actionness label as $g_i^a = 1$, else we set it as $g_i^a = 0$. P^a consists of two actionness probability sequences, we can construct CFG actionness classification loss as the average of them, denoted as $L_{CFG}^a = \frac{1}{2L} \Sigma_{j=1}^2 L_{bl}(P^a, g^a)$.

We adopt binary logistic regression loss function L_{bl} for both two actionness sequences losses, where $L_{bl}(P^a, g^a)$ is denoted as $L_{bl}(P^a, g^a) = \Sigma_{i=1}^L (g_i^a \log(p_i^{a_j}) + (1 - g_i^a) \log(1 - p_i^{a_j}))$

Loss of BP. In BP, we need to generate temporal boundary probability sequence $P_S, P_E \in R^T$. In order to solve the problem of imbalance between positive and negative samples and difficult samples during training, we propose the Free-Focal loss to construct the classification loss function of BP for starting and ending sequence separately, denoted as:

$$L_{PBC}^s = \frac{1}{L} \Sigma_{i=1}^L (\alpha^+ \cdot b_i^s (1 - P_i^S)^\gamma) \log(P_i^S) + (\alpha^- \cdot (1 - b_i^s)(P_i^S)^\gamma) \log(1 - P_i^E)$$

$$L_{PBC}^e = \frac{1}{L} \Sigma_{i=1}^L (\alpha^+ \cdot b_i^e (1 - P_i^E)^\gamma) \log(P_i^E) + (\alpha^- \cdot (1 - b_i^e)(P_i^E)^\gamma) \log(1 - P_i^E)$$

Where $b_i = sign(g_i - \theta)$ is a two-value function used to convert g_i from $[0, 1]$ to $\{0, 1\}$ based on overlap threshold $\theta = 0.5$. Denoting $l^+ = \Sigma b_i$ and $l^- = L - l^+$, the weighted terms are $\alpha^+ = \frac{L}{l^+}$ and $\alpha^- = \frac{L}{l^-}$. They are used to balance the proportion imbalance between positive and negative samples in a batch.

Loss of PE. Following BMN [20], we generate BM confidence map m_{CC} and m_{CR}. We use BM label map g^c to train both of them simultaneously. For proposal $\varphi(i, j) = (t_s = t_j, t_e = t_j + t_i)$, we calculate the maximum Intersection-over-Union (IoU) with all φ_g to generate confidence label $g_{i,j}^c$. With the BM confidence map m_{CC} and m_{CR} from PE, classification and regression problems are solved simultaneously under the guidance of a multi-task loss, which is the sum of binary classification loss and regression loss, denoted as $L_{PEM}^C = L_C(m_{CC}, g^c) + \lambda \cdot L_R(m_{CR}, g^c)$.

As described in Libra R-CNN [12], the model is more sensitive to difficult samples in the regression loss, and the large gradient generated in the backpropagation process is harmful to the training process. Considering these issues, we adopt Balanced L1 Loss for regression loss L_R. Finally, a promoted gradient formulation is designed as:

$$\frac{\partial L_R}{\partial x} = \begin{cases} \alpha ln(b|x| + 1) & \text{if } |x| < 0.7 \\ \gamma & \text{other} \end{cases}$$

Balanced L1 loss increases the gradients of easy samples under the control of a factor denoted as α. By integrating the gradient formulation proposed above, we can get the balanced L1 loss, denoted as:

$$L_R(x) = \begin{cases} \frac{a}{b}(b|x| + 1)ln(b|x| + 1 - a|x| & \text{if } |x| < 0.7 \\ \gamma|x| + C & \text{other} \end{cases}$$

2.4   Inference of Context-BMN

Candidate Proposals Generation. Following BMN [20], we combining temporal locations with high boundary probabilities to generate candidate proposals. Firstly, we select the locations in boundary probability sequences that satisfy any of the following conditions to generate the set of starting and ending boundary points. (1) The probability higher than $0.5max(p)$ or (2) being a probability peak, where $max(p)$ is the maximum starting probability in this video. Then we generate starting locations set $B_S = \{t_i\}_{i=1}^{N_S}$ and ending locations set $B_E = \{t_j\}_{j=1}^{N_E}$, where N_S and N_E are the number of locations in the set separately. We combine each starting location with each ending location to generate candidate proposal. We denote the starting and ending probabilities of a proposal as $p_{t_s}^s$ and $p_{t_e}^e$.

Score Fusion. In order to get a more reliable proposal confidence score for retrieval, we fuse the boundary probabilities and action confidence scores of each proposal to get the final proposal score p_f.

In this way, we get candidate proposal set $\psi_p = \{\varphi_i = (t_s, t_e, p_f)\}_{i=1}^{N_p}$, where p_f is the final proposal score used to retrieve in the redundant proposal suppression phase.

Proposal Retrieving. We want to achieve higher recall with fewer number of proposals, so we need to suppress redundant candidate proposals obtained in the previous stage. We follow BMN and adopt Soft-NMS method [15], which is a non-maximum suppression through a score decaying function. After Soft-NMS, we get the final candidate proposals set as $\psi_p = \{\varphi_n = (t_s, t_e, p_f)\}_{n=1}^N$, where N is the final number of proposals used for retrieving.

3   Experiments

3.1   Datasets and Setup

ActivityNet-1.3. ActivityNet-1.3 is collected for action recognition, temporal detection and temporal proposal generation. It is a large-scale dataset containing 19994 temporal annotated untrimmed videos with 200 activity classes. The overall dataset is divided into training set, validation set and testing set with ratio of 2:1:1.

3.2 Temporal Action Proposal Generation (TAPG)

We adopt Average Recall (AR) with average number of proposals (AN) under different IoU thresholds following previous works [14,18,20], The IoU thresholds are [0.5:0.05:0.95]. The metric name is abbreviated as AR@AN. Besides, the Area Under the AR/AN Curve (AUC) is also calculated as an evaluation metric on ActivityNet-1.3 with AN varying from 0 to 100.

Table 1. Comparison with the state-of-the art on ActivityNet-1.3.

Method	[9]	[10]	[18]	[19]	[20]	[21]	Ours
AR@100(val)	73.01	73.17	74.16	74.54	75.01	**76.75**	76.56
AUC(val)		64.40	65.72	66.17	66.43	67.10	**68.50**	68.20

Comparison with State-of-the-Art Methods. The results of the proposed Context-BMN and the other methods on the validation set of ActivityNet-1.3 is shown in Table 1. The validation set is not as usual one in machine learning. All the researchers use this validation set for evaluation on this dataset. The validation set is not used during training in our experiment. As can be seen from Table 1, the proposed method achieves satisfactory results under both metrics. Specifically, comparing to the recent baseline method of BMN [20], the proposed method improves the AUC from 67.10% to 68.20% with a clear margin of 1.1%. This demonstrates the effectiveness of the proposed Context-BMN. And in comparison with the current state-of-the-art work [21], our proposed innovation is very different from it, and we believe that by integrating the two works, we can achieve better results.

Ablation Comparison with BMN. In order to show the effectiveness of the newly designed modules comparing with the ones in the baseline method of BMN [20], we further conduct detailed ablation studies. The following module combination settings are evaluated.

BMN with CFG: We replace the Base Module in BMN with our CFG to extract local semantic information.

BMN with (CFG + BP): We add BM layer into TEM to verify that the proposal-level feature is useful for predicting boundary probability.

Context-BMN without CFG: We replace the CFG network with a BMN-like Base Module.

Context-BMN without BP: We replace the BP module with several convolution layers like TEM in BMN.

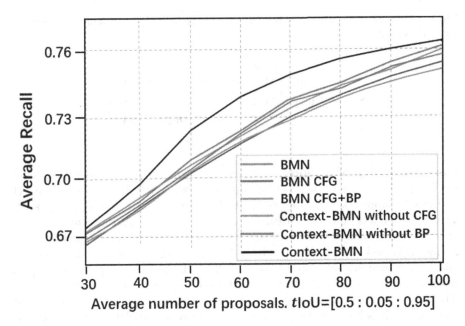

Fig. 3. Comparison of different module combination between BMN and Context-BMN on validation set of ActivityNet-1.3.

The results of different settings are shown in Fig. 3 for comparison. From Fig. 3, one can see that Context-BMN achieves the best results comparing with all the other settings.

Analysis of Free-Focal Loss. In order to investigate the effectiveness of the proposed Free-Focal loss, we compare the results of the three models learned with weighted binary logistic regression loss, focal loss [11] and Free-Focal loss. The results are shown in Table 2. From Table 2 can see that Free-Focal loss always ranks in the first place under different metrics. Focal loss always ranks in the second place and weighted binary logistic regression loss always ranks in the last place. This clearly tells us that to balance both of positive/negative samples and difficult/easy samples with the proposed scheme is very necessary.

Table 2. Comparison of weighted binary logistic regression (Wblr), Focal loss and Free-Focal loss(F-Focal loss).

Method	AR@10	AR@100	AUC
Wblr	56.24	75.21	67.20
Focal loss [11]	56.95	76.03	67.87
F-Focal loss	**57.28**	**76.56**	**68.20**

Table 3. Generalizability evaluation of Context-BMN on validation set of ActivityNet-1.3.

	Seen		Unseen	
Training data	AR@100	AUC	AR@100	AUC
Seen + Unseen	73.12	66.31	66.98	64.30
Seen	72.88	66.04	**66.54**	**63.22**

Generalizability of Proposals. To evaluate the ability of generating high-quality proposals for unseen action categories, we follow BMN [20] and select two un-overlapped action subsets on ActivityNet-1.3 for generalizability analysis. The (Sports, Exercise, Recreation) and (Socializing, Relaxing, Leisure) are the seen and unseen subsets separately. There are 87 and 38 action categories, 4455 and 1903 training videos, 2198 and 896 validation videos on seen and unseen subsets separately. We use the C3D network [16] pre-trained on Sports-1M dataset [17] for video representation. The results are shown in Table 3. The results on unseen subset shows a very slight AUC drop, which proves that Context-BMN achieves great generalizability to generate high-quality proposals for unseen actions, and can understand the general concept of actions.

4   Conclusion

This article introduces a novel temporal action proposal generation method called Context-BMN. It consists of three modules: Context feature generator (CFG), Boundary Prediction (BP) and Proposal Evaluation (PE). CFG is used to extract local features with rich action semantic information from video feature sequences and generate two different levels of features. Then through the BM layer, the two local-level features are converted into proposal-level features and feed to BP and PE respectively. The BP module is used to accurately predict the starting and ending probabilities of each location in feature sequence and then associate the starting and ending into pairs. The PE module generates a reliable confidence score for each candidate proposal for retrieving. Extensive experiments on popular benchmarks prove that the proposed Context-BMN achieves state-of-the-art result in temporal action proposal generation task.

References

1. Buch, S., Escorcia, V., Shen, C., et al.: SST: single-stream temporal action proposals. In: IEEE Conference on Computer Vision and Pattern Recognition, pp. 2911–2920 (2017)
2. Heilbron, F.C., Niebles, J.C., Ghanem, B.: Fast temporal activity proposals for efficient detection of human actions in untrimmed videos. In: IEEE Conference on Computer Vision and Pattern Recognition, pp. 1914–1923 (2016)

3. Feichtenhofer, C., Pinz, A., Zisserman, A.: Convolutional two-stream network fusion for video action recognition. In: IEEE Conference on Computer Vision and Pattern Recognition, pp. 623–634 (2016)
4. Simonyan, K., Zisserman, A.: Two-stream convolutional networks for action recognition in videos. In: IEEE Conference on Computer Vision and Pattern Recognition, pp. 3422–3431 (2016)
5. Wang, L., Xiong, Y., Wang, Z., et al.: Temporal segment networks: towards good practices for deep action recognition. In: IEEE International Conference on Computer Vision, pp. 2546–2555 (2016)
6. Tran, D., Bourdev, L., Fergus, R., et al.: Learning spatiotemporal features with 3D convolutional networks. In: IEEE International Conference on Computer Vision, pp. 4489–4497 (2015)
7. Gao, J., Yang, Z., Chen, K., et al.: Turn tap: temporal unit regression network for temporal action proposals. In: IEEE International Conference on Computer Vision, pp. 3628–3636 (2017)
8. Qiu, Z., Yao, T., Mei, T.: Learning spatio-temporal representation with pseudo-3D residual networks. In: IEEE International Conference on Computer Vision, pp. 2343–2354 (2017)
9. Lin, T., Zhao, X., Shou, Z.: Temporal convolution based action proposal: submission to activitynet. In: IEEE Conference on Computer Vision and Pattern Recognition, pp. 367–378 (2017)
10. Gao, J., Chen, K., Nevatia, R.: CTAP: complementary temporal action proposal generation. In: Ferrari, V., Hebert, M., Sminchisescu, C., Weiss, Y. (eds.) ECCV 2018. LNCS, vol. 11206, pp. 70–85. Springer, Cham (2018). https://doi.org/10.1007/978-3-030-01216-8_5
11. Lin, T., Goyal, P., Girshick, R., et al.: Focal loss for dense object detection. IEEE Trans. Pattern Anal. Mach. Intell. 345–353 (2018)
12. Pang, J., Chen, K., Shi, J., et al.: Libra R-CNN: towards balanced learning for object detection. In: IEEE Conference on Computer Vision and Pattern Recognition, pp. 821–830 (2019)
13. Zhao, Y., Xiong, Y., Wang, L., et al.: Temporal action detection with structured segment networks. In: IEEE International Conference on Computer Vision, pp. 2914–2923 (2017)
14. Lin, T., Zhao, X., Shou, Z.: Single shot temporal action detection. In: ACM International Conference on Multimedia, pp. 988–996 (2017)
15. Bodla, N., Singh, B., Chellappa, R., et al.: Soft-NMS-improving object detection with one line of code. In: IEEE International Conference on Computer Vision, pp. 5561–5569 (2017)
16. Du, T., Ray, J., Shou, Z., et al.: ConvNet architecture search for spatiotemporal feature learning. In: IEEE conference on Computer Vision and Pattern Recognition, pp. 273–285 (2017)
17. Karpathy, A., Toderici, G., Shetty, S., et al.: Large-scale video classification with convolutional nueral network. In: IEEE Conference on Computer Vision and Pattern Recognition, pp. 1725–1732 (2014)
18. Lin, T., Zhao, X., Su, H., Wang, C., Yang, M.: BSN: boundary sensitive network for temporal action proposal generation. In: Ferrari, V., Hebert, M., Sminchisescu, C., Weiss, Y. (eds.) ECCV 2018. LNCS, vol. 11208, pp. 3–21. Springer, Cham (2018). https://doi.org/10.1007/978-3-030-01225-0_1
19. Liu, Y., Ma, L., Zhang, Y., et al.: Multi-granularity generator for temporal action proposal. In: IEEE Conference on Computer Vision and Pattern Recognition, pp. 3604–3613 (2019)

20. Lin, T., Liu, X., Li, X., et al.: BMN: boundary-matching network for temporal action proposal generation. In: IEEE International Conference on Computer Vision, pp. 3889–3898 (2019)
21. Chang, S., Wang, P., Wang, F., et al.: Augmented transformer with adaptive graph for temporal action proposal generation, pp. 7–19 (2021)

Revisiting Knowledge Distillation for Image Captioning

Jingjing Dong, Zhenzhen Hu[✉], and Yuanen Zhou

Hefei University of Technology, Hefei 230601, Anhui, China

Abstract. Knowledge Distillation (KD) [6], as an effective technique for model compression and improving a model's performance, has been widely studied and adopted. However, most previous researches focus on image classification and few on sequence generation (such as Neural Machine Translation). We also note that few works for image captioning have incorporated KD, but they mainly treat it as a training trick. In contrast, we thoroughly investigate KD in the context of the image captioning task by conducting a series of experiments in this work. Specifically, we first apply the standard word-level KD to the image captioning model and explore cross-model distillation and self-distillation. We find that self-distillation is a practical choice that can achieve competitive performance while without spending time on choosing teacher's architecture. Inspired by the sequence-level distillation for Neural Machine Translation (NMT) [11], we secondly adopt and modify it for image captioning and observe that competitive performance can be obtained using only one-fifth of resources and the speed of inference can be significantly improved by eliminating the need for beam search at the cost of slight performance degradation. Inspired by distilling BERT [19] for NMT, we finally try to distill VL-BERT [12] to make the captioning model look ahead by leveraging its bidirectional nature.

Keywords: Image captioning · Knowledge Distillation · VL-BERT.

1 Introduction

Knowledge Distillation (KD) [6] is an effective technique for model compression and improving the model's performance. In KD, a student model is additionally supervised by a teacher model in addition to learning from the ground truth label. The main idea is that the student model acquires additional "dark knowledge" by mimicking the teacher model. However, most previous researches focus on image classification [26–29] and few on sequence generation [11,17,19].

To the best of our knowledge, [11] is the pioneering work that applies KD to NMT (one of sequence generation tasks). We also note that few works [20–23] for captioning have incorporated KD, but they mainly treat it as a training trick. For example, Dognin et al. [20] proposed to alleviate noisy data in image captioning with KD. In [21], KD is used to conduct data augmentation by generating pseudo

© Springer Nature Switzerland AG 2021
L. Fang et al. (Eds.): CICAI 2021, LNAI 13069, pp. 613–625, 2021.
https://doi.org/10.1007/978-3-030-93046-2_52

target captions for unlabeled images. In [22], language knowledge of the external language model is integrated into the video caption model by KD to alleviate the "long-tailed" problem of the caption corpus. In this work, we focus on the image domain and aim to fully investigate KD in the context of image captioning.

Image captioning [4,5,14,15] is a fundamental task that connects computer vision with Natural Language Processing (NLP). It aims at generating a natural language description of an image and has important practical applications, such as helping visually impaired people see. Recent methods typically follow the encoder/decoder paradigm where a Convolutional Neural Network (CNN) encodes the input image, and a sequence decoder, e.g. Recurrent Neural Networks (RNNs) and Transformer [1], generates a caption. Image captioning model is frequently trained by cross-entropy loss and then an optional self-critical [18] loss. Since we aim to fully investigate KD in the context of image captioning, we don't use the self-critical loss in this work and leave it as our future work.

Specifically, we firstly apply standard word-level KD [6] to three representative image captioning models [1,4,7] and explore self-distillation and cross-model distillation (i.e., teacher and student models have the same or different type of structures, with a little abuse for convenience). Through extensive experiments, we find that teacher with much better performance but different architecture from the student only show slight performance gain compared with teacher with lower performance but the same architecture as student. This suggests that self-distillation is a practical choice which can achieve comparative performance without spending time on choosing teacher's architecture.

Secondly, inspired by sequence-level KD for NMT [11], we adopt and modify it for image captioning. The steps are as follows: (1) train a teacher model, (2) run beam search over the training set with the teacher model and obtain the generated dataset then concatenate the generated dataset with the original training set to form a new training set, (3) train the student model on the new training set. During the experiment, we find that using only one-fifth of resources, the model trained only on the generated dataset shows competitive performance than the one trained on the original full training set but much better performance than the one trained on one-fifth of the original full training set. This indicates that sequence-level KD can serve as a dataset compression technique. Additionally, the model trained on the new dataset without beam search can obtain similar performance than the model trained on the original training set with beam search. As we known, beam search is time-consuming during inference and this property of sequence-level KD can be used to significantly accelerate the speed of inference with similar performance during deployment.

Thirdly, inspired by distilling BERT for NMT [19], we try to distill VL-BERT [12] to make the captioning model look ahead by leveraging its bidirectional nature. Specifically, we first fine-tune pre-trained VL-BERT on the target dataset then leverage the finetuned VL-BERT as a teacher model that generates sequences of word probability logits on the training samples for student model to imitate. Compared with the auto-regressive teacher, VL-BERT as a teacher can exploit both the left and the right context and thus provide a good estimation on word probability distribution for distilling. During the experiment, we try two manners to fine-tune the teacher: the one is Conditional Masked Language Modeling [19], which can leverage VL-BERT's bidirectional nature, and the other is left-to-right masked prediction as in the conventional sequence-to-sequence (seq2seq) model, which serves as a baseline for comparison. Different from the observation in [19], we find that both types of teacher can boost the student's performance and the former doesn't show an obvious advantage over the latter. One hypothesis is that the source and target side information is equivalent in NMT task while source (image) side contains much more information than target (text) side in image captioning task, so ignoring the right text context doesn't have too much impact in image captioning. In summary, this work serves as the first try to distill VL-BERT for image captioning.

2 Related Work

2.1 Image Captioning

Earlier methods for image captioning are template-based [31, 32]. These methods tend to produce captions that are relevant to the image but not natural sounding. Recent methods [4,5,7,15,33,34]typically follow the encoder/decoder paradigm. Based on the architectures of decoder, image captioning models can roughly be divided into three categories: LSTM-based decoder [4], LSTM with attention as decoder [7], Transformer-based decoder [1]. Image captioning model is frequently trained by cross-entropy loss and then an optional self-critical [18] loss. Since we aim to investigate KD in the context of image captioning, we don't use the self-critical loss in this work and leave it as our future work. In this work, we select three representative models [1,4,7] based on the above taxonomy for experiment.

2.2 Knowledge Distillation

Hinton et al. [6] first proposed the concept of KD. By introducing the soft-target related to the teacher network as part of the total loss, it can induce the training of the student network and realize the knowledge transfer. In terms of knowledge form, there are three main categories: 1) response-based knowledge [6,43], which refers to the neural response of the last output layer of the teacher model, 2) feature-based knowledge [44,45], in which the output of the intermediate layer (i.e., feature map) is used as knowledge to guide the training of the student model, 3) relationship-based knowledge [46,47], in which relationship between different layers or data samples is used as knowledge. The first one can directly imitate the final prediction of the teacher model and is easy to understand, especially in the context of "dark knowledge". In this work, we adopt response-based knowledge and leave others as our future works. In terms of the learning schemes, there are also three main categories: 1) offline distillation [6,37], in which the teacher is pre-trained, 2) online distillation [10,35,48], in which both the teacher model and the student model are updated simultaneously, 3) self-distillation [13,36,49], in which the same networks are used for the teacher and student models. In terms of applications, most previous researches focus on visual classification [26–29] and few [11,17,19] on sequence generation (e.g. NMT) For example, Kim et al. [11] first applied vanilla KD to NMT and then proposed a sequence-level KD tailored for NMT. We also note that few works [20–23] for captioning have incorporated KD, but they mainly treat it as a training trick. For example, Dognin et al. [20] proposed to alleviate noisy data in image captioning with KD. In [21], KD is used to conduct data augmentation by generating pseudo target captions for unlabeled images. In [22], language knowledge of the external language model is integrated into video caption model by KD to alleviate the "long-tailed" problem of video caption corpus. In contrast, we aim to fully investigate KD in the context of image captioning.

2.3 VL-BERT

Inspired by the recent success of pre-trained language models such as BERT [30], there is a growing interest in extending these models to the vision-language research field and putting forward VL-BERT [12,41,42]. These models use a two-stage training scheme. In the pre-training stage, contextualized vision-language representations are learned by predicting the masked words or image regions based on their intra-modality or cross-modality relationships on large amounts of image-text pairs. In the finetune stage, the pre-trained model is fine-tuned to adapt to the downstream task. Both BERT and VL-BERT have bidirectional nature, which means each token in a sentence can simultaneously consume both the left and the right context. Few attempts have been made to exploit this characteristic to provide rich word-level knowledge during KD. Chen et al. [19] tried to distill BERT to improve the performance of auto-regression models on NMT. Similarly, in this work, we try to distill VL-BERT to improve the performance of image captioning model.

3   Knowledge Distillation for Image Captioning

In this section, we first briefly formulate image captioning and then explore three different ways to apply KD to image captioning. Figure 1 gives an illustration of our distillation schemes.

3.1   Image Captioning

In the standard task of image captioning, model is given an image I to be described with a natural-language sentence $Y_{1:T}$. The sentence $Y_{1:T} = \{y_1, y_2, ..., y_T\}$ is a sequence of T words. A captioning model typically learns parameters θ to estimate the conditional likelihood $P_\theta(Y|I)$ by minimizing the cross-entropy loss:

$$L_{xe}(\theta) = -\log P_\theta(Y|I) = -\sum_{t=1}^{T} \log p_\theta(y_t|y_{1:t-1}, I), \tag{1}$$

where each conditional probability can be calculated via vanilla LSTM [4], attention-based LSTM [7], or Transformer [1].

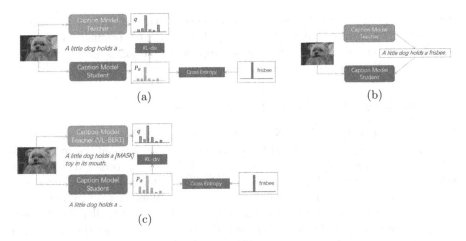

Fig. 1. Illustration of three kinds of knowledge distillation schemes. (a) is word-level knowledge distillation, (b) is sequence-level knowledge distillation, and (c) is distilling VL-BERT for image captioning.

3.2 Word-Level Knowledge Distillation for Image Captioning

We generally assume that the teacher has previously been trained and we are estimating parameters for the student. Standard KD [6] suggests training by matching the student's predictions to the teacher's predictions. So the straightforward approach to applying KD to image captioning is at word-level. Specifically, besides minimizing cross-entropy with the ground truth data, we also minimize the KL-divergence between student's and teacher's probability distribution at each word position, as shown in Fig. 1(a). The final loss function is:

$$L_{word-kd}(\theta) = L_{xe} + \lambda * L_{kd} = - \sum_{t=1}^{T} \{\log p_\theta(y_t|y_{1:t-1}, I) \tag{2}$$
$$+ \lambda * KL(p_\theta(y|y_{1:t-1}, I), q(y|y_{1:t-1}, I))\},$$

where $q(y|y_{1:t-1}, I)$ is the output distribution of a pre-trained teacher at time step t, KL denotes the KL-divergence loss and λ is a hyper-parameter for tuning the relative importance of the two losses.

In terms of teacher's architecture, we try two settings. The one is self-distillation where teacher has the same architecture with student and the other is cross-model distillation where teacher has a different architecture with student.

3.3 Sequence-Level Knowledge Distillation for Image Captioning

The motivation of sequence-level distillation is to match the sequence-level distribution of the teacher. Inspired by sequence-level distillation for NMT [11], we adopt and modify it for image captioning. The steps are as follows: 1)train a teacher model on the training set, 2) run beam search over the training set with the teacher model (only the generated sentences with the highest probability are reserved) and concatenate the generated dataset with original training set to form a new training set, 3) the cross-entropy loss function is used to train the student model on the new dataset, as shown in Fig. 1(b).

3.4   Distilling VL-BERT for Image Captioning

Inspired by distilling BERT for NMT [19], we try to distill VL-BERT [12] to make the captioning model look ahead by leveraging its bidirectional nature. Specifically, we first fine-tune the pre-trained VL-BERT on the target dataset then leverage the finetuned VL-BERT as a teacher model that generates sequences of word probability logits on the training samples for student model to imitate, as shown in Fig. 1(c). Compared with auto-regressive teacher, VL-BERT as teacher can potentially exploit both the left and the right context and thus provide a good estimation on the word probability distribution for distilling.

4   Experiments

4.1   Datasets and Evaluation Metrics

We conduct experiments on two widely-used image captioning datasets: MS-COCO [2] and Flickr30 k [24]. MS-COCO has $123, 287$ images and each image is assigned with 5 captions. We adopt the offline "Karpathy" data split [50] where $5, 000$ images are used for validation, $5, 000$ images for testing, and the rest for training. Flickr30k has $31, 000$ images and each image is assigned with 5 captions. We also adopt the offline "Karpathy" data split where $29, 000$ images are used for training, $1, 000$ images for testing, and $1, 000$ images for training. We use the common evaluation metrics to evaluate the quality of image captioning, including BLEU [3], METEOR [16], ROUGE_L [8], CIDEr [9], and SPICE [25].

4.2   Implementation Details

For word-level and sequence-level KD, we experimented on the open-source code-base[1]. Specifically, for Show-Tell [4] and Up-Down [7] model, the image feature embedding size and LSTM hidden state size were set to $1, 024$. Model was optimized with Adam [51] for 30 epochs. The learning rate was initialized to 0.0005 and decayed by a factor of 0.8 every three epochs. The batch size was set to 32. For Transformer [1] model, the decoder is composed of a stack of 6 identical layers. All sub-layers as well as the embedding layers produce outputs of dimension 512. The size of the feed-forward network's inner layer was set to $2, 048$. Model was also optimized with Adam [51] for 15 epochs. The learning rate was initialized to 0.0005 and the warmup step was set to $20, 000$. The batch size was set to 10. The beam search size was set to 1 during validation and 3 during testing. We perform light model hyper-parameter search with $\lambda \in \{0.1, 0.2, 0.4, 0.8, 1.5, 3.0\}$.

---

[1] https://github.com/ruotianluo/self-critical.

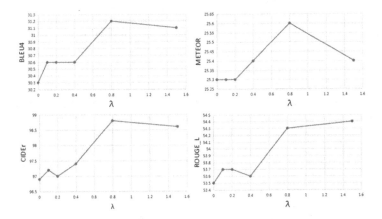

Fig. 2. The effect of λ on MS-COCO validation set. Both student and teacher models are Show-Tell [4].

For distilling VL-BERT, we conduct experiments on the open-source code[2] since it can support both Seq2Seq and bidirectional training simultaneously. We choose the model pre-trained on Conceptual Captions dataset [52] by full bidirectional objective as our starting point. Then we finetune the pre-trained model on Flickr30k using the directional objective as the bidirectional teacher (dubbed as VL-BERT$_{bi}$). We also finetune it by Seq2Seq objective as the conventional auto-regressive teacher (dubbed as VL-BERT$_{s2s}$) for comparison. For convenience, the model trained on Flickr30k by Seq2Seq objective serves as our conventional auto-regressive student. The search range of λ is set as above. We also tune the temperature τ for the softmax applied at the teacher's logits following the practice in [19]. The beam search size was set to 1 during validation. During testing, beam search size ranges from 1 to 5 and we choose the best one.

4.3 Results and Analysis

In this section, we will give some analysis based on the experimental results by answering the following questions.

Q1: What is The Effect of λ During Word-Level KD? The λ is used to balance the cross-entropy loss and KD loss. We show the changing trend of evaluation metrics with λ in Fig. 2. We adopt a self-distillation scheme and both teacher and student are Show-Tell model [4] in Fig. 2. We can see that all language metrics benefit from word-level KD and an appropriate λ is also important to achieve optimal performance. We observed similar results in both Up-Down [7] and Transformer [1] models and don't present it due to space limited.

---

[2] https://github.com/LuoweiZhou/VLP.

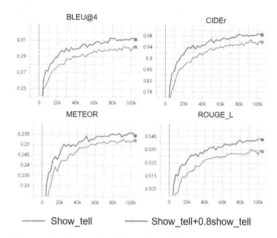

Fig. 3. Word-level self-distillation performance of Show_Tell model on MS-COCO validation set. The value of λ is 0.8.

Q2: Is The Training Stable During Word-Level KD? In Fig. 3, we show the validation curve of the Show-Tell model's word-level self-distillation and we can see that the training is stable and the model equipped with word-level self-distillation (Show_Tell+0.8Show_Tell) can outperform the baseline model (Show_Tell) by a large margin at every epoch. Similar results can also be observed from other models [1, 7] and are not shown due to space limitations.

Q3: How Does Word-Level KD Compare with Label Smoothing? As claimed in [26], label smoothing [53] is equivalent to word-level KD with a uniform distribution teacher. By comparing the 5th row with other rows in each section of Table 1, we can observe that KD is better than label smoothing in most cases even if the temperature τ is set to 1 by default. A reasonable explanation is that the output distribution of KD contains more information than the one of label smoothing. It is interesting to find that the Transformer-based decoder can benefit more from label smoothing than the LSTM-based decoder. A possible explanation is that Transformer has more capacity and label smoothing can prevent it from being over-confidence and then improve generalization.

Q4: How Does Cross-Model Distillation Compare with Self-Distillation During Word-Level KD? Besides self-distillation, we also try cross-model distillation where the student and teacher have different architectures. Let's first focus on the first section of Table 1 and we can observe that though Up-Down and Transformer teachers have much better performance (e.g. almost 10 points in CIDEr) than the Show-Tell teacher when the student is Show-Tell model, the final distillation performance gap is marginal. One possible explanation is that different architectures have different solution spaces and the student has not enough capacity to mimic the teacher. This suggests that, compared with cross-model distillation, self-distillation is a practical choice that can achieve comparative performance while without spending time on choosing teacher's architecture. With label smoothing

Table 1. Performance of word-level KD on MS-COCO test set. The number after _ is the value of λ. None denotes the model is only trained by cross-entropy loss. 'S' denotes label smoothing.

Student model	Teacher model	B@4	METEOR	CIDEr	SPICE
Show-Tell	None	32.9	26.0	101.1	18.7
	Show-Tell_0.8	33.8	26.3	103.0	**19.2**
	Up-Down_1.5	**34.0**	26.4	104.1	**19.2**
	Transformer_1.5	33.8	26.3	**104.6**	**19.2**
	LS_0.8	33.4	25.8	102.7	18.8
Up-Down	None	36.3	27.7	113.2	20.6
	Up-Down_0.8	**37.1**	27.8	115.2	20.8
	Show-Tell_0.2	36.3	27.8	114.0	20.8
	Transformer_0.8	36.8	**27.9**	**115.3**	**20.9**
	LS_0.2	36.2	27.7	113.3	20.7
Transformer	None	34.8	27.5	111.5	20.7
	Transformer_1.5	36.3	**28.0**	115.5	**21.2**
	Show-Tell_0.4	36.0	27.6	113.1	20.7
	Up-Down_1.5	**36.7**	**28.0**	115.4	21.0
	LS_0.8	36.6	27.6	**115.5**	20.7

discussed above, it is no surprise to find that an inferior teacher can still guide the learning of a superior student to some extent, as shown in the second and third sections of Table 1.

Q5: How About Sequence-Level KD for Image Captioning? From Table 2, we find that, with using only one-fifth of resources, model (i.e.,*-one-seqkd, * denotes Show-Tell or Up-Down or Transformer) trained only on the generated dataset shows competitive performance than the one (i.e.,*-baseline) trained on the original full training set but much better performance than the one (i.e.,*-one-gt) trained on one-fifth of the original full training set. This indicates that sequence-level KD can serve as a dataset compression technique. Additionally, model (i.e.,*-six-seqkd) trained on the new dataset can obtain better performance (for three out of four metrics) than the one (i.e.,*-baseline) trained on original training set when not using beam search (i.e.,beam_size=1). It is worth noting that model (i.e.,*-six-seqkd) trained on the new dataset without the need of beam search can obtain slightly lower but closer performance than model (i.e.,*-baseline) trained on original training set with beam_size=3. As we have known, beam search is time-consuming during inference and this property of sequence-level KD can be used to significantly accelerate the speed of inference with similar performance during deployment. We also find that model trained on data generated by sequence-level KD can NOT benefit from beam search and the reason needs further exploring.

Q6: How About Distilling VL-BERT for Image Captioning? We show the preliminary results in Table 3. We can find that both types of teacher can boost the student's performance by comparing the first row with others. Different from the observation in [19], we can see that the bidirectional teacher doesn't show an obvious advantage over the conventional auto-regressive Seq2Seq teacher by comparing the third (fourth) row with the second(fifth) row. One hypothesis

Table 2. Performance of sequence-level KD on MS-COCO test set. 'one' denotes only one caption per image is used and 'six' denotes one generated caption plus five ground truth captions. 'gt' denotes ground truth caption and 'seqkd' denotes caption generated by sequence-level KD.

Beam size	Model	B@4	METEOR	CIDEr	SPICE
1	Show-Tell-baseline	30.9	25.4	98.5	**18.6**
	Show-Tell-one-gt	29.2	24.3	91.1	17.2
	Show-Tell-one-seqkd	31.8	25.2	95.6	17.7
	Show-Tell-six-seqkd	**32.6**	**25.7**	**100.0**	18.4
3	Show-Tell-baseline	**32.9**	**26.0**	**101.1**	**18.7**
	Show-Tell-six-seqkd	32.4	25.6	98.2	18.1
1	Transformer-baseline	33.2	27.2	110.3	20.6
	Transformer-one-gt	31.3	25.7	101.3	19.1
	Transformer-one-seqkd	33.7	26.8	105.0	19.6
	Transformer-six-seqkd	**34.8**	**27.6**	**112.7**	**20.7**
3	Transformer-baseline	34.8	27.5	**111.5**	**20.7**
	Transformer-six-seqkd	**35.2**	27.5	110.8	20.4
1	Up-Down-baseline	34.0	27.1	109.9	**20.3**
	Up-Down-one-gt	33.0	26.4	105.8	19.7
	Up-Down-one-seqkd	35.1	27.2	108.5	19.8
	Up-Down-six-seqkd	**35.5**	**27.4**	**111.6**	**20.3**
3	Up-Down-baseline	**36.3**	**27.7**	**113.2**	**20.6**
	Up-Down-six-seqkd	35.2	27.3	109.6	20.1

Table 3. Performance on Flickr30 k test split. The number after _ is the value of λ. $\tau5$ denotes the temperature is set to 5.

Model	B@4	METEOR	CIDEr	SPICE
VL-BERT$_{s2s}$(base)	29.8	23.6	65.9	17.7
base+ VL-BERT$_{s2s\_1.5}$	30.5	23.6	67.7	17.5
base+ VL-BERT$_{bi\_0.2}$	29.8	23.7	66.8	18.0
base+ VL-BERT$_{bi\_1.5\_\tau5}$	**31.0**	23.9	68.5	**18.1**
base+ VL-BERT$_{s2s\_0.8\_\tau5}$	30.9	**24.1**	**69.0**	18.0

is that the source and target side information is equivalent in NMT task while the source (image) side contains much more information than the target (text) side in image captioning task, so ignoring part right text context doesn't have too much impact in image captioning compared with in NMT.

5   Conclusion

In this work, we thoroughly investigate KD in the context of image captioning task by conducting three types of distillation schemes(i.e., word-level distillation, sequence level distillation and distilling VL-BERT for image captioning) and get some new interesting findings. In the future, we will try to explore how to use knowledge distillation in the context of self-critical loss [18] and apply these findings to state-of-the-art captioning models.

References

1. Vaswani, A., et al.: Attention is all you need. In arXiv (2017)
2. Lin, T.-Y., et al.: Microsoft coco: common objects in context. In: ECCV (2014)
3. Papineni, K., et al.: Bleu: a method for automatic evaluation of machine translation. In: ACL (2002)
4. Vinyals, O., et al.: Show and tell: a neural image caption generator. In: CVPR (2015)
5. Xu, K., et al.: Show, attend and tell: neural image caption generation with visual attention. In: ICML (2015)
6. Hinton, G.E., et al.: Distilling the knowledge in a neural network. In arXiv (2015)
7. Anderson, P., et al.: Bottom-up and top-down attention for image captioning and visual question answering. In: CVPR (2018)
8. Lin, C.-Y.: Rouge: a package for automatic evaluation of summaries. In: Text Summarization Branches Out (2004)
9. Vedantam, R., Lawrence, Z.C., Parikh, D. Cider: consensus-based image description evaluation. In: CVPR (2015)
10. Zhang, Y., et al.: Deep mutual learning. In: CVPR (2018)
11. Kim, Y., Rush, A.M.: Sequence-level knowledge distillation. In arXiv (2016)
12. Zhou, L., et al.: Unified vision-language pre-training for image captioning and vqa. In: AAAI (2020)
13. Zhang, L., et al.: Be your own teacher: improve the performance of convolutional neural networks via self distillation. In: ICCV (2019)
14. Zhou, Y., et al.: More grounded image captioning by distilling image-text matching model. In: CVPR (2020)
15. Pan, Y., et al.: X-linear attention networks for image captioning. In: CVPR (2020)
16. Denkowski, M., Alon, L.: Meteor universal: language specific translation evaluation for any target language. In: Proceedings of the Ninth Workshop on Statistical Machine Translation, pp. 376–380 (2014)
17. Hahn, S., Choi, H.: Self-knowledge distillation in natural language processing. In arXiv (2019)
18. Rennie, S.J., et al.: Self-critical sequence training for image captioning. In: CVPR (2017)

19. Chen, Y.-C., et al.: Distilling knowledge learned in BERT for text generation. In arXiv (2019)
20. Dognin, P.L., et al.: Alleviating noisy data in image captioning with cooperative distillation. In: arXiv (2020)
21. Guo, L., et al.: Non-autoregressive image captioning with counterfactuals-critical multi-agent learning. In arXiv (2020)
22. Zhang, Z., et al.: Object relational graph with teacher-recommended learning for video captioning. In: CVPR (2020)
23. Pan, B., et al.: Spatio-temporal graph for video captioning with knowledge distillation. In: CVPR (2020)
24. Plummer, B.A., et al.: Flickr30k entities: collecting region-to-phrase correspondences for richer image-to-sentence models. In: ICCV (2015)
25. Anderson, P., et al.: SPICE: Semantic Propositional Image Caption Evaluation. In: ECCV (2016)
26. Yuan, L., et al.: Revisiting knowledge distillation via label smoothing regularization. In: CVPR (2020)
27. Li, J., et al.: Learning to learn from noisy labeled data. In: CVPR (2019)
28. He, Y.-Y., Jianxin, W., Wei, X.-S.: Distilling virtual examples for long-tailed recognition. In arXiv (2021)
29. Furlanello, T., et al.: Born again neural networks. In: ICML (2018)
30. Devlin, J., et al.: Bert: pre-training of deep bidirectional transformers for language understanding. In arXiv (2018)
31. Dhar, G.K.V.P.S., et al.: Baby Talk: Understanding and Generating Simple Image Descriptions (2013)
32. Mitchell, M., et al.: Midge: generating image descriptions from computer vision detections. In: ECACL (2012)
33. Huang, L., et al.: Attention on attention for image captioning. In: ICCV (2019)
34. Cornia, M., et al.: Meshed-memory transformer for image captioning. In: CVPR (2020)
35. Chen, D., Mei, J.P., Wang, C., Feng, Y., Chen, C.: Online knowledge distillation with diverse peers. In: AAAI (2020)
36. Yuan, L., Tay, F.E., Li, G., Wang, T., Feng, J.: Revisit knowledge distillation: a teacher-free framework. In: CVPR (2020)
37. Huang, Z., Wang, N.: Like what you like: Knowledge distill via neuron selectivity transfer. In arXiv (2017)
38. Wei, H.R., Huang, S., Wang, R., Dai, X., Chen, J.: Online distilling from checkpoints for neural machine translation. In: NAACL-HLT (2019)
39. Freitag, M., Al-Onaizan, Y., Sankaran, B.: Ensemble distillation for neural machine translation. In arXiv (2017)
40. Su, W., et al.: VL-BERT: pre-training of generic visual-linguistic representations. In arXiv (2019)
41. Lu, J., et al.: ViLBERT: pretraining task-agnostic visiolinguistic representations for vision-and-language tasks. In arXiv (2019)
42. Li, L.H., et al.: VisualBERT: a simple and performant baseline for vision and language. In arXiv (2019)
43. Kim, J., Park, S.U.K., Kwak, N.: Paraphrasing complex network: network compression via factor transfer. In arXiv (2018)
44. Romero, A., et al.: Fitnets: hints for thin deep nets. In arXiv (2014)
45. Zagoruyko, S., Nikos, K.: Paying more attention to attention: improving the performance of convolutional neural networks via attention transfer. In arXiv (2016)

46. Park, W., et al.: Relational knowledge distillation. In: CVPR (2019)
47. Chen, H., et al.: Learning student networks via feature embedding. IEEE TNNLS (2020)
48. Xie, J., et al.: Training convolutional neural networks with cheap convolutions and online distillation. In arXiv (2019)
49. Bagherinezhad, H., et al.: Label refinery: improving imagenet classification through label progression. In arXiv (2018)
50. Karpathy, A., Li, F.-F.: Deep visual-semantic alignments for generating image descriptions. In: CVPR (2015)
51. Kingma, D.P., Jimmy, B.: Adam: a method for stochastic optimization. In arXiv (2014)
52. Sharma, P., et al.: Conceptual captions: a cleaned, hypernymed, image alt-text dataset for automatic image captioning. In: ACL (2018)
53. Szegedy, C., et al.: Rethinking the inception architecture for computer vision. In: CVPR (2016)

Enhanced Attribute Alignment Based on Semantic Co-Attention for Text-Based Person Search

Hao Wang[✉] and Zhenzhen Hu[✉]

Hefei University of Technology, Hefei 230601, Anhui, China
`2019170905@mail.hfut.edu.cn`

Abstract. Person search by natural language description aims to retrieve the most related person in the image gallery according to the given textual descriptions. This task is challenging due to the gap of cross-domain and cross-modality. Previous methods align the local visual-textual features based on the global matching score while ignoring capturing the fine-grained cross-modal correspondence between image and text. In this paper, we propose a novel framework named Enhanced Attributes Alignment based on Semantic Co-Attention (EAA-SCA) for text-based person search. The proposed SCA consists of Self-Attention (SA) modules and Relationships Attention (RA) modules cascaded in depth. SA module takes visual attribute features and textual features as input respectively to learn the internal dependencies of single modality. Then self-attended visual attribute features and self-attended textual features are feed into RA module to learn more fine-grained visual attribute features rich in semantic relationships between visual attributes and textual description, which contributes to more precise attributes alignment. Experimental results on CUHK-PEDES dataset demonstrate the effectiveness of the proposed method. With assistance from SCA, the performance improves 2.43% on Rank-1 in text-based person search.

Keywords: Text-based person search · Semantic co-attention · Enhanced Attributes Alignment

1 Introduction

Person search has received a wide attention in recent years because of its extensive applications in video surveillance, missing people search and et al. Comparing with image queries, person search by natural language makes the retrieval form more open and more humanized because it identifies the same person in the image database only according to natural language description related to a person.

Although natural language description can provide a wide range of information including semantic composition and potential relationships, the challenge still remains. In the traditional person search, the query and search galleries are homologous and the algorithms cannot be directly transferred to the

© Springer Nature Switzerland AG 2021
L. Fang et al. (Eds.): CICAI 2021, LNAI 13069, pp. 626–637, 2021.
https://doi.org/10.1007/978-3-030-93046-2_53

cross-domain and cross-modality text-based person search task. There are various kinds of cross-media challenges in the visual-textual feature alignment. In the image-text matching task, many methods [8,9,22] have recently made great progress on some popular benchmarks such as MSCOCO [23], but they usually fail to show better performance on text-based person search that is similar to image-text matching. The fundamental reason for this phenomenon is that the different quality of pictures in each dataset. Compared with other datasets for image-text matching task, pictures of CUHK-PEDES dataset [1] are less distinguishable or even highly ambiguous. What's more, MSCOCO contains many high-definition pictures about all kinds of objects, not just pedestrians like CUHK-PEDES dataset. This leads to the pursuit of accurate alignment of global visual-textual features in terms of image-text matching, while neglecting the corresponding relationship between the local visual cues and attribute descriptions in the text. Therefore, we should pay more attention to the local key features of pedestrians under the better matching of global features considering the quality of the images in CUHK-PEDES dataset. Now some related work has overcome the above challenge. In terms of visual processing, [27,28] aim to learn posture related features from human key point map, while [11,29,30] extract human part features through auxiliary segmentation as supervision. In particular, ViTAA [11] utilizes semantic segmentation network to divide people into five parts, and then matches these five parts one by one with the attribute description in the text by k-sampling algorithm, where the local align loss is designed so that the similarity of matched visual-textual attributes(positive attributes) must be greater than 0.6, and the similarity of the mismatched (negative attributes) is less than 0.4 at least, resulting in promote visual-textual attribute alignment to some degree.

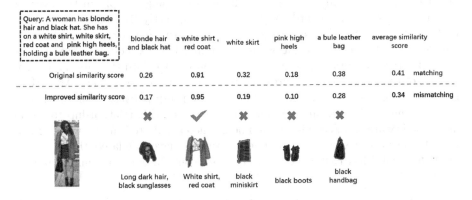

Fig. 1. Illustration of the enhanced attribute alignment. When the average similarity score is greater than 0.4, it may be mistaken for positive attributes. We deal with hard negative attributes alignment by obtaining enhanced attribute features based on semantic co-attention mechanism.

In view of the above solutions to the challenges, we have found areas that can be improved to enhance visual attribute alignment. Although ViTAA has achieved the better results in the aforementioned methods, its final attribute similarity is the average value after the sum of the similarity among the five attributes as the problem follows. For example in Fig. 1, all samples are negative attributes(similarity < 0.4) except that the second pair of attribute features is matched (similarity > 0.6) in original similarity. We can find that query text and image belong to the negative sample pair while the average similarity is $0.41(>0.4)$. Therefore, semantic co-attention is used to build strong relationships between visual attribute features and query text. Then we attach this relationship to the visual attribute feature to get the more fine-grained attribute feature. After getting the more fine-grained attribute features, we can find that the positive attributes are more similar because the query text contains the semantics corresponding to the visual attributes such as "white shirt, red coat", otherwise the similarity of the negative attributes is smaller. The increase of positive attributes similarity only has a small impact because the upper limit of similarity is 1, while the similarity of other negative attributes is reduced as much as possible, which leads to a sharp decrease in average similarity to $0.34(<0.4)$. It proves that we can effectively deal with the hard negative samples through this method.

In this work, we propose a novel Enhanced Attributes Alignment based on Semantic Co-Attention (EAA-SCA) for text-based person search according to the aforementioned example, towards realizing the more precise attribute matching of fine-grained visual attribute features rich in semantic relationships. As shown in Fig. 2, EAA-SCA brings global textual features and visual attribute features into semantic co-attention mechanism to get more fine-grained attribute features, which contributes to obtaining greater/smaller similarity of positive/negative attributes. That results in decreasing sharply in the average similarity so as to handle hard negative samples correctly. To be specific, Semantic Co-Attention (SCA) mechanism is made up of the Self-Attention (SA) module and the Relationship-Attention (RA) module. The SA module is built on the basis of attention mechanism in [12]. Its purpose is to learn the internal dependencies of visual attribute features and text description respectively. After that, the RA module is used to build a strong relationship between visual attribute features and textual features. Meanwhile, we attach this relationship to visual attribute features for achieving more fine-grained attribute features with semantic relationships. Extensive experimental results have validated the proposed method on CUHK-PEDES dataset. The main contributions are summarized as follow:

1. We design a novel Enhanced Attribute Alignment based on Semantic CoAttention(EAA-SCA) network for dealing with hard negative samples effectively in the text-based person search, which reduces the local average similarity value of negative samples greatly to enhance attribute alignment in essence.

2. We utilize the SA modules and the RA modules to build SCA mechanism, the SA module is adopted to analyze the internal dependencies of each mode, and the RA module is used to generate enhanced fine-grained visual attribute features with semantic relationships.
3. The results of experiments demonstrate the effectiveness of EAA-SCA on CUHK-PEDES. With the help of SCA, we achieve the 2.43% Rank-1 improvements in the text-based person search.

2 Related Work

Attention Mechanism. Attention mechanism is divided into soft attention and hard attention in general. Soft attention averages weight graph and selects a part of high weight in attention graph as input, while hard attention samples input and ignores other parts. Therefore, since the soft attention has achieved extraordinary results in transformer [12], soft attention mechanism has been widely used in various fields, such as [12] in natural language tasks, [13] in visual question answering, [6,33] in person search. For cross modal tasks, in addition to understanding the visual content of images, these tasks also requires a complete understanding of visual-textual semantic relationships. Thus it is indispensable to use semantic co-attention mechanism [14,15] that combines visual attention with textual attention for the problem.

Person Search. Given a pedestrian data, the relevant pedestrian data in the database is found by the technology of pedestrian re-identification. According to form of query data, we can divide pedestrian re-identification into two categories: image-based pedestrian re-identification and text-based pedestrian re-identification. In general, these retrieval technologies are both to calculate the greatest similarity between the query data and image galleries. However, compared with image-based person research, the image retrieval based on text is more difficult due to modal heterogeneity. What's more, it is non-trivial to address the cross-modal problem in the text-based person Re-id. Li et al. [1] firstly establish a large-scaled person identification dataset with detailed natural language annotations named CUHK Person Description(CUHK-PEDES). At the same time, they propose the Recurrent Neural Network with Gated Neural Attention mechanism model (GNA-RNN) to capture the similarity between textual feature and visual feature. Afterwards, Chen et al. [2] improve the unit-level attentions in the GNA-RNN model by setting adaptive threshold. Zheng et al. [3] propose a dual-path model in order to learn the visual-textual embedding, which sets the instance loss so that the model can control the fine-grained visual-textual distance of intra-modality. Many methods like [4,5] imitate the idea that learn the potential semantic space mapping pedestrian attribute space through loss function. There are also some attempts to learn modal invariant feature representation according to adversarial learning such as [6,7,7]. [10,11] extract multi-granularity pedestrian limb features to promote the alignment between pedestrian limb features and noun phrases through pedestrian posture analysis. Some soft attention based person re-identification technology [8,9,33] have also obtained satisfactory results in text retrieval tasks in the manner of realizing the semantic alignment between pedestrian attribute features and noun phrases in the text, especially AXM-Net [33] utilizes complementary intra modal attention learning mechanisms for robust feature matching, becoming a trend to fine-grained attribute alignment.

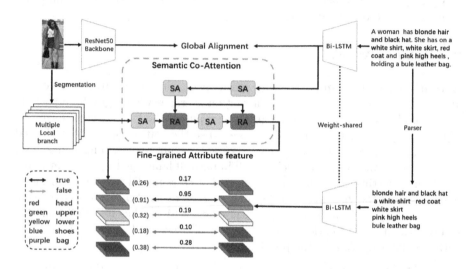

Fig. 2. The overall framework of Enhanced Attribute Alignment based on Semantic Co-Attention (EAA-SCA). It utilizes SCA mechanism to extract fine-grained attributes features rich in semantic relationship for enhanced attribute alignment.

3   Approach

The overall framework with Enhanced Attribute Alignment based on Semantic Co-Attention (EAA-SCA) model is shown in Fig. 2. The framework consists of three parts: (a) global visual-textual alignment. (b) visual-textual attribute alignment and (c) semantic co-attention mechanism. Our core contribution is the semantic co-attention mechanism that adds the semantic relationship between visual attribute features and textual features to each visual attribute feature in order to get more fine-grained attribute features, which contributes to more precise attribute alignment.

3.1   Background

Global Visual-Textual Alignment. Given a person image I and its textual description T, for the global visual-textual alignment module based on ViTAA model [11], we first use ResNet-50 [16] and Bi-LSTM to extract global visual-textual representations v_i, t_i separately. Then $\langle v^i, t^+, t^- \rangle$ and $\langle t^i, v^+, v^- \rangle$ are taken as inputs into the designed global alignment loss function on the basis of Triplet loss [17]. We take $\langle v^i, t^+, t^- \rangle$ as example here, $\langle t^i, v^+, v^- \rangle$ can be obtained in the same way. Firstly, the cosine similarity of positive/negative pairs is defined as the affinity between visual and textual features:

$$S = \frac{v^T \cdot t}{\|v\| \cdot \|t\|}, S^+ = S(v^i, t^+), S^- = S(v^i, t^-) \tag{1}$$

Then we forcibly add a standard to ranges of S^+ and S^-:

$$(S^+ - \alpha) > 0, -(S^- - \beta) > 0 \tag{2}$$

Finally, the alignment loss can be unrolled as follows, more details related to the improved triplet loss is introduced in [11].

$$\mathcal{L}_{align} = \frac{1}{N} \sum_{i=1}^{N} \left\{ log \left[1 + e^{-\tau_p(S^+ - \alpha)} \right] + log \left[1 + e^{\tau_n(S^- - \beta)} \right] \right\} \tag{3}$$

Local Visual-Textual Alignment. We divide pedestrian characteristics into five attributes: head, upper clothes, lower clothes, shoes, bag. On the one hand, we make use of semantic segmentation network as an auxiliary tool to get a stack of visual attribute features. On the other hand, the whole language stream is divided into a list of the attributes phrases by standard natural language parser [18] to generate phrases features. Finally, we utilize K-reciprocal Sampling arithmetic [11] for attributes alignment, which means that when they belong to the positive attributes, the following loss is calculated: $log \left[1 + e^{-\tau_p(S_i^+ - \alpha)} \right]$, otherwise it is calculated like this: $log \left[1 + e^{\tau_n(S_i^- - \beta)} \right]$.

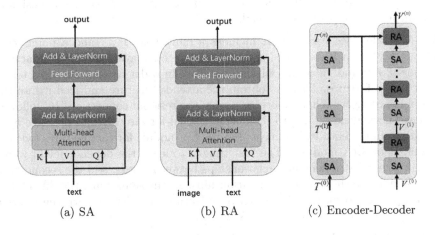

(a) SA   (b) RA   (c) Encoder-Decoder

Fig. 3. Semantic Co-Attention

3.2   Semantic Co-Attention Mechanism

With the aim of enhanced attributes alignment in the person search task, we attend semantic relationships between the text and visual attributes features to visual attributes features by semantic co-attention mechanism (SCA). We feed visual attributes features and global textual features into SCA, which consists of a framework with encoder-decoder to perform semantic co-attention learning. As shown in Fig. 3(c), the encoder consists of n SA modules to learn the attended textual feature $T^{(n)}$ while the decoder contains n SRA modules that is made up of SA modules and RA modules, towards learning semantic relationship between text description and visual attributes, and attaching it to visual attribute feature in order to get $V^{(n)}$. The Scaled Dot-Product attention mechanism [12] is used in the SA module and RA module but their inputs are different. We take the SA module as an example to illustrate in detail. The input of SA module contains queries(Q), keys(K) and values(V). The Scaled Dot-Product attention mechanism can be expressed by the following formula:

$$ f = Attention(Q, K, V) = softmax \left(\frac{QK^T}{\sqrt{d_k}} V \right) \tag{4} $$

Where d_k denotes V of dimension. In order to obtain a variety of feature representations, we can get several groups of transformed V, K, Q by making different linear changes to V, K, Q, and then realize multi-head attention that consists of h paralleled heads. The multi-head attention is given by:

$$ head_i = Attention \left(QW_i^Q, KW_i^K, VW_i^V \right) \tag{5} $$

$$ Multihead\,(Q, K, V) = Concat(head_1, ..., head_h)W^o \tag{6} $$

Where $W_i^Q, W_i^K, W_i^V \in \mathbb{R}^{d \times d_h}$ are the transformation matrix for the i-th head, $W^o \in \mathbb{R}^{h*d_h \times d}$. d is the dimension of raw input features. d_h is the dimension of the output features from each head.

SA Module. (see Fig. 3(a)) It includes a multi-head layer and a point feed-forward layer that is composed of two fully connected layers and ReLU function. Its query, key and value are all features itself in order to capture the internal structure of features. Then we obtain the attended feature and feed it into the feed-forward layer. What's more, we apply the residual connection [16] followed by layer normalization [21] to the output of feed-forward layer to promote optimization. In the encoder, we have used the SA module for text features twice as the input of SRA modules. The first time is to learn the dependency of words in sentences, that is semantic relationships between words, and the second time is to summarize these semantic relationships. At the same time, the SA module is also performed on the visual attribute feature in order to learn the internal relationship of features in each SRA module.

RA Module. (see Fig. 3(b)) Although Similar to the SA module, the RA module has two groups of input features. Its query is attended textual feature while its key and value are both attended visual attributes feature. More specifically, $Multihead\,(T, v_i, v_i)$ for $v_i \in V$ reconstructs v_i by all attended word features related to visual attribute feature in the textual feature T with respect to their normalized similarity between T and local visual feature v_i. In other words, the RA module establishes strong connection between visual attributes and related textual content through cross modal co-attention.

3.3   Joint Training

We train the whole network in an end-to-end manner. The cross-entropy loss(ID loss) is used to extract the discriminative features for each instance. When extracting local visual features, the pixel-level cross-entropy loss(Seg loss) is adopted as an assistant to classify five kinds of attributes. Furthermore, We learn the alignment of visual-textual features learning on both global and local level with the improved triple loss(Align Loss), but local align loss takes the enhanced fine-grained attribute features as the input, which further solves the difficult problem about mismatching of negative samples. Therefore, the total loss is calculated as follows:

$$L = L_{id} + L_{seg} + L_{align}^{global} + L_{align}^{local} \tag{7}$$

4   Experiment

4.1   Experimental Setting

Datasets. We evaluate the performance of the proposed Enhanced Attributes Alignment based on Semantic Co-Attention (EAA-SCA) model on the text-based person search dataset CUHK-PEDES [1]. The dataset contains 40,206 images with 13,003 identities. The official split method is adopted on this dataset that is split into 11,003 identities with 34,054 images in the training set, 1,000 identities with 3,078 images in validating set, and 1,000 identities with 3,074 images in testing set.

Evaluation Metric. Following [1], we measure performance by Rank-K (K=1, 5, 10). Rank-k indicates the accuracy of the at least one correct images among the top-K results.

Implementation Details. We resize all the images to 384×128 and flip the images horizontally to perform data augmenting. We make use of the Adam optimizer with weight decay set as 4×10^{-5}, and involve 32 image-language pairs each batch. The number of SA in the encoder and SRA in the decoder are both set to 2, the learning rate is initialized at 2×10^{-4} at the first 40 epochs during training, then set as 2×10^{-5} for the remaining 5 epochs. We set $\alpha = 0.6, \beta = 0.4, \tau_p = 10, \tau_n = 40$ for hyper-parameters in the align loss. Finally, we conduct the experiment on the GTX 1080 GPU machine.

4.2   Comparison to Other Methods

As Table 1 shows, we summarize the performance of EAA-SCA model and compare with other methods on the CUHK-PEDES test set. The compared

Table 1. Performance comparison to other methods on CUHK-PEDES. * denotes the experimental results we reproduced according to the code provided by the author.

Method	Rank-1	Rank-5	Rank-10
GNA-RNN	19.05	–	53.64
CMCE	25.94	–	60.48
PWM-ATH	27.14	49.45	61.02
Dual Path	44.40	66.26	75.07
CMPM+CMPC	49.37	–	79.27
MCCL	50.58	–	79.06
ViTAA*	53.02	73.84	81.25
A-GANet	53.14	74.03	81.95
EAA-SCA (ours)	**55.57**	**74.64**	**82.42**

Table 2. Ablation studies to $V^{(n)}$. $V^{(n)}$ denotes the fine-grained visual attribute features extracted by n SRA modules.

$V^{(n)}$	Rank-1	Rank-5	Rank-10
$V^{(1)}$	54.66	73.97	82.21
$V^{(2)}$	**55.57**	74.64	82.42
$V^{(3)}$	54.25	74.51	82.36
$V^{(4)}$	54.22	74.56	82.00
$V^{(5)}$	54.01	**74.77**	**82.68**
$V^{(6)}$	53.85	74.50	81.95

methods include GNA-RNN [1], CMCE [24], PWM-ATH [2], Dual Path [3], CMPM+CMPC [4], MCCL [25], ViTAA* [11], A-GANet [6]. The proposed model EAA-SCA achieves 55.57%, 74.64%, 82.42% of Rank-1, Rank-5, Rank-10 accuracy respectively, which is 2.55% higher accuracy on Rank-1 than ViTAA* [11] that our code is based on. It proves that there are many hard negative samples make the model locally misaligned as described in the Introduction and the fine-grained visual attribute features with semantic relations generated by SCA mechanism enhance attribute alignment indeed. Even, EAA-SCA model outperforms the A-GANet [6] by a margin of 2.43%, 0.61%, 0.47%. That demonstrates the effectiveness of the more fine-grained attribute features for enhanced attribute alignment, which shows a consistent lead on all metrics.

4.3   Ablation Study

Influence of $V^{(n)}$. The extraction of visual attribute features $V^{(n)}$ plays an important role in the enhancement of attribute alignment, which is analyzed quantitatively. As shown in Table 2, $V^{(2)}$ achieves 1.56% improvement in Rank-1 compared with $V^{(5)}$ while $V^{(5)}$ only has a slight lead in Rank-5 and Rank-10. We think $V^{(2)}$ show better performance after comprehensive consideration.

Qualitative Analysis. We visualize the test results of pedestrian re-identification in order to provide more in-depth research. As shown in Fig. 4, the first three pictures are all consistent with the attribute phrases in the above example. What's more, in the below example, images can still be detected successfully in the case of luminance interference. Not only that, it is worth mentioning that alignment on certain attributes can also be found in other failed cases. The below example clearly shows that almost all mismatched persons have the attributes of a white shirt, dark trousers and a black bag. The last seven wrong pictures in the above example are aligned with the relevant attributes in the text to some degree, such as "green pants", "stripe tank top" or "pink shoes". Especially, the sixth picture may be misled by the red carpet. In summary, the model shows robust performance on fine-grained attribute alignment.

Fig. 4. Examples of top-10 retrieved images from textual description, green/red boxes are indicated the true/false matching results. (Color figure online)

5 Conclusion

In this work, we propose an Enhanced Attributes Alignment based on Semantic Co-Attention (EAA-SCA) network For Text-based Person Search, which solves the mismatched problem of visual-textual negative attributes features to a greater extent. EAA-SCA utilizes semantic co-attention mechanism to build potential relationships between visual attribute feature and textual feature in order to obtaining more fine-grained visual attribute feature with semantic relationships, which enhances visual attributes alignment with textual description. Experimental results on CUHK-PEDES dataset have demonstrated better performance of the model and the effectiveness of semantic co-attention mechanism.

References

1. Li, S., Xiao, T., Li, H., et al.: Person search with natural language description. In: Proceedings of the IEEE Conference on Computer Vision and Pattern Recognition, pp. 1970–1979 (2017)
2. Chen, T., Xu, C., Luo, J.: Improving text-based person search by spatial matching and adaptive threshold. In: 2018 IEEE Winter Conference on Applications of Computer Vision (WACV), pp. 1879–1887. IEEE (2018)
3. Zheng, Z., Zheng, L., Garrett, M., et al.: Dual-path convolutional image-text embedding with instance loss. arXiv preprint arXiv:1711.05535 (2017)
4. Zhang, Y., Lu, H.: Deep cross-modal projection learning for image-text matching. In: Ferrari, V., Hebert, M., Sminchisescu, C., Weiss, Y. (eds.) ECCV 2018. LNCS, vol. 11205, pp. 707–723. Springer, Cham (2018). https://doi.org/10.1007/978-3-030-01246-5_42
5. Aggarwal, S., Radhakrishnan, V.B., Chakraborty, A.: Text-based person search via attribute-aided matching. In: Proceedings of the IEEE/CVF Winter Conference on Applications of Computer Vision, pp. 2617–2625 (2020)
6. Liu, J., Zha, Z.J., Hong, R., et al.: Deep adversarial graph attention convolution network for text-based person search. In: Proceedings of the 27th ACM International Conference on Multimedia, pp. 665–673 (2019)
7. Sarafianos, N., Xu, X., Kakadiaris, I.A.: Adversarial representation learning for text-to-image matching. In: Proceedings of the IEEE/CVF International Conference on Computer Vision, pp. 5814–5824 (2019)
8. Lee, K.-H., Chen, X., Hua, G., Hu, H., He, X.: Stacked cross attention for image-text matching. In: Ferrari, V., Hebert, M., Sminchisescu, C., Weiss, Y. (eds.) ECCV 2018. LNCS, vol. 11208, pp. 212–228. Springer, Cham (2018). https://doi.org/10.1007/978-3-030-01225-0_13
9. Liu, Y., Guo, Y., Bakker, E.M., et al.: Learning a recurrent residual fusion network for multimodal matching. In: Proceedings of the IEEE International Conference on Computer Vision, pp. 4107–4116 (2017)
10. Jing, Y., Si, C., Wang, J., et al.: Pose-guided multi-granularity attention network for text-based person search. In: Proceedings of the AAAI Conference on Artificial Intelligence, vol. 34, no. 07, pp. 11189–11196 (2020)
11. Wang, Z., Fang, Z., Wang, J., Yang, Y.: *ViTAA*: visual-textual attributes alignment in person search by natural language. In: Vedaldi, A., Bischof, H., Brox, T., Frahm, J.-M. (eds.) ECCV 2020. LNCS, vol. 12357, pp. 402–420. Springer, Cham (2020). https://doi.org/10.1007/978-3-030-58610-2_24
12. Vaswani, A., Shazeer, N., Parmar, N., et al.: Attention is all you need. arXiv preprint arXiv:1706.03762 (2017)
13. Jing, Y., Si, C., Wang, J., et al.: Cascade attention network for person search: both image and text-image similarity selection **2**(3), 5. arXiv preprint arXiv:1809.08440 (2018)
14. Kim, J.H., Jun, J., Zhang, B.T.: Bilinear attention networks. arXiv preprint arXiv:1805.07932 (2018)
15. Yu, Z., Yu, J., Cui, Y., et al.: Deep modular co-attention networks for visual question answering. In: Proceedings of the IEEE/CVF Conference on Computer Vision and Pattern Recognition, pp. 6281–6290 (2019)
16. He, K., Zhang, X., Ren, S., et al.: Deep residual learning for image recognition. In: Proceedings of the IEEE Conference on Computer Vision and Pattern Recognition, pp. 770–778 (2016)

17. Hermans, A., Beyer, L., Leibe, B.: In defense of the triplet loss for person re-identification. arXiv preprint arXiv:1703.07737 (2017)

18. Klein, D., Manning, C.D.: Fast exact inference with a factored model for natural language parsing. In: Advances in Neural Information Processing Systems, pp. 3–10 (2003)

19. Sun, K., Xiao, B., Liu, D., et al.: Deep high-resolution representation learning for human pose estimation. In: Proceedings of the IEEE/CVF Conference on Computer Vision and Pattern Recognition, pp. 5693–5703 (2019)

20. Manning, C.D., Surdeanu, M., Bauer, J., et al.: The Stanford CoreNLP natural language processing toolkit. In: Proceedings of 52nd Annual Meeting of the Association for Computational Linguistics: System Demonstrations, pp. 55–60 (2014)

21. Ba, J.L., Kiros, J.R., Hinton, G.E.: Layer normalization. arXiv preprint arXiv:1607.06450 (2016)

22. Yan, F., Mikolajczyk, K.: Deep correlation for matching images and text. In: Proceedings of the IEEE Conference on Computer Vision and Pattern Recognition, pp. 3441–3450 (2015)

23. Lin, T.-Y., et al.: Microsoft COCO: common objects in context. In: Fleet, D., Pajdla, T., Schiele, B., Tuytelaars, T. (eds.) ECCV 2014. LNCS, vol. 8693, pp. 740–755. Springer, Cham (2014). https://doi.org/10.1007/978-3-319-10602-1_48

24. Li, S., Xiao, T., Li, H., et al.: Identity-aware textual-visual matching with latent co-attention. In: Proceedings of the IEEE International Conference on Computer Vision, pp. 1890–1899 (2017)

25. Wang, Y., Bo, C., Wang, D., et al.: Language person search with mutually connected classification loss. In: ICASSP 2019–2019 IEEE International Conference on Acoustics, Speech and Signal Processing (ICASSP), pp. 2057–2061. IEEE (2019)

26. Veličković, P., Cucurull, G., Casanova, A., et al.: Graph attention networks. arXiv preprint arXiv:1710.10903 (2017)

27. Su, C., Li, J., Zhang, S., et al.: Pose-driven deep convolutional model for person re-identification. In: Proceedings of the IEEE International Conference on Computer Vision, pp. 3960–3969 (2017)

28. Zheng, L., Huang, Y., Lu, H., et al.: Pose-invariant embedding for deep person re-identification. IEEE Trans. Image Process. 28(9), 4500–4509 (2019)

29. Kalayeh, M.M., Basaran, E., Gökmen, M., et al.: Human semantic parsing for person re-identification. In: Proceedings of the IEEE Conference on Computer Vision and Pattern Recognition, pp. 1062–1071 (2018)

30. Liang, X., Gong, K., Shen, X., et al.: Look into person: joint body parsing & pose estimation network and a new benchmark. IEEE Trans. Pattern Anal. Mach. Intell. 41(4), 871–885 (2018)

31. Yin, Z., Zheng, W.S., Wu, A., et al.: Adversarial attribute-image person re-identification. arXiv preprint arXiv:1712.01493 (2017)

32. Layne, R., Hospedales, T.M., Gong, S.: Attributes-based re-identification. In: Gong, S., Cristani, M., Yan, S., Loy, C.C. (eds.) Person Re-Identification. ACVPR, pp. 93–117. Springer, London (2014). https://doi.org/10.1007/978-1-4471-6296-4_5

33. Farooq, A., Awais, M., Kittler, J., et al.: AXM-Net: cross-modal context sharing attention network for person Re-ID. arXiv preprint arXiv:2101.08238 (2021)

ARShape-Net: Single-View Image Oriented 3D Shape Reconstruction with an Adversarial Refiner

Hao Xu[1] and Jing Bai[1,2(✉)]

[1] North Minzu University, Yinchuan 750021, Ningxia, China
[2] The Key Laboratory of Images and Graphics Intelligent Processing of State Ethnic Affairs Commission, Yinchuan 750021, Ningxia, China

Abstract. In this paper, we propose a novel method of reconstructing 3D shapes from single-view images based on an adversarial refiner. Generative Adversarial mechanism is adopted between the coarse-volumes generation stage and the refinement stage. In the coarse-volumes generation stage, a Context Aware Channel Attention Module (CA-CAM) and a VoxFocal Loss are designed to reconstruct the coarse-volume shapes as complete as possible. Furthermore, an adversarial refiner is proposed to adaptively optimize the coarse-volume shapes and remove redundant voxels by adding the discriminator into refiner. On the challenging large synthesis-image dataset ShapeNet and the real-world dataset Pix3D, ARShape-Net demonstrated significant quantitative and qualitative improvements compared with the state-of-the-art methods.

Keywords: 3D shape reconstruction · Generative adversarial · Single-view

1 Introduction

With the development of deep learning, researchers try to overcome the inherent limitations of 3D reconstruction with its powerful learning ability. Pix2Vox [6] proposed by xie et al. is a carefully designed two-stage voxel model generation network. The encoder accepts multi-view input in parallel, and the context fusion module in the decoder selects high-quality reconstruction parts among different views. In terms of fusing the latent spatial information of multiple views, Pix2vox eliminates the sensitivity of LSTM [17] methods (such as 3DR2N2 [2]) to the view input sequence, and selectively merges the high-quality reconstruction parts of different views. But when dealing with single-view reconstruction tasks, this module does not contribute to the refined reconstruction results.

Theoretically, single-view 3D reconstruction is an ill-posed problem. Single-view RGB images lack depth information, and it is difficult for traditional convolution to focus on the global structure information of the target in the process of

This work was supported in part by the National Natural Science Foundation of China under Grant 61762003, Grant 62162001 and Grant 61972121, in part by CAS "Light of West China" Program, and in part by Ningxia Excellent Talent Program.

© Springer Nature Switzerland AG 2021
L. Fang et al. (Eds.): CICAI 2021, LNAI 13069, pp. 638–649, 2021.
https://doi.org/10.1007/978-3-030-93046-2_54

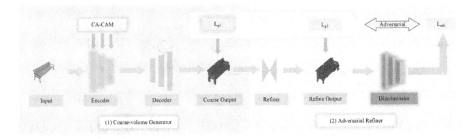

Fig. 1. Network architecture: (1) Coarse-volume Generator: The encoder based on the CNNs takes single-view images as input and output the corresponding 2D feature maps, then the decoder based on the 3D transposed convolutional layers is responsible for transforming information of 2D feature maps into 3D coarse-volumes. (2) Adversarial Refiner: The refiner can be regarded as a 3D encoder-decoder (U-net connected), which works with the 3D discriminator to refine the coarse volumes.

extracting features from the images. Building a memory storage module requires storing a huge number of shape priors in the training set, which will cause huge hardware costs. Based on the above factors, the 3D shape reconstructed from a single RGB image usually does not have a complete structure. Therefore, under the premise of single-view RGB image as input, how to extract the depth and structure information of single-view RGB image to the maximum extent, and ensure the structural integrity of the reconstruction results, is the key problem of single-view 3D reconstruction.

Further, most of the existing 3D reconstruction methods based on voxel representations predict the occupancy probability of the occupancy grid. Most approaches use BCE loss to constrain the occupation probability to 0 or 1. However, the 3D data in the spatial grid representation is sparse, and constraining the occupied and unoccupied grids with the same penalty will lead to erroneous reconstruction results (structural discontinuity caused by missing voxels).

In order to solve the above problems, we propose a method dedicated to single-view 3D reconstruction based on a Generative Adversarial mechanism. Our contributions include:

- We propose a gradually refined single-view 3D reconstruction network based on the adversarial learning between the generator and the adversarial refiner. A well designed generator reconstruct coarse-volumes with integrity and continuity. An adversarial refiner is designed to eliminate unreasonable redundant voxels and generate more realistic 3D objects.
- We design CA-CAM in the image feature extraction stage to perform weight fusion of different scales. The fusion of global features and local features helps the generation of the overall structure and local details of the 3D target.
- We design VoxFocal Loss based on Focal Loss [13] for the decoder. With the settings of single-view image as input, the occupied grid is assigned a larger weight to promote voxel generation, thereby reducing or even eliminating the lack of 3D shape structure in the reconstruction process, and ensuring the continuity of generated voxels.

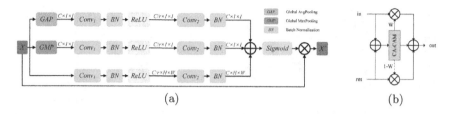

Fig. 2. (a) Illustration of the proposed CA-CAM. (b) Illustration of how CA-CAM works. "res" represents the residual and "w" represents the attention weight.

2   Relate Works

The traditional methods of ShapeFromX [8,11,16] estimate the 3D shape of the object by matching feature descriptors (such as texture, contour, etc.) between images, however, when the intervals between multiple viewpoints are too large, the matching relationship between features will be weakened. Therefore, these methods require a lot of geometric constraints and hand-made geometric features. When there is occlusion on the surface of the object, the reconstructed 3D shape will inevitably be incomplete.

With the mature development of convolutions, researchers began to be dissatisfied with obtaining information only from 2D data. VoxNet [12] and 3D ShapeNets [1] proposed in 2015 greatly promoted the progress of using 3D convolution to process 3D voxel grid data. As a pioneer of 3D reconstruction with voxel grids representation, 3DR2N2 regards the reconstruction as a sequence problem with multiple views as inputs, and introduces LSTM to handle the self-occlusion problem. However, due to the structural characteristics of LSTM, the reconstruction results of 3DR2N2 are inevitably affected by the number and order of input views. To eliminate the influence from the order of input views, Pix2Vox is proposed to automatically select the best part from the reconstruction results of multiple views for fusion. Further, on the basis of Pix2Vox, Pix2Vox++ [20] updates the backbone network of the encoder and achieves better results. However, both above methods implicitly utilize multi-view spatial information and are difficult to reconstruct a complete 3D shape from a single-view image.

For single-view 3D reconstruction, a few works [15,21] are based on the point cloud. Point cloud data is difficult to process and has limited representation capabilities, so more work is based on the voxel: 3D-VAE-GAN [3] establishes a mapping between 2D images and latent vector representations. DRC [14] developes a differentiable formula suitable for the consistency between the 3D shape and the 2D view of various input forms. MarrNet [5] and its variants [4,10] assist 3D reconstruction by estimating intermediate information (such as the depth) from a single-view image. In all, the existing work is dedicated to recovering as complete a 3D shape as possible from a single-view image.

3 Method

3.1 Overview

We propose a gradual refinement model based on a Generative Adversarial mechanism specifically for the 3D shapes reconstruction from a single-view image. Figure 1 illustrates the overview of the proposed model. First, we design a coarse-volume generator to reconstruct the 3D shapes as complete as possible based on the proposed CA-CAM and VoxFocal Loss. Second, the refiner and the discriminator work together to form an adversarial refiner, which is utilized to adaptively dropping out extra voxels by the adversarial learning and retain the true 3D structure of the reconstruction result. The overall loss of our proposed network can be expressed as: $L_{total} = (\lambda_1 L_{g1}, \lambda_2 L_{g2}, \lambda_3 L_{adv})$.

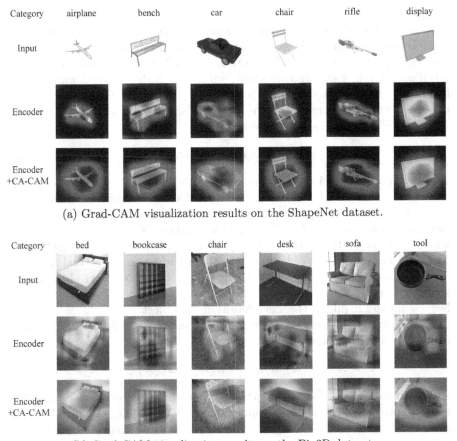

(a) Grad-CAM visualization results on the ShapeNet dataset.

(b) Grad-CAM visualization results on the Pix3D dataset.

Fig. 3. Grad-CAM [9] visualization results verifying the effectiveness of CA-CAM on ShapeNet and Pix3D test sets.

10.28%   11.41%   9.36%

Fig. 4. The Sparsity characteristics of 3D volume. The density shown in the figure is defined as $\frac{|occupied\_grid|}{|total\_grid|}$.

3.2   Coarse-Volume Generator

In the first stage, coarse-volume 3D shapes are generated as completely as possible based on an encoder with CA-CAM and a decoder using VoxFocal Loss.

Encoder via CA-CAM. Compared with multi-view, the reconstruction from a single view is difficult to obtain potential spatial information. Aimed at the problem, as shown in Fig. 2, CA-CAM is designed and added into the encoder specifically for fine feature extraction, which can realize context awareness of features by changing the receptive field and type of pooling. Concretely, in order to obtain detailed information of the target 3D shapes, the local channel context $L(X) \in R^{C*H*W}$ can be calculated as:

$$L(X) = \beta\left(Conv_2\left(\delta\left(\beta\left(Conv_1\left(X\right)\right)\right)\right)\right) \tag{1}$$

where β represents the Batch Normalization (BN) [18], and δ represents the Rectified Linear Unit (ReLU) [7]. Similarly, two global channel contexts used to learn salient features of the object and the position information in the background can be expressed as $G_1(X) \in R^{C*1*1} = \varepsilon(L(X))$ and $G_2(X) \in R^{C*1*1} = \psi(L(X))$, where ε represents the global average pooling and ψ represents the global max pooling. In the process of obtaining attention information, the kernel sizes used by $Conv_1$ and $Conv_2$ are $\frac{C}{r} \times C \times 1 \times 1$, $C \times \frac{C}{r} \times 1 \times 1$ respectively, and their step size is 1. $L(X)$ is consistent with the size of the input feature, which can help retain and highlight the local details of the object.

Consequently, the context-aware channel attentional weights $C(X)$ generated by CA-CAM can be expressed as:

$$X' = X \otimes C(X) = X \otimes \sigma\left(L(X) \oplus G_1(X) \oplus G_2(X)\right) \tag{2}$$

where σ represents the Sigmoid function, $\oplus$ represents the broadcasting addition and $\otimes$ represents the matrix multiplication. $G_1(X)$ and $G_2(X)$ that highlight salient features (such as contours) and location features respectively. From the visualization results (Fig. 3), we can see that CA-CAM pays more attention to the features we expect to focus on.

Decoder Based on VoxFocal Loss. Since the reconstruction result is represented by a 3D voxel grid [1,12], the reconstruction task is essentially a binary classification problem for the state of the grids (occupied: 1, unoccupied: 0). Most reconstruction networks use binary cross-entropy loss, which gives the same loss weight ($\lambda = 0.5$) to the two categories. However, from Fig. 4, we can observe that the proportion of occupied and unoccupied grids are seriously out of balance, therefore, the methods based on binary cross-entropy loss may result in incomplete 3D structures due to the lack of attention on occupied girds. To solve the above problem, a VoxFocal Loss is proposed based on Focal Loss [13] and applied into the coarse-volumes generation stage to promote the integrity and continuity of the 3D structures:

$$L_{vfl} = \begin{cases} -\zeta \left(1 - \hat{p_n}\right)^\gamma log\hat{p_n} & , y = 1 \\ -\left(1 - \zeta\right)\hat{p_n}^\gamma log\left(1 - \hat{p_n}\right) & , y = 0 \end{cases} \tag{3}$$

where $\hat{p_n} \in [0,1]$ represents the model's estimated probability for the class with label $y = 1$. We hope that the sparse occupied grid and the parts that are difficult to rebuild (such as the mast of a ship) get a larger loss weight. After experimental verification, we found that when $\zeta = 0.75$ and $\gamma = 1$, a complete reconstruction result can be obtained in the coarse voxel generation stage.

3.3 Adversarial Refiner

Inputting a single-view image, a more complete coarse-volume 3D shapes are generated after the encoder-decoder stage. In this stage, we focus on how to eliminate redundant voxels. An adversarial refiner is designed by adding a discriminator into the refiner network to generate more realistic 3D objects. The adversarial loss is expressed as:

$$L_{adv} = logD\left(x\right) + log\left(1 - D\left(V\right)\right) \tag{4}$$

where x is a ground truth in a 32^3 space, V is the reconstruction result generated by the refiner.

4   Experiments

In this section, we first introduce the datasets used in the experiment, evaluation indicators and experimental details (Sect. 4.1 and 4.2). Then we demonstrated the effectiveness of the proposed method through ablation experiments in Sect. 4.3. Finally, quantitative and qualitative comparisons to the state-of-the-art methods are presented in Sect. 4.4.

4.1   Datasets and Metrics

Datasets. We use both synthetic image dataset ShapeNet and real-world image dataset Pix3D to evaluate the effects of our proposed method. In the experiments, we use a subset of ShapeNet dataset and split 4/5 for training and the remaining for testing following the settings in [2], and use the Pix3D dataset following the settings in [6].

Table 1. Single-view reconstruction using our different versions model compared using Intersection-over-Union (IoU).

Ours	Component			Dataset	
	CA-CAM	Vox-Focal Loss	Discriminator	Pix3D [19]	ShapeNet [1]
Baseline	×	×	×	0.286	0.662
v1	✓	×	×	0.292	0.676
v2	✓	✓	×	0.298	0.679
v3	✓	✓	✓	0.305	0.680

Evaluation Metrics. Recognized evaluation index of Intersection-over-Union (IoU) is used to evaluate the reconstruction quality. More formally,

$$IoU = \frac{\sum_{i,j,k} I(p_{i,j,k} > t) I(y_{i,j,k})}{\sum_{i,j,k} I(p_{i,j,k} > t) + I(y_{i,j,k})} \tag{5}$$

where $p_{i,j,k}$ represents the occupancy probability and $y_{i,j,k}$ represents the ground truth. $I(\cdot)$ is an indicator function and t denotes a voxelization threshold. Higher $IoU \in [0, 1]$ means better reconstruction results.

4.2 Implementation Details

We use part of ResNext50 as our encoder. Our network use 224×224 images as input and output 32^3 3D volumes. The voxelization threshold t is set to 0.3, the initial learning rate of the Adam optimizer is set to 0.001 and decayed by 2 after $[100, 175, 225, 250, 275]$ epochs. Since the generative adversarial network is difficult to fit, the training process is divided into two steps: we train the model for the first 300 epochs without discrminator by setting the weights of losses as $\lambda_1 = 10, \lambda_2 = 20, \lambda_3 = 0$, and then train the model for 200 epochs to fine-tune the network with the discriminator by setting the weights of losses as $\lambda_1 = 10, \lambda_2 = 20, \lambda_3 = 10$. In the second stage, the initial learning rate of the discriminator's optimizer is set to 0.001 and decayed by 2 after $[50, 100, 150]$ epochs.

4.3 Ablation Study

In this section, we conduct a series of ablation experiments to verify the effectiveness of the proposed CA-CAM, Vox-Focal Loss and the 3D discriminator. Table 1 shows the IoU values of different versions of our model.

To facilitate comparison, we use ARShape-Net without adding any components as the baseline model. From the results it can be observed that, compared with baseline model, model v1 uses CA-CAM in the encoder improves IoU by

Input   GT   Baseline   v1   v2   v3

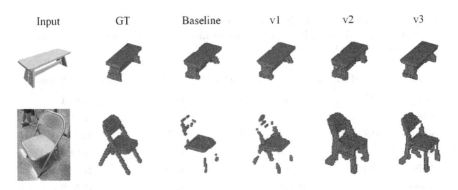

Fig. 5. Two visual examples of the ablation experiment (the top is the sample in ShapeNet [1], and the bottom is in Pix3D [19]).

0.014 for the ShapeNet dataset and 0.006 for the Pix3D dataset. Compared with v1 model, v2 model that uses Vox-Focal Loss improves IoU by 0.003 for the ShapeNet dataset and 0.006 for the Pix3D dataset. Compared with v2 model, the v3 model after adding a 3D discriminator into the refiner gives the best results with the IoU improvements of 0.007 and 0.001 for the two datasets.

Furthermore, we make a qualitative comparison of model effects. Figure 5 shows two visual examples. From the results we can clearly observe the performance improvements from v1 model to v3 model. Concretely, the reconstructed results of v1 model is more complete than the results of the baseline by adding the proposed CA-CAM. Furthermore, the results of v2 model are the most complete 3D shapes by using both the CA-CAM and the VoxFocal Loss. In addition, after adding discriminator into the refiner, v3 model generates more accurate results by eliminating redundant voxels from the results of v2 model.

Specially, although v3 model is not significantly improved in quantitative comparison, the visual effect of v3 model is far better than v2 model. We analyze and believe that this is because only a few redundant voxels are eliminated after adding the discriminator, which only leads to a small change in quantity but the reconstructed results are more accurate.

4.4   Comparison with State-of-the-Art Methods

Since we focus on the 3D shape reconstruction based on a single-view image without any preconditions of storing shape priors, in this experiment, the state-of-the-art methods based on single-view images without memory blocks are chosen for comparison. Table 2 shows the comparison results on ShapeNet dataset. Observing the experimental results, we can see that our method achieves the best quantitative result to the existing state-of-the-art methods in overall, and is also superior to these methods in most object categories.

Table 2. Comparison of single-view 3D object reconstruction on ShapeNet at 32^3 resolution compared using Intersection-over-Union (IoU). The best number for each category is highlighted in bold.

Category	3D-R2N2 [2]	DRC [14]	PSGN [15]	Pix2Vox++ [20]	ARShape-Net
airplane	0.513	0.571	0.601	0.674	**0.691**
bench	0.421	0.453	0.550	0.608	**0.621**
cabinet	0.716	0.635	0.771	0.799	**0.816**
car	0.798	0.755	0.831	0.858	**0.863**
chair	0.466	0.469	0.544	0.581	**0.588**
display	0.468	0.419	**0.552**	0.548	**0.552**
lamp	0.381	0.415	0.462	0.457	**0.472**
speaker	0.662	0.609	**0.737**	0.721	0.721
rifle	0.544	0.608	0.604	0.617	**0.635**
sofa	0.628	0.606	0.708	0.725	**0.749**
table	0.513	0.424	0.606	0.620	**0.627**
telephone	0.661	0.413	0.749	**0.809**	0.767
watercraft	0.513	0.556	0.611	0.603	**0.633**
Overall	0.560	0.545	0.640	0.670	**0.680**

Figure 6 shows more visual comparison results on the ShapeNet and Pix3D datasets. For the synthetic images from dataset ShapeNet in Fig. 6a, some of the results from 3D-R2N2, OGN and DRC include holes, while the results of Pix2Vox and ARShape-Net are complete. Compared with Pix2Vox, ARShape-Net s more accurate local structures, such as the armer of the bench and the leg of the chair. From Fig. 6b, we can find the reconstruction on the real-world image dataset Pix3D is more challenging. For the first two input images, our results have more complete shapes. About the others, our methods have both complete shapes and accurate local details. In all, our method achieve better reconstruction results in both synthetic-image dataset and real-word-image dataset than existing methods.

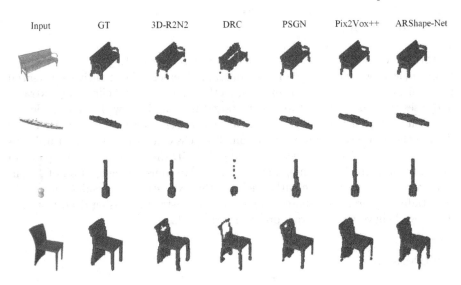

(a) Reconstructions on the ShapeNet dataset.

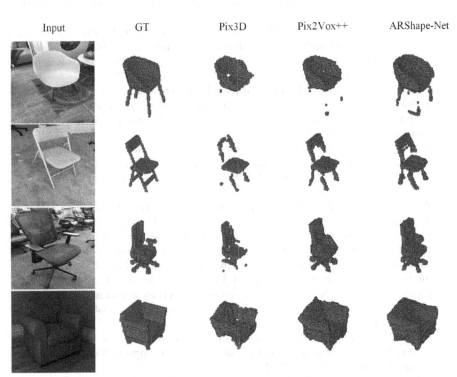

(b) Reconstructions on the Pix3D dataset.

Fig. 6. GT represents the ground truth of the 3D object. It can be seen from (a) and (b) that the 3D model reconstructed by our method is more superior in structural integrity and continuity, whether it is in the synthetic data set or the real data set.

5 Conclusion

In this paper, we propose a novel method of reconstructing 3D object shape from single-view image based on the gradual refinement of generative adversarial mechanism. Different from the existing methods, our method effectively extracts and fuses the geometric features of the target in a single-view through the learnable context attention weight. VoxFocal Loss is designed for the sparsity of 3D data in the occupied grid representation. This loss can ensure the structural continuity and integrity after reconstruction. The 3D discriminator participates in model training in a fine-tuning manner, which weakens the generation of redundant voxels and ensures the authenticity of the reconstruction results. Our study essentially explores voxel-based single-view reconstruction using deep learning, which we believe will inspire more future research.

References

1. Wu, Z., et al.: 3D ShapeNets: a deep representation for volumetric shapes. In: Proceedings of the IEEE Conference on Computer Vision and Pattern Recognition, pp. 1912–1920 (2015)
2. Choy, C.B., Xu, D., Gwak, J.Y., Chen, K., Savarese, S.: 3D-R2N2: a unified approach for single and multi-view 3D object reconstruction. In: Leibe, B., Matas, J., Sebe, N., Welling, M. (eds.) ECCV 2016. LNCS, vol. 9912, pp. 628–644. Springer, Cham (2016). https://doi.org/10.1007/978-3-319-46484-8_38
3. Wu, J., Zhang, C., Xue, T., Freeman, W. T., Tenenbaum, J. B.: Learning a probabilistic latent space of object shapes via 3D generative-adversarial modeling. In: Proceedings of the 30th International Conference on Neural Information Processing Systems, pp. 82–90 (2016)
4. Zhang, X., Zhang, Z., Zhang, C., Tenenbaum, J.B., Freeman, W.T., Wu, J.: Learning to reconstruct shapes from unseen classes. In: Proceedings of the 32nd International Conference on Neural Information Processing Systems, pp. 2263–2274 (2018)
5. Wu, J., Wang, Y., Xue, T., Sun, X., Freeman, W.T., Tenenbaum, J.B.: MarrNet: 3D shape reconstruction via 2.5 d sketches. In: Proceedings of the 31st International Conference on Neural Information Processing Systems, pp. 540–550 (2017)
6. Xie, H., Yao, H., Sun, X., Zhou, S., Zhang, S.: Pix2vox: context-aware 3D reconstruction from single and multi-view images. In: Proceedings of the IEEE/CVF International Conference on Computer Vision, pp. 2690–2698 (2019)
7. Glorot, X., Bordes, A., Bengio, Y.: Deep sparse rectifier neural networks. In: Proceedings of the Fourteenth International Conference on Artificial Intelligence and Statistics, pp. 315–323 (2011)
8. Richter, S.R., Roth, S.: Discriminative shape from shading in uncalibrated illumination. In: Proceedings of the IEEE Conference on Computer Vision and Pattern Recognition, pp. 1128–1136 (2015)
9. Selvaraju, R.R., Cogswell, M., Das, A., Vedantam, R., Parikh, D., Batra, D.: Grad-CAM: visual explanations from deep networks via gradient-based localization. In: Proceedings of the IEEE International Conference on Computer Vision, pp. 618–626 (2017)

10. Wu, J., Zhang, C., Zhang, X., Zhang, Z., Freeman, W.T., Tenenbaum, J.B.: Learning shape priors for single-view 3D completion and reconstruction. In: Ferrari, V., Hebert, M., Sminchisescu, C., Weiss, Y. (eds.) ECCV 2018. LNCS, vol. 11215, pp. 673–691. Springer, Cham (2018). https://doi.org/10.1007/978-3-030-01252-6_40

11. Witkin, A.P.: Recovering surface shape and orientation from texture. Artif. Intell. **17**(1–3), 17–45 (1981)

12. Maturana, D., Scherer, S.: VoxNet: a 3D convolutional neural network for real-time object recognition. In: 2015 IEEE/RSJ International Conference on Intelligent Robots and Systems, pp. 922–928 (2015)

13. Lin, T.Y., Goyal, P., Girshick, R., He, K., Dollár, P.: Focal loss for dense object detection. In: Proceedings of the IEEE International Conference on Computer Vision, pp. 2980–2988 (2017)

14. Tulsiani, S., Zhou, T., Efros, A.A., Malik, J.: Multi-view supervision for single-view reconstruction via differentiable ray consistency. In: Proceedings of the IEEE conference on Computer Vision and Pattern Recognition, pp. 2626–2634 (2017)

15. Fan, H., Su, H., Guibas, L.J.: A point set generation network for 3D object reconstruction from a single image. In: Proceedings of the IEEE Conference on Computer Vision and Pattern Recognition, pp. 605–613 (2017)

16. Dibra, E., Jain, H., Oztireli, C., Ziegler, R., Gross, M.: Human shape from silhouettes using generative HKS descriptors and cross-modal neural networks. In: Proceedings of the IEEE Conference on Computer Vision and Pattern Recognition, pp. 4826–4836 (2017)

17. Zaremba, W., Sutskever, I., Vinyals, O.: Recurrent neural network regularization. arXiv preprint arXiv:1409.2329 (2014)

18. Ioffe, S., Szegedy, C.: Batch normalization: accelerating deep network training by reducing internal covariate shift. In: International Conference on Machine Learning, pp. 448–456 (2015)

19. Sun, X., et al.: Pix3d: dataset and methods for single-image 3D shape modeling. In: Proceedings of the IEEE Conference on Computer Vision and Pattern Recognition, pp. 2974–2983 (2018)

20. Xie, H., Yao, H., Zhang, S., Zhou, S., Sun, W.: Pix2Vox++: multi-scale context-aware 3D object reconstruction from single and multiple images. Int. J. Comput. Vision **128**(12), 2919–2935 (2020). https://doi.org/10.1007/s11263-020-01347-6

21. Mandikal, P., Babu, R.V.: Dense 3D point cloud reconstruction using a deep pyramid network. In: Proceedings-2019 IEEE Winter Conference on Applications of Computer Vision, pp. 1052–1060 (2019)

Training Few-Shot Classification via the Perspective of Minibatch and Pretraining

Meiyu Huang⑩, Yao Xu, Wei Bao, and Xueshuang Xiang[✉]

Qian Xuesen Laboratory of Space Technology, China Academy of Space Technology,
Beijing, China
{huangmeiyu,xuyao,xiangxueshuang}@qxslab.cn

Abstract. Few-shot classification is a challenging task which aims to formulate the ability of humans to learn concepts from limited prior data. Recent progress in few-shot classification has featured meta-learning, in which a parameterized model for a learning algorithm is trained to learn the ability of handling classification tasks on extremely large episodes. In this work, we advance this few-shot classification paradigm by formulating it as a regular classification learning problem. We further propose multi-episode and cross-way training techniques, which respectively correspond to the minibatch and pretraining in regular classification problems for speeding up convergence in training. Experimental results on a state-of-the-art few-shot classification method (prototypical networks) demonstrate that both the proposed training strategies can highly accelerate the training process without accuracy loss for varying few-shot classification problems on Omniglot and *mini*ImageNet.

Keywords: Few-shot classification · Multi-episode training · Cross-way training

1 Introduction

Few-shot classification problems [1,2] have drawn much attention, since they can formulate the ability of humans to learn concepts from limited prior data. Formally, few-shot classification is a challenging task that aims to learn information about object categories from one or only a few labeled samples. To overcome the drawbacks of adopting the deep learning techniques to address few-shot classification, a well-established paradigm is to train few-shot classification in an auxiliary meta-learning [3,4] or learning-to-learn [5,6] phase, where transferrable knowledge is learned using optimization based methods [7–10], memory based methods [11–13] and metric based methods [14–22]. The target few-shot

Supported by the Beijing Nova Program of Science and Technology under Grant Z191100001119129 and the National Natural Science Foundation of China 61702520.

Supplementary Information The online version contains supplementary material available at https://doi.org/10.1007/978-3-030-93046-2_55.

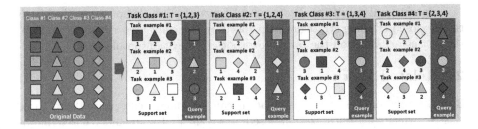

Fig. 1. An illustration of task classes and task examples for a 3-way 1-shot classification problem on a dataset with 4 classes, where each class has 6 examples. From the view of supervised learning, we may analogize the task class and task examples of few-shot classification problems (Right) to the class and examples of regular classification problems (Left), respectively.

classification problem is then learned by fine-tuning [7,9,10] with the learned optimization strategy [8] or computed in a feed-forward pass [11,12,14–19] without updating network weights.

These various meta-learning formulations have led to significant progress recently in few-shot classification. And the best performing methods prescribed by meta-learning use the training framework based on episodes [15], each with a small labeled support set and its corresponding query set generated from large quantities of available labeled data, to mimic the few-shot setting in the test environment for improving generalization. In this episodic training framework, few-shot classification can be viewed as learning the ability of *classifying an unlabeled query example given a small labeled support set* (a classification task) by training on a large number of classification tasks (C_{1200}^5 kinds of tasks if we consider the 5-way few-shot classification problem on Omniglot [1] with 1200 training classes). From this point of view, the training data is not limited but extremely massive. This paper advances this view by explaining it in a way that is more explicit or formal, and further transfers the advanced training approach of classification problem into few-shot learning area. The main contribution of this paper can be summarized as follows: **1)** Inspired by the episodic training paradigm [15], we introduce a formal parallel between regular supervised classification and few-shot classification, as shown in Fig. 1 and see Table 1 in the supplementary material for detailed comparison, which further motivates us to improve the training strategies of few-shot classification by imitating acceleration learning strategy of regular supervised classification for faster convergence; **2)** Compared to minibatch training (several examples in each class in each iteration) in regular classification problems, we first suggest using multi-episode training (several task examples in multiple task class in each iteration) in metric-based few-shot classification methods; **3)** Compared to the pretraining (training the model on a similar dataset with large-scale data) technique in regular classification problems, such as ImageNet pretraining [23], we first suggest using cross-way training (pretraining the model on a task with a higher way) in few-shot classification problems.

Experimental results on Prototypical Networks [17] demonstrate that both the proposed training strategies help speed up the convergence or even improve the testing accuracy on the target few-shot classification problems.

2   Related Work

Recent works on few-shot classification can be mainly categorized into three classes, which are optimization-based methods [7–10], memory-based methods [11–13] and metric-based methods [14–18, 20–22].

The approach within which our work falls is that of metric-based methods. Previous work in metric-learning for few-shot-classification includes Deep Siamese Networks [14], Matching Networks [15], Relation Networks [18], and Prototypical Networks [17], which is the model we implement the two proposed training strategies in our work. The main idea here is to learn an embedding function that embeds examples belonging to the same class close together while keeping embeddings from different classes far apart. Distances between embeddings of examples from the support set and query set are then used as a notion of similarity to do classification. Lastly, closely related to our work, Matching Networks notably introduced the training framework based on episodes representing different classification tasks, which inspires us to formulate classification tasks as examples and parallel few-shot classification with regular classification. On top of the formal parallel, we propose the multi-episode training strategy, which can reduce training iterations before convergence without accuracy loss compared with the one-episode training strategy used in Matching Networks and the follow-up metric-based methods [17, 18].

The other two kinds of few-shot classification approaches, namely optimization-based methods and memory-based methods include learning how to use the support set to update a learner model so as to generalize to the query set. Specifically, optimization-based approaches aim to optimize the model for fast adaptability, allowing it to adapt to new tasks with only a few examples. MAML [7] and REPTILE [9] reach this target by learning a set of parameters of a given neural network for sensitivity on a given task distribution, so that it can be efficiently fine-tuned for a sparse data problem within a few gradient-descent update steps. LEO [10] learns a data-dependent latent generative representation of model parameters and then performs gradient-based meta-learning in a low dimensional latent space. Ravi et al. [8] introduces an LSTM [24]-based optimizer that is trained to be specifically effective for fine-tuning. Memory-based methods [11–13], on the other hand, exploit memory neural network architectures such as the RNN [25] to store and retrieve knowledge in their memories to fulfill the given tasks. For instance, MANN [11] learns quickly from data presented sequentially with an LSTM architecture.

3   Methodology

3.1   Background

Episodic Training Paradigm. Suppose we consider a few-shot classification problem on a large labeled dataset with L classes and each class of H examples denoted by $\mathcal{D} = \{(\mathbf{x}_i, y_i)\}_{i=1}^{LH} = \cup_{j=1}^{L}\mathcal{D}_j$, where $\mathbf{x}_i \in \mathbb{R}^D$ is an input vector of dimension D, $y_i \in \{1, 2, \cdots, L\}$ is a class label, $\mathcal{D}_j$ denotes the subset of $\mathcal{D}$ containing all elements $(\mathbf{x}_i, y_i)$ such that $y_i = j$. The idea behind the episodic paradigm is to simulate the types of few-shot problems that will be encountered at test for a disjoint set $\mathcal{D}_{test}$, taking advantage of the large quantities of available labeled data from $\mathcal{D}$. Specifically, models are trained on K-way S-shot episodes constructed by first sampling a small subset V of K classes from $\mathcal{D}$ and then generating: 1) a support set $\mathcal{S}_V$ containing S examples from each of the K classes in the sampled subset V and 2) a query set $\mathcal{Q}_V$ of different examples from the same K classes. Let $\text{RANDOMSAMPLE}(\mathcal{C}, N)$ denote a set of N elements chosen uniformly at random from set $\mathcal{C}$ without replacement. Then, $V = \text{RANDOMSAMPLE}(\{1, \cdots, L\}, K)$, $\mathcal{S}_V = \cup_{k=1}^K \mathcal{S}_{V_k}$, and $\mathcal{Q}_V = \cup_{k=1}^K \mathcal{Q}_{V_k}$, where $\mathcal{S}_{V_k} = \text{RANDOMSAMPLE}(\mathcal{D}_{V_k}, S)$, $\mathcal{Q}_{V_k} = \text{RANDOMSAMPLE}(\mathcal{D}_{V_k} \setminus \mathcal{S}_{V_k}, Q)$, and Q is the number of query examples in each of the K classes.

Prototypical Networks. Prototypical Network [17] learns an embedding function $f_\phi : \mathbb{R}^D \to \mathbb{R}^M$ with learnable parameters ϕ, that maps examples into a space where examples from the same class are close and those from different classes are far. To compute the prototype $\mathbf{c}_{V_k}$ of each class k in the selected subset V, a per-class average of the embedded examples is performed:

$$\mathbf{c}_{V_k} = \frac{1}{|\mathcal{S}_{V_k}|} \sum_{(\mathbf{x}_{i'}, y_{i'}) \in \mathcal{S}_{V_k}} f_\phi(\mathbf{x}_{i'}) \tag{1}$$

These prototypes define a predictor for the class of any new (query) example $\mathbf{x}_i$, which assigns a probability over any class V_k based on the distances between $\mathbf{x}_i$ and each prototype $\mathbf{c}_{V_k}$, as follows:

$$p_\phi(y = V_k \mid \mathcal{S}_V, \mathbf{x}_i) = \frac{\exp(-d(f_\phi(\mathbf{x}_i), \mathbf{c}_{V_k}))}{\sum_{k'} \exp(-d(f_\phi(\mathbf{x}_i), \mathbf{c}_{V_{k'}}))}, \tag{2}$$

where $d : \mathbb{R}^M \times \mathbb{R}^M \to [0, +\infty)$ is a distance function. The loss function used to update Prototypical Network for a query example of a given episode is then simply the negative log-probability of the true class y_i:

$$J(f_\phi; \mathcal{S}_V, \mathbf{x}_i, y_i) = -\log p_\phi(y = y_i \mid \mathcal{S}_V, \mathbf{x}_i) \tag{3}$$

For each test episode, we use the predictor produced by the Prototypical Network for the provided support set $\mathcal{S}_V$ to classify each of query input $\mathbf{x}_i$ into the most likely class $\hat{y} = \arg\max_k p_\phi(y = V_k \mid \mathcal{S}_V, \mathbf{x}_i)$.

3.2 Formal Parallel

Supervised Learning. Suppose we consider a supervised learning problem on a labeled training dataset $\mathcal{D}^s = \{(\mathbf{s}_i, y_i)\}_{i=1}^N$ with the following objective function:

$$\min_\phi \mathcal{L}(f_\phi) := \sum_i l(f_\phi; \mathbf{s}_i, y_i), \tag{4}$$

where f_ϕ is a specified network with parameters ϕ, and $l(\cdot; \cdot, \cdot)$ is a predefined loss function.

Regular Classification. For a regular classification problem on the above defined training dataset $\mathcal{D} = \{(\mathbf{x}_i, y_i)\}_{i=1}^{LH} = \cup_{j=1}^{L}\mathcal{D}_j$, f_ϕ is the classifier to be learned, and a plain example of the loss function $l(f_\phi; \mathbf{x}_i, y_i)$ is cross entropy, which takes the form:

$$l(f_\phi; \mathbf{x}_i, y_i) = -\log p(y = y_i|\mathbf{x}_i),$$
$$p(y = j|\mathbf{x}_i) = \frac{\exp\left(-f_\phi(\mathbf{x}_i)_j\right)}{\sum_{j'=1}^{L}\exp\left(-f_\phi(\mathbf{x}_i)_{j'}\right)}, \tag{5}$$

where $f_\phi(\mathbf{x}_i)_j$ denotes the j-th output of $f_\phi(\mathbf{x}_i)$.

Few-Shot Classification. Suppose we consider the K-way S-shot classification problem on the above training dataset $\mathcal{D}$. Motivated by the episodic training paradigm, we can define a **task class** as a class label subset $V \in \mathcal{T}$ that contains K indexes of the L classes. Then we can define a **task example** (τ_i, y_i) of task class V as a pair of a *support* set $\mathcal{S}_V$, and a *query* example $(\mathbf{x}_i, y_i)$ from the corresponding query set $\mathcal{Q}_V$. To be specific, each task example (τ_i, y_i) can be denoted by $(\tau_i = \{\mathcal{S}_V, \mathbf{x}_i\}, y_i)$, where $(\mathbf{x}_i, y_i) = \text{RANDOMSAMPLE}(\mathcal{Q}_V, 1)$. Thus, the total number of task classes $|\mathcal{T}|$ is C_L^K, and each task class V will have $|\mathcal{G}(V)| = (C_H^S)^K C_K^1 (H - S)$ task examples. As shown in Fig. 1, we give an instance of task classes and task examples for a 3-way 1-shot classification problem on a dataset with 4 classes, and each class has 6 examples. On top of the above formalism of task classes and task examples, the few-shot classification problem can be also formulated as a supervised learning problem represented in Eq. (4) like the regular classification problem. Particularly, the regular supervised classification aims to learn a classifier f_ϕ ($f_\phi(\mathbf{x})$ can estimate the label of example $\mathbf{x}$) given **a large number of examples** $\{(\mathbf{x}_i, y_i)\}$, and the few-shot classification problem aims to learn a tasker (the one that can handle a task) f_ϕ ($f_\phi(\tau)$ can estimate whether we complete the task τ or not) given **a large number of task examples** $\{(\tau_i, y_i)\}$. To clarify the formulation of the few-shot classification problem, the loss function $l(f_\phi; \tau_i, y_i)$ of Prototypical Networks [17] represented in Eq. (3) is used for instance, which has a well correspondence with the cross-entropy loss in the regular classification problem given the definition of $\tau_i = \{\mathcal{S}_V, \mathbf{x}_i\}$.

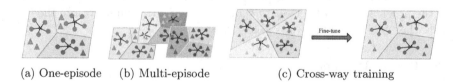

(a) One-episode   (b) Multi-episode   (c) Cross-way training

Fig. 2. (a) and (b) illustrate the comparison between the one-episode and multi-episode training strategy for a 3-way 5-shot problem at each iteration. Support and query examples are shaped in circle and square respectively. (c) illustrates the cross-way training strategy for a 3-way 5-shot problem pretrained by a 5-way 5-shot problem.

3.3 Minibatch Training

We discuss the minibatch training from the view of stochastic gradient descent (SGD) [26]. To solve the supervised learning problem in Eq. (4), minibatch SGD performs the following update:

$$\phi_{t+1} = \phi_t - \alpha \sum_{(\mathbf{s}_i, y_i) \in \mathcal{B}_t} \frac{\partial l(f_\phi; \mathbf{s}_i, y_i)}{\partial \phi} |_{\phi=\phi_t}, \tag{6}$$

where α is the learning rate, t is the iteration index, and $\mathcal{B}_t$ is a minibatch randomly sampled from the whole dataset $\mathcal{D}^s$. Minibatch SGD is proven to be both efficient and effective [27].

Regular Classification. Formally, for a regular classification problem on the training dataset $\mathcal{D}$, at each training step represented by Eq. (6), we randomly select several examples in $\mathcal{D}$ uniformly as $\mathcal{B}_t$. Suppose $|\mathcal{B}_t| = 100$ and $L = 10$; then, from the perspective of probability, $\mathcal{B}_t$ will have approximately 10 examples from each $\mathcal{D}_j$.

Few-shot Classification. For a K-way S-shot classification problem with $|\mathcal{T}| = C_L^K$ task classes and $|\mathcal{G}(V)| = (C_H^S)^K C_K^1 (H-S)$ task examples in each task class $V \in \mathcal{T}$, we have the dataset denoted as $\mathcal{D}^f = \{(\tau_i, y_i)\}_{i=1}^{|\mathcal{T}||\mathcal{G}(V)|} = \cup_{V \in \mathcal{T}} \mathcal{G}(V)$, where $\tau_i = \{\mathcal{S}_V, \mathbf{x}_i\}$, $(\mathbf{x}_i, y_i) = \mathrm{RANDOMSAMPLE}(\mathcal{Q}_V, 1)$. Here, the minibatch training for few-shot classification is that at each training step represented by Eq. (6), we should randomly select several task examples in $\mathcal{D}^f$ as $\mathcal{B}_t$. Apparently, the number of the whole set of task examples of $\mathcal{D}^f$ is extremely massive, as that calculated in the above Sect. 3.2. Thus it is almost impossible to explicitly generate $\mathcal{D}^f$, which is definitely memory- and time- consuming. Here, we recommend **multi-episode training**: sampling several task classes in $\mathcal{T}$ and then sampling several task examples of the sampled task classes as a minibatch. From this point of view, the episodic training paradigm proposed by matching nets [15], which samples an episode that consists of a pair of a support set $\mathcal{S}_V$ and a query set $\mathcal{Q}_V$ at each training iteration, can be seen as randomly selecting *only one* task class V in $\mathcal{T}$ and then sampling KQ task examples of the same support set $\mathcal{S}_V$ in the selected task class V as $\mathcal{B}_t$, namely $\mathcal{B}_t \subset \mathcal{G}(V)$. Obviously, it is not a reasonable choice because it is almost impossible that the task examples in $\mathcal{B}_t$ just located in one task class given $\mathcal{B}_t$ are exactly randomly sampled from $\mathcal{D}^f$ uniformly. Multi-episode training is proposed to relieve this issue by using multiple episodes to construct $\mathcal{B}_t$. Denote E-episode training such that we use minibatch $\mathcal{B}_t := \cup_{e=1}^E \mathcal{B}_t^e$, where $\mathcal{B}_t^e \subset \mathcal{G}(V^e)$ is a randomly sampled episode, and V^e, $e = 1, \cdots, E$ are E task classes first randomly sampled from $\mathcal{T}$. Figure 2 shows a comparison instance between the one-episode and multi-episode training strategy for a 3-way 5-shot problem at each iteration.

Relation with MAML [7]. The idea of multi-episode training has already been used in optimization based few-shot classification methods, such as MAML [7], but with different motivation. In MAML, sampling multiple episodes aims to optimize the performance across different kinds of tasks, while in this paper, the idea is directly motivated by the minibatch training in regular classification problems and aims to reduce the number of iterations before convergence.

3.4   Pretraining

Another critical point of iteratively solving the supervised learning problem represented by Eq. (4) is the initial value, ϕ_0 in Eq. (6). The pretraining strategy suggests a choice of ϕ_0, which comes from solving another supervised learning problem with a similar or more complicated data distribution. Specifically, suppose we have another data distribution, $\mathcal{D}_{\mathrm{pre}}$. Then, we set the initial value ϕ_0 for solving Eq. (4) as:

$$\phi_0 = \mathrm{argmin}_\phi \sum_{(\mathbf{s}_i, y_i) \in \mathcal{D}_{\mathrm{pre}}} l(f_\phi; \mathbf{s}_i, y_i). \tag{7}$$

Regular Classification. We usually set $\mathcal{D}_{\mathrm{pre}}$ to be a dataset of large-scale data, that is, $|\mathcal{D}| < |\mathcal{D}_{\mathrm{pre}}|$. The most famous pretraining approach is ImageNet pretraining [23] for computer vision tasks. ImageNet pretraining has achieved state-of-the-art results on many computer vision tasks, such as object detection [28] and image segmentation [29]. Recently, ImageNet pretraining has been found to speed up the convergence but not necessarily improve the final accuracy [30].

Few-Shot Classification. Similar to using large-scale data to pretrain in classification problems, here we suggest using the $\hat{K}$-way S-shot classification problem to pretrain the K-way S-shot classification problem with $K < \hat{K} < L - K$, because obviously we have the number of task classes $C_L^K < C_L^{\hat{K}}$ and the total number of task examples $C_L^K (C_H^S)^K C_K^1 (H - S) < C_L^{\hat{K}} (C_H^S)^{\hat{K}} C_{\hat{K}}^1 (H - S)$. We named this kind of pretraining for few-shot classification the **cross-way training** strategy[1]. Figure 2(c) shows a cross-way training strategy instance for a 3-way 5-shot problem, pretrained by a 5-way 5-shot problem.

Relation with the Training Idea in Prototypical Networks [17]. Prototypical Networks also suggested to train on a different "way", but they do not explore its actual impact and not expand it with fine-tuning. Particularly, different from the conclusion in [17], empirical evaluation conducted in this paper verify that pretraining employing a higher way without fine-tuning cannot always achieve a better test accuracy on the target problem with a lower way than training from random initialization if given a slower learning rate decaying policy and more iteration steps.

---

[1] It is noted that the network in pretraining does not need to be the same as that in the target supervised learning problem. Therefore, the cross-way training strategy can also work for optimization or memory-based methods where we can optionally just pretrain several feature layers. Related work can be explored in the future.

4 Experiments

Baselines. We implement the proposed training strategies based on the open source code of Prototypical Networks [17][2].

Datasets. We perform experiments on the two related datasets: Omniglot [1] and the *mini*ImageNet version of ILSVRC-2012 [23] with the splits proposed by Ravi and Larochelle [8].

Training Settings. Following Prototypical Networks, we consider the 1-shot and 5-shot scenarios, 5-way and 20-way situations under Euclidean distance for Omniglot, and 5 way only under cosine[3] and Euclidean distance for *mini*ImageNet. We consider multi-episode training with the number of episodes $E = 1, 3, 5$. The maximum number of iterations for $E = 1, 3, 5$ are set as 450000, 150000, 90000, respectively, to make sure all models are trained with the same size of data. In each episode, we set the number of query points per class in the selected task class as 15. Regarding cross-way training, we fixedly set the number of episodes in each iteration as 1. We then consider training with a higher way of 60 for Omniglot and set the number of query points per class as 5. For *mini*ImageNet, we consider training with higher ways of 20, 30 and set the number of query points per class as 15. The maximum number of iterations for fine-tuning the pretrained models is set as 20000. All of the models were trained via SGD with Adam [31]. We used an initial learning rate of 10^{-3}. The original Prototypical Networks cut the learning rate in half every 2000 iterations (namely, "1× schedule"). For models in this paper, we investigate the slower learning rate scheduling strategy[4], and we use a similar terminology, e.g., a so-called "3× (5×) schedule" to cut the learning rate in half every 6000 (10000) iterations. No regularization was used other than batch normalization.

Testing Settings. For all tasks considered in our experiments, we set the number of test points per class in each testing episode as 15. We computed few-shot classification accuracy for our models on Omniglot (*mini*ImageNet) by averaging over 1000 (600) randomly generated episodes from the testing set with 95% confidence intervals.

4.1 Multi-Episode Training

The optimum convergence accuracy-iterations results of multi-episode training with different episode numbers for Omniglot and *mini*ImageNet are shown in Table 1. The rows where the episode number is set as 1* and 1 report the results presented in [17], and we rerun the open source code the paper provided, respectively[5].

---

[2] https://github.com/jakesnell/prototypical-networks.git.

[3] See results of cosine distance in supplementary material.

[4] See results of different learning rate scheduling strategy in supplementary material.

[5] Results are slightly different on *mini*ImageNet because the open source code does not contain the implementations of training settings and data processing and we re-implement these by ourselves.

These results demonstrate that with the increasing of the number of episodes in each iteration, models can converge faster for most considered tasks. Specifically, for Omniglot 5-way 1-shot, 20-way 5-shot tasks and *mini*ImageNet 5-way 1-shot tasks, the iteration number of the multi-episode training with 5 episodes reduces nearly or more than half compared with only 1 episode. It should be noticed that the optimal number of episodes are not consistent for different tasks. This result is in line with what usually happens in regular supervised learning [27]. Regarding the accuracy performance, models trained with multiple episodes in each iteration appear to be superior to those trained with one episode on most tasks. Specifically, for the Omniglot 5-way 1-shot problem, the multi-episode training with 5 episodes can achieve approximately 0.28% accuracy improvement compared with only 1 episode on a very high baseline accuracy of 98.28%. In total, training with more episodes helps to speed up convergence on the target task and improves the final classification accuracy on most tasks. This may because that multi-episode training can well relieve the problem of imbalanced task class sampling of one-episode training, or it may improve the behavior of Hessian spectrum and make the optimization more robust [32], see Fig. 3.

Table 1. The optimum convergence accuracy-iterations results of multi-episode training on Prototypical Networks [17] for Omniglot and *mini*ImageNet. * Results reported in the original paper [17].

E	Omniglot								MiniImageNet			
	5 Way				20 Way				5 Way			
	1 shot		5 shot		1 shot		5 shot		1 shot		5 shot	
	Acc.	Iters.(10³)	Acc.	Iters.(10²)	Acc.	Iters.(10²)	Acc.	Iters.(10²)	Acc.	Iters.(10²)	Acc.	Iters.(10²)
1*	97.40%	–	99.30%	–	95.40%	–	98.70%	–	46.61 ± 0.78%	–	65.77 ± 0.70%	–
1	98.28 ± 0.19%	1094	99.53 ± 0.07%	935	95.10 ± 0.17%	506	98.70 ± 0.06%	506	48.39 ± 0.80%	483	66.24 ± 0.65%	458
3	98.49 ± 0.17%	812	99.59 ± 0.07%	440	**95.11 ± 0.17%**	477	**98.75 ± 0.06%**	519	48.81 ± 0.79%	301	65.85 ± 0.65%	122
5	**98.56 ± 0.16%**	517	**99.61 ± 0.07%**	760	94.98 ± 0.17%	468	98.70 ± 0.06%	265	**49.00 ± 0.80%**	225	65.77 ± 0.67%	273

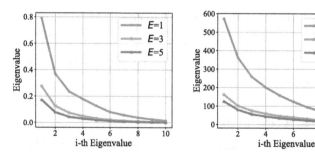

Fig. 3. Top 10 eigenvalues of the Hessian of the loss function w.r.t weights for multi-episode training on Prototypical Networks (with Euclidean distance) for Omniglot (left) and *mini*ImageNet (right) 5 way 1 shot task. The spectrum is computed using power iteration [33] with relative error of 1E-4. This figure shows that multi-episode training converges to points with noticeably smaller Hessian spectrum compared with one-episode training. As discussed in [32], points with small or flat Hessian spectrum show robustness to adversarial perturbation and yield accuracy improvement.

4.2 Cross-way Training

The optimum convergence accuracy-iterations results of cross-way training for Omniglot and *mini*ImageNet are shown in Table 2. These results demonstrate that different from the conclusion in the original paper [17], pretraining on a few-shot problem of a higher way without fine-tuning does not necessarily improve the testing accuracy on the target problem of a lower way. As shown in Table 2, for the *mini*ImageNet dataset, the testing accuracy of models trained with a higher way is similar or even worse than that trained with a lower way. In the original paper [17], the authors claimed that it is advantageous to use more classes (higher "way") per training episode rather than fewer because a higher way always achieves higher accuracy than a lower way. Through our experiments, we found that this claim was biased because the authors only studied one learning rate decaying policy, which is too fast to converge to a near optimum for models trained with a lower way. When trained with a slow learning rate decaying policy, models trained with a lower way can catch up with or even surpass those trained with a higher way. Meanwhile, pretraining with a higher way may generate a more "universal" feature representation, which helps to greatly speed up the convergence of the target problem with a lower-way and may improve the testing accuracy on some tasks. All considered models with pretraining can converge in less than 20000 iterations, which is much less than that of the target problems. In addition, for the *mini*ImageNet 5-way 1-shot classification problem under Euclidean distance, pretraining on the 20-way 1-shot classification problem may achieve approximately 1% accuracy improvement. However, we should also notice that the accuracy of the fine-tuned version of cross-way training are lower than those of non-fine-tuned versions on most tasks of Omniglot, which may due to the overfitting in fine-tuning the few-shot problems on this dataset.

Table 2. The optimum convergence accuracy-iterations results of cross-way training on Prototypical Networks [17] for Omniglot and *mini*ImageNet. FT is short for fine-tune.

K	Omniglot								MiniImageNet			
	5 Way($K=5$)				20 Way($K=20$)				5 Way($K=5$)			
	1 SHOT		5 SHOT		1 SHOT		5 SHOT		1 SHOT		5 SHOT	
	Acc.	Iters.(10^2)	Acc.	Iters.(10^2)	Acc.	Iters.(10^2)	Acc.	Iters.(10^2)	Acc.	Iters.(10^3)	Acc.	Iters.(10^2)
5	98.28 ± 0.19%	1094	99.53 ± 0.07%	935	93.89 ± 0.19%	1094	98.36 ± 0.06%	935	48.39 ± 0.79%	483	66.24 ± 0.65%	458
20	98.70 ± 0.16%	506	99.63 ± 0.07%	506	95.10 ± 0.17%	506	98.70 ± 0.06%	506	48.20 ± 0.80%	153	65.68 ± 0.66%	453
20-FT	98.45 ± 0.17%	121	99.56 ± 0.08%	157	-	-	-	-	49.35 ± 0.82%	144	66.88 ± 0.66%	150
60(30)	**98.73 ± 0.15%**	326	**99.64 ± 0.07%**	402	95.21 ± 0.17%	326	**98.77 ± 0.05%**	402	48.37 ± 0.77%	138	65.24 ± 0.69%	63
60(30)-FT	98.45 ± 0.17%	112	99.57 ± 0.07%	144	**95.24 ± 0.17%**	191	98.72 ± 0.06%	176	49.20 ± 0.80%	91	66.41 ± 0.65%	102

5 Conclusion and Future Work

This paper introduced a formal parallel between the regular classification problem and the few-shot classification problem from the perspective of supervised learning. On top of this formalism of parallel, we further propose multi-episode and cross-way training techniques, which correspond to the minibatch training and pretraining, respectively. The performance of multi-episode and cross-way training is guaranteed by the numerical experimental results on Prototypical Networks [17] for varying few-shot classification problems of Omniglot and *mini*ImageNet. This research is in its early stage. There are several aspects that deserve deeper investigation: 1) theoretically analyze the performance of the two proposed training techniques on an artificial few-shot learning problem; 2) exploit the performance on more few-shot classification approaches, more challenging dataset and more complicated network architectures.

References

1. Lake, B., Salakhutdinov, R., Gross, J., Tenenbaum, J.: One shot learning of simple visual concepts. In: Proceedings of AMCSS, vol. 33, pp. 2568–2573 (2011)
2. Li, F.F., Rob, F., Pietro, P.: One-shot learning of object categories. IEEE Trans. PAMI **28**(4), 594–611 (2006)
3. Schmidhuber, J.: Evolutionary principles in self-referential learning, On learning how to learn: The meta-meta-... hook.) Diploma thesis, Institut f. Informatik, Tech. Univ. Munich (1987)
4. Naik, D.K., Mammone, R.J.: Meta-neural networks that learn by learning. In: Proceedings of IJCNN, vol. 1, pp. 437–442. IEEE (1992)
5. Thrun, S., Pratt, L.: Learning to Learn. Springer, Heidelberg (2012). https://doi.org/10.1007/978-1-4615-5529-2
6. Hochreiter, S., Younger, A.S., Conwell, P.R.: Learning to learn using gradient descent. In: Dorffner, G., Bischof, H., Hornik, K. (eds.) ICANN 2001. LNCS, vol. 2130, pp. 87–94. Springer, Heidelberg (2001). https://doi.org/10.1007/3-540-44668-0_13
7. Finn, C., Abbeel, P., Levine, S.: Model-agnostic meta-learning for fast adaptation of deep networks, CoRR, vol. abs/1703.03400 (2017)
8. Ravi, S., Larochelle, H.: Optimization as a model for few-shot learning. In: Proceedings of ICLR (2017)
9. Nichol, A., Achiam, J., Schulman, J.: On first-order meta-learning algorithms, CoRR, vol. abs/1803.02999 (2018)
10. Rusu, A.A., Rao, D., Sygnowski, J., Vinyals, O., Pascanu, R., Osindero, S., Hadsell, R.: Meta-learning with latent embedding optimization, arXiv preprint arXiv:1807.05960 (2018)
11. Santoro, A., Bartunov, S., Botvinick, M., Wierstra, D., Lillicrap, T.: Meta-learning with memory-augmented neural networks. In: Proceedings of ICML, pp. 1842–1850 (2016)
12. Munkhdalai, T., Yu, H.: Meta networks. In: Proceedings of ICML, pp. 2554–2563. JMLR. org (2017)
13. Mishra, N., Rohaninejad, M., Chen, X., Abbeel, P.: Meta-learning with temporal convolutions, CoRR, vol. abs/1707.03141 (2017)
14. Koch, G., Zemel, R., Salakhutdinov, R.: Siamese neural networks for one-shot image recognition. In: ICML Deep Learning Workshop, vol. 2 (2015)
15. Vinyals, O., Blundell, C., Lillicrap, T., Wierstra, D., et al.: Matching networks for one shot learning. In: NIPS, pp. 3630–3638 (2016)
16. Shyam, P., Gupta, S., Dukkipati, A.: Attentive recurrent comparators. In: Proceedings of ICML, pp. 3173–3181. JMLR. org (2017)
17. Snell, J., Swersky, K., Zemel, R.S.: Prototypical networks for few-shot learning. In: NIPS, pp. 4077–4087 (2017)
18. Sung, F., Yang, Y., Zhang, L., Xiang, T., Torr, P.H., Hospedales, T.M.: Learning to compare: relation network for few-shot learning. In: Proceedings of IEEE CVPR, pp. 1199–1208 (2018)

19. Ren, M., et al.: Meta-learning for semi-supervised few-shot classification, CoRR, vol. abs/1803.00676 (2018)
20. Zhang, C., Cai, Y., Lin, G., Shen, C.: DeepEMD: few-shot image classification with differentiable earth mover's distance and structured classifiers. In: Proceedings of the IEEE/CVF Conference on Computer Vision and Pattern Recognition, pp. 12203–12213 (2020)
21. Chen, Y., Wang, X., Liu, Z., Xu, H., Darrell, T.: A new meta-baseline for few-shot learning, arXiv preprint arXiv:2003.04390 (2020)
22. Li, A., Huang, W., Lan, X., Feng, J., Li, Z., Wang, L.: Boosting few-shot learning with adaptive margin loss. In: Proceedings of the IEEE/CVF Conference on Computer Vision and Pattern Recognition, pp. 12576–12584 (2020)
23. Russakovsky, O., et al.: ImageNet large scale visual recognition challenge. IJCV **115**(3), 211–252 (2015). https://doi.org/10.1007/s11263-015-0816-y
24. Hochreiter, S., Schmidhuber, J.: Long short-term memory. Neural Comput. **9**(8), 1735–1780 (1997)
25. Mikolov, T., Karafiát, M., Burget, L., Černocký, J., Khudanpur, S.: Recurrent neural network based language model. In: Eleventh Annual Conference of the International Speech Communication Association (2010)
26. Robbins, H., Monro, S.: A stochastic approximation method. Ann. Math. Stat. **22**(3), 400–407 (1951)
27. Dekel, O., Ran, G.B., Shamir, O., Xiao, L.: Optimal distributed online prediction using mini-batches. JMLR **13**(1), 165–202 (2012)
28. Ren, S., He, K., Girshick, R., Sun, J.: Faster R-CNN: towards real-time object detection with region proposal networks. In: NIPS, pp. 91–99 (2015)
29. He, K., Gkioxari, G., Dollár, P., Girshick, R.: Mask R-CNN. In: Proceedings of IEEE ICCV, pp. 2961–2969 (2017)
30. He, K., Girshick, R., Dollár, P.: Rethinking ImageNet pre-training, arXiv preprint arXiv:1811.08883 (2018)
31. Kingma, D.P., Ba, J.: Adam: a method for stochastic optimization, arXiv preprint arXiv:1412.6980 (2014)
32. Yao, Z., Gholami, A., Lei, Q., Keutzer, K., Mahoney, M.W.: Hessian-based analysis of large batch training and robustness to adversaries. In: NeurIPS (2018)
33. Lee, J.D., Panageas, I., Piliouras, G., Simchowitz, M., Jordan, M.I., Recht, B.: First-order methods almost always avoid saddle points, ArXiv, vol. abs/1710.07406 (2017)

Classification Beats Regression: Counting of Cells from Greyscale Microscopic Images Based on Annotation-Free Training Samples

Xin Ding[⊠], Qiong Zhang, and William J. Welch

Department of Statistics, University of British Columbia, Vancouver, Canada
{xin.ding,qiong.zhang,will}@stat.ubc.ca

Abstract. Modern methods often formulate the counting of cells from microscopic images as a regression problem and more or less rely on expensive, manually annotated training images (e.g., dot annotations indicating the centroids of cells or segmentation masks identifying the contours of cells). This work proposes a supervised learning framework based on classification-oriented convolutional neural networks (CNNs) to count cells from greyscale microscopic images without using annotated training images. In this framework, we formulate the cell counting task as an image classification problem, where the cell counts are taken as class labels. This formulation has its limitation when some cell counts in the test stage do not appear in the training data. Moreover, the ordinal relation among cell counts is not utilized. To deal with these limitations, we propose a simple but effective data augmentation (DA) method to synthesize images for the unseen cell counts. We also introduce an ensemble method, which can not only moderate the influence of unseen cell counts but also utilize the ordinal information to improve the prediction accuracy. This framework outperforms many modern cell counting methods and won the data analysis competition (https://ssc.ca/en/case-study/case-study-1-counting-cells-microscopic-images) of the 47th Annual Meeting of the Statistical Society of Canada (SSC). Our code is available at https://github.com/UBCDingXin/CellCount_TinyBBBC005.

Keywords: Annotation-free cell counting · Microscopic images

1 Introduction

Modern methods [5,11,12,16–18] often formulate the counting of cells from microscopic images as a regression problem, where the cell count is regressed

---

X. Ding and Q. Zhang—Equal contribution.

Supplementary Information The online version contains supplementary material available at https://doi.org/10.1007/978-3-030-93046-2_56.

L. Fang et al. (Eds.): CICAI 2021, LNAI 13069, pp. 662–673, 2021.
https://doi.org/10.1007/978-3-030-93046-2_56

on some image-related covariates. Most of these regression-based methods [5, 11, 12, 16] can be generalized as a two-step procedure: extract some high-level features as the covariates from a microscopic image, and then regress the cell count on these covariates. At the first step, [16] and [12] extract a dot density map [9] from an image via a U-net [14], while [5] generates a segmentation mask for cells in an image via a Feature Pyramid Network (FPN) [10]. At the second step, [16] directly sums up the dot density map to fit the cell count; [12] and [5] regress the cell count on the dot density map and the segmentation mask, respectively, by a VGG-19 [15]. VGG-19 [15] is also utilized by [11] to regress the cell count on an integration of the dot density map and the segmentation mask. These two-step methods require manual annotations (i.e., dot annotations indicating cells' centroids or segmentation masks identifying cells' contours) on training images. Unfortunately, it is usually difficult and expensive to obtain such annotations in practice. To avoid these expensive manual annotations, [18] and [17] propose to directly regress the cell count on the microscopic image via residual neural networks (ResNets) [4]. However, all these regression-based approaches have the drawback of rarely making a precise prediction, i.e., the predicted cell counts often deviate from the ground truth even for some simple test images.

Instead of the regression-based formulation, we can formulate the cell counting problem as one of classification, where the cell counts are taken as class labels. In this formulation, we predict the cell count (i.e., class label) directly from the greyscale microscopic images by using classification-oriented CNNs. This formulation has two advantages. First, it does not require any manual annotation (e.g., dot annotation or segmentation mask) on the training images that is expensive to obtain in practice. Second, as long as a test image is correctly classified, the prediction error on it is exactly zero. However, besides these two advantages, there are also two limitations of this formulation which explain why the modern cell counting methods are all regression-oriented. First, if a test image has a cell count not seen in the training set, then a prediction error is inevitable. Second, since the ordinal information in the cell counts is not utilized by the classification-oriented CNNs (e.g., counts 10 and 11 are taken as far apart as counts 10 and 100), even when the classification loss (e.g., cross entropy) on a test image is small, the predicted cell count may still be far from the ground truth.

We therefore introduce a novel framework to count cells from greyscale microscopic images to tackle the drawbacks of existing methods and the limitations of the classification-based formulation. Our contributions is summarized as follows:

- We propose in Sect. 3 a novel framework to count cells from greyscale microscopic images in which the cell counting problem is formulated as an image classification. This framework consists of a simple but effective data augmentation (DA) to synthesize images for unseen cell counts. An ensemble scheme (i.e., combine a classification-oriented CNN with a regression-oriented CNN) is also included in this framework to not only deal with the unseen cell counts but also utilize the ordinal information to avoid large prediction errors.

- In Sect. 4, we introduce the Tiny-BBBC005 dataset (used by the data analysis competition of the 47th Annual Meeting of the SSC), on which the proposed framework outperforms several modern cell counting methods. The simple data augmentation and the ensemble scheme can effectively alleviate the two limitations of the classification-based formulation.

2   Related Works

In this section, we review some modern cell counting methods, which are empirically compared with our proposed framework in Sect. 4.

DRDCNN [12]: DRDCNN is a two-step method. A U-Net is first trained to extract the dot density map with minimum Mean Square Error (MSE) from a given microscopic image. A VGG-19 is then attached to the trained U-Net to predict the cell count based on the extracted dot density map and trained to minimize the MSE loss.

FPNCNN [5]: FPNCNN is another two-step method which first uses a FPN to generate the segmentation mask for cells in a given microscopic image, and then regresses the cell count on this mask via a VGG-19. The FPN is trained to minimize the sum of the aleatoric loss [6] and the total-variational (TV) loss [1]. Similar to DRDCNN, the VGG-19 is trained to minimize the MSE loss.

ERDCNN [11]: ERDCNN is a combination of DRDCNN and FPNCNN, where the cell count is regressed on an integration of the dot density maps and the segmentation masks. Different from FPNCNN, the segmentation masks are generated by a U-Net instead of a FPN. ERDCNN also uses a VGG-19 to predict cell counts with MSE loss.

Regression-Oriented ResNets [17,18]: [18] and [17] propose to directly predict the cell count from a microscopic image by using regression-oriented ResNets, which are trained to minimize the MSE loss.

3   Method

In this section, we propose a novel framework to count cells from greyscale microscopic images. We first formulate the cell counting task as a classification problem, where the cell counts are taken as class labels. Then, we use modern classification CNNs (e.g., ResNets) as the backbone to predict cell counts from greyscale microscopic images. A simple but effective data augmentation and an ensemble scheme are also proposed to deal with the two limitations of the classification CNNs (see Sect. 1). The workflows of our proposed framework in the training and testing stages are visualized, respectively, in Figs. 1(a) and 1(b).

3.1 Counting Cells by Classification-Oriented CNNs

As the backbone of our framework, we count cells from greyscale microscopic images by classification-oriented ResNets which are trained to minimize the Cross Entropy (CE) loss. These ResNets take the greyscale microscopic image as input and output the cell counts (i.e., class labels). To distinguish between the regression-oriented ResNets in [17,18] and the classification-oriented ResNets in our framework, we denote all ResNets in this paper as ResNet-XX (YY), where XX and YY, respectively, represent the number of convolutional or linear layers and the loss function. For example, the ResNet-34 (MSE) and ResNet-34 (CE) in Sect. 4 are trained for regression and classification respectively.

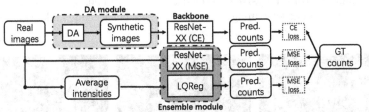

(a) Training stage. Please see Section 3.1 and 3.3 for the definitions of ResNet-XX (CE), ResNet-XX (MSE), and LQReg.

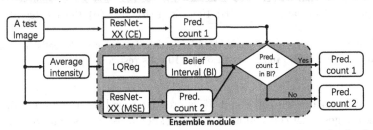

(b) Testing stage. If the ensemble module is disabled, then the final prediction is Pred. count 1.

Fig. 1. The workflows for our proposed framework in the training and testing stages. The data augmentation (DA) module is enabled if we know which cell counts are missing. The ensemble module is enabled if ResNet-XX (CE) does not work well due to either missing cell counts (known or unknown) or insufficient training samples.

Two Limitations: As we discussed in Sect. 1, there are two limitations of the classification-oriented formulation. First, some cell counts in the test set may be missing in the training set, so prediction errors on these test samples are inevitable. Second, the ordinal information in the cell counts is not utilized, which may consequently lead to large prediction errors on some test images.

3.2   A Simple but Effective Data Augmentation

If we know which cell counts in the test set do not appear in the training data, we propose a simple but effective data augmentation (DA) to synthesize greyscale microscopic images for these missing cell counts. Given distinct images $X^{(1)}, \ldots, X^{(n)}$ and their cell counts $y^{(1)}, \cdots, y^{(n)}$, a synthetic image Z with cell count $\sum_{k=1}^{n} y^{(k)}$ can be created via $Z_{ij} = \max\{X_{ij}^{(1)}, X_{ij}^{(2)}, \cdots, X_{ij}^{(n)}\}$, where Z_{ij} is the (i, j)-th pixel of Z. We propose to use the max operation rather than a convex combination to overlay multiple images since the synthetic images obtained via the convex combination usually lack contrast. Additionally, the max operation guarantees the output pixel values do not exceed the bit depth of real images. An example of creating a synthetic image with 15 cells by overlaying two real images from Tiny-BBBC005 with 5 and 10 cells respectively is shown in Fig. 2 and the synthetic image (i.e., Fig. 2(c)) with 15 cells looks very realistic.

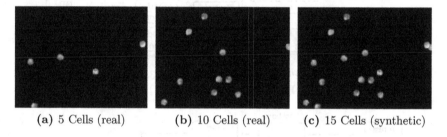

(a) 5 Cells (real)   (b) 10 Cells (real)   (c) 15 Cells (synthetic)

Fig. 2. Creating a synthetic greyscale microscopic image with 15 cells by overlaying two real Tiny-BBBC005 images with 5 and 10 cells respectively.

In Fig. 2, an unseen cell count 15 is created based on a combination of two existing images with cell counts 5 and 10 (known as "basis cell counts"). Such a synthesis can be written as a formula, i.e., $15 = 5 \times (1) + 10 \times (1)$, where the first number in a product is a basis cell count and the associated number in parentheses is the number of distinct real images with that count. In addition to which operation should be used for overlaying multiple images, another question is which formula should be selected to create an unseen cell count? Often there will be more than one possible formula. For example, to create 15-cell images, we can use the following formulae: $15 = 1 \times (15)$, $15 = 1 \times (5) + 10 \times (1)$, $15 = 5 \times (1) + 10 \times (1)$, $15 = 1 \times (10) + 5 \times (1)$, etc. If there is enough computation budget, we suggest taking into account as many potential formulae as possible to increase the variety of synthetic images. For a given unseen cell count, we can create a pool of potential formulae. One synthetic image with this unseen cell count is synthesized at a time by randomly choosing one formula from the pool.

3.3   Ensembling Classification and Regression Methods

To further improve the prediction accuracy of our framework, we also propose an ensemble scheme which combines the high precision of classification-oriented ResNets on seen cell counts with the high stability of regression-oriented ResNets on both seen and unseen cell counts. To be specific, for a test image, we first predict the cell count by ResNet-XX (CE); however, if the predicted cell count from ResNet-XX (CE) is outside a certain interval (termed the *belief interval*), then we use ResNet-XX (MSE) to make the prediction. The proposed ensemble scheme has two benefits. First, it moderates the influence of unseen cell counts on ResNet-XX (CE), even when we do not know which counts are missing. Second, the belief interval implicitly utilizes the ordinal information in the cell counts and ensures that the ResNet-XX (CE) does not make "big" mistakes.

We use Tiny-BBBC005 as an example to show how to build the belief interval for the ensemble, which may be generalized to other greyscale microscopic image datasets. Specifically, from Fig. 2, we can see that greyscale images with larger cell counts usually have higher average intensity (i.e., the average pixel value of an image). Figure 3(a) shows a scatter plot of the nuclei stained images and blur level 1 in Tiny-BBBC005, with average intensity on the x-axis and cell count on the y-axis (the different types of stain and the blur levels are introduced in Sect. 4.1). Figure 3(b) shows the analogous plot for body stained images with blur level 1. We can see that Fig. 3(a) implies a linear relation between average intensity and cell count, while Fig. 3(b) implies a quadratic relation. Moreover, in both Fig. 3(a) and Fig. 3(b), we can see there is a smallest average intensity and a largest average intensity for each cell count. Based on these findings, for each of the three nuclei stained image groups in the training set of Tiny-BBBC005, we fit two linear regression models, i.e., the green and red regression lines in Fig. 3(a). The green regression line is fitted on images with the smallest average intensities (i.e., data points close to the y-axis) while the red regression line is fitted on images with the largest average intensities (i.e., data points close to the x-axis). Similarly, for each of the three body stained image groups, we fit two quadratic regression models. After fitting these linear/quadratic regression models, given a test image along with its stain type and blur level, we first compute the average intensity of this image and plug it into the linear/quadratic regression models to get a predicted upper bound and a predicted lower bound (shown in Fig. 3) for the ground truth cell count of this image. These lower and upper bounds form the belief intervals in the ensemble.

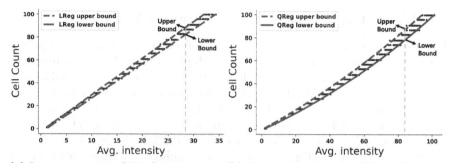

(a) Linear regression (LReg) lines for nu- (b) Quadratic regression (QReg) lines for
clei stained and blur level 1 images   body stained and blur level 1 images

Fig. 3. Scatter plots (blue dots) of the nuclei/body stained and blur level 1 Tiny-BBBC005 images with linear/quadratic regression lines. The green regression line is fitted to data points close to the y-axis while the red regression line is fitted to data points close to the x-axis. The green and red regression lines provide a belief interval for the ground truth cell count of any given image. (Color figure online)

4   Experiment

We first introduce the Tiny-BBBC005 dataset, some implementation details of our experiments, and two evaluation metrics. Then, we compare our proposed framework with several modern methods (summarized in Sect. 2) under four experimental scenarios: (1) all cell counts in the test set appear in the training set; (2) some randomly selected cell counts along with their images from the training set are deleted; (3) five consecutive cell counts along with their images from the training set are deleted; and (4) half of the training images, chosen at random, are deleted.

4.1   Dataset: Tiny-BBBC005

Tiny-BBBC005, used in Case Study 1 of the 47th Annual Meeting of the SSC, is a subset of the Broad Bioimage Benchmark Collection (BBBC005) [13] and consists of 3600 simulated greyscale microscopic images [7,8] of size 696×520 for 600 plates of cells. There are 24 distinct cell counts (i.e., 1, 5, 10, 14, 18, 23, 27, 31, 35, 40, 44, 48, 53, 57, 61, 66, 70, 74, 78, 83, 87, 91, 96, 100) that are evenly distributed across 1 to 100. For each image, a ground truth segmentation mask that identify the contours of cells is also provided, but Tiny-BBBC005 does not have ground truth dot density maps.

To separate cells from the background and facilitate counting, cells are usually dyed in practice. There are two common methods: nuclei stain and cell body stain. In Tiny-BBBC005, all the cells of each plate are dyed in both ways. For example, Fig. 4a and Fig. 4b are respectively the nuclei stained and body stained image of the same plate with 78 cells. For the nuclei stained images, the cells are better separated, whereas cell overlapping is more severe for body stained

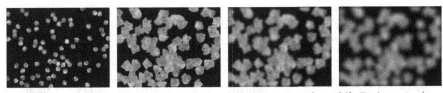

(a) Nuclei stain (in-focus; blur level 1) **(b)** Body stain (in-focus; blur level 1) **(c)** Body stain (out-of-focus; blur level 23) **(d)** Body stain (out-of-focus; blur level 48)

Fig. 4. Four simulated microscopic images from Tiny-BBBC005 for the same plate of 78 cells with different stain type and blur level. Figures 4a and 4b are in-focus images with blur level 1. Figures 4c and 4d are out-of-focus images with blur level 23 and 48 respectively.

images. There are also 3 levels (i.e., 1, 23 and 48) of focus blur for an image. Focus blur was simulated by applying Gaussian filters to in-focus images. For example, Fig. 4c and Fig. 4d are the out-of-focus images simulated from the in-focus image in Fig. 4b. Therefore, each plate of cells has 6 images which correspond to the combinations of 3 blur levels and 2 stain types. For each combination of blur level and stain, the 600 images are divided equally between the 24 distinct cell counts, i.e., 25 images per distinct cell count. Note that the blur level and stain type of each image in Tiny-BBBC005 are known to us.

The 600 images for each stain type and blur level combination are randomly split into two parts; 400 images form a training set and the remaining 200 comprise the test set. Overall, then, the training set has 2,400 images while the test set has 1,200 images, and these two sets contain the same 24 distinct cell counts.

4.2 Implementation Details

We resize all Tiny-BBBC005 images to 256 × 256 with the Lanczos filter [3] by `Pillow` [2]. Since Tiny-BBBC005 does not provide the ground truth dot density maps, the U-Net for density extraction in DRDCNN and ERDCNN is pre-trained on the VGG dataset [9]. The formulae for the DA scheme in Experiment 2 and 3 are shown in Table S.I.1 and S.I.2 in the supplementary material.

In the following experiments, all methods are evaluated on Tiny-BBBC005's test set by Root Mean Square Error (RMSE), i.e., $\sqrt{\frac{1}{1200}\sum_{i=1}^{1200}(c_i - \hat{c}_i)^2}$ and Mean Absolute Error (MAE), i.e., $\frac{1}{1200}\sum_{i=1}^{1200}|c_i - \hat{c}_i|$, where c_i is the true cell count of test image i, and $\hat{c}_i$ is the predicted cell count.

4.3 Experiment 1: No Unseen Counts

In the first experiment, all images in the training set of Tiny-BBBC005 are available for training. For regression-oriented ResNets [17,18], we include ResNet-34 (MSE), ResNet-50 (MSE), and ResNet-101 (MSE) in the comparison. We do not implement the data augmentation and ensemble schemes, because there are

Table 1. Test RMSE and MAE in Experiment 1. In our framework, the DA and ensemble modules are disabled since ResNet-XX (CE) already performs very well and there are no missing cell counts.

Method	Annot. type	Pred. type	RMSE	MAE
DRDCNN [12]	density	Regression	3.067	2.230
FPNCNN [5]	masks	Regression	2.817	1.727
ERDCNN [11]	density + masks	Regression	2.877	2.114
ResNet-34 (MSE) [18]	None	Regression	1.378	1.001
ResNet-50 (MSE) [18]	None	Regression	1.512	1.114
ResNet-101 (MSE) [18]	None	Regression	2.140	1.551
Ours (only ResNet-34 (CE))	None	Classification	**0.400**	**0.040**
Ours (only ResNet-50 (CE))	None	Classification	0.757	0.093
Ours (only ResNet-101 (CE))	None	Classification	0.841	0.098

no unseen cell counts in this experiment and each distinct cell count has enough samples. The experiment is designed to show that, under these conditions, the classification-oriented ResNets are already good enough to make precise predictions. For our framework, we only include ResNet-34 (CE), ResNet-50 (CE), and ResNet-101 (CE) in the comparison.

The performance of all candidate methods is summarized in Table 1. We can see our proposed classification method substantially outperforms others regardless of the ResNet architecture. Moreover, we find that ResNet-34 performs better than ResNet-50 and ResNet-101 in both regression and classification. Therefore, in the following experiments, we only use ResNet-34.

4.4   Experiment 2: Randomly Missing Counts

To test the effectiveness of the proposed data augmentation and the ensemble scheme, we perform a three-round experiment, where, in each round, we randomly remove five cell counts along with their images from the training set. The five deleted cell counts in each round are shown in Table 2. The data augmentation and the ensemble scheme in the proposed framework is applied. When conducting the data augmentation, for each missing count and each combination of stain type and blur level, we create 20 synthetic images. Each synthetic image is created based on a randomly selected formula from a pool of 3, 4, or 5 formulae for each missing count. The experimental results averaged over three rounds are shown in Table 4. From Table 4, we can see the proposed framework still outperforms the other five methods. In this experiment, an ablation study is conducted to test the effectiveness of each component of our proposed framework and the results are reported in Table 3. ResNet-34 (CE) does not perform well due to the missing counts; however, both the data augmentation and the ensemble reduce the impact of these missing counts and their combination leads to the largest performance gain.

Table 2. Deleted cell counts in each round of Experiment 2 and 3.

	Random (Exp. 2)					Consecutive (Exp. 3)				
Round 1	14	35	57	66	83	61	66	70	74	78
Round 2	10	31	70	83	91	70	74	78	83	87
Round 3	18	27	44	53	91	83	87	91	96	100

Table 3. An ablation study of our method in Experiment 2 and Experiment 3.

Method	Exp. 2		Exp. 3	
	RMSE	MAE	RMSE	MAE
ResNet-34 (CE)	3.045 ± 0.143	1.238 ± 0.056	6.153 ± 1.071	2.575 ± 0.477
DA	2.120 ± 0.105	0.615 ± 0.134	2.335 ± 0.269	0.792 ± 0.078
Ensemble	1.359 ± 0.032	0.556 ± 0.016	1.983 ± 0.454	0.843 ± 0.188
DA+Ensemble	$\mathbf{1.103 \pm 0.041}$	$\mathbf{0.350 \pm 0.031}$	$\mathbf{1.664 \pm 0.275}$	$\mathbf{0.621 \pm 0.083}$

Table 4. Average test RMSE and MAE over three rounds in Experiment 2 and Experiment 3 with standard deviations after the "$\pm$" symbol. All modules in our framework are enabled.

Method	Exp. 2		Exp. 3	
	RMSE	MAE	RMSE	MAE
DRDCNN [12]	4.103 ± 0.213	3.405 ± 0.261	4.480 ± 0.484	3.509 ± 0.522
FPNCNN [5]	2.503 ± 0.195	1.902 ± 0.186	3.606 ± 0.702	2.529 ± 0.325
ERDCNN [11]	3.620 ± 1.300	2.845 ± 1.258	3.706 ± 0.495	2.785 ± 0.470
ResNet-34 (MSE) [18]	1.707 ± 0.096	1.242 ± 0.101	2.200 ± 0.399	1.461 ± 0.162
Ours	$\mathbf{1.103 \pm 0.041}$	$\mathbf{0.350 \pm 0.031}$	$\mathbf{1.664 \pm 0.275}$	$\mathbf{0.621 \pm 0.083}$

Table 5. Average test RMSE and MAE over three rounds in Experiment 4 with standard deviations after the "$\pm$" symbol. The DA module in our framework is disabled because there is no missing cell counts.

Methods	RMSE	MAE
DRDCNN [12]	16.139 ± 22.767	13.669 ± 19.772
FPNCNN [5]	3.342 ± 0.516	2.556 ± 0.381
ERDCNN [11]	3.531 ± 0.440	2.715 ± 0.374
ResNet-34 (MSE) [18]	2.863 ± 0.614	2.124 ± 0.458
Ours (only ResNet-34 (CE))	2.753 ± 0.274	1.017 ± 0.224
Ours (Ensemble)	$\mathbf{1.969 \pm 0.348}$	$\mathbf{0.868 \pm 0.196}$

4.5   Experiment 3: Consecutively Missing Counts

This experiment is similar to Experiment 2 except that at each round, we delete five consecutive cell counts along with their images from the training set (shown in Table 2). This experiment is also designed to show the effectiveness of the proposed data augmentation and the ensemble scheme. Since the missing cell counts are consecutive, this setup is more challenging than Experiment 2. The main comparison in Table 4 shows that our proposed framework is far better than the existing methods. The ablation study in Table 3 shows that again both the data augmentation and the ensemble scheme are effective.

4.6   Experiment 4: Reduced Training Set

It is known that the performance of classification deteriorates when the number of training examples decreases. Therefore, this experiment is designed to test the effectiveness of the ensemble scheme when there are few training images for each distinct cell count, so the data augmentation is not used. In this experiment, we randomly delete half of the training images instead of removing all images for a certain cell count. Compared to Experiment 1, there are fewer training images for each distinct cell count under this setup. The whole experiment is repeated three times and the average performance of the candidate methods is shown in Table 5. From Table 3 and Table 5, we can see the ensemble scheme is able to improve the performance of ResNet-34 (CE) on both seen and unseen cell counts.

5   Conclusion

In this work, we propose a novel framework to count cells from greyscale microscopic images without using manual annotations. We first formulate the cell counting problem as one of image classification and use ResNets to predict cell counts from images. Then, to deal with the two limitations of this formulation, we introduce data augmentation and ensemble schemes. Our proposed framework achieves the state of the art on the Tiny-BBBC005 dataset and won the Case Study 1 competition of the annual meeting of SSC.

References

1. Chambolle, A.: An algorithm for total variation minimization and applications. J. Math. Imaging Vis. **20**(1–2), 89–97 (2004)
2. Clark, A.: Pillow (pil fork) documentation (2015). https://buildmedia.readthedocs. org/media/pdf/pillow/latest/pillow.pdf
3. Duchon, C.E.: Lanczos filtering in one and two dimensions. J. Appl. Meteorol. **18**(8), 1016–1022 (1979)
4. He, K., Zhang, X., Ren, S., Sun, J.: Deep residual learning for image recognition. In: Proceedings of the IEEE Conference on Computer Vision and Pattern Recognition, pp. 770–778 (2016)

5. Hernández, C.X., Sultan, M.M., Pande, V.S.: Using deep learning for segmentation and counting within microscopy data. arXiv preprint arXiv:1802.10548 (2018)
6. Kendall, A., Gal, Y.: What uncertainties do we need in Bayesian deep learning for computer vision? In: Advances in Neural Information Processing Systems, pp. 5574–5584 (2017)
7. Lehmussola, A., Ruusuvuori, P., Selinummi, J., Huttunen, H., Yli-Harja, O.: Computational framework for simulating fluorescence microscope images with cell populations. IEEE Trans. Med. Imaging **26**(7), 1010–1016 (2007)
8. Lehmussola, A., Ruusuvuori, P., Selinummi, J., Rajala, T., Yli-Harja, O.: Synthetic images of high-throughput microscopy for validation of image analysis methods. Proc. IEEE **96**(8), 1348–1360 (2008)
9. Lempitsky, V., Zisserman, A.: Learning to count objects in images. In: Advances in Neural Information Processing Systems, pp. 1324–1332 (2010)
10. Lin, T.Y., Dollár, P., Girshick, R., He, K., Hariharan, B., Belongie, S.: Feature pyramid networks for object detection. In: Proceedings of the IEEE Conference on Computer Vision and Pattern Recognition, pp. 2117–2125 (2017)
11. Liu, Q., Junker, A., Murakami, K., Hu, P.: Automated counting of cancer cells by ensembling deep features. Cells **8**(9), 1019 (2019)
12. Liu, Q., Junker, A., Murakami, K., Hu, P.: A novel convolutional regression network for cell counting. In: 2019 IEEE 7th International Conference on Bioinformatics and Computational Biology (ICBCB), pp. 44–49. IEEE (2019)
13. Ljosa, V., Sokolnicki, K.L., Carpenter, A.E.: Annotated high-throughput microscopy image sets for validation. Nat. Methods **9**(7), 637 (2012)
14. Ronneberger, O., Fischer, P., Brox, T.: U-Net: convolutional networks for biomedical image segmentation. In: Navab, N., Hornegger, J., Wells, W.M., Frangi, A.F. (eds.) MICCAI 2015. LNCS, vol. 9351, pp. 234–241. Springer, Cham (2015). https://doi.org/10.1007/978-3-319-24574-4_28
15. Simonyan, K., Zisserman, A.: Very deep convolutional networks for large-scale image recognition. arXiv preprint arXiv:1409.1556 (2014)
16. Xie, W., Noble, J.A., Zisserman, A.: Microscopy cell counting and detection with fully convolutional regression networks. Comput. Methods Biomech. Biomed. Eng.: Imaging Visual. **6**(3), 283–292 (2018)
17. Xue, Y.: Cell counting and detection in microscopy images using deep neural network. Ph.D. thesis, University of Alberta, Edmonton, AB (2018)
18. Xue, Y., Ray, N., Hugh, J., Bigras, G.: Cell counting by regression using convolutional neural network. In: Hua, G., Jégou, H. (eds.) ECCV 2016. LNCS, vol. 9913, pp. 274–290. Springer, Cham (2016). https://doi.org/10.1007/978-3-319-46604-0_20

Adaptive Learning Rate and Spatial Regularization Background Perception Filter for Visual Tracking

Kai Lv[1], Liang Yuan[1,2](✉)(iD), L. He[1](iD), Ran Huang[2](iD), and Jie Mei[3](iD)

[1] School of Mechanical Engineering, Xinjiang University, Urumqi, China
yuanliang@mail.buct.edu.cn
[2] College of Information Science and Technology, Beijing University of Chemical Technology, Beijing, China
[3] School of Mechanical Engineering and Automation, Harbin Institute of Technology, Shenzhen, China

Abstract. In recent years, the correlation filter (CF) has excellent accuracy and speed in the field of visual object tracking. Training samples for CF are usually generated by circular shifts. Although such training samples combined with Fourier transform can be effective in reducing computational effort. They also give rise to boundary effects. Spatial regularization can effectively suppress the boundary effect, but the learning rate are fixed. They cannot be adaptively adjusted to match environmental changes, and the background information is not suppressed. In this paper, we propose a new Correlation filter model, namely Adaptive Learning Rate and Spatial Regularization Background Perception Filter for Visual Tracking (SRAL). Firstly, the SRAL uses real background information as negative samples to train the filter model. Secondly, we use the Average Peak to Correlation Energy (APCE) and the response value error between the two frames to adjust the learning rate together. In addition, the introduction of the regular term destroys the closed solution of CF, and this problem can be effectively solved by the use of the alternating direction method of multipliers (ADMM). Extensive experimental evaluations on three large tracking benchmarks are performed, which demonstrate the good performance of the proposed method over some of the state-of-the-art trackers.

Keywords: Visual object tracking · Correlation filter · Adaptive learning rate · Background perception

1 Introduction

Visual object tracking is a popular research direction in the field of computer vision. Its purpose is to be able to accurately determine the location of a target

This work was supported by the National Natural Science Foundation of China [grant number U1813220] and the Natural Science Foundation of Xinjiang Uygur Autonomous Region [grant number 2019D01C02].

in an image sequence without the need to identify what the target is. It has been widely used in areas such as intelligent visual surveillance [1,2], unmanned vehicles [3] and human-computer interaction [4], etc. Although in the past decades, visual object tracking algorithms have developed rapidly and in a wide variety of ways, there are still many challenges. For example, the tracking process is often disturbed by scale variation deformation, fast movements or target occlusion. At the same time, achieving high-speed and high-precision target localization has always been a difficult task.

In CF tracking, the use of circular shifts and Fast Fourier Transform (FFT) for efficient training and detection can greatly improve computational efficiency, however it also causes boundary effects. This problem leads to degraded tracking performance, especially in the case of fast moving targets. Recently, there are two schemes which can effectively reduce the influence of boundary effects. The first scheme is the use of cropping operations to collect real negative samples in order to improve samples quality, such as CFLB [5], BACF [6], etc. The second scheme is to use spatial regularization to constrain the weight of the filter coefficients, such as SRDCF [7], CSR-DCF [8], etc. However, firstly SRDCF uses circular shifts to obtain negative samples instead of using real negative samples, so it is prone to drift when the target is similar to the background information. Secondly, the learning rate of SRDCF is fixed and cannot be adaptively adjusted as the scene changes, and finally SRDCF uses Gauss-Seidel solver filters, which are computationally expensive.

In this paper, for these problems mentioned above, we propose a novel visual object tracking algorithm, namely Adaptive Learning Rate and Spatial Regularization Background Perception Filter for Visual Tracking (SRAL). The main contributions of this paper are summarized as follows:

- We propose a new framework for visual target tracking that uses realistic background information to train filters, so that our framework can better resist background interference.
- We use the APEC indicator [9] and the response error between two frames to adaptively adjust the learning rate to give the filter better robustness.
- Our SRAL is non-closed solution. To reduce computational complexity, we use ADMM algorithm [10] to transform the SRAL into two sub-problems with globally optimal solutions, because both sub-problems are convex. Therefore, the two sub-problems have their own closed solution and globally optimal solutions.
- Experimental results on three benchmarks, i.e., OTB-2015 [11], TC-128 [12] and VOT-2018 [13] validate that the proposed approach obviously improves the tracking accuracy of CF based trackers.

2 Related Work

2.1 Correlation Filter for Tracking

Correlation filter (CF) was first applied in signal processing. Then it was not until 2010 that it was used for visual object tracking by Bolme et al. proposed the Minimum Output Sum of Squared Error (MOSSE) filter [14], which uses grayscale feature to establish the target appearance model. It uses the fast Fourier transform to cleverly transform the relevant calculations from the spatial domain to the frequency domain, which greatly reducing the computational effort and showing the advantages of the CF framework in the field of visual target tracking, i.e., a well-balanced between accuracy and speed. In recent years, CF tracking algorithms have been improved rapidly, and it can be roughly divided into two typical strategies to improve CF tracking performance. The first strategy is to use a more effective feature or combination of features. In the first strategy, multi-channel features such as HOG (Histogram of Oriented Gradient) [15], CN (Color Names) [16], CNN (Convolutional Neural Network) [17,18] etc. are incorporated into the CF tracking instead of simply using grayscale feature. Henriques et al. proposed the KCF tracker [19] with HOG feature. The CN tracker [20] is proposed by Danelljan et al. uses CN feature. The HCF tracker [21] is proposed by Ma et al. adopts CNN features. The SAMF tracker [22] is proposed by Li and Zhu combines HOG, CN, and grayscale features. Danelljan et al. proposed the C-COT tracker [23] that merges features of multiple resolutions. The second strategy is to improve the tracker function. These include the KCF tracker which uses kernel function mapping to solve the nonlinearity problem. The DSST tracker [24] and the SAMF tracker adopt the idea of scale pooling to solve the problem of scale variation of the target. Li et al. proposed the LCT tracker [25] that adds a re-detection mechanism on the basis of the DSST tracker. In terms of template updating, the MOSSE tracker uses the Peak to Sidelobe Ratio (PSR) indicator and the LMCF tracker [9] uses the Average Peak to Correlation Energy (APCE) indicator to determine whether to update the model. Although these trackers can effectively improve the tracking accuracy, they cannot solve the boundary effect.

2.2 Spatial Regularization for CF Tracking

The boundary effect of the CF tracker is caused due to the non-realistic training samples generated by the circular shifts. In recent years, several methods were proposed to reduce the impact of the boundary effect on tracking performance [5–7,26,27]. Both the CFLB [5] is proposed by Galoogahi et al. and the SRDCF tracker [7] is proposed by Danelljan et al. expands the search area. However, the difference is that the CFLB uses a mask matrix to increase the proportion of real training samples, while the SRDCF added spatial regularization to suppress the response of background regions. Based on CFLB, the BACF tracker [6] is proposed by Galoogahi et al. trains CF with real negative training samples extracted from background information, and extends the single-channel grayscale feature to multi-channel HOG features. Similarly, based on SRDCF, Danelljan et al. proposed a CCOT tracker [23], which extends feature maps of different resolutions to the periodic continuous space domain through cubic spline interpolation to achieve high-precision positioning. To improve the CCOT tracker, Danelljan et al. proposed the ECO tracker [28]. It greatly reduces the computational effort by decomposing the convolution operator, simplifying the training samples of the hybrid Gaussian model and sparsely updating the model. The CSRDCF tracker [8] is proposed by Lukezic et al. uses the spatial reliability map to adaptively select target area.

The learning rate parameters of SRDCF are fixed after filter initialisation and cannot be adaptively adjusted when the scene changes at any time during tracking. To solve these problems, we propose SRAL, which senses changes in the scene and adaptively adjusts the learning rate parameters. At the same time, the filter is trained using real background information, which enhances the robustness of the filter.

3 Our Method

3.1 Review BACF [6]

CF trackers use cyclic shifts to collect training samples. This approach relies on the assumption of sample period expansion, which allows model training and target localization to be efficiently accomplished with the fast Fourier transform. However, it also brings negative boundary effects. The main reason is that negative samples generated by the circular shift are non-realistic, which is difficult to express the real image content, thus reducing the discriminative ability of filters. To address the above issues, the BACF filter uses a cropping matrix to collect true negative samples for training, which improves the robustness of the filter.

First, review the energy function of the correlation filter algorithm. The formula in the spatial domain is as follows:

$$E_{CF}(h) = \frac{1}{2} \sum_{j=1}^{D} \left\| y(j) - \sum_{k=1}^{K} h_k^\mathsf{T} x_k \right\|_2^2 + \frac{\lambda}{2} \sum_{k=1}^{K} \|h_k\|_2^2, \tag{1}$$

where K is the number of feature channels, k is the k-th channel, $y \in \mathbb{R}^D$ represents the desired response value, $x \in \mathbb{R}^D$ and $h \in \mathbb{R}^D$ represent the training sample and the filter template respectively, λ denotes the regularization parameter. $y(j)$ is the j-th element of y, T is a transposition symbol. the BACF filter is improved on the basis of the correlation filter algorithm, that is, the cropping matrix P is added to Eq. 1. The formula is as follows:

$$E_{BA}(h) = \frac{1}{2} \sum_{j=1}^{T} \left\| y(j) - \sum_{k=1}^{K} h_k^\mathsf{T} P x_k [\Delta \tau_j] \right\|_2^2 + \frac{\lambda}{2} \sum_{k=1}^{K} \|h_k\|_2^2, \tag{2}$$

where $[\Delta \tau_j]$ is the circular shift operator, and $x_k [\Delta \tau_j]$ denotes the training sample $x_k \in \mathbb{R}^T$ obtained from the j-th step of cyclic shift. P is a binary matrix of $D \times T$, as a cropping matrix to crop the middle D elements of the training sample x_k, $y \in \mathbb{R}^T$ and $h_k \in \mathbb{R}^D$, where $T \geq D$.

3.2 Review SRDCF [7]

In this section, our baseline SRDCF is revisited. The SRDCF filter adds spatial regularization on the basis of Eq. 1, and the basic principle is to use spatial weights to constrain filter template so that it suppresses the interference of background information. The formula is expressed as follows:

$$E_{SR}(h) = \frac{1}{2}\left\|y - \sum_{k=1}^{K} h_k * x_k\right\|_2^2 + \frac{\lambda}{2}\sum_{k=1}^{K}\|\mathcal{W}_{SR} \odot h_k\|_2^2, \tag{3}$$

where $\mathcal{W}_{SR}$ is the spatial weight, which is calculated in the first frame and does not change during subsequent tracking. $\odot$ denotes the element-wise product.

3.3 Our SRAL

Overall Objective of SRAL. We propose a new energy function to replace Eq. 3.

$$E_{AL}(h) = \frac{1}{2}\sum_{j=1}^{T}\left\|y(j) - \sum_{k=1}^{K} h_k^{\mathsf{T}}Px_k\right\|_2^2 + \frac{\lambda}{2}\sum_{k=1}^{K}\|\mathcal{W}_{SR} \odot h_k\|_2^2, \tag{4}$$

where P is the cropping matrix from BACF [6], which is used to improve the quality of the training samples. $y \in \mathbb{R}^T$, $x_k \in \mathbb{R}^T$, $\mathcal{W}_{SR} \in \mathbb{R}^D$ and $h_k \in \mathbb{R}^D$. To improve computational efficiency, the correlation filter is usually learned in the frequency domain. By applying Parseval's theorem, Eq. 4 can be expressed in the frequency domain as:

$$E(H, \hat{G}) = \frac{1}{2T}\|\hat{y} - \hat{X} \odot \hat{G}\|_2^2 + \frac{\lambda}{2}\|\mathcal{W}_{SR} \odot H\|_2^2$$
$$\text{s.t. } \hat{G} = \sqrt{T}\left(FP^{\mathsf{T}} \otimes I_K\right)H, \tag{5}$$

where $\hat{G}$ is an auxiliary variable. $\hat{G} = \left[\hat{G}_1, \ldots, \hat{G}_K\right]^{\mathsf{T}} \in \mathbb{C}^{KT\times 1}$ stands for the complete expression of $\hat{G}$. $H = \left[H_1^{\mathsf{T}}, \ldots, H_K^{\mathsf{T}}\right]^{\mathsf{T}} \in \mathbb{R}^{KD\times 1}$ shows the complete expression of H. The matrix $\hat{X}$ is defined as $\hat{X} = \left[\text{diag}\left(\hat{x}_1\right)^{\mathsf{T}}, \ldots, \text{diag}\left(\hat{x}_K\right)^{\mathsf{T}}\right] \in \mathbb{C}^{T\times KT}$, I_K is a $K \times K$ identity matrix, and $\otimes$ indicates the Kronecker product. The symbol $\hat{\bullet}$ denotes the discrete Fourier transform (DFT) of a signal. The energy function in Eq. 5 is convex. We can be minimized to obtain the globally optimal solution via ADMM [10]. To solve for Eq. 5, we employ an Augmented Lagrangian Method (ALM) to express:

$$\mathbb{L}(H, \hat{G}, \hat{\zeta}) = \frac{1}{2T}\|\hat{y} - \hat{X} \odot \hat{G}\|_2^2 + \frac{\lambda}{2}\|\mathcal{W}_{SR} \odot H\|_2^2$$
$$+ \hat{\zeta}^{\mathsf{T}}\left(\hat{G} - \sqrt{T}\left(FP^{\mathsf{T}} \otimes I_K\right)H\right) \tag{6}$$
$$+ \frac{\mu}{2}\left\|\hat{G} - \sqrt{T}\left(FP^{\mathsf{T}} \otimes I_K\right)H\right\|_2^2,$$

where μ denotes stepsize parameter, $\hat{\zeta} = \left[\hat{\zeta}_1^\top, \ldots, \hat{\zeta}_K^\top\right]^\top \in \mathbb{C}^{KT \times 1}$ denotes the Lagrange multiplier in the Fourier domain. We solve the following subproblems using the ADMM algorithm. Each of the subproblems $\hat{G}^*$, H^* and $\hat{\zeta}^*$ have closed form solution. We detail the solution to each subproblem as follows:

Subproblem 1: $\hat{G}^*$

$$
\begin{aligned}
\hat{G}^* = \arg\min \frac{1}{2T}\|\hat{y} - \hat{X} \odot \hat{G}\|_2^2 + \hat{\zeta}^\top \left(\hat{G} - \sqrt{T}\left(FP^\top \otimes I_K\right)H\right) \\
+ \frac{\mu}{2}\left\|\hat{G} - \sqrt{T}\left(FP^\top \otimes I_K\right)H\right\|_2^2
\end{aligned}
\tag{7}
$$

Solving Eq. 7 directly is computationally intensive. Fortunately, we consider that $\hat{y}\left(\hat{y}_j, j = 1, \ldots, T\right)$ each element depends only on K channels of $\hat{x} = [\mathcal{V}_1(\hat{x}), \ldots \mathcal{V}_T(\hat{x})]^\top$ and $\hat{G} = \left[\mathcal{V}_1(\hat{G})^\top, \ldots \mathcal{V}_T(\hat{G})^\top\right]^\top$. The symbol $\mathcal{V}_j(\bullet)$ denotes the vector containing values of all K channels of $\bullet$ on pixel $j(j = 1, 2, \ldots, T)$. So can be decomposed into T independent objectives to solve $\hat{G}^*$. We can get the closed form solution for $\mathcal{V}_j(\hat{G})$:

$$
\mathcal{V}_j^*(\hat{G}) = \left(\mathcal{V}_j(\hat{X})\mathcal{V}_j(\hat{X})^\top + T\mu I_K\right)^{-1}\varpi,
\tag{8}
$$

where $\varpi = \mathcal{V}_j(\hat{X})\hat{y}_j - T\mathcal{V}_j(\hat{\zeta}) + \mu T\mathcal{V}_j(\hat{H})$. Since Eq. 8 has reversible calculations, we simplify it by the Sherman Morrsion formula.

$$
\mathcal{V}_j^*(\hat{G}) = \frac{1}{\mu T}\left(I_K - \frac{\mathcal{V}_j(\hat{X})\mathcal{V}_j(\hat{X})^\top}{\mu T + \mathcal{V}_j(\hat{X})^\top \mathcal{V}_j(\hat{X})}\right)\varpi
\tag{9}
$$

Subproblem 2: H^*

$$
\begin{aligned}
H^* = \arg\min_H \frac{\lambda}{2}\|W_{SR} \odot H\|_2^2 + \hat{\zeta}^\top\left(\hat{G} - \sqrt{T}\left(FP^\top \otimes I_K\right)H\right) \\
+ \frac{\mu}{2}\left\|\hat{G} - \sqrt{T}\left(FP^\top \otimes I_K\right)H\right\|_2^2
\end{aligned}
\tag{10}
$$

Taking the derivative of Eq. 10 be zero, we can get the closed form solution for H^*:

$$
H^* = \left(\lambda\left(\tilde{W}_{SR}^\top \tilde{W}_{SR}\right) + \mu T I_K\right)^{-1}(\mu T G + T\zeta),
\tag{11}
$$

where $G = \frac{1}{\sqrt{T}}\left(PF^\top \otimes I_K\right)\hat{G}$ and $\zeta = \frac{1}{\sqrt{T}}\left(PF^\top \otimes I_K\right)\hat{\zeta}$. $\tilde{W}_{SR} = \text{diag}(W_{AS})$ represents diagonal matrix.

Update of Lagrangian parameter $\hat{\zeta}^*$:

$$
\hat{\zeta}^{(i+1)} = \hat{\zeta}^{(i)} + \delta^{(i)}\left(\hat{G}^{(i+1)} - \hat{H}^{(i+1)}\right),
\tag{12}
$$

where $\delta^{(i+1)} = \min\left(\delta^{\max}, \rho\delta^{(i)}\right)$, $\delta^{\max}$ denotes the maximum value of δ and ρ is the scale factor.

Adaptive Learning Rate. For the purpose of a better robustness of filter, we use the APEC indicators [9] and the response error between two frames [29,30] to adaptively adjust the learning rate. Specifically, in the APEC indicator, we set two thresholds Φ_1 and Φ_2 such that the target template is updated when both the APEC value and the $F_{\max}$ are proportionally greater than the historical average; conversely, this indicates that the target is obscured and the target template is contaminated, at which point the template stops being updated. In the target template update process, we use the response error value between two frames to adjust the learning rate of the target template, so that the filter can better adapt to the changes in the environment.

$$F_{APCE} = \frac{|F_{\max} - F_{\min}|^2}{\text{mean}\left(\sum_{w,h}\left(F_{w,h} - F_{\min}\right)^2\right)}, \tag{13}$$

where $F_{\max}$ and $F_{\min}$ denotes highest response and lowest response respectively. $F_{w,h}$ stands for the response at the position of (w, h). Similar to the other filters, we use linear interpolation to update the target template.

$X_{\text{model}}^{(i+1)} = (1 - \eta)X_{\text{model}}^{(i)} + \eta X_{\text{model}}^{(i+1)}$, where η represents the learning rate, which is not fixed and is determined by the response error between two frames, the formula is expressed as follows:

$$\eta = (1 + \alpha \log\left(\|\varepsilon_t - \varepsilon_{t-1}\|_2^2\right))\eta_0, \tag{14}$$

where α is hyper parameter. η_0 represents the initial value of the learning rate. $\varepsilon_t = \frac{\mathbb{S}_t[\Psi_\Delta] - \mathbb{S}^*}{\mathbb{S}^*}$ denotes the response error at frame t. $[\Psi_\Delta]$ is the shift operator, its function is to shift the peak of the response map to the center. $\mathbb{S}_t$ represents the Response map of the t-th frame and $\mathbb{S}^*$ denotes the expected response map.

Target Localization. In the target localization phase, we use the previous ADMM to solve for the $\hat{G}_{t-1}$, and then perform correlation operations with the current frame z_t^k to obtain the response map. The position of the maximum response value in the response map is used as the target position. The formula is expressed as follows:

$$\mathbb{S}(z_t) = F^{-1}\left(\text{conj}(\hat{z}_t) \odot \hat{G}_{t-1}\right), \tag{15}$$

where $\text{conj}(\bullet)$ indicates conjugate operation. For scale estimation in the algorithm, following the most previous CF-based trackers [7,22,27], we use learning filters on multiple resolutions of the search area to estimate scale changes, and then select the optimal scale with the largest response. During tracking, we employ a scale pool $S = \{s_1, \ldots, s_n\}$ to obtain n different search regions, where the searching regions have been resized into the same size as the filter. We calculate the response maps of n search areas, and finally we take the highest response value in the n response map as the target position and scale.

4 Experiments

4.1 Implementation Details

The experimental hardware environment is a computer with a CPU Intel Core i5-7500 and a single NVIDIA GTX 1030 GPU, a main frequency of 3.40 GHz, and a memory with 8 GB configuration. The algorithm development platform is MATLAB R2018a. We used HOG features and depth features to build the target appearance model. For scale estimation, we chose $n = 5$. The initialized learning rate in SRAL is $\eta_0 = 0.0185$, $\alpha = 3 \times 10^{-3}$, and regularization parameter is $\lambda = 1.2$. thresholds $\Phi_1 = 0.5$ and $\Phi_2 = 0.9$ in APCE indicators. In the ADMM iteration parameters, the number of iterations is 2, $\delta^{\max} = 10^4$ and $\rho = 10$.

4.2 Quantitive Evaluation

OTB-2015 Dataset. The OTB-2015 dataset is one of the most popular tracking benchmarks and it includes 100 video sequences with 11 interference attributes for the challenge. We chose to validate the performance of the tracking algorithm using the OPE (One Pass Evaluation) model, where the tracking algorithm is run once in each video and evaluation results are obtained. We compared our algorithm to the state-of-the-art tracking algorithms, which include ECO [28], CFWCR [31], CCOT [23], ECO-HC [28], STRCF [26], BACF [6], SRDCF [7]. Figure 1(a) and Fig. 1(b) reports precision and success graphs for different trackers according to OPE rules. The graph shows that SRAL is the best with a precision of 0.910 and a success rate of 0.862. Table 1 shows the success rate and accuracy rate of 11 interference attributes. The value in parentheses indicates the tracking accuracy rate, and the bold symbol indicates ranking first in a certain attribute. As can be seen from the table, SRAL is the best in almost all of the 11 interference attributes. Figure 2 visually demonstrates the best performance of our algorithm.

TC128 Dataset. We perform experimental analysis on the TC128 dataset. This dataset contains 128 colour video sequences. We compared our algorithm to the state-of-the-art tracking algorithms, which include ECO [28], CFWCR [31], CCOT [23], ECO-HC [28], STRCF [26], BACF [6], SRDCF [7]. Figure 1(c) and Fig. 1(d) reports precision and success graphs for different trackers according to OPE rules. It can be seen from the figure that the success rate of SRAL is 0.727 ranked first, and the accuracy of 0.784 is second only to ECO.

VOT2018 Dataset. We also employ VOT2018 as an experimental benchmark, which contains 60 video sequences. We used accuracy, robustness, and expected average overlap(EAO) to evaluate the performance of tracking algorithms. We compare tracking algorithms including ECO [28], STRCF [26], BACF [6], SRDCF [7]. The Table 2 shows that our tracking algorithm has better performance. Although the EAO and Robustness indicators are second only to ECO, our average running speed is faster than ECO.

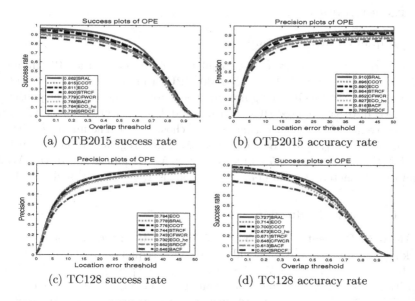

(a) OTB2015 success rate   (b) OTB2015 accuracy rate

(c) TC128 success rate   (d) TC128 accuracy rate

Fig. 1. Precision curve and success rate curve of the overall attributes of the OTB2015 datasets and TC128 datasets.

Table 1. Tracking accuracy and success rate of 11 interference attributes. Tracking accuracy values in brackets, bold indicates top ranking.

Tracker	SRAL	ECO	CCOT	CFWCR	ECO-HC	STRCF	BACF	SRDCF
IV	**0.887**	0.808	0.824	0.780	0.754	0.778	0.780	0.735)
	(0.904)	(0.876)	(0.871)	(0.840)	(0.789)	(0.837)	(0.803)	(0.781)
SV	**0.807**	0.773	0.787	0.750	0.710	0.760	0.698	0.661
	(0.878)	(0.872)	**(0.881)**	(0.834)	(0.791)	(0.840)	(0.767)	(0.742)
OCC	**0.837**	0.818	0.819	0.738	0.725	0.750	0.692	0.674
	(0.871)	**(0.890)**	(0.883)	(0.793)	(0.776)	(0.810)	(0.730)	(0.727)
DEF	**0.815**	0.752	0.745	0.670	0.721	0.732	0.691	0.659
	(0.889)	(0.854)	(0.851)	(0.754)	(0.791)	(0.841)	(0.764)	(0.730)
MB	0.841	**0.861**	0.853	0.759	0.745	0.794	0.735	0.729
	(0.859)	**(0.890)**	(0.886)	(0.808)	(0.775)	(0.826)	(0.741)	(0.767)
FM	**0.819**	0.804	0.807	0.754	0.756	0.757	0.757	0.717
	(0.857)	(0.863)	**(0.876)**	(0.838)	(0.800)	(0.802)	(0.787)	(0.769)
IPR	**0.803**	0.750	0.750	0.703	0.664	0.733	0.711	0.658
	(0.884)	(0.860)	(0.866)	(0.809)	(0.756)	(0.811)	(0.792)	(0.742)
OPR	**0.843**	0.783	0.787	0.722	0.719	0.768	0.709	0.660
	(0.903)	(0.883)	(0.889)	(0.817)	(0.798)	(0.850)	(0.779)	(0.740)
OV	**0.796**	0.758	0.738	0.618	0.696	0.693	0.689	0.558
	(0.892)	(0.887)	(0.879)	(0.751)	(0.759)	(0.766)	(0.748)	(0.602)
BC	**0.886**	0.766	0.810	0.795	0.773	0.801	0.767	0.701
	(0.910)	(0.864)	(0.896)	(0.874)	(0.818)	(0.872)	(0.801)	(0.775)
LR	**0.732**	0.680	0.705	0.734	0.697	0.652	0.663	0.625
	(0.849)	(0.841)	**(0.869)**	(0.853)	(0.801)	(0.737)	(0.841)	(0.663)

Table 2. Comparison of 5 tracking algorithms on the VOT2018 dataset. All tested with the same equipment.

	SRAL	ECO	STRCF	BACF	SRDCF
EAO	0.1931	0.2666	0.1727	0.1351	0.1166
Accuracy	0.5083	0.4884	0.4885	0.5174	0.4788
Robustness	0.3373	0.2251	0.4548	0.6201	0.6952
FPS	4.0255	2.1472	12.447	20.220	5.6225

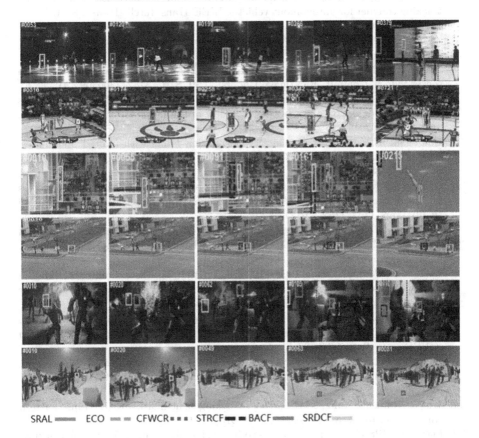

SRAL ▬▬ ECO ▬ ▬ CFWCR ▪ ▪ ▪ STRCF ▬ ▪ ▬ BACF ▬▬▬ SRDCF ▬▬▬

Fig. 2. Quantitative comparison of our algorithm with other state-of-the-art algorithms in skating1, basketball, diving, Human3, ironman and skating. Our SRAL performance shows the best performance.

5   Conclusion

In this work, we propose Adaptive Learning Rate and Spatial Regularization Background Perception Filter for Visual Tracking (SRAL). We use real background information as training samples and use the APEC indicator and the error value between two frames together to adjust the learning rate of the target model in addition our SRAL is optimised using the ADMM algorithm to reduce the complexity of the computation. Extensive experimental results show the high performance of our SRAL in comparison to many excellent tracking algorithms.

References

1. Gao, M., Jin, L., Jiang, Y., Guo, B.: Manifold Siamese network: a novel visual tracking convnet for autonomous vehicles. IEEE Trans. Intell. Transp. Syst. **21**(4), 1612–1623 (2020)
2. Zg, A., Gz, A., Hd, B., Xy, A.: Extended geometric models for stereoscopic 3D with vertical screen disparity. Displays **65**, 101972 (2020)
3. Manafifard, M., Ebadi, H., Moghaddam, H.A.: A survey on player tracking in soccer videos. Comput. Vis. Image Underst. **159**, S1077314217300309 (2017)
4. Bouget, D., Allan, M., Stoyanov, D., Jannin, P.: Vision-based and marker-less surgical tool detection and tracking: a review of the literature. Med. Image Anal. **35**, 633–654 (2017)
5. Galoogahi, H.K., Sim, T., Lucey, S.: Correlation filters with limited boundaries. In: 2015 IEEE Conference on Computer Vision and Pattern Recognition (CVPR), pp. 4630–4638 (2015)
6. Galoogahi, H.K., Fagg, A., Lucey, S.: Learning background-aware correlation filters for visual tracking. In: 2017 IEEE International Conference on Computer Vision (ICCV), pp. 1144–1152 (2017)
7. Danelljan, M., Häger, G., Khan, F.S., Felsberg, M.: Learning spatially regularized correlation filters for visual tracking. In: 2015 IEEE International Conference on Computer Vision (ICCV), pp. 4310–4318 (2015)
8. LukeŽic, A., Vojír, T., Zajc, L.C., Matas, J., Kristan, M.: Discriminative correlation filter with channel and spatial reliability. In: 2017 IEEE Conference on Computer Vision and Pattern Recognition (CVPR), pp. 4847–4856 (2017)
9. Wang, M., Liu, Y., Huang, Z.: Large margin object tracking with circulant feature maps. In: 2017 IEEE Conference on Computer Vision and Pattern Recognition (CVPR), pp. 4800–4808 (2017)
10. Boyd, S., Parikh, N., Chu, E.: Distributed Optimization and Statistical Learning via the Alternating Direction Method of Multipliers. Now Publishers Inc., Norwell (2011)
11. Wu, Y., Lim, J., Yang, M.H.: Object tracking benchmark. IEEE Trans. Pattern Anal. Mach. Intell. **37**(9), 1834–1848 (2015)
12. Liang, P., Blasch, E., Ling, H.: Encoding color information for visual tracking: algorithms and benchmark. IEEE Trans. Image Process. **24**(12), 5630–5644 (2015)
13. Kristan, M., et al.: The sixth visual object tracking VOT2018 challenge results. In: Leal-Taixé, L., Roth, S. (eds.) ECCV 2018. LNCS, vol. 11129, pp. 3–53. Springer, Cham (2019). https://doi.org/10.1007/978-3-030-11009-3_1
14. Bolme, D.S., Beveridge, J.R., Draper, B.A., Lui, Y.M.: Visual object tracking using adaptive correlation filters. In: 2010 IEEE Computer Society Conference on Computer Vision and Pattern Recognition, pp. 2544–2550 (2010)
15. Dalal, N., Triggs, B.: Histograms of oriented gradients for human detection. In: 2005 IEEE Computer Society Conference on Computer Vision and Pattern Recognition (CVPR'05), vol. 1, pp. 886–893 (2005)

16. van de Weijer, J., Schmid, C., Verbeek, J., Larlus, D.: Learning color names for real-world applications. IEEE Trans. Image Process. **18**(7), 1512–1523 (2009)
17. Chatfield, K., Simonyan, K., Vedaldi, A., Zisserman, A.: Return of the devil in the details: delving deep into convolutional nets. Computer Science (2014)
18. Simonyan, K., Zisserman, A.: Very deep convolutional networks for large-scale image recognition. Computer Science (2014)
19. Henriques, J.F., Caseiro, R., Martins, P., Batista, J.: High-speed tracking with kernelized correlation filters. IEEE Trans. Pattern Anal. Mach. Intell. **37**(3), 583–596 (2015)
20. Danelljan, M., Khan, F.S., Felsberg, M., Van De Weijer, J.: Adaptive color attributes for real-time visual tracking. In: 2014 IEEE Conference on Computer Vision and Pattern Recognition, pp. 1090–1097 (2014)
21. Ma, C., Huang, J., Yang, X., Yang, M.: Hierarchical convolutional features for visual tracking. In: 2015 IEEE International Conference on Computer Vision (ICCV), pp. 3074–3082 (2015)
22. Li, Y., Zhu, J.: A scale adaptive kernel correlation filter tracker with feature integration. In: Agapito, L., Bronstein, M.M., Rother, C. (eds.) ECCV 2014. LNCS, vol. 8926, pp. 254–265. Springer, Cham (2015). https://doi.org/10.1007/978-3-319-16181-5_18
23. Danelljan, M., Robinson, A., Shahbaz Khan, F., Felsberg, M.: Beyond correlation filters: learning continuous convolution operators for visual tracking. In: Leibe, B., Matas, J., Sebe, N., Welling, M. (eds.) ECCV 2016. LNCS, vol. 9909, pp. 472–488. Springer, Cham (2016). https://doi.org/10.1007/978-3-319-46454-1_29
24. Danelljan, M., Häger, G., Khan, F.S., Felsberg, M.: Discriminative scale space tracking. IEEE Trans. Pattern Anal. Mach. Intell. **39**(8), 1561–1575 (2017). https://doi.org/10.1109/TPAMI.2016.2609928
25. Ma, C., Yang, X., Zhang, C., Yang, M.: Long-term correlation tracking. In: 2015 IEEE Conference on Computer Vision and Pattern Recognition (CVPR), pp. 5388–5396 (2015)
26. Li, F., Tian, C., Zuo, W., Zhang, L., Yang, M.: Learning spatial-temporal regularized correlation filters for visual tracking. In: 2018 IEEE/CVF Conference on Computer Vision and Pattern Recognition, pp. 4904–4913 (2018)
27. Dai, K., Wang, D., Lu, H., Sun, C., Li, J.: Visual tracking via adaptive spatially-regularized correlation filters. In: 2019 IEEE/CVF Conference on Computer Vision and Pattern Recognition (CVPR), pp. 4665–4674 (2019)
28. Danelljan, M., Bhat, G., Khan, F.S., Felsberg, M.: Eco: efficient convolution operators for tracking. In: 2017 IEEE Conference on Computer Vision and Pattern Recognition (CVPR), pp. 6931–6939 (2017)
29. Huang, Z., Fu, C., Li, Y., Lin, F., Lu, P.: Learning aberrance repressed correlation filters for real-time UAV tracking. In: 2019 IEEE/CVF International Conference on Computer Vision (ICCV), pp. 2891–2900 (2019)
30. Li, Y., Fu, C., Ding, F., Huang, Z., Lu, G.: AutoTrack: towards high-performance visual tracking for UAV with automatic spatio-temporal regularization. In: 2020 IEEE/CVF Conference on Computer Vision and Pattern Recognition (CVPR), pp. 11920–11929 (2020)
31. He, Z., Fan, Y., Zhuang, J., Dong, Y., Bai, H.: Correlation filters with weighted convolution responses. In: 2017 IEEE International Conference on Computer Vision Workshops (ICCVW), pp. 1992–2000 (2017)

Data Mining

Estimating Treatment Effect via Differentiated Confounder Matching

Zhao Ziyu$^{(\boxtimes)}$, Kun Kuang, and Fei Wu

College of Computer Science and Technology, Zhejiang University, Hangzhou, China
kunkuang@zju.edu.cn, wufei@cs.zju.edu.cn

Abstract. For causal inference, an important issue is to estimate the treatment effect from observational data where variables are confounded. The matching method is a classical algorithm for controlling the confounding bias via matching units with different treatments but similar variables. But traditional matching methods fail to do selection and differentiation among the pool of a large number of potential confounders, leading to possible underperformance in high dimensional settings. In this paper, we give a new theoretical analysis on confounder selection and differentiation, and propose a novel Differentiated Confounder Matching (DCM) algorithm for both individual and average treatment effect estimation by optimizing confounder weights and units matching. With extensive experiments on both synthetic and real-world datasets, we demonstrate that our DCM algorithm achieves significantly better performance than other matching methods on both individual and average treatment effect estimation.

Keywords: Treatment effect · Matching method · Confounder differentiation · Causal inference

1 Introduction

Causal inference [6] is a powerful statistical modeling tool for explanatory analysis on many decision making applications. Treatment effect estimation is one fundamental problem in causal inference and its main challenge is to remove the confounding bias induced by the different variables' distribution between treated and control units. The golden standard approaches for removing confounding bias are randomized experiments [12], where different treatments are randomly assigned to units. In real applications, however, the fully randomized experiments are usually extremely expensive [9] or sometimes even infeasible [2]. Hence, it is of paramount importance to infer treatment effect from observational data.

Matching is a classical and interpretable approach for treatment effect, especially individual treatment effect estimation in observational studies, which removes the confounding bias by matching units with different treatments but similar covariates. Matching methods [13], especially exactly (or almost exactly)

L. Fang et al. (Eds.): CICAI 2021, LNAI 13069, pp. 689–699, 2021.
https://doi.org/10.1007/978-3-030-93046-2_58

matching methods, brings the interpretability of causal analysis since the raw covariates are almost exactly the same between the matched pair units. Exactly matching achieves good performance in early applications, but quick ran into issues of insufficient sample size in many applications with continuous or high-dimensional variables, where few such "identical units" exist.

To address the challenges from continuous and high-dimensional variables, [7] proposed the coarsened exact matching method to coarsen each variable by recording for applying exact matching algorithm. [15] proposed propensity score matching algorithm to project the entire dimensions of variables to one dimension of propensity score. [14] introduced an "optimal matching" to choose matched units according to a pre-defined distance measure. These methods perform matching or distance calculation based on all observed variables, but in real applications, not all observed variables are confounders that need to be matched and different confounders might bring different confounding bias [10]. Hence, these methods generally suffer in the presence of many irrelevant variables, leading to incorrect matches.

Recently, GenMatch algorithm [5] was proposed to learn a suitable distance measure via evolutionary search on variables' weight. GenMatch can easily combine both propensity score matching and Mahalanobis distance, but its complexity grows exponentially with the number of observed variables. [13] proposed a weighted Hamming distance with considering confounder selection for matching, and achieved good performance on causal inference. But it ignores the differentiation of confounders, moreover, it only focuses on categorical variables and cannot be applied on matching with continuous variables.

In this paper, we focus on individual and average treatment effect estimation via interpretable matching method, taking into account the selection and differentiation of confounders. Firstly, we theoretically proved that some variables are not confounders and different confounders should be differentiated for individual treatment effect estimation in matching process. Motivated by this, then, we propose a data-driven method, named Differentiated Confounder Matching (DCM) algorithm, by optimizing confounder selection, differentiation and units matching for treatment effect estimation. Specifically, the confounder weights for confounder selection and differentiation are learned by regression with theoretical guarantee. Then, the weights are used for weighted matching so that improves the accuracy of units matching and precise of treatment effect estimation. We demonstrate the advantages of our DCM algorithm with extensive experiments on both synthetic and real-world datasets.

To summarize, we make the following contributions:

- We investigate the problem of individual and average treatment effect estimation via matching method with considering the confounder selection and differentiation, which is beyond the capability of previous matching methods.
- We propose a novel DCM algorithm to jointly select confounders, optimize confounder weights for weighted matching on units, and simultaneously estimate individual and average treatment effect.

– Extensive experiments on both synthetic and real world datasets demonstrate the superior performance of our proposed algorithms on units matching and treatment effect estimation.

2   Problem and Assumption

Our goal is to estimate the treatment effect, including individual and average treatment effect from observational data. With the potential outcome framework proposed by [8], we define the treatment as a random variable T and a potential outcome as $Y(t)$ which corresponds to a specific treatment assignment $T = t$. In this paper, we focus on estimating the causal effect of binary treatment, which is $t \in \{0, 1\}$. We define the units which received treatment $(T = 1)$ as treated units and the other units with $T = 0$ as control units. Then, for each unit indexed by $i = 1, 2, \cdots, n$, we observe a treatment T_i, an outcome Y_i^{obs} and a vector of observed variables $X_i \in \mathbb{R}^{p \times 1}$, where the observed outcome Y_i^{obs} of unit i denotes by:

$$Y_i^{obs} = Y_i(T_i) = T_i \cdot Y_i(1) + (1 - T_i) \cdot Y_i(0). \tag{1}$$

The numbers of treated and control units are equal to n_t and n_c, and the dimension of all observed variables is p.

The important goal of causal inference in observational studies is to evaluate the casual effect of treatment T on outcome Y, including Individual Treatment effect on Treated (ITT) and Average Treatment effect on Treated (ATT). ITT of a treated unit i refers to the difference between the potential outcome of units i under treated and control status. Formally, the ITT of treated unit i is defined as:

$$ITT_i = Y_i(1) - Y_i(0). \tag{2}$$

ATT represents the average ITT over all treated units. Formally, the ATT is defined as:

$$ATT = E(ITT_i) = E(Y(1) - Y(0)|T = 1), \tag{3}$$

where $Y(1)$ and $Y(0)$ represent the potential outcome of units with treatment status as treated $T = 1$ and control $T = 0$, respectively. $E(\cdot)$ refers to the expectation function.

The Eq. (2) and Eq. (3) are infeasible because of the counterfactual problem [3], that for each treated unit i, we can only observe one of the two potential outcomes $Y_i(1)$, the other potential outcome $Y_i(0)$ is unobserved or counterfactual. One can address this counterfactual problem by approximate the unobserved potential outcome. The simplest approach is to directly compare the average outcome between the treated and control units. However, in observational studies, comparing two samples directly is likely to have bias if the treatment assignment is not random, as confounding bias is not taken into account [3].

In this paper, we focus on matching methods for treatment effect estimation, including ITT_i and ATT. Specifically, for each treated units i, we try to find a control unit j to match with guarantee that the bias between the match units pair (i, j) is removed. Then, we can estimate the ITT of treated unit i as:

$$\widehat{ITT}_i = Y_i^{obs} - Y_j^{obs}. \tag{4}$$

With the matched treated-control units pair set $S = \{(i, j)|T_i = 1, T_j = 0\}$, one can easily evaluate the ATT as follows:

$$\widehat{ATT} = \sum_{(i,j)\in S} \frac{1}{n_t}(Y_i^{obs} - Y_j^{obs}). \tag{5}$$

Throughout this paper, we assume following standard assumptions [15] are satisfied.

Assumption 1: Stable Unit Treatment Value. Given the observed variables, the distribution of potential outcome for one unit is assumed to be unaffected by the particular treatment assignment of another unit.

Assumption 2: Unconfoundedness. Given the observed variables, the distribution of treatment is independent of potential outcome. Formally, $T \perp (Y(0), Y(1))|\mathbf{X}$.

Assumption 3: Overlap. Every unit has a nonzero probability to receive either treatment status when given the observed variables. Formally, $0 < p(T = 1|\mathbf{X}) < 1$.

3 Our Algorithm

In this section, we first introduce the traditional matching methods for treatment effect estimation and analysis the their limitations in scenario of big data. Then, we propose a differentiated confounder matching methods for treatment effect with theoretical analysis.

3.1 Traditional Matching Method

To unbiasedly estimate the ATT in observational studies, one usually used way is matching method, including exact matching,coarsened exact matching and many distance measure based matching. Specifically, for each treated unit i, matching methods try to find its closet match among control units as follow:

$$match(i) = \underset{j:T_j=0}{\arg\min} \, d(X_i, X_j), \tag{6}$$

where function $d(a, b)$ measures the distance between the vector of variables a and b. Based on Eq. (6), exact matching constrains the match unit pair (i, j)

to satisfy that $X_i = X_j$, and other distance based matching methods focus on proposing more appropriate distance metric $d(\cdot)$ for units matching. With the matched units pairs, one can easily estimate the ITT and ATT with Eq. (4) & (5). But these traditional matching methods match units based on all observed variables without confounder selection and confounder differentiation, learning to poor performance in the setting of high dimensional variables.

3.2 Differentiated Confounder Matching

To fully remove the confounding bias for precise treatment effect estimation, we propose to learn confounder weights to determine which variables are confounders and differentiate different confounders during matching process. To be specific, for each treated unit i, we find its closet match among control units as follow:

$$match(i) = \arg \min_{j:T_j=0} d(X_i \odot \beta, X_j \odot \beta), \qquad (7)$$

where $\odot$ refers to Hadamard product and $\beta \in \mathbb{R}^{p \times 1}$ is the confounder weights to differentiate the roles of each confounder in the matching process, which helps for better removing the confounding bias.

Next we will give theoretical analysis on how to learn that confounder weight with following proposition.

Proposition 1. *In matching, not all observed variables are confounders and different confounders make unequal confounding bias on treatment effect with their own weights, and the weights can be learned via regressing potential outcome $Y(0)$ on observed variables* **X**.

The general relationship among observed variables **X**, treatment T and outcome Y can be represented as:

$$Y = f(\mathbf{X}) + T \cdot g(\mathbf{X}) + \epsilon, \qquad (8)$$

where the *true* ITT_i for a treated units i is $g(\mathbf{X}_i)$, and the potential outcome $Y(0)$ can be represented by:

$$Y(0) = f(\mathbf{X}) + \epsilon. \qquad (9)$$

We prove Proposition 1 with following assumption.

Assumption 4: Linearity. The regression of potential outcome $Y(0)$ on observed variables **X** is linear, that is $f(\mathbf{X}) = c + \mathbf{X}\beta$.

Under Assumption 4, we can rewrite the estimator of $\widehat{ITT}_i$ of a treated unit i with matched control unit j as:

$$
\begin{aligned}
\widehat{ITT}_i &= Y_i^{obs} - Y_j^{obs} \\
&= (c + X_i\beta + g(X_i) + \epsilon_i) - (c + X_j\beta + \epsilon_j) \\
&= g(\mathbf{X}_i) + (X_i\beta - X_j\beta) + \phi(\epsilon) \\
&= ITT_i + \sum_{k=1}^{p} \beta_k(X_{i,k} - X_{j,k}) + \phi(\epsilon).
\end{aligned}
$$

where $\phi(\epsilon) = \epsilon_i - \epsilon_j$ refers to the difference of noises between the matched treated and control units pair. In order to reduce the bias of estimated ITT, we have to regulate the term $\sum_{k=1}^{p} \beta_k (X_{i,k} - X_{j,k})$, where $(X_{i,k} - X_{j,k})$ means the difference of the kth confounder between treated and control units, and the parameter β_k represents the confounding bias weight of the kth confounder.

Therefore, different confounders make unequal confounding bias with their own weights, and those variables with weight $\beta_k = 0$ are non-confounders since they would not bring any bias. Fortunatelly, the confounder weight β_k is exactly the coefficient of X_k in the function $f(\mathbf{X})$. Hence, we can learn the confounder weights from the regression of potential outcome $Y(0)$ on observed variables $\mathbf{X}$ under *Linearity* assumption[1].

3.3   Algorithm and Optimization

Based on Proposition 1 and Assumption 4, we propose to learn the confounder weight for confounder selection and differentiation before units matching as follow:

$$\beta = \arg\min_{\beta} \sum_{j:T_j=0} (Y_j - X_j\beta)^2 \tag{10}$$

$$s.t. \ \|\beta\|_1 \leq \lambda \quad and \quad \|\beta\|_2^2 \leq \delta,$$

where β is the confounder weights. With the constraints $\|\beta\|_1 \leq \lambda$ and $\|\beta\|_2^2 \leq \delta$, we can remove the non-confounders and smooth the confounder weights.

With the confounder weight β learned from Eq. (10), we propose to match units with differentiated confounder matching algorithm in Eq. (6). Specifically, we adopt absolute distance to measure the similarity between two units, then, for each treated unit i, we match it to a control unit:

$$match(i) = \arg\min_{j:T_j=0} |\beta \cdot (X_i - X_j)|. \tag{11}$$

Then, for each treated unit i, we obtain a matched units pair (i, j), where $j = match(i)$. To bound the bias during matching process, we drop units pair if $|\beta \cdot (X_i - X_j)| > \epsilon$. Finally, we obtain a matched treated and control units pairs set $S = \{(i, j) | T_i = 1, T_j = 0\}$, and one can easily estimate individual treatment effect ITT_i for each treated unit i with Eq. (4) and average treatment effect ATT with Eq. (5).

4   Experiments

In this section, we apply our algorithm on both synthetic and real-world dataset to demonstrate the advantages of our algorithm for treatment effect estimation.

---

[1] The linearity assumption can be relaxed by including high order terms of $\mathbf{X}$ in regression.

4.1   Baselines

In this work, we focus on the interpretable matching methods for treatment effect (ITT and ATT) estimation, so we implement following matching baselines for comparison, including (1) Naive estimator, which evaluates the ATT by directly comparing the average outcome between the treated and control units, ignoring the confounding bias in data; (2) Propensity Score Matching (PSM) [1], which matches units based on the distance of their propensity score, regarding all variables as confounders; (3) Genetic Matching (genMatch) [5], which matches units based on weighted Mahalanobis metric, where the weight is learned by evolutionary search, ignoring the differentiation of confounders; (4) Dynamic Almost Matching Exactly matching (DAME) [13], which matches units based on a weighted Hamming distance with considering the selection of confounders and irrelevant variables, ignoring confounder differentiation.

The Naive estimator cannot be applied for estimating ITT, hence, we compare our algorithm with PSM, Genetic matching and DAME for ITT estimation.

4.2   Experiments on Synthetic Data

Dataset. We generate the synthetic datasets with considering two settings, including a categorical setting for comparing with DAME and a continuous setting.

Categorical Setting: In this setting, we set the observed variables as categorical. Specifically, we consider two sample sizes $n = \{2000, 5000\}$ and also vary the dimension of observed variables $p = \{10, 15, 20\}^2$. To bring the confounding bias, we generate the observed variables $\mathbf{X} = \{x_1, x_2, \ldots, x_p\}$ with independent Gaussian distributions as:

$$\mathbf{x}_1, \mathbf{x}_2, \cdots, \mathbf{x}_p \overset{iid}{\sim} \mathcal{N}(0.3, 1), \quad \text{for treated units}$$

$$\mathbf{x}_1, \mathbf{x}_2, \cdots, \mathbf{x}_p \overset{iid}{\sim} \mathcal{N}(-0.3, 1), \quad \text{for control units}$$

To make $\mathbf{X}$ categorical, we let $\mathbf{x}_i = 1$ if $\mathbf{x}_i = 1 \geq 0$, otherwise $\mathbf{x}_i = 0$.

Continuous Setting: In this setting, we set the observed variables as continuous. We also consider two sample sizes $n = \{2000, 5000\}$ but vary the dimension of observed variables $p = \{10, 50, 100\}$. And we generate the observed variables $\mathbf{X} = \{x_1, x_2, \ldots, x_p\}$ with independent Gaussian distributions as:

$$\mathbf{x}_1, \mathbf{x}_2, \cdots, \mathbf{x}_p \overset{iid}{\sim} \mathcal{N}(0.5, 1), \quad \text{for treated units}$$

$$\mathbf{x}_1, \mathbf{x}_2, \cdots, \mathbf{x}_p \overset{iid}{\sim} \mathcal{N}(-0.5, 1), \quad \text{for control units}$$

Finally, for both categorical and continuous settings, we generate the outcome Y as follows:

$$Y = f(\mathbf{X}) + T \cdot g(\mathbf{X}) + \epsilon,$$

---

^{2} High dimension brings NULL matching in DAME method, we compare our algorithm with other baselines in high dimensional continuous setting.

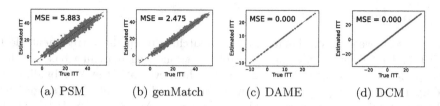

Fig. 1. Estimated ITT v.s. true ITT in categorical setting with $n = 5000$, $p = 15$. Each blue dot represents the results of a treated unit and the red line $y = x$ represents the estimated ITT exactly equals the true ITT.

where $f(\mathbf{X}) = \mathbf{X}\alpha$, $g(\mathbf{X}) = \mathbf{X}\gamma$, and the coefficients $\alpha, \gamma \in [0, 1]$ are randomly generated.

In synthetic data, we know the *true ITT$_i$* for each treated unit i and *ATT* over data. We evaluate the *ITT$_i$* and *ATT* with our algorithm, comparing with baselines.

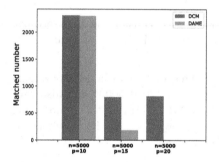

Fig. 2. No. of matched units pairs in categorical setting.

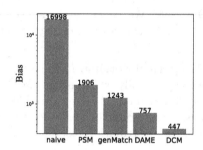

Fig. 3. Bias of ATT estimation on Lalonde dataset.

Results. We evaluate the performance of our proposed method on both ITT and ATT estimation.

Figure 1 plots the results of ITT estimation in categorical setting with $n = 5000$, $p = 15$. The MSE refers to the mean square error between the estimated and true ITT over all matched units.

DAME achieve good performance in the categorical setting. However, this method is not suitable to be extended into continuous and high-dimensional settings. To demonstrate the advantages of our methods over DAME and CEM, we also compared the number of matched unit pairs in Fig. 2, which shows that our method can consistently obtain more high-quality matched units than DAME under all settings, especially in settings with higher dimension of variables. From

Fig. 1, we conclude that our algorithms have a significant improvement over other methods on ITT estimation.

Table 1 demonstrates the results on ATT estimation in different settings, where the *Bias* refers to the absolute error between the true and estimated ATT. The *SD*, *MAE* and *RMSE* represent the standard deviations, mean absolute errors and root mean square errors of estimated ATT ($\widehat{ATT}$) after 15 times independently experiments, respectively. The smaller *Bias*, *SD*, *MAE* and *RMSE*, the better. Form Table 1, we have the similar observations and analyses that: (1) Naive methods make huge error on ATT estimation since it ignores the confounding bias in data. (2) With considering confounding bias, PSM, Gen-Match and DAME achieved better performance, but worse than our method since all of them ignore the differentiation of confounder during matching. (3) With simultaneously considering on confounder selection and differentiation, our DCM method achieved the best performance in most of settings.

Table 1. Results of ATT estimation in different settings. The "NA" represents the number of matched units is *zero*. We did not compare with DAME in continuous setting since it cannot be applied in continuous setting.

Categorical setting									
n	p	$p = 10$			$p = 15$			$p = 20$		
	Estimator	*Bias* (SD)	MAE	RMSE	*Bias* (SD)	MAE	RMSE	*Bias* (SD)	MAE	RMSE
$n = 2000$	$\widehat{ATT}_{naive}$	0.568(0.78)	0.684	0.78	0.451(1.182)	0.924	1.182	0.498(1.21)	1.017	1.21
	$\widehat{ATT}_{PSM}$	0.076(0.164)	0.143	**0.164**	0.191(0.442)	0.329	0.442	0.576(2.205)	1.906	2.205
	$\widehat{ATT}_{GenMatch}$	**0.023(0.19)**	0.152	0.19	0.185(0.442)	0.329	0.442	0.294(0.593)	0.456	0.593
	$\widehat{ATT}_{DAME}$	0.075(0.19)	0.157	0.19	0.047(0.74)	0.61	0.74	NA(NA)	NA	NA
	$\widehat{ATT}_{DCM}$	0.056(0.176)	**0.137**	0.176	**0.035(0.203)**	**0.168**	**0.203**	**0.099(0.256)**	**0.205**	**0.256**
$n = 5000$	$\widehat{ATT}_{naive}$	0.168(0.93)	0.825	0.93	0.066(1.011)	0.925	1.011	0.348(0.801)	0.68	0.801
	$\widehat{ATT}_{PSM}$	0.043(0.149)	0.113	0.149	0.02(0.311)	0.264	0.311	0.109(0.295)	0.261	0.295
	$\widehat{ATT}_{GenMatch}$	0.073(0.223)	0.159	0.223	0.023(0.31)	0.266	0.31	0.109(0.295)	0.261	0.295
	$\widehat{ATT}_{DAME}$	0.052(0.167)	0.123	0.167	0.063(0.526)	0.447	0.526	NA(NA)	NA	NA
	$\widehat{ATT}_{DCM}$	**0.027(0.128)**	**0.091**	**0.128**	**0.008(0.131)**	**0.109**	**0.131**	**0.069(0.107)**	**0.087**	**0.107**
Continuous setting									
n	p	$p = 10$			$p = 50$			$p = 100$		
	Estimator	*Bias* (SD)	MAE	RMSE	*Bias* (SD)	MAE	RMSE	*Bias* (SD)	MAE	RMSE
$n = 2000$	$\widehat{ATT}_{naive}$	0.818(2.796)	2.414	2.796	0.45(4.59)	4.299	4.59	0.306(11.406)	9.505	11.406
	$\widehat{ATT}_{PSM}$	0.371(1.268)	1.097	1.268	**0.01(3.751)**	3.366	3.751	1.615(9.2)	7.525	9.2
	$\widehat{ATT}_{GenMatch}$	0.782(1.976)	1.663	1.976	0.094(4.022)	3.623	4.022	3.22(9.397)	7.367	9.397
	$\widehat{ATT}_{DCM}$	**0.052(0.104)**	**0.085**	**0.104**	0.041(0.168)	**0.13**	**0.168**	**0.027(0.401)**	**0.251**	**0.401**
$n = 5000$	$\widehat{ATT}_{naive}$	0.103(2.748)	1.95	2.748	1.497(6.663)	5.225	6.663	2.379(10.748)	8.761	10.748
	$\widehat{ATT}_{PSM}$	0.025(0.999)	0.753	0.999	0.833(4.798)	3.608	4.798	1.938(7.769)	6.347	7.769
	$\widehat{ATT}_{GenMatch}$	0.372(1.384)	1.095	1.384	1.36(5.478)	4.737	5.478	3.007(8.537)	6.949	8.537
	$\widehat{ATT}_{DCM}$	**0.043(0.127)**	**0.076**	**0.127**	**0.18(0.467)**	**0.212**	**0.467**	**0.058(0.363)**	**0.195**	**0.363**

4.3 Experiments on Real-World Data

Dataset. We apply the algorithm to the LaLonde dataset [11], an authoritative dataset in the field of causal inference. The LaLonde dataset used in our paper consists of two parts. The first part comes from a randomized trial based on a large-scale vocational training program National Support Work Demonstration(NSW). In the second part, as in the literature, we replaced the control group with the control group obtained by CPS-1 sampling, which contains the same observed variables as in the previous experiment. In this data set, the treatment variable is whether the survey participant participated in this particular vocational training program, and the outcome variable is the survey participant's income in 1978. There are 10 raw observed variables in the data, including income and employment status, education status (years of high school education and availability), age, race, and marital status from 1974 to 1975.

We adopted the dataset analogous to [4], and replaced the control group with the control group obtained by PSID (Population Survey of Income Dynamics) sampling and evaluated the ATT on the LaLonde dataset.

Results. The result of ATT estimation of Lalonde dataset is plotted in Fig. 3. Due to the existence of confounding bias, directly compare the treated and control group even leads to a huge bias on ATT estimation. The other baseline methods effectively reduce confounding bias, however not good enough compared with our methods. Our algorithm achieve the best performance on ATT estimation.

In real applications, we can hardly know the ground truth of ITT even with randomized experiments. Hence, we cannot evaluate the performance of all algorithms in real world dataset. In future work, we will apply our work in real online recommendation system to check its advantages for interpretable individual recommendation.

5   Conclusion

In this work, we focus on how to estimate the individual and average treatment effect more precisely by interpretable matching methods. We argue that traditional matching methods do not consider the difference among confounders, leading to poor-quality matched units pair and underperformance on treatment effect estimation. Therefore, we proposed a differentiated confounder matching algorithm with theoretical guarantee for treatment effect estimation. Extensive experiments on both synthetic and real world datasets clearly demonstrate that our proposed algorithm outperforms the start-of-the-art methods in matching on both individual and average treatment effect estimation.

Acknowledgement. This work was supported in part by Zhejiang Province Natural Science Foundation (No. LQ21F020020), National Key Research and Development Program of China (No. 2018AAA0101900), National Natural Science Foundation of China (No. 62006207), and the Fundamental Research Funds for the Central Universities.

References

1. Austin, P.C.: An introduction to propensity score methods for reducing the effects of confounding in observational studies. Multivar. Behav. Res. **46**(3), 399–424 (2011)
2. Bottou, L., et al.: Counterfactual reasoning and learning systems: the example of computational advertising. J. Mach. Learn. Res. **14**(1), 3207–3260 (2013)
3. Chan, D., Ge, R., Gershony, O., Hesterberg, T., Lambert, D.: Evaluating online ad campaigns in a pipeline: causal models at scale. In: KDD, pp. 7–16 (2010)
4. Dehejia, R.H., Wahba, S.: Causal effects in nonexperimental studies: reevaluating the evaluation of training programs. J. Am. Stat. Assoc. **94**(448), 1053–1062 (1999)
5. Diamond, A., Sekhon, J.S.: Genetic matching for estimating causal effects: a general multivariate matching method for achieving balance in observational studies. Rev. Econ. Stat. **95**(3), 932–945 (2013)
6. Holland, P.W.: Statistics and causal inference. J. Am. Stat. Assoc. **81**(396), 945–960 (1986)
7. Iacus, S.M., King, G., Porro, G.: Causal inference without balance checking: coarsened exact matching. Polit. Anal. **20**(1), 1–24 (2012)
8. Imbens, G.W., Rubin, D.B.: Causal Inference in Statistics, Social, and Biomedical Sciences. Cambridge University Press, Cambridge (2015)
9. Kohavi, R., Longbotham, R.: Unexpected results in online controlled experiments. ACM SIGKDD Explor. Newsl. **12**(2), 31–35 (2011)
10. Kuang, K., Cui, P., Li, B., Jiang, M., Yang, S.: Estimating treatment effect in the wild via differentiated confounder balancing. In: Proceedings of the 23rd ACM SIGKDD International Conference on Knowledge Discovery and Data Mining, pp. 265–274. ACM (2017)
11. LaLonde, R.J.: Evaluating the econometric evaluations of training programs with experimental data. Am. Econ. Rev. 604–620 (1986)
12. Lewis, R.A., Reiley, D.: Does retail advertising work? Measuring the effects of advertising on sales via a controlled experiment on yahoo! Measuring the Effects of Advertising on Sales Via a Controlled Experiment on Yahoo (2008)
13. Liu, Y., Dieng, A., Roy, S., Rudin, C., Volfovsky, A.: Interpretable almost matching exactly for causal inference. AISTATS (2019)
14. Rosenbaum, P.R.: Imposing minimax and quantile constraints on optimal matching in observational studies. J. Comput. Graph. Stat. **26**(1), 66–78 (2017)
15. Rosenbaum, P.R., Rubin, D.B.: The central role of the propensity score in observational studies for causal effects. Biometrika **70**(1), 41–55 (1983)

End-to-End Anomaly Score Estimation for Contaminated Data via Adversarial Representation Learning

Daoming Li⬤, Jiahao Liu⬤, and Huangang Wang(✉)⬤

Department of Automation, Tsinghua University, Beijing 100084, China
{ldm18,ujiaha19}@mails.tsinghua.edu.cn, hgwang@tsinghua.edu.cn

Abstract. In recent years, deep learning has been widely used in the field of anomaly detection. Existing deep anomaly detection methods mostly focus on extracting feature representations that represent the essence of the data, then constructing anomaly detection models based on the learned representations. These indirect methods often cause the learned anomaly scores to be suboptimal. At the same time, in many real problems, the training set is usually mixed with unwanted label noise, and the model trained on the contaminated data might jeopardize detection performance. In response to the above problems, we propose a novel robust anomaly detection method for contaminated data, called ARL-RAD. ARL-RAD combines adversarial representation learning with anomaly detection, which can directly optimize the anomaly score end-to-end. Considering that there are anomalies in the training set, ARL-RAD leverages an autoencoder and a discriminator to achieve essential information preservation and prior distribution constraints in the latent space based on the adversarial training mechanism. Furthermore, ARL-RAD proposes a pseudo label adjusting strategy, which dynamically updates pseudo labels during the training phase by the probabilistic description and geometric structure of input data. To enhance the robustness of the model to contaminated data, the inputs with pseudo labels can be used as supervision information to train the anomaly score estimator, and the anomaly score can be optimized directly. The experimental results on four benchmark data sets can verify that the proposed method obtains better anomaly detection results and is more robust to contaminated data.

Keywords: Robust anomaly detection · Adversarial representation learning · End-to-End

1 Introduction

Anomaly detection is often considered to find data targets that are inconsistent with the majority of data [1]. Anomaly detection is a research hotspot in the

Supported by National Science and Technology Innovation 2030 Major Project (2018AAA0101604) of the Ministry of Science and Technology of China.

field of data mining, and currently has applications in many fields. It is often difficult to obtain a large number of labeled anomaly samples when training anomaly detection models in practice. Therefore, the anomaly detection task is often assumed to learn the pattern of normal data distribution under the premise that only normal samples are obtained, and an anomaly score function is designed to measure the degree of deviation of the test data from the normal pattern. This view of unsupervised learning makes anomaly detection methods pay more attention to learning meaningful feature representations from input data. In recent years, deep learning [2] has been widely used in the mining of complex and high-dimensional data under its advantages such as layer-by-layer abstraction, end-to-end modeling, and features self-learning. The representations of input data learned by neural networks can preserve the essential structure, and then provide meaningful semantic information for downstream tasks.

The existing anomaly detection methods based on deep learning [3] mostly focus on exploring the advantages of neural networks to learn feature representations of input data, and the learned representations are leveraged to construct anomaly detection models. Autoencoders (AEs) are the basis of many deep anomaly detection methods. By minimizing the mean square error between the input data and the reconstruction, it can learn essential representations from input data. At the same time, the reconstruction error can be taken as an anomaly score. However, these methods that use the learned representations to design anomaly scores indirectly are often irrelevant to anomaly detection tasks, and the learned features may be suboptimal [4]. Therefore, some methods [5,6] integrated the traditional anomaly detection targets into representation learning to improve the expression ability of the neural network on anomaly detection tasks. For example, [5] proposed a Deep SVDD method, which trains the encoder to bring the representation of each training sample close to the center of all representations in latent space, to provide semantic information for anomaly detection by compacting the representations of normal data. However, the above methods often aim at optimizing feature representation and do not directly learn anomaly scores, which will cause inefficiency and instability of the anomaly detection model [7].

It is worth noting that in practice, the training set for anomaly detection often fails to satisfy the assumption that only normal samples are included. The training set might be contaminated due to the presence of noise in the labels, which means it not only contains normal samples, but also a small number of anomaly samples. If the model learns rashly on the contaminated training set, the ability to describe the distribution of normal data will be affected, which causing impairing the effect of anomaly detection. [8] found that continuous training of the autoencoder on the contaminated training set will reduce the reconstruction error of anomaly samples, so the reconstruction error cannot be used to accurately measure the difference between normal samples and anomaly samples. Therefore, when facing contaminated data, it is necessary to consider enhancing the robustness of the model for anomaly detection.

To solve the above problems, we aim to find a flexible and robust method that can not only use deep learning technologies to learn meaningful feature representations in contaminated data scenarios but also directly estimate anomaly scores to detect anomalies. Generative adversarial networks (GANs) [9] are deep generative models that have attracted much attention in recent years, which have been gradually applied to anomaly detection under their superior learning ability on complex data distribution [10]. Here, we propose adversarial representation learning (ARL), which refers to construct feature representation models to automatically obtain meaningful representations from input data based on the GAN architecture. ARL can integrate different neural network modules (such as encoders). Using adversarial representation learning methods, we can mine the semantic information contained in the latent representation of contaminated data, and flexibly design an anomaly score estimator to achieve direct optimization of the anomaly score.

Specifically, we propose an Adversarial Representation Learning-based method for Robust Anomaly Detection, which is called ARL-RAD. Given a contaminated training set, ARL-RAD can use an autoencoder and a discriminator to learn the mapping from the original input space to the low-dimensional latent space based on the adversarial representation learning method. Besides, ARL-RAD imposes a prior probability distribution in the latent space to constrain the location of latent representations and describes the distribution of the input data from a probabilistic perspective. To reduce the negative impact of anomalies in the training set on the detection performance, a pseudo label adjusting strategy is proposed based on the probabilistic description and geometric structure, which dynamically updates pseudo labels during the training phase. Combining adversarial representation learning and anomaly detection, we use pseudo-labeled data to train the designed anomaly score estimator to achieve end-to-end optimization of the anomaly score.

The rest of this paper is organized as follows. In Sect. 2, we discuss related works on adversarial representation learning and robust anomaly detection. In Sect. 3, ARL-RAD is introduced in detail. The experimental results and discussion are given in Sect. 4. Finally, we conclude in Sect. 5.

2   Related Work

2.1   Adversarial Representation Learning

Generative adversarial networks (GANs), as representative deep generative models, have shown great potential in the application of representation learning. GAN treats the problem of learning data distribution as a zero-sum game, and it learns complex data distributions by the adversarial training mechanism. In order to apply the ability to learn the complex data distribution to representation learning, some methods [11,12] propose to introduce the neural network modules (such encoders) into the GAN architecture and design the mapping relationship between the generator and the encoder, which can help learn the feature representation from the original space to the latent space. This kind of representation learning method based on the GAN architecture, namely adversarial representation learning (ARL) in this paper, can make full use of GAN's ability to mine high-level semantic information in the data. By integrating a variety of neural network modules to realize the flexible design of feature representation models, ARL can be used in different application scenarios. The proposition of ARL not only injects fresh development momentum into the field of representation learning, but also motivates more researchers to study anomaly detection problems.

2.2   Robust Anomaly Detection

It is a challenging task to establish a robust anomaly detection model on the contaminated training set. The existing research ideas can be divided into two categories. The first focuses on building a model that is robust to noise, which is dedicated to designing more robust algorithms without changing the original data set to reduce the negative effects of label noise, such as choosing more robust loss functions [13] and transforming feature extraction models [14]. The second argues the modeling of pseudo label prediction, which aims to assign pseudo labels to all training samples by designing a label prediction function. In this way, the training set is divided into a suspected normal set and a suspected abnormal set, and we can eliminate or adjust incorrectly labeled samples in the training set. The modeling of pseudo label prediction has better applicability, because it can be completed before the model training, or dynamically performed during the training phase.

Our method combines adversarial representation learning and anomaly detection, and the pseudo-label prediction is embedded into the optimization process of the anomaly score. By dividing latent representations of the training samples into suspected normal and suspected abnormal during the training phase, we achieve an end-to-end approach to directly learn the anomaly score.

3   Proposed Methods

3.1   Problem Formulation

We propose a novel robust anomaly detection method for contaminated data, called ARL-RAD. Compared with methods that aim to optimize feature representations, ARL-RAD focuses on directly optimize anomaly scores using pseudo-labeled data, and strives to make suspected anomaly samples have higher scores than suspected normal samples. By combining adversarial representation learning with anomaly detection, the model is expected to obtain more generalized anomaly scores while improving the efficiency of data set utilization.

Specifically, given the training set $X = \{x^1, ..., x^N\}$, where $x^i \in R^{d_x}$, $i \in \{1, ..., N\}$. Define the mapping function $\phi : R^{d_x} \mapsto R^{d_z} (d_z \ll d_x)$, which represents the mapping from the original space to the latent space. Given x^i, its latent representation is $z^i = \phi(x^i)$. Although robust anomaly detection is essentially unsupervised, we consider the label noise in the training set and define a pseudo label set $Y = \{y^1, ..., y^N\}$, where $y^i \in \{y_+, y_-\}$. y_+ indicates that the data is suspected as normal, and y_- indicates that the data is suspected as abnormal. Our goal is to learn an end-to-end anomaly score function $f : R^{d_z} \mapsto R$ for a specific anomaly detection task. The anomaly score function ensures that normal samples and anomaly samples can be easily distinguished in the latent space. In the training phase, if the pseudo label of x^i is $y^i = y_-$ and the pseudo label of x^j is $y^i = y_+$, we expect $f(\phi(x^i)) > f(\phi(x^j))$. In the testing phase, given the test sample x^{new}, we directly obtain its anomaly score $f(\phi(x^{new}))$ to measure the degree of deviation from the description of normal data.

3.2   ARL-RAD

The framework of ARL-RAD is shown in Fig. 1. In this paper, the Adversarial Autoencoder (AAE) [15] is taken as the network backbone, which is one of the representatives of adversarial representation learning. By introducing the encoder module into the generative discriminative network, any prior distribution can be imposed to the latent space based on the adversarial training mechanism, so as to mine the semantic information from input data. ARL-RAD includes an encoder E, a decoder De, a discriminator D, and a specially designed anomaly score estimator f. The output of f can be directly used as the anomaly score.

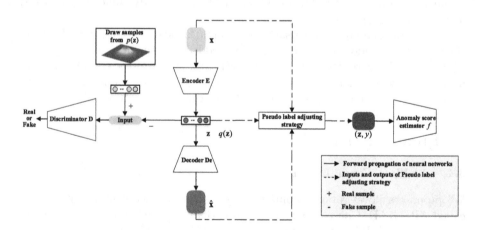

Fig. 1. Framework of ARL-RAD

Considering that a robust anomaly detection task assumes that we can't obtain the label information in the training set, we construct an autoencoder (AE) network to obtain the latent representation of the input data. The AE is composed of the encoder E and the decoder De. Given the input data x, the encoder E can output its representation $z = E(x)$ in the latent space, and the decoder De receives z and outputs the corresponding reconstructed $\hat{x} = De(z)$. By minimizing the mean square error of input samples and reconstructed samples, the AE can be trained. Let the data distribution is $p_d(x)$, and the reconstruction loss is shown as follows

$$l_{re} = E_{x \sim p_d(x)} \|x - \hat{x}\|_2^2. \tag{1}$$

As shown in Fig. 1, the latent representation z of the encoder output is not only used to preserve the essential information of the input data, but also expected to describe the distribution of the input data in the latent space from the perspective of probability. Specifically, when the latent space of input data is constrained by a prior probability distribution, latent representations of normal data and anomaly data can be located in different probability density regions. The representation of normal data is generally located in the high probability region, while the representation of anomaly data is located in the low probability region.

To achieve this purpose, we set the discriminator D in the latent space based on the adversarial representation learning method, which forms the AAE network with the encoder E and the decoder De. A priori probability distribution is imposed on the latent space. Let the standard Gaussian distribution $p(z) = N(0, I)$ as a prior distribution, which is generally suitable for describing the latent representation distribution of the data set. The aggregate posterior distribution of encoder output is $q(z) = \int_x q(z|x)p_d(x)dx$, where $q(z|x)$ is the encoding distribution. To deceive the discriminator D, the encoder E can be regarded as a generator to optimize the latent representation to obey the prior distribution. D is required to distinguish the false samples of encoder output from the real samples of the prior distribution. In the training phase, the encoder E and the discriminator D are trained alternately, and the distribution of input data in the latent space is gradually approaching the prior probability distribution. Therefore, the adversarial loss can be described as follows:

$$l_{adv} = E_{z \sim p(z)} \log(D(z)) + E_{z \sim q(z)} \log(1 - D(z)). \tag{2}$$

Based on the pseudo label adjusting strategy to be introduced in Sect. 3.3, the anomaly score estimator f can be trained by receiving the data with pseudo labels as supervised information. Specifically, we can obtain the latent representation of $z = E(x)$ and pseudo label y of given input x before optimizing the anomaly score. The anomaly score estimator f can receive z as input and output the anomaly score $f(z)$ in the training phase. Under the condition of given pseudo labels, the loss function of the two classification tasks can be applied to the training of the network f. To ensure that the anomaly score estimator f can give the sample with the suspected normal class lower output, and give the sample with the suspected abnormal class higher output, Hinge loss [16] is selected as the loss function. In this paper, we call the loss function of the network f as estimation loss, which can be defined as follows:

$$l_e = E_{x \sim p_d(x), y=y_-} \max(0, 1 - f(E(x))) + E_{x \sim p_d(x), y=y_+} \max(0, 1 + f(E(x))). \tag{3}$$

Under the proposed ARL-RAD framework, a total loss function as follows:

$$l_{total} = l_{re} + \alpha_0 l_{adv} + \alpha_1 l_e, \tag{4}$$

where α_0 and α_1 are the trade-off coefficients. We can optimize different network modules by alternating iterative training method until Eq. (4) converges.

3.3   Pseudo Label Adjusting Strategy

To improve the robustness of the model to contaminated data, we propose to predict the pseudo label of each sample based on the pseudo label adjusting strategy in the training phase, and the training set can be dynamically divided into a suspected normal set and a suspected abnormal set.

Due to the role of adversarial representation learning, the latent space is constrained by the standard Gaussian distribution. Therefore, the positional relationship between the latent representation of the input data and the origin of the latent space affects the possibility of belonging to the normal class [17]. We define the following normal class membership function:

$$\mu(\boldsymbol{x}) = e^{-\frac{E(\boldsymbol{x})^T E(\boldsymbol{x})}{r}}, \tag{5}$$

where r is the flat coefficient, which controls the influence of the position change of the latent representation to the origin on the degree of membership, $0 < \mu(\boldsymbol{x}) \leq 1$. The closer the latent representation of the training sample is to the origin, the closer the membership degree of the corresponding normal class is to 1. At the same time, it can be considered that the latent representation is in the high probability area, and the corresponding sample is more likely to belong to the normal class [17]. Therefore, the normal class membership function can be used for label evaluation from the perspective of probability.

Besides, the reconstruction error is also applied to the design of the label evaluation function. When the training set is contaminated, [8] found that in the early phase of training, reconstruction errors of normal samples are smaller than those of anomaly samples. However, in the later phase of training, the reconstruction error will lose the ability to distinguish between normal samples and anomaly samples. Therefore, the reconstruction error can guide the discovery of suspected anomalies in the early phase of training, and provide a basis for pseudo-label prediction from the perspective of geometric structure. Given the training set $X = \{\boldsymbol{x}^1, ..., \boldsymbol{x}^N\}$, we calculate the error $r(\boldsymbol{x}) = \|\boldsymbol{x} - \hat{\boldsymbol{x}}\|_2^2$ between each sample $\boldsymbol{x}$ and its reconstructed sample $\hat{\boldsymbol{x}}$. The smaller $r(\boldsymbol{x})$, the more likely the sample belongs to the normal class. The inverse normalized reconstruction error can be defined as follows:

$$\bar{r}(\boldsymbol{x}) = \frac{\max_{\boldsymbol{x}^i \in X}(r(\boldsymbol{x}^i)) - r(\boldsymbol{x})}{\max_{\boldsymbol{x}^i \in X}(r(\boldsymbol{x}^i)) - \min_{\boldsymbol{x}^i \in X}(r(\boldsymbol{x}^i))}, \tag{6}$$

where $\bar{r}(\boldsymbol{x})$ represents mapping reconstruction errors to [0,1], and the closer $\bar{r}(\boldsymbol{x})$ is to 1, the more normal the sample $\boldsymbol{x}$ is.

Based on the above analysis, the label evaluation function can be formulated as

$$t(\boldsymbol{x}) = \lambda \bar{r}(\boldsymbol{x}) + (1 - \lambda)\mu(\boldsymbol{x}), \tag{7}$$

where $\lambda \in [0, 1]$ is the trade-off coefficient of the two label evaluation functions, $0 \le t(\boldsymbol{x}) \le 1$. The label evaluation value set of the training set is $T = \{t(\boldsymbol{x}^1), ..., t(\boldsymbol{x}^N)\}$. The closer $t(\boldsymbol{x})$ is to 1, the more likely it is that the sample belongs to the normal class. We let the contamination rate be the proportion of anomaly data in the training set. Based on the given contamination rate $\beta\%$, through the distribution of the label evaluation value on the training set, the discrimination threshold T_y of the pseudo label can be obtained. Specifically, the discrimination threshold is usually defined as such that the label evaluation values corresponding to the samples with the proportion of $\beta\%$ in the training set are all less than the threshold, that is, $T_y = \beta\%$ quantile of $\{t(\boldsymbol{x})|\boldsymbol{x} \in X\}$. Given a sample $\boldsymbol{x}$, the pseudo label can be judged based on its label evaluation value $t(\boldsymbol{x})$ relative to T_y. If $t(\boldsymbol{x}) > T_y$, then $y = y_+$; if $t(\boldsymbol{x}) <= T_y$, then $y = y_-$. In the initial phase of training, the pseudo labels of samples are defined as the normal class.

The pseudo label adjusting strategy can help to reduce the negative impact of the mixed anomalies in the training set on the performance of the model. On the one hand, the anomaly score can be optimized end-to-end and more suitable for specific tasks. On the other hand, the representation of encoder output can be improved better, and drive the supervised information to be constantly adjusted in the iterative.

4   Experiments

4.1   Datasets and Evaluation Metrics

We select four benchmark data sets to verify the effectiveness of the proposed method. All data sets are from the odds database [18]. The details of each dataset are shown in Table 1, and the names of some datasets are represented by abbreviations in brackets. In each group of experiments, the training set includes 80% normal samples randomly selected from normal data and a specified number of anomaly samples randomly selected from anomaly data based on a given contamination rate. For the design of the test set, we compare the number of the remaining normal samples and the number of the remaining anomaly samples. All the samples of the corresponding category with a smaller number are included in the test set, and the same number of samples are randomly selected from another class to be included in the test set. Through the above operations, we can ensure that the number of normal class samples in the test set is equal to the number of anomaly class samples, and improve the utilization of the data set as much as possible.

We select the area under receiver operating characteristic curve (ROC-AUC) and the average precision (AP) to evaluate the detection performance. The ROC-AUC and AP reported are the average results of 10 independent runs.

Table 1. Data statistics

Data	Size	D	Anomaly Percents(%)
Arrhythmia(Arr.)	452	274	14.602
Breastw(Bre.)	683	9	34.993
Pima	768	8	34.896
Satellite(Sat.)	6435	36	31.640

4.2 Parameter Settings and Competing Methods

We use multilayer perceptrons to build the networks of ARL-RAD. Specifically, the middle layer of encoder E, decoder De, discriminator D and anomaly score estimator f use LeakyReLU activation function with a negative slope of 0.01. The output layer of encoder E and anomaly score estimator f have no activation function, while the output layer of decoder De and discriminator D use Sigmoid activation function. In the setting of hyper parameters, $r = 100$, $\lambda = 0.6$, $\alpha_0 = 1$ and $\alpha_1 = 1$. Moreover, the encoder output dimension of each experiment is set to 6 to achieve low dimensional compression.

For each group of experiments, the training process is set to 1000 epochs, and the batch size of each epoch is 128. Each training set is normalized to $[0,1]$, and the test set is transformed according to the corresponding normalization operation. Adam optimizer [19] is used in all experiments, and the learning rate of encoder E and decoder De is set to 0.0004, the learning rate of discriminator D and anomaly score estimator f is set to 0.0002.

We select a series of popular methods as baselines to compare with ARL-RAD, including traditional methods and deep learning-based methods. Traditional methods, including OCSVM [20], IForest [21] and LOF [22], are implemented by using the PyOD library [23], and default parameters are used in experiments. The deep learning-based methods, including AE and AAE, are implemented with the same network structure and training method as ARL-RAD, and their reconstruction errors are taken as anomaly scores.

4.3 Experimental Results

We evaluate the robust detection performance on Sat. data sets with different contamination rates. The contamination rate of Sat. data set is selected from $\{10\%, 15\%, 20\%, 25\%, 30\%\}$, and the corresponding training set and test set are built according to the design idea in Sect. 4.1. Figure 2 shows the ROC-AUC and AP of each method on Sat. data sets under different contamination rates. We can find that ARL-RAD has better detection performance than other methods under different contamination rates. It is worth noting that the evaluation value of ARL-RAD can always be greater than 0.70. These results show that the proposed method can better reduce the negative impact of the contaminated training set, and has a more stable detection effect.

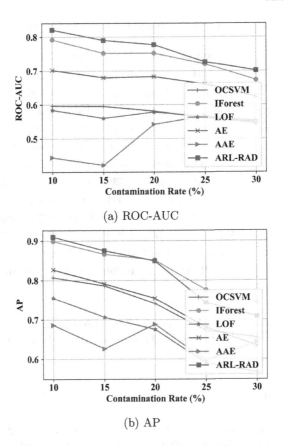

(a) ROC-AUC

(b) AP

Fig. 2. Comparison of detection performance on Sat. data sets with different contamination rates.

We compared the detection results of all methods on each data set with a 10% contamination rate. Table 2 shows the detection results based on ROC-AUC and AP. In this paper, "Avg." represents the average value, and the elements marked black in each line represent the best detection result. It is worth noting that the proposed ARL-RAD outperforms all the compared methods in seven of the eight comparisons, and the best results are obtained in both average values. Table 2 shows that ARL-RAD is effective in robust anomaly detection and competitive compared with other comparison methods. In these experiments, OCSVM, IForest, and LOF can accept the prior contamination rate, and use their respective algorithms to reduce the negative impact of the contaminated training set. However, the detection result of the ARL-RAD method is generally higher than them, which shows that the proposed pseudo label adjusting strategy is effective. Compared with the detection results of AE and AAE, ARL-RAD achieves better detection results by directly optimizing the anomaly score end-to-end, which indicates that it may be more suitable for anomaly detection tasks

Table 2. Evaluation metrics comparisons between the baselines and ARL-RAD.

Metric	Method	Arr.	Bre.	Pima	Sat.	Avg.
ROC-AUC	OCSVM	0.731	0.602	0.599	0.596	0.632
	IForest	0.731	0.994	0.678	0.792	0.799
	LOF	0.745	0.578	0.631	0.584	0.634
	AE	0.744	0.978	0.622	0.702	0.762
	AAE	0.781	0.096	0.363	0.444	0.421
	ARL-RAD	**0.800**	**0.999**	**0.724**	**0.821**	**0.836**
AP	OCSVM	0.687	0.739	0.600	0.807	0.708
	IForest	0.720	0.994	0.672	0.899	0.821
	LOF	0.706	0.524	0.618	0.755	0.651
	AE	0.705	0.970	0.621	0.827	0.781
	AAE	**0.814**	0.337	0.413	0.686	0.563
	ARL-RAD	0.806	**0.999**	**0.691**	**0.910**	**0.852**

to learn the anomaly score rather than feature representation directly. Therefore, we prove that the proposed ARL-RAD is effective and has better performance than the existing methods.

5   Conclusion

This paper proposes a novel robust anomaly detection method ARL-RAD for contaminated data, which combines adversarial representation learning and anomaly detection to achieve end-to-end learning. To enhance the robustness against data contamination, a pseudo label adjusting strategy based on probability description and geometric structure is proposed, which can dynamically update pseudo labels during the training phase. A series of experiments proved that the proposed ARL-RAD can obtain better detection results. For future work, exploring the application of adversarial representation learning in other areas of anomaly detection is interesting.

References

1. Chandola, V., Banerjee, A., Kumar, V.: Anomaly detection: a survey. ACM Comput. Surv. (CSUR) **41**(3), 1–58 (2009)
2. LeCun, Y., Bengio, Y., Hinton, G.: Deep learning. Nature **521**(7553), 436–444 (2015)
3. Pang, G., Shen, C., Cao, L., et al.: Deep learning for anomaly detection: a review. arXiv preprint arXiv:2007.02500 (2020)
4. Pang, G., Shen, C., van den Hengel, A.: Deep anomaly detection with deviation networks. In: Proceedings of the 25th ACM SIGKDD International Conference on Knowledge Discovery & Data Mining, pp. 353–362 (2019)

5. Ruff, L., Vandermeulen, R., Goernitz, N., et al.: Deep one-class classification. In: International Conference on Machine Learning, pp. 4393–4402. PMLR (2018)

6. Wu, P., Liu, J., Shen, F.: A deep one-class neural network for anomalous event detection in complex scenes. IEEE Trans. Neural Netw. Learn. Syst. **31**(7), 2609–2622 (2019)

7. Pang, G., Cao, L., Chen, L., et al.: Learning representations of ultrahigh-dimensional data for random distance-based outlier detection. In: Proceedings of the 24th ACM SIGKDD International Conference on Knowledge Discovery & Data Mining, pp. 2041–2050 (2018)

8. Beggel, L., Pfeiffer, M., Bischl, B.: Robust anomaly detection in images using adversarial autoencoders. In: Joint European Conference on Machine Learning and Knowledge Discovery in Databases, pp. 206–222 (2019)

9. Goodfellow, I.J., Pouget-Abadie, J., Mirza, M., et al.: Generative adversarial nets. In: Advances in Neural Information Processing Systems, pp. 2672–2680 (2014)

10. Perera, P., Nallapati, R., Xiang, B.: OCGAN: one-class novelty detection using GANs with constrained latent representations. In: Proceedings of the IEEE/CVF Conference on Computer Vision and Pattern Recognition, pp. 2898–2906 (2019)

11. Donahue, J., Krähenbühl, P., Darrell, T.: Adversarial feature learning. arXiv preprint arXiv:1605.09782 (2016)

12. Donahue, J., Simonyan, K.: Large scale adversarial representation learning. In: Advances in Neural Information Processing Systems, pp. 10542–10552 (2019)

13. Wang, Y., Ma, X., Chen, Z., et al.: Symmetric cross entropy for robust learning with noisy labels. In: Proceedings of the IEEE/CVF International Conference on Computer Vision, pp. 322–330 (2019)

14. Gao, Y., Shi, B., Dong, B., et al.: RVAE-ABFA: robust anomaly detection for high dimensional data using variational autoencoder. In: 2020 IEEE 44th Annual Computers, Software, and Applications Conference, pp. 334–339. IEEE (2020)

15. Makhzani, A., Shlens, J., Jaitly, N., et al.: Adversarial autoencoders. arXiv preprint arXiv:1511.05644 (2015)

16. Lim, J.H., Ye, J.C.: Geometric GAN. arXiv preprint arXiv:1705.02894 (2017)

17. Cao, V.L., Nicolau, M., McDermott, J.: Learning neural representations for network anomaly detection. IEEE Trans. Cybern. **49**(8), 3074–3087 (2018)

18. Rayana, S.: ODDS library (2016). http://odds.cs.stonybrook

19. Kingma, D.P., Ba, J.: Adam: a method for stochastic optimization. arXiv preprint arXiv:1412.6980 (2014)

20. Schölkopf, B., Platt, J.C., Shawe-Taylor, J., et al.: Estimating the support of a high-dimensional distribution. Neural Comput. **13**(7), 1443–1471 (2001)

21. Liu, F.T., Ting, K.M., Zhou, Z.H.: Isolation forest. In: 2008 Eighth IEEE International Conference on Data Mining, pp. 413–422. IEEE (2008)

22. Breunig, M.M., Kriegel, H.P., Ng, R.T., et al.: LOF: identifying density-based local outliers. In: Proceedings of the 2000 ACM SIGMOD International Conference on Management of Data, pp. 93–104 (2000)

23. Zhao, Y., Nasrullah, Z., Li, Z.: PyOD: a python toolbox for scalable outlier detection. J. Mach. Learn. Res. **20**(96), 1–7 (2019)

Legal Judgment Prediction with Multiple Perspectives on Civil Cases

Lili Zhao, Linan Yue, Yanqing An, Ye Liu, Kai Zhang, Weidong He,
Yanmin Chen, Senchao Yuan, and Qi Liu[✉]

Anhui Province Key Laboratory of Big Data Analysis and Application, School of
Data Science and School of Computer Science and Technology, University of Science
and Technology of China, Hefei, China
{liliz,lnyue,anyq,liuyer,sa517494,hwd,ymchen16,yuansc}@mail.ustc.edu.cn,
qiliuql@ustc.edu.cn

Abstract. Legal Judgment Prediction, which aims at predicting the
judgment result based on case materials, is an essential task in Legal
Intelligence. Most existing studies have analyzed and modeled criminal
cases as a whole, while a small part of the research focuses on civil cases
which are also significant in the legal system. In these studies, most model
on a certain type of civil causes and make the judgment prediction based
on the ascertained fact from the perspective of the court. However, in
real-world scenarios, there are different civil cases on various causes, and
every case is judged from multiple perspectives (i.e., plaintiff, defendant,
and the court). It is difficult to make judgment predictions on various
civil causes. To address the above challenges, in this paper, we propose
a novel Civil Case Judgment (CCJudge) prediction method by simulating the logic of judges. Following this logic, we construct an external
knowledge base that contains the explanations and applications of every
cause, it helps make the judgment on various causes. Furthermore, a special encoder layer and interaction layer are designed for learning linguistic
semantics from multiple perspectives. We conduct extensive experiments
on a real-world dataset. The experimental results demonstrate the effectiveness of our method.

1 Introduction

Legal Judgment Prediction (**LJP**) has been a critical research topic and a challenging problem in the legal field, aiming to predict the judgment results of legal
cases. LJP could not only reduce heavy and redundant work for legal professionals but also provide reliable references for the masses who are unfamiliar
with the laws [1,26,28]. In recent years, many efforts [3,12,23,27] and datasets
[2,6,21] have been proposed to promote the development of LJP. However, most
of them pay more attention to make judgment predictions on criminal cases and
neglect civil ones which are equally essential in the legal system.

The judgment prediction on a civil case is mainly to support or reject the
pleas of the plaintiff. Figure 1 illustrates the six steps when a judge handles a

© Springer Nature Switzerland AG 2021
L. Fang et al. (Eds.): CICAI 2021, LNAI 13069, pp. 712–723, 2021.
https://doi.org/10.1007/978-3-030-93046-2_60

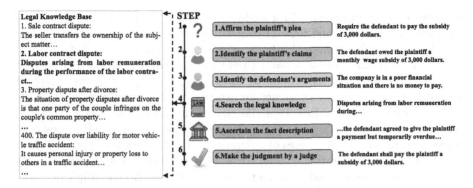

Fig. 1. An example of concerning a labor contract dispute.

civil case. In this example, the *defendant* is a company and the *plaintiff* used to work there. Specifically, the *judge* first affirms that the plaintiff pleas the court to order the defendant to return the money (step 1). Subsequently, the judge identifies the case statements by the plaintiff and defendant respectively. In detail, the judge confirms the claims of the plaintiff where the defendant owes the plaintiff a month's salary and never returns (step 2). And the judge identifies the arguments of the defendant where the company is in a poor financial situation and unable to afford it (step 3). Then, the judge considers all with the relevant legal knowledge (step 4) and ascertains the fact through the trial (step 5). Finally, the judgment is determined on the plea of the plaintiff that the defendant should return the money (step 6).

In the literature, some studies have been proposed for civil case judgment prediction. They focused on a specific type of civil cases (e.g., the divorce cases [11] and the private lending ones [20]), and made the judgment prediction based on the ascertained fact. Although these methods have achieved some effects, they still suffer from the limitations on two major challenges as detailed below:

First, as shown in the left part of Fig. 1, there exist more than 400 causes[1] (i.e., types of civil cases) during the actual trial. Different causes vary widely such as the labor contract cause and the divorce one. It is challenging that how to handle various causes in a unified framework. Besides, there exist many elements from multiple perspectives, which complicate the judgment prediction on civil cases. Specifically, as the actual trial is shown in Fig. 1, the judgment of a civil case should consider the ascertained fact from the perspective of the court, the claims and pleas from the perspective of the plaintiff, and the arguments from the defendant. It is difficult for civil case judgment prediction to model the multi-perspective elements.

In real-world scenarios, the human judges can handle different civil cases on various causes and take all legal elements into consideration to make the final judgment. Thus, learning to simulate the logic of judges in our structure will help

---

[1] http://www.court.gov.cn/fabu-xiangqing-282031.html.

to solve the above problems. In a well-known book [30], the author elaborates the judicial experience and logic of judges in the trial. We summarize the logic of judges into six steps from this book, which have been discussed before.

Accordingly, we propose a novel Civil Case Judgment method (denoted by CCJudge) for judgment prediction by integrating the logic of judges. Inspired by the logic of judges, we construct an external legal knowledge base for dealing with various causes. Based on the claims and arguments, we extract the relevant knowledge which contains the legal explanations and applications that correspond to the specific causes of different cases and adopt the knowledge into our method. The integrating of prior knowledge could help us to handle various causes well. Besides, CCJudge interacts with the elements from multiple perspectives and predicts the final judgment result in a logical order where a judge deals with a civil case. Specifically, it adopts self-attention [17] and co-attention [22] mechanisms to obtain more information from multiple perspectives. First, the claims and arguments are connected with the fact respectively for considering all perspectives. Subsequently, the plea is integrated into connected elements to capture relationships among them for final judgment. For experiments, we collect and construct a real-world dataset that contains 123,084 civil cases. And the experimental results show the effectiveness of our method CCJudge.

2   Related Work

With the development of legalAI and inspired by the success of neural networks [8,18]. A lot of studies [19,25] have been proposed for LJP. In this section, we review the legal judgment prediction on criminal cases and civil cases.

LJP on Criminal Cases. Recent research pays much attention to LJP on criminal cases. Luo et al. [12] presented a network to extract the relevant law articles for predicting charges of criminal cases. Except for the prediction of charges [7], Chen et al. [3] proposed the task of charge-based prison terms prediction. Simultaneously, some researchers [23,24,27] studied multi-task learning which contains three subtasks as the predictions on charges, law articles, and terms of penalty. Extensive studies have been succeeded for LJP on criminal cases.

LJP on Civil Cases. In addition to criminal cases, some studies concentrate on civil cases. Long et al. [11] proposed a legal reading comprehension framework and incorporated law articles to make judgment predictions on a divorce dataset. Zhou et al. [29] found that e-commerce dispute cases could be judged not only by the fact of the current transaction, but also the historical transaction dispute records of the target sellers and buyers, and designed a multiview dispute representation technique for e-commerce lawsuit judgment prediction. Wu et al. [20] mainly studied for court's view generation with a claim-aware encoder for synergistic judgment prediction on a private lending dataset. However, they all focused on a particular civil cause. The LJP for civil cases on various causes has not been studied up to now. In this paper, we try to make up for that.

3   Problem Definition

Table 1. The main mathematical notations.

Symbol	Description
$s^c = \left\{ w_1^c, \ldots, w_{l_c}^c \right\}$	A word sequence of a plaintiff's claims
$s^a = \left\{ w_1^a, \ldots, w_{l_a}^a \right\}$	A word sequence of a defendant's arguments
$s^f = \left\{ w_1^f, \ldots, w_{l_f}^f \right\}$	A word sequence of the ascertained fact
$s^p = \left\{ w_1^p, \ldots, w_{l_p}^p \right\}$	A word sequence of a plaintiff's first plea
$D = \{ d_1, \ldots, d_k \}$	The k pieces of knowledge from the knowledge base
$d_i = \left\{ w_1^{d_i}, \ldots, w_{l_{d_i}}^{d_i} \right\}$	A word sequence of the i-th knowledge
$Y = \{0, 1\}$	The judgment label on the plaintiff's first plea

In this section, we focus on the problem of civil case judgment prediction. First, we formulate the problem as a binary classification task. In Table 1, we list the main mathematical notations about the input and the output. Specifically, given the claims s^c, the arguments s^a, the fact s^f, and the top k knowledge we get from the legal knowledge base, our goal is to learn a classifier ξ which is able to get the judgment result with label 0 or 1 on the plaintiff's first plea s^p (i.e., $\{y\} \Leftarrow \xi \left(s^c, s^a, s^f, s^p, D \right)$). Among them, 0 means the rejection, 1 means the support. Taking the civil case in Fig. 1 for an example, our classifier ξ aims to predict the result with label 1 which indicates the plea is supported.

In this paper, we only consider the first plea s^p because plaintiffs always put the most important plea first, and it could be obtained easily by regular expressions. The prediction of other pleas will leave for future work.

4   Model

In this section, we first introduce the logic of judges in dealing with civil cases and how that logic is reflected in our framework. Then, we describe our CCJudge via exploiting external knowledge from multiple perspectives in detail. Figure 2 shows the overall framework which consists of a legal knowledge extractor, an encoder layer, an interaction layer, and the final predictor one.

4.1   The Logical Judgment in Dealing with Civil Cases

As discussed before, simulating the logic of judges in our framework could help us to address the challenges in civil case judgment prediction. Specifically, the logic we adopted is based on the book **"The Nine Steps of Trial of Essential Items"** [30].

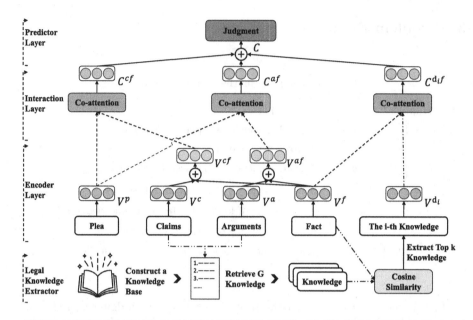

Fig. 2. The architecture of the CCJudge.

The book describes the mindset of a human judge, breaking down the process of dealing with **civil cases** and making judgment documents into nine steps. On account that we make the judgment prediction on the text analysis of legal judgment documents, some steps for making judgment documents are filtered out, and we summarize the nine steps on dealing with civil cases into six steps. As shown in Fig. 1, the six steps respectively represent the search, confirmation, and analysis of elements by the judge during the trial of the civil case. We construct an external knowledge base for searching the legal points. The confirmation is mapped in the encoder layer. The final judgment is obtained through rigorous analysis, the interaction and predictor layer correspond to that.

4.2   Legal Knowledge Extraction

Following the logic of judges, the relevant legal knowledge which contains the explanations and applications of each cause helps to make judgments on different cases. To better model civil cases on various causes, we construct a knowledge base as depicted in the left part of Fig. 1 according to the work [14], the relevant legal knowledge is retrieved from the base.

For searching the relevant legal knowledge, we first tokenize claims s^c and arguments s^a, and put them into the elasticsearch[2] to retrieve the relevant G pieces of knowledge, respectively. Then, we transform each word of s^f and each knowledge d_i into their word embeddings. The word embedding sequences are

---

[2] https://www.elastic.co/.

defined as E^f and E^{d_i} respectively. Next, we compute the cosine similarity of each word on e_i^f with $e_i^{d_i}$ to re-rank the retrieved knowledge. The k highest-ranked pieces of knowledge are stored to form a candidate set. Every piece of knowledge is encoded sharing the same manipulation in Sect. 4.3, which is put into the encoder and generate the vector representation $V^{d_i} = \left\{ v_1^{d_i}, \ldots, v_{l_{d_i}}^{d_i} \right\} \in \mathbb{R}^{l_{d_i} \times d_s}$.

4.3   Encoder Layer

After obtaining the legal knowledge to assist the judgment, the judge needs to confirm the claims, arguments, fact, and legal knowledge in a case. We need an encoder to capture the information among them adequately.

A prominent type of encoder is the recurrent neural network (RNN) which is often used in LJP [7,10]. In order to capture more information among so many elements, we adopt the Transformer [17] as our encoder to address specific long-term dependencies that RNN cannot address. First, given a word sequence of claims s^c, we map each word of s^c into its word embeddings by adopting pre-trained word vectors, the word2vec [13], and get the word embedding sequences $E^c = \left\{ e_1^c, \ldots, e_{l_c}^c \right\}$, $e_i^c \in \mathbb{R}^{d_w}$, where d_w is the dimension of the word embedding. For capturing the positional information of words in a sentence, a positional encoding with dimension d_{model} is added to the original input embedding. We denote the positional embedding sequence of s^c as $PE^c = \left\{ pe_1^c, \ldots, pe_{l_c}^c \right\}$, $pe_i^c \in \mathbb{R}^{d_{model}}$. The word embeddings and positional embeddings are combined to obtain the input embeddings as $IE^c = \left\{ e_1^c + pe_1^c, \ldots, e_{l_c}^c + pe_{l_c}^c \right\}$. We embed each of them into the continuous vector by the encoder of the Transformer.

$$V^c = \text{Transformer\_Encoder}\left(IE^c\right), \tag{1}$$

where $V^c = \left\{ v_1^c, \ldots, v_{l_c}^c \right\} \in \mathbb{R}^{l_c \times d_s}$. As well, we can also obtain the representations of the arguments, fact, and plea as $V^a \in \mathbb{R}^{l_a \times d_s}$, $V^f \in \mathbb{R}^{l_f \times d_s}$, $V^p \in \mathbb{R}^{l_p \times d_s}$, d_s is the size of the hidden dimension. Then, we concat the V^c, V^a with the fact vector V^f respectively to acquire $V^{cf} \in \mathbb{R}^{(l_c+l_f) \times d_s}$ and $V^{af} \in \mathbb{R}^{(l_a+l_f) \times d_s}$ as essential elements of the civil case.

4.4   Interaction Layer

For judges, it is significant to analyze and group all the relationships of essential elements which are from multiple perspectives to make the final judgment. Here we regard the plaintiff's plea as a question, we need to find the final answer which is supported or rejected to this question. The co-attention [22] mechanism is utilized to solve the problem.

After encoding the context and get the representations as V^{cf}, V^{af}, V^p, we first compute the affinity matrix which contains affinity scores corresponding to all pairs of concatenation words (i.e., the fact and claims) and words of the plea:

$$L = V^{cf}(V^p)^{\text{T}} \in \mathbb{R}^{(l_c+l_f) \times l_p}. \tag{2}$$

The affinity matrix is normalized row-wise to produce attention weights A^p across the concatenation for each word in the plea, and column-wise to produce attention weights A^{cf} across the plea for each word in the concatenation words:

$$A^p = \text{softmax}(L) \in \mathbb{R}^{(l_c+l_f)\times(l_p)} \text{ and } A^{cf} = \text{softmax}\left(L^\top\right) \in \mathbb{R}^{(l_p)\times(l_c+l_f)}. \quad (3)$$

Next, we compute attention contexts of the concatenation in light of each word of the plea:

$$C^p = (V^{cf})^\text{T}(A^p), C^p \in \mathbb{R}^{(d_s)\times(l_p)}. \quad (4)$$

Finally, we get the co-attention representation of the concatenation with the plea:

$$C^{cf} = \left(A^{cf}\right)^\text{T}[V^\text{p}; (C^p)^\text{T}], C^{cf} \in \mathbb{R}^{(l_c+l_f)\times(2d_s)}. \quad (5)$$

Similarly, given the concatenation of the fact and arguments V^{af} and the plea representation V^p, we can obtain the co-attention representation C^{af} between them. Following the judicial logic which assists in combining the legal knowledge with the civil case, we capture the co-attention representation $C^{d_i f}$ between the fact and the i-th legal knowledge.

4.5   Predictor Layer

For making the final judgment, we first apply per-dimension mean-pooling over the concated representation C (i.e., $[C^{cf}; C^{af}; C^{d_1 f}; ...; C^{d_k f}]$) to obtain the final presentation c. Then, we apply an affine transformation followed by softmax and obtain the final prediction as

$$P = \text{softmax}\left(W_o c + b_o\right). \quad (6)$$

Here, W_o and b_o are parameters to learned. We use cross-entropy as the loss function:

$$\mathcal{L}_{\text{pred}} = -\hat{j}\log P - (1 - \hat{j})\log(1 - P), \quad (7)$$

where $\hat{j}$ is the real judgment. In practice, we employ Adam [9] for optimization and dropout [15] on the final representations to prevent overfitting.

5   Experiments

5.1   Dataset Construction

Since there are no publicly available judgment prediction datasets for civil cases on various causes, we first construct a dataset based on raw civil legal documents[3]. Then, as the documents are well-structured and human-annotated, we could split legal documents into five parts: claims, arguments, fact, pleas, and the judgment result on the first plea. Next, the dataset is randomly separated into a training set, a validation set, and testing set according to a ratio of 7:2:1.

---

[3] https://wenshu.court.gov.cn.

Table 2. Statistics of civil case dataset.

Type	Result
#Supported case	$92,812(75.4\%)$
#Unsupported case	$30,236(24.6\%)$
#Supported case in un-arguments	$28,663(85.95\%)$
#Suppoted case in arguments	$64,149(71.51\%)$
Avg. # tokens in claims	109.8
Avg. # tokens in arguments	75.7
Avg. # tokens in fact	198.7
Avg. # tokens in plea	38.7

The statistics of the datasets are shown in Table 2. Among them, (1) the ratio of support is about 75% in each set. In [20], authors also describe such imbalanced data on civil cases; (2) We collect 238 common civil causes in the dataset, and the distribution of civil cases on different causes is roughly the same on each set; (3) There are some plaintiffs and defendants who have not clarified their cases, and about 1% of claims and 27% of arguments are none. The proportion of the un-arguments data is heavy. In the 33,346 un-arguments cases, the 28,663 cases are supported. When arguments exist, the 64,149 cases are supported in the 89,702 cases. This shows the ratio of supported cases falls 14.44% when arguments exist. The join of arguments plays a role in the judgment of the case. In the following experiments, we set claims and arguments in the un-claims and un-arguments cases as "No claims" and "No arguments" separately.

5.2 Experimental Setup

In CCJudge, we set the word embedding size d_w to 64, our Transformer encoder with hidden state size as 1024. In the training process, the learning rate is set as 0.001, mini batches as 32, and dropout as 0.3. Finally, we employ accuracy (Accuracy), weighted-precision (Precision), weighted-recall (Recall), and weighted-F1 (F1) as evaluation metrics to evaluate the model on the testing set.

5.3 Baselines

For comparison, we implement some baselines. The **SVM+Word2Vec** utilizes the word2vec [13] to represent the word features and SVM [16] for text classification. For verifying the effectiveness of our introducing mechanisms, we introduce the variant **CCJudge-BiGRU** of CCJudge by replacing the Transformer encoder with BiGRU [4]. We also implement and make some fine-tuning on the model of dynamic co-attention network (**DCN**) [22]. Specifically, we regard the mutil-perspective elements as contexts, and the plea as a question to predict whether the judgment is supported or not. We also adopt the framework **Auto-Judge** proposed by [11] which makes judgment prediction on the divorce cause. Besides, BERT outperforms state-of-the-art models on a wide range of NLP tasks. We also fine-tune Chinese **BERT** [5] as our benchmark method.

Table 3. Experimental results (%).

Models	Accuracy	Precision	Recall	F1
SVM+Word2Vec	48.4	69.9	48.4	50.8
CCJudge-BiGRU	76.0	57.1	76.0	65.1
DCN	75.6	57.0	76.0	65.0
AutoJudge	75.9	71.4	75.9	67.7
BERT	**80.5**	77.1	74.7	75.9
CCJudge	80.1	**78.2**	**80.2**	**78.1**

5.4 Experimental Results

Table 3 reports the results of all models for making judgment predictions on civil cases. There are several observations show:

(1) CCJudge performs the best overall which demonstrates CCJudge could effectively make predictions on various causes and capture the relationships from multiple perspectives on the logic of judges.
(2) The SVM+Word2Vec does not perform as well as all deep learning based models. It is possible SVM ignores the deep interaction between contexts and labels. We also find the Transformer performs better than BiGRU since the Transformer is better able to capture long sequence dependencies when the input contexts are complicated and heterogeneous.
(3) The performance of DCN is close to CCJudge-BiGRU on evaluation metrics. Although the frameworks of them are different, they both utilize RNN for encoding and attention mechanisms to do the interaction, perhaps similar results are from analogous interactions. AutoJudge performs worse than us, which indicates although AutoJudge performs well on the divorce cause, but could not model well on various causes. Besides, AutoJudge makes judgment predictions on the ascertained fact, ignoring the elements from other perspectives.
(4) Due to the truncated data processing and the limit of the maximum sequence length, BERT does not perform as well as we thought, which indicates the performance of CCJudge benefits from the overall framework.

5.5 Comparative Analysis

To further illustrate the significance of our framework, we make some ablation tests to evaluate the effectiveness of CCJudge: CCJudge/logic simply inputs all elements regardless of the order in which legal elements are dealt with; CCJudge/knowledge misses the legal knowledge extraction and the input of legal knowledge; CCJudge/co-attention ignores the co-attention mechanism to concat the presentations directly.

The results of the designed ablation tests are shown in Fig. 3 (a). We find that the performance drops obviously on metrics of Accuracy and F1 after taking off

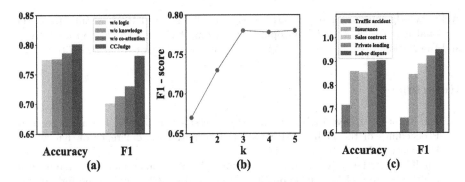

Fig. 3. (a) The experimental results of ablation tests. (b) Experiments with different k legal knowledge. (c) The experimental results on five causes.

the logical framework, the legal knowledge, and the mechanism of co-attention. Therefore, it can be seen that they all play irreplaceable roles in our model.

Except for the above ablation tests, we also make experiments on the knowledge base as summarized in Fig. 3 (b). In Sect. 4.2, we describe the k highest-ranked knowledge was encoded and interacted with the case fact. We find the best performance of the model when $k=3$. With the increase of the k value, the model effect does not significantly improve. This proves that our legal knowledge extraction effectively searches relevant information from the knowledge base by inputting the claims and arguments and extracts useful knowledge by interacting with case facts. So, we set $k=3$ in the all above experiments.

Furthermore, we choose five common civil causes for verifying the effect of CCJudge. Specifically, CCJudge performs well on most causes as shown in Fig. 3 (c). However, on some causes as the traffic accident dispute, due to the absence of the claims and arguments in most cases, CCJudge could not capture enough information from the perspectives of the plaintiff and defendant. The results indicate that utilizing elements from multiple perspectives effectively could better help the model to make judgment predictions.

6   Conclusion

In this paper, we proposed a novel method, CCJudge, for legal judgment prediction on civil cases. We simulated the judicial logic of human judges from multiple perspectives to form a robust architecture. As well as the legal knowledge extractor effectively extracted the relevant knowledge from an external legal knowledge base, which effectively helped model on various causes. Besides, we designed an encoder layer and an interaction layer to confirm and capture relationships of legal elements from multiple perspectives. And the final judgment was achieved by a predictor layer. The experimental results showed the effectiveness of CCJudge.

Acknowledgements. This research was partially supported by grants from the National Key Research and Development Program of China (No. 2018YFC0832101), and the National Natural Science Foundation of China (Grant No. 61922073).

References

1. An, Y., et al.: LawyerPAN: a proficiency assessment network for trial lawyers. In: Proceedings of the 27th ACM SIGKDD International Conference on Knowledge Discovery & Data Mining (2021)
2. Chalkidis, I., Fergadiotis, M., Malakasiotis, P., Androutsopoulos, I.: Large-scale multi-label text classification on EU legislation. In: ACL. Association for Computational Linguistics (2019)
3. Chen, H., Cai, D., Dai, W., Dai, Z., Ding, Y.: Charge-based prison term prediction with deep gating network. In: Proceedings of the 2019 Conference on Empirical Methods in Natural Language Processing and the 9th International Joint Conference on Natural Language Processing (EMNLP-IJCNLP) (2019)
4. Chung, J., Gulcehre, C., Cho, K., Bengio, Y.: Empirical evaluation of gated recurrent neural networks on sequence modeling. arXiv preprint arXiv:1412.3555 (2014)
5. Cui, Y., et al.: Pre-training with whole word masking for Chinese BERT. arXiv preprint arXiv:1906.08101 (2019)
6. Duan, X., et al.: CJRC: a reliable human-annotated benchmark DataSet for Chinese judicial reading comprehension. In: Sun, M., Huang, X., Ji, H., Liu, Z., Liu, Y. (eds.) CCL 2019. LNCS (LNAI), vol. 11856, pp. 439–451. Springer, Cham (2019). https://doi.org/10.1007/978-3-030-32381-3_36
7. Hu, Z., Li, X., Tu, C., Liu, Z., Sun, M.: Few-shot charge prediction with discriminative legal attributes. In: Proceedings of the 27th International Conference on Computational Linguistics, pp. 487–498 (2018)
8. Kim, Y.: Convolutional neural networks for sentence classification. In: Proceedings of the 2014 Conference on Empirical Methods in Natural Language Processing, EMNLP (2014)
9. Kingma, D.P., Ba, J.: Adam: a method for stochastic optimization. In: 3rd International Conference on Learning Representations, ICLR 2015, San Diego, CA, USA, 7–9 May 2015, Conference Track Proceedings (2015)
10. Li, S., Zhang, H., Ye, L., et al.: Mann: a multichannel attentive neural network for legal judgment prediction. IEEE Access **7**, 151144–151155 (2019)
11. Long, S., Tu, C., Liu, Z., Sun, M.: Automatic judgment prediction via legal reading comprehension. In: Sun, M., Huang, X., Ji, H., Liu, Z., Liu, Y. (eds.) CCL 2019. LNCS (LNAI), vol. 11856, pp. 558–572. Springer, Cham (2019). https://doi.org/10.1007/978-3-030-32381-3_45
12. Luo, B., Feng, Y., Xu, J., Zhang, X., Zhao, D.: Learning to predict charges for criminal cases with legal basis. In: Proceedings of the 2017 Conference on Empirical Methods in Natural Language Processing, EMNLP. Association for Computational Linguistics (2017)
13. Mikolov, T., Sutskever, I., Chen, K., Corrado, G.S., Dean, J.: Distributed representations of words and phrases and their compositionality. In: Advances in Neural Information Processing Systems 26: 27th Annual Conference on Neural Information Processing Systems (2013)
14. Press, P.C.: Guidelines on the Applicable Rules of Civil Cases and the Right of Claim of the Supreme People's Court. People's Court Press (2019)

15. Srivastava, N., Hinton, G., Krizhevsky, A., et al.: Dropout: a simple way to prevent neural networks from overfitting. J. Mach. Learn. Res. **15**(1), 1929–1958 (2014)
16. Suykens, J.A., Vandewalle, J.: Least squares support vector machine classifiers. Neural Process. Lett. **9**, 293–300 (1999)
17. Vaswani, A., et al.: Attention is all you need. In: Advances in Neural Information Processing Systems 30: Annual Conference on Neural Information Processing Systems (2017)
18. Wang, H., et al.: MCNE: an end-to-end framework for learning multiple conditional network representations of social network. In: Proceedings of the 25th ACM SIGKDD International Conference on Knowledge Discovery & Data Mining, pp. 1064–1072 (2019)
19. Wang, Y., et al.: Equality before the law: legal judgment consistency analysis for fairness. arXiv preprint arXiv:2103.13868 (2021)
20. Wu, Y., et al.: De-biased court's view generation with causality. In: Proceedings of the 2020 Conference on Empirical Methods in Natural Language Processing (EMNLP) (2020)
21. Xiao, C., et al.: Cail 2018: a large-scale legal dataset for judgment prediction. arXiv preprint arXiv:1807.02478 (2018)
22. Xiong, C., Zhong, V., Socher, R.: Dynamic coattention networks for question answering. arXiv preprint arXiv:1611.01604 (2016)
23. Xu, Z., Li, X., Li, Y., Wang, Z., Fanxu, Y., Lai, X.: Multi-task legal judgement prediction combining a subtask of the seriousness of charges. In: Sun, M., Li, S., Zhang, Y., Liu, Y., He, S., Rao, G. (eds.) CCL 2020. LNCS (LNAI), vol. 12522, pp. 415–429. Springer, Cham (2020). https://doi.org/10.1007/978-3-030-63031-7_30
24. Yang, W., Jia, W., Zhou, X., Luo, Y.: Legal judgment prediction via multi-perspective bi-feedback network. In: Proceedings of the Twenty-Eighth International Joint Conference on Artificial Intelligence, IJCAI (2019)
25. Yue, L., et al.: NeurJudge: a circumstance-aware neural framework for legal judgment prediction. In: Proceedings of the 44th International ACM SIGIR Conference on Research and Development in Information Retrieval (2021)
26. Yue, L., et al.: Circumstances enhanced criminal court view generation. In: Proceedings of the 44th International ACM SIGIR Conference on Research and Development in Information Retrieval (2021)
27. Zhong, H., Guo, Z., Tu, C., Xiao, C., Liu, Z., Sun, M.: Legal judgment prediction via topological learning. In: Proceedings of the 2018 Conference on Empirical Methods in Natural Language Processing (2018)
28. Zhong, H., Xiao, C., Tu, C., Zhang, T., Liu, Z., Sun, M.: How does NLP benefit legal system: a summary of legal artificial intelligence. In: Proceedings of the 58th Annual Meeting of the Association for Computational Linguistics, ACL 2020, Online, 5–10 July 2020 (2020)
29. Zhou, X., Zhang, Y., Liu, X., Sun, C., Si, L.: Legal intelligence for e-commerce: multi-task learning by leveraging multiview dispute representation. In: Proceedings of the 42nd International ACM SIGIR Conference on Research and Development in Information Retrieval (2019)
30. Zou, B.: The Nine Steps of Trial of Essential Items. Law Press (2010)

Multi-view Relevance Matching Model of Scientific Papers Based on Graph Convolutional Network and Attention Mechanism

Jie Song, Zhe Xue$^{(\boxtimes)}$, Junping Du, Feifei Kou, Meiyu Liang, and Mingying Xu

Beijing Key Laboratory of Intelligent Telecommunication Software and Multimedia,
School of Computer Science, Beijing University of Posts and Telecommunications,
Beijing 100876, China
{songs,xuezhe,koufeifei000,meiyu1210,xumingying0612}@bupt.edu.cn

Abstract. Deep learning has been widely used in text matching tasks. However, the existing deep learning models are mainly designed for short texts matching and cannot be directly applied to the search of scientific papers. The main reason is that the differences between long and short texts in scientific paper search have not been fully considered, and the structural information of the text will be lost when the length difference is large. In order to solve the above long-short scientific text matching problem, we propose a multi-view relevance matching model (MVRM) of scientific papers based on graph convolutional network and attention mechanism. First, we use scientific papers abstract to construct interactive graph to retain the structural information in the long text. Each vertex denotes the keyword in the abstract and the edge weight denotes similarity between the keywords. Second, we propose a matching network for interactive graph based on the graph convolution networks. Multiple keywords in the search term form multiple views, and each keyword under each view interacts with the interactive graph. Then the interaction feature vectors from multiple views are generated through graph convolution network. Finally, attention mechanism is used for fusion, and the final matching result is output through the multilayer perceptron. Experiments on several representative scientific paper search datasets demonstrate that our model achieves better performance.

Keywords: Relevance matching · Graph convolutional network · Attention mechanism · Multi-view · Long-short text matching

1 Introduction

Text matching is a core problem in natural language processing, and many natural language processing tasks can be abstracted into text matching problems. For example, the search of scientific papers can be boiled down to the matching of search sentences and scientific paper documents. Designing different matching

© Springer Nature Switzerland AG 2021
L. Fang et al. (Eds.): CICAI 2021, LNAI 13069, pp. 724–734, 2021.
https://doi.org/10.1007/978-3-030-93046-2_61

models for different task scenarios is of vital importance to improve the matching accuracy.

Traditional relevance matching is mainly based on the literal matching degree of search term to calculate the relevance, such as literal hit, coverage, TF-IDF, BM25 [1], etc. But literal matching has its limitations: It cannot deal with synonyms and polysemous words. Deep learning is also applied to relevance matching. Most relevance matching methods, such as DSSM [2], SimNet, and MV-LSTM [3], use deep models to represent the search sentences of scientific papers (hereinafter called Query) and scientific paper documents (hereinafter called Doc), and calculate the vector similarity as relevance matching score. The advantage is fast while disadvantage is that there is no interaction between Query and Doc, and the fine-grained matching signals of Query and Doc cannot be fully utilized. The relevance matching methods represented by ARC-I [4], ARC-II [4] and MatchPyramid [5] learn the text vectors after interaction between Query and Doc, then obtain relevance matching score through neural network. However, it is difficult to deploy these methods online due to calculation of the vector. In addition, when obtaining the text vector, all the above methods have a shorter optimal sentence length. When this length is exceeded, the validity of the text vector representation will be affected.

Therefore, this paper proposes a Multi-View Relevance Matching Model (MVRM) of scientific papers based on graph convolutional network and attention mechanism to improve the accuracy of scientific papers search. The model uses a graph structure to represent the Doc, which solves the problem that the word vector model characterizes the text with a limited length, and the graph structure can retain interactive relationship between keywords in Doc to a certain extent. For Query, in order to fully consider the user's intentions, we assign each keyword to a view, and let each keyword interact with the Doc in the corresponding view. Then, we use the graph convolutional neural network to spread the node features on the Doc represented by graph to each other, and aggregate them into the interaction vector of Query and Doc in each view. Finally, we re-aggregate the interaction vectors of multiple views through the attention mechanism to obtain the final matching feature vector of Query and Doc, and use the multi-layer perceptron to match and predict the feature vector to obtain the matching score of Query and Doc. The experimental results on several representative paper datasets verify the effectiveness of our proposed method. The main contributions of this paper include three aspects:

1. We propose a text representation method for the abstracts of scientific papers based on graph structure, which sufficiently, retains structured information in scientific paper abstracts, and makes the semantic representation of Doc more comprehensive.
2. We propose a matching network for scientific papers based on graph convolutional neural networks. By using graph convolutional neural network, the matching of keywords in Query and Doc is globally integrated, and the degree of information loss of the long and short text matching can be effectively reduced.

3. We propose MVRM, introducing a multi-view mechanism to convert possible user intentions into multiple views, so that user intentions can be well captured and more accurate search results can be obtained.

2   Related Work

The purpose of relevance matching is to determine whether two texts are related, or to infer the score of relevance between the two texts. In the search scene of scientific papers, this is a core issue. Early relevance matching is mainly based on the literal matching score of Query and Doc to calculate relevance. The relevance characteristics of literal matching play an important role in the search of scientific papers. However literal matching has its limitations, such as the inability to deal with synonyms and polysemous words, and when the vocabulary is completely overlapped but the semantics expressed are completely different, the literal matching cannot be achieved to a good effect.

Text matching methods of deep learning mainly include representation-based matching methods and interaction-based matching methods.

The representation-based matching method uses a deep learning model to represent Query and Doc respectively, and obtains semantic matching scores by calculating vector similarity. One of the common methods is to use pre-training and transfer to obtain the text representation. A typical model such as the Gensen [6] can generalize sentence representation in a variety of tasks. Quick-thought [7] uses the meaning of the current sentence to predict the meaning of connected sentences, which can learn sentence representation more effectively. BERT learns a good feature representation for words by running a self-supervised learning method on the basis of massive corpus, refreshing many records of natural language processing. The Sentence-BERT [8] pre-training model adopts a double or triple BERT network structure to ensure accuracy while greatly reducing computational overhead.

Another interaction-based matching method does not directly learn the text representation vectors of Query and Doc, but lets Query and Doc interact in advance at the bottom of the neural network to obtain a better text vector representation, and finally obtain a matching score through a multi-layer perceptron network. This type of model usually contains an interactive layer. For example, DIIN [9] performs element product interaction on the obtained Query and Doc vector text vector representations at the interaction layer, and then encodes the vector after the interaction. MCAN [10] uses multiple attentions to model multiple views to improve performance. The model introduces a multi-cast attention mechanism to interact and aggregate Query and Doc on different views. Match^2 [11] proposes a novel matching strategy, which compares the matching score of two Query on the same Doc for similarity matching, and generates the final similarity score based on the representation and matching mode. Also paying attention to the two matching modes to get the final result is the HCAN [12], which integrates semantic matching (emphasis on meaning correspondence and component structure) results and relevance matching (emphasis on keyword matching) results, using full connection to get the final matching result. RE2 [13] designs an enhanced residual network, which retains the original meaning of the text to the greatest extent, prevents it from changing in the process of network transmission, and uses the traditional attention mechanism to achieve interaction.

The above methods are mainly used for matching between short texts. In the search scenario of scientific papers, the length difference between Query and Doc needs to be considered. CIG-GCN-BERT [14] proposes a method to construct a long text into a concept graph, and interacts with another long text through graph convolution, and finally obtains the final matching result through a multilayer perceptron. Based on the above description, we propose MVRM for the matching of Query and Doc in scientific paper search.

3   Method

The structure of MVRM is shown in Fig. 1. MVRM is mainly divided into three modules: Interaction module, multi-view convolution module and aggregation module. Interaction module encodes Query and Doc into feature vectors, where Doc will be transformed into graph structure. Feature vectors of Query and Doc interact in different views to obtain the interactive vector. Multi-view convolution module mainly uses graph convolutional networks to synthesize graph node matching scores. Aggregation module aggregates the graph network features from different views through the attention mechanism, and the aggregated feature vector is passed through the multilayer perceptron to obtain the final matching score.

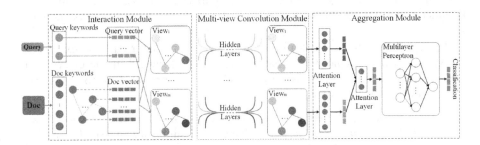

Fig. 1. The structure of MVRM

3.1   Data Preprocessing

For a given Query and Doc, we use word segmentation tools to segment the text, and use the keyword extraction algorithm TextRank [15] to extract the keywords and the corresponding weights in the text. Then, we use a pre-trained word vector model to obtain the keyword embedding representation of Query and Doc.

3.2   Problem Definition

Suppose the keyword set of Query is $Q = \{query_1, query_2, ..., query_m\}$, the weight set obtained by TextRank corresponding to the Query keyword is $Q_{weight} = \{w_{q1}, w_{q2}, ..., w_{qm}\}$, the corresponding word vector set is $Q_{feature} = \{\boldsymbol{q}_1, \boldsymbol{q}_2, ..., \boldsymbol{q}_m\}$. Similarly, the keyword set of Doc obtained by TextRank is $D = \{doc_1, doc_2, ..., doc_n\}$, the weight set corresponding to the Doc keyword is $D_{weight} = \{w_{d1}, w_{d2}, ..., w_{dn}\}$, the corresponding word vector set is $D_{feature} = \{\boldsymbol{d}_1, \boldsymbol{d}_2, ..., \boldsymbol{d}_n\}$, where m denotes the number of keywords in Query, n denotes the number of keywords in Doc, the dimensions of the word vector of Query and Doc remain the same, initially 300. Our goal is to determine whether a given set of Query and Doc match.

3.3   Interaction Module

To store Doc text information, a scientific paper interactive graph is defined in Definition 1. This graph decomposes content of Doc, and the match between Query and Doc is converted to match between the keywords on the graph nodes and the keywords in the Query, so that our method can sufficiently retain the relationship and structural information to the greatest extent.

Definition 1. *Given an undirected graph $C = (V, E)$. V denotes node set and E denotes edge set. $V = \{v_1, v_2, ..., v_n\}$, v_c denotes the c-th keyword in Doc. Any edge e_{ij} in E denotes the similarity weight between the i-th keyword and the j-th keyword in Doc.*

Each node in the graph is a keyword extracted from Doc. According to the similarity, the text similarity, which is represented by the reciprocal of the Euclidean distance of the vertex vector, of the two nodes is used as the edge weight.

For Query, due to its short and capable general characteristics, we extract all the keywords in the Query and match every single keyword in the Query with the keywords on the undirected graph node constructed by Doc to obtain the interaction vector. The specific steps are as follows:

– Assuming that word vectors of Query keyword q_i and Doc keyword d_j are $\boldsymbol{q}_i \in R^{1 \times k}$ and $\boldsymbol{d}_j \in R^{1 \times k}$ respectively. The similarity matrix $\boldsymbol{U} \in R^{k \times k}$ between Query and Doc is calculated as follows:

$$U = q^T d \tag{1}$$

– Combining $\boldsymbol{q}_i$, $\boldsymbol{d}_j$ and $\boldsymbol{U}$, we get similarity-weighted word vector $\boldsymbol{p}_{ij} \in R^{1 \times k}$, each element p_v in $\boldsymbol{p}_{ij}$ is as follows:

$$p_v = \sum_{j=1}^{k} U_{vj} \cdot U_{jv} \tag{2}$$

– Since Query contains m keywords, an interactive graph of scientific papers between Query and Doc from m views will be generated.

3.4   Multi-view Convolution Module

In order to fully consider the impact of each keyword in Query on the matching results, we introduce multi-view convolution module. Scientific papers interactive graph after the interaction of graph C and each keyword $query_i(i = 1, 2, ..., m)$ in Q is regarded as a match under a perspective, and this perspective is recorded as $view_i(i = 1, 2, ..., m)$.

For each perspective $view_i$, calculate $q_u(u = 1, 2, ..., m)$ and $d_v(\text{v} = 1, 2, ..., n)$ in the word vector set $Q_{feature}$ and $D_{feature}$ according to formulas (2) and (3) to get the interaction vector p_{ij}, where j = 1, 2, ..., n. We define P_i as the vector set in $view_i$'s perspective, and $P_i = \{p_{i1}, p_{i2}, ..., p_{in}\}$. The vector set P_i is attached to the corresponding node in the graph C, and the Query and Doc interaction graph $G_i = \{V, E, P_i\}$ under $view_i$ is obtained.

We apply graph convolutional neural network to the obtained interaction graph G_i, calculating the weighted adjacency matrix $A \in R^{n \times n}$ of the interaction graph, where A_{ij} denotes the similarity between i-th keyword and j-th keyword in interactive graph. The degree matrix of A is $S \in R^{n \times n}$, S can be calculated as follows:

$$S_{ii} = \sum_j A_{ij} \tag{3}$$

In order to solve the problem that the vertex feature's own information will be lost after propagation, we set $Z = A + I$, where I is the identity matrix. In the graph convolutional neural network, the convolution propagation formula of the l-th layer is as follows:

$$H_i^{(l)} = \sigma(S^{-\frac{1}{2}} Z S^{-\frac{1}{2}} H_i^{(l-1)} W^{(l)}) \tag{4}$$

where $W^{(l)}$ denotes the training parameters of the l-th layer, and σ denotes the activation function. When $l = 0$, $H_i^{(l)}$ denotes the initial feature matrix P_i of the undirected graph under the $view_i$ perspective. When $l = L$, $H_i^{(l)}$ denotes the output H_i of the graph convolutional neural network.

3.5   Aggregation Module

After obtaining the convolution output $H_i \in R^{n \times r}$ from $view_i$, we build an attention network, combine the weight set D_{weight}, output the aggregation vector $h_i \in R^{1 \times r}$, where $i = (1, 2, ..., m)$. The process is as follows:

$$\alpha = (\alpha_1, \alpha_2, ..., \alpha_n) \tag{5}$$

$$h_i = \sigma(\sum_{j=1}^{n} \alpha_j H_{ij}) \tag{6}$$

$$\alpha_j = \frac{exp(ReLU(b[h_j||w_{dj}H_{ij}]))}{\sum_{j=1}^{n} exp(ReLU(b[h_j||w_{dj}H_{ij}]))} \tag{7}$$

where H_{ij} denotes the j-th row of H_i, α and b are parameters to be learned. We use attention layer to integrate the output of each view, and now we have $h = \{h_1, h_2, ..., h_m\} \in R^{m \times r}$. Similarly, the weight set Q_{weight} is used to aggregate all views to obtain the final matching feature vector $z \in R^{1 \times r}$ between Query and Doc. The process is similar to the above method, by using sigmod function, σ of Doc maps n dimension to 1 and σ of Query maps m dimension to 1.

We define a multi-layer perceptron to perform a binary classification problem on the matching feature vector z of Query and Doc.

$$y' = \sigma(\sum_{i=1}^{r} w_i z_i) \tag{8}$$

where w is parameter to be learned. The final loss function is as follows:

$$Loss = -(y \cdot \log(y') + (1 - y) \cdot \log(1 - y')) \tag{9}$$

where y denotes the real label and y' denotes the predicted label.

4   Experiments

4.1   Experimental Settings

Metric. We adopt the following metrics to evaluate the performance of our method: Accuracy (ACC), F1-Score (F1) and Mean Average Precision (MAP).

Dataset. We crawl the title and abstract of scientific papers from the two open platforms, "CNKI" and "AMiner". We randomly shuffle part of the titles and abstracts of scientific papers in a certain proportion ($\theta = 0.4$), and combine the titles and abstracts of scientific papers in different fields into a pair of datasets, so that the pair of long and short texts does not match, and the undisturbed titles and abstracts are between matched. Then we have CNKI-Dataset and AMiner-Dataset.

Each dataset is divided into training set and test set, the ratio is 8:2. Each pair of scientific papers are labeled with 0 and 1 between the title and abstract, where 1 denotes a match, and 0 denotes no match, the detailed description of datasets is shown in the Table 1 below.

Table 1. Dataset corpus structure

Dataset	Pos	Neg	Train	Test
CNKI-Dataset	60000	40000	80000	20000
AMiner-Dataset	30000	20000	40000	10000

Parameter Settings. The length of the encoded word vector is 300, the graph convolutional neural network is divided into three layers, and the mapping dimensions are 300, 200, and 128 respectively. The output vector dimension of the two-layer attention network is 128, and the mapping dimension of the multilayer perceptron network is 128, 1.

In addition, the learning rate of MVRM during the above experiments is set to 0.01 and the dimension of the interaction vector output by the multi-view convolution module is set to 128.

Compared Methods. We compare eight methods with our method on two datasets: ARC-I [4], ARC-I [4], DSSM [2], C-DSSM [16], MV-LSTM [3], Match-Pyramid [5], DRMM [17], ESIM [18].

4.2   Results and Analysis

Experimental Analysis. Experimental results of ACC, F1 and MAP on the two datasets are shown in the following table. From Table 2 we can observe that:

- The results on the AMiner-Dataset are generally better than those on the CNKI-Dataset on ACC. There may be two reasons for this. Firstly, the size of the AMiner-Dataset is smaller. Secondly, the AMiner-Dataset is mainly in English, while the CNKI-Dataset is mainly in Chinese, which may be affected by different word segmentation processing.
- It can be observed that our method MVRM achieves better accuracy and F1-score compared to all the other methods on each dataset. Abstracts of scientific papers contain keywords in more than one field. The compared method cannot obtain all the semantics of the abstract, and our method represents the text by constructing a graph, which sufficiently retains structured information and achieves a higher accuracy rate.

Table 2. Comparison results on CNKI-Dataset and AMiner-Datase

Method	CNKI-Dataset			AMiner-Dataset		
	ACC	F1	MAP	ACC	F1	MAP
ARC-I	0.6364	0.6789	0.5995	0.6045	0.6463	0.5439
ARC-II	0.6978	0.7326	0.6210	0.6829	0.7035	0.5861
DSSM	0.6696	0.6342	0.5286	0.6547	0.6157	0.5123
CDSSM	0.7263	0.6587	0.5316	0.6892	0.6514	0.5227
MV-LSTM	0.6602	0.6734	0.6528	0.7106	0.6583	0.6284
MatchPyramid	0.7136	0.7267	0.5643	0.6946	0.6921	0.5513
DRMM	0.7258	0.7154	0.6401	0.7624	0.7332	0.5931
ESIM	0.7488	0.7675	0.6624	0.7968	0.7946	0.6184
MVRM	**0.8567**	**0.8622**	**0.6814**	**0.8639**	**0.8601**	**0.6213**

Also, we plot the training accuracy and training loss while MVRM runs on the CNKI-Dataset, line charts of accuracy and loss are shown in Fig. 2.

Module Analysis. We also test several model variants for ablation study. For each model variant, we remove one module from our complete module and compare its performance with our complete model on both two datasets to evaluate the impact of the removed component.

(a) Training Accuracy   (b) Training Loss

Fig. 2. Training accuracy and loss during training epochs on CNKI-Dataset

Table 3. ACC, F1 and MAP results of complete model and it's variants

Algorithm	CNKI-Dataset			AMiner-Dataset		
	ACC	F1	MAP	ACC	F1	MAP
No Interaction Module	0.7624	0.7833	0.6521	0.7815	0.8044	0.5976
No Multi-View Convolution Module	0.7952	0.8124	0.6645	0.8243	0.8279	0.6013
No Attention Module	0.8354	0.8427	0.6682	0.8418	0.8367	0.5964
Full Module	**0.8567**	**0.8622**	**0.6814**	**0.8639**	**0.8601**	**0.6213**

In Table 3, No interaction module means the word vectors of Query and Doc are directly spliced without interactive operation. No multi-view convolution module means graph neural network without performing convolution operation. No attention module means we directly add the vectors according to the Query and Doc weights, and then get the results through the multilayer perceptron.

From Table 3 we can observe that the three modules have a certain effect on the results, of which the interactive module has the greatest effect. The interaction between Query and Doc has a great impact on the matching result, which is also the core of the interactive matching method. In addition, how to aggregate the feature vectors of the vertices of the interaction graph and aggregate the interaction vectors under multiple views also has a significant impact on the matching results. Finally, the graph convolutional neural network can make the local matching features of Query and Doc spread globally, taking into account the influence of the difference in length of long and short texts on the matching results to the greatest extent.

Parameters Analysis. In order to verify the rationality of the datasets, we analyze the scale parameter θ of the randomly scattered dataset. The above experiments are all carried out under the condition of $\theta = 0.4$. Now we set the θ value from 0.1 to 0.9, and the step size is 0.1. Within this range, we conduct experiments on both CNKI-Datasets and AMiner-Dataset on ACC indicators, and the results are shown in Fig. 3. We can observe that when θ is between 0.3 and 0.7, MVRM can still achieve good results after training, but when it is not in this range, MVRM's effect is significantly reduced. This shows that the appropriate negative samples can play a certain role in training, but if the proportion of negative samples is too high or too low, the performance of our method will degrade.

In order to test the sensitivity of MVRM to the parameters, we experiment on the learning rate (lr) which is chosen from $\{10^{-1}, 10^{-2}, 10^{-3}, 10^{-4}, 10^{-5}\}$ and the dimension (η) of the interaction vector output by the multi-view convolution module which is chosen from $\{256, 128, 64, 32\}$. We select the CNKI-Dataset and evaluate it with ACC and the sensitivity test results are shown in Fig. 4. We can observe that when $lr = 0.01$ and $\eta = 128$, ACC achieves the maximum value, so our experiment is also completed based on this condition. Moreover, parameter experiments show that MVRM is not sensitive to parameters, and a certain degree of parameter fluctuation will not affect the overall results of the model.

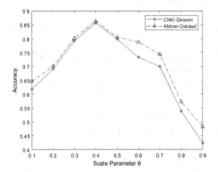
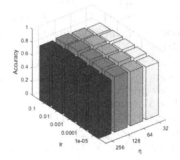

Fig. 3. The impact of different θ on ACC of both datasets

Fig. 4. Parameter analysis on CNKI-Dataset

5 Conclusion

In this paper, we propose a multi-view relevance matching model for scientific papers based on graph convolutional networks and attention mechanism. We model the abstract of scientific papers as scientific paper interactive graph. On this basis, we further propose a multi-view scientific paper matching model based on GCN, which integrates the matching results of all keywords in search term and scientific papers. Then, based on the attention mechanism, we sequentially aggregate the vectors in the interaction graph and the interaction vectors in the multi-view to obtain the final feature vector, and then output the final result through the multilayer perceptron. We compare the model with the other methods on real paper datasets, and the results show that our method is better than the other methods in ACC, F1 and MAP indicators.

Acknowledgements. This work was supported by National Key R&D Program of China (2018YFB1402600), and by the National Natural Science Foundation of China (61802028, 61772083, 61877006, 62002027), and sponsored by CCF-Baidu Open Fund.

References

1. Robertson, S., Zaragoza, H.: The Probabilistic Relevance Framework: BM25 and Beyond. Now Publishers Inc. (2009)
2. Huang, P.S., He, X., Gao, J., et al.: Learning deep structured semantic models for web search using clickthrough data. In: Proceedings of the 22nd ACM International Conference on Information & Knowledge Management, pp. 2333–2338 (2013)
3. Wan, S., Lan, Y., Guo, J., et al.: A deep architecture for semantic matching with multiple positional sentence representations. In: Proceedings of the AAAI Conference on Artificial Intelligence, vol. 30, no. 1 (2016)
4. Hu, B., Lu, Z., Li, H., et al.: Convolutional neural network architectures for matching natural language sentences. arXiv preprint arXiv:1503.03244 (2015)
5. Pang, L., Lan, Y., Guo, J., et al.: Text matching as image recognition. In: Proceedings of the AAAI Conference on Artificial Intelligence, vol. 30, no. 1 (2016)
6. Subramanian, S., Trischler, A., Bengio, Y., et al.: Learning general purpose distributed sentence representations via large scale multi-task learning. arXiv preprint arXiv:1804.00079 (2018)
7. Logeswaran, L., Lee, H.: An efficient framework for learning sentence representations. arXiv preprint arXiv:1803.02893 (2018)
8. Reimers, N., Gurevych, I.: Sentence-BERT: sentence embeddings using Siamese BERT-networks. arXiv preprint arXiv:1908.10084 (2019)
9. Gong, Y., Luo, H., Zhang, J.: Natural language inference over interaction space. arXiv preprint arXiv:1709.04348 (2017)
10. Tay, Y., Tuan, L.A., Hui, S.C.: Multi-cast attention networks. In: Proceedings of the 24th ACM SIGKDD International Conference on Knowledge Discovery & Data Mining, pp. 2299–2308 (2018)
11. Wang, Z., Fan, Y., Guo, J., et al.: Match^2: a matching over matching model for similar question identification. In: Proceedings of the 43rd International ACM SIGIR Conference on Research and Development in Information Retrieval, pp. 559–568 (2020)
12. Rao, J., Liu, L., Tay, Y., et al.: Bridging the gap between relevance matching and semantic matching for short text similarity modeling. In: Proceedings of the 2019 Conference on Empirical Methods in Natural Language Processing and the 9th International Joint Conference on Natural Language Processing (EMNLP-IJCNLP), pp. 5373–5384 (2019)
13. Yang, R., Zhang, J., Gao, X., et al.: Simple and effective text matching with richer alignment features. arXiv preprint arXiv:1908.00300 (2019)
14. Liu, B., Niu, D., Wei, H., et al.: Matching article pairs with graphical decomposition and convolutions. arXiv preprint arXiv:1802.07459 (2018)
15. Mihalcea, R., Tarau, P.: TextRank: bringing order into text. In: Proceedings of the 2004 Conference on Empirical Methods in Natural Language Processing, pp. 404–411 (2004)
16. Shen, Y., He, X., Gao, J., et al.: Learning semantic representations using convolutional neural networks for web search. In: Proceedings of the 23rd International Conference on World Wide Web, pp. 373–374 (2014)
17. Guo, J., Fan, Y., Ai, Q., et al.: A deep relevance matching model for ad-hoc retrieval. In: Proceedings of the 25th ACM International Conference on Information and Knowledge Management, pp. 55–64 (2016)
18. Chen, Q., Zhu, X., Ling, Z., et al.: Enhanced LSTM for natural language inference. arXiv preprint arXiv:1609.06038 (2016)

A Hierarchical Multi-label Classification Algorithm for Scientific Papers Based on Graph Attention Networks

Changwei Zheng, Zhe Xue$^{(\boxtimes)}$, Junping Du, Feifei Kou, Meiyu Liang, and Mingying Xu

Beijing Key Laboratory of Intelligent Telecommunication Software and Multimedia, School of Computer Science, Beijing University of Posts and Telecommunications, Beijing 100876, China
{zhengchangwei,xuezhe,koufeifei000,meiyu1210,xumingying}@bupt.edu.cn

Abstract. Scientific paper classification refers to assigning one or more subject categories to papers. This task requires a lot of domain knowledge and heavy manual annotation. With the gradual increase in interdisciplinary research, a paper often has multiple categories. For instance, both Chinese Library Classification (http://www.ztflh.com/) and Engineering Village (EI) have a complete classification system, and there is a hierarchical relationship between the categories. The category of the paper has a hierarchical structure, so the paper classification can be converted into a hierarchical classification problem. However, the existing methods cannot effectively classify papers due to the following two reasons: First, these methods cannot well capture the semantic relationship between papers. Second, they neglect to model the hierarchical structure of labels. In this paper, we propose a hierarchical label attention model based on graph attention network, which utilizes word co-occurrence to model the semantic relationship of papers. We use multiple linear layers to model the category hierarchy and combine every hierarchy of labels through an attention mechanism. The experiments are conducted on CNKI (https://www.cnki.net/) and RCV1 datasets. The experimental results demonstrate that our method is superior to the other methods in the task of scientific paper classification.

Keywords: Graph convolutional network · Hierarchical classification · Multi-label classification

1 Introduction

Scientific papers are an important source for scholars to obtain the latest research results. However, due to the wide variety of paper databases and the different classification standards adopted by different institutions, it is usually necessary for staff to rely on professional knowledge to manually classify papers. Such manual classification undoubtedly requires heavy manual annotation. Some institutions allow authors to provide classifications when submitting papers. Although

© Springer Nature Switzerland AG 2021
L. Fang et al. (Eds.): CICAI 2021, LNAI 13069, pp. 735–746, 2021.
https://doi.org/10.1007/978-3-030-93046-2_62

this way can save a certain amount of manpower, the authors are often unfamiliar with the existing classification system. In addition, the stratification make the authors confused, which is difficult for authors to provide accurate and complete paper classification.

The Chinese Library Classification (CLC), which is a classification standard widely adopted in China and contains a variety of publications including papers. CLC is divided into 22 major categories, 51,881 categories (including general categories). There is a hierarchical relationship between each category, and the categories are coded using letters and numbers. For example, TP181 means 'Artificial Intelligence Theory', where T represents 'industrial technology' in 22 categories, TP represents 'automation technology, computer technology' under the category of 'industrial technology', and so on. With the increasing frequency of interdisciplinary, the CLC category of the paper is often more than one. For example, the combination of artificial intelligence and medicine, biology, transportation and other fields has become frequently. Moreover, the category of the paper can adopt hierarchical names. For example, TP18 is 'Artificial Intelligence Theory' and its subcategories such as TP183 'Artificial Neural Network and Computing' can be used as the category of the paper. Therefore, the task of automatic paper classification can be converted into a hierarchical multi-label text classification problem.

The characteristics of the paper and the classification standards of the CLC bring new challenges to the multi-label task. First, the keywords of the paper are closely related to the paper category, but it is difficult to extract semantic information due to its short and sparse text content. Therefore, it is necessary to comprehensively utilize the semantic information of keywords and paper titles. The existing methods do not consider the association between papers with the same keywords. Second, there are a large number of categories in CLC, and the difference between categories is small. It is difficult to accurately classify papers from a large number of similar categories.

To solve the above problems, in this paper, we propose a Hierarchical Multi-Label Attention classification method with Graph attention network (HMLAG). First, we use Graph Attention Network (GAT) to aggregate keywords and titles of papers. Second, we use a multiple-output deep neural network to model the structure of labels which can obtain local output and global output. Considering the characteristics of labels from different levels, our method adaptively aggregates local labels and global labels to obtain the final label representation. Our contributions are summarized as follows:

(1) We use the GAT network to aggregate the keywords and title features of the paper. The title information of scientific papers can be aggregated into the keyword node to enrich the semantic representation of the keyword. On this basis, the paper node can obtain the semantic features of words and titles jointly by aggregating keyword information.

(2) We propose a hierarchical multi-label attention network for paper classification. With the help of hierarchical relationship, each layer of the network only pays attention to the label of the corresponding layer. The number of classes needed to be classified for each layer is reduced. Then we use an attention network to combine the global labels and local labels of each level adaptively.

(3) We conduct extensive experiments to evaluate our model. Experimental results demonstrate that our method outperforms several state-of-the-art methods in the task of scientific paper classification tasks.

2   Related Work

The associations between labels can be leveraged in the multi-label classification task. Zhang et al. [1] attempt to model the label space by building the label graph. Zhang et al. [2] propose a global optimization method with the goal of considering feature relevance, label relevance (i.e., label correlation), and feature redundancy for feature evaluation. Feng et al. [3] learn the label correlations via sparse reconstruction in the label space, integrating the learned label correlations into model training. Many labels lack sufficient samples, Lv et al. [4] use the structural information in the feature space and the local correlation in the label space to enhance the label. Xing et al. [5] leverage information concerning the co-occurrence of pairwise labels to communicate labels of selected samples among co-training classifiers. You et al. [6] utilize LSTM to capture long-distance word dependencies, and use attention mechanism to make different words have different effects on labels. Xun et al. [7] develops the correlation networks architecture to learn the label correlations, enhance raw label predictions with correlation knowledge and output augmented label predictions. Shi et al. [8] propose a deep generative model to describe the label generation process for semi-supervised multi-label learning by incorporating latent variables to describe the labeled and unlabeled data

In recent years, graph learning has developed rapidly, Velikovi and Petar et al. [9] use the attention mechanism to calculate the weights of different nodes in the neighborhood, without relying on the global structure of the graph. Yao et al. [10] build a single text graph for a corpus based on word co-occurrence and document word relations, then learn a text graph convolutional network. Based on the GraphSage, Tang et al. [11] take advantage of BiLSTM as the aggregator functions get the Second-order feature to capture dependencies. Wang et al. [12] utilize the co-occurrence information to model the label graph, then apply multi-layer graph convolutions on the final superimposed graph for label embedding abstraction.

Different from traditional multi-label classification task, labels are organized into a hierarchical structure in hierarchical multi-label task. Considering that the conceptual relationships between words can also form a hierarchical structure, Chen et al. [13] learn mappings from word hierarchies to label hierarchies. Wehrmann et al. [14] utilize multiple linear layers, corresponding to the number of category layers, and have outputs locally in each layer. It optimizes the loss of the local layer and the global loss of the final output. Yan et al. [15] incorporate the potential contribution of ancestor and descendant labels to estimate the informativeness of each candidate query.

However, the existing methods do not take into account the association of papers of labels and the hierarchical structure jointly. Inspired by Wehrmann's work, we proposed HMLAG which utilizes graph attention network to aggregate keywords and titles of papers and uses a multiple-output deep neural network to model the structure of labels.

3 Methodology

HMLAG is composed of two components: Graph attention module and hierarchical multi-label attention module. The structure of HMLAG is shown in Fig. 1. Graph attention module learns the relationship between papers and keywords to get the paper representation on text graphs. Hierarchical multi-label attention module models the hierarchical structure of labels and obtains the multi-label classification results by applying a self-attention network. We will introduce the two modules in the following parts.

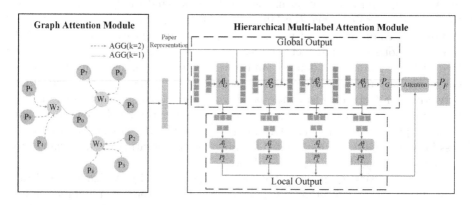

Fig. 1. The overall architecture of hierarchical multi-label classification based on graph attention network (HMLAG).

3.1 Paper Representation Based on Graph Attention Network

In our task, it is very important to capture the keyword co-occurrence relationship between papers. First, we construct an undirected graph of papers and keywords $G_{pw} = (V_p \cup V_w, E_{pw})$, V_p, V_w represent the paper nodes and the keyword nodes, respectively. E_{pw} represents the edges between papers and keywords. For a keyword w_i, if a paper p_i contains it, there will be an edge between w_i and p_i. The input of the model is $\mathbf{X} \in \mathbf{R}^{s \times d}$, where s is the number of keywords and titles, d is the dimension of features.

Spectral-based GCN model [16] relies on the complete structure of the graph, so it is difficult to train on large-scale data. In addition, each keyword of the paper and other related papers have different effects on the category of the paper, and GCN cannot provide different weights to nodes. Therefore, we use GAT to learn graph node embedding. GAT does not depend on the global structure, so batch training can be used for large data sets. For node v, $N(v), u \in N(v)$ is the immediate neighbors of v. The node feature h_v is updated by the following process. First, we perform self-attention on nodes, which is calculated as follows,

$$e_{vu} = LeakyReLU\left(\mathbf{a}^T\left[\mathbf{W}h_v\|\mathbf{W}h_u\right]\right) \tag{1}$$

where $LeakyReLU$ is the activation function, $\mathbf{W} \in \mathbf{R}^{d \times d}$ is a shared linear transformation, $\mathbf{a}^T$ is a shared attentional mechanism, $\|$ is the concatenation operation. Second, we get the attention factor between u and v by Eq. (2)

$$\alpha_{vu} = softmax\left(e_{vu}\right) = \frac{\exp\left(e_{vu}\right)}{\sum_{k \in N_v} \exp\left(e_{vk}\right)} \tag{2}$$

Finally, we get the updated feature of v

$$h'_v = \sigma\left(\sum_{u \in \mathcal{N}_v} \alpha_{vu}\mathbf{W}h_u\right) \tag{3}$$

To obtain a more stable output, we introduce the multi-head attention network, where K means the number of heads as follows,

$$h'_v = \|_{k=1}^K \sigma\left(\sum_{j \in \mathcal{N}_v} \alpha_{vu}^k \mathbf{W}^k h_u\right) \tag{4}$$

Through the GAT network, we use the structure of the graph and combine the semantic feature of the neighbor nodes to update the node representation. Finally, the feature matrix of the paper node is represented as $X' \in \mathbf{R}^{s \times d}$.

3.2 Hierarchical Multi-label Attention Network

We apply a multiple-output deep neural network, corresponding to the number of category layers to model the hierarchical structure of labels. There are two kinds of flows through the network. The global flow propagates from the input to the global. The local flow propagates with the global flow until it reaches respective FC layers and then ends at the corresponding local output. It optimizes the loss of the local output and the global output at every epoch. In addition, to get the consistent hierarchical path, a punishment for predictions with hierarchical violations is used. m is the serial number of the layer, $|M|$ is the total number of layers, C is the set of all labels. C^m is the label set of layer m. $\mathbf{A}_G^m$ is the global output of layer m, used to obtain the global label representation. $\mathbf{A}_L^m$ is the local output of layer m, which captures the local features of the layer through $\mathbf{A}_G^m$ to obtain the local label representation of the layer. Let x is a row vector of X'. The output of the first layer is obtained by Eq. (5),

$$\mathbf{A}_G^1 = \sigma\left(\mathbf{W}_G^1 x + \mathbf{b}_G^1\right) \tag{5}$$

We can get $\mathbf{A}_G^m$ from $\mathbf{A}_G^{m-1}$ by

$$\mathbf{A}_G^m = \sigma\left(\mathbf{W}_G^m \mathbf{A}_G^{m-1}\|x + \mathbf{b}_G^m\right) \tag{6}$$

where $\mathbf{W}_G^m \in \mathbf{R}^{|\mathbf{A}_G^m| \times |\mathbf{A}_G^{m-1}|}$ is the global weight matrix, $\mathbf{b}_G^m$ is the bias vector. The global output is

$$\mathbf{P}_G = \sigma \left(\mathbf{W}_G^{|M|+1} \mathbf{A}_G^{|M|} + \mathbf{b}_G^{|M|+1} \right) \tag{7}$$

where $\mathbf{P}_G^i$ denotes the probability for $C_i \in \mathbf{C}$.

For every $\mathbf{A}_G^m$, there will also be a local propagation. We use a local weight matrix $\mathbf{W}_T^m \in \mathbf{R}^{|\mathbf{A}_L^m| \times |\mathbf{A}_G^m|}$ to map $\mathbf{A}_G^m$ to $\mathbf{A}_L^m$,

$$\mathbf{A}_L^m = \sigma \left(\mathbf{W}_T^m \mathbf{A}_G^m + \mathbf{b}_T^m \right) \tag{8}$$

We use another linear layer $\mathbf{W}_L^m \in \mathbf{R}^{|c^m| \times |\mathbf{A}_L^m|}$ to map $\mathbf{A}_L^m$ to $\mathbf{P}_L^m \in \mathbf{R}^{|C^m|}$,

$$\mathbf{P}_L^m = \sigma \left(\mathbf{W}_L^m \mathbf{A}_L^m + \mathbf{b}_L^m \right) \tag{9}$$

where $\mathbf{P}_L^i$ denotes the probability for $C_i \in \mathbf{C}^m$. In the process of combining the global label and local label, the dimension of the global label is the sum of the dimensions of each level. We divide the global label into multiple parts, which correspond to the local labels of each layer, then we use an attention network to combine the local labels and global labels of each level.

$$\alpha_{FL} = \frac{\exp \left(ReLU \left(\mathbf{a}^T \left[\mathbf{WP}_F^m \| \mathbf{WP}_L^m \right] \right) \right)}{\exp \left(ReLU \left(\mathbf{a}^T \left[\mathbf{WP}_F^m \| \mathbf{WP}_L^m \right] \right) \right) + \exp \left(ReLU \left(\mathbf{a}^T \left[\mathbf{WP}_F^m \| \mathbf{WP}_G^m \right] \right) \right)} \tag{10}$$

where $\mathbf{a}$ is an attention parameter, $\mathbf{W} \in \mathbf{R}^{|C^m| \times |C^m|}$ is a shared linear transformation. We can get α_{FG} by the same way. The final output is

$$\mathbf{P}_F = \left(a_{FL}^1 \mathbf{P}_L^1 + a_{FG}^1 \mathbf{P}_G^1 \right) \| \left(a_{FL}^2 \mathbf{P}_L^2 + a_{FG}^2 \mathbf{P}_G^2 \right) \dots \| \left(a_{FL}^M \mathbf{P}_L^M + a_{FG}^M \mathbf{P}_G^M \right) \tag{11}$$

When the confidence of the subcategory is greater than the parent category, we add a loss function $\mathcal{L}_{M_i}$ for label i to punish this violation. Compared to the sublabels, it is easier to classify on the parent labels and the confidence should be higher.

$$\mathcal{L}_{M_i} = \max \left\{ 0, \mathbf{Y}_{in} - \mathbf{Y}_{ip} \right\}^2 \tag{12}$$

where $\mathbf{Y}_{ip}$ is the probability for the parent lable of label i.

The total loss function is formulated by integrating the global loss and local loss as follows,

$$\mathcal{L}_F = \mathcal{E} \left(\mathbf{P}_G, \mathbf{Y}_G \right) + \lambda_L \sum_{m=1}^{|M|} \left[\mathcal{E} \left(\mathbf{P}_L^m, \mathbf{Y}_L^m \right) \right] + \lambda_M \mathcal{L}_M \tag{13}$$

where λ_L is the tradeoff parameter for local loss, λ_M is the tradeoff parameter for violation loss, $\mathcal{E}(X, Y)$ is the binary cross entropy loss which is commonly used in multi-label classification and is defined as,

$$\mathcal{E}(X, Y) = -\frac{1}{N} \sum_{i=1}^{N} \sum_{j=1}^{|C|} \left[\mathbf{Y}_{ij} \times \log \left(\mathbf{X}_{ij} \right) + \left(1 - \mathbf{Y}_{ij} \right) \times \log \left(1 - \mathbf{X}_{ij} \right) \right] \tag{14}$$

4   Experiment

4.1   Dataset

We use CNKI and RCV1 [17] datasets as the experimental datasets. We collected 80,000 papers from CNKI with 265 categories. The maximum depth of the label level is 4 layers. Among these papers, there are 73,920 multi-labeled papers in total. Each sample contains the title, keywords, and label of the paper. We divide the dataset into a training set and a test set with a ratio of 10:1, We use the BERT [18] Chinese pre-training model for word embedding. We also use RCV1 dataset to evaluate our method, the size of training set and test set is 66285 and 25905, respectively. Since the dataset has no title and keywords, we use NLTK to preprocess the data. We remove words appearing less than 5 times. We build the graph based on the keyword co-occurrence relationship and embed the content to get document representation.

4.2   Experimental Setup and Baselines

We use BERT to get the initial feature and set the dimension to 768 dimensions. In the graph attention network, we use a two-layer attention network and keep the output dimension to 768. For the activation function leakyrelu, we set negative input slope $\alpha = 0.2$, for the hierarchical network, we set four hierarchical classification layers according to the hierarchy of categories. For each layer, the number of units is set to $\{384, 384, 384, 384\}$, and the local output dimension of each layer to $\{32,128,128,128\}$. We set $\lambda_M = 10^{-2}$, $\lambda_L = 1$. Adam is used as the optimizer, the learning rate is set to 10^{-3}, and the size of each batch is set to 64. The epoch is 200 for every model. We compare our model with the popular methods TEXTRNN [19], AttentiveConvNet [20], DRNN [21], DPCNN [22] and HMCN on our dataset. We employ the ranking-based metrics, which are widely used in the multi-label classification task. Precision@k (P@k) counts the fraction of correct label predictions in the top k scoring labels from the predicted labels list. Micro-F1 is the harmonic mean of the precision and recall. Macro-F1 is the arithmetic mean of all the F1 scores of different classes. We present results when k = 1, 3, 5 in our experiments.

4.3   Result Analysis

It can be seen from the Table 1 that our method HMLAG outperforms the baselines by 8.19%, 14.86%, and 10.7% on P@1, P@3, and P@5 respectively. In micro-F1, macro-F1 indicators, our method outperforms the baselines by 11.69% and 12.75% respectively. The results indicate that our method is more effective on the paper dataset. In Table 2, TEXTRNN gets the best results among the non-hierarchical classification model, our method performs similar to TEXTRNN due to the lack of natural keyword features in RCV1. With the gradual increase of P@k, compared with other methods, our method has a slower rate of decline than other methods. This shows that our method can not only get the vector

Table 1. Results of multi-label classification on CNKI papers

	P@1	P@3	P@5	micro-F1@3	macro-F1@3
TEXTRNN	0.7897	0.4251	0.2851	0.3961	0.2149
AttentiveConvNet	0.7279	0.4142	0.2382	0.3343	0.1686
DRNN	0.8105	0.4162	0.2732	0.3270	0.1842
DPCNN	0.7092	0.3974	0.2947	0.2162	0.1321
HMCN	0.8037	0.5130	0.3196	0.3925	0.2786
GAT-FC	0.7952	0.4655	0.2474	0.4153	0.2615
GAT-HMCN	0.8763	0.5572	0.4021	0.5021	0.3944
HMLAG (Ours)	**0.8924**	**0.5737**	**0.4266**	**0.5130**	**0.4061**

Table 2. Results of multi-label classification on RCV1

	P@1	P@3	P@5	micro-F1@3	macro-F1@3
TEXTRNN	0.9597	**0.9080**	0.8843	**0.7694**	0.4332
AttentiveConvNet	0.9462	0.8717	0.8208	0.7294	0.3509
DRNN	0.9216	0.8437	0.7738	0.6309	0.1894
DPCNN	0.9288	0.8369	0.7945	0.6808	0.2795
HMCN	0.9047	0.8572	0.8169	0.6188	0.4245
GAT-FC	0.9253	0.8471	0.8072	0.6542	0.3373
GAT-HMCN	0.9418	0.8952	0.8663	0.7561	0.4363
HMLAG (Ours)	**0.9614**	0.9053	**0.8850**	0.7627	**0.4492**

representation of the document by combining its own title and keyword information, but also the data information of other papers with the same keyword node is aggregated based on the graph attention network, so that the document representation contains more abundant multi-label information.

4.4   Ablation Study

Since our method is divided into two parts: Document representation and hierarchical classification, in the ablation study, we compare HMLAG with GAT-FC, HMCN and GAT-HMCN. For GAT-FC, we directly use two full connection layers and a SoftMax normalization to predict the classification results. For GAT-HMCN, we use HMCN as the classifier after GAT. We first compare HMLAG and GAT-FC to show how the hierarchical label classification network improves the final performance. We can observe that HMLAG outperforms GAT-FC by 10.62% and 5.82% in CNKI and RCV1, respectively. In hierarchical label classification task, it is important to capture the relationship between different levels, the result shows that our model effectively captures such features. Then we compare HMLAG with HMCN, it can be observed that our method outperforms HMCN by 6.07% and 4.81%, which demonstrates that our method successfully aggregates the feature of keywords and titles of papers. Finally, compared with GAT-HMCN, our method has an improvement on P@3 by 1.65% and 1.01%, which shows that the attention network in HMLAG which combines the local labels and global labels can effectively improve the performance of classification.

4.5 Parameter Sensitivity Analysis

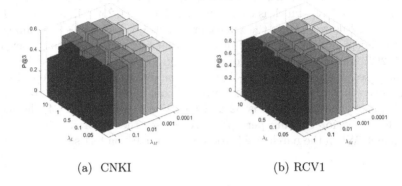

(a) CNKI   (b) RCV1

Fig. 2. Parameter sensitivity on P@3

In this section, we evaluate the performance under different parameter settings. Results are illustrated in Fig. 2. We report parameter sensitivity for P@3. We make 25 combinations by changing λ_M and λ_L. We choose λ_M from $\{10^0, 10^{-1}, 10^{-2}, 10^{-3}, 10^{-4}, 10^{-5}\}$ and choose λ_L from $\{10, 1, 0.5, 0.1, 0.05\}$. We conduct experiments on CNKI and RCV1. It can be observed that our method performs best when $\lambda_M = 10^{-2}$ and $\lambda_L = 1$ on CNKI from Fig. 2. In addition, our model can obtain 0.55 in P@3 in most parameter combinations, which proves that our model is not sensitive to parameters. One can note that when $\lambda_M = 1$ or 0.1, the results fluctuate greatly with the change of λ_L.

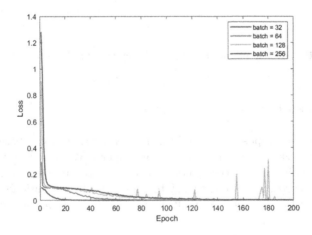

Fig. 3. The impact of different batch size on loss of CNKI

We apply the same settings on RCV1, the results in Fig. 2 show that our method gets the best performance when $\lambda_M = 10^{-2}$ and $\lambda_L = 1$. Compared with CNKI, different combinations have less impact on our method. We can still observe that the results are not stable when λ_M is too high, which indicate that the excessive punishment for violation make the model unstable.

We evaluate the performance of our method with different batch-size on training set of CNKI, which is choose from $\{32, 64, 128, 256\}$, fixing $\lambda_M = 10^{-2}$ and $\lambda_L = 1$. Figure 3 shows the binary cross-entropy loss values of training set across different epochs. It can be observed that our method usually converges within 20 iterations. The speed of model convergence increases as the batch size increases. Figure 4 shows the P@3 on test set across different epochs. We can observe that after our model converges, our method achieves the similar performance when batch size is 32 and 64. When batch size is 64, the model needs less time for training per epoch, so we set the batch size to 64 in our experiment. When the batch size is too large, the P@3 on test set drops sharply.

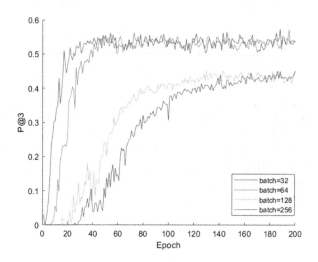

Fig. 4. The impact of different batch size on P@3 of CNKI

5   Conclusion

In this paper, we propose a hierarchical label attention model based on graph attention network to get multi-label for papers. We use the keyword co-occurrence relationship of the paper to construct the topological structure of the paper keywords, and use the GAT to aggregate the semantic features of the keywords and titles in papers. In multi-label classification, we use multiple linear layers to model the hierarchical classification features of the papers, and use the attention mechanism to adaptively adjust the weights of local labels and global labels. We obtain local output to predict labels for the corresponding hierarchical labels. The experimental results show that compared with the state-of-the-art methods, our model performs better on multi-label scientific paper classification.

Acknowledgements. This work was supported by National Key R&D Program of China (2018YFB1402600), and by the National Natural Science Foundation of China (61802028, 61772083, 61877006, 62002027), and sponsored by CCF-Baidu Open Fund.

References

1. Zhang, W., Yan, J., Wang, X., Zha, H.: Deep extreme multi-label learning. In: Proceedings of the 2018 ACM on International Conference on Multimedia Retrieval, ICMR 2018, pp. 100–107. Association for Computing Machinery, New York (2018). https://doi.org/10.1145/3206025.3206030
2. Zhang, J., Lin, Y., Jiang, M., Li, S., Tang, Y., Tan, K.C.: Multi-label feature selection via global relevance and redundancy optimization. In: Bessiere, C. (ed.) Proceedings of the Twenty-Ninth International Joint Conference on Artificial Intelligence, IJCAI-20, pp. 2512–2518. International Joint Conferences on Artificial Intelligence Organization, July 2020. Main track
3. Feng, L., An, B., He, S.: Collaboration based multi-label learning. In: Proceedings of the AAAI Conference on Artificial Intelligence, vol. 33, no. 01, pp. 3550–3557 (2019)
4. Lv, J., Xu, N., Zheng, R., Geng, X.: Weakly supervised multi-label learning via label enhancement. In: Proceedings of the Twenty-Eighth International Joint Conference on Artificial Intelligence, IJCAI-19, pp. 3101–3107. International Joint Conferences on Artificial Intelligence Organization, July 2019. https://doi.org/10.24963/ijcai.2019/430
5. Xing, Y., Yu, G., Domeniconi, C., Wang, J., Zhang, Z.: Multi-label co-training. In: Proceedings of the Twenty-Seventh International Joint Conference on Artificial Intelligence, IJCAI-18, pp. 2882–2888. International Joint Conferences on Artificial Intelligence Organization, July 2018. https://doi.org/10.24963/ijcai.2018/400
6. You, R., Zhang, Z., Wang, Z., Dai, S., Mamitsuka, H., Zhu, S.: AttentionXML: label tree-based attention-aware deep model for high-performance extreme multi-label text classification. arXiv preprint arXiv:1811.01727 (2018)
7. Xun, G., Jha, K., Sun, J., Zhang, A.: Correlation networks for extreme multi-label text classification. In: Proceedings of the 26th ACM SIGKDD International Conference on Knowledge Discovery & Data Mining, KDD 2020, pp. 1074–1082. Association for Computing Machinery, New York (2020). https://doi.org/10.1145/3394486.3403151
8. Shi, W., Sheng, V.S., Li, X., Gu, B.: Semi-supervised multi-label learning from crowds via deep sequential generative model. In: Proceedings of the 26th ACM SIGKDD International Conference on Knowledge Discovery & Data Mining, KDD 2020, pp. 1141–1149. Association for Computing Machinery, New York (2020). https://doi.org/10.1145/3394486.3403167
9. Veličković, P., Cucurull, G., Casanova, A., Romero, A., Lio, P., Bengio, Y.: Graph attention networks. arXiv preprint arXiv:1710.10903 (2017)

10. Yao, L., Mao, C., Luo, Y.: Graph convolutional networks for text classification. In: Proceedings of the AAAI Conference on Artificial Intelligence, vol. 33, no. 01, pp. 7370–7377 (2019)
11. Tang, P., Jiang, M., Xia, B.N., Pitera, J.W., Welser, J., Chawla, N.V.: Multi-label patent categorization with non-local attention-based graph convolutional network. In: Proceedings of the AAAI Conference on Artificial Intelligence, vol. 34, no. 05, pp. 9024–9031 (2020)
12. Wang, Y., et al.: Multi-label classification with label graph superimposing. In: Proceedings of the AAAI Conference on Artificial Intelligence, vol. 34, no. 07, pp. 12 265–12 272 (2020)
13. Chen, B., Huang, X., Xiao, L., Cai, Z., Jing, L.: Hyperbolic interaction model for hierarchical multi-label classification. In: Proceedings of the AAAI Conference on Artificial Intelligence, vol. 34, no. 05, pp. 7496–7503 (2020)
14. Wehrmann, J., Cerri, R., Barros, R.: Hierarchical multi-label classification networks. In: International Conference on Machine Learning, pp. 5075–5084. PMLR (2018)
15. Yan, Y.-F., Huang, S.-J.: Cost-effective active learning for hierarchical multi-label classification. In: Proceedings of the Twenty-Seventh International Joint Conference on Artificial Intelligence, IJCAI-18, pp. 2962–2968. International Joint Conferences on Artificial Intelligence Organization, July 2018. https://doi.org/10.24963/ijcai.2018/411
16. Kipf, T.N., Welling, M.: Semi-supervised classification with graph convolutional networks. In: 5th International Conference on Learning Representations, ICLR 2017, Toulon, France, 24–26 April 2017. Conference Track Proceedings. OpenReview.net (2017). https://openreview.net/forum?id=SJU4ayYgl
17. Lewis, D.D., Yang, Y., Rose, T.G., Li, F.: RCV1: a new benchmark collection for text categorization research. J. Mach. Learn. Res. 5, 361–397 (2004). http://jmlr.org/papers/volume5/lewis04a/lewis04a.pdf
18. Devlin, J., Chang, M.-W., Lee, K., Toutanova, K.: BERT: pre-training of deep bidirectional transformers for language understanding. In: Proceedings of the 2019 Conference of the North American Chapter of the Association for Computational Linguistics: Human Language Technologies, Volume 1 (Long and Short Papers), pp. 4171–4186. Association for Computational Linguistics, Minneapolis, June 2019. https://www.aclweb.org/anthology/N19-1423
19. Liu, P., Qiu, X., Huang, X.: Recurrent neural network for text classification with multi-task learning. In: Kambhampati, S. (ed.) Proceedings of the Twenty-Fifth International Joint Conference on Artificial Intelligence, IJCAI 2016, New York, NY, USA, 9–15 July 2016, pp. 2873–2879. IJCAI/AAAI Press (2016). http://www.ijcai.org/Abstract/16/408
20. Wang, B.: Disconnected recurrent neural networks for text categorization. In: Proceedings of the 56th Annual Meeting of the Association for Computational Linguistics (Volume 1: Long Papers), pp. 2311–2320. Association for Computational Linguistics, Melbourne, July 2018. https://www.aclweb.org/anthology/P18-1215
21. Johnson, R., Zhang, T.: Deep pyramid convolutional neural networks for text categorization. In: Proceedings of the 55th Annual Meeting of the Association for Computational Linguistics (Volume 1: Long Papers), pp. 562–570. Association for Computational Linguistics, Vancouver, July 2017. https://www.aclweb.org/anthology/P17-1052
22. Yin, W., Schütze, H.: Attentive convolution: equipping CNNs with RNN-style attention mechanisms. Trans. Assoc. Comput. Linguist. 6, 687–702 (2018)

HNECV: Heterogeneous Network Embedding via Cloud Model and Variational Inference

Ming Yuan[1], Qun Liu[1(✉)], Guoyin Wang[1(✉)], and Yike Guo[2,3]

[1] Chongqing Key Laboratory of Computational Intelligence,
Chongqing University of Posts and Telecommunications, ChongQing, China
s180231080@stu.cqupt.edu.cn, {liuqun,wanggy}@cqupt.edu.cn
[2] Hong Kong Baptist University, HongKong, China
yikeguo@hkbu.edu.hk
[3] Imperial College London, London, UK

Abstract. Deep learning has been successfully used in heterogeneous network embedding. Although it shows excellent performance on preserving the structure and semantic characteristics of network while a large scale of training data is provided, it is still challenging to model complex structured representations that effectively perform on diverse network tasks. In this work, a new heterogeneous network embedding learning method is presented based on cloud model and variational inference, called HNECV. The model uses meta-path random walks to obtain structural information of original network which can capture abundant semantics of networks from different views. In addition, a novel framework is put forward to build an excellent embedding. We employ the forward cloud transformation algorithm to improve the sampling method of the variational autoencoder in its hidden space, and then a self-supervised learning module is constructed to guide the cluster of node vectors in the hidden space of variational autoencoder. Experimental results indicate that the proposed model can achieve better performance than those of state-of-the-art algorithms. Furthermore, HNECV shows better robustness and steadiness on different network tasks when different ratio of edges are disconnected at training.

Keywords: Heterogeneous network · Representation learning · Variational autoencoder · Cloud model · Meta-path

1 Introduction

Network embedding can map the nodes in the network to low-dimensional space and capture the structural information of the network. Recent work has confirmed that this kind of node representation can bring significant performance improvements to tasks such as link prediction [1–3], node classification [4–6], and node clustering [7–9].

However, the traditional network embedding method only focuses on homogeneous network embedding, and the network only owns the same type of nodes

© Springer Nature Switzerland AG 2021
L. Fang et al. (Eds.): CICAI 2021, LNAI 13069, pp. 747–758, 2021.
https://doi.org/10.1007/978-3-030-93046-2_63

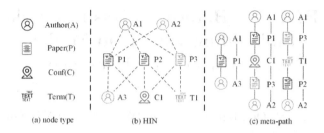

Fig. 1. Example of DBLP heterogeneous information network.

and links. In real scenarios, the types of nodes and links in the network are often different, and they construct a heterogeneous information network (HIN). Compared with homogeneous networks, HIN has more complex network relationships and contain rich semantic information. As shown in Fig. 1, the DBLP academic citation network contains four different types of nodes, such as Author (A), Paper (P), Conferences (C) and Term (T), and three different types of link relations, that is Paper-Author (PA), Paper-Conference (PC), and Paper-Term (PT). Obviously, the use of homogeneous network embedding in such a network will inevitably lead to a decline in embedding performance.

Therefore, in order to overcome the challenges brought by HIN, Some methods have been studied from the perspective of heterogeneous neighbors and different links, such as Metapath2vec [10], HIN2vec [11], HERec [12]. In addition, some researchers use the decomposition method to simplify the HIN [13,14], which eases the difficulty in the modeling process to a certain extent. Most of the above methods make preprocessing designs for HIN, and then learn the representation of nodes in combination with shallow neural networks.

SHINE [15] uses multiple deep autoencoders to map user information. MCRec [16] designed a co-attention mechanism to learn the importance of nodes and meta-paths. HAN [17] is the first expansion of graph neural network on heterogeneous graphs. HetGAN [18] tries the structure of GAN to learn embedding. RHINE [19] maps different relationships between nodes into different spaces. Besides, there are some works that explore how to model attributes of HIN [20–22] or use the GCNs method to aggregate the features of nodes [23–25] to learn the latent semantics and high-order neighbor features of the network.

Most of the above methods consider the characteristics of the network structure and semantics, and rarely consider the original real distribution information of the HIN. For example, although some nodes in the real network do not have direct links, they may still have a high similarity. Based on VAE, we can improve the quality of node representation by inducing the distribution of latent space with some restrictions rather than by relying on the structure of networks. In fact, if the distribution information of network data cannot be used, the low-dimensional embedding of nodes learned by the model may not conform to the real network situation, and it will also affect the accuracy of subsequent tasks. To address the above problems, the main contributions of this work are summarized as following:

- We provide a key insight to learn heterogeneous information network embeddings based on variational autoencoders. In order to make better use of the real distribution information of network data, it provides a feasible idea and promotes the application of HIN embedding.
- In this framework, cloud model, which is also known as a "recognition" model, is introduced to approximate the true posterior. And then a self supervised learning module is constructed to guide the cluster of similar nodes in the hidden space. Through the above joint optimization, HNECV closely integrates inference and clustering to learn high quality heterogeneous network embedding.
- We have conducted comprehensive experiments on three real datasets, and the experimental results show that the method in this paper is more superiord and robustness than state-of-the-art algorithms.

2   Preliminaries

Definition 1. *Heterogeneous information network (HIN)* [26]. *A heterogeneous information network is defined as* $G = (V, E)$, *including a set of nodes V and a set of links E. The mapping functions of node type and link type in the network are $\varphi : V \to \mathcal{A}$ and $\psi : E \to \mathcal{R}$ respectively. $\mathcal{A}$ and $\mathcal{R}$ represent the pre-defined node type and link type, where $|\mathcal{A}| + |\mathcal{R}| > 2$. The network schema is defined as $S = (\mathcal{A}, \mathcal{R})$, which is the basic prototype of HIN, and can represent a graph with node type $\mathcal{A}$ and link type $\mathcal{R}$.*

Definition 2. *Meta-path* [27]. *The meta-path P is a path instance defined on the network schema $S = (\mathcal{A}, \mathcal{R})$, which is denoted as $\mathcal{A}_1 \xrightarrow{\mathcal{R}_1} \mathcal{A}_2 \xrightarrow{\mathcal{R}_2} \dots \xrightarrow{\mathcal{R}_l} \mathcal{A}_{l+1}$. $\mathcal{R} = \mathcal{R}_1 \circ \mathcal{R}_2 \circ \dots \circ \mathcal{R}_l$ describes the composite relationship between $\mathcal{A}_1, \mathcal{A}_2, \dots, \mathcal{A}_{l+1}$, and $\circ$ represents the composite operator on the relationship.*

Figure 1(c) shows the meta-path relationship in the DBLP network, each meta-path represents a different semantic. For example, the meta-path APA indicates the co-author relationship between two authors, APCPA indicates the co-conferences relationship, and APTPA indicates the co-term relationship.

3   The Proposed Model

In this section, our model (HNECV) is introduced in detail. The overall framework of the model is shown in Fig. 2. It is mainly composed of three parts: fusion heterogeneous graph structure, forward cloud inference, and self-supervised learning module. Our dataset and codes can be available at website[1].

---

[1] https://github.com/benym/HNECV.

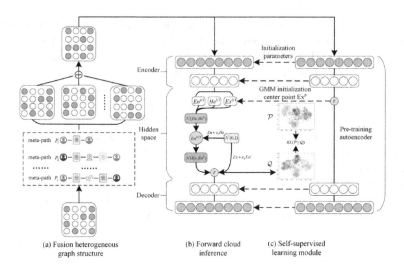

Fig. 2. The framework of HNECV.

3.1 Fusion Heterogeneous Graph Structure

In heterogeneous information networks, meta-paths can describe different semantic information, and the node sequence generated by random walks of meta-paths can well retain the structure and semantics of HIN. As shown in Fig. 2(a), we use multiple meta-paths $P_1, P_2, \ldots, P_i$ to guide the random walk to obtain the multi-view information of the original HIN. Random walks under different meta-paths can obtain different node sequences $H_1, H_2, \ldots, H_i$, which reflect the structural characteristics of HIN in a specific semantic environment. Hence, the multiple adjacency matrices $G_1, G_2, \ldots, G_i$ are reconstructed according to the node sequences of different meta-paths. Furthermore, we merge these matrices as follows:

$$G_{in} = G_1 \oplus G_2, \ldots \oplus G_i \tag{1}$$

where $\oplus$ is the element-wise addition, and G_{in} is the matrix after fusion.

3.2 Forward Cloud Inference

Generally in variational autoencoder (VAE) [28], the input of the decoder is sampled from the latent space depending on Gaussian distribution. But the reconstructed input data usually lose a lot of information. In order to solve this problem, we extend the sampling process in VAE by introducing the cloud model to obtain the embeddings of nodes. Cloud models algorithm has been widely used in various research fields [29, 30]. It can realize the bidirectional transformations between concepts and data based on probability statistics and fuzzy set theory. The probability distribution in the cloud model is also called the Gaussian cloud distribution, which can be described by Expected Value Ex, Entropy En, and

Hyper Entropy He. Compared with the Gaussian distribution, the Gaussian cloud distribution describes the distribution of data more accurately.

As same as the structure of the VAE, our model uses MLP as the encoder and decoder. We use the fused adjacency matrix G_{in} as the input of the encoder, suppose G_{in} contains N nodes, the representation of each hidden layer is as following:

$$h_N^c = f\left(W^c h_N^{(c-1)} + b^c\right), c = 1, 2, \ldots, C \tag{2}$$

where $f(\cdot)$ is the Relu function, W^c and b^c are the weight and bias parameters of the model in the c-th layer, C is the number of layers of the encoder or decoder, and input data x_n is denoted as h_N^0.

Here, the latent variable Z in the VAE is no longer described by the mean and variance, but is represented by the Gaussian cloud parameters Ex, En, He. The Ex and En can be compared to the mean and variance of the original Gaussian distribution, He can reflect the thickness of the Gaussian cloud, it can be used to adjust the thickness of Gaussian cloud by sampling more data from the distribution of space. Their formal descriptions in our model are given as follows:

$$Ex = W^c h_N^c + b^c \tag{3}$$

$$En = W^c h_N^c + b^c \tag{4}$$

$$He = W^c h_N^c + b^c \tag{5}$$

Inspired by the forward cloud transformation (FCT) algorithm [30], HNECV leverages two sampling steps to obtain the latent variable Z, which expands the sampling space of the original VAE. Meanwhile, due to the sampling operation cannot be derivable, we employ reparameterization trick, and take the sampling results into the training process to ensure that the model can be optimized. The forward cloud inference of HNECV is shown in Fig. 2(b), and this process can be defined as follows:

$$\varepsilon_1 \sim \mathcal{N}(0, 1) = En' \sim \mathcal{N}\left(En, He^2\right) \tag{6}$$

$$En' = \varepsilon_1 \odot He + En \tag{7}$$

$$\varepsilon_2 \sim \mathcal{N}(0, 1) = Z \sim \mathcal{N}\left(Ex, En'^2\right) \tag{8}$$

$$Z = \varepsilon_2 \odot En' + Ex \tag{9}$$

The latent variable Z can be obtained by combining Eqs. (7) and (9):

$$Z = Ex + \varepsilon_1 \odot En + \varepsilon_1 \odot \varepsilon_2 \odot He \tag{10}$$

where ε_1 and ε_2 represent noise variables sampled from the standard Gaussian distribution, and $\odot$ denotes Hadamard product.

Assuming that the latent variable Z obeys the standard Gaussian distribution $\mathcal{N}(0, 1)$, the distance between the two distributions can be calculated by KL divergence as follows:

$$D_{KL}\left(\mathcal{N}\left(Ex, En^2\right) \| \mathcal{N}(0, 1)\right) =$$
$$\mathcal{L}_{KL} = \frac{1}{2} \sum_{d=1}^{D} \left[1 + \ln\left((En_d)^2\right) - (Ex_d)^2 - (En_d)^2\right] \tag{11}$$

where D is the number of dimensions of the hidden space, Ex_d and En_d are the Ex and En of the d-dimension respectively.

After obtaining the latent variable Z, HNECV can generate an adjacency matrix containing N nodes through the following equations:

$$h_N^{(c-1)} = f\left(W^c Z + b^c\right) \tag{12}$$

$$h_N^c = f\left(W^c h_N^{(c-1)} + b^c\right) \tag{13}$$

$$\hat{x} = W^c h_N^c + b^c \tag{14}$$

Then, we can calculate the distance between ground truth x and the generation $\hat{x}$ to get the reconstruction error of the model. Due to the sparsity of network data, we impose greater penalties on more meaningful non-zero elements. The reconstruction objective function of HNECV is shown as follows:

$$\mathcal{L}_{rec} = \sum_{n=1}^{|N|} \|(\hat{x}_n - x_n) \odot B_n\|_2^2 \tag{15}$$

where $B_i = \{B_{i,j}\}_{j=1}^{|N|}$ is a penalty item. If the i-th row and j-th column element of the adjacency matrix G_{in} is 0, $B = 1$, otherwise $B > 1$.

3.3   Self-supervised Learning Module

Aforementioned HNECV can represent nodes as dense vectors. In fact, different nodes have different categories in the networks. In order to achieve the quality node vector in the latent space, it is important to enhance the cohesiveness in the hidden space. Therefore, as shown in Fig. 2(c), we designed a self-supervised learning module to integrate the clustering learning process naturally into the model learning process without any supervision information.

In particular, for the low-dimensional representation Z_i of the node object x_i, the certainty degree that it belongs to the k-th category in the hidden space can be calculated by FCT [30]:

$$\eta_{ik} = e^{-\frac{\left(Z_i - Ex_k^p\right)^2}{2En_k'^2}} \tag{16}$$

where Ex_k^p is the expectation of the k-th Gaussian distribution, which is initialized with the mean μ learned by GMM in our model, it will be used in the self-supervised learning. En_k' is the random number sampled from the k-th Gaussian distribution initially. In order to calculate the probability that the vector representation Z_i belongs to each category, the Eq. (16) can be rewritten as the Eq. (17), which is used to measure the similarity between the node vector representing Z_i and the cluster center vector:

$$Q_{ik} = \frac{e^{-\frac{\tau + \left(Z_i - Ex_k^p\right)^2}{\tau + 2En_k'^2}}}{\sum_{k=1}^{K} e^{-\frac{\tau + \left(Z_i - Ex_k^p\right)^2}{\tau + 2En_k'^2}}} \tag{17}$$

where $\tau = 1$ is used to prevent the model collapse caused by the minimum value. $\mathcal{Q}_{ik}$ is the probability that the vector Z_i is assigned to the cluster Ex_k^p.

Aiming to strengthen the confidence of the clustering task and enhance the cohesion of each category in the hidden space, we introduced an auxiliary distribution $\mathcal{P}$ as follows [31]:

$$\mathcal{P}_{ik} = \frac{\mathcal{Q}_{ik}^2/f_k}{\sum_{k'} \mathcal{Q}_{ik'}^2/f_{k'}} \tag{18}$$

where $f_k = \sum_i \mathcal{Q}_{ik}$ are soft cluster frequencies, which standardizes the contribution of cluster centers. Then, we leverage KL divergence to calculate the difference between the two distributions:

$$\mathcal{L}_{self} = D_{KL}(\mathcal{P}\|\mathcal{Q}) = \sum_i \sum_k \mathcal{P}_{ik} \log \frac{\mathcal{P}_{ik}}{\mathcal{Q}_{ik}} \tag{19}$$

During the optimization procedure, a novel strategy of self-supervised learning [32] is used, where the distribution $\mathcal{P}$ depends on the distribution $\mathcal{Q}$, and the $\mathcal{Q}$ distribution is supervised by the $\mathcal{P}$ distribution.

Therefore, the joint optimization loss function is as following:

$$\begin{aligned} \mathcal{L} &= \mathcal{L}_{rec} + \mathcal{L}_{KL} + \mathcal{L}_{self} \\ &= \sum_{n=1}^{|N|} \left\| (\hat{x}_n - x_n) \odot B_n \right\|_2^2 \\ &\quad + \frac{1}{2} \sum_{d=1}^{D} \left[1 + \ln\left((En_d)^2 \right) - (Ex_d)^2 - (En_d)^2 \right] \\ &\quad + \sum_i \sum_k \mathcal{P}_{ik} \log \frac{\mathcal{P}_{ik}}{\mathcal{Q}_{ik}} \end{aligned} \tag{20}$$

4 Experiment

To verify the effectiveness of HNECV, we conducted several experiments on three real data sets and compared some state-of-the-art baselines, such as Deepwalk (DW) [5], self-supervised learning method DEC [29], SDCN [9] and VAE-based network embedding method VGAE [4], Metapath2vec (MP2V) [11], HERec [13], HAN [18]. Here, we mainly show the performance of the model on three different network tasks. The brief datasets are described as following:

- DBLP[2]: Contains 14376 papers (P), 14475 authors (A), 20 conferences (C), and 8920 Terms (T), average degree of the network is 4.73. The nodes are divided into 4 categories according to the author's research field.
- AMiner[3]: We extracted a subset of 13978 papers (P), 16543 authors (A), and 2,152 conferences (C), average degree of the network is 2.05. The nodes are divided into 8 categories according to the author's research field.
- Yelp[4]: Contains 2614 businesses (B), 1286 users (U), 8 star (St), and 2 services (S), average degree of the network is 9.22. We label according to the type of business, divided into 3 categories.

---

[2] https://dblp.uni-trier.de.
[3] https://www.aminer.cn/citation.
[4] https://www.yelp.com/dataset/.

4.1   Classification

In this section, we adopt the KNN classifier with K = 5 as the evaluation algorithm for node classification tasks, and use Micro-F1 and Macro-F1 as evaluation metrics. We perform the classification task 10 times and take the average value. The classifier selects representations of nodes in the network generated by the model randomly at a ratio of 30%, 50%, 70%, and 90% as the training sets.

Table 1. Experimental results of node classification task.

Datasets	Metrics	Train	DW	DEC	SDCN	VGAE	MP2V	HERec	HAN	HNECV
DBLP	Micro-F1	30%	0.6077	0.7832	0.6873	0.8444	0.9055	0.9088	0.9126	**0.9311**
		50%	0.6566	0.7992	0.7051	0.8603	0.9122	0.9106	0.9181	**0.9313**
		70%	0.6838	0.8105	0.7094	0.8686	0.9159	0.9173	0.9203	**0.9341**
		90%	0.7131	0.8305	0.7108	0.8815	0.9131	0.9224	0.9161	**0.9337**
	Macro-F1	30%	0.5880	0.7544	0.6798	0.8301	0.8984	0.9021	0.9010	**0.9261**
		50%	0.6399	0.7758	0.6983	0.8474	0.9054	0.9031	0.9075	**0.9269**
		70%	0.6682	0.7896	0.7019	0.8568	0.9105	0.9107	0.9094	**0.9292**
		90%	0.6984	0.8111	0.7060	0.8693	0.9052	0.9145	0.9053	**0.9288**
AMiner	Micro-F1	30%	0.6855	0.6757	0.2504	0.6497	0.6751	0.7036	0.5902	**0.7123**
		50%	0.7006	0.6853	0.2768	0.6665	0.6836	0.7068	0.6329	**0.7196**
		70%	0.7160	0.6906	0.3018	0.6774	0.6940	0.7070	0.6605	**0.7251**
		90%	0.7112	0.6978	0.3301	0.6876	0.6942	0.7147	0.6772	**0.7383**
	Macro-F1	30%	0.6790	0.6630	0.1890	0.6371	0.6553	0.6944	0.5662	**0.7069**
		50%	0.6947	0.6718	0.2209	0.6570	0.6766	0.6978	0.6162	**0.7130**
		70%	0.7101	0.6768	0.2507	0.6674	0.6840	0.6987	0.6474	**0.7186**
		90%	0.7052	0.6829	0.2846	0.6773	0.6848	0.7076	0.6601	**0.7289**
Yelp	Micro-F1	30%	0.7050	0.3556	0.3013	0.6711	0.6565	0.6601	**0.7342**	0.7253
		50%	0.7198	0.3577	0.3533	0.6732	0.6839	0.6720	0.7270	**0.7372**
		70%	0.7234	0.3706	0.3803	0.6757	0.6757	0.6605	0.7253	**0.7361**
		90%	0.7313	0.3691	0.3927	0.6840	0.6782	0.6599	0.7312	**0.7590**
	Macro-F1	30%	0.6447	0.3059	0.2169	0.5848	0.5770	0.5961	0.5999	**0.6742**
		50%	0.6678	0.3149	0.2129	0.5873	0.5907	0.5927	0.5916	**0.6900**
		70%	0.6711	0.3113	0.2304	0.5860	0.5905	0.5859	0.5919	**0.6887**
		90%	0.6763	0.3088	0.2802	0.5900	0.5953	0.5798	0.5809	**0.7160**

As shown in Table 1, HNECV outperforms all baselines in most cases. The Micro-F1 and Macro-F1 have increased by 1.3% and 4.6% respectively. For the network with small average degree, like the AMiner, the classification results of various methods almost are same because of its sparsity. Compared with AMiner, DBLP has additional Term nodes, HIN embedding exhibits better performances than homogeneous network embedding method. In addition, because Yelp is the network with larger average degree and the nodes in it have more neighbors. The models that use multiple meta-paths, such as HNECV and HAN, show good results due to the use of multi-view information. Since the node classification task focuses on the use of network structure information, the models that cannot capture the structure information of networks, such as DEC, SDCN and VGAE, have achieved poor classification results.

4.2 Clustering

Table 2. Experimental results of node clustering task.

Algorithms	DBLP		AMiner		Yelp	
	NMI	ARI	NMI	ARI	NMI	ARI
Deepwalk	0.5841	0.4960	0.3160	0.2227	0.2940	0.3179
DEC	0.7075	0.7686	0.1967	0.0355	0.0012	0.0009
SDCN	0.5977	0.5724	0.0033	0.0051	0.0005	0.0007
VGAE	0.6737	0.7275	0.1318	0.0474	0.1522	0.0855
Metapath2vec	0.6395	0.6369	0.2645	0.2083	0.3540	0.4047
HERec	0.6844	0.7104	0.3230	0.2322	0.3511	0.4018
HAN	0.5987	0.5929	0.0375	0.0165	**0.3635**	**0.4255**
HNECV	**0.7950**	**0.8471**	**0.3438**	**0.2765**	0.3584	0.4119

In this section, K-means algorithm is used as the clustering method to test the node clustering task, then NMI and ARI are used as the evaluation metrics. In the DBLP, AMiner, and Yelp networks, the values of K are set to 4, 8, and 3 respectively. We also perform the clustering task 10 times and record the average of the results. The results are shown in Table 2.

From the Table 2, it shows that HNECV has an average increase of 3.4% and 3.74% on NMI and ARI. It is worth noting that the HNECV in the Yelp dataset is slightly lower than the HAN method. This may be due to the fact that in the Yelp network with greater node average and more neighborhood information, it is difficult for the traditional random walk of the meta-path to fully consider the structure information of the network.

4.3 Robustness

In order to verify the stability of HNECV, we randomly deleted 30% of P-A links in the DBLP dataset and compared our method with some typical algorithms. Specifically, when we delete the P-A type links, we need also delete the author-related P-C and P-T links. Note that due to the particularity of HIN, it is difficult for us to randomly delete the links from the overall data. As we know, when an link is lost, its related links are needed to be deleted too. For simplicity, we start to delete the P-A type link. We compare ours with all above baselines, and calculate the average decline ratios of each metrics for every algorithm. The experimental results are shown in Table 3.

From the Table 3, we find that those algorithms which rely on the network structure have a large performance drop, such as DeepWalk and VGAE. The performance degradations of DEC and HAN in the classification task is moderate, but DEC has a sharp decline in the clustering task, which shows that it is not enough to learn quality node vector representations just by considering the clustering characteristics of the network. On the other hand, it also verifies the effectiveness of HAN and HNECV by considering multi-view information. In addition, because HNECV expands the sampling range of the hidden space, a lot of information in the original data can be captured in the hidden space. After combining with self-supervised clustering, the similar low dimension vectors will be cohesive more and more closely. It promises HNECV to achieve the most robust results in the entire comparison algorithm.

Table 3. Stability experiments with 30% link deleted.

Node classfication						
Metrics	Traning	DW	DEC	VGAE	HAN	HNECV
Micro-F1	30%	0.2820	0.6026	0.3574	0.7327	**0.8373**
	50%	0.2759	0.6310	0.4060	0.7376	**0.8450**
	70%	0.2831	0.6410	0.4202	0.7410	**0.8485**
	90%	0.2874	0.6477	0.4360	0.7444	**0.8536**
Macro-F1	30%	0.2443	0.5824	0.3356	0.7186	**0.8307**
	50%	0.2392	0.6122	0.3838	0.7273	**0.8393**
	70%	0.2008	0.6314	0.4001	0.7298	**0.8419**
	90%	0.1974	0.6317	0.4159	0.7241	**0.8481**
Avg decline ratio	/	61.80%	21.65%	53.99%	19.68%	**9.42%**
Node clustering						
NMI	100%	0.0212	0.0091	0.0081	0.3913	**0.5769**
ARI	100%	0.0224	0.0054	0.0053	0.3801	**0.5878**
Avg decline ratio	/	95.92%	99.00%	99.03%	35.27%	**29.02%**

5   Conclusion

In this paper, we compress the cloud model into the sampling procedure for hidden space of VAE framework to expand the sampling space. In addition, we leverage self-supervised learning module to promote the compactness of the sampling for hidden space. Experiments show that our model excels compared with various state-of-the-art algorithms. In particular, our method exhibits better robustness and steadiness. In the future, we will continue to work on the disentangling control of hidden space of VAE based on HNECV and cloud model.

References

1. Grover, A., Leskovec, J.: node2vec: scalable feature learning for networks. In: Proceedings of the 22nd ACM SIGKDD International Conference on Knowledge Discovery and Data Mining, pp. 855–864. ACM, New York (2016)

2. Cui, P., Wang, X., Pei, J., Zhu, W.: A survey on network embedding. IEEE Trans. Knowl. Data Eng. **31**(5), 833–852 (2018)
3. Kipf, T.N., Welling, M.: Variational graph auto-encoders. arXiv preprint arXiv:1611.07308 (2016)
4. Perozzi, B., Al-Rfou, R., Skiena, S.: DeepWalk: online learning of social representations. In: Proceedings of the 20th ACM SIGKDD International Conference on Knowledge Discovery and Data Mining, pp. 701–710. ACM, New York (2014)
5. Ribeiro, L.F., Saverese, P.H., Figueiredo, D.R.: struc2vec: learning node representations from structural identity. In: Proceedings of the 23rd ACM SIGKDD International Conference on Knowledge Discovery and Data Mining, pp. 385–394. ACM, New York (2017)
6. Kipf, T.N., Welling, M.: Semi-supervised classification with graph convolutional networks. arXiv preprint arXiv:1609.02907 (2016)
7. Wang, C., Pan, S., Hu, R., Long, G., Jiang, J., Zhang, C.: Attributed graph clustering: a deep attentional embedding approach. arXiv preprint arXiv:1906.06532 (2019)
8. Fan, S., Wang, X., Shi, C., Lu, E., Lin, K., Wang, B.: One2multi graph autoencoder for multi-view graph clustering. In: Proceedings of The Web Conference 2020, pp. 3070–3076. ACM, New York (2020)
9. Bo, D., Wang, X., Shi, C., Zhu, M., Lu, E., Cui, P.: Structural deep clustering network. In: Proceedings of The Web Conference 2020, pp. 1400–1410. ACM, New York (2020)
10. Dong, Y., Chawla, N.V., Swami, A.: metapath2vec: scalable representation learning for heterogeneous networks. In: Proceedings of the 23rd ACM SIGKDD International Conference on Knowledge Discovery and Data Mining, pp. 135–144. ACM, New York (2017)
11. Fu, T.Y., Lee, W.C., Lei, Z.: Hin2vec: explore meta-paths in heterogeneous information networks for representation learning. In: Proceedings of the 2017 ACM on Conference on Information and Knowledge Management, pp. 1797–1806. ACM, New York (2017)
12. Shi, C., Hu, B., Zhao, W.X., Philip, S.Y.: Heterogeneous information network embedding for recommendation. IEEE Trans. Knowl. Data Eng. **31**(2), 357–370 (2018)
13. Tang, J., Qu, M., Mei, Q.: PTE: predictive text embedding through large-scale heterogeneous text networks. In: Proceedings of the 21th ACM SIGKDD International Conference on Knowledge Discovery and Data Mining, pp. 1165–1174. ACM, New York (2015)
14. Xu, L., Wei, X., Cao, J., Yu, P.S.: Embedding of embedding (EOE) joint embedding for coupled heterogeneous networks. In: Proceedings of the Tenth ACM International Conference on Web Search and Data Mining, pp. 741–749. ACM, New York (2017)
15. Wang, H., Zhang, F., Hou, M., Xie, X., Guo, M., Liu, Q.: SHINE: signed heterogeneous information network embedding for sentiment link prediction. In: Proceedings of the Eleventh ACM International Conference on Web Search and Data Mining, pp. 592–600. ACM, New York (2018)
16. Hu, B., Shi, C., Zhao, W.X., Yu, P.S.: Leveraging meta-path based context for top-n recommendation with a neural co-attention model. In: Proceedings of the 24th ACM SIGKDD International Conference on Knowledge Discovery & Data Mining, pp. 1531–1540. ACM, New York (2018)

17. Wang, X., Ji, H., Shi, C., Wang, B., Ye, Y., Cui, P., Yu, P.S.: Heterogeneous graph attention network. In: The World Wide Web Conference, pp. 2022–2032. ACM, New York (2019)

18. Hu, B., Fang, Y., Shi, C.: Adversarial learning on heterogeneous information networks. In: Proceedings of the 25th ACM SIGKDD International Conference on Knowledge Discovery & Data Mining, pp. 120–129. ACM, New York (2019)

19. Shi, C., Lu, Y., Hu, L., Liu, Z., Ma, H.: RHINE: relation structure-aware heterogeneous information network embedding. IEEE Trans. Knowl. Data Eng. **99**(1), 1–15 (2020)

20. Cen, Y., Zou, X., Zhang, J., Yang, H., Zhou, J., Tang, J.: Representation learning for attributed multiplex heterogeneous network. In: Proceedings of the 25th ACM SIGKDD International Conference on Knowledge Discovery & Data Mining, pp. 1358–1368. ACM, New York (2019)

21. Zhang, C., Song, D., Huang, C., Swami, A., Chawla, N.V.: Heterogeneous graph neural network. In: Proceedings of the 25th ACM SIGKDD International Conference on Knowledge Discovery & Data Mining, pp. 793–803. ACM, New York (2019)

22. Hu, B., Zhang, Z., Shi, C., Zhou, J., Li, X., Qi, Y.: Cash-out user detection based on attributed heterogeneous information network with a hierarchical attention mechanism. In: Proceedings of the AAAI Conference on Artificial Intelligence, vol. 33, pp. 946–953. AAAI, Palo Alto (2019)

23. Li, J., et al.: Higher-order attribute-enhancing heterogeneous graph neural networks. arXiv preprint arXiv:2104.07892 (2021)

24. Wu, L., et al.: Learning the implicit semantic representation on graph-structured data. arXiv preprint arXiv:2101.06471 (2021)

25. Li, X., Wen, L., Qian, C., Wang, J.: GAHNE: graph-aggregated heterogeneous network embedding. In: 2020 IEEE 32nd International Conference on Tools with Artificial Intelligence, pp. 1012–1019. IEEE, Baltimore (2020)

26. Shi, C., Li, Y., Zhang, J., Sun, Y., Philip, S.Y.: A survey of heterogeneous information network analysis. IEEE Trans. Knowl. Data Eng. **29**(1), 17–37 (2016)

27. Sun, Y., Han, J., Yan, X., Yu, P.S., Wu, T.: PathSim: meta path-based top-k similarity search in heterogeneous information networks. Proc. VLDB Endow. **4**(11), 992–1003 (2011)

28. Kingma, D.P., Welling, M.: Auto-encoding variational bayes. arXiv preprint arXiv:1312.6114 (2013)

29. Li, D., Han, J., Shi, X., Chan, M.C.: Knowledge representation and discovery based on linguistic atoms. Knowl.-Based Syst. **10**(7), 431–440 (1998)

30. Wang, G., Xu, C., Li, D.: Generic normal cloud model. Inf. Sci. **280**, 1–15 (2014)

31. Xie, J., Girshick, R., Farhadi, A.: Unsupervised deep embedding for clustering analysis. In: International Conference on Machine Learning, pp. 478–487. PMLR, ACM, New York (2016)

32. Nigam, K., Ghani, R.: Analyzing the effectiveness and applicability of co-training. In: Proceedings of the Ninth International Conference on Information and Knowledge Management, pp. 86–93. ACM, New York (2000)

DRPEC: An Evolutionary Clustering Algorithm Based on Dynamic Representative Points

Peng Li, Haibin Xie[✉], and Zhiyong Ding

National University of Defense Technology, Changsha 410073, China
lipeng@nudt.edu.cn

Abstract. This paper discusses an evolutionary clustering algorithm that uses dynamic representative points as the core of sample cluster (DRPEC). DRPEC algorithm calculates the similarity between samples and representative points by Gaussian function, and splits the winning representative points according to the principle of "Winner-take-all", to construct a representative point spanning tree that can represent the cluster relation. DRPEC algorithm takes a representative point as the starting point, realizes the dynamic evolution of the representative points in an incremental way, and merges the sub-clusters represented by the nodes in the representative point spanning tree according to our designed measuring function, in order to effectively find the natural clusters existing in the data space. Finally, numerous experiments were conducted on UCI datasets, and compared with the current popular clustering algorithm, the results show that the DRPEC algorithm has excellent clustering performance and strong robustness.

Keywords: Incremental clustering · Dynamic representative points · Spanning tree · Measuring function · Sub-cluster merging

1 Introduction

Clustering ability is the premise and foundation for people to understand the world [1]. Through interaction with the environment, complex information is abstracted and classified, to enhance people's adaptability in a complex environment [2,3].

At present, the commonly used K-means [4–6] and K-means++ algorithms based on partition method [7,8] firstly select k initial clustering centers, and solve the clustering results by minimizing the objective function, which can quickly find the clustering structure of sample distribution. The density-based DBSCAN algorithm [9–12] determines the cluster center by the density of the neighborhood of the sample, and connects the density core points according to the principle of density reachability, so that the cluster with complex shapes can be found. However, the two parameters involved in the DBSCAN algorithm are highly sensitive to the final clustering results. Therefore, Rodriguez et al. [13] proposed DPC algorithm to determine the number of clusters based on the decision graph, assuming that the distance between cluster centers is relatively far under the premise of

© Springer Nature Switzerland AG 2021
L. Fang et al. (Eds.): CICAI 2021, LNAI 13069, pp. 759–770, 2021.
https://doi.org/10.1007/978-3-030-93046-2_64

high cluster center density. SPC algorithm based on spectral graph theory [14, 15] only needs the similarity matrix between data to realize clustering. SOM clustering algorithm based on neuron method [16, 17] uses competitive learning training to find the active node of input sample, optimizes the parameters of the active node according to the random gradient descent method, and can adaptively change the network structure to adapt to the data contained pattern.

Although the above algorithms can achieve good clustering results, there are still many problems. For example, partition-based algorithms and SPC usually need to specify the number of clusters artificially, which is often difficult to obtain information about the number of clusters in practical applications. Although the DPC algorithm allows users to determine the number of clusters according to the decision graph, it still needs users' input. SOM clustering results usually do not correspond to a single natural cluster, and the SOM algorithm is very sensitive to network parameters.

Therefore, to solve the above problems, this paper proposes a DRPEC algorithm, which uses dynamic representative points to represent sample clusters, and realizes clustering by splitting and merging representative points. DRPEC algorithm calculates the similarity between a single sample and all the representative points according to the Gaussian function, judges the winning representative points according to the principle of 'Winner-take-all', and performs parameter adjustment or splitting operation on the winning representative points, so as to construct a representative point spanning tree that matches the sample pattern. On this basis, the DRPEC algorithm performs aggregation operation on the nodes in the spanning tree, and merges the sub-clusters according to the designed measuring function, to obtain the final clustering result. DRPEC algorithm finds the cluster structure in the sample space through the evolution mechanism of representative points, and achieves excellent clustering performance.

2   The Idea of Algorithm

In most algorithms, a few sample points are usually used to represent the cluster contained in the sample set, i.e., the method of representative points. For example, in the K-means algorithm, firstly, k points are randomly selected as the start item of the algorithm. In the chameleon algorithm [18, 19], the k-nearest neighbor graph is constructed first, and then the initial sub-cluster set is obtained by dividing the graph. But these algorithms are very sensitive to the setting of parameter k, which directly affects the final clustering effect.

DRPEC algorithm adopts the idea of dynamic representative point, which imitates people's memory process of things. When we constantly contact the same kind of object, the memory of this kind of object will be continuously strengthened, and the memory neurons related to this kind of object will be continuously stimulated, which will lead to the division of the neuron into new memory neurons. If memory neurons are not stimulated for a long time, they will gradually die out, and the memory related to such objects will be gradually forgotten. Inspired by this, the DRPEC algorithm takes data samples as objects that neurons need to remember. If the samples belong to the same class, the memory neurons corresponding to the samples will be continuously stimulated with the increase of the samples, to split and generate new neurons.

DRPEC algorithm designs a dynamic representation point based evolutionary mechanism by simulating the changes of neurons in human memory, i.e., the evolution of representative points is realized through the stimulation of representative points by samples (the greater the similarity, the higher the stimulation degree). The similarity between samples and representative points is calculated according to Gaussian function, and then the representative point with the highest similarity is selected as the winning representative point, and the relevant evolution operation is performed on it.

After the evolution, the spanning tree is constructed by the splitting and generating relation of the representative points, and the nodes on the tree are merged according to the designed measuring function, so as to better discover the natural clusters. In the design of measuring function, drpec algorithm borrows the relative nearest neighbor proposed in chameleon algorithm and modifies it as the basis of merging sub-clusters.

3   DRPEC Algorithm

In this section, we will introduce the detailed process of the DRPEC algorithm, and give the pseudo-code of key steps. Finally, the time complexity of the DRPEC algorithm is analyzed.

3.1   Symbol Description and Definition

Firstly, we define the related symbols and definitions in DRPEC algorithm. Suppose that there are n samples to be clustered in the data space D, and each sample $x_i = (x_{i1}, x_{i2}, ..., x_{is})$ has s-dimensional characteristics. After clustering by the DRPEC algorithm, (x_i, c_j) means that sample x_i belongs to cluster j, and c_j means the set of samples belonging to cluster j. $C = \{c_1, c_2, ..., c_k\}$ is the set of classes in the sample space, where $c_i \cap c_j|_{i \neq j} = \varnothing$, and k is the number of clusters. $dist(x_i, x_j)$ is the similarity between sample x_i and sample x_j, which is calculated by Euclidean distance.

We use a ternary array $Core = (\eta, \rho, s)$ to represent the representative point, where η represents the center vector of the representative point, i.e., the position of the representative point in the data space. ρ represents the coverage area of the representative point, i.e., the range that the representative point can affect in the data space. And the larger ρ is, the more concentrated the distribution of sample cluster represented by representative points is. The center vector η and the coverage domain ρ of the representative points satisfy the Gaussian normal distribution, i.e., the probability of the sample distribution in $(\mu - 3\rho, \mu + 3\rho)$ is 0.9973. Each representative point corresponds to a Gaussian function. For example, the Gaussian function corresponding to the representative point A is $\frac{1}{\sqrt{2\pi}\rho_A}e^{-\frac{(x_i - \eta_A)^2}{2\rho_A{}^2}}$, where x_i represents the sample of the i-th input.

Definition 1 (Maturity). In the ternary array $Core = (\eta, \rho, s)$, s represents the maturity of the representative point, i.e., the degree of information carried by the representative point. If a representative point wins many times in the competition, its maturity will increase until it reaches the splitting threshold and splits to produce a new representative point.

Definition 2 (Meta-representative point). Meta-representative point is the starting item in the evolution process of representative point. The meta-representative point's ternary array is expressed as $Core_{meta} = (\eta_m, \rho_m, s_m)$. Where η_m represents the center of all samples to be clustered, and ρ_m represents the coverage of the whole space, i.e., $\rho_m = \max\limits_{i,j} dist\,(x_i, x_j)\,/6$, which covers all the samples to be clustered to the maximum extent within $3\rho_m$ of the meta-representative point.

Definition 3 (Spanning tree). Assume that the representative point A is the parent node, and the new representative point B generated by the splitting of A is the child node, and construct the representative point spanning tree according to the parent-child node relation. The first layer of the spanning tree contains only meta-representative points. The spanning tree of representative points is represented by n_tree.

In the DRPEC algorithm, maturity involves reset threshold s_r and saturation threshold s_s, which determine the splitting time of representative points. s_r and s_s of all representative points belong to the structural parameters of the algorithm, and the settings in the experiment are the same, i.e., $s_s = 1, s_r = 0.9$.

With the increase of samples, assuming that representative point A wins in many competitions, i.e., s_A will gradually increase. When s_A exceeds the saturation threshold s_s, A will split and a new representative point B will be generated. At this time, the maturity $s_B = 0$ of B and the maturity of A will change to the reset threshold s_r, i.e., $s_A = s_r$. If the representative point A fails in the competition, but the maturity of A meets the condition: $s_r < s_A < s_s$, then s_A decays to the reset threshold according to the beat (referring to the Ebbinghaus forgetting curve in the experiment, the decaying is completed after 7 beats). The maturity s_m of meta-representative points is set to saturation threshold s_s, $s_m = s_s = 1$, i.e., in the process of competition, as long as the meta-representative points win, it will directly split and generate new representative points.

3.2 Evolutionary Mechanism of Representative Points

Based on the above definition, DRPEC algorithm designs the ternary array update rules of representative points. When the new sample x_i is input, all the representative points respond according to the Gaussian function, and the winning representative points are determined according to the Winner-take-all principle, and the parameters are updated or representative points split according to the following rules:

(1) If the meta-representative points win, the meta-representative points are directly split to generate new representative points. Suppose that the meta-representative point splits to generate a new representative point A, then set $\mu_A = (x_{i1}, x_{i2}, ..., x_{is})$, $\rho_A = \frac{1}{3}dist(\eta_A, \eta_m)$, and $s_A = 0$. The center vector, coverage area and maturity of the meta-representative points of the element remain unchanged;

(2) Suppose that the representative point N wins and s_N reaches the saturation threshold, then point N splits to generate a new representative point B. Then set $\mu_B = (x_{i1}, x_{i2}, ..., x_{is})$, $\rho_B = \frac{1}{3}dist(\eta_B, \eta_N)$, and $s_B = 0$. Because of the split of representative point N, it is necessary to update N's maturity, and set s_N to reset threshold s_r;

(3) Assuming that the representative point N wins, but s_N does not reach the saturation threshold, the maturity s_N and center vector μ_N of N need to be updated according to the new information introduced by the new sample x_i. The formula is updated to $s_N' = s_N + o(1 - o)$, $\mu_N' = s_N'\mu_N + (1 - s_N')x_i$, where $o = e^{\frac{-(x_i - \eta_N)^2}{2\rho_N{}^2}}$.

When all the samples are processed by the algorithm, the set of representative points is represented by $ns = \{n_1, n_2, ..., n_p\}$, $Core_{n_i} = (\eta_{n_i}, \rho_{n_i}, s_{n_i})$, $n_i \in ns$, where p is the number of representative points finally generated. We give the pseudo-code representing the evolution process of the representative point, as shown in Algorithm 1.

Algorithm 1. Evolution

Input: D;
Output: ns, n_tree;
1: Initializing $Core_m = (\eta_m, \rho_m, s_m)$;
2: **for** $i = 1 \rightarrow n$ **do**
3:      add i-th sample;
4:      Judgment winning representative point;
5:      **if** meta-representative point wins **then**
6:          Generate new representative point, update ns, Construct the n_tree;
7:      **else**
8:          **if** $s_{n_i} > s_s$ (suppose n_i wins) **then**
9:              Generate new representative point, update ns, $s_{n_i} = s_r$, Construct the n_tree;
10:         **else**
11:             $s_{n_i}' = s_{n_i} + o(1 - o)$, $\mu_{n_i}' = s_{n_i}'\mu_{n_i} + (1 - s_{n_i}')x_i$;
12:         **end if**
13:     **end if**
14:     The s of the unsuccessful representative point decays according to the beat;
15: **end for**

3.3   Merge Sub-clusters

All samples distributed in the representative point coverage area can be clustered into the same class. But in fact, the coverage areas of representative points overlap with each other. Therefore, according to the principle of nearest distance, DRPEC algorithm clusters the samples to be clustered and their nearest representative points into a cluster, i.e., each representative point represents a sub-cluster. In order to merge sub-clusters, we define two variables: relative closeness rc and relative distance rd.

Definition 4 (Relative closeness, rc). rc is the degree of approximation between two clusters, and the formula is: $rc = \frac{(|n_i|+|n_j|)E(n_i,n_j)}{|n_i|E(n_j)+|n_j|E(n_i)}$. Where $|n_i|$ represents the number of samples contained in the sub-cluster represented by the representative point n_i, $E(n_i, n_j)$ represents the sum of weights (i.e., distances) of all edges connecting sub-cluster n_i and n_j, and $E(n_i)$ represents the sum of weights of all edges connecting all samples in sub-cluster n_i. The closer the sub-cluster are, the smaller rc is.

Definition 5 (Relative distance, rd). rd is the Euclidean distance between the centroids of two sub-clusters, $rd = dist(n_i\_center, n_j\_center)$, where n_i_center represents the centroid position of the sub-cluster represented by the representative point n_i.

The sub-cluster reflects the local characteristics of the sample set represented by each representative point, but the degree of connection between the sub-clusters is still high. Therefore, we use the measuring function f as the basis to judge whether the clusters should be merged, where the measuring function is set to: $f = rc * rd$. When the measure function f of two sub-clusters is greater than the set threshold γ, the two sub-clusters can be merged. In the experimental part, we can observe that the algorithm is not sensitive to the value of the parameter.

3.4   DRPEC

According to the parent-child relation between the representative points in the spanning tree, we can find the internal relation between the representative points. Different from the tree with data objects as nodes in hierarchical clustering algorithm, the nodes of the representative point spanning tree can represent a sub-cluster. The construction of representative point spanning tree only depends on the structural parameters in the maturity of representative points, but these parameters are fixed in any dataset.

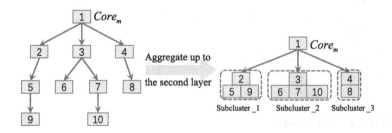

Fig. 1. Aggregate to the second layer.

Spanning tree n_tree often contains many layers, and each layer has several representative points. The lower the level of representative point, the smaller its coverage and the fewer points it contains. This will affect the calculation of the measuring function. Therefore, DRPEC algorithm first aggregates all the bottom representative points in n_tree to the second layer, as shown in Fig. 1. Then judge whether it should be merged or not according to the measuring function relation among the aggregated Subcluster_1, Subcluster_2, and Subcluster_3.

DRPEC algorithm creates the spanning tree n_tree according to its parent-child relation after the representative point evolution, and aggregates the bottom representative points in the spanning tree up to the second layer, and finally merges the sub-clusters according to the measuring function. The pseudo-code of DRPEC algorithm is shown in Algorithm 2.

Algorithm 2. DRPEC

Input: D, γ;
Output: $C = \{c_1, c_2, ..., c_k\}$
1: $[ns, n\_tree] = Evolution(D)$
2: $subcluster\_set = Aggregate(ns, n\_tree)$
3: $C = Merge\_subclusters(subcluster\_set, \gamma)$

The time complexity of DRPEC algorithm mainly includes the time complexity in the process of evolutionary and the time complexity of merging subclusters. The process of evolutionary is shown in Algorithm 1, and the time complexity is $O(n)$. When merging sub-clusters, it is necessary to calculate the relative closeness and distance between sub-clusters, and all samples are required to participate in the calculation, so the time complexity may reach $O(n^2)$ in the worst case. So, the time complexity of DRPEC algorithm is $O(n^2)$.

4   Experiment

This section mainly tests the performance of DRPEC algorithm, and compares it with the current popular clustering algorithm. At the same time, the sensitivity of the parameters involved in the algorithm is analyzed. All algorithms are implemented on MATLAB2020.

4.1   Dataset and Evaluation Index

Datasets: We use synthetic datasets DS1, DS2 and UCI datasets to verify the characteristics of the algorithm. UCI dataset [20] contains high-dimensional datasets in the real world, as shown in the Table 1.

Evaluation Index: We select four common external clustering indexes as the criteria to evaluate the clustering performance, including ACC [21], NMI [22], ARI [23] and F-measure [24]. The higher their scores, the better the clustering performance of the algorithm.

Table 1. Dataset

Dataset	Number of samples (Number of clusters)	Dimension	Features
DS1	500(5)	2	Obeys normal distribution with same variances
DS2	500(5)	2	Obeys normal distribution with different variances
Compound	399(6)	2	Embedded and connected
Liver	345(2)	6	Real, High dimensional
Wpbc	198(2)	33	
Breast	277(2)	9	
Vehicle	846(4)	18	

4.2   Analysis of Experimental Results

We show the results of DRPEC algorithm on DS2, as shown in Fig. 2. The clustering result after the representative points are generated and aggregated to the second layer is shown in Fig. 2(a), where '*' represents the position of the center vector of the representative points. When agglomerating sub-clusters, the clusters whose measuring function f is greater than the threshold γ are combined to generate the final clustering result, as shown in Fig. 2(b).

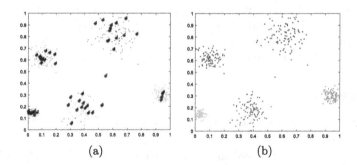

(a)   (b)

Fig. 2. Clustering results on DS2. (a) Aggregate to the second layer. (b) Merge sub-clusters.

We compare DRPEC algorithm with K-means, K-means++ algorithm, density DPC algorithm and spectral clustering (SPC algorithm). The results are shown in Table 2.

It can be observed that on DS1 and DS2 datasets based on two-dimensional and normal distribution, the four indexes of the five algorithms are close to 1, but the performance of DRPEC algorithm is still the best. The performance of DRPEC algorithm is better than the other four algorithms on two-dimensional

Table 2. Algorithm comparison

ACC	K-means	K-means++	DPC	SPC	DRPEC	NMI	K-means	K-means++	DPC	SPC	DRPEC
DS1	0.9743	0.9318	1	1	1	DS1	0.9844	0.9584	1	1	1
DS2	0.9488	0.9002	0.998	0.998	0.998	DS2	0.9646	0.9364	0.993	0.993	0.9931
Compound	0.6585	0.6573	0.5564	0.5564	0.8722	Compound	0.7047	0.7048	0.6108	0.6108	0.7899
Liver	0.5474	0.5453	0.513	0.5246	0.5797	Liver	0	0	0	0	0
Wpbc	0.5942	0.6	0.6768	0.6993	0.7626	Wpbc	0.0225	0.0239	0.0238	0.0382	0.0494
Breast	0.6149	0.6326	0.509	0.509	0.6859	Breast	0.0395	0.0454	0.0012	0.0012	0.0363
Vehicle	0.3704	0.3706	0.3605	0.3746	0.3984	Vehicle	0.1132	0.1127	0.1	0.1157	0.1477
ARI	K-means	K-means++	DPC	SPC	DRPEC	**F-Measure**	K-means	K-means++	DPC	SPC	DRPEC
DS1	0.9748	0.9328	1	1	1	DS1	0.983	0.9579	1	1	1
DS2	0.9478	0.9009	0.995	0.995	0.9975	DS2	0.9656	0.9336	0.998	0.998	0.999
Compound	0.6105	0.6006	0.4667	0.4667	0.8125	Compound	0.7103	0.7085	0.6304	0.6303	0.8513
Liver	−0.003	−0.004	−0.004	−0.0071	0	Liver	0.6282	0.6267	0.5621	0.6109	0.7339
Wpbc	0.0304	0.0346	−0.069	0.1087	0.1396	Wpbc	0.6271	0.6301	0.7114	0.7074	0.732
Breast	0.077	0.091	−0.03	−0.0031	0.108	Breast	0.6265	0.642	0.5315	0.5315	0.6768
Vehicle	0.0826	0.0824	0.0675	0.0808	0.1025	Vehicle	0.425	0.4248	0.4374	0.4204	0.4613

non-convex dataset compound, which shows that DRPEC algorithm can achieve better clustering results in datasets with complex shapes. At the same time, in the four real and high-dimensional datasets, the index values of DRPEC are higher than the other four algorithms, which shows that DRPEC algorithm is also suitable for real and high-dimensional data clustering.

4.3 Parameter Sensitivity Analysis

In the process of merging sub-clusters, the value of threshold γ will affect the final merging effect. Taking DS2 as an example, we show the impact on the final clustering when the threshold γ changes, as shown in Fig. 3. Figure 3(a) shows the influence of γ changes on indicators when the algorithm generates eight representative points, and Fig. 3(b) shows the influence of γ changes on indicators when nine representative points are generated. It can be observed that although the change of γ has an impact on the clustering results, the results will remain above 0.8. In the experiment, $\gamma = 1$ is usually set.

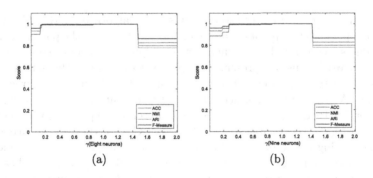

(a)   (b)

Fig. 3. The influence of the change of γ on the algorithm. (a) 8 representative points. (b) 9 representative points.

In the process of generating representative points, the reset threshold of maturity is set differently, which will lead to different number of representative points generated, which will affect the clustering effect of merging sub-clusters. Therefore, based on the fixed threshold $\gamma = 1$, we analyzed the impact of different maturity reset thresholds on the number of generated representative points and the final clustering effect, as shown in Fig. 4.

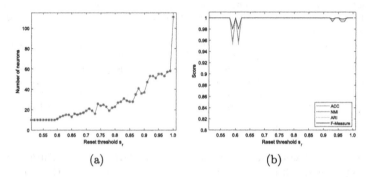

(a)   (b)

Fig. 4. The influence of the change of reset threshold s_r on the algorithm. (a) The number of generated representative points. (b) The change of index.

When the reset threshold s_r of maturity increases from 0.5 to 1, the number of representative points generated by splitting is shown in Fig. 4(a), and the effect of final clustering is shown in Fig. 4(b). It can be observed that the number of representative points will increase when the reset threshold s_r of maturity increases, but the increase of the number of representative points has little effect on the final clustering results. The four indexes are all above 0.94, and the change degree is small, which indicates that DRPEC algorithm is not sensitive to the change of reset threshold s_r.

5   Conclusion

This paper proposes an evolutionary clustering algorithm DRPEC based on dynamic representative points, which can adaptively match the pattern classes in the sample space through the generation and splitting of representative points. DRPEC algorithm uses representative points to represent the set of samples in the sub-cluster, which can effectively improve the clustering accuracy of the algorithm. At the same time, according to the measuring function designed in this paper, DRPEC algorithm merges the representative points, so as to find the natural clusters in the sample space. The DRPEC algorithm is insensitive to the threshold setting in the process of representative point generation and merging, and has good robustness. Future research work will expand the application of DRPEC algorithm in larger real datasets, and improve the clustering accuracy of the algorithm.

References

1. Xu, D., Tian, Y.: A comprehensive survey of clustering algorithms. Ann. Data Sci. **2**(2), 165–193 (2015)
2. Suo, M., Zhu, B., Ding, Z., An, R., Li, S.: Neighborhood grid clustering and its application in fault diagnosis of satellite power system. Proc. Inst. Mech. Eng. Part G J. Aerosp. Eng. **233**(4), 095441001775199 (2018)
3. Xu, K.S., Kliger, M., Iii, A.H.: Adaptive evolutionary clustering. Data Min. Knowl. Disc. **28**(2), 304–336 (2014)
4. Xu, J., Lange, K.: Power k-means clustering. In: International Conference on Machine Learning, PMLR, vol. 97, pp. 6921–6931 (2019)
5. Bagirov, A.M., Ugon, J., Webb, D.: Fast modified global k-means algorithm for incremental cluster construction. Pattern Recognit. **44**(4), 866–876 (2011)
6. Franti, P., Sieranoja, S.: How much k-means can be improved by using better initialization and repeats? Pattern Recognit. **93**, 95–112 (2019)
7. Arthur, D., Vassilvitskii, S.: K-Means++: the advantages of carefull seeding. In: Proceedings of the Eighteenth Annual ACM-SIAM Symposiumon Discrete algorithms, Society for Industrial and Applied Mathematics, vol. 11, no. 6, pp. 1027–1035 (2007)
8. Lattanzi, S., Sohler, C.: A better k-means++ algorithm via local search. In: International Conference on Machine Learning, PMLR, pp. 3662–3671 (2019)
9. Ester, M.: A density-based algorithm for discovering clusters in large spatial databases with noise. In: Proceedings of the Second International Conference on Knowledge Discovery and Data Mining, pp. 226–231 (1996)
10. Zhu, Ye., Ting, M.K., Carman, M.J.: Density-ratio based clustering for discovering clusters with varying densities. Pattern Recognit. **60**, 983–997 (2016)
11. Bechini, A., Marcelloni, F., Renda, A.: TSF-DBSCAN: a novel fuzzy density-based approach for clustering unbounded data streams. IEEE Trans. Fuzzy Syst. **99**, 1 (2020)
12. Chen, Y., Zhou, L., Bouguila, N., Wang, C., Du, J.: BLOCK-DBSCAN: fast clustering for large scale data. Pattern Recognit. **109**, 107624 (2020)
13. Rodriguez, A., Laio, A.: Clustering by fast search and find of density peaks. Science **344**(6191), 1492 (2014)
14. Ng, A.Y., Jordan, M.I., Weiss, Y.: On spectral clustering: analysis and an algorithm. Adv. Neural. Inf. Process. Syst. **2**, 849–856 (2002)
15. Ding, S., Cong, L., Hu, Q., Jia, H., Shi, Z.: A multiway p-spectral clustering algorithm. Knowl.-Based Syst. **164**(15), 849–856 (2019)
16. Vesanto, J., Alhoniemi, E.: Clustering of the self-organizing map. IEEE Trans. Neural Netw. **11**(3), 586–600 (2000)
17. Xu, G., Zhang, L., Ma, C., Liu, Y.: A mixed attributes oriented dynamic SOM fuzzy cluster algorithm for mobile user classification. Inf. Sci. **515**(3), 280–293 (2019)
18. Karypis, G., Han, E.H., Kumar, V.: Chameleon: hierarchical clustering using dynamic modeling. Computer-Los Alamos **32**(8), 68–75 (1999)
19. Zhang, Y., Ding, S., Wang, Y., Hou, H.: Chameleon algorithm based on improved natural neighbor graph generating sub-clusters. Appl. Intell., 1–17 (2021)
20. Dua, D., Graff, C.: UCI machine learning repository (2017). http://archive.ics.uci.edu/ml
21. Li, T., Ding, C.: The relationships among various nonnegative matrix factorization methods for clustering. In: International Conference on Data Mining, pp. 362–371 (2006)

22. Strehl, A., Ghosh, J.: Cluster ensembles-a knowledge reuse framework for combining multiple partitions. J. Mach. Learn. Res. **3**(3), 583–617 (2002)
23. Lerman, I.C., Peter, P.: Comparing partitions. Czech J. Phys. **8**(10), 742–748 (1988)
24. Soleymani, R., Granger, E., Fumera, G.: F-measure curves: a tool to visualize classifier performance under imbalance. Pattern Recognit. **100**, 107146 (2019)

User Reviews Based Rating Prediction in Recommender System

Wenchuan Shi, Liejun Wang$^{(\boxtimes)}$, Shuli Cheng, and Yongming Li

College of Information Science and Engineering, Xinjiang University, Ürümqi, China
{wencs,slcaydxju}@stu.xju.edu.cn, wljxju@xju.edu.cn

Abstract. The user feedback information based Collaborative Filtering algorithm is often used to discover the hidden preferences of users and potential features of items in Recommender System for the past few years. Nevertheless, the potential relationship between different users is often ignored in the current Collaborative Filtering algorithm which contained in the user feedback information. To enhance the precision of Rating Prediction task in the Recommender System, this paper structures a new Rating Prediction method named the Review-based Rating Prediction (RRP) to explore the potential relationship among the different users. Through analyzing the reviews text, the method can derive the users' potential relationship. Moreover, The resulting potential user relationship data was fused into the rating prediction task. The results of our experiments on open data sets suggest that our proposed model has a performance ascension over the traditional rating prediction methods.

Keywords: Data mining · Reviews · Rating prediction · Recommender system

1 Introduction

This is an era where life is influenced by the recommender system (RS) everywhere, and it has changed the way users discover and evaluate items or services online [1]. The rapid development of the Internet has greatly facilitated the formation of social networks, and the social networks have become an important platform for users to create and share their own information. Based on the user reviews or ratings generated on the platform, the RS summarizes the key points of user feedback and not only recommends items that a user might like, but also identifies other users who have similar preferences to a particular user. With the increasing of user engagement, a large amount of user feedback has been generated in social networking platforms, and this information has opened up new opportunities for the development of RS. How to use this information efficiently and exploit its potential resources has become one of the research hotspots for optimizing RS.

© Springer Nature Switzerland AG 2021
L. Fang et al. (Eds.): CICAI 2021, LNAI 13069, pp. 771–782, 2021.
https://doi.org/10.1007/978-3-030-93046-2_65

More and more recommender methods have been proposed one after another in recent decades. These methods can be broadly classified into two broad categories based on how they are constructed: Collaborative Filtering based method (CF) [2,3] and Content-based Recommendation method [4]. The CF methods have received a lot of attention due to the fact that they only use explicit rating information, and although they can achieve better recommendation results, there are characteristics such as high data sparsity and uneven data distribution, which will lead to low accuracy performance of the model and Cold Start (CS) of users. The Content-based recommendation method is based on mining items with the same or similar attributes to make recommendations, and the recommendations generated by this method suffer from the problem of monolithic results. With the iterative evolution of recommendation techniques, the new recommendation methods such as Reinforcement learning (RL) [5], Knowledge Graph (KG) [17], Graph Embedding (GE) [18], and Generative Adversarial Networks (GAN) [19] have emerged. The RS based on RL defines the process of making List-wise recommendations as a problem of sequential decision making. The KG based RS can combine the rich data semantic information from multiple data sources to discover user interests at a deeper level, and can serve users with implicit information from inference. The basic principle of the RS based on GE is to generate a sequence of nodes based on sampling the nodes in the graph by random wandering and other algorithms. Then, the sequence of nodes and edges is mapped to a low-dimensional vector space. The GAN based RS uses the adversarial model of generators and discriminators to find items of possible interest for users. There has been a lot of research into modeling based on user rating data, but another form of feedback on review sites, the reviews themselves, has been overlooked. The recommendations will be more accurate and scientific by combining information from user reviews, which can explain why the users rate in a certain way.

The recommender algorithms based on user rating data are effective in improving the quality of RS currently. However, the problems such as sparsity and uneven distribution of rating data still exist. Therefore, more and more researchers have introduced the additional user information into recommender algorithms to ease the low recommender accuracy and user CS. And good results have been achieved to some extent. Social relationships provide potential connections between different users [6]. And some methods around the users' trust relationship between users in social networks have proved that they perform well in social recommendations.

To sum up, this paper structures a Rating Prediction (RP) method by the user reviews information. This method aims to improve the accuracy of RP. Compared with the previous work, the characteristics of our method are mainly reflected in the following aspects: 1). We have extracted an element that affect the underlying relationships between users from the user reviews text information and integrate them into the recommender model to enhance the precision of user RP. 2). We quantify the influence of implicit relationship between users on the RP. The emotional co-occurrence matrix calculated based on the user's reviews text can prove that: the more users contain emotional words in the reviews text, the greater the mutual information between them and other users, the higher the degree of availability and the greater the affect on others. 3). We conducted many experiment researches on the Yelp datase, and the experimental finding proved the validity of our method in enhancing the precision of RP.

2   Related Work

2.1   Recommender System

The task of the CF algorithm based on Matrix Factorization (MF) is to predict user predilections for unrated items, and then the model can recommend a list of its favorite items to the user. The specific approach of the model is to stand for the user's rating information on item expressed in matrix form, mine the low dimensional implicit feature space by decomposition operations on the matrix, re-represent the user and item on this low-dimensional space, then portray the association between the user and item.

The basic idea behind the user-based CF algorithm structured in the literature [20] is that people who had similar interests in the past were more likely to buy the same items in later life. In addition, the item-based CF algorithm [21] generates user rating of unrated items by the mean scores of similar or related items by the particular user, which has been effective in calculating the similarity between items. However, the above CF algorithms suffer from the poor recommender performance and user CS. The purpose is to increase the prediction performance of RS, many new CF algorithms have been proposed, such as Non-negative Matrix Factorization (NMF) [7], Probabilistic Matrix Factorization (PMF) [8]. The methods mentioned above aims to derive a personalized list of items by learning from the user's historical behavior to construct potential associations between the user and the project.

2.2   Social Recommender System

Users can create social relationships with other users based on social networks, as well as rate and review on items. The CF method works best when users share a lot of the same items and ratings. However, when it comes to solving problems such as CS and rating sparsity, such a similarity-based approach is unlikely to find similar users, and its recommendation effect is poor. Therefore, the recommendation methods based on social network use a large amount of contact information among users to solve this similarity problem, thus providing an effective means to solve the problem of CS and sparse rating.

The CF based social recommendation methods can be divided into two categories: the MF based recommendation method and the neighborhood based recommendation method. The MF based social recommendation method integrates users' social trust information and user-item feedback historical information (such as rating, click, purchase, etc.) to improve the accuracy of the traditional MF based RS. The typical methods include: Social-MF, Trust-MF [9],

Trust-SVD [22], etc. The SNT method traverses the adjacent users of direct or indirect links in the social network, and then generates recommendations for the users.

2.3   Reviews Based Applications for Recommender System

Although at present, the user rating matrix is still the main behavioral preference information used by most RS, the information obtained in practice does not always provide structured information, such as the reviews posted by users. However, the rich information contained in these review texts can effectively alleviate such problems as the sparsity of rating data. The reason is that the reason why users assign such ratings to items is implicit in the review texts, which can help the model learn the implicit characteristics representing user preferences and commodity attributes, and has great reference value. Jakob et al. [23] found that the narration about movie evaluation in users' comments on movies could increase the RP efficiency of the model. However, this work only stops at the explicit features of the commentary text and fails to dig out the implicit features. Jordan et al. [10] proposed the Latent Dirichlet Allocation (LDA) model, which is used to find the topic distribution in a text to construct Latent factor characteristics for scoring prediction, and thus becomes the most influential text topic mining model. Li et al. [24] fused the review text theme with the rating MF model to improve the recommendation accuracy by manually establishing part of the subject words. The semantic model of Bag of Words Latent Factor (BoWLF) proposed by Almahairi et al. [25] which used the commodity characteristic vector to produce the word probability distribution of the review document, and the LDA part used the likelihood degree generated under the specified commodity characteristic parameter as the regularization term, so that the model could reflect the information of the review. Ma et al. [11] combined the user reviews and ratings information to study RS and discuss the recommendation problems of social media. Lou et al. [26] attempted to categorize users' entire reviews into positive, negative, or neutral emotional polarities.

3   The Proposed Method

The proposed method aims to find the effective clues to influence user relationship from user reviews information, and to predict the users' rating of unrated items based on the above clues. This chapter firstly extracts the influencing factors of user relationship from the user reviews corpus, and then we add the above factors into the SVD++ [27] model to perform the RP task.

3.1   Extracting the User Influence Factor from Reviews

In this section, we extract and quantify how much the users like item from the user reviews text based on the HowNet Sentiment Dictionary [12,28]. As for the positive emotion and evaluation words in the HowNet Sentiment Dictionary, they are collectively called the positive words list (Pos-W), which contains 4363 positive words. The negative emotion words and negative evaluation words are collectively called the negative words list (Neg-W), which contains 4574 negative words. In addition, we rate the 137 words in the dictionary of emotion into five levels based on how emotional they are. Specifically, the first-level word set contains 11 words which representing the lowest level of emotion, such as "merely" and "slight". The second-level word set consists of 15 words that indicate a lower level of emotion, such as "fairly" and "pretty". The third-level word set contains 22 words, such as "further" and "even". There are 25 words such as "awfully" and "extremely" that are associated with higher levels of emotion in the fourth-level word set. The fifth-level word set, which represents the highest level of emotion, is made up of 64 words such as "absolutely" and "awfully". The Table 1 provides a brief introduction to the representative words for the sentiment dictionary.

Table 1. The brief introduction to the dictionary of sentiment words.

Dictionaries	Representative words
Sentiment Dictionary (Sen-D)	**Positive-Words(Pos-W)**: abstemious, affirmative, apropos, baronial, delicate, domesticate, slippery, tenderly, unzealous
	Negative-Words(Neg-W): abandoned, acerbity, airless, barbarian, dangerous, debauched, dirtiness, uncouthness, wordiness
Sentiment Degree Dictionary (Sen-DD)	**Level-5**: absolutely, awfully, bitterly, completely, deeply, extremely, greatly, immensely, most, best, greatest, 100%
	Level-4: awfully, extremely, really, very, super, pretty, especially, better, disastrously, particularly
	Level-3: further, even, more, relatively, increasingly, comparatively, insanely, intensely, far, rather
	Level-2: fairly, pretty, passably, slightly, somewhat, kind of, a trifle, just, relative
	Level-1: merely, slight, less, not very, bit, little, passably, insufficiently, not too, just

In this paper, we first process a user's review text information for a particular item into a set of words, and then we look for the corresponding words in the emotion dictionary based on the words in the set. Specifically, a corresponding positive word has an initial value of $+1.0$, and a corresponding negative word has an initial value of -1.0. In addition, we search for the corresponding word in the emotion level dictionary according to the words in the set. Since the emotion level dictionary is divided into five levels, we set the initial values as 5.0, 4.0, 3.0, 2.0 and 1.0 based on the degree of emotion. Specifically, a word with the highest degree of emotion starts with a value of 5.0, and a word with the lowest degree of emotion starts with a value of 1.0. Finally, based on the review r published by user u for the item i, we can get the sentiment score of user u for item i $\text{Sen}(r)_{u,i}$:

$$\text{Sen}(r)_{u,i} = \left(\sum_{w \in r} D_w \cdot R_w \right) / N_w \tag{1}$$

Where, parameter w represents the emotional word in user u's reviews information on item i, the meaning of N_w is amount of emotional words, the meaning of D_w is the initial assignment of emotional degree words [13], and R_w represents the initial assignment of emotional words. Then, we get the user-item sentiment score matrix $\Phi_{u,i}^{M \times N}$. Specifically, the rows of the matrix represent users, the columns represent items, and the fill value is the sentiment score $\text{Sen}(r)$. We explore the impact factors between users based on the User-wise Mutual Information (UMI) [14,15]. The $UMI(u,v)$ can be described by the following equation:

$$UMI(u,v) = \log\{P(u,v)/P(u) * P(v)\} \tag{2}$$

First of all, we only keep the value not less than 70% of the maximum $\text{Sen}(r)_{u,i}$, then the corresponding user u will be regarded as a strong like user of the item i. Then, we extract the strong like user set for each item, and the total number of times the observed user u appears in the strong like user list for a given item together with another user v is denoted by L. $P(u,v)$ represents the possibility that user u and user v appear together in L $(P(u,v) = \#(u,v)/|L|)$, $P(u)$ is the possibility that user u appears in L alone $(P(u) = \#(u)/|L|)$, $P(v)$ is the possibility that user v appears alone in L $(P(v) = \#(v)/|L|)$. Furthermore, the $UMI(u,v)$ can be expressed as:

$$UMI(u,v) = \log\{[\#(u,v) * |L|]/[\#(u) * \#(v)]\} \tag{3}$$

Then, we can construct a matrix with dimensions of $M \times M$, where M represents a total of M users in the dataset. We define this square matrix as the impact factor matrix between users $\Omega_{u,v}^{M \times M}$. The filling element value is $UMI(u,v)$, and the greater the $UMI(u,v)$ value is, the richer the potential connections between user u and user v.

3.2   Rating Prediction Model

The classical RP equation based on CF is as follows:

$$\widehat{R}_{u,i} = \bar{R} + B_u + B_i + \left(P_u + |N_u|^{-1/2} \sum_{j \in N_u} Y_j \right) Q_i^T \tag{4}$$

$$E_{u,i} = R_{u,i} - \widehat{R}_{u,i} \tag{5}$$

Where, $R_{u,i}$ stands for the user u's true rating of item i, $R_{u,i} \in R_{M \times N}$; $\widehat{R}_{u,i}$ stands for the unknown predicted rating given by user u for item i. $\bar{R}$ stands for the mean of the ratings. B_u stands for the user bias. B_i stands for the item bias. For a user u, the collection of items that it provides implicit feedback is defined as N_u. Y_n stands for the implicit impact of items that user u rated in the past on the unrated items in the future.

Based on the analysis of the user impact factor $\Omega_{u,v} M \times M$ obtained from user reviews text information, we define the object function of the RP method proposed in this paper as follows:

$$
\begin{aligned}
\Psi(R, P, Q) = {} & \tfrac{1}{2} \sum_{u,i} E_{u,i}^2 + \tfrac{\alpha}{2} \left(\|P_u\|_F^2 + \|Q_i\|_F^2 + \|B_u\|_F^2 + \|B_i\|_F^2 + \sum_{j \in N_u} \|Y_j\|_F^2 \right) \\
& + \tfrac{\beta}{2} \sum_u \left\{ \left(1^{M \times M} P_u - \sum_v \Omega_{u,v}{}^{M \times M} P_v \right) \left(1^{M \times M} P_u - \sum_v \Omega_{u,v}{}^{M \times M} P_v \right)^T \right\}
\end{aligned}
\tag{6}
$$

Where, P_u and Q_i stand for the potential element matrix of users and items. $P_{M \times K}$ and $Q_{K \times N}$ stand for the K-dimensional vectors of user u and item i. The first half of the formula stands for the error between the existing factual score value $R_{u,I}$ and the unknown predicted score value $\widehat{R}_{u,I}$. The middle part of the formula is the regular term set to prevent the model from overfitting. The third part shows the influence of impact factor $\Omega_{u,v}^{M \times M}$ among users on the RP task.

3.3   Model Training

We presented the object function of the RP model in the previous section. In this section, we use the gradient descent method to minimize the object function. Specifically, the gradient of user bias vector B_u, project bias vector B_i, user implicit feedback vector Y_j, and k-dimension potential factor vector P_u and Q_i of user and item are shown as follows:

$$
\partial\psi / \partial B_u = \sum_i E_{u,i} + \alpha B_u
\tag{7}
$$

$$
\partial\psi / \partial B_i = \sum_u E_{u,i} + \alpha B_i
\tag{8}
$$

$$
\partial\psi / \partial Q_i = \sum_i E_{u,i} P_u + \alpha Q_i
\tag{9}
$$

$$
\partial\psi / \partial Y_j = \sum_u E_{u,i} |N_u|^{-1/2} Q_i + \alpha \sum_{j \in N_u} Y_j
\tag{10}
$$

$$
\partial\psi / \partial P_u = \sum_i E_{u,i} Q_i + \alpha P_u + \beta \left(P_u - \sum_v \Omega_{u,v} P_v \right) - \beta \sum_v \Omega_{u,v} \left(P_u - \sum_v \Omega_{u,v} P_v \right)
\tag{11}
$$

Moreover, the initial values of B_u and B_i are set to the zero vector, and we conduct random sampling based on normal distribution data with zero mean to get the initial values of P_u and Q_i. The learning rate ζ of the RP model is set to 0.003, and the total number of iterations τ is set to 10000 to ensure that the object function keeps decreasing, and an early stop identifier is set.

4   Experiments

4.1   Datasets

Since this paper is based on the user reviews text information to extract the influence factors between different users, we use the Yelp dataset [16] which contain the user reviews and rating information to test the performance of our method. Specifically, the Yelp data set consists of 28,630 users, 96,975 items, 300,848 ratings, 66,992 reviews, and each review contains an average of 134 words. They are divided into 8 different subsets: Active Life, Beauty&Spa, Home, Service, Hotel&Travel, Night Life, Restaurants, Shopping, and pets. In the experiments of this paper, we select three subsets for verification, they are Hotel&Travel, Restaurants and Shopping.

4.2   Evaluation Metrics

Two evaluation indicators used in the experiments are Root Mean Squared Error (RMSE) and Mean Absolute Error (MAE) [29].These two metrics measure the performance of the RP model by calculating the error between the user's existing factual score and the predicted score. And the smaller the value, the higher the performance. Their formula is defined as follows:

$$RMSE = \sqrt{\sum_{u,i \in R_{\text{test}}} \left(R_{u,i} - \widehat{R}_{u,i} \right)^2 / R_{\text{test}}} \tag{12}$$

$$MAE = \sum_{u,i \in R_{test}} \left| R_{u,i} - \widehat{R}_{u,i} \right| / R_{\text{test}} \tag{13}$$

where, the parameter R_{test} stands for the amount of rating records in the testset, $R_{u,i}$ stands for the already existed rating, and $\hat{R}_{u,i}$ stands for the predicted rating.

4.3   Comparative Methods

In this subsection, we conduct a series of experiments to verify the performance of the method proposed in this paper and the existing RP methods. The comparison methods used in the experiments are as follows:

PRM: This method explored and extracted three social factors based on the user's historical behavior: interpersonal influence, personal interest and interpersonal interest similarity, and adds the above factors to the MF model to improve the accuracy of RP.

CUNE: [30] This method was dedicated to extracting the reliable social implicit information from user feedback information, exploring the top N semantic level companies of each user, and adding them to the MFmodel to improve the accuracy of user RP.

IS: This method firstly identified the subject and user sentiment from the review text, and then grouped similar users based on the soft clustering technology to improve the quality of RP.

EFM: [31] This method constructed the user characteristic attention matrix and the item characteristic quality matrix on the basis of the MF framework. Specifically, each element in the user characteristic attention matrix measures the degree of user attention to the corresponding item characteristic, and each element in the item characteristic quality matrix measures the quality of the corresponding item characteristic.

RRP: We extract the user's preference for a specific item by the user review text information, and then quantify the correlation element on different users by the *UMI* between users, and finally add it into the MF model to promote the accuracy degree of RP task.

Table 2. The predictive performance comparison between our method (RRP) and the comparison methods in the 3 subsets of Yelp dataset (Dimension K = 10).

Datasets	PRM		CUNE		IS		EFM		RRP	
	RMSE	MAE	RMSE	MAE	RMSE	MAE	RMSE	MAE	**RMSE**	**MAE**
	Improve	*Improve*	*Improve*	*Improve*	*Improve*	*Improve*	*Improve*	*Improve*		
Hotel&Travel	1.321	1.042	1.139	1.026	1.181	0.997	1.267	1.024	**1.102**	**0.938**
	16.62%	9.98%	3.25%	8.58%	6.69%	5.92%	13.02%	8.39%		
Restaurants	1.094	0.873	1.126	0.894	1.133	0.902	1.113	0.886	**1.027**	**0.851**
	6.12%	2.52%	8.79%	4.81%	9.36%	5.65%	7.73%	3.95%		
Shopping	1.201	1.016	1.068	0.997	1.224	1.053	1.158	0.989	**1.013**	**0.912**
	15.71%	10.24%	5.15%	8.53%	17.24%	13.39%	12.52%	7.79%		
Average	1.205	0.977	1.111	0.972	1.179	0.984	1.176	0.966	**1.047**	**0.901**
	13.11%	7.78%	5.76%	7.31%	11.19%	8.43%	10.97%	6.73%		

4.4 Performance Comparison

We compare the RRP method with the above-mentioned methods. In all comparison method experiments, we set the potential feature dimension K to 10, and parameter β to optimize the degree of influence between users. Specifically, we first set the parameter α to 1, and Find the best value for the parameter β in the interval $[10^{-2}, 10^{-1}, 1, 10]$. Then, when the fixed parameter β is the optimal value, we find the optimal value of the parameter α in the interval $[10^{-2}, 10^{-1}, 1, 10]$. In addition, if the model parameter has an optimal value on the value boundary, then we extend the boundary appropriately to obtain the model optimization.

We show the performance of the structured method and other comparative RP methods based on 3 Yelp subsets in Table 2. The percentage figures in the table stand for the improvement of RRP relative to various other comparison methods. It can be clearly seen that the performance of our structured RP method (RRP) which considers the user reviews information factors on each

Yelp subset is better than the baseline method for comparison. Compared with the baseline methods: PRM, CUNE, IS, and EFM, the average RMSE value of our method is reduced by 13.11%, 5.76%, 11.19%, and 10.97%; the average MAE value is reduced by 7.78%, 7.31%, 8.43%, and 6.73%. In general, the results of the experiment show the importance of the inter-user influence factors implied in the user reviews information in expressing user preferences and improving the accuracy of RP task.

5   Conclusion

In this paper, we structure a new RP method by the users' review text information. Specifically, we first quantify the user's predilection on a specific item by the user review information. Then we calculate the impact factor between users based on the value of between different users. Finally, we add the calculated inter-user influence factor matrix into the MF model to perform the task. We conduct a series of experimental studies on the 3 subsets in the Yelp. The experimental finding show that the overall performance of the method structured in this paper decreases by at least 5.76% and 6.73% in the RMSE index and the MAE index, respectively.

Ackonwledgment. This research was funded by the Natural Science Foundation of Xinjiang Uygur Autonomous Region grant number 2020D01C034, Tianshan Innovation Team of Xinjiang Uygur Autonomous Region grant number 2020D14044, National Science Foundation of China under Grant U1903213, 61771416 and 62041110, the National Key R&D Program of China under Grant 2018YFB1403202, Creative Research Groups of Higher Education of Xinjiang Uygur Autonomous Region under Grant XJEDU2017T002.

References

1. Ng, J.P.: Recommender systems handbook. Comput. Rev. **57**(8), 470–474 (2016)
2. Wang, W., Chen, Z., Liu, J., Qi, Q., Zhao, Z.: User-based collaborative filtering on cross domain by tag transfer learningUMI. In: Proceedings of the 1st International Workshop on Cross Domain Knowledge Discovery in Web and Social Network Mining, vol. 2, pp. 10–17 (2012)
3. Deng, X., Deng, Z.R., Liang, X.U., Xie, P.: Optimized collaborative filtering recommendation algorithm. Comput. Eng. Des. **37**(5), 1259–1264 (2016)
4. Chen, T., Hong, L., Shi, Y., Sun, Y.: Joint text embedding for personalized content-based recommendation. arXiv preprint arXiv:1706.01084 (2017)
5. Zhao, X., Zhang, L., Xia, L., Ding, Z., Yin, D., Tang, J.: Deep reinforcement learning for list-wise recommendations. arXiv preprint arXiv:1801.00209 (2017)
6. Zhao, G., Qian, X., Lei, X., Mei, T.: Service quality evaluation by exploring social users' contextual information. IEEE Trans. Knowl. Data Eng. **28**(12), 3382–3394 (2016)
7. Févotte, C., Idier, J.: Algorithms for nonnegative matrix factorization with the beta-divergence. Neural Comput. **23**(9), 2421–2456 (2010)

8. Mnih, A., Salakhutdinov, R.R.: Probabilistic matrix factorization. Adv. Neural. Inf. Process. Syst. **20**, 1257–1264 (2007)
9. Yang, B., Lei, Y., Liu, J., Li, W.: Social collaborative filtering by trust. IEEE Trans. Pattern Anal. Mach. Intell. **39**(8), 1633–1647 (2016)
10. Blei, D.M., Ng, A.Y., Jordan, M.I.: Latent dirichlet allocation. J. Mach. Learn. Res. **3**, 993–1022 (2003)
11. Ma, T., et al.: Social network and tag sources based augmenting collaborative recommender system. IEEE Trans. Inf. Syst. **98**(4), 902–910 (2015)
12. Ganu, G., Kakodkar, Y., Marian, A.: Improving the quality of predictions using textual information in online user reviews. Inf. Syst. **38**(1), 1–15 (2013)
13. Lei, X., Qian, X., Zhao, G.: Rating prediction based on social sentiment from textual reviews. IEEE Trans. Multimed. **18**(9), 1910–1921 (2016)
14. Hui, N., Zhe, R.: Review helpfulness prediction research based on review sentiment feature sets. Data Anal. Knowl. Discov. **31**(7–8), 113–121 (2015)
15. Shi, W., Wang, L., Qin, J.: User embedding for rating prediction in SVD++-based collaborative filtering. Symmetry **12**(1), 121 (2020)
16. Shi, W., Wang, L., Qin, J.: Extracting user influence from ratings and trust for rating prediction in recommendations. Sci. Rep. **10**(1), 1–13 (2020)
17. Wang, H., et al.: Ripplenet: propagating user preferences on the knowledge graph for recommender systems. In: Proceedings of the 27th ACM International Conference on Information and Knowledge Management, pp. 417–426. ACM (2018)
18. Quispe, L.C., Luna, J.E.O.: A content-based recommendation system using TrueSkill. In: 2015 Fourteenth Mexican International Conference on Artificial Intelligence (MICAI), pp. 203–207. IEEE (2015)
19. Chae, D.K., Kang, J.S., Kim, S.W., Lee, J.T.: Cfgan: a generic collaborative filtering framework based on generative adversarial networks. In: Proceedings of the 27th ACM International Conference on Information and Knowledge Management, pp. 137–146. ACM (2018)
20. Resnick, P., Iacovou, N., Suchak, M., Bergstrom, P., Riedl, J.: Grouplens: an open architecture for collaborative filtering of netnews. In: Proceedings of the 1994 ACM Conference on Computer Supported Cooperative Work, pp. 175–186. ACM (1994)
21. Sarwar, B., Karypis, G., Konstan, J., Riedl, J.: Item-based collaborative filtering recommendation algorithms. In: Proceedings of the 10th International Conference on World Wide Web, pp. 285–295 (2001)
22. Guo, G., Zhang, J., Yorke-Smith, N.: Trustsvd: collaborative filtering with both the explicit and implicit influence of user trust and of item ratings. In: Proceedings of the AAAI Conference on Artificial Intelligence, pp. 124–132 (2015)
23. Jakob, N., Weber, S.H., Müller, M.C., Gurevych, I.: Trustsvd: beyond the stars: exploiting free-text user reviews to improve the accuracy of movie recommendations. In: Proceedings of the 1st International CIKM Workshop on Topic-sentiment Analysis for Mass Opinion, pp. 57–64 (2009)
24. Li, X., Xu, G., Chen, E., Li, L.: Learning user preferences across multiple aspects for merchant recommendation. In: 2015 IEEE International Conference on Data Mining, pp. 865–870 (2015)
25. Almahairi, A., Kastner, K., Cho, K., Courville, A.: Learning distributed representations from reviews for collaborative filtering. In: Proceedings of the 9th ACM Conference on Recommender Systems, pp. 147–154 (2015)
26. Lou, P., Zhao, G., Qian, X., Wang, H., Hou, X.: Schedule a rich sentimental travel via sentimental POI mining and recommendation. In: 2016 IEEE Second International Conference on Multimedia Big Data (BigMM), pp. 33–40 (2016)

27. Rendle, S.: Factorization machines. In: 2010 IEEE International Conference on Data Mining, pp. 995–1000 (2010)
28. Zhang, W., Ding, G., Chen, L., Li, C., Zhang, C.: Generating virtual ratings from Chinese reviews to augment online recommendations. In: ACM Transactions on Intelligent Systems and Technology (TIST), pp. 1–17 (2013)
29. Yang, X., Steck, H., Liu, Y.: Circle-based recommendation in online social networks. In: Proceedings of the 18th ACM SIGKDD International Conference on Knowledge Discovery and Data Mining, pp. 1267–1275 (2012)
30. Chawla, N., Wang, W.: Collaborative user network embedding for social recommender systems. In: Proceedings of the 2017 SIAM International Conference on Data Mining, pp. 381–389 (2017)
31. Zhang, Y., Lai, G., Zhang, M., Zhang, Y., Liu, Y., Ma, S.: Explicit factor models for explainable recommendation based on phrase-level sentiment analysis. In: Proceedings of the 37th International ACM SIGIR Conference on Research & Development in Information Retrieval, pp. 83–92 (2014)

Exploiting Visual Context and Multi-grained Semantics for Social Text Emotion Recognition

Wei Cao[1,2], Kun Zhang[3], Hanqing Tao[1], Weidong He[1], Qi Liu[1],
Enhong Chen[1(✉)], and Jianhui Ma[1]

[1] University of Science and Technology of China, Hefei 230027, China
cw0808@mail.ustc.edu.cn, cheneh@ustc.edu.cn
[2] Xinjiang Normal University, Urumqi 830054, China
[3] Hefei University of Technology, Hefei 230009, China

Abstract. Social text is a kind of user-generated data on social media, which can reflect the opinions and emotions of netizens in their social activities. The study about emotion recognition for social text could help us clarify netizens' emotional position on certain issues, products, or services to support opinion monitoring, marketing management and so on. But with the continuous improvement of information technology, the mode of emotional expression has become increasingly complex and diverse. For the sake of concise and comprehensive implications, social texts are usually very short and noisy, which are often accompanied with visual context and pictorial multi-grained semantics. Therefore, traditional research strategies based on plain text analysis have great limitations faced with those contents. To this end, we in this article focus on the semantic and emotional uncertainty in social texts through taking into account the textual content of social text and its related non-text information to improve emotion semantic representations for social text emotion recognition. Specifically, to realize the visual context modeling, we first leverage the visual information associated with social text as the contextual supplement to enhance the emotional semantics of short social text. Then, we model the semantics of social text with different granularity to fully mine the limited information of social text. After that, with the help of visual context enhancement and multi-grained semantic mining, we are capable of alleviating the limited expression of social text and its uncertainty of semantics and emotions. This could represent the emotion semantics of social text effectively for its emotion recognition. Finally, extensive experiments on the real multi-modal dataset demonstrate that our proposed method has promising results with high efficiency.

Keywords: Text emotion · Visual · Semantics · Multi-grained

© Springer Nature Switzerland AG 2021
L. Fang et al. (Eds.): CICAI 2021, LNAI 13069, pp. 783–795, 2021.
https://doi.org/10.1007/978-3-030-93046-2_66

Fig. 1. Some texts on social platforms. Manifestly, social text is often very short. Thus, there are some uncertainties in social text, such as "darlings" in the 2-th case and so on. Furthermore, social text may be accompanied by image information sometimes.

1   Introduction

Social text emotion recognition, which aims to identify the emotional categories of text on social networks, has been widely applied in data mining, information retrieval, man-machine emotional interaction, and so on [3–5]. Due to the importance of emotion in human communication, especially for social network activities, social text emotion recognition has become one of the most active research branches in natural language processing (NLP) and attracted many researchers to do efforts in this area [17,20]. Among these studies, the most mainstream method is to use the deep neural network to mine emotion semantics for social text emotional recognition. For example, Quan et al. [24] proposed an emotion model based on Long Short Term Memory (LSTM) [12] to mine emotion semantics for text emotional recognition. After that, Luo et al. [19] combined Gated Recurrent Unit (GRU) [7] and Convolutional Neural Networks (CNN) [16] to identify text emotion. These studies are devoted to the emotional semantic understanding of text content and have achieved good recognition results.

However, since people tend to use visual information such as pictures to help convey emotions, social text is often accompanied by short length and noise problems, which is shown in Fig. 1. And this issue often makes the semantics and emotion of social text uncertain. Most significantly, this uncertainty has brought great difficulties to social text emotion recognition, while few researchers have considered and solved this problem. Fortunately, social platforms often contain some image data that exists simultaneously with social text. Taking the images shown in Fig. 1 as an example, those contents have a time-series correlation with the corresponding text and can serve as textual context enhancement to alleviate the uncertainty of semantics and emotion for social text. But the mainstream investigations are concerned solely with the text content of social text, ignoring the effect of the associated multi-modal data on social text. Furthermore, social text is usually so short that its content is limited. Consequently, compared with the emotion classification of other texts, it is necessary to fully explore the fuzzy emotion information hidden behind social texts. To this end, we focus on solving the semantic and emotional problems for social text emotion recognition. The specific solution includes two aspects: on the one hand, we introduce the associated image data to enhance the text context of social text at the data level; on the other hand, we employ multi-grained semantics to enrich the limited text content of social text at the method level. In the process of implementation, there are two main challenges: 1) How to use the associated images to enhance the context of social text at the data level; 2) How to conduct the multi-granularity semantic modeling for the limited information of social text at the method level.

To conquer the above challenges, we propose a novel model based on **V**isual **C**ontext **E**hancement and **M**ulti-grained **S**emantics **E**xpression (**VCEMSE**) for social text emotion recognition. Firstly, we design a context enhancement unit to fuse the associated visual information into both the sentence embedding and word embeddings for context enhancement of social text. Then, VCEMSE adopts a text fine-grained expression unit to model the fine-grained semantics of the above word embeddings for a new sentence representation. Finally, this new sentence embedding containing fine-grained semantic expression would be fused with the previous sentence embedding for the final representation of social text. This final representation involves the enhanced visual context and multi-grained semantics, which can represent sentence semantics accurately. The experiments demonstrate that VCEMSE can identify the emotion of social text efficiently.

2   Related Work

Generally speaking, there are three kinds of approaches to social text emotion recognition: the emotion dictionary-based approach, the machine learning-based approach, and the deep learning method.

Dictionary-Based Approach. This method analyzes emotion words and calculates sentiment scores to identify text emotion [13,40]. Here, emotion dictionary plays a important role, such as WordNetAffect [30], HowNet [9], NTudSD [15] and so on. In the initial studies, emotion dictionaries rely on manual tagging, which is time-consuming and labor-intensive. Then, scholars tried to construct emotion dictionaries automatically for efficiency improvement. They expanded emotion dictionaries by comparing and calculating the relation between the words to be processed and the known emotion seed words [29]. This method is operable and requires no manual labels, so it is still used today, such as the work about sentence emotion detection [27]. But it has low adaptability since language is so complex that emotion rules cannot cover all language expressions.

Machine Learning-Based Approach. With the development of machine learning technology, scholars have tried to use machine learning algorithms to carry out text emotion recognition and achieved good results. Different from the dictionary-based approach, this method relies on feature engineering and appropriate classifiers [41]. Related features involves n-gram [33], syntax information [2], topic information [31], emoji [14] and so on. For example, Abbasi et al. [1] used the n-gram feature to address the multilingual sentiment analysis task. Subsequently, Abbasi et al. [2] improved the above work by a feature relation network that leverages both syntactic relationships and n-gram features. These machine learning methods are widely used for the small computation.

However, these studies have certain limitations because it relies on the quality of feature engineering and cannot understand the emotion by text semantics.

Deep Learning-Based Approach. Due to the excellent representation ability of deep neural networks, many deep learning techniques have been introduced into text sentiment recognition and achieved considerable results. Rakhlin et al. [25] used CNN to classify text emotion for the first time. Vateekul et al. [35] built the deep learning model DCNN for this task and performed well. Considering the sequentiality of text semantics, scholars preferred to use Recursive Neural Networks (RNN) [10] and its derived models for text emotion recognition [19,24]. Pal et al. [22] designed a multiple layers LSTM to improve text representations and realize text emotion classification. With the success of the attention mechanism in computer vision, researchers also introduced this mechanism into text emotion recognition and gained good performance [6,38]. For example, Basiri et al. [6] used the attention mechanism to emphasize different words to analyze text emotion accurately. All these studies focus on the semantic understanding of text content and have gained good results. As the research progresses, some scholars have noted the unique role of multimodal data in emotion understanding and introduced other non-text forms into social text emotion recognition [18,32]. Go et al. [11] used emoticons as natural annotation and predicted text emotion by the remote monitoring method. But these studies only involve emoticons, Moreover, they focus only on addressing the lack of data labels through emoticons.

Unlike the above studies, our work introduces the external visual information to enhance text context and expands the semantic granularity to explore limited text content for social text emotion recognition. And this solution has proven to be effective because it can alleviate the uncertainty of social text more pertinently for accurate semantic representation.

3   Emotion Recognition of Social Text

In this section, we introduce the whole architecture of our designed model VCEMSE and describe its each unit in detail.

3.1   Problem Definition

For the given multimodal emotion dataset $C_e = \{< c^m, f^m, l_e^m >\}$, c^m is the m-th text sentence with n words, f^m is the image data corresponding to c^m, and l_e^m is the emotion category of c^m. The model input is text c^m with its corresponding and our goal is to predict the emotion category of c^m.

3.2   The Details of VCEMSE Model

Figure 2 shows the whole framework of VCEMSE, including the units of feature embedding, visual context enhancement, fine-grained semantics expression and multi-grained semantics fusion. The related details will be elaborated as below.

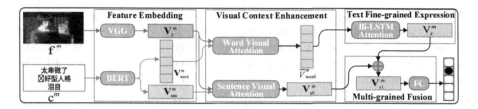

Fig. 2. The model of Visual Context Enhancement and Multi-grained Semantics Expression for Social Text Emotion Recognition (VCEMSE).

Feature Embedding. This unit aims to vectorize the original inputs of text c^m and image f^m. For text c^m, we leverage the pre-trained language model BERT [8] to represent c^m as embedding vectors. Moreover, considering the strong semantic representation capability of BERT, we obtain both the word-level semantic representations V_{word}^m and the sentence-level semantic representations V_{sen}^m of c^m. These two vectors can represent text semantics at different dimensions. For image f^m, we adopt VGG19 [28] to process its visual data. Specifically, this unit extracts the results of the last convolutional layer from VGG19 as the visual representations V_f^m of image f^m. The formulas are as follows:

$$(V_{word}^m, V_{sen}^m) = BERT(C^m), \tag{1}$$
$$V_f^m = VGG(f^m).$$

Visual Context Enhancement. To alleviate the uncertainty of semantics and emotions in social text for text emotion recognition accurately, this unit enhances the text context by the associated visual information. What's more, to fully explore the limited text content, we conduct the context enhancement at the word-level and sentence-level respectively through different attention networks. The word-level visual context attention for word embedding V_{word}^m is as below:

$$M_1 = \tanh\left(W_1 V_f^m + W_2 V_{word}^m\right),$$
$$\alpha = softmax\left(W_3 M_1\right), \tag{2}$$
$$\overline{V}_{word}^m = \alpha \cdot V_{word}^m,$$

where W_1, W_2 and W_3 are trainable parameters, M_1 is the intermediate variable, α is the attention weight between each word and visual information, $\overline{V}_{word}^m$ is the word representations with the visual context information. By the word-level visual attention, VEMSE can enhance word context and pay more attention to the words that are more relevant to the visual context of visual information V_f^m.

The sentence-level visual context attention of sentence embedding V_{sen}^m is relatively simple. It can be realized by the dot product as below:

$$V_{s0}^m = V_{sen}^m \cdot V_f^m. \tag{3}$$

Through the sentence-level visual context enhancement, we can obtain the new sentence embedding V_{s0}^m that contains the associated visual context information.

Fine-Grained Semantics Expression. This unit aims to mine fine-grained semantics expression of the above word embedding $\overline{V}^m_{word}$ through BiLSTM network [26] and self-attention mechanism. Firstly, we use BiLSTM to model sequence semantics of text and acquire the sentence context for each word. The new word embeddings $V^m_{h\_word}$ that output from BiLSTM is formulated as below:

$$V^m_{h\_word} = BiLSTM\left(\overline{V}^m_{word}\right),$$

$$V^m_{h\_word} = \left(V^m_{h\_word\_1}, ..., V^m_{h\_word\_j}, ..., V^m_{h\_word\_n}\right). \tag{4}$$

Then, we use the self-attention mechanism to differentiate the importance of each word in the above word embeddings $V^m_{h\_word}$. Finally, we fuse the word importances α_1 into word embeddings to obtain new sentence representations:

$$M_2 = \tanh\left(W_4 V^m_{h\_word}\right),$$

$$\alpha_1 = softmax\left(W_5 M_2\right), \tag{5}$$

$$V^m_{s1} = \sum \alpha_1 \cdot V^m_{h\_word}.$$

The new sentence representation V^m_{s1} contains word-level visual context and fine-grained semantic expression.

Multi-grained Semantics Fusion. This unit is designed to mine the limited information of text by multi-grained semantics fusion. Specifically, the sentence embedding V^m_{s1}, which contains word-level visual context and fine-grained semantics, will be fused with the previous sentence embedding V^m_{s0} that contains the sentence-level visual context for multi-grained semantics representation V^m_s:

$$V^m_s = V^m_{s1} + V^m_{s0}. \tag{6}$$

Based on the above units, we could acquire the final representation V^m_s which can represent social text semantics very well. V^m_s enhances the text context by the associated visual information. Furthermore, it obtains the multi-grained semantics information through the textual fine-grained expression at word-level and the coarse-grained expression at sentence-level. Finally, V^m_s would be fed into a Fully Connected (FC) Layer and the softmax function for emotion prediction:

$$P_s = softmax\left(FC\left(V^m_s\right)\right), \tag{7}$$

where FC is a single-layer fully connected network, P_s is the emotional category probability of sentence representation V^m_s. Considering VCEMSE contains the multi-grained semantics modeling, we can also obtain the emotional category probabilities P_{s0} and P_{s1} for the other two text representations V^m_{s0} and V^m_{s1}:

$$P^m_{s0} = softmax\left(FC\left(V^m_{s0}\right)\right),$$

$$P^m_{s1} = softmax\left(FC\left(V^m_{s1}\right)\right). \tag{8}$$

3.3 Model Training

Since our task is a classification problem, we choose to employ the *cross_entropy* as our loss function. Additionally, to improve recognition efficiency, we expect the text representations of each granularity to make emotion prediction as correctly as possible. So we calculate the loss functions for the text representations on each grained and fuse these losses into the final loss functions L for model training:

$$
\begin{aligned}
L &= Loss(V_s^M) + Loss(V_{s0}^M) + Loss(V_{s1}^M) \\
&= -\frac{1}{M}\sum_{m=1}^{M} l_e^m log P_s^m - \frac{1}{M}\sum_{m=1}^{M} l_e^m log P_{s0}^m - \frac{1}{M}\sum_{i=m}^{M} l_e^m log P_{s1}^m,
\end{aligned}
\tag{9}
$$

where l_e^m is the true label of c^m, m and M are the subscript and total of training text data. To minimize L, we apply Adam optimizer to update all the parameters. And we conduct the dropout operation to prevent VCEMSE from overfitting.

4 Experiments Study

In this part, we will explain the experimental preparation in detail, including the dataset, experimental setup, benchmark models, evaluation criteria, etc. Then, we analyze experimental results to demonstrate the superiority of VCEMSE.

4.1 Construction of Our Multi-modal Emotion Dataset

As we know, bullet-screen comment (danmu) is currently a typical social text prevailing in various media platforms. Because danmu is sent by viewers to express instant feelings while watching videos, it is rich in emotional information. In particular, danmu is synchronized with the corresponding videos. Each danmu corresponds to a video frame, which can be seen as the context of danmu. Thus we construct the multimodal dataset C_e by danmu and the corresponding frames.

To reduce the cost of labeling, we use emotion dictionaries to acquire the emotion labels of text. Notably, to ensure the accuracy of labels, we limit the length of danmu to 15, and recognize emotion from emotional polarities to fine-grained categories. Firstly, we use the mainstream emotion polarity dictionary[1] from How-Net to identify emotional polarities of danmu. In addition, we employ two emotional dictionaries special for danmu to extend How-Net to suit the expressions of danmu. One is from Baidu Wenku[2], another is from [23]. Then, we construct a fine-grained emotion dictionary to identify the emotion categories of the danmu with definite emotion polarities. This fine-grained dictionary evolves from Chinese emotion ontology database [39] and the above two emotion dictionaries special for danmu. The ontology database describes many emotional phrases based on emotional category, emotional polarity, etc. The emotional categories

---

[1] http://www.keenage.com/html/c_index.html.
[2] https://wenku.baidu.com/view/22191501b9d528ea81c779dd.html.

Table 1. The details of emotion categories in dataset C_e before and after sampling.

Dataset state	Total numbers	Glad	Amazed	Disliked	Sad	Afraid
Before sampling	1,500,000	1,122,833	89,406	281,613	106,052	55,622
After sampling	278,110	55,622	55,622	55,622	55,622	55,622

involve "glad", "good", "angry", "sad", "afraid", "disliked" and "amazed". To alleviate the imbalance of categories of the dataset, we combined the "anger" category into the "disliked" category and the "good" category into the "glad" category according to the proximity of emotion semantics. In this way, we can acquire the text with emotion labels and construct dataset C_e.

4.2 Experiment Setup

The input of VCEMSE is the text in C_e and the corresponding images in F_e. We leverage the RandomUnderSampler method to overcome the issue of category imbalance. And the sampled data is split into a training set, a valid set, and a test set by (0.6, 0.3, 0.1). The details of emotion categories in dataset C_e before and after sampling can be seen in Table 1. Before training, we use the pre-trained model BERT and VGG to process text and image data into vectors of $1,024$ and $4,096$ dimensions, respectively. In training, the hidden state size of BiLSTM is set as 256, the initialize weights follow the uniform distribution suggested in [21], all the biases are initialized as zeros, and the learning rate is set to 10^{-4}.

4.3 Benchmark Models

To compare the experimental performance of the proposed model VCEMSE, the following baselines are constructed:

1) **ETransformer.** Considering the Transformer [34] can model text semantics well, we design ETransformer that evolves from Transformer and classifies text emotion through position encoding and multi-head attention mechanism.
2) **ABiLSTM.** ABiLSTM identifies text emotion by sequence semantics modeling of BiLSTM and words importance capturing of attention mechanisms.
3) **PABiLSTM.** PABiLSTM is evolved from ABiLSTM by introducing word position manipulation with the purpose of text semantics understanding well.
4) **BABiLSTM.** BABiLSTM is evolved from ABiLSTM by changing the text pre-trained model from Word2Vec to BERT for better text embeddings.
5) **VCEMSE.** VCEMSE is our model that integrates the visual context and multi-grained semantics to model the emotional semantics of social text well.

4.4 Performance Metrics

Considering that our dataset involves 5 emotional categories: "glad", "sad", "afraid", "disliked" and "amazed", this work is a multi-classification task. Hence,

Table 2. The performance comparison of social text emotion recognition.

Category	VCEMSE (Ours)			BABiLSTM			PABiLSTM			ABiLSTM			Etransformer		
	P	R	F_1	P	R	F_1	P	R	F_1	P	R	F_1	P	R	F_1
glad	0.91	0.91	**0.90**	0.92	0.92	0.89	0.81	0.81	0.85	0.82	0.82	0.86	0.82	0.82	0.80
amazed	0.97	0.97	**0.96**	0.93	0.93	0.94	0.96	0.96	0.88	0.92	0.92	0.87	0.76	0.76	0.80
disliked	0.85	0.85	0.88	0.81	0.81	0.84	0.91	0.91	**0.91**	0.91	0.91	**0.91**	0.84	0.84	0.81
sad	0.90	0.90	**0.91**	0.90	0.90	0.90	0.87	0.87	0.89	0.90	0.90	0.89	0.81	0.81	0.82
afraid	0.96	0.96	0.93	0.93	0.93	0.91	0.96	0.96	**0.96**	0.97	0.97	**0.96**	0.91	0.91	0.90
Accuracy	**0.9159**			0.8956			0.8976			0.8992			0.8246		

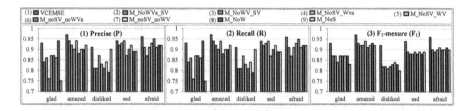

Fig. 3. The ablation performance of the proposed model VCEMSE.

we adopt *Precision* (*P*), *Recall* (*R*), and $F_1 - measure$ (*F*₁) for each category to evaluate the classification performance. Besides, we use the indicator *Accuracy* to evaluate the overall performance of social text emotion recognition.

4.5 Experimental Results Analysis

As shown in Table 2, the overall accuracy of our model VCEMSE achieves nearly 91.6%. Although our task is a fine-grained emotion classification task, it is generally more difficult than traditional emotion polarity classification. Nonetheless, the performance of the VCEMSE model is still very considerable.

We also evaluate the performance of all models on the evaluation criterias of *Precision* (P), *Recall* (R), and $F_1 - measure$ (F₁). Specifically, Etransformer performed the worst in all baselines. The probable cause is that Transformer is good at capturing similar structures among words, but not so good at modeling semantic context that is important for emotion understanding. By contrast, the method ABiLSTM, PABiLSTM, BABiLSTM all perform better than ETransformer. It may be because these models can use RNN and attention mechanisms to model bidirectional semantics and word importance based on sentence context for a good understanding of text emotion semantics. Intriguingly, it can be noted the results difference between PABiLSTM and ABiLSTM are small. It suggests the advantage of position-coding is not striking here. It may be because social text is short that sequence modeling is enough to mining its emotion semantics. It is known that the text pre-train model BERT is superior to Word2Vec in word embeddings for its operation of masked LM and next sentence prediction. But the results of BABiLSTM with BERT do not perform better than ABiLSTM with Word2Vec. It could indicate the difficulties of our task are not the quality of

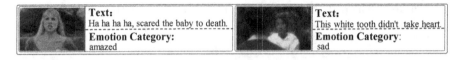

Fig. 4. The case study of social text emotion recognition by VCEMSE.

semantics embeddings. Obviously, VCEMSE performs better than all the baselines. The superiority is due to the context enhancement of visual information and the content supplement of multi-grained semantics, which can alleviate the uncertainty of semantics and emotion in social text for emotion recognition.

4.6 Ablation Performance

As shown in Fig. 3, we examine the effectiveness of each component in our proposed model VCEMSE by an ablation study. Experiments (2)–(5) utilize only partial visual attention (word-level or sentence-level visual attention). Experiments (6)–(7) consider no visual information but textual information with or without the attention mechanism. Experiments (8)–(9) involve single one granularity (word-level or sentence-level granularity) of text semantics. It is can be observed the indicators of P and F_1 in ablation models are not very good in most cases. Especially, without some critical components of VCEMSE, the overall performance of the ablation models on F_1 is clearly worse than that of VCEMSE. This fully demonstrates the visual context, multi-grained semantic fusion, and emotional attention of fine-grained semantic expression are helpful for this task. It also can validate that VCEMSE is effective for social text emotion recognition.

4.7 Case Study

We provide some intuitive demonstrations to show the effectiveness of VCEMSE in Fig. 4. Obviously, these texts are very short and their contents are simple. What's more, the text in the first case has uncertain semantics and emotion due to its expressions "ha ha" and "scared". While VCEMSE can mine the "scared" semantics from the case and predict its emotion category as "amazed" accurately. It may be because its associated image could convey the information unrelated to the emotion in the expression "ha ha". In the second case, VCEMSE can also identifies text emotion accurately. These cases show VCEMSE could address the uncertainty of social text to improve its emotion classification accurately.

5   Conclusion

In this study, we presented a novel emotion recognition model (VCEMSE) which exploits Visual Context and Multi-grained Semantics Expression to alleviate the uncertainty of semantics and emotions in social text emotion recognition. Specifically, VCEMSE utilized the associated images to enhance the text context both at sentence-level and word-level and incorporate multi-grained semantic representations to enrich the limited text content of social text. Experiments on the real-world dataset clearly demonstrated that VCEMSE could utilize the associated image and its multi-grained text content to represent emotion semantics of social text well and realize text emotion recognition accurately. In the future, we will refer to some deep representation models such as SANE [36] or MCNE [37], to explore deep representations of the relationship between image and text.

Acknowledgements. This research was supported by the National Key Research and Development Program of China (No. 2016YFB1000904), the National Natural Science Foundation of China (No. 61727809) and the Scientific Program of the Higher Education Institution of Xinjiang (No. XJEDU2016S067).

References

1. Abbasi, A., Chen, H., Salem, A.: Sentiment analysis in multiple languages: feature selection for opinion classification in web forums. ACM Trans. Inf. Syst. (TOIS) **26**(3), 1–34 (2008)
2. Abbasi, A., France, S., Zhang, Z., Chen, H.: Selecting attributes for sentiment classification using feature relation networks. TKDE **23**(3), 447–462 (2010)
3. Acheampong, F.A., Wenyu, C., Nunoo-Mensah, H.: Text-based emotion detection: advances, challenges, and opportunities. Eng. Rep. **2**(7), e12189 (2020)
4. Alswaidan, N., Menai, M.E.B.: A survey of state-of-the-art approaches for emotion recognition in text. Knowl. Inf. Syst. **62**(8), 1–51 (2020)
5. Bakshi, R.K., Kaur, N., Kaur, R., Kaur, G.: Opinion mining and sentiment analysis. In: 2016 3rd International Conference on Computing for Sustainable Global Development (INDIACom), pp. 452–455. IEEE (2016)
6. Basiri, M.E., Nemati, S., Abdar, M., Cambria, E., Acharya, U.R.: ABCDM: an attention-based bidirectional CNN-RNN deep model for sentiment analysis. Futur. Gener. Comput. Syst. **115**, 279–294 (2021)
7. Chung, J., Gulcehre, C., Cho, K., Bengio, Y.: Empirical evaluation of gated recurrent neural networks on sequence modeling. arXiv preprint arXiv:1412.3555 (2014)
8. Devlin, J., Chang, M.W., Lee, K., Toutanova, K.: Bert: pre-training of deep bidirectional transformers for language understanding. arXiv preprint arXiv:1810.04805 (2018)
9. Dong, Z., Dong, Q., Hao, C.: Hownet and its computation of meaning. In: COLING 2010, pp. 53–56 (2010)
10. Elman, J.L.: Finding structure in time. Cogn. Sci. **14**(2), 179–211 (1990)
11. Go, A., Bhayani, R., Huang, L.: Twitter sentiment classification using distant supervision. CS224N project report, Stanford 1(12), 2009 (2009)
12. Hochreiter, S., Schmidhuber, J.: Long short-term memory. Neural Comput. **9**(8), 1735–1780 (1997)
13. Hu, M., Liu, B.: Mining and summarizing customer reviews. In: SIGKDD 2004, pp. 168–177 (2004)
14. Kouloumpis, E., Wilson, T., Moore, J.: Twitter sentiment analysis: the good the bad and the OMG! In: AAAI 2011, vol. 5 (2011)

15. Ku, L.W., Liang, Y.T., Chen, H.H., et al.: Opinion extraction, summarization and tracking in news and blog corpora. In: AAAI 2006, vol. 100107, pp. 1–167 (2006)
16. LeCun, Y., et al.: Backpropagation applied to handwritten zip code recognition. Neural Comput. **1**, 541–551 (1989)
17. Lin, C., He, Y.: Joint sentiment/topic model for sentiment analysis. In: CIKM 2009, pp. 375–384 (2009)
18. Liu, K.L., Li, W.J., Guo, M.: Emoticon smoothed language models for twitter sentiment analysis. In: AAAI 2012, vol. 26 (2012)
19. Luo, L.: Network text sentiment analysis method combining LDA text representation and GRU-CNN. Pers. Ubiquitous Comput. **23**(3), 405–412 (2018). https://doi.org/10.1007/s00779-018-1183-9
20. Mishne, G., De Rijke, M., et al.: Capturing global mood levels using blog posts. In: AAAI 2006, vol. 6, pp. 145–152 (2006)
21. Montavon, G., Orr, G.B., Müller, K.-R. (eds.): Neural Networks: Tricks of the Trade. LNCS, vol. 7700. Springer, Heidelberg (2012). https://doi.org/10.1007/978-3-642-35289-8
22. Pal, S., Ghosh, S., Nag, A.: Sentiment analysis in the light of LSTM recurrent neural networks. Int. J. Synth. Emot. (IJSE) **9**(1), 33–39 (2018)
23. Ping, Q., Chen, C.: Video highlights detection and summarization with lag-calibration based on concept-emotion mapping of crowd-sourced time-sync comments. arXiv preprint arXiv:1708.02210 (2017)
24. Quan, X., Wang, Q., Zhang, Y., Si, L., Wenyin, L.: Latent discriminative models for social emotion detection with emotional dependency. ACM Trans. Inf. Syst. (TOIS) **34**(1), 1–19 (2015)
25. Rakhlin, A.: Convolutional neural networks for sentence classification. GitHub (2016)
26. Schuster, M., Paliwal, K.K.: Bidirectional recurrent neural networks. IEEE Trans. Signal Process. **45**(11), 2673–2681 (1997)
27. Seal, D., Roy, U.K., Basak, R.: Sentence-level emotion detection from text based on semantic rules. In: Tuba, M., Akashe, S., Joshi, A. (eds.) Information and Communication Technology for Sustainable Development. AISC, vol. 933, pp. 423–430. Springer, Singapore (2020). https://doi.org/10.1007/978-981-13-7166-0_42
28. Simonyan, K., Zisserman, A.: Very deep convolutional networks for large-scale image recognition. In: Bengio, Y., LeCun, Y. (eds.) 3rd International Conference on Learning Representations, ICLR, San Diego, CA, USA, May 7–9 (2015)
29. Song, X.Y., Zhao, Y., Jin, L.T., Sun, Y., Liu, T.: Research on the construction of sentiment dictionary based on word2vec. In: Proceedings of the 2018 International Conference on Algorithms, Computing and Artificial Intelligence, pp. 1–6 (2018)
30. Strapparava, C., Valitutti, A., et al.: Wordnet affect: an affective extension of wordnet. In: Lrec, vol. 4, p. 40. Citeseer (2004)
31. Tang, D.: Sentiment-specific representation learning for document-level sentiment analysis. In: ICDM 2015, pp. 447–452 (2015)
32. Tang, D., Wei, F., Qin, Bing, et al.: Building large-scale twitter-specific sentiment lexicon: a representation learning approach. In: COLING, pp. 172–182 (2014)
33. Tripathi, G., Singh, G.: Sentiment analysis approach based N-gram and KNN classifier. Int. J. Adv. Res. Comput. Sci. **9**(3), 209–212 (2018)
34. Vaswani, A., et al.: Attention is all you need. In: Advances in Neural Information Processing Systems, pp. 5998–6008 (2017)
35. Vateekul, P., Koomsubha, T.: A study of sentiment analysis using deep learning techniques on Thai Twitter data. In: 2016 13th International Joint Conference on Computer Science and Software Engineering (JCSSE), pp. 1–6. IEEE (2016)

36. Wang, H., Chen, E., Liu, Q., Xu, Tong, et al.: A united approach to learning sparse attributed network embedding. In: ICDM, pp. 557–566. IEEE (2018)
37. Wang, H., et al.: MCNE: an end-to-end framework for learning multiple conditional network representations of social network. In: SIGKDD 2019, pp. 1064–1072 (2019)
38. Wang, Y., Huang, M., Zhu, X., Zhao, L.: Attention-based LSTM for aspect-level sentiment classification. In: EMNLP 2016, pp. 606–615 (2016)
39. Xu, L., Lin, H.: Ontology-driven affective Chinese text analysis and evaluation method. In: Affective Computing & Intelligent Interaction, Second International Conference, Acii, Lisbon, Portugal, September (2007)
40. Yu, H., Hatzivassiloglou, V.: Towards answering opinion questions: separating facts from opinions and identifying the polarity of opinion sentences. In: EMNLP 2003, pp. 129–136 (2003)
41. Zagibalov, T., Carroll, J.A.: Automatic seed word selection for unsupervised sentiment classification of Chinese text. In: COLING 2008, pp. 1073–1080 (2008)

Correction to: Selected Sample Retraining Semi-supervised Learning Method for Aerial Scene Classification

Ye Tian, Jun Li, Liguo Zhang, Jianguo Sun, and Guisheng Yin

Correction to:
Chapter "Selected Sample Retraining Semi-supervised
Learning Method for Aerial Scene Classification"
in: L. Fang et al. (Eds.): *Artificial Intelligence*, LNAI 13069,
https://doi.org/10.1007/978-3-030-93046-2_9

In the originally published version of chapter 9 the name of the author was spelled incorrectly. The author name has been corrected as "Jun Li".

The updated version of this chapter can be found at
https://doi.org/10.1007/978-3-030-93046-2_9

Author Index